EFFECTIVE

A powerful way for students to learn how to apply and use core concepts covered in the text chapters.
More and more professors who teach strategy courses are finding that simulations are every bit as effective as case analysis in providing students with a means of applying what they have read about in the text chapters.

Students are assigned a senior executive role.
Students' strategy-making and decision making skills are put to the test. In this learn-by-doing exercise, students gain hands-on experience in crafting a competitive strategy and in making decisions relating to product quality, production, workforce compensation and training, pricing and marketing, and financing of company operations.

Assurance of Learning.
Wonder how well your students perform globally, or perform against accreditation standards? A Learning Assurance Report is automatically produced and displays how well each student performed relative to all other students worldwide.

See what the buzz is all about

Visit the Web site **www.mhhe.com/thompsonsims** to register for a demonstration and to read what your colleagues are saying about BSG and GLO-BUS.

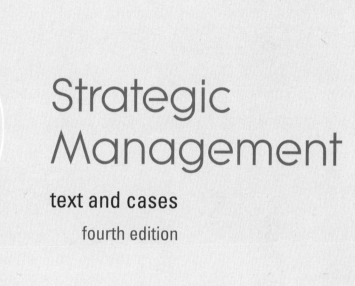

Strategic Management

text and cases

fourth edition

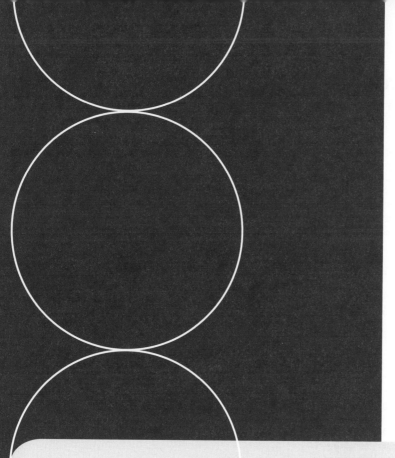

Gregory G. Dess
University of Texas
at Dallas

G. T. Lumpkin
Texas Tech University

Alan B. Eisner
Pace University

Strategic Management

text and cases

fourth edition

 **McGraw-Hill
Irwin**

Boston   Burr Ridge, IL   Dubuque, IA   New York   San Francisco   St. Louis
Bangkok   Bogotá   Caracas   Kuala Lumpur   Lisbon   London   Madrid   Mexico City
Milan   Montreal   New Delhi   Santiago   Seoul   Singapore   Sydney   Taipei   Toronto

McGraw-Hill
Irwin

STRATEGIC MANAGEMENT: TEXT AND CASES

Published by McGraw-Hill/Irwin, a business unit of The McGraw-Hill Companies, Inc., 1221 Avenue of the Americas, New York, NY, 10020. Copyright © 2008, 2007, 2006, 2004 by The McGraw-Hill Companies, Inc. All rights reserved. No part of this publication may be reproduced or distributed in any form or by any means, or stored in a database or retrieval system, without the prior written consent of The McGraw-Hill Companies, Inc., including, but not limited to, in any network or other electronic storage or transmission, or broadcast for distance learning.

Some ancillaries, including electronic and print components, may not be available to customers outside the United States.

This book is printed on acid-free paper.

1 2 3 4 5 6 7 8 9 QPD/QPD 0 9 8 7

ISBN-13: 978-0-07-340498-1
ISBN-10: 0-07-340498-5

Senior sponsoring editor: *Doug Hughes*
Developmental editor: *Laura Griffin*
Marketing manager: *Anke Braun Weekes*
Senior project manager: *Harvey Yep*
Production supervisor: *Debra Sylvester*
Design coordinator: *Jillian Lindner*
Lead media project manager: *Susan Lombardi*
Cover design: *Pam Verros*
Interior design: *Pam Verros*
Photo researcher: *Jeremy Cheshareck*
Typeface: *10/12 Times Roman*
Compositor: *Aptara, Inc.*
Printer: *Quebecor World Dubuque Inc.*

Library of Congress Cataloging-in-Publication Data

Dess, Gregory G.
    Strategic management : text and cases / Gregory G. Dess, G.T. Lumpkin, Alan B. Eisner. — 4th ed.
      p. cm.
    Includes index.
    ISBN-13: 978-0-07-340498-1 (alk. paper)
    ISBN-10: 0-07-340498-5 (alk. paper)
    1. Strategic planning. I. Lumpkin, G. T. II. Eisner, Alan B. III. Title.
HD30.28.D4743 2008
658.4′012—dc22
                                                               2007034045

Dedication

To my family, Margie and Taylor;
my parents, Bill and Mary Dess;
and Walter and Eleanor Descovich
–Greg

To my lovely wife, Vicki, and my colleagues
at Texas Tech University
–Tom

To my family, Helaine,
Rachel, and Jacob
–Alan

About the Authors

Gregory G. Dess is the Andrew R. Cecil Endowed Chair in Management at the University of Texas at Dallas. His primary research interests are in strategic management, organization–environment relationships, and knowledge management. He has published numerous articles on these subjects in both academic and practitioner-oriented journals. In August 2000, he was inducted into the *Academy of Management Journal's* Hall of Fame as one of its charter members. Professor Dess has conducted executive programs in the United States, Europe, Africa, Hong Kong, and Australia. During 1994 he was a Fulbright Scholar in Oporto, Portugal. He received his PhD in Business Administration from the University of Washington (Seattle).

G. T. (Tom) Lumpkin is the Kent Hance Regents Endowed Chair and Professor of Entrepreneurship at Texas Tech in Lubbock, Texas. He received his PhD in management from the University of Texas at Arlington and MBA from the University of Southern California. His research interests include entrepreneurial orientation, opportunity recognition, strategy-making processes, and innovative forms of organizing work. He has published numerous research articles and book chapters. He is a member of Editorial Review Boards of *Entrepreneurship Theory & Practice* and the *Journal of Business Venturing.* Professor Lumpkin also conducts executive programs in strategic and entrepreneurial applications of e-commerce and digital business technologies.

Alan B. Eisner is Professor of Management and Graduate Management Program Chair at the Lubin School of Business, Pace University. He received his PhD in management from the Stern School of Business, New York University. His primary research interests are in strategic management, technology management, organizational learning, and managerial decision making. He has published research articles and cases in journals such as *Advances in Strategic Management, International Journal of Electronic Commerce, International Journal of Technology Management, American Business Review, Journal of Behavioral and Applied Management,* and *Journal of the International Academy for Case Studies.* He is the Associate Editor of the Case Association's peer reviewed journal, *The CASE Journal.*

Preface

We welcome you to the Fourth Edition of *Strategic Management: Text and Cases!* The author team and our colleagues at McGraw-Hill/Irwin are very gratified with the positive market response that our three previous editions have received. And we are most appreciative of the constructive and extensive feedback that many strategy professionals, who have taken the time to carefully review and critique our work, have provided. We are always striving to improve our product and many of their ideas have been incorporated into the book. We're pleased to acknowledge these many contributors later in the Preface.

In a few words we'd like to revisit the fundamental question: Why did we write the book in the first place? After all, there are already some good strategy textbooks available. The author team felt that there was a need for a book that students would find both relevant and readable, but at the same time challenging. In essence, our tagline could be: "Strong enough for the professor, but made for the student." Perhaps, one of our reviewers, Professor Stephen Vitucci (Tarleton State University–Central Texas), said it best: "I want it to be rigorous but something they can read and understand. The Dess, Lumpkin, and Eisner text I am currently using is exactly what I like and, more importantly, what my students need and like."

To earn such praise, we have endeavored to use an engaging writing style free of unnecessary jargon, to cover all the traditional bases, and to integrate some central themes throughout the book that are vital to understanding strategic management in today's global economy. Among these themes are globalization, technology, ethics, and entrepreneurship. We bring concepts to life with short examples from business practice to illustrate virtually every strategy concept in the book, and we have provided over 90 Strategy Spotlights—more detailed examples—to drive home key points.

We have also included three separate chapters that other strategy texts usually do not have. These chapters focus on timely topics about which all business students should have a solid understanding: the role of intellectual assets and knowledge in value creation (Chapter 4), entrepreneurial strategy and competitive dynamics (Chapter 8), and the value of fostering entrepreneurship in established organizations (Chapter 12). We also provide an excellent set of cases to help students analyze, integrate, and apply strategic management concepts.

When we developed *Strategic Management: Text and Cases*, we did not, of course, forget the instructors. You certainly have a very challenging (but rewarding) job. And we want to do our best to help you. We provide a variety of supplementary materials that should help you in class preparation and delivery. In our chapter notes, for example, we did not simply summarize the material. Rather, we always kept in mind (consistent with the strategy concept) value added. To that end, we always asked ourselves: What can we do to add value to the process of teaching and learning? Thus, we provide numerous questions to guide discussion and at least 12 boxed examples to supplement material that is already in the chapter. And, we might add, the author team completed the entire test bank themselves. We have worked hard to provide instructors with a complete package that should make your classes relevant, rigorous, and rewarding for both you and your students. We felt so strongly about this that we developed almost all of these materials ourselves; that is, we didn't "farm them out" to others, as many textbook writers often do. We really believe that this enables us to ensure a high level of quality and consistency in all of our materials.

We'd now like to address some of the major substantive changes in the Fourth Edition. New features we have added we feel "add value" for both instructors and students. And what remains the same—are key features that have been consistent throughout all of our editions.

What's New: Highlights of the Fourth Edition

We have endeavored to add new material to the chapters that reflect both the feedback that we have received from reviewers and the challenges faced by today's managers. While we have added chapter material, we have been careful to avoid "chapter creep." That is, we've worked hard to tighten our writing style and cut redundant examples to illustrate concepts. Thus, our chapters have remained about the same length—and in some cases, have been shortened.

Here are some of our major changes for the Fourth Edition:

- **Ten of the 13 opening Learning from Mistakes "minicases" that lead off the chapters are totally new.** And others have been carefully updated. Unique to this text, these vignettes are all examples of what can go wrong, and they serve as an excellent vehicle for clarifying and reinforcing strategy concepts. After all, what can be learned if we simply admire perfection? **In addition, about half of our 90 Strategy Spotlights are new and many others have been updated.**

- **Four to six "Reflecting on Career Implications" for each chapter.** This feature will help instructors drive home to students the immediate relevance/value of strategy concepts. It focuses on how an understanding of key concepts helps business students early in their careers. This should dramatically enhance the relevance of course material.

- Approximately a dozen key terms for each chapter are defined in the margins of the pages. This was in response to reviewer feedback and should improve students' understanding of core strategy concepts.

- Content (Strategy Spotlights and Exhibits) has been broken out into art or tables to aid learning and improve the visual appeal of our chapters. Further, we strive to avoid long paragraphs, instead focusing on shorter paragraphs with many indented examples. All of these efforts are directed at improving readability and impact.

- The addition of two detailed experiential exercises in the Instructor's Manual that were co-authored by one of the textbook's authors. Atkinson Company deals with managers facing a retrenchment situation in which they have to determine a "rank order of layoff." Plastico is about a management team that must make a quick decision on how to address a serious quality problem that has arisen. But all of the key players have conflicting roles and expectations! These exercises have been used in many contexts, including executive education. They both have a strong game component that makes it enjoyable for students. But, more importantly, Atkinson and Plastico are excellent mechanisms to drive home key course concepts.

Our major content changes for each chapter include:

- **Chapter 1 introduces the concept of "ambidextrous behaviors."** Such behaviors enable managers to help their firms take advantages of existing opportunities as well as explore new opportunities. Among the four ambidextrous behaviors that we discuss is taking initiative and being alert to opportunities beyond the confines of one's own job. This topic has immediate relevance for business graduates.

- **Chapter 3 addresses some of the potential downsides of the balanced scorecard.** Too often, books only focus on the advantages and benefits of concepts that are popular in the business world. Here, as with other concepts in the book (for example, five forces analysis and emotional intelligence), we take a more even-handed approach. This provides a more realistic, critical mind-set for students.

- **Chapter 4 has many useful additions. We provide a detailed discussion of social networks and their implications for knowledge management and career success.** We'd all probably agree that this is a real hot topic in strategic management (and related fields), and it is supported by a substantial amount of research. We discuss the relative advantages of being part of multiple unconnected networks in a network (i.e., bridging structural holes) and being central to a single network. For example, being a key part of multiple networks (which may represent several departments in a firm) helps individuals gain a greater variety of information sources and contacts which enables them to add more value to their organization and enhance their career success. **We address how many firms are developing effective strategies to attract, develop, and retain Generation Y employees.** This is a contemporary issue that all types of organizations face. And of course, it is very relevant to today's students. **And the closing section discusses the importance of firms protecting their intellectual property.** To this end, firms often rely on patents, trademarks, copyrights, and noncompete clauses. However, managers must ensure that their firms develop dynamic capabilities to ensure that they are able to reconfigure knowledge and activities to attain sustainable advantages in the marketplace.

- **Chapter 5 expands our discussion of the industry life cycle.** We discuss how firms can avoid the maturity phase and establish a growth trajectory through "reverse" or "breakaway" positioning. At times, the industry life cycle (the S-curve) is taken as a given. However, our presentation provides insights into how the concept can be addressed more creatively.

- **Chapter 7 introduces the concept of "regionalization" to supplement our discussion of the globalization of the world's economy.** Most multinationals compete in only one or two regions (i.e., North America, Europe, Asia). Why? There are substantial differences (such as language, culture, political/legal institutions) across regions that pose significant challenges for managers. We address the strategic implications, which should spur students' interests in international issues.

- **Chapter 8 (Entrepreneurial Strategy and Competitive Dynamics)** has been completely reconfigured. Part of the chapter (competitive dynamics) is entirely new and addresses the cycle of actions and responses that are initiated when a new player enters a competitive marketplace. This is a "hot issue" in strategy and has important implications for competitive advantage—the core topic of our book. We address competitive dynamics for such rivals as XM and Sirius (satellite radio) and AMD and Intel (chip-makers). The first part of the chapter draws on material that was previously part of Chapter 13 on creating new ventures.

- **In our first three editions, Chapter 8 focused on digital and Internet strategies.** Based on reviewer feedback and the salience of the Internet in the business world and society in general, we have distributed the material that was formerly in Chapter 8 throughout the book: **Chapter 2** addresses how the Internet affects the five forces, **Chapter 3** (appendix) discusses how the Internet adds value, and **Chapter 5** discusses the impact the Internet has on competitive advantage.

- **Chapter 9 addresses one of today's major governance issues—the "backdating" of stock options.** This topic raises critical ethical concerns. By March 2007, about 140 U.S. companies were under investigation by the SEC; 75 firms planned to restate earnings because of backdating, and 66 executives have lost their jobs. Clearly, this issue should raise both emotions and discussion among business students!

- **In Chapter 12, we draw on McGrath and Keil's work on the value captor's processes.** We address how employment practices such as finding the optimal mix of experienced players with new talented and diverse employees can spur experimentation in new venture teams. Given Generation Y's urge to work in progressive and innovative organizations, this topic will be highly relevant.

- **Alan Eisner, our case author, has worked hard to further enhance our excellent case package.** These include:
  - 25 author-written cases (much more than our competition)
  - updating our users' favorite cases (based on extensive market feedback) with new information and data to minimize instructor preparation time and "maximize freshness"

- 11 new cases and significant updates on 19 cases, including World Wide Entertainment (WWE), The Casino Industry, JetBlue Airways, Southwest Airlines, Wal-Mart, Panera Bread Company, FreshDirect, and many others.
- providing an excellent mix of "tried and true classics" as well as shorter favorites.
- drawing on multiple prestigious sources such as Harvard and Ivey (University of Western Ontario).
- a major focus on fresh and current cases about familiar firms.
- cases of varying lengths to best fit instructor needs.
- more videos to match cases than ever before.

What Remains the Same: Key Features from Earlier Editions

We've discussed some of the most important changes that we have made to improve *Strategic Management* and keep it fresh and up-to-date. Now, let's briefly address some of the exciting features that remain from the earlier editions.

- *Traditional organizing framework with three other chapters on timely topics.* Crisply written chapters cover all of the strategy bases and address contemporary topics. First, the chapters are divided logically into the traditional sequence: strategy analysis, strategy formulation, and strategy implementation. Second, we include three chapters on such timely topics as intellectual capital/knowledge management, entrepreneurial strategy and competitive dynamics; and, fostering corporate entrepreneurship, and new ventures.
- *"Learning from Mistakes" chapter-opening cases.* To enhance student interest, we begin each chapter with a case that depicts an organization that has suffered a dramatic performance drop, or outright failure, by failing to adhere to sound strategic management concepts and principles. We believe that this feature serves to underpin the value of the concepts in the course and that it is a preferred teaching approach to merely providing examples of outstanding companies that always seem to get it right! After all, isn't it better (and more challenging) to diagnose problems than admire perfection? As Dartmouth's Sydney Finkelstein, author of *Why Smart Executives Fail,* notes: "We live in a world where success is revered, and failure is quickly pushed to the side. However, some of the greatest opportunities to learn—both for individuals and organizations—come from studying what goes wrong."[1] We'll see how, for example, Ford Motor Company's strategic misfires doomed the best-selling car in the United States—the Taurus; how Coors' inability to recognize and act on health trends left its low-carb product, Aspen Edge, in Anheuser-Busch's dust; and, how major flaws in corporate governance has enabled executives like KB Homes' CEO, Bruce Karatz, to enrich themselves—via the backdating of stock options—at shareholder expense.
- *Consistent chapter format and features to reinforce learning.* We have included several features in each chapter to add value and create an enhanced learning experience. First, each chapter begins with an overview and a set of bullets pointing to key learning objectives. Second, as previously noted, the opening case describes a situation in which a company's performance eroded because of a lack of proper application of strategy concepts. Third, at the end of each chapter there are five different types of questions/exercises that should help students assess their understanding and application of material:

1. Implications of chapter material for career success.
2. Summary review questions.
3. Experiential exercises.
4. Application questions and exercises.
5. Ethics questions

[1]Personal communication, June 20, 2005.

Given the emergence of Internet and e-commerce, each chapter contains at least one exercise that involves the use of the Internet.

- *Clear articulation and illustration of key concepts.* Key strategy concepts are introduced in a clear and concise manner and are followed by timely and interesting examples from business practice. Such concepts include value-chain analysis, the resource-based view of the firm, Porter's five forces model, competitive advantage, boundaryless organizational designs, digital strategies, corporate governance, ethics, and entrepreneurship.
- *Extensive use of sidebars.* We include over 90 sidebars (or about six per chapter) called "Strategy Spotlights." The Strategy Spotlights not only illustrate key points but also increase the readability and excitement of new strategy concepts.
- *Integrative themes.* The text provides a solid grounding in ethics, globalization, and technology. These topics are central themes throughout the book and form the basis for many of the Strategy Spotlights.
- *Implications of concepts for small businesses.* Many of the key concepts are applied to start-up firms and smaller businesses, which is particularly important since many students have professional plans to work in such firms.
- *Not just a textbook but an entire package. Strategic Management* features the best chapter teaching notes available today. Rather than merely summarizing the key points in each chapter, we focus on value-added material to enhance the teaching (and learning) experience. Each chapter includes dozens of questions to spur discussion, teaching tips, in-class group exercises, and about a dozen detailed examples from business practice to provide further illustrations of key concepts.
- **Case Studies** We have selected an outstanding collection of current and classic cases for this edition, carefully including a wide variety of cases matched to key strategic concepts and organized to create maximum flexibility. We now have a balance of short, consice and longer, comprehensive cases while maintaining currency and name recognition of our cases with many new and updated classroom tested cases. We also have updated many of the favorites from the Third Edition such as Southwest Airlines, JetBlue Airways, Panera Bread Company, World Wrestling Entertainment, and many others to further engage students. New cases include: Ann Taylor, Apple, Caribou Coffee, Claire's Stores, eBay in Asia, Nintendo, Rocky Mountain Chocolate Factory, and United Way. We are once again pleased to include several cases from The Harvard Business School and *The Harvard Business Review,* including Crown Cork and Seal, and Automation Consulting.

Student Support Materials

- **Online Learning Center (OLC)** The following resources are available to students via the publisher's OLC at www.mhhe.com/dess4e:
  - Chapter quizzes students can take to gauge their understanding of material covered in each chapter.
  - A selection of PowerPoint slides for each chapter.
  - Links to strategy simulations the Business Strategy Game & GLO-BUS. Both provide a powerful and constructive way of connecting students to the subject matter of the course with a competition among classmates on campus and around the world.

  And purchasing access to our premium learning resources right on the OLC Web site provides student with the following value-added resources:
  - Pre- and Post-tests. Students can access the online pretest prior to reading the chapter, answer the questions, study the chapter, and then take the posttest to see what they have learned.
  - A handful of content (for instance, quizzes, Pre- and Post-tests, narrated slides, and videos) is also available for iPod download to help students prepare for exams on the go.

Instructor Support Materials

- **Instructor's Manual (IM)** Prepared by the textbook authors, the accompanying IM contains summary/objectives, lecture/discussion outlines, discussion questions, extra examples not included in the text, teaching tips, reflecting on career implications, experiential exercises, and more.

- **Test Bank** Prepared by the authors, the test bank contains more than 1,000 true/false, multiple-choice, and essay questions. It has now been tagged with learning objectives as well as Bloom's Taxonomy and AACSB criteria. **Assurance of Learning Ready** Many educational institutions today are focused on the notion of assurance of learning, an important element of some accreditation standards. Dess 4e is designed specifically to support your assurance of learning initiatives with a simple, yet powerful, solution. Each test bank question for Dess 4e maps to a specific chapter learning outcome/objective listed in the text. You can use our test bank software, EZ Test to easily query for learning outcomes/objectives that directly relate to the learning objectives for your course. You can then use the reporting features of EZ Test to aggregate student results in similar fashion, making the collection and presentation of assurance of learning data simple and easy. **AACSB Statement** McGraw-Hill Companies is a proud corporate member of AACSB International. Recognizing the importance and value of AACSB accreditation, the authors of Dess 4e have sought to recognize the curricula guidelines detailed in AACSB standards for business accreditation by connecting selected questions in Dess 4e the general knowledge and skill guidelines found in the AACSB standards. It is important to note that the statements contained in Dess 4e are provided only as a guide for the users of this text. The statements contained in Dess 4e are provided only as a guide for the users of this text. The AACSB leaves content coverage and assessment clearly within the realm and control of individual schools, the mission of the school, and the faculty. The AACSB does also charge schools with the obligation of doing assessment against their own content and learning goals. While Dess 4e and its teaching package make no claim of any specific AACSB qualification or evaluation, we have, within Dess 4e labeled selected questions according to the six general knowledge and skills areas. The labels or tags within Dess 4e are as indicated. There are of course, many more within the test bank, the text, and the teaching package which might be used as a 'standard' for your course. However, the labeled questions are suggested for your consideration. **EZ Test,** a computerized version of the test bank, can also be found on the Instructor's Resource CD-ROM. This flexible and easy-to-use electronic testing program allows instructors to create multiple versions of tests from book-specific items with a wide range of question types, including adding their own. And any test can be exported for use with course management systems. And now **McGraw-Hill EZ Test Online** is accessible to busy instructors virtually anywhere—in their office, at home or while traveling—and eliminates the need for software installation. It gives instructors access to hundreds of textbook question banks and millions of questions when creating tests. Instructors can view question banks associated with their textbook or easily create their own questions. Multiple versions of tests can be saved for future delivery as a paper test or online. When created and delivered with EZ Test Online, individual tests are immediately scored, saving instructors valuable time and providing prompt test feedback to students. To register please visit http://www.eztestonline.com/.

- **PowerPoint Presentation** for the text consists of more than 400 slides incorporating an outline for the chapters tied to learning objectives. Also included are multiple choice and discussion Classroom Performance System (CPS) questions as well as additional examples outside of the text. And Case Study PowerPoint slides are available to facilitate case study coverage.

- **Instructor's Resource CD-ROM** All instructor supplements are available in this one-stop multimedia resource, which includes the Instructor's Manual, Test Bank, PowerPoint Presentations, and Case Study Teaching Notes.
- **Case Videos** A set of videos related to selected cases accompanies the text to support your classroom, student lab, or for home viewing. These thought-provoking video clips are available upon adoption of this text.
- **Online Learning Center (OLC)** The instructor section of www.mhhe.com/dess4e also includes the Instructor's Manual, PowerPoint Presentations, Interactive Case Grid, and Case Study Teaching Notes as well as additional resources.
- **Enhanced Cartridge for Blackboard and WebCT*** The Enhanced Cartridge is the perfect tool for instructors teaching a hybrid course or a course completely online requiring substantial online content. Resources such as Pre- and Post-tests, iPod content, interactive skills exercises, and self-assessments help students to learn and apply concepts and allow you to monitor their progress.
- **The Business Strategy Game and GLO-BUS Online Simulations** Both allow teams of students to manage companies in a head-to-head contest for global market leadership. These simulations give students the immediate opportunity to experiment with various strategy options and to gain proficiency in applying the concepts and tools they have been reading about in the chapters. To find out more or to register, please visit www.mmhe.com/thompsonsims.

Additional Resources

- **McGraw-Hill/Primis Custom Publishing** You can customize this text. McGraw-Hill/Primis Online's digital database offers you the flexibility to customize your course including material from the largest online collection of textbooks, readings, and cases. Primis leads the way in customized eBooks with hundreds of titles available at prices that save your students over 20 percent off bookstore prices. For more information, please visit www.primisonline.com/dess or call 800-228-0634.
- **Group and Video Resource Manual** is an instructor's guide to an active classroom. This electronic manual for instructors includes a menu of items you can use as teaching tools in class. Included are detailed teaching notes and PowerPoints for self-assessments, test your knowledge exercises, and the Manager's Hot Seat DVD as well as new group exercises, complete with any handouts or worksheets you'll need to accompany them.
- **Manager's Hot Seat** This interactive, video-based software puts students in the manager's hot seat where they have to apply their knowledge to make decisions on the spot on hot issues such as ethics, diversity, working in teams, and the virtual workplace. This resource is available for student purchase with the Dess text. Resources to support these videos are located in the Group and Video Resource Manual.
- **Dess in eBook** format. Real texts—Real Savings! Are you interested in giving your students the option to access the textbook contents digitally, with interactive, dynamic features and save your students some money? If so, our eBooks are for you. They are identical to our printed textbooks and cost about half as much. Your students will be able to search, highlight, bookmark, annotate, and print the eBook! McGraw-Hill Higher Education's eBooks can be viewed online on any computer with an Internet connection or downloaded to an individual's computer. For more information, please visit http://ebooks.primisonline.com/ or contact your McGraw-Hill representative.

*Please ask your McGraw-Hill representative about the availability of our Enhanced Cartridge materials for other course management platforms.

- ***BusinessWeek*** subscription. Students can subscribe to *BusinessWeek* for a special rate in addition to the price of the text. Students will receive a passcode card shrink-wrapped with their new text. The card directs students to a Web site where they enter the code and then gain access to *BusinessWeek*'s registration page to enter their address information and set up their print and online subscription. Please ask your McGraw-Hill/Irwin representative for more information.
- **Standard & Poor's Educational Version of Market Insight.** McGraw-Hill/Irwin is proud to partner with Standard & Poor's Market Insight ©. This rich online resource provides six years of financial data, key ratio summary reports, and S&P's exclusive "Industry Surveys" that offer an in-depth look at industry trends, projections, and competitive analysis for 500 top U.S. companies in the renowned COMPUSTAT® database. The password-protected Web site is the perfect way to bring real data into today's classroom for use in case analysis, industry analysis, and research for team and individual projects. Learn more at www.mhhe.com/edumarketinsight.

Acknowledgments

Strategic Management represents far more than just the joint efforts of the three co-authors. Rather, it is the product of the collaborative input of many people. Some of these individuals are academic colleagues, others are the outstanding team of professionals at McGraw-Hill/Irwin, and still others are those who are closest to us—our families. It is time to express our sincere gratitude.

First, we'd like to acknowledge the thorough, constructive reviews that we received from our superb team of reviewers and symposia participants. Their input was very helpful in both pointing out errors in the manuscript and suggesting areas that needed further development as additional topics. We sincerely believe that the incorporation of their ideas was critical to improving the final product. These professionals and their affiliations are:

Reviewers for the 4th Edition

George S. Cole, *Shippensburg University*

Keith Credo, *Auburn University*

Tracy Ethridge, *Tri-County Technical College*

Naomi A. Gardberg, *Baruch College, CUNY*

Stephen V. Horner, *Arkansas State University*

Jay J. Janney, *University of Dayton*

Helaine J. Korn, *Baruch College, CUNY*

Zhiang (John) Lin, *University of Texas at Dallas*

Kevin Lowe, *University of North Carolina–Greensboro*

Rickey Madden, Ph.D., *Presbyterian College*

John R. Massaua, *University of Southern Maine*

Fatma Mohamed, *Morehead State University*

Floyd Ormsbee, *Clarkson University*

Ralph W. Parrish, Ph.D., *University of Central Oklahoma*

Annette L. Ranft, *Florida State University*

William W. Sannwald, *San Diego State University*

Mark Shanley, *University of Illinois at Chicago*

Alan Theriault, *University of California–Riverside*

Karen Torres, *Angelo State University*

Craig A. Turner, Ph.D., *East Tennessee State University*

S. Stephen Vitucci, *Tarleton State University–Central Texas*

N. Wasilewski, *Pepperdine University*

Marta Szabo White, *Georgia State University*

John E. Wroblewski, *State University of New York–Fredonia*

Second, the authors would like to thank several faculty colleagues who were particularly helpful in the review, critique, and development of the book and supplementary materials. While Greg was at the University of Kentucky, faculty in the strategic management area were extremely generous with their time. They provided many excellent ideas and contributions for the book's first edition. Accordingly, he would like to thank Wally Ferrier, Gordon Holbein, Dan Lockhart, and Bruce Skaggs. His colleagues at the University of Texas at Dallas also have been helpful and supportive. These individuals include Mike Peng, Joe Picken, Kumar Nair, John Lin, Seung-Hyun Lee, Tev Dalgic, and Jane Salk. His administrative assistant, Mary Vice, has been extremely helpful. Former MBA student Naga Damaraju, along with two doctoral students, Ted Khoury and Erin Pleggenkuhle-Miles, have provided many useful inputs and ideas. He also appreciates the support of his dean and associate dean, Hasan Pirkul and Varghese Jacob, respectively. Tom would like to thank Gerry Hills, Abagail McWilliams, Darold Barnum, Mike Miller, Rod Shrader, James Gillespie, Lou Coco, and other colleagues at the University of Illinois at Chicago, for their continued support. Tom also thanks Keith Brigham, Rod Magee, Todd Moss, Tyge Payne, Jeremy Short, Bill Wan, Abby Wang, and Andy Yu at Texas Tech University, as well as Tammy Branham, Claudia Cogliser, Bill Gardner, Liana Guajardo, Ron Mitchell, Morag Nairn, and Ritch Sorenson for their support. Special thanks also to Jeff Stambaugh for his vital contribution to new materials prepared for the Fourth Edition. Tom also extends a special thanks to Benyamin Lichtenstein for his support and encouragement. Both Greg and Tom wish to thank a special colleague, Abdul Rasheed at the University of Texas at Arlington, who certainly has been a valued source of friendship and ideas for us for many years. He provided many valuable contributions to the Fourth Edition. Alan thanks his colleagues at Pace University and the Case Association for their support in developing these fine case selections. Special thanks go to Jamal Shamsie at Michigan State University for his support in developing the case selections for this edition. And we appreciate Doug Sanford, at Towson State University, for his expertise with one of our new pedagogical features—the key terms in each chapter.

Third, we would like to thank the team at McGraw-Hill/Irwin for their outstanding support throughout the process. This begins with John Biernat, formerly Publisher, who signed us to our original contract. John was always available to provide support and valued input during the entire process. In editorial, Doug Hughes and Laura Griffin kept things on track, responded quickly to our never-ending needs and requests, and offered insights and encouragement. Once the manuscript was completed and revised, project manager Harvey Yep expertly guided us through the production process. Susan Lombardi did an outstanding job in helping us with the supplementary materials. Design Coordinator Jillian Lindner and freelance designer Pam Verros provided excellent design and art work. And finally, we thank Krista Bettino, Anke Braun Weekes, and Mike Gedatus for their energetic, competent, and thorough marketing efforts.

Finally, we would like to thank our families. For Greg this includes his parents, William and Mary Dess, who have always been there for him. His wife Margie and daughter, Taylor, have been a constant source of love and companionship. Greg would also like to recognize two very special people—Walter and Eleanor Descovich, his uncle and aunt, who live in Massapequa, Long Island. They have been a constant source of love and encouragement to him through the years and have raised four wonderful children. They might not write about such ideas as leadership and trust, but they sure practice it! Tom thanks his wife Vicki for her constant love and companionship. Tom also thanks Lee Hetherington and Thelma Lumpkin for their inspiration, as well as his mom Katy, and his sister Kitty, for a lifetime of support. Alan thanks his family—his wife Helaine and his children Rachel and Jacob—for their love and support. He also thanks his parents, Gail Eisner and the late Marvin Eisner, for their support and encouragement.

guided tour

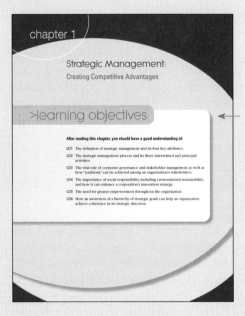

Learning Objectives
Learning Objectives now numbered LO1, LO2, LO3, etc. with corresponding icons in the margins to indicate where learning objectives are covered in the text.

Learning from Mistakes
Learning from Mistakes are examples of where things went wrong. Failures are not only interesting but also sometimes easier to learn from. And students realize strategy is not just about "right or wrong" answers, but requires critical thinking.

Learning from Mistakes

Robert Atkins, a cardiologist, was the founder of the original low-carbohydrate, high-protein diet.[1] He wrote several books that popularized his Atkins diet, including his best seller, *Dr. Atkins New Diet Revolution*, that sold over 10 million copies worldwide. As we will see below, in the beer industry, one firm—Anheuser-Busch—took quick action and benefited from this popular diet trend. Others, including Coors Brewing, were slow to react and paid the price.

In September 2002, Anheuser Busch became one of the pioneers in the low-carb category by launching Michelob Ultra. The brand rapidly became the leader, capturing 5.7 percent of the light beer market by March 2004. The company had jumped on the wave early and rode it during the upsurge of the low-carb trend, which peaked during that year. Clearly, this was an attractive market segment: Beer experts had estimated that about half of the $60 to $70 billion U.S. beer market is from light beer sales as Americans continue to seek out beers that won't add to their waistline.

Coors, in contrast, didn't enter the low-carb market until March 2004—after Michelob Ultra had begun to erode Coors Light's market share. The Coors low-carb brand, Aspen Edge, was too little, too late. By the time Aspen Edge was launched, it faced very stiff competition. In addition to a powerful leader in the segment, Michelob Ultra (which, of course, benefited from Anheuser Busch's deep pockets and marketing prowess), there were already over a dozen other low-carb rivals. These included Rolling Rock, which had introduced Rock Green Light, and Miller Brewing, which had begun to promote the fact that its staple, Miller Lite, had only 3.2 carbs. Further, there were several imported beers, including Martens Low Carbohydrate, brewed by Brouwerij Martens in Belgium.

Even though Coors invested $30 million in Aspen Edge's launch, its sales peaked at just 0.4 percent of the beer market in July 2004. Then its market share began to slide and it was discontinued in April 2006.

Strategy Spotlight
These boxes weave themes of ethics, globalization, and technology into every chapter of the text, providing students with a thorough grounding necessary for understanding strategic management.

Key Terms

Key Terms defined in the margins have been added to improve students' understanding of core strategy concepts.

strategic management the analyses, decisions, and actions an organization undertakes in order to create and sustain competitive advantages.

Exhibit 2.7 Porter's Five-Forces Model of Industry Competition
Source: Reprinted with permission of The Free Press, a division of Simon & Schuster Adult Publishing Group, from *Competitive Strategy: Techniques for Analyzing Industries and Competitors* by Michael E. Porter. Copyright © 1980, 1998 by The Free Press. All rights reserved.

Reflecting on Career Implications

This new section before the summary of every chapter consists of examples on how understanding of key concepts helps business students early in their careers.

Reflecting on Career Implications . . .

- **The Value Chain:** Carefully analyze where you can add value in your firm's value chain. How might your firm's support activities (e.g., information technology, human resource practices) help you accomplish your assigned tasks more effectively?
- **The Value Chain:** Consider important relationships among activities both within your firm as well as between your firm and its suppliers, customers, and alliance partners.
- **Resource Based View of the Firm:** Are your skills and talents rare, valuable, difficult to imitate, and have few substitutes? If so, you are in a better position to add value for your firm—and earn rewards and incentives. How can your skills and talents be enhanced to help satisfy these criteria to a greater extent? More training? Change positions within the firm? Consider career options at other organizations?
- **Balanced Scorecard:** In your decision making, strive to "balance" the four perspectives: customer, internal business, innovation and learning, and financial. Do not focus too much on short-term profits. Do your personal career goals provide opportunities to develop your skills in all four directions?

Exhibits

Both new and improved exhibits in every chapter provide visual presentations of the most complex concepts covered to support student comprehension.

Cases

Updated case lineup provides 11 new cases. The remaining have been revised to "maximize freshness" and minimize instructor preparation time. New cases for this edition include well-known companies such as Whole Foods, Ann Taylor, Rocky Mountain Chocolate Factory, Caribou Coffee, eBay in Asia, Apple, and Nintendo.

support materials

Online Learning Center (OLC)

Online Learning Center (OLC):
www.mhhe.com/dess4e is a Web site that follows the text chapter-by-chapter. OLC content is ancillary and supplementary germane to the textbook. As students read the book, they can go online to take self-grading quizzes, review material, or work through interactive exercises. It includes chapter quizzes, student PowerPoint slides, and links to strategy simulations The *Business Strategy Game* and GLO-BUS. Additional value-added resources are available by purchasing premium content via the OLC. These include Pre- and Post-Tests, narrated slides, and videos—all of which are available for iPod download.

The instructor section also includes the Instructor's Manual, PowerPoint Presentations, Case Study Teaching Notes, Interactive Case Grid, Video Guide, and Case Web Links as well as all student resources.

Enhanced Cartridge

The Enhanced Cartridge walks students through each chapter with Pre- and Post- Tests, iPod content, interactive skills exercises, and self-assessments helping them learn and apply concepts while also allowing instructors to monitor their progress along the way by feeding directly into the gradebook.

Brief Contents

Contents

Cases

ement

Strategic Analysis

Chapter 1
Introduction and Analyzing Goals and Objectives

Chapter 2
Analyzing the External Environment

Chapter 3
Analyzing the Internal Environment

Chapter 4
Assessing Intellectual Capital

Strategic Formulation

Chapter 5
Formulating Business-Level Strategies

Chapter 6
Formulating Corporate-Level Strategies

Chapter 7
Formulating International Strategies

Chapter 8
Entrepreneurial Strategy and Competitive Dynamics

Strategic Implementation

Chapter 9
Strategic Control and Corporate Governance

Chapter 10
Creating Effective Organizational Designs

Chapter 11
Strategic Leadership Excellence, Ethics and Change

Chapter 12
Fostering Corporate Entrepreneurship

Case Analysis

Chapter 13
Case Analysis

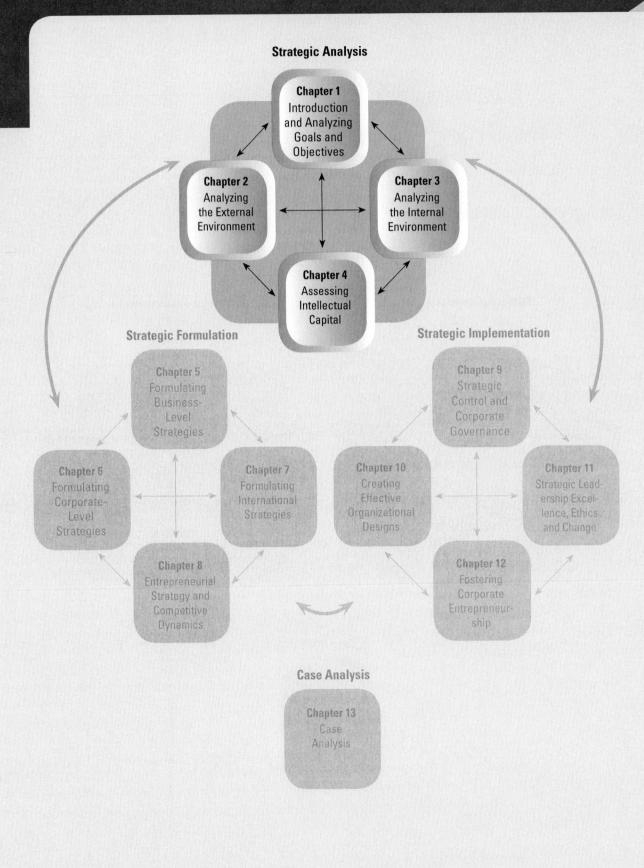

Strategic Analysis

Chapter 1 Introduction and Analyzing Goals and Objectives

Chapter 2 Analyzing the External Environment

Chapter 3 Analyzing the Internal Environment

Chapter 4 Assessing Intellectual Capital

Strategic Formulation

Chapter 5 Formulating Business-Level Strategies

Chapter 6 Formulating Corporate-Level Strategies

Chapter 7 Formulating International Strategies

Chapter 8 Entrepreneurial Strategy and Competitive Dynamics

Strategic Implementation

Chapter 9 Strategic Control and Corporate Governance

Chapter 10 Creating Effective Organizational Designs

Chapter 11 Strategic Leadership Excellence, Ethics and Change

Chapter 12 Fostering Corporate Entrepreneurship

Case Analysis

Chapter 13 Case Analysis

Strategic Analysis

chapter 1

Strategic Management:

Creating Competitive Advantages

>learning objectives

After reading this chapter, you should have a good understanding of:

LO1 The definition of strategic management and its four key attributes.

LO2 The strategic management process and its three interrelated and principal activities.

LO3 The vital role of corporate governance and stakeholder management as well as how "symbiosis" can be achieved among an organization's stakeholders.

LO4 The importance of social responsibility, including environmental sustainability, and how it can enhance a corporation's innovation strategy.

LO5 The need for greater empowerment throughout the organization.

LO6 How an awareness of a hierarchy of strategic goals can help an organization achieve coherence in its strategic direction.

*W*e define strategic management as *consisting of the analyses, decisions, and actions an organization undertakes in order to create and sustain competitive advantages.* At the heart of strategic management is the question: How and why do some firms outperform others? Thus, the challenge to managers is to decide on strategies that provide advantages that can be sustained over time. There are four key attributes of strategic management. It is directed at overall organizational goals, includes multiple stakeholders, incorporates short-term as well as long-term perspectives, and recognizes trade-offs between effectiveness and efficiency. We discuss the above definition and the four key attributes in the first section.

The second section addresses the strategic management process. The three major processes are strategy analysis, strategy formulation, and strategy implementation. These three components parallel the analyses, decisions, and actions in the above definition. We discuss how each of the 13 chapters addresses these three processes and provide examples from each chapter.

The third section discusses two important and interrelated concepts: corporate governance and stakeholder management. Corporate governance addresses the issue of who "governs" the corporation and determines its direction. It consists of three primary participants: stockholders (owners), management (led by the chief executive officer), and the board of directors (elected to monitor management). Stakeholder management recognizes that the interests of various stakeholders, such as owners, customers, and employees, can often conflict and create challenging decision-making dilemmas for managers. However, we discuss how some firms have been able to achieve "symbiosis" among stakeholders wherein their interests are considered interdependent and can be achieved simultaneously. We also discuss the important role of social responsibility, including the need for corporations to incorporate environmental sustainability in their strategic actions.

The fourth section addresses factors in the business environment that have increased the level of unpredictable change for today's leaders. Such factors have also created the need for a greater strategic management perspective and reinforced the role of empowerment throughout the organization.

The final section focuses on the need for organizations to ensure consistency in their vision, mission, and strategic objectives which, collectively, form a hierarchy of goals. While visions may lack specificity, they must evoke powerful and compelling mental images. Strategic objectives are much more specific and are essential for driving toward overall goals.

Learning from Mistakes

One of the things that makes the study of strategic management so interesting is that struggling firms can become stars, while high flyers can become earthbound very rapidly. For example, consider Ford Motor Company. As this pioneer of the auto industry begins its second century of existence, it is struggling for answers to a variety of problems.[1]

> Ford Motor Company's losses for the year 2006 alone were a staggering $12.7 billion! And even by the company's own projections, they do not see a return to profitability until at least 2009. Along with continuing losses, the company is also experiencing shrinking market share and a stock price that has not risen above single-digit levels in many years. According to analysts at Morgan Stanley, Renault-Nissan may overtake Ford as the world's number three automaker as early as 2007. As the company struggles to avoid drowning in a sea of red ink, one cannot but help wonder how this pioneer of the auto industry went into a downward financial spiral after years of comfortable profits and innovative products. While a number *[continued]*

of errors may have contributed to this decline, nothing illustrates their poor strategy and mismanagement more compellingly than the decision to discontinue the production of the popular Taurus sedan.

Introduced in 1985, the Taurus won acclaim as a symbol of American automotive renaissance. It was admired for its sleek aerodynamic design which was revolutionary for its time. Often referred to as a "jellybean" or a "flying potato" for its futuristic styling, the car was an instant hit, selling 263,000 units in its first year of production. The designers at Ford had spotted an interesting trend among North American car buyers: They were moving away from big, cushy American cars to better handling European models. They catered to this trend by offering a car with stiffer suspension, more interior room, firmer seats, better ergonomics, and more trunk space. They also added a number of "surprise and delight" features such as a cargo net to hold grocery bags in the trunk, and rear seat head rests and heat ducts. In 1989, the Taurus SHO (Super High Output) model was introduced.

After a very successful six-year run, the car was revamped for the 1992 model year, maintaining the overall oval shape, but adding new body panels, slimmer headlights and smoothed-out body sides. The result was a less controversial, more refined design, which catapulted Taurus to the position of the highest-selling passenger car in the United States with sales of nearly half a million units that year. From 1992 to 1996, Taurus was America's best-selling car, instilling a sense of pride in American manufacturers that they could indeed compete with their Japanese rivals and win. It also reversed Ford's financial losses of the early 1980s, contributing immensely to its profitability.

The signs of the decline of Taurus began in the late 1990s. In 1997, Toyota Camry edged out Taurus for the number one spot in the passenger car segment. By 2006, the Camry was outselling the Taurus two to one and Taurus sales had slid below 200,000 annual units. By October 2006, after 21 years and sales of 7.5 million cars (not counting its sibling Mercury Sable), Ford announced the decision to discontinue production of the Taurus.

The obvious question in the minds of millions of loyal customers was: How did the proudest brand of the last two decades come to such an inglorious end? "It didn't keep pace. That's the whole story in four words," claims Joel Pitcoff, Taurus' marketing manager of the mid 1990s. For nearly a decade, Ford treated the Taurus strictly as a cash cow, leaving the car virtually unchanged and with little advertising support. Instead, the company's focus was on high-margin products such as big-size trucks and sport utility vehicles. Meanwhile, competitors had copied and refined many of the attractive features of the Taurus. While the increasingly sophisticated American customers who had plenty of choice in the overcrowded passenger sedan market walked away from the product, Ford focused mainly on the volume intensive but less demanding fleet sales to rental car companies. When the sudden spike in oil prices in mid-2005 sent customers scurrying for more fuel efficient vehicles, Ford was caught flat-footed with virtually no desirable product to offer. "They put no money into the product for the last several years," said Jack Telnack, the original Taurus' chief designer, who retired in 1998. "They just let it wither on the vine. It's criminal. The car had a great reputation, a good name. I don't understand what they were waiting for."

While all of Ford's financial woes cannot be attributed to the demise of the Taurus, it is symptomatic of the many ills that have brought this once proud company to the brink of losing the industry leader position it had enjoyed for decades. Some of the causes of their problems are external in nature, such as the high retiree health benefit costs, the saturation of American markets by numerous producers from Japan and Korea, and the sudden doubling of oil prices. But, in the final analysis, most of Ford's wounds are self-inflicted. Their excessive reliance on trucks and SUVs for profits showed that they had forgotten all the lessons they learned from the oil price increases of the early 1980s. Ford spent $5 billion in the late 1990s in their ill-conceived effort to introduce a "world car." Introduced as the Ford Contour *[continued]* and its sibling the Mercury Mystique, the cars were an instant flop. To starve a successful brand that had captured the imagination of the public and contributed to the resurgence of the company was perhaps the biggest mistake of all.

Responding to the public uproar in the aftermath of the discontinuation of the Taurus brand, the company announced in early 2007 that it would reintroduce the brand by renaming the Ford Five Hundred the Taurus. Only time will tell how customers will respond to this reincarnated Taurus.

Today's leaders, such as those at Ford, face a large number of complex challenges in the global marketplace. In considering how much credit (or blame) they deserve, two perspectives of leadership come immediately to mind: the "romantic" and "external control" perspectives.[2] First, let's look at the **romantic view of leadership.** Here, the implicit assumption is that the leader is the key force in determining an organization's success—or lack thereof.[3] This view dominates the popular press in business magazines such as *Fortune, Business-Week,* and *Forbes,* wherein the CEO is either lauded for his or her firm's success or chided for the organization's demise. Consider, for example, the credit that has been bestowed on leaders such as Jack Welch, Andrew Grove, and Herb Kelleher for the tremendous accomplishments of their firms, General Electric, Intel, and Southwest Airlines, respectively.

> **romantic view of leadership** situations in which the leader is the key force determining the organization's success—or lack thereof.

More recently, Carlos Ghosn has been lionized in the business press for turning around Nissan's fortunes in the worldwide automobile industry. He transformed huge losses into a $7 billion profit, eliminated $23 billion of debt, and made Nissan the world's most profitable volume producer.[4] And, in the world of sports, managers and coaches, such as Bill Belichick of the New England Patriots in the National Football League, get a lot of credit for their team's outstanding success on the field.

On the other hand, when things don't go well, much of the failure of an organization can also, rightfully, be attributed to the leader. For example, when Carly Fiorina was fired as CEO of Hewlett Packard, the firm enjoyed an immediate increase in its stock price of 7 percent—hardly a strong endorsement of her leadership! The failure of Ford's top management to halt their continuing losses and market erosion finally led the company's board to hire an industry outsider—Boeing's Alan Mulally.

However, this reflects only part of the picture. Consider another perspective called **external view of leadership.** Here, rather than making the implicit assumption that the leader is the most important factor in determining organizational outcomes, the focus is on external factors that may positively or negatively affect a firm's success. We don't have to look far to support this perspective. For example, Ford Motor Company's decline can be attributed partly to a number of external factors. The rising healthcare costs in the United States and the company's pension obligations make it practically impossible to make a profit. Further, the sudden increase in the cost of gasoline after years of steady or declining prices caused a sudden reversal of consumer preferences from high margin SUVs to more efficient vehicles. These developments had serious negative effects not just on Ford, but also on General Motors and Daimler Chrysler.

> **external view of leadership** situations in which external forces— where the leader has limited influence— determine the organization's success.

The point, of course, is that, while neither the romantic nor the external control perspective is entirely correct, we must acknowledge both in the study of strategic management. Our premise is that leaders can make a difference, but they must be constantly aware of the opportunities and threats that they face in the external environment and have a thorough understanding of their firm's resources and capabilities.

Clearly, the fortunes of the U.S. automobile manufacturers have declined in recent years. However, the Japanese automakers, led by Toyota and Honda, have been steadily gaining market share in the United States and have established a strong position in the rest of the world. According to some estimates, Toyota may become the world's biggest automotive company as early as 2009, unseating General Motors from the number one spot that it has occupied for more than 70 years. What explains the ascendancy of the Japanese companies? Consider four factors:

- They are miles ahead of their U.S. counterparts when it comes to fuel efficiency. Toyota's hybrid car, the Prius, already sells more than 170,000 units in the United States per year while the U.S. companies have no competing product. Gasoline prices are significantly higher in other countries compared to the United States. Therefore, the Japanese automakers' smaller and more fuel efficient vehicles have greater global appeal.

● An aerial view of the extensive damage caused by Hurricane Katrina taken the day after the hurricane hit (August 30, 2005).

- Despite recent improvements by U.S. auto companies, the Japanese manufacturers still lead in quality and reliability. This is based not only on customer perceptions but also on surveys by J. D. Power & Company, although the gap has narrowed in recent years.
- They have avoided the excessive product proliferation that reduces the effectiveness of the U.S. manufacturers.
- Their recently built manufacturing plants in the United States have lower healthcare and pension costs because of their younger workforce and few retirees.

Before moving on, we'd like to provide a rather dramatic example of the external control perspective at work. On August 29, 2005, Hurricane Katrina had a devastating impact with the loss of many lives and much property damage. Strategy Spotlight 1.1 shares some insights on how this natural disaster placed tremendous constraints on the influence that leaders had on their firms' performance in a variety of industries.

What Is Strategic Management?

Given the many challenges and opportunities in the global marketplace, today's managers must do more than set long-term strategies and hope for the best.[5] They must go beyond what some have called "incremental management," whereby they view their job as making a series of small, minor changes to improve the efficiency of their firm's operations.[6] That is fine if your firm is competing in a very stable, simple, and unchanging industry. But there aren't many of those left. As we shall discuss in this chapter and throughout the book, the pace of change is accelerating, and the pressure on managers to make both major and minor changes in a firm's strategic direction is increasing.

Rather than seeing their role as merely custodians of the status quo, today's leaders must be proactive, anticipate change, and continually refine and, when necessary, make dramatic changes to their strategies. The strategic management of the organization must become both a process and a way of thinking throughout the organization.

Defining Strategic Management

strategic management the analyses, decisions, and actions an organization undertakes in order to create and sustain competitive advantages.

Strategic management consists of the analyses, decisions, and actions an organization undertakes in order to create and sustain competitive advantages. This definition captures two main elements that go to the heart of the field of strategic management.

First, the strategic management of an organization entails three ongoing processes: *analyses, decisions,* and *actions.* That is, strategic management is concerned with the *analysis* of strategic goals (vision, mission, and strategic objectives) along with the analysis of

The Impact of Hurricane Katrina on Some Industries

August 29, 2005, Hurricane Katrina resulted in the loss of several thousands lives and hundreds of billions of dollars in lost property. Below, we discuss some of the industries that have been particularly hard hit and a few that will benefit.

- Immediately after the hurricane, lumber prices surged. Katrina devastated sawmills and plywood plants on the Gulf Coast and wiped out "vast inventories of wood products," according to one industry newsletter. Up to 1 million board feet of lumber on the docks of New Orleans was destroyed.

- Coffee futures soared. About 27 percent of all U.S. green coffee stocks, some 1.6 million 60 kilogram bags, were stored in New Orleans.

- The nation's breadbasket is also reeling. Katrina knocked out ports where grain-filled barges go upstream to be reloaded, pushing demand and prices up. One company, Colusa Elevator Company in Illinois (which has five grain elevators), has seen the price of corn soar from 42 cents per bushel to 71 cents.

- The tourist and convention business has been hard hit. The tourist business employs 84,300 people in New Orleans. Airlines have been forced to cancel flights, and hotels have halted bookings. Officials at the Omni Hotels in Irving, Texas (which owns two New Orleans hotels) canceled all reservations during the month following Katrina. And the convention business has suffered. The American Association of Retired Persons (AARP) which was scheduled to hold its annual meeting in late September in New Orleans was canceled. Registration had hit 25,000.

- Clearly, some industries will benefit once the rebuilding begins. "From a bank's perspective . . . it's good economically in the same paradoxical way that war is good economically for a lot of people," according to bank research analyst Eric Reinford of SNL Financial in Charlottesville, Virginia. "Natural disasters historically have been a boon for banks because they'll be lending and speeding up the processing of loans." Other big industry winners are construction companies and materials makers. The stocks of these companies soared immediately after Katrina hit.

Sources: Woellert, L., Palmeri, C., & Reed, S. 2005. Katrina's wake. *Business-Week*, September 12: 32–40; and, Lavelle, M. 2005. The (big) ripple effect. *U.S. News & World Report*, September 12: 33–35.

---

the internal and external environment of the organization. Next, leaders must make strategic decisions. These *decisions,* broadly speaking, address two basic questions: What industries should we compete in? How should we compete in those industries? These questions also often involve an organization's domestic as well as its international operations. And last are the *actions* that must be taken. Decisions are of little use, of course, unless they are acted on. Firms must take the necessary actions to implement their strategies. This requires leaders to allocate the necessary resources and to design the organization to bring the intended strategies to reality. As we will see in the next section, this is an ongoing, evolving process that requires a great deal of interaction among these three processes.

Second, the essence of strategic management is the study of why some firms outperform others.[7] Thus, managers need to determine how a firm is to compete so that it can obtain advantages that are sustainable over a lengthy period of time. That means focusing on two fundamental questions. First: *How should we compete in order to create competitive advantages in the marketplace?* For example, managers need to determine if the firm should position itself as the low-cost producer, develop products and services that are unique and will enable the firm to charge premium prices, or some combination of both.

Second, managers must ask how to make such advantages sustainable, instead of highly temporary, in the marketplace. That is: *How can we create competitive advantages in the marketplace that are not only unique and valuable but also difficult for competitors to copy or substitute?*[8,9]

Ideas that work are almost always copied by rivals immediately. In the 1980s, American Airlines tried to establish a competitive advantage by introducing the frequent flyer program. Within weeks, all the airlines did the same thing. Overnight, frequent flyer programs became a necessary tool for competitive parity instead of a competitive advantage. The challenge, therefore, is to create competitive advantages that are sustainable.

Michael Porter argues that sustainable competitive advantage cannot be achieved through operational effectiveness alone.[10] Most of the popular management innovations of the last two decades—total quality, just-in-time, benchmarking, business process reengineering, outsourcing—all are about operational effectiveness. **Operational effectiveness** means performing similar activities better than rivals. Each of these is important, but none lead to sustainable competitive advantage for the simple reason that everyone is doing them. Strategy is all about being different from everyone else. Sustainable competitive advantage is possible only through performing different activities from rivals or performing similar activities in different ways. Companies such as Wal-Mart, Southwest Airlines, and IKEA have developed unique, internally consistent, and difficult-to-imitate activity systems that have provided them with sustained competitive advantages. A company with a good strategy must make clear choices about what it wants to accomplish. Trying to do everything that your rivals do eventually leads to mutually destructive price competition, not long-term advantage.

operational effectiveness performing similar activities better than rivals.

The Four Key Attributes of Strategic Management

Before discussing the strategic management process in more detail, let's briefly talk about four attributes of strategic management.[11] In doing so, it will become clear how this course differs from other courses that you have had in functional areas, such as accounting, marketing, operations, and finance. Exhibit 1.1 provides a definition and the four attributes of strategic management.

First, strategic management is *directed toward overall organizational goals and objectives.* That is, effort must be directed at what is best for the total organization, not just a single functional area. Some authors have referred to this perspective as "organizational versus individual rationality."[12] That is, what might look "rational" or most appropriate for one functional area, such as operations, may not be in the best interest of the overall firm. For example, operations may decide to schedule long production runs of similar products in order to lower unit costs. However, the standardized output may be counter to what the marketing department needs in order to appeal to a sophisticated and demanding target market. Similarly, research and development may "overengineer" the product in order to develop a far superior offering, but the design may make the product so expensive that market demand is minimal. Therefore, in this course you will look at cases and strategic issues from the perspective of the organization

Exhibit 1.1

Strategic Management Concepts

Definition: Strategic management consists of the analyses, decisions, and actions an organization undertakes in order to create and sustain competitive advantages.

Key Attributes of Strategic Management

- Directs the organization toward overall goals and objectives.
- Includes multiple stakeholders in decision making.
- Needs to incorporate short-term and long-term perspectives.
- Recognizes trade-offs between efficiency and effectiveness.

rather than that of the functional area(s) in which you have had the most training and experience.

Second, strategic management *includes multiple stakeholders in decision making.* Managers must incorporate the demands of many stakeholders when making decisions.[13] **Stakeholders** are those individuals, groups, and organizations who have a "stake" in the success of the organization, including owners (shareholders in a publicly held corporation), employees, customers, suppliers, the community at large, and so on. We'll discuss this in more detail later in this chapter. Managers will not be successful if they continually focus on a single stakeholder. For example, if the overwhelming emphasis is on generating profits for the owners, employees may become alienated, customer service may suffer, and the suppliers may become resentful of continual demands for pricing concessions. As we will see, however, many organizations have been able to satisfy multiple stakeholder needs simultaneously. For example, financial performance may actually be greater because employees who are satisfied with their jobs make a greater effort to enhance customer satisfaction, thus leading to higher profits.

stakeholders individuals, groups, and organizations who have a stake in the success of the organization, including owners (shareholders in a publicly held corporation), employees, customers, suppliers, and the community at large.

Third, strategic management *requires incorporating both short-term and long-term perspectives.* Peter Senge, a leading strategic management author at the Massachusetts Institute of Technology, has referred to this need as a "creative tension."[14] That is, managers must maintain both a vision for the future of the organization as well as a focus on its present operating needs. However, financial markets can exert significant pressures on executives to meet short-term performance targets. Studies have shown that corporate leaders often take a short-term approach to the detriment of creating long-term shareholder value. Consider the following:

> According to recent studies, only 59 percent of financial executives say they would pursue a positive net present value project if it meant missing the quarter's consensus earnings per-share estimate. Worse, 78 percent say they would sacrifice value—often a great deal of value—to smooth earnings. Similarly, managers are more likely to cut R&D to reverse an earning slide if a significant amount of the company's equity is owned by institutions with high portfolio turnover. Many companies have the same philosophy about long-term investments such as infrastructure and employee training.[15]

Fourth, strategic management *involves the recognition of trade-offs between effectiveness and efficiency.* Closely related to the third point above, this recognition means being aware of the need for organizations to strive to act effectively and efficiently. Some authors have referred to this as the difference between "doing the right thing" **(effectiveness)** and "doing things right" **(efficiency)**.[16] While managers must allocate and use resources wisely, they must still direct their efforts toward the attainment of overall organizational objectives. Managers who are totally focused on meeting short-term budgets and targets may fail to attain the broader goals of the organization. Consider the following amusing story told by Norman Augustine, former CEO of defense giant, Martin Marietta (now Lockheed Martin):

effectiveness tailoring actions to the needs of an organization rather than wasting effort, or "doing the right thing."

> I am reminded of an article I once read in a British newspaper which described a problem with the local bus service between the towns of Bagnall and Greenfields. It seemed that, to the great annoyance of customers, drivers had been passing long queues of would-be passengers with a smile and a wave of the hand. This practice was, however, clarified by a bus company official who explained, "It is impossible for the drivers to keep their timetables if they must stop for passengers."[17]

efficiency performing actions at a low cost relative to a benchmark, or "doing things right."

Clearly, the drivers who were trying to stay on schedule had ignored the overall mission. As Augustine noted, "Impeccable logic but something seems to be missing!"

Successful managers must make many trade-offs. It is central to the practice of strategic management. At times, managers must focus on the short term and efficiency; at other times the emphasis is on the long term and expanding a firm's product-market scope in order to

Four Ambidextrous Behaviors: Combining Alignment and Adaptability

Julian Birkinshaw and Christina Gibson studied a wide variety of employees, ranging from senior executives to front-line workers. Their research was a collaboration of the University of Southern California, Booz Allen Hamilton, Inc., and the World Economic Forum. There were a total of 4,195 respondents from 41 business units in 10 multinational companies.

The research identified four ambidextrous behaviors in individuals:

They take the initiative and are alert to opportunities beyond the confines of their own jobs. For example, a regional sales manager for a large computer company, in discussions with one large client, became aware of the need for a new software module that no company currently offered. Rather than try to sell the client something else or just pass the lead on to the business development team, he took it upon himself to work up a business case for the new module. Once he received the go-ahead, he began working full time on the development of the product.

They are cooperative and seek out opportunities to combine their efforts with others. A large beverage company's marketing manager for Italy was primarily involved in supporting a newly acquired subsidiary. She was frustrated with the lack of contact she had with her peers in the other countries. Rather than wait for someone at headquarters to act, she began discussions with peers in other countries that led to the creation of a European marketing

forum. This group met quarterly to discuss issues, share best practices, and collaborate on the marketing plans.

They are brokers, always looking to build internal linkages. On a routine visit to the head office in St. Louis, a Canadian plant manager for a large consumer products company heard discussions about plans for a $10 million investment for a new tape manufacturing plant. He inquired further into these plans, and on his return to Canada, he called a regional manager in Manitoba, who he knew was looking for ways of building his business. With some generous support from the Manitoba government, the regional manager bid for, and ultimately won, the $10 million investment.

They are multitaskers who are comfortable wearing more than one hat. For example, the operations manager in France for a major coffee and tea distributor was initially charged with making the plant run as efficiently as possible. However, he took it upon himself to identify new value-added services for his clients. He developed a dual role for himself, managing operations four days a week and on the fifth day developing a promising electronic module that automatically reported impending problems inside a coffee vending machine. He arranged corporate funding, found a subcontractor to develop the software, and then piloted the module in his own operations. The module worked so well that operations managers in several other countries subsequently adopted it.

In summary, such ambidextrous behaviors encourage action that involves adaptation to new opportunities but is clearly aligned with the overall strategy of the business. Such behaviors are the essence of ambidexterity, and they illustrate how a dual capacity for alignment and adaptability can be woven into the fabric of an organization on the individual level.

anticipate opportunities in the competitive environment. For example, consider Kevin Sharer's perspective. He is CEO of Amgen, the giant $12 billion biotechnology firm:

> A CEO must always be switching between what I call different altitudes—tasks of different levels of abstraction and specificity. At the highest altitude you're asking the big questions: What are the company's mission and strategy? Do people understand and believe in these aims? Are decisions consistent with them? At the lowest altitude, you're looking at on-the-ground operations: Did we make that sale? What was the yield on that last lot in the factory? How many days of inventory do we have for a particular drug? And then there's everything in between: How many chemists do we need to hire this quarter? What should we pay for a small biotech company that has a promising new drug? Is our production capacity adequate to roll out a product in a new market?[18]

ambidexterity the challenge managers face of both aligning resources to take advantage of existing product markets as well as proactively exploring new opportunities.

Some authors have developed the concept of **"ambidexterity"** which refers to a manager's challenge to both align resources to take advantage of existing product markets as well as proactively explore new opportunities. Strategy Spotlight 1.2 discusses ambidextrous behaviors that are required for success in today's challenging marketplace.

The Strategic Management Process

>LO2
The strategic management process and its three interrelated and principal activities.

We've identified three ongoing processes—analyses, decisions, and actions—that are central to strategic management. In practice, these three processes—often referred to as strategy analysis, strategy formulation, and strategy implementation—are highly interdependent. Further, these three processes do not take place one after the other in a sequential fashion in most companies.

Intended versus Realized Strategies

Henry Mintzberg, a very influential management scholar at McGill University, argues that conceptualizing the strategic management process as one in which analysis is followed by optimal decisions and their subsequent meticulous implementation neither describes the strategic management process accurately nor prescribes ideal practice.[19] In his view, the business environment is far from predictable, thus limiting our ability for analysis. Further, decisions in an organization are seldom based on optimal rationality alone, given the political processes that occur in all organizations.

Taking into consideration the limitations discussed above, Mintzberg proposed an alternative model of strategy development. As depicted in Exhibit 1.2, decisions following from analysis, in this model, constitute the ***intended* strategy** of the firm. For a variety of reasons, the intended strategy rarely survives in its original form. Unforeseen environmental developments, unanticipated resource constraints, or changes in managerial preferences may result in at least some parts of the intended strategy remaining *unrealized*. On the other hand, good managers will want to take advantage of a new opportunity presented by the environment, even if it was not part of the original set of intentions. For example, consider the wind energy industry.[20] In September 2004 the United States Congress renewed the wind tax credit. Legislation in 19 states now requires that electricity providers offer a certain percentage of "green" (i.e., renewable) energy. Such legislation, combined with falling clean energy costs and rising prices for coal, oil, and gas, have created a surge in demand for competitors such as GE Wind Energy, which makes large turbines and fan blades. Not surprisingly, such businesses have increased hiring and research and development, as well as revenue and profit forecasts. The final ***realized* strategy** of any firm is thus a combination of *deliberate* and *emergent* strategies.

In the next three subsections, we will address each of the three key strategic management processes: strategy analysis, strategy formulation, and strategy implementation.

Exhibit 1.3 depicts the strategic management process and indicates how it ties into the chapters in the book. Consistent with our discussion above, we use two-way arrows to convey the interactive nature of the processes.

intended strategy
strategy in which organizational decisions are determined only by analysis.

realized strategy
strategy in which organizational decisions are determined by both analysis and unforeseen environmental developments, unanticipated resource constraints, and/or changes in managerial preferences.

Exhibit 1.2 **Realized Strategy and Intended Strategy: Usually Not the Same**

Source: From Mintzberg, H. & Waters, J. A., "Of Strategies: Deliberate and Emergent," *Strategic Management Journal*, Vol. 6, 1985, pp. 257–272. Copyright © John Wiley & Sons Limited. Reproduced with permission.

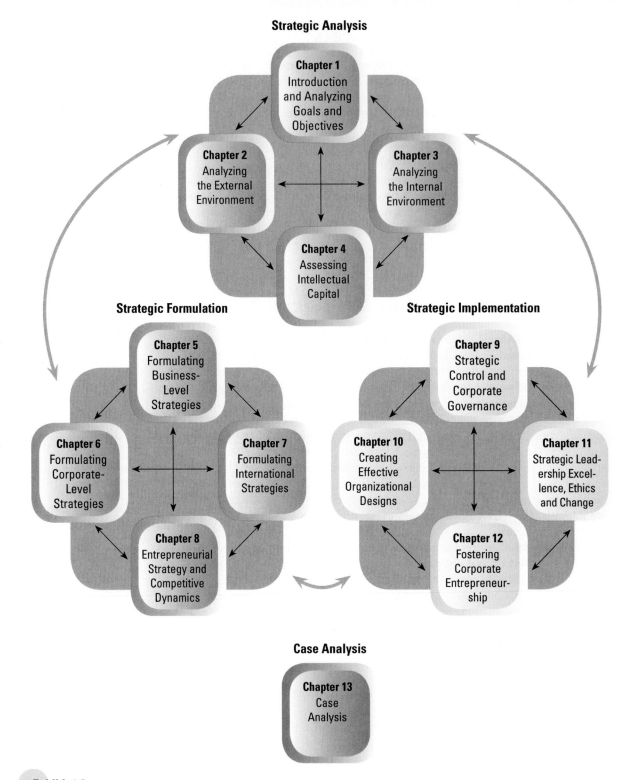

Strategic Analysis

Chapter 1
Introduction and Analyzing Goals and Objectives

Chapter 2
Analyzing the External Environment

Chapter 3
Analyzing the Internal Environment

Chapter 4
Assessing Intellectual Capital

Strategic Formulation

Chapter 5
Formulating Business-Level Strategies

Chapter 6
Formulating Corporate-Level Strategies

Chapter 7
Formulating International Strategies

Chapter 8
Entrepreneurial Strategy and Competitive Dynamics

Strategic Implementation

Chapter 9
Strategic Control and Corporate Governance

Chapter 10
Creating Effective Organizational Designs

Chapter 11
Strategic Leadership Excellence, Ethics and Change

Chapter 12
Fostering Corporate Entrepreneurship

Case Analysis

Chapter 13
Case Analysis

Exhibit 1.3 The Strategic Management Process

Strategy Analysis

Strategy analysis may be looked upon as the starting point of the strategic management process. It consists of the "advance work" that must be done in order to effectively formulate and implement strategies. Many strategies fail because managers may want to formulate and implement strategies without a careful analysis of the overarching goals of the organization and without a thorough analysis of its external and internal environment.

Analyzing Organizational Goals and Objectives (Chapter 1)   Later in this chapter, we will address how organizations must have clearly articulated goals and objectives in order to channel the efforts of individuals throughout the organization toward common ends. Goals and objectives also provide a means of allocating resources effectively. A firm's vision, mission, and strategic objectives form a hierarchy of goals that range from broad statements of intent and bases for competitive advantage to specific, measurable strategic objectives.

As indicated in Exhibit 1.3, this hierarchy of goals is not developed in isolation. Rather, it is developed in concert with a rigorous understanding of the opportunities and threats in the external environment (Chapter 2) as well as a thorough understanding of the firm's strengths and weaknesses (Chapters 3 and 4).

Analyzing the External Environment of the Firm (Chapter 2)   Managers must monitor and scan the environment as well as analyze competitors. Such information is critical in determining the opportunity and threats in the external environment. Two frameworks of the external environment are provided. First, the general environment consists of several elements, such as demographic, technological, and economic segments, from which key trends and events can have a dramatic impact on the firm. Second, the industry environment consists of competitors and other organizations that may threaten the success of a firm's products and services.

Assessing the Internal Environment of the Firm (Chapter 3)   Useful frameworks are provided to identify both strengths and weaknesses that can, in part, determine how well a firm will succeed in an industry. Analyzing the strengths and relationships among the activities that constitute a firm's value chain (e.g., operations, marketing and sales, and human resource management) can be a means of uncovering potential sources of competitive advantage for the firm.

Assessing a Firm's Intellectual Assets (Chapter 4)   The knowledge worker and a firm's other intellectual assets (e.g., patents, trademarks) are becoming increasingly important as the drivers of competitive advantages and wealth creation. In addition to human capital, we assess how well the organization creates networks and relationships among its employees as well as its customers, suppliers, and alliance partners. Further, technology can enhance collaboration among employees as well as provide a means of accumulating and storing knowledge.

Strategy Formulation

A firm's strategy formulation is developed at several levels. First, business-level strategy addresses the issue of how to compete in a given business to attain competitive advantage. Second, corporate-level strategy focuses on two issues: (a) what businesses to compete in and (b) how businesses can be managed to achieve synergy; that is, they create more value by working together than if they operate as stand-alone businesses. Third, a firm must determine the best method to develop international strategies as it ventures beyond its national boundaries. Fourth, managers must formulate effective entrepreneurial initiatives to succeed in highly competitive and dynamic environments.

Formulating Business-Level Strategy (Chapter 5)   The question of how firms compete and outperform their rivals and how they achieve and sustain competitive advantages goes to the heart of strategic management. Successful firms strive to develop bases for competitive advantage, which can be achieved through cost leadership and/or differentiation as well as by focusing on a narrow or industrywide market segment. We'll also discuss why some advantages can be more sustainable (or durable) over time and how a firm's business-level strategy changes with the industry life cycle—that is, the stages of introduction, growth, maturity, and decline.

Formulating Corporate-Level Strategy (Chapter 6)   Corporate-level strategy addresses a firm's portfolio (or group) of businesses, asking (1) What business (or businesses) should we compete in? and (2) How can we manage this portfolio of businesses to create synergies among the businesses? We explore the relative advantages and disadvantages of firms pursuing strategies of related or unrelated diversification. We also discuss the various means that firms can employ to diversify—internal development, mergers and acquisitions, and joint ventures and strategic alliances—as well as their relative advantages and disadvantages.

Formulating International Strategy (Chapter 7)   When firms enter foreign markets, they face both opportunities and pitfalls. Managers must decide not only on the most appropriate entry strategy but also how they will go about attaining competitive advantages in international markets. Many successful international firms have been able to attain both lower costs and higher levels of differentiated products and services via a "transnational strategy."

Entrepreneurial Strategy and Competitive Dynamics (Chapter 8)   Entrepreneurial activity aimed at new value creation is a major engine for economic growth. For entrepreneurial initiatives to succeed viable opportunities must be recognized and effective strategies must be formulated. Actions by new, entrepreneurial entrants threaten existing players and evoke competitive responses designed to maintain a strong competitive position. Such competitively dynamic environments provide both opportunities and significant challenges for entrepreneurial firms.

Strategy Implementation

Clearly, sound strategies are of no value if they are not properly implemented. Strategy implementation involves ensuring proper strategic controls and organizational designs, which includes establishing effective means to coordinate and integrate activities within the firm as well as with its suppliers, customers, and alliance partners. Leadership plays a central role, including ensuring that the organization is committed to excellence and ethical behavior. It also promotes learning and continuous improvement and acts entrepreneurially in creating and taking advantage of new opportunities.

Strategic Control and Corporate Governance (Chapter 9)   Firms must exercise two types of strategic control. First, informational control requires that organizations continually monitor and scan the environment and respond to threats and opportunities. Second, behavioral control involves the proper balance of rewards and incentives as well as cultures and boundaries (or constraints). Further, successful firms (those that are incorporated) practice effective corporate governance. They must create mechanisms to ensure that the actions of the managers are consistent with the interests of the owners (shareholders) of the firm. These include an effective board of directors, actively engaged shareholders, and proper managerial reward and incentive systems. Various external mechanisms such as the market for corporate control, auditors, banks, analysts, and the financial press often help to ensure good governance.

Creating Effective Organizational Designs (Chapter 10)   To succeed, firms must have organizational structures and designs that are consistent with their strategy. For example, firms that diversify into related product-market areas typically decentralize decision making by implementing divisional structures. In today's rapidly changing competitive environments, firms must ensure that their organizational boundaries—those internal to the firm and external—are more flexible and permeable. Often, organizations develop strategic alliances to capitalize on the capabilities of other organizations.

Creating a Learning Organization and an Ethical Organization (Chapter 11)
Effective leaders set a direction, design the organization, and develop an organization that is committed to excellence and ethical behavior. In addition, given rapid and unpredictable change, leaders must create a "learning organization." This ensures that the entire organization can benefit from individual and collective talents.

Fostering Corporate Entrepreneurship (Chapter 12) With rapid and unpredictable change in the global marketplace, firms must continually improve and grow as well as find new ways to renew their organizations. Corporate entrepreneurship and innovation provide firms with new opportunities, and strategies should be formulated that enhance a firm's innovative capacity. Within corporations, proactiveness and autonomous entrepreneurial behavior by product champions and other organizational members are needed to turn new ideas into corporate ventures.

We've discussed the strategic management process. In addition, Chapter 13, "Analyzing Strategic Management Cases," provides guidelines and suggestions on how to evaluate cases in this course. Thus, the concepts and techniques discussed in these 12 chapters can be applied to real-world organizations.

Let's now address two concepts—corporate governance and stakeholder management—that are critical to the strategic management process.

The Role of Corporate Governance and Stakeholder Management

>LO3
The vital role of corporate governance and stakeholder management as well as how "symbiosis" can be achieved among an organization's stakeholders.

Most business enterprises that employ more than a few dozen people are organized as corporations. As you recall from your finance classes, the overall purpose of a corporation is to maximize the long-term return to the owners (shareholders). Thus, we may ask: Who is really responsible for fulfilling this purpose? Robert Monks and Neil Minow, in addressing this issue, provide a useful definition of **corporate governance** as "the relationship among various participants in determining the direction and performance of corporations. The primary participants are (1) the shareholders, (2) the management (led by the chief executive officer), and (3) the board of directors."[21] This relationship is illustrated in Exhibit 1.4.

corporate governance the relationship among various participants in determining the direction and performance of corporations. The primary participants are (1) the shareholders, (2) the management (led by the chief executive officer), and (3) the board of directors.

Management
(Headed by the chief executive officer)

Shareholders
(Owners)

Board of Directors
(Elected by the shareholders to represent their interests)

Exhibit 1.4 The Key Elements of Corporate Governance

The board of directors (BOD) are the elected representatives of the shareholders. They are charged with ensuring that the interests and motives of management are aligned with those of the owners (i.e., shareholders). In many cases, the BOD is diligent in fulfilling its purpose. For example, Intel Corporation, the giant $35 billion maker of microprocessor chips, is widely recognized as an excellent example of sound governance practices. Its BOD has established guidelines to ensure that its members are independent (i.e., not members of the executive management team and do not have close personal ties to top executives) so that they can provide proper oversight, it has explicit guidelines on the selection of director candidates (to avoid "cronyism"), and it provides detailed procedures for formal evaluations of both directors and the firm's top officers.[22] Such guidelines serve to ensure that management is acting in the best interests of shareholders.[23]

Recently, there has been much criticism as well as cynicism by both citizens and the business press about the poor job that management and the BODs of large corporations are doing. We only have to look at the recent scandals at firms such as Arthur Andersen, WorldCom, Enron, Tyco, and ImClone Systems.[24] Such malfeasance has led to an erosion of the public's trust in the governance of corporations. For example, a recent Gallup poll found that 90 percent of Americans felt that people leading corporations could not be trusted to look after the interests of their employees, and only 18 percent thought that corporations looked after their shareholders. Forty-three percent, in fact, believed that senior executives were in it only for themselves. In Britain, that figure, according to another poll, was an astonishing 95 percent.[25] Perhaps worst of all, in another study, 60 percent of directors (the very people who decide how much executives should earn) felt that executives were "dramatically overpaid"![26]

To drive home the point, consider the humorous perspective of Russell T. Lewis, CEO of the New York Times Company, in a recent speech:[27]

> Not long ago, CEOs were regarded as captains of industry—among the country's best and brightest talents—at least that's what I've been telling my parents, and they seem to have bought the line. Today, however, CEOs and their CFOs are highly reviled defendants in felony criminal proceedings. And their companies are the subjects of billion-dollar shareholder lawsuits. Things have gotten so bad that any day now I expect *Fortune* magazine to come out with its list of "Most Wanted CEOs." No doubt this will soon be followed by a spin-off of a popular TV program. I can see the promo now: "Tonight at 8 PM—Help us catch America's Most Wanted CEOs . . . they could be hiding in our hometown."
>
> But, folks, the final indignity for this particular CEO concerns my own parents: my loving 87-year-old mother—a former public school teacher and my unfailingly supportive 94-year-old father. They no longer brag about me to the clerks at the Lake Worth, Florida, Publix supermarket. Yes, folks, it has gotten that bad.

Clearly, there is a strong need for improved corporate governance, and we will address this topic in Chapter 9. We focus on three important mechanisms to ensure effective corporate governance: an effective and engaged board of directors, shareholder activism, and proper managerial rewards and incentives.[28] In addition to these internal controls, a key role is played by various external control mechanisms.[29] These include the auditors, banks, analysts, an active financial press, and the threat of hostile takeovers.

Zero Sum or Symbiosis? Two Alternate Perspectives of Stakeholder Management

Generating long-term returns for the shareholders is the primary goal of a publicly held corporation. As noted by former Chrysler vice chairman Robert Lutz, "We are here to serve the shareholder and create shareholder value. I insist that the only person who owns the company is the person who paid good money for it."[30]

Stakeholder Group	Nature of Claim
Stockholders	Dividends, capital appreciation
Employees	Wages, benefits, safe working environment, job security
Suppliers	Payment on time, assurance of continued relationship
Creditors	Payment of interest, repayment of principal
Customers	Value, warranties
Government	Taxes, compliance with regulations
Communities	Good citizenship behavior such as charities, employment, not polluting the environment

Exhibit 1.5
An Organization's Key Stakeholders and the Nature of Their Claims

Despite the primacy of generating shareholder value, managers who focus solely on the interests of the owners of the business will often make poor decisions that lead to negative, unanticipated outcomes. For example, decisions such as mass layoffs to increase profits, ignoring issues related to conservation of the natural environment to save money, and exerting excessive pressure on suppliers to lower prices can certainly harm the firm in the long run. Such actions would likely lead to negative outcomes such as alienated employees, increased governmental oversight and fines, and disloyal suppliers.

Clearly, in addition to *shareholders,* there are other *stakeholders* (e.g. suppliers, customers) who must be explicitly taken into account in the strategic management process.[31] A stakeholder can be defined as an individual or group, inside or outside the company, that has a stake in and can influence an organization's performance. Each stakeholder group makes various claims on the company. Exhibit 1.5 provides a list of major stakeholder groups and the nature of their claims on the company.

There are two opposing ways of looking at the role of stakeholder management in the strategic management process.[32] The first one can be termed "zero sum." In this view, the role of management is to look upon the various stakeholders as competing for the organization's resources. In essence, the gain of one individual or group is the loss of another individual or group. For example, employees want higher wages (which drive down profits), suppliers want higher prices for their inputs and slower, more flexible delivery times (which drive up costs), customers want fast deliveries and higher quality (which drive up costs), the community at large wants charitable contributions (which take money from company goals), and so on. This zero-sum thinking is rooted, in part, in the traditional conflict between workers and management, leading to the formation of unions and sometimes ending in adversarial union–management negotiations and long, bitter strikes.

Although there will always be some conflicting demands, there is value in exploring how the organization can achieve mutual benefit through *stakeholder symbiosis,* which recognizes that stakeholders are dependent upon each other for their success and well-being.[33] That is, managers acknowledge the interdependence among employees, suppliers, customers, shareholders, and the community at large. Consider Outback Steakhouse:[34]

Outback Steakhouse asked their employees to identify on a six-point scale how strongly they agreed or disagreed that Outback's principles and beliefs (P&Bs) were practiced in their particular restaurants. The turnover rate of the hourly employees in the group most strongly agreeing that the P&Bs were their stores' guiding ethos was half what it was in the group most strongly disagreeing. Five times as many customers in the strongly agreeing group indicated that they were likely to return. Further, at the strongly agreeing group's restaurants, revenues were 8.9 percent higher, cash flow was 27 percent higher, and pretax profit was 48 percent higher. Not surprisingly, it is now mandatory that Outback managers conduct this survey.

Social Responsibility and Environmental Sustainability: Moving beyond the Immediate Stakeholders

Organizations cannot ignore the interests and demands of stakeholders such as citizens and society in general that are beyond its immediate constituencies—customers, owners, suppliers, and employees. That is, they must consider the needs of the broader community at large and act in a socially responsible manner.[35]

social responsibility
the expectation that businesses or individuals will strive to improve the overall welfare of society.

Social responsibility is the expectation that businesses or individuals will strive to improve the overall welfare of society.[36] From the perspective of a business, this means that managers must take active steps to make society better by virtue of the business being in existence.[37] Similar to norms and values, actions that constitute socially responsible behavior tend to change over time. In the 1970s affirmative action was a high priority and during the 1990s and up to the present time, the public has been concerned about environmental quality. Many firms have responded to this by engaging in recycling and reducing waste. And in the wake of terrorist attacks on New York City and the Pentagon, as well as the continuing threat from terrorists worldwide, a new kind of priority has arisen: the need to be vigilant concerning public safety.

>LO4
The importance of social responsibility, including environmental sustainability, and how it can enhance a corporation's innovation strategy.

Today, demands for greater corporate responsibility have accelerated.[38] These include corporate critics, social investors, activists, and, increasingly, customers who claim to assess corporate responsibility when making purchasing decisions. Such demands go well beyond product and service quality.[39] They include a focus on issues such as labor standards, environmental sustainability, financial and accounting reporting, procurement, and environmental practices. At times, a firm's reputation can be tarnished by exceedingly poor judgment on the part of one of its managers.

> In 2006, Judith Regan, a publisher at HarperCollins, was set to publish a book by O. J. Simpson called *If I Did It,* detailing how he would have committed the 1995 murder of his ex-wife Nicole Brown Simpson and her friend, Ron Goldman. The book was characterized by Regan as O. J.'s "confession," and it earned the world's outrage as an "evil sweeps stunt" that will likely be remembered as a low point in American culture. Regan's boss, News Corporation Chairman Rupert Murdoch cancelled the book and the TV special that was also planned. But this was not before pre-orders for *If I Did It* cracked the Top 20 on Amazon.com. Not surprisingly, Judith Regan was fired.[40]

A key stakeholder group that appears to be particularly susceptible to corporate social responsibility (CSR) initiatives is its customers.[41] Surveys indicate a strong positive relationship between CSR behaviors and consumers' reactions to a firm's products and services. For example:

- Corporate Citizenship's poll conducted by Cone Communications found that "84 percent of Americans say they would be likely to switch brands to one associated with a good cause, if price and quality are similar."[42]
- Hill & Knowlton/Harris's Interactive poll reveals that "79 percent of Americans take corporate citizenship into account when deciding whether to buy a particular company's product and 37 percent consider corporate citizenship an important factor when making purchasing decisions."[43]

Such findings are consistent with a large body of research that confirms the positive influence of CSR on consumers' company evaluations and product purchase intentions across a broad range of product categories.

Cause-related marketing is another example of the growing link between corporate social responsibility and financial objectives. Such marketing generally features promotions in which a portion of the purchase price of a product or service is donated to a social cause: It essentially links marketing and corporate philanthropy. Strategy Spotlight 1.3 discusses how American Express became one of the pioneers of this emerging trend and significantly benefited.

American Express: Using Cause-Related Marketing Effectively

American Express (AmEx) has benefited from favorable public relations, and financially, from its cause-related marketing initiatives. Back in 1983, in connection with the restoration of the Statue of Liberty project, it promised that it would contribute to this initiative a portion of the amount that consumers charged on their American Express cards. The resulting campaign made marketing history. It eventually donated $1.7 million to the cause. But AmEx card use increased 28 percent and new card applications increased 17 percent. Cause-related marketing has grown significantly from $125 million in 1990 to $991 million in 2004, and the figure is expected to continue to increase.

According to a recent Cone Corporate Citizenship Study, cause-related marketing can both reinforce consumer relationships as well as strengthen employee morale. For example, 84 percent of respondents said they would like to switch brands to one associated with a good cause, and 92 percent of Americans said that they have a more positive image of companies and products that support good causes. Similarly, 57 percent of employees wish that their company would do more to support a social issue, and 75 percent of Americans would consider a company's commitment to social issues when deciding where to work.

Sources: Vogel, D. J. 2005. Is there a market for virtue? The business case for corporate social responsibility. *California Management Review,* 47(4): 19–36; 2002 Cone Corporate Citizenship Study, Cone, Inc.

The Triple Bottom Line: Incorporating Financial as well as Environmental and Social Costs   Many companies are now measuring what has been called a **"triple bottom line,"** which involves assessing financial, social, and environmental performance. Shell, NEC, and Procter & Gamble, among other corporations, have recognized that failing to account for the environmental and social costs of doing business poses risks to the company and its community.[44]

The environmental revolution has been almost four decades in the making.[45] It has changed forever how companies do business. In the 1960s and 1970s, companies were in a state of denial regarding their firms' impact on the natural environment. However, a series of visible ecological problems created a groundswell for strict governmental regulation. In the United States, Lake Erie was "dead," and in Japan, people were dying of mercury poisoning. Clearly, the effects of global warming are being felt throughout the world. Some other examples include the following:

- Ice roads are melting, so Canadian diamond miners must airlift equipment at great cost instead of trucking it in.
- More severe storms and rising seas mean oil companies must build stronger rigs, and cities must build higher seawalls.
- The loss of permafrost and protective sea ice may force villages like Alaska's Shismaref to relocate.
- Yukon River salmon and fisheries are threatened by a surge of parasites associated with a jump in water temperature.

● Solar cells can be organized into arrays, such as this one, to provide electric power for industrial, commercial, and residential customers. Solar power is a more sustainable, environmentally friendly option than nuclear power plants or coal- and oil-fired power plants.

triple bottom line
the assessment of
a company's
performance in
financial, social, and
environmental
dimensions.

- Later winters have let beetles spread in British Columbia killing 22 million acres of pine forests, an area the size of Maine.
- In Mali, Africa, crops are threatened. The rainy season is now too short for rice, and the dry season is too hot for potatoes.[46]

Stuart Hart, writing in the *Harvard Business Review*, addresses the magnitude of problems and challenges associated with the natural environment:

> The challenge is to develop a *sustainable global economy:* an economy that the planet is capable of supporting indefinitely. Although we may be approaching ecological recovery in the developed world, the planet as a whole remains on an unsustainable course. Increasingly, the scourges of the late twentieth century—depleted farmland, fisheries, and forests; choking urban pollution; poverty; infectious disease; and migration—are spilling over geopolitical borders. The simple fact is this: in meeting our needs, we are destroying the ability of future generations to meet theirs . . . corporations are the only organizations with the resources, the technology, the global reach, and, ultimately, the motivation to achieve sustainability.[47]

Environmental sustainability is now a value embraced by the most competitive and successful multinational companies.[48] The McKinsey Corporation's survey of more than 400 senior executives of companies around the world found that 92 percent agreed with former Sony President Akio Morita's contention that the environmental challenge will be one of the central issues in the 21st century.[49] Virtually all executives acknowledged their firm's responsibility to control pollution, and 83 percent agreed that corporations have an environmental responsibility for their products even after they are sold.

For many successful firms, environmental values are now becoming a central part of their cultures and management processes. And, as noted earlier, environmental impacts are being audited and accounted for as the "third bottom line." According to one 2004 corporate report, "If we aren't good corporate citizens as reflected in a Triple Bottom Line that takes into account social and environmental responsibilities along with financial ones—eventually our stock price, our profits, and our entire business could suffer."[50] And, according to a KPMG study of 350 firms: "More big multinational firms are seeing the benefits of improving their environmental performance. . . . Firms are saving money and boosting share performance by taking a close look at how their operations impact the environment . . . Companies see that they can make money as well." Strategy Spotlight 1.4 discusses how Adobe Systems benefits financially from its environmental initiatives.

The Strategic Management Perspective: An Imperative throughout the Organization

>LO5
The need for greater
empowerment
throughout the
organization.

Strategic management requires managers to take an integrative view of the organization and assess how all of the functional areas and activities fit together to help an organization achieve its goals and objectives. This cannot be accomplished if only the top managers in the organization take an integrative, strategic perspective of issues facing the firm and everyone else "fends for themselves" in their independent, isolated functional areas. Marketing and sales will generally favor broad, tailor-made product lines, production will demand standardized products that are relatively easy to make in order to lower manufacturing costs, research and development will design products to demonstrate technical elegance, and so on. Instead, people throughout the organization must strive toward overall goals.

The need for such a perspective is accelerating in today's increasingly complex, interconnected, ever-changing, global economy. As noted by Peter Senge of MIT, the days when

How Adobe Systems Benefits from "Being Green"

In June 2006, Adobe Systems, the $2 billion software maker, became the first firm to receive a platinum award from the nonprofit U.S. Green Building Council. Platinum certification of Adobe's buildings was based on ratings in six categories: sustainability; water efficiency; energy efficiency and atmospheric quality; use of materials and resources; indoor environmental quality; and innovations in upgrades, operations, and maintenance.

Thus, Adobe's San Jose headquarters is the greenest corporate site on record in the United States. What is more impressive is that Adobe earned the honor by retrofitting its two existing office towers (approximately 1 million square feet). Most of the 151 buildings that have received the council's gold ratings (a "step" down from platinum) are new structures.

By installing everything from motion detectors to waterless urinals, the firm has reduced its electricity use by 35 percent and its gas consumption by 41 percent since 2001. In addition, it conserves 295,000 gallons of water each month. And, during this time, the company's headcount has shot up 80 percent!

Adobe is proving that building "green" isn't just good citizenship—it is profitable. Adobe has invested approximately $650,000 for energy and environmental retrofits since 2001. The retrofits on the two office towers have resulted in approximately $720,000 in savings to date, for a total return on investment of approximately 115 percent. Randy Knox III, Adobe's director of real estate, facilities, and security, comments, "This isn't some pie-in-the-sky kind of thing the enviros are pushing. It really works."

Sources: Nachtigal, J. 2006. It's easy and cheap being green. *BusinessWeek,* October 16: 53; Warner, J. 2006. Adobe headquarters awarded highest honors from U.S. green building council. *Adobe Press Release,* December 6; and, Juran, K. 2006. Adobe wins top California Flex Your Power! Award for energy efficiency. *Adobe Press Release,* July 3.

Henry Ford, Alfred Sloan, and Tom Watson (top executives at Ford, General Motors, and IBM, respectively) "learned for the organization are gone." He goes on to say:

> In an increasingly dynamic, interdependent, and unpredictable world, it is simply no longer possible for anyone to "figure it all out at the top." The old model, "the top thinks and the local acts," must now give way to integrating thinking and acting at all levels. While the challenge is great, so is the potential payoff. "The person who figures out how to harness the collective genius of the people in his or her organization," according to former Citibank CEO Walter Wriston, "is going to blow the competition away."[51]

Managers need to anticipate and respond to dramatic and unpredictable changes in the competitive environment. With the emergence of the knowledge economy, human capital (as opposed to financial and physical assets) has become the key to securing advantages in the marketplace that persist over time.

To develop and mobilize people and other assets, leaders are needed throughout the organization.[52] No longer can organizations be effective if the top "does the thinking" and the rest of the organization "does the work." Everyone must be involved in the strategic management process. There is a critical need for three types of leaders:

- Local line leaders who have significant profit-and-loss responsibility.
- Executive leaders who champion and guide ideas, create a learning infrastructure, and establish a domain for taking action.
- Internal networkers who, although they have little positional power and formal authority, generate their power through the conviction and clarity of their ideas.[53]

Sally Helgesen, author of *The Web of Inclusion: A New Architecture for Building Great Organizations,* also expressed the need for leaders throughout the organization. She asserted that many organizations "fall prey to the heroes-and-drones syndrome, exalting the value of those in powerful positions while implicitly demeaning the contributions of those who fail to achieve top rank."[54] Culture and processes in which leaders emerge at all levels, both up and down as well as across the organization, typify today's high-performing firms.[55]

Top-level executives are key in setting the tone for the empowerment of employees. Consider Richard Branson, founder of the Virgin Group, whose core businesses include retail operations, hotels, communications, and an airline. He is well known for creating a culture and an informal structure where anybody in the organization can be involved in generating and acting upon new business ideas. In an interview, he stated,

> [S]peed is something that we are better at than most companies. We don't have formal board meetings, committees, etc. If someone has an idea, they can pick up the phone and talk to me. I can vote "done, let's do it." Or, better still, they can just go ahead and do it. They know that they are not going to get a mouthful from me if they make a mistake. Rules and regulations are not our forte. Analyzing things to death is not our kind of thing. We very rarely sit back and analyze what we do.[56]

To inculcate a strategic management perspective throughout the organization, many large traditional organizations must often make a major effort to effect transformational change. This involves extensive communication, incentives, training, and development to strengthen a strategic perspective throughout the organization. For example, under the direction of Nancy Snyder, a corporate vice president, Whirlpool, the world's largest producer of household appliances, brought about a significant shift in the firm's reputation as an innovator.[57] This five-year initiative included both financial investments in capital spending as well as a series of changes in management processes, including training innovation mentors, making innovation a significant portion of leadership development programs, enrolling all salaried employees in online courses in business innovation, and providing employees with an innovation portal that allows them access to multiple innovation tools and data. We discuss Whirlpool's initiatives in more detail in Chapter 11.

We'd like to close with our favorite example of how inexperience can be a virtue. It further reinforces the benefits of having broad involvement throughout the organization in the strategic management process (see Strategy Spotlight 1.5)

>LO6

How an awareness of a hierarchy of strategic goals can help an organization achieve coherence in its strategic direction.

Ensuring Coherence in Strategic Direction

Employees and managers throughout the organization must strive toward common goals and objectives. By specifying desired results, it becomes much easier to move forward. Otherwise, when no one knows what the firm is striving to accomplish, they have no idea of what to work toward. As the old nautical expression puts it, "No wind favors the ship that has no charted course."

hierarchy of goals organizational goals ranging from, at the top, those that are less specific yet able to evoke powerful and compelling mental images, to, at the bottom, those that are more specific and measurable.

Organizations express priorities best through stated goals and objectives that form a **hierarchy of goals,** which includes its vision, mission, and strategic objectives. What visions may lack in specificity, they make up for in their ability to evoke powerful and compelling mental images. On the other hand, strategic objectives tend to be more specific and provide a more direct means of determining if the organization is moving toward broader, overall goals.[58] Visions, as one would expect, also have longer time horizons than either mission statements or strategic objectives. Exhibit 1.6 depicts the hierarchy of goals and its relationship to two attributes: general versus specific and time horizon.

Organizational Vision

vision organizational goal(s) that evoke(s) powerful and compelling mental images.

A **vision** is a goal that is "massively inspiring, overarching, and long term."[59] It represents a destination that is driven by and evokes passion. A vision may or may not succeed; it depends on whether everything else happens according to a firm's strategy. As Mark Hurd, Hewlett-Packard's CEO, humorously pointed out, "Without execution, vision is just another word for hallucination."[60]

1.5 strategy spotlight

Strategy and the Value of Inexperience

Peter Gruber, chairman of Mandalay Entertainment, explained how his firm benefited from the creative insights of an inexperienced intern.

Sometimes life is all about solving problems. In the movie business, at least, there seems to be one around every corner. One of the most effective lessons I've learned about tackling problems is to start by asking not "How to?" but rather "What if?" I learned that lesson from a young woman who was interning on a film I was producing. She actually saved the movie from being shelved by the studio.

The movie, *Gorillas in the Mist,* had turned into a logistical nightmare. We wanted to film at an altitude of 11,000 feet, in the middle of the jungle, in Rwanda—then on the verge of a revolution—and to use more than 200 animals. Warner Brothers, the studio financing the movie, worried that we would exceed our budget. But our biggest problem was that the screenplay required the gorillas to do what we wrote—in other words, to "act." If they couldn't or wouldn't, we'd have to fall back on a formula that the studio had seen fail before: using dwarfs in gorilla suits on a soundstage.

Source: Gruber, P. 1998. My greatest lesson. *Fast Company* 15: 88, 90.

We called an emergency meeting to solve these problems. In the middle of it, a young intern asked, "What if you let the gorillas write the story?" Everyone laughed and wondered what she was doing in the meeting with experienced filmmakers. Hours later, someone casually asked her what she had meant. She said, "What if you sent a really good cinematographer into the jungle with a ton of film to shoot the gorillas. Then you could write a story around what the gorillas did on film." It was a brilliant idea. And we did exactly what she suggested: We sent Alan Root, an Academy Award–nominated cinematographer, into the jungle for three weeks. He came back with phenomenal footage that practically wrote the story for us. We shot the film for $20 million—half of the original budget!

This woman's inexperience enabled her to see opportunities where we saw only boundaries. This experience taught me three things. First, ask high-quality questions, like "What if?" Second, find people who add new perspectives and create new conversations. As experienced filmmakers, we believed that our way was the only way—and that the intern lacked the experience to have an opinion. Third, pay attention to those with new voices. If you want unlimited options for solving a problem, engage the what if before you lock onto the how to. You'll be surprised by what you discover.

Leaders must develop and implement a vision. In a survey of 1,500 senior leaders, 870 of them CEOs from 20 different countries, respondents were asked what they believed were a leader's key traits. Ninety-eight percent responded that "a strong sense of vision" was the most important. Similarly, when asked about the critical knowledge skills, the leaders cited "strategy formulation to achieve a vision" as the most important skill. In other words, managers need to have not only a vision but also a plan to implement it. Regretfully, 90 percent reported a lack of confidence in their own skills and ability to conceive a vision. For example, T. J. Rogers, CEO of Cypress Semiconductor, an electronic chipmaker that

Exhibit 1.6 A Hierarchy of Goals

faced some difficulties in 1992, lamented that his own shortsightedness caused the danger, "I did not have the 50,000-foot view, and got caught."[61]

One of the most famous examples of a vision is Disneyland's: "To be the happiest place on earth." Other examples are:

- "Restoring patients to full life." (Medtronic)
- "We want to satisfy all of our customers' financial needs and help them succeed financially." (Wells Fargo)
- "Our vision is to be the world's best quick service restaurant." (McDonald's)

Although such visions cannot be accurately measured by a specific indicator of how well they are being achieved, they do provide a fundamental statement of an organization's values, aspirations, and goals. Such visions go well beyond narrow financial objectives, of course, and strive to capture both the minds and hearts of employees.

The vision statement may also contain a slogan, diagram, or picture—whatever grabs attention.[62] The aim is to capture the essence of the more formal parts of the vision in a few words that are easily remembered, yet that evoke the spirit of the entire vision statement. In its 20-year battle with Xerox, Canon's slogan, or battle cry, was "Beat Xerox." Motorola's slogan is "Total Customer Satisfaction." Outboard Marine Corporation's slogan is "To Take the World Boating." And Chevron strives "To Become Better than the Best."

Clearly, vision statements are not a cure-all. Sometimes they backfire and erode a company's credibility. Visions fail for many reasons, including those discussed in the following paragraphs.[63]

The Walk Doesn't Match the Talk   An idealistic vision can arouse employee enthusiasm. However, that same enthusiasm can be quickly dashed if employees find that senior management's behavior is not consistent with the vision. Often, vision is a sloganeering campaign of new buzzwords and empty platitudes like "devotion to the customer," "teamwork," or "total quality" that aren't consistently backed by management's action.

Irrelevance   Visions created in a vacuum—unrelated to environmental threats or opportunities or an organization's resources and capabilities—often ignore the needs of those who are expected to buy into them. Employees reject visions that are not anchored in reality.

Not the Holy Grail   Managers often search continually for the one elusive solution that will solve their firm's problems—that is, the next "holy grail" of management. They may have tried other management fads only to find that they fell short of their expectations. However, they remain convinced that one exists. Visions support sound management, but they require everyone to walk the talk and be accountable for their behavior. A vision simply cannot be viewed as a magic cure for an organization's illness.

Too Much Focus Leads to Missed Opportunities   Clearly, one of the benefits of a sound vision statement is that it can focus efforts and excite people. However, the downside is that in directing people and resources toward a grandiose vision, losses can be devastating. Consider, Samsung's ambitious venture into automobile manufacturing:

> In 1992, Kun-Hee Lee, chairman of South Korea's Samsung Group, created a bold strategy to become one of the 10 largest car makers by 2010. Seduced by the clarity of the vision, Samsung bypassed staged entry through a joint venture or initial supply contract. Instead, Samsung borrowed heavily to build a state-of-the-art research and design facility and erect a greenfield factory, complete with cutting-edge robotics. Samsung Auto suffered operating losses and crushing interest charges from the beginning. And within a few years the business was divested for a fraction of the initial investment.[64]

An Ideal Future Irreconciled with the Present   Although visions are not designed to mirror reality, they must be anchored somehow in it. People have difficulty identifying with a vision that paints a rosy picture of the future but does not account for the often hostile environment in which the firm competes or that ignores some of the firm's weaknesses.

Mission Statements

A company's **mission statement** differs from its vision in that it encompasses both the purpose of the company as well as the basis of competition and competitive advantage.

Exhibit 1.7 contains the vision statement and mission statement of WellPoint Health Network, a giant $57 billion managed health care organization. Note that while the vision statement is broad based, the mission statement is more specific and focused on the means by which the firm will compete. This includes providing branded products that will be tailor-made to customers in order to create long-term customer relationships.

Effective mission statements incorporate the concept of stakeholder management, suggesting that organizations must respond to multiple constituencies if they are to survive and prosper. Customers, employees, suppliers, and owners are the primary stakeholders, but others may also play an important role. Mission statements also have the greatest impact when they reflect an organization's enduring, overarching strategic priorities and competitive positioning. Mission statements also can vary in length and specificity. The two mission statements below illustrate these issues.

- To produce superior financial returns for our shareholders as we serve our customers with the highest quality transportation, logistics, and e-commerce. (Federal Express)
- To be the very best in the business. Our game plan is status go . . . we are constantly looking ahead, building on our strengths, and reaching for new goals. In our quest of these goals, we look at the three stars of the Brinker logo and are reminded of the basic values that are the strength of this company . . . People, Quality and Profitability. Everything we do at Brinker must support these core values. We also look at the eight golden flames depicted in our logo, and are reminded of the fire that ignites our mission and makes up the heart and soul of this incredible company. These flames are: Customers, Food, Team, Concepts, Culture, Partners, Community, and Shareholders. As keeper of these flames, we will continue to build on our strengths and work together to be the best in the business. (Brinker International, whose restaurant chains include Chili's and On the Border)[65]

Few mission statements identify profit or any other financial indicator as the sole purpose of the firm. Indeed, many do not even mention profit or shareholder return.[66] Employees of organizations or departments are usually the mission's most important audience. For them, the mission should help to build a common understanding of purpose and commitment to nurture.

mission statement
a set of organizational goals that include both the purpose of the organization, its scope of operations, and the basis of its competitive advantage.

Vision
WellPoint *will redefine our industry:*
Through a new generation of consumer-friendly products that puts individuals back in control of their future.

Mission
The WellPoint companies provide health *security* by offering a *choice* of quality branded health and related financial services *designed* to meet the *changing* expectations of individuals, families, and their sponsors throughout a *lifelong* relationship.

Source: WellPoint Health Network company records.

Exhibit 1.7
Comparing WellPoint Health Network's Vision and Mission

NextJet's Change of Mission

The dot-com crash was only the first blow to NextJet, Inc., a Dallas-based business launched in 1999 to ship packages overnight. The bigger blow came with the September 11 terrorist attacks, when passenger airlines were forced to add security and reduce flights. One of NextJet's strengths was its nationwide network of local courier services that got packages to and from airports, all coordinated through their proprietary software that could determine the optimal routing. However, the company's business model fell apart when it could not rely on the airlines to get packages between cities quickly enough to make the added cost for same-day delivery worthwhile.

Rather than give up, NextJet reinvented the business around the idea that its most important asset was the software itself. The company's new mission received almost immediate validation when its software was deployed successfully at United Parcel Service (UPS).

NextJet's software provides Atlanta-based UPS with tools for setting online rates and tracking packages. While a lot of same-day business did evaporate when corporations tightened the reins on spending, some things can't wait overnight to be shipped. For example, makers of hospital equipment may need to ship critical parts within a few hours. NextJet's software can help shippers make important decisions in less than a second, finding the fastest and most economical route among air, truck, and courier operations. In addition to UPS, its customers include FedEx, Greyhound, and Menlo Worldwide.

NextJet serves a very large industry segment—Service Parts & Logistics (SPL). The annual expenditures for spare parts in the United States are estimated to be $500 billion. And managers have increased their focus on the importance of effective logistics operations, given its potential impact on a firm's income. After all, whether or not a production line is running can often depend on the quick and effective installation of relatively inexpensive spare parts.

NextJet currently has 50 employees and four offices in the United States, and it seems to be on the right track with its new mission. Although executives at the privately held company will not disclose financial results, they say they are about to complete their third consecutive profitable quarter.

Sources: Goldstein, A. 2002. NextJet is hoping that its software can deliver. *Dallas Morning News*, December 4: 1–3; Nelson, M. G. 2001. NextJet network adds wireless. *Information Week*, April 30: 34; Anonymous. 2004. Who's who in e-logistics. www.americanshipper.com, September; and Hudspeth, B., & Jones, J. 2004. Service parts and logistics: Should you in-source or outsource? *3pl line*, www.inboundlogistics.com, October.

Profit maximization not only fails to motivate people but also does not differentiate between organizations. Every corporation wants to maximize profits over the long term. A good mission statement, by addressing each principal theme, must communicate why an organization is special and different. Two studies that linked corporate values and mission statements with financial performance found that the most successful firms mentioned values other than profits. The less successful firms focused almost entirely on profitability.[67] In essence, profit is the metaphorical equivalent of oxygen, food, and water that the body requires. They are not the point of life, but without them, there is no life.

Although vision statements tend to be quite enduring and seldom change, a firm's mission can and should change when competitive conditions dramatically change or the firm is faced with new threats or opportunities. Strategy Spotlight 1.6 provides an example of a firm, NextJet, that changed its mission in order to realize new opportunities.

strategic objectives
A set of organizational goals that are used to operationalize the mission statement and that are specific and cover a well-defined time frame.

Strategic Objectives

Thus far, we have discussed both visions and missions. Statements of vision tend to be quite broad and can be described as a goal that represents an inspiring, overarching, and emotionally driven destination. Mission statements tend to be more specific and address questions concerning the organization's reason for being and the basis of its competitive advantage. Strategic objectives are used to operationalize the mission statement.[68] That is,

Exhibit 1.8
Strategic Objectives

Strategic Objectives (Financial)

- Increase sales growth 6 percent to 8 percent and accelerate core net earnings growth from 13 percent to 15 percent per share in each of the next 5 years. (Procter & Gamble)
- Generate Internet-related revenue of $1.5 billion. (AutoNation)
- Increase the contribution of Banking Group earnings from investments, brokerage, and insurance from 16 percent to 25 percent. (Wells Fargo)
- Cut corporate overhead costs by $30 million per year. (Fortune Brands)

Strategic Objectives (Nonfinancial)

- We want a majority of our customers, when surveyed, to say they consider Wells Fargo the best financial institution in the community. (Wells Fargo)
- We want to operate 6,000 stores by 2010—up from 3,000 in the year 2000. (Walgreen's)
- We want to be the top-ranked supplier to our customers. (PPG)
- Reduce greenhouse gases by 10 percent (from a 1990 base) by 2010. (BP Amoco)

Sources: Company documents and annual reports.

they help to provide guidance on how the organization can fulfill or move toward the "higher goals" in the goal hierarchy—the mission and vision. Thus, they are more specific and cover a more well-defined time frame.

Setting objectives demands a yardstick to measure the fulfillment of the objectives.[69] If an objective lacks specificity or measurability, it is not very useful, simply because there is no way of determining whether it is helping the organization move toward its mission and vision.

Exhibit 1.8 lists several firms' strategic objectives, divided into financial and nonfinancial categories. While most of these strategic objectives are directed toward generating greater profits and returns for the owners of the business, others are directed at customers or society at large.

For objectives to be meaningful, they need to satisfy several criteria. They must be:

- *Measurable.* There must be at least one indicator (or yardstick) that measures progress against fulfilling the objective.
- *Specific.* This provides a clear message as to what needs to be accomplished.
- *Appropriate.* It must be consistent with the vision and mission of the organization.
- *Realistic.* It must be an achievable target given the organization's capabilities and opportunities in the environment. In essence, it must be challenging but doable.
- *Timely.* There needs to be a time frame for accomplishing the objective. After all, as the economist John Maynard Keynes once said, "In the long run, we are all dead!"

When objectives satisfy the above criteria, there are many benefits for the organization. First, they help to channel employees throughout the organization toward common goals. This helps the organization concentrate and conserve valuable resources and work collectively in a more timely manner.

Second, challenging objectives can help to motivate and inspire employees throughout the organization to higher levels of commitment and effort. A great deal of research has supported the notion that individuals work harder when they are striving toward specific goals instead of being asked simply to "do their best."

Third, as we noted earlier in the chapter, there is always the potential for different parts of an organization to pursue their own goals rather than overall company goals. Although well intentioned, these may work at cross-purposes to the organization as a whole. Meaningful objectives thus help to resolve conflicts when they arise.

Finally, proper objectives provide a yardstick for rewards and incentives. Not only will they lead to higher levels of employee motivation but they will also help to ensure a greater sense of equity or fairness when rewards are allocated.

In summary, an organization must take care to ensure consistency throughout in how it implements strategic objectives. Otherwise, employees and organizational units will be acting at cross purposes, resources will be wasted, and people will become unmotivated. Consider how Textron, a $10 billion conglomerate, ensures that its corporate goals are effectively implemented:

> At Textron, each business unit identifies "improvement priorities" that it must act upon to realize the performance outlined in the firm's overall strategic plan. Each improvement priority is translated into action items with clearly defined accountabilities, timetables, and key performance indicators (KPIs) that enable executives to tell how a unit is delivering on a priority. Improvement priorities and action items cascade to every level at the firm—from the management committee (consisting of Textron's top five executives) down to the lowest levels in each of the company's 10 business units. Says Lewis Campbell, Textron's CEO, "Everyone needs to know: 'If I have only one hour to work, here's what I'm going to focus on.' Our goal deployment process makes each individual's accountabilities and priorities clear."[70]

As indicated in this example, organizations have lower-level objectives that are more specific than the strategic objectives that we have focused on in this section. These are often referred to as short-term objectives—essential components of a firm's "action plan" that are critical in implementing the firm's chosen strategy. We discuss these issues in detail in Chapter 9.

Reflecting on Career Implications . . .

- *Attributes of Strategic Management:* How do your activities and actions contribute to the goals of your organization? Observe the decisions you make on the job. What are the short-term and long-term implications of your decisions and actions? Have you recently made a decision that might yield short-term profits but might negatively impact the long-term goals of the organization (e.g., cutting maintenance expenses to meet a quarterly profit target)?
- *Intended versus Emergent Strategies:* Don't be too inflexible in your career strategies; strive to take advantage of new opportunities as they arise. Many promising career opportunities may "emerge" that were not part of your intended career strategy or your specific job assignment. Take initiative by pursuing opportunities to get additional training (e.g., learn a software or a statistical package), volunteering for a short-term overseas assignment, etc.
- *Ambidexterity:* Avoid defining your role in the organization too narrowly; look for opportunities to leverage your talents and your organization's resources to create value for your organization. This often involves collaborating with people in other departments or with your organization's customers and suppliers.
- *Strategic Coherence:* Focus your efforts on the "big picture" in your organization. In doing this, you should always strive to assure that your efforts are directed toward your organization's vision, mission, and strategic objectives.

Summary

We began this introductory chapter by defining strategic management and articulating some of its key attributes. Strategic management is defined as "consisting of the analyses, decisions, and actions an organization undertakes to create and sustain competitive advantages." The issue of how and why some firms outperform others in the marketplace is central to the study of strategic management. Strategic management has four key attributes: It is directed at overall organizational goals, includes multiple stakeholders, incorporates both short-term and long-term perspectives, and incorporates trade-offs between efficiency and effectiveness.

The second section discussed the strategic management process. Here, we paralleled the above definition of strategic management and focused on three core activities in the strategic management process—strategy analysis, strategy formulation, and strategy implementation. We noted how each of these activities is highly interrelated to and interdependent on the others. We also discussed how each of the 12 chapters in this text fits into the three core activities.

Next, we introduced two important concepts—corporate governance and stakeholder management—which must be taken into account throughout the strategic management process. Governance mechanisms can be broadly divided into two groups: internal and external. Internal governance mechanisms include shareholders (owners), management (led by the chief executive officer), and the board of directors. External control is exercised by auditors, banks, analysts, and an active business press as well as the threat of takeovers. We identified five key stakeholders in all organizations: owners, customers, suppliers, employees, and society at large. Successful firms go beyond an overriding focus on satisfying solely the interests of owners. Rather, they recognize the inherent conflicts that arise among the demands of the various stakeholders as well as the need to endeavor to attain "symbiosis"—that is, interdependence and mutual benefit—among the various stakeholder groups. Managers must also recognize the need to act in a socially responsible manner which, if done effectively, can enhance a firm's innovativeness. They also should recognize and incorporate issues related to environmental sustainability in their strategic actions.

In the fourth section, we discussed factors that have accelerated the rate of unpredictable change that managers face today. Such factors, and the combination of them, have increased the need for managers and employees throughout the organization to have a strategic management perspective and to become more empowered.

The final section addressed the need for consistency among a firm's vision, mission, and strategic objectives. Collectively, they form an organization's hierarchy of goals. Visions should evoke powerful and compelling mental images. However, they are not very specific. Strategic objectives, on the other hand, are much more specific and are vital to ensuring that the organization is striving toward fulfilling its vision and mission.

Summary Review Questions

1. How is "strategic management" defined in the text, and what are its four key attributes?
2. Briefly discuss the three key activities in the strategic management process. Why is it important for managers to recognize the interdependent nature of these activities?
3. Explain the concept of "stakeholder management." Why shouldn't managers be solely interested in stockholder management, that is, maximizing the returns for owners of the firm—its shareholders?
4. What is "corporate governance"? What are its three key elements and how can it be improved?
5. How can "symbiosis" (interdependence, mutual benefit) be achieved among a firm's stakeholders?
6. Why do firms need to have a greater strategic management perspective and empowerment in the strategic management process throughout the organization?
7. What is meant by a "hierarchy of goals"? What are the main components of it, and why must consistency be achieved among them?

Key Terms

romantic view of
  leadership, 7
external view of
  leadership, 7
strategic management, 8
operational
  effectiveness, 10
stakeholders, 11
effectiveness, 11
efficiency, 11

ambidexterity, 12
intended strategy, 13
realized strategy, 13
corporate governance, 17
social responsibility, 20
triple bottom line, 22
hierarchy of goals, 24
vision, 24
mission statement, 27
strategic objectives, 28

Experiential Exercise

Using the Internet or library sources, select four organizations—two in the private sector and two in the public sector. Find their mission statements. Complete the following exhibit by identifying the stakeholders that are mentioned. Evaluate the differences between firms in the private sector and those in the public sector.

Name			
Mission Statement			
Stakeholders (✓ = mentioned)			
1. Customers			
2. Suppliers			
3. Managers/employees			
4. Community-at-large			
5. Owners			
6. Others?			
7. Others?			

Application Questions Exercises

1. Go to the Internet and look up one of these company sites: www.walmart.com, www.ge.com, or www.fordmotor.com. What are some of the key events that would represent the "romantic" perspective of leadership? What are some of the key events that depict the "external control" perspective of leadership?

2. Select a company that competes in an industry in which you are interested. What are some of the recent demands that stakeholders have placed on this company? Can you find examples of how the company is trying to develop "symbiosis" (interdependence and mutual benefit) among its stakeholders? (Use the Internet and library resources.)

3. Provide examples of companies that are actively trying to increase the amount of empowerment in the strategic management process throughout the organization. Do these companies seem to be having positive outcomes? Why? Why not?

4. Look up the vision statements and/or mission statements for a few companies. Do you feel that they are constructive and useful as a means of motivating employees and providing a strong strategic direction? Why? Why not? (*Note:* Annual reports, along with the Internet, may be good sources of information.)

Ethics Questions

1. A company focuses solely on short-term profits to provide the greatest return to the owners of the business (i.e., the shareholders in a publicly held firm). What ethical issues could this raise?

2. A firm has spent some time—with input from managers at all levels—in developing a vision statement and a mission statement. Over time, however, the behavior of some executives is contrary to these statements. Could this raise some ethical issues?

References

1. This section draws from the following articles: Maynard, M. 2006. Gone but not forgotten. *New York Times*, October 28: C1; McCracken, J. 2007. Big three face new obstacles in restructuring. *Wall Street Journal*, January 26: A1 & A8; Edmondson, G. 2007. Putting Ford in the rearview mirror. *BusinessWeek*, February 12: 44; and, McClellan, B. 2006. The Ford Taurus is dead, but what an amazing run. *Ward's Dealer Business*, December 1, np.

2. For a discussion of the "romantic" versus "external control" perspective, refer to Meindl, J. R. 1987. The romance of leadership and the evaluation of organizational

performance. *Academy of Management Journal* 30: 92–109; and Pfeffer, J., & Salancik, G. R. 1978. *The external control of organizations: A resource dependence perspective.* New York: Harper & Row.

3. A recent perspective on the "romantic view" of leadership is provided by Mintzberg, H. 2004. Leadership and management development: An afterword. *Academy of Management Executive,* 18(3): 140–142.

4. Anonymous. 2005. Face value: The 10 billion dollar man. *The Economist.* February 26: 66. Interestingly, this article speculated that Mr. Ghosn could add approximately $10 billion to the market value of Ford or General Motors if he were to sign on as Chief Executive Officer. Such a perspective is clearly consistent with the "romantic view" of leadership. For an insightful perspective on the challenges faced by Mr. Ghosn as he assumes the roles of CEO for both Nissan and Renault (which owns 44 percent of Nissan), refer to: Edmondson, G. 2005. What Ghosn will do with Renault. *BusinessWeek,* April 25: 54.

5. For an interesting perspective on the need for strategists to maintain a global mind-set, refer to Begley, T. M., & Boyd, D. P. 2003. The need for a global mind-set. *MIT Sloan Management Review* 44(2): 25–32.

6. Porter, M. E. 1996. What is strategy? *Harvard Business Review* 74(6): 61–78.

7. See, for example, Barney, J. B., & Arikan, A. M. 2001. The resource-based view: Origins and implications. In Hitt, M. A., Freeman, R. E., & Harrison, J. S. (Eds.), *Handbook of strategic management:* 124–189. Malden, MA: Blackwell.

8. Barney, J. 1991. Firm resources and sustained competitive advantage. *Journal of Management,* 17(1): 99–120.

9. Much of Gary Hamel's work advocates the importance of not focusing on incremental change. For example, refer to Hamel, G., & Prahalad, C. K. 1994. *Competing for the future.* Boston: Harvard Business School Press; see also Christensen, C. M. 2001. The past and future of competitive advantage. *Sloan Management Review,* 42(3): 105–109.

10. Porter, M. E. 1996. What is strategy? *Harvard Business Review,* 74(6): 61–78; and Hammonds, K. H. 2001. Michael Porter's big ideas. *Fast Company,* March: 55–56.

11. This section draws upon Dess, G. G., & Miller, A. 1993. *Strategic management.* New York: McGraw-Hill.

12. See, for example, Hrebiniak, L. G., & Joyce, W. F. 1986. The strategic importance of managing myopia. *Sloan Management Review,* 28(1): 5–14.

13. For an insightful discussion on how to manage diverse stakeholder groups, refer to Rondinelli, D. A., & London, T. 2003. How corporations and environmental groups cooperate: Assessing cross-sector alliances and collaborations. *Academy of Management Executive,* 17(1): 61–76.

14. Senge, P. 1996. Leading learning organizations: The bold, the powerful, and the invisible. In Hesselbein, F., Goldsmith, M., & Beckhard, R. (Eds.), *The leader of the future:* 41–58. San Francisco: Jossey-Bass.

15. Samuelson, J. 2006. A critical mass for the long term. *Harvard Business Review,* 84(2): 62, 64; and, Anonymous. 2007. Power play. *The Economist,* January 20: 10–12.

16. Loeb, M. 1994. Where leaders come from. *Fortune,* September 19: 241 (quoting Warren Bennis).

17. Address by Norman R. Augustine at the Crummer Business School, Rollins College, Winter Park, FL, October 20, 1989.

18. Hemp, P. 2004. An Interview with CEO Kevin Sharer. *Harvard Business Review,* 82(7/8): 66–74.

19. Mintzberg, H. 1985. Of strategies: Deliberate and emergent. *Strategic Management Journal,* 6: 257–272.

20. Carey, J. 2005. Tax credits put wind in the sails of renewables. *BusinessWeek.* January 10: 94.

21. Monks, R., & Minow, N. 2001. *Corporate governance* (2nd ed.). Malden, MA: Blackwell.

22. Intel Corp. 2007. *Intel corporation board of directors guidelines on significant corporate governance issues.* www.intel.com

23. Jones, T. J., Felps, W. & Bigley, G. A. 2007. Ethical theory and stakeholder-related decisions: The role of stakeholder culture. *Academy of Management Review,* 32(1): 137–155.

24. For example, see The best (& worst) managers of the year, 2003. *BusinessWeek,* January 13: 58–92; and Lavelle, M. 2003. Rogues of the year. *Time,* January 6: 33–45.

25. Handy, C. 2002. What's a business for? *Harvard Business Review,* 80(12): 49–55.

26. Anonymous, 2007. In the money. *Economist,* January 20: 3–6.

27. From Lewis, Russel T., "The CEO's Lot is Not a Happy One . . ." *Academy of Management Executive: The Thinking Manager's Source,* 16(4): 38–39, Copyright © 2002 by Academy of Management. Reproduced by permission of Academy of Management via Copyright Clearance Center.

28. For an interesting perspective on the changing role of boards of directors, refer to Lawler, E., & Finegold, D. 2005. Rethinking governance. *MIT Sloan Management Review,* 46(2): 67–70.

29. Benz, M. & Frey, B. S. 2007. Corporate governance: What can we learn from public governance? *Academy of Management Review,* 32(1): 92–104.

30. Stakeholder symbiosis. 1998. *Fortune,* March 30: S2.

31. For a definitive, recent discussion of the stakeholder concept, refer to Freeman, R. E., & McVae, J. 2001. A stakeholder approach to strategic management. In Hitt, M. A., Freeman, R. E., & Harrison, J. S. (Eds.). *Handbook of strategic management:* 189–207. Malden, MA: Blackwell.

32. For an insightful discussion on the role of business in society, refer to Handy, op. cit.

33. Stakeholder symbiosis. op. cit., p. S3.

34. Sullivan, C. T. 2005. A stake in the business. *Harvard Business Review,* 83(9): 57–67.

35. An excellent theoretical discussion on stakeholder activity is Rowley, T. J., & Moldoveanu, M. 2003. When will stakeholder groups act? An interest- and identity-based model of stakeholder group mobilization. *Academy of Management Review,* 28(2): 204–219.

36. Thomas, J. G. 2000. Macroenvironmetal forces. In Helms, M. M. (Ed.), *Encyclopedia of management.* (4th ed.): 516–520. Farmington Hills, MI: Gale Group.

37. For a strong advocacy position on the need for corporate values and social responsibility, read Hollender, J. 2004. What matters most: Corporate values and social responsibility. *California Management Review,* 46(4): 111–119.

38. Waddock, S. & Bodwell, C. 2004. Managing responsibility: What can be learned from the quality movement. *California Management Review,* 47(1): 25–37.

39. For a discussion of the role of alliances and collaboration on corporate social responsibility initiatives, refer to Pearce, J. A. II., & Doh, J. P. 2005. The high impact of collaborative social initiatives. *MIT Sloan Management Review,* 46(3): 30–40.

40. Anonymous, 2006. If I did it. *BusinessWeek.* December 18: 108.

41. Bhattacharya, C. B., & Sen, S. 2004, Doing better at doing good: When, why, and how consumers respond to corporate social initiatives. *California Management Review,* 47(1): 9–24.

42. Cone Corporate Citizenship Study, 2002, www.coneinc.com.

43. Refer to www.bsr.org.

44. An insightful discussion of the risks and opportunities associated with global warming, refer to: Lash, J. & Wellington, F. 2007. Competitive advantage on a warming planet. *Harvard Business Review,* 85(3): 94–102.

45. This section draws on Hart, S. L. 1997. Beyond greening: Strategies for a sustainable world. *Harvard Business Review,* 75(1): 66–76, and Berry, M. A. & Rondinelli, D. A. 1998. Proactive corporate environmental management: A new industrial revolution. *Academy of Management Executive,* 12(2): 38–50.

46. Carey, J. 2006. Business on a warmer planet. *BusinessWeek,* July 17: 26–29.

47. Hart, op. cit., p. 67.

48. For a creative perspective on environmental sustainability and competitive advantage as well as ethical implications, read Ehrenfeld, J. R. 2005. The roots of sustainability. *MIT Sloan Management Review,* 46(2): 23–25.

49. McKinsey & Company. 1991. *The corporate response to the environmental challenge.* Summary Report, Amsterdam: McKinsey & Company.

50. Vogel, D. J. 2005. Is there a market for virtue? The business case for corporate social responsibility. *California Management Review,* 47(4): 19–36.

51. Senge, P. M. 1990. The leader's new work: Building learning organizations. *Sloan Management Review,* 32(1): 7–23.

52. For an interesting perspective on the role of middle managers in the strategic management process, refer to Huy, Q. H. 2001. In praise of middle managers. *Harvard Business Review,* 79(8): 72–81.

53. Senge, 1996, op. cit., pp. 41–58.

54. Helgesen, S. 1996. Leading from the grass roots. In Hesselbein, F., Goldsmith, M., & Beckhard, R. (Eds.), *The leader of the future:* 19–24. San Francisco: Jossey-Bass.

55. Wetlaufer, S. 1999. Organizing for empowerment: An interview with AES's Roger Sant and Dennis Blake. *Harvard Business Review,* 77(1): 110–126.

56. Kets de Vries, M. F. R. 1998. Charisma in action: The transformational abilities of Virgin's Richard Branson and ABB's Percy Barnevik. *Organizational Dynamics,* 26(3): 7–21.

57. Hamel, G. 2006. The why, what, and how of management innovation. *Harvard Business Review,* 84(2): 72–84.

58. Our discussion draws on a variety of sources. These include Lipton, M. 1996. Demystifying the development of an organizational vision. *Sloan Management Review,* 37(4): 83–92; Bart, C. K. 2000. Lasting inspiration. *CA Magazine,* May: 49–50; and Quigley, J. V. 1994. Vision: How leaders develop it, share it, and sustain it. *Business Horizons,* September–October: 37–40.

59. Lipton, op. cit.

60. Hardy, Q. 2007. The uncarly. *Forbes,* March 12: 82–90.

61. Quigley, op. cit.

62. Ibid.

63. Lipton, op. cit. Additional pitfalls are addressed in this article.

64. Sull, D. N. 2005. Strategy as active waiting. *Harvard Business Review,* 83(9): 120–130.

65. Company records.

66. Lipton, op. cit.

67. Sexton, D. A., & Van Aukun, P. M. 1985. A longitudinal study of small business strategic planning. *Journal of Small Business Management,* January: 8–15, cited in Lipton, op. cit.

68. For an insightful perspective on the use of strategic objectives, refer to Chatterjee, S. 2005. Core objectives: Clarity in designing strategy. *California Management Review,* 47(2): 33–49.

69. Ibid.

70. Mankins, M. M. & Steele, R. 2005. Turning great strategy into great performance. *Harvard Business Review,* 83(5): 66–73.

chapter 2

Analyzing the External Environment of the Firm

>learning objectives

After reading this chapter, you should have a good understanding of:

LO1 The importance of developing forecasts of the business environment.

LO2 Why environmental scanning, environmental monitoring, and collecting competitive intelligence are critical inputs to forecasting.

LO3 Why scenario planning is a useful technique for firms competing in industries characterized by unpredictability and change.

LO4 The impact of the general environment on a firm's strategies and performance.

LO5 How forces in the competitive environment can affect profitability, and how a firm can improve its competitive position by increasing its power vis-à-vis these forces.

LO6 How the Internet and digitally based capabilities are affecting the five competitive forces and industry profitability.

LO7 The concept of strategic groups and their strategy and performance implications.

*S*trategies are not and should not be developed in a vacuum. They must be responsive to the external business environment. Otherwise, your firm could become, in effect, the most efficient producer of buggy whips, leisure suits, or slide rules. To avoid such strategic mistakes, firms must become knowledgeable about the business environment. One tool for analyzing trends is forecasting. In the development of forecasts, environmental scanning and environmental monitoring are important in detecting key trends and events. Managers also must aggressively collect and disseminate competitor intelligence. The information gleaned from these three activities is invaluable in developing forecasts and scenarios to minimize present and future threats as well as to exploit opportunities. We address these issues in the first part of this chapter. We also introduce a basic tool of strategy analysis—the concept of SWOT analysis (strengths, weaknesses, opportunities, and threats).

In the second part of the chapter, we present two frameworks for analyzing the external environment—the general environment and the competitive environment. The general environment consists of six segments—demographic, sociocultural, political/legal, technological, economic, and global. Trends and events in these segments can have a dramatic impact on your firm.

The competitive environment is closer to home. It consists of five industry-related factors that can dramatically affect the average level of industry profitability. An awareness of these factors is critical in making decisions such as which industries to enter and how to improve your firm's current position within an industry. This is helpful in neutralizing competitive threats and increasing power over customers and suppliers. We also address how industry and competitive practices are being affected by the capabilities provided by Internet technologies. In the final part of this section, we place firms within an industry into strategic groups based on similarities in resources and strategies. As we will see, the concept of strategic groups has important implications for the intensity of rivalry and how the effects of a given environmental trend or event differ across groups.

Learning from Mistakes

Robert Atkins, a cardiologist, was the founder of the original low-carbohydrate, high-protein diet.[1] He wrote several books that popularized his Atkins diet, including his best seller, *Dr. Atkins New Diet Revolution,* that sold over 10 million copies worldwide. As we will see below, in the beer industry, one firm—Anheuser-Busch—took quick action and benefited from this popular diet trend. Others, including Coors Brewing, were slow to react and paid the price.

In September 2002, Anheuser Busch became one of the pioneers in the low-carb category by launching Michelob Ultra. The brand rapidly became the leader, capturing 5.7 percent of the light beer market by March 2004. The company had jumped on the wave early and rode it during the upsurge of the low-carb trend, which peaked during that year. Clearly, this was an attractive market segment: Beer experts had estimated that about half of the $60 to $70 billion U.S. beer market is from light beer sales as Americans continue to seek out beers that won't add to their waistline.

Coors, in contrast, didn't enter the low-carb market until March 2004—after Michelob Ultra had begun to erode Coors Light's market share. The Coors low-carb brand, Aspen Edge, was too little, too late. By the time Aspen Edge was launched, it faced very stiff competition. In addition to a powerful leader in the segment, Michelob Ultra (which, of course, benefited from Anheuser Busch's deep pockets and marketing prowess), there were already over a dozen other low-carb rivals. These included Rolling Rock, which had introduced Rock Green Light, and Miller Brewing, which had begun to promote the fact that its staple, Miller Lite, had only 3.2 carbs. Further, there were several imported beers, including Martens Low Carbohydrate, brewed by Brouwerij Martens in Belgium.

Even though Coors invested $30 million in Aspen Edge's launch, its sales peaked at just 0.4 percent of the beer market in July 2004. Then its market share began to slide and it was discontinued in April 2006.

Successful managers must recognize opportunities and threats in their firm's external environment. They must be aware of what's going on outside their company. If they focus exclusively on the efficiency of internal operations, the firm may degenerate into the world's most efficient producer of buggy whips or carbon paper. But if they miscalculate the market, opportunities will be lost—hardly an enviable position for their firm.

In *Competing for the Future,* Gary Hamel and C. K. Prahalad suggest that "every manager carries around in his or her head a set of biases, assumptions, and presuppositions about the structure of the relevant 'industry,' about how one makes money in the industry, about who the competition is and isn't, about who the customers are and aren't, and so on."[2] Environmental analysis requires you to continually question such assumptions. Peter Drucker labeled these interrelated sets of assumptions the "theory of the business."[3] Most would agree that Coors would have benefited from a more rigorous environmental analysis—in particular the growing popularity of low-carb products. By the time Coors took action, the low-carb boom had already peaked.

A firm's strategy may be good at one point in time, but it may go astray when management's frame of reference gets out of touch with the realities of the actual business situation. This results when management's assumptions, premises, or beliefs are incorrect or when internal inconsistencies among them render the overall "theory of the business" invalid. As Warren Buffett, investor extraordinaire, colorfully notes, "Beware of past performance 'proofs.' If history books were the key to riches, the Forbes 400 would consist of librarians." And Arthur Martinez, former chairman of Sears, Roebuck & Co., states, "Today's peacock is tomorrow's feather duster."

In the business world, many peacocks have become feather dusters or at least had their plumage dulled. Consider the high-tech company Novell, which went head-to-head with Microsoft. Novell bought market-share loser WordPerfect to compete with Microsoft Word. The result? A $1.3 billion loss when Novell sold WordPerfect to Corel. And today we may wonder who will be the next Wang, Delta Airlines, or *Encyclopaedia Britannica.*

Creating the Environmentally Aware Organization

>LO1

The importance of developing forecasts of the business environment.

So how do managers become environmentally aware?[4] We will now address three important processes—scanning, monitoring, and gathering competitive intelligence—used to develop forecasts. Exhibit 2.1 illustrates relationships among these important activities. We also discuss the importance of scenario planning in anticipating major future changes in the external environment and the role of SWOT analysis.[5]

Exhibit 2.1 Inputs to Forecasting

The Role of Scanning, Monitoring, Competitive Intelligence, and Forecasting

Environmental Scanning   **Environmental scanning** involves surveillance of a firm's external environment to predict environmental changes and detect changes already under-way.[6] Successful environmental scanning alerts the organization to critical trends and events before the changes have developed a discernible pattern and before competitors recognize them.[7] Otherwise, the firm may be forced into a reactive mode.[8]

Sir John Browne, former chief executive officer of petroleum company BP Amoco, described the kind of environmental changes his company was experiencing.

> The next element of the change we've experienced is the growth in demand, and the changing nature of that demand. The world uses eight million more barrels of oil and 30 billion more cubic feet of natural gas every day than it did in the spring of 1990. The growth of natural gas in particular has been and continues to be spectacular, and I believe that change can legitimately be seen as part of a wider, longer-term shift to lighter, cleaner, less carbon-intensive fuels.[9]

Consider how difficult it would be for BP Amoco to develop strategies and allocate resources if it did not scan the external environment for such emerging changes in demand.

At times, your company may benefit from studies conducted by outside experts in a particular industry. A. T. Kearney, a large international consulting company, identified several key issues in the automobile industry, including.[10]

- *Globalization.* This is not a new trend but it has intensified, with enormous opportunities opening up in Asia, central and eastern Europe, and Latin America.
- *Time to Market.* Despite recent improvements, there's still a gap between product development cycles in the United States and Europe compared to Japan. This gap may be widening as Japanese companies continue to make improvements.
- *Shifting Roles and Responsibilities.* Design responsibility, purchasing, and even project management and systems engineering are shifting from original equipment manufacturers to integrators/suppliers.

Consider how disadvantaged you would be as an executive in the global automobile industry if you were unaware of such trends.

Environmental Monitoring   **Environmental monitoring** tracks the evolution of environmental trends, sequences of events, or streams of activities. They may be trends that the firm came across by accident or ones that were brought to its attention from outside the organization. Consider the automobile industry. While environmental scanning may make you aware of the trends, they require close monitoring, which involves closer ongoing scrutiny. For example, you should closely monitor sales in Asia, central and eastern Europe, and Latin America. You should observe how fast Japanese companies and other competitors bring products to market compared with your firm. You should also study trends with your own suppliers/integrators in purchasing, project management, and systems engineering. Monitoring enables firms to evaluate how dramatically environmental trends are changing the competitive landscape.

One of the authors of this text has conducted on-site interviews with executives from several industries to identify indicators that firms monitor as inputs to their strategy process. Examples of such indicators included:

- *A Motel 6 executive.* The number of rooms in the budget segment of the industry in the United States and the difference between the average daily room rate and the consumer price index (CPI).
- *A Pier 1 Imports executive.* Net disposable income (NDI), consumer confidence index, and housing starts.

>LO2

Why environmental scanning, environmental monitoring, and collecting competitive intelligence are critical inputs to forecasting.

environmental scanning surveillance of a firm's external environment to predict environmental changes and detect changes already under way.

environmental monitoring a firm's analysis of the external environment that tracks the evolution of environmental trends, sequences of events, or streams of activities.

- **A Johnson & Johnson medical products executive.** Percentage of gross domestic product (GDP) spent on health care, number of active hospital beds, and the size and power of purchasing agents (indicates the concentration of buyers).

Such indices are critical for managers in determining a firm's strategic direction and resource allocation.

competitive intelligence a firm's activities of collecting and interpreting data on competitors, defining and understanding the industry, and identifying competitors' strengths and weaknesses.

Competitive Intelligence Competitive intelligence (CI) helps firms define and understand their industry and identify rivals' strengths and weaknesses.[11] This includes the intelligence gathering associated with collecting data on competitors and interpreting such data. Done properly, competitive intelligence helps a company avoid surprises by anticipating competitors' moves and decreasing response time.[12]

Examples of competitive analysis are evident in daily newspapers and periodicals such as *The Wall Street Journal, BusinessWeek,* and *Fortune.* For example, banks continually track home loan, auto loan, and certificate of deposit (CD) interest rates charged by peers in a given geographic region. Major airlines change hundreds of fares daily in response to competitors' tactics. Car manufacturers are keenly aware of announced cuts or increases in rivals' production volume, sales, and sales incentives (e.g., rebates and low interest rates on financing). They use this information to plan their own marketing, pricing, and production strategies. Exhibit 2.2 provides some insights on what CI is (and what it isn't).

The Internet has dramatically accelerated the speed at which firms can find competitive intelligence. Leonard Fuld, founder of the Cambridge, Massachusetts, training and consulting firm Fuld & Co., specializes in competitive intelligence.[13] His firm often profiles top company and business group managers and considers these issues: What is their background? What is

Exhibit 2.2
What Competitive Intelligence Is and Is Not!

Competitive Intelligence Is . . .	Competitive Intelligence Is Not . . .
1. **Information** that has been analyzed to the point where you can make a decision.	1. **Spying.** Spying implies illegal or unethical activities. It is a rare activity, since most corporations do not want to find themselves in court or to upset shareholders.
2. **A tool** to alert management to early recognition of both threats and opportunities.	2. **A crystal ball.** CI gives corporations good approximations of short- and long-term reality. It does not predict the future.
3. **A means to deliver reasonable assessments.** CI offers approximations of the market and competition. It is not a peek at a rival's financial books. Reasonable assessments are what modern entrepreneurs need and want on a regular basis.	3. **Database search.** Databases offer just that—data. They do not massage or analyze the data in any way. They certainly don't replace human beings who make decisions by examining the data and applying their common sense, experience, and intuition.
4. **A way of life, a process.** If a company uses CI the way it should be used, it becomes everyone's job, not just the strategic planning or marketing staff's. It is a process by which critical information is available to those who need it.	4. **A job for one smart person.** A CEO may appoint one person as the CI ringmaster, but one person cannot do it all. At best, the ringmaster can keep management informed and ensure that others become trained to apply this tool within their business units.

Sources: Imperato, G. 1998. Competitive intelligence—Get smart! *Fast Company,* April: 26–29; and Fuld, F. M. What competitive intelligence is and is not! www.fuld.com/whatCI.html.

strategy spotlight

Ethical Guidelines on Competitive Intelligence: United Technologies

United Technologies (UT) is a $28 billion global conglomerate composed of world-leading businesses with rich histories of technological pioneering, such as Otis Elevator, Carrier Air Conditioning, and Sikorsky (helicopters). It was founded in 1853 and has an impressive history of technological accomplishments. UT built the first working helicopter, developed the first commercially available hydrogen cells, and designed complete life support systems for space shuttles. UT believes strongly in a robust code of ethics. In the last decade, they have clearly articulated their principles governing business conduct. These include an antitrust guide, an ethics guide when contracting with the U.S. government and foreign governments, a policy on accepting gifts from suppliers, and guidelines for proper usage of e-mail. One such document is the Code of Ethics Guide on Competitive Intelligence. This encourages managers and workers to ask themselves these five questions whenever they have ethical concerns.

Sources: Nelson, B. 2003. The thinker. *Forbes,* March 3: 62–64; and The Fuld war room—Survival kit 010. Code of Ethics (printed 2/26/01).

1. Have I done anything that coerced somebody to share this information? Have I, for example, threatened a supplier by indicating that future business opportunities will be influenced by the receipt of information with respect to a competitor?

2. Am I in a place where I should not be? If, for example, I am a field representative with privileges to move around in a customer's facility, have I gone outside the areas permitted? Have I misled anybody in order to gain access?

3. Is the contemplated technique for gathering information evasive, such as sifting through trash or setting up an electronic "snooping" device directed at a competitor's facility from across the street?

4. Have I misled somebody in a way that the person believed sharing information with me was required or would be protected by a confidentiality agreement? Have I, for example, called and misrepresented myself as a government official who was seeking some information for some official purpose?

5. Have I done something to evade or circumvent a system intended to secure or protect information?

their style? Are they marketers? Are they cost cutters? Fuld has found that the more articles he collects and the more biographies he downloads, the better he can develop profiles.

One of Fuld & Co.'s clients needed to know if a rival was going to start competing more aggressively on costs. Fuld's analysts tracked down articles from the Internet and a local newspaper profile of the rival firm's CEO. The profile said the CEO had taken a bus to a nearby town to visit one of the firm's plants. Fuld claimed, "Those few words were a small but important sign to me that this company was going to be incredibly cost-conscious." Another client retained Fuld to determine the size, strength, and technical capabilities of a privately held company. Initially, it was difficult to get detailed information. Then one analyst used Deja News (www.dejanews.com), now part of Google, to tap into some online discussion groups. The analyst's research determined that the company had posted 14 job openings on one Usenet group. That posting was a road map to the competitor's development strategy.

At times, a firm's aggressive efforts to gather competitive intelligence may lead to unethical or illegal behaviors.[14] Strategy Spotlight 2.1 provides an example of a company, United Technologies, that has set clear guidelines to help prevent unethical behavior.

A word of caution: Executives must be careful to avoid spending so much time and effort tracking the actions of traditional competitors that they ignore new competitors. Further, broad environmental changes and events may have a dramatic impact on a firm's viability. Peter Drucker, often considered the father of modern management, wrote:

> Increasingly, a winning strategy will require information about events and conditions outside the institution: noncustomers, technologies other than those currently used by the company and its present competitors, markets not currently served, and so on.[15]

● The sales of printed encyclopedias were decimated by CD-ROMs.

Consider the fall of the once-mighty *Encyclopaedia Britannica*.[16] Its demise was not caused by a traditional competitor in the encyclopedia industry. It was caused by new technology. CD-ROMs came out of nowhere and devastated the printed encyclopedia industry. Why? A full set of the *Encyclopaedia Britannica* sells for about $2,000, but an encyclopedia on CD-ROM, such as Microsoft *Encarta,* sells for about $50. To make matters worse, many people receive *Encarta* free with their personal computers.

Environmental Forecasting   Environmental scanning, monitoring, and competitive intelligence are important inputs for analyzing the external environment. However, they are of little use unless they provide raw material that is reliable enough to help managers make accurate forecasts. **Environmental forecasting** involves the development of plausible projections about the direction, scope, speed, and intensity of environmental change.[17] Its purpose is to predict change. It asks: How long will it take a new technology to reach the marketplace? Will the present social concern about an issue result in new legislation? Are current lifestyle trends likely to continue?

Some forecasting issues are much more specific to a particular firm and the industry in which it competes. Consider how important it is for Motel 6 to predict future indicators, such as the number of rooms, in the budget segment of the industry. If its predictions are low, it will build too many units, creating a surplus of room capacity that would drive down room rates. Similarly, if Pier 1 Imports is overly optimistic in its forecast of future net disposable income and U.S. housing starts, it will order too much inventory and later be forced to discount merchandise drastically.

A danger of forecasting is that managers may view uncertainty as black and white and ignore important gray areas. Either they assume that the world is certain and open to precise predictions, or they assume it is uncertain and completely unpredictable.[18] The problem is that underestimating uncertainty can lead to strategies that neither defend against threats nor take advantage of opportunities. In 1977 one of the colossal underestimations in business history occurred when Kenneth H. Olsen, then president of Digital Equipment Corp., announced, "There is no reason for individuals to have a computer in their home." The explosion in the personal computer market was not easy to detect in 1977, but it was clearly within the range of possibilities that industry experts were discussing at the time. And, historically, there have been underestimates of the growth potential of new telecommunication services. The electric telegraph was derided by Ralph Waldo Emerson, and the telephone had its skeptics. More recently, an "infamous" McKinsey study in the early 1980s predicted that there would be fewer than 1 million cellular users in the United States by the year 2000. Actually, there were nearly 100 million.[19] As humorously noted by Jane Bryant Quinn, a business writer: "The rule on staying alive as a forecaster is to give 'em a number or give 'em a date, but never give 'em both at once."[20]

At the other extreme, if managers assume the world is unpredictable, they may abandon the analytical rigor of their traditional planning process and base strategic decisions on gut instinct. Such a "just do it" approach may cause executives to place misinformed bets on emerging products or markets that result in record write-offs. Entrepreneurs and venture capitalists who took the plunge and invested in questionable Internet ventures in the late 1990s provide many examples.

A more in-depth approach to forecasting involves scenario analysis. **Scenario analysis** draws on a range of disciplines and interests, among them economics, psychology, sociology, and demographics. It usually begins with a discussion of participants' thoughts on ways in

environmental forecasting the development of plausible projections about the direction, scope, speed, and intensity of environmental change.

>LO3

Why scenario planning is a useful technique for firms competing in industries characterized by unpredictability and change.

scenario analysis an in-depth approach to environmental forecasting that involves experts' detailed assessments of societal trends, economics, politics, technology, or other dimensions of the external environment.

Scenario Planning at Shell Oil Company

Preparing to cope with uncertainty is one of the biggest strategic challenges faced by most businesses. There are few tools for coping with strategic uncertainty, especially over medium- to long-term horizons. One technique that has proved its usefulness is scenario planning.

Scenario planning is different from other tools for strategic planning such as trend analysis or high and low forecasts. The origins of scenario planning lie with the military, which used it to cope effectively with multiple challenges and limited resources.

In the 1960s and 1970s, Shell combined analytical tools with information to create scenarios of possible outcomes. The result of the 1973 oil embargo was a sharp increase in crude oil prices, short supplies of gasoline for consumers, and a depressed world economy. However, Shell's strategic planning, including the use of scenarios, had strongly suggested that a more unstable environment was coming, with a shift of power from oil companies to oil producers. As a result of the precautionary actions it took, Shell was in a better position than most oil companies when the 1973 embargo occurred. Shell also uses scenario planning to plan major new oil field investments because elements of risk can be identified and explored over a considerable period of time.

Sources: Martin, R. 2002. The oracles of oil. *Business 2.0,* January: 35–39; www.touchstonerenard.co.uk/Expertise/Strategy/Scenario_Planning/ scenario_planning.htm; and Epstein, J. 1998. Scenario planning: An introduction. *The Futurist,* September: 50–52.

The Shell process of scenario planning involves the following stages:

1. Interviews with people both inside and outside the business, using an open-ended questioning technique to encourage full and frank answers.

2. Analysis of interviews by issue in order to build a "natural agenda" for further processing.

3. Synthesis of each agenda to draw out underlying areas of uncertainty/dispute and possible interrelationships among issues.

4. A small number of workshops to explore key issues to improve understanding and identify gaps for further research. These generate a wide range of strategy options.

5. A workshop to identify and build a small number of scenarios that may occur in the next 10 to 15 years or even later.

6. A testing of strategy options against the scenarios in order to assess robustness (i.e., whether or not a given strategy is effective under more than one scenario).

Other practitioners of scenario planning include Levi Strauss, which uses scenario planning to consider potential impacts of everything from cotton deregulation to the total disappearance of cotton from this planet. Also, a German insurance company anticipated the fall of the Berlin wall and made plans to expand in central Europe. And in 1990 when Nelson Mandela was released from a South African prison, he met with a panel that helped him create scenarios to chart out the country's future. Scenario planning helps by considering not just trends or forecasts but also how they could be upset by events and the outcomes that may result.

which societal trends, economics, politics, and technology may affect the issue under discussion.[21] For example, consider Lego. The popular Danish toy manufacturer has a strong position in the construction toys market. But what would happen if this broadly defined market should change dramatically? After all, Lego is competing not only with producers of similar products but also on a much broader canvas for a share of children's playtime. In this market, Lego has a host of competitors, many of them computer based; still others have not yet been invented. Lego may end up with an increasing share of a narrow, shrinking market (much like IBM in the declining days of the mainframe computer). To avoid such a fate, managers must consider their future in a wider context than their narrow, traditional markets. They need to lay down guidelines for at least 10 years in the future to anticipate rapid change. Strategy Spotlight 2.2 provides an example of scenario planning at Shell Oil Company.

SWOT Analysis

To understand the business environment of a particular firm, you need to analyze both the general environment and the firm's industry and competitive environment. Generally, firms compete with other firms in the same industry. An industry is composed of a set of firms that produce similar products or services, sell to similar customers, and use similar methods of production. Gathering industry information and understanding competitive dynamics among the different companies in your industry is key to successful strategic management.

One of the most basic techniques for analyzing firm and industry conditions is **SWOT analysis.** SWOT stands for strengths, weaknesses, opportunities, and threats. SWOT analysis provides a framework for analyzing these four elements of a company's internal and external environment. It provides "raw material"—a basic listing of conditions both inside and surrounding your company.

SWOT analysis a framework for analyzing a company's internal and external environment and that stands for strengths, weaknesses, opportunities, and threats.

The Strengths and Weaknesses portion of SWOT refers to the internal conditions of the firm—where your firm excels (strengths) and where it may be lacking relative to competitors (weaknesses). Opportunities and Threats are environmental conditions external to the firm. These could be factors either in the general environment or in the competitive environment. In the general environment, one might experience developments that are beneficial for most companies such as improving economic conditions, that cause lower borrowing costs or trends that benefit some companies and harm others. An example is the heightened concern with fitness, which is a threat to some companies (e.g., tobacco) and an opportunity to others (e.g., health clubs). Opportunities and threats are also present in the competitive environment among firms competing for the same customers.

The general idea of SWOT analysis is that a firm's strategy must:

- build on its strengths,
- try to remedy the weaknesses or work around them,
- take advantage of the opportunities presented by the environment, and,
- protect the firm from the threats.

Despite its apparent simplicity, the SWOT approach has been immensely popular for a number of reasons. First, it forces managers to consider both internal and external factors simultaneously. Second, its emphasis on identifying opportunities and threats makes firms act proactively rather than reactively. Third, it raises awareness about the role of strategy in creating a match between the environmental conditions and the firm's internal strengths and weaknesses. Finally, its conceptual simplicity is achieved without sacrificing analytical rigor.

We discuss the analysis of the external environment in the following sections of this chapter. We will also address some of the limitations of SWOT analysis in Chapter 3.

general environment factors external to an industry, and usually beyond a firm's control, that affect a firm's strategy.

>LO4

The impact of the general environment on a firm's strategies and performance.

The General Environment

The **general environment** is composed of factors that can have dramatic effects on firm strategy.[22] Typically, a firm has little ability to predict trends and events in the general environment and even less ability to control them. When listening to CNBC, for example, you can hear many experts espouse totally different perspectives on what action the Federal Reserve Board may take on short-term interest rates—an action that can have huge effects on the valuation of entire economic sectors. Also, it's difficult to predict future political events such as the ongoing Middle East peace negotiations and tensions on the Korean peninsula. In addition, who would have guessed the Internet's impact on national and global economies in the past decade or two? Such dramatic innovations in information technology (e.g., the Internet) have helped keep inflation in check by lowering the cost of doing business in the United States at the beginning of the 21st century.

We divide the general environment into six segments: demographic, sociocultural, political/legal, technological, economic, and global. First, we discuss each segment and provide a summary of the segment and examples of how events and trends can impact industries. Second, we address relationships among the general environment segments. Third, we consider how trends and events can vary across industries. Exhibit 2.3 provides examples of key trends and events in each of the six segments of the general environment.

The Demographic Segment

Demographics are the most easily understood and quantifiable elements of the general environment. They are at the root of many changes in society. Demographics include elements such as the aging population,[23] rising or declining affluence, changes in ethnic composition, geographic distribution of the population, and disparities in income level.

The impact of a demographic trend, like all segments of the general environment, varies across industries. The aging of the U.S. population has had a positive effect on the health care industry but a negative impact on the industry that produces diapers and baby food. Rising levels of affluence in many developed countries bode well for brokerage services as well as for upscale pets and supplies. However, these same trends may have an adverse effect on fast food restaurants because people can afford to dine at higher-priced restaurants. Fast-food restaurants depend on minimum-wage employees to operate efficiently, but the competition for labor intensifies as more attractive employment opportunities become prevalent, thus threatening the employment base for restaurants. Let's look at the details of one of these trends.

The aging population in the United States and other developed countries has important implications. The U.S. Bureau of Statistics states that only 14 percent of American workers were 55 and older in 2002.[24] However, by 2012 that figure will increase to 20 percent, or one in five, of all U.S. workers. At the same time, the United States is expected to experience a significant drop in the percentage of younger workers aged 25 to 44, making it increasingly important for employers to find ways to recruit and retain older workers. Similarly, the National Association of Manufacturing estimates that as baby boomers continue retiring and the economy grows, the United States will have 7 million more jobs than workers by 2010.

The Sociocultural Segment

Sociocultural forces influence the values, beliefs, and lifestyles of a society. Examples include a higher percentage of women in the workforce, dual-income families, increases in the number of temporary workers, greater concern for healthy diets and physical fitness, greater interest in the environment, and postponement of having children. Such forces enhance sales of products and services in many industries but depress sales in others. The increased number of women in the workforce has increased the need for business clothing merchandise but decreased the demand for baking product staples (since people would have less time to cook from scratch). A greater concern for health and fitness has had differential effects. This trend has helped industries that manufacture exercise equipment and healthful foods but harmed industries that produce unhealthful foods.

The trend toward increased educational attainment by women in the workplace has led to an increase in the number of women in upper management positions. U.S. Department of Education statistics show that women have become the dominant holders of college degrees. Based on figures of a recent graduating class, women with bachelor's degrees will outnumber their male counterparts by 27 percent. By the class of 2006–2007, the gap should surge to 38 percent. Additionally, throughout the 1990s the number of women earning MBAs increased by 29 percent compared to only 15 percent for men.[25] Given these educational attainments, it is hardly surprising that companies owned by women have been one of the driving forces of the U.S. economy; these companies (now more than 9 million in number) account for 40 percent of all U.S. businesses and have generated more than $3.6 trillion in annual revenue. In addition, women have a tremendous impact on consumer spending decisions. Not surprisingly,

Exhibit 2.3

General Environment:
Key Trends and Events

Demographic

- Aging population
- Rising affluence
- Changes in ethnic composition
- Geographic distribution of population
- Greater disparities in income levels

Sociocultural

- More women in the workforce
- Increase in temporary workers
- Greater concern for fitness
- Greater concern for environment
- Postponement of family formation

Political/Legal

- Tort reform
- Americans with Disabilities Act (ADA) of 1990
- Repeal of Glass-Steagall Act in 1999 (banks may now offer brokerage services)
- Deregulation of utility and other industries
- Increases in federally mandated minimum wages
- Taxation at local, state, federal levels
- Legislation on corporate governance reforms in bookkeeping, stock options, etc. (Sarbanes-Oxley Act of 2002)

Technological

- Genetic engineering
- Emergence of Internet technology
- Computer-aided design/computer-aided manufacturing systems (CAD/CAM)
- Research in synthetic and exotic materials
- Pollution/global warming
- Miniaturization of computing technologies
- Wireless communications
- Nanotechnology

Economic

- Interest rates
- Unemployment rates
- Consumer Price Index
- Trends in GDP
- Changes in stock market valuations

Global

- Increasing global trade
- Currency exchange rates
- Emergence of the Indian and Chinese economies
- Trade agreements among regional blocs (e.g., NAFTA, EU, ASEAN)
- Creation of WTO (leading to decreasing tariffs/free trade in services)

The Sarbanes-Oxley Act: A Boon for Accountants

Government regulation is often prompted as elected officials respond to voters' expectations. When faced with a crisis, voters often demand a solution and expect elected officials to provide one. If the politicians fail to deliver, they suffer in the next election. Consider some of the historical examples of how the U.S. government has reacted to ethical disasters with the blunt force of increased legislation.

- The creation of the Securities and Exchange Commission (SEC) and other legislation following the stock market crash of 1929.

- The Foreign Corrupt Practices Act of 1977, which followed Lockheed's bribes to government officials.

- In the wake of the Enron, WorldCom, and Andersen debacles, Congress passed the Sarbanes-Oxley Act on July 30, 2002. (The law was passed just 35 days after WorldCom announced that it had overstated its revenues by at least $3.8 billion.)

Accounting firms have really benefited from the Sarbanes-Oxley Act. They had lobbied hard to keep the act from being passed. But, fortunately for them, they lost!

Companies are working hard to comply with Section 404 of the act. The provision requires publicly traded corporations to vouch for internal financial controls and remedy problems. A recent survey by Financial Executives International (FEI) finds that, on average, companies will spend $3.1 million and 30,700 hours to comply—nearly double the estimates of an earlier poll.

Much of that expense goes to privately held accounting firms. Audit fees are expected to surge more than 50 percent, according to FEI. To deal with the increased business, the Big Four accounting firms are in a hiring frenzy and logging lots of overtime. For example, KPMG has added 850 auditors in 2004, while PricewaterhouseCoopers (PWC) has hired 400 people from English-speaking foreign countries as temporary employees. "It's a scramble," say Dennis Nally, PWC's U.S. senior partner. It seems every cloud has a silver lining.

Sources: Arndt, M. 2004. A boon for bean counters. *BusinessWeek,* November 22: 13; and Thomas, T., Schermerhorn, R. R., Jr., & Dienhart, J. W. 2004. Strategic leadership of ethical behavior in business. *The Academy of Management Executive,* 18(2): 56–68.

many companies have focused their advertising and promotion efforts on female consumers. Consider, for example, Wilkesboro (North Carolina)–based Lowe's efforts to attract female shoppers: Lowe's has found that women prefer to do larger home-improvement projects with a man—be it a boyfriend, husband, or neighbor.[26] As a result, in addition to its "recipe card classes" (that explain various projects that take only one weekend), Lowe's offers co-ed store clinics for projects like sink installation. "Women like to feel they're given the same attention as a male customer," states Lowe's spokespersons Julie Valeant-Yenichek, who points out that most seminar attendees, whether male or female, are inexperienced.

Not surprisingly, Home Depot has recently spent millions of dollars to add softer lighting and brighter signs in 300 stores. Why? It is an effort to match rival Lowe's long-standing appeal to women.

The Political/Legal Segment

Political processes and legislation influence the environmental regulations with which industries must comply.[27] Some important elements of the political/legal arena include tort reform, the Americans with Disabilities Act (ADA) of 1990, the repeal of the Glass-Steagall Act in 1999 (banks may now offer brokerage services), deregulation of utilities and other industries, and increases in the federally mandated minimum wage.

Government legislation can also have a significant impact on the governance of corporations. The U.S. Congress passed the Sarbanes-Oxley Act in 2002, which greatly increases the accountability of auditors, executives, and corporate lawyers. This act was a response to the widespread perception that existing governance mechanisms have failed to protect the interests of shareholders, employees, and creditors. Perhaps it is not too surprising that Sarbanes-Oxley has also created a tremendous demand for professional accounting services. We address this trend in Strategy Spotlight 2.3.

Legislation also helps companies in the high-tech sector of the economy by expanding the number of temporary visas available for highly skilled foreign professionals. For example, a bill passed in October 2000 allows 195,000 H-1B visas in each of the next three years, up from the cap of only 115,000 in 2000. The allotment for the year 2000 was used up by March, and the cap decreased to 107,500 for 2001 and a mere 65,000 each year thereafter. Almost half of the visas are for professionals from India, and most of them are computer or software specialists.[28] For U.S. labor and workers' rights groups, however, the issue was a political hot potato.

The Technological Segment

Developments in technology lead to new products and services and improve how they are produced and delivered to the end user. Innovations can create entirely new industries and alter the boundaries of existing industries.[29] Examples of technological developments and trends are genetic engineering, Internet technology, computer-aided design/computer-aided manufacturing (CAD/CAM), research in artificial and exotic materials, and, on the downside, pollution and global warming. Firms in the petroleum and primary metals industries incur significant expenses to reduce the amount of pollution they produce. Engineering and consulting firms that work with polluting industries derive financial benefits from solving such problems.

Another important technological development is the combination of information technology (IT) and the Internet, which has played a key role in productivity improvement.[30] In the United States, for example, improvement in productivity rates is running at an all-time high. For the 20-year period ending in 1990, U.S. worker productivity grew at less than 1.7 percent annually. In contrast, from 2001 to 2005, it grew at an annual rate of 3.6 percent. In recent years, productivity around the world has also increased by, for example, nearly 6 percent in Taiwan and nearly 10 percent in South Korea. Better productivity means that more work can be done by fewer people.

Nanotechnology is becoming a very promising area of research with many potentially useful applications.[31] Nanotechnology takes place at industry's tiniest stage: one billionth of a meter. Remarkably, this is the size of 10 hydrogen atoms in a row.

Researchers have discovered that matter at such a tiny scale behaves very differently. While some of the science behind this phenomenon is still shrouded in mystery, the commercial potential is coming sharply into focus. Familiar materials—from gold to carbon soot—display startling and useful new properties. Some transmit light or electricity. Others become harder than diamonds or turn into potent chemical catalysts. What's more, researchers have found that a tiny dose of nanoparticles can transform the chemistry and nature of far bigger things, creating everything from stronger fenders to superefficient fuel cells. Exhibit 2.4 lists a few of the potential ways in which nanotechnology could revolutionize industries.

There are downsides to technology. In addition to ethical issues in biotechnology, there are threats to our environment associated with the emission of greenhouse gases. In response,

Exhibit 2.4

How Nanotechnology Might Revolutionize Various Industries

- **To fight cancer,** sensors will be able to detect a single cancer cell and will help guide nanoparticles that can burn tumors from the inside out, leaving healthy cells alone.
- **To transform energy,** nano-enhanced solar panels will feed cheap electricity onto superconducting power lines made of carbon nanotubes.
- **To replace silicon,** carbon nanotubes will take over when silicon peters out, leading to far faster chips that need less power than today's chips.
- **For space travel,** podlike crawlers will carry cargo thousands of miles up a carbon-nanotube cable to a space station for billions less than rocket launches.

Source: Baker, S. & Aston, A. 2004. Universe in a grain of sand. *BusinessWeek,* October 11: 139–140.

some firms have taken a proactive approach. BP Amoco plans to decrease its greenhouse gas emissions by giving each of its 150 business units a quota of emission permits and encouraging the units to trade them. If a unit cuts emissions and has leftover permits, it can sell them to other units that are having difficulty meeting their goals. For example, Julie Hardwick, manager at the Naperville, Illinois, petrochemical division, saved up permits by fast-tracking a furnace upgrade that allowed elimination of a second furnace.[32]

The Economic Segment

The economy has an impact on all industries, from suppliers of raw materials to manufacturers of finished goods and services, as well as all organizations in the service, wholesale, retail, government, and nonprofit sectors. Key economic indicators include interest rates, unemployment rates, the Consumer Price Index, the gross domestic product, and net disposable income. Interest-rate increases have a negative impact on the residential home construction industry but a negligible (or neutral) effect on industries that produce consumer necessities such as prescription drugs or common grocery items.

Other economic indicators are associated with equity markets. Perhaps the most watched is the Dow Jones Industrial Average (DJIA), which is composed of 30 large industrial firms. When stock market indexes increase, consumers' discretionary income rises and there is often an increased demand for luxury items such as jewelry and automobiles. But when stock valuations decrease, demand for these items shrinks.

The Global Segment

There is an increasing trend for firms to expand their operations and market reach beyond the borders of their "home" country. Globalization provides both opportunities to access larger potential markets and a broad base of production factors such as raw materials, labor, skilled managers, and technical professionals. However, such endeavors also carry many political, social, and economic risks.

Examples of key elements include currency exchange rates, increasing global trade, the economic emergence of China, trade agreements among regional blocs (e.g., North American Free Trade Agreement, European Union), and the General Agreement on Tariffs and Trade (GATT) (lowering of tariffs). Increases in trade across national boundaries also provide benefits to air cargo and shipping industries but have a minimal impact on service industries such as bookkeeping and routine medical services. The emergence of China as an economic power has benefited many industries, such as construction, soft drinks, and computers. However, it has had a negative impact on the defense industry in the United States as diplomatic relations between the two nations improve.

Few industries are as global as the automobile industry. Consider just a few examples of how some of the key players expanded their reach into Latin America during the 1990s. Fiat built a new plant in Argentina, Volkswagen retooled a plant in Mexico to launch the New Beetle, DaimlerChrysler built a new plant as a joint venture with BMW to produce engines in Brazil, and General Motors built a new car factory in Brazil. Why the interest? In addition to the region's low wage rates and declining trade barriers, the population of 400 million is very attractive. But the real bonus lies in the 9-to-1 ratio of people to cars in the region compared to a 2-to-1 ratio in developed countries. With this region's growth expected to be in the 3 to 4 percent range for the first part of the century, sales should increase at a healthy rate.[33]

Finally, consider the cost of terrorism. A recent survey indicates that for S&P 500 firms, the threat has caused direct and indirect costs of $107 billion a year. This figure includes extra spending (on insurance and redundant capacity, for instance) as well as lost revenues (from fearful consumers' decreased activity). Another finding in a 2006 survey of CFOs: Some 21 percent of U.S. companies have reduced employees' air travel since September 11 (as have 17 percent of European companies).[34]

Relationships among Elements of the General Environment

In our discussion of the general environment, we see many relationships among the various elements.[35] For example, a demographic trend in the United States, the aging of the population, has important implications for the economic segment (in terms of tax policies to provide benefits to increasing numbers of older citizens). Another example is the emergence of information technology as a means to increase the rate of productivity gains in the United States and other developed countries. Such use of IT results in lower inflation (an important element of the economic segment) and helps offset costs associated with higher labor rates.

The effects of a trend or event in the general environment vary across industries. Governmental legislation (political/legal) to permit the importation of prescription drugs from foreign countries is a very positive development for drugstores but a very negative event for U.S. drug manufacturers. Exhibit 2.5 provides other examples of how the impact of trends or events in the general environment can vary across industries.

Exhibit 2.5

The Impact of General Environmental Trends on Various Industries

Segment/Trends and Events	Industry	Positive	Neutral	Negative
Demographic				
Aging population	Health care	✓		
	Baby products			✓
Rising affluence	Brokerage services	✓		
	Fast foods			✓
	Upscale pets and supplies	✓		
Sociocultural				
More women in the workforce	Clothing	✓		
	Baking products (staples)			✓
Greater concern for health and fitness	Home exercise equipment	✓		
	Meat products			✓
Political/legal				
Tort reform	Legal services			✓
	Auto manufacturing	✓		
Americans with Disabilities Act (ADA)	Retail			✓
	Manufacturers of elevators, escalators, and ramps	✓		
Technological				
Genetic engineering	Pharmaceutical	✓		
	Publishing		✓	
Pollution/global warming	Engineering services	✓		
	Petroleum			✓
Economic				
Interest rate increases	Residential construction			✓
	Most common grocery products		✓	
Global				
Increasing global trade	Shipping	✓		
	Personal service		✓	
Emergence of China as an economic power	Soft drinks	✓		
	Defense			✓

The Internet and Digital Technologies: Affecting Many Environmental Segments

The Internet has dramatically changed the way business is conducted in every corner of the globe. According to digital economy visionary Don Tapscott:

> The Net is much more than just another technology development; the Net represents something qualitatively new—an unprecedented, powerful, universal communications medium. Far surpassing radio and television, this medium is digital, infinitely richer, and interactive. . . . Mobile computing devices, broadband access, wireless networks, and computing power embedded in everything from refrigerators to automobiles are converging into a global network that will enable people to use the Net just about anywhere and anytime.

The Internet provides a platform or staging area for the application of numerous technologies, rapid advances in knowledge, and unprecedented levels of global communication and commerce. Even technologies that don't require the Internet to function, such as wireless phones and GPS, rely on the Internet for data transfer and communications.

Growth in Internet usage has surged in recent years both among individual users as well as businesses. Exhibit 2.6 illustrates current usage levels as well as worldwide growth trends in Internet use. Business use of the Internet has become nearly ubiquitous throughout the economy. Major corporations all have a Web presence, and many companies use the Internet to interact with key stakeholders. For example, some companies have direct links with suppliers through online procurement systems that automatically reorder inventories and supplies. Companies such as Cisco Systems even interact with their own employees

Sources: Anonymous. 2005. SMBs believe in the Web. *eMarketer.com,* www.emarketer.com, May 16. Downes, L. & Mui, C. 1998. *Unleashing the killer app.* Boston: Harvard Business School Press. Green, H. 2003. Wi-Fi means business. *BusinessWeek,* April 28: 86–92; McGann, R. 2005. Broadband: High speed, high spend. *ClickZ Network,* www.clickz.com, January 24; Tapscott, D. 2001. Rethinking strategy in a Networked World. *Strategy and Business,* Third Quarter: 34–41; and, Yang, C. 2003. Beyond wi-fi: A new wireless age. *BusinessWeek,* December 15: 84–88.

Internet Users (in millions)		
Geographic Region	2005	2010 (estimated)
North America	219,650	259,390
Western Europe	215,734	319,528
Eastern Europe/Russia	70,381	130,888
Asia-Pacific	420,999	745,421
South/Central America	83,724	155,590
Middle East/Africa	64,245	146,624
Total Internet Users	1,074,733	1,785,941

Source: Computer Industry Almanac.

Exhibit 2.6 Growth in Internet Activity

using the Internet to update employment records, such as health care information and benefits.

Small and medium-sized enterprises (SMEs) are also relying on the Internet more than ever. A recent study found that 87 percent of SMEs are receiving monthly revenue from their Web site, and 42 percent derive more than a quarter of their monthly revenue from their Internet presence. According to Joel Kocher, CEO of Interland, "We are getting to the point in most small-business categories where it will soon be safe to say that if you're not online, you're not really serious about being in business."

Despite these advances, the Internet and digital technologies still face numerous challenges. For example, international standards for digital and wireless communications are still in flux. As a result, cell phones and other devices that work in the United States are often useless in many parts of Europe and Asia. And, unlike analog systems, electronic bits of data that are zooming through space can be more easily lost, stolen, or manipulated. However, even with these problems, Internet and digital technologies will continue to be a growing global phenomenon. As Andy Grove, former chairman of Intel, stated, "The world now runs on Internet time."

Before moving on, let's consider a recent event that has had a strong influence on many segments of the environment—the Internet. The Internet has been a leading and highly visible component of a broader technological phenomenon—the emergence of digital technology. These technologies are altering the way business is conducted and having an impact on nearly every business domain. Strategy Spotlight 2.4 addresses the impact of the Internet and digital technologies on the business environment.

>LO5

How forces in the competitive environment can affect profitability, and how a firm can improve its competitive position by increasing its power vis-à-vis these forces.

competitive environment

factors that pertain to an industry and affect a firm's strategies.

The Competitive Environment

In addition to the general environment, managers must also consider the competitive environment (also sometimes referred to as the task or industry environment). The nature of competition in an industry, as well as the profitability of a firm, is often more directly influenced by developments in the competitive environment.

The **competitive environment** consists of many factors that are particularly relevant to a firm's strategy. These include competitors (existing or potential), customers, and suppliers. Potential competitors may include a supplier considering forward integration, such as an automobile manufacturer acquiring a rental car company, or a firm in an entirely new industry introducing a similar product that uses a more efficient technology.

In the following sections, we will discuss key concepts and analytical techniques that managers should use to assess their competitive environments. First, we examine Michael Porter's five-forces model that illustrates how these forces can be used to explain low profitability in an industry.[36] Second, we discuss how the five forces are being affected by the capabilities provided by Internet technologies. Third, we address some of the limitations, or "caveats" that managers should be familiar with when conducting industry analysis. Finally, we address the concept of strategic groups. This concept demonstrates that even within an industry it is often useful to group firms on the basis of similarities of their strategies. As we will see, competition tends to be more intense among firms *within* a strategic group than between strategic groups.

Porter's Five-Forces Model of Industry Competition

The "five-forces" model developed by Michael E. Porter has been the most commonly used analytical tool for examining the competitive environment. It describes the competitive environment in terms of five basic competitive forces.[37]

1. The threat of new entrants.
2. The bargaining power of buyers.
3. The bargaining power of suppliers.
4. The threat of substitute products and services.
5. The intensity of rivalry among competitors in an industry.

Each of these forces affects a firm's ability to compete in a given market. Together, they determine the profit potential for a particular industry. The model is shown in Exhibit 2.7 on page 53. As a manager, you should be familiar with the five-forces model for several reasons. It helps you decide whether your firm should remain in or exit an industry. It provides the rationale for increasing or decreasing resource commitments. The model helps you assess how to improve your firm's competitive position with regard to each of the five forces. For example you can use insights provided by the five-forces model to create higher entry barriers that discourage new rivals from competing with you.[38] Or you may develop strong relationships with your distribution channels. You may decide to find suppliers who satisfy the price/performance criteria needed to make your product or service a top performer.

The Threat of New Entrants   The threat of new entrants refers to the possibility that the profits of established firms in the industry may be eroded by new competitors.[39] The extent of the threat depends on existing barriers to entry and the combined reactions from existing competitors. If entry barriers are high and/or the newcomer can anticipate a sharp retaliation from established competitors, the threat of entry is low. These circumstances discourage new competitors. There are six major sources of entry barriers.

> ***Economies of Scale*** Economies of scale refers to spreading the costs of production over the number of units produced. The cost of a product per unit declines as the absolute volume per period increases. This deters entry by forcing the entrant to come

Exhibit 2.7 Porter's Five-Forces Model of Industry Competition

Source: Reprinted with permission of The Free Press, a division of Simon & Schuster Adult
Publishing Group, from *Competitive Strategy: Techniques for Analyzing Industries and Competitors*
by Michael E. Porter. Copyright © 1980, 1998 by The Free Press. All rights reserved.

in at a large scale and risk strong reaction from existing firms or come in at a small
scale and accept a cost disadvantage. Both are undesirable options.

Product Differentiation When existing competitors have strong brand identification
and customer loyalty, differentiation creates a barrier to entry by forcing entrants to
spend heavily to overcome existing customer loyalties.

Capital Requirements The need to invest large financial resources to compete creates
a barrier to entry, especially if the capital is required for risky or unrecoverable up-
front advertising or research and development (R&D).

Switching Costs A barrier to entry is created by the existence of one-time costs that
the buyer faces when switching from one supplier's product or service to another.

Access to Distribution Channels The new entrant's need to secure distribution for its
product can create a barrier to entry.

Cost Disadvantages Independent of Scale Some existing competitors may have
advantages that are independent of size or economies of scale. These derive from:

- Proprietary products
- Favorable access to raw materials
- Government subsidies
- Favorable government policies

In an environment where few, if any, of these entry barriers are present, the threat of
new entry is high. For example, if a new firm can launch its business with a low capital
investment and operate efficiently despite its small scale of operation, it is likely to be a
threat. One company that failed because of low entry barriers in an industry is ProCD.[40]
You probably never heard of this company. It didn't last very long. ProCD provides an example of a firm that failed because it entered an industry with very low entry barriers.

The story begins in 1986 when Nynex (a former Baby Bell company) issued the first electronic phone book, a compact disk containing all listings for the New York City area. It charged $10,000 per copy and sold the CDs to the FBI, IRS, and other large commercial and government organizations. James Bryant, the Nynex executive in charge of the project, smelled a fantastic business opportunity. He quit Nynex and set up his own firm, ProCD, with the ambitious goal of producing an electronic directory covering the entire United States.

As expected, the telephone companies, fearing an attack on their highly profitable Yellow Pages business, refused to license digital copies of their listings to this upstart. Bryant was not deterred. He traveled to Beijing and hired Chinese workers at $3.50 a day to type every listing from every U.S. telephone book into a database. The result contained more than 70 million phone numbers and was used to create a master disk that enabled ProCD to make hundreds of thousands of copies. Each CD sold for hundreds of dollars and cost less than a dollar each to produce.

It was a profitable business indeed! However, success was fleeting. Competitors such as Digital Directory Assistance and American Business Information quickly launched competing products with the same information. Since customers couldn't tell one product from the next, the players were forced to compete on price alone. Prices for the CD soon plummeted to a few dollars each. A high-priced, high-margin product just months earlier, the CD phone book became little more than a cheap commodity.

The Bargaining Power of Buyers   Buyers threaten an industry by forcing down prices, bargaining for higher quality or more services, and playing competitors against each other. These actions erode industry profitability.[41] The power of each large buyer group depends on attributes of the market situation and the importance of purchases from that group compared with the industry's overall business. A buyer group is powerful under the following conditions:

- ***It is concentrated or purchases large volumes relative to seller sales.*** If a large percentage of a supplier's sales are purchased by a single buyer, the importance of the buyer's business to the supplier increases. Large-volume buyers also are powerful in industries with high fixed costs (e.g., steel manufacturing).
- ***The products it purchases from the industry are standard or undifferentiated.*** Confident they can always find alternative suppliers, buyers play one company against the other, as in commodity grain products.
- ***The buyer faces few switching costs.*** Switching costs lock the buyer to particular sellers. Conversely, the buyer's power is enhanced if the seller faces high switching costs.
- ***It earns low profits.*** Low profits create incentives to lower purchasing costs. On the other hand, highly profitable buyers are generally less price sensitive.
- ***The buyers pose a credible threat of backward integration.*** If buyers are either partially integrated or pose a credible threat of backward integration, they are typically able to secure bargaining concessions.
- ***The industry's product is unimportant to the quality of the buyer's products or services.*** When the quality of the buyer's products is not affected by the industry's product, the buyer is more price sensitive.

At times, a firm or set of firms in an industry may increase its buyer power by using the services of a third party. FreeMarkets Online is one such third party.[42] Pittsburgh-based FreeMarkets has developed software enabling large industrial buyers to organize online auctions for qualified suppliers of semistandard parts such as fabricated components, packaging materials, metal stampings, and services. By aggregating buyers, FreeMarkets increases the buyers' bargaining power. The results are impressive. In its first 48 auctions, most participating companies saved over 15 percent; some saved as much as 50 percent.

The Bargaining Power of Suppliers   Suppliers can exert bargaining power over participants in an industry by threatening to raise prices or reduce the quality of purchased goods and services. Powerful suppliers can squeeze the profitability of firms in an industry so far that they can't recover the costs of raw material inputs.[43] The factors that make suppliers powerful tend to mirror those that make buyers powerful. A supplier group will be powerful in the following circumstances:

- *The supplier group is dominated by a few companies and is more concentrated (few firms dominate the industry) than the industry it sells to.* Suppliers selling to fragmented industries influence prices, quality, and terms.
- *The supplier group is not obliged to contend with substitute products for sale to the industry.* The power of even large, powerful suppliers can be checked if they compete with substitutes.
- *The industry is not an important customer of the supplier group.* When suppliers sell to several industries and a particular industry does not represent a significant fraction of its sales, suppliers are more prone to exert power.
- *The supplier's product is an important input to the buyer's business.* When such inputs are important to the success of the buyer's manufacturing process or product quality, the bargaining power of suppliers is high.
- *The supplier group's products are differentiated or it has built up switching costs for the buyer.* Differentiation or switching costs facing the buyers cut off their options to play one supplier against another.
- *The supplier group poses a credible threat of forward integration.* This provides a check against the industry's ability to improve the terms by which it purchases.

When considering supplier power, we focus on companies that supply raw materials, equipment, machinery, and associated services. But the supply of labor is also an important input to businesses, and labor's power varies over time and across occupations and industries. Currently, the outlook is not very good for semiskilled and unskilled laborers. When annual wage gains before inflation are taken into account—typically a good measure of workers' bargaining clout in the labor market—wages have remained in the 3 percent range for much of the 1990s.[44] When the CPI averaged around 2 percent, that provided employees with pay increases that exceeded inflation. With higher consumer prices, however, real wage gains (wage increases above the inflation rate) have been virtually nonexistent recently.

Strategy Spotlight 2.5 discusses how catfish farmers were able to enhance their bargaining power vis-à-vis their customers—large agribusiness firms—by banding together to form a cooperative.

The Threat of Substitute Products and Services   All firms within an industry compete with industries producing substitute products and services. Substitutes limit the potential returns of an industry by placing a ceiling on the prices that firms in that industry can profitably charge. The more attractive the price/performance ratio of substitute products, the tighter the lid on an industry's profits.

Identifying substitute products involves searching for other products or services that can perform the same function as the industry's offerings. This is a subtle task, one that leads a manager into businesses seemingly far removed from the industry. For example, the airline industry might not consider video cameras much of a threat. But as digital technology has improved and wireless and other forms of telecommunication have become more efficient, teleconferencing has become a viable substitute for business travel for many executives. That is, the rate of improvement in the price–performance relationship of the substitute product (or service) is high.

Teleconferencing can save both time and money, as IBM found out with its "Manager Jam" idea.[45] Currently, with 319,000 employees scattered around six continents,

Enhancing Supplier Power: The Creation of Delta Pride Catfish

The formation of Delta Pride Catfish in 1981 is an example of the power that a group of suppliers can attain if they exercise the threat of forward integration. Catfish farmers in Mississippi had historically supplied their harvest to processing plants run by large agribusiness firms such as ConAgra and Farm Fresh. When the farmers increased their production of catfish in response to growing demand in the early 1970s, they found, much to their chagrin, that processors were holding back on their plans to increase their processing capabilities in hopes of higher retail prices for catfish.

Source: Cargile, D. 2005. Personal communication. (Vice President of Sales, Delta Pride Catfish, Inc.), February 2; Anonymous. 2003. Delta Pride Catfish names Steve Osso President and CEO. www.deltabusiness.journal.com, February; and Fritz, M. 1988. Agribusiness: Catfish story. *Forbes*, December 12: 37.

What action did the farmers take? They responded by forming a cooperative, raising $4.5 million, and constructing their own processing plant, which they supplied themselves. Within two years, ConAgra's market share had dropped from 35 percent to 11 percent, and Farm Fresh's market share fell by over 20 percent.

By the late 1980s, Delta Pride controlled over 40 percent of the 280-million-pound-per-year U.S. catfish market. It has continued to grow by including value-added products such as breaded and marinated catfish products. Recently it introduced Country Crisp Catfish Strips, a bakeable, breaded product with country-style seasoning. By 2005, Delta Pride had more than 500 employees. Its approximately 100 shareholders are mostly catfish farmers who own more than 60,000 acres of catfish production ponds and produce more than 200 million pounds of live catfish each year.

---

it is one of the world's largest businesses (including 32,000 managers) and can be a pretty confusing place. The shift to an increasingly mobile workplace means many managers supervise employees they rarely see face-to-face. To enhance coordination, Samuel Palmisano, IBM's new CEO, launched one of his first big initiatives: a two-year program exploring the role of the manager in the 21st century. "Manager Jam," as the project was nicknamed, was a 48-hour real-time Web event in which managers from 50 different countries swapped ideas and strategies for dealing with problems shared by all of them, regardless of geography. Some 8,100 managers logged on to the company's intranet to participate in the discussion forums.

Renewable energy resources are also a promising substitute product and are rapidly becoming more economically competitive with fossil fuels. Strategy Spotlight 2.6 addresses this critical issue.

The Intensity of Rivalry among Competitors in an Industry   Rivalry among existing competitors takes the form of jockeying for position. Firms use tactics like price competition, advertising battles, product introductions, and increased customer service or warranties. Rivalry occurs when competitors sense the pressure or act on an opportunity to improve their position.

Some forms of competition, such as price competition, are typically highly destabilizing and are likely to erode the average level of profitability in an industry.[46] Rivals easily match price cuts, an action that lowers profits for all firms. On the other hand, advertising battles expand overall demand or enhance the level of product differentiation for the benefit of all firms in the industry. Rivalry, of course, differs across industries. In some instances it is characterized as warlike, bitter, or cutthroat, whereas in other industries it is referred to as polite and gentlemanly. Intense rivalry is the result of several interacting factors, including the following:

- ***Numerous or equally balanced competitors.*** When there are many firms in an industry, the likelihood of mavericks is great. Some firms believe they can make moves without being noticed. Even when there are relatively few firms, and they are nearly

The Growing Viability of Renewable Resources as Substitutes for Fossil Fuels

Renewable resources currently provide just over 6 percent of total U.S. energy. However, that figure could increase rapidly in the years ahead, according to a joint report issued in September 2006 by the Worldwatch Institute and the Center for Progress, entitled "American Energy: The Renewable Path to Energy Security."

The report indicates that many of the new technologies that harness renewables are, or soon will be, economically competitive with fossil fuels. Dynamic growth rates are driving down costs and spurring rapid advances in technologies. And, since 2000, global wind energy generation has more than tripled, solar cell production has risen six-fold, production of fuel ethanol from crops has more than doubled, and biodiesel production has expanded nearly four-fold. Annual global investment in

Sources: Clayton, M. 2006. Greener, cleaner . . . and competitive. www.csmonitor.com. December 4; and, Anonymous. 2006. Renewables becoming cost-competitive with fossil fuels in the U.S. www.worldwatch.org. September 18.

"new" renewable energy has risen almost six-fold since 1995, with cumulative investment over the period nearly $180 billion. The report claims: "With oil prices soaring, the security risks of petroleum dependence growing, and the environmental costs of today's fuels becoming more apparent, the country faces compelling reasons to put these technologies to use on a larger scale."

A November 2006 study by the RAND Corporation is consistent with the aforementioned report. It asserts that the economy of the United States would likely benefit, rather than be slowed, if the nation attained the goal of supplying 25 percent of its energy needs from renewable sources by 2025. The RAND study also says that while most renewable fuels cannot yet compete with fossil fuels, their costs of production are falling steadily. If the trend continues, America's energy mix by 2025 could be far greener and cleaner—without damaging the economy—than most analysts could have anticipated a few years ago. Such developments would also reduce U.S. dependence on oil, which would mean a substantial start on capping greenhouse gas emissions, which most scientists link to global warming.

equal in size and resources, instability results from fighting among companies having the resources for sustained and vigorous retaliation.

- **Slow industry growth.** Slow industry growth turns competition into a fight for market share, since firms seek to expand their sales.
- **High fixed or storage costs.** High fixed costs create strong pressures for all firms to increase capacity. Excess capacity often leads to escalating price cutting.
- **Lack of differentiation or switching costs.** Where the product or service is perceived as a commodity or near commodity, the buyer's choice is typically based on price and service, resulting in pressures for intense price and service competition. Lack of switching costs, described earlier, has the same effect.
- **Capacity augmented in large increments.** Where economies of scale require that capacity must be added in large increments, capacity additions can be very disruptive to the industry supply/demand balance.
- **High exit barriers.** Exit barriers are economic, strategic, and emotional factors that keep firms competing even though they may be earning low or negative returns on their investments. Some exit barriers are specialized assets, fixed costs of exit, strategic interrelationships (e.g., relationships between the business units and others within a company in terms of image, marketing, shared facilities, and so on), emotional barriers, and government and social pressures (e.g., governmental discouragement of exit out of concern for job loss).

Rivalry between firms is often based solely on price, but it can involve other factors. Take Pfizer's market position in the impotence treatment market. Pfizer was the first pharmaceutical firm to develop Viagra, a drug that treats impotence. International sales of Viagra were $332 million during a recent quarter. There are currently 30 million prescriptions for the drug. Pfizer would like to keep competitors from challenging this lucrative position.

In several countries, the United Kingdom among them, Pfizer faced a lawsuit by Eli Lilly & Co. and Icos Corp. challenging its patent protection. These two pharmaceutical firms recently entered into a joint venture to market Cialis, a drug to compete with Viagra. The U.K. courts agreed and lifted the patent.

This opened the door for Eli Lilly and Icos to proceed with challenging Pfizer's market position. Because Cialis has fewer side effects than Viagra, the drug has the potential to rapidly decrease Pfizer's market share in the United Kingdom if physicians switch prescriptions from Viagra to Cialis. If future patent challenges are successful, Pfizer may see its sales of Viagra erode rapidly. With projected annual sales of Cialis at $1 billion, Pfizer has reason to worry. With FDA approval, sales of Cialis could cause those of Viagra to plummet in the United States, further eroding Pfizer's market share.[47] But Pfizer is hardly standing still. It recently doubled its advertising expenditures on Viagra.

Exhibit 2.8 summarizes our discussion of industry five-forces analysis. It points out how various factors such as economies of scale and capital requirements affect each "force."

How the Internet and Digital Technologies Are Affecting the Five Competitive Forces

>LO6

How the Internet and digitally based capabilities are affecting the five competitive forces and industry profitability.

The Internet and other digital technologies are having a significant impact on nearly every industry. These technologies have fundamentally changed the ways businesses interact with each other and with consumers. In most cases, these changes have affected industry forces in ways that have created many new strategic challenges. In this section, we will evaluate Michael Porter's five-forces model in terms of the actual use of the Internet and the new technological capabilities that it makes possible.

The Threat of New Entrants In most industries, the threat of new entrants has increased because digital and Internet-based technologies lower barriers to entry. For example, businesses that reach customers primarily through the Internet may enjoy savings on other traditional expenses such as office rent, sales-force salaries, printing, and postage. This may encourage more entrants who, because of the lower start-up expenses, see an opportunity to capture market share by offering a product or performing a service more efficiently than existing competitors. Thus, a new cyber entrant can use the savings provided by the Internet to charge lower prices and compete on price despite the incumbent's scale advantages.

Alternatively, because digital technologies often make it possible for young firms to provide services that are equivalent or superior to an incumbent, a new entrant may be able to serve a market more effectively, with more personalized services and greater attention to product details. A new firm may be able to build a reputation in its niche and charge premium prices. By so doing, it can capture part of an incumbent's business and erode profitability. Consider Voice Over Internet Protocol (VOIP), a fast growing alternative to traditional phone service, which is expected to reach 12.1 million U.S. households by 2009.[48] Savings of 20 to 30 percent are common for VOIP consumers. This is driving prices down and lowering telecom industry profits. A more sweeping implication is that it threatens the value of the phone line infrastructure that the major carriers have invested in so heavily. Clearly, VOIP represents a major new entrant threat to incumbent phone service providers.

Another potential benefit of Web-based business is access to distribution channels. Manufacturers or distributors that can reach potential outlets for their products more efficiently by means of the Internet may be encouraged to enter markets that were previously closed to them. Such access is not guaranteed, however, because of the strong barriers to entry that may exist in certain industries.[49] Nevertheless, Internet and digital technologies are providing many new entrants with more efficient and lower cost methods of accessing customers.

Threat of New Entrants Is High When:	High	Low
Economies of scale are		X
Product differentiation is		X
Capital requirements are		X
Switching costs are		X
Incumbent's control of distribution channels is		X
Incumbent's proprietary knowledge is		X
Incumbent's access to raw materials is		X
Incumbent's access to government subsidies is		X

Power of Buyers Is High When:	High	Low
Concentration of buyers relative to suppliers is	X	
Switching costs are		X
Product differentiation of suppliers is		X
Threat of backward integration by buyers is	X	
Extent of buyer's profits is		X
Importance of the supplier's input to quality of buyer's final product is		X

Power of Suppliers Is High When:	High	Low
Concentration relative to buyer industry is	X	
Availability of substitute products is		X
Importance of customer to the supplier is		X
Differentiation of the supplier's products and services is	X	
Switching costs of the buyer are	X	
Threat of forward integration by the supplier is	X	

Threat of Substitute Products Is High When:	High	Low
The differentiation of the substitute product is	X	
Rate of improvement in price–performance relationship of substitute product is	X	

Intensity of Competitive Rivalry Is High When:	High	Low
Number of competitors is	X	
Industry growth rate is		X
Fixed costs are	X	
Storage costs are	X	
Product differentiation is		X
Switching costs are		X
Exit barriers are	X	
Strategic stakes are	X	

Exhibit 2.8 Competitive Analysis Checklist

Buyer Power in the Book Industry: The Role of the Internet

The $25 billion book publishing industry illustrates some of the changes brought on by the Internet that have affected buying power among two types of buyers—end users and buyer channel intermediaries. Prior to the Internet, book publishers worked primarily through large distributors. These intermediaries such as Tennessee-based Ingram, one of the largest and most powerful distributors, exercised strong control over the movement of books from publishers to bookstores. This power was especially strong relative to small, independent publishers who often found it difficult to get their books into bookstores and in front of potential customers.

The Internet has significantly changed these relationships. Publishers can now negotiate distribution agreements directly with online retailers such as Amazon and Books-A-Million. Such online bookstores now account for about $4 billion in annual sales. And small publishers can use the Internet to sell directly to end users and publicize new titles, without depending on buyer channel intermediaries to handle their books. By using the Internet to appeal to niche markets, 63,000 small publishers with revenues of less than $50 million each generated $14.2 billion in sales in 2005—over half of the industry's total sales.

Sources: Hoynes, M. 2002. Is it the same for book sales? *BookWeb.org*, www.bookweb.org, March 20; www.parapublishing.com; Teague, D. 2005. U.S. book production reaches new high of 195,000 titles in 2004; Fiction soars. *Bowker.com*, www.bowker.com, May 24; and Teicher, C. M. 2007. March of the small presses. *Publishers Weekly*, www.publishersweekly.com, March 26.

The Bargaining Power of Buyers   The Internet and wireless technologies may increase buyer power by providing consumers with more information to make buying decisions and by lowering switching costs. But these technologies may also suppress the power of traditional buyer channels that have concentrated buying power in the hands of a few, giving buyers new ways to access sellers. To sort out these differences, let's first distinguish between two types of buyers: end users and buyer channel intermediaries.

End users, as the name implies, are the final customers in a distribution channel. They are the consumers who actually buy a product and put it to use. Internet sales activity that is labeled "B2C"—that is, business-to-consumer—is concerned with end users. The Internet is likely to increase the power of these buyers for several reasons. First, a large amount of consumer information is available on the Internet. This gives end users the information they need to shop for quality merchandise and bargain for price concessions. The automobile industry provides an excellent example of this phenomenon. For a small fee, agencies such as Consumers Union (publishers of *Consumer Reports*) will provide customers with detailed information about actual automobile manufacturer costs.[50] This information, available online, can be used to bid down dealers' profits. Second, an end user's switching costs are also potentially much lower because of the Internet. Switching may involve only a few clicks of the mouse to find and view a competing product or service online.

In contrast, the bargaining power of distribution channel buyers may decrease because of the Internet. *Buyer channel intermediaries* are the wholesalers, distributors, and retailers who serve as intermediaries between manufacturers and end users. In some industries, they are dominated by powerful players that control who gains access to the latest goods or the best merchandise. The Internet and wireless communications, however, make it much easier and less expensive for businesses to reach customers directly. Thus, the Internet may increase the power of incumbent firms relative to that of traditional buyer channels. Strategy Spotlight 2.7 illustrates some of the changes brought on by the Internet that have affected the industry's two types of buyers.

The Bargaining Power of Suppliers   Use of the Internet and digital technologies to speed up and streamline the process of acquiring supplies is already benefiting many sectors of the economy. But the net effect of the Internet on supplier power will depend on the nature of competition in a given industry. As with buyer power, the extent to which the Internet is a benefit or a detriment may also hinge on the supplier's position along the supply chain.

The role of suppliers typically involves providing products or services to other businesses. Thus, the term "B2B"—that is, business-to-business—is often used to refer to businesses that supply or sell to other businesses. The effect of the Internet on the bargaining power of suppliers is a double-edged sword. On the one hand, suppliers may find it difficult to hold onto customers because buyers can do comparative shopping and price negotiations so much faster on the Internet and can turn to other suppliers with a few clicks of the mouse. This is especially damaging to supply-chain intermediaries, such as product distributors, who may not be able to stop suppliers from directly accessing other potential business customers. In addition, one of the greatest threats to supplier power is that the Internet inhibits the ability of suppliers to offer highly differentiated products or unique services. Most procurement technologies can be imitated by competing suppliers, and the technologies that make it possible to design and customize new products rapidly are being used by all competitors.

On the other hand, several factors may also contribute to stronger supplier power. First, the growth of new Web-based business in general may create more downstream outlets for suppliers to sell to. Second, suppliers may be able to create Web-based purchasing arrangements that make purchasing easier and discourage their customers from switching. Online procurement systems, for example, create a direct link between suppliers and customers that reduces transaction costs and paperwork.[51] Third, the use of proprietary software that links buyers to a supplier's Web site may create a rapid, low-cost ordering capability that discourages the buyer from seeking other sources of supply. Amazon.com, for example, created and patented One-Click purchasing technology that speeds up the ordering process for customers who enroll in the service.[52]

Finally, suppliers will have greater power to the extent that they can reach end users directly without intermediaries. Previously, suppliers often had to work through intermediaries who brought their products or services to market for a fee. But a process known as *disintermediation* is removing the organizations or business process layers responsible for intermediary steps in the value chain of many industries.[53] Just as the Internet is eliminating some business functions, it is creating an opening for new functions. These new activities are entering the value chain by a process known as *reintermediation*—the introduction of new types of intermediaries. Many of these new functions are affecting traditional supply chains. For example, delivery services are enjoying a boom because of the Internet. Many more consumers are choosing to have products delivered to their door rather than going out to pick them up. Electronic delivery of products such as tickets to sporting events and electronic postage stamps is also becoming common.

The Threat of Substitutes   Along with traditional marketplaces, the Internet has created a new marketplace; along with traditional channels, it has become a new channel. In general, therefore, the threat of substitutes is heightened because the Internet introduces new ways to accomplish the same tasks.

Consumers will generally choose to use a product or service until a substitute that meets the same need becomes available at a lower cost. The economies created by Internet technologies have led to the development of numerous substitutes for traditional ways of doing business. For example, a company called Conferenza is offering an alternative way to participate in conferences for people who don't want to spend the time and money to attend. The Web site provides summaries of many conference events, quality ratings using an "event intelligence" score, and schedules of upcoming events.[54]

Another example of substitution is in the realm of electronic storage. With expanded desktop computing, the need to store information electronically has increased dramatically. Until recently, the trend has been to create increasingly larger desktop storage capabilities and techniques for compressing information that create storage efficiencies. But a viable substitute has recently emerged: storing information digitally on the Internet. Companies such as My Docs Online Inc. are providing Web-based storage that firms can access simply by leasing space online. Since these storage places are virtual, they can be accessed anywhere the Web can be accessed. This makes it possible for a traveler to access important documents and files without transporting them physically from place to place. Cyberstorage is not free, but it is still cheaper and more convenient than purchasing and carrying additional disk storage.[55]

The Intensity of Competitive Rivalry   Because the Internet creates more tools and means for competing, rivalry among competitors is likely to be more intense. Only those competitors that can use digital technologies and the Web to give themselves a distinct image, create unique product offerings, or provide "faster, smarter, cheaper" services are likely to capture greater profitability with the new technology. Such gains are hard to sustain, however, because in most cases the new technology can be imitated quickly. Thus, the Internet tends to increase rivalry by making it difficult for firms to differentiate themselves and by shifting customer attention to issues of price.

Rivalry is more intense when switching costs are low and product or service differentiation is minimized. Because the Internet makes it possible to shop around with a few clicks of the mouse, it has "commoditized" products that might previously have been regarded as rare or unique. Since the Internet eliminates the importance of location, products that previously had to be sought out in geographically distant outlets are now readily available online. This makes competitors in cyberspace seem more equally balanced, thus intensifying rivalry.

The problem is made worse for marketers by the presence of shopping robots ("bots") and infomediaries that search the Web for the best possible prices. Consumer websites like mySimon and PriceSCAN seek out all the Web locations that sell similar products and provide price comparisons.[56] Obviously, this hinders a firm's ability to establish unique characteristics and focuses the consumer exclusively on price. Some shopping infomediaries, such as BizRate and CNET, not only search for the lowest prices on many different products but also rank the customer service quality of different sites that sell similarly priced items.[57] Such infomediary services are good for consumers because they give them the chance to compare services as well as price. For businesses, however, they increase rivalry by consolidating the marketing message that consumers use to make a purchase decision to a few key pieces of information over which the selling company has little control.

Exhibit 2.9 summarizes many of the ways the Internet is affecting industry structure. These influences will also change how companies develop and deploy strategies to generate above-average profits and sustainable competitive advantage.

Using Industry Analysis: A Few Caveats

For industry analysis to be valuable, a company must collect and evaluate a wide variety of information from many sources. As the trend toward globalization accelerates, information on foreign markets as well as on a wider variety of competitors, suppliers, customers, substitutes, and potential new entrants becomes more critical. Industry analysis helps a firm not only to evaluate the profit potential of an industry, but also to consider various ways to strengthen its position vis-à-vis the five forces. However, we'd like to address a few caveats. First, *managers must not always avoid low profit industries (or low profit segments in profitable industries).* Such industries can still yield high returns for some players who

	Benefits to Industry (+)	Disadvantages to Industry (−)
Threat of New Entrants		• Lower barriers to entry increases number of new entrants. • Many Internet-based capabilities can be easily imitated.
Bargaining Power of Buyers	• Reduces the power of buyer intermediaries in many distribution channels.	• Switching costs decrease. • Information availability online empowers end users.
Bargaining Power of Suppliers	• Online procurement methods can increase bargaining power over suppliers.	• The Internet gives suppliers access to more customers and makes it easier to reach end users. • Online procurement practices deter competition and reduce differentiating features.
Threat of Substitutes	• Internet-based increases in overall efficiency can expand industry sales.	• Internet-based capabilities create more opportunities for substitution.
Intensity of Rivalry		• Since location is less important, the number of competitors increases. • Differences among competitors are harder to perceive online. • Rivalry tends to focus on price and differentiating features are minimized.

Sources: Bodily, S., & Venkataraman, S. 2004. Not walls, windows: Capturing value in the digital age. *Journal of Business Strategy,* 25(3): 15–25; Lumpkin, G. T., Droege, S. B., & Dess, G. G. 2002. E-commerce strategies: Achieving sustainable competitive advantage and avoiding pitfalls. *Organizational Dynamics,* 30 (Spring): 1–17.

Exhibit 2.9 How the Internet and Digital Technologies Influence Industry

pursue sound strategies. As examples, consider Paychex, a payroll-processing company, and WellPoint Health Network, a huge health care insurer:[58]

> Paychex, with $1.6 billion in revenues, became successful by serving small businesses. Existing firms had ignored them because they assumed that such businesses could not afford the service. When Paychex's founder, Tom Golisano, failed to convince his bosses at Electronic Accounting Systems that they were missing a great opportunity, he launched the firm. It now serves 550,000 businesses—each employing about 17 employees. Paychex's after-tax-return on sales is a stunning 28 percent.
>
> In 1986, WellPoint Health Network (when it was known as Blue Cross of California) suffered a loss of $160 million. That year, Leonard Schaeffer became CEO and challenged the conventional wisdom that individuals and small firms were money losers. (This was certainly "heresy" at the time—the firm was losing $5 million a year insuring 65,000 individuals!) However, by the early 1990s, the health insurer was leading the industry in profitability. The firm has continued to grow and outperform its rivals even during economic downturns. By 2006, its revenues and profits were nearly $60 billion and $3 billion, respectively—each figure representing an *annual* increase of over 35 percent for the most recent five-year period.

Second, five-forces analysis implicitly *assumes a zero-sum game, determining how a firm can enhance its position relative to the forces.* Yet such an approach can often be shortsighted; that is, it can overlook the many potential benefits of developing constructive win–win relationships with suppliers and customers. Establishing long-term mutually beneficial relationships with suppliers improves a firm's ability to implement just-in-time (JIT) inventory systems, which let it manage inventories better and respond quickly to market demands. A recent study found that if a company exploits its powerful position against a supplier, that action may come back to haunt the company. Consider, for example, General Motors's heavy-handed dealings with its suppliers:[60]

> GM has a reputation for particularly aggressive tactics. Although it is striving to crack down on the most egregious of these, it continues to rank dead last in the annual supplier satisfaction survey. "It's a brutal process," says David E. Cole, who is head of the Center for Automotive Research in Ann Arbor. "There are bodies lying by the side of the road."
>
> Suppliers point to one particularly nasty tactic: shopping their technology out the back door to see if rivals can make it cheaper. In one case, a GM purchasing manager showed a supplier's new brake design to Delphi Corporation. He was fired. However, in a recent survey, parts executives said they tend to bring hot new technology to other carmakers first. This is yet another reason GM finds it hard to compete in an intensely competitive industry.

Third, the five-forces analysis also has been criticized for *being essentially a static analysis*. External forces as well as strategies of individual firms are continually changing the structure of all industries. The search for a dynamic theory of strategy has led to greater use of game theory in industrial organization economics research and strategy research. Based on game-theoretic considerations, Brandenburger and Nalebuff recently introduced the concept of the value net,[61] which in many ways is an extension of the five-forces analysis. It is illustrated in Exhibit 2.10. The value net represents all the players in the game and analyzes how their interactions affect a firm's ability to generate and appropriate value. The vertical dimension of the net includes suppliers and customers. The firm has direct transactions with them. On the horizontal dimension are substitutes and complements, players with whom a firm interacts but may not necessarily transact. The concept of complementors is perhaps the single most important contribution of value net analysis and is explained in more detail below.

Complements typically are products or services that have a potential impact on the value of a firm's own products or services. Those who produce complements are usually referred to as complementors.[62] Powerful hardware is of no value to a user unless there is software that runs on it. Similarly, new and better software is possible only if the hardware on which it can be run is available. This is equally true in the video game industry, where the sales of game

complements
products or services that have an impact on the value of a firm's products or services.

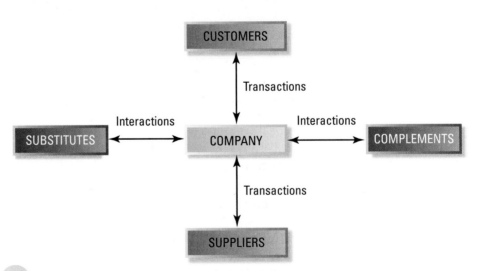

Exhibit 2.10 The Value Net

Source: Adapted and reprinted by permission of *Harvard Business Review.* Exhibit from "The Right Game: Use Game Theory to Shape Strategy," by A. Brandenburger and B. J. Nalebuff, July–August 1995. Copyright © 1995 by the Harvard Business School Publishing Corporation. All rights reserved.

Apple's iPod: Relationships with its Complementors

In 2002, Steve Jobs began his campaign to cajole the major music companies into selling tracks to iPod users through the iTunes Music Store, an online retail site. Most industry executives, after being burned by illegal file-sharing services like Napster and Kazaa, just wanted digital music to disappear. However, Jobs's passionate vision persuaded them to climb on board. He promised to reduce the risks that they faced by offering safeguards against piracy, as well as a hip product (iPod) that would drive sales.

However, Apple had a much stronger bargaining position when its contracts with the music companies came up for renewal in April 2005. By then, iTunes had captured 80 percent of the market for legal downloads. The music companies, which were receiving between 60 and 70 cents per download, wanted more. Their reasoning: If the iTunes Music Store would only charge $1.50 or $2.00 per track, they could double or triple their revenues and profits. Since Jobs knew that he could sell more iPods if the music was cheap, he was determined to keep the price of a download at 99 cents and to maintain Apple's margins. Given iTunes dominant position, the music companies had little choice but to relent.

Apple's venture into music has been tremendously successful. For the fiscal year ending September 30, 2006, iPod sales had increased to $7.4 billion, and other music-

related products and services totaled $1.9 billion. These figures represent increases of 69 percent and 110 percent, respectively, over the previous year.

- A female employee sits at her desk equipped with both an iMac and an iPod. She works on a spreadsheet, uses iTunes and listens to an iPod.

Source: Apple Computer Inc. 10-K, December 29, 2006; and, Yoffie, D. B. & Kwak, M. 2006. With friends like these: The art of managing complementors. *Harvard Business Review*, 84(9): 88–98.

---

consoles and video games complement each other. Nintendo's success in the early 1990s was a result of their ability to manage their relationship with their complementors. They built a security chip into the hardware and then licensed the right to develop games to outside firms. These firms paid a royalty to Nintendo for each copy of the game sold. The royalty revenue enabled Nintendo to sell game consoles at close to their cost, thereby increasing their market share, which, in turn, caused more games to be sold and more royalties to be generated.[63]

Despite efforts to create win–win scenarios, conflict among complementors is inevitable.[64] After all, it is naive to expect that even the closest of partners will do you the favor of abandoning their own interests. And even the most successful partnerships are seldom trouble free. Power is a factor that comes into play as we see in Strategy Spotlight 2.8 with the example of Apple's iPod—an enormously successful product.

> **>LO7**
> The concept of strategic groups and their strategy and performance implications.

Strategic Groups within Industries

In an industry analysis, two assumptions are unassailable: (1) No two firms are totally different, and (2) no two firms are exactly the same. The issue becomes one of identifying groups of firms that are more similar to each other than firms that are not, otherwise known as **strategic groups**.[65] This is important because rivalry tends to be greater among firms

> **strategic groups**
> clusters of firms that share similar strategies.

that are alike. Strategic groups are clusters of firms that share similar strategies. After all, is Kmart more concerned about Nordstrom or Wal-Mart? Is Mercedes more concerned about Hyundai or BMW? The answers are straightforward.[66]

These examples are not meant to trivialize the strategic groups concept.[67] Classifying an industry into strategic groups involves judgment. If it is useful as an analytical tool, we must exercise caution in deciding what dimensions to use to map these firms. Dimensions include breadth of product and geographic scope, price/quality, degree of vertical integration, type of distribution (e.g., dealers, mass merchandisers, private label), and so on. Dimensions should also be selected to reflect the variety of strategic combinations in an industry. For example, if all firms in an industry have roughly the same level of product differentiation (or R&D intensity), this would not be a good dimension to select.

What value is the strategic groups concept as an analytical tool? *First, strategic groupings help a firm identify barriers to mobility that protect a group from attacks by other groups*.[68] Mobility barriers are factors that deter the movement of firms from one strategic position to another. For example, in the chainsaw industry, the major barriers protecting the high-quality/dealer-oriented group are technology, brand image, and an established network of servicing dealers.

The second value of strategic grouping is that it *helps a firm identify groups whose competitive position may be marginal or tenuous*. We may anticipate that these competitors may exit the industry or try to move into another group. This has been the case in recent years in the retail department store industry, where firms such as JCPenney and Sears have experienced extremely difficult times because they were stuck in the middle, neither an aggressive discount player like Wal-Mart nor a prestigious upscale player like Neiman Marcus.

Third, strategic groupings *help chart the future directions of firms' strategies*. Arrows emanating from each strategic group can represent the direction in which the group (or a firm within the group) seems to be moving. If all strategic groups are moving in a similar direction, this could indicate a high degree of future volatility and intensity of competition. In the automobile industry, for example, the competition in the minivan and sport utility segments has intensified in recent years as many firms have entered those product segments.

Fourth, strategic groups are *helpful in thinking through the implications of each industry trend for the strategic group as a whole*. Is the trend decreasing the viability of a group? If so, in what direction should the strategic group move? Is the trend increasing or decreasing entry barriers in a given group? Will the trend decrease the ability of one group to separate itself from other groups? Such analysis can help in making predictions about industry evolution. A sharp increase in interest rates, for example, would tend to have less impact on providers of higher-priced goods (e.g., Porsches) than on providers of lower-priced goods (e.g., Chevrolet Cobalt). The Chevrolet Cobalt customer base is much more price sensitive.

Exhibit 2.11 provides a strategic grouping of the worldwide automobile industry.[69] The firms in each group are representative; not all firms are included in the mapping. We have identified four strategic groups. In the top left-hand corner are high-end luxury auto-makers who focus on a very narrow product market. Most of the cars produced by the members of this group cost well over $100,000. Some cost many times that amount. The Ferrari F50 costs roughly $550,000 and the Lamborghini L147 $300,000[70] (in case you were wondering how to spend your employment signing bonus). Players in this market have a very exclusive clientele and face little rivalry from other strategic groups. At the other extreme, in the lower left-hand corner is a strategic group that has low-price/quality attributes and targets a narrow market. These players, Hyundai and Kia, limit competition from other strategic groups by pricing their products very low. The third group (near the middle) consists of firms high in product pricing/quality and average in their product-line breadth. The final group (at the far right) consists of firms with a broad range of products

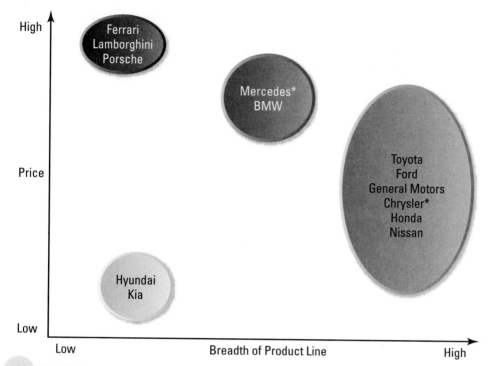

Exhibit 2.11 The World Automobile Industry: Strategic Groups

*Chrysler and Mercedes (part of DaimlerChrysler) are separated for purposes of illustration.

Note: Members of each strategic group are not inclusive, only illustrative.

and multiple price points. These firms have entries that compete at both the lower end of the market (e.g., the Ford Focus) and the higher end (e.g., Chevrolet Corvette).

The auto market has been very dynamic and competition has intensified in recent years. Many firms in different strategic groups compete in the same product markets, such as minivans and sport utility vehicles. In the late 1990s Mercedes entered the fray with its M series, and Porsche has a recent entry as well with its Cayenne, a 2004 model. Some players are also going more upscale with their product offerings. Recently, Hyundai introduced its XG300, priced at over $25,000 for a fully loaded model. This brings Hyundai into direct competition with entries from other strategic groups such as Toyota's Camry and Honda's Accord. Hyundai is offering an extensive warranty (10 years, 100,000 miles) in an effort to offset customer perceptions of their lower quality. Perhaps Ford has made the most notable efforts to go upscale. Not content to rely solely on the Lincoln nameplate to attract high-ticket buyers, Ford, like other large players, recently went on an acquisition binge, acquiring Volvo, Land Rover, Jaguar, and Aston Martin. Ford is aggressively accelerating its forecasted sales for each of these brands.[71] To further intensify competition, some key automakers are providing offerings in lower-priced segments. Mercedes and BMW, with their C-class and 3-series, respectively, are well-known examples. Such cars, priced in the low $30,000s, compete more directly with products from broad-line manufacturers like Ford, General Motors, and Toyota.

These new products are competing in an industry that has experienced relatively flat unit sales in the first half of this decade.[72] In addition, high-incentive–laden offerings appear to be losing some of their appeal to consumers, and there are higher levels of inventory at dealerships. Further, since manufacturers have maintained, if not increased, production schedules and plant capacity, overall competition should intensify. Don't be surprised, therefore, if rebates and discounting continue on most models.

Reflecting on Career Implications . . .

- *Creating the Environmentally Aware Organization:* In your career, what are some ways in which you can engage in scanning, monitoring, and intelligence gathering for future job opportunities? Consider, for example, subscribing to your field's professional publications and becoming actively involved in relevant professional organizations.
- *SWOT Analysis:* From a career standpoint, periodically evaluate your strengths and weaknesses as well as potential opportunities and threats to your career. In addition, strive to seek input from trusted peers and superiors.
- *General Environment:* Carefully evaluate the elements of the general environment facing your firm. Identify factors (e.g., rapid technological change) that can provide promising career opportunities as well as possibilities for you to add value for your organization. In doing this, don't focus solely on "internal factors" of your organization.
- *Five-forces analysis:* Consider the five-forces affecting the industry within which your organization competes. If the "forces" are unfavorable, the long-term profit potential of the industry may be unattractive. And, there will likely be fewer resources available and—all other things being equal—fewer career opportunities.

Summary

Managers must analyze the external environment to minimize or eliminate threats and exploit opportunities. This involves a continuous process of environmental scanning and monitoring as well as obtaining competitive intelligence on present and potential rivals. These activities provide valuable inputs for developing forecasts. In addition, many firms use scenario planning to anticipate and respond to volatile and disruptive environmental changes.

We identified two types of environments: the general environment and the competitive environment. The six segments of the general environment are demographic, sociocultural, political/legal, technological, economic, and global. Trends and events occurring in these segments, such as the aging of the population, higher percentages of women in the workplace, governmental legislation, and increasing (or decreasing) interest rates, can have a dramatic effect on a firm. A given trend or event may have a positive impact on some industries and a negative, neutral, or no impact at all on others.

The competitive environment consists of industry-related factors and has a more direct impact than the general environment. Porter's five-forces model of industry analysis includes the threat of new entrants, buyer power, supplier power, threat of substitutes, and rivalry among competitors. The intensity of these factors determines, in large part, the average expected level of profitability in an industry. A sound awareness of such factors, both individually and in combination, is beneficial not only for deciding what industries to enter but also for assessing how a firm can improve its competitive position. We discuss how many of the changes brought about by the digital economy can be understood in the context of five-forces analysis. The limitations of five-forces analysis include its static nature and its inability to acknowledge the role of complementors. Although we addressed the general environment and competitive environment in separate sections, they are quite interdependent. A given environmental trend or event, such as changes in the ethnic composition of a population or a technological innovation, typically has a much greater impact on some industries than on others.

The concept of strategic groups is also important to the external environment of a firm. No two organizations are completely different nor are they exactly the same. The question is how to group firms in an industry on the basis of similarities in their resources and strategies. The strategic groups concept is valuable for determining mobility barriers across groups, identifying groups with marginal competitive positions, charting the future directions of firm strategies, and assessing the implications of industry trends for the strategic group as a whole.

Summary Review Questions

1. Why must managers be aware of a firm's external environment?

2. What is gathering and analyzing competitive intelligence and why is it important for firms to engage in it?

3. Discuss and describe the six elements of the external environment.

4. Select one of these elements and describe some changes relating to it in an industry that interests you.

5. Describe how the five forces can be used to determine the average expected profitability in an industry.

6. What are some of the limitations (or caveats) in using five-forces analysis?

7. Explain how the general environment and industry environment are highly related. How can such interrelationships affect the profitability of a firm or industry?

8. Explain the concept of strategic groups. What are the performance implications?

Key Terms

environmental scanning, 39
environmental monitoring, 39
competitive intelligence, 40
environmental, forecasting, 42
scenario analysis, 42
SWOT analysis, 44
general environment, 44
competitive environment, 52
complements, 64
strategic groups, 65

Experiential Exercise

Select one of the following industries: personal computers, airlines, or automobiles. For this industry, evaluate the strength of each of Porter's five forces as well as complementors.

Industry Force	High? Medium? Low?	Why?
1. Threat of new entrants		
2. Power of buyers		
3. Power of suppliers		
4. Power of substitutes		
5. Rivalry among competitors		
6. Complementors		

Application Questions Exercises

1. Imagine yourself as the CEO of a large firm in an industry in which you are interested. Please (1) identify major trends in the general environment, (2) analyze their impact on the firm, and (3) identify major sources of information to monitor these trends. (Use Internet and library resources.)

2. Analyze movements across the strategic groups in the U.S. retail industry. How do these movements within this industry change the nature of competition?

3. What are the major trends in the general environment that have impacted the U.S. pharmaceutical industry?

4. Go to the Internet and look up www.kroger.com. What are some of the five forces driving industry competition that are affecting the profitability of this firm?

Ethics Questions

1. What are some of the legal and ethical issues involved in collecting competitor intelligence in the following situations?

   a. Hotel A sends an employee posing as a potential client to Hotel B to find out who Hotel B's major corporate customers are.

b. A firm hires an MBA student to collect information directly from a competitor while claiming the information is for a course project.

c. A firm advertises a nonexistent position and interviews a rival's employees with the intention of obtaining competitor information.

2. What are some of the ethical implications that arise when a firm tries to exploit its power over a supplier?

References

1. Pirovano, T. 2006. Health & wellness trends—The speculation is over. *Retailing Insights,* Spring, 10–15; Anonymous. 2003. Coors goes low carb. November 19, www.realbeer.com; Anonymous. 2004. The "Atkins Effect"—Shrinking waistlines, expanding wallets. January 23, www.frost.com; Lin, J. 2003. Low-carb beer may become the biggest thing since light beer. *Oakland Tribune,* np; Cordova, N. N. 2007. Personal communication. January 12 (Consumer Relations, Coors); and, Day, G. S. & Schoemaker, P. J. H. 2005. Scanning the periphery, *Harvard Business Review,* 83(11): 135–149.

2. Hamel, G., & Prahalad, C. K. 1994. *Competing for the future.* Boston: Harvard Business School Press.

3. Drucker, P. F. 1994. Theory of the business. *Harvard Business Review,* 72: 95–104.

4. For an insightful discussion on managers' assessment of the external environment, refer to Sutcliffe, K. M., & Weber, K. 2003. The high cost of accurate knowledge. *Harvard Business Review,* 81(5): 74–86.

5. Charitou, C. D., & Markides, C. C. 2003. Responses to disruptive strategic innovation. *MIT Sloan Management Review,* 44(2): 55–64.

6. Our discussion of scanning, monitoring, competitive intelligence, and forecasting concepts draws on several sources. These include Fahey, L., & Narayanan, V. K. 1983. *Macroenvironmental analysis for strategic management.* St. Paul, MN: West; Lorange, P., Scott, F. S., & Ghoshal, S. 1986. *Strategic control.* St. Paul, MN: West; Ansoff, H. I. 1984. *Implementing strategic management.* Englewood Cliffs, NJ: Prentice Hall; and Schreyogg, G., & Stienmann, H. 1987. Strategic control: A new perspective. *Academy of Management Review,* 12: 91–103.

7. Elenkov, D. S. 1997. Strategic uncertainty and environmental scanning: The case for institutional influences on scanning behavior. *Strategic Management Journal,* 18: 287–302.

8. For an interesting perspective on environmental scanning in emerging economies see May, R. C.,

Stewart, W. H., & Sweo, R. 2000. Environmental scanning behavior in a transitional economy: Evidence from Russia. *Academy of Management Journal,* 43(3): 403–27.

9. Browne, Sir John. The new agenda. Keynote speech delivered to the World Petroleum Congress in Calgary, Canada, June 13, 2000.

10. Bowles, J. 1997. Key issues for the automotive industry CEOs. *Fortune,* August 18: S3.

11. Walters, B. A., & Priem, R. L. 1999. Business strategy and CEO intelligence acquisition. *Competitive Intelligence Review,* 10(2): 15–22.

12. Prior, V. 1999. The language of competitive intelligence, Part 4. *Competitive Intelligence Review,* 10(1): 84–87.

13. Zahra, S. A., & Charples, S. S. 1993. Blind spots in competitive analysis. *Academy of Management Executive* 7(2): 7–27.

14. Wolfenson, J. 1999. The world in 1999: A battle for corporate honesty. *The Economist* 38: 13–30.

15. Drucker, P. F. 1997. The future that has already happened. *Harvard Business Review,* 75(6): 22.

16. Evans, P. B., & Wurster, T. S. 1997. Strategy and the new economics of information. *Harvard Business Review,* 75(5): 71–82.

17. Fahey & Narayanan, op. cit., p. 41.

18. Courtney, H., Kirkland, J., & Viguerie, P. 1997. Strategy under uncertainty. *Harvard Business Review,* 75(6): 66–79.

19. Odlyzko, A. 2003. False hopes. *Red Herring,* March: 31.

20. Rosne, B. 2007. The little guy. abcnews.com. January 12:4.

21. For an interesting perspective on how Accenture practices and has developed its approach to scenario planning, refer to Ferguson, G., Mathur, S., & Shah, B. 2005. Evolving from information to insight. *MIT Sloan Management Review,* 46(2): 51–58.

22. Dean, T. J., Brown, R. L., & Bamford, C. E. 1998. Differences in large and small firm responses to environmental context: Strategic implications from a comparative analysis of business formations. *Strategic Management Journal,* 19: 709–728.

23. Colvin, G. 1997. How to beat the boomer rush. *Fortune,* August 18: 59–63.

24. Guntner, T. 2006. Still working and loving it. *BusinessWeek,* October 16: 108; Warner, M. 2004. Home Depot goes old school. *Business 2.0,* June: 74; and, O'Brien, S. 2005. Over 50 and looking for work? *www.seniorliving.about.com.*

25. Challenger, J. 2000. Women's corporate rise has reduced relocations. *Lexington* (KY) *Herald-Leader,* October 29: D1.

26. Tsao, A. 2005. Retooling home improvement, Businesssweek.com, February, 14; and, Grow, B. 2004. Who wears the wallet in the family? *BusinessWeek,* August 16:10.

27. Watkins, M. D. 2003. Government games. *MIT Sloan Management Review* 44(2): 91–95.

28. Davies, A. 2000. The welcome mat is out for nerds. *BusinessWeek,* October 16: 64.

29. Anonymous. Business ready for Internet revolution. 1999. *Financial Times,* May 21: 17.

30. Lataif, L. E. 2006. B-Schools and the common good. *BizEd,* March/April: 36–39.

31. Baker, S., & Aston, A. 2005. The business of nanotech. *BusinessWeek,* February 14: 64–71.

32. Ginsburg, J. 2000. Letting the free market clear the air. *BusinessWeek,* November 6: 200, 204.

33. Smith, G., Wheatley, J., & Green, J. 2000. Car power. *BusinessWeek,* October 23: 72–80.

34. Byrnes, N. 2006. The high cost of fear. *BusinessWeek,* November 6: 16.

35. Goll, I., & Rasheed, M. A. 1997. Rational decision-making and firm performance: The moderating role of environment. *Strategic Management Journal,* 18: 583–591.

36. This discussion draws heavily on Porter, M. E. 1980. *Competitive strategy:* Chapter 1. New York: Free Press.

37. Ibid.

38. Fryer, B. 2001. Leading through rough times: An interview with Novell's Eric Schmidt. *Harvard Business Review,* 78(5): 117–123.

39. For a discussion on the importance of barriers to entry within industries, read Greenwald, B., & Kahn, J. 2005. *Competition demystified: A radically simplified approach to business strategy.* East Rutherford, NJ: Portfolio.

40. The ProCD example draws heavily upon Shapiro, C., & Varian, H. R. 2000. Versioning: The smart way to sell information. *Harvard Business Review,* 78(1): 106–114.

41. Wise, R., & Baumgarter, P. 1999. Go downstream: The new profit imperative in manufacturing. *Harvard Business Review,* 77(5): 133–141.

42. Salman, W. A. 2000. The new economy is stronger than you think. *Harvard Business Review,* 77(6): 99–106.

43. Mudambi, R., & Helper, S. 1998. The "close but adversarial" model of supplier relations in the U.S.

auto industry. *Strategic Management Journal,* 19: 775–792.

44. Bernstein, A. 2000. Workers are doing well, but will it last? *BusinessWeek,* October 9: 48.

45. Tischler, L. 2002. IBM: Manager jam. *Fast Company,* October: 48.

46. For an interesting perspective on the intensity of competition in the supermarket industry, refer to Anonymous. 2005. Warfare in the aisles. *The Economist,* April 2: 6–8.

47. Marcial, G. 2000. Giving Viagra a run for its money. *BusinessWeek,* October 23: 173.

48. McGann, R. 2005. VOIP poised to take flight? ClickZ.com, February 23, www.clickz.com.

49. For an interesting perspective on changing features of firm boundaries, refer to Afuah, A. 2003. Redefining firm boundaries in the face of Internet: Are firms really shrinking? *Academy of Management Review,* 28(1): 34–53.

50. www.consumerreports.org.

51. Time to rebuild. 2001. *Economist,* May 19: 55–56.

52. www.amazon.com.

53. For more on the role of the Internet as an electronic intermediary, refer to Carr, N. G. 2000. Hypermediation: Commerce as clickstream. *Harvard Business Review,* 78(1): 46–48.

54. Olofson, C. 2001. The next best thing to being there. *Fast Company,* April: 175; and www.conferenza.com.

55. Lelii, S. R. 2001. Free online storage a thing of the past? *eWEEK,* April 22.

56. www.mysimon.com; and www.pricescan.com.

57. www.cnet.com; and www.bizrate.com.

58. Foust, D. 2007. The best performers. *BusinessWeek,* March 26: 58–95; Rosenblum, D., Tomlinson, D. & Scott, L. 2003. Bottom-feeding for blockbuster businesses. *Harvard Business Review,* 81(3): 52–59; Paychex 2006 Annual Report; and, WellPoint Health Network 2005 Annual Report.

59. Kumar, N. 1996. The power of trust in manufacturer-retailer relationship. *Harvard Business Review,* 74(6): 92–110.

60. Welch, D. 2006. Renault-Nissan: Say hello to Bo. *BusinessWeek,* July 31: 56–57.

61. Brandenburger, A., & Nalebuff, B. J. 1995. The right game: Use game theory to shape strategy. *Harvard Business Review,* 73(4): 57–71.

62. For a scholarly discussion of complementary assets and their relationship to competitive advantage, refer to Stieglitz, N., & Heine, K. 2007. Innovations and

the role of complementarities in a strategic theory of the firm. *Strategic Management Journal,* 28(1): 1–15.

63. A useful framework for the analysis of industry evolution has been proposed by Professor Anita McGahan of Boston University. Her analysis is based on the identification of the core activities and the core assets of an industry and the threats they face. She suggests that an industry may follow one of four possible evolutionary trajectories—radical change, creative change, intermediating change, or progressive change—based on these two types of threats of obsolescence. Refer to: McGahan, A. M. 2004. How industries change. *Harvard Business Review,* 82(10): 87–94.

64. Yoffie, D. B., & Kwak, M. 2006. With friends like these: The art of managing complementors. *Harvard Business Review*, 84(9): 88–98.

65. Peteraf, M., & Shanley, M. 1997. Getting to know you: A theory of strategic group identity. *Strategic Management Journal,* 18 (Special Issue): 165–186.

66. An interesting scholarly perspective on strategic groups may be found in Dranove, D., Perteraf, M., & Shanley, M. 1998. Do strategic groups exist? An economic framework for analysis. *Strategic Management Journal,* 19(11): 1029–1044.

67. For an empirical study on strategic groups and predictors of performance, refer to Short, J. C., Ketchen, D. J., Jr., Palmer, T. B., & Hult, T. M. 2007. Firm, strategic group, and industry influences on performance. *Strategic Management Journal,* 28(2): 147–167.

68. This section draws on several sources, including Kerwin, K. R., & Haughton, K. 1997. Can Detroit make cars that baby boomers like? *BusinessWeek,* December 1: 134–148; and Taylor, A., III. 1994. The new golden age of autos. *Fortune,* April 4: 50–66.

69. Csere, C. 2001. Supercar supermarket. *Car and Driver,* January: 118–127.

70. Healey, J. R. 1999. Groomed so as not to marry. *USA Today,* August 6: B1.

71. Csere, op. cit.

72. Smith, J. A. 2005. Auto & Truck Industry. *Value Line,* March 4: 101.

chapter 3

Assessing the Internal Environment of the Firm

>learning objectives

After reading this chapter, you should have a good understanding of:

LO1 The benefits and limitations of SWOT analysis in conducting an internal analysis of the firm.

LO2 The primary and support activities of a firm's value chain.

LO3 How value-chain analysis can help managers create value by investigating relationships among activities within the firm and between the firm and its customers and suppliers.

LO4 The resource-based view of the firm and the different types of tangible and intangible resources, as well as organizational capabilities.

LO5 The four criteria that a firm's resources must possess to maintain a sustainable advantage and how value created can be appropriated by employees and managers.

LO6 The usefulness of financial ratio analysis, its inherent limitations, and how to make meaningful comparisons of performance across firms.

LO7 The value of the "balanced scorecard" in recognizing how the interests of a variety of stakeholders can be interrelated.

LO8 How firms are using Internet technologies to add value and achieve unique advantages. (Appendix) *t*wo firms compete in the same industry and both have many strengths in a variety of functional areas: marketing, operations, logistics, and so on. However, one of these firms outperforms the other by a wide margin over a long period of time. How can this be so? This chapter endeavors to answer that question.

We begin with two sections that include frameworks for gaining key insights into a firm's internal environment: value-chain analysis and the resource-based view of the firm. In value-chain analysis, we divide a firm's activities into a series of value-creating steps. We then explore how individual activities within the firm add value, and also how *interrelationships* among activities within the firm, and between the firm and its suppliers and customers, create value.

In the resource-based view of the firm, we analyze the firm as a collection of tangible and intangible resources as well as organizational capabilities. Advantages that tend to be sustainable over time typically arise from creating *bundles* of resources and capabilities that satisfy four criteria: they are valuable, rare, difficult to imitate, and difficult to substitute. Not all of the value created by a firm will necessarily be kept (or appropriated) by the owners. We discuss the four key factors that determine how profits will be distributed between owners as well as employees and managers.

In the closing sections, we discuss how to evaluate a firm's performance and make comparisons across firms. We emphasize both the inclusion of financial resources and the interests of multiple stakeholders. Central to our discussion is the concept of the balanced scorecard, which recognizes that the interests of different stakeholders can be interrelated. We also consider how a firm's performance evolves over time and how it compares with industry norms and key competitors.

In an appendix to this chapter, we explore how Internet-based businesses and incumbent firms are using digital technologies to add value. We consider four activities—search, evaluation, problem solving, and transaction—as well as three types of content—customer feedback, expertise, and entertainment programming. Such technology-enhanced capabilities are providing new means with which firms can achieve competitive advantages.

 Learning from Mistakes

In the late 1980s, Goodyear Tire & Rubber Co., then the largest tire company in the world, began an organizationwide initiative to adopt the principles of total quality management (TQM).[1] Like so many other companies that embraced TQM, Goodyear's operations, logistics, procurement, and research and development were reengineered with the objective of producing "defect-free" products. So far, so good? Read on. . . .

Unfortunately, sales and distribution, which had always been central to Goodyear's success, were demoted to secondary status because TQM focused almost entirely on the manufacturing process. Not surprisingly, relationships began to sour between manufacturing people and the sales and distribution staff.

Resources to support the highly successful existing U.S. dealer network, which had taken nearly a century to develop and perfect, were reallocated to operations. With fewer resources, Goodyear had little choice but to cannibalize its existing distribution arrangement. Wholesalers became dealers and vice versa. Multiple sales outlets appeared everywhere where there had previously been only one or two Goodyear dealers for years. Thus, Goodyear's control over the sale and distribution of its products began to crumble.

For Goodyear's consumers, this was good news. They could now have Wrangler or American Eagle tires mounted on their cars while they shopped at the mall or purchased dry goods at large, powerful retailers such as Wal-Mart and Sears, which *[continued]* began selling Goodyear tires in the early 1990s. Retailers also came out ahead. Since such new retailers were not exclusive dealers, they placed Goodyear tires next to competing brands, giving their customers more choices. Not surprisingly, the price of Goodyear's tires sharply declined. And, with a large number of outlets competing for the same customer base, price wars became inevitable.

In the long run, the only loser was Goodyear and its employees. The firm's competitive position and profitability began to erode. Unable to raise its prices through a compromised distribution network, Goodyear faced inevitable plant closures. This was done to compensate for steady losses from the ill-conceived dissolution of its dealer network. By early 2003, the company was carrying a huge debt burden, and its pension fund was underfunded by $2 billion. What's worse, Goodyear's once-loyal dealers were in open revolt because the company could not even fill the orders from dealers—mainly because of the disconnect between the factories and the distributor network.

Goodyear's problems began when it failed to invest in its valuable resources in its downstream activities—sales and distribution. Instead, it "followed the herd" and became a TQM disciple by focusing its resources on improving its operations, logistics, and research and development activities. Thus, its performance suffered when its key strength began to wither. Without its superb distribution network, the firm was forced to sell its products through mass merchandisers such as Wal-Mart and Sears, and its customers began perceiving its products, in essence, as a commodity. Clearly, firms benefit from assessing the internal environment to address what value-creating activities lead to their competitive advantages and developing strategies accordingly. Overemphasizing one part of the value chain and neglecting others may result in a failure to maintain and enhance overall organizational effectiveness.[2]

>LO1

The benefits and limitations of SWOT analysis in conducting an internal analysis of the firm.

value chain analysis
a strategic analysis of an organization that uses value-creating activities.

primary activities
sequential activities of the value chain that refer to the physical creation of the product or service, its sale and transfer to the buyer, and its service after sale, including inbound logistics, operations, outbound logistics, marketing and sales, and service.

Before moving ahead to value-chain analysis, let's briefly revisit SWOT analysis to discuss some of its benefits and limitations. As discussed in Chapter 2, a SWOT analysis consists of a careful listing of a firm's strengths, weaknesses, opportunities, and threats. While we believe SWOT analysis is very helpful as a starting point, it should not form the primary basis for evaluating a firm's internal strengths and weaknesses or the opportunities and threats in the environment. Strategy Spotlight 3.1 elaborates on the limitations of the traditional SWOT approach.

We will now turn to value-chain analysis. As you will see, it provides greater insights into analyzing a firm's competitive position than SWOT analysis does by itself.

Value-Chain Analysis

Value-chain analysis views the organization as a sequential process of value-creating activities. The approach is useful for understanding the building blocks of competitive advantage. Value-chain analysis was described in Michael Porter's seminal book *Competitive Advantage*.[3] In competitive terms, value is the amount that buyers are willing to pay for what a firm provides them. Value is measured by total revenue, a reflection of the price a firm's product commands and the quantity it can sell. A firm is profitable to the extent that the value it receives exceeds the total costs involved in creating its product or service. Creating value for buyers that exceeds the costs of production (i.e., margin) is a key concept used in analyzing a firm's competitive position.

Porter described two different categories of activities. First, five **primary activities**—inbound logistics, operations, outbound logistics, marketing and sales, and service—contribute to the physical creation of the product or service, its sale and transfer to

The Limitations of SWOT Analysis

SWOT analysis is a tried-and-true tool of strategic analysis. SWOT (strengths, weaknesses, opportunities, threats) analysis is used regularly in business to initially evaluate the opportunities and threats in the business environment as well as the strengths and weaknesses of a firm's internal environment. Top managers rely on SWOT to stimulate self-reflection and group discussions about how to improve their firm and position it for success.

But SWOT has its limitations. It is just a starting point for discussion. By listing the firm's attributes, managers have the raw material needed to perform more in-depth strategic analysis. However, SWOT cannot show them how to achieve a competitive advantage. They must not make SWOT analysis an end in itself, temporarily raising awareness about important issues but failing to lead to the kind of action steps necessary to enact strategic change.

Consider the ProCD example from Chapter 2, page 54. A brief SWOT analysis might include the following:

Strengths	Opportunities
First-mover advantage	Demand for electronic phone books
Low labor cost	Sudden growth in use of digital technology

Weaknesses	Threats
Inexperienced new company	Easily duplicated product
No proprietary information	Market power of incumbent firms

The combination of low production costs and an early-mover advantage in an environment where demand for CD-based phone books was growing rapidly seems to indicate that ProCD founder James Bryant had a golden opportunity. But the SWOT analysis did not reveal how to turn those strengths into a competitive advantage, nor did it highlight how rapidly the environment would change, allowing imitators to come into the market and erode his first-mover advantage. Let's look at some of the limitations of SWOT analysis.

Strengths May Not Lead to an Advantage

A firm's strengths and capabilities, no matter how unique or impressive, may not enable it to achieve a competitive advan-

tage in the marketplace. It is akin to recruiting a concert pianist to join a gang of thugs—even though such an ability is rare and valuable, it hardly helps the organization attain its goals and objectives! Similarly, the skills of a highly creative product designer would offer little competitive advantage to a firm that produces low-cost commodity products. Indeed, the additional expense of hiring such an individual could erode the firm's cost advantages. If a firm builds its strategy on a capability that cannot, by itself, create or sustain competitive advantage, it is essentially a wasted use of resources. ProCD had several key strengths, but it did not translate them into lasting advantages in the marketplace.

SWOT's Focus on the External Environment Is Too Narrow

Strategists who rely on traditional definitions of their industry and competitive environment often focus their sights too narrowly on current customers, technologies, and competitors. Hence they fail to notice important changes on the periphery of their environment that may trigger the need to redefine industry boundaries and identify a whole new set of competitive relationships. Reconsider the example from Chapter 2 of *Encyclopaedia Britannica*, whose competitive position was severely eroded by a "nontraditional" competitor—CD-based encyclopedias (e.g., Microsoft *Encarta*) that could be used on home computers.

SWOT Gives a One-Shot View of a Moving Target

A key weakness of SWOT is that it is primarily a static assessment. It focuses too much of a firm's attention on one moment in time. Essentially, this is like studying a single frame of a motion picture. You may be able to identify the principal actors and learn something about the setting, but it doesn't tell you much about the plot. Competition among organizations is played out over time. As circumstances, capabilities, and strategies change, static analysis techniques do not reveal the dynamics of the competitive environment. Clearly, ProCD was unaware that its competitiveness was being eroded so quickly.

SWOT Overemphasizes a Single Dimension of Strategy

Sometimes firms become preoccupied with a single strength or a key feature of the product or service they are offering and ignore other factors needed for competitive success. For example, Food Lion, a large grocery retailer, paid a heavy price for its excessive emphasis on cost control. The resulting problems with labor and the negative publicity led to its eventual withdrawal from several markets.

SWOT analysis has much to offer, but only as a starting point. By itself, it rarely helps a firm develop competitive advantages that it can sustain over time.

Sources: Shapiro, C., & Varian, H. R. 2000. Versioning: The smart way to sell information. *Harvard Business Review*, 78(1): 99–106; and Picken, J. C., & Dess, G. G. 1997. *Mission Critical*. Burr Ridge, IL: Irwin Professional Publishing.

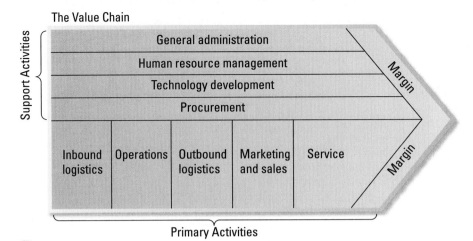

The Value Chain

Exhibit 3.1 **The Value Chain: Primary and Support Activities**

>LO2

The primary and support activities of a firm's value chain.

support activities
activities of the value chain that either add value by themselves or add value through important relationships with both primary activities and other support activities; including procurement, technology development, human resource management, and general administration.

the buyer, and its service after the sale. Second, **support activities**—procurement, technology development, human resource management, and general administration—either add value by themselves or add value through important relationships with both primary activities and other support activities. Exhibit 3.1 illustrates Porter's value chain.

To get the most out of value-chain analysis, you need to view the concept in its broadest context, without regard to the boundaries of your own organization. That is, place your organization within a more encompassing value chain that includes your firm's suppliers, customers, and alliance partners. Thus, in addition to thoroughly understanding how value is created within the organization, you must become aware of how value is created for other organizations that are involved in the overall supply chain or distribution channel in which your firm participates.[4]

Next, we'll describe and provide examples of each of the primary and support activities. Then, we'll provide examples of how companies add value by means of relationships among activities within the organization as well as activities outside the organization, such as those activities associated with customers and suppliers.[5]

Primary Activities

Five generic categories of primary activities are involved in competing in any industry, as shown in Exhibit 3.2. Each category is divisible into a number of distinct activities that depend on the particular industry and the firm's strategy.[6]

Inbound Logistics   Inbound logistics is primarily associated with receiving, storing, and distributing inputs to the product. It includes material handling, warehousing, inventory control, vehicle scheduling, and returns to suppliers.

Just-in-time (JIT) inventory systems, for example, were designed to achieve efficient inbound logistics. In essence, Toyota epitomizes JIT inventory systems, in which parts deliveries arrive at the assembly plants only hours before they are needed. JIT systems will play a vital role in fulfilling Toyota's commitment to fill a buyer's new car order in just five days.[7] This standard is in sharp contrast to most competitors that require approximately 30 days' notice to build vehicles. Toyota's standard is three times faster than even Honda Motors, considered to be the industry's most efficient in order follow-through. The five days represent the time from the company's

Inbound Logistics	Operations	Outbound Logistics	Marketing and Sales	Service
• Location of distribution facilities to minimize shipping times. • Excellent material and inventory control systems. • Systems to reduce time to send "returns" to suppliers. • Warehouse layout and designs to increase efficiency of operations for incoming materials.	• Efficient plant operations to minimize costs. • Appropriate level of automation in manufacturing. • Quality production control systems to reduce costs and enhance quality. • Efficient plant layout and workflow design.	• Effective shipping processes to provide quick delivery and minimize damages. • Efficient finished goods warehousing processes. • Shipping of goods in large lot sizes to minimize transportation costs. • Quality material handling equipment to increase order picking.	• Highly motivated and competent sales force. • Innovative approaches to promotion and advertising. • Selection of most appropriate distribution channels. • Proper identification of customer segments and needs. • Effective pricing strategies.	• Effective use of procedures to solicit customer feedback and to act on information. • Quick response to customer needs and emergencies. • Ability to furnish replacement parts as required. • Effective management of parts and equipment inventory. • Quality of service personnel and ongoing training. • Appropriate warranty and guarantee policies.

Source: Adapted with permission of The Free Press, a division of Simon & Schuster Adult Publishing Group, from *Competitive Advantage: Creating and Sustaining Superior Performance* by Michael E. Porter. Copyright © 1985, 1998 by Michael E. Porter. All rights reserved.

Exhibit 3.2 The Value Chain: Some Factors to Consider in Assessing a Firm's Primary Activities

receipt of an order to the time the car leaves the assembly plant. Actual delivery may take longer, depending on where a customer lives. How can Toyota achieve such fast turnaround?

- Its 360 key suppliers are now linked to the company by way of computer on a virtual assembly line.
- Suppliers load parts onto trucks in the order in which they will be installed.
- Parts are stacked on trucks in the same place each time to help workers unload them quickly.
- Deliveries are required to meet a rigid schedule with as many as 12 trucks a day and no more than four hours between trucks.

Operations Operations include all activities associated with transforming inputs into the final product form, such as machining, packaging, assembly, testing, printing, and facility operations.

Creating environmentally friendly manufacturing is one way to use operations to achieve competitive advantage. Shaw Industries (now part of Berkshire Hathaway), a world-class competitor in the floor-covering industry, is well known for its concern for the environment.[8] It has been successful in reducing the expenses associated with the disposal of dangerous chemicals and other waste products from its manufacturing operations. Its environmental endeavors have multiple payoffs. Shaw has received many awards for its recycling efforts—awards that enhance its reputation.

Outbound Logistics   Outbound logistics is associated with collecting, storing, and distributing the product or service to buyers. These activities include finished goods, warehousing, material handling, delivery vehicle operation, order processing, and scheduling.

Campbell Soup uses an electronic network to facilitate its continuous-replenishment program with its most progressive retailers.[9] Each morning, retailers electronically inform Campbell of their product needs and of the level of inventories in their distribution centers. Campbell uses that information to forecast future demand and to determine which products require replenishment (based on the inventory limits previously established with each retailer). Trucks leave Campbell's shipping plant that afternoon and arrive at the retailers' distribution centers the same day. The program cuts the inventories of participating retailers from about a four- to a two-weeks' supply. Campbell Soup achieved this improvement because it slashed delivery time and because it knows the inventories of key retailers and can deploy supplies when they are most needed.

The Campbell Soup example also illustrates the win–win benefits of exemplary value-chain activities. Both the supplier (Campbell) and its buyers (retailers) come out ahead. Since the retailer makes more money on Campbell products delivered through continuous replenishment, it has an incentive to carry a broader line and give the company greater shelf space. After Campbell introduced the program, sales of its products grew twice as fast through participating retailers as through all other retailers. Not surprisingly, supermarket chains love such programs. For example, Wegman's Food Markets in upstate New York has augmented its accounting system to measure and reward suppliers whose products cost the least to stock and sell.

Marketing and Sales   These activities are associated with purchases of products and services by end users and the inducements used to get them to make purchases.[10] They include advertising, promotion, sales force, quoting, channel selection, channel relations, and pricing.[11]

It is not always enough to have a great product.[12] The key is to convince your channel partners that it is in their best interests not only to carry your product but also to market it in a way that is consistent with your strategy. Consider Monsanto's efforts at educating distributors to improve the value proposition of its line of Saflex® windows.[13] The products introduced in the early 1990s had a superior attribute: The window design permitted laminators to form an exceptional type of glass by sandwiching a plastic sheet interlayer between two pieces of glass. This product is not only stronger and offers better ultraviolet protection than regular glass, but also when cracked, it adheres to the plastic sheet—an excellent safety feature for both cars and homes.

Despite these benefits, Monsanto had a hard time convincing laminators and window manufacturers to carry products made with Saflex. According to Melissa Toledo, brand manager at Monsanto, "Saflex was priced at a 30 percent premium above traditional glass, and the various stages in the value chain (distributors and retailers) didn't think there would be a demand for such an expensive glass product." What was Monsanto's solution? Subsequently, it reintroduced Saflex as KeepSafe® and worked to coordinate the product's value propositions. By analyzing the experiences of all of the players in the supply chain, it was able to create marketing programs that helped each build a business aimed at selling its products. Said Toledo, "We want to know how they go about selling those types of products, what challenges they face, and what they think they need to sell our products. This helps us a lot when we try to provide them with these needs." Thus, marketing is often a key element of competitive advantage.[14]

Coach's Effective Marketing Strategy

Coach has put its leather in Lexus cars and insignias on Canon Elph digital camera cases. However, the firm has turned down offers to lend its name to hotels and athletic drinks. It calls the strategy "focus," and the firm admits that it had a rather stodgy image a decade ago. How things have changed!

Coach now has 443 stores and has made a fortune selling stylish but fairly affordable handbags. Revenue has quadrupled since the company went public in 2000. At the time, Coach bags were most often bought by women looking for well-made totes. In the year ending July 1, 2006, sales rose 23 percent to $2.1 billion, and income before interest and taxes rose 34 percent to $765 million. The company's stock also hit an all-time high of $46 in January 2007.

A key element of Coach's success is its knowledge of customers' buying habits. It spends $4 million to $5 million a year on market research, including talking to 15,000 women on the phone, in stores, or via the Internet or regular mail. Analyzing that information has enabled Coach to know that the biggest spenders visit their stores every four to five weeks. Thus, Coach rolls out its new products and store designs to keep pace with this "rhythm."

In addition to market timing, the proprietary information that it gathers provides the basis for market experiments that record the effect of changing such variables as price, features, and offers from competing brands. Based on such data, Coach quickly alters product designs, drops items that test poorly, creates new lines in a wider range of fabrics and colors, changes prices, and tailors mer-

● Coach has dramatically improved its competitive position through effective marketing strategies.

chandise presentation to fit customer demographics at specific stores. Several years ago, Coach had customers preview its Hampton satchel and learned that they would willingly pay $30 more than the company had thought. In the case of another bag, Coach solicited customer feedback on the design and, learning that customers found it "tippy," responded by widening the bag's base.

Sources: Fass, A. 2007. Trading up. *Forbes*. January 29: 48–49; Slywotzky, A. J., & Drzik, J. 2005. Countering the biggest risk of all. *Harvard Business Review*, 83(4): 78–88; and Fass. A. 2005. Thank you for spending $300. *Forbes*. January 10: 150.

Strategy Spotlight 3.2 addresses a vital aspect of marketing—marketing research. We discuss Coach, the high-end producer of leather handbags and other leather products.

At times, a firm's marketing initiatives may become overly aggressive and lead to actions that are both unethical and illegal.[15] For example:

- **Burdines.** This department store chain is under investigation for allegedly adding club memberships to its customers' credit cards without prior approval.
- **Fleet Mortgage.** This company has been accused of adding insurance fees for dental coverage and home insurance to its customers' mortgage loans without the customers' knowledge.
- **HCI Direct.** Eleven states have accused this direct-mail firm with charging for panty hose samples that customers did not order.
- **Juno Online Services.** The Federal Trade Commission brought charges against this Internet service provider for failing to provide customers with a telephone number to cancel service.

Service   This primary activity includes all actions associated with providing service to enhance or maintain the value of the product, such as installation, repair, training, parts supply, and product adjustment.

Let's see how two retailers are providing exemplary customer service. At Sephora.com, a customer service representative taking a phone call from a repeat customer has instant access to what shade of lipstick she likes best. This will help the rep cross-sell by suggesting a matching shade of lip gloss. CEO Jim Wiggett expects such personalization to build loyalty and boost sales per customer. Nordstrom, the Seattle-based department store chain, goes even a step further. It offers a cyber-assist: A service rep can take control of a customer's Web browser and literally lead her to just the silk scarf that she is looking for. CEO Dan Nordstrom believes that such a capability will close enough additional purchases to pay for the $1 million investment in software.

Ritz-Carlton, the luxury hotelier and two-time winner of the prestigious Baldrige Award (1992, 1999) provides an example of exemplary customer service.[16] Its credo includes the goal of fulfilling "even the unexpected wishes and needs" of its guests. According to John Collins, Ritz-Carlton's human resource director, "If you go to a good hotel and ask for something, you get it. If you go to a great hotel, you don't even have to ask." To fulfill this goal, Ritz-Carlton uses its chainwide guest-recognition database to track guest preferences such as preferred floor and newspaper. It also gathers data from employees such as housekeepers, who track events like a guest's moving a desk to get a better view. That observation is placed on a guest recognition slip so that furniture can be arranged according to a guest's preference on his or her next visit.

Support Activities

Support activities in the value chain can be divided into four generic categories, as shown in Exhibit 3.3. As with primary activities, each category of the support activity is divisible into a number of distinct value activities that are specific to a particular industry. For example, technology development's discrete activities may include component design, feature design, field testing, process engineering, and technology selection. Similarly, procurement may be divided into activities such as qualifying new suppliers, purchasing different groups of inputs, and monitoring supplier performance.

Procurement   Procurement refers to the function of purchasing inputs used in the firm's value chain, not to the purchased inputs themselves.[17] Purchased inputs include raw materials, supplies, and other consumable items as well as assets such as machinery, laboratory equipment, office equipment, and buildings.[18]

Microsoft has improved its procurement process (and the quality of its suppliers) by providing formal reviews of its suppliers. One of Microsoft's divisions has extended the review process used for employees to its outside suppliers.[19] The employee services group, which is responsible for everything from travel to 401(k) programs to the on-site library, outsources more than 60 percent of the services it provides. Unfortunately, the employee services group was not providing them with enough feedback on how well Microsoft thought they were doing. This was feedback that the suppliers wanted to get and that Microsoft wanted to give. The evaluation system that Microsoft developed helped clarify its expectations to suppliers. An executive noted: "We had one supplier—this was before the new system—that would have scored a 1.2 out of 5. After we started giving this feedback, and the supplier understood our expectations, its performance improved dramatically. Within six months, it scored a 4. If you'd asked me before we began the feedback system, I would have said that was impossible."

Technology Development   Every value activity embodies technology.[20] The array of technologies employed in most firms is very broad, ranging from technologies used to prepare documents and transport goods to those embodied in processes and equipment or the product itself. Technology development related to the product and its features supports the entire value chain, while other technology development is associated with particular primary or support activities.

The 2000 merger of Allied Signal and Honeywell brought together roughly 13,000 scientists and an $870 million R&D budget that promises to lead to some innovative products and services in two major areas: performance materials and control systems. Some of the possible innovations include:

- **Performance materials.** The development of uniquely shaped fibers with very high absorption capability. When employed in the company's Fram oil filters, they capture 50 percent more particles than ordinary filters. This means that cars can travel further with fewer oil changes.
- **Control systems.** Working with six leading oil companies, Honeywell developed software using "self-learning" algorithms that predict when something might go wrong in an oil refinery before it actually does. Examples include a faulty gas valve or hazardous spillage.[21]

Exhibit 3.3

The Value Chain: Some Factors to Consider in Assessing a Firm's Support Activities

General Administration

- Effective planning systems to attain overall goals and objectives.
- Ability of top management to anticipate and act on key environmental trends and events.
- Ability to obtain low-cost funds for capital expenditures and working capital.
- Excellent relationships with diverse stakeholder groups.
- Ability to coordinate and integrate activities across the "value system."
- High visibility to inculcate organizational culture, reputation, and values.
- Effective information technology to integrate value-creating activities.

Human Resource Management

- Effective recruiting, development, and retention mechanisms for employees.
- Quality relations with trade unions.
- Quality work environment to maximize overall employee performance and minimize absenteeism.
- Reward and incentive programs to motivate all employees.

Technology Development

- Effective research and development activities for process and product initiatives.
- Positive collaborative relationships between R&D and other departments.
- State-of-the art facilities and equipment.
- Culture that enhances creativity and innovation.
- Excellent professional qualifications of personnel.
- Ability to meet critical deadlines.

Procurement

- Procurement of raw material inputs to optimize quality and speed, and to minimize the associated costs.
- Development of collaborative "win–win" relationships with suppliers.
- Effective procedures to purchase advertising and media services.
- Analysis and selection of alternate sources of inputs to minimize dependence on one supplier.
- Ability to make proper lease-versus-buy decisions.

strategy spotlight

Commuter Power: A New Meaning

How many Japanese commuters does it take to light a bulb? On October 16, 2006, East Japan Railway, or JR East, began testing rubber floor mats that generate electricity when walked on. The mats, which will be at several turnstiles inside Tokyo Station for two months, work by converting vibrations into energy.

Presently, they certainly don't produce much energy: just 100 milliwatts with each commuter's steps.

With about 700,000 commuters entering and leaving Tokyo Station each day, that translates to about 70 kilowatts of power—barely enough to light a 100-watt lightbulb for 10 minutes.

However, officials aren't discouraged. They claim that if the technology gets refined over the years those stomping feet could generate much more energy—providing electricity for a train station's lighting and other needs. "The mats could power machines and signs that don't require much energy," claims JR East spokesman Takaki Nemoto. "But that's far into the future."

Source: Hall, K. 2006. Now that's commuter power. *BusinessWeek*, November 13: 10.

Strategy Spotlight 3.3 addresses a unique application of technology—using rubber floor mats at a railway station to generate electricity!

Human Resource Management   Human resource management consists of activities involved in the recruiting, hiring, training, development, and compensation of all types of personnel.[22] It supports both individual primary and support activities (e.g., hiring of engineers and scientists) and the entire value chain (e.g., negotiations with labor unions).

Like all great service companies, JetBlue Airways Corporation is obsessed with hiring superior employees.[23] But they found it difficult to attract college graduates to commit to careers as flight attendants. JetBlue developed a highly innovative recruitment program for flight attendants—a one-year contract that gives them a chance to travel, meet lots of people, and then decide what else they might like to do. They also introduced the idea of training a friend and employee together so that they could share a job. With such employee-friendly initiatives, JetBlue has been very successful in attracting talent.

Employees often leave a firm because they reach a plateau and begin to look for new opportunities.[24] AT&T strives to retain such people with Resource Link, an in-house temporary service that enables employees with diverse management, technical, or professional skills to market their abilities to different departments for short-term assignments. This enables professionals to broaden their experience base as well as provide a mechanism for other parts of the organization to benefit from new sources of ideas.

Jeffrey Immelt, GE's chairman, addresses the importance of effective human resource management:[25]

> Human resources has to be more than a department. GE recognized early on—50 or 60 years ago—that in a multibusiness company, the common denominators are people and culture. From an employee's first day at GE, she discovers that she's in the people-development business as much as anything else. You'll find that most good companies have the same basic HR processes that we have, but they're discrete. HR at GE is not an agenda item; it is the agenda.

Strategy Spotlight 3.4 describes how SAS Institute's innovative approach to human resources provides an insightful financial justification for the broad array of benefits it provides to employees.

General Administration   General administration consists of a number of activities, including general management, planning, finance, accounting, legal and government affairs, quality management, and information systems. Administration (unlike the other support activities) typically supports the entire value chain and not individual activities.

SAS and Employee Turnover

Jeffrey Pfeffer, professor of organizational behavior at Stanford University, asked a managing partner at a San Francisco law firm about its employee turnover rate. Turnover had increased from 25 percent to 30 percent over the last few years. The law firm's solution was to increase recruitment of new employees. Pfeffer's response was, "What kind of doctor would you be if your patient was bleeding faster and faster, and your only response was to increase the rate of transfusion?"

It's not difficult to calculate the cost of a new hire, but what does it cost a firm when employees leave? Software developer SAS Institute puts the cost at around $50 million. David Russo, director of human resources at SAS, a $1.7 billion company suggested that keeping employees is not just about caring for your employees, it also provides a strong economic advantage to the company.

Consider Russo's example: Average employee turnover in the software business is 20 percent per year. SAS's turnover rate is 4 percent. SAS has 5,200 employees earning an average of $80,000 a year. The difference between turnover in the industry and turnover at SAS is 16 percent. Multiplying 16 percent by SAS's 5,200 employees at $80,000

Sources: Karlgaard, R. 2006. Who wants to go public? *Forbes.* October 19:31; Fisher, A. 2007. Playing for Keeps. *Fortune,* January 22:85–88; Levering, R., & Moskowitz, M. 2003. The 100 best companies to work for. *Fortune,* January 20: 127–152; and Webber, A. M. 1998. Danger: Toxic Company. *Fast Company,* November: 152–161.

a year, SAS has a cost savings of nearly $70 million. SAS estimates the total cost of turnover per employee to equal the employee's annual salary.

What can a firm do with an extra $70 million? SAS spends a large portion of this sum on its employees. The SAS gym, cafeteria (with pianist), on-site medical and child care, flexible work schedules, employer retirement contributions of 15 percent of an employee's pay, and a host of other family-friendly programs help keep SAS's employee turnover level well below the industry average. Even after all these perks, SAS still has money left over.

Russo's message? "This is not tree-huggery. This is money in the bank." The bottom line is it pays to retain employees.

A final note: During the 1990s go–go stock market, a privately held technology firm like SAS seemed an anachronism. For a few weeks in 1999, SAS's cofounder, Jim Goodnight (who ranks 52nd on The Forbes 400 list), considered doing an initial public offering (IPO). He was concerned about losing his top tech people to local highfliers such as Red Hat, who were doling out stock options like candy. Goodnight once said, "Morgan Stanley and Goldman Sachs called me up (about an IPO). I asked, 'What's your fee?' They said 7 percent. I said, 'Make it 0.7 percent and we'll do a deal.'" Richard Karlgaard, *Forbes'* publisher, who heard Goodnight make these comments, recalls, "Goodnight snickered at his punch line. I knew then that SAS would never go public."

Although general administration is sometimes viewed only as overhead, it can be a powerful source of competitive advantage. In a telephone operating company, for example, negotiating and maintaining ongoing relations with regulatory bodies can be among the most important activities for competitive advantage. In a similar vein, effective information systems can contribute significantly to cost position, while in some industries top management plays a vital role in dealing with important buyers.[26]

The strong and effective leadership of top executives can also make a significant contribution to an organization's success. As we discussed in Chapter 1, chief executive officers (CEOs) such as Herb Kelleher, Andrew Grove, and Jack Welch have been credited with playing critical roles in the success of Southwest Airlines, Intel, and General Electric. And Carlos Ghosn is considered one of today's top corporate leaders after his turnaround of Nissan, the Japan-based automobile manufacturer.

Information systems can also play a key role in increasing operating efficiencies and enhancing a firm's performance.[27] Consider Walgreen Co.'s introduction of Intercom Plus, a computer-based prescription management system. Linked by computer to both doctors' offices and third-party payment plans, the system automates telephone refills, store-to-store prescription transfers, and drug reordering. It also provides information on drug interactions and, coupled with revised workflows, frees up pharmacists from administrative tasks to devote more time to patient counseling.

>LO3

How value-chain analysis can help managers create value by investigating relationships among activities within the firm and between the firm and its customers and suppliers.

Interrelationships among Value-Chain Activities within and across Organizations

We have defined each of the value-chain activities separately for clarity of presentation. Managers must not ignore, however, the importance of relationships among value-chain activities.[28] There are two levels: (1) interrelationships among activities within the firm and (2) relationships among activities within the firm and with other organizations (e.g., customers and suppliers) that are part of the firm's expanded value chain.[29]

With regard to the first level, recall AT&T's innovative Resource Link program wherein employees who have reached their plateau may apply for temporary positions in other parts of the organization. Clearly, this program has the potential to benefit all activities within the firm's value chain because it creates opportunities for top employees to lend their expertise to all of the organization's value-creating activities.

With regard to the second level, Campbell Soup's use of electronic networks enabled it to improve the efficiency of outbound logistics.[30] However, it also helped Campbell manage the ordering of raw materials more effectively, improve its production scheduling, and help its customers better manage their inbound logistics operations.

An example of how a firm's value-creating activity can enhance customer value is provided by Ciba Specialty Chemicals (which merged with Sandoz in 1996 to form Novartis), a Swiss manufacturer of textile dyes.[31] The firm's research and development experts have created dyes that fix more readily to the fabric and therefore require less salt. How does this innovation add value for Ciba's customers? There are three ways. First, it lowers the outlays for salt. Textile companies using the new dyes are able to reduce their costs for salt by up to 2 percent of revenues, a significant drop in an industry with razor thin profit margins. Second, it reduces manufacturers' costs for water treatment. Used bathwater full of salt and unfixed dye must be treated before it is released into rivers or streams (even in low-income countries where environmental standards are typically lax). Simply put, less salt and less unfixed dye mean lower water-treatment costs. Third, the higher fixation rates of the new dyes make quality control easier, lowering the costs of rework.

We conclude this section with Strategy Spotlight 3.5. It addresses how Cardinal Health expertly integrates several value activities to create value for its suppliers and customers.

Applying the Value Chain to Service Organizations

The concepts of inbound logistics, operations, and outbound logistics suggest managing the raw materials that might be manufactured into finished products and delivered to customers. However, these three steps do not apply only to manufacturing. They correspond to any transformation process in which inputs are converted through a work process into outputs that add value. For example, accounting is a sort of transformation process that converts daily records of individual transactions into monthly financial reports. In this example, the transaction records are the inputs, accounting is the operation that adds value, and financial statements are the outputs.

What are the "operations," or transformation processes, of service organizations? These could be many different things. At times, the difference between manufacturing and service is in providing a customized solution rather than the kind of mass production that is common in manufacturing. For example, a travel agent adds value by creating an itinerary that includes transportation, accommodations, and activities that are customized to your budget and your dates of travel. A law firm renders services that are specific to a client's needs and circumstances. In both cases, the work process (operation) involves the application of specialized knowledge based on the specifics of a situation (inputs) and the outcome that the client seeks to achieve (outputs).

The application of the value chain to service organizations suggests that the value-adding process may be configured differently depending on the type of business a firm is engaged in. As the preceding discussion on support activities suggests, activities such as procurement and

Cardinal Health: Creating Value through the Extended Value Chain

Cardinal Health is a wholesale drug distributor that buys sprays, pills, and capsules from pharmaceutical companies and puts them on the shelves in pharmacies or into the hands of emergency-room nurses. Profitability is a problem in this business, because the company is caught between powerful manufacturers and cost-conscious customers. Cardinal, for example, buys pharmaceuticals from the likes of Pfizer (its biggest supplier) and sells them to the likes of CVS (its largest customer).

Cardinal responded to the profitability challenge by trying to add value for both customers and suppliers. It understood how urgent it was for one of its customer groups (hospitals) to control costs, so it began to offer services to hospital pharmacies. Rather than shipping medications to the hospitals' front door, it "followed the pill" into the hospital and right to the patient's room, offering pharmacy-management services and extending those services to customized surgical kits.

Sources: Slywotzky, A., & Wise, R. 2003. Double digit growth in no-growth times. *Fast Company,* April: 66–70; Stewart, T. 2002. Fueling drug growth during an economic drought. *Business 2.0,* May: 17–21; and Lashinsky, A. 2003. Big man in the "middle." *Fortune,* April 14: 161–162.

As the knowledgeable intermediary, Cardinal realized it could bring significant value to its suppliers (the pharmaceutical manufacturers) by providing services in drug formulation, testing, manufacturing, and packaging, freeing those companies to concentrate on the discovery of the next round of blockbuster medicines. Cardinal even used its position to develop new services for commercial pharmacies. Cardinal's drug-chain customers depend on third-party payments for most of the prescriptions it fills. It worked with a number of leading chains to develop a system called ScriptLINE that automates the reimbursement process for pharmacies and updates rates daily.

The result of this stream of innovations is a wave of growth and profits. Cardinal, with annual sales of $65 billion, has registered compound annual earnings growth of approximately 20 percent or better for the past 15 years.

The Cardinal Health story is a powerful example of extending the value chain and adding value to the many players involved—from the suppliers to the customers. The company found opportunities in an unpromising business landscape by identifying new customer needs related to the activities that surround the products it sells.

legal services are critical for adding value. Indeed, the activities that may only provide support to one company may be critical to the primary value-adding activity of another firm.

Exhibit 3.4 provides two models of how the value chain might look in service industries. In the retail industry, there are no manufacturing operations. A firm, such as Circuit City, adds value by developing expertise in the procurement of finished goods and by displaying

Retail: Primary Value-Chain Activities

Engineering Services: Primary Value-Chain Activities

Exhibit 3.4 Some Examples of Value Chains in Service Industries

them in their stores in a way that enhances sales. Thus, the value chain makes procurement activities (i.e., partnering with vendors and purchasing goods) a primary rather than a support activity. Operations refer to the task of operating Circuit City's stores.

For an engineering services firm, research and development provides inputs, the transformation process is the engineering itself, and innovative designs and practical solutions are the outputs. Arthur D. Little, for example, is a large consulting firm with offices in 30 countries. In its technology and innovation management practice, A. D. Little strives to make the best use of the science, technology and knowledge resources available to create value for a wide range of industries and client sectors. This involves activities associated with research and development, engineering, and creating solutions as well as downstream activities such as marketing, sales, and service. These examples suggest that how the primary and support activities of a given firm are configured and deployed will often depend on industry conditions and the extent to which the company is service and/or manufacturing oriented.

Resource-Based View of the Firm

resource-based view of the firm perspective that firms' competitive advantages are due to their endowment of strategic resources that are valuable, rare, costly to imitate, and costly to substitute.

The **resource-based view (RBV) of the firm** combines two perspectives: (1) the internal analysis of phenomena within a company and (2) an external analysis of the industry and its competitive environment.[32] It goes beyond the traditional SWOT (strengths, weaknesses, opportunities, threats) analysis by integrating internal and external perspectives. The ability of a firm's resources to confer competitive advantage(s) cannot be determined without taking into consideration the broader competitive context. That is, a firm's resources must be evaluated in terms of how valuable, rare, and hard they are for competitors to duplicate. Otherwise, at best, the firm would be able to attain only competitive parity. As noted earlier in the chapter (in Strategy Spotlight 3.1), a firm's strengths and capabilities—no matter how unique or impressive—do not necessarily lead to competitive advantages in the marketplace. The criteria for whether advantages are created and whether or not they can be sustained over time will be addressed later in this section. Thus, the RBV is a very useful framework for gaining insights as to why some competitors are more profitable than others. As we will see later in the book, the RBV is also helpful in developing strategies for individual businesses and diversified firms by revealing how core competencies embedded in a firm can help it exploit new product and market opportunities.

>LO4

The resource-based view of the firm and the different types of tangible and intangible resources, as well as organizational capabilities.

In the two sections that follow, we will discuss the three key types of resources that firms possess (summarized in Exhibit 3.5): tangible resources, intangible resources, and organizational capabilities. Then we will address the conditions under which such assets and capabilities can enable a firm to attain a sustainable competitive advantage.[33]

It is important to note that resources by themselves typically do not yield a competitive advantage. Even if a basketball team recruited an all-star center, there would be little chance of victory if the other members of the team were continually outplayed by their opponents or if the coach's attitude was so negative that everyone, including the center, became unwilling to put forth their best efforts. And imagine how many World Series titles Joe Torre would have won as manager of the New York Yankees if none of the pitchers on his team could throw fastballs over 70 miles per hour. Although the all-star center and the baseball manager are unquestionably valuable resources, they would *not* enable the organization to attain advantages under these circumstances.

In a business context, Cardinal Health's excellent value-creating activities (e.g., logistics, drug formulation) would not be a source of competitive advantage if those activities were not integrated with other important value-creating activities such as marketing and sales. Thus, a central theme of the resource-based view of the firm is that competitive advantages are created (and sustained) through the bundling of several resources in unique combinations.

Tangible Resources

Financial	• Firm's cash account and cash equivalents. • Firm's capacity to raise equity. • Firm's borrowing capacity.
Physical	• Modern plant and facilities. • Favorable manufacturing locations. • State-of-the-art machinery and equipment.
Technological	• Trade secrets. • Innovative production processes. • Patents, copyrights, trademarks.
Organizational	• Effective strategic planning processes. • Excellent evaluation and control systems.

Intangible Resources

Human	• Experience and capabilities of employees. • Trust. • Managerial skills. • Firm-specific practices and procedures.
Innovation and creativity	• Technical and scientific skills. • Innovation capacities.
Reputation	• Brand name. • Reputation with customers for quality and reliability. • Reputation with suppliers for fairness, non–zero-sum relationships.

Organizational Capabilities

- Firm competencies or skills the firm employs to transfer inputs to outputs.
- Capacity to combine tangible and intangible resources, using organizational processes to attain desired end.

  EXAMPLES:
  - Outstanding customer service.
  - Excellent product development capabilities.
  - Innovativeness of products and services.
  - Ability to hire, motivate, and retain human capital.

Source: Adapted from Barney, J. B. 1991. Firm resources and sustained competitive advantage. *Journal of Management:* 17: 101; Grant, R. M. 1991. *Contemporary Strategy Analysis:* 100–102. Cambridge England: Blackwell Business and Hitt, M. A., Ireland, R. D., & Hoskisson, R. E. 2001. *Strategic management: Competitiveness and globalization* (4th ed.). Cincinnati: South-Western College Publishing.

Types of Firm Resources

We define firm resources to include all assets, capabilities, organizational processes, information, knowledge, and so forth, controlled by a firm that enable it to develop and implement value-creating strategies.

Tangible Resources   **Tangible resources** are assets that are relatively easy to identify. They include the physical and financial assets that an organization uses to create value for its

tangible resources organizational assets that are relatively easy to identify, including physical assets, financial resources, organizational resources, and technological resources.

customers. Among them are financial resources (e.g., a firm's cash, accounts receivable, and its ability to borrow funds); physical resources (e.g., the company's plant, equipment, and machinery as well as its proximity to customers and suppliers); organizational resources (e.g., the company's strategic planning process and its employee development, evaluation, and reward systems); and technological resources (e.g., trade secrets, patents, and copyrights).

Many firms are finding that high-tech, computerized training has dual benefits: It develops more effective employees and reduces costs at the same time. Employees at FedEx take computer-based job competency tests every 6 to 12 months.[34] The 90-minute computer-based tests identify areas of individual weakness and provide input to a computer database of employee skills—information the firm uses in promotion decisions.

Intangible Resources   Much more difficult for competitors (and, for that matter, a firm's own managers) to account for or imitate are **intangible resources,** which are typically embedded in unique routines and practices that have evolved and accumulated over time. These include human resources (e.g., experience and capability of employees, trust, effectiveness of work teams, managerial skills), innovation resources (e.g., technical and scientific expertise, ideas), and reputation resources (e.g., brand name, reputation with suppliers for fairness and with customers for reliability and product quality). A firm's culture may also be a resource that provides competitive advantage.[35]

For example, you might not think that motorcycles, clothes, toys, and restaurants have much in common. Yet Harley-Davidson has entered all of these product and service markets by capitalizing on its strong brand image—a valuable intangible resource.[36] It has used that image to sell accessories, clothing, and toys, and it has licensed the Harley-Davidson Café in New York City to provide further exposure for its brand name and products.

Organizational Capabilities   **Organizational capabilities** are not specific tangible or intangible assets, but rather the competencies or skills that a firm employs to transform inputs into outputs.[37] In short, they refer to an organization's capacity to deploy tangible and intangible resources over time and generally in combination, and to leverage those capabilities to bring about a desired end.[38] Examples of organizational capabilities are outstanding customer service, excellent product development capabilities, superb innovation processes, and flexibility in manufacturing processes.[39]

Gillette's capability to combine several technologies has been one of the keys to its unparalleled success in the wet-shaving industry. Key technologies include its expertise concerning the physiology of facial hair and skin, the metallurgy of blade strength and sharpness, the dynamics of a cartridge moving across skin, and the physics of a razor blade severing the hair—highly specialized areas for which Gillette has unique capabilities. Combining these technologies has helped the company to develop innovative products such as the Excel, Sensor Excel, MACH 3, and Fusion shaving systems.

In 1984, Michael Dell started Dell Inc. in a University of Texas dorm room with an investment of $1,000. By 2006, Dell had attained annual revenues of $56 billion and a net income of $3.5 billion. Dell achieved this meteoric growth by differentiating itself through the direct sales approach that it pioneered. Its user-configurable products enabled it to satisfy the diverse needs of its corporate and institutional customer base. Exhibit 3.6 summarizes the Dell recipe for its remarkable success by integrating its tangible resources, intangible resources, and organizational capabilities.

Dell has continued to maintain this competitive advantage by further strengthening its value-chain activities and interrelationships that are critical to satisfying the largest market opportunities. They achieved this by (1) implementing e-commerce direct sales and support processes that accounted for the sophisticated buying habits of the largest markets and (2) matching their operations to the purchase options by adopting flexible assembly processes, while leaving inventory management to its extensive supplier network. Dell has sustained these advantages by investing in intangible resources such as proprietary assembly methods

intangible resources organizational assets that are difficult to identify and account for and are typically embedded in unique routines and practices, including human resources, innovation resources, and reputation resources.

organizational capabilities the competencies and skills that a firm employs to transform inputs into outputs.

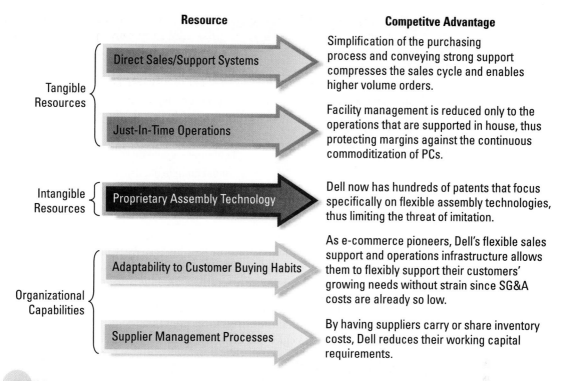

Exhibit 3.6 Dell's Tangible Resources, Intangible Resources, and Organizational Capabilities

and packaging configurations that help to protect against the threat of imitation. Dell recognizes that the PC is a complex product with components sourced from several different technologies and manufacturers. Thus, in working backwards from the customer's purchasing habits, Dell saw that they could build valuable solutions by organizing their resources and capabilities around the build-to-specification tastes, making both the sales and integration processes flexible, and passing on overhead expenses to their suppliers. As the PC industry has become further commoditized, Dell has been one of the few competitors that has retained solid margins. They have accomplished this by adapting their manufacturing and assembly capabilities to match the PC market's trend toward user compatibility.

Firm Resources and Sustainable Competitive Advantages

As we have mentioned, resources alone are not a basis for competitive advantages, nor are advantages sustainable over time. In some cases, a resource or capability helps a firm to increase its revenues or to lower costs but the firm derives only a temporary advantage because competitors quickly imitate or substitute for it. Many e-commerce businesses in the early 2000s have seen their profits seriously eroded because new (or existing) competitors easily duplicated their business model. For example, Priceline.com, expanded its offerings from enabling customers to place bids online for airline tickets to a wide variety of other products. However, it was easy for competitors (e.g., a consortium of major airlines) to duplicate Priceline's products and services. Ultimately, its market capitalization had plummeted roughly 98 percent from its all-time high.

For a resource to provide a firm with the potential for a sustainable competitive advantage, it must have four attributes.[40] First, the resource must be valuable in the sense that it exploits opportunities and/or neutralizes threats in the firm's environment. Second, it must be rare among the firm's current and potential competitors. Third, the resource must be difficult for competitors to imitate. Fourth, the resource must have no strategically equivalent

>LO5
The four criteria that a firm's resources must possess to maintain a sustainable advantage and how value created can be appropriated by employees and managers.

Exhibit 3.7

Four Criteria for Assessing Sustainability of Resources and Capabilities

Is the resource or capability . . .	Implications
Valuable?	• Neutralize threats and exploit opportunities
Rare?	• Not many firms possess
Difficult to imitate?	• Physically unique
	• Path dependency (how accumulated over time)
	• Causal ambiguity (difficult to disentangle what it is or how it could be re-created)
	• Social complexity (trust, interpersonal relationships, culture, reputation)
Difficult to substitute?	• No equivalent strategic resources or capabilities

substitutes. These criteria are summarized in Exhibit 3.7. We will now discuss each of these criteria. Then, we will examine how Dell's competitive advantage, which seemed secure just a few years ago, has eroded.

Is the Resource Valuable?   Organizational resources can be a source of competitive advantage only when they are valuable. Resources are valuable when they enable a firm to formulate and implement strategies that improve its efficiency or effectiveness. The SWOT framework suggests that firms improve their performance only when they exploit opportunities or neutralize (or minimize) threats.

The fact that firm attributes must be valuable in order to be considered resources (as well as potential sources of competitive advantage) reveals an important complementary relationship among environmental models (e.g., SWOT and five-forces analyses) and the resource-based model. Environmental models isolate those firm attributes that exploit opportunities and/or neutralize threats. Thus, they specify what firm attributes may be considered as resources. The resource-based model then suggests what additional characteristics these resources must possess if they are to develop a sustained competitive advantage.

Is the Resource Rare?   If competitors or potential competitors also possess the same valuable resource, it is not a source of a competitive advantage because all of these firms have the capability to exploit that resource in the same way. Common strategies based on such a resource would give no one firm an advantage. For a resource to provide competitive advantages, it must be uncommon, that is, rare relative to other competitors.

This argument can apply to bundles of valuable firm resources that are used to formulate and develop strategies. Some strategies require a mix of multiple types of resources—tangible assets, intangible assets, and organizational capabilities. If a particular bundle of firm resources is not rare, then relatively large numbers of firms will be able to conceive of and implement the strategies in question. Thus, such strategies will not be a source of competitive advantage, even if the resource in question is valuable.

Can the Resource Be Imitated Easily?   Inimitability (difficulty in imitating) is a key to value creation because it constrains competition.[41] If a resource is inimitable, then any profits generated are more likely to be sustainable. Having a resource that competitors can easily copy generates only temporary value. This has important implications. Since managers often fail to apply this test, they tend to base long-term strategies on resources that are imitable. IBP (Iowa Beef Processors) became the first meatpacking company in the United States to modernize by building a set of assets (automated plants located in cattle-producing states) and capabilities (low-cost "disassembly" of carcasses) that earned returns on assets of 1.3 percent in the 1970s. By the late 1980s, however, ConAgra and Cargill had imitated these resources, and IBP's profitability fell by nearly 70 percent, to 0.4 percent.

Monster.com entered the executive recruiting market by providing, in essence, a substitute for traditional bricks-and-mortar headhunting firms. Although Monster.com's resources are rare and valuable, they are subject to imitation by new rivals—other dot-com firms. Why? There are very low entry barriers for firms wanting to try their hand at recruitment. For example, many job search dot-coms have emerged in recent years, including jobsearch.com, headhunter.com, nationjob.com, and hotjobs.com. In all, there are approximately 30,000 online job boards available to job seekers. It would be most difficult for a firm to attain a sustainable advantage in this industry.

Clearly, an advantage based on inimitability won't last forever. Competitors will eventually discover a way to copy most valuable resources. However, managers can forestall them and sustain profits for a while by developing strategies around resources that have at least one of the following four characteristics.[42]

Physical Uniqueness The first source of inimitability is physical uniqueness, which by definition is inherently difficult to copy. A beautiful resort location, mineral rights, or Pfizer's pharmaceutical patents simply cannot be imitated. Many managers believe that several of their resources may fall into this category, but on close inspection, few do.

Path Dependency A greater number of resources cannot be imitated because of what economists refer to as **path dependency.** This simply means that resources are unique and therefore scarce because of all that has happened along the path followed in their development and/or accumulation. Competitors cannot go out and buy these resources quickly and easily; they must be built up over time in ways that are difficult to accelerate.

The Gerber Products Co. brand name for baby food is an example of a resource that is potentially inimitable. Re-creating Gerber's brand loyalty would be a time-consuming process that competitors could not expedite, even with expensive marketing campaigns. Similarly, the loyalty and trust that Southwest Airlines employees feel toward their firm and its cofounder, Herb Kelleher, are resources that have been built up over a long period of time. Also, a crash R&D program generally cannot replicate a successful technology when research findings cumulate. Clearly, these path-dependent conditions build protection for the original resource. The benefits from experience and learning through trial and error cannot be duplicated overnight.

Causal Ambiguity The third source of inimitability is termed **causal ambiguity.** This means that would-be competitors may be thwarted because it is impossible to disentangle the causes (or possible explanations) of either what the valuable resource is or how it can be re-created. What is the root of 3M's innovation process? You can study it and draw up a list of possible factors. But it is a complex, unfolding (or folding) process that is hard to understand and would be hard to imitate.

Often, causally ambiguous resources are organizational capabilities, involving a complex web of social interactions that may even depend on particular individuals. When Continental and United tried to mimic the successful low-cost strategy of Southwest Airlines, the planes, routes, and fast gate turnarounds were not the most difficult aspects for them to copy. Those were all rather easy to observe and, at least in principle, easy to duplicate. However, they could not replicate Southwest's culture of fun, family, frugality, and focus since no one can clearly specify exactly what that culture is or how it came to be.

Social Complexity A firm's resources may be imperfectly inimitable because they reflect a high level of **social complexity.** Such phenomena are typically beyond the ability of firms to systematically manage or influence. When competitive advantages are based on social complexity, it is difficult for other firms to imitate them.

A wide variety of firm resources may be considered socially complex. Examples include interpersonal relations among the managers in a firm, its culture, and its reputation with its suppliers and customers. In many of these cases, it is easy to specify how these socially complex resources add value to a firm. Hence, there is little or no causal ambiguity

path dependency a characteristic of resources that is developed and/or accumulated through a unique series of events.

casual ambiguity a characteristic of a firm's resources that is costly to imitate because a competitor cannot determine what the resource is and/or how it can be re-created.

social complexity a characteristic of a firm's resources that is costly to imitate because the social engineering required is beyond the capability of competitors, including interpersonal relations among managers, organizational culture, and reputation with suppliers and customers.

surrounding the link between them and competitive advantage. But an understanding that certain firm attributes, such as quality relations among managers, can improve a firm's efficiency does not necessarily lead to systematic efforts to imitate them. Such social engineering efforts are beyond the capabilities of most firms.

Although complex physical technology is not included in this category of sources of imperfect inimitability, the exploitation of physical technology in a firm typically involves the use of socially complex resources. That is, several firms may possess the same physical technology, but only one of them may have the social relations, culture, group norms, and so on to fully exploit the technology in implementing its strategies. If such complex social resources are not subject to imitation (and assuming they are valuable and rare and no substitutes exist), this firm may obtain a sustained competitive advantage from exploiting its physical technology more effectively than other firms.

Are Substitutes Readily Available?   The fourth requirement for a firm resource to be a source of sustainable competitive advantage is that there must be no strategically equivalent valuable resources that are themselves not rare or inimitable. Two valuable firm resources (or two bundles of resources) are strategically equivalent when each one can be exploited separately to implement the same strategies.

Substitutability may take at least two forms. First, though it may be impossible for a firm to imitate exactly another firm's resource, it may be able to substitute a similar resource that enables it to develop and implement the same strategy. Clearly, a firm seeking to imitate another firm's high-quality top management team would be unable to copy the team exactly. However, it might be able to develop its own unique management team. Though these two teams would have different ages, functional backgrounds, experience, and so on, they could be strategically equivalent and thus substitutes for one another.

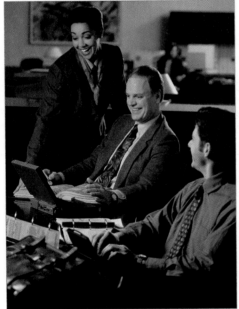

Second, very different firm resources can become strategic substitutes. For example, Internet booksellers such as Amazon.com compete as substitutes for bricks-and-mortar booksellers such as B. Dalton. The result is that resources such as premier retail locations become less valuable. In a similar vein, several pharmaceutical firms have seen the value of patent protection erode in the face of new drugs that are based on different production processes and act in different ways, but can be used in similar treatment regimes. The coming years will likely see even more radical change in the pharmaceutical industry as the substitution of genetic therapies eliminates certain uses of chemotherapy.[43]

To recap this section, recall that resources and capabilities must be rare and valuable as well as difficult to imitate or substitute in order for a firm to attain competitive advantages that are sustainable over time.[44] Exhibit 3.8 illustrates the relationship among the four criteria of sustainability and shows the competitive implications.

In firms represented by the first row of Exhibit 3.8, managers are in a difficult situation. When their resources and capabilities do not meet any of the four criteria, it would be difficult to develop any type of competitive advantage, in the short or long term. The resources and capabilities they possess enable the firm

● Dell's competitive position in personal computers—including desktops and laptops—has eroded in recent years.

neither to exploit environmental opportunities nor neutralize environmental threats. In the second and third rows, firms have resources and capabilities that are valuable as well as rare, respectively. However, in both cases the resources and capabilities are not difficult for competitors to imitate or substitute. Here, the firms could attain some level of competitive parity. They could perform on par with equally endowed rivals or attain a temporary competitive advantage. But their advantages would be easy for competitors

Is a resource or capability . . .				
Valuable?	Rare?	Difficult to Imitate?	Without Substitutes?	Implications for Competitiveness?
No	No	No	No	Competitive disadvantage
Yes	No	No	No	Competitive parity
Yes	Yes	No	No	Temporary competitive advantage
Yes	Yes	Yes	Yes	Sustainable competitive advantage

Source: Adapted from Barney, J. B. 1991. Firm resources and sustained competitive advantage. *Journal of Management,* 17: 99–120.

to match. It is only in the fourth row, where all four criteria are satisfied, that competitive advantages can be sustained over time.

Revisiting Dell   For many years, it looked as if Dell's competitive advantage over its rivals would be sustainable for a very long period of time. However, by early 2007, Dell was falling behind its rivals in market share. This led to a significant decline in its stock price—followed by a complete shake-up of the top management team. But what led to Dell's competitive decline in the first place?[45]

- Dell had become so focused on cost that it failed to pay attention to the design of the brand. Customers increasingly began to see the product as a commodity.
- Much of the growth in the PC industry today is in laptops. Customers demand a sleeker, better-designed machine instead of just the cheapest laptop. Also, they often want to see the laptop before they buy it.
- When Dell outsourced its customer service function to foreign locations, it led to a decline in customer support. This eroded Dell's brand value.
- Dell's efforts to replicate its made-to-order, no middleman strategy to other products such as printers and storage devices proved to be a failure because customers saw very little need for customization of these products. Meanwhile, rivals such as Hewlett-Packard have been improving their product design and reducing their costs. Thus, they now have cost parity with Dell, while enjoying a better brand image and the support of an extensive dealer network.

The Generation and Distribution of a Firm's Profits: Extending the Resource-Based View of the Firm

Many scholars would agree that the resource-based view of the firm has been useful in determining when firms will create competitive advantages and enjoy high levels of profitability. However, it has not been developed to address how a firm's profits (often referred to as "rents" by economists) will be distributed to a firm's management and employees.[46] This becomes an important issue because firms may be successful in creating competitive advantages that can be sustainable for a period of time but much of the profits can be retained (or "appropriated") by its employees and managers instead of flowing to the owners of the firm (i.e., the stockholders).*

Consider Viewpoint DataLabs International, a Salt Lake City–based company that makes sophisticated three-dimensional models and textures for film production houses,

---

* Economists define rents as profits (or prices) in excess of what is required to provide a normal return.

video games, and car manufacturers. This example will help to show how employees are often able to obtain (or "appropriate") a high proportion of a firm's profits:

> Walter Noot, head of production, was having trouble keeping his highly skilled Generation X employees happy with their compensation. Each time one of them was lured away for more money, everyone would want a raise. "We were having to give out raises every six months—30 to 40 percent—then six months later they'd expect the same. It was a big struggle to keep people happy."[47]

At Viewpoint DataLabs, it is apparent that much of the profits are being generated by the highly skilled professionals working together on a variety of projects. They are able to exercise their power by successfully demanding more financial compensation. In part, management has responded favorably because they are united in their demands, and their work involves a certain amount of social complexity and causal ambiguity—given the complex, coordinated efforts that their work entails.

Four factors help explain the extent to which employees and managers will be able to obtain a proportionately high level of the profits that they generate:[48]

- **Employee Bargaining Power.** If employees are vital to forming a firm's unique capability, they will earn disproportionately high wages. For example, marketing professionals may have access to valuable information that helps them to understand the intricacies of customer demands and expectations, or engineers may understand unique technical aspects of the products or services. Additionally, in some industries such as consulting, advertising, and tax preparation, clients tend to be very loyal to individual professionals employed by the firm, instead of to the firm itself. This enables them to "take the clients with them" if they leave. This enhances their bargaining power.
- **Employee Replacement Cost.** If employees' skills are idiosyncratic and rare (a source of resource-based advantages), they should have high bargaining power based on the high cost required by the firm to replace them. For example, Raymond Ozzie, the software designer who was critical in the development of Lotus Notes, was able to dictate the terms under which IBM acquired Lotus.
- **Employee Exit Costs.** This factor may tend to reduce an employee's bargaining power. An individual may face high personal costs when leaving the organization. Thus, that individual's threat of leaving may not be credible. In addition, some of an employee's expertise may be firm-specific, that is, of limited value to other firms. A related factor is that of causal ambiguity, which would make it difficult for the employee to explain his or her specific contribution to a given project. Thus, a rival firm might be less likely to pay a high wage premium since it would be unsure of the employee's unique contribution.
- **Manager Bargaining Power.** Like other members of the firm, managers' power would be based on how well they create resource-based advantages. They are generally charged with creating value through the process of organizing, coordinating, and leveraging employees as well as other forms of capital such as plant, equipment, and financial capital (issues that we will address in more detail in Chapter 4). Such activities provide managers with sources of information that may not be readily available to others. Thus, although managers may not know as much about the specific nature of customers and technologies, they are in a position to have a more thorough, integrated understanding of the total operation.

Chapter 9 addresses the conditions under which top-level managers (such as CEOs) of large corporations have been, at times, able to obtain levels of total compensation that would appear to be significantly disproportionate to their contributions to wealth generation as well as to top executives in peer organizations. Here, corporate governance becomes a critical control mechanism. For example, William Esrey and Ronald T. LeMay (the former two top executives at

Sprint Corporation) were able to earn more than $130 million in stock options primarily because of "cozy" relationships with members of their board of directors, who tended to approve with little debate huge compensation packages.[49] Such diversion of profits from the owners of the business to top management is far less likely when the board does not consist of a high proportion of the firm's management and board members are truly independent outsiders (i.e., they do not have close ties to management). In general, given the external market for top talent, the level of compensation that executives receive is based on factors similar to the ones just discussed that determine the level of their bargaining power.[50]

Evaluating Firm Performance: Two Approaches

This section addresses two approaches to use when evaluating a firm's performance. The first is financial ratio analysis, which, generally speaking, identifies how a firm is performing according to its balance sheet, income statement, and market valuation. As we will discuss, when performing a financial ratio analysis, you must take into account the firm's performance from a historical perspective (not just at one point in time) as well as how it compares with both industry norms and key competitors.[51]

The second perspective takes a broader stakeholder view. Firms must satisfy a broad range of stakeholders, including employees, customers, and owners, to ensure their long-term viability. Central to our discussion will be a well-known approach—the balanced scorecard—that has been popularized by Robert Kaplan and David Norton.[52]

Financial Ratio Analysis

The beginning point in analyzing the financial position of a firm is to compute and analyze five different types of financial ratios:

- Short-term solvency or liquidity
- Long-term solvency measures
- Asset management (or turnover)
- Profitability
- Market value

Exhibit 3.9 summarizes each of these five ratios.

The Appendix to Chapter 13 (the Case Analysis chapter) provides detailed definitions for and discussions of each of these types of ratios as well as examples of how each is calculated. Refer to pages 470 to 484.

A meaningful ratio analysis must go beyond the calculation and interpretation of financial ratios.[53] It must include an analysis of how ratios change over time as well as how they are interrelated. For example, a firm that takes on too much long-term debt to finance operations will see an immediate impact on its indicators of long-term financial leverage. The additional debt will also have a negative impact on the firm's short-term liquidity ratio (i.e., current and quick ratios) since the firm must pay interest and principal on the additional debt each year until it is retired. Additionally, the interest expenses must be deducted from revenues, reducing the firm's profitability.

>LO6
The usefulness of financial ratio analysis, its inherent limitations, and how to make meaningful comparisons of performance across firms.

A firm's financial position should not be analyzed in isolation. Important reference points are needed. We will address some issues that must be taken into account to make financial analysis more meaningful: historical comparisons, comparisons with industry norms, and comparisons with key competitors.

Historical Comparisons   When you evaluate a firm's financial performance, it is very useful to compare its financial position over time. This provides a means of evaluating trends. For example, Microsoft reported revenues of $44.3 billion and net income of $12.6 billion in 2006. Almost all firms—except a few of the largest and most profitable companies

I. Short-term solvency, or liquidity, ratios

$$\text{Current ratio} = \frac{\text{Current assets}}{\text{Current liabilities}}$$

$$\text{Quick ratio} = \frac{\text{Current assets} - \text{Inventory}}{\text{Current liabilities}}$$

$$\text{Cash ratio} = \frac{\text{Cash}}{\text{Current liabilities}}$$

II. Long-term solvency, or financial leverage, ratios

$$\text{Total debt ratio} = \frac{\text{Total assets} - \text{Total equity}}{\text{Total assets}}$$

$$\text{Debt-equity ratio} = \text{Total debt/Total equity}$$

$$\text{Equity multiplier} = \text{Total assets/Total equity}$$

$$\text{Times interest earned ratio} = \frac{\text{EBIT}}{\text{Interest}}$$

$$\text{Cash coverage ratio} = \frac{\text{EBIT} + \text{Depreciation}}{\text{Interest}}$$

III. Asset utilization, or turnover, ratios

$$\text{Inventory turnover} = \frac{\text{Cost of goods sold}}{\text{Inventory}}$$

$$\text{Days' sales in inventory} = \frac{365 \text{ days}}{\text{Inventory turnover}}$$

$$\text{Receivables turnover} = \frac{\text{Sales}}{\text{Accounts receivable}}$$

$$\text{Days' sales in receivables} = \frac{365 \text{ days}}{\text{Receivables turnover}}$$

$$\text{Total asset turnover} = \frac{\text{Sales}}{\text{Total assets}}$$

$$\text{Capital intensity} = \frac{\text{Total assets}}{\text{Sales}}$$

IV. Profitability ratios

$$\text{Profit margin} = \frac{\text{Net income}}{\text{Sales}}$$

$$\text{Return on assets (ROA)} = \frac{\text{Net income}}{\text{Total assets}}$$

$$\text{Return on equity (ROE)} = \frac{\text{Net income}}{\text{Total equity}}$$

$$\text{ROE} = \frac{\text{Net income}}{\text{Sales}} \times \frac{\text{Sales}}{\text{Assets}} \times \frac{\text{Assets}}{\text{Equity}}$$

V. Market value ratios

$$\text{Price-earnings ratio} = \frac{\text{Price per share}}{\text{Earnings per share}}$$

$$\text{Market-to-book ratio} = \frac{\text{Market value per share}}{\text{Book value per share}}$$

Exhibit 3.9 A Summary of Five Types of Financial Ratios.

in the world—would be very happy with such financial success. These figures reflect an annual growth in revenue and net income of 10 percent and 24 percent, respectively for the 2004 to 2006 time period. Clearly, had Microsoft's revenues and net income in 2006 been $35 billion and $10 billion, respectively, it would still be a very large and highly profitable enterprise. However, such performance would have resulted in significant damage to Microsoft's market valuation and reputation as well as to the careers of many of its executives. Exhibit 3.10 illustrates a 10-year period of return on sales (ROS) for a hypothetical company. As indicated by the dotted trend lines, the rate of growth (or decline) differs substantially over time periods.

Comparison with Industry Norms When you are evaluating a firm's financial performance, remember also to compare it with industry norms. A firm's current ratio or profitability may appear impressive at first glance. However, it may pale when compared with industry standards or norms.

By comparing your firm with all other firms in your industry, you can assess relative performance. Banks often use such comparisons when evaluating a firm's creditworthiness. Exhibit 3.11 includes a variety of financial ratios for three industries: semiconductors, grocery stores, and skilled-nursing facilities. Why is there such variation among the financial ratios for these three industries? There are several reasons. With regard to the collection period, grocery stores operate mostly on a cash basis, hence a very short collection period. Semiconductor manufacturers sell their output to other manufacturers (e.g., computer makers) on terms such as 2/15 net 45, which means they give a 2 percent discount on bills paid within

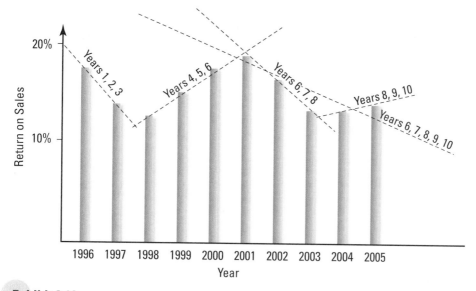

Exhibit 3.10 Historical Trends: Return on Sales (ROS) for a Hypothetical Company

15 days and start charging interest after 45 days. Skilled-nursing facilities would also have a longer collection period than grocery stores because they typically rely on payments from insurance companies.

The industry norms for return on sales also highlight some differences among these industries. Grocers, with very slim margins, have a lower return on sales than either skilled-nursing facilities or semiconductor manufacturers. But how might we explain the differences between skilled-nursing facilities and semiconductor manufacturers? Health care facilities, in general, are limited in their pricing structures by Medicare/Medicaid regulations and by insurance reimbursement limits, but semiconductor producers have pricing structures determined by the market. If their products have superior performance, semiconductor manufacturers can charge premium prices.

Comparison with Key Competitors   Recall from Chapter 2 that firms with similar strategies are members of a strategic group in an industry. Furthermore, competition tends to be more intense among competitors within groups than across groups. Thus, you can gain valuable insights into a firm's financial and competitive position if you make comparisons between a firm and its most direct rivals. Consider Procter & Gamble's ill-fated efforts to enter

Exhibit 3.11

How Financial Ratios Differ across Industries

Financial Ratio	Semiconductors	Grocery Stores	Skilled-Nursing Facilities
Quick ratio (times)	1.9	0.5	1.1
Current ratio (times)	4.0	1.6	1.6
Total liabilities to net worth (%)	30.7	92.0	163.5
Collection period (days)	49.6	2.9	31.2
Assets to sales (%)	187.8	20.2	101.6
Return on sales (%)	5.8	0.8	1.6

Source: Dun & Bradstreet. *Industry Norms and Key Business Ratios, 2003–2004.* One Year Edition, SIC #2000-3999 (Semiconductors); SIC #5200-5499 (Grocery Stores); SIC #6100-8999 (Skilled-Nursing Facilities). New York: Dun & Bradstreet Credit Services.

Exhibit 3.12

Comparison of Procter & Gamble's and Key Competitors' Drug Revenues and R&D Expenditures

Company (or division)	Sales* ($ billions)	R&D Budget ($ billions)
P&G Drug Division	$ 0.8	$0.38
Bristol-Myers Squibb	20.2	1.80
Pfizer	27.4	4.00
Merck	32.7	2.10

Source: Berner, R. 2000. Procter & Gamble: Just say no to drugs. *BusinessWeek*, October 9: 128; data courtesy of Lehman Brothers and Procter & Gamble.

*Data: Lehman Brothers, Procter & Gamble Co.

the highly profitable pharmaceutical industry. Although P&G is a giant in consumer products, its efforts over two decades have produced nominal profits at best. In 1999 P&G spent $380 million on R&D in drugs—22 percent of its total corporate R&D budget. However, its drug unit produced only 2 percent of the company's $40 billion sales. Why? While $380 million is hardly a trivial amount of capital, its key competitors dwarf P&G. Consider the drug revenues and R&D budgets of P&G compared to its main rivals as shown in Exhibit 3.12. *BusinessWeek*'s take on P&G's chances in an article entitled "Just Say No to Drugs" was this: "Don't bet on it. P&G may be a giant in detergent and toothpaste, but the consumer-products maker is simply outclassed by the competition."[54]

Integrating Financial Analysis and Stakeholder Perspectives: The Balanced Scorecard

It is useful to see how a firm is performing over time in terms of the several ratios. However, such traditional approaches to performance assessments can be a double-edged sword.[55] Many important transactions that managers make—investments in research and development, employee training and development, and, advertising and promotion of key brands—may greatly expand a firm's market potential and create significant long-term shareholder value. But such critical investments are not reflected positively in short-term financial reports. Why? Because financial reports typically measure expenses, not the value created. Thus, managers may be penalized for spending money in the short term to improve their firm's long-term competitive viability!

Now consider the other side of the coin. A manager may be destroying the firm's future value by operating in a way that makes customers dissatisfied, depletes the firm's stock of good products coming out of R&D, or damages the morale of valued employees. Such budget cuts, however, may lead to very good short-term financials. The manager may look good in the short run and even receive credit for improving the firm's performance. In essence, such a manager has mastered "denominator management," whereby decreasing investments makes the return on investment (ROI) ratio larger, even though the actual return remains constant or shrinks.

The Balanced Scorecard: Description and Benefits To provide a meaningful integration of the many issues that come into evaluating a firm's performance, Kaplan and Norton developed a **"balanced scorecard."**[56] This is a set of measures that provide top managers with a fast but comprehensive view of the business. In a nutshell, it includes financial measures that reflect the results of actions already taken, but it complements these indicators with operational measures of customer satisfaction, internal processes, and the organization's innovation and improvement activities—operational measures that drive future financial performance.

> **>LO7**
>
> The value of the "balanced scorecard" in recognizing how the interests of a variety of stakeholders can be interrelated.

balanced scorecard a method of evaluating a firm's performance using performance measures from the customers', internal, innovation and learning, and financial perspectives.

Exhibit 3.13
The Balanced Scorecard's Four Perspectives

- How do customers see us? (customer perspective)
- What must we excel at? (internal business perspective)
- Can we continue to improve and create value? (innovation and learning perspective)
- How do we look to shareholders? (financial perspective)

The balanced scorecard enables managers to consider their business from four key perspectives: customer, internal, innovation and learning, and financial. These are briefly described in Exhibit 3.13.

Customer Perspective Clearly, how a company is performing from its customers' perspective is a top priority for management. The balanced scorecard requires that managers translate their general mission statements on customer service into specific measures that reflect the factors that really matter to customers. For the balanced scorecard to work, managers must articulate goals for four key categories of customer concerns: time, quality, performance and service, and cost. For example, lead time may be measured as the time from the company's receipt of an order to the time it actually delivers the product or service to the customer.

Internal Business Perspective Although customer-based measures are important, they must be translated into indicators of what the firm must do internally to meet customers' expectations. Excellent customer performance results from processes, decisions, and actions that occur throughout organizations in a coordinated fashion, and managers must focus on those critical internal operations that enable them to satisfy customer needs. The internal measures should reflect business processes that have the greatest impact on customer satisfaction. These include factors that affect cycle time, quality, employee skills, and productivity. Firms also must identify and measure the key resources and capabilities they need to ensure continued strategic success.

Innovation and Learning Perspective Given the rapid rate of markets, technologies, and global competition, the criteria for success are constantly changing. To survive and prosper, managers must make frequent changes to existing products and services as well as introduce entirely new products with expanded capabilities. A firm's ability to improve, innovate, and learn is tied directly to its value. Simply put, only by developing new products and services, creating greater value for customers, and increasing operating efficiencies can a company penetrate new markets, increase revenues and margins, and enhance shareholder value. A firm's ability to do well from an innovation and learning perspective is more dependent on its intangible than tangible assets. Three categories of intangible assets are critically important: human capital (skills, talent, and knowledge), information capital (information systems, networks), and organization capital (culture, leadership).

Financial Perspective Measures of financial performance indicate whether the company's strategy, implementation, and execution are indeed contributing to bottom-line improvement. Typical financial goals include profitability, growth, and shareholder value. Periodic financial statements remind managers that improved quality, response time, productivity, and innovative products benefit the firm only when they result in improved sales, increased market share, reduced operating expenses, or higher asset turnover.[57]

We now provide an example that illustrates the causal relationships among the multiple perspectives in the model. Sears, the huge retailer, found a strong causal relationship between employee attitudes, customer attitudes, and financial outcomes.[58] Through an ongoing study, Sears developed (and continues to refine) what it calls its total performance indicators, or TPI—a set of indicators that shows how well the company is doing with customers, employees, and investors. Sears's quantitative model has shown that a 5.0 percent improvement in employee attitudes leads to a 1.3 percent improvement in customer satisfaction, which in turn will drive a 0.5 percent improvement in revenue. Thus, if a single store improved its employee attitude by 5.0 percent on a survey scale, Sears could predict with confidence that if the revenue growth in the district as a whole were 5.0 percent, the revenue growth in this particular store would be 5.5 percent. Interestingly, Sears's managers consider such numbers as rigorous as any others that they work with every year. The company's accounting firm audits management as closely as it audits the financial statements.

A key implication of the balanced scorecard is that managers do not need to look at their job as primarily balancing stakeholder demands. They need to avoid the following mind-set: "How many units in employee satisfaction do I have to give up to get some additional units of customer satisfaction or profits?" Instead, when done properly, the balanced scorecard provides a win–win approach—a means of simultaneously increasing satisfaction among a wide variety of organizational stakeholders, including employees (at all levels), customers, and stockholders.

Limitations and Potential Downsides of the Balanced Scorecard   There is general agreement that there is nothing inherently wrong with the concept of the balanced scorecard.[59] The key limitation is that some executives may view it as a "quick fix" that can be easily installed in their organization. However, implementing a balanced metrics system is an evolutionary process. It is not a one-time task that can be quickly checked off as "completed." If managers do not recognize this from the beginning and fail to commit to it long term, the organization will be disappointed with the results. Poor execution becomes the cause of such performance outcomes. And organizational scorecards must be aligned with individuals' scorecards to turn the balanced scorecards into a powerful tool for sustained organizational performance.

In a recent study of 50 Canadian medium-size and large organizations, the number of users expressing skepticism about scorecard performance was much greater than the number claiming positive results. However, the overwhelming perspective was that balanced scorecards can be worthwhile in clarifying an organization's strategy, and if this can be accomplished, better results will follow. A few companies stated categorically that scorecards have improved their firm's financial results. For example, one respondent claimed that, "We did not meet our financial goals previously, but since implementing our balanced scorecard, we have now met our goals three years running."

On the other hand, a greater number of respondents agreed with the statement, "Balanced scorecards don't really work." Some representative comments included: "It became just a number-crunching exercise by accountants after the first year," "It is just the latest management fad and is already dropping lower on management's list of priorities as all fads eventually do," and, "If scorecards are supposed to be a measurement tool, why is it so hard to measure their results?" Few would argue that there is much work to do before scorecards can become a viable framework for the measurement of sustained strategic performance.

Problems often occur in the balanced scorecard implementation efforts when there is an insufficient commitment to learning and the inclusion of employees' personal ambitions. If there is not a set of rules for employees that address continuous process improvement and the personal improvement of individual employees, there will be limited employee buy-in and insufficient cultural change. Thus, many improvements may be temporary and superficial. Often, scorecards that failed to attain alignment and improvements

---

* Building on the concepts that are the foundation of the balanced scorecard approach, Kaplan and Norton have recently developed a useful tool called the strategy map. Strategy maps show the cause and effect links by which specific improvements in different areas lead to a desired outcome. Strategy maps also help employees see how their jobs are related to the overall objectives of the organization. They also help us understand how an organization can convert its assets—both tangible and intangible—into tangible outcomes. Refer to Kaplan, R. S., & Norton, D. P. 2000. Having trouble with your strategy? Then map it. *Harvard Business Review,* 78(10): 167–176.

Exhibit 3.14
Potential Limitations of the Balanced Scorecard

Most agree that the balanced scorecard concept is a useful and an appropriate management tool. However, there are many design and implementation issues that may short circuit its value, including the following:

- **Lack of a Clear Strategy.** A scorecard can be developed without the aid of a strategy. However, it then becomes a key performance indicator or stakeholder system, lacking in many of the attributes offered from a true balanced scorecard.

- **Limited or Ineffective Executive Sponsorship.** Although training and education is important, without tenacious leadership and support of a scorecard project, the effort is most likely doomed.

- **Too Much Emphasis on Financial Measures Rather than Nonfinancial Measures.** This leads to measures that do not connect to the drivers of the business and are not relevant to performance improvement.

- **Poor Data on Actual Performance.** This can negate most of the effort invested in defining performance measures because a company can't monitor actual changes in results from changes in behavior.

- **Inappropriate Links of Scorecard Measures to Compensation.** Although this can focus managerial and employee attention, exercising it too soon can produce many unintended side effects such as dysfunctional decision making by managers looking to cash in.

- **Inconsistent or Inappropriate Terminology.** Everyone must speak the same language if measurement is to be used to guide change within an organization. Translating strategy into measures becomes even more difficult if everyone cannot agree on (or understand) the same language and terminology.

Sources: Angel, R., & Rampersad, H. 2005. Do scorecards add up? *Camagazine.com*. May: np; and Niven, P. 2002. *Balanced scorecard step by step: Maximizing performance and maintaining results*. New York: John Wiley & Sons.

dissipated very quickly. And, in many cases, management's efforts to improve performance were seen as divisive. That is, it was viewed by employees as aimed at benefiting senior management compensation which fostered a "what's in it for me?" attitude among employees. Exhibit 3.14 summarizes some of the primary limitations and potential downsides of the balanced scorecard.

Reflecting on Career Implications . . .

- **The Value Chain:** Carefully analyze where you can add value in your firm's value chain. How might your firm's support activities (e.g., information technology, human resource practices) help you accomplish your assigned tasks more effectively?
- **The Value Chain:** Consider important relationships among activities both within your firm as well as between your firm and its suppliers, customers, and alliance partners.
- **Resource Based View of the Firm:** Are your skills and talents rare, valuable, difficult to imitate, and have few substitutes? If so, you are in a better position to add value for your firm—and earn rewards and incentives. How can your skills and talents be enhanced to help satisfy these criteria to a greater extent? More training? Change positions within the firm? Consider career options at other organizations?
- **Balanced Scorecard:** In your decision making, strive to "balance" the four perspectives: customer, internal business, innovation and learning, and financial. Do not focus too much on short-term profits. Do your personal career goals provide opportunities to develop your skills in all four directions?

Summary

In the traditional approaches to assessing a firm's internal environment, the primary goal of managers would be to determine their firm's relative strengths and weaknesses. Such is the role of SWOT analysis, wherein managers analyze their firm's strengths and weaknesses as well as the opportunities and threats in the external environment. In this chapter, we discussed why this may be a good starting point but hardly the best approach to take in performing a sound analysis. There are many limitations to SWOT analysis, including its static perspective, its potential to overemphasize a single dimension of a firm's strategy, and the likelihood that a firm's strengths do not necessarily help the firm create value or competitive advantages.

We identified two frameworks that serve to complement SWOT analysis in assessing a firm's internal environment: value-chain analysis and the resource-based view of the firm. In conducting a value-chain analysis, first divide the firm into a series of value-creating activities. These include primary activities such as inbound logistics, operations, and service as well as support activities such as procurement and human resources management. Then analyze how each activity adds value as well as how *interrelationships* among value activities in the firm and among the firm and its customers and suppliers add value. Thus, instead of merely determining a firm's strengths and weaknesses per se, you analyze them in the overall context of the firm and its relationships with customers and suppliers—the value system.

The resource-based view of the firm considers the firm as a bundle of resources: tangible resources, intangible resources, and organizational capabilities. Competitive advantages that are sustainable over time generally arise from the creation of bundles of resources and capabilities. For advantages to be sustainable, four criteria must be satisfied: value, rarity, difficulty in imitation, and difficulty in substitution. Such an evaluation requires a sound knowledge of the competitive context in which the firm exists. The owners of a business may not capture all of the value created by the firm. The appropriation of value created by a firm between the owners and employees is determined by four factors: employee bargaining power, replacement cost, employee exit costs, and manager bargaining power.

An internal analysis of the firm would not be complete unless you evaluate its performance and make the appropriate comparisons. Determining a firm's performance requires an analysis of its financial situation as well as a review of how well it is satisfying a broad range of stakeholders, including customers, employees, and stockholders. We discussed the concept of the balanced scorecard, in which four perspectives must be addressed: customer, internal business, innovation and learning, and financial. Central to this concept is the idea that the interests of various stakeholders can be interrelated. We provide examples of how indicators of employee satisfaction lead to higher levels of customer satisfaction, which in turn lead to higher levels of financial performance. Thus, improving a firm's performance does not need to involve making trade-offs among different stakeholders. Assessing the firm's performance is also more useful if it is evaluated in terms of how it changes over time, compares with industry norms, and compares with key competitors.

In the Appendix to Chapter 3, we discuss how Internet and digital technologies have created new opportunities for firms to add value. Four value-adding activities that have been enhanced by Internet capabilities are search, evaluation, problem solving, and transaction. These four activities are supported by three different types of content that Internet businesses often use—customer feedback, expertise, and entertainment programming. Seven business models have been identified that are proving successful for use by Internet firms. These include commission, advertising, markup, production, referral, subscription, and fee-for-service–based models. Firms also are finding that combinations of these business models can contribute to greater success.

Summary Review Questions

1. SWOT analysis is a technique to analyze the internal and external environment of a firm. What are its advantages and disadvantages?
2. Briefly describe the primary and support activities in a firm's value chain.
3. How can managers create value by establishing important relationships among the value-chain activities both within their firm and between the firm and its customers and suppliers?
4. Briefly explain the four criteria for sustainability of competitive advantages.
5. Under what conditions are employees and managers able to appropriate some of the value created by their firm?
6. What are the advantages and disadvantages of conducting a financial ratio analysis of a firm?
7. Summarize the concept of the balanced scorecard. What are its main advantages?

Key Terms

Experiential Exercise

Dell Computer is a leading firm in the personal computer industry, with annual revenues of $56 billion during its 2006 fiscal year. Dell has created a very strong competitive position via its "direct model," whereby it manufactures its personal computers to detailed customer specifications.

Below we address several questions that focus on Dell's value-chain activities and interrelationships among them as well as whether they are able to attain sustainable competitive advantage(s). (We discuss Dell in this chapter on pages 90–91.)

1. Where in Dell's value chain are they creating value for their customer?

Value-Chain Activity	Yes/No	How Does Dell Create Value for the Customer?
Primary:		
Inbound logistics		
Operations		
Outbound logistics		
Marketing and sales		
Service		
Support:		
Procurement		
Technology development		
Human resource management		
General administration		

2. What are the important relationships among Dell's value-chain activities? What are the important interdependencies? For each activity, identify the relationships and interdependencies.

	Inbound logistics	Operations	Outbound logistics	Marketing and sales	Service	Procurement	Technology development	Human resource management	General administration
Inbound logistics									
Operations									
Outbound logistics									
Marketing and sales									
Service									
Procurement									
Technology development									
Human resource management									
General administration									

3. What resources, activities, and relationships enable Dell to achieve a sustainable competitive advantage?

Resource/Activity	Is It Valuable?	Is It Rare?	Are There Few Substitutes?	Is It Difficult to Make?
Inbound logistics				
Operations				
Outbound logistics				
Marketing and sales				
Service				
Procurement				
Technology development				
Human resource management				
General administration				

Application Questions Exercises

1. Using published reports, select two CEOs who have recently made public statements regarding a major change in their firm's strategy. Discuss how the successful implementation of such strategies requires changes in the firm's primary and support activities.

2. Select a firm that competes in an industry in which you are interested. Drawing upon published financial reports, complete a financial ratio analysis. Based on changes over time and a comparison with industry norms, evaluate the firm's strengths and weaknesses in terms of its financial position.

3. How might exemplary human resource practices enhance and strengthen a firm's value-chain activities?

4. Using the Internet, look up your university or college. What are some of its key value-creating activities that provide competitive advantages? Why?

Ethics Questions

1. What are some of the ethical issues that arise when a firm becomes overly zealous in advertising its products?

2. What are some of the ethical issues that may arise from a firm's procurement activities? Are you aware of any of these issues from your personal experience or businesses you are familiar with?

References

1. Thomas, A. R., & Wilkinson, T. J. 2006. The outsourcing compulsion. *MIT Sloan Management Review,* 48(1): 10–14; and Fahey, J. 2005. Rolling, rolling, rolling. *Forbes.com.* November 28: np.

2. As a postscript, the Goodyear story does have the making of a happy ending. In early 2003, Robert Keegan, a former president of Eastman Kodak, replaced 37-year veteran Samir Gibara as chief executive officer at Goodyear. At the time, Goodyear's stock was struggling at around $5 per share (reaching a low of $3.57 on February 3 of that year). Keegan began a restructuring plan to reposition the company as a consumer-products firm rather than a rust belt manufacturer. For years, Goodyear had chased volume, selling low-margin tires to auto manufacturers and replacement tires to the middle of the market. In contrast, under Keegan's leadership the firm began developing expensive tires aimed at performance and luxury-car drivers. Production of low-end tires was being moved offshore to Goodyear plants in lower-wage countries in Latin America, Asia, and Eastern Europe. Says Jonathan Rich, head of North American operations: "We owned the wrong real estate." After a long period of losses for 2001 through 2004, Goodyear turned a net profit of $228 million in 2005. And, in the beginning of 2007, its stock is back up to more than $21 per share—far above the level it was at when Keegan took over. Source: Fahey, J. 2005. Rolling, rolling, rolling. Forbes.com, November 28.

3. Our discussion of the value chain will draw on Porter, M. E. 1985. *Competitive advantage:* chap. 2. New York: Free Press.

4. Dyer, J. H. 1996. Specialized supplier networks as a source of competitive advantage: Evidence from the auto industry. *Strategic Management Journal,* 17: 271–291.

5. For an insightful perspective on value-chain analysis, refer to Stabell, C. B., & Fjeldstad, O. D. 1998. Configuring value for competitive advantage: On chains, shops, and networks. *Strategic Management Journal,* 19: 413–437. The authors develop concepts of value chains, value shops, and value networks to extend the value-creation logic across a broad range of industries. Their work builds on the seminal contributions of Porter, 1985, op. cit., and others who have addressed how firms create value through key interrelationships among value-creating activities.

6. Ibid.

7. Maynard, M. 1999. Toyota promises custom order in 5 days. *USA Today,* August 6: B1.

8. Shaw Industries. 1999. Annual report: 14–15.

9. Fisher, M. L. 1997. What is the right supply chain for your product? *Harvard Business Review,* 75(2): 105–116.

10. Jackson. M. 2001. Bringing a dying brand back to life. *Harvard Business Review,* 79(5): 53–61.

11. Anderson, J. C., & Nmarus, J. A. 2003. Selectively pursuing more of your customer's business. *MIT Sloan Management Review,* 44(3): 42–50.

12. An insightful discussion of the role of identity marketing—that is, the myriad labels that people use to express who they are—in successful marketing activities is found in Reed, A., II, & Bolton, L. E. 2005. The complexity of identify. *MIT Sloan Management Review,* 46(3): 18–22.

13. Berggren, E., & Nacher, T. 2000. Why good ideas go bust. *Management Review,* February: 32–36.

14. For an insightful perspective on creating effective brand portfolios, refer to Hill, S., Ettenson, R., & Tyson, D. 2005. Achieving the ideal brand portfolio. *MIT Sloan Management Review,* 46(2): 85–90.

15. Haddad, C., & Grow, B. 2001. Wait a second—I didn't order that! *BusinessWeek,* July 16: 45.

16. Berman, B. 2005. How to delight your customers. *California Management Review*, 48(1): 129–151.

17. For a scholarly discussion on the procurement of technology components, read Hoetker, G. 2005. How much you know versus how well I know you: Selecting a supplier for a technically innovative component. *Strategic Management Journal*, 26(1): 75–96.

18. For a discussion on criteria to use when screening suppliers for back-office functions, read Feeny, D., Lacity, M., & Willcocks, L. P. 2005. Taking the measure of outsourcing providers. *MIT Sloan Management Review*, 46(3): 41–48.

19. Imperato, G. 1998. How to give good feedback. *Fast Company*, September: 144–156.

20. Bensaou, B. M., & Earl, M. 1998. The right mindset for managing information technology. *Harvard Business Review*, 96(5): 118–128.

21. Donlon, J. P. 2000. Bonsignore's bid for the big time. *Chief Executive*, March: 28–37.

22. Ulrich, D. 1998. A new mandate for human resources. *Harvard Business Review*, 96(1): 124–134.

23. Wood, J. 2003. Sharing jobs and working from home: The new face of the airline industry. *AviationCareer. net*, February 21.

24. Follow AT&T's lead in this tactic to retain "plateaued" employees. n.d. *Recruitment & Retention:* 1.

25. Green, S., Hasan, F., Immelt, J. Marks, M., & Meiland, D. 2003. In search of global leaders. *Harvard Business Review*, 81(8): 38–45.

26. For a cautionary note on the use of IT, refer to McAfee, A. 2003. When too much IT knowledge is a dangerous thing. *MIT Sloan Management Review*, 44(2): 83–90.

27. Walgreen Co. 1996. *Information technology and Walgreens: Opportunities for employment,* January; and Dess, G. G., & Picken, J. C. 1997. *Beyond productivity.* New York: AMACOM.

28. For an interesting perspective on some of the potential downsides of close customer and supplier relationships, refer to Anderson, E., & Jap, S. D. 2005. The dark side of close relationships. *MIT Sloan Management Review*, 46(3): 75–82.

29. Day, G. S. 2003. Creating a superior customer-relating capability. *MIT Sloan Management Review*, 44(3): 77–82.

30. To gain insights on the role of electronic technologies in enhancing a firm's connections to outside suppliers and customers, refer to Lawrence, T. B., Morse, E. A., & Fowler, S. W. 2005. Managing your portfolio of connections. *MIT Sloan Management Review*, 46(2): 59–66.

31. Reinhardt, F. L. 1999. Bringing the environment down to earth. *Harvard Business Review*, 77(4): 149–157.

32. Collis, D. J., & Montgomery, C. A. 1995. Competing on resources: Strategy in the 1990's. *Harvard Business Review*, 73(4): 119–128; and Barney, J. 1991. Firm resources and sustained competitive advantage. *Journal of Management*, 17(1): 99–120.

33. For recent critiques of the resource-based view of the firm, refer to: Sirmon, D. G., Hitt, M. A., & Ireland, R. D. 2007. Managing firm resources in dynamic environments to create value: Looking inside the black box. *Academy of Management Review*, 32(1): 273–292; and Newbert, S. L. Empirical research on the resource-based view of the firm: An assessment and suggestions for future research. *Strategic Management Journal*, 28(2): 121–146.

34. Henkoff, R. 1993. Companies that train the best. *Fortune,* March 22: 83; and Dess & Picken, *Beyond productivity*, p. 98.

35. Barney, J. B. 1986. Types of competition and the theory of strategy: Towards an integrative framework. *Academy of Management Review*, 11(4): 791–800.

36. Harley-Davidson. 1993. Annual report.

37. For a rigorous, academic treatment of the origin of capabilities, refer to Ethiraj, S. K., Kale, P., Krishnan, M. S., & Singh, J. V. 2005. Where do capabilities come from and how do they matter? A study of the software services industry. *Strategic Management Journal*, 26(1): 25–46.

38. For an academic discussion on methods associated with organizational capabilities, refer to Dutta, S., Narasimhan, O., & Rajiv, S. 2005. Conceptualizing and measuring capabilities: Methodology and empirical application. *Strategic Management Journal*, 26(3): 277–286.

39. Lorenzoni, G., & Lipparini, A. 1999. The leveraging of interfirm relationships as a distinctive organizational capability: A longitudinal study. *Strategic Management Journal*, 20: 317–338.

40. Barney, J. 1991. Firm resources and sustained competitive advantage. *Journal of Management*, 17(1): 99–120.

41. Barney, 1986, op. cit. Our discussion of inimitability and substitution draws upon this source.

42. Deephouse, D. L. 1999. To be different, or to be the same? It's a question (and theory) of strategic balance. *Strategic Management Journal*, 20: 147–166.

43. Yeoh, P. L., & Roth, K. 1999. An empirical analysis of sustained advantage in the U.S. pharmaceutical industry: Impact of firm resources and capabilities. *Strategic Management Journal*, 20: 637–653.

44. Robins, J. A., & Wiersema, M. F. 2000. Strategies for unstructured competitive environments: Using scarce resources to create new markets. In Bresser, R. F., et al., (Eds.), *Winning strategies in a deconstructing world:* 201–220. New York: John Wiley.

45. Byrnes, N., & Burrows, P. 2007. Where Dell went wrong. *BusinessWeek,* February 18: 62–63; and Smith, A. D. 2007. Dell's moves create buzz. *Dallas Morning News.* Februrary 21: D1.

46. Amit, R., & Schoemaker, J. H. 1993. Strategic assets and organizational rent. *Strategic Management Journal,* 14(1): 33–46; Collis, D. J., & Montgomery, C. A. 1995. Competing on resources: Strategy in the 1990's. *Harvard Business Review,* 73(4): 118–128; Coff, R. W. 1999. When competitive advantage doesn't lead to performance: The resource-based view and stakeholder bargaining power. *Organization Science,* 10(2): 119–133; and Blyler, M., & Coff, R. W. 2003. Dynamic capabilities, social capital, and rent appropriation: Ties that split pies. *Strategic Management Journal,* 24: 677–686.

47. Munk, N. 1998. The new organization man. *Fortune,* March 16: 62–74.

48. Coff, op. cit.

49. Lavelle, L. 2003. Sprint's board needs a good sweeping, too. *BusinessWeek,* February 24: 40; Anonymous. 2003. Another nail in the coffin. *The Economist,* February 15: 69–70; and Byrnes, N., Dwyer, P., & McNamee, M. 2003. Hacking away at tax shelters, *BusinessWeek,* February 24: 41.

50. We have focused our discussion on how internal stakeholders (e.g., employees, managers, and top executives) may appropriate a firm's profits (or rents). For an interesting discussion of how a firm's innovations may be appropriated by external stakeholders (e.g., customers, suppliers) as well as competitors, refer to Grant, R. M. 2002. *Contemporary strategy analysis* (4th ed.): 335–340. Malden, MA: Blackwell.

51. Luehrman, T. A. 1997. What's it worth? A general manager's guide to valuation. *Harvard Business Review,* 45(3): 132–142.

52. See, for example, Kaplan, R. S., & Norton, D. P. 1992. The balanced scorecard: Measures that drive performance. *Harvard Business Review,* 69(1): 71–79.

53. Hitt, M. A., Ireland, R. D., & Stadter, G. 1982. Functional importance of company performance: Moderating effects of grand strategy and industry type. *Strategic Management Journal,* 3: 315–330.

54. Berner, R. 2000. Procter & Gamble: Just say no to drugs. *BusinessWeek,* October 9: 128.

55. Kaplan & Norton, op. cit.

56. Ibid.

57. For a discussion of the relative value of growth versus increasing margins, read Mass, N. J. 2005. The relative value of growth. *Harvard Business Review,* 83(4): 102–112.

58. Rucci, A. J., Kirn, S. P., & Quinn, R. T. 1998. The employee-customer-profit chain at Sears. *Harvard Business Review,* 76(1): 82–97.

59. Our discussion draws upon: Angel, R., & Rampersad, H. 2005. Do scorecards add up? *camagazine.com.* May: np.; and Niven, P. 2002. *Balanced scorecard step by step: Maximizing performance and maintaining results.* New York: John Wiley & Sons.

APPENDIX TO CHAPTER 3

How the Internet and Digital Technologies Add Value

The Internet has changed the way business is conducted. By providing new ways to interact with customers and using digital technologies to streamline operations, the Internet is helping companies create new value propositions. Let's take a look at several ways these changes have added new value. Exhibit 3A.1 illustrates four related activities that are being revolutionized by the Internet—search, evaluation, problem solving, and transactions.[1]

> **>LO8**
>
> How firms are using Internet technologies to add value and achieve unique advantages. (Appendix)

Search Activities

Search refers to the process of gathering information and identifying purchase options. The Internet has enhanced both the speed of information gathering and the breadth of information that can be accessed. This enhanced search capability is one of the key reasons the Internet has lowered switching costs—by

[1]The ideas in this section draw on several sources, including Zeng, M., & Reinartz, W. 2003. Beyond online search: The road to profitability. *California Management Review,* Winter: 107–130; and Stabell, C. B., & Fjeldstad, O. D. 1998. Configuring value for competitive advantage: On chains, shops, and networks. *Strategic Management Journal,* 19: 413–437.

Exhibit 3A.1 **Internet Activities that Add Value**

Sources: Adapted from Zeng, M., & Reinartz, W. 2003. Beyond online search: The road to profitability. *California Management Review.* Winter: 107–130; and Stabell, C. B., & Fjeldstad, O. D. 1998. Configuring value for competitive advantage: On chains, shops, and networks. *Strategic Management Jounral,* 19: 413–437.

decreasing the cost of search. These efficiency gains have greatly benefited buyers. Suppliers also have benefited. Small suppliers that had difficulty getting noticed can be found more easily, and large suppliers can publish thousands of pages of information for a fraction of the cost that hard-copy catalogs once required. Additionally, online search engines have accelerated the search process to incredible speeds. Consider the example of Google:

> Google, a search engine developed as a project by two graduate students, became the number one search service in just four years. Why? Because it is capable of incredible things. Using over 10,000 networked computers, it searches 3 billion Web pages in an average of 500 milliseconds. To do the same search manually, by thumbing through 3 billion pages at the rate of one minute per page, would take 5,707 years. This ability has made Google an essential tool for many businesses. As a result, Google has built a powerful advertising business. Mark Kini, who runs a small limousine service in Boston, spends 80 percent of his advertising budget on Google and other search engines. "It's how we survive," says Kini.[2]

Evaluation Activities

Evaluation refers to the process of considering alternatives and comparing the costs and benefits of various options. Online services that facilitate comparative shopping, provide product reviews, and catalog customer evaluations of performance have made the Internet a valuable resource.[3] For example, BizRate.com offers extensive product ratings that can help evaluate products. Sites such as CNET that provide comparative pricing have helped lower prices even for quality products that have traditionally maintained premium prices. Opinion-based sites such as ePinions.com and PlanetFeedback.com provide reports of consumer experiences with various vendors.

Many Internet businesses, according to digital business experts Ming Zeng and Werner Reinartz, could improve their performance by making a stronger effort to help buyers evaluate purchases.[4] Even so, only certain types of products can be evaluated online. Products such as CDs that appeal primarily to the sense of sound sell well on the Internet. But products that appeal to multiple senses are harder to evaluate online. This explains why products such as furniture and fashion have never been strong online sellers. It's one thing to look at a leather sofa, but to be able to sit on it, touch, and smell the leather online are impossible.

Problem-Solving Activities

Problem solving refers to the process of identifying problems or needs and generating ideas and action plans to address those needs. Whereas evaluation is primarily product-related, problem solving is typically used in the context of services. Customers usually have unique problems that are handled one at a time. For example, online travel services such as Travelocity help customers select from many options to form a unique travel package. Furthermore, problem solving often involves providing

[2]Hardy, Q. 2003. All eyes on Google. *Forbes,* May 26, www.forbes.com.
[3]For an interesting discussion of how successful Internet-based companies are using evaluation to add value see Weiss, L. M., Capozzi, M. M., & Prusak, L. 2004. Learning from the Internet giants. *Sloan Management Review,* 45(4): 79–84.
[4]Zeng & Reinartz, *op.cit.*

answers immediately (compared to the creation of a new product). Firms in industries such as medicine, law, and engineering are using the Internet and digital technologies to deliver many new solutions.

Many products involve both a service and a product component; therefore, both problem solving and evaluation may be needed. Dell Computer's website is an example of a site that has combined the benefits of both. By creating a website that allows for customization of individual computers, they address the unique concerns of customers "one computer at a time." But the site also features a strong evaluative component because it allows users to compare the costs and features of various options. Shoppers can even compare their customized selection to refurbished Dell computers that are available at a substantially lower cost.

Transaction Activities

Transaction refers to the process of completing the sale, including negotiating and agreeing contractually, making payments, and taking delivery. Numerous types of Internet-enabled activities have contributed to lowering this aspect of overall transaction costs. Auctions of various sorts, from raw materials used in manufacturing to collectibles sold on eBay, facilitate the process of arriving at mutually agreed-on prices. Services such as PayPal provide a third-party intermediary that facilitates transactions between parties who never have (and probably never will) meet. Amazon.com's One-Click technology allows for very rapid purchases, and Amazon's overall superiority in managing order fulfillment has made its transactions process rapid and reliable. Amazon's success today can be attributed to a large extent to its having sold this transaction capability to other companies such as Target, Toys "R" Us and even Borders (another bookseller!).[5]

Other Sources of Competitive Advantage

There are other factors that can be important sources of competitive advantage. One of the most important of these is content. The Internet makes it possible to capture vast amounts of content at a very low cost. Three types of content can improve the value proposition of a Web site—customer feedback, expertise, and entertainment programming.

- ***Customer Feedback.*** Buyers often trust what other buyers say more than a company's promises. One type of content that can enhance a Web site is customer testimonials. Remember the leather sofa online? The testimonials of other buyers can build confidence and add to the chances that the purchaser will buy online sight unseen. This is one way that content can be a source of competitive advantage. Being able to interact with like-minded customers by reading their experiences or hearing how they have responded to a new product offering builds a sense of belonging that is otherwise hard to create.
- ***Expertise.*** The Internet has emerged as a tremendously important learning tool. Fifty-one percent of users compare the Internet to a library.[6] The prime reason many users go to the Web is to gain expertise. Web sites that provide new knowledge or unbiased information are highly valuable. Additionally the problem-solving function often involves educating consumers regarding options and implications of various choices. For example, LendingTree.com, the online loan company, provides a help center that includes extensive information and resources about obtaining loans, maintaining good credit, and so forth. Further, the expertise function is not limited to consumer sites. In the case of B2B businesses, Web sites that facilitate sharing expert knowledge help build a sense of community in industry or professional groups.
- ***Entertainment Programming.*** The Internet is being used by more and more people as an entertainment medium. With technologies such as streaming media, which allows the Internet to send televisionlike images and sound, computers can provide everything from breaking news to video games to online movies. A study by the Pew Internet and American Life Project indicates that among people using high-speed broadband service, TV viewing is down and online activity has increased. One reason is that the technology is interactive, which means that viewers don't just passively watch, but they use the Web to create art or play online games. Businesses have noticed this trend, of course, and are creating Web content that is not just informative but entertaining.

These three types of content—customer feedback, expertise, and entertainment programming—are potential sources of competitive advantage. That is, they create advantages by making the value creation process even stronger. Or, if they are handled poorly, they diminish performance.

[5]Bayers, C. 2002. The last laugh. *Business 2.0,* September: 86–93.
[6]Greenspan, R. 2003. Internet not for everyone. *CyberAtlas,* April 16, www.cyberatlas.com.

Business Models

The Internet provides a unique platform or staging area for business activity, which has become, in some ways, like a new marketplace. How do firms conduct business in this new arena? One way of addressing this question is by describing various Internet business models. A business model is a method and a set of assumptions that explain how a business creates value and earns profits in a competitive environment. Some of these models are quite simple and traditional even when applied in an Internet context. Others have features that are unique to the digitally networked, online environment. In this section, we discuss seven Internet business models that account for the vast majority of business conducted online.[7]

- *Commission-Based* **Models** are used by businesses that provide services for a fee. The business is usually a third-party intermediary, and the commission charged is often based on the size of the transaction. The most common type is a brokerage service, such as a stockbroker (e.g., Schwab.com), real estate broker (e.g., Remax.com), or transaction broker (e.g., PayPal.com). This category also includes auction companies such as eBay. In exchange for putting buyers and sellers together, eBay earns a commission.
- *Advertising-Based* **Models** are used by companies that provide content and/or services to visitors and sell advertising to businesses that want to reach those visitors. It is similar to the broadcast television model, in which viewers watch shows produced with advertising dollars. A key difference is that online visitors can interact with both the ads and the content. Large portals such as Yahoo.com are in this category as well as specialty portals such as iNest.com, which provides services for buyers of newly constructed homes. Epinions.com, a recommender system, is just one example of the many types of content that are often available.
- *Markup-Based* **Models** are used by businesses that add value in marketing and sales (rather than production) by acquiring products, marking up the price, and reselling them at a profit. Also known as the merchant model, it applies to both wholesalers and retailers. Amazon.com is the best-known example in this category. It also includes bricks-and-mortar companies such as Wal-Mart, which has a very successful online operation, and vendors whose products are purely digital such as Fonts.com, which sells downloadable fonts and photographs.
- *Production-Based* **Models** are used by companies that add value in the production process by converting raw materials into value-added products. Thus, it is also referred to as the manufacturing model. The Internet adds value to this model in two key ways. First, it lowers marketing costs by enabling direct contact with end users. Second, such direct contact facilitates customization and problem solving. Dell's online ordering system is supported by a state-of-the-art customized manufacturing process. Travelocity uses its rich database of travel options and customer profiles to identify, produce, and deliver unique solutions.
- *Referral-Based* **Models** are used by firms that steer customers to another company for a fee. One type is the affiliate model, in which a vendor pays an affiliate a fee each time a visitor clicks through the affiliate's Web site and makes a purchase from the vendor. Many name-brand companies use affiliate programs. For example, WeddingChannel.com, which provides a bridal registry where wedding guests can buy gifts from companies such as Tiffany's, Macy's, or Crate & Barrel, receives a fee each time a sale is made through its Web Site. Another referral-based example is Yesmail.com, which generates leads using e-mail marketing.
- *Subscription-Based* **Models** are used by businesses that charge a flat fee for providing either a service or proprietary content. Internet service providers are one example of this model. Companies such as America Online and Earthlink supply Internet connections for fees that are charged whether buyers use the service or not. Subscription-based models are also used by content creators such as the *Economist* or the *New York Times*. Although these recognizable brands often provide free content, only a small portion is available free. The *Economist,* for example, advertises that 70 percent of its content is available only to subscribers.
- *Fee-For-Service–Based* **Models** are used by companies that provide ongoing services similar to a utility company. Unlike the commission-based model, the fee-for-service model involves a pay-as-you-go system. That is, activities are metered and companies pay only for the amount of service

---

[7]Afuah, A., & Tucci, C.L. 2003. *Internet business models and strategies* (2nd ed). New York: McGraw-Hill; and, Timmers, P. 1999. *Electronic commerce.* New York: Wiley.

used. Application service providers fall in this category. For example, eProject.com provides virtual work space where people in different physical locations can collaborate online. Users essentially rent Internet space, and a host of tools that make it easy to interact, for a fee based on their usage.

Exhibit 3A.2 summarizes the key feature of each Internet business model, suggest what role content may play in the model, and addresses how the four value-adding activities—search, evaluation, problem solving, and transaction—can be sources of competitive advantage.

Exhibit 3A.2
Internet Business Models

Type	Features and Content	Sources of Competitive Advantage
Commission-Based	Charges commissions for brokerage or intermediary services. Adds value by providing expertise and/or access to a wide network of alternatives.	Search Evaluation Problem solving Transaction
Advertising-Based	Web content paid for by advertisers. Adds value by providing free or low-cost content—including customer feedback, expertise, and entertainment programming—to audiences that range from very broad (general content) to highly targeted (specialized content).	Search Evaluation
Markup-Based	Resells marked-up merchandise. Adds value through selection, through distribution efficiencies, and by leveraging brand image and reputation. May use entertainment programming to enhance sales.	Search Transaction
Production-Based	Sells manufactured goods and custom services. Adds value by increasing production efficiencies, capturing customer preferences, and improving customer service.	Search Problem solving
Referral-Based	Charges fees for referring customers. Adds value by enhancing a company's product or service offering, tracking referrals electronically, and generating demographic data. Expertise and customer feedback often included with referral information.	Search Problem solving Transaction
Subscription-Based	Charges fees for unlimited use of service or content. Adds value by leveraging strong brand name, providing high-quality information to specialized markets, or providing access to essential services. May consist entirely of entertainment programming.	Evaluation Problem solving
Fee-for-service–Based	Charges fees for metered services. Adds value by providing service efficiencies, expertise, and practical outsourcing solutions.	Problem solving Transaction

Sources: Afuah, A., & Tucci, C. L. 2003. *Internet business models and strategies* (2nd ed). New York: McGraw-Hill; Rappa, M. 2005. *Business models on the Web,* digitalenterprise.org/models/models.html; and Timmers, P. 1999. *Electronic commerce.* New York: Wiley.

chapter 4

Recognizing a Firm's Intellectual Assets:

Moving beyond a Firm's Tangible Resources

>learning objectives

After reading this chapter, you should have a good understanding of:

LO1 Why the management of knowledge professionals and knowledge itself are so critical in today's organizations.

LO2 The importance of recognizing the interdependence of attracting, developing, and retaining human capital.

LO3 The key role of social capital in leveraging human capital within and across the firm.

LO4 The importance of social networks in knowledge management and in promoting career success.

LO5 The vital role of technology in leveraging knowledge and human capital.

LO6 Why "electronic" or "virtual" teams are critical in combining and leveraging knowledge in organizations and how they can be made more effective.

LO7 The challenge of protecting intellectual property and the importance of a firm's dynamic capabilities.

LO8 How leveraging human capital is critical to strategy formulation for business-level, corporate-level, international, and entrepreneurial strategies.

One of the most important trends that managers must consider is the significance of the knowledge worker in today's economy. Managers must both recognize the importance of top talent and provide mechanisms to leverage human capital to innovate and, in the end, develop products and services that create value.

The first section addresses the increasing role of knowledge as the primary means of wealth generation in today's economy. A company's value is not derived solely from its physical assets, such as plant, equipment, and machinery. Rather, it is based on knowledge, know-how, and intellectual assets—all embedded in people.

The second section discusses the key resource itself, human capital, which is the foundation of intellectual capital. We explore ways in which the organization can attract, develop, and retain top talent—three important, interdependent activities. With regard to attracting human capital, we address issues such as "hiring for attitude, training for skill." One of the issues regarding developing human capital is encouraging widespread involvement throughout the organization. Our discussion on retaining human capital addresses issues such as the importance of having employees identify with an organization's mission and values. We also address the value of a diverse workforce.

The attraction, development, and retention of human capital are necessary but not sufficient conditions for organizational success. In the third section we address social capital—networks of relationships among a firm's members. This is especially important where collaboration and sharing information are critical. In this section we address why social capital can be particularly important in attracting human capital and making teams effective. We also address the vital role of social networks—both in improving knowledge management and in promoting career success.

The fourth section addresses the role of technology in leveraging human capital. Examples range from e-mail and the use of networks to facilitate collaboration among individuals to more complex forms of technologies, such as sophisticated knowledge management systems. We discuss how electronic teams can be effectively managed. We also address how technology can help to retain knowledge.

The fifth section discusses the differences between protection of physical property and intellectual property. We suggest that the development of dynamic capabilities may be one of the best ways that a firm can protect its intellectual property.

The sixth and final section discusses how leveraging human capital is vital to each of the four levels of strategy formulation—business, corporate, international, and Internet.

Learning from Mistakes

Some companies excel in attracting top talent and leveraging such talent. This often leads to positive relationships among individuals within the firm, promoting a social infrastructure that is critical for gaining consensus on major decisions, sharing information, and promoting cooperation. However, at times, hiring top talent or "stars" can have a big downside. Consider the experience of The Wildflower Group, a New York–based licensing and marketing group that represents the trademark owners of such products as home furnishings, giftware, and popular characters, including ALF and Newton's Law (a small bear extremely popular in Great Britain).

> To Michael Carlisle, one of Wildflower's partners, it seemed like the coup of a lifetime.[1] Although his firm was just three years old and had only 10 employees, it was able to recruit a highly regarded salesperson from one of the industry's largest and *[continued]*

most prestigious companies. She was a bona fide superstar, with a blue-chip resume, a Rolodex brimming with contacts, and a track record for landing top-dollar clients. The excited Carlisle remembers thinking, "She could do a lot for us."

But that was then . . . and things didn't work out as planned. The new employee was accustomed to the comforts and amenities of a large corporation. She became testy and unpleasant when asked to, for example, troubleshoot her own computer problems or alter her travel plans to take advantage of cheaper airfares. And she hardly created warm, positive feelings among her co-workers by trying to fob off administrative chores such as sending faxes. To make matters worse, she was not bringing in new business for Wildflower. Finally, and not too surprisingly, she did not take direction very well. Carlisle would lay out Wildflower's sales plan, and she'd argue about it.

Carlisle and his partner, Fred Paprin, spent many unproductive hours discussing how to best salvage the situation. However, as the complaints mounted, Carlisle began to worry about losing other employees. The final straw came when Carlisle noticed that several younger employees were beginning to emulate the star's poor behavior. The partners agreed it was time for the company to cut its losses. Wildflower's big "hiring coup" lasted less than 10 months.

Managers are always hunting for stellar employees who can raise the organization to the next level. Unfortunately, as Carlisle discovered, bulletproof credentials are far from a "happily ever after" guarantee. Just the opposite may come true instead.

We will discuss how attracting, developing, and retaining talent is a necessary but not sufficient condition for success. Many firms have experienced problems leveraging talent and technologies into successful products and services. In today's knowledge economy, it doesn't matter too much how big your stock of resources is—whether it be top talent, physical resources, or financial capital. Rather, the question becomes: How good is the organization at attracting top talent and leveraging that talent to produce a stream of products and services valued by the marketplace?

The Central Role of Knowledge in Today's Economy

Central to our discussion is an enormous change that has accelerated over the past few decades and its implications for the strategic management of organizations.[2] That is, for most of the 20th century, managers were primarily concerned with tangible resources such as land, equipment, and money as well as intangibles such as brands, image, and customer loyalty. Most efforts were directed more toward the efficient allocation of labor and capital—the two traditional factors of production.

How times have changed. Today, more than 50 percent of the gross domestic product (GDP) in developed economies is knowledge-based; that is, it is based on intellectual assets and intangible people skills.[3] In the United States, intellectual and information processes create most of the value for firms in large service industries (e.g., software, medical care, communications, and education), which make up 76 percent of the U.S. GDP. In the manufacturing sector, intellectual activities like R&D, process design, product design, logistics, marketing, or technological innovation produce the preponderance of value added.[4] To drive home the point, consider the perspective of Gary Hamel and C. K. Prahalad, two leading writers in strategic management:

> The machine age was a physical world. It consisted of things. Companies made and distributed things (physical products). Management allocated things (capital budgets); management invested in things (plant and equipment).

In the machine age, people were ancillary, and things were central. In the information age, things are ancillary, knowledge is central. A company's value derives not from things, but from knowledge, know-how, intellectual assets, competencies—all embedded in people.[5]

In the **knowledge economy,** wealth is increasingly created through the effective management of knowledge workers instead of by the efficient control of physical and financial assets. The growing importance of knowledge, coupled with the move by labor markets to reward knowledge work, tells us that someone who invests in a company is, in essence, buying a set of talents, capabilities, skills, and ideas—intellectual capital—not physical and financial resources.[6]

Let's provide a few examples. People don't buy Microsoft's stock because of its software factories; it doesn't own any. Rather, the value of Microsoft is bid up because of its ability to set standards for personal-computing software, exploit the value of its name, and forge alliances with other companies. Similarly, Merck didn't become the "Most Admired" company, for seven consecutive years in *Fortune*'s annual survey, because it can manufacture pills, but because its scientists can discover medicines. P. Roy Vagelos, who was CEO of Merck, the $22 billion pharmaceutical giant, during its long run atop the "Most Admired" survey, said, "A low-value product can be made by anyone anywhere. When you have knowledge no one else has access to—that's dynamite. We guard our research even more carefully than our financial assets."[7]

To apply some numbers to our arguments, let's ask, What's a company worth?[8] Start with the "big three" financial statements: income statement, balance sheet, and statement of cash flow. If these statements tell a story that investors find useful, then a company's market value* should roughly (but not precisely, because the market looks forward and the books look backward) be the same as the value that accountants ascribe to it—the book value of the firm. However, this is not the case. A study compared the market value with the book value of 3,500 U.S. companies over a period of two decades. In 1978 the two were similar: Book value was 95 percent of market value. However, market values and book values have diverged significantly. By 1998, book value was just 28 percent of market value. A colorful commentary comes from Robert A. Howell, an expert on the changing role of finance and accounting, "The big three financial statements . . . are about as useful as an 80-year-old Los Angeles road map."

The gap between a firm's market value and book value is far greater for knowledge-intensive corporations than for firms with strategies based primarily on tangible assets. Exhibit 4.1 shows the ratio of market-to-book value for some well-known companies. In firms where knowledge and the management of knowledge workers are relatively important contributors to developing products and services—and physical resources are less critical—the ratio of market-to-book value tends to be much higher. Many writers have defined **intellectual capital** as the difference between a firm's market value and book value—that is, a measure of the value of a firm's intangible assets.[9] This broad definition includes assets such as reputation, employee loyalty and commitment, customer relationships, company values, brand names, and the experience and skills of employees.[10] Thus, simplifying, we have:

Intellectual capital = Market value of firm − Book value of the firm

The issue becomes: How do companies create value in the knowledge-intensive economy? As we stated above, the general answer is to attract and leverage human capital effectively through mechanisms that create products and services of value over time. Let's articulate a few of the basic concepts that we will be talking about in this chapter.

>LO1
Why the management of knowledge professionals and knowledge itself are so critical in today's organizations.

knowledge economy an economy where wealth is created through the effective management of knowledge workers instead of by the efficient control of physical and financial assets.

intellectual capital the difference between the market value of the firm and the book value of the firm, including assets such as reputation, employee loyalty and commitment, customer relationships, company values, brand names, and the experience and skills of employees.

* The market value of a firm is equal to the value of a share of its common stock times the number of shares outstanding. The book value of a firm is primarily a measure of the value of its tangible assets. It can be calculated by the formula: total assets − total liabilities.

Exhibit 4.1

Ratio of Market Value to
Book Value for Selected
Companies

Company	Annual Sales ($ billions)	Market Value ($ billions)	Book Value ($ billions)	Ratio of Market to Book Value
Genentech	9.3	86.5	9.5	9.1
Google	10.7	142.5	17.0	8.4
Yahoo!	6.4	42.5	9.2	4.6
eBay	6.0	45.4	10.9	4.2
Southwest Airlines	9.1	11.6	6.4	1.8
Union Pacific (Railroad)	15.6	27.5	15.3	1.8
General Motors	192.6	17.3	14.6	1.2

Note: The data on market valuations are as of March 30, 2007. All other financial data is based on the most recently available balance sheets and income statements.

human capital the individual capabilities, knowledge, skills, and experience of a company's employees and managers.

First, consider human capital. **Human capital** is the "*individual* capabilities, knowledge, skills, and experience of the company's employees and managers."[11] This is knowledge that is relevant to the task at hand, as well as the capacity to add to this reservoir of knowledge, skills, and experience through learning.[12]

Second, **social capital** can be defined as "the network of relationships that individuals have throughout the organization." Such relationships are critical in sharing and leveraging knowledge and in acquiring resources.[13] Social capital also can extend beyond the organizational boundaries to include relationships between the firm and its suppliers, customers, and alliance partners.[14]

social capital the network of relationships that individuals have both inside and outside the organization.

Third is the concept of "knowledge," which comes in two different forms. First, there is **explicit knowledge** that is codified, documented, easily reproduced, and widely distributed. Examples include engineering drawings, software code, and patents.[15] The other type of knowledge is **tacit knowledge.** That is, in essence, in the minds of employees and is based on their experiences and backgrounds.[16] Tacit knowledge is shared only with the consent and participation of the individual.

explicit knowledge knowledge that is codified, documented, easily reproduced, and widely distributed.

New knowledge is constantly being created. It involves the continual interaction of explicit and tacit knowledge. Consider, for example, two software engineers working together on a computer code. The computer code is the explicit knowledge. However, through their sharing of ideas based on each individual's experience—that is, their tacit knowledge—new knowledge is created when they make modifications to the code. Another important issue is the role of "socially complex processes," which include leadership, culture, and trust.[17] These processes play a central role in the creation of knowledge.[18] They represent the "glue" that holds the organization together and helps to create a working environment where individuals are more willing to share their ideas, work in teams, and, in the end, create products and services of value. In a later section, we will address the importance of social capital in the value creation process.

tacit knowledge knowledge that is in the minds of employees and is based on their experiences and backgrounds.

Numerous books have been written on the subject of knowledge management and the central role that it has played in creating wealth in organizations and countries throughout the developed world.[19] Here, we focus on some of the key issues that organizations must address to compete through knowledge.

We will now turn our discussion to the central resource itself—human capital—and some guidelines on how it can be attracted/selected, developed, and retained. Tom Stewart, editor of the *Harvard Business Review,* noted that organizations must also undergo significant efforts to protect their human capital. A firm may "diversify the ownership of vital knowledge by emphasizing teamwork, guard against obsolescence by developing learning programs, and shackle key people with golden handcuffs."[20] In addition, people are less likely to leave an organization if there are effective structures to promote teamwork and information sharing, strong leadership that encourages innovation, and cultures that demand excellence and ethical behavior. Such issues are also central to the topic of this chapter. Although we touch on these issues throughout this chapter, we provide more detail in later chapters. We discuss organizational controls (culture, rewards, and boundaries) in Chapter 9, organization structure and design in Chapter 10, and a variety of leadership and entrepreneurship topics in Chapters 11 and 12.

Human Capital: The Foundation of Intellectual Capital

Organizations must recruit talented people—employees at all levels with the proper sets of skills and capabilities coupled with the right values and attitudes. Such skills and attitudes must be continually developed, strengthened, and reinforced, and each employee must be motivated and her efforts focused on the organization's goals and objectives.

The rise to prominence of the knowledge worker as a vital source of competitive advantage is changing the balance of power in today's organization. Knowledge workers place professional development and personal enrichment (financial and otherwise) above company loyalty. Attracting, recruiting, and hiring the "best and the brightest," is a critical first step in the process of building intellectual capital. At a symposium for CEOs, Bill Gates said, "The thing that is holding Microsoft back . . . is simply how [hard] we find it to go out and recruit the kind of people we want to grow our research team."[21]

Hiring is only the first of three key processes in which all successful organizations must engage to build and leverage their human capital. Firms must also *develop* employees at all levels and specialties to fulfill their full potential to maximize their joint contributions. Finally, the first two processes are for naught if firms can't provide the working environment and intrinsic and extrinsic rewards to *retain* their best and brightest.[22]

These three activities are highly interrelated. We would like to suggest the imagery of a three-legged stool (see Exhibit 4.2).[23] If one leg is weak or broken, the stool collapses.

To illustrate such interdependence, poor hiring impedes the effectiveness of development and retention processes. In a similar vein, ineffective retention efforts place additional

>LO2
The importance of recognizing the interdependence of attracting, developing, and retaining human capital.

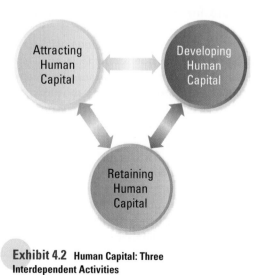

Exhibit 4.2 **Human Capital: Three Interdependent Activities**

burdens on hiring and development. Consider the following anecdote, provided by Jeffrey Pfeffer of the Stanford University Business School:

> Not long ago, I went to a large, fancy San Francisco law firm—where they treat their associates like dog doo and where the turnover is very high. I asked the managing partner about the turnover rate. He said, "A few years ago, it was 25 percent, and now we're up to 30 percent." I asked him how the firm had responded to that trend. He said, "We increased our recruiting." So I asked him, "What kind of doctor would you be if your patient was bleeding faster and faster, and your only response was to increase the speed of the transfusion?"[24]

Clearly, stepped-up recruiting is a poor substitute for weak retention. Although there are no simple, easy-to-apply answers, we can learn from what leading-edge firms are doing to attract, develop, and retain human capital in today's highly competitive and rapidly changing marketplace. Let's begin by discussing hiring and selection practices.

Attracting Human Capital

> All we can do is bet on the people we pick. So my whole job is picking the right people.
>
> **Jack Welch,** former chairman, General Electric Company[25]

The first step in the process of building superior human capital is input control: attracting and selecting the right person. Many human resource professionals still approach employee selection from a "lock and key" mentality—that is, fit a key (a job candidate) into a lock (the job). Such an approach involves a thorough analysis of both the person and the job. Only then can the right decision be made as to how well the two will fit together. How can you fail, the theory goes, if you get a precise match of knowledge, ability, and skill profiles? Frequently, however, the precise matching approach places its emphasis on task-specific skills (e.g., motor skills, specific information processing capabilities, and communication skills) and puts less emphasis on the broad general knowledge and experience, social skills, values, beliefs, and attitudes of employees.

Many have questioned the precise matching approach. Instead, they argue that firms can identify top performers by focusing on key employee mind-sets, attitudes, social skills, and general orientations. These firms reason that if they get these elements right, the task-specific skills can be learned in relatively short order. (This does not imply, however, that task-specific skills are unimportant; rather, it suggests that the requisite skill sets must be viewed as a necessary but not sufficient condition.) This leads us to a popular phrase today and serves as the title of the next section.

"Hire for Attitude, Train for Skill" Organizations are increasingly placing their emphasis on the general knowledge and experience, social skills, values, beliefs, and attitudes of employees. Consider Southwest Airlines's hiring practices, with their strong focus on employee values and attitudes. Given its strong team orientation, Southwest uses an "indirect" approach. For example, the interviewing team asks a group of employees to prepare a five-minute presentation about themselves. During the presentations, the interviewers observe which candidates are enthusiastically supporting their peers and which candidates are focused on polishing their own presentations while the others are presenting.[26] The former are, of course, favored.

Alan Cooper, president of Cooper Software, Inc., in Palo Alto, California, goes further. He cleverly *uses technology* to hone in on the problem-solving ability of his applicants and their attitudes before an interview even takes place. He has devised a "Bozo Filter," a test administered online (see Strategy Spotlight 4.1) that can be applied to any industry. Before you spend time figuring out whether job candidates will work out satisfactorily, find out how their minds work. Cooper advised, "Hiring was a black hole. I don't talk to bozos anymore because 90 percent of them turn away when they see our test. It's a self-administering bozo filter."[27]

Cooper Software's "Bozo Filter"

Hiring is often easier than firing. Even when unemployment rates are low and labor is scarce, it's still easier to find employees than it is to get them out the door if they don't work out. Not only do poor employees affect the morale of better talent, but they also cost the company money in lost productivity.

Cooper Software has found an innovative way to prevent the problem of hiring bad employees. CEO Alan Cooper asks job applicants to visit the company's Web site, where the applicants will find a test that takes between two and five hours to complete. The test asks questions designed to see how prospective employees approach problem-solving tasks. For example, one key question asks software engineer applicants to design a new table-creation software program for Microsoft Word. Candidates provide pencil sketches and a description of the new user interface. Another question is used for design communicators. They are asked to develop a marketing strategy for a new touchtone phone—directed at consumers in the year 1850. Candidates e-mail their answers back to the company, and the answers are circulated around the firm to solicit feedback. Only candidates with the highest marks get interviews.

Jonathan Korman, a design communicator, suggested that the test "told me more about real job duties than any description could." Josh Seiden, a software designer, is even more positive: "It was a fun puzzle—much more engaging than most of what I was doing at my previous job."

That's exactly the kind of attitude Cooper wants. "We get e-mail from some people saying, 'Before I take this test, is the position still open?' I say no, because I don't want anybody who sees it as an effort," claims Cooper. "People who really care take the test and love it. Other people say it's hard. We don't want those people."

Sources: Cardin, R. 1997. Make your own bozo filter. *Fast Company*, October–November: 56; Coop, A. 1997. Getting design across. Unpublished manuscript, November 23: 1–8; and www.cooper.com.

Sound Recruiting Approaches and Networking   Companies that take hiring seriously must also take recruiting seriously. The number of jobs that successful knowledge-intensive companies must fill is astonishing. Ironically, many companies still have no shortage of applicants. Southwest Airlines typically gets 150,000 résumés a year, yet hires only about 5,000 new employees. And, Google, named in 2007 as the "Best Company to Work For" by *Fortune* magazine, gets an astounding 1,300 résumés a *day!* [28] Netscape (now part of Time Warner) reviews 60 résumés for every hire.[29] The challenge becomes having the right job candidates, not the greatest number of them.

GE Medical Systems, which builds CT scanners and magnetic resonance imaging (MRI) systems, relies extensively on networking. They have found that current employees are the best source for new ones. Recently, Steven Patscot, head of staffing and leadership development, made a few simple changes to double the number of referrals. First, he simplified the process—no complex forms, no bureaucracy, and so on. Second, he increased incentives. Everyone referring a qualified candidate received a gift certificate from Sears. For referrals who were hired, the "bounty" was increased to $2,000 (or $3,000 if the referral was a software engineer). Although this may sound like a lot of money, it is "peanuts" compared to the $15,000 to $20,000 fees that GE typically pays to headhunters for each person hired.[30] Also, when someone refers a former colleague or friend for a job, his or her credibility is on the line. Thus, employees will tend to be careful in recommending people for employment unless they are reasonably confident that these people are good candidates. This provides a good "screen" for the firm in deciding whom to hire. After all, hiring the right people makes things a lot easier: fewer rules and regulations, less need for monitoring and hierarchy, and greater internalization of organizational norms and objectives.

Before moving on, it is useful to point out some of the approaches that companies are currently using to recruit and retain young talent. As more of the baby boomers retire,

Exhibit 4.3

What Companies are Doing to Attract and Keep Young Talent

Here are some "best practices" that companies are using to help recruit and retain today's high-maintenance Millennials. This generation has also been termed "Generation Y" or "Echo Boom" and includes people born after 1982:

- ***Don't Fudge the Sales Pitch.*** High-tech presentations and one-on-one attention may be attractive to undergrads, but the pitch better match the experience. Today's ultra-connected students can get the lowdown on a company by spending five minutes on a social networking site.

- ***Let Them Have a Life.*** Wary of their parents' 80-hour workweeks, Millennials strive for more balance, so liberal vacations are a must. They also want assurances they'll be able to use it. At KPMG, 80 percent of employees used 40 hours of paid time off in the six months through May 2006.

- ***No Time Clocks, Please.*** Recent grads don't mind long hours if they can work them on their own time. Lockheed Martin and its comptroller of the currency allow employees to work nine-hour days and take every other Friday off.

- ***Give Them Responsibility.*** A chance to work on fulfilling projects and develop ones of their own is important to Millennials. Google urges entry-level employees to spend 20 percent of their time developing new ideas. PepsiCo allows promising young employees to manage small teams in six months.

- ***Feedback and More Feedback.*** Career planning advice and frequent performance appraisals are keys to holding on to young hires. Lehman Brothers provides new hires with two mentors—a slightly older peer to help them get settled and a senior employee to give long-term guidance.

- ***Giving Back Matters.*** Today's altruistic young graduates expect to have opportunities for community service. Wells Fargo encourages its employees to teach financial literacy classes in the community. Accenture and Bain allow employees to consult for nonprofits.

Source: Gerdes, L. 2006. The top 50 employers for new college grads. *BusinessWeek,* September 18: 64–81.

people in this demographic group are becoming more and more important in today's workforce. We address this issue in Exhibit 4.3.

Developing Human Capital

It is not enough to hire top-level talent and expect that the skills and capabilities of those employees remain current throughout the duration of their employment. Rather, training and development must take place at all levels of the organization.[31] For example, Solectron assembles printed circuit boards and other components for its Silicon Valley clients.[32] Its employees receive an average of 95 hours of company-provided training each year. Chairman Winston Chen observed, "Technology changes so fast that we estimate 20 percent of an engineer's knowledge becomes obsolete each year. Training is an obligation we owe to our employees. If you want high growth and high quality, then training is a big part of the equation." Although the financial returns on training may be hard to calculate, most experts believe it is not only real, but also essential. One company that has calculated the benefit from training is Motorola. This high-technology firm has calculated that every dollar spent on training returns $30 in productivity gains over the following three years.

In addition to the importance of training and developing human capital, let's now discuss three other related topics: encouraging widespread involvement, monitoring and tracking employee development, and evaluating human capital.[33]

Encouraging Widespread Involvement   Developing human capital requires the active involvement of leaders at all levels. It won't be successful if it is viewed only as the responsibility of the human resources department. Each year at General Electric, 200 facilitators, 30 officers, 30 human resource executives, and many young managers actively participate in GE's orientation program at Crotonville, its training center outside New York City. Topics include global competition, winning on the global playing field, and personal examination of the new employee's core values vis-à-vis GE's values. As a senior manager once commented, "There is nothing like teaching Sunday school to force you to confront your own values."

Transferring Knowledge   Often in our lives, we need to either transfer our knowledge to someone else (a child, a junior colleague, a peer) or access accumulated bits of wisdom—someone else's tacit knowledge.[34] A vital aspect of developing human capital is transferring unique and specialized knowledge. However, before we can even begin to plan such a transfer, we need to understand how our brains process incoming information. According to Dorothy A. Leonard of Harvard University:

> Our existing tacit knowledge determines how we assimilate new experiences. Without receptors—hooks on which to hang new information—we may not be able to perceive and process the information. It is like being sent boxes of documents but having no idea how they could or should be organized.

This cognitive limitation also applies to the organizational level as well. For example, when GE Healthcare sets up or transfers operations from one location to another, it appoints an experienced manager to be the "pitcher" and a team in the receiving plant to be the "catcher." These two teams work together, often over a period of years—first at the pitcher's location and then at the catcher's. In order to ensure a smooth transition, the pitching team needs to be sensitive to the catching team's level of experience and familiarity with GE Healthcare procedures.

Strategy Spotlight 4.2 discusses Intel's Mentoring Program. It is a very effective way to share information throughout an organization.

Monitoring Progress and Tracking Development   Whether a firm uses on-site formal training, off-site training (e.g., universities), or on-the-job training, tracking individual progress—and sharing this knowledge with both the employee and key managers—becomes essential. At Citibank (part of Citigroup, the large financial services organization), a talent inventory program keeps track of roughly 10,000 employees worldwide—how they're doing, what skills they need to work on, and where else in the company they might thrive. Larry Phillips, head of human resources, considers the program critical to the company's global growth.[35]

Like many leading-edge organizations, GlaxoSmithKline places strong emphasis on broader experiences over longer time periods. Dan Phelan, senior vice president and director of human resources, explained, "We ideally follow a two-plus-two-plus-two formula in developing people for top management positions." This reflects the belief that SmithKline's best people should gain experience in two business units, two functional units (such as finance and marketing), in two countries.

Evaluating Human Capital   In today's competitive environment, collaboration and interdependence have become vital to organizational success. Individuals must share their knowledge and work together constructively to achieve collective, not just individual, goals. However, traditional evaluation systems evaluate performance from a single perspective (i.e., "top down") and generally don't address the "softer" dimensions of communications and social skills, values, beliefs, and attitudes.[36]

To address the limitations of the traditional approach, many organizations have begun to use 360-degree evaluation and feedback systems.[37] Here, superiors, direct reports, colleagues, and even internal and external customers rate a person's performance. Managers also rate themselves in order to have a personal benchmark. The 360-degree feedback system complements teamwork, employee involvement, and organizational flattening.

strategy spotlight

4.2

How Intel Shares Information through Its Mentoring Program

Mentor relationships are often stereotyped as one-way transfers from older experienced employees to the young for the purposes of professional development and career advancement. However, that's not the case at Intel, where the partner may outrank the mentor. Thus, an administrative assistant who is an expert at navigating informal internal networks may be selected to mentor an executive. Or a young technology-savvy employee may be chosen to share his knowledge with an older, more senior employee.

Intel's mentoring program began in a chip-making factory in New Mexico in 1997. At the time, Intel was growing rapidly and many of the factory's managers were being transferred to new locations. The company needed to develop new experts in a variety of fields. Thus, the factory's top managers started matching partners with mentors who had the needed skills and knowledge.

Sources: Morrison, R., Erickson, T., & Dychtwald, K. 2006. Managing middlescence. *Harvard Business Review,* 84(3): 78–86; Hill, R. P., & Stephens, D. L. 2003. The compassionate organization of the 21st century. *Organizational Dynamics,* 32(4): 331–341; www.intel.com; and Warner, R. 2002. Inside Intel's mentoring movement. *Fast Company,* April: 67–69.

Today Intel's program uses an intranet-based questionnaire to match partners with the right mentor, creating relationships that stretch across state lines and national boundaries. The system works by having potential mentors list their top skills at Circuit, Intel's internal employee site. Partners click on topics they want to master. Then an algorithm computes all of the variables and the database hashes out a list of possible matches. Once a match is made, an automatic e-mail goes to the mentor asking her to set up a time to meet and talk. The mentor and partner learn and follow some simple guidelines:

1. The partner controls the relationship.
2. A mentoring contract is drawn up to outline what needs to be accomplished by the end of the mentoring.
3. Both the partner and the mentor decide what to talk about.

Unlike many corporations, Intel does not use its mentoring for career advancement. Its style is all about learning and sharing the knowledge pool of someone whom you have probably never met.

As organizations continue to push responsibility downward, traditional top-down appraisal systems become insufficient. For example, a manager who previously managed the performance of 3 supervisors might now be responsible for 10 and might be less likely to have the in-depth knowledge needed to appraise and develop them adequately. Exhibit 4.4 provides a portion of GE's 360-degree evaluation system.

Evaluation systems must also ensure that a manager's success does not come at the cost of compromising the organization's core values. Clearly, such behavior generally leads to only short-term wins for both the manager and the organization. The organization typically suffers long-term losses in terms of morale, turnover, productivity, and so on. Accordingly, Merck's chairman, Ray Gilmartin, told his employees, "If someone is achieving results but not demonstrating the core values of the company, at the expense of our people, that manager does not have much of a career here."

Retaining Human Capital

It has been said that talented employees are like "frogs in a wheelbarrow."[38] They can jump out at any time! By analogy, the organization can either try to force employees to stay in the firm or try to keep them from wanting to jump out by creating incentives. In other words, today's leaders can either provide the work environment and incentives to keep productive employees and management from wanting to bail out, or they can rely on legal means such as employment contracts and noncompete clauses.[39] Clearly, firms must provide mechanisms that prevent the transfer of valuable and sensitive information outside the organization. Failure to do so would be the neglect of a leader's fiduciary responsibility to shareholders. However, greater efforts should be directed at the former (e.g., good work

Vision	• Has developed and communicated a clear, simple, customer-focused vision/direction for the organization.
	• Forward-thinking, stretches horizons, challenges imaginations.
	• Inspires and energizes others to commit to Vision. Captures minds. Leads by example.
	• As appropriate, updates Vision to reflect constant and accelerating change affecting the business.

Customer/Quality Focus

Integrity

Accountability/Commitment

Communication/Influence

Shared Ownership/Boundaryless

Team Builder/Empowerment

Knowledge/Expertise/Intellect

Initiative/Speed

Global Mind-Set

Source: Adapted from Slater, R. 1994. *Get better or get beaten:* 152–155. Burr Ridge, IL: Irwin Professional Publishing.

Note: This evaluation system consists of 10 "characteristics"—Vision, Customer/Quality Focus, Integrity, and so on. Each of these characteristics has four "performance criteria." For illustrative purposes, the four performance criteria of "Vision" are included.

environment and incentives), but, as we all know, the latter (e.g., employment contracts and noncompete clauses) have their place.[40]

Identifying with an Organization's Mission and Values   People who identify with and are more committed to the core mission and values of the organization are less likely to stray or bolt to the competition. Consider Medtronic, Inc., an $11 billion medical products firm based in Minneapolis.[41] Former CEO Bill George stated, "Shareholder value is a hollow notion as the sole source of employee motivation. If you do business that way, you'll end up like ITT." What motivates its workers to go well beyond Medtronic's excellent financial performance? Simply put, it's helping sick people get well. The company's motto is "Restoring patients to full life," and its symbol is an image of a supine human rising toward upright wellness. That sounds good, but how does the "resurrection" imagery come to life?

> Each December, at the company's holiday party, patients, their families, and their doctors are flown in to tell their survival stories. It's for employees—who are moved to tears year after year—and journalists are generally not invited. President Art Collins, a strapping guy with a firm handshake who is not prone to crying fits, said, "I remember my first holiday party and someone asked me if I had brought my Kleenex. I assumed I'd be fine, but these parents got up with their daughter who was alive because of our product. Even surgeons who see this stuff all the time were crying." Collins calls it "our most important meeting of the year."

So much for the all-consuming emphasis on profits.

In addition to identifying with the organization, "tribal loyalty" is another key factor that links people to the organization.[42] A tribe is not the organization as a whole (unless it is very small). Rather, it is teams, communities of practice, and other groups within an organization or occupation.

Brian Hall, CEO of Values Technology in Santa Cruz, California, documented a shift in people's emotional expectations from work. From the 1950s on, a "task first" relationship—"tell me what the job is, and let's get on with it"—dominated employee attitudes. Emotions and personal life were checked at the door. In the past few years, a "relationship-first" set of values has challenged the task orientation. Hall believes that it will become dominant. Employees want to share attitudes and beliefs as well as workspace.

Challenging Work and a Stimulating Environment   Arthur Schawlow, winner of the 1981 Nobel Prize in physics, was asked what made the difference between highly creative and less creative scientists. His reply: "The labor of love aspect is very important. The most successful scientists often are not the most talented. But they are the ones impelled by curiosity. They've got to know what the answer is."[43] Such insights highlight the importance of intrinsic motivation: the motivation to work on something because it is exciting, satisfying, or personally challenging.[44]

One way successful firms keep highly mobile employees motivated and challenged is through an internal market for opportunities that lower the barriers to an employee's mobility within a company. For example, Shell Oil Company has created an "open sourcing" model for talent. Jobs are listed on Shell's intranet, and, with a two-month notice, employees can go to work on anything that interests them. Monsanto[45] has developed a similar approach. According to one executive:

> Because we don't have a lot of structure, people will flow toward where success and innovation are taking place. We have a free-market system where people can move, so you have an outflow of people in areas where not much progress is being made. Before, the HR function ran processes like management development and performance evaluation. Now it also facilitates this movement of people.

Exhibit 4.5 lists some of the best practices that leading-edge organizations are using to create a challenging and stimulating work environment to help attract and retain top young

Exhibit 4.5

Creating a Challenging and Stimulating Workplace: *BusinessWeek*'s "Best Places to Launch a Career"

Company (Industry)	Comments
Lockheed Martin (Defense)	Offers leadership programs in communications, engineering, finance, human resources, information systems, and operations.
Enterprise Rent-a-Car (Transportation)	Management training program amounts to an MBA crash course for executive wannabes. New hires get to run their own business.
Verizon Wireless (Telecommunications)	Verizon Wireless recently launched a retail training program where participants work in as many as three locations over two years.
National Instruments (Technology)	NI puts its money where its mouth is, spending over $30,000 a year to train each participant in its engineering leadership program.
L'Oreal (Consumer Goods)	Rising entry-level marketing stars are put through a fast-paced training program that lasts between 18 months and two years.
Vanguard (Financial Services)	Four extensive rotational training and development programs range from 12 to 24 months in length with three to six rotations.

Source: Gerdes, L. 2006. The top 50 employers for new college grads. *BusinessWeek*, September 18: 64–81.

talent. It draws upon an in-depth study conducted by *BusinessWeek* to identify the "Best Places to Launch a Career."

Financial and Nonfinancial Rewards and Incentives   Without a doubt, financial rewards are a vital organizational control mechanism (as we will discuss in Chapter 9). Money—whether in the form of salary, bonus, stock options, and so forth—can mean many different things to people. For some it might mean security, to others recognition, and to still others, a sense of freedom and independence.

Paying people more is seldom the most important factor in attracting and retaining human capital.[46] Most surveys show that money is not the most important reason why people take or leave jobs, and that money, in some surveys, is not even in the top 10. Consistent with these findings, Tandem Computers (now part of Hewlett-Packard) typically doesn't tell people being recruited what their salaries would be. People who asked were told that their salaries were competitive. If they persisted along this line of questioning, they would not be offered a position. Why? Tandem realized a rather simple idea: People who come for money will leave for money. Clearly, money can't be ignored, but it shouldn't be the primary mechanism to attract and retain talent.

Another nonfinancial reward involves accommodating working families with children. Coping with the conflicting demands of family and work is a problem at some point for virtually all employees.

Strategy Spotlight 4.3 discusses some of the challenges (and solutions) with the use of flextime. With this popular employment practice, flextime allows employees greater flexibility in when and where they do their work.

Enhancing Human Capital: The Role of Diversity in the Workforce

Today, a combination of demographic trends and accelerating globalization of business has made the management of cultural differences a critical issue.[47] Workforces, which reflect demographic changes in the overall population, will be increasingly heterogeneous along dimensions such as gender, race, ethnicity, and nationality. For example, demographic trends in the United States indicate a growth in Hispanic Americans from 6.9 million in 1960 to over 35 million in 2000. This figure also is expected to increase to over 55 million by 2020. Similarly, the Asian-American population should grow to 20 million in 2020 from 12 million in 2000 and only 1.5 million in 1970. And the African-American population is becoming more ethnically heterogeneous. Census estimates project that by 2010 as many as 10 percent of Americans of African descent will be immigrants from Africa or the Caribbean.[48]

Such demographic changes have implications not only for the labor pool but also for customer bases, which are also becoming more diverse. This creates important organizational challenges and opportunities.

The effective management of diversity can enhance the social responsibility goals of an organization.[49] However, there are many other benefits as well. Six other areas where sound management of diverse workforces can improve an organization's effectiveness and competitive advantages are: (1) cost, (2) resource acquisition, (3) marketing, (4) creativity, (5) problem-solving, and (6) organizational flexibility.

- *Cost Argument.* As organizations become more diverse, firms effective in managing diversity will have a cost advantage over those that are not.
- *Resource Acquisition Argument.* Firms with excellent reputations as prospective employers for women and ethnic minorities will have an advantage in the competition for top talent. As labor pools shrink and change in composition, such advantages will become even more important.

Solving the Challenges of Flextime

A recently study by Hewitt Associates, a human resources consulting firm, found that 75 percent of companies offered some kind of flexible work arrangement. However, these policies have earned mixed results. Working remotely can leave employees feeling isolated and managers feeling they lack control. Further, flextimers often find themselves squeezed into policies that are anything but flexible. "The work–life movement has always had a heavy layer of one-size-fits-all-ism," says Stewart D. Friedman, head of the Work/Life Integration Project and the Wharton School at the University of Pennsylvania.

Such a complaint is prompting many organizations to change their policies, says Hewitt's Carol Sladek, who heads the firm's work–life practice. Now more and more managers are using a template of questions to help them design their most fitting arrangement. "There's definitely a focus away from the structure of rigid flextime policies" says Sladek.

In a sense, flexibility is becoming more flexible. At Deloitte & Touche, years of stagnant enrollment in formal flexibility programs have led managers to help teams create flexible schedules among themselves. Staffers fill out a survey that helps them set goals as a group (reducing the number of times they interrupt co-workers off-hours, for instance) and jointly keep track of people's schedules so they know, say, when someone has reserved time with their kids. Deloitte is also experimenting with something called "mass career customization" that redefines flexibility over the course of a career rather than by the hours in a week. This helps employees to adjust their pace, workload, schedule, and work roles during various life stages.

Below are some suggested best practices or tips for making flextime programs work:

Source: Conlin, M. 2006. Smashing the clock. *BusinessWeek*, December 11: 60–68.

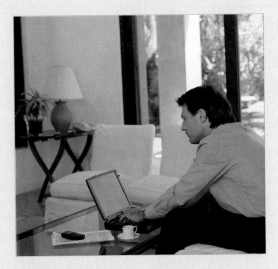

● Flextime and telecommuting can be an effective way to attract and retain talent. Here a man works from home on his laptop.

- **Measure.** Before unplugging workers, metrics are key to ensuring that productivity, engagement, and turnover improve.
- **Tailor.** Imposing new work rules rarely pays because managers and workers need to tailor schedules to their needs.
- **Trust.** Inevitably, some untethered workers will slack off. Managers need to trust, then rely on data to assess performance.
- **Educate.** Location-agnostic work is a hard concept to grasp. Thus, refresher courses are a must for managers and workers.
- **Gather.** When workers are nomads, regular gatherings, in person or by videoconference, help retain a team dynamic.

- *Marketing Argument.* For multinational firms, the insight and cultural sensitivity that members with roots in other countries bring to marketing efforts will be very useful. A similar rationale applies to subpopulations within domestic operations.
- *Creativity Argument.* Less emphasis on conformity to norms of the past and a diversity of perspectives will improve the level of creativity.
- *Problem-Solving Argument.* Heterogeniety in decision-making and problem-solving groups potentially produces better decisions because of a wider range of perspectives as well as more thorough and critical analysis of issues. To illustrate, Jim Schiro, CEO of PriceWaterhouseCoopers, explains, "When you make a genuine commitment

MTV: Benefiting from a Diverse Workforce

Managers know that heterogeneous workforces are rich seedbeds for ideas. However, companies seldom tap employees for insights and experiences specific to their cultures. Further, barriers of language, geography, and association often prevent diverse employees from collaborating on innovation efforts.

Chief Diversity Officers (CDOs) are probably more familiar with the cultural breadth and variety of their companies' talent than anyone. Consequently, they are in an excellent position to bring together different groups to produce innovation.

On October 28, 2006, MTV Networks, a unit of Viacom International Inc. announced that Billy Dexter was appointed the firm's first Executive Vice President and Chief Diversity Officer. He will lead MTV's global initiatives to foster the highest levels of diversity throughout every aspect of the business.

Source: Johansson, F. 2005. Masters of the multicultural. *Harvard Business Review*, 83(10): 18–19; and Anonymous. 2006. MTV Networks names Billy Dexter as Chief Diversity Officer. *PRNewswire*. October 28. np.

Judy McGrath, Chairman and CEO of MTV Networks states:

> We are completely committed to diversity and inclusion, because it's the most creative and vibrant thing we can do for our future. The audience for our content is increasingly global, diverse in thought, demographic, and lifestyle. Over the years, no other initiative has so enriched MTV Networks, or made us more relevant and successful.

How has MTV Networks benefited from their diversity?

One cross-cultural group discovered marketing opportunities in the similarities between North American country music and Latin American music, which use many of the same instruments, feature singers with similar vocal styles, and—in the U.S. Sunbelt—appeal to much the same audience. Other groups have influenced the multicultural content of Nickelodeon's children's programming. Says Tom Freston, MTV's former CEO, "Those teams are diverse by design to generate innovation. The probability that you will get a good, original, innovative idea with that type of chemistry is simply much higher."

---

to diversity, you bring a greater diversity of ideas, approaches, and experiences and abilities that can be applied to client problems. After all, six people with different perspectives have a better shot at solving complex problems than sixty people who all think alike."[50]

- *System Flexibility Argument.* With effective programs to enhance workplace diversity, systems become less determinant, less standardized, and therefore more fluid. Such fluidity should lead to greater flexibility to react to environmental changes. Reactions should be faster and less costly.

In the past, the role of the diversity officer was mostly to ensure compliance with EEOC (Equal Employment Opportunity Commission) requirements or, at best, to make minimal efforts to produce the appearance of diversity. Today many companies are realizing that the role of the Chief Diversity Officer (CDO) can add real value to a company. Strategy Spotlight 4.4 discusses how the role of the CDO at MTV Networks (part of Viacom) has evolved and how its business has benefited from a diverse workforce.

The Vital Role of Social Capital

>LO3
The key role of social capital in leveraging human capital within and across the firm.

Successful firms are well aware that the attraction, development, and retention of talent *is a necessary but not sufficient condition* for creating competitive advantages.[51] In the knowledge economy, it is not the stock of human capital that is important, but the extent to which it is combined and leveraged. In a sense, developing and retaining human capital becomes less important as key players (talented professionals, in particular) take the role of "free agents" and bring with them the requisite skill in many cases. Rather, the development of social capital (that is, the friendships and working relationships among talented individuals) gains importance, because it helps tie knowledge workers to a given firm.[52] Knowledge workers often exhibit greater loyalties to their colleagues and their profession than their employing organization, which may be "an amorphous, distant, and sometimes threatening entity."[53] Thus, a firm must find ways to create "ties" among its knowledge workers.

To illustrate, let's look at a hypothetical example. Two pharmaceutical firms are fortunate enough to hire Nobel Prize–winning scientists.[54] In one case, the scientist is offered a very attractive salary, outstanding facilities and equipment, and told to "go to it!" In the second case, the scientist is offered approximately the same salary, facilities, and equipment plus one additional ingredient. He or she will be working in a laboratory with 10 highly skilled and enthusiastic scientists. Part of the job is to collaborate with these peers and jointly develop promising drug compounds. There is little doubt as to which scenario will lead to a higher probability of retaining the scientist. Clearly, the interaction, sharing, and collaboration will create a situation in which the scientist will develop firm-specific ties and be less likely to "bolt" for a higher salary offer. Such ties are critical because knowledge-based resources tend to be more tacit in nature, as we mentioned early in this chapter. Therefore, they are much more difficult to protect against loss (i.e., the individual quitting the organization) than other types of capital, such as equipment, machinery, and land.

Another way to view this situation is in terms of the resource-based view of the firm that we discussed in Chapter 3. That is, competitive advantages tend to be harder for competitors to copy if they are based on "unique bundles" of resources.[55] So, if employees are working effectively in teams and sharing their knowledge and learning from each other, not only will they be more likely to add value to the firm, but they also will be less likely to leave the organization, because of the loyalties and social ties that they develop over time.

Next, we'll address a key concept in the New Economy—the Pied Piper Effect. Here, groups of professionals join (or leave) organizations en masse, not one at a time. Then, we will discuss the vital role of social networks in promoting knowledge management and enhancing career success.

How Social Capital Helps Attract and Retain Talent

The importance of social ties among talented professionals is creating a significant challenge (and opportunity) for organizations today. In *The Wall Street Journal,* Bernard Wysocki described the increasing prevalence of a type of "Pied Piper Effect," in which teams or networks of people are leaving one company for another.[56] The trend is to recruit job candidates at the crux of social relationships in organizations, particularly if they are seen as having the potential to bring with them a raft of valuable colleagues. This is a process that is referred to as "hiring via personal networks." Let's look at one instance of this practice.

> Gerald Eickhoff, founder of an electronic commerce company called Third Millennium Communications, tried for 15 years to hire Michael Reene. Why? Mr. Eickhoff says that he has "these Pied Piper skills." Mr. Reene was a star at Andersen Consulting in the 1980s and at IBM in the 1990s. He built his businesses and kept turning down overtures from Mr. Eickhoff.
>
> However, in early 2000, he joined Third Millennium as chief executive officer, with a salary of just $120,000 but with a 20 percent stake in the firm. Since then, he has brought in a raft of former IBM colleagues and Andersen subordinates. One protégé from his time at Andersen, Mary Goode, was brought on board as executive vice president. She promptly tapped her own network and brought along a half-dozen friends and former colleagues.

Company	What It Does	Defectors from Microsoft
Crossgain	Builds software around XML computer language	23 of 60 employees
ViAir	Makes software for wireless providers	Company declines to specify
CheckSpace	Builds online payment service for small businesses	Company says "a good chunk" of its 30 employees
digiMine	Sells data mining service	About 15% of 62 employees in addition to the 3 founders
Avogadro	Builds wireless notification software	8 of 25 employees
Tellme Networks	Offers information like stock quotes and scores over the phone	About 40 of 250 employees; another 40 from the former Netscape

Source: Buckman, R. 2000. "Tech Defectors from Microsoft Resettle Together," *The Wall Street Journal,* Eastern Edition, 2000. Copyright © 2000 by Dow Jones & Company, Inc. Reproduced with permission of Dow Jones & Company, Inc. via Copyright Clearance Center.

Wysocki considers the Pied Piper effect one of the underappreciated factors in the war for talent today. This is because one of the myths of the New Economy is rampant individualism, wherein individuals find jobs on the Internet career sites and go to work for complete strangers. Perhaps, instead of Me Inc., the truth is closer to We Inc.[57]

Another example of social relationships causing human capital mobility is the emigration of talent from an organization to form start-up ventures. Microsoft is perhaps the best-known example of this phenomenon.[58] Professionals have frequently left Microsoft en masse to form venture capital and technology start-ups built around teams of software developers. One example is Ignition Corporation, of Bellevue, Washington, which was formed by Brad Silverberg, a former Microsoft senior vice president. Eight former Microsoft executives, among others, founded the company. Exhibit 4.6 provides a partial listing of other companies that have been formed by groups of former Microsoft employees.

Social relationships can provide an important mechanism for obtaining both resources and information from individuals and organizations outside the boundary of a firm.[59] Strategy Spotlight 4.5 touts the benefits of firms' alumni programs. It describes how eBay's general counsel became an excellent source of business for his prior employer.

Social Networks: Implications for Knowledge Management and Career Success

Today, managers face a myriad of challenges driven by such factors as rapid changes in globalization and technology. Clearly, leading a successful company is more than a one-person job. As Tom Malone recently put it in *The Future of Work,* "As managers, we need to shift our thinking from command and control to coordinate and cultivate—the best way to gain power is sometimes to give it away." The move away from top-down bureaucratic control to more open, decentralized network models of organization makes it more difficult for managers to understand how work is actually getting done, who is interacting with whom both within and outside the organization, and the consequences of these

strategy spotlight

Alumni Programs: A Great Way to Stay in Touch

Michael Jacobson had worked in securities practices at Cooley Godward, a Palo Alto, California law firm, for a dozen years. Nobody was happy when he gave notice in 1998. Everyone felt that it would be difficult to get along without him.

However, a few months later, Cooley Godward's managers couldn't have been happier. Why? Jacobson's new job was as general counsel at a little-known online auction site called eBay! When the site needed outside counsel, Jacobsen tapped his former employer. A few months later, Cooley Godward was lead counsel for eBay's record-breaking $1.3 billion initial public offering. "It's a great relationship," says Mark Pitchford, partner and chief operating officer of the firm.

With such a "lucky break," Cooley Godward no longer leaves such matters to chance. In January 2004, it launched an alumni program to help the firm stay in touch with its former attorneys. Such programs are not particularly new to corporate America. Firms such as McKinsey & Company, Ernst & Young, and Procter & Gamble have had them in place for years. However, as partners at Cooley Godward have found, smaller firms can also benefit from alumni initiatives. "Former employees are a resource," says John Izzo, president of Izzo Consulting, a firm based in Vancouver, Washington. The firm advises small businesses on employee training and retention issues.

Despite the potential benefits of maintaining active contact with former employees, many employers treat them as just another name in the Rolodex—or even worse, as a competitive threat. Izzo warns that this can be a big mistake. Often, he claims, former staffers can act as goodwill ambassadors for their former employers, helping to refer new talent and clients. They may even return at a later point and will requiring little training. And with the job market now showing signs of improvement and many employees more likely to move on, alumni programs could become very important, especially at firms that have a hard time recruiting and retaining qualified professionals.

Source: Rich, L. 2005. Don't be a stranger. *Inc.*, January: 32–33.

>LO4

The importance of social networks in knowledge management and in promoting career success.

social network analysis analysis of the pattern of social interactions among individuals.

interactions for the long-term health of the organization. In short, coordination, cultivation, and collaboration are increasingly becoming the mode of work at every level throughout organizations.[60]

But how can this be done? One approach that has provided valuable insights is social network analysis.[61] **Social network analysis** depicts the pattern of interactions among individuals and helps to diagnose effective and ineffective patterns. It can be used to help identify groups or clusters of individuals that comprise the network, individuals who link the clusters, and other network members. It helps diagnose communication patterns and, consequently, communication effectiveness.[62] Such analysis of communication patterns is helpful because the configuration of group members' social ties within and outside the group affects the extent to which members connect to individuals who:

- convey needed resources,
- have the opportunity to exchange information and support,
- have the motivation to treat each other in positive ways, and,
- have the time to develop trusting relationships that might improve the groups' effectiveness.

However, such relationships don't "just happen."[63] Developing and protecting social capital requires interdependence among members in a group. Social capital erodes when people in the network become more independent of each other. And increased interactions between members aid in the development and maintenance of mutual obligations in a social network.

Let's take a brief look at a simplified network analysis to get a grasp of the key ideas. In Exhibit 4.7, the links are used to depict informal relationships among individuals

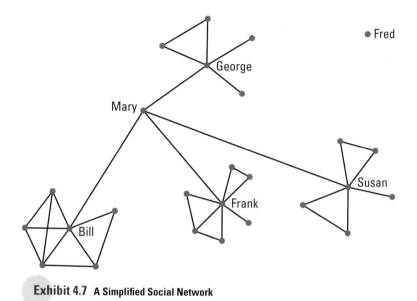

Exhibit 4.7 A Simplified Social Network

involving communication flows, personal support, and advice networks. There may be some individuals with literally no linkages, such as Fred. These individuals are typically labeled "isolates." However, most people do have some linkages with others.

To simplify, there are two primary types of mechanisms through which social capital will flow: *closure relationships* (depicted by Bill, Frank, George, and Susan) and *bridging relationships* (depicted by Mary). As we can see, in the former relationships one member is central to the communication flows in a group. In contrast, in the latter relationship, one person "bridges" or brings together groups that would have been otherwise unconnected.

Both closure and bridging relationships have important implications for the effective flow of information in organizations and for the management of knowledge. We will now briefly discuss each of these types of relationships. We will also address some of the implications that understanding social networks has for one's career success.

Closure   With **closure,** each group has a high level of connectedness. That is, many members have relationships (or ties) with other members. As indicated in Exhibit 4.7, Bill's group would have a higher level of closure than Frank, Susan, or George's groups because more group members are connected to each other. Through closure, group members develop strong relationships with each other, high levels of trust, and greater solidarity. High levels of trust help to ensure that informal norms in the group will be more easily enforced and there will tend to be less "free riding." Social pressure will prevent people from withholding effort or shirking their responsibilities. In addition, people in the network are more willing to extend favors and "go the extra mile" on a colleague's behalf because they are confident that their efforts will be reciprocated by another member in their group. Another benefit of a network with closure is that there is a high level of emotional support. This becomes particularly valuable when setbacks occur that may destroy morale or an unexpected tragedy happens that might cause the group to lose its focus. Social support helps the group to rebound from misfortune and get back on track.

But high levels of closure often come with a price. Groups that become too closed can become insular. They cut themselves off from learning about what is happening in the rest of the organization and fail to share what they are learning from people outside their group. Research shows that while managers need to encourage closure up to a point, if there is too much closure, they need to encourage people to open up their groups and infuse new ideas through bridging relationships.[64]

closure the degree to which all members of a social network have relationships (or ties) with other group members.

Bridging Relationships   The closure perspective rests on an assumption that there is a high level of similarity among group members. However, members can be quite heterogeneous with regard to their positions in either the formal or informal structures of the group or the organization. Such heterogeneity exists because of, for example, vertical boundaries (different levels in the hierarchy) and horizontal boundaries (different functional areas).

Bridging relationships, in contrast to closure, stresses the importance of ties connecting heterogeneous people. Employees who bridge otherwise disconnected people tend to receive timely, diverse information because of their access to a wide range of heterogeneous information flows. Such bridging relationships can serve to span a number of different types of boundaries within an organization.

The University of Chicago's Ron Burt originally coined the term **"structural holes"** to refer to the social gap between two groups. Structural holes are common in organizations. When they occur in business, managers typically refer to them as "silos" or "stovepipes." Sales and engineering are a classic example of two groups whose members traditionally interact with their peers rather than across groups.

Let's briefly review a study that Burt conducted at Raytheon, a $20 billion U.S. electronics company and military contractor, that provides further insight into the benefits of bridging.[65]

> Burt studied several hundred managers within Raytheon's supply chain group and asked each manager to write down ideas to improve the company's supply chain management. Then he asked two Raytheon executives to rate the ideas. The conclusion: *The best suggestions consistently came from managers who discussed ideas outside their regular work group.*
>
> Burt found that Raytheon managers were good at thinking of ideas but bad at developing them. Too often, Burt said, the managers discussed their ideas with colleagues already in their informal discussion network. Instead, he said, they should have had discussions outside their typical contacts, particularly with an informal boss, or someone with enough power to be an ally but not an actual supervisor.

Strategy Spotlight 4.6 addresses the value of informal friendships as an effective source of social capital. Interestingly, it also discusses the downside of insular, self-reliant groups.

Before we address the implications of social network theory for managers' career success, one might ask: Which is the more valuable mechanism to develop and nurture social capital—closure or bridging relationships? As with many aspects of strategic management, the answer becomes: "It all depends." So let's consider a few contingent issues.[66] First, consider firms in competitive environments characterized by rapidly changing technology and market factors. These firms should bridge relationships across networks because they need a wide variety of timely sources of information. Also, innovation is facilitated if there are multiple, interdisciplinary perspectives. On the other hand, firms competing in a stable environment would typically face a rather small amount of unpredictability. Thus, the cohesive ties associated with network closure would help to ensure the timely and effective implementation of strategies.

A second contingent factor would be the type of business strategies that a firm may choose to follow (a topic that we address next in Chapter 5). Managers with social networks characterized by closure would be in a preferred position if their firm is following an overall low cost strategy.[67] Here, there is a need for control and coordination to implement strategies that are rather constrained by pressures to reduce costs. Alternatively, the uncertainties generally associated with differentiation strategies (i.e., creating products that are perceived by customers as unique and highly valued) would require a broad range of information sources and inputs. Social networks characterized by bridging relationships across groups would access the diverse informational sources needed to deal with more complex, multifaceted strategies.

A caveat: In both contingencies that we have discussed—competitive environment and business strategy—closure and bridging relationships across groups are necessary. Our purpose is to address where one type should be more dominant.

The Value (and Limitations) of Informal Friendships in Organizations

Rope courses and Outward Bound-type activities help white-collar workers develop corporate collegiality through socializing, sweating and sharing stressful situations. People go in as co-workers and come out as friends. However, wholesale congeniality can actually make teams *less* effective.

Recently, Joe Labianca (now at the University of Kentucky) and two colleagues studied 60 teams in 11 companies representing a wide variety of industries. In the most effective teams, about half of the relationships among members were close enough to be considered friendships. However, in teams where the number of friendships approached 100 percent, performance dropped dramatically. Why? Such groups suffered because they were insular, impermeable to outside influences, and unhealthily self-reliant. Members may have developed a high level of trust and commitment with each other but they were too dependent on their own members for new insights and initiatives. At times, those problems can be avoided by brainstorming or by assigning someone in the group to be a devil's advocate. But where friendships are especially close, even those techniques are unlikely to produce dramatically differing perspectives.

Sources: Labianca, J. 2004. The ties that bind. *Harvard Business Review,* 82(10): 19; Oh, H. Chung, M., & Labianca, G. 2004. Group social capital and group effectiveness: The role of informal socializing ties. *Academy of Management Journal,* 47(6): 86–875; and Labianca, J. 2007. Personal communication. February 28.

The friendships that benefit teams most are formed *outside the group.* Business-centered relationships with people in other parts of the company are important for transmitting simple work flow information. But even more important are relationships that extend into the social sphere—to lunches and dinners and after-work drinks. Such interactions are especially valuable sources of social capital. Team members who socialize in this way, particularly with top managers and with leaders of other teams play a key role in bridging groups and individuals who otherwise would be unconnected to their own group. This enables them to bring back to their groups strategic information, task-related advice, and political and social support.

Higher-level managers can't require employees to befriend people outside their own domains. However, they can encourage it. Team leaders should be told that developing a broad social network is part of their job. Managers should set aside funds for cross-functional social activities and create opportunities for employees to bond around common hobbies or pursuits. When composing teams, leaders should consider whom—as well as what—potential members know. And mentoring programs should aim to place company fledglings beneath the wings of veterans from other departments rather than with people they work with every day.

To sum up, there is nothing wrong with Outward Bound activities. However, instead of braving the wilderness, teams should venture into the far corners of their own organization!

Implications for Career Success   Clearly, effective social networks can provide many advantages for an organization. They can also play a key role in an individual's career advancement and success. From an individual's perspective, social networks deliver three unique advantages: private information, access to diverse skill sets, and power.[68] Managers see these advantages at work every day but might not pause to consider how their networks regulate them.

Private Information   When we make judgments, we use both public and private information. Today, public information is easily available from a variety of sources, including the Internet. However, since it is so accessible, public information offers significantly less competitive advantage than it used to.

In contrast, private information is gathered from personal contacts who can offer something unique that cannot be found in publicly available sources, such as the release date of a new product or knowledge about what a particular interviewer looks for in candidates. Private information, therefore, can give managers an edge, though it is more subjective than public information since it cannot be easily verified by independent sources, such as Dunn & Bradstreet. Consequently the value of your private information to others—and the value of others' private information to you—depends on how much trust exists in the network of relationships.

Access to Diverse Skill Sets Linus Pauling, one of only two people to win a Nobel Prize in two different areas and considered one of the towering geniuses of the 20th century, attributed his creative success not to his immense brainpower or luck but to his diverse contacts. He said, "The best way to have a good idea is to have a lot of ideas."

While expertise has become more specialized during the past 15 years, organizational, product, and marketing issues have become more interdisciplinary. This means that success is tied to the ability to transcend natural skill limitations through others. Highly diverse network relationships, therefore, can help you develop more complete, creative, and unbiased perspectives on issues. And when you trade information or skills with people whose experiences differ from your own, you provide one another with unique, exceptionally valuable resources. It is common for people in relationships to share their problems with each other. If you know enough people, you will begin to see how the problems that another person is struggling with can be solved by the solutions being developed by others. If you can bring together problems and solutions, it will greatly benefit your career.

Power Traditionally, a manager's power was embedded in a firm's hierarchy. But, when corporate organizations became flatter, more like pancakes than pyramids, that power was repositioned in the network's brokers (people who bridged multiple networks), who could adapt to changes in the organization, develop clients, and synthesize opposing points of view. Such brokers weren't necessarily at the top of the hierarchy or experts in their fields, but they linked specialists in the firm with trustworthy and informative relationships.

Most personal networks are highly clustered; that is, an individual's friends are likely to be friends with one another as well. Most corporate networks are made up of several clusters that have few links between them. Brokers are especially powerful because they connect separate clusters, thus stimulating collaboration among otherwise independent specialists.

The Potential Downside of Social Capital

We'd like to close our discussion of social capital by addressing some of its limitations; that is, how social capital can impede an organization's effectiveness. First, some firms have been adversely affected by very high levels of social capital because it may breed **"groupthink"**—a tendency not to question shared beliefs.[69] Such thinking may occur in networks with high levels of closure where there is little input from people outside of the network. In effect, too many warm and fuzzy feelings among group members prevent people from rigorously challenging each other with tough questions. People are discouraged from engaging in the "creative abrasion" that Dorothy Leonard of Harvard University describes as a key source of innovation.[70] Two firms that were well known for their collegiality, strong sense of employee membership, and humane treatment—Digital Equipment (now part of Hewlett-Packard) and Polaroid—suffered greatly from market misjudgments and strategic errors. The aforementioned aspects of their culture contributed to their problems.

The second potential limitation is an outcome of the first one. If there are deep-rooted mindsets, there would be a tendency to develop dysfunctional human resource practices. That is, the organization (or group) would continue to hire, reward, and promote like-minded people who tend to further intensify organizational inertia and erode innovation. Such homogeneity would increase over time and decrease the effectiveness of decision-making processes.

Third, the socialization processes (orientation, training, etc.) can be expensive in terms of both financial resources and managerial commitment. Such investments can represent a

groupthink a tendency in an organization for individuals not to question shared beliefs.

significant opportunity cost that should be evaluated in terms of the intended benefits. If such expenses become excessive, profitability would be adversely affected.

Finally, individuals may use the contacts they develop to pursue their own interests and agendas that may be inconsistent with the organization's goals and objectives. Thus, they may distort or selectively use information to favor their preferred courses of action or withhold information in their own self-interest to enhance their power in the organization to the detriment of the common good. Drawing on our discussion of social networks, this is particularly true in an organization that has too many bridging relationships but not enough closure relationships. When people are involved in high closure groups, it is easy for them to watch each other to make certain that illegal or unethical acts don't occur. By contrast, bridging relationships make it easier for a person to play one group or individual off on another, with no one being the wiser.[71] We will discuss some behavioral control mechanisms in Chapter 9 (rewards, control, boundaries) that serve to reduce such dysfunctional behaviors and actions.[72]

Using Technology to Leverage Human Capital and Knowledge

Sharing knowledge and information throughout the organization can be a means of conserving resources, developing products and services, and creating new opportunities. In this section we will discuss how technology can be used to leverage human capital and knowledge within organizations as well as with customers and suppliers beyond their boundaries.

>LO5
The vital role of technology in leveraging knowledge and human capital.

Using Networks to Share Information

As we all know, e-mail is an effective means of communicating a wide variety of information. It is quick, easy, and almost costless. Of course, it can become a problem when employees use it extensively for personal reasons. And we all know how fast jokes or rumors can spread within and across organizations!

Below is an example of how a CEO curbed what he felt was excessive e-mail use in his firm.[73]

> Scott Dockter, CEO of PBD Worldwide Fulfillment Services in Alpharetta, Georgia, launched "no e-mail Friday." Why? He suspected that overdependence on e-mail at PBD, which offers services such as call center management and distribution, was hurting productivity and, perhaps, sales. Accordingly, he instructed his 275 employees to pick up the phone or meet in person each Friday, and reduce e-mail use the rest of the time.
>
> That was tough to digest, especially for the younger staffers. "We discovered a lot of introverts . . . who had drifted into a pattern of communicating by e-mail," says Dockter. However, in less than four months, the simple directive resulted in quicker problem-solving, better teamwork, and, best of all, happier customers." "Our relationship with PBD is much stronger," says Cynthia Fitzpatrick of Crown Financial Ministries. "You can't get to know someone through e-mail."

E-mail can, however, be a means for top executives to communicate information efficiently. For example, Martin Sorrell, chairman of WPP Group PLC, a $2.4 billion advertising and public relations firm, is a strong believer in the use of e-mail.[74] He e-mails all of his employees once a month to discuss how the company is doing, address specific issues, and offer his perspectives on hot issues, such as new business models for the Internet. He believes that it keeps people abreast of what he is working on.

Technology can also enable much more sophisticated forms of communication in addition to knowledge sharing. Buckman Laboratories is a $300 million specialty chemicals company based in Memphis, Tennessee, with approximately 1,300 employees in over

100 countries. Buckman has successfully used its global knowledge sharing network—known as K'Netix—to enhance its competitive advantages:[75]

> Here's an example of how the network can be applied. One of Buckman's paper customers in Michigan realized that the peroxide it was adding to remove ink from old magazines was no longer working. A Buckman sales manager presented this problem to the knowledge network. Within two days, salespeople from Belgium and Finland identified a likely cause: Bacteria in the paper slurry was producing an enzyme that broke down the peroxide. The sales manager recommended a chemical to control the bacteria, solving the problem. You can imagine how positive the customer felt about Buckman. And with the company and the customer co-creating knowledge, a new level of trust and value can emerge.

Electronic Teams: Using Technology to Enhance Collaboration

>LO6

Why "electronic" or "virtual" teams are critical in combining and leveraging knowledge in organizations and how they can be made more effective.

The use of technology has also enabled professionals to work as part of electronic, or virtual, teams to enhance the speed and effectiveness with which products are developed. For example, Microsoft has concentrated much of its development on **electronic teams** (or e-teams) that are networked together throughout the company.[76] This helps to accelerate design and testing of new software modules that use the Windows-based framework as their central architecture. Microsoft is able to foster specialized technical expertise while sharing knowledge rapidly throughout the organization. This helps the firm learn how its new technologies can be applied rapidly to new business ventures such as cable television, broadcasting, travel services, and financial services.

electronic teams a team of individuals that completes tasks primarily through e-mail communication.

What are electronic teams (or e-teams)? There are two key differences between e-teams and more traditional teams.[77] First, e-team members either work in geographically separated work places or they may work in the same space but at different times. E-teams may have members working in different spaces and time zones, as is the case with many multinational teams. Second, most of the interactions among members of e-teams occur through electronic communication channels such as fax machines and groupware tools such as e-mail, bulletin boards, chat, and videoconferencing.

E-teams have expanded exponentially in recent years.[78] Organizations face increasingly high levels of complex and dynamic change. E-teams are also effective in helping businesses cope with global challenges. Most e-teams perform very complex tasks and most knowledge-based teams are charged with developing new products, improving organizational processes, and satisfying challenging customer problems. For example, Eastman Kodak's e-teams design new products, Hewlett Packard's e-teams solve clients' computing problems, and Sun Microsystems' e-teams generate new business models.

Advantages   There are multiple advantages of e-teams.[79] In addition to the rather obvious use of technology to facilitate communications, the potential benefits parallel the other two major sections in this chapter—human capital and social capital. First, e-teams are less restricted by the geographic constraints that are placed on face-to-face teams. Thus, e-teams have the potential to acquire a broader range of "human capital" or the skills and capacities that are necessary to complete complex assignments. So, e-team leaders can draw upon a greater pool of talent to address a wider range of problems since they are not constrained by geographic space. Once formed, e-teams can be more flexible in responding to unanticipated work challenges and opportunities because team members can be rotated out of projects when demands and contingencies alter the team's objectives.

Second, e-teams can be very effective in generating "social capital"—the quality of relationships and networks that leaders and team members form. Such capital is a key lubricant in work transactions and operations. Given the broader boundaries associated with e-teams, members and leaders generally have access to a wider range of social contacts than would be typically available in more traditional face-to-face teams. Such contacts are often connected to a broader scope of clients, customers, constituents, and other key stakeholders.

Challenges   However, there are challenges associated with making e-teams effective. Successful action by both traditional teams and e-teams requires that:

- Members *identify* who among them can provide the most appropriate knowledge and resources, and,
- E-team leaders and key members know how to *combine* individual contributions in the most effective manner for a coordinated and appropriate response.

Group psychologists have termed such activities "identification and combination" activities and teams that fail to perform them face a "process loss."[80] Process losses prevent teams from reaching high levels of performance because of inefficient interaction dynamics among team members. Such poor dynamics require that some collective energy, time, and effort be devoted to dealing with team inefficiencies, thus diverting the team away from its objectives. For example, if a team member fails to communicate important information at critical phases of a project, other members may waste time and energy. This can lead to conflict and resentment as well as to decreased motivation to work hard to complete tasks. Clearly, team leaders and other members must expend collective energy to repair the breach, resulting in a process loss.

The potential for process losses tends to be more prevalent in e-teams than in traditional teams because the geographical dispersion of members increases the complexity of establishing effective interaction and exchanges. Generally, teams suffer process loss because of low cohesion, low trust among members, a lack of appropriate norms or standard operating procedures, or a lack of shared understanding among team members about their tasks. With e-teams, members are more geographically or temporally dispersed, and the team becomes more susceptible to the risk factors that can create process loss. Such problems can be exacerbated when team members have less than ideal competencies and social skills. This can erode problem-solving capabilities as well as the effective functioning of the group as a social unit.

Codifying Knowledge for Competitive Advantage

As we discussed early in this chapter, there are two different kinds of knowledge. Tacit knowledge is embedded in personal experience and shared only with the consent and participation of the individual. Explicit (or codified) knowledge, on the other hand, is knowledge that can be documented, widely distributed, and easily replicated. One of the challenges of knowledge-intensive organizations is to capture and codify the knowledge and experience that, in effect, resides in the heads of its employees. Otherwise, they will have to constantly "reinvent the wheel," which is both expensive and inefficient. Also, the "new wheel" may not necessarily be superior to the "old wheel."[81]

Once a knowledge asset (e.g., a software code or processes, routines for a consulting firm) is developed and paid for, it can be reused many times at very low cost, assuming that it doesn't have to be substantially modified each time. Let's take the case of a consulting company, such as Accenture (formerly Andersen Consulting).[82] Since the knowledge of its consultants has been codified and stored in electronic repositories, it can be employed in many jobs by a huge number of consultants. Additionally, since the work has a high level of standardization (i.e., there are strong similarities across the numerous client engagements), there generally tends to be a rather high ratio of consultants to partners. For example, the ratio of consultants to partners is roughly 30, which is quite high. As one might expect, there must be extensive training of the newly hired consultants for such an approach to work. The recruits are trained at Accenture's Center for Professional Education, a 150-acre campus in St. Charles, Illinois. Using the center's knowledge-management respository, the consultants work through many scenarios designed to improve business processes. In effect, the information technologies enable the consultants to be "implementers, not inventors."

Access Health, a call-in medical center, also uses technology to capture and share knowledge. When someone calls the center, a registered nurse uses the company's "clinical decision architecture" to assess the caller's symptoms, rule out possible conditions, and

How Context Integration Developed an Effective Knowledge Management System

Bruce Strong, founder and CEO of Context Integration, a Web consulting firm, decided to develop a knowledge-management system. Six months and a half million dollars later, he unveiled IAN (Intellectual Assets Network). The objective was to provide a medium for his consultants to share ideas, ask questions, and trace earlier journeys on similar projects. In theory it was fine. But Strong was disappointed with the lack of involvement by his employees. Why didn't the consultants embrace IAN? There were many reasons:

- Consultants saw depositing notes or project records into the database as one more task in a busy day.
- The task didn't appear to have any urgency.
- Consultants generally did not like to admit that they couldn't solve a problem.
- They resented management trying to impose what consultants perceived as a rigid structure on their work.

What did Strong decide to do? He began to reinforce the many benefits of the system, such as providing better and more consistent service. He also publicly recognized people who stood out as strong IAN contributors, and he made this part of everyone's job description. Perhaps most important, he began paying people to use it. He assigned points when people used the system—for example, one point for posting a résumé on the system, five points for creating a project record, and so on. The results were tallied every three months and the score accounted for 10 percent of a consultant's quarterly bonus. Over a two-month period, overall IAN usage almost doubled. However, more importantly, many consultants became enthusiastic converts once they had a positive experience with IAN. Not only does IAN continue to help many of them provide excellent service to their clients, but it also allows the firm to retain some of their knowledge when they leave.

Bruce Strong's initial disappointment was hardly surprising. According to Carla O'Dell, president of the American Productivity and Quality Center, of the companies trying knowledge management, fewer than 10 percent succeeded in making it part of their culture. She suggests:

> Technology plays a laggard role, not a leadership role. You need to establish relationships, the communities, the networks, the habits of sharing, the agreements about what we're going to share, and why it's important. All of that has to be working first before you automate it.

Sources: O'Dell, C. 2005. Knowledge Management: Identify, capture, share, and reuse key information. *EMA Communicator*. Fall: 4–5; and Koudsi, S. 2000. Actually, it is brain surgery. *Fortune*. March 20: 233.

recommend a home remedy, doctor's visit, or trip to the emergency room. The company's knowledge repository contains algorithms of the symptoms of more than 500 illnesses. According to CEO Joseph Tallman, "We are not inventing a new way to cure disease. We are taking available knowledge and inventing processes to put it to better use." The software algorithms were very expensive to develop, but the investment has been repaid many times over. The first 300 algorithms that Access Health developed have each been used an average of 8,000 times a year. Further, the company's paying customers—insurance companies and provider groups—save money because many callers would have made expensive trips to the emergency room or the doctor's office had they not been diagnosed over the phone.

Motivation is often a key issue in making knowledge management systems effective. That is, what are the incentives for people to contribute their knowledge? Some organizations have found that such systems work best when they are incorporated into the firm's evaluation and reward systems. Strategy Spotlight 4.7 discusses some of the challenges faced by Context Integration's CEO in developing his firm's knowledge management system.

We close this section with a series of questions managers should consider in determining (1) how effective their organization is in attracting, developing, and retaining human capital and (2) how effective they are in leveraging human capital through social capital and technology. These questions, included in Exhibit 4.8, summarize some of the key issues addressed in this chapter.

Human Capital

Recruiting "Top-Notch" Human Capital

- Does the organization assess attitude and "general makeup" instead of focusing primarily on skills and background in selecting employees at all levels?
- How important are creativity and problem-solving ability? Are they properly considered in hiring decisions?
- Do people throughout the organization engage in effective networking activities to obtain a broad pool of worthy potential employees? Is the organization creative in such endeavors?

Enhancing Human Capital through Employee Development

- Does the development and training process inculcate an "organizationwide" perspective?
- Is there widespread involvement, including top executives, in the preparation and delivery of training and development programs?
- Is the development of human capital effectively tracked and monitored?
- Are there effective programs for succession at all levels of the organization, especially at the top-most levels?
- Does the firm effectively evaluate its human capital? Is a 360-degree evaluation used? Why? Why not?
- Are mechanisms in place to assure that a manager's success does not come at the cost of compromising the organization's core values?

Retaining the Best Employees

- Are there appropriate financial rewards to motivate employees at all levels?
- Do people throughout the organization strongly identify with the organization's mission?
- Are employees provided with a stimulating and challenging work environment that fosters professional growth?
- Are valued amenities provided (e.g., flex time, child-care facilities, telecommuting) that are appropriate given the organization's mission, strategy, and how work is accomplished?
- Is the organization continually devising strategies and mechanisms to retain top performers?

Social Capital

- Are there positive personal and professional relationships among employees?
- Is the organization benefiting (or being penalized) by hiring (or by voluntary turnover) en masse?
- Does an environment of caring and encouragement rather than competition enhance team performance?
- Do the social networks within the organization have the appropriate levels of closure and bridging relationships?
- Does the organization minimize the adverse effects of excessive social capital, such as excessive costs and "groupthink"?

Technology

- Has the organization used technologies such as e-mail and networks to develop products and services?
- Does the organization effectively use technology to transfer best practices across the organization?
- Does the organization use technology to leverage human capital and knowledge both within the boundaries of the organization and among its suppliers and customers?
- Has the organization effectively used technology to codify knowledge for competitive advantage?
- Does the organization try to retain some of the knowledge of employees when they decide to leave the firm?

Source: Adapted from Dess, G. G., & Picken, J. C. 1999. *Beyond Productivity:* 63–64. New York: AMACON.

Exhibit 4.8 Issues to Consider in Creating Value through Human Capital, Social Capital, and Technology

Protecting the Intellectual Assets of the Organization: Intellectual Property and Dynamic Capabilities

>LO7

The challenge of protecting intellectual property and the importance of a firm's dynamic capabilities.

In today's dynamic and turbulent world, unpredictability and fast change dominate the business environment. Economic prosperity rests upon the useful application of knowledge. Firms can use technology, attract human capital, or tap into research and design networks to get access to pretty much the same information as their competitors. So what would give firms a sustainable competitive advantage?[83] Protecting a firm's intellectual property requires a concerted effort on the part of the company. After all, employees become disgruntled and patents expire. The management of intellectual property involves, besides patents, contracts with confidentiality and noncompete clauses, copyrights, and the development of trademarks. Moreover, developing dynamic capabilities is the only avenue providing firms with the ability to reconfigure their knowledge and activities to achieve a sustainable competitive advantage.

Intellectual property rights are more difficult to define and protect than property rights for physical assets (e.g., plant, equipment, and land). However, if intellectual property rights are not reliably protected by the state, no individuals will have the incentive to develop new products and services. Property rights have been enshrined in constitutions and rules of law in many countries. In the information era, though, adjustments need to be made to accommodate the new realities of knowledge. Knowledge and information are fundamentally different assets from the physical ones that property rights have been designed to protect.

The protection of intellectual rights raises unique issues, compared to physical property rights. Much of the production of intellectual property is characterized by significant development costs and very low marginal costs. Indeed, it may take a substantial investment to develop a software program, an idea, or a digital music tune. Once developed, though, their reproduction and distribution cost may be almost zero, especially if the Internet is used. Effective protection of intellectual property is necessary before any investor will finance such an undertaking. Appropriation of their returns is harder to police since possession and deployment are not as readily observable. Unlike physical assets, intellectual property can be stolen by simply broadcasting it. Recall Napster and MP3 as well as the debates about counterfeit software, music CDs, and DVDs coming from developing countries such as China. Part of the problem is that using an idea does not prevent others from simultaneously using it for their own benefit, which is typically impossible with physical assets. Moreover, new ideas are frequently built on old ideas and are not easily traceable. Strategy Spotlight 4.8 describes the many legal battles fought by a Canadian firm, Research in Motion of Waterloo, the developer of the popular Blackberry. This example illustrates the high stakes that ride on intellectual property rights.

Countries are attempting to pass new legislation to cope with developments in such diverse fields as new pharmaceutical compounds, stem cell research, and biotechnology. However, a firm that is faced with this challenge today cannot wait for the legislation to catch up. It has to embark on the next technological development, drug, software solution, electronic game, online service, or any of a myriad of other products and services to contribute to our economic prosperity and the creation of wealth for those entrepreneurs who have the idea first and risk bringing it to the market.

Related to the above, dynamic capabilities entail the capacity to build and protect a competitive advantage. This rests on knowledge, assets, competencies, and complementary assets and technologies as well as the ability to sense and seize new opportunities, generate new knowledge, and reconfigure existing assets and capabilities. According to

4.8 strategy spotlight

Research in Motion, Maker of the Blackberry, Loses an Intellectual Property Lawsuit

Research in Motion (RIM) is a Waterloo, Ontario–based company that is best known for developing the Blackberry, a wireless device that integrates the functionalities of a cell phone with the ability to receive e-mail messages. During its brief history, it has beccome one of the fastest growing companies in North America. Founded by Mike Lazaridis, a former University of Waterloo student in 1984, Research in Motion was a competent but obscure technology firm until 1999 when the first Blackberry was released. Through the development of integrated hardware, software, and services that support multiple wireless network standards, the Blackberry has enabled RIM to grow from less than $50 million in sales revenue in 1999 to $2 billion by 2006. Even more impressive, by 2007 the company can boast a market capitalization in excess of $25 billion. RIM's commitment to their slogan "always on, always connected" has won them a legion of dedicated followers around the globe.

Interestingly, legal challenges have been the biggest obstacles that Research in Motion has faced in the eight years since the introduction of the first Blackberry. In 2002, Virginia-based NTP sued the company alleging patent infringement. Although RIM tried to demonstrate that NTP's patents were invalid because wireless e-mail technology existed prior to NTP's filing of patent applications, the court found them guilty of willfully infringing NTP's patents. While the appeal process dragged on

through higher courts, the fear that the court might issue an injunction against Blackberry greatly slowed the growth of RIM's subscriber base. Given the need to allay the anxieties of the subscribers, who could not imagine life without their Blackberries, RIM decided to settle its dispute with NTP in March, 2006. The settlement amount was a staggering $612.5 million in "full and final settlement of all claims"!

In a bizarre postscript to the settlement with NTP, in May 2006, RIM was sued by Redwood Shores, California–based Visto for infringement of its patents. Visto has a history of suing, and occasionally winning, patent infringement lawsuits against companies such as Good Technology, Microsoft, and Seven. Interestingly, NTP holds an equity stake in Visto!

● Research in Motion (RIM) has faced litigation over its highly acclaimed Blackberry.

Sources: Hesseldahl, A. 2006. RIM's latest patent problem. *BusinessWeek Online,* May 2: np; Anonymous. 2006. Settlement reached in Blackberry patent case. (The Associated Press) MSNBC.Com. March 3: np; and Wolk, M. 2006. RIM pays up, taking "one for the team." MSNBC.Com. March 3.

David Teece, an economist at the University of California at Berkeley, dynamic capabilities are related to the entrepreneurial side of the firm and are built within a firm through its environmental and technological "sensing" apparatus, its choices of organizational form, and its collective ability to strategize. Dynamic capabilities are about the ability of an organization to challenge the conventional wisdom within its industry and market, learn and innovate, adapt to the changing world, and continuously adopt new ways to serve the evolving needs of the market.

The Central Role of Leveraging Human Capital in Strategy Formulation

>LO8

How leveraging human capital is critical to strategy formulation for business-level, corporate-level, international, and entrepreneurial strategies.

In this chapter we have emphasized the importance of human capital and how such intangible assets can create the greatest value in today's successful organizations. As we have noted throughout the chapter, attracting top talent is a necessary, but not a sufficient, condition for competitive advantage. It must be not only developed and retained, but also leveraged through effective use of social capital and technology. In this section we will discuss how leveraging human capital is vital to each of the levels of strategy that we will address in the next four chapters (5, 6, 7, and 8) of the book.

Leveraging Human Capital and Business-Level Strategy

At the business level (Chapter 5), firms strive to create advantages that are sustainable over time. To do this, managers must integrate the primary and support activities in their firm's value chain (discussed in Chapter 3). We will discuss how FedEx has provided its drivers with handheld computers—a valuable technology—to help them effectively track customer packages. The FedEx example points out how technology can help a firm enhance business-level strategies by leveraging its human capital.

Leveraging Human Capital and Corporate-Level Strategy

In Chapter 6 on corporate-level strategy, we will discuss how firms can create value by managing their business to create synergy; that is, how more value can be created by working together across business units than if they were freestanding units. Managers must determine what important relationships (products, markets, technologies) exist across businesses and how they can be leveraged. For such knowledge transfer to occur, managers must be aware of not only their human capital (tacit knowledge), but also their organization's codified knowledge and relationships among key professionals and across business units.

Leveraging Human Capital and International-Level Strategy

In Chapter 7 we will address how companies create value by leveraging resources and knowledge across national boundaries. Here firms are faced with two opposing forces: how to achieve economies of scale and how to adapt to local market needs. We will discuss how some leading-edge firms are able to successfully attain a "transnational strategy" wherein not only do the firms achieve lower costs through economies of scale, but also they are able to adapt successfully to local markets. To do so, firms must facilitate the flow of information and knowledge between business units in different countries. This requires not only attracting, developing, and retaining superior talent, but also leveraging their knowledge and skills through effective working relationships (i.e., social capital) and use of technology.

Leveraging Human Capital and Entrepreneurial Strategies

One of the key resources that entrepreneurial firms use to foster new value creation is technology. Technology knowledge provides managers who use it with the ability to lower costs, enhance customer service, and improve performance. Human resources and knowledge are also used to exploit market uncertainties and launch preemptive strategies aimed at achieving first-mover advantages. Such competitive actions require sophisticated knowledge by talented professionals as well as strong, positive working relationships between managers and technology experts. We provide the example of SkyTower Telecommunications, a pioneering entrepreneurial firm that received NASA backing and $80 million in investment capital for combining unmanned aircraft technology with knowledge of wireless communications to create solar-powered, flying wing-style airplanes designed to replace the radio towers and satellites presently being used to send out Internet, mobile phone, and high-definition TV signals.

Reflecting on Career Implications . . .

- *Human Capital:* Does your organization effectively attract, develop, and retain talent? If not, you may have fewer career opportunities to enhance your human capital at your organization. Take advantage of your organization's human resource programs such as tuition reimbursement, mentoring, etc.
- *Human Capital:* Does your organization value diversity? What kinds of diversity seems to be encouraged (e.g., age-based or ethnicity-based)? If not, there may be limited perspectives on strategic and operational issues and a career at this organization may be less attractive to you.
- *Social Capital:* Does your organization have effective programs to build and develop social capital such that professionals develop strong "ties" to the organization? Alternatively, is social capital so strong that you see effects occur such as "groupthink"? From your perspective, how might you better leverage social capital towards pursuing other career opportunities?
- *Technology:* Does your organization provide and effectively use technology (e.g., groupware, knowledge management systems) to help you leverage your talents and expand your knowledge base?

Summary

Firms throughout the industrial world are recognizing that the knowledge worker is the key to success in the marketplace. However, we also recognize that human capital, although vital, is still only a necessary, but not a sufficient, condition for creating value. We began the first section of the chapter by addressing the importance of human capital and how it can be attracted, developed, and retained. Then we discussed the role of social capital and technology in leveraging human capital for competitive success. We pointed out that intellectual capital—the difference between a firm's market value and its book value—has increased significantly over the past few decades. This is particularly true for firms in knowledge-intensive industries, especially where there are relatively few tangible assets, such as software development.

The second section of the chapter addressed the attraction, development, and retention of human capital. We viewed these three activities as a "three-legged stool"—that is, it is difficult for firms to be successful if they ignore or are unsuccessful in any one of these activities. Among the issues we discussed in *attracting* human capital were "hiring for attitude, training for skill" and the value of using social networks to attract human capital. In particular, it is important to attract employees who can collaborate with others, given the importance of collective efforts such as teams and task forces. With regard to *developing* human capital, we discussed the need to encourage widespread involvement throughout the organization, monitor progress and track the development of human capital, and evaluate human capital. Among the issues that are widely practiced in evaluating human capital is the 360-degree evaluation system. Employees are evaluated by their superiors, peers, direct reports, and even internal and external customers. We also addressed the value of maintaining a diverse workforce. Finally, some mechanisms for retaining human capital are employees' identification with the organization's mission and values, providing challenging work and a stimulating environment, the importance of financial and nonfinancial rewards and incentives, and providing flexibility and amenities. A key issue here is that a firm should not overemphasize financial rewards. After all, if individuals join an organization for money, they also are likely to leave for money. With money as the primary motivator, there is little chance that employees will develop firm-specific ties to keep them with the organization.

The third section of the chapter discussed the importance of social capital in leveraging human capital. Social capital refers to the network of relationships that individuals have throughout the organization as well as with customers and suppliers. Such ties can be critical in obtaining both information and resources. With regard to recruiting, for example, we saw how some firms are able to hire en masse groups of individuals who are part of social networks. Social relationships can also be very important in the effective functioning of groups. Finally, we discussed some of the potential downsides of social capital. These include the expenses that firms may bear when promoting social and working relationships among individuals as well as the potential for "groupthink," wherein individuals are reluctant to express divergent (or opposing) views on an issue because of social pressures to conform. We also introduced the concept of social networks. The relative advantages of being central in a network versus bridging multiple networks was discussed. We addressed the key role that social networks can play in both improving knowledge management and promoting career success.

The fourth section addressed the role of technology in leveraging human capital. We discussed relatively simple means of using technology, such as e-mail and networks where individuals can collaborate by way of personal computers. We provided suggestions and guidelines on how electronic teams can be effectively managed. We also addressed more sophisticated uses of technology, such as sophisticated management systems. Here knowledge can be codified and reused at very low cost, as we saw in the examples of firms in the consulting, health care, and high-technology industries.

In the fifth section we discussed the increasing importance of protecting a firm's intellectual property. Although traditional approaches such as patents, copyrights, and trademarks are important, the development of dynamic capabilities may be the best protection in the long run.

The final section addressed how the leveraging of human capital is critical in strategy formulation at all levels. This includes business-level, corporate-level, international, and entrepreneurial strategies.

Summary Review Questions

1. Explain the role of knowledge in today's competitive environment.
2. Why is it important for managers to recognize the interdependence in the attraction, development, and retention of talented professionals?
3. What are some of the potential downsides for firms that engage in a "war for talent"?
4. Discuss the need for managers to use social capital in leveraging their human capital both within and across their firm.
5. Discuss the key role of technology in leveraging knowledge and human capital.

Key Terms

knowledge economy, 117
intellectual capital, 117
human capital, 118
social capital, 118
explicit knowledge, 118
tacit knowledge, 118
social network analysis, 132
closure, 133
bridging relationships, 134
structural holes, 134
groupthink, 136
electronic teams, 138

Experiential Exercise

Johnson & Johnson, a leading health care firm with $47 billion in 2004 revenues, is often rated as one of *Fortune*'s "Most Admired Firms." It is also considered an excellent place to work and has generated high return to shareholders. Clearly, they value their human capital. Using the Internet and/or library resources, identify some of the actions/strategies Johnson & Johnson has taken to attract, develop, and retain human capital. What are their implications?

Activity	Actions/Strategies	Implications
Attracting human capital		
Developing human capital		
Retaining human capital		

Application Questions Exercises

1. Look up successful firms in a high-technology industry as well as two successful firms in more traditional industries such as automobile manufacturing and retailing. Compare their market values and book values. What are some implications of these differences?
2. Select a firm for which you believe its social capital—both within the firm and among its suppliers and customers—is vital to its competitive advantage. Support your arguments.
3. Choose a company with which you are familiar. What are some of the ways in which it uses technology to leverage its human capital?
4. Using the Internet, look up a company with which you are familiar. What are some of the policies and procedures that it uses to enhance the firm's human and social capital?

Ethics Questions

1. Recall an example of a firm that recently faced an ethical crisis. How do you feel the crisis and management's handling of it affected the firm's human capital and social capital?
2. Based on your experiences or what you have learned in your previous classes, are you familiar with any companies that used unethical practices to attract talented professionals? What do you feel were the short-term and long-term consequences of such practices?

References

1. Wellner, A. S. 2004. The perils of hiring stars. *Inc.,* August: 32–33; Molaro, R. 2005. Bear season. *The Art of Licensing,* Winter: S-11–S13; and personal communication with Michael Carlisle and the authors, February 10, 2005.
2. Parts of this chapter draw upon some of the ideas and examples from Dess, G. G., & Picken, J. C. 1999. *Beyond Productivity.* New York: AMACOM.
3. An acknowledged trend: The world economic survey. 1996. *The Economist,* September 28: 25–28.
4. Quinn, J. B., Anderson, P., & Finkelstein, S. 1996. Leveraging intellect. *Academy of Management Executive,* 10(3): 7–27.
5. Hamel, G., & Prahalad, C. K. 1996. Competing in the new economy: Managing out of bounds. *Strategic Management Journal,* 17: 238.
6. Stewart, T. A. 1997. *Intellectual capital: The new wealth of organizations.* New York: Doubleday/Currency.
7. Leif Edvisson and Michael S. Malone have a similar, more detailed definition of *intellectual capital:* "the combined knowledge, skill, innovativeness, and ability to meet the task at hand." They consider intellectual capital to equal human capital plus structural capital. *Structural capital* is defined as "the hardware, software, databases, organization structure, patents, trademarks, and everything else of organizational capability that supports those employees' productivity—in a word, everything left at the office when the employees go home." Edvisson, L., &

Malone, M. S. 1997. *Intellectual capital: Realizing your company's true value by finding its hidden brainpower:* 10–14. New York: HarperBusiness.

8. Stewart, T. A. 2001. Accounting gets radical. *Fortune,* April 16: 184–194.

9. Thomas Stewart has suggested this formula in his book *Intellectual Capital.* He provides an insightful discussion on pages 224–225, including some of the limitations of this approach to measuring intellectual capital. We recognize, of course, that during the late 1990s and in early 2000, there were some excessive market valuations of high-technology and Internet firms. For an interesting discussion of the extraordinary market valuation of Yahoo!, an Internet company, refer to Perkins, A. B. 2001. The Internet bubble encapsulated: Yahoo! *Red Herring,* April 15: 17–18.

10. Roberts, P. W., & Dowling, G. R. 2002. Corporate reputation and sustained superior financial performance. *Strategic Management Journal,* 23(12): 1077–1095.

11. For a recent study on the relationships between human capital, learning, and sustainable competitive advantage, read Hatch, N. W., & Dyer, J. H. 2005. Human capital and learning as a source of sustainable competitive advantage. *Strategic Management Journal,* 25: 1155–1178.

12. One of the seminal contributions on knowledge management is Becker, G. S. 1993. *Human capital: A theoretical and empirical analysis with special reference to education* (3rd ed.). Chicago: University of Chicago Press.

13. For an excellent overview of the topic of social capital, read Baron, R. A. 2005. Social capital. In Hitt, M. A., & Ireland, R. D. (Eds.), *The Blackwell encyclopedia of management* (2nd ed.): 224–226. Malden, MA: Blackwell.

14. For an excellent discussion of social capital and its impact on organizational performance, refer to Nahapiet, J., & Ghoshal, S. 1998. Social capital, intellectual capital, and the organizational advantage. *Academy of Management Review,* 23: 242–266.

15. An interesting discussion of how knowledge management (patents) can enhance organizational performance can be found in Bogner, W. C., & Bansal, P. 2007. Knowledge management as the basis of sustained high performance. *Journal of Management Studies,* 44(1): 165–188.

16. Polanyi, M. 1967. *The tacit dimension.* Garden City, NY: Anchor Publishing.

17. Barney, J. B. 1991. Firm resources and sustained competitive advantage. *Journal of Management,* 17: 99–120.

18. For an interesting perspective of empirical research on how knowledge can adversely affect performance, read Haas, M. R., & Hansen, M. T. 2005. When using knowledge can hurt performance: The value of organizational capabilities in a management consulting company. *Strategic Management Journal,* 26(1): 1–24.

19. Some of the notable books on this topic include Edvisson & Malone, op. cit.; Stewart, op. cit.; and Nonaka, I., & Takeuchi, I. 1995. *The knowledge creating company.* New York: Oxford University Press.

20. Stewart, T. A. 2000. Taking risk to the marketplace. *Fortune,* March 6: 424.

21. Dutton, G. 1997. Are you technologically competent? *Management Review,* November: 54–58.

22. For a discussion of attracting, developing, and retaining top talent, refer to Goffee, R., & Jones, G. 2007. Leading clever people. *Harvard Business Review,* 85(3): 72–89.

23. Dess & Picken, op. cit.: 34.

24. Webber, A. M. 1998. Danger: Toxic company. *Fast Company,* November: 152–161.

25. Morris, B. 1997. Key to success: People, people, people. *Fortune,* October 27: 232.

26. Martin, J. 1998. So, you want to work for the best. . . . *Fortune,* January 12: 77.

27. Cardin, R. 1997. Make your own Bozo Filter. *Fast Company,* October–November: 56.

28. Lavering, R., & Muskowitz. M. 2007. In good company. *Fortune,* January 22: 94–114.

29. Martin, op. cit.; Henkoff, R. 1993. Companies that train best. *Fortune,* March 22: 53–60.

30. Ibid.

31. An interesting perspective on developing new talent rapidly when they join an organization can be found in Rollag, K., Parise, S., & Cross, R. 2005. Getting new hires up to speed quickly. *MIT Sloan Management Review,* 46(2): 35–41.

32. Stewart, T. A. 1998. Gray flannel suit? moi? *Fortune,* March 18: 80–82.

33. An interesting perspective on how Cisco Systems develops its talent can be found in Chatman, J., O'Reilly, C., & Chang, V. 2005. Cisco Systems: Developing a human capital strategy. *California Management Review,* 47(2): 137–166.

34. This section is based on Leonard, D. A., & Swap, W. 2004. Deep smarts. *Harvard Business Review,* 82(9): 88–97.

35. Morris, B. op. cit.

36. For an innovative perspective on the appropriateness of alternate approaches to evaluation and rewards, refer to Seijts, G. H., & Lathan, G. P. 2005. Learning versus performance goals: When should each be used? *Academy of Management Executive,* 19(1): 124–132.

37. The discussion of the 360-degree feedback system draws on the article UPS. 1997. 360-degree feedback: Coming from all sides. *Vision* (a UPS Corporation internal company publication), March: 3; Slater, R. 1994. *Get better or get beaten: Thirty-one leadership secrets from Jack Welch.* Burr Ridge, IL: Irwin; Nexon, M. 1997. General Electric: The secrets of the finest company in the world. *L'Expansion,* July 23: 18–30; and Smith, D. 1996. Bold new directions for human resources. *Merck World* (internal company publication), October: 8.

38. Kets de Vries, M. F. R. 1998. Charisma in action: The transformational abilities of Virgin's Richard Branson and ABB's Percy Barnevik. *Organizational Dynamics,* Winter: 20.

39. We have only to consider the most celebrated case of industrial espionage in recent years, wherein José Ignacio Lopez was indicted in a German court for stealing sensitive product planning documents from his former employer, General Motors, and sharing them with his executive colleagues at Volkswagen. The lawsuit was dismissed by the German courts, but Lopez and his colleagues were investigated by the U.S. Justice Department. Also consider the recent litigation involving noncompete employment contracts and confidentiality clauses of *International Paper v. Louisiana-Pacific, Campbell Soup v. H. J. Heinz Co.,* and *PepsiCo v. Quaker Oats's Gatorade.* In addition to retaining valuable human resources and often their valuable network of customers, firms must also protect proprietary information and knowledge. For interesting insights, refer to Carley, W. M. 1998. CEO gets hard lesson in how not to keep his lieutenants. *The Wall Street Journal,* February 11: A1, A10; and Lenzner, R., & Shook, C. 1998. Whose Rolodex is it, anyway? *Forbes,* February 23: 100–103.

40. For an insightful discussion of retention of knowledge workers in today's economy, read Davenport, T. H. 2005. *The care and feeding of the knowledge worker.* Boston, MA: Harvard Business School Press.

41. Lieber, R. B. 1998, Why employees love these companies. *Fortune,* January 12: 72–74.

42. Stewart, T. A. 2001. *The wealth of knowledge.* New York: Currency.

43. Amabile, T. M. 1997. Motivating creativity in organizations: On doing what you love and loving what you do. *California Management Review,* Fall: 39–58.

44. For an insightful perspective on alternate types of employee–employer relationships, read Erickson, T. J., & Gratton, L. 2007. What it means to work here. *Harvard Business Review,* 85(3): 104–112.

45. Monsanto has been part of Pharmacia since 2002. *Hoover's Handbook of Am. Bus. 2004:* 562.

46. Pfeffer, J. 2001. Fighting the war for talent is hazardous to your organization's health. *Organizational Dynamics,* 29(4): 248–259.

47. Cox, T. L. 1991. The multinational organization. *Academy of Management Executive,* 5(2): 34–47. Without doubt, a great deal has been written on the topic of creating and maintaining an effective diverse workforce. Some excellent, recent books include: Harvey, C. P., & Allard, M. J. 2005. *Understanding and managing diversity: Readings, cases, and exercises.* (3rd ed.). Upper Saddle River, NJ: Pearson Prentice-Hall; Miller, F. A., & Katz, J. H. 2002. *The inclusion breakthrough: Unleashing the real power of diversity.* San Francisco: Berrett Koehler; and Williams, M. A. 2001. *The 10 lenses: Your guide to living and working in a multicultural world.* Sterling, VA: Capital Books.

48. www.rand.org/publications/RB/RB/5050.

49. This section, including the six potential benefits of a diverse workforce, draws on Cox, T. H., & Blake, S. 1991. Managing cultural diversity: Implications for organizational competitiveness. *Academy of Management Executive,* 5(3): 45–56.

50. www.pwcglobal.com/us/eng/careers/diversity/index.html.

51. This discussion draws on Dess, G. G., & Lumpkin, G. T. 2001. Emerging issues in strategy process research. In Hitt, M. A., Freeman, R. E., & Harrison, J. S. (Eds.). *Handbook of strategic management:* 3–34. Malden, MA: Blackwell.

52. Adler, P. S., & Kwon, S. W. 2002. Social capital: Prospects for a new concept. *Academy of Management Review,* 27(1): 17–40.

53. Capelli, P. 2000. A market-driven approach to retaining talent. *Harvard Business Review,* 78(1): 103–113.

54. This hypothetical example draws on Peteraf, M. 1993. The cornerstones of competitive advantage. *Strategic Management Journal,* 14: 179–191.

55. Wernerfelt, B. 1984. A resource-based view of the firm. *Strategic Management Journal,* 5: 171–180.

56. Wysocki, B., Jr. 2000. Yet another hazard of the new economy: The Pied Piper Effect. *The Wall Street Journal,* March 20: A1–A16.

57. Ibid.

58. Buckman, R. C. 2000. Tech defectors from Microsoft resettle together. *The Wall Street Journal,* October: B1–B6.

59. An insightful discussion of the interorganizational aspects of social capital can be found in Dyer, J. H., & Singh, H. 1998. The relational view: Cooperative strategy and sources of interorganizational competitive advantage. *Academy of Management Review,* 23: 66–79.

60. Hoppe, B. 2005. Structural holes, Part one. connectedness.blogspot.com. January 18: np.

61. There has been a tremendous amount of theory building and empirical research in recent years in the area of social network analysis. Unquestionably, two of the major contributors to this domain have been Ronald Burt and J. S. Coleman. For excellent background discussions, refer to: Burt, R. S. 1992. *Structural holes: The social structure of competition.* Cambridge, MA: Harvard University Press; Coleman, J. S. 1990. *Foundations of social theory.* Cambridge, MA: Harvard University Press; and Coleman, J. S. 1988. Social capital in the creation of human capital. *American Journal of Sociology.* 94: S95–S120. For a more recent review and integration of current thought on social network theory, consider: Burt, R. S. 2005. *Brokerage & closure: An introduction to social capital.* Oxford Press: New York.

62. Our discussion draws on the concepts developed by Burt, 1992, op. cit.; Coleman, 1990, op. cit.; Coleman, 1988, op. cit.; and Oh, H., Chung, M. & Labianca, G. 2004. Group social capital and group effectiveness: The role of informal socializing ties. *Academy of Management Journal,* 47(6): 860–875. We would like to thank Joe Labianca (University of Kentucky) for his helpful feedback and ideas in our discussion of social networks.

63. Arregle, J. L., Hitt, M. A., Sirmon, D. G., & Very, P. 2007. The development of organizational social capital: Attributes of family firms. *Journal of Management Studies,* 44(1): 73–95.

64. Oh, et. al., op. cit.

65. Hoppe, op. cit.

66. The discussion of these two contingent factors draws on Dess, G. G., & Shaw, J. D. 2001. Voluntary turnover, social capital, and organizational performance. *Academy of Management Review,* 26(3): 446–456.

67. The business-level strategies of overall low cost and differentiation draws upon Michael E. Porter's classic work and will be discussed in more detail in Chapter 5. Source: Porter, M. E. 1985. *Competitive advantage.* Free Press: New York.

68. Our discussion of the three advantages of social networks draws on Uzzi, B., & Dunlap. S. 2005. How to build your network. *Harvard Business Review,* 83(12): 53–60. For a recent, excellent review on the research exploring the relationship between social capital and managerial performance, read Moran, P. 2005. Structural vs. relational embeddedness: Social capital and managerial performance. *Strategic Management Journal,* 26(12): 1129–1151.

69. Prusak, L., & Cohen, D. 2001. How to invest in social capital. *Harvard Business Review,* 79(6): 86–93.

70. Leonard, D., & Straus, S. 1997. Putting your company's whole brain to work. *Harvard Business Review,* 75(4): 110–122.

71. For an excellent discussion of public (i.e., the organization) versus private (i.e., the individual manager) benefits of social capital, refer to Leana, C. R., & Van Buren, H. J. 1999. Organizational social capital and employment practices. *Academy of Management Review,* 24(3): 538–555.

72. The authors would like to thank Joe Labianca, University of Kentucky, and John Lin, University of Texas at Dallas, for their very helpful input in our discussion of social network theory and its practical implications.

73. Brady, D. 2006. *!#?@ the e-mail. Can we talk?. *BusinessWeek,* December 4: 109.

74. Taylor, W. C. 1999. Whatever happened to globalization? *Fast Company,* December: 228–236.

75. Prahalad, C. K., & Ramaswamy, V. 2004. *The future of competition: Co-creating value with customers.* Boston: Harvard Business School Press.

76. Lei, D., Slocum, J., & Pitts, R. A. 1999. Designing organizations for competitive advantage: The power of unlearning and learning. *Organizational Dynamics,* Winter: 24–38.

77. This section draws upon Zaccaro, S. J., & Bader, P. 2002. E-Leadership and the challenges of leading

e-teams: Minimizing the bad and maximizing the good. *Organizational Dynamics,* 31(4): 377–387.

78. Kirkman, B. L., Rosen, B., Tesluk, P. E., & Gibson, C. B. 2004. The impact of team empowerment on virtual team performance: The moderating role of face-to-face interaction. *Academy of Management Journal,* 47(2): 175–192.

79. The discussion of the advantages and challenges associated with e-teams draws on Zacarro & Bader, op. cit.

80. For a recent study exploring the relationship between team empowerment, face-to-face interaction, and performance in virtual teams, read Kirkman, Rosen, Tesluk, & Gibson, op. cit.

81. For an innovative study on how firms share knowledge with competitors and the performance implications, read Spencer, J. W. 2003. Firms' knowledge sharing strategies in the global innovation system: Empirical evidence from the flat panel display industry. *Strategic Management Journal,* 24(3): 217–235.

82. The examples of Andersen Consulting and Access Health draw upon Hansen, M. T., Nohria, N., & Tierney, T. 1999. What's your strategy for managing knowledge? *Harvard Business Review,* 77(2): 106–118.

83. This discussion draws on Conley, J. G. 2005. Intellectual capital management, Kellogg School of Management and Schulich School of Business, York University, Toronto, KS 2003; Conley, J. G., & Szobocsan, J. 2001. Snow White shows the way. *Managing Intellectual Property,* June: 15–25; Greenspan, A. 2004. Intellectual property rights, The Federal Reserve Board, Remarks by the chairman, February 27; and Teece, D. J. 1998. Capturing value from knowledge assets, *California Management Review,* 40(3): 54–79. The authors would like to thank Professor Theo Peridis, York University, for his contribution to this section.

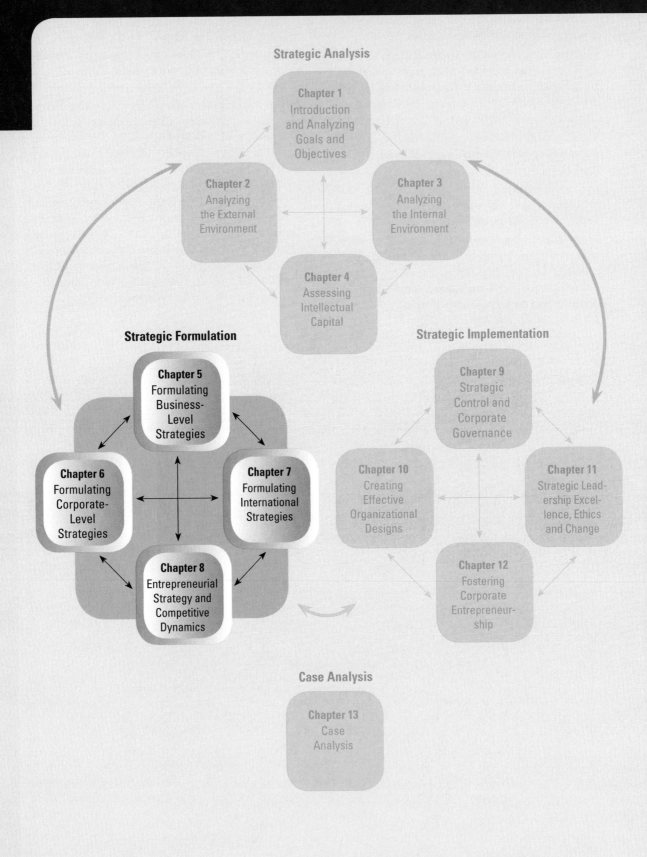

Strategic Analysis

Chapter 1
Introduction and Analyzing Goals and Objectives

Chapter 2
Analyzing the External Environment

Chapter 3
Analyzing the Internal Environment

Chapter 4
Assessing Intellectual Capital

Strategic Formulation

Chapter 5
Formulating Business-Level Strategies

Chapter 6
Formulating Corporate-Level Strategies

Chapter 7
Formulating International Strategies

Chapter 8
Entrepreneurial Strategy and Competitive Dynamics

Strategic Implementation

Chapter 9
Strategic Control and Corporate Governance

Chapter 10
Creating Effective Organizational Designs

Chapter 11
Strategic Leadership Excellence, Ethics and Change

Chapter 12
Fostering Corporate Entrepreneurship

Case Analysis

Chapter 13
Case Analysis

part two

2

Strategic Formulation

chapter 5

Business-Level Strategy:
Creating and Sustaining Competitive Advantages

>learning objectives

After reading this chapter, you should have a good understanding of:

LO1 The central role of competitive advantage in the study of strategic management.

LO2 The three generic strategies: overall cost leadership, differentiation, and focus.

LO3 How the successful attainment of generic strategies can improve a firm's relative power vis-à-vis the five forces that determine an industry's average profitability.

LO4 The pitfalls managers must avoid in striving to attain generic strategies.

LO5 How firms can effectively combine the generic strategies of overall cost leadership and differentiation.

LO6 How Internet-enabled business models are being used to improve strategic positioning.

LO7 The importance of considering the industry life cycle to determine a firm's business-level strategy and its relative emphasis on functional area strategies and value-creating activities.

LO8 The need for turnaround strategies that enable a firm to reposition its competitive position in an industry.

*h*ow firms compete with each other and how they attain and sustain competitive advantages go to the heart of strategic management. In short, the key issue becomes: Why do some firms outperform others and enjoy such advantages over time? This subject, business-level strategy, is the focus of Chapter 5.

The first part of the chapter draws on Michael Porter's framework of generic strategies. He identifies three strategies—overall cost leadership, differentiation, and focus—that firms may apply to outperform their rivals in an industry. We begin by describing each of these strategies and providing examples of firms that have successfully attained them as a means of outperforming competitors in their industry. Next, we address how these strategies help a firm develop a favorable position vis-à-vis the "five forces" (Chapter 2). We then suggest some of the pitfalls that managers must avoid if they are to successfully pursue these generic strategies and discuss the conditions under which firms may effectively combine generic strategies to outperform rivals. We close this section by addressing how competitive strategies should be revised and redeployed in light of the shifts in industry and competitive forces caused by Internet and digital strategies. Here, combination strategies are the most solid because they integrate the new capabilities with sound principles.

The second part of Chapter 5 discusses a vital consideration in the effective use of business-level strategies: industry life cycles. The four stages of the industry life cycle—introduction, growth, maturity, and decline—are indicative of an evolving management process that affects factors such as the market growth rate and the intensity of competition. Accordingly, the stages of an industry's life cycle are an important contingency that managers should take into account when making decisions concerning the optimal overall business-level strategies and the relative emphasis to place on functional capabilities and value-creating activities. At times, firms are faced with performance declines and must find ways to revitalize their competitive positions. The actions followed to do so are referred to as turnaround strategies, which may be needed at any stage of the industry life cycle. However, they occur more frequently during the maturity and decline stages.

Learning from Mistakes

Few companies have been as successful as Starbucks. What began in 1985 as a small coffee shop in Seattle's Pike Place Market has emerged as a megabrand, with almost $8 billion in revenues and more than 13,000 retail outlets worldwide. And, by early 2007, its market capitalization was approaching that of Ford and General Motors *combined*.[1] By doing what? Selling cups of consistent, although richly priced coffee. But as we will see below, even hugely successful companies can stumble.

> Starbucks's strategy is driven by innovation—a promise that is implicit in its well-known and complicated menu. To spur growth, Starbucks places a tremendous amount of effort and expense in developing new products. Also, it continually researches various metrics to determine customer attitudes about new beverages.
>
> However, Starbucks found that there was an unexpected cost to such complex, innovative offerings. Such added complexity increased the time required to serve customers. And, not too surprisingly, demand for its labor-intensive customized drinks declined. *[continued]*

According to Starbucks's research, a "highly satisfied customer" spent $4.42 on average during each visit and visited an average of 7.2 times a month. In contrast, although "unsatisfied customers" spent about the same amount per visit ($3.88), they only averaged about half as many visits (3.9) each month. Further, the company's research found that 75 percent of customers valued friendly, fast, convenient service, while only 15 percent considered new, innovative beverages to be highly important. Clearly, although innovation is a key part of Starbucks's strategy, it loses its value if people must wait too long.*

Since all firms endeavor to enjoy above-average returns (or profits), the question of how management should go about this is a core issue in strategic management. Organizations that have created sustainable competitive advantages don't rely too much on a single strength—as Starbucks apparently did with its overemphasis on innovation. Instead they strive for well-rounded strategies that recognize the tradeoffs associated with their competitive positions. Tradeoffs occur when activities are incompatible (e.g., innovation and fast customer service).[2] Managers who recognize tradeoffs in their strategies and activities enhance the chance that their firm's advantages will be more lasting, or sustainable.

Starbucks's competitive advantage is based on the unique "Starbucks experience"—a superior product served by a knowledgeable salesperson in a friendly social environment with short wait times. Obviously, it is this uniqueness that enables the company to charge a premium price.

In this chapter, we address several forms that competitive advantage may take: overall cost leadership, differentiation, and focus. Next we discuss how Michael Porter's three generic strategies contribute to a firm's competitive advantage and how firms can successfully combine multiple strategies.

Types of Competitive Advantage and Sustainability

Michael Porter presented three generic strategies that a firm can use to overcome the five forces and achieve competitive advantage.[3] Each of Porter's generic strategies has the potential to allow a firm to outperform rivals in their industry. The first, *overall cost leadership*, is based on creating a low-cost-position. Here, a firm must manage the relationships throughout the value chain and lower costs throughout the entire chain. On the other hand, *differentiation* requires a firm to create products and/or services that are unique and valued. Here, the primary emphasis is on "nonprice" attributes for which customers will gladly pay a premium. Finally, with a *focus* strategy, firms must direct their attention (or "focus") toward narrow product lines, buyer segments, or targeted geographic markets and they must attain advantages either through differentiation or cost leadership. Whereas the overall cost leadership and differentiation strategies strive to attain advantages industrywide, focusers build their strategy with a narrow target market in mind. Exhibit 5.1 illustrates these three strategies on two dimensions: competitive advantage and strategic target.

Both casual observation and research support the notion that firms that identify with one or more of the forms of competitive advantage outperform those that do not.[4] There has been a rich history of strategic management research addressing this topic. One study analyzed 1,789 strategic business units and found that businesses combining multiple

---

*As one would expect, Starbucks promptly took corrective action. It streamlined its artisan approach to making drinks by automating and standardizing various elements of the latte manufacturing process. Further, the firm spent $40 million adding staff to cut wait times. It also introduced the Starbucks Card to speed payment. The result: 85 percent of customers were served within three minutes (compared to the prior 54 percent), and customer satisfaction levels increased 20 percent.

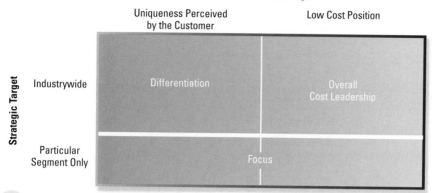

Competitive Advantage

Exhibit 5.1 **Three Generic Strategies**

Source: Adepted with the permission of The Free Press, a division of Simon & Schuster Adult Publishing Group, from *Competitive Strategy: Techniques for Analyzing Industries and Competitors* by Michael E. Porter. Copyright © 1980, 1998 by The Free Press. All rights reserved.

forms of competitive advantage (differentiation and overall cost leadership) outperformed businesses that used only a single form. The lowest performers were those that did not identify with any type of advantage. They were classified as "stuck in the middle." Results of this study are presented in Exhibit 5.2.[5]

Overall Cost Leadership

The first generic strategy is overall cost leadership. Overall cost leadership requires a tight set of interrelated tactics that include:

- Aggressive construction of efficient-scale facilities.
- Vigorous pursuit of cost reductions from experience.
- Tight cost and overhead control.
- Avoidance of marginal customer accounts.
- Cost minimization in all activities in the firm's value chain, such as R&D, service, sales force, and advertising.

Exhibit 5.3 draws on the value-chain concept (see Chapter 3) to provide examples of how a firm can attain an overall cost leadership strategy in its primary and support activities.

overall cost leadership a firm's generic strategy based on appeal to the industrywide market using a competitive advantage based on low cost.

	Competitive Advantage					
	Differentiation and Cost	Differentiation	Cost	Differentiation and Focus	Cost and Focus	Stuck in the Middle
Performance						
Return on investment (%)	35.5	32.9	30.2	17.0	23.7	17.8
Sales growth (%)	15.1	13.5	13.5	16.4	17.5	12.2
Gain in market share (%)	5.3	5.3	5.5	6.1	6.3	4.4
Sample size	123	160	100	141	86	105

Exhibit 5.2 **Competitive Advantage and Business Performance**

	Firm infrastructure	Few management layers to reduce overhead costs.	Standardized accounting practices to minimize personnel required.			

Firm infrastructure: Few management layers to reduce overhead costs. | Standardized accounting practices to minimize personnel required.

Human resource management: Minimize costs associated with employee turnover through effective policies. | Effective orientation and training programs to maximize employee productivity.

Technology development: Effective use of automated technology to reduce scrappage rates. | Expertise in process engineering to reduce manufacturing costs.

Procurement: Effective policy guidelines to ensure low-cost raw materials (with acceptable quality levels). | Shared purchasing operations with other business units.

Margin

Inbound logistics	Operations	Outbound logistics	Marketing and sales	Service
Effective layout of receiving dock operations.	Effective use of quality control inspectors to minimize rework on the final product.	Effective utilization of delivery fleets.	Purchase of media in large blocks. Sales force utilization is maximized by territory management.	Thorough service repair guidelines to minimize repeat maintenance calls. Use of single type of repair vehicle to minimize costs.

Margin

Exhibit 5.3 Value-Chain Activities: Examples of Overall Cost Leadership

Source: Adapted with the permission of The Free Press, a division of Simon & Schuster Adult Publishing Group, from *Competitive Advantage: Creating and Sustaining Superior Performance* by Michael E. Porter. Copyright © 1985, 1998 by Michael E. Porter. All rights reserved.

An important concept related to an overall cost leadership strategy is the experience curve, which refers to how business "learns" to lower costs as it gains experience with production processes. That is, with experience, unit costs of production decline as output increases in most industries. The experience curve concept is discussed in Strategy Spotlight 5.1 and Exhibit 5.4 (page 160).

To generate above-average performance, a firm following an overall cost leadership position must attain **competitive parity** on the basis of differentiation relative to competitors. In other words, a firm achieving parity is similar to its competitors, or "on par," with respect to differentiated products.[6] Competitive parity on the basis of differentiation permits a cost leader to translate cost advantages directly into higher profits than competitors. Thus, the cost leader earns above-average returns.[7]

The failure to attain parity on the basis of differentiation can be illustrated with an example from the automobile industry—the ill-fated Yugo. Below is an excerpt from a speech by J. W. Marriott, Jr., Chairman of the Marriott Corporation:[8]

competitive parity a firm's achievement of similarity, or being "on par," with competitors with respect to low cost, differentiation, or other strategic product characteristic.

> . . . money is a big thing. But it's not the only thing. In the 1980s, a new automobile reached North America from behind the Iron Curtain. It was called the Yugo, and its main attraction was price. About $3,000 each. But the only way they caught on was as the butt of jokes. Remember the guy who told his mechanic, "I want a gas cap for my Yugo." "OK," the mechanic replied, "that sounds like a fair trade."

strategy spotlight

The Experience Curve

The experience curve, developed by the Boston Consulting Group in 1968, is a way of looking at efficiencies developed through a firm's cumulative experience. In its basic form, the experience curve relates production costs to production output. As output doubles, costs decline by 10 percent to 30 percent. For example, if it costs $1 per unit to produce 100 units, the per unit cost will decline to between 70 to 90 cents as output increases to 200 units.

What factors account for this increased efficiency? First, the success of an experience curve strategy depends on the industry life cycle for the product. Early stages of a product's life cycle are typically characterized by rapid gains in technological advances in production efficiency. Most experience curve gains come early in the product life cycle.

Second, the inherent technology of the product offers opportunities for enhancement through gained experience. High-tech products give the best opportunity for gains in production efficiencies. As technology is developed, "value engineering" of innovative production processes is implemented, driving down the per unit costs of production.

Third, a product's sensitivity to price strongly affects a firm's ability to exploit the experience curve. Cutting the price of a product with high demand elasticity—where demand increases when price decreases—rapidly creates consumer purchases of the new product. By cutting prices, a firm can increase demand for its product. The increased demand in turn increases product manufacture, thus increasing the firm's experience in the manufacturing process. So by decreasing price and increasing demand, a firm gains manufacturing experience in that particular product, which drives down per unit production costs.

Fourth, the competitive landscape factors into whether or not a firm might benefit from an experience curve strategy. If other competitors are well positioned in the market, have strong capital resources, and are known to promote their product lines aggressively to gain market share, an experience curve strategy may lead to nothing more than a price war between two or more strong competitors. But if a company is the first to market with the product and has good financial backing, an experience curve strategy may be successful.

In an article in the *Harvard Business Review,* Pankaj Ghemawat recommended answering several questions when considering an experience curve strategy.

- Does my industry exhibit a significant experience curve?
- Have I defined the industry broadly enough to take into account interrelated experience?
- What is the precise source of cost reduction?
- Can my company keep cost reductions proprietary?
- Is demand sufficiently stable to justify using the experience curve?
- Is cumulated output doubling fast enough for the experience curve to provide much strategic leverage?
- Do the returns from an experience curve strategy warrant the risks of technological obsolescence?
- Is demand price-sensitive?
- Are there well-financed competitors who are already following an experience curve strategy or are likely to adopt one if my company does?

Michael Porter suggested, however, that the experience curve is not useful in all situations. Whether or not to base strategy on the experience curve depends on what specifically causes the decline in costs. For example, if costs drop from efficient production facilities and not necessarily from experience, the experience curve is not helpful. But as Sharon Oster pointed out in her book on competitive analysis, the experience curve can help managers analyze costs when efficient learning, rather than efficient machinery, is the source of cost savings.

Sources: Ghemawat, P. 1985. Building strategy on the experience curve. *Harvard Business Review,* March–April: 143–149; Porter, M. E. 1996. *On competition.* Boston: Harvard Business Review Press; and Oster, S. M. 1994. *Modern competitive analysis* (2nd ed.). New York: Oxford University Press.

Yugo was offering a lousy value proposition. The cars literally fell apart before your eyes. And the lesson was simple. Price is just one component of value. No matter how good the price, the most cost-sensitive consumer won't buy a bad product.

Next, we discuss some examples of how firms enhance cost leadership position.

While other managed care providers were having a string of weak years, WellPoint, based in Thousand Oaks, California, has had a number of banner years and recently enjoyed an annual profit growth of over 50 percent to $3.1 billion over the past three years.[9] Chairman Leonard Schaeffer credits the company's focus on innovation for both

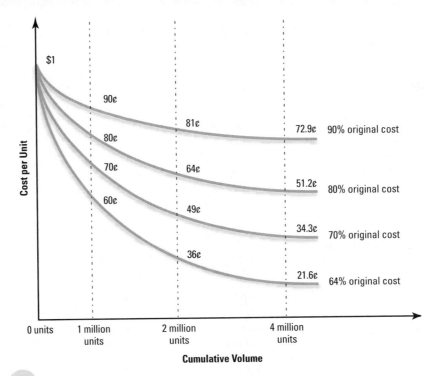

Exhibit 5.4 Comparing Experience Curve Effects

expanding revenues and cutting costs. Recently, for example, WellPoint asked the Food and Drug Administration (FDA) to make the allergy drug Claritin available over the counter. Surprisingly, this may be the first time that an insurer has approached the FDA with this type of request. Schaeffer claimed, "They were kind of stunned," but the FDA agreed to consider it. It was a smart move for WellPoint. If approved as an over-the-counter drug, Claritin would reduce patient visits to the doctor and eliminate the need for prescriptions—two reimbursable expenses for which WellPoint would otherwise be responsible.

Stephen Sanger, CEO of General Mills, recently came up with an idea that helped his firm cut costs.[10] To improve productivity, he sent technicians to watch pit crews during a NASCAR race. That experience inspired the techies to figure out how to reduce the time it takes to switch a plant line from five hours to 20 minutes. This provided an important lesson: Many interesting benchmarking examples can take place far outside of an industry. Often, process improvements involve identifying the best practices in other industries and adapting them for implementation in your own firm. After all, when firms benchmark competitors in their own industry, the end result is often copying and playing catch-up.[11]

A business that strives for a low-cost advantage must attain an absolute cost advantage relative to its rivals. This is typically accomplished by offering a no-frills product or service to a broad target market using standardization to derive the greatest benefits from economies of scale and experience. However, such a strategy may fail if a firm is unable to attain parity on important dimensions of differentiation such as quick responses to customer requests for services or design changes. Strategy Spotlight 5.2 discusses Ryanair—a firm that has developed a very unique overall cost leadership strategy. One might say that it "one upped" Southwest Airlines!

Ryanair: A Highly Effective Overall Cost Leadership Strategy

Michael O'Leary, CEO of Ryanair Holdings PLC, makes no apologies for his penny-pinching. Want to check luggage? You'll pay up to $9.50 per bag for the privilege. Expecting free drinks and snacks? You'll be disappointed. Even a bottle of water will cost you $3.40. And it is not just the passengers who are affected. Flight crews buy their own uniforms, and staff at Ryanair's Spartan Dublin Airport headquarters must supply their own pens. After a customer sued Ryanair for charging $34 for the use of a wheelchair, the company added a 63 cent "wheelchair levy" to every ticket!

Low-fare U.S. carriers have taken the opposite approach of Ryanair by adding perks such as leather seats, live television, and business class. "All of the low-cost carriers' costs have gotten a little out of control," says Tim Sieber, general manager of The Boyd Group, an Evergreen (Colorado) aviation consultant. Clearly Ryanair hasn't followed its industry peers.

Ryanair has been extremely successful. For 2006, its revenues were $2.1 billion—only one-seventh the size of British Airways (BA). However, its operating margins are 22.7 percent—three times as large as BA's. Not too surprisingly, Ryanair's market capitalization of nearly $14 billion (in early 2007) is more than that of British Airways ($12.5 billion), and, incidentally, even more than Southwest Airlines ($12.1 billion). The latter, of course, has been the industry role model of low-cost strategies.

What is O'Leary's secret? He thinks like a retailer and charges for every little thing. Imagine the seat as a cell phone: It comes free, or nearly free, but its owner winds up spending money on all sorts of services.

However, what O'Leary loses in seat revenue he more than makes up by turning both his planes and the Ryanair Web site into stores brimming with irresistible goodies, even as he charges for such "perks" as priority boarding and assigned seating.

Sounds outrageous? Probably so, but the strategy is clearly working. Although its average fare is $53, compared with $92 for Southwest Airlines, Ryanair's net margins are, at 18 percent—more than double the 7 percent achieved by Southwest. Says Nick van den Brul, an aviation analyst: "Ryanair is Wal-Mart with wings." As O'Leary says, "You want luxury? Go somewhere else."

A few other Ryanair practices include:

- Flight attendants sell digital cameras ($137.50) and iPocket MP3 players ($165). Soon-to-come is on-board gaming and cell-phone service.

- The seats don't recline, seat-back pockets have been removed to cut cleaning time and speed turnaround of the planes, there's no entertainment, and seat-back trays will soon carry ads.

- Ryanair sells more than 98 percent of its tickets online. Its Web site offers insurance, hotels, car rentals, and more—even online bingo.

Sources: Capell, K. 2006. Wal-Mart with Wings. *BusinessWeek*. November 27: 44–45; Kumar, N. 2006. Strategies to fight low-cost rivals. *Harvard Business Review*, 84(12): 104–113; and, *Ryanair Annual Report*, 2006.

Overall Cost Leadership: Improving Competitive Position vis-à-vis the Five Forces   An overall low-cost position enables a firm to achieve above-average returns despite strong competition. It protects a firm against rivalry from competitors, because lower costs allow a firm to earn returns even if its competitors eroded their profits through intense rivalry. A low-cost position also protects firms against powerful buyers. Buyers can exert power to drive down prices only to the level of the next most efficient producer. Also, a low-cost position provides more flexibility to cope with demands from powerful suppliers for input cost increases. The factors that lead to a low-cost position also provide substantial entry barriers from economies of scale and cost advantages. Finally, a low-cost position puts the firm in a favorable position with respect to substitute products introduced by new and existing competitors.

A few examples will illustrate these points. Ryanair's close attention to costs helps to protect them from buyer power and intense rivalry from competitors. Thus, they are able to drive down costs and enjoy relatively high power over their customers. By increasing its productivity and lowering unit costs, General Mills (and its competitors in that industry) enjoy greater scale economies and erect higher entry barriers for others who want to enter the industry. Finally, as competitors such as WellPoint lower costs through means such as

> **>LO3**
>
> How the successful attainment of generic strategies can improve a firm's relative power vis-à-vis the five forces that determine an industry's average profitability.

petitioning the FDA to make certain drugs available over the counter, they become less vulnerable to substitutes such as Internet-based competitors.

Potential Pitfalls of Overall Cost Leadership Strategies   Potential pitfalls of overall cost leadership strategy include:

>LO4

The pitfalls managers must avoid in striving to attain generic strategies.

- ***Too much focus on one or a few value-chain activities.*** Would you consider a person to be astute if he cancelled his newspaper subscription and quit eating out to save money, but then "maxed out" several credit cards, requiring him to pay hundreds of dollars a month in interest charges? Of course not. Similarly, firms need to pay attention to all activities in the value chain. Too often managers make big cuts in operating expenses, but don't question year-to-year spending on capital projects. Or managers may decide to cut selling and marketing expenses but ignore manufacturing expenses. Managers should explore *all* value-chain activities, including relationships among them, as candidates for cost reductions.

- ***All rivals share a common input or raw material.*** Here, firms are vulnerable to price increases in the factors of production. Since they're competing on costs, they are less able to pass on price increases, because customers can take their business to rivals who have lower prices. Consider the hardship experienced by fertilizer producers in early 2001 when energy prices spiked.[12] A quadrupling of prices to $10 per thousand cubic feet of natural gas forced firms to shut down nearly half of their production capacity. Why? Natural gas accounts for over 70 percent of the fertilizer's cost. According to Betty-Ann Hegge, senior vice president of Potash Corporation of Saskatchewan, Inc., North America's second largest producer, "Many companies are not even covering their cash costs at these prices."

- ***The strategy is imitated too easily.*** One of the common pitfalls of a cost-leadership strategy is that a firm's strategy may consist of value-creating activities that are easy to imitate.[13] Such was the case with online brokers in recent years.[14] As of early 2001, there were about 140 online brokers, hardly symbolic of an industry where imitation is extremely difficult. But according to Henry McVey, financial services analyst at Morgan Stanley, "We think you need five to ten" online brokers.

  What are some of the dynamics? First, although online brokers were geared up to handle 1.2 million trades a day, volume had shrunk to about 834,000—a 30 percent drop. Thus, competition for business intensified. Second, when the stock market is down, many investors trust their instincts less and seek professional guidance from brokerages that offer differentiated services. Eric Rajendra of A. T. Kearney, an international consulting company, claimed, "The current (online broker) model is inadequate for the pressures the industry is facing now."

- ***A lack of parity on differentiation.*** As noted earlier, firms striving to attain cost leadership advantages must obtain a level of parity on differentiation. Organizations providing online degree programs to adults working full-time may offer low prices. However, they may not be successful unless they can offer instruction that is perceived as comparable to traditional providers. For them, parity can be achieved on differentiation dimensions such as reputation and quality and through signaling mechanisms such as national and regional accreditation agencies.

- ***Erosion of cost advantages when the pricing information available to customers increases.*** This is becoming a more significant challenge as the Internet dramatically increases both the quantity and volume of information available to consumers about pricing and cost structures. Life insurance firms offering whole life insurance provide an interesting example.[15] One study found that for each 10 percent increase in consumer use of the Internet, there is a corresponding reduction in insurance prices to consumers of 3 to 5 percent. Recently, the nationwide savings (or, alternatively, reduced revenues to providers) was between $115 and $125 million annually.

Differentiation

As the name implies, a **differentiation strategy** consists of creating differences in the firm's product or service offering by creating something that is perceived *industrywide* as unique and valued by customers. Differentiation can take many forms:

> **differentiation strategy** a firm's generic strategy based on creating differences in the firm's product or service offering by creating something that is perceived *industrywide* as unique and valued by customers.

- Prestige or brand image (Adam's Mark hotels, BMW automobiles).[16]
- Technology (Martin guitars, Marantz stereo components, North Face camping equipment).
- Innovation (Medtronic medical equipment, Nokia cellular phones).
- Features (Cannondale mountain bikes, Honda Goldwing motorcycles).
- Customer service (Nordstrom department stores, Sears lawn equipment retailing).
- Dealer network (Lexus automobiles, Caterpillar earthmoving equipment).

Exhibit 5.5 draws on the concept of the value chain as an example of how firms may differentiate themselves in primary and support activities.

Firms may differentiate themselves along several different dimensions at once. For example, BMW is known for its high prestige, superior engineering, and high-quality automobiles. And, Harley-Davidson differentiates on image and dealer services.[17]

Firm infrastructure	Superior MIS—To integrate value-creating activities to improve quality.	Facilities that promote firm image.	Widely respected CEO enhances firm reputation.	
Human resource management	Programs to attract talented engineers and scientists.		Provide training and incentives to ensure a strong customer service orientation.	
Technology development	Superior material handling and sorting technology.		Excellent applications engineering support.	
Procurement	Purchase of high-quality components to enhance product image.		Use of most prestigious outlets.	

Inbound logistics	Operations	Outbound logistics	Marketing and sales	Service
Superior material handling operations to minimize damage. Quick transfer of inputs to manufacturing process.	Flexibility and speed in responding to changes in manufacturing specifications. Low defect rates to improve quality.	Accurate and responsive order processing. Effective product replenishment to reduce customer inventory.	Creative and innovative advertising programs. Fostering of personal relationship with key customers.	Rapid response to customer service requests. Complete inventory of replacement parts and supplies.

Margin

Exhibit 5.5 Value-Chain Activities: Examples of Differentiation

Source: Adapted with the permission of The Free Press, a division of Simon & Schuster Adult Publishing Group, from *Competitive Advantage: Creating and Sustaining Superior Performance* by Michael E. Porter. Copyright © 1985, 1998 by Michael E. Porter. All rights reserved.

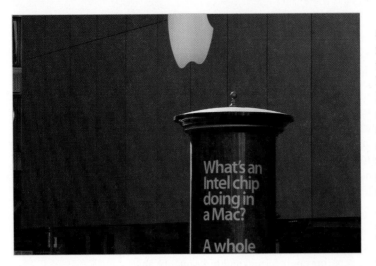

● Through effective advertising, Intel strives to further differentiate its products. This advertisement touts Apple's use of its processors in their newest line of computers. An Apple store is behind the ad.

Firms achieve and sustain differentiation advantages and attain above-average performance when their price premiums exceed the extra costs incurred in being unique.[18] For example, both BMW and Harley-Davidson must increase consumer costs to offset added marketing expenses. Thus, a differentiator will always seek out ways of distinguishing itself from similar competitors to justify price premiums greater than the costs incurred by differentiating. Clearly, a differentiator cannot ignore costs. After all, its premium prices would be eroded by a markedly inferior cost position. Therefore, it must attain a level of cost *parity* relative to competitors. Differentiators can do this by reducing costs in all areas that do not affect differentiation. Porsche, for example, invests heavily in engine design—an area in which its customers demand excellence—but it is less concerned and spends fewer resources in the design of the instrument panel or the arrangement of switches on the radio.[19]

Many companies successfully follow a differentiation strategy.[20] For example, FedEx's CEO and founder, Fred Smith, claims that the key to his firm's success is innovation.[21] He contends his management team didn't understand their real goal when they started the firm in 1971: "We thought that we were selling the transportation of goods; in fact, we were selling peace of mind." To that end, they now provide each driver with a handheld computer and a transmitting device that makes it possible for customers to track their packages right from their desktop PCs.

Lexus, a division of Toyota, provides an example of how a firm can strengthen its differentiation strategy by *achieving integration at multiple points along the value chain.*[22] Although the luxury car line was not introduced until the late 1980s, by the early 1990s the cars had already soared to the top of J. D. Power & Associates's customer satisfaction ratings.

> In the spirit of benchmarking, one of Lexus's competitors hired Custom Research Inc. (CRI), a marketing research firm, to find out why Lexus owners were so satisfied. CRI conducted a series of focus groups in which Lexus drivers eagerly offered anecdotes about the special care they experienced from their dealers. It became clear that, although Lexus was manufacturing cars with few mechanical defects, it was the extra care shown by the sales and service staff that resulted in satisfied customers. Such pampering is reflected in the feedback from one customer who claimed she never had a problem with her Lexus. However, upon further probing, she said, "Well, I suppose you could call the four times they had to replace the windshield a 'problem.' But frankly, they took care of it so well and always gave me a loaner car, so I never really considered it a problem until you mentioned it now." An insight gained in CRI's research is that perceptions of product quality (design, engineering, and manufacturing) can be strongly influenced by downstream activities in the value chain (marketing and sales, service).

Strategy Spotlight 5.3 discusses how three firms have been successful through effective differentiation strategies. Similar to Starbucks, these firms have taken commodity-type products and converted them to high-priced goods.

Differentiation: Improving Competitive Position vis-à-vis the Five Forces   Differentiation provides protection against rivalry since brand loyalty lowers customer sensitivity to price and raises customer switching costs. By increasing a firm's margins, differentiation also avoids the need for a low-cost position. Higher entry barriers result because of customer

Successful Differentiators Who Follow the Starbucks Model

Starbucks has been extremely successful in turning the purchase of coffee into a gourmet event. Others have copied the model and several café concepts have sprung up. Here are three of them:

- Ten high-end **Ethel's Chocolate Lounges** located in the Chicago area now sell individual chocolates with flavors such as mojito, expresso, and cinna-swirl for $1.50 apiece. When customers visit the frilly pink-and-chocolate-brown cafes, they can spend $15 for a chocolate fondue for two or enjoy tea and truffles. Some of the cache might erode if customers knew that Ethel's was owned by M&M maker Mars Inc.

Sources: Danigelis, A. 2006. Customers find local hereo: Cereality. www.fastcompany.com. np; Caplan, J. 2006. In a real crunch. *Inside Business*, July: A37–A38; Luna, N. 2006. Sprinkles bakery to open in Corona del Mar. *The Orange County Register*, May 18, np; and Gottfried, M. 2006. What hath Starbucks wrought? *Forbes*. April 10: 52.

- **Sprinkles Cupcakes** opened a chic, minimalist store in Beverly Hills, California. It sells flavors like lemon coconut and chai latte for $3.25 a cupcake. Here, the ingredients are not low-priced commodities—the vanilla is not just vanilla but rather Madagascar Bourbon Vanilla. The cupcakes were featured on "The Oprah Winfrey Show." The next day, cupcake sales increased 50 percent!

- **Cereality,** a new chain with locations in Illinois, Pennsylvania, and Arizona has happily found that people are willing to pay $3.50 for a bowl of breakfast cereal. For that, its pajama-clad employees will serve you two scoops of cereal, one topping (fruit, nuts, marshmallows, etc.) and milk. The cereal is blended to order and is served in containers similar to Chinese food-style paper cartons. The most popular blend is a $4 concoction of Life cereal, almonds, bananas, and honey.

loyalty and the firm's ability to provide uniqueness in its products or services. Differentiation also provides higher margins that enable a firm to deal with supplier power. And it reduces buyer power, because buyers lack comparable alternatives and are therefore less price sensitive. Supplier power is also decreased because there is a certain amount of prestige associated with being the supplier to a producer of highly differentiated products and services. Last, differentiation enhances customer loyalty, thus reducing the threat from substitutes.

Our examples illustrate these points. Lexus has enjoyed enhanced power over buyers because its top J. D. Power ranking makes buyers more willing to pay a premium price. This lessens rivalry, since buyers become less price-sensitive. The prestige associated with its brand name also lowers supplier power since margins are high. Suppliers would probably desire to be associated with prestige brands, thus lessening their incentives to drive up prices. Finally, the loyalty and "peace of mind" associated with a service provider such as FedEx makes such firms less vulnerable to rivalry or substitute products and services.

Potential Pitfalls of Differentiation Strategies   Potential pitfalls of differentiation strategy include:

- *Uniqueness that is not valuable.* A differentiation strategy must provide unique bundles of products and/or services that customers value highly. It's not enough just to be "different." An example is Gibson's Dobro bass guitar. Gibson came up with a unique idea: Design and build an acoustic bass guitar with sufficient sound volume so that amplification wasn't necessary. The problem with other acoustic bass guitars was that they did not project enough volume because of the low-frequency bass notes. By adding a resonator plate on the body of the traditional acoustic bass, Gibson increased the sound volume. Gibson believed this product would serve a particular niche market—bluegrass and folk artists who played in small group "jams" with other acoustic musicians. Unfortunately, Gibson soon discovered that its targeted market was content with their existing options: an upright bass amplified with a microphone or an acoustic electric guitar. Thus, Gibson developed a unique product, but it was not perceived as valuable by its potential customers.[23]

- *Too much differentiation.* Firms may strive for quality or service that is higher than customers desire. Thus, they become vulnerable to competitors who provide an appropriate level of quality at a lower price. For example, consider the expensive Mercedes-Benz S-Class, which ranges in price between $75,000 and $125,000.[24] *Consumer Reports* described it as "sumptuous," "quiet and luxurious," and a "delight to drive." The magazine also considered it to be the least reliable sedan available in the United States. According to David Champion, who runs their testing program, the problems are electronic. "The engineers have gone a little wild," he says. "They've put every bell and whistle that they think of, and sometimes they don't have the attention to detail to make these systems work." Some features include: a computer-driven suspension that reduces body roll as the vehicle whips around a corner; cruise control that automatically slows the car down if it gets too close to another car; and seats that are adjustable 14 ways and that are ventilated by a system that uses eight fans.

- *Too high a price premium.* This pitfall is quite similar to too much differentiation. Customers may desire the product, but they are repelled by the price premium. For example, Duracell (a division of Gillette) recently charged too much for batteries.[25] The firm tried to sell consumers on its superior quality products, but the mass market wasn't convinced. Why? The price differential was simply too high. At a CVS drugstore just one block from Gillette's headquarters, a four-pack of Energizer AA batteries was on sale at $2.99 compared with a Duracell four-pack at $4.59. Duracell's market share dropped 2 percent in a recent two-year period, and its profits declined over 30 percent. Clearly, the price/performance proposition Duracell offered customers was not accepted.

- *Differentiation that is easily imitated.* As we noted in Chapter 3, resources that are easily imitated cannot lead to sustainable advantages. Similarly, firms may strive for, and even attain, a differentiation strategy that is successful for a time. However, the advantages are eroded through imitation. In Strategy Spotlight 5.3 we discussed Cereality's innovative differentiation strategy of offering a wide variety of cereals.[26] As one would expect, once their idea proved successful, competitors entered the market because much of the initial risk had already been taken. Rivals include an Iowa City restaurant named the Cereal Cabinet, the Cereal Bowl in Miami, and Bowls: A Cereal Joint in Gainesville, Florida. Says David Roth, one of Cereality's founders: "With any good business idea, you're faced with people who see you've cracked the code and who try to cash in on it."

- *Dilution of brand identification through product-line extensions.* Firms may erode their quality brand image by adding products or services with lower prices and less quality. Although this can increase short-term revenues, it may be detrimental in the long run. Consider Gucci.[27] In the 1980s Gucci wanted to capitalize on its prestigious brand name by launching an aggressive strategy of revenue growth. It added a set of lower-priced canvas goods to its product line. It also pushed goods heavily into department stores and duty-free channels and allowed its name to appear on a host of licensed items such as watches, eyeglasses, and perfumes. In the short term, this strategy worked. Sales soared. However, the strategy carried a high price. Gucci's indiscriminate approach to expanding its products and channels tarnished its sterling brand. Sales of its high-end goods (with higher profit margins) fell, causing profits to decline.

- *Perceptions of differentiation may vary between buyers and sellers.* The issue here is that "beauty is in the eye of the beholder." Companies must realize that although they may perceive their products and services as differentiated, their customers may view them as commodities. Indeed, in today's marketplace, many products and services have been reduced to commodities.[28] Thus, a firm could overprice its offerings and lose margins altogether if it has to lower prices to reflect market realities.

Overall Cost Leadership:

- Too much focus on one or a few value-chain activities.
- All rivals share a common input or raw material.
- The strategy is imitated too easily.
- A lack of parity on differentiation.
- Erosion of cost advantages when the pricing information available to customers increases.

Differentiation:

- Uniqueness that is not valuable.
- Too much differentiation.
- The price premium is too high.
- Differentiation that is easily imitated.
- Dilution of brand identification through product-line extensions.
- Perceptions of differentiation may vary between buyers and sellers.

Exhibit 5.6
Potential Pitfalls of Overall Cost Leadership and Differentiation Strategies

Exhibit 5.6 summarizes the pitfalls of overall cost leadership and differentiation strategies. In addressing the pitfalls associated with these two generic strategies there is one common, underlying theme. Managers must be aware of the dangers associated with concentrating so much on one strategy that they fail to attain parity on the other.

Focus

A **focus strategy** is based on the choice of a narrow competitive scope within an industry. A firm following this strategy selects a segment or group of segments and tailors its strategy to serve them. The essence of focus is the exploitation of a particular market niche. As you might expect, narrow focus itself (like merely "being different" as a differentiator) is simply not sufficient for above-average performance. The focus strategy, as indicated in Exhibit 5.1, has two variants. In a cost focus, a firm strives to create a cost advantage in its target segment. In a differentiation focus, a firm seeks to differentiate in its target market. Both variants of the focus strategy rely on providing better service than broad-based competitors who are trying to serve the focuser's target segment. Cost focus exploits differences in cost behavior in some segments, while differentiation focus exploits the special needs of buyers in other segments.

Let's look at examples of two firms that have successfully implemented focus strategies. Network Appliance (NA) has developed a more cost-effective way to store and distribute computer files.[29] Its larger rival, EMC, makes mainframe-style products priced over $1 million that store files and accommodate Internet traffic. NA makes devices that cost under $200,000 for particular storage jobs such as caching (temporary storage) of Internet content. Focusing on such narrow segments has certainly paid off for NA; it has posted a remarkable 20 straight quarters of revenue growth.

Bessemer Trust competes in the private banking industry.[30] A differentiation focuser, it targets families with a minimum of $5 million in assets, who desire both capital preservation and wealth accumulation. In other words, these are not people who want to put all their "eggs in a dot-com basket." Bessemer configures its activities for highly personalized service by assigning one account officer for every 14 families. Meetings are more likely to be held at a client's ranch or yacht than in Bessemer's office. Bessemer offers a wide range of customized services, such as investment management, estate administration, oversight of oil and gas investments, and accounting for race horses and aircraft. Despite the industry's most generous compensation of account officers and the highest personnel cost as a percentage of operating expenses, Bessemer's focused differentiation strategy is estimated to yield the highest return on equity in the industry.

focus strategy a firm's generic strategy based on appeal to a narrow market segment within an industry.

Focus: Improving Competitive Position vis-à-vis the Five Forces Focus requires that a firm either have a low-cost position with its strategic target, high differentiation, or both. As we discussed with regard to cost and differentiation strategies, these positions provide defenses against each competitive force. Focus is also used to select niches that are least vulnerable to substitutes or where competitors are weakest.

Let's look at our examples to illustrate some of these points. First, Bessemer Trust experienced less rivalry and lower buyer bargaining power by providing products and services to a targeted market segment that was less price-sensitive. New rivals would have difficulty attracting customers away from Bessemer based only on lower prices. Similarly, the brand image and quality that this brand evoked heightened rivals entry barriers. Additionally, we could reasonably speculate that Bessemer Trust enjoyed some protection against substitute products and services because of their relatively high reputation, brand image, and customer loyalty. With regard to the strategy of cost focus, Network Appliances, the successful rival to EMC in the computer storage industry, was better able to absorb pricing increases from suppliers as a result of its lower cost structure, reducing supplier power.

Potential Pitfalls of Focus Strategies Potential pitfalls of focus strategies include:

- ***Erosion of cost advantages within the narrow segment.*** The advantages of a cost focus strategy may be fleeting if the cost advantages are eroded over time. For example, Dell's pioneering direct selling model in the personal computer industry, while still the industry standard, is constantly being challenged and eroded by rivals such as Hewlett Packard as they gain experience with Dell's distribution method. Similarly, other firms have seen their profit margins drop as competitors enter their product segment.
- ***Even product and service offerings that are highly focused are subject to competition from new entrants and from imitation.*** Some firms adopting a focus strategy may enjoy temporary advantages because they select a small niche with few rivals. However, their advantages may be short-lived. A notable example is the multitude of dot-com firms that specialize in very narrow segments such as pet supplies, ethnic foods, and vintage automobile accessories. The entry barriers tend to be low, there is little buyer loyalty, and competition becomes intense. And since the marketing strategies and technologies employed by most rivals are largely nonproprietary, imitation is easy. Over time, revenues fall, profits margins are squeezed, and only the strongest players survive the shakeout.
- ***Focusers can become too focused to satisfy buyer needs.*** Some firms attempting to attain competitive advantages through a focus strategy may have too narrow a product or service. Examples include many retail firms. Hardware chains such as Ace and True Value are losing market share to rivals such as Lowe's and Home Depot who offer a full line of home and garden equipment and accessories. And given the enormous purchasing power of the national chains, it would be difficult for such specialty retailers to attain parity on costs.

Combination Strategies: Integrating Overall Low Cost and Differentiation

>LO5

How firms can effectively combine the generic strategies of overall cost leadership and differentiation.

There has been ample evidence—in the popular press and in research studies—about the strategic benefits of combining generic strategies. In the beginning of this section, we provided some evidence from a study of nearly 1,800 strategic business units (see Exhibit 5.2) to support this contention. As you will recall, the highest performers were businesses that attained both cost and differentiation advantages, followed by those that had either one or the other. Those strategic business units that had the lowest performance identified with neither generic strategy; that is, they were "stuck in the middle." Results from other studies are consistent with these findings across a wide variety of industries including low-profit industries, the paints and allied products industry, the Korean electronics industry, the apparel industry, and the screw machine products industry.[31]

Perhaps the primary benefit to firms that integrate low-cost and differentiation strategies is that it is generally harder for rivals to duplicate or imitate. This strategy enables a firm to provide two types of value to customers: differentiated attributes (e.g., high quality, brand identification, reputation) and lower prices (because of the firm's lower costs in value-creating activities). The goal becomes one of providing unique value to customers in an efficient manner.[32] Some firms are able to attain both types of advantages simultaneously. For example, superior quality can lead to lower costs because of less need for rework in manufacturing, fewer warranty claims, a reduced need for customer service personnel to resolve customer complaints, and so forth. Thus, the benefits of combining advantages can be additive, instead of merely involving trade-offs. Next, we consider three approaches to combining overall low-cost and differentiation.

Automated and Flexible Manufacturing Systems   Given the advances in manufacturing technologies such as CAD/CAM (computer aided design and computer aided manufacturing) as well as information technologies, many firms have been able to manufacture unique products in relatively small quantities at lower costs—a concept known as "mass customization."[33]

Let's consider Andersen Windows of Bayport, Minnesota—a $1 billion manufacturer of windows for the building industry.[34] Until about 20 years ago, Andersen was a mass producer, in small batches, of a variety of standard windows. However, to meet changing customer needs, Andersen kept adding to its product line. The result was catalogs of ever-increasing size and a bewildering set of choices for both homeowners and contractors. Over a 6-year period, the number of products tripled, price quotes took several hours, and the error rate increased. This not only damaged the company's reputation, but also added to its manufacturing expenses.

To bring about a major change, Andersen developed an interactive computer version of its paper catalogs that it sold to distributors and retailers. Salespersons can now customize each window to meet the customer's needs, check the design for structural soundness, and provide a price quote. The system is virtually error free, customers get exactly what they want, and the time to develop the design and furnish a quotation has been cut by 75 percent. Each showroom computer is connected to the factory, and customers are assigned a code number that permits them to track the order. The manufacturing system has been developed to use some common finished parts, but it also allows considerable variation in the final products. Despite its huge investment, Andersen has been able to lower costs, enhance quality and variety, and improve its response time to customers.

Below are some other examples of how flexible production systems have enabled firms to successfully engage in mass customization for their customers:[35]

- At Nikeid.com, customers can design an athletic or casual shoe to their specifications online, selecting almost every element of the shoe from the material of the sole to the color of the shoelace.
- Eleuria sells custom perfumes. Each product is created in response to a user profile constructed from responses to a survey about habits and preferences. Eleuria provides a sample at modest cost to verify fit.
- Lands' End offers customized shirts and pants. Consumers specify style parameters, measurements, and fabrics through the company's Web site. These settings are saved so that returning users can easily order a duplicate item.
- Cannondale permits consumers to specify the parameters that define a road bike frame, including custom colors and inscriptions. The user specifies the parameters on the company's Web site and then arranges for delivery through a dealer.

Exploiting the Profit Pool Concept for Competitive Advantage   A profit pool can be defined as the total profits in an industry at all points along the industry's value chain.[36] Although the concept is relatively straightforward, the structure of the profit pool

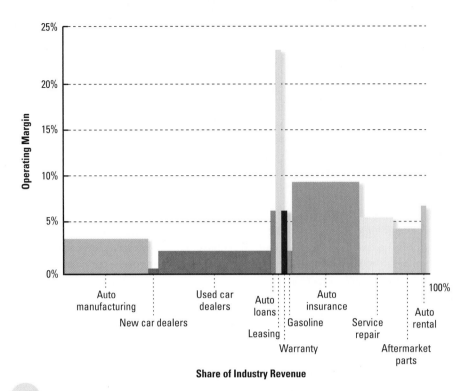

Share of Industry Revenue

Exhibit 5.7 The U.S. Automobile Industry's Profit Pool

Source: Adapted and reprinted by permission of *Harvard Business Review,* Exhibit from "Profit Pools: A Fresh Look at Strategy," by O. Gadiesh and J. L. Gilbert, May–June 1998. Copyright © 1999 by the Harvard Business School Publishing Corporation; all rights reserved.

can be complex. The potential pool of profits will be deeper in some segments of the value chain than in others, and the depths will vary within an individual segment. Segment profitability may vary widely by customer group, product category, geographic market, or distribution channel. Additionally, the pattern of profit concentration in an industry is very often different from the pattern of revenue generation.

Consider the automobile industry profit pool in Exhibit 5.7. Here we see little relationship between the generation of revenues and capturing of profits. While manufacturing generates most of the revenue, this value activity is far smaller profitwise than other value activities such as financing and extended warranty operations. So while a car manufacturer may be under tremendous pressure to produce cars efficiently, much of the profit (at least proportionately) can be captured in the aforementioned downstream operations. Thus, a carmaker would be ill-advised to focus solely on manufacturing and leave downstream operations to others through outsourcing.

Coordinating the "Extended" Value Chain by Way of Information Technology

Many firms have achieved success by integrating activities throughout the "extended value chain" by using information technology to link their own value chain with the value chains of their customers and suppliers. As noted in Chapter 3, this approach enables a firm to add value not only through its own value-creating activities, but also for its customers and suppliers.

Such a strategy often necessitates redefining the industry's value chain. A number of years ago, Wal-Mart took a close look at its industry's value chain and decided to reframe the competitive challenge.[37] Although its competitors were primarily focused on retailing—merchandising and promotion—Wal-Mart determined that it was not so much in the retailing industry as in the transportation logistics and communications industries. Here, linkages in the extended value chain became central. That became Wal-Mart's chosen battleground. By redefining the rules of competition that played to its strengths, Wal-Mart has attained competitive advantages and dominates its industry.

Integrated Overall Low-Cost and Differentiation Strategies: Improving Competitive Position vis-à-vis the Five Forces   Firms that successfully integrate both differentiation and cost advantages create an enviable position. For example, Wal-Mart's integration of information systems, logistics, and transportation helps it to drive down costs and provide outstanding product selection. This dominant competitive position, serves to erect high entry barriers to potential competitors that have neither the financial nor physical resources to compete head-to-head. Wal-Mart's size—$316 billion in 2006 sales—provides the chain with enormous bargaining power over suppliers. Its low pricing and wide selection reduce the power of buyers (its customers), because there are relatively few competitors that can provide a comparable cost/value proposition. This reduces the possibility of intense head-to-head rivalry, such as protracted price wars. Finally, Wal-Mart's overall value proposition makes potential substitute products (e.g., Internet competitors) a less viable threat.

Pitfalls of Integrated Overall Cost Leadership and Differentiation Strategies   The pitfalls of integrated overall cost leadership and differentiation include:

- ***Firms that fail to attain both strategies may end up with neither and become "stuck in the middle."*** A key issue in strategic management is the creation of competitive advantages that enable a firm to enjoy above-average returns. Some firms may become "stuck in the middle" if they try to attain both cost and differentiation advantages. An example that we are all familiar with would be the Big 3 U.S. automobile makers. They are plagued by very expensive "legacy costs" associated with pension and health care obligations. And, they suffer from long-term customer perceptions of mediocre quality—inferior to their European and Japanese rivals. The troubling quality perceptions persist despite the fact that the Big 3 has attained approximate parity with their Japanese and European competitors in recent J. D. Power surveys.

- ***Underestimating the challenges and expenses associated with coordinating value-creating activities in the extended value chain.*** Successfully integrating activities across a firm's value chain with the value chain of suppliers and customers involves a significant investment in financial and human resources. Managers must not underestimate the expenses linked to technology investment, managerial time and commitment, and the involvement and investment required by the firm's customers and suppliers. The firm must be confident that it can generate a sufficient scale of operations and revenues to justify all associated expenses.

- ***Miscalculating sources of revenue and profit pools in the firm's industry.*** Firms may fail to accurately assess sources of revenue and profits in their value chain. This can occur for several reasons. For example, a manager may be biased due to his or her functional area background, work experiences, and educational background. If the manager's background is in engineering, he or she might perceive that proportionately greater revenue and margins were being created in manufacturing, product, and process design than a person whose background is in a "downstream" value-chain activity such as marketing and sales. Or politics could make managers "fudge" the numbers to favor their area of operations. This would make them responsible for a greater proportion of the firm's profits, thus improving their bargaining position.

A related problem is directing an overwhelming amount of managerial time, attention, and resources to value-creating activities that produce the greatest margins—to the detriment of other important, albeit less profitable, activities. For example, car manufacturer may focus too much on downstream activities, such as warranty fulfillment and financing operations, to the detriment of differentiation and cost of the cars themselves.

How the Internet and Digital Technologies Are Affecting the Competitive Strategies

>LO6
How Internet-enabled business models are being used to improve strategic positioning.

Internet and digital technologies have swept across the economy and now have an impact on how nearly every company conducts its business. These changes have created new cost efficiencies and avenues for differentiation that never existed before. However, the presence of these technologies is so widespread that it is questionable how any one firm can use them effectively in ways that genuinely set them apart from rivals. Thus, to stay competitive, firms must update their strategies to reflect the new possibilities and constraints that these phenomena represent. In this section, we address both the opportunities and the pitfalls that Internet and digital technologies offer to companies using overall cost leadership, differentiation, and focus strategies. We also briefly consider two major impacts that the Internet is having on business: lowering transaction costs and enabling mass customization.

Overall Cost Leadership

The Internet and digital technologies are creating new opportunities for firms to achieve low-cost advantages by enabling them to manage costs and achieve greater efficiencies. Managing costs, and even changing the cost structures of certain industries, is a key feature of the new digital economy. Most analysts agree that the Internet's ability to lower transaction costs is transforming business. Broadly speaking, *transaction costs* refer to all the various expenses associated with conducting business. It applies not just to buy/sell transactions but to the costs of interacting with every part of a firm's value chain, within and outside the firm. Think about it. Hiring new employees, meeting with customers, ordering supplies, addressing government regulations—all of these exchanges have some costs associated with them. Because business can be conducted differently on the Internet, new ways of saving money are changing the competitive landscape.

Other factors also help to lower transaction costs. The process of disintermediation, described briefly in Chapter 2, has a similar effect. Each time intermediaries are used in a transaction, additional costs are added. Removing those intermediaries lowers transaction costs. The Internet reduces the costs of traveling to a location to search for a product or service, whether it is a retail outlet (as in the case of consumers) or a trade show (as in the case of business-to-business shoppers). Not only is the need for travel eliminated but so is the need to maintain a physical address, whether it's a permanent retail location or a temporary presence at a trade show.

Exhibit 5.8 identifies several types of cost leadership strategies that are made possible by Internet and digital technologies. These cost savings are available throughout a firm's value chain, in both primary and support activities.

Exhibit 5.8
Internet-Enabled Low Cost Leader Strategies

- Online bidding and order processing are eliminating the need for sales calls and are minimizing sales force expenses.
- Online purchase orders are making many transactions paperless, thus reducing the costs of procurement and paper.
- Direct access to progress reports and the ability for customers to periodically check work in progress is minimizing rework.
- Collaborative design efforts using Internet technologies that link designers, materials suppliers, and manufacturers are reducing the costs and speeding the process of new product development.

Potential Internet-Related Pitfalls for Low-Cost Leaders   One of the biggest threats to low-cost leaders is imitation. This problem is intensified for business done on the Internet. Most of the advantages associated with contacting customers directly, and even capabilities that are software driven (e.g., customized ordering systems or real-time access to the status of work in progress), can be duplicated quickly and without threat of infringement on proprietary information. Another pitfall relates to companies that become overly enamored with using the Internet for cost-cutting. Companies that do so may suffer if they place too much attention on one business activity and ignore others. They may jeopardize customer relations or neglect other cost centers, such as providing services or controlling turnover and recruiting expenses, which then dig into their cost advantages.

Differentiation

For many companies, Internet and digital technologies have enhanced their ability to build brand, promote a favorable reputation, offer quality products and services, and achieve other differentiation advantages. Among the most striking trends that the new technologies foster are new ways to interact with consumers. In particular, the Internet is creating new ways of differentiating by enabling *mass customization,* which improves the response of companies to customer wishes. Mass customization is not a new phenomenon; it has been growing for years as flexible manufacturing systems have made manufacturing more adaptable and electronic data interchange has made communications more direct. But the Internet has generated a giant leap forward in the amount of control customers can have in influencing the process. Such capabilities are changing the way companies develop unique product and service offerings, build their reputation, and preserve their brand image.

Methods like mass customization, which are changing the way companies go to market, are challenging some of the tried-and-true techniques of differentiation. Traditionally, companies reached customers using high-end catalogs, the showroom floor, the personal sales calls and made products more inviting using prestige packaging, celebrity endorsements, and charity sponsorships. All of these avenues are still available and may still be effective, depending on a firm's competitive environment. But many customers now judge the quality and uniqueness of a product or service by their ability to be involved in its planning and design, combined with speed of delivery and reliable results. Internet and digitally based capabilities are thus changing the way differentiators make exceptional products and achieve superior service. And these improvements are being made at a reasonable cost, allowing firms to achieve parity on the basis of overall cost leadership relative to competitors.

Exhibit 5.9 identifies differentiation activities that are made possible by Internet and digital technologies. Opportunities to differentiate are available in all parts of a company's value chain—both primary and support activities.

Exhibit 5.9
Internet-Enabled Differentiation Strategies

- Personalized online access provides customers with their own "site within a site" in which their prior orders, status of current orders, and requests for future orders are processed directly on the supplier's website.
- Online access to real-time sales and service information is being used to empower the sales force and continually update R&D and technology development efforts.
- Internet-based knowledge management systems that link all parts of the organization are shortening response times and accelerating organization learning.
- Quick online responses to service requests and rapid feedback to customer surveys and product promotions are enhancing marketing efforts.

Potential Internet-Related Pitfalls for Differentiators   Traditional differentiation strategies such as building strong brand identity and prestige pricing have been undermined by Internet-enabled capabilities such as the ability to compare product features side-by-side or bid online for competing services. As applications of these technologies become part of the mainstream, it will become harder to use the Web to differentiate. The sustainability of Internet-based gains from differentiation will deteriorate if companies offer differentiating features that customers don't want or create a sense of uniqueness that customers don't value. The result can be a failed value proposition—the value companies thought they were offering, does not translate into sales. Other problems can result from overpricing products and services or developing brand extensions that dilute a company's image or reputation.

Focus

A focus strategy involves targeting a narrow market segment with customized products and/or specialized services. For companies that pursue focus strategies, the Internet offers new avenues in which to compete because they can access markets less expensively (low cost) and provide more services and features (differentiation). Some claim that the Internet has opened up a new world of opportunities for niche players who seek to access small markets in a highly specialized fashion.[38] Niche businesses are among the most active users of digital technologies and e-business solutions. According to the ClickZ.com division of Jupitermedia Corporation, 77 percent of small businesses agree that a Web site is essential for small business success. Small businesses also report that the Internet has helped them grow (58 percent), made them more profitable (51 percent), and helped reduce business costs (49 percent).[39] Clearly niche players and small businesses are using the Internet and digital technologies to create more viable focus strategies.

Many aspects of the Internet economy favor focus strategies because niche players and small firms have been able to extend their reach and effectively compete with larger competitors using Internet and digital technologies. For example, niche firms have been quicker than Fortune 1000 firms to adopt blogging as a way to create a community and gather customer feedback.[40] Effective use of blogs is a good example of how focusers are using the new technology to provide the kinds of advantages that have been the hallmark of a focus strategy in the past—specialized knowledge, rapid response, and strong customer service. Thus, the Internet has provided many companies that pursue focus strategies with new tools for creating competitive advantages.

Exhibit 5.10 outlines several approaches to strategic focusing that are made possible by Internet and digital technologies. Both primary and support activities can be enhanced using the kind of singlemindedness that is characteristic of a focus strategy.

Exhibit 5.10
Internet-Enabled Focus Strategies

- Permission marketing techniques are focusing sales efforts on specific customers who opt to receive advertising notices.
- Niche portals that target specific groups are providing advertisers with access to viewers with specialized interests.
- Virtual organizing and online "officing" are being used to minimize firm infrastructure requirements.
- Procurement technologies that use Internet software to match buyers and sellers are highlighting specialized buyers and drawing attention to smaller suppliers.

Potential Internet-Related Pitfalls for Focusers   A key danger for focusers using the Internet relates to correctly assessing the size of the online marketplace. Focusers may misstep if they misread the scope and interests of their target markets. This can cause them to focus on segments that are too narrow to be profitable or to lose their uniqueness by going after overly broad niches, making them vulnerable to imitators or new entrants. What happens when an e-business focuser tries to overextend its niche? Efforts to appeal to a broader audience by carrying additional inventory, developing additional content, or offering additional services can cause it to lose the cost advantages associated with a limited product or service offering. Conversely, when focus strategies become too narrow, the e-business may have trouble generating enough activity to justify the expense of operating the Web site.

Are Combination Strategies the Key to E-Business Success?

Because of the changing dynamics presented by digital and Internet-based technologies, new strategic combinations that make the best use of the competitive strategies just described may hold the greatest promise for future success.[41] Many experts agree that the net effect of the digital economy is fewer rather than more opportunities for sustainable advantages.[42] This means strategic thinking is even more important in the Internet age.

More specifically, the Internet has provided all companies with greater tools for managing costs. So it may be that cost management and control will become more important management tools. In general, this may be good if it leads to an economy that makes more efficient use of its scarce resources. However, for individual companies, it may shave critical percentage points off profit margins and create a climate that makes it impossible to survive, much less achieve sustainable above-average profits.

Many differentiation advantages are also diminished by the Internet. The ability to comparison shop—to check product reviews and inspect different choices with a few clicks of the mouse—is depriving some companies, such as auto dealers, of the unique advantages that were the hallmark of their success in a previous time. Differentiating is still an important strategy, of course. But how firms achieve it may change, and the best approach may be to combine a differentiation strategy with other competitive strategies.

Perhaps the greatest beneficiaries are the focusers who can use the Internet to capture a niche that previously may have been inaccessible. Even this is not assured, however, because the same factors that make it possible for a small niche player to be a contender may make that same niche attractive to a big company. That is, an incumbent firm that previously thought a niche market was not worth the effort may use Internet technologies to enter that segment for a lower cost than in the past. The larger firm can then bring its market power and resources to bear in a way that a smaller competitor cannot match.

A combination strategy, by definition, challenges a company to carefully blend alternative strategic approaches and remain mindful of the impact of different decisions on the firm's value-creating processes and its extended value-chain activities. Strong leadership is needed to maintain a bird's-eye perspective on a company's overall approach and to coordinate the multiple dimensions of a combination strategy.

Strategy Spotlight 5.4 describes the efforts of Liberty Mutual, a company that used Internet and digital technologies to successfully combine both differentiation and overall low-cost advantages.

Liberty Mutual's Electronic Invoice System: Combining Low Cost and Differentiation Advantages

Boston-based Liberty Mutual Group is a leading global insurer and the sixth largest property and casualty insurer in the United States. Its largest line of business is personal automobile insurance. Liberty Mutual has $85.5 billion in assets and $23.5 billion in annual revenues—ranking the firm 102nd on the Fortune 500 list of the largest corporations.

In 2000, Liberty Mutual became one of the first companies to experiment with electronic invoices. It set up a pilot program with a few law firms to submit its bills through a secured Web site. These firms, for the most part, handle claims litigation for Liberty, defending its policyholders in lawsuits. Its success with this program convinced Liberty that it could achieve significant cost savings and also pass along differentiating features to its customers and strategic partners. Liberty now processes nearly 400,000 electronic legal-services invoices a year—70 percent of the total invoices that the firm receives.

As expected, the initial transition was quite expensive. The company invested nearly $1 million in the first four years. However, Liberty estimates that the electronic invoice program saves the company $750,000 a year in direct costs by streamlining the distribution, payment, storage, and retrieval of invoices. E-invoices enable Liberty to move from intake to payment with half the staff that it had taken to process paper invoices. The firm has also created new efficiencies by cutting costs resulting from data entry errors, late payments, and overpayments. As a relatively minor issue, Liberty saves more than $20,000 per year on postage, photocopying, archiving, and retrieval costs.

The legal invoices are organized by litigation phase or task—for example, taking a deposition or reporting a witness statement. Work is diced into tiny increments of six minutes

or less. A single invoice that covers a month of complex litigation, for example, can include well over 1,000 lines. However, by building and mining a database of law firm billing practices, Liberty is able to generate a highly granular report card about law firm activities and performance. The new knowledge generated by this system not only increases internal effectiveness but also allows Liberty to provide detailed feedback to clients and other external stakeholders.

Online invoicing has also helped speed up both processing and response time. Liberty can instantaneously see how firms deploy and bill for partners, paralegals, and other staff, how they compare with each other on rates, hours, and case outcomes; and whether, how, and how often they send duplicate invoices or charge for inappropriate services. The system also allows Liberty to instantly review all of the time billed for a particular attorney across many cases, enabling the firm to reconstruct the total time billed to Liberty during a single day. More than once they have found that attorneys have billed more than 24 hours in a day. Liberty is also able to easily expose prohibited formula billing patterns (wherein, for example, they are billed a set amount for a service instead of actual time spent). In two cases in which formula billing was used, Liberty found that there were more than $28,000 in suspected overcharges.

Liberty Mutual is in the process of developing a large database of law firms' billing practices on different types of cases. The database should eventually enable Liberty to evaluate a law firm's billing activities and compare them to the norms of all of its partner firms. With such intelligence, it will be a rather straightforward matter to rate each firm's cost effectiveness in handling certain types of cases and match firms with cases accordingly.

Liberty's decision to use electronic invoices was initially based on the potential for cost savings. But the differentiating advantages it has achieved in terms of rapid feedback, decreased response time, and a knowledge trove in databases that can be electronically mined has provided the company with a fruitful combination of Internet-based strategic advantages.

Sources: Coyle, M., & Angevine, R. 2007. Liberty Mutual Group reports fourth quarter 2006 results. February 26, www.libertymutual.com; and Smunt, T. L., & Sutcliffe, C. L., 2004. There's gold in them bills. *Harvard Business Review*, 82(9): 24–25.

Industry Life Cycle Stages: Strategic Implications

industry life cycle
the stages of introduction, growth, maturity, and decline that typically occur over the life of an industry.

The **industry life cycle** refers to the stages of introduction, growth, maturity, and decline that occur over the life of an industry. In considering the industry life cycle, it is useful to think in terms of broad product lines such as personal computers, photocopiers, or long-distance telephone service. Yet the industry life cycle concept can be explored from several levels, from the life cycle of an entire industry to the life cycle of a single variation or model of a specific product or service.

Why is it important to consider industry life cycles?[43] The emphasis on various generic strategies, functional areas, value-creating activities, and overall objectives varies over the course of an industry life cycle. Managers must become even more aware of their firm's strengths and weaknesses in many areas to attain competitive advantages. For example, firms depend on their research and development (R&D) activities in the introductory stage of the life cycle. R&D is the source of new products and features that everyone hopes will appeal to customers. Firms develop products and services to stimulate consumer demand. Later, during the maturity phase, the functions of the product have been defined, more competitors have entered the market, and competition is intense. Managers then place greater emphasis on production efficiencies and process (as opposed to the product) engineering in order to lower manufacturing costs. This helps to protect the firm's market position and to extend the product life cycle because the firm's lower costs can be passed on to consumers in the form of lower prices, and price-sensitive customers will find the product more appealing.

>LO7
The importance of considering the industry life cycle to determine a firm's business-level strategy and its relative emphasis on functional area strategies and value-creating activities.

Exhibit 5.11 illustrates the four stages of the industry life cycle and how factors such as generic strategies, market growth rate, intensity of competition, and overall objectives change over time. As we noted earlier, managers must strive to emphasize the key functional areas during each of the four stages and to attain a level of parity in all functional areas and value-creating activities. For example, even though controlling production costs may be a primary concern during the maturity stage, managers should not totally ignore other functions such as marketing and R&D. If they do, they can become so focused on lowering costs that they miss market trends or fail to incorporate important product or process designs. In such cases, the firm may attain low-cost products that have limited market appeal.

It is important to point out a caveat. While the life cycle idea is analogous to a living organism (i.e., birth, growth, maturity, and death), the comparison does have limitations.[44] Products and services go through many cycles of innovation and renewal. For the most part, only fad products have a single life cycle. Maturity stages of an industry can be "transformed" or followed by a stage of rapid growth if consumer tastes change, technological innovations take place, or new developments occur in the general environment. The cereal industry is a good example. When medical research indicated that oat consumption reduced a person's cholesterol, sales of Quaker Oats increased dramatically.[45]

Next we discuss each stage of the industry life cycle. Then, we will discuss turnaround strategies—that is, strategies that are necessary in order to reverse performance erosion and regain competitive position.

Strategies in the Introduction Stage

In the **introduction stage,** products are unfamiliar to consumers.[46] Market segments are not well defined, and product features are not clearly specified. The early development of an industry typically involves low sales growth, rapid technological change, operating losses, and the need for strong sources of cash to finance operations. Since there are few players and not much growth, competition tends to be limited.

Success requires an emphasis on research and development and marketing activities to enhance awareness. The challenge becomes one of (1) developing the product and finding a way to get users to try it, and (2) generating enough exposure so the product emerges as the "standard" by which all other rivals' products are evaluated.

There's an advantage to being the "first mover" in a market.[47] Consider Coca-Cola's success in becoming the first soft-drink company to build a recognizable global brand. Moving first enabled Caterpillar to get a lock on overseas sales channels and service capabilities. Being a first mover allowed Matsushita to establish Video Home Source (VHS) as the global standard for videocassette recorders.

introduction stage the first stage of the industry life cycle characterized by (1) new products that are not known to customers, (2) poorly defined market segments, (3) unspecified product features, (4) low sales growth, (5) rapid technological change, (6) operating losses, and (7) a need for financial support.

Stage / Factor	Introduction	Growth	Maturity	Decline
Generic strategies	Differentiation	Differentiation	Differentiation Overall cost leadership	Overall cost leadership Focus
Market growth rate	Low	Very large	Low to moderate	Negative
Number of segments	Very few	Some	Many	Few
Intensity of competition	Low	Increasing	Very intense	Changing
Emphasis on product design	Very high	High	Low to moderate	Low
Emphasis on process design	Low	Low to moderate	High	Low
Major functional area(s) of concern	Research and development	Sales and marketing	Production	General management and finance
Overall objective	Increase market awareness	Create consumer demand	Defend market share and extend product life cycles	Consolidate, maintain, harvest, or exit

Exhibit 5.11 Stages of the Industry Life Cycle

However, there can also be a benefit to being a "late mover." Target carefully thought out the decision to delay its Internet strategy. Compared to its competitors Wal-Mart and Kmart, Target was definitely the industry laggard. But things certainly turned out well for Target:[48]

> By waiting, Target gained a late mover advantage. The store was able to use competitors' mistakes as its own learning curve. This saved money, and customers didn't seem to mind the wait: When Target finally opened its Web site, it quickly captured market share from both Kmart and Wal-Mart Internet shoppers. Forrester Research Internet analyst Stephen Zrike commented, "There's no question, in our mind, that Target has a far better understanding of how consumers buy online."

Examples of products currently in the introductory stages of the industry life cycle include electric vehicles, digital cameras, and high-definition television (HDTV).

Strategies in the Growth Stage

The **growth stage** is characterized by strong increases in sales. The potential for strong sales (and profits) attracts other competitors. In the growth stage, the primary key to success is to build consumer preferences for specific brands. This requires strong brand recognition, differentiated products, and the financial resources to support a variety of value-chain activities such as marketing and sales, customer service, and research and development. Whereas marketing and sales initiatives were mainly directed at spurring *aggregate* demand—that is, demand for all such products in the introduction stage—efforts in the growth stage are directed toward stimulating *selective* demand, in which a firm's product offerings are chosen instead of those of its rivals.

Revenues in the growth stage increase at an accelerating rate because (1) new consumers are trying the product and (2) a growing proportion of satisfied consumers are making repeat purchases.[49] In general, as a product moves through its life cycle, the proportion of repeat buyers to new purchasers increases. Conversely, new products and services often fail if there are relatively few repeat purchases. This is especially true with many consumer products that are characterized by relatively low price and frequent purchase. For example, Alberto-Culver introduced Mr. Culver's Sparklers, which were solid air fresheners that looked like stained glass. Although the product quickly went from the introductory to the growth stage, sales then plummeted. Why? Unfortunately, there were few repeat purchasers because buyers treated them as inexpensive window decorations, left them there, and felt little need to purchase new ones. Examples of products currently in the growth stage of the industry life cycle include Internet servers and personal digital assistants (e.g., Palm Pilots).

Strategies in the Maturity Stage

In the **maturity stage** aggregate industry demand begins to slow. Since markets are becoming saturated, there are few opportunities to attract new adopters. It's no longer possible to "grow around" the competition, so direct competition becomes predominant.[50] With few attractive prospects, marginal competitors begin to exit the market. At the same time, rivalry among existing rivals intensifies because there is often fierce price competition at the same time that expenses associated with attracting new buyers are rising. Advantages based on efficient manufacturing operations and process engineering become more important for keeping costs low as customers become more price sensitive. It also becomes more difficult for firms to differentiate their offerings, because users have a greater understanding of products and services.

An article in *Fortune* magazine that addressed the intensity of rivalry in mature markets was aptly titled "A Game of Inches." It stated, "Battling for market share in a slowing industry can be a mighty dirty business. Just ask laundry soap archrivals Unilever and Procter & Gamble."[51] These two firms have been locked in a battle for market share since 1965. Why is the competition so intense? There is not much territory to gain. In 2000, total sales for the industry were flat at $6 billion a year. A Lehman Brothers analyst noted, "People aren't getting any dirtier." Thus, the only way to win is to take market share from the competition. To increase its share, Procter & Gamble (P&G) spends $100 million a year promoting its Tide brand on television, billboards, subways, buses, magazines, and the Internet. But Unilever isn't standing still. Armed with a new $80 million budget, it recently launched a soap tablet product named Wisk Dual Action Tablets. For example, it delivered samples of this product to 24 million U.S. homes in Sunday newspapers, followed by a series of TV ads. P&G launched a counteroffensive with Tide

growth stage the second stage of the product life cycle characterized by (1) strong increases in sales; (2) growing competition; (3) developing brand recognition; and (4) a need for financing complementary value-chain activities such as marketing, sales, customer service, and research and development.

maturity stage the third stage of the product life cycle characterized by (1) slowing demand growth, (2) saturated markets, (3) direct competition, (4) price competition, and (5) strategic emphasis on efficient operations.

Rapid Action Tablets ads showed in side-by-side comparisons of the two products dropped into beakers of water. In the promotion, P&G claimed that its product is superior because it dissolves faster than Unilever's product. A minor point, but Unilever is challenging P&G in court. And the beat goes on. . . .

Although this is only one example, many product classes and industries, including consumer products such as beer, automobiles, and televisions, are in the maturity stage.

Studies have shown that firms do not need to be "held hostage" to the life-cycle curve. By positioning or repositioning their products in unexpected ways, firms can change how customers mentally categorize them. Thus, firms are able to rescue products floundering in the maturity phase of their life cycles and return them to the growth phase.

Two positioning strategies that managers can use to affect consumers' mental shifts are **reverse positioning,** which strips away "sacred" product attributes while adding new ones, and **breakaway positioning,** which associates the product with a radically different category.[52] We discuss each of these positioning strategies below and then provide an example of each in Strategy Spotlight 5.5.

Reverse Positioning Reverse positioning assumes that although customers don't desire more than the baseline product, they also don't necessarily want an endless list of features. Such companies make the creative decision to step off the augmentation treadmill and shed product attributes that the rest of the industry considers sacred. Then, once a product is returned to its baseline state, reverse positioners supplement the stripped-down product with one or more carefully selected attributes that would usually be found only in a highly augmented product. Such an unconventional combination of attributes allows the product to assume a new competitive position within the category and move backwards from maturity into a growth position on the life-cycle curve.

Breakaway Positioning As noted above, with reverse positioning, a product establishes a unique position in its category but retains a clear category membership. However, with breakaway positioning, a product escapes its category by deliberately associating with a different one. Thus, managers leverage the new category's conventions to change both how products are consumed and with whom they compete. Instead of merely seeing the breakaway product as simply an alternative to others in its category, consumers perceive it as altogether different.

When a breakaway product is successful in leaving its category and joining a new one, it is able to redefine its competition. Similar to reverse positioning, this strategy permits the product to shift backward on the life-cycle curve, moving from the rather dismal maturity phase to a thriving growth opportunity.

Strategy Spotlight 5.5 provides examples of reverse and breakaway positioning.

Strategies in the Decline Stage

Although all decisions in the phases of an industry life cycle are important, they become particularly difficult in the **decline stage.** Hard choices must be made, and firms must face up to the fundamental strategic choices of either exiting or staying and attempting to consolidate their position in the industry.[53]

The decline stage occurs when industry sales and profits begin to fall. Typically, changes in the business environment are at the root of an industry or product group entering this stage.[54] Changes in consumer tastes or a technological innovation can push a product into decline. Typewriters have entered into the decline stage because of the word processing capabilities of personal computers. Compact disks have forced cassette

reverse positioning a break in industry tendency to continuously augment products, characteristic of the product life cycle, by offering products with fewer product attributes and lower prices.

breakaway positioning a break in industry tendency to incrementally improve products along specific dimensions, characteristic of the product life cycle, by offering products that are still in the industry but that are perceived by customers as being different.

decline stage the fourth stage of the product life cycle characterized by (1) falling sales and profits, (2) increasing price competition, and (3) industry consolidation.

Reverse and Breakaway Positioning: How to Avoid Being Held Hostage to the Life-Cycle Curve

When firms adopt a reverse or breakaway positioning strategy, there is typically no pretense about what they are trying to accomplish. In essence, they subvert convention through unconventional promotions, prices, and attributes. That becomes a large part of their appeal—a cleverly positioned product offering. Next we discuss Commerce Bank's reverse positioning and Swatch's breakaway positioning.

Commerce Bank

While most banks offer dozens of checking and savings accounts and compete by trying to offer the highest interest rates, Commerce Bank takes a totally different approach. It pays among the lowest rates in its market. Further, it offers a very limited product line—just four checking accounts, for example. One would think that such a stingy approach would seem to scare off customers. However, Commerce Bank has been very successful. Between 1999 and 2005, it expanded from 120 to 373 branches and its total assets have soared from $5.6 billion to $39 billion.

How has it been so successful? It has stripped away all of what customers expect—lots of choices and peak interest rates and it has *reverse positioned* itself as "the most convenient bank in America." It's open seven days a week, including evenings until 8 p.m. You can get a debit card while you wait. And, when it rains, an escort with an umbrella will escort you to your car. Further, the bank offers free coffee,

Sources: Moon, Y. 2005. Break free from the product life cycle. *Harvard Business Review,* 83(5): 87–94; Commerce Bancorp, Inc. www.hoovers.com; Swatch. en.wikipedia.org; and, www.commercebank.com.

newspapers, and most of the branches have free coin-counting machines that customers love (in one recent week, customers fed the machines a total of $28 million in loose change). Not too surprisingly, despite the inferior rates and few choices, new customers are flocking to the bank.

Swatch

Interestingly, the name "Swatch" is often misconstrued as a contraction of the words *Swiss watch.* However, Nicholas Hayek, Chairman, affirms that the original contraction was "Second Watch"—the new watch was introduced as a new concept of watches as casual, fun, and relatively disposable accessories. And therein lies Swatch's *breakaway positioning.*

When Swatch was launched in 1983, Swiss watches were marketed as a form of jewelry. They were serious, expensive, enduring, and discreetly promoted. Once a customer purchased one, it lasted a lifetime. Swatch changed all of that by defining its watches as playful fashion accessories which were showily promoted. They inspired impulse buying—customers would often purchase half a dozen in different designs. Their price—$40 when the brand was introduced—expanded Swatch's reach beyond its default category (watches as high-end jewelry) and moved it into the fashion accessory category, where it has different customers and competitors. Swatch was the official timekeeper of the 1996, 2000, and 2004 Summer Olympics.

Today, The Swatch Group is the largest watch company in the world. It has acquired many brands over the years including Omega, Longines, Calvin Klein, and Hamilton. Revenues have grown to $3.6 billion in 2005 and net income has increased to $500 million. And it remains on a roll. As of February 2007, its stock had soared 42 percent over the prior 52-week period.

---

tapes into decline in the prerecorded music industry, and digital video disks (DVDs) are replacing compact disks. About 20 years earlier, of course, cassette tapes had led to the demise of long-playing records (LPs).

When a product enters the decline stage, it often consumes a large share of management time and financial resources relative to its potential worth. Not only are sales and profits declining, but also competitors may start drastically cutting their prices to raise cash and remain solvent in the short term. The situation is further aggravated by the wholesale liquidation of assets, including inventory, of some of the competitors that have failed. This further intensifies price competition.

In the decline stage, a firm's strategic options become dependent on the actions of rivals. If many competitors decide to leave the market, sales and profit opportunities increase. On the other hand, prospects are limited if all competitors remain.[55] If some

● Many consumer food products such as cereal are in the mature stage of the product life cycle. However, some organic products are enjoying high rates of growth.

competitors merge, their increased market power may erode the opportunities for the remaining players. Managers must carefully monitor the actions and intentions of competitors before deciding on a course of action.

Four basic strategies are available in the decline phase: *maintaining, harvesting, exiting,* or *consolidating.*[56]

- ***Maintaining*** refers to keeping a product going without significantly reducing marketing support, technological development, or other investments, in the hope that competitors will eventually exit the market. Many offices, for example, still use typewriters for filling out forms and other purposes that cannot be completed on a personal computer. In some rural areas, rotary (or dial) telephones persist because of the older technology used in central switching offices. Thus, if a firm remains in the business and others exit, there may still be the potential for revenues and profits.

- ***Harvesting*** involves obtaining as much profit as possible and requires that costs be reduced quickly. Managers should consider the firm's value-creating activities and cut associated budgets. Value-chain activities to consider are primary (e.g., operations, sales and marketing) and support (e.g., procurement, technology development). The objective is to wring out as much profit as possible.

- ***Exiting the market*** involves dropping the product from a firm's portfolio. Since a residual core of consumers may still use the product, eliminating it should be considered carefully. If the firm's exit involves product markets that affect important relationships with other product markets in the corporation's overall portfolio, an exit could have repercussions for the whole corporation. For example, it may involve the loss of valuable brand names or human capital with a broad variety of expertise in many value-creating activities such as marketing, technology, and operations.

- ***Consolidation*** involves one firm acquiring at a reasonable price the best of the surviving firms in an industry. This enables firms to enhance market power and acquire valuable assets. One example of a consolidation strategy took place in the defense industry in the early 1990s. As the cliché suggests, "peace broke out" at the end of the Cold War and overall U.S. defense spending levels plummeted.[57] Many companies that make up the defense industry saw more than 50 percent of their market disappear. Only one-quarter of the 120,000 companies that once supplied the Department of Defense still serve in that capacity; the others have shut down their defense business or dissolved altogether. But one key player, Lockheed Martin, became a dominant rival by pursuing an aggressive strategy of consolidation. During the 1990s, it purchased 17 independent entities, including General Dynamics's tactical aircraft and space systems divisions, GE Aerospace, Goodyear Aerospace, and Honeywell ElectroOptics. These combinations enabled Lockheed Martin to emerge as the top provider to three governmental customers: the Department of Defense, the Department of Energy, and NASA. Despite several downsizing initiatives, the firm was ranked for the first time in the Fortune 25 (the largest 25 industrial concerns in the United States). Clearly, the prospects for industry prosperity have increased in the aftermath of the September 11, 2001, terrorist attacks, the wars in Iraq and Afghanistan, and the "War on Terror."

Examples of products currently in the decline stage of the industry life cycle include automotive spark plugs (replaced by electronic fuel ignition), videocassette recorders (replaced by digital video disk recorders), and personal computer zip drives (replaced by compact disk read-write drives). As we mentioned previously, compact disks are being replaced by digital video disks (DVDs).

Turnaround Strategies

A **turnaround strategy** involves reversing a firm's decline in performance and reinvigorating it back to growth and profitability. A need for turnaround may occur at any stage in the life cycle. However, it is more likely to occur during the maturity or decline stage.

turnaround strategy
a strategy that reverses a firm's decline in performance and returns it to growth and profitability.

Most turnarounds require a firm to carefully analyze the external and internal environments.[58] The external analysis leads to identification of market segments or customer groups that may still find the product attractive. Internal analysis results in actions aimed at reduced costs and higher efficiency. Typically, a firm needs to undertake a mix of both internally and externally oriented actions to effect a turnaround.[59]

A study of 260 mature businesses in need of a turnaround identified three strategies used by successful companies.[60]

>LO8
The need for turnaround strategies that enable a firm to reposition its competitive position in an industry.

- *Asset and cost surgery.* Very often, mature firms tend to have assets that do not produce any returns. These include real estate, buildings, etc. Outright sales or sale and leaseback free up considerable cash and improve returns. Investment in new plants and equipment can be deferred. Firms in turnaround situations try to aggressively cut administrative expenses and inventories and speed up collection of receivables. Costs also can be reduced by outsourcing production of various inputs for which market prices may be cheaper than in-house production costs.
- *Selective product and market pruning.* Most mature or declining firms have many product lines that are losing money or are only marginally profitable. One strategy is to discontinue these product lines and focus all resources on a few core profitable areas. For example, in the early 1980s, faced with possible bankruptcy, Chrysler Corporation sold off all its nonautomotive businesses as well as all its production facilities abroad. Focus on the North American market and identification of a profitable niche—namely, minivans—were keys to their eventual successful turnaround.
- *Piecemeal productivity improvements.* There are hundreds of ways in which a firm can eliminate costs and improve productivity. Although individually these are small gains, they cumulate over a period of time to substantial gains. Improving business processes by reengineering them, benchmarking specific activities against industry leaders, encouraging employee input to identify excess costs, reducing R&D and marketing expenses, increasing capacity utilization, and improving employee productivity lead to a significant overall gain.

The turnaround of software maker Intuit is an interesting case of a quick but well-implemented turnaround strategy. After stagnating and stumbling during the dot-com boom, Intuit, which is known for its Quickbook and Turbotax software, hired Stephen M. Bennett, a 22-year GE veteran, in 1999. He immediately discontinued Intuit's online finance, insurance, and bill-paying operations that were losing money. Instead, he focused on software for small businesses that employ less than 250 people. He also instituted a performance-based reward system that greatly improved employee productivity. Within a few years, Intuit was once again making substantial profits and its stock was up 42 percent.[61]

Mitchell Caplan's Successful Turnaround at E*Trade

Mitchell Caplan is an optimist. He was confident that E*Trade Financial Corporation would survive and prosper. However, such optimism seemed to be misplaced given the fact that the shares of the online broker and bank had plunged from $60 at the peak of the Internet frenzy to a low of $3 in 2002. In 2001 and 2002, the firm lost a total of $428 million.

Fortunately for E*Trade (and their shareholders), Mr. Caplan was elevated to the CEO position in 2003, and he initiated what became a very successful turnaround. Let's take a look at how he did it.

First, Caplan had to change the firm's general approach to business. E*Trade had traditionally ignored the red ink as long as the stock price climbed. However, Caplan realized that he had to cut costs and sell off unrelated businesses. This included sharply reducing marketing and advertising expenses. E*Trade no longer splurges on $2 million Super Bowl commercials. In fact, one year, the company spent $500 million on marketing—more than the entire U.S. liquor industry! Now it only spends about $140 million a year. There are also fewer employees—down to about 4,000 now from a peak of 5,000. He also sold off businesses and assets that were unrelated to E*Trade's core. This included a national ATM network, kiosks in Target stores, a palatial New York retail branch that sold

Source: Weber, J. 2005. E*Trade rises from the ashes. *BusinessWeek*, January 17: 58–59; and Schmerken, I. 2004. Innovation in motion. *Wall Street & Technology*, October: 22–26.

E*Trade souvenirs, and a TV business-news service. In addition, new ventures, such as a string of small storefront offices in major cities, are now rigorously analyzed for profitability. Notes Caplan, "I am adamant—and as a team we are adamant—about financial returns."

Mitch Caplan also felt that he needed to change the organization's culture and instill more discipline. He moved the headquarters from Menlo Park, California, to New York City. In effect, he left behind the propeller beanies, rubber chickens, and geeky props that made the firm's atmosphere rather loose. In its place are jackets and ties.

In addition to cutting costs and changing the culture, Caplan also focused E*Trade on leveraging its core banking operations. Here, it had a clear edge over rivals Charles Schwab Corp. and Ameritrade Inc. By offering banking products such as checking accounts and loans at reduced rates to customers who had brokerage accounts, E*Trade has built the nation's eighth-largest thrift. It also has become a big profit center, accounting for 40 percent of all revenues and 48 percent of profits. Now the company has about 632,000 bank accounts and 2.9 million active brokerage accounts—up from 170,00 bank accounts and 2.4 million brokerage accounts in early 2000.

By focusing on its core business, E*Trade's revenues were only $1.6 billion for the year 2004, which is less than the roughly $2 billion for the years 2003, 2002, 2001. However, profits have soared to $389 million in 2004 compared to an average *loss* of about $75 million for the three previous years. And E*Trade was recently recognized by *InformationWeek* as one of the 40 top firms in the financial services industry for delivering IT solutions to solve business problems.

Even when an industry is in overall decline, pockets of profitability remain. These are segments with customers who are relatively price insensitive. For example, the replacement demand for vacuum tubes affords its manufacturers an opportunity to earn above normal returns although the product itself is technologically obsolete. Surprisingly, within declining industries, there may still be segments that are either stable or growing. Cigars and chewing tobacco are examples of profitable segments within the tobacco industry. Although fountain pens ceased to be the writing instrument of choice a long time ago, the fountain pen industry has successfully reconceptualized the product as a high margin luxury item that signals accomplishment, success, and appreciation of the finer things in life. In the final analysis, every business has the potential for rejuvenation. But it takes creativity, persistence, and most of all a clear strategy to translate that potential into reality.

Strategy Spotlight 5.6 summarizes how Mitchell Caplan conducted a successful turnaround at E*Trade. He was able to effectively cut costs and sell off unrelated businesses, change the firm's general approach to business and its culture, and leverage its core banking operations.

Reflecting on Career Implications . . .

- *Types of Competitive Advantage:* Always be aware of your organization's business-level strategy. What do you do to help your firm either increase differentiation or lower costs? What are some ways that your role in the firm can help realize these outcomes?
- *Combining Sources of Competitive Advantage:* Are you engaged in activities that simultaneously help your organization increase differentiation and lower costs?
- *Industry Life Cycle:* If your firm is in the mature stage of the industry life cycle, can you think of ways to enhance your firm's level of differentiation in order to make customers less price sensitive to your organization's goods and services?
- *Industry Life Cycle:* If you sense that your career is maturing (or in the decline phase!), what actions can you take to restore career growth and momentum (e.g., training, mentoring, professional networking)? Should you actively consider professional opportunities in other industries?

Summary

How and why firms outperform each other goes to the heart of strategic management. In this chapter, we identified three generic strategies and discussed how firms are able not only to attain advantages over competitors, but also to sustain such advantages over time. Why do some advantages become long-lasting while others are quickly imitated by competitors?

The three generic strategies—overall cost leadership, differentiation, and focus—form the core of this chapter. We began by providing a brief description of each generic strategy (or competitive advantage) and furnished examples of firms that have successfully implemented these strategies. Successful generic strategies invariably enhance a firm's position vis-à-vis the five forces of that industry—a point that we stressed and illustrated with examples. However, as we pointed out, there are pitfalls to each of the generic strategies. Thus, the sustainability of a firm's advantage is always challenged because of imitation or substitution by new or existing rivals. Such competitor moves erode a firm's advantage over time.

We also discussed the viability of combining (or integrating) overall cost leadership and generic differentiation strategies. If successful, such integration can enable a firm to enjoy superior performance and improve its competitive position. However, this is challenging, and managers must be aware of the potential downside risks associated with such an initiative.

The way companies formulate and deploy strategies is changing because of the impact of the Internet and digital technologies in many industries. Further, Internet technologies are enabling the mass customization capabilities of

greater numbers of competitors. Focus strategies are likely to increase in importance because the Internet provides highly targeted and lower-cost access to narrow or specialized markets. These strategies are not without their pitfalls, however, and firms need to understand the dangers as well as the potential benefits of Internet-based approaches.

The concept of the industry life cycle is a critical contingency that managers must take into account in striving to create and sustain competitive advantages. We identified the four stages of the industry life cycle—introduction, growth, maturity, and decline—and suggested how these stages can play a role in decisions that managers must make at the business level. These include overall strategies as well as the relative emphasis on functional areas and value-creating activities.

When a firm's performance severely erodes, turnaround strategies are needed to reverse its situation and enhance its competitive position. We have discussed three approaches—asset cost surgery, selective product and market pruning, and piecemeal productivity improvements.

Summary Review Questions

1. Explain why the concept of competitive advantage is central to the study of strategic management.
2. Briefly describe the three generic strategies—overall cost leadership, differentiation, and focus.
3. Explain the relationship between the three generic strategies and the five forces that determine the average profitability within an industry.

4. What are some of the ways in which a firm can attain a successful turnaround strategy?

5. Describe some of the pitfalls associated with each of the three generic strategies.

6. Can firms combine the generic strategies of overall cost leadership and differentiation? Why or why not?

7. Explain why the industry life cycle concept is an important factor in determining a firm's business-level strategy.

Key Terms

overall low-cost leadership, 157
competitive parity, 158
differentiation strategy, 163
focus strategy, 167
industry life cycle, 176
introduction stage, 177
growth stage, 179
maturity stage, 179
decline stage, 180
reverse positioning, 180
breakaway positioning, 180
turnaround strategy, 183

Experiential Exercise

What are some examples of primary and support activities that enable Nucor, an $11 billion steel manufacturer, to achieve a low-cost strategy?

Application Questions Exercises

1. Go to the Internet and look up www.walmart.com. How has this firm been able to combine overall cost leadership and differentiation strategies?

2. Choose a firm with which you are familiar in your local business community. Is the firm successful in following one (or more) generic strategies? Why or why not? What do you think are some of the challenges it faces in implementing these strategies in an effective manner?

3. Think of a firm that has attained a differentiation focus or cost focus strategy. Are their advantages sustainable? Why? Why not? (*Hint:* Consider its position vis-à-vis Porter's five forces.)

4. Think of a firm that successfully achieved a combination overall cost leadership and differentiation strategy. What can be learned from this example? Are these advantages sustainable? Why? Why not? (*Hint:* Consider its competitive position vis-à-vis Porter's five forces.)

Value-Chain Activity	Yes/No	How Does Nucor Create Value for the Customer?
Primary:		
Inbound logistics		
Operations		
Outbound logistics		
Marketing and sales		
Service		
Support:		
Procurement		
Technology development		
Human resource management		
General administration		

Ethics Questions

1. Can you think of a company that suffered ethical consequences as a result of an overemphasis on a cost leadership strategy? What do you think were the financial and nonfinancial implications?

2. In the introductory stage of the product life cycle, what are some of the unethical practices that managers could engage in to enhance their firm's market position? What could be some of the long-term implications of such actions?

References

1. The Starbucks example draws upon the following sources: Crane, M. 2007. How to run a restaurant: Best role model. www.forbes.com. February 2: np.; McGovern, G. J., Court, D., Quelch, J. A., & Crawford, B. 2004. Bringing customers into the boardroom. *Harvard Business Review*, 82(11): 70–80; Gottfrendson, M., & Aspinall, K. 2005. Innovation and complexity. *Harvard Business Review*, 83(11); 62–71; and Francis, D. 2005. The secret of successful marketing. *Financial Post*. November 25: FP2.

2. For a seminal discussion on competitive advantage and the importance of recognizing tradeoffs, refer to Porter, M. 1996. What is strategy? *Harvard Business Review*, 74(6): 61–78.

3. For a recent perspective by Porter on competitive strategy, refer to Porter, M. E. 1996. What is strategy? *Harvard Business Review*, 74(6): 61–78.

4. Some useful ideas on maintaining competitive advantages can be found in Ma, H., & Karri, R. 2005. Leaders beware: Some sure ways to lose your competitive advantage. *Organizational Dynamics*, 343(1): 63–76.

5. Miller, A., & Dess, G. G. 1993. Assessing Porter's model in terms of its generalizability, accuracy, and simplicity. *Journal of Management Studies*, 30(4): 553–585.

6. For a scholarly discussion and analysis of the concept of competitive parity, refer to Powell, T. C. 2003. Varieties of competitive parity. *Strategic Management Journal*, 24(1): 61–86.

7. Rao, A. R., Bergen, M. E., & Davis, S. 2000. How to fight a price war. *Harvard Business Review*, 78(2): 107–120.

8. Marriot, J. W. Jr. Our competitive strength: Human capital. A speech given to the Detroit Economic Club on October 2, 2000.

9. Whalen, C. J., Pascual, A. M., Lowery, T., & Muller, J. 2001. The top 25 managers. *BusinessWeek*, January 8: 63.

10. Ibid.

11. For an interesting perspective on the need for creative strategies, refer to Hamel, G., & Prahalad, C. K. 1994. *Competing for the Future*. Boston: Harvard Business School Press.

12. Symonds, W. C., Arndt, M., Palmer, A. T., Weintraub, A., & Holmes, S. 2001. Trying to break the choke hold. *BusinessWeek*, January 22: 38–39.

13. For a perspective on the sustainability of competitive advantages, refer to Barney, J. 1995. Looking inside for competitive advantage. *Academy of Management Executive*, 9(4): 49–61.

14. Thornton, E., 2001, Why e-brokers are broker and broker. *BusinessWeek*, January 22: 94.

15. Koretz, G. 2001. E-commerce: The buyer wins. *BusinessWeek*, January 8: 30.

16. For an interesting perspective on the value of corporate brands and how they may be leveraged, refer to Aaker, D. A. 2004, *California Management Review*, 46(3): 6–18.

17. MacMillan, I., & McGrath, R. 1997. Discovering new points of differentiation. *Harvard Business Review*, 75(4): 133–145; Wise, R., & Baumgarter, P. 1999. Beating the clock: Corporate responses to rapid change in the PC industry. *California Management Review*, 42(1): 8–36.

18. For a discussion on quality in terms of a company's software and information systems, refer to Prahalad, C. K., & Krishnan, M. S. 1999. The new meaning of quality in the information age. *Harvard Business Review*, 77(5): 109–118.

19. Taylor, A., III. 2001. Can you believe Porsche is putting its badge on this car? *Fortune*, February 19: 168–172.

20. Ward, S., Light, L., & Goldstine, J. 1999. What high-tech managers need to know about brands. *Harvard Business Review*, 77(4): 85–95.

21. Rosenfeld, J. 2000. Unit of one. *Fast Company*, April: 98.

22. Markides, C. 1997. Strategic innovation. *Sloan Management Review*, 38(3): 9–23.

23. The authors would like to thank Scott Droege, a faculty member at Western Kentucky University, for providing this example.

24. Flint, J. 2004. Stop the nerds. *Forbes*, July 5: 80; and, Fahey, E. 2004. Over-engineering 101. *Forbes*, December 13: 62.

25. Symonds, W. C. 2000. Can Gillette regain its voltage? *BusinessWeek,* October 16: 102–104.

26. Caplan, J. 2006. In a real crunch. *Inside Business,* July: A37–A38.

27. Gadiesh, O., & Gilbert, J. L. 1998. Profit pools: A fresh look at strategy. *Harvard Business Review,* 76(3): 139–158.

28. Colvin, G. 2000. Beware: You could soon be selling soybeans. *Fortune,* November 13: 80.

29. Whalen et al., op. cit.: 63.

30. Porter, M. E. 1996. What is Strategy? *Harvard Business Review,* 74(6): 61–78.

31. Hall, W. K. 1980. Survival strategies in a hostile environment, *Harvard Business Review,* 58: 75–87; on the paint and allied products industry, see Dess, G. G., & Davis, P. S. 1984. Porter's (1980) generic strategies as determinants of strategic group membership and organizational performance. *Academy of Management Journal,* 27: 467–488; for the Korean electronics industry, see Kim, L., & Lim, Y. 1988. Environment, generic strategies, and performance in a rapidly developing country: A taxonomic approach. *Academy of Management Journal,* 31: 802–827; Wright, P., Hotard, D., Kroll, M., Chan, P., & Tanner, J. 1990. Performance and multiple strategies in a firm: Evidence from the apparel industry. In Dean, B. V., & Cassidy, J. C. (Eds.). *Strategic management: Methods and studies:* 93–110. Amsterdam: Elsevier-North Holland; and Wright, P., Kroll, M., Tu, H., & Helms, M. 1991. Generic strategies and business performance: An empirical study of the screw machine products industry. *British Journal of Management,* 2: 1–9.

32. Gilmore, J. H., & Pine, B. J., II. 1997. The four faces of customization. *Harvard Business Review,* 75(1): 91–101.

33. Ibid. For interesting insights on mass customization, refer to Cattani, K., Dahan, E., & Schmidt, G. 2005. Offshoring versus "spackling." *MIT Sloan Management Review,* 46(3): 6–7.

34. Goodstein, L. D., & Butz, H. E. 1998. Customer value: The linchpin of organizational change. *Organizational Dynamics,* Summer: 21–34.

35. Randall, T., Terwiesch, C., & Ulrich, K. T. 2005. Principles for user design of customized products. *California Management Review,* 47(4): 68–85.

36. Gadiesh & Gilbert, op. cit.: 139–158.

37. This example draws on Dess & Picken. 1997. op. cit.

38. Seybold, P. 2000. Niches bring riches. *Business 2.0,* June 13: 135.

39. Greenspan, R. 2004. Net drives profits to small biz. *ClickZ.com,* March 25, www.clickz.com. Greenspan, R. 2002. Small biz benefits from Internet tools. *ClickZ.com,* March 28, www.clickz.com.

40. Burns, E. 2006. Executives slow to see value of corporate blogging. *ClickZ.com,* May 9, www.clickz.com

41. Empirical support for the use of combination strategies in an e-business context can be found in Kim, E., Nam, D., & Stimpert, J. L. 2004. The applicability of Porter's generic strategies in the Digital Age: Assumptions, conjectures, and suggestions. *Journal of Management,* 30(5): 569–589.

42. Porter, M. E. 2001. Strategy and the Internet. *Harvard Business Review,* 79: 63–78.

43. For an interesting perspective on the influence of the product life cycle and rate of technological change on competitive strategy, refer to Lei, D., & Slocum, J. W. Jr. 2005. Strategic and organizational requirements for competitive advantage. *Academy of Management Executive,* 19(1): 31–45.

44. Dickson, P. R. 1994. *Marketing Management:* 293. Fort Worth, TX: Dryden Press; Day, G. S. 1981. The product life cycle: Analysis and application. *Journal of Marketing Research,* 45: 60–67.

45. Bearden, W. O., Ingram, T. N., & LaForge, R. W. 1995. *Marketing principles and practices.* Burr Ridge, IL: Irwin.

46. MacMillan, I. C. 1985. Preemptive strategies. In Guth, W. D. (Ed.). *Handbook of Business Strategy:* 9-1–9-22. Boston: Warren, Gorham & Lamont; Pearce, J. A., & Robinson, R. B. 2000. *Strategic management* (7th ed.). New York: McGraw-Hill; Dickson, op. cit.: 295–296.

47. Bartlett, C. A., & Ghoshal, S. 2000. Going global: Lessons for late movers. *Harvard Business Review,* 78(2): 132–142.

48. Neuborne, E. 2000. E-tailers hit the relaunch key. *BusinessWeek,* October 17: 62.

49. Berkowitz, E. N., Kerin, R. A., & Hartley, S. W. 2000. *Marketing* (6th ed.). New York: McGraw-Hill.

50. MacMillan, op. cit.

51. Brooker, K. 2001. A game of inches. *Fortune,* February 5: 98–100.

52. Our discussion of reverse and breakaway positioning draws on Moon, Y. 2005. Break free from the product life cycle. *Harvard Business Review,* 83(5): 87–94. This article also discusses stealth positioning as a means of overcoming consumer resistance and advancing a product from the introduction to the growth phase.

53. MacMillan, op. cit

53. Berkowitz et al., op. cit.

55. Bearden et al., op. cit.

56. The discussion of these four strategies draws on MacMillan, op. cit.; Berkowitz et al., op. cit.; and Bearden et al., op. cit.

57. Augustine, N. R. 1997. Reshaping an industry: Lockheed Martin's survival story. *Harvard Business Review,* 75(3): 83–94.

58. A study that draws on the resource-based view of the firm to investigate successful turnaround strategies is: Morrow, J. S., Sirmon, D. G., Hitt, M. A., & Holcomb, T. R. 2007. *Strategic Management Journal,* 28(3): 271–284.

59. For some useful ideas on effective turnarounds and handling downsizings, refer to Marks, M. S., & De Meuse, K. P. 2005. Resizing the organization: Maximizing the gain while minimizing the pain of layoffs, divestitures and closings. *Organizational Dynamics,* 34(1): 19–36.

60. Hambrick, D. C., & Schecter, S. M. 1983. Turnaround strategies for mature industrial product business units. *Academy of Management Journal,* 26(2): 231–248.

61. Mullaney, T. J. 2002. The wizard of Intuit. *BusinessWeek,* October 28: 60–63.

chapter 6

Corporate-Level Strategy:

Creating Value through Diversification

>learning objectives

After reading this chapter, you should have a good understanding of:

LO1 The reasons for the failure of many diversification efforts.

LO2 How managers can create value through diversification initiatives.

LO3 How corporations can use related diversification to achieve synergistic benefits through economies of scope and market power.

LO4 How corporations can use unrelated diversification to attain synergistic benefits through corporate restructuring, parenting, and portfolio analysis.

LO5 The various means of engaging in diversification—mergers and acquisitions, joint ventures/strategic alliances, and internal development.

LO6 Managerial behaviors that can erode the creation of value.

orporate-level strategy addresses two related issues: (1) what businesses should a corporation compete in, and (2) how can these businesses be managed so they create "synergy"—that is, more value by working together than if they were freestanding units? As we will see, these questions present a key challenge for today's managers. Many diversification efforts fail or, in many cases, provide only marginal returns to shareholders. Thus, determining how to create value through entering new markets, introducing new products, or developing new technologies is a vital issue in strategic management.

We begin by discussing why diversification initiatives, in general, have not yielded the anticipated benefits. Then, in the next three sections of the chapter, we explore the two key alternative approaches: related and unrelated diversification. With related diversification, corporations strive to enter product markets that share some resources and capabilities with their existing business units or increase their market power. Here we suggest four means of creating value: leveraging core competencies, sharing activities, pooled negotiating power, and vertical integration. With unrelated diversification, there are few similarities in the resources and capabilities among the firm's business units, but value can be created in multiple ways. These include restructuring, corporate parenting, and portfolio analysis approaches. Whereas the synergies to be realized with related diversification come from *horizontal relationships* among the business units, the synergies from unrelated diversification are derived from *hierarchical relationships* between the corporate office and the business units.

The last two sections address (1) the various means that corporations can use to achieve diversification and (2) managerial behaviors (e.g., self-interest) that serve to erode shareholder value. We address merger and acquisitions (M&A), divestitures, joint ventures/strategic alliances, and internal development. Each of these involves the evaluation of important trade-offs. Detrimental managerial behaviors, often guided by a manager's self-interest, are "growth for growth's sake," egotism, and antitakeover tactics. Some of these behaviors raise ethical issues because managers, in some cases, are not acting in the best interests of a firm's shareholders.

Learning from Mistakes

In what *Fortune* magazine claimed was the second biggest merger and acquisition blunder of all time (next only to AOL/Time Warner), Boston Scientific acquired Guidant for $27.3 billion in late 2006. Why did Boston Scientific offer such a huge amount for what at best was a "dubious prize"? In retrospect, this seems like a classic case of the "winner's curse," where in the heat of a bidding war, the winner ends up paying a price that is well above the rest of the market's valuation of an asset. The chances are that the market is right and the winner is wrong.[1] Let's take a brief look at what happened.[2]

On a warm August 2006 evening in Manhattan, the former leaders of medical-device maker Guidant joined their investment bankers in a private room at the tony Bouley restaurant to celebrate the sale of their company to Boston Scientific. Sipping rare Bordeaux, they marveled over the wild bidding war between Boston Scientific and rival Johnson & Johnson, which had netted them $27.3 billion, a premium price for their company—at the time reeling from a series of damaging product failures and lawsuits. (Astonishingly, about nine months earlier, on November 15, 2005, Johnson & Johnson and Guidant had agreed on a much lower price of $21.5 billion! But at that point Boston Scientific entered the fray and a bidding war began.) *[continued]*

Boston Scientific had held its own bash on May 1, 2006, just after the deal had closed (on April 21). Boston Scientific's investment bankers, Merrill Lynch and Bank of America, organized the feast at the St. Regis Hotel in New York City. However, the day of the event, thunderstorms in the New York area played havoc with the arriving flight schedules. Boston Scientific co-founder Pete Nicholas, CEO Jim Tobin, and CFO Larry Best sat for hours in a drafty hanger on Hanscomb Field in Bedford, Massachusetts, while their lawyers and investment bankers, as well as lower-level executives, partied into the night. The stormy weather turned out to be an omen: While the lawyers and bankers were, of course, well paid for their efforts, the deal turned into to a deluge of bad days for Boston Scientific's top executives.

About two months later, in late June, Boston Scientific issued recalls or warnings on almost 50,000 Guidant cardiac devices and acknowledged that it could take as long as two years to fix the safety problems. Then, on September 21, Boston issued a profit warning that shocked Wall Street, sending its already beaten-down shares plunging another 9.2 percent in a single day.

Since it announced the bid for Guidant on December 2005, Boston's stock had dropped a stunning 46 percent, wiping out $18 billion in shareholder value in a matter of months.

Indeed the deal is arguably the second-worst ever, trailing only the spectacular AOL Time Warner debacle. "It's like the movie The Money Pit," Matthew Dodds, an analyst at Citigroup, says of Boston Scientific's handling of the deal. "Once you've put enough in, you'll go all the way till it's done, regardless of the value."

>LO1

The reasons for the failure of many diversification efforts.

Boston Scientific is not alone in having a disappointing experience with an acquisition. Many large multinational firms and recent big acquirers have also failed to effectively integrate their acquisitions, paid too high a premium for the target's common stock, or were unable to understand how the acquired firm's assets would fit with their own lines of business. And, at times, top executives may not have acted in the best interests of shareholders. That is, the motive for the acquisition may have been to enhance the executives' power and prestige rather than to improve shareholder returns. At times, the only other people who may have benefited were the shareholders of the *acquired* firms—or the investment bankers who advise the acquiring firm because they collect huge fees upfront regardless of what happens afterwards!

There have been several studies that were conducted over a variety of time periods that show how disappointing acquisitions have typically turned out. For example:

- A study evaluated the stock market reaction of 600 acquisitions over the period between 1975 and 1991. The results indicated that the acquiring firms suffered an average 4 percent drop in market value (after adjusting for market movements) in the three months following the acquisitions announcement.[3]
- In a study by Solomon Smith Barney of U.S. companies acquired since 1997 in deals for $15 billion or more, the stocks of the acquiring firms have, on average, underperformed the S&P stock index by 14 percentage points and underperformed their peer group by 4 percentage points after the deals were announced.[4]

Exhibit 6.1 lists some well-known examples of failed acquisitions and mergers.

Many acquisitions ultimately result in divestiture—an admission that things didn't work out as planned. In fact, some years ago, a writer for *Fortune* magazine lamented, "Studies show that 33 percent to 50 percent of acquisitions are later divested, giving corporate marriages a divorce rate roughly comparable to that of men and women."[5]

Admittedly, we have been rather pessimistic so far. Clearly, many diversification efforts have worked out very well—whether through mergers and acquisitions, strategic alliances and joint ventures, or internal development. We will discuss many success stories throughout this chapter. Next, we will discuss the primary rationales for diversification.

Exhibit 6.1

**Some Examples
of Well-Known
Unsuccessful Mergers
and Acquisitions**

The chapter began with Boston Scientific's acquisition of Guidant. Here are examples of some other very expensive blunders:

- AOL paid $114 billion to acquire Time Warner in 2001. Over the next two years, AOL Time Warner lost $150 billion in market valuation.

- Conseco paid $5.8 billion to buy Green Tree, a mobile home mortgage lender, in 1998 though the company's net worth was not even $1 billion. In the next two years, Conseco lost 90 percent of its market value!

- Quaker Oats' acquisition of the once high-flying Snapple for $1.8 billion in 1994 was followed by its divestment for $300 million three years later.

- AT&T bought computer equipment maker NCR for $7.4 billion in 1991, only to spin it off for $3.4 billion six years later.

- Sony acquired Columbia Pictures in 1989 for $4.8 billion although it had no competencies in movie production. Five years later, Sony was forced to take a $2.7 billion write-off on the acquisition.

Source: Tully, S. 2006. The (second) worst deal ever. *Fortune.* October 16: 102–119.

Making Diversification Work: An Overview

Clearly, not all diversification moves, including those involving mergers and acquisitions, erode performance. For example, acquisitions in the oil industry, such as British Petroleum's purchases of Amoco and Arco, are performing well as is the Exxon-Mobil merger. In the automobile industry, the Renault-Nissan alliance, under CEO Carlos Ghosn's leadership, has led to a quadrupling of its collective market capitalization—from $20.4 billion to $84.9 billion—by the end of 2006.[6] Many leading high-tech firms such as Microsoft, Cisco Systems, and Intel have dramatically enhanced their revenues, profits, and market values through a wide variety of diversification initiatives, including acquisitions, strategic alliances, and joint ventures, as well as internal development.*

So the question becomes: Why do some diversification efforts pay off and others produce disappointing results? In this chapter we will address this question. Whereas Chapter 5 focused on business-level strategy—that is, how to achieve sustainable advantages in a given business or product market—this chapter addresses two related issues: (1) What businesses should a corporation compete in? and (2) How should these businesses be managed to jointly create more value than if they were freestanding units?

Diversification initiatives—whether through mergers and acquisitions, strategic alliances and joint ventures, or internal development—must be justified by the creation of value for shareholders. But this is not always the case. As noted earlier, acquiring firms typically pay high premiums when they acquire a target firm. For example, in 2006 Freeport-McMoran paid a 30 percent premium to acquire Phelps Dodge in order to create the largest metals and mining concern in the United States. In contrast, you and I, as private investors, can diversify our portfolio of stocks very cheaply. With

>LO2

How managers can create value through diversification initiatives.

---

* Many high-tech firms, such as Motorola, IBM, Qualcomm, and Intel have also diversified through company-owned venture capital arms. Intel Capital, for example, has invested $4 billion in 1,000 companies over 15 years. Some 160 of those companies have been sold to other firms, while another 150 of them have been publicly listed. In 2006, Intel Capital's investments added $214 million to the parent company's net income. For an insightful discussion of how Apple might benefit from a venture capital initiative, refer to Hesseldahl, A. 2007. What to do with Apple's cash. *BusinessWeek,* March 19: 80.

an intensely competitive online brokerage industry, we can acquire hundreds (or thousands) of shares for a transaction fee of as little as $10.00 or less—a far cry from the 30 to 40 percent (or higher) premiums that corporations typically must pay to acquire companies.

Given the seemingly high inherent downside risks and uncertainties, it might be reasonable to ask why companies should even bother with diversification initiatives. The answer, in a word, is *synergy*, derived from the Greek word *synergos*, which means "working together." This can have two different, but not mutually exclusive, meanings. First, a firm may diversify into *related* businesses. Here, the primary potential benefits to be derived come from *horizontal relationships*; that is, businesses sharing intangible resources (e.g., core competences such as marketing) and tangible resources (e.g., production facilities, distribution channels). Additionally, firms can enhance their market power through pooled negotiating power and vertical integration. For example, Procter & Gamble enjoys many synergies from having businesses that share distribution resources.

Second, a corporation may diversify into *unrelated* businesses. In these instances, the primary potential benefits are derived largely from *hierarchical relationships*; that is, value creation derived from the corporate office. Examples of the latter would include leveraging some of the support activities in the value chain that we discussed in Chapter 3, such as information systems or human resource practices. Cooper Industries has followed a successful strategy of unrelated diversification. There are few similarities in the products it makes or the industries in which it competes. However, the corporate office adds value through such activities as superb human resource practices as well as planning and budgeting systems.

Please note that the aforementioned benefits derived from horizontal (related diversification) and hierarchical (unrelated diversification) relationships are not mutually exclusive. Many firms that diversify into related areas benefit from information technology expertise in the corporate office. Similarly, firms diversifying into unrelated areas often benefit from the "best practices" of sister businesses even though their products, markets, and technologies may differ dramatically.

Exhibit 6.2 provides an overview of how we will address the various means by which firms create value through both related and unrelated diversification and also include a summary of some examples that we will address in this chapter.[7]

Related Diversification: Economies of Scope and Revenue Enhancement

As discussed earlier, **related diversification** enables a firm to benefit from horizontal relationships across different businesses in the diversified corporation by leveraging core competencies and sharing activities (e.g., production facilities and distribution facilities). This enables a corporation to benefit from economies of scope. **Economies of scope** refers to cost savings from leveraging core competencies or sharing related activities among businesses in the corporation. A firm can also enjoy greater revenues if two businesses attain higher levels of sales growth combined than either company could attain independently.

For example, a sporting goods store with one or several locations may acquire retail stores carrying other product lines. This enables it to leverage, or reuse, many of its key resources—favorable reputation, expert staff and management skills, efficient purchasing operations—the basis of its competitive advantage(s), over a larger number of stores.[8] Let's next address how to create value by leveraging core competencies.

---

related diversification
a firm entering a different business in which it can benefit from leveraging core competencies, sharing activities, or building market power.

economies of scope
cost savings from leveraging core competencies or sharing related activities among businesses in a corporation.

>LO3
How corporations can use related diversification to achieve synergistic benefits through economies of scope and market power.

Exhibit 6.2

Creating Value through Related and Unrelated Diversification

Related Diversification: Economies of Scope

Leveraging core competences
- 3M leverages its competencies in adhesives technologies to many industries, including automotive, construction, and telecommunications.

Sharing activities
- McKesson, a large distribution company, sells many product lines, such as pharmaceuticals and liquor, through its superwarehouses.

Related Diversification: Market Power

Pooled negotiating power
- The Times Mirror Company increases its power over customers by providing "one-stop shopping" for advertisers to reach customers through multiple media—television and newspapers—in several huge markets such as New York and Chicago.

Vertical integration
- Shaw Industries, a giant carpet manufacturer, increases its control over raw materials by producing much of its own polypropylene fiber, a key input to its manufacturing process.

Unrelated Diversification: Parenting, Restructuring, and Financial Synergies

Corporate restructuring and parenting
- The corporate office of Cooper Industries adds value to its acquired businesses by performing such activities as auditing their manufacturing operations, improving their accounting activities, and centralizing union negotiations.

Portfolio management
- Novartis, formerly Ciba-Geigy, uses portfolio management to improve many key activities, including resource allocation and reward and evaluation systems.

Leveraging Core Competencies

The concept of core competencies can be illustrated by the imagery of the diversified corporation as a tree.[9] The trunk and major limbs represent core products; the smaller branches are business units; and the leaves, flowers, and fruit are end products. The core competencies are represented by the root system, which provides nourishment, sustenance, and stability. Managers often misread the strength of competitors by looking only at their end products, just as we can fail to appreciate the strength of a tree by looking only at its leaves. Core competencies may also be viewed as the "glue" that binds existing businesses together or as the engine that fuels new business growth.

Core competencies reflect the collective learning in organizations—how to coordinate diverse production skills, integrate multiple streams of technologies, and market and merchandise diverse products and services. The theoretical knowledge necessary to put a radio on a chip does not in itself assure a company of the skill needed to produce a miniature radio approximately the size of a business card. To accomplish this, Casio, a giant electronic products producer, must synthesize know-how in miniaturization, microprocessor design, material science, and ultrathin precision castings. These are the same skills that it applies in its miniature card calculators, pocket TVs, and digital watches.

core competencies
a firm's strategic resources that reflect the collective learning in the organization.

For a core competence to create value and provide a viable basis for synergy among the businesses in a corporation, it must meet three criteria.[10]

- **_The core competence must enhance competitive advantage(s) by creating superior customer value._** It must enable the business to develop strengths relative to the competition. Every value-chain activity has the potential to provide a viable basis for building on a core competence.[11] At Gillette, for example, scientists developed the Fusion and Mach 3 after the introduction of the tremendously successful Sensor System because of a thorough understanding of several phenomena that underlie shaving. These include the physiology of facial hair and skin, the metallurgy of blade strength and sharpness, the dynamics of a cartridge moving across skin, and the physics of a razor blade severing hair. Such innovations are possible only with an understanding of such phenomena and the ability to combine such technologies into innovative products. Customers have consistently been willing to pay more for such technologically differentiated products.

- **_Different businesses in the corporation must be similar in at least one important way related to the core competence._** It is not essential that the products or services themselves be similar. Rather, at least one element in the value chain must require similar skills in creating competitive advantage if the corporation is to capitalize on its core competence. At first glance you might think that cars and houses have little in common. However, Strategy Spotlight 6.1 discusses how Toyota creates synergies in a business—manufactured homes—that has little to do with its core business—automobiles.

- **_The core competencies must be difficult for competitors to imitate or find substitutes for._** As we discussed in Chapter 5, competitive advantages will not be sustainable if the competition can easily imitate or substitute them. Similarly, if the skills associated with a firm's core competencies are easily imitated or replicated, they are not a sound basis for sustainable advantages. Consider Sharp Corporation, a $26 billion consumer electronics giant.[12] It has a set of specialized core competencies in optoelectronics technologies that are difficult to replicate and contribute to its competitive advantages in its core businesses. Its most successful technology has been liquid crystal displays (LCDs) that are critical components in nearly all of Sharp's products. Its expertise in this technology enabled Sharp to succeed in videocassette recorders (VCRs) with its innovative LCD viewfinder and led to the creation of its Wizard, a personal electronic organizer.

Sharing Activities

As we saw above, leveraging core competencies involves transferring accumulated skills and expertise across business units in a corporation. When carried out effectively, this leads to advantages that can become quite sustainable over time. Corporations also can achieve synergy by **sharing activities** across their business units. These include value-creating activities such as common manufacturing facilities, distribution channels, and sales forces. As we will see, sharing activities can potentially provide two primary payoffs: cost savings and revenue enhancements.

sharing activities
having activities of two or more businesses' value chains done by one of the businesses.

Deriving Cost Savings through Sharing Activities   Typically, this is the most common type of synergy and the easiest to estimate. Peter Shaw, head of mergers and acquisitions at the British chemical and pharmaceutical company ICI, refers to cost savings as "hard synergies" and contends that the level of certainty of their achievement is quite high. Cost savings come from many sources, including elimination of jobs, facilities, and related expenses that are no longer needed when functions are consolidated, or from economies of scale in purchasing. Cost savings are generally highest when one company acquires another from the same industry in the same country. Shaw Industries, recently acquired by

Toyota's Diversification into Home Manufacturing

Looking for the biggest Toyota on the market? It's not the Tundra pickups and Sequoia SUVs down at your local dealer. Instead, you'll have to travel to the Toyota factory in Kasugai, a city of 300,000 about three hours west of Tokyo. There you won't see much in the way of horsepower or acceleration. But they are very roomy—as in multiple bedrooms, a living room, kitchen, bath, and patio.

At Kasugai, Toyota's houses are 85 percent completed at the plant before being transported by road and built in just six hours. To improve efficiency, Toyota borrows know-how from its fabled Toyota Production System with its principles of just-in-time delivery and *kaizen*, or continuous improvement. Using methods adopted from car production, anticorrosive paint is applied evenly to the houses' steel frames. Just as in all of Toyota's Japan automobile factories, a banner proclaiming "good thinking, good products" hangs from the roof. "We follow the Toyota way in housing," says Senta Morioka, a managing officer at Toyota.

Source: Rowley, I. 2006. Way, way, off-road. *BusinessWeek*, July 17: 36–37.

● Toyota is a world-class automobile producer. Above is a Scion, one of its popular products. Toyota has also diversified into many areas, including manufactured homes.

Toyota currently builds about 5,000 prefabricated houses a year. And, in 2005, it took a 13 percent stake in Misawa Homes, another maker of prefabs.

Berkshire Hathaway, is the nation's largest carpet producer. Over the years, it has dominated the competition through a strategy of acquisition which has enabled Shaw, among other things, to consolidate its manufacturing operations in a few, highly efficient plants and to lower costs through higher capacity utilization.

Sharing activities inevitably involve costs that the benefits must outweigh such as the greater coordination required to manage a shared activity. Even more important is the need to compromise on the design or performance of an activity so that it can be shared. For example, a salesperson handling the products of two business units must operate in a way that is usually not what either unit would choose if it were independent. If the compromise erodes the unit's effectiveness, then sharing may reduce rather than enhance competitive advantage.

Enhancing Revenue and Differentiation through Sharing Activities Often an acquiring firm and its target may achieve a higher level of sales growth together than either company could on its own. Shortly after Gillette acquired Duracell, it confirmed its expectation that selling Duracell batteries through Gillette's existing channels for personal care products would increase sales, particularly internationally. Gillette sold Duracell products in 25 new markets in the first year after the acquisition and substantially increased sales in established international markets. Also, a target company's distribution channel can be used to escalate the sales of the acquiring company's product. Such was the case when Gillette acquired Parker Pen. Gillette estimated that it could gain an additional $25 million in sales of its own Waterman pens by taking advantage of Parker's distribution channels.

Firms also can enhance the effectiveness of their differentiation strategies by means of sharing activities among business units. A shared order-processing system, for example, may permit new features and services that a buyer will value. Also, sharing can reduce the cost of differentiation. For instance, a shared service network may make more advanced, remote service technology economically feasible. To illustrate the potential for enhanced differentiation though sharing, consider $7 billion VF Corporation—producer of such well-known brands as Lee, Wrangler, Vanity Fair, and Jantzen.

> VF's acquisition of Nutmeg Industries and H. H. Cutler provided it with several large customers that it didn't have before, increasing its plant utilization and productivity. But more importantly, Nutmeg designs and makes licensed apparel for sports teams and organizations, while Cutler manufactures licensed brand-name children's apparel, including Walt Disney kids' wear. Such brand labeling enhances the differentiation of VF's apparel products. According to VF President Mackey McDonald, "What we're doing is looking at value-added knitwear, taking our basic fleece from Basset-Walker [one of its divisions], embellishing it through Cutler and Nutmeg, and selling it as a value-added product." Additionally, Cutler's advanced high-speed printing technologies will enable VF to be more proactive in anticipating trends in the fashion-driven fleece market. Claims McDonald, "Rather than printing first and then trying to guess what the customer wants, we can see what's happening in the marketplace and then print it up."[13]

As a cautionary note, managers must keep in mind that sharing activities among businesses in a corporation can have a negative effect on a given business's differentiation. For example, with the merger of Chrysler and Daimler-Benz, many consumers may lower their perceptions of Mercedes's quality and prestige because they felt that common production components and processes were being used across the two divisions. And Ford's Jaguar division was adversely affected as consumers came to understand that it shared many components with its sister divisions at Ford, including Lincoln.

Strategy Spotlight 6.2 discusses how Freemantle Media leverages its hit television show *American Idol* through its core competences and shared activities to create multiple revenue streams.

Related Diversification: Market Power

In the previous section, we explained how leveraging core competencies and sharing activities help firms create economies of scale and scope through related diversification. In this section, we discuss how companies achieve related diversification through **market power.** We also address the two principal means by which firms achieve synergy through market power: *pooled negotiating power* and *vertical integration.* It is important to recognize that managers have limits on their ability to use market power for diversification, because government regulations can sometimes restrict the ability of a business to gain very large shares of a particular market.

market power firms' abilities to profit through restricting or controlling supply to a market or coordinating with other firms to reduce investment.

When General Electric announced a $41 billion bid for Honeywell, the European Union stepped in. GE's market clout would have expanded significantly with the deal: GE would supply over one-half the parts needed to build several aircraft engines. The commission's concern, causing them to reject the acquisition, was that GE could use its increased market power to dominate the aircraft engine parts market and crowd out rivals.[14] Thus, while managers need to be aware of the strategic advantages of market power, they must at the same time be aware of regulations and legislation.

Pooled Negotiating Power

Similar businesses working together or the affiliation of a business with a strong parent can strengthen an organization's bargaining position relative to suppliers and customers and enhance its position vis-à-vis competitors. Compare, for example, the position of an independent food manufacturer with the same business within Nestlé. Being part of Nestlé

American Idol: Far More than Just a Television Show

American Idol is one of several of FremantleMedia's (FM) hit television shows. FM is a division of German media giant Bertlesmann, which has approximately $26 billion in revenues. Some of FM's other well-known television shows are *The Apprentice, The Swan,* and at a ripe old age of 48—*The Price Is Right.*

First shown in the United States in June 2002, *American Idol* became a tremendous overnight success. Although the show may be crass and occasionally cruel, it is undeniably brilliant. It's become the ultimate testament to a singular business achievement: FM has become extremely successful at creating truly global programming. In part, that is due to the creative minds at Fremantle. It has some of the best professionals in the business who have a talent for developing shows that appeal to huge populations with different backgrounds and circumstances.

Amazingly, FM, which created *Pop Idol* in Britain in 2001, is now rolling out the show in its 30th country. There's *Belgium Idool, Portugal Idolos, Deutschland Sucht den SuperStar* (Germany), *SuperStar KZ* (Kazakhstan), and of course, the largest and best-known show, *American Idol,* in the United States. *American Idol* is the primary reason that Fremantle's revenue is up 9 percent to more than $1 billion since the show was launched. According to Fremantle's CEO Tony Cohen, "*Idol* has become a national institution in lots of countries." To illustrate, fans cast more than 65 million votes for the *American Idol* finale in May, 2004—that is two-thirds as many people as voted in the 2004 U.S. presidential election.

The real key to Fremantle's success is not just adapting its television hits to other countries, but systematically leveraging its core product—television shows—to create multiple revenue streams. In essence, the "Fremantle Way" holds lessons not just for show business but for all business. It enables a company to use its core competence of making products of mass appeal and then to customize them for places with widely varying languages, cultures, and mores. It then milks the hits for every penny through tie-ins, spinoffs, innovative uses of technology, and marketing masterstrokes.

The *Idol* franchise has created a wide variety of new revenue streams for Fremantle's German parent, Bertelsmann. Here's how much *American Idol* has generated in its first two years since its June 2002 launch:

- *Products ($50 million).* Brand extensions range from videogames and fragrances to a planned micro-phone-shaped soap-on-a-rope. Fremantle receives a licensing fee from manufacturers.

- *TV Licensing ($75 million).* For its rights fee, Fox gets to broadcast the show and, in turn, sell ads and lucrative sponsorships.

- *Compact Discs (CDs) ($130 million).* The most successful performers on the *Idols* shows have sold millions of CDs; more than one-third of the revenue goes to BMG, which, like Fremantle, is an affiliate of Bertelsmann.

- *Concerts ($35 million).* Although artists and their management get the bulk of the take, concerts sell records and merchandise and promote the next *Idol* show.

In addition, Fremantle Licensing Worldwide signed Warner Brothers Publications to produce and distribute *Idol* audition books with CDs for the United States, Canada, United Kingdom, and Australia. The new books/CDs—*Pop Idol* (UK), *Australian Idol,* and *Canadian Idol*—join the *American Idol* book/CD.

Sources: Sloan, P. 2004. The reality factory. *Business 2.0,* August: 74–82; Cooney, J. 2004. In the news. *License!,* March: 48; and, Anonymous. 2005. Fox on top in Feb; NBC languishing at the bottom. www.indiantelevision.com, March 2.

Corporation provides the business with significant clout—greater bargaining power with suppliers and customers—since it is part of a firm that makes large purchases from suppliers and provides a wide variety of products to its customers. Access to the parent's deep pockets increases the business's strength relative to rivals. Further, the Nestlé unit enjoys greater protection from substitutes and new entrants. Not only would rivals perceive the unit as a more formidable opponent, but the unit's association with Nestlé would also provide greater visibility and improved image.

Consolidating an industry can also increase a firm's market power. This is clearly an emerging trend in the multimedia industry.[15] All of these mergers and acquisitions have a common goal: to control and leverage as many news and entertainment channels as possible. In total, more than $261 billion in mergers and acquisitions in the media industry were announced in 2000—up 12 percent from 1999. For example, consider the Tribune Company's $8 billion purchase of the Times Mirror Company.

> The merger doubled the size of the Tribune and secured its position among the top tier of major media companies. The enhanced scale and scope helped it to compete more effectively and grow more rapidly in two consolidating industries—newspaper and television broadcasting. The combined company would increase its power over customers by providing a "one-stop shop" for advertisers desiring to reach consumers through multiple media in enormous markets such as Chicago, Los Angeles, and New York. The company had estimated its incremental revenue from national and cross-media advertising will grow from $40 to $50 million in 2001 to $200 million over four years. The combined company should also increase its power relative to its suppliers. The company's enhanced size is expected to lead to increased efficiencies when purchasing newsprint and other commodities.[16]

When acquiring related businesses, a firm's potential for pooled negotiating power vis-à-vis its customers and suppliers can be very enticing. However, managers must carefully evaluate how the combined businesses may affect relationships with actual and potential customers, suppliers, and competitors. For example, when PepsiCo diversified into the fast-food industry with its acquisitions of Kentucky Fried Chicken, Taco Bell, and Pizza Hut (now part of Yum! Brands), it clearly benefited from its position over these units that served as a captive market for its soft-drink products. However, many competitors such as McDonald's have refused to consider PepsiCo as a supplier of its own soft-drink needs because of competition with Pepsi's divisions in the fast-food industry. Simply put, McDonald's did not want to subsidize the enemy! Thus, although acquiring related businesses can enhance a corporation's bargaining power, it must be aware of the potential for retaliation.

Strategy Spotlight 6.3 discusses how 3M's actions to increase its market power led to a lawsuit (which 3M lost) by a competitor.

Vertical Integration

vertical integration
an expansion or extension of the firm by integrating preceding or successive production processes.

Vertical integration occurs when a firm becomes its own supplier or distributor. That is, it represents an expansion or extension of the firm by integrating preceding or successive production processes.[17] The firm incorporates more processes toward the original source of raw materials (backward integration) or toward the ultimate consumer (forward integration). For example, an automobile manufacturer might supply its own parts or make its own engines to secure sources of supply. Or it might control its own system of dealerships to ensure retail outlets for its products. Similarly, an oil refinery might secure land leases and develop its own drilling capacity to ensure a constant supply of crude oil. Or it could expand into retail operations by owning or licensing gasoline stations to guarantee customers for its petroleum products.

Clearly, vertical integration can be a viable strategy for many firms. Strategy Spotlight 6.4 discusses Shaw Industries, a carpet manufacturer that has attained a dominant position in the industry via a strategy of vertical integration. Shaw has successfully implemented strategies of both forward and backward integration. Exhibit 6.3 depicts the stages of Shaw's vertical integration.

Benefits and Risks of Vertical Integration   Although vertical integration is a means for an organization to reduce its dependence on suppliers or its channels of distribution to end users, it represents a major decision that an organization must carefully consider. The benefits associated with vertical integration—backward or forward—must be carefully weighed against the risks.[18]

The *benefits* of vertical integration include (1) a secure supply of raw materials or distribution channels that cannot be "held hostage" to external markets where costs can

How 3M's Efforts to Increase its Market Power Backfired

In the spring and summer of 2006, 3M found itself in court facing three class-action lawsuits launched by consumers and retailers of transparent and invisible adhesive tape (often generically known as "Scotch tape"). The suits all alleged that 3M had unlawfully bullied its way into a monopoly position in the tape market and that, as a result, consumers had been deprived of their rightful amount of choice and often paid up to 40 percent too much for their tape.

One rival that is particularly interested in these cases is LaPage's Inc. of North York, Ontario—3M's only significant competitor in the home and office adhesive tape market. LaPage's has everything to gain from court penalties against 3M's selling practices. This includes greater access to the lucrative North American market. The Canadian company started 3M's legal travails in the first place: all of the current class-action suits were initiated by LePage's.

Back in 1997, LePage's (then based in Pittsburgh) filed a complaint in the Pennsylvania District Court against 3M's practice of selling its various tape products using what was called "bundled rebates." LePage's argued that it violated the Sherman Act, the century-old U.S. legislation that limited monopoly power. 3M's bundled rebate program offered significant rebates—sometimes in the millions of dollars—to retailers as a reward for selling targeted amounts of six product lines. LePage's claimed that such selling targets were so large that retailers could only meet them by excluding competing products—in this case LePage's tape—from store shelves. For example, LePage's argued that Kmart, which had constituted 10% of LePage's sales dropped the account when 3M started offering the discount chain $1 million in rebates in return for selling more than $15 million worth of 3M products each year. Further, LePage's offered its own conspiracy theory: 3M introduced rebates not simply to grow its sales, but to eliminate LePage's—its only significant competitor.

A jury awarded LePage's $68.5 million in damages (the amount after trebling)—almost 15 percent of the 3M Consumer and Office Business unit's operating income in 2000. The Court of Appeals for the Third Circuit rejected 3M's appeal and upheld the judgment. It concluded that rebate bundling, even if above cost, may exclude equally efficient competitors from offering product (in this case, tape). In the ruling, Judge Dolores K. Sloviter wrote that "they may foreclose portions of the market to a potential competitor who does not manufacture an equally diverse group of products and who therefore cannot make a comparable offer." Therefore, the bundled rebates were judged to be an exploitation of 3M's monopoly power.

Sources: Bush, D., & Gelb, B. D. 2005. When marketing practices raise antitrust concerns. *MIT Sloan Management Review,* 46(4): 73–81; Campbell, C. 2006. Tale of the tape. *Canadian Business.* April 24: 39–40; and Bergstrom, B. 2003. $68M jury award upheld against 3M in antitrust case. *The Associated Press:* March 26.

---

fluctuate over time, (2) protection and control over assets and services required to produce and deliver valuable products and services, (3) access to new business opportunities and new forms of technologies, and (4) simplified procurement and administrative procedures since key activities are brought inside the firm, eliminating the need to deal with a wide variety of suppliers and distributors.

Winnebago, the leader in the market for drivable recreational vehicles with a 19.3 percent market share, illustrates some of vertical integration's benefits.[19] The word Winnebago means "big RV" to most Americans. And the firm has a sterling reputation for great quality.

Exhibit 6.3 Simplified Stages of Vertical Integration: Shaw Industries

strategy spotlight

6.4

Vertical Integration at Shaw Industries

Shaw Industries (now part of Berkshire Hathaway) is an example of a firm that has followed a very successful strategy of vertical integration. By relentlessly pursuing both backward and forward integration, Shaw has become the dominant manufacturer of carpeting products in the United States. According to CEO Robert Shaw, "We want to be involved with as much of the process of making and selling carpets as practical. That way, we're in charge of costs." For example, Shaw acquired Amoco's polypropylene fiber manufacturing facilities in Alabama and Georgia. These new plants provide carpet fibers for internal use and for sale to other manufacturers. With this backward integration, fully one-quarter of Shaw's carpet fiber needs are now met in-house. In early 1996 Shaw began to integrate forward, acquiring seven floor-covering retailers in a move that suggested a strategy to consolidate the fragmented industry and increase its influence over retail pricing. Exhibit 6.3 provides a simplified depiction of the stages of vertical integration for Shaw Industries.

Sources: White, J. 2003. Shaw to home in on more with Georgia Tufters deal. *HFN: The Weekly Newspaper for the Home Furnishing Network*, May 5: 32; Shaw Industries. 1993, 2000. Annual reports; and Server, A. 1994. How to escape a price war. *Fortune*, June 13: 88.

The firm's huge northern Iowa factories do everything from extruding aluminum for body parts to molding plastics for water and holding tanks to dashboards. Such vertical integration at the factory may appear to be outdated and expensive, but it guarantees excellent quality. The Recreational Vehicle Dealer Association started giving a quality award in 1996, and Winnebago has won it every year.

The *risks* of vertical integration include (1) the costs and expenses associated with increased overhead and capital expenditures to provide facilities, raw material inputs, and distribution channels inside the organization; (2) a loss of flexibility resulting from the inability to respond quickly to changes in the external environment because of the huge investments in vertical integration activities that generally cannot be easily deployed elsewhere; (3) problems associated with unbalanced capacities or unfilled demand along the value chain; and (4) additional administrative costs associated with managing a more complex set of activities. Exhibit 6.4 summarizes the benefits and risks of vertical integration.

Exhibit 6.4
Benefits and Risks of Vertical Integration

Benefits

- A secure source of raw materials or distribution channels.
- Protection of and control over valuable assets.
- Access to new business opportunities.
- Simplified procurement and administrative procedures.

Risks

- Costs and expenses associated with increased overhead and capital expenditures.
- Loss of flexibility resulting from large investments.
- Problems associated with unbalanced capacities along the value chain.
- Additional administrative costs associated with managing a more complex set of activities.

In making vertical integration decisions, six issues should be considered.[20]

1. *Is the company satisfied with the quality of the value that its present suppliers and distributors are providing?* If the performance of organizations in the vertical chain—both suppliers and distributors—is satisfactory, it may not, in general, be appropriate for a company to perform these activities themselves. Firms in the athletic footwear industry such as Nike and Reebok have traditionally outsourced the manufacture of their shoes to countries such as China and Indonesia where labor costs are low. Since the strengths of these companies are typically in design and marketing, it would be advisable to continue to outsource production operations and continue to focus on where they can add the most value.

2. *Are there activities in the industry value chain presently being outsourced or performed independently by others that are a viable source of future profits?* Even if a firm is outsourcing value-chain activities to companies that are doing a credible job, it may be missing out on substantial profit opportunities. To illustrate, consider the automobile industry's profit pool. As you may recall from Chapter 5, there is much more potential profit in many downstream activities (e.g., leasing, warranty, insurance, and service) than in the manufacture of automobiles. Not surprising, carmakers such as Ford and General Motors are undertaking forward integration strategies to become bigger players in these high-profit activities.

3. *Is there a high level of stability in the demand for the organization's products?* High demand or sales volatility would not be conducive to a vertical integration strategy. With the high level of fixed costs in plant and equipment as well as operating costs that accompany endeavors toward vertical integration, widely fluctuating sales demand can either strain resources (in times of high demand) or result in unused capacity (in times of low demand). The cycles of "boom and bust" in the automobile industry are a key reason why the manufacturers have increased the amount of outsourced inputs in recent years.

4. *How high is the proportion of additional production capacity actually absorbed by existing products or by the prospects of new and similar products?* The smaller the proportion of production capacity to be absorbed by existing or future products, the lower is the potential for achieving scale economies associated with the increased capacity—either in terms of backward integration (toward the supply of raw materials) or forward integration (toward the end user). Alternatively, if there is excess capacity in the near term, the strategy of vertical integration may be viable if there is the anticipation of future expansion of products.

5. *Does the company have the necessary competencies to execute the vertical integration strategies?* As many companies would attest, successfully executing strategies of vertical integration can be very difficult. For example, Unocal, a major petroleum refiner, which once owned retail gas stations, was slow to capture the potential grocery and merchandise side of the business that might have resulted from customer traffic to its service stations. Unocal lacked the competencies to develop a separate retail organization and culture. The company eventually sold the assets and brand to Tosco (now part of Phillips Petroleum).

6. *Will the vertical integration initiative have potential negative impacts on the firm's stakeholders?* Managers must carefully consider the impact that vertical integration may have on existing and future customers, suppliers, and competitors. After Lockheed Martin, a dominant defense contractor, acquired Loral Corporation, an electronics supplier, for $9.1 billion, it had an unpleasant and unanticipated surprise. Loral, as a captive supplier of Lockheed, is now viewed as a rival by many of its previous customers. Thus, before Lockheed Martin can realize any net synergies from this acquisition, it must make up for the substantial business that it has lost.

Analyzing Vertical Integration: The Transaction Cost Perspective   Another approach that has proved very useful in understanding vertical integration is the **transaction cost perspective**.[21] According to this perspective, every market transaction involves some *transaction costs.* First, a decision to purchase an input from an outside source leads to *search* costs (i.e., the cost to find where it is available, the level of quality, etc.). Second, there are costs associated with *negotiating.* Third, a *contract* needs to be written spelling out future possible contingencies. Fourth, parties in a contract have to *monitor* each other. Finally, if a party does not comply with the terms of the contract, there are *enforcement* costs. Transaction costs are thus the sum of search costs, negotiation costs, contracting costs, monitoring costs, and enforcement costs. These transaction costs can be avoided by internalizing the activity, in other words, by producing the input in-house.

A related problem with purchasing a specialized input from outside is the issue of *transaction-specific investments.* For example, when an automobile company needs an input specifically designed for a particular car model, the supplier may be unwilling to make the investments in plant and machinery necessary to produce that component for two reasons. First, the investment may take many years to recover but there is no guarantee the automobile company will continue to buy from them after the contract expires, typically in one year. Second, once the investment is made, the supplier has no bargaining power. That is, the buyer knows that the supplier has no option but to supply at ever-lower prices because the investments were so specific that they cannot be used to produce alternative products. In such circumstances, again, vertical integration may be the only option.

Vertical integration, however, gives rise to a different set of costs. These costs are referred to as *administrative costs.* Coordinating different stages of the value chain now internalized within the firm causes administrative costs to go up. Decisions about vertical integration are, therefore, based on a comparison of transaction costs and administrative costs. If transaction costs are lower than administrative costs, it is best to resort to market transactions and avoid vertical integration. For example, McDonald's may be the world's biggest buyer of beef, but they do not raise cattle. The market for beef has low transaction costs and requires no transaction-specific investments. On the other hand, if transaction costs are higher than administrative costs, vertical integration becomes an attractive strategy. Most automobile manufacturers produce their own engines because the market for engines involves high transaction costs and transaction-specific investments.

Unrelated Diversification: Financial Synergies and Parenting

With unrelated diversification, unlike related diversification, few benefits are derived from *horizontal relationships*—that is, the leveraging of core competencies or the sharing of activities across business units within a corporation. Instead, potential benefits can be gained from *vertical (or hierarchical) relationships*—the creation of synergies from the interaction of the corporate office with the individual business units. There are two main sources of such synergies. First, the corporate office can contribute to "parenting" and restructuring of (often acquired) businesses. Second, the corporate office can add value by viewing the entire corporation as a family or "portfolio" of businesses and allocating resources to optimize corporate goals of profitability, cash flow, and growth. Additionally, the corporate office enhances value by establishing appropriate human resource practices and financial controls for each of its business units.

Corporate Parenting and Restructuring

So far, we have discussed how firms can add value through related diversification by exploring sources of synergy *across* business units. Here, we will discuss how value can be created *within* business units as a result of the expertise and support provided by the corporate office. Thus, we look at these as *hierarchical* sources of synergy.

Parenting   The positive contributions of the corporate office have been referred to as the **"parenting advantage."**[22] Many firms have successfully diversified their holdings without strong evidence of the more traditional sources of synergy (i.e., horizontally across business units). Diversified public corporations such as BTR, Emerson Electric, and Hanson and leveraged buyout firms such as Kohlberg, Kravis, Roberts & Company, and Clayton, Dublilier & Rice are a few examples.[23] These parent companies create value through management expertise. How? They improve plans and budgets and provide especially competent central functions such as legal, financial, human resource management, procurement, and the like. Additionally, they help subsidiaries make wise choices in their own acquisitions, divestitures, and new internal development decisions. Such contributions often help business units to substantially increase their revenues and profits. Consider Texas-based Cooper Industries' acquisition of Champion International, the spark plug company, as an example of corporate parenting:[24]

> Cooper applies a distinctive parenting approach designed to help its businesses improve their manufacturing performance. New acquisitions are "Cooperized"—Cooper audits their manufacturing operations; improves their cost accounting systems; makes their planning, budgeting, and human resource systems conform with its systems; and centralizes union negotiations. Excess cash is squeezed out through tighter controls and reinvested in productivity enhancements, which improve overall operating efficiency. As one manager observed, "When you get acquired by Cooper, one of the first things that happens is a truckload of policy manuals arrives at your door." Such active parenting has been effective in enhancing the competitive advantages of many kinds of manufacturing businesses.

Restructuring   **Restructuring** is another means by which the corporate office can add substantial value to a business.[25] The central idea can be captured in the real estate phrase "buy low and sell high." Here, the corporate office tries to find either poorly performing firms with unrealized potential or firms in industries on the threshold of significant, positive change. The parent intervenes, often selling off parts of the business; changing the management; reducing payroll and unnecessary sources of expenses; changing strategies; and infusing the company with new technologies, processes, reward systems, and so forth. When the restructuring is complete, the firm can either "sell high" and capture the added value or keep the business in the corporate family and enjoy the financial and competitive benefits of the enhanced performance.[26]

Loews Corporation, a conglomerate with $18 billion in revenues competes in such industries as oil and gas, tobacco, watches, insurance, and hotels. It provides an exemplary example of how firms can successfully "buy low and sell high" as part of their corporate strategy.[27]

> Energy accounts for 33 percent of Loews' $30 billion in total assets. In the 1980s it bought six oil tankers for only $5 million each during a sharp slide in oil prices. The downside was limited. After all these huge hulks could easily have been sold as scrap steel. However, that didn't have to happen. Eight years after Loews purchased the tankers, they sold them for $50 million each.
>
> Loews was also extremely successful with its next energy play—drilling equipment. Although wildcatting for oil is very risky, selling services to wildcatters is not, especially if the assets are bought during a down cycle. Loews did just that. It purchased 10 offshore drilling rigs for $50 million in 1989 and formed Diamond Offshore Drilling. In 1995 Loews received $338 million after taking a 30 percent piece of this operation public!

For the restructuring strategy to work, the corporate management must have both the insight to detect undervalued companies (otherwise the cost of acquisition would be too high) or businesses competing in industries with a high potential for transformation.[28] Additionally,

parenting advantage the positive contributions of the corporate office to a new business as a result of expertise and support provided and not as a result of substantial changes in assets, capital structure, or management.

restructuring the intervention of the corporate office in a new business that substantially changes the assets, capital structure, and/or management, including selling off parts of the business, changing the management, reducing payroll and unnecessary sources of expenses, changing strategies, and infusing the new business with new technologies, processes, and reward systems.

of course, they must have the requisite skills and resources to turn the businesses around, even if they may be in new and unfamiliar industries.

Restructuring can involve changes in assets, capital structure, or management.

- *Asset restructuring* involves the sale of unproductive assets, or even whole lines of businesses, that are peripheral. In some cases, it may even involve acquisitions that strengthen the core business.
- *Capital restructuring* involves changing the debt-equity mix, or the mix between different classes of debt or equity. Although the substitution of equity with debt is more common in buyout situations, occasionally the parent may provide additional equity capital.
- *Management restructuring* typically involves changes in the composition of the top management team, organizational structure, and reporting relationships. Tight financial control, rewards based strictly on meeting short- to medium-term performance goals, and reduction in the number of middle-level managers are common steps in management restructuring. In some cases, parental intervention may even result in changes in strategy as well as infusion of new technologies and processes.

Hanson, plc, a British conglomerate, made numerous such acquisitions in the United States in the 1980s, often selling these firms at significant profits after a few years of successful restructuring efforts. Hanson's acquisition and subsequent restructuring of the SCM group is a classic example of the restructuring strategy. Hanson acquired SCM, a diversified manufacturer of industrial and consumer products (including Smith-Corona typewriters, Glidden paints, and Durkee Famous Foods), for $930 million in 1986 after a bitter takeover battle. In the next few months, Hanson sold SCM's paper and pulp operations for $160 million, the chemical division for $30 million, Glidden paints for $580 million, and Durkee Famous Foods for $120 million, virtually recovering the entire original investment. In addition, Hanson also sold the SCM headquarters in New York for $36 million and reduced the headquarters staff by 250. They still retained several profitable divisions, including the titanium dioxide operations and managed them with tight financial controls that led to increased returns.[29]

Exhibit 6.5 summarizes the three primary types of restructuring activities.

Portfolio Management

During the 1970s and early 1980s, several leading consulting firms developed the concept of **portfolio management** to achieve a better understanding of the competitive position of an overall portfolio (or family) of businesses, to suggest strategic alternatives for each of the businesses, and to identify priorities for the allocation of resources. Several studies have reported widespread use of these techniques among American firms.[30]

Description and Potential Benefits   The key purpose of portfolio models is to assist a firm in achieving a balanced portfolio of businesses.[31] This consists of businesses whose profitability, growth, and cash flow characteristics complements each other and adds up to a satisfactory overall corporate performance. Imbalance, for example, could be caused either by excessive cash generation with too few growth opportunities or by insufficient cash

portfolio management a method of a) assessing the competitive position of a portfolio of businesses within a corporation, b) suggesting strategic alternatives for each business, and c) to identify priorities for the allocation of resources across the businesses.

Exhibit 6.5
The Three Primary Types of Restructuring Activities

Asset Restructuring: The sale of unproductive assets, or even whole lines of businesses, that are peripheral.

Capital Restructuring: Changing the debt-equity mix, or the mix between different classes of debt or equity.

Management Restructuring: Changes in the composition of the top management team, organization structure, and reporting relationships.

Exhibit 6.6 The Boston Consulting Group (BCG) Portfolio Matrix

generation to fund the growth requirements in the portfolio. Monsanto, for example, used portfolio planning to restructure its portfolio, divesting low-growth commodity chemicals businesses and acquiring businesses in higher-growth industries such as biotechnology.

The Boston Consulting Group's (BCG) growth/share matrix is among the best known of these approaches.[32] In the BCG approach, each of the firm's strategic business units (SBUs) is plotted on a two-dimensional grid in which the axes are relative market share and industry growth rate. The grid is broken into four quadrants. Exhibit 6.6 depicts the BCG matrix. Following are a few clarifications:

1. Each circle represents one of the corporation's business units. The size of the circle represents the relative size of the business unit in terms of revenues.
2. Relative market share, measured by the ratio of the business unit's size to that of its largest competitor, is plotted along the horizontal axis.
3. Market share is central to the BCG matrix. This is because high relative market share leads to unit cost reduction due to experience and learning curve effects and, consequently, superior competitive position.

Each of the four quadrants of the grid has different implications for the SBUs that fall into the category:

- **Stars** are SBUs competing in high-growth industries with relatively high market shares. These firms have long-term growth potential and should continue to receive substantial investment funding.
- **Question Marks** are SBUs competing in high-growth industries but having relatively weak market shares. Resources should be invested in them to enhance their competitive positions.
- **Cash Cows** are SBUs with high market shares in low-growth industries. These units have limited long-run potential but represent a source of current cash flows to fund investments in "stars" and "question marks."
- **Dogs** are SBUs with weak market shares in low-growth industries. Because they have weak positions and limited potential, most analysts recommend that they be divested.

In using portfolio strategy approaches, a corporation tries to create synergies and shareholder value in a number of ways.[33] Since the businesses are unrelated, synergies that develop are those that result from the actions of the corporate office with the individual units (i.e., hierarchical relationships) instead of among business units (i.e., horizontal relationships). First, portfolio analysis provides a snapshot of the businesses in a corporation's portfolio. Therefore, the corporation is in a better position to allocate resources among the business units according to prescribed criteria (e.g., use cash flows from the "cash cows" to fund promising "stars"). Second, the expertise and analytical resources in the corporate office provide guidance in determining what firms may be attractive (or unattractive) acquisitions. Third, the corporate office is able to provide financial resources to the business units on favorable terms that reflect the corporation's overall ability to raise funds. Fourth, the corporate office can provide high-quality review and coaching for the individual businesses. Fifth, portfolio analysis provides a basis for developing strategic goals and reward/evaluation systems for business managers. For example, managers of cash cows would have lower targets for revenue growth than managers of stars, but the former would have higher threshold levels of profit targets on proposed projects than the managers of star businesses. Compensation systems would also reflect such realities. Cash cows understandably would be rewarded more on the basis of cash that their businesses generate than would managers of star businesses. Similarly, managers of star businesses would be held to higher standards for revenue growth than managers of cash cow businesses.

To see how companies can benefit from portfolio approaches, consider Ciba-Geigy.

In 1994 Ciba-Geigy adopted portfolio planning approaches to help it manage its business units, which competed in a wide variety of industries, including chemicals, dyes, pharmaceuticals, crop protection, and animal health.[34] It placed each business unit in a category corresponding to the BCG matrix. The business unit's goals, compensation programs, personnel selection, and resource allocation were strongly associated with the category within which the business was placed. For example, business units classified as "cash cows" had much higher hurdles for obtaining financial resources (from the corporate office) for expansion than "question marks" since the latter were businesses for which Ciba-Geigy had high hopes for accelerated future growth and profitability. Additionally, the compensation of a business unit manager in a cash cow would be strongly associated with its success in generating cash to fund other businesses, whereas a manager of a question mark business would be rewarded on his or her ability to increase revenue growth and market share. The portfolio planning approaches appear to be working. In 2006, Ciba-Geigy's (now Novartis) revenues and net income stood at $26 billion and $8 billion, respectively. This represents a 22 percent increase in revenues and a most impressive 40 percent growth in net income over the past two years.

Limitations   Despite the potential benefits of portfolio models, there are also some notable downsides. First, they compare SBUs on only two dimensions, making the implicit but erroneous assumption that (1) those are the only factors that really matter and (2) every unit can be accurately compared on that basis. Second, the approach views each SBU as a stand-alone entity, ignoring common core business practices and value-creating activities that may hold promise for synergies across business units. Third, unless care is exercised, the process becomes largely mechanical, substituting an over-simplified graphical model for the important contributions of the CEO's (and other corporate managers's) experience and judgment. Fourth, the reliance on "strict rules" regarding resource allocation across SBUs can be detrimental to a firm's long-term viability. For example, according to one study, over one-half of all the businesses that should have been cash users (based on the BCG matrix) were instead cash providers.[35]

Finally, while colorful and easy to comprehend, the imagery of the BCG matrix can lead to some troublesome and overly simplistic prescriptions. According to one author:

> The dairying analogy is appropriate (for some cash cows), so long as we resist the urge to oversimplify it. On the farm, even the best-producing cows eventually begin to dry up. The farmer's solution to this is euphemistically called "freshening" the cow: The farmer arranges a date for the cow with a bull, she has a calf, the milk begins flowing again. Cloistering the cow—isolating her from everything but the feed trough and the milking machines—assures that she will go dry.[36]

- "Cows" in the BCG matrix as well as "live" cows need nourishment to be productive. Corporations will falter if they "milk" their cows excessively and fail to invest in these business units.

To see what can go wrong, consider Cabot Corporation.

> Cabot Corporation supplies carbon black for the rubber, electronics, and plastics industries. Following the BCG matrix, Cabot moved away from its cash cow, carbon black, and diversified into stars such as ceramics and semiconductors in a seemingly overaggressive effort to create more revenue growth for the corporation. Predictably, Cabot's return on assets declined as the firm shifted away from its core competence to unrelated areas. The portfolio model failed by pointing the company in the wrong direction in an effort to spur growth—away from their core business. Recognizing its mistake, Cabot Corporation returned to its mainstay carbon black manufacturing and divested unrelated businesses. Today the company is a leader in its field with $2.5 billion in 2006 revenues.[37]

Exhibit 6.7 summarizes the limitations of portfolio model analysis.

Caveat: Is Risk Reduction a Viable Goal of Diversification?

Analysts and academics have suggested that one of the purposes of diversification is to reduce the risk that is inherent in a firm's variability in revenues and profits over time. In essence, the argument is that if a firm enters new products or markets that are affected differently by seasonal or economic cycles, its performance over time will be more stable. For example, a firm manufacturing lawn mowers may diversify into snow blowers to even out its annual sales. Or a firm manufacturing a luxury line of household furniture may introduce a lower-priced line since affluent and lower-income customers are affected differently by economic cycles.

At first glance the above reasoning may make sense, but there are some problems with it. First, a firm's stockholders can diversify their portfolios at a much lower cost than a corporation. As we have noted in this chapter, individuals can purchase their shares with almost no premium (e.g., only a small commission is paid to a discount broker), and they don't have to worry about integrating the acquisition into their portfolio. Second, economic cycles as well as their impact on a given industry (or firm) are difficult to predict with any degree of accuracy.

- They are overly simplistic; consisting of only two dimensions (growth and market share).
- They view each business as separate, ignoring potential synergies across businesses.
- The process may become overly largely mechanical, minimizing the potential value of managers' judgment and experience.
- The reliance on strict rules for resource allocation across SBUs can be detrimental to a firm's long-term viability.
- The imagery (e.g., cash cows, dogs) while colorful, may lead to troublesome and overly simplistic prescriptions.

Exhibit 6.7
Limitations of Portfolio Models

Notwithstanding the above, some firms have benefited from diversification by lowering the variability (or risk) in their performance over time. Consider Emerson Electronic.

Emerson Electronic is a $16 billion manufacturer that has enjoyed an incredible run—43 consecutive years of earnings growth![38] It produces a wide variety of products, including measurement devices for heavy industry, temperature controls for heating and ventilation systems, and power tools sold at Home Depot. Recently, many analysts questioned Emerson's purchase of companies that sell power systems to the volatile telecommunications industry. Why? This industry is expected to experience, at best, minimal growth. However, CEO David Farr maintained that such assets could be acquired inexpensively because of the aggregate decline in demand in this industry. Additionally, he argued that the other business units, such as the sales of valves and regulators to the now-booming oil and natural gas companies, were able to pick up the slack. Therefore, while net profits in the electrical equipment sector (Emerson's core business) sharply decreased, Emerson's overall corporate profits increased 1.7 percent.

In summary, risk reduction in and of itself is rarely viable as a means to create shareholder value. It must be undertaken with a view of a firm's overall diversification strategy.

The Means to Achieve Diversification

>LO5

The various means of engaging in diversification—mergers and acquisitions, joint ventures/strategic alliances, and internal development.

In the prior two sections, we have addressed the types of diversification (e.g., related and unrelated) that a firm may undertake to achieve synergies and create value for its shareholders. In this section, we address the means by which a firm can go about achieving these desired benefits.

We will address three basic means. First, through acquisitions or mergers, corporations can directly acquire a firm's assets and competencies. Although the terms *mergers* and *acquisitions* are used quite interchangeably, there are some key differences. With **acquisitions,** one firm buys another either through a stock purchase, cash, or the issuance of debt. **Mergers,** on the other hand, entail a combination or consolidation of two firms to form a new legal entity. Mergers are relatively rare and entail a transaction among two firms on a relatively equal basis. Despite such differences, we consider both mergers and acquisitions to be quite similar in terms of their implications for a firm's corporate-level strategy.

acquisitions the incorporation of one firm into another through purchase.

Second, corporations may agree to pool the resources of other companies with their resource base, commonly known as a joint venture or strategic alliance. Although these two forms of partnerships are similar in many ways, there is an important difference. Joint ventures involve the formation of a third-party legal entity where the two (or more) firms each contribute equity, whereas strategic alliances do not.

Third, corporations may diversify into new products, markets, and technologies through internal development. This approach, sometimes called corporate entrepreneurship, involves the leveraging and combining of a firm's own resources and competencies to create synergies and enhance shareholder value.

mergers the combining of two or more firms into one new legal entity.

Mergers and Acquisitions

The rate of mergers and acquisitions (M&A) had dropped off beginning in 2001. This trend was largely a result of a recession, corporate scandals, and a declining stock market. However, the situation has changed dramatically. Recently, several large mergers and acquisitions were announced. These include:[39]

- Mittal Steel's acquisition of Arcelor for $33 billion.
- Freeport-McMoRan's acquisition of Phelps Dodge for $26 billion.
- BellSouth's acquisition of AT&T for $86.0 billion.
- Sprint's merger with Nextel for $39 billion.
- Boston Scientific's $27 billion acquisition of medical device maker Guidant.

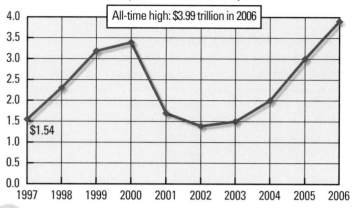

Global Value of Mergers and Acquisitions

Global mergers and acquisitions soared past their previous record and nearly hit $4 trillion for the year 2006.

Exhibit 6.8 Global Value of Mergers and Acquistions

Source: Bloomberg; Dealogic.

- Exelon's acquisition of Public Service Enterprise Group for $12 billion.
- Procter & Gamble's purchase of Gillette for $54 billion.
- Kmart Holding Corp.'s acquisition of Sears, Roebuck & Co. for $11 billion.

Exhibit 6.8 illustrates the dramatic increase in worldwide merger and acquisition activity in the United States in the past few years. Several factors help to explain the recent rise. First, there is the robust economy and the increasing corporate profits that have boosted stock prices and cash. For example, the Standard & Poor's 500 stock index companies, including financial companies, have a record of over $2 trillion in cash and other short-term assets, according to S&P Compustat.

Second, the weak U.S. dollar makes U.S. assets more attractive to other countries. That is, from the perspective of a foreign acquirer, compared to any other period in recent memory, U.S. companies are "cheap" today. For example, a Euro which was worth only 80 cents in 1999 was worth $1.35 by mid 2007. This makes U.S. companies a relative bargain for a European acquirer. And third, stricter governance standards are requiring poorly performing CEOs and boards of directors to consider unsolicited offers. In essence, top executives and board members are less likely to be protected by anti-takeover mechanisms such as greenmail, poison pills and golden parachutes (which we will discuss at the end of the chapter).

Next, we will address some of the motives and potential benefits of mergers and acquisitions as well as their potential limitations.

Motives and Benefits Growth through mergers and acquisitions has played a critical role in the success of many corporations in a wide variety of high-technology and knowledge-intensive industries. Here, market and technology changes can occur very quickly and unpredictably.[40] Speed—speed to market, speed to positioning, and speed to becoming a viable company—is critical in such industries. For example, Alex Mandl, then AT&T's president, was responsible for the acquisition of McCaw Cellular. Although many industry experts felt the price was too steep, he believed that cellular technology was a critical asset for the telecommunications business and that it would have been extremely difficult to build that business from the ground up. Mandl claimed, "The plain fact is that acquiring is much faster than building."[41]

As we discussed earlier in the chapter, mergers and acquisitions also can be a means of *obtaining valuable resources that can help an organization expand its product offerings and services*. For example, Cisco Systems, a dominant player in networking equipment, acquired more than 70 companies over a recent seven-year period.[42] This provides Cisco with access to the latest in networking equipment. Then it uses its excellent sales force to market the new technology to its corporate customers and telephone companies. Cisco also provides strong incentives to the staff of acquired companies to stay on. In order to realize the greatest value from its acquisitions, Cisco also has learned to integrate acquired companies efficiently and effectively.[43]

Mergers and acquisitions also can *provide the opportunity for firms to attain the three bases of synergy that were addressed earlier in the chapter—leveraging core competencies, sharing activities, and building market power.* Consider Procter & Gamble's $57 billion acquisition of Gillette.[44] First, it helps Procter & Gamble to leverage its core competencies in marketing and product positioning in the area of grooming and personal care brands. For example, P&G has experience in repositioning brands such as Old Spice in this market (which recently passed Gillette's Right Guard brand to become No. 1 in the deodorant market). Gillette has very strong brands in razors and blades. Thus, P&G's marketing expertise enhances its market position. Second, there are opportunities to share value-creating activities. Gillette will benefit from P&G's stronger distribution network in developing countries where the potential growth rate for the industry's products remains higher than in the United States, Europe, or Japan. Consider the insight of A. F. Lafley, P&G's CEO:

> When I was in Asia in the 90s, we had already gone beyond the top 500 cities in China. Today, we're way down into the rural areas. So we add three, four, five Gillette brands, and we don't even have to add a salesperson.

Third, the addition of Gillette increases P&G's market power. In recent years, the growth of powerful global retailers such as Wal-Mart, Carrefour, and Costco has eroded much of the consumer goods industry's pricing power. A central part of P&G's recent strategy has been to focus its resources on enhancing its core brands. Today, 16 of its brands (each with revenues of over $1 billion) account for $30 billion of the firm's $51.4 billion in total revenues. Gillette, with $10.5 billion in total revenues, adds five brands which also have revenues of over $1 billion. P&G anticipates that its growing stable of "superbrands" will help it to weather the industry's tough pricing environment and enhance its power relative to large, powerful retailers such as Wal-Mart and Target.

Merger and acquisition activity also can *lead to consolidation within an industry and can force other players to merge.*[45] In the pharmaceutical industry, the patents for many top-selling drugs are expiring and M&A activity is expected to heat up.[46] For example, a few years ago SG Cowen Securities predicted that between 2000 and 2005, U.S. patents would expire on pharmaceutical products with annual domestic sales of approximately $34.6 billion. Clearly, this is an example of how the political—legal segment of the general environment (discussed in Chapter 2) can affect a corporation's strategy and performance. Although health care providers and patients are happy about the lower-cost generics that will arrive, drug firms are being pressed to make up for lost revenues. Combining top firms such as Pfizer Inc. and Warner-Lambert Co. as well as Glaxo Wellcome and SmithKline Beecham has many potential long-term benefits. They not only promise significant postmerger cost savings, but also the increased size of the combined companies brings greater research and development possibilities.

Two other industries where consolidation is the primary rationale are telecommunications and software.[47] In 2004, Cingular Wireless became number one in the industry by acquiring AT&T Wireless Communications. Subsequently, Sprint agreed to buy Nextel to form a stronger number three. In software, the primary motive for mergers is to offer customers a fuller portfolio of products. Many niche players are selling out to serial buyers like Oracle Corp., which recently acquired PeopleSoft Inc. after a long and heated struggle. Symantec Corp. agreed to acquire Veritas Software Corporation for $13.5 billion. Such consolidation raises questions about whether smaller players such as McAfee, BEA Systems, and Siebel Systems are big enough to remain independent. According to Joseph M. Tucci, president and CEO of data-storage giant EMC, "This is going to be a big boys' game. They're going to move very aggressively and quickly."

Corporations can also *enter new market segments by way of acquisitions.* Although Charles Schwab & Co. is best known for providing discount trading services for middle America, it clearly is interested in other target markets.[48] In late 2000 Schwab surprised its rivals by paying $2.7 billion to acquire (divested in 2006) U.S. Trust Corporation, a 147-year-old financial services institution that is a top estate planner for the wealthy. However, Schwab is in no way ignoring its core market. The firm also purchased Cybercorp Inc., a Texas brokerage company, for $488 million. That firm offers active online traders sophisticated quotes and stock-screening tools.

Potential Limitations   As noted in the previous section, mergers and acquisitions provide a firm with many potential benefits. However, at the same time, there are many potential drawbacks or limitations to such corporate activity.[49]

First, *the takeover premium that is paid for an acquisition is very high.* Two times out of three, the stock price of the acquiring company falls once the deal is made public. Since the acquiring firm often pays a 30 percent to 40 percent premium for the target company, the acquirer must create synergies and scale economies that result in sales and market gains exceeding the premium price. Firms paying higher premiums set the performance hurdle even higher. For example, Household International paid an 82 percent premium to buy Beneficial, and Conseco paid an 83 percent premium to acquire Green Tree Financial. Historically, paying a high premium over the stock price has been a largely unprofitable strategy.

Second, *competing firms often can imitate any advantages realized or copy synergies that result from the M&A.* Thus, a firm can often see its advantages quickly evaporate if it plans to achieve competitive advantage through M&A activity. Unless the advantages are sustainable and difficult to copy, investors will not be willing to pay a high premium for the stock. Similarly, the time value of money must be factored into the stock price. M&A costs are paid up front. Conversely, firms pay for research and development, ongoing marketing, and capacity expansion over time. This stretches out the payments needed to gain new competencies. The M&A argument is that a large initial investment is worthwhile because it creates long-term advantages. However, stock analysts want to see immediate results from such a large cash outlay. If the acquired firm does not produce results quickly, investors often sell the stock, driving the price down.

Third, *managers' credibility and ego can sometimes get in the way of sound business decisions.* If the M&A does not perform as planned, managers who pushed for the deal find that their reputation may be at stake. Sometimes, this can lead these managers to protect their credibility by funneling more money, or escalating their commitment, into an inevitably doomed operation. Further, when a merger fails and a firm tries to unload the acquisition, managers often find that they must sell at a huge discount. These problems further compound the costs and weaken the stock price.

Fourth, *there can be many cultural issues that may doom the intended benefits from M&A endeavors.* Consider, for example, the insights of Joanne Lawrence, who played an important role as vice president and director of communications and investor relations at SmithKline Beecham, in the merger between SmithKline and the Beecham Group, a diversified consumer-oriented group headquartered in the United Kingdom.[50]

> The key to a strategic merger is to create a new culture. This was a mammoth challenge during the SmithKline Beecham merger. We were working at so many different cultural levels, it was dizzying. We had two national cultures to blend—American and British—that compounded the challenge of selling the merger in two different markets with two different shareholder bases. There were also two different business cultures: One was very strong, scientific, and academic; the other was much more commercially oriented. And then we had to consider within both companies the individual businesses, each of which has its own little culture.[51]

Divestment: The Other Side of the "M&A Coin" When firms acquire other businesses it typically generates quite a bit of "press" in business publications such as *The Wall Street Journal, BusinessWeek,* and *Fortune.* It makes for exciting news and one thing is for sure—large acquiring firms automatically improve their standing in the Fortune 500 rankings (since it is based solely on total revenues). However, managers must also carefully consider the strategic implications of exiting businesses.

Divestments, the exit of a business from a firm's portfolio, are quite common. One study found that large, prestigious U.S. companies divested more acquisitions than they had kept.[52] Well-known divestitures in business history include (1) Novell's purchase of WordPerfect for stock valued at $1.4 billion and later sold to Corel for $124 million, and (2) Quaker Oats unloading of the Snapple Beverage Company to Triarc for only $300 million in 1997—three years after it had bought it for $1.8 billion! Also, in early 2007, DaimlerChrysler announced that they are looking for a buyer for its Chrysler unit, which they had acquired a decade earlier.[53]

Divesting a business can accomplish many different objectives.* As the examples above demonstrate, it can be used to help a firm reverse an earlier acquisition that didn't work out as planned. Often, this is simply to help "cut their losses." Other objectives include: (1) enabling managers to focus their efforts more directly on the firm's core businesses,[54] (2) providing the firm with more resources to spend on more attractive alternatives; and, (3) raising cash to help fund existing businesses.

In summary, divesting can enhance a firm's competitive position only to the extent that it reduces its tangible (e.g., maintenance, investments, etc.) or intangible (e.g., opportunity costs, managerial attention) costs without sacrificing a current competitive advantage or the seeds of future advantages.[55] To be effective, divesting requires a thorough understanding of a business unit's current ability and future potential to contribute to a firm's value creation. However, since such decisions involve a great deal of uncertainty, it is very difficult to make such evaluations. In addition, because of managerial self-interests and organizational inertia, firms often delay divestments of underperforming businesses.

Strategy Spotlight 6.5 addresses how Royal Philips Electronics NV, a bastion of European business with $35 billion in revenues, has gone about divesting businesses over the past several years.

Strategic Alliances and Joint Ventures

A **strategic alliance** is a cooperative relationship between two (or more) firms. Alliances may be either informal or formal—that is, involving a written contract. **Joint ventures** represent a special case of alliances, wherein two (or more) firms contribute equity to form a new legal entity.

Strategic alliances and joint ventures are assuming an increasingly prominent role in the strategy of leading firms, both large and small.[56] Such cooperative relationships have many potential advantages.[57] Among these are entering new markets, reducing manufacturing (or other) costs in the value chain, and developing and diffusing new technologies.[58]

Entering New Markets Often a company that has a successful product or service wants to introduce it into a new market. However, it may not have the requisite marketing

---

> **divestment** the exit of a business from a firm's portfolio.

> **strategic alliances** a cooperative relationship between two or more firms.

> **joint ventures** new entities formed within a strategic alliance in which two or more firms, the parents, contribute equity to form the new legal entity.

---

* Firms can divest their businesses in a number of ways. Sell-offs, spin-offs, equity carve-outs, asset sales/dissolution, and split-ups are some such modes of divestment. In a sell-off, the divesting firm privately negotiates with a third party to divest a unit/subsidiary for cash/stock. In a spin-off, a parent company distributes shares of the unit/subsidiary being divested pro-rata to its existing shareholders and a new company is formed. Equity carve-outs are similar to spin-offs except that shares in the unit/subsidiary being divested are offered to new shareholders. Dissolution involves sale of redundant assets, not necessarily as an entire unit/subsidiary as in sell-offs but a few bits at a time. A split-up, on the other hand, is an instance of divestiture where the parent company is split into two or more new companies and the parent ceases to exist. Shares in the parent company are exchanged for shares in new companies and the exact distribution varies case by case.

strategy spotlight

6.5

Philips Divests Some of its Businesses

Royal Philips Electronics NV started making lightbulbs in Eindhoven in the Netherlands in 1891. In the first half of the 20th century it produced X-ray machines and radio equipment, and in the 1970s it moved into the record business. By 2007, it employed 122,000 people in 60 countries in its diversified businesses.

Until recently, however, Philips wasn't like most big companies. It was a huge, unwieldy conglomerate that made everything from lightbulbs, consumer electronics, mobile phones, microprocessors, and electric shavers to less-well-known products such as defibrillators and MRI machines. In fact, at one time, Philips was even in the music business, with internationally known artists like Sting and Elton John recording on its PolyGram label. Not surprisingly, the company even confused analysts. "Can You Tell What It Is Yet?" asked Citigroup's Simon Smith in a report on Philips that touted the company as "one of the last great misunderstood conglomerates of Europe."

Sources: Anonymous. 2007. Home and abroad. *The Economist*. February 10: 7–8; Sterling, T. 2007. Philips 4Q doubles, sales slip, bizyahoo.com. January 22; Schwartz, N. D. 2007. Europe businessman of the year: Gerard Kleisterlee. Money.cnn.com. January 12; and Reihardt, A. 2004. Philips: Back on the beam. www.businessweek.com. May 3.

In recent years, Philips has been undergoing an endless round of restructuring in an effort to make it more competitive. Things came to a head in the 2001 recession when the company suffered huge losses and had to shed 55,000 jobs—about one-fourth of its workforce. Thirty separate divisions were reduced to only five—domestic appliances, lighting, medical, consumer electronics, and semiconductors. A net loss of $4.2 billion in 2002 turned into a net profit of $3.6 billion by 2004.

Philips has continued its effective divestment strategy. It has been steadily exiting electronics markets where it doesn't hold a first- or second-place position—most notably divesting its mobile phones operation after being eclipsed by Nokia Corp.

Its biggest divestiture was its sale of its microprocessor division for $5.6 billion in August 2006 to a consortium of private investors led by Kohlberg Kravis Roberts & Co. The proceeds were used to focus on faster growing lines like lighting and medical devices and to reward investors with a multibillion-dollar share buyback. The streamlined company's goal is now to refocus on its fastest-growing and most profitable sectors, such as medical systems. "No question, it's a much more focused company," says Rene Verhaef of Fortis Bank in Amsterdam.

Philip's performance has continued to soar. Its 2006 earnings hit $7 billion on revenues of $35 billion.

expertise because it does not understand customer needs, know how to promote the product, or have access to the proper distribution channels.

The partnerships formed between Time-Warner, Inc., and three African American–owned cable companies in New York City are examples of joint ventures created to serve a domestic market. Time-Warner built a 185,000-home cable system in the city and asked the three cable companies to operate it. Time-Warner supplied the product, and the cable companies supplied the knowledge of the community and the know-how to market the cable system. Joining with the local companies enabled Time-Warner to win the acceptance of the cable customers and to benefit from an improved image in the black community.

Reducing Manufacturing (or Other) Costs in the Value Chain Strategic alliances (or joint ventures) often enable firms to pool capital, value-creating activities, or facilities in order to reduce costs. For example, Molson Companies and Carling O'Keefe Breweries in Canada formed a joint venture to merge their brewing operations. Although Molson had a modern and efficient brewery in Montreal, Carling's was outdated. However, Carling had the better facilities in Toronto. In addition, Molson's Toronto brewery was located on the waterfront and had substantial real estate value. Overall, the synergies gained by using their combined facilities more efficiently added $150 million of pretax earnings during the initial year of the venture. Economies of scale were realized and facilities were better utilized.

Developing and Diffusing New Technologies   Strategic alliances also may be used to build jointly on the technological expertise of two or more companies in order to develop products technologically beyond the capability of the companies acting independently. STMicroelectronics (ST) is a high-tech company based in Geneva, Switzerland, that has thrived—largely due to the success of its strategic alliances.[59] The firm develops and manufactures computer chips for a variety of applications such as mobile phones, set-top boxes, smart cards, and flash memories. In 1995 it teamed up with Hewlett-Packard to develop powerful new processors for various digital applications that are now nearing completion. Another example was its strategic alliance with Nokia to develop a chip that would give Nokia's phones a longer battery life. Here, ST produced a chip that tripled standby time to 60 hours—a breakthough that gave Nokia a huge advantage in the marketplace.

The firm's CEO, Pasquale Pistorio, was among the first in the industry to form R&D alliances with other companies. Now ST's top 12 customers, including HP, Nokia, and Nortel, account for 45 percent of revenues. According to Pistorio, "Alliances are in our DNA." Such relationships help ST keep better-than-average growth rates, even in difficult times. That's because close partners are less likely to defect to other suppliers. ST's financial results are most impressive. During 2000 its revenues grew 55 percent—nearly double the industry average.

Potential Downsides   Despite their promise, many alliances and joint ventures fail to meet expectations for a variety of reasons.[60] First, without the proper partner, a firm should never consider undertaking an alliance, even for the best of reasons. Each partner should bring the desired complementary strengths to the partnership. Ideally, the strengths contributed by the partners are unique; thus synergies created can be more easily sustained and defended over the longer term. The goal must be to develop synergies between the contributions of the partners, resulting in a win–win situation for both. Moreover, the partners must be compatible and willing to trust each other. Unfortunately, often little attention is given to nurturing the close working relationships and interpersonal connections that bring together the partnering organizations. The human or people factors are not carefully considered or, at worst, they are dismissed as an unimportant consideration.

Internal Development

Firms can also diversify by means of corporate entrepreneurship and new venture development. **In today's economy, internal development is such an important means by which companies expand their businesses that we have devoted a whole chapter to it (see Chapter 12).** Sony and the Minnesota Mining & Manufacturing Co. (3M), for example, are known for their dedication to innovation, R&D, and cutting-edge technologies. For example, 3M has developed its entire corporate culture to support its ongoing policy of generating at least 25 percent of total sales from products created within the most recent four-year period. During the 1990s, 3M exceeded this goal by achieving about 30 percent of sales per year from new internally developed products.

Many companies use some form of internal development to extend their product lines or add to their service offerings. This approach to internal development is used by many large publicly held corporations as well as small firms. An example of the latter is Rosa Verde, a small but growing business serving the health care needs of San Antonio, Texas.

> This small company began with one person who moved from Mexico to San Antonio, Texas, to serve the health care needs of inner-city residents.[61] Beginning as a sole proprietor, Dr. Lourdes Pizana started Rosa Verde Family Health Care Group in 1995 with only $10,000 obtained from credit card debt. She has used a strategy of internal development to propel the company to where it is today—six clinics, 30 doctors, and a team of other health care professionals.
>
> How was Dr. Pizana able to accomplish this in such a short time? She emphasizes the company's role in the community, forging links with community leaders. In addition, she hires nearly all her professional staff as independent contractors to control

The Ritz-Carlton Leadership Center: A Successful Internal Venture

Companies worldwide often strive to be the "Ritz-Carlton" of their industries. Ritz-Carlton, the large luxury hotel chain, is the only service company to have won the prestigious Malcolm Baldrige National Quality Award twice—in 1992 and 1999 (one year after being acquired by Marriott). It also has placed first in guest satisfaction among luxury hotels in the most recent J.D. Power & Associates hotel survey.

Until a few years ago, being "Ritz-Carlton-like" was just a motivational simile. However, in 2000, the company launched the Ritz-Carlton Leadership Center, where it offers 12 leadership development programs for its employees and seven benchmarking seminars and workshops to outside companies. It also conducts 35 off-site presentations on such topics as "Creating a Dynamic Employee Orientation," and "The Key to Retaining and Selecting Talented

Employees." (Incidentally, Ritz-Carlton's annual turnover rate among nonmanagement employees is 25 percent— roughly half the average rate for U.S. luxury hotels.)

Within its first four years of operation, 800 different companies from such industries as health care, banking and finance, hospitality, and the automotive industries have participated in the Leadership Center's programs. And to date it has generated over $2 million in revenues. Ken Yancey, CEO of the nonprofit small-business consultancy, Score, says the concepts he learned, like "the three steps of service," apply directly to his business. "Hotels are about service to a client," he says. "And we are too."

To give a few specifics on one of the Leadership Center's programs, consider its "Legendary Service I" course. The topics that are covered include empowerment, using customer recognition to boost loyalty, and Ritz-Carlton's approach to quality. The course lasts two days and costs $2,000 per attendee. Well-known companies that have participated include Microsoft, Morgan Stanley, and Starbucks.

Sources: McDonald, D. 2004. Roll out the blue carpet. *Business 2.0*, May: 53; and Johnson, G. 2003. Nine tactics to take your corporate university from good to GREAT. *Training*, July/August: 38–41.

costs. These professionals are paid based on the volume of work they do rather than a set salary; Pizana splits her revenue with them, thus motivating them to work efficiently. Her strategy is to grow the company from the inside out through high levels of service, commitment to the community she serves, and savvy leadership. By committing to a solid plan, Pizana has proven that internal growth and development can be a successful strategy.

The luxury hotel chain Ritz-Carlton has long been recognized for its exemplary service. In fact, it is the only service company ever to win two Malcolm Baldrige National Quality Awards. It has built on this capability by developing a highly successful internal venture to offer leadership development programs—both to its employees as well as to outside companies. We address this internal venture in Strategy Spotlight 6.6.

Compared to mergers and acquisitions, firms that engage in internal development are able to capture the value created by their own innovative activities without having to "share the wealth" with alliance partners or face the difficulties associated with combining activities across the value chains of several companies or merging corporate cultures. Another advantage is that firms can often develop new products or services at a relatively lower cost and thus rely on their own resources rather than turning to external funding. There are also potential disadvantages. Internal development may be time consuming; thus, firms may forfeit the benefits of speed that growth through mergers or acquisitions can provide. This may be especially important among high-tech or knowledge-based organizations in fast-paced environments where being an early mover is critical. Thus, firms that choose to diversify through internal development must develop capabilities that allow them to move quickly from initial opportunity recognition to market introduction.

How Managerial Motives Can Erode Value Creation

>LO6

Managerial behaviors that can erode the creation of value.

Thus far in the chapter we have implicitly assumed that CEOs and top executives are "rational beings"; that is, they act in the best interests of shareholders to maximize long-term shareholder value. In the real world, however, this is not the case. Frequently, they may act in their own self-interest. Next, we address some managerial motives that can serve to erode, rather than enhance, value creation. These include "growth for growth's sake," excessive egotism, and the creation of a wide variety of antitakeover tactics.

Growth for Growth's Sake

There are huge incentives for executives to increase the size of their firm, and many of these are hardly consistent with increasing shareholder wealth. Top managers, including the CEO, of larger firms typically enjoy more prestige, higher rankings for their companies on the Fortune 500 list (which is based on revenues, not profits), greater incomes, more job security, and so on. There is also the excitement and associated recognition of making a major acquisition. As noted by Harvard's Michael Porter, "There's a tremendous allure to mergers and acquisitions. It's the big play, the dramatic gesture. With one stroke of the pen you can add billions to size, get a front-page story, and create excitement in markets."[62]

In recent years many high-tech firms have suffered from the negative impact of their uncontrolled growth. Consider, for example, Priceline.com's ill-fated venture into an online service to offer groceries and gasoline.[63] A myriad of problems—perhaps most importantly, a lack of participation by manufacturers—caused the firm to lose more than $5 million a *week* prior to abandoning these ventures. Similarly, many have questioned the profit potential of Amazon.com's recent ventures into a variety of products such as tools and hardware, cell phones, and service. Such initiatives are often little more than desperate moves by top managers to satisfy investor demands for accelerating revenues. Unfortunately, the increased revenues often fail to materialize into a corresponding hike in earnings.

At times, executives' overemphasis on growth can result in a plethora of ethical lapses, which can have disastrous outcomes for their companies. A good example (of bad practice) is Joseph Bernardino's leadership at Andersen Worldwide. Bernardino had a chance early on to take a hard line on ethics and quality in the wake of earlier scandals at clients such as Waste Management and Sunbeam. Instead, according to former executives, he put too much emphasis on revenue growth. Consequently, the firm's reputation quickly eroded when it audited and signed off on the highly flawed financial statements of such infamous firms as Enron, Global Crossing, and WorldCom. WorldCom, in fact, is recognized as the biggest financial fraud of all time. Bernardino ultimately resigned in disgrace in March 2002, and his firm was dissolved later that year.[64]

Egotism

Most would agree that there is nothing wrong with ego, per se. After all, a healthy ego helps make a leader confident, clearheaded, and able to cope with change. CEOs, by their very nature, are typically fiercely competitive people in the office as well as on the tennis court or golf course. However, sometimes when pride is at stake, individuals will go to great lengths to win. Such behavior, of course, is not a new phenomenon. We discuss the case of Cornelius Vanderbilt, one of the original American moguls, in Strategy Spotlight 6.7.

Egos can get in the way of a "synergistic" corporate marriage. Few executives (or lower-level managers) are exempt from the potential downside of excessive egos. Consider, for

Cornelius Vanderbilt: Going to Great Lengths to Correct a Wrong!

Cornelius Vanderbilt's legendary ruthlessness set a bar for many titans to come. Back in 1853, the Commodore took his first vacation, an extended voyage to Europe aboard his yacht. He was in for a big surprise when he returned. Two of his associates had taken the power of attorney that he had left them and sold his interest in his steamship concern, Accessory Transit Company, to themselves.

"Gentlemen," he wrote, in a classic battle cry, "you have undertaken to cheat me. I won't sue you, for the law is too slow. I'll ruin you." He converted his yacht to a passenger ship to compete with them and added other vessels. He started a new line, appropriately named *Opposition*. Before long, he bought his way back in and regained control of the company.

Source: McGregor, J. 2007. Sweet revenge. *BusinessWeek*, January 22: 64–70.

example, the reflections of General Electric's former CEO Jack Welch, considered by many to be the world's most admired executive. He admitted to his regrettable decision for GE to acquire Kidder Peabody.[65] According to Welch, "My hubris got in the way in the Kidder Peabody deal. [He was referring to GE's buyout of the soon-to-be-troubled Wall Street firm.] I got wise advice from Walter Wriston and other directors who said, 'Jack, don't do this.' But I was bully enough and on a run to do it. And I got whacked right in the head." In addition to poor financial results, Kidder Peabody was wracked by a widely publicized trading scandal that tarnished the reputations of both GE and Kidder Peabody. Welch ended up selling Kidder in 1994.

The business press has included many stories of how egotism and greed have infiltrated organizations. Some incidents are considered rather astonishing, such as Tyco's former (and now convicted) CEO Dennis Kozlowski's well-chronicled purchase of a $6,000 shower curtain and vodka-spewing, full-size replica of Michaelangelo's David.[66] Other well-known examples of power grabs and extraordinary consumption of compensation and perks include executives at Enron, the Rigas family who were convicted of defrauding Adelphia of roughly $1 billion, former CEO Bernie Ebbers's $408 million loan from WorldCom, and so on. However, executives in the United States clearly don't have a monopoly on such deeds. Consider, for example, Jean-Marie Messier, former CEO of Vivendi Universal.[67]

> In striving to convert a French utility into a global media conglomerate, Messier seldom passed up a chance for self-promotion. Although most French executives have a preference for discreet personal lives, Messier hung out with rock stars and moved his family into a $17.5 million Park Avenue spread paid for by Vivendi. He pushed the company to the brink of collapse by running up $19 billion in debt from an acquisition spree and confusing investors with inconsistent financial transactions which are now under investigation by authorities in both the United States and France. Not one to accept full responsibility, less than five months after his forced resignation, he published a book, *My True Diary*, that blames a group of French business leaders for plotting against him. And his ego is clearly intact: At a recent Paris press conference, he described his firing as a setback for French capitalism!

Antitakeover Tactics

Unfriendly or hostile takeovers can occur when a company's stock becomes undervalued. A competing organization can buy the outstanding stock of a takeover candidate in sufficient quantity to become a large shareholder. Then it makes a tender offer to gain full

strategy spotlight

6.8

Poison Pills: How Antitakeover Strategies Can Raise Ethical Issues

Poison pills are almost always good for managers but not always so good for shareholders. They present managers with an ethical dilemma: How can they balance their own interests with their fiduciary responsibility to shareholders?

Here's how poison pills work. In the event of a take-over bid, existing shareholders have the option to buy additional shares of stock at a discount to the current market price. This action is typically triggered when a new shareholder rapidly accumulates more than a set percentage of ownership (usually 20 percent) through stock purchases. When this happens, managers fear that the voting rights and increased proportional ownership of the new shareholder might be a ploy to make a takeover play.

To protect existing shareholders, stock is offered at a discount, but only to existing shareholders. As the existing owners buy the discounted stock, the stock is diluted (i.e., there are now more shares, each with a lower value). If there has been a takeover offer at a set price per share,

the overall price for the company immediately goes up since there are now more shares. This assures stockholders of receiving a fair price for the company.

Sounds good, but here's the problem. Executives on the company's board of directors retain the right to allow the stock discount. The discounted stock price for existing shareholders may or may not be activated when a take-over is imminent. This brings in the issue of motive: Why did the board enact the poison pill provision in the first place? At times, it may have been simply to protect the existing shareholders. At other times, it may have been to protect the interests of those on the board of directors. In other words, the board may have enacted the rule not to protect shareholders, but to protect their own jobs.

When the board receives a takeover offer, the offering company will be aware of the poison pill provision. This gives negotiating power to board members of the takeover target. They may include as part of the negotiation that the new company keep them as members of the board. In exchange, the board members would not enact the discounted share price; existing stockholders would lose, but the jobs of the board members would be protected.

When a company offers poison pill provisions to shareholders, the shareholders should keep in mind that things are not always as they seem. The motives may reflect concern for shareholders. But on the other hand....

Sources: Vicente, J. P. 2001. Toxic treatment: Poison pills proliferate as Internet firms worry they've become easy marks. *Red Herring,* May 1 and 15: 195; Chakraborty, A., & Baum, C. F. 1998. Poison pills, optimal contracting and the market for corporate control: Evidence from Fortune 500 firms. *International Journal of Finance,* 10(3): 1120–1138; Sundaramurthy, C. 1996. Corporate governance within the context of antitakeover provisions. *Strategic Management Journal,* 17: 377–394.

control of the company. If the shareholders accept the offer, the hostile firm buys the target company and either fires the target firm's management team or strips them of their power. For this reason, antitakeover tactics are common. Three of these are greenmail, golden parachutes, and poison pills.[68]

The first, *greenmail,* is an effort by the target firm to prevent an impending takeover. When a hostile firm buys a large block of outstanding target company stock and the target firm's management feels that a tender offer is impending, they offer to buy the stock back from the hostile company at a higher price than the unfriendly company paid for it. The positive side is that this often prevents a hostile takeover. On the downside, the same price is not offered to preexisting shareholders. However, it protects the jobs of the target firm's management.

The second strategy is a *golden parachute.* A golden parachute is a prearranged contract with managers specifying that, in the event of a hostile takeover, the target firm's managers will be paid a significant severance package. Although top managers lose their jobs, the golden parachute provisions protect their income.

Strategy Spotlight 6.8 illustrates how poison pills are used to prevent takeovers. *Poison pills* are means by which a company can give shareholders certain rights in the event of a takeover by another firm. In addition to "poison pills," they are also known as shareholder rights plans.

As you can see, antitakeover tactics can often raise some interesting ethical issues.

Reflecting on Career Implications . . .

- **Corporate-level strategy:** Be aware of your firm's corporate-level strategy. Can you come up with an initiative that will create value both within and across business units?
- **Core Competencies:** What do you see as your core competencies? How can you leverage them both within your business unit as well as across other business units?
- **Sharing Infrastructures:** What infrastructure activities and resources (e.g., information systems, legal) are available in the corporate office that would help you add value for your business unit—or other business units?
- **Diversification:** From your career perspective, what actions can you take to diversify your employment risk (e.g., coursework at a local university, obtain professional certification such as a C.P.A., networking through professional affiliation, etc.)? For example, in periods of retrenchment, such actions will provide you with a greater number of career options.

Summary

A key challenge for today's managers is to create "synergy" when engaging in diversification activities. As we discussed in this chapter, corporate managers do not, in general, have a very good track record in creating value in such endeavors when it comes to mergers and acquisitions. Among the factors that serve to erode shareholder values are paying an excessive premium for the target firm, failing to integrate the activities of the newly acquired businesses into the corporate family, and undertaking diversification initiatives that are too easily imitated by the competition.

We addressed two major types of corporate-level strategy: related and unrelated diversification. With *related diversification* the corporation strives to enter into areas in which key resources and capabilities of the corporation can be shared or leveraged. Synergies come from horizontal relationships between business units. Cost savings and enhanced revenues can be derived from two major sources. First, economies of scope can be achieved from the leveraging of core competencies and the sharing of activities. Second, market power can be attained from greater, or pooled, negotiating power and from vertical integration.

When firms undergo *unrelated diversification* they enter product markets that are dissimilar to their present businesses. Thus, there is generally little opportunity to either leverage core competencies or share activities across business units. Here, synergies are created from vertical relationships between the corporate office and the individual business units. With unrelated diversification, the primary ways to create value are corporate restructuring and parenting, as well as the use of portfolio analysis techniques.

Corporations have three primary means of diversifying their product markets—mergers and acquisitions, joint ventures/strategic alliances, and internal development. There are key trade-offs associated with each of these. For example, mergers and acquisitions are typically the quickest means to enter new markets and provide the corporation with a high level of control over the acquired business. However, with the expensive premiums that often need to be paid to the shareholders of the target firm and the challenges associated with integrating acquisitions, they can also be quite expensive. Not surprisingly, many poorly performing acquisitions are subsequently divested. At times, however, divestitures can help firms refocus their efforts and generate resources. Strategic alliances and joint ventures between two or more firms, on the other hand, may be a means of reducing risk since they involve the sharing and combining of resources. But such joint initiatives also provide a firm with less control (than it would have with an acquisition) since governance is shared between two independent entities. Also, there is a limit to the potential upside for each partner because returns must be shared as well. Finally, with internal development, a firm is able to capture all of the value from its initiatives (as opposed to sharing it with a merger or alliance partner). However, diversification by means of internal development can be very time-consuming—a disadvantage that becomes even more important in fast-paced competitive environments.

Finally, some managerial behaviors may serve to erode shareholder returns. Among these are "growth for growth's sake," egotism, and antitakeover tactics. As we discussed, some of these issues—particularly antitakeover tactics—raise ethical considerations because the managers of the firm are not acting in the best interests of the shareholders.

Summary Review Questions

1. Discuss how managers can create value for their firm through diversification efforts.
2. What are some of the reasons that many diversification efforts fail to achieve desired outcomes?
3. How can companies benefit from related diversification? Unrelated diversification? What are some of the key concepts that can explain such success?
4. What are some of the important ways in which a firm can restructure a business?
5. Discuss some of the various means that firms can use to diversify. What are the pros and cons associated with each of these?
6. Discuss some of the actions that managers may engage in to erode shareholder value.

Key Terms

related diversification, 194
economies of scope, 194
core competencies, 195
sharing activities, 196
market power, 198
vertical integration, 200
transaction cost
  perspective, 204
parenting advantage, 205
restructuring, 205
portfolio management, 206
acquisitions, 210
mergers, 210
divestment, 214
strategic alliances, 214
joint ventures, 214

Experiential Exercise

Time Warner (formerly AOL Time Warner) is a firm that follows a strategy of related diversification. Evaluate its success (or lack thereof) with regard to how well it has: (1) built on core competencies, (2) shared infrastructures, and (3) increased market power.

Application Questions Exercises

1. What were some of the largest mergers and acquisitions over the last two years? What was the rationale for these actions? Do you think they will be successful? Explain.
2. Discuss some examples from business practice in which an executive's actions appear to be in his or her self-interest rather than the corporation's well-being.
3. Discuss some of the challenges that managers must overcome in making strategic alliances successful. What are some strategic alliances with which you are familiar? Were they successful or not? Explain.
4. Use the Internet and select a company that has recently undertaken diversification into new product markets. What do you feel were some of the reasons for this diversification (e.g., leveraging core competencies, sharing infrastructures)?

Ethics Questions

1. In recent years there has been a rash of corporate downsizing and layoffs. Do you feel that such actions raise ethical considerations? Why or why not?
2. What are some of the ethical issues that arise when managers act in a manner that is counter to their firm's best interests? What are the long-term implications for both the firms and the managers themselves?

Rationale for Related Diversification	Successful/Unsuccessful?	Why?
1. Build on core competencies		
2. Share infrastructures		
3. Increase market power		

References

1. For a detailed discussion of the phenomenon of winner's curse, refer to Thaler, R. H. 1992. *The Winner's Curse*. The Free Press: New York.

2. This example draws upon Tully, S. 2006. The (second) worst deal ever. *Fortune,* October 2006: 102–119; and Levenson, E. 2006. Buyer's remorse. *Fortune,* October 16: 12.

3. Dr. G. William Schwert, University of Rochester study cited in Pare, T. P. 1994. The new merger boom. *Fortune.* November 28: 96.

4. Lipin, S. & Deogun, N. 2000. Big mergers of the 1990's prove disappointing to shareholders. *The Wall Street Journal.* October 30: C1.

5. Pare, T. P. 1994. The new merger boom. *Fortune,* November 28: 96.

6. Ghosn, C. 2006. Inside the alliance: The win–win nature of a unique business mode. *Address to the Detroit Economic Club,* November 16.

7. Our framework draws upon a variety of sources, including Goold, M., & Campbell, A. 1998. Desperately seeking synergy. *Harvard Business Review,* 76(5): 131–143; Porter, M. E. 1987. From advantage to corporate strategy. *Harvard Business Review,* 65(3): 43–59; and Hitt, M. A., Ireland, R. D., & Hoskisson, R. E. 2001. *Strategic management: competitiveness and globalization* (4th ed.). Cincinnati, OH: South-Western.

8. Collis, D. J., & Montgomery, C. A. 1987. *Corporate strategy: Resources and the scope of the firm.* New York: McGraw-Hill.

9. This imagery of the corporation as a tree and related discussion draws on Prahalad, C. K., & Hamel, G. 1990. The core competence of the corporation. *Harvard Business Review,* 68(3): 79–91. Parts of this section also draw on Picken, J. C., & Dess, G. G. 1997. *Mission critical:* chap. 5. Burr Ridge, IL: Irwin Professional Publishing.

10. This section draws on Prahalad & Hamel, op. cit.; and Porter, op. cit.

11. A recent study that investigates the relationship between a firm's technology resources, diversification, and performance can be found in Miller, D. J. 2004. Firms' technological resources and the performance effects of diversification. A longitudinal study. *Strategic Management Journal,* 25: 1097–1119.

12. Collis & Montgomery, op. cit.

13. Henricks, M. 1994. VF seeks global brand dominance. *Apparel Industry Magazine,* August: 21–40; VF Corporation. 1993. First quarter corporate summary report. *1993 VF Annual Report.*

14. Hill, A., & Hargreaves, D. 2001. Turbulent times for GE-Honeywell deal. *Financial Times,* February 28: 26.

15. Lowry, T. 2001. Media. *BusinessWeek,* January 8: 100–101.

16. The Tribune Company. 1999. *Annual report.*

17. This section draws on Hrebiniak, L. G., & Joyce, W. F. 1984. *Implementing strategy.* New York: MacMillan; and Oster, S. M. 1994. *Modern competitive analysis.* New York: Oxford University Press.

18. The discussion of the benefits and costs of vertical integration draws on Hax, A. C., & Majluf, N. S. 1991. *The strategy concept and process: A pragmatic approach:* 139. Englewood Cliffs, NJ: Prentice Hall.

19. Fahey, J. 2005. Gray winds. *Forbes.* January 10: 143.

20. This discussion draws on Oster, op. cit.; and Harrigan, K. 1986. Matching vertical integration strategies to competitive conditions. *Strategic Management Journal,* 7(6): 535–556.

21. For a scholarly explanation on how transaction costs determine the boundaries of a firm, see Oliver E. Williamson's pioneering books *Markets and Hierarchies: Analysis and Antitrust Implications* (New York: Free Press, 1975) and *The Economic Institutions of Capitalism* (New York: Free Press, 1985).

22. Campbell, A., Goold, M., & Alexander, M. 1995. Corporate strategy: The quest for parenting advantage. *Harvard Business Review,* 73(2): 120–132; and Picken & Dess, op. cit.

23. Anslinger, P. A., & Copeland, T. E. 1996. Growth through acquisition: A fresh look. *Harvard Business Review,* 74(1): 126–135.

24. Campbell et al., op. cit.

25. This section draws on Porter, op. cit.; and Hambrick, D. C. 1985. Turnaround strategies. In Guth, W. D. (Ed.). *Handbook of business strategy:* 10-1–10-32. Boston: Warren, Gorham & Lamont.

26. There is an important delineation between companies that are operated for a long-term profit and those that are bought and sold for short-term gains. The latter are sometimes referred to as "holding companies" and are generally more concerned about financial issues than strategic issues.

27. Lenzner, R. 2007. High on Loews. *Forbes,* February 26: 98–102.

28. Casico. W. F. 2002. Strategies for responsible restructuring. *Academy of Management Executive,* 16(3): 80–91; and Singh, H. 1993. Challenges in researching

corporate restructuring. *Journal of Management Studies,* 30(1): 147–172.

29. Cusack, M. 1987. *Hanson Trust: A review of the company and its prospects.* London: Hoare Govett.

30. Hax & Majluf, op. cit. By 1979, 45 percent of Fortune 500 companies employed some form of portfolio analysis, according to Haspelagh, P. 1982. Portfolio planning: Uses and limits. *Harvard Busines Review,* 60: 58–73. A later study conducted in 1993 found that over 40 percent of the respondents used portfolio analysis techniques, but the level of usage was expected to increase to more than 60 percent in the near future: Rigby, D. K. 1994. Managing the management tools. *Planning Review,* September–October: 20–24.

31. Goold, M., & Luchs, K. 1993. Why diversify? Four decades of management thinking. *Academy of Management Executive,* 7(3): 7–25.

32. Other approaches include the industry attractiveness–business strength matrix developed jointly by General Electric and McKinsey and Company, the life-cycle matrix developed by Arthur D. Little, and the profitability matrix proposed by Marakon. For an extensive review, refer to Hax & Majluf, op. cit.: 182–194.

33. Porter, op. cit.: 49–52.

34. Collis, D. J. 1995. Portfolio planning at Ciba-Geigy and the Newport investment proposal. Harvard Business School Case No. 9-795-040. Novartis AG was created in 1996 by the merger of Ciba-Geigy and Sandoz.

35. Buzzell, R. D., & Gale, B. T. 1987. *The PIMS Principles: Linking Strategy to Performance.* New York: Free Press; and Miller, A., & Dess, G. G. 1996. *Strategic Management,* (2nd ed.). New York: McGraw-Hill.

36. Seeger, J. 1984. Reversing the images of BCG's growth share matrix. *Strategic Management Journal,* 5(1): 93–97.

37. Picken & Dess, op. cit.; Cabot Corporation. 2001. 10-Q filing, Securities and Exchange Commission, May 14.

38. Koudsi, S. 2001. Remedies for an economic hangover. *Fortune,* June 25: 130–139.

39. Coy, P., Thornton, E., Arndt, M., & Grow, B. 2005. Shake, rattle, and merge. *BusinessWeek,* January 10: 32–35; and Anonymous. 2005. Love is in the air. *Economist,* February 5: 9.

40. For an interesting study of the relationship between mergers and a firm's product-market strategies, refer to Krisnan, R. A., Joshi, S., & Krishnan, H. 2004. The influence of mergers on firms' product-mix strategies. *Strategic Management Journal,* 25: 587–611.

41. Carey, D., moderator. 2000. A CEO roundtable on making mergers succeed. *Harvard Business Review,* 78(3): 146.

42. Shinal, J. 2001. Can Mike Volpi make Cisco sizzle again? *BusinessWeek,* February 26: 102–104; Kambil, A. Eselius, E. D., & Monteiro, K. A. 2000. Fast venturing: The quick way to start Web businesses. *Sloan Management Review,* 41(4): 55–67; and Elstrom, P. 2001. Sorry, Cisco: The old answers won't work. *BusinessWeek,* April 30: 39.

43. Like many high-tech firms during the economic slump that began in mid-2000, Cisco Systems has experienced declining performance. On April 16, 2001, it announced that its revenues for the quarter closing April 30 would drop 5 percent from a year earlier—and a stunning 30 percent from the previous three months—to about $4.7 billion. Furthermore, Cisco announced that it would lay off 8,500 employees and take an enormous $2.5 billion charge to write down inventory. By late October 2002, its stock was trading at around $10, down significantly from its 52-week high of $70. Elstrom, op. cit.: 39.

44. Coy, P., Thornton, E., Arndt, M. & Grow, B. 2005. Shake, rattle, and merge. *BusinessWeek,* January 10: 32–35; and, Anonymous. 2005. The rise of the superbrands. *Economist.* February 5: 63–65; and, Sellers, P. 2005. It was a no-brainer. *Fortune,* February 21: 96–102.

45. For a discussion of the trend toward consolidation of the steel industry and how Lakshmi Mittal is becoming a dominant player, read Reed, S., & Arndt, M. 2004. The Raja of steel. *BusinessWeek,* December 20: 50–52.

46. Barrett, A. 2001. Drugs. *BusinessWeek,* January 8: 112–113.

47. Coy, P., et al. 2005, op. cit.

48. Whalen, C. J., Pascual, A. M., Lowery, T., & Muller, J. 2001. The top 25 managers. *BusinessWeek,* January 8: 63.

49. This discussion draws upon Rappaport, A., & Sirower, M. L. 1999. Stock or cash? The trade-offs for buyers and sellers in mergers and acquisitions. *Harvard Business Review,* 77(6): 147–158; and Lipin, S., & Deogun, N. 2000. Big mergers of 90s prove disappointing to shareholders. *Wall Street Journal,* October 30: C1.

50. Mouio, A. (Ed.). 1998. Unit of one. *Fast Company,* September: 82.

51. Ibid.

52. Porter, M. E. 1987. From competitive advantage to corporate strategy. *Harvard Business Review,* 65(3): 43.

53. This was originally termed a "merger of equals." However, as noted in *The Economist* and elsewhere, it has turned out to be "just another disastrous car-industry takeover." For an interesting, recent discussion, see Anonymous. 2007. Dis-assembly. *The Economist.* February 17: 63–64.

54. The divestiture of a business which is undertaken in order to enable managers to better focus on its core business has been termed "downscoping." Refer to Hitt, M. A., Harrison, J. S., & Ireland, R. D. 2001. *Mergers and acquisitions: A guide to creating value for stakeholders.* Oxford Press: New York.

55. Sirmon, D. G., Hitt, M. A., & Ireland, R. D. 2007. Managing firm resources in dynamic environments to create value: Looking inside the black box. *Academy of Management Review,* 32(1): 273–292.

56. For scholarly perspectives on the role of learning in creating value in strategic alliances, refer to Anard, B. N., & Khanna, T. 2000. Do firms learn to create value? *Strategic Management Journal,* 12(3): 295–317; and Vermeulen, F., & Barkema, H. P. 2001. Learning through acquisitions. *Academy of Management Journal,* 44(3): 457–476.

57. For a detailed discussion of transaction cost economics in strategic alliances, read Reuer, J. J., & Arno, A. 2007. Strategic alliance contracts: Dimensions and determinants of contractual complexity. *Strategic Management Journal,* 28(3): 313–330.

58. This section draws on Hutt, M. D., Stafford, E. R., Walker, B. A., & Reingen, P. H. 2000. Case study: Defining the strategic alliance. *Sloan Management Review,* 41(2): 51–62; and Walters, B. A., Peters, S., & Dess, G. G. 1994. Strategic alliances and joint ventures: Making them work. *Business Horizons,* 4: 5–10.

59. Edmondson, G., & Reinhardt, A. 2001. From niche player to Goliath. *BusinessWeek,* March 12: 94–96.

60. For an institutional theory perspective on strategic alliances, read: Dacin, M. T., Oliver, C., & Roy, J. P. 2007. The legitimacy of strategic alliances: An institutional perspective. *Strategic Management Journal,* 28(2): 169–187.

61. Clayton, V. 2000. Lourdes Pizana's passions: Confessions and lessons of an accidental business owner. *E-Merging Business,* Fall–Winter: 73–75.

62. Porter, op. cit.: 43–59.

63. Angwin, J. S., & Wingfield, N. 2000. How Jay Walker built WebHouse on a theory that he couldn't prove. *The Wall Street Journal,* October 16: A1, A8.

64. *BusinessWeek.* 2003. The fallen. January 13: 80–82.

65. The Jack Welch example draws upon Sellers, P. 2001. Get over yourself. *Fortune,* April 30: 76–88.

66. Polek, D. 2002. The rise and fall of Dennis Kozlowski. *BusinessWeek,* December 23: 64–77.

67. *BusinessWeek.* 2003. op. cit.: 80.

68. This section draws on Weston, J. F., Besley, S., & Brigham, E. F. 1996. *Essentials of Managerial Finance* (11th ed.): 18–20. Fort Worth, TX: Dryden Press, Harcourt Brace.

chapter 7

International Strategy:

Creating Value in Global Markets

>learning objectives

After reading this chapter, you should have a good understanding of:

LO1 The importance of international expansion as a viable diversification strategy.

LO2 The sources of national advantage; that is, why an industry in a given country is more (or less) successful than the same industry in another country.

LO3 The motivations (or benefits) and the risks associated with international expansion, including the emerging trend for greater offshoring and outsourcing activity.

LO4 The two opposing forces—cost reduction and adaptation to local markets—that firms face when entering international markets.

LO5 The advantages and disadvantages associated with each of the four basic strategies: international, global, multidomestic, and transnational.

LO6 The difference between regional companies and truly global companies.

LO7 The four basic types of entry strategies and the relative benefits and risks associated with each of them.

*t*he global marketplace provides many opportunities for firms to increase their revenue base and their profitability. Furthermore, in today's knowledge-intensive economy, there is the potential to create advantages by leveraging firm knowledge when crossing national boundaries to do business. At the same time, however, there are pitfalls and risks that firms must avoid in order to be successful. In this chapter we will provide insights on how to be successful and create value when diversifying into global markets.

After some introductory comments on the global economy, we address the question: What explains the level of success of a given industry in a given country? To provide a framework for analysis, we draw on Michael Porter's "diamond of national advantage," in which he identified four factors that help to explain performance differences.

In the second section of the chapter, we shift our focus to the level of the firm and discuss some of the major motivations and risks associated with international expansion. Recognizing such potential benefits and risks enables managers to better assess the growth and profit potential in a given country. We also address important issues associated with a topic of growing interest in the international marketplace—offshoring and outsourcing.

Next, in the third section—the largest in this chapter—we address how firms can attain competitive advantages in the global marketplace. We discuss two opposing forces firms face when entering foreign markets: cost reduction and local adaptation. Depending on the intensity of each of these forces, they should select among four basic strategies: international, global, multidomestic, and transnational. We discuss both the strengths and limitations of each of these strategies. We also present a recent perspective which posits that even the largest multinational firms are more regional than global even today.

The final section addresses the four categories of entry strategies that firms may choose in entering foreign markets. These strategies vary along a continuum from low investment, low control (exporting) to high investment, high control (wholly owned subsidiaries and greenfield ventures). We discuss the pros and cons associated with each.

Learning from Mistakes

Wal-Mart, the world's largest retailer, certainly didn't have a good year in 2006.[1] There were executive turnover problems, such as the resignation of Sam's Clubs marketing head Mark Goodman and the embarrassing firing of Julie Roehm, the young advertising whiz who Wal-Mart had hired away from DaimlerChrysler. Also, there were ongoing legal problems—a Philadelphia jury ordered Wal-Mart to pay $78 million to a class of 185,000 workers who claimed that they were denied breaks and forced to work off the clock.

There were also business setbacks: same-store sales were only up 1.6 percent (while those of Costco and Target were up 9 percent and 4.1 percent, respectively). Wal-Mart's stock was flat in an otherwise strong year for equities. In fact, from January 2000 (when Lee Scott took over for David Glass as CEO) to early 2007, the stock has fallen 22 percent. *[continued]*

The company has also had its share of setbacks overseas. Wal-Mart suffered a $900 million loss after its forays into Germany and South Korea failed. Let's take a closer look at what might explain its 2006 exit from South Korea—a market it entered in 1998.

Wal-Mart was never successful in South Korea. They were slow in opening stores—failing not only to win customers but also to build enough market share to press suppliers on pricing. The core of their problem was an inability to adapt to local markets. As noted by Na Hong Seok, an analyst in Seoul: "Wal-Mart is a typical example of a global giant who has failed to localize its operations in South Korea."

Wal-Mart put off South Korean consumers by sticking to Western marketing strategies that concentrated on dry goods, from electronics to clothing. Their rivals, on the other hand, focused on food and beverages, the segment that specialists say attracts South Koreans to hypermarkets. In South Korea, fresh, quality food is a key ingredient of success. It typically generates half of a store's revenues. To make matters worse, one of Wal-Mart's competitors, E-Mart, even owned its own farms that supplied its stores.

Wal-Mart also ran into problems with a membership approach that was similar to the one used by its Sam's warehouses. According to Song Kye-Hyon, a financial analyst: "It turned out to be a strategic flaw of Wal-Mart when it first adopted the Western policy of the membership where customers were required to pay a membership fee for shopping privileges."

Further, Wal-Mart had difficulty overcoming mechanisms that some of its rivals had developed to create greater customer loyalty. Some employed green-capped young men who helped bring the shopping carts to the customers' cars in the parking lot. Further, rivals operated shuttle buses to go through neighborhoods to pick up customers and drop them off at their homes after they completed their shopping. Simply put, Wal-Mart did not adapt to the local market conditions by investing the resources necessary to achieve some level of parity on such customer-service initiatives.

In the end, Wal-Mart continued to flounder until it sold all 16 of its South Korean outlets in May 2006 to Shinsgae, a local retailer. Consistent with its long-term problems in the South Korean market, Wal-Mart lost $10.4 million on revenues of $787 million in 2005—its last full year of operations in South Korea. Wal-Mart's vice chairman, Michael Duke, summed up the situation quite well: "As we continue to focus our efforts where we have the greatest impact on our growth strategy, it became increasingly clear that in South Korea's environment it would be difficult for us to reach the scale we desired."

In this chapter we discuss how firms can create value and achieve competitive advantage in the global marketplace. We also discuss how firms can avoid pitfalls such as those experienced by Wal-Mart in South Korea. In addition, we address factors that can influence a nation's success in a particular industry. In our view, this is an important context in determining how well firms might eventually do when they compete beyond their nation's boundaries.

The Global Economy: A Brief Overview

> **>LO1**
> The importance of international expansion as a viable diversification strategy.

Managers face many opportunities and risks when they diversify abroad.[2] The trade among nations has increased dramatically in recent years and it is estimated that by 2015, the trade *across* nations will exceed the trade within nations. In a variety of industries such as semiconductors, automobiles, commercial aircraft, telecommunications, computers, and consumer electronics, it is almost impossible to survive unless firms scan the world for competitors, customers, human resources, suppliers, and technology.[3]

GE's wind energy business illustrates the benefits of tapping into talent around the world. The firm has built research centers in China, Germany, India, and the United States.

"We did it," says CEO Jeffrey Immelt, "to access the best brains everywhere in the world." All four centers have played a key role in GE's development of huge 92-ton turbines. How did each contribute?[4]

- Chinese researchers in Shanghai designed the microprocessors that control the pitch of the blade.
- Mechanical engineers from India (Bangladore) devised mathematical models to maximize the efficiency of materials in the turbine.
- Power-systems experts in the United States (Niskayuna, New York), which has researchers from 55 countries, do the design work.
- Technicians in Munich, Germany have created a "smart" turbine that can calculate wind speeds and signal sensors in other turbines to pitch their blades to produce maximum electricity.

The rise of globalization—meaning the rise of market capitalism around the world—has undeniably contributed to the economic boom in America's New Economy, where knowledge is the key source of competitive advantage and value creation. It is estimated that it has brought phone service to about 300 million households in developing nations and a transfer of nearly $2 trillion from rich countries to poor countries through equity, bond investments, and commercial loans.[5]

Without doubt, there have been extremes in the effect of global capitalism on national economies and poverty levels around the world.[6] Clearly, the economies of East Asia have attained rapid growth, but there has been comparatively little progress in other areas of the world. For example, income in Latin America grew by only 6 percent in the past two decades when the continent was opening up to global capitalism. Average incomes in sub-Saharan Africa and the old Eastern European bloc have actually declined. Indeed, the World Bank estimates that the number of people living on $1 per day has *increased* to 1.3 billion over the past decade.

Such disparities in wealth among nations raise an important question: Why do some countries and their citizens enjoy the fruits of global capitalism while others are mired in poverty? Or why do some governments make the best use of inflows of foreign investment and know-how and others do not? There are many explanations. Among these are the need of governments to have track records of business-friendly policies to attract multinationals and local entrepreneurs to train workers, invest in modern technology, and nurture local suppliers and managers. Also, it means carefully managing the broader economic factors in an economy, such as interest rates, inflation, and unemployment, as well as a good legal system that protects property rights, strong educational systems, and a society where prosperity is widely shared.

The above policies are the type that East Asia—in locations such as Hong Kong, Taiwan, South Korea, and Singapore—has employed to evolve from the sweatshop economies of the 1960s and 1970s to industrial powers today. On the other hand, many countries have moved in the other direction. For example, in Guatemala only 52.0 percent of males complete fifth grade and an astonishing 39.8 percent of the population subsists on less than $1 per day.[7] (By comparison, the corresponding numbers for South Korea are 98 percent and less than 2 percent, respectively.)

Strategy Spotlight 7.1 provides an interesting perspective on global trade—marketing to the "bottom of the pyramid." This refers to the practice of a multinational firm targeting its goods and services to the nearly 5 billion poor people in the world who inhabit developing countries. Collectively, this represents a very large market with $14 trillion in purchasing power.

Next, we will address in more detail the question of why some nations and their industries are more competitive. This establishes an important context or setting for the remainder of the chapter. After we discuss why some *nations and their industries* outperform others, we will be better able to address the various strategies that *firms* can take to create competitive advantage when they expand internationally.

strategy spotlight

7.1

Marketing to the "Bottom of the Pyramid"

Many executives wrongly believe that profitable opportunities to sell consumer goods exist only in countries where income levels are high. Even when they expand internationally, they often tend to limit their marketing to only the affluent segments within the developing countries. Such narrow conceptualizations of the market cause them to ignore the vast opportunities that exist at "the bottom of the pyramid," according to University of Michigan professor C. K. Prahalad. The *bottom of the pyramid* refers to the nearly 5 billion poor people who inhabit the developing countries. Surprisingly, they represent $14 trillion in purchasing power! And they are looking for products and services that can improve the quality of their lives such as clean energy, personal-care products, lighting, and medicines. Multinationals are missing out on growth opportunities if they ignore this vast segment of the market.

Other innovative firms have found creative ways to serve the poor and still make a profit. Grameen Bank in Bangladesh is very different from the money center banks of London or New York. Pioneers of the concept of microcredit, Grameen Bank (whose founder, Muhammad Yunus, won the 2006 Nobel Peace Prize) extends small loans—sometimes as small as $20—to thousands of struggling micro-entrepreneurs who have no collateral to offer. The value of microcredit loans has soared from $4 million to $1.3 billion between 1996 and 2006. Not only are their loan recovery rates comparable to big banks, but they are also

changing the lives of thousands of people while making a profit as well. Casas Bahias, the Brazilian retailer, has built a $2.5 billion-a-year chain selling to the poor who live in the *favelas,* the illegal shanty towns. Another amazing example is Aravind Eye Care, an Indian hospital that specializes in cataract surgeries. Today, they are the largest eye care facility in the world, performing more than 200,000 surgeries per year. The secret of their volume: The surgeries cost only about $25! A comparable surgery in the West costs $3,000. And best of all, Aravind has a return on equity of more than 75 percent!

As the above examples demonstrate, in order to sell to the bottom of the pyramid, managers must rethink their costs, quality, scale of operations, and even their use of capital. What prevents managers from selling to this vast market? Often they are victims of their own false assumptions. First, they think that the poor have no purchasing power. But $14 trillion can buy a lot. Second, they assume that poor people have no need for new technologies. We only have to see the demand for cell phones from entrepreneurs who run microbusinesses in villages in India to dispel this myth. Third, they assume that the poor have no use for their products and services. Shampoo, detergents, and banking satisfy universal needs, not just the needs of the rich. Fourth, they assume that managers may not be excited about working in these markets. Recent experience shows that this may be a more exciting environment than dogs fighting for fractions of market shares in the mature markets of the developed countries.

No one is helped by viewing the poor as the wretched of the earth. Instead, they are the latest frontier of opportunity for those who can meet their needs. A vast market that is barely tapped, the bottom of the pyramid offers enormous opportunities.

Sources: Miller, C. C. 2006. Easy money. *Forbes,* November 27: 134–138; Prahalad, C. K. 2004. Why selling to the poor makes for good business. *Fortune,* 150(9): 32–33; Overholt, A. 2005. A new path to profit. *Fast Company,* January: 25–26; and Prahalad, C. K. 2005. *The fortune at the bottom of the pyramid: Eradicating poverty through profits.* Philadelphia: Wharton School Publishing.

Factors Affecting a Nation's Competitiveness

factor conditions (national advantage)
a nation's position in factors of production.

Michael Porter of Harvard University conducted a four-year study in which he and a team of 30 researchers looked at the patterns of competitive success in 10 leading trading nations. He concluded that there are four broad attributes of nations that individually, and as a system, constitute what is termed "the diamond of national advantage." In effect, these attributes jointly determine the playing field that each nation establishes and operates for its industries. These factors are:

demand conditions (national advantage)
the nature of home-market demand for the industry's product or service.

- *Factor conditions.* The nation's position in factors of production, such as skilled labor or infrastructure, necessary to compete in a given industry.
- *Demand conditions.* The nature of home-market demand for the industry's product or service.

- *Related and supporting industries.* The presence or absence in the nation of supplier industries and other related industries that are internationally competitive.
- *Firm strategy, structure, and rivalry.* The conditions in the nation governing how companies are created, organized, and managed, as well as the nature of domestic rivalry.

We will now briefly discuss each of these factors.[8] Then we will provide an integrative example—the Indian software industry—to demonstrate how these attributes interact to explain India's high level of competitiveness in this industry.

>LO2
The sources of national advantage; that is, why an industry in a given country is more (or less) successful than the same industry in another country.

Factor Conditions[9]

Classical economics suggests that factors of production such as land, labor, and capital are the building blocks that create usable consumer goods and services.[10] But this tells only part of the story when we consider the global aspects of economic growth. Companies in advanced nations seeking competitive advantage over firms in other nations *create* many of the factors of production. For example, a country or industry dependent on scientific innovation must have a skilled human resource pool to draw upon. This resource pool is not inherited; it is created through investment in industry-specific knowledge and talent. The supporting infrastructure of a country—that is, its transportation and communication systems as well as its banking system—are also critical.

To achieve competitive advantage, factors of production must be developed that are industry and firm specific. In addition, the pool of resources a firm or a country has at its disposal is less important than the speed and efficiency with which these resources are deployed. Thus, firm-specific knowledge and skills created within a country that are rare, valuable, difficult to imitate, and rapidly and efficiently deployed are the factors of production that ultimately lead to a nation's competitive advantage.

For example, the island nation of Japan has little land mass, making the warehouse space needed to store inventory prohibitively expensive. But by pioneering just-in-time inventory management, Japanese companies managed to create a resource from which they gained advantage over companies in other nations that spent large sums to warehouse inventory.

Demand Conditions

Demand conditions refer to the demands that consumers place on an industry for goods and services. Consumers who demand highly specific, sophisticated products and services force firms to create innovative, advanced products and services to meet the demand. This consumer pressure presents challenges to a country's industries. But in response to these challenges, improvements to existing goods and services often result, creating conditions necessary for competitive advantage over firms in other countries.

Demanding consumers push firms to move ahead of companies in other countries where consumers are less demanding and more complacent. Countries with demanding consumers drive firms in that country to meet high standards, upgrade existing products and services, and create innovative products and services. Thus, the conditions of consumer demand influence how firms view a market, with more demanding consumers stimulating advances in products and services. This, in turn, helps a nation's industries to better anticipate future global demand conditions and proactively respond to product and service requirements.

Denmark, for instance, is known for its environmental awareness. Demand from consumers for environmentally safe products has spurred Danish manufacturers to become leaders in water pollution control equipment—products it successfully exported.

related and supporting industries (national advantage) the presence, absence, and quality in the nation of supplier industries and other related industries that supply services, support, or technology to firms in the industry value chain.

firm strategy, structure, and rivalry (national advantage) the conditions in the nation governing how companies are created, organized, and managed, as well as the nature of domestic rivalry.

Related and Supporting Industries

Related and supporting industries enable firms to manage inputs more effectively. For example, countries with a strong supplier base benefit by adding efficiency to downstream activities. A competitive supplier base helps a firm obtain inputs using cost-effective, timely methods, thus reducing manufacturing costs. Also, close working relationships with suppliers provide the potential to develop competitive advantages through joint research and development and the ongoing exchange of knowledge.

Related industries offer similar opportunities through joint efforts among firms. In addition, related industries create the probability that new companies will enter the market, increasing competition and forcing existing firms to become more competitive through efforts such as cost control, product innovation, and novel approaches to distribution. Combined, these give the home country's industries a source of competitive advantage.

In the Italian footwear industry the supporting industries show how they can lead to national competitive advantage. In Italy, shoe manufacturers are geographically located near their suppliers. The manufacturers have ongoing interactions with leather suppliers and learn about new textures, colors, and manufacturing techniques while a shoe is still in the prototype stage. The manufacturers are able to project future demand and gear their factories for new products long before companies in other nations become aware of the new styles. Similarly, geographic proximity of industries related to the pharmaceutical industry (e.g., the dye industry) in Switzerland has given that nation a leadership position in this market, with firms such as Novartis, Hoffman LaRoche, and Sandoz using dyes from local manufacturers in many pharmaceutical products.

Firm Strategy, Structure, and Rivalry

Rivalry is particularly intense in nations with conditions of strong consumer demand, strong supplier bases, and high new entrant potential from related industries. This competitive rivalry in turn increases the efficiency with which firms develop, market, and distribute products and services within the home country. Domestic rivalry thus provides a strong impetus for firms to innovate and find new sources of competitive advantage.

Interestingly, this intense rivalry forces firms to look outside their national boundaries for new markets, setting up the conditions necessary for global competitiveness. Among all the points on Porter's diamond of national advantage, domestic rivalry is perhaps the strongest indicator of global competitive success. Firms that have experienced intense domestic competition are more likely to have designed strategies and structures that allow them to successfully compete in world markets.

In the United States, for example, intense rivalry has spurred companies such as Dell Computer to find innovative ways to produce and distribute its products. This is largely a result of competition from IBM and Hewlett-Packard.

Strategy Spotlight 7.2 discusses India's software industry. It provides an integrative example of how Porter's "diamond" can help to explain the relative degree of success of an industry in a given country. Exhibit 7.1 illustrates India's "software diamond."

Concluding Comment on Factors Affecting a Nation's Competitiveness

Porter drew his conclusions based on case histories of firms in more than 100 industries. Despite the differences in strategies employed by successful global competitors, a common theme emerged: Firms that succeeded in global markets had first succeeded in intensely competitive home markets. We can conclude that competitive advantage for global firms typically grows out of relentless, continuing improvement, and innovation.

Now that we have talked about the important role that nations play in international strategy, let's turn to the level of the individual firm.[11] In the next section, we will discuss a company's motivations and the risks associated with international expansion.

India and the Diamond of National Advantage

Consider the following facts:

- SAP, the German software company, has developed new applications for notebook PCs at its 500-engineer Bangladore facility.

- General Electric plans to invest $100 million and hire 2,600 scientists to create the world's largest research and development lab in Bangalore, India.

- Microsoft plans to invest $400 million in new research partnerships in India.

- Over one-fifth of Fortune 1000 companies outsource their software requirements to firms in India.

Sources: Kripalani, M. 2002. Calling Bangladore: Multinationals are making it a hub for high-tech research *BusinessWeek*, November 25: 52–54; Kapur, D., & Ramamurti, R. 2001. India's emerging competitive advantage in services. 2001. *Academy of Management Executive*, 15(2): 20–33; World Bank. *World development report:* 6. New York: Oxford University Press. Reuters. 2001. Oracle in India push, taps software talent. *Washington Post Online*, July 3.

- McKinsey & Co. projects that the Indian software and services industry will be an $87 billion business by 2008; $50 billion of this will be exported.

- For the past decade, the Indian software industry has grown at a 50 percent annual rate.

- More than 800 firms in India are involved in software services as their primary activity.

- Software and information technology firms in India are projected to employ 2.2 million people by 2008.

What is causing such global interest in India's software services industry? Porter's diamond of national advantage helps clarify this question. See Exhibit 7.1.

First, *factor conditions* are conducive to the rise of India's software industry. Through investment in human resource development with a focus on industry-specific knowledge, India's universities and software firms have literally created this essential factor of production. For example, India produces the second largest annual output of scientists and engineers in the world, behind only the United States. In a knowledge-intensive industry *(continued)*

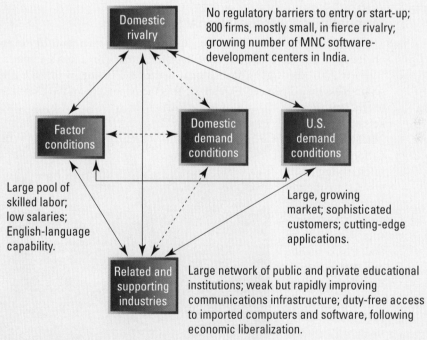

No regulatory barriers to entry or start-up; 800 firms, mostly small, in fierce rivalry; growing number of MNC software-development centers in India.

Large pool of skilled labor; low salaries; English-language capability.

Large, growing market; sophisticated customers; cutting-edge applications.

Large network of public and private educational institutions; weak but rapidly improving communications infrastructure; duty-free access to imported computers and software, following economic liberalization.

Note: Dashed lines represent weaker interactions.

Exhibit 7.1 India's Diamond in Software

Source: From Kampur D. and Ramamurti R., "India's Emerging Competition Advantage in Services," *Academy of Management Executive: The Thinking Manager's Source.* Copyright © 2001 by Academy of Management. Reproduced with permission of Academy of Management via Copyright Clearance Center.

(continued) such as software, development of human resources is fundamental to both domestic and global success.

Second, *demand conditions* require that software firms stay on the cutting edge of technological innovation. India has already moved toward globalization of its software industry; consumer demand conditions in developed nations such as Germany, Denmark, parts of Southeast Asia, and the United States created the consumer demand necessary to propel India's software makers toward sophisticated software solutions.*

Third, India has the *supplier base as well as the related industries* needed to drive competitive rivalry and enhance competitiveness. In particular, information technology (IT)

* Although India's success cannot be explained in terms of its home market demand (according to Porter's model), the nature of the industry enables software to be transferred among different locations simultaneously by way of communications links. Thus, competitiveness of markets outside India can be enhanced without a physical presence in those markets.

hardware prices declined rapidly in the 1990s. Furthermore, rapid technological change in IT hardware meant that latecomers like India were not locked into older-generation technologies. Thus, both the IT hardware and software industries could "leapfrog" older technologies. In addition, relationships among knowledge workers in these IT hardware and software industries offer the social structure for ongoing knowledge exchange, promoting further enhancement of existing products. Further infrastructure improvements are occurring rapidly.

Fourth, with over 800 firms in the software services industry in India, *intense rivalry forces firms to develop competitive strategies and structures.* Although firms like TCS, Infosys, and Wipro have become large, they were quite small only five years ago. And dozens of small and midsized companies are aspiring to catch up. This intense rivalry is one of the primary factors driving Indian software firms to develop overseas distribution channels, as predicted by Porter's diamond of national advantage.

International Expansion: A Company's Motivations and Risks

Motivations for International Expansion

There are many motivations for a company to pursue international expansion. The most obvious one is to *increase the size of potential markets* for a firm's products and services.[12] By early 2007, the world's population exceeded 6.5 billion, with the United States representing less than 5 percent. Exhibit 7.2 lists the population of the United States compared to other major markets abroad.

Many multinational firms are intensifying their efforts to market their products and services to countries such as India and China as the ranks of their middle class have increased over the past decade. These include Procter & Gamble's success in achieving a 50 percent share in China's shampoo market as well as

>LO3

The motivations (or benefits) and the risks associated with international expansion, including the emerging trend for greater offshoring and outsourcing activity.

● Starbucks, based in Seattle, Washington, has aggressively expanded its international operations. By 2007 it had several thousand coffeehouses in 36 countries outside of the United States. Above is one of its coffeehouses in Bangkok, Thailand.

Exhibit 7.2
Populations of Selected
Nations and the World

Country	March 2007 (in millions) (estimated)
China	1,320
India	1,107
United States	300
Japan	127
Germany	82
World Total	6,580

Source: www.geohive.com/global/pop_data2.php.

PepsiCo's impressive inroads in the Indian soft-drink market.[13] Let's take a brief look at China's emerging middle class:[14]

- China's middle class has finally attained a critical mass—between 35 million and 200 million people, depending on what definition is used. The larger number is preferred by Fan Gong, director of China's National Economic Research Institute, who fixes the lower boundary of "middle" as a family income of $10,000.
- The central government's emphasis on science and technology has boosted the rapid development of higher education, which is the incubator of the middle class.
- China may be viewed as a new example of economies of scale. Many American companies already have factories in China exporting goods. Now that there is a domestic market to go along with the export market, those factories can increase their output with little additional cost. That is one reason why many foreign companies' profits in China have been so strong in recent years.

Expanding a firm's global presence also automatically increases its scale of operations, providing it with a larger revenue and asset base. As we noted in Chapter 5 in discussing overall cost leadership strategies, such an increase in revenues and asset base potentially enables a firm to *attain economies of scale.* This provides multiple benefits. One advantage is the spreading of fixed costs such as research and development over a larger volume of production. Examples include the sale of Boeing's commercial aircraft and Microsoft's operating systems in many foreign countries.

A second advantage would be *reducing the costs of research and development as well as operating costs.* Recall, Microsoft's software development operations and other firms in talent-rich India (see Strategy Spotlight 7.2). A final advantage would be the attainment of greater purchasing power by pooling purchases. For example, as McDonald's increases the number of outlets it has all over the world, it can place larger orders for equipment and supplies, thus increasing its bargaining power with suppliers.

International expansion can also *extend the life cycle of a product* that is in its maturity stage in a firm's home country but that has greater demand potential elsewhere. As we noted in Chapter 5, products (and industries) generally go through a four-stage life cycle of introduction, growth, maturity, and decline. In recent decades, U.S. soft-drink producers such as Coca-Cola and PepsiCo have aggressively pursued international markets to attain levels of growth that simply would not be available in the United States. Similarly, personal computer manufacturers such as Dell and Hewlett-Packard have sought out foreign markets to offset the growing saturation in the U.S. market.

Finally, international expansion can enable a firm to *optimize the physical location for every activity in its value chain.* Recall from our discussions in Chapters 3 and 5 that the value chain represents the various activities in which all firms must engage to produce products and services. They include primary activities, such as inbound logistics, operations, and marketing, as well as support activities, such as procurement, research and development, and human resource management. All firms have to make critical decisions as to where each activity will take place.[15] Optimizing the location for every activity in the value chain can yield one or more of three strategic advantages: performance enhancement, cost reduction, and risk reduction. We will now discuss each of these.

Performance Enhancement   Microsoft's decision to establish a corporate research laboratory in Cambridge, England, is an example of a location decision that was guided mainly by the goal of building and sustaining world-class excellence in selected value-creating activities.[16] This strategic decision provided Microsoft with access to outstanding technical and professional talent. Location decisions can affect the quality with which any activity is performed in terms of the availability of needed talent, speed of learning, and the quality of external and internal coordination.

Cost Reduction   Two location decisions founded largely on cost-reduction considerations are (1) Nike's decision to source the manufacture of athletic shoes from Asian countries such as China, Vietnam, and Indonesia, and (2) the decision of many multinational companies to set up production operations just south of the United States–Mexico border to access lower-cost labor. These operations are called *maquiladoras.* Such location decisions can affect the cost structure in terms of local manpower and other resources, transportation and logistics, and government incentives and the local tax structure.

Performance enhancement and cost-reduction benefits parallel the business-level strategies (discussed in Chapter 5) of differentiation and overall cost leadership. They can at times be attained simultaneously. Consider our example in the previous section on the Indian software industry. When Oracle set up a development operation in that country, the company benefited both from lower labor costs and operational expenses as well as from performance enhancements realized through the hiring of superbly talented professionals.

Managing across borders can lead to challenging ethical dilemmas. One issue that has received a good deal of attention in the recent business press is the issue of child labor. Strategy Spotlight 7.3 discusses how two multinational companies have taken different approaches to address this issue.

Risk Reduction   Given the erratic swings in the exchange ratios between the U.S. dollar and the Japanese yen (in relation to each other as well as other major currencies), an important basis for cost competition between Ford and Toyota has been their relative ingenuity at managing currency risks. One of the ways for such competitors to manage currency risks has been to spread the high-cost elements of their manufacturing operations across a few select and carefully chosen locations around the world. Location decisions such as these can affect the overall risk profile of the firm with respect to currency, economic, and political risks.[17]

Potential Risks of International Expansion

When a company expands its international operations, it does so to increase its profits or revenues. As with any other investment, however, there are also potential risks.[18] To help companies assess the risk of entering foreign markets, rating systems have been developed to evaluate political, economic, and financial and credit risks.[19] *Euromoney* magazine publishes a semiannual "Country Risk Rating" that evaluates political, economic, and other risks that entrants potentially face. Exhibit 7.3 depicts a sample of country risk ratings, published by the World Bank, from the 178 countries that *Euromoney* evaluates. Note that the lower the score, the higher the country's expected level of risk.

Child Labor: How Two Companies Have Addressed This Issue

It is interesting to consider how multinational companies have taken different approaches to address the issue of child labor in their overseas operations. Nike, for example, has revised its code of conduct a few times since 1992, including increasing the minimum age from 14 to 18 years for footwear factory workers and from 14 to 16 for equipment and apparel, which is quite a bit higher than other company codes and the International Labor Organization's (ILO) convention. The company also has started an internal compliance program, supplemented with external monitoring. However, this does not seem to have silenced the staunchest critics. Nike's Web site reflects the way in which the company tries to openly address this critique, providing ample information about the monitoring of facilities and the dilemmas the company faces after the introduction of its latest code.

Chiquita Banana almost completely follows the SA 8000 standard, including all references to international conventions, but with a few modifications, primarily to take account of workplace issues specific to agriculture. (The SA 8000 standard is developed by the Council on Economic Priorities Accreditation Agency and is widely recognized and accepted. It is based on ILO and United Nations conventions.) The company's strict child labor provisions do not apply to family farms or to small-scale holdings in the seasonal, nonbanana business, which do not regularly employ hired workers. This is also meant to allow for employment of a farmer's own children in seasonal activities. In line with its standard, Chiquita Banana tries to address the problem associated with children found to be working in supplying factories by giving "adequate support to enable such children to attend and remain in school until no longer a child."

Source: Kolk, A., & Tulder, R. V. 2004. Ethics in international business: Multinational approaches to child labor. *Journal of World Business*, 39: 49–60.

Next we will discuss the four main types of risk: political risk, economic risk, currency risk, and management risk.

Political and Economic Risk   Generally speaking, the business climate in the United States is very favorable. However, some countries around the globe may be hazardous to

Exhibit 7.3
A Sample of International Country Risk Rankings

Rank	Country	Total Risk Assessment	Economic Performance	Political Risk	Total of Debt Indicators	Total of Credit and Access to Finance Indicators
1	Luxembourg	99.51	25.00	24.51	20.00	30.00
2	Switzerland	98.84	23.84	25.00	20.00	30.00
3	United States	98.37	23.96	24.41	20.00	30.00
40	China	71.27	18.93	16.87	19.73	15.74
55	Poland	57.12	18.56	13.97	9.36	15.23
63	Vietnam	52.04	14.80	11.91	18.51	6.82
86	Russia	42.62	11.47	8.33	17.99	4.83
114	Albania	34.23	8.48	5.04	19.62	1.09
161	Mozambique	21.71	3.28	2.75	13.85	1.83
178	Afghanistan	3.92	0.00	3.04	0.00	0.88

Source: Adapted from worldbank.org/html/prddr/trans/so96/art7.htm.

Piracy: A Key Threat to World Trade

Counterfeiting has grown up and has become a major threat to multinational corporations. "We've seen a massive increase in the last five years, and there is a risk that it will spiral out of control," claims Anthony Simon, marketing chief of Unilever Bestfoods. "It is no longer a cottage industry."

The figures are astounding. The World Customs Organization estimates that counterfeiting accounts for about 5 percent to 7 percent of global merchandise trade—equivalent to as much as $512 billion. Seizures of fakes by United States customs jumped 46 percent last year as counterfeiters boosted exports to Western markets. Unilever Groups says that knockoffs of its shampoos, soaps, and teas are growing at a rate of 30 percent annually.

Such counterfeiting can also have health and safety implications as well. The World Health Organization says up to 10 percent of medicines worldwide are counterfeit—a deadly hazard that could be costing the pharmaceutical industry $46 billion a year. "You won't die from purchasing a pair of counterfeit blue jeans or a counterfeit golf club.

Source: Engardio, P., & Yang, C. 2006. The runaway trade giant. *BusinessWeek.* April 24: 30–32; Letzing, J. 2007. Antipiracy group make's list of worst-offendor nations. www.marketwatch. February 12: np. Balfour, F. 2005. Fake! *Business-Week*, February 7: 54–64; Anonymous. 2005. Editorial. *BusinessWeek,* February 7: 96; and Simon, B. 2004. The world's greatest fakes. www.cbsnews.com, August 8.

You can die from taking counterfeit pharmaceutical products. And there's no doubt that people have died in China from bad medicine," says John Theirault, head of global security for American pharmaceutical giant, Pfizer. And, sadly, cases like the one in China, where fake baby formula recently killed 60 infants, have investigators stepping up enforcement at U.S. ports. Injuries from overheating counterfeit cell phone batteries purchased right on Verizon store shelves sparked a recall. According to Hal Stratton, of the Consumer Product Safety Commission, "We know of at least one apartment fire that's occurred. We know of at least one burn situation of someone's face that's occurred." And bogus car parts are a $12 billion market worldwide. "Counterfeiting has gone from a local nuisance to a global threat," says Hanns Glatz, DaimlerChrysler's point man on intellectual property.

China is the key to any solution. Given the country's economic power, its counterfeiting is turning into quite the problem itself, accounting for nearly two-thirds of all fake and pirated goods worldwide. Dan Chow, a law professor at Ohio State University who specializes in Chinese counterfeiting provides some perspective: "We have never seen a problem of this size and magnitude in world history. There's more counterfeiting going on in China now than we've ever seen anywhere. We know that 15 to 20 percent of all goods in China are counterfeit."

---

political risk
potential threat to a firm's operations in a country due to ineffectiveness of the domestic political system.

the health of corporate initiatives because of **political risk.**[20] Forces such as social unrest, military turmoil, demonstrations, and even violent conflict and terrorism can pose serious threats.[21] Consider, for example, the ongoing tension and violence in the Middle East between Israelis and Palestinians, and the social and political unrest in Indonesia.[22] Because such conditions increase the likelihood of destruction of property and disruption of operations as well as nonpayment for goods and services, countries that are viewed as high risk are less attractive for most types of business. Typical exceptions include providers of munitions and counterintelligence services.

economic risk
potential threat to a firm's operations in a country due to economic policies and conditions, including property rights laws and enforcement of those laws.

The laws, and the enforcement of laws, associated with the protection of intellectual property rights can be a major potential **economic risk** in entering new countries.[23] Microsoft, for example, has lost billions of dollars in potential revenue through piracy of its software products in many countries, including China. Other areas of the globe, such as the former Soviet Union and some eastern European nations, have piracy problems as well. Firms rich in intellectual property have encountered financial losses as imitations of their products have grown due to a lack of law enforcement of intellectual property rights.[24]

Strategy Spotlight 7.4 discusses a problem that presents a severe threat to global trade—piracy. As we will see, estimates are that counterfeiting accounts for between 5 percent and 7 percent of global merchandise trade—the equivalent of as much as $512 billion a year. And the potential corrosive effects include health and safety, not just economic, damage.

Currency Risks   Currency fluctuations can pose substantial risks. A company with operations in several countries must constantly monitor the exchange rate between its own currency and that of the host country to minimize **currency risks.** Even a small change in the exchange rate can result in a significant difference in the cost of production or net profit when doing business overseas. When the U.S. dollar appreciates against other currencies, for example, U.S. goods can be more expensive to consumers in foreign countries. At the same time, however, appreciation of the U.S. dollar can have negative implications for American companies that have branch operations overseas. The reason for this is that profits from abroad must be exchanged for dollars at a more expensive rate of exchange, reducing the amount of profit when measured in dollars. For example, consider an American firm doing business in Italy. If this firm had a 20 percent profit in euros at its Italian center of operations, this profit would be totally wiped out when converted into U.S. dollars if the euro had depreciated 20 percent against the U.S. dollar. (U.S. multinationals typically engage in sophisticated "hedging strategies" to minimize currency risk. The discussion of this is beyond the scope of this section.)

It is important to note that even when government intervention is well intended, the macroeconomic effects of such action can be very negative for multinational corporations. Such was the case in 1997 when Thailand suddenly chose to devalue its currency, the baht, after months of trying to support it at an artificially high level. This, in effect, made the baht worthless compared to other currencies. And in 1998 Russia not only devalued its ruble but also elected not to honor its foreign debt obligations.

currency risk
potential threat to a firm's operations in a country due to fluctuations in the local currency's exchange rate.

Management Risks   **Management risks** may be considered the challenges and risks that managers face when they must respond to the inevitable differences that they encounter in foreign markets. These take a variety of forms: culture, customs, language, income levels, customer preferences, distribution systems, and so on.[25] As we will note later in the chapter, even in the case of apparently standard products, some degree of local adaptation will become necessary.

Differences in cultures across countries can also pose unique challenges for managers.[26] Cultural symbols can evoke deep feelings.[27] For example, in a series of advertisements aimed at Italian vacationers, Coca-Cola executives turned the Eiffel Tower, Empire State Building, and the Tower of Pisa into the familiar Coke bottle. So far, so good. However, when the white marble columns of the Parthenon that crowns the Acropolis in Athens were turned into Coke bottles, the Greeks became outraged. Why? Greeks refer to the Acropolis as the "holy rock," and a government official said the Parthenon is an "international symbol of excellence" and that "whoever insults the Parthenon insults international culture." Coca-Cola apologized for the ad. Below are a few examples of how culture varies across nations and some of the implications for business.[28]

management risk
potential threat to a firm's operations in a country due to the problems that managers have making decisions in the context of foreign markets.

- *Ecuador.* Dinners at Ecuadorian homes last for many hours. Expect drinks and appetizers around 8:00 p.m., with dinner not served until 11:00 p.m. or midnight. You will dismay your hosts if you leave as early as 1:00 a.m. A party at an Ecuadorian home will begin late and end around 4:00 a.m. or 5:00 a.m. Late guests may sometimes be served breakfast before they leave.
- *France.* Words in French and English may have the same roots but different meanings or connotations. For example, a French person might "demand" something because demander in French means "to ask."
- *Hong Kong.* Negotiations occur over cups of tea. Always accept an offer of tea whether you want it or not. When you are served, wait for the host to drink first.
- *Singapore.* Singaporeans associate all of the following with funerals, so do not give them as gifts: straw sandals, clocks, a stork or crane, handkerchiefs, or gifts or wrapping paper where the predominant color is white, black, or blue.

How a Local Custom Can Affect a Manufacturing Plant's Operations

At times, a lack of understanding and awareness of local customs can provide some frustrating and embarrassing situations. Such customs can raise issues that must be taken into account in order to make good decisions.

For example, consider the unique problem that Larry Henderson, plant manager, and John Lichthental, manager

Source: Harvey, M., & Buckley, M. R. 2002. Assessing the "conventional wisdoms" of management for the 21st century organization. *Organizational Dynamics*, 30(4): 368–378.

of human resources, were faced with when they were assigned by Celanese Chemical Corp. to build a new plant in Singapore. The $125 million plant was completed in July, but according to local custom, a plant should only be christened on "lucky" days. Unfortunately, the next "lucky" day was not until September 3.

Henderson and Lichthental had to convince executives at Celanese's Dallas headquarters to delay the plant opening. It wasn't easy. But after many heated telephone conversations and flaming e-mails, the president agreed to open the new plant on the "lucky" day—September 3.

Strategy Spotlight 7.5 addresses a rather humorous example of how a local custom can affect operations at a manufacturing plant.

We have addressed several of the motivations and risks associated with international expansion. A major recent trend has been the dispersion of the value chains of multinational corporations across different countries; that is, the various activities that constitute the value chain of a firm are now spread across several countries and continents. Such dispersion of value occurs mainly through increasing offshoring and outsourcing. We now address some of the primary associated benefits and costs.

Global Dispersion of Value Chains: Outsourcing and Offshoring

A report issued by the World Trade Organization describes the production of a particular U.S. car as follows: "30 percent of the car's value goes to Korea for assembly, 17.5 percent to Japan for components and advanced technology, 7.5 percent to Germany for design, 4 percent to Taiwan and Singapore for minor parts, 2.5 percent to U.K. for advertising and marketing services, and 1.5 percent to Ireland and Barbados for data processing. This means that only 37 percent of the production value is generated in the U.S."[29] Similarly, in the production of a Barbie doll, Mattel purchases plastic and hair from Taiwan and Japan, the molds from the United States, the doll clothing from China, and paint from the U.S. and assembles the product in Indonesia and Malaysia for sales worldwide. In today's economy these are not isolated examples. Instead, we are increasingly witnessing two interrelated trends: outsourcing and offshoring.

Outsourcing occurs when a firm decides to utilize other firms to perform value-creating activities that were previously performed in-house.[30] In some cases, it may be a new activity that the firm is perfectly capable of doing, but it still chooses to have someone else perform the function for cost or quality reasons. Outsourcing can be to either a domestic company or a foreign firm.

Offshoring takes place when a firm decides to shift an activity that they were previously performing in a domestic location to a foreign location. For example, both Microsoft and Intel now have R&D facilities in India, employing a large number of Indian scientists and engineers. In many cases, offshoring and outsourcing go together; that is, a firm

outsourcing using other firms to perform value-creating activities that were previously performed in-house.

offshoring shifting a value-creating activity from a domestic location to a foreign location.

may outsource an activity to a foreign supplier, thereby causing the work to be off-shored as well.

Spending on offshore information technology will nearly triple between 2004 and 2010 to $60 billion, according to research firm Gartner.[31] And offshore employment in information technology (IT), banking, and six other areas will double to 1.2 million from 2003 to 2008, says the McKinsey Global Institute.

The recent explosion in the volume of outsourcing and offshoring is due to a variety of factors. Up until the 1960s, for most companies, the entire value chain was in one location. Further, the production took place close to where the customers were in order to keep transportation costs under control. In the case of service industries, it was generally believed that offshoring was not possible because the producer and consumer had to be present at the same place at the same time. After all, a haircut could not be performed if the barber and the client were separated!

In the case of manufacturing industries, the rapid decline in transportation and coordination costs has enabled firms to disperse their value chains over different locations. For example, Nike's R&D takes place in the United States, raw materials are procured from a multitude of countries, actual manufacturing takes place in China or Indonesia, advertising is produced in the United States, and sales and service take place in practically all the countries. Each value-creating activity is performed in the location where the cost is the lowest or the quality is the best. Without finding optimal locations for each activity and the resultant dispersion of the value chain, Nike could not have attained its position as the world's largest shoe company.

The experience of the manufacturing sector was repeated in the service sector as well by the mid-1990s. A trend that began with the outsourcing of low-level programming and data entry work to countries such as India and Ireland suddenly grew manyfold, encompassing a variety of white collar and professional activities ranging from call-centers to R&D. Now, the technical support lines of a large number of U.S. firms are answered from call centers in faraway locations. The cost of a long distance call from the United States to India has decreased from about $3 to $0.03 in the last 20 years, thereby making it possible to have call centers located in countries like India where a combination of low labor costs and English proficiency presents an ideal mix of factor conditions. Bangalore, India, in recent years, has emerged as a location where more and more U.S. tax returns are prepared. In India, U.S.–trained and licensed radiologists interpret chest X-rays and CT scans from U.S. hospitals for half the cost. The advantages from offshoring go beyond mere cost savings today. In many specialized occupations in science and engineering, there is a shortage of qualified professionals in developed countries whereas countries like India, China, and Singapore have what seems like an inexhaustible supply.[32]

For most of the 20th century, domestic companies catered to the needs of local populations. However, with the increasing homogenization of customer needs around the world and the institutionalization of free trade and investment as a global ideology (especially after the creation of the WTO), competition has become truly global. Each company has to keep its costs low in order to survive. They also must find the best suppliers and the most skilled workers as well as locate each stage of the value chain in places where factor conditions are most conducive. Thus, outsourcing and offshoring are no longer mere options to consider, but an imperative for competitive survival.

While there is a compelling logic for companies to engage in offshoring, there are many pitfalls associated with it. Strategy Spotlight 7.6 discusses the experience of Misiu Systems, a U.S. alarm systems manufacturer that found out the hard way that offshoring is not for everyone.

Let's now look at how firms can attain competitive advantages when they move beyond the boundaries of their home nation.

Misiu Systems: Outsourcing Is Not for Everyone

When Todd Hodgen, CEO of Misiu Systems, a Bothell, Washington–based manufacturer of alarm systems, learned that he could save 65 percent of his design costs by outsourcing it to a Taiwanese firm, he was really excited. In addition to cost savings, an added bonus was that the Taiwanese engineers would be working after Misiu's engineers had gone home because of the time differences. This meant that the product development cycle could be greatly accelerated. For a start-up financed mostly with loans from friends and family, the twin advan-tages of cost savings and reduced cycle time were too much to resist.

After several months of discussions with the contrac-tor and a visit to Taiwan, Hodgen signed the outsourcing agreement. However, things did not quite work out as he had expected. His feedback to the design team in Taiwan often went unheeded. The design was eventually delivered eight months late and the quality fell well short of expecta-tions. Why? The Taiwanese engineers who were supposed to be working solely for him were also working for other clients. Business from a small firm like Misiu was not given the same priority that was given to bigger clients. Eventu-ally Hodgen ended up terminating the agreement with the Taiwanese firm and hiring a U.S. firm to finish the project!

Source: Wahlgren, E. 2004. The outsourcing dilemma. *Inc.*, April: 41–43.

Achieving Competitive Advantage in Global Markets

We now discuss the two opposing forces that firms face when they expand into global mar-kets: cost reduction and adaptation to local markets. Then we address the four basic types of international strategies that they may pursue: international, global, multidomestic, and transnational. The selection of one of these four types of strategies is largely dependent on a firm's relative pressure to address each of the two forces.

Two Opposing Pressures: Reducing Costs and Adapting to Local Markets

>LO4

The two opposing forces—cost reduction and adaptation to local markets—that firms face when entering international markets.

Many years ago, the famed marketing strategist Theodore Levitt advocated strategies that favored global products and brands. That is, he suggested that firms should standardize all of their products and services for all of their worldwide markets. Such an approach would help a firm lower its overall costs by spreading its investments over as large a market as possible. Levitt's approach rested on three key assumptions:

1. Customer needs and interests are becoming increasingly homogeneous worldwide.
2. People around the world are willing to sacrifice preferences in product features, func-tions, design, and the like for lower prices at high quality.
3. Substantial economies of scale in production and marketing can be achieved through supplying global markets.[33]

However, there is ample evidence to refute these assumptions.[34] Regarding the first assumption—the increasing worldwide homogeneity of customer needs and interests—consider the number of product markets, ranging from watches and handbags to soft drinks and fast foods. Here, companies have successfully identified global customer seg-ments and developed global products and brands targeted to those segments. In addition, many other companies adapt lines to idiosyncratic country preferences and develop local brands targeted to local market segments. For example, Nestlé's line of pizzas marketed in the United Kingdom includes cheese with ham and pineapple topping on a French bread crust. Similarly, Coca-Cola in Japan markets Georgia (a tonic drink) as well as Classic Coke and Hi-C.

Consider the second assumption—the sacrifice of product attributes for lower prices. While there is invariably a price-sensitive segment in many product markets, there is no indication that this is increasing. In contrast, in many product and service markets—ranging from watches, personal computers, and household appliances, to banking and insurance—there is a growing interest in multiple product features, product quality, and service.

Finally, the third assumption is that significant economies of scale in production and marketing could be achieved for global products and services. Although standardization may lower manufacturing costs, such a perspective does not consider three critical and interrelated points. First, as we discussed in Chapter 5, technological developments in flexible factory automation enable economies of scale to be attained at lower levels of output and do not require production of a single standardized product. Second, the cost of production is only one component, and often not the critical one, in determining the total cost of a product. Third, a firm's strategy should not be product-driven. It should also consider other activities in the firm's value chain, such as marketing, sales, and distribution.

Based on the above, we would have a hard time arguing that it is wise to develop the same product or service for all markets throughout the world. While there are some exceptions, such as Harley-Davidson motorcycles and some of Coca-Cola's soft-drink products, managers must also strive to tailor their products to the culture of the country in which they are attempting to do business. Few would argue that "one size fits all" generally applies.

What we have briefly discussed so far are two opposing pressures that managers face when they compete in markets beyond their national boundaries. These forces place conflicting demands on firms as they strive to be competitive.[35] On the one hand, competitive pressures require that firms do what they can to *lower unit costs* so that consumers will not perceive their product and service offerings as too expensive. This may lead them to consider locating manufacturing facilities where labor costs are low and developing products that are highly standardized across multiple countries.

In addition to responding to pressures to lower costs, managers also must strive to be *responsive to local pressures* in order to tailor their products to the demand of the local market in which they do business. This requires differentiating their offerings and strategies from country to country to reflect consumer tastes and preferences and making changes to reflect differences in distribution channels, human resource practices, and governmental regulations. However, since the strategies and tactics to differentiate products and services to local markets can involve additional expenses, a firm's costs will tend to rise.

The two opposing pressures result in four different basic strategies that companies can use to compete in the global marketplace: international, global, multidomestic, and transnational. The strategy that a firm selects depends on the degree of pressure that it is facing for cost reductions and the importance of adapting to local markets. Exhibit 7.4 shows the conditions under which each of these strategies would be most appropriate. As we would expect, there are advantages and disadvantages associated with each of these strategies. In the following sections we will summarize each strategy, discuss where each is most appropriate, and identify relative advantages and disadvantages.

It is important to note that we consider these strategies to be "basic" or "pure"; that is, in practice, all firms will tend to have some elements of international, global, multidomestic, and transnational strategies.

International Strategy

There are a small number of industries in which pressures for both local adaptation and lowering costs are rather low. An extreme example of such an industry is the "orphan" drug industry. These are medicines for diseases that are severe but affect only a small number of people. Diseases such as the Gaucher disease and Fabry disease fit into this category. Companies such as Genzyme and Oxford GlycoSciences are active in this segment of the drug industry. There is virtually no need to adapt their products to the local markets. And the

> **>LO5**
> The advantages and disadvantages associated with each of the four basic strategies: international, global, multidomestic, and transnational.

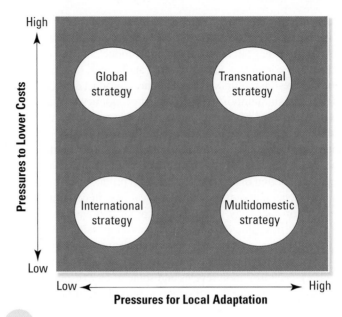

Exhibit 7.4 Opposing Pressures and Four Strategies

pressures to reduce costs are low; even though only a few thousand patients are affected, the revenues and margins are significant because patients are charged up to $100,000 per year.

An international strategy is based on diffusion and adaptation of the parent company's knowledge and expertise to foreign markets. Country units are allowed to make some minor adaptations to products and ideas coming from the head office, but they have far less independence and autonomy compared to multidomestic companies. The primary goal of the strategy is worldwide exploitation of the parent firm's knowledge and capabilities. All sources of core competencies are centralized.

For most of its history, Ericsson, a Swedish telecommunications firm, has followed this strategy. Because its home market (Sweden) was too small to support the required R&D effort, Ericsson built its strategy on its ability to transfer and adapt its innovative products and process technologies to international markets. This strategy of sequential diffusion of innovation developed at home helped it compete successfully against NEC, which followed a global strategy, and ITT, which followed a multidomestic strategy.[36]

The majority of large U.S. multinationals pursued the international strategy in the decades following World War II. These companies centralized R&D and product development but established manufacturing facilities as well as marketing organizations abroad. Companies such as McDonald's and Kellogg are examples of firms following such a strategy. Although these companies do make some local adaptations, they are of a very limited nature. With increasing pressures to reduce costs due to global competition, especially from low-cost countries, opportunities to successfully employ international strategy are becoming more limited. This strategy is most suitable in situations where a firm has distinctive competencies that local companies in foreign markets lack.

Risks and Challenges   Below, are some of the risks and challenges associated with an international strategy.

• Different activities in the value chain typically have different optimal locations. That is, R&D may be optimally located in a country with an abundant supply of scientists and engineers, whereas assembly may be better conducted in a low-cost location. Nike, for example, designs its shoes in the United States, but all the manufacturing is

Exhibit 7.5

Strengths and
Limitations of
International Strategies
in the Global
Marketplace

Strengths	Limitations
• Leverage and diffusion of a parent firm's knowledge and core competencies. • Lower costs because of less need to tailor products and services.	• Limited ability to adapt to local markets • Inability to take advantage of new ideas and innovations occurring in local markets.

done in countries like China or Thailand. The international strategy, with its tendency to concentrate most of its activities in one location, fails to take advantage of the benefits of an optimally distributed value chain.

• The lack of local responsiveness may result in the alienation of local customers. Worse still, the firm's inability to be receptive to new ideas and innovation from its foreign subsidiaries may lead to missed opportunities.

Exhibit 7.5 summarizes the strengths and weaknesses of international strategies in the global marketplace.

Global Strategy

As indicated in Exhibit 7.4, a firm whose emphasis is on lowering costs tends to follow a global strategy. Competitive strategy is centralized and controlled to a large extent by the corporate office. Since the primary emphasis is on controlling costs, the corporate office strives to achieve a strong level of coordination and integration across the various businesses.[37] Firms following a global strategy strive to offer standardized products and services as well as to locate manufacturing, R&D, and marketing activities in only a few locations.[38]

A global strategy emphasizes economies of scale due to the standardization of products and services, and the centralization of operations in a few locations. As such, one advantage may be that innovations that come about through efforts of either a business unit or the corporate office can be transferred more easily to other locations. Although costs may be lower, the firm following a global strategy may, in general, have to forgo opportunities for revenue growth since it does not invest extensive resources in adapting product offerings from one market to another.

Consistent with Exhibit 7.4, a global strategy is most appropriate when there are strong pressures for reducing costs and comparatively weak pressures for adaptation to local markets. Identifying potential economies of scale becomes an important consideration.[39] Advantages to increased volume may come not only from larger production plants or runs but also from more efficient logistics and distribution networks. Worldwide volume is also especially important in supporting high levels of investment in research and development. As we would expect, many industries requiring high levels of R&D, such as pharmaceuticals, semiconductors, and jet aircraft, follow global strategies.

Another advantage of a global strategy is that it can enable a firm to create a standard level of quality throughout the world. Let's look at what Tom Siebel, chairman of Siebel Systems (now part of Oracle), the $2 billion developer of e-business application software, has to say about global standardization.

> Our customers—global companies like IBM, Zurich Financial Services, and Citicorp—expect the same high level of service and quality, and the same licensing policies, no matter where we do business with them around the world. Our human resources and legal departments help us create policies that respect local cultures and requirements worldwide, while at the same time maintaining the highest standards. We have one brand, one image, one set of corporate colors, and one set of messages, across every place on the planet. An organization needs central quality control to avoid surprises.[40]

Exhibit 7.6
Strengths and Limitations
of Global Strategies

Strengths	Limitations
• Strong integration across various businesses.	• Limited ability to adapt to local markets.
• Standardization leads to higher economies of scale, which lowers costs.	• Concentration of activities may increase dependence on a single facility.
• Helps create uniform standards of quality throughout the world.	• Single locations may lead to higher tariffs and transportation costs.

Risks and Challenges   There are, of course, some risks associated with a global strategy.[41]

- A firm can enjoy scale economies only by concentrating scale-sensitive resources and activities in one or few locations. Such concentration, however, becomes a "double-edged sword." For example, if a firm has only one manufacturing facility, it must export its output (e.g., components, subsystems, or finished products) to other markets, some of which may be a great distance from the operation. Thus, decisions about locating facilities must weigh the potential benefits from concentrating operations in a single location against the higher transportation and tariff costs that result from such concentration.
- The geographic concentration of any activity may also tend to isolate that activity from the targeted markets. Such isolation may be risky since it may hamper the facility's ability to quickly respond to changes in market conditions and needs.
- Concentrating an activity in a single location also makes the rest of the firm dependent on that location. Such dependency implies that, unless the location has world-class competencies, the firm's competitive position can be eroded if problems arise. A European Ford executive, reflecting on the firm's concentration of activities during a global integration program in the mid-1990s, lamented, "Now if you misjudge the market, you are wrong in 15 countries rather than only one."

Exhibit 7.6 summarizes the strengths and weaknesses of global strategies.

Multidomestic Strategy

According to Exhibit 7.4, a firm whose emphasis is on differentiating its product and service offerings to adapt to local markets follows a multidomestic strategy. Decisions evolving from a multidomestic strategy tend to be decentralized to permit the firm to tailor its products and respond rapidly to changes in demand. This enables a firm to expand its market and to charge different prices in different markets. For firms following this strategy, differences in language, culture, income levels, customer preferences, and distribution systems are only a few of the many factors that must be considered. Even in the case of relatively standardized products, at least some level of local adaptation is often necessary. Consider, for example, Honda motorcycles.

> Although we could argue that a good product knows no national boundaries, there are subtle differences in ways that a product is used and what customers expect of it. Thus, while Honda uses a common basic technology, it must develop different types of motorcycles for different regions of the world. For example, North Americans primarily use motorcycles for leisure and sports; thus aggressive looks and high horsepower are key. Southeast Asians provide a counterpoint. Here, motorcycles are a basic means of transportation. Thus, they require low cost and ease of maintenance. And, in Australia and New Zealand, shepherds use motorcycles to herd sheep. Therefore, they demand low-speed torque, rather than high speed and maintenance.[42]

strategy spotlight

Dealing with Bribery Abroad

Most multinational firms experience difficult dilemmas when it comes to the question of adapting rules and guidelines, both formal and informal, while operating in foreign countries. A case in point is the Foreign Corrupt Practices Act of 1977, which makes it illegal for U.S. companies to bribe foreign officials to gain business or facilitate approvals and permissions. Unfortunately, in many parts of the world, bribery is a way of life, with large payoffs to government officials and politicians the norm to win government contracts. At a lower level, goods won't clear customs unless routine illegal, but well-accepted, payments, are made to officials. What is an American company to do in such situations?

Source: Begley, T. M., & Boyd, D. P. 2003. The need for a corporate global mind-set. *MIT Sloan Management Review*, Winter: 25–32.

Intel follows a strict rule-based definition of bribery as "a thing of value given to someone with the intent of obtaining favorable treatment from the recipient." The company strictly prohibits payments to expedite a shipment through customs if the payment did not "follow applicable rules and regulations, and if the agent gives money or payment in kind to a government official for personal benefit." Texas Instruments, on the other hand, follows a middle approach. They require employees to "exercise good judgment" in questionable circumstances "by avoiding activities that could create even the appearance that our decisions could be compromised." And Analog Devices has set up a policy manager as a consultant to overseas operations. The policy manager does not make decisions for country managers. Instead, the policy manager helps country managers think through the issues and provides information on how the corporate office has handled similar situations in the past.

In addition to the products themselves, how they are packaged must sometimes be adapted to local market conditions. Some consumers in developing countries are likely to have packaging preferences very different from western consumers. For example, single-serve packets, or sachets, are very popular in India.[43] They permit consumers to purchase only what they need, experiment with new products, and conserve cash. Products as varied as detergents, shampoos, pickles, and cough syrup are sold in sachets in India. It is estimated that they make up 20 percent to 30 percent of the total sold in their categories. In China, sachets are spreading as a marketing device for such items as shampoos. This reminds us of the importance of considering all activities in a firm's value chain (discussed in Chapters 3 and 5) in determining where local adaptations may be required.

Cultural differences may also require a firm to adapt its personnel practices when it expands internationally.[44] For example, some facets of Wal-Mart stores have been easily "exported" to foreign operations, while others have required some modifications.[45] When the retailer entered the German market in 1997, it took along the company "cheer"—Give me a W! Give me an A! Give me an L! Who's Number One? The Customer!—which suited German employees. However, Wal-Mart's 10-Foot Rule, which requires employees to greet any customer within a 10-foot radius, was not so well received in Germany, where employees and shoppers alike weren't comfortable with the custom. (As noted in this chapter's opening case, Wal-Mart exited the German market in 2006.)

Strategy Spotlight 7.7 describes how U.S. multinationals have adapted to the problem of bribery in various countries while adhering to strict federal laws on corrupt practices abroad.

Risks and Challenges   As you might expect, there are some risks associated with a multidomestic strategy. Among these are the following:

- Typically, local adaptation of products and services will increase a company's cost structure. In many industries, competition is so intense that most firms can ill afford any competitive disadvantages on the dimension of cost. A key challenge of managers is to determine the trade-off between local adaptation and its cost structure. For example, cost considerations led Procter & Gamble to standardize its diaper design across all European markets. This was done despite research data indicating that

Exhibit 7.7

Strengths and Limitations of Multidomestic Strategies

Strengths	Limitations
• Ability to adapt products and services to local market conditions. • Ability to detect potential opportunities for attractive niches in a given market, enhancing revenue.	• Decreased ability to realize cost savings through scale economies. • Greater difficulty in transferring knowledge across countries. • May lead to "overadaptation" as conditions change.

Italian mothers, unlike those in other countries, preferred diapers that covered the baby's navel. Later, however, P&G recognized that this feature was critical to these mothers, so the company decided to incorporate this feature for the Italian market despite its adverse cost implications.

- At times, local adaptations, even when well intentioned, may backfire. When the American restaurant chain TGI Fridays entered the South Korean market, it purposely incorporated many local dishes, such as kimchi (hot, spicy cabbage), in its menu. This responsiveness, however, was not well received. Company analysis of the weak market acceptance indicated that Korean customers anticipated a visit to TGI Fridays as a visit to America. Thus, finding Korean dishes was inconsistent with their expectations.

- Consistent with other aspects of global marketing, the optimal degree of local adaptation evolves over time. In many industry segments, a variety of factors, such as the influence of global media, greater international travel, and declining income disparities across countries, may lead to increasing global standardization. On the other hand, in other industry segments, especially where the product or service can be delivered over the Internet (such as music), the need for even greater customization and local adaptation may increase over time. Firms must recalibrate the need for local adaptation on an ongoing basis; excessive adaptation extracts a price as surely as underadaptation.

Exhibit 7.7 summarizes the strengths and limitations of multidomestic strategies.

Transnational Strategy

A *transnational strategy* strives to optimize the trade-offs associated with efficiency, local adaptation, and learning.[46] It seeks efficiency not for its own sake, but as a means to achieve global competitiveness. It recognizes the importance of local responsiveness but as a tool for flexibility in international operations.[47] Innovations are regarded as an outcome of a larger process of organizational learning that includes the contributions of everyone in the firm.[48] Also, a core tenet of the transnational model is that a firm's assets and capabilities are dispersed according to the most beneficial location for each activity. Thus, managers avoid the tendency to either concentrate activities in a central location (a global strategy) or disperse them across many locations to enhance adaptation (a multidomestic strategy). Peter Brabeck, CEO of Nestlé, the giant food company, provides such a perspective.

> We believe strongly that there isn't a so-called global consumer, at least not when it comes to food and beverages. People have local tastes based on their unique cultures and traditions—a good candy bar in Brazil is not the same as a good candy bar in China. Therefore, decision making needs to be pushed down as low as possible in the organization, out close to the markets. Otherwise, how can you make good brand decisions? That said, decentralization has its limits. If you are too decentralized, you can become too complicated—you get too much complexity in your production system. The closer we come to the consumer, in branding, pricing, communication, and product adaptation, the more we decentralize. The more we are dealing with production, logistics, and supply-chain management, the more centralized decision making becomes. After all, we want to leverage Nestlé's size, not be hampered by it.[49]

The Nestlé example illustrates a common approach in determining whether or not to centralize or decentralize a value-chain activity. Typically, primary activities that are "downstream" (e.g., marketing, sales, and service), or closer to the customer, tend to require more decentralization in order to adapt to local market conditions. On the other hand, primary activities that are "upstream" (e.g., logistics and operations), or further away from the customer, tend to be centralized. This is because there is less need for adapting these activities to local markets and the firm can benefit from economies of scale. Additionally, many support activities, such as information systems and procurement, tend to be centralized in order to increase the potential for economies of scale.

A central philosophy of the transnational organization is enhanced adaptation to all competitive situations as well as flexibility by capitalizing on communication and knowledge flows throughout the organization.[50] A principal characteristic is the integration of unique contributions of all units into worldwide operations. Thus, a joint innovation by headquarters and by one of the overseas units can lead potentially to the development of relatively standardized and yet flexible products and services that are suitable for multiple markets.

Asea Brown Boveri (ABB) is a firm that successfully follows a transnational strategy. ABB, with its home bases in Sweden and Switzerland, illustrates the trend toward cross-national mergers that lead firms to consider multiple headquarters in the future. It is managed as a flexible network of units, and one of management's main functions is the facilitation of information and knowledge flows between units. ABB's subsidiaries have complete responsibility for product categories on a worldwide basis. Such a transnational strategy enables ABB to benefit from access to new markets and the opportunity to utilize and develop resources wherever they may be located.

Risks and Challenges   As with the other strategies, there are some unique risks and challenges associated with a transnational strategy.

- *The choice of a seemingly optimal location cannot guarantee that the quality and cost of factor inputs (i.e., labor, materials) will be optimal.* Managers must ensure that the relative advantage of a location is actually realized, not squandered because of weaknesses in productivity and the quality of internal operations. Ford Motor Co., for example, has benefited from having some of its manufacturing operations in Mexico. While some have argued that the benefits of lower wage rates will be partly offset by lower productivity, this does not always have to be the case. Since unemployment in Mexico is higher than in the United States, Ford can be more selective in its hiring practices for its Mexican operations. And, given the lower turnover among its Mexican employees, Ford can justify a high level of investment in training and development. Thus, the net result can be not only lower wage rates but also higher productivity than in the United States.
- *Although knowledge transfer can be a key source of competitive advantage, it does not take place "automatically."* For knowledge transfer to take place from one subsidiary to another, it is important for the source of the knowledge, the target units, and the corporate headquarters to recognize the potential value of such unique know-how. Given that there can be significant geographic, linguistic, and cultural distances that typically separate subsidiaries, the potential for knowledge transfer can become very difficult to realize. Firms must create mechanisms to systematically and routinely uncover the opportunities for knowledge transfer.

Exhibit 7.8 summarizes the relative advantages and disadvantages of transnational strategies.

Global or Regional? A Second Look at Globalization

>LO6
The difference between regional companies and truly global companies.

Thus far, we have suggested four possible strategies from which a firm must choose once it has decided to compete in the global marketplace. In recent years, many writers have asserted that the process of globalization has caused national borders to become increasingly

Exhibit 7.8
Strengths and Limitations of Transnational Strategies

Strengths	Limitations
• Ability to attain economies of scale. • Ability to adapt to local markets. • Ability to locate activities in optimal locations. • Ability to increase knowledge flows and learning.	• Unique challenges in determining optimal locations of activities to ensure cost and quality. • Unique managerial challenges in fostering knowledge transfer.

irrelevant. However, some scholars have recently questioned this perspective, and they have argued that it is unwise for companies to rush into full scale globalization.[51]

Before answering questions about the extent of firms' globalization, let's try to clarify what "globalization" means. Traditionally, a firm's globalization is measured in terms of its foreign sales as a percentage of total sales. However, this measure can be misleading. For example, consider a U.S. firm that has expanded its activities into Canada. Clearly, this initiative is qualitatively different from achieving the same sales volume in a distant country such as China. Similarly, if a Malaysian firm expands into Singapore or a German firm starts selling its products in Austria, this would represent an expansion into a geographically adjacent country. Such nearby countries would often share many common characteristics in terms of language, culture, infrastructure, and customer preferences. In other words, this is more a case of regionalization than globalization.

Extensive analysis of the distribution data of sales across different countries and regions led Alan Rugman and Alain Verbeke to conclude that there is a stronger case to be made in favor of regionalization than globalization. According to their study, a company would have to have at least 20 percent of its sales in each of the three major economic regions—North America, Europe, and Asia—to be considered a global firm. However, they found that only nine of the world's 500 largest firms met this standard! Even when they relaxed the criterion to 20 percent of sales each in at least two of the three regions, the number only increased to 25. *Thus, most companies are regional or, at best, biregional—not global—even today.* Exhibit 7.9 provides a listing of the large firms that met each of these two criteria.

One might ask: In a world of instant communication, rapid transportation, and governments that are increasingly willing to open up their markets to trade and investment, why are so few firms "global"? The most obvious answer is that distance still matters. After all, it is easier to do business in a neighboring country than in a far away country, all else being equal. Distance, in the final analysis, may be viewed as a concept with many dimensions, not just a measure of geographical distance. For example, both Canada and Mexico are the same distance from the United States. However, U.S. companies find it easier to expand operations into Canada than into Mexico. Why? Canada and the United States share many commonalities in terms of language, culture, economic development, legal and political systems, and infrastructure development. Thus, if we view distance as having many dimensions, the United States and Canada are very close, whereas there is greater distance between the United States and Mexico. Similarly, when we look at what we might call the "true" distance between the United States and China, the effects of geographic distance is multiplied by distance in terms of culture, language, religion, and legal and political systems between the two countries. On the other hand, although United States and Australia are geographically distant, the "true" distance is somewhat less when one considers distance along the other dimensions.

Another reason for regional expansion is the rise of the trading blocs. The European Union originally started in the 1950s as a regional trading bloc. However, recently it has achieved a large degree of economic and political integration in terms of common currency

Exhibit 7.9

Global or Regional? Sales Distribution of the *Fortune* Global 500 Firms

Firms with at least 20 percent sales in Asia, Europe, and North America each but with less than 50 percent sales in any one region:

IBM	Nokia	Coca-Cola
Sony	Intel	Flextronics
Philips	Canon	LVMH

Firms with at least 20 percent sales in at least two of the three regions (Asia, Europe, North America) but with less than 50 percent sales in any one region:

BP Amoco	Alstom	Michelin
Toyota	Aventis	Kodak
Nissan	Daigeo	Electrolux
Unilever	Sun Microsystems	BAE
Motorola	Bridgestone	Alcan
GlaxoSmithKline	Roche	L'Oreal
EADS	3M	Lafarge
Bayer	Skanska	
Ericsson	McDonald's	

Sources: Peng, M.W. 2006. *Global strategy:* 387. Mason, OH: Thomson Southwestern; and Rugman, A.M., & Verbeke, A. 2004. A perspective on regional and global strategies of multinational enterprises. *Journal of International Business Studies.* 35: 3–18.

and common standards that many thought infeasible, if not impossible, only 20 years ago. The resulting economic benefits have led other regions also to consider similar moves. For example, the North American Free Trade Agreement (NAFTA) has the eventual abolition of all barriers to the free movement of goods and services among Canada, the United States, and Mexico as its goal. Other regional trading blocks include MERCOSUR (consisting of Argentina, Brazil, Paraguay, and Uruguay) and the Association of Southeast Asian Nations (ASEAN) (consisting of about a dozen Southeast Asian countries).

Regional economic integration has progressed at a faster pace than global economic integration and the trade and investment patterns of the largest companies reflect this reality. After all, regions represent the outcomes of centuries of political and cultural history that results not only in commonalities but also mutual affinity. For example, stretching from Algeria and Morocco in the West to Oman and Yemen in the East, more than 30 countries share the Arabic language and the Muslim religion, making these countries a natural regional bloc. Similarly, the countries of South and Central America share the Spanish language (except Brazil), Catholic religion, and a shared history of Spanish colonialism. No wonder firms find it easier and less risky to expand within their region than to other regions.

Let's now turn to the types of entry modes that companies may use to enter international markets.

Entry Modes of International Expansion

A firm has many options available to it when it decides to expand into international markets. Given the challenges associated with such entry, many firms first start on a small scale and then increase their level of investment and risk as they gain greater experience with the overseas market in question.[52]

Exhibit 7.10 illustrates a wide variety of modes of foreign entry, including exporting, licensing, franchising, joint ventures, strategic alliances, and wholly owned subsidiaries.[53]

>LO7
The four basic types of entry strategies and the relative benefits and risks associated with each of them.

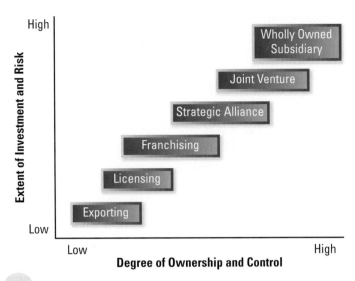

Exhibit 7.10 Entry Modes for International Expansion

As the exhibit indicates, the various types of entry form a continuum ranging from exporting (low investment and risk, low control) to a wholly owned subsidiary (high investment and risk, high control).[54]

There can be frustrations and setbacks as a firm evolves its international entry strategy from exporting to more expensive types, including wholly owned subsidiaries. For example, according to the CEO of a large U.S. specialty chemical company:

> In the end, we always do a better job with our own subsidiaries; sales improve, and we have greater control over the business. But we still need local distributors for entry, and we are still searching for strategies to get us through the transitions without battles over control and performance.[55]

Let's discuss each of these international entry modes.[56]

Exporting

exporting producing goods in one country to sell to residents of another country.

Exporting consists of producing goods in one country to sell in another. This entry strategy enables a firm to invest the least amount of resources in terms of its product, its organization, and its overall corporate strategy. Many host countries dislike this entry strategy because it provides less local employment than other modes of entry.[57]

Multinationals often stumble onto a stepwise strategy for penetrating markets, beginning with the exporting of products. This often results in a series of unplanned actions to increase sales revenues. As the pattern recurs with entries into subsequent markets, this approach, named a "beachhead strategy," often becomes official policy.

Benefits   Such an approach definitely has its advantages. After all, firms start from scratch in sales and distribution when they enter new markets. Because many foreign markets are nationally regulated and dominated by networks of local intermediaries, firms need to partner with local distributors to benefit from their valuable expertise and knowledge of their own markets. Multinationals, after all, recognize that they cannot master local business practices, meet regulatory requirements, hire and manage local personnel, or gain access to potential customers without some form of local partnership.

In addition to the need to partner with local firms, multinationals also want to minimize their own risk. They do this by hiring local distributors and investing very little in the undetaking. In essence, the firm gives up control of strategic marketing decisions to the local partners—much more control than they would be willing to give up in their home market.

Risks and Limitations   As we might expect, exporting is a relatively inexpensive way to enter foreign markets. However, it can still have significant downsides. In a study of 250 instances in which multinational firms used local distributors to implement their exporting entry strategy, the results were dismal. In the vast majority of the cases, the distributors were bought (to increase control) by the multinational firm or fired. In contrast, successful distributors shared two common characteristics:

- They carried product lines that complemented, rather than competed with, the multinational's products.
- They behaved as if they were business partners with the multinationals. They shared market information with the corporations, they initiated projects with distributors in neighboring countries, and they suggested initiatives in their own or nearby markets. Additionally, these distributors took on risk themselves by investing in areas such as training, information systems, and advertising and promotion in order to increase the business of their multinational partners.

The key point is the importance of developing collaborative, win–win relationships.

To ensure more control over operations without incurring significant risks, many firms have used licensing and franchising as a mode of entry. Let's now discuss these and their relative advantages and disadvantages.

Licensing and Franchising

Licensing and franchising are both forms of contractual arrangements. **Licensing** enables a company to receive a royalty or fee in exchange for the right to use its trademark, patent, trade secret, or other valuable item of intellectual property.[58]

Franchising contracts generally include a broader range of factors in an operation and have a longer time period during which the agreement is in effect. Franchising remains a primary form of American business. According to a recent survey, more than 400 U.S. franchisers have international exposure.[59] This is greater than the combined totals of the next four largest franchiser home countries—France, the United Kingdom, Mexico, and Austria.

Benefits   In international markets, an advantage of licensing is that the firm granting a license incurs little risk, since it does not have to invest any significant resources into the country itself. In turn, the licensee (the firm receiving the license) gains access to the trademark, patent, and so on, and is able to potentially create competitive advantages. In many cases, the country also benefits from the product being manufactured locally. For example, Yoplait yogurt is licensed by General Mills from Sodima, a French cooperative, for sale in the United States. The logos of college and professional athletic teams in the United States are another source of trademarks that generate significant royalty income domestically and internationally.

Franchising has the advantage of limiting the risk exposure that a firm has in overseas markets. At the same time, the firm is able to expand the revenue base of the company.

● While Australia is geographically distant from the United States, it is much closer when other dimensions are considered such as income levels, language, culture, and political/legal systems.

licensing a contractual arrangement in which a company receives a royalty or fee in exchange for the right to use its trademark, patent, trade secret, or other valuable intellectual property.

franchising a contractual arrangement in which a company receives a royalty or fee in exchange for the right to use its intellectual property; it usually involves a longer time period than licensing and includes other factors, such as monitoring of operations, training, and advertising.

Risks and Limitations   There are, of course, some important disadvantages with this type of entry. For example, the licensor gives up control of its product and forgoes potential revenues and profits. Furthermore, the licensee may eventually become so familiar with the patent and trade secrets that it may become a competitor; that is, the licensee may make some modifications to the product and manufacture and sell it independently of the licensor without having to pay a royalty fee. This potential situation is aggravated in countries that have relatively weak laws to protect intellectual property. Additionally, if the licensee selected by the multinational firm turns out to be a poor choice, the brand name and reputation of the product may be tarnished.[60]

With franchising, the multinational firm receives only a portion of the revenues, in the form of franchise fees. Had the firm set up the operation itself (e.g., a restaurant through direct investment), it would have had the entire revenue to itself.

Companies often desire a closer collaboration with other firms in order to increase revenue, reduce costs, and enhance their learning—often through the diffusion of technology. To achieve such objectives, they enter into strategic alliances or joint ventures, two entry modes we will discuss next.

Strategic Alliances and Joint Ventures

Joint ventures and strategic alliances have recently become increasingly popular. These two forms of partnership differ in that joint ventures entail the creation of a third-party legal entity, whereas strategic alliances do not. In addition, strategic alliances generally focus on initiatives that are smaller in scope than joint ventures.

Benefits   As we discussed in Chapter 6, these strategies have been effective in helping firms increase revenues and reduce costs as well as enhance learning and diffuse technologies. These partnerships enable firms to share the risks as well as the potential revenues and profits. Also, by gaining exposure to new sources of knowledge and technologies, such partnerships can help firms develop core competencies that can lead to competitive advantages in the marketplace.[61] Finally, entering into partnerships with host country firms can provide very useful information on local market tastes, competitive conditions, legal matters, and cultural nuances.[62]

Joint ventures can often include more than two different parties. Strategy Spotlight 7.8 discusses a joint venture that involved companies from the United States, China, and India.

Risks and Limitations   Managers must be aware of the risks associated with strategic alliances and joint ventures and how they can be minimized.[63] First, there needs to be a clearly defined strategy that is strongly supported by the organizations that are party to the partnership. Otherwise, the firms may work at cross-purposes and not achieve any of their goals. Second, and closely allied to the first issue, there must be a clear understanding of capabilities and resources that will be central to the partnership. Without such clarification, there will be fewer opportunities for learning and developing competencies that could lead to competitive advantages. Third, trust is a vital element. Phasing in the relationship between alliance partners permits them to get to know each other better and develop trust. According to Philip Benton, Jr., former president of Ford Motor Co. (which has been involved in multiple international partnerships over the years), "The first time two companies work together, the chances of succeeding are very slight. But once you find ways to work together, all sorts of opportunities arise." Without trust, one party may take advantage of the other by, for example, withholding its fair share of resources and gaining access to privileged information through unethical (or illegal) means. Fourth, cultural issues that can potentially lead to conflict and dysfunctional behaviors need to be addressed. An organization's culture is the set of values,

7.8

strategy spotlight

A Joint Venture with Partners from Three Countries

A joint venture has been formed with partners from China, India, and the United States. In December 2006, Tata Consulting Services (TCS), India's largest information technology outsourcing company, joined forces with three Chinese state-owned companies and Microsoft to form a new software development center based in Beijing, China.

The development has been hailed as one of the most striking steps forward in bilateral IT relations between India and China, which for many years have been marred by mutual suspicions. Political leaders, especially in India, have traditionally been skeptical about the export of technology skills from India to China. Why? India had concerns about assisting an economic rival.

One sign of the complexities in establishing such a partnership in China is the time that it has taken to set up

TCS China: The parties had signed the initial agreement to go ahead with the project 17 months earlier in June 2005. Under the agreement, TCS will hold 65 percent of the venture while the three Chinese partners will hold 25 percent. Microsoft will hold the remaining 10 percent. The three Chinese partners are organized under the National Development and Reform Commission, the powerful central government planning agency.

The joint venture will leverage the complementary strengths of the investing parties in technology, software development management, and talent training. Of particular value will be TCS's best processes and practices as well as its experience in handling large and industrial-scale projects. It will also benefit from the resources of the Chinese partners, which run the national software development parks.

Microsoft should also benefit. According to Jonathan Spira, chief analyst of a Basex, an IT research firm: "Microsoft is a global company so it makes sense for them to invest and participate in global partnerships, especially in markets as large as China's. China is a region where Microsoft does not have anything close to resembling a foothold."

Sources: Leahy, J. 2006. Asian partnership takes off. www.ft.com, December 5: 3; Anonymous. 2005. TCS and Microsoft intend to establish joint venture with Chinese firms. Microsoft Press Release. June 30, np.; and Anonymous. 2005. Microsoft sets up JV with Tata. www.basex.com. July 1, np.

---

beliefs, and attitudes that influence the behavior and goals of its employees. Thus, recognizing cultural differences as well as striving to develop elements of a "common culture" for the partnership is vital. Without a unifying culture, it will become difficult to combine and leverage resources that are increasingly important in knowledge-intensive organizations (discussed in Chapter 4).[64]

As we know, not all partnerships are successful, for a variety of reasons. One of the most famous in recent business history was the joint venture formed by General Motors and Daewoo Motor Co.

> In the mid-1980s General Motors sought cheap labor in Korea while Daewoo (of Korea) wanted to export automobiles. Thus, the two companies joined forces in 1986 to manufacture the ill-fated Pontiac LeMans. Things did not work out as planned. The LeMans experienced a sales decline of 39 percent from 1988 to 1990 and further declines in 1990 until the partnership was dissolved shortly thereafter.
>
> What went wrong? The first cars had quality problems: GM sent engineers to Korea to correct them. Korea's cheap labor didn't materialize because of economic improvement, devaluation of the dollar, and increasingly strong demands from the newly formed labor unions for higher wages. However, the biggest problem was the differing goals of the two firms. While Daewoo wanted to upgrade the models to gain a larger share of the domestic market, GM wanted to keep costs down.
>
> In effect, the alliance failed from the start, due to minimal understanding of each other's objectives and a lack of effort to reevaluate plans when problems appeared.[65]

Finally, the success of a firm's alliance should not be left to chance.[66] To improve their odds of success, many companies have carefully documented alliance-management knowledge by creating guidelines and manuals to help them manage specific aspects of the entire alliance life cycle (e.g., partner selection and alliance negotiation and contracting). For example, Lotus Corp. (part of IBM) created what it calls its "35 rules of thumb" to manage each phase of an alliance from formation to termination. Hewlett-Packard developed 60 different tools and templates, which it placed in a 300-page manual for guiding decision making. The manual included such tools as a template for making the business case for an alliance, a partner evaluation form, a negotiation template outlining the roles and responsibilities of different departments, a list of the ways to measure alliance performance, and an alliance termination checklist.

When a firm desires the highest level of control, it develops wholly owned subsidiaries. Although wholly owned subsidiaries can generate the greatest returns, they also have the highest levels of investment and risk. We will now discuss them.

Wholly Owned Subsidiaries

wholly owned subsidiary a business in which a multinational company owns 100 percent of the stock.

A **wholly owned subsidiary** is a business in which a multinational company owns 100 percent of the stock. Two ways a firm can establish a wholly owned subsidiary are to (1) acquire an existing company in the home country or (2) develop a totally new operation (often referred to as a "greenfield venture").

Benefits   Establishing a wholly owned subsidiary is the most expensive and risky of the various entry modes. However, it can also yield the highest returns. In addition, it provides the multinational company with the greatest degree of control of all activities, including manufacturing, marketing, distribution, and technology development.[67]

Wholly owned subsidiaries are most appropriate where a firm already has the appropriate knowledge and capabilities that it can leverage rather easily through multiple locations in many countries. Examples range from restaurants to semiconductor manufacturers. To lower costs, for example, Intel Corporation builds semiconductor plants throughout the world—all of which use virtually the same blueprint. In establishing wholly owned subsidiaries, knowledge can be further leveraged by the hiring of managers and professionals from the firm's home country, often through hiring talent from competitors.

Risks and Limitations   As noted, wholly owned subsidiaries are typically the most expensive and risky of the various entry modes. With franchising, joint ventures, or strategic alliances, the risk is shared with the firm's partners. With wholly owned subsidiaries, the entire risk is assumed by the parent company. The risks associated with doing business in a new country (e.g., political, cultural, and legal) can be lessened by hiring local talent.

For example, Wendy's was saved from committing two separate blunders in Germany by hiring locals to its advertising staff.[68] In one case, the firm wanted to promote its "old-fashioned" qualities. However, a literal translation would have resulted in the company promoting itself as "outdated." In another situation, Wendy's wanted to emphasize that its hamburgers could be prepared 256 ways. The problem? The German word that Wendy's wanted to use for "ways" usually meant "highways" or "roads." Although such errors may sometimes be entertaining to the public, it is certainly preferable to catch these mistakes before they confuse the consumer or embarrass the company.

In this closing section, we have addressed entry strategies as a progression from exporting through the creation of wholly owned subsidiaries. However, we must point out that many firms do not follow such an evolutionary approach. Instead, such firms follow rather unique entry strategies; see the discussion of Häagen-Dazs in Strategy Spotlight 7.9.

Häagen-Dazs's Unique Entry Strategy

The ice-cream and frozen yogurt company Häagen-Dazs (now a subsidiary of General Mills) has taken a unique route for cross-border entry. Rather than follow traditional entry modes, the Bronx, New York–based company has an unconventional way of moving beyond the boundaries of the United States.

The company uses a three-step process. First, it uses high-end retailers to introduce the brand. Next, it finds high-traffic areas to build company-owned stores. The last step is to sell Häagen-Dazs products in convenience stores and supermarkets.

Häagen-Dazs is quick to adapt to local needs. For instance, freezers in some European stores are notorious for their unreliability. Clearly, a freezer malfunction would ruin a store's stock of Häagen-Dazs products. So Häagen-Dazs buys high-quality freezers for stores willing to carry its brand. Small sacrifices such as this have grown the company from a small ice-cream manufacturer in the Bronx to a worldwide franchiser with 650 stores in 55 countries, including Belgium, France, Japan, and the United Kingdom.

Sources: Meremenot, M. 1991. Screaming for Häagen-Dazs. *BusinessWeek,* October 14: 121; Häagen-Dazs. 2001. Information for franchisees. Häagen-Dazs company document: 1–24.

Reflecting on Career Implications . . .

- *International Strategy:* Be aware of your organization's international strategy. What percentage of the total firm activity is international? What skills are needed to enhance your company's international efforts? How can you get more involved in your organization's international strategy? For your career, what conditions in your home country might cause you to seek careers abroad?
- *Outsourcing and Offshoring:* What activities in your organization can/should be outsourced or offshored? Be aware that you are competing in the global marketplace for employment and professional advancement. Continually take inventory of your talents, skills, and competencies.
- *International Career Opportunities:* Work assignments in other countries can often provide a career boost. Be proactive in pursuing promising career opportunities in other countries. Anticipate how such opportunities will advance your short- and long-term career aspirations.
- *Management Risks:* Develop cultural sensitivity. This applies, of course, to individuals from different cultures in your home-based organization as well as in your overseas experience.

Summary

We live in a highly interconnected global community where many of the best opportunities for growth and profitability lie beyond the boundaries of a company's home country. Along with the opportunities, of course, there are many risks associated with diversification into global markets.

The first section of the chapter addressed the factors that determine a nation's competitiveness in a particular industry. The framework was developed by Professor Michael Porter of Harvard University and was based on a four-year study that explored the competitive success of 10 leading trading nations. The four factors, collectively termed the "diamond of national advantage," were factor conditions, demand characteristics, related and supporting industries, and firm strategy, structure, and rivalry.

The discussion of Porter's "diamond" helped, in essence, to set the broader context for exploring competitive advantage at the firm level. In the second section, we discussed the primary motivations and the potential risks associated with international expansion. The primary motivations included increasing the size of the potential market for the firm's products and services, achieving economies of scale, extending the life cycle of the firm's products, and optimizing the location for every activity in the value chain. On the other hand, the key risks included political and economic risks, currency risks, and management risks. Management risks are the challenges associated with responding to the inevitable differences that exist across countries such as customs, culture, language, customer preferences, and distribution systems. We also addressed some of the managerial challenges and opportunities associated with offshoring and outsourcing.

Next, we addressed how firms can go about attaining competitive advantage in global markets. We began by discussing the two opposing forces—cost reduction and adaptation to local markets—that managers must contend with when entering global markets. The relative importance of these two factors plays a major part in determining which of the four basic types of strategies to select: international, global, multidomestic, or transnational. The chapter covered the benefits and risks associated with each type of strategy. We also presented a recent perspective by Alan Rugman who argues that despite all the talk of globalization, most of the large multinationals are regional or at best biregional (in terms of geographical diversification of sales) rather than global.

The final section discussed the four types of entry strategies that managers may undertake when entering international markets. The key trade-off in each of these strategies is the level of investment or risk versus the level of control. In order of their progressively greater investment/risk and control, the strategies range from exporting to licensing and franchising, to strategic alliances and joint ventures, to wholly owned subsidiaries. The relative benefits and risks associated with each of these strategies were addressed.

Summary Review Questions

1. What are some of the advantages and disadvantages associated with a firm's expansion into international markets?

2. What are the four factors described in Porter's diamond of national advantage? How do the four factors explain why some industries in a given country are more successful than others?

3. Explain the two opposing forces—cost reduction and adaptation to local markets—that firms must deal with when they go global.

4. There are four basic strategies—international, global, multidomestic, and transnational. What are the advantages and disadvantages associated with each?

5. What is the basis of Alan Rugman's argument that most multinationals are still more regional than global? What factors inhibit firms from becoming truly global?

6. Describe the basic entry strategies that firms have available when they enter international markets. What are the relative advantages and disadvantages of each?

Key Terms

factor conditions (national advantage), 230
demand conditions (national advantage), 230
related and supporting industries (national advantage), 231
firm strategy, structure, and rivalry (national advantage), 231
political risk, 238
economic risk, 238
currency risk, 239
management risk, 239
outsourcing, 240
offshoring, 240
exporting, 252
licensing, 253
franchinsing, 253
wholly owned subsidiary, 256

Experiential Exercise

The United States is considered a world leader in the motion picture industry. Using Porter's diamond framework for national competitiveness, explain the success of this industry.

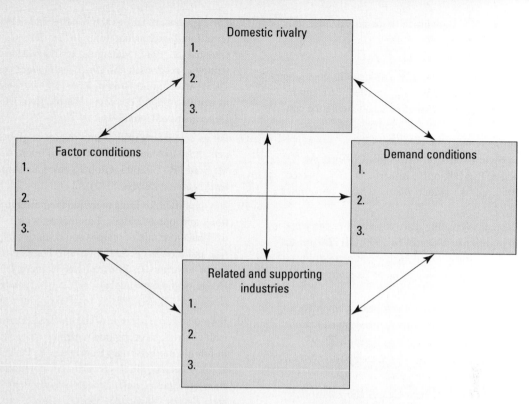

Domestic rivalry
1.
2.
3.

Factor conditions
1.
2.
3.

Demand conditions
1.
2.
3.

Related and supporting industries
1.
2.
3.

Application Questions Exercises

1. Data on the "competitiveness of nations" can be found at www.imd.ch/wcy/ranking/. This Web site provides a ranking on a variety of criteria for 49 countries. How might Porter's diamond of national advantage help to explain the rankings for some of these countries for certain industries that interest you?

2. The Internet has lowered the entry barriers for smaller firms that wish to diversify into international markets. Why is this so? Provide an example.

3. Many firms fail when they enter into strategic alliances with firms that link up with companies based in other countries. What are some reasons for this failure? Provide an example.

4. Many large U.S.–based management consulting companies such as McKinsey and Company and the BCG Group have been very successful in the international marketplace. How can Porter's diamond explain their success?

Ethics Questions

1. Over the past few decades, many American firms have relocated most or all of their operations from the United States to countries such as Mexico and China that pay lower wages. What are some of the ethical issues that such actions may raise?

2. Business practices and customs vary throughout the world. What are some of the ethical issues concerning payments that must be made in a foreign country to obtain business opportunities?

References

1. Birger, J. 2007. The unending woes of Lee Scott. *Fortune.* January 27: 118, 122; Berner, R. 2007. My year at Wal-Mart. *BusinessWeek,* February 12: 70–74; Anonymous. 2006. Wal-Mart in Japan sees losses. www.sptimes.com, August 23, np; and Mi-Young, A. 2000. Wal-Mart has to adapt to the South Korean customer. *Deutsche Presse-Agentur.* November 8: 1–3.

2. For a recent discussion on globalization by one of international business's most respected authors, read Ohmae, K. 2005. *The next global stage: Challenges and opportunities in our borderless world.* Philadelphia: Wharton School Publishing.

3. Our discussion of globalization draws upon Engardio, P., & Belton, C. 2000. Global capitalism: Can it be made to work better? *BusinessWeek,* November 6: 72–98.

4. Sellers, P. 2005. Blowing in the wind. *Fortune,* July 25: 63.

5. Engardio & Belton, op. cit.

6. For insightful perspectives on strategy in emerging economies, refer to the article entitled: Strategy research in emerging economies: Challenging the conventional wisdom in the January 2005 issue of *Journal of Management Studies,* 42(1).

7. The above discussion draws on Clifford, M. L., Engardio, P., Malkin, E., Roberts, D., & Echikson, W. 2000. Up the ladder. *BusinessWeek,* November 6: 78–84.

8. For another interesting discussion on a country perspective, refer to Makino, S. 1999. MITI Minister Kaora Yosano on reviving Japan's competitive advantages. *Academy of Management Executive,* 13(4): 8–28.

9. The following discussion draws heavily upon Porter, M. E. 1990. The competitive advantage of nations. *Harvard Business Review,* March–April: 73–93.

10. Landes, D. S. 1998. *The wealth and poverty of nations.* New York: W. W. Norton.

11. A recent study that investigates the relationship between international diversification and firm performance is Lu, J. W., & Beamish, P. W. 2004. International diversification and firm performance: The s-curve hypothesis. *Academy of Management Journal,* 47(4): 598–609.

12. Part of our discussion of the motivations and risks of international expansion draws upon Gregg, F. M. 1999. International strategy. In Helms, M. M. (Ed.). *Encyclopedia of management:* 434–438. Detroit: Gale Group.

13. These two examples are discussed, respectively, in Dawar, N., & Frost, T. 1999. Competing with giants: Survival strategies for local companies in emerging markets. *Harvard Business Review,* 77(2): 119–129; and Prahalad, C. K., & Lieberthal, K. 1998. The end of corporate imperialism. *Harvard Business Review,* 76(4): 68–79.

14. Meredith, R. 2004. Middle kingdom, middle class. *Forbes,* November 15: 188–192; and Anonymous. 2004. Middle class becomes rising power in China. www.Chinadaily.com. November 6.

15. This discussion draws upon Gupta, A. K., & Govindarajan, V. 2001. Converting global presence into global competitive advantage. *Academy of Management Executive,* 15(2): 45–56.

16. Stross, R. E. 1997. Mr. Gates builds his brain trust. *Fortune,* December 8: 84–98.

17. For a good summary of the benefits and risks of international expansion, refer to Bartlett, C. A., & Ghoshal, S. 1987. Managing across borders: New strategic responses. *Sloan Management Review,* 28(5): 45–53; and Brown, R. H. 1994. *Competing to win in a global economy.* Washington, DC: U.S. Department of Commerce.

18. For an interesting insight into rivalry in global markets, refer to MacMillan, I. C., van Putten, A. B., & McGrath, R. G. 2003. Global gamesmanship. *Harvard Business Review,* 81(5): 62–73.

19. It is important for firms to spread their foreign operations and outsourcing relationships with a broad, well-balanced mix of regions and countries to reduce risk and increase potential reward. For example, refer to Vestring, T., Rouse, T., & Reinert, U. 2005. Hedge your offshoring bets. *MIT Sloan Management Review,* 46(3): 27–29.

20. For a discussion of some of the challenges associated with government corruption regarding entry strategies in foreign markets, read Rodriguez, P., Uhlenbruck, K., & Eden, L. 2005. Government corruption and entry strategies of multinationals. *Academy of Management Review,* 30(2): 383–396.

21. For a discussion of the political risks in China for United States companies, refer to Garten, J. E. 1998. Opening the doors for business in China. *Harvard Business Review,* 76(3): 167–175.

22. Shari, M. 2001. Is a holy war brewing in Indonesia? *BusinessWeek,* October 15: 62.

23. For an interesting perspective on the relationship between diversification and the development of a nation's institutional environment, read Chakrabarti, A., Singh, K., & Mahmood, I. 2007. Diversification and performance: Evidence from East Asian firms. *Strategic Management Journal,* 28(2): 101–120.

24. Gikkas, N. S. 1996. International licensing of intellectual property: The promise and the peril. *Journal of Technology Law & Policy,* 1(1): 1–26.

25. For an excellent theoretical discussion of how cultural factors can affect knowledge transfer across national boundaries, refer to Bhagat, R. S., Kedia, B. L., Harveston, P. D., & Triandis, H. C. 2002. Cultural variations in the cross-border transfer of organizational knowledge: An integrative framework. *Academy of Management Review,* 27(2): 204–221.

26. To gain insights on the role of national and regional cultures on knowledge management models and frameworks, read Pauleen, D. J., & Murphy, P. 2005.

In praise of cultural bias. *MIT Sloan Management Review,* 46(2): 21–22.

27. Berkowitz, E. N. 2000. *Marketing* (6th ed.). New York: McGraw-Hill.

28. Morrison, T. Conaway, W., & Borden, G. 1994. *Kiss, bow, or shake hands.* Avon, MA: Adams Media; and www.executiveplanet.com/business-culture.

29. World Trade Organization. *Annual Report 1998.* Geneva: World Trade Organization.

30. Lei, D. 2005. Outsourcing. In Hitt, M. A., & Ireland, R. D. (Eds.). *The Blackwell encyclopedia of management.* Entrepreneurship: 196–199. Malden, MA: Blackwell.

31. Dolan, K.A. 2006. Offshoring the offshorers. *Forbes.* April 17: 74–78.

32. The discussion above draws from Colvin, J. 2004. Think your job can't be sent to India? Just watch. *Fortune,* December 13: 80; Schwartz, N. D. 2004. Down and out in white collar America. *Fortune,* June 23: 321–325; Hagel, J. 2004. Outsourcing is not just about cost cutting. *The Wall Street Journal,* March 18: A3.

33. Levitt, T. 1983. The globalization of markets. *Harvard Business Review,* 61(3): 92–102.

34. Our discussion of these assumptions draws upon Douglas, S. P., & Wind, Y. 1987. The myth of globalization. *Columbia Journal of World Business,* Winter: 19–29.

35. Ghoshal, S. 1987. Global strategy: An organizing framework. *Strategic Management Journal,* 8: 425–440.

36. Bartlett, C. A., & Ghoshal, S. 1989. *Managing across borders: The transnational solution.* Boston: Harvard Business School Press.

37. For insights on global branding, refer to Aaker, D. A., & Joachimsthaler, E. 1999. The lure of global branding. *Harvard Business Review,* 77(6): 137–146.

38. For an interesting perspective on how small firms can compete in their home markets, refer to Dawar & Frost, op. cit.: 119–129.

39. Hout, T., Porter, M. E., & Rudden, E. 1982. How global companies win out. *Harvard Business Review,* 60(5): 98–107.

40. Fryer, B. 2001. Tom Siebel of Siebel Systems: High tech the old-fashioned way. *Harvard Business Review,* 79(3): 118–130.

41. The risks that are discussed for the global, multidomestic, and transnational strategies draw upon Gupta & Govindarajan, op. cit.

42. Sigiura, H. 1990. How Honda localizes its global strategy. *Sloan Management Review,* 31: 77–82.

43. Prahalad & Lieberthal, op. cit.: 68–79. Their article also discusses how firms may have to reconsider their brand management, costs of market building, product design, and approaches to capital efficiency when entering foreign markets.

44. Hofstede, G. 1980. *Culture's consequences: International differences in work-related values.* Beverly Hills, CA: Sage; Hofstede, G. 1993. Cultural constraints in management theories. *Academy of Management Executive,* 7(1): 81–94; Kogut, B., & Singh, H. 1988. The effect of national culture on the choice of entry mode. *Journal of International Business Studies,* 19: 411–432; and Usinier, J. C. 1996. *Marketing across cultures.* London: Prentice Hall.

45. McCune, J. C. 1999. Exporting corporate culture. *Management Review,* December: 53–56.

46. Prahalad, C. K., & Doz, Y. L. 1987. *The multinational mission: Balancing local demands and global vision.* New York: Free Press.

47. Kidd, J. B., & Teramoto, Y. 1995. The learning organization: The case of Japanese RHQs in Europe. *Management international review,* 35 (Special Issue): 39–56.

48. Gupta, A. K., & Govindarajan, V. 2000. Knowledge flows within multinational corporations. *Strategic Management Journal,* 21(4): 473–496.

49. Wetlaufer, S. 2001. The business case against revolution: An interview with Nestlé's Peter Brabeck. *Harvard Business Review,* 79(2): 112–121.

50. Nobel, R., & Birkinshaw, J. 1998. Innovation in multinational corporations: Control and communication patterns in international R&D operations. *Strategic Management Journal,* 19(5): 461–478.

51. This section draws upon Ghemawat, P. 2005. Regional strategies for global leadership. *Harvard Business Review.* 84(12): 98–108; Ghemawat, P. 2006. Apocalypse now? *Harvard Business Review.* 84(12): 32; Ghemawat, P. 2001. Distance still matters: The hard reality of global expansion. *Harvard Business Review,* 79(8): 137–147; Peng, M.W. 2006. *Global strategy:* 387. Mason, OH: Thomson Southwestern; and Rugman, A. M., & Verbeke, A. 2004. A perspective on regional and global strategies of multinational enterprises. *Journal of International Business Studies.* 35: 3–18.

52. For a rigorous analysis of performance implications of entry strategies, refer to Zahra, S. A., Ireland, R. D., & Hitt, M. A. 2000. International expansion by new venture firms: International diversity, modes of entry, technological learning, and performance. *Academy of Management Journal,* 43(6): 925–950.

53. Li, J. T. 1995. Foreign entry and survival: The effects of strategic choices on performance in international markets. *Strategic Management Journal,* 16: 333–351.

54. For a discussion of how home-country environments can affect diversification strategies, refer to Wan, W. P., & Hoskisson, R. E. 2003. Home country environments, corporate diversification strategies, and firm performance. *Academy of Management Journal,* 46(1): 27–45.

55. Arnold, D. 2000. Seven rules of international distribution. *Harvard Business Review,* 78(6): 131–137.

56. Sharma, A. 1998. Mode of entry and ex-post performance. *Strategic Management Journal,* 19(9): 879–900.

57. This section draws upon Arnold, op. cit.: 131–137; and Berkowitz, op. cit.

58. Kline, D. 2003. Strategic licensing. *MIT Sloan Management Review,* 44(3): 89–93.

59. Martin, J. 1999. Franchising in the Middle East. *Management Review.* June: 38–42.

60. Arnold, op. cit.; and Berkowitz, op. cit.

61. Manufacturer–supplier relationships can be very effective in global industries such as automobile manufacturing. Refer to Kotabe, M., Martin, X., & Domoto, H. 2003. Gaining from vertical partnerships: Knowledge transfer, relationship duration, and supplier performance improvement in the U.S. and Japanese automotive industries. *Strategic Management Journal,* 24(4): 293–316.

62. For a good discussion, refer to Merchant, H., & Schendel, D. 2000. How do international joint ventures create shareholder value? *Strategic Management Journal,* 21(7): 723–738.

63. This discussion draws upon Walters, B. A., Peters, S., & Dess, G. G. 1994. Strategic alliances and joint ventures: Making them work. *Business Horizons,* 37(4): 5–11.

64. For a rigorous discussion of the importance of information access in international joint ventures, refer to Reuer, J. J., & Koza, M. P. 2000. Asymmetric information and joint venture performance: Theory and evidence for domestic and international joint ventures. *Strategic Management Journal,* 21(1): 81–88.

65. Treece, J. 1991. Why Daewoo wound up on the road to nowhere. *BusinessWeek,* September 23: 55.

66. Dyer, J. H., Kale, P., & Singh, H. 2001. How to make strategic alliances work. *MIT Sloan Management Review,* 42(4): 37–43.

67. For a discussion of some of the challenges in managing subsidiaries, refer to O'Donnell, S. W. 2000. Managing foreign subsidiaries: Agents of headquarters, or an independent network? *Strategic Management Journal,* 21(5): 525–548.

68. Ricks, D. 2006. *Blunders in international business* (4th ed.). Malden, MA: Blackwell Publishing.

Entrepreneurial Strategy and Competitive Dynamics

>learning objectives

After reading this chapter, you should have a good understanding of:

LO1 The role of new ventures and small businesses in the U.S. economy.

LO2 The role of opportunities, resources, and entrepreneurs in successfully pursuing new ventures.

LO3 Three types of entry strategies—pioneering, imitative, and adaptive—commonly used to launch a new venture.

LO4 How the generic strategies of overall cost leadership, differentiation, and focus are used by new ventures and small businesses.

LO5 How competitive actions, such as the entry of new competitors into a market-place, may launch a cycle of actions and reactions among close competitors.

LO6 The components of competitive dynamics analysis—new competitive action, threat analysis, motivation and capability to respond, types of competitive actions, and likelihood of competitive reaction.

*n*ew technologies, shifting social and demographic trends, and sudden changes in the business environment create opportunities for entrepreneurship. New ventures, which often emerge under such conditions, face unique strategic challenges if they are going to survive and grow. Young and small businesses, which are a major engine of growth in the U.S. economy because of their role in job creation and innovation, must rely on sound strategic principles to be successful.

This chapter addresses how new ventures and entrepreneurial firms can achieve competitive advantages. It also examines how entrepreneurial activity influences a firm's strategic priorities and intensifies the rivalry among an industry's close competitors.

In the first section, we discuss the role of opportunity recognition in the process of new venture creation. Three factors that are important in determining whether a value-creating opportunity should be pursued are highlighted—the nature of the opportunity, the resources available to undertake it, and the characteristics of the entrepreneur(s) pursuing it.

The second section addresses three different types of new entry strategies—pioneering, imitative, and adaptive. Then, the generic strategies (discussed in Chapter 5) as well as combination strategies are addressed in terms of how they apply to new ventures and entrepreneurial firms. Additionally, some of the pitfalls associated with each of these strategic approaches are presented.

In section three, we explain how new entrants and other competitors often set off a series of actions and reactions that affect the competitive dynamics of an industry. In determining how to react to a competitive action, firms must analyze whether they are seriously threatened by the action, how important it is for them to respond, and what resources they can muster to mount a response. They must also determine what type of action is appropriate—strategic or tactical—and whether their close competitors are likely to counterattack. Taken together, these actions often have a strong impact on the strategic choices and overall profitability of an industry.

Learning from Mistakes

The success of an entrepreneurial venture—whether it is undertaken by a small start-up or a major corporation—depends on many factors. The right combination of resources, know-how, and strategic action can lead to above-average profitability and value-creating advantages. However, many things can go wrong. To see how a firm's efforts to launch an entrepreneurial new entry can turn sour, consider the example of ESPN's foray into the cell phone business.[1]

> ESPN, the giant sports network, has grown to an impressive $5 billion-a-year business since it was launched just 27 years ago. Today it shows up everywhere in the world of sports and seems as if it has been around forever. That impression stems in part from ESPN's great ability to know sports fans and to deliver what its customers want. The company has leveraged its brand "with the ferocity of a linebacker on steroids" according to *BusinessWeek* media expert Tom Lowry.[2] The result has been a number of successful brand extensions including *ESPN Magazine* with a circulation of nearly 2 million, ESPN Zone Restaurants, and ESPN2, a second cable TV station that scrolls sports scores and plays rock music.
>
> With such an impressive track record, it's no surprise that ESPN, the high-flying unit of the Walt Disney Co., would attempt to extend its reach into the fast-growing world of wireless communications. On Super Bowl Sunday 2006, ESPN *[continued]*

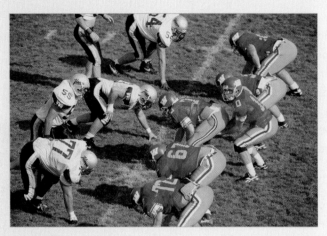

● Football is one of many sports that ESPN has aggressively promoted through its broadcasts.

announced that it was launching its own cell phone service, Mobile ESPN. The service was targeted at sports fanatics—the kind who can't stand to miss "Sports Center" or not know the latest scores. Through an expensive $40 million ad campaign that ran on ESPN.com as well as TV and radio stations, Mobile ESPN promised unique sports content on a 24/7 basis.

The effort was troubled from the start. Despite extensive advertising, ". . . it was tough to tell where you could get their phones," observed wireless industry expert Peter Gorham in *Red Herring*.[3] The phones, which critics described as "very plain," cost up to $199, and monthly service ran from $65 to as much as $225 for premium content. Except for the sports content, no incentives were offered to customers who were being asked to switch carriers and abandon their family calling plans.

Behind the scenes, the hurdles facing ESPN's new entry proved insurmountable. Although ESPN was primarily targeting existing customers, the move into cell phones represented entry into a new industry where it was one of 175 MVNOs (mobile virtual network operators) in the United States. To make this move, it had to pay Sprint to lease its network infrastructure. In addition, because ESPN is a secondary rights holder to most sports content, it has to pay the leagues for the clips it broadcasts. It was this "double whammy" of expenses that led ESPN to charge such high fees.

In the end, the cost of switching was too high and only 30,000 users signed up for the service. ESPN had projected that 500,000 were needed to break even so after just eight months, it pulled the plug. Overall, the experiment cost ESPN nearly $150 million.

Despite ESPN's large base of dedicated customers, the company misread how easy it would be to leverage its brand. The entrepreneurial entry it attempted involved using its strong reputation and differentiated content to attract users of its new service. But unlike other ESPN brand extensions such as clothing and publications, cell phones are more of a necessity than a luxury for millions of users. ESPN did not recognize that most customers would prefer reliable service at competitive prices over highly specialized content at premium prices. ESPN also failed to assess the competitive environment correctly. The sports network was simply no match for well-known, reliable MVNO companies capable of offering multiple phone plans, buyer incentives, and 24/7 customer service.[4] Given that ESPN had to pay for both sports content and network access to offer the service, its profit margin was too narrow to react to these competitive pressures. To its credit, ESPN cut its losses and got out quickly once it realized its new venture was failing.

The ESPN case illustrates how important it is for new entrepreneurial entrants—whether they are start-ups or incumbents—to think and act strategically. Even with a strong resource base and good track record, an ill-conceived strategy and strong competitive forces may prevent what seems like a good idea from taking off.

In this chapter we address entrepreneurial strategies. The previous three chapters have focused primarily on the business-level, corporate-level, and international strategies of incumbent firms. Here we ask: What about the strategies of those entering into a market or industry for the first time? Whether it's a small, young start-up or an existing company seeking growth opportunities such as ESPN, new entrants need effective strategies. In the first part of this chapter, we discuss how companies recognize opportunities and improve their chances of success by effectively using entrepreneurial strategy.

Companies wishing to launch new ventures must also be aware that, consistent with the five forces model in Chapter 2, new entrants are a threat to existing firms in an industry. Entry into a new market arena is intensely competitive from the perspective of incumbents in that arena. Therefore, new entrants can nearly always expect a competitive response from other companies in the industry it is entering. Knowledge of the competitive dynamics that are at work in the business environment is an aspect of entrepreneurial new entry that will be addressed later in this chapter.

Before moving on, it is important to highlight the role that entrepreneurial start-ups and small business play in entrepreneurial value creation. Young and small firms are responsible for more innovations and more new job creation than any other type of business.[5] As such, they are the primary users of entrepreneurial strategies. Strategy Spotlight 8.1 addresses some of the reasons why small business and entrepreneurship are viewed favorably in the United States.

>LO1
The role of new ventures and small businesses in the U.S. economy.

Recognizing Entrepreneurial Opportunities

Defined broadly, **entrepreneurship** refers to new value creation. As noted earlier, even though entrepreneurial activity is usually associated with start-up companies, new value can be created in many different contexts including:

- *Start-up ventures*
- *Major corporations*
- *Family-owned businesses*
- *Non-profit organizations*
- *Established institutions*

entrepreneurship
the creation of new value by an existing organization or new venture that involves the assumption of risk.

For an entrepreneurial venture to create new value, three factors must be present—an entrepreneurial opportunity, the resources to pursue the opportunity, and an entrepreneur or entrepreneurial team willing and able to undertake the opportunity.[6] The entrepreneurial strategy that an organization uses will depend on these three factors. Thus, beyond merely identifying a venture concept, the opportunity recognition process also involves organizing the key people and resources that are needed to go forward. Exhibit 8.2 on page 269 depicts the three factors that are needed to successfully proceed—opportunity, resources, and entrepreneur(s). In the sections that follow, we address each of these factors.

>LO2
The role of opportunities, resources, and entrepreneurs in successfully pursuing new ventures.

Entrepreneurial Opportunities

The starting point for any new venture is the presence of an entrepreneurial opportunity. Where do opportunities come from? For new business start-ups, opportunities come from many sources—current or past work experiences, hobbies that grow into businesses or lead to inventions, suggestions by friends or family, or a chance event that makes an entrepreneur aware of an unmet need. For established firms, new business opportunities come from the needs of existing customers, suggestions by suppliers, or technological developments that lead to new advances.[7] For all firms, there is a major, overarching factor behind all viable opportunities that emerge in the business landscape: change. Change creates opportunities. Entrepreneurial firms make the most of changes brought about by new technology, sociocultural trends, and shifts in consumer demand.

The Contribution of Small Businesses to the U.S. Economy

In the late 1970s, MIT professor David Birch launched a study to explore the sources of business growth. "I wasn't really looking for anything in particular," says Birch. But the findings surprised him: Small businesses create the most jobs. Since then, Birch and others have shown that it's not just big companies that power the economy. Small business and entrepreneurship have become a major component of new job creation.

Sources: Small Business Administration. 2005. *The small business economy.* Washington, DC: U.S. Government Printing Office; Small Business Administration. 2006. Small business by the numbers. *SBA Office of Advocacy,* June, www.sba.gov/advo/; *Inc.* 2001. Small business 2001: Where we are now? May 29: 18–19; Minniti, M., & Bygrave, W. D. 2004. *Global entrepreneurship monitor—National entrepreneurship assessment: United States of America 2004, executive report.* Kansas City, MO: Kauffman Center for Entrepreneurial Leadership; and *Fortune.* 2001. The heroes: A portfolio. October 4: 74.

Here are the facts:

- In the United States, there are approximately 5.6 million companies with fewer than 100 employees. Another 100,000 companies have 100 to 500 employees. In addition, approximately 17.0 million individuals are nonemployer sole proprietors.

- Small businesses create the majority of new jobs. According to recent data, small business created three-quarters of U.S. net new jobs in a recent period (2.5 million of the 3.4 million total). A small percentage of the fastest growing entrepreneurial firms (5 to 15 percent) account for a majority of the new jobs created.

- Small businesses (fewer than 500 employees) employ more than half of the private sector work-force (56 million in 2002) and account for more than 50 percent of nonfarm private gross domestic product (GDP). *(continued)*

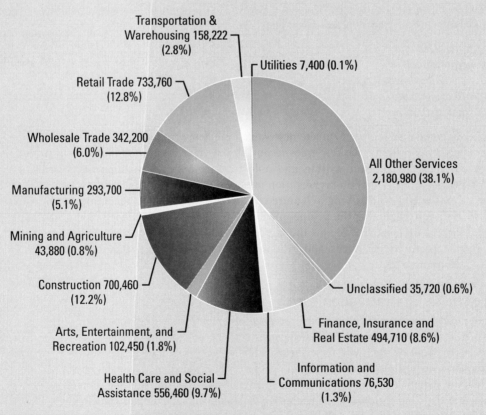

Exhibit 8.1 All U.S. Small Companies by Industry*

*Businesses with 500 or fewer employees in 2002.

Source: Small Business Administration's Office of Advocacy, based on data provided by the U.S. Census Bureau, statistics of U.S. businesses. (Percentages don't add to 100% because of rounding.)

(continued)

- Small firms produce 13 to 14 times more patents per employee than large patenting firms and employ 39 percent of high-tech workers (such as scientists and engineers). In addition, smaller entrepreneurial firms account for 55 percent of all innovations.

- Small businesses make up 97 percent of all U.S. exporters and accounted for 29 percent of known U.S. export value in 2001.

Exhibit 8.1 shows the number of small businesses in the United States and how they are distributed through different sectors of the economy.

How do changes in the external environment lead to new business creation? They spark creative new ideas and innovation. Businesspeople often have ideas for entrepreneurial ventures. However, not all such ideas are good ideas—that is, viable business opportunities. To determine which ideas are strong enough to become new ventures, entrepreneurs must go through a process of identifying, selecting, and developing potential opportunities. This is the process of **opportunity recognition**.[8]

Opportunity recognition refers to more than just the "Eureka!" feeling that people sometimes experience at the moment they identify a new idea. Although such insights are often very important, the opportunity recognition process involves two phases of activity—discovery and evaluation—that lead to viable new venture opportunities.[9]

The discovery phase refers to the process of becoming aware of a new business concept.[10] Many entrepreneurs report that their idea for a new venture occurred to them in an instant, as a sort of "Aha!" experience—that is, they had some insight or epiphany, often based on their prior knowledge, that gave them an idea for a new business. This may occur unintentionally, because the discovery of new opportunities is often spontaneous and unexpected. For example, Howard Schultz, CEO of Starbucks, was in Milan, Italy, when he suddenly realized that the coffee-and-conversation café model that was common in Europe would work in the United States as well. According to Schultz, he didn't need to do research to find out if Americans would pay $3 for a

opportunity recognition the process of discovering and evaluating changes in the business environment, such as a new technology, socio-cultural trends, or shifts in consumer demand, that can be exploited.

Exhibit 8.2 **Opportunity Analysis Framework**

Sources: Based on Timmons, J. A., & Spinelli, S. 2004. *New venture creation* (6th ed.). New York: McGraw-Hill/Irwin; and Bygrave, W. D. 1997. The entrepreneurial process. In W. D. Bygrave (Ed.), *The portable MBA in entrepreneurship* (2nd ed.). New York: Wiley.

Opportunity Recognition: Great Businesses that Started with a Simple Idea

In the founding of a business, there is always a moment when the opportunity is first recognized. The recognition may unfold in tiny steps over time or appear suddenly as an Aha! experience. When founding entrepreneurs act on such realizations, the rest, as they say, is history. And speaking of history, here are a few examples of the initial sparks that eventually resulted in some very big businesses.

Carl Westcott, founder of 1-800-Flowers

While visiting Los Angeles in 1979, Carl Westcott decided to send flowers back home to his wife. It was late but he finally found a florist that was open. The only problem was, it wouldn't take his credit card over the phone. "Bottom line," recalls Westcott, "I didn't send the flowers." While trying to get the florist to take his order, however, he noticed that the word "flowers" had seven digits. The next day he dialed 1-800-356-9377. The backhaul trucker that answered wasn't too surprised—he had already heard from FTD. But Westcott persisted and offered the man $15,000 and 3 percent of the 1-800-FLOWERS business. Both the trucker and Westcott made out pretty well when he sold the business for $4 million just 18 months later.

David Cook, founder of TollTags

When David Cook heard that the Los Alamos National Laboratories in New Mexico was going to implant miniaturized radio frequency chips under the skin of cattle to track their

Sources: Hall, C. 2004. The big ideas that started here. *Dallas Morning News*, December 26: 1D–6D. www.eds.com; www.hoovers.com; and, www.ntta.org.

location, he laughed and thought, "That's just insane—and tough to market." Soon after, while driving on a toll road, he realized the same technology could be used to enable drivers to pay tolls automatically. To prove that TollTags would work, he raised $6 million from investors to build an electronic payment system on a toll road in Dallas, Texas, with the agreement that the tollway authority could scrap the system with just 24 hours notice. "It was by far the riskiest thing I've ever done in my life," recalls Cook. But it paid off. Today the North Texas Tollway Authority sells nearly 1 million TollTags annually. As for opportunity recognition, Cook says, "You have to believe in your idea and your ability to take your accumulated knowledge and intuition and apply that as you build your business."

Ross Perot, founder of Electronic Data Systems (EDS)

Ross Perot was a salesman at IBM when he had his epiphany: Computer customers don't especially care about computer hardware. What they really need is computing *power*. "It was obvious to me . . . that people wanted a system that worked, which included the computer, the software, the whole package," recalls Perot. He took the idea to his bosses who weren't interested. At the time, 80 cents of every dollar spent on computing was for hardware and IBM dominated the market. But Perot knew he was onto something. "I was sitting in a barbershop reading an old *Reader's Digest* that had a quote from Thoreau that said, 'The mass of men lead lives of quiet desperation.' That's when I made the decision that I had to try it." With $1,000 of his wife's money, he launched EDS in 1962. Today, this provider of information technology and business process outsourcing services enjoys annual revenues of about $20 billion.

cup of coffee—he just *knew*. Starbucks was just a small business at the time but Schultz began literally shaking with excitement about growing it into a bigger business.[11] Strategy Spotlight 8.2 tells how three other highly successful entrepreneurs identified their business opportunities.

Opportunity discovery also may occur as the result of a deliberate search for new venture opportunities or creative solutions to business problems. New venture ideas often emerge only after a concerted effort to identify good opportunities or realistic solutions. It is very similar to a creative process, which may be unstructured and "chaotic" at first but eventually leads to a practical solution or business innovation. To stimulate the discovery of new opportunities, companies often encourage creativity, out-of-the-box thinking, and brainstorming.

Opportunity evaluation, which occurs after an opportunity has been identified, involves analyzing an opportunity to determine whether it is viable and strong enough to be developed into a full-fledged new venture. Ideas that have been developed by new-product groups or in brainstorming sessions are tested by various methods, including talking to potential target customers and discussing operational requirements with production or logistics managers. A technique known as feasibility analysis is used to evaluate these and other critical success factors. This type of analysis often leads to the decision that a new venture project should be discontinued. If the venture concept continues to seem viable, a more formal business plan may be developed.

Among the most important factors to evaluate is the market potential for the product or service. Established firms tend to operate in established markets. They have to adjust to market trends and to shifts in consumer demand, of course, but they usually have a customer base for which they are already filling a marketplace need. New ventures, in contrast, must first determine whether a market exists for the product or service they are contemplating. Thus, a critical element of opportunity recognition is assessing to what extent the opportunity is viable *in the marketplace.*

For an opportunity to be viable, it needs to have four qualities.[12]

- *Attractive.* The opportunity must be attractive in the marketplace; that is, there must be market demand for the new product or service.
- *Achievable.* The opportunity must be practical and physically possible.
- *Durable.* The opportunity must be attractive long enough for the development and deployment to be successful; that is, the window of opportunity must be open long enough for it to be worthwhile.
- *Value creating.* The opportunity must be potentially profitable; that is, the benefits must surpass the cost of development by a significant margin.

If a new business concept meets these criteria, two other factors must be considered before the opportunity is launched as a business: the resources available to undertake it, and the characteristics of the entrepreneur(s) pursuing it. In the next section, we address the issue of entrepreneurial resources; following that, we address the importance of entrepreneurial leaders and teams.

Entrepreneurial Resources

As Exhibit 8.2 indicates, resources are an essential component of a successful entrepreneurial launch. For start-ups, the most important resource is usually money because a new firm typically has to expend substantial sums just to start the business. However, financial resources are not the only kind of resource a new venture needs. Human capital and social capital are also important. Many firms also rely on government resources to help them thrive. In this section we will address some of the resource requirements of entrepreneurial firms and how they can meet their needs.

Financial Resources   Hand-in-hand with the importance of markets (and marketing) to new-venture creation, entrepreneurial firms must also have financing. In fact, the level of available financing is often a strong determinant of how the business is launched and its eventual success. Cash finances are, of course, highly important. But access to capital, such as a line of credit or favorable payment terms with a supplier, can also help a new venture succeed.

In general, financial resources will take one of two forms—debt or equity. Exhibit 8.3 highlights the differences between debt and equity funding and provides examples of each.

The types of financial resources that may be needed depend on two factors: the stage of venture development and the scale of the venture.[13] Entrepreneurial firms that are starting from scratch—start-ups—are at the earliest stage of development. Most start-ups also begin on a relatively small scale. The funding that is available to young and small firms tends to be

Exhibit 8.3

Sources of Venture
Financing

Type	Definition	Examples
Equity	Funds invested in ownership shares such as stock. The value of equity funding increases or decreases depending on firm performance. To obtain it usually requires that business founders give up some ownership and control of the business.	• Personal savings • Investments by family and friends • Private investors • Venture capital • Public stock offerings
Debt	Borrowed funds such as interest-bearing loans. In general, debt funding must be repaid regardless of firm performance. To obtain it usually requires that some business or personal assets be used as collateral.	• Bank loans • Credit cards • Loans by family and friends • Mortgaged property • Supplier financing • Public financing

Sources: Comaford-Lynch, C. 2007. Show me the money, part I. *BusinessWeek*, www.businessweek.com, March 12; and Fraser, J. A. 1998. A hitchhiker's guide to capital resources. *Inc.*, February: 74–82.

quite limited. In fact, the vast majority of new firms are low-budget start-ups launched with personal savings and the contributions of family and friends.[14] Even among firms included in the *Entrepreneur* list of the 100 fastest-growing new businesses in a recent year, 61 percent reported that their start-up funds came from personal savings.[15] Although bank financing, public financing, and venture capital are important sources of small business finance, these types of financial support are typically available only after a company has started to conduct business and generate sales. Therefore, the founders usually carry the initial burden of financing most new firms. And the burdens are many: renting space, buying inventory, installing phones and equipment, obtaining insurance, and paying salaries. Strategy Spotlight 8.3 identifies a technique known as bootstrapping that helps start-ups minimize their need for financial resources.

Once a young venture has established itself as a going concern, other sources of financing become readily available.[16] Later-stage financing is also readily available to incumbents that launch entrepreneurial initiatives. Banks, for example, are more likely to loan funds to companies with a track record of sales or other cash-generating activity.

Even "angel" investors—private individuals who provide equity investments for seed capital during the early stages of a new venture—favor companies that already have a winning business model and dominance in a market niche.[17] According to Cal Simmons, coauthor of *Every Business Needs an Angel,* "I would much rather talk to an entrepreneur who has already put his money and his effort into proving the concept.[18]

Start-ups that involve large capital investments or extensive development costs—such as manufacturing or engineering firms that are trying to commercialize an innovative product—may have high cash requirements soon after they are founded. Others need financing only when they are on the brink of rapid growth. To obtain such funding, entrepreneurial firms often seek venture capital. Venture capital is a form of private equity financing through which entrepreneurs raise money by selling shares in the new venture. In contrast to angel investors, who are actively engaged in investing their own money, venture capital companies are organized to place the funds of private investors into lucrative business opportunities. Venture capitalists nearly always have high performance expectations

How Stacy's Pita Chip Co. Bootstrapped Its Way to a Big Pay-off

How does a cash-strapped entrepreneur make ends meet? One way is by *bootstrapping*. This term is used to describe a company that relies on the owner's personal resources and resourcefulness to succeed. Applied to entrepreneurs, it refers to techniques used to minimize borrowing and avoid selling parts of a business to investors or venture capitalists. For the young start-up, this involves getting the most out of every dollar and doing without anything but the bare necessities. It may mean buying used equipment, operating out of a basement, or forgoing a new car purchase in order to reinvest in the business.

To successfully bootstrap, a new firm may have to get cash-generating products or services to market quickly in order to jump start cash flow. Consider the example of Stacy's Pita Chip Co.:

In 1996, founders Mark and Stacy Andrus were operating a successful pita-wrap sandwich business that was ready to grow. But customers kept asking for the baked chips they made every night from leftover pita bread and handed out free to customers waiting in line. "We thought we could get bigger faster with the chips," said Stacy. The couple, who were still paying off six-figure student loans, decided to take their chips nationwide. The business they created is a model of bootstrapping efficiency. The paper sign on the door, folding tables, and used dining room chairs are the first signs of their spartan approach to business. They also saved over $250,000 buying used equipment. "Everything goes into the business," said Stacy, who takes home a scavenger-level salary.

Has it paid off? Absolutely. Within just a few years, their baked pita chips were generating annual revenues over $1.3 million with sales in 37 states. In 2006, just 10 years after starting, the company was acquired by snack food giant PepsiCo for $60 million.

Sources: Anonymous. 2006. PepsiCo completes acquisition of Stacy's Pita Chip. *Boston Business Journal*, www.bizjournals.com/boston, January 13; Stuart, A. 2001. The pita principle. *Inc. Magazine*, August: 58–64; and www.stacyssnacks.com.

---

from the companies they invest in, but they also provide important managerial advice, and links to key contacts in an industry.

Despite the importance of venture capital to many fast-growing firms, the vast majority of external funding for young and small firms comes from informal sources such as family and friends. Exhibit 8.4, based on the *Global Entrepreneurship Monitor* survey of entrepreneurial firms, demonstrates this dramatic difference. A closer look, however, reveals an interesting fact: Firms that obtain venture capital receive funding of about $2.6 million each. In contrast, companies that obtain funding from informal sources typically receive only about $10,000 each. Although relatively few companies receive venture funding, they are attractive to venture capitalists because their profit potential and impact on innovation, job growth, and wealth creation tends to be much greater.

Clearly, financial resources are essential for entrepreneurial ventures.[19] But other types of resources are also vitally important. Next we address the role of human capital, social capital, and government resources in the entrepreneurial value creation process.

Human Capital Bankers, venture capitalists, and angel investors who invest in entrepreneurial firms and small businesses agree that the most important asset an entrepreneurial firm can have is strong and skilled management. According to Stephen Gaal, founding member of Walnut Venture Associates, venture investors do not invest in businesses; instead "We invest in people . . . very smart people with very high integrity." Managers need to have a strong base of experience and extensive domain knowledge, as well as an ability to make rapid decisions and change direction as shifting circumstances may require. In the case of start-ups, more is better. New ventures that are started by teams of three, four, or five entrepreneurs are more likely to succeed in the long run than are ventures launched by "lone wolf" entrepreneurs.[20]

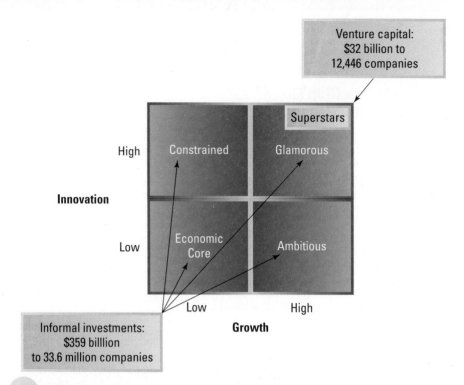

Exhibit 8.4 **How Different Types of New Ventures Are Financed:**
Informal Investment versus Venture Capital

Source: Reynolds, P. D., Bygrave, W. D., & Autio, E. 2004. *Global Entrepreneurship Monitor: 2003 executive report.* Babson College, London Business School, and the Kauffman Foundation. The classification of the company system used by GEM is based on Kirchhoff, B. 1994. *Entrepreneurship and dynamic capitalism.* London: Praeger.

Social Capital   New ventures founded by entrepreneurs who have extensive social contacts are more likely to succeed than are ventures started without the support of a social network.[21] Even though a venture may be new, if the founders have contacts who will vouch for them, they gain exposure and build legitimacy faster.[22] This support can come from several sources: prior jobs, industry organizations, and local business groups such as the chamber of commerce. These contacts can all contribute to a growing network that provides support for the entrepreneurial firm. Janina Pawlowski, co-founder of the online lending company E-Loan, attributes part of her success to the strong advisors she persuaded to serve on her board of directors, including Tim Koogle, former CEO of Yahoo![23]

Strategic alliances represent a type of social capital that can be especially important to young and small firms.[24] Strategy Spotlight 8.4 presents a few examples of alliances and some potential pitfalls of using alliances.

Government Resources   In the United States, the federal government provides support for entrepreneurial firms in two key arenas—financing and government contracting. The Small Business Administration (SBA) has several loan guarantee programs designed to support the growth and development of entrepreneurial firms. The government itself does not lend money but underwrites loans made by banks to small businesses, thus reducing the risk associated with lending to firms with unproven records. The SBA also offers training, counseling, and support services through its local offices and Small Business Development Centers.[25] State and local governments also

Strategic Alliances:
A Key Entrepreneurial Resource

Strategic alliances provide a key avenue for growth by entrepreneurial firms. By partnering with other companies, young or small firms can expand or give the appearance of entering numerous markets and/or handling a range of operations. Here are several types of alliances that have been used to extend or strengthen entrepreneurial firms:

Technology Alliances

Tech-savvy entrepreneurial firms often benefit from forming alliances with older incumbents. The alliance allows the larger firm to enhance its technological capabilities and expands the revenue and reach of the smaller firm.

Manufacturing Alliances

The use of outsourcing and other manufacturing alliances by small firms has grown dramatically in recent years. Internet-enabled capabilities such as collaborating online about delivery and design specifications has greatly simplified doing business, even with foreign manufacturers.

Sources: Copeland, M. V., & Tilin, A. 2005. Get someone to build it. *Business 2.0*, 6(5): 88–90; Monahan, J. 2005. All systems grow. *Entrepreneur*, March: 78–82; Prince, C. J. 2005. Foreign affairs. *Entrepreneur*, March: 56; and, Weaver, K. M., & Dickson, P. 2004. Strategic alliances. In W. J. Dennis, Jr. (Ed.), *NFIB national small business poll*. Washington, DC: National Federation of Independent Business.

Retail Alliances

Licensing agreements allow one company to sell the products and services of another in different markets, including overseas. Specialty products—the types sometimes made by entrepreneurial firms—often seem more exotic when sold in another country.

According to the National Federation of Independent Business (NFIB), nearly two-thirds of small businesses currently hold or have held some type of alliance. Strategic alliances among entrepreneurial firms can take many different forms. Exhibit 8.5 shows the different types of partnering that small businesses and small manufacturers in the NFIB study often use.

Although such alliances often sound good, there are also potential pitfalls. Lack of oversight and control is one danger of partnering with foreign firms. Problems with product quality, timely delivery, and receiving payments can also sour an alliance relationship if it is not carefully managed. With technology alliances, there is a risk that big firms may take advantage of the technological know-how of their entrepreneurial partners. However, even with these potential problems, strategic alliances provide a good means for entrepreneurial firms to develop and grow.

Type of Alliance and/or Long-Term Agreement*	Small Manufacturers	Small Businesses
Licensing	20.0%	32.5%
Export/Import	14.4%	7.3%
Franchise	5.0%	5.3%
Marketing	18.0%	25.2%
Distribution	20.1%	20.5%
Production	26.5%	11.3%
Product/Services R&D	12.2%	12.6%
Process R&D	6.7%	5.3%
Purchaser/Supplier	23.5%	13.9%
Outside Contracting	23.2%	28.5%

*Columns add to over 100 percent because firms may use multiple alliances.

Exhibit 8.5 Use of Strategic Alliances by Small Businesses and Small Manufacturers

Source: From Weaver, K. M., & Dickson, P. 2004. Strategic Alliances. In W. J. Dennis, Jr. (Ed.), *NFIB National Small Business Poll*. Washington, DC: National Federation of Independent Business. Reprinted with permission.

have hundreds of programs to provide funding, contracts, and other support for new ventures and small businesses.

Another key area of support is in government contracting. Programs sponsored by the SBA and other government agencies ensure that small businesses have the opportunity to bid on contracts to provide goods and services to the government. Although working with the government sometimes has its drawbacks in terms of issues of regulation and time-consuming decision making, programs to support small businesses and entrepreneurial activity constitute an important resource for entrepreneurial firms.

Entrepreneurial Leadership

Whether a venture is launched by an individual entrepreneur or an entrepreneurial team, effective leadership is needed. Launching a new venture requires a special kind of leadership. It involves courage, belief in one's convictions, and the energy to work hard even in difficult circumstances. Yet these are the very challenges that motivate most business owners. Entrepreneurs put themselves to the test and get their satisfaction from acting independently, overcoming obstacles, and thriving financially. To do so, they must embody three characteristics of leadership—vision, dedication and drive, and commitment to excellence—and pass these on to all those who work with them:

- **Vision.** This may be an entrepreneur's most important asset. Entrepreneurs envision realities that do not yet exist. Not all new businesses succeed. But without a vision, most entrepreneurs would never even get their venture off the ground. With a vision, entrepreneurs are able to exercise a kind of transformational leadership that creates something new and, in some way, changes the world. Just having a vision, however, is not enough. To develop support, get financial backing, and attract employees, entrepreneurial leaders must share their vision with others.
- **Dedication and drive.** Dedication and drive are reflected in hard work. Drive involves internal motivation; dedication calls for an intellectual commitment that keeps an entrepreneur going even in the face of bad news or poor luck. They both require patience, stamina, and a willingness to work long hours. However, a business built on the heroic efforts of one person may suffer in the long run. That's why the dedicated entrepreneur's enthusiasm is also important—like a magnet, it attracts others to the business to help with the work.
- **Commitment to excellence.** Excellence requires entrepreneurs to develop a commitment to knowing the customer, providing quality goods and services, paying attention to details, and continuously learning. Entrepreneurs who achieve excellence are sensitive to how these factors work together and devote themselves to surpassing the performance of competitors. However, entrepreneurs may flounder if they think they are the only ones who can create excellent results. The most successful, by contrast, often report that they owe their success to hiring people smarter than themselves.

In his book *Good to Great*, Jim Collins makes another important point about entrepreneurial leadership: Ventures that are built on the charisma of a single person may have trouble growing "from good to great" once that person leaves.[26] Thus, the leadership that is needed to build a great organization is usually exercised by a team of dedicated people working together rather than a single leader. Another aspect of this team approach is attracting team members who fit with the company's culture, goals, and work ethic. "Those people who do not share the company's core values," Collins says, "find themselves surrounded by corporate antibodies and ejected like a virus."[27] Thus, for a venture's leadership to be a valuable resource and not a liability it must be cohesive in its vision, drive and dedication, and commitment to excellence.

Once an opportunity has been recognized, and an entrepreneurial team and resources have been assembled, a new venture must craft a strategy. Prior chapters have addressed the strategies of incumbent firms. In the next section, we highlight the types of strategies and strategic considerations faced by new entrants.

Entrepreneurial Strategy

Successfully creating new ventures requires several ingredients. As indicated in Exhibit 8.2, three factors are necessary—a viable opportunity, sufficient resources, and a skilled and dedicated entrepreneur or entrepreneurial team. Once these elements are in place, the new venture needs a strategy. In this section, we consider several different strategic factors that are unique to new ventures and also how the generic strategies introduced in Chapter 5 can be applied to entrepreneurial firms. We also indicate how combination strategies might benefit entrepreneurial firms and address the potential pitfalls associated with launching new venture strategies.

To be successful new ventures must evaluate industry conditions, the competitive environment, and market opportunities in order to position themselves strategically. However, a traditional strategic analysis may have to be altered somewhat to fit the entrepreneurial situation. For example, five-forces analysis (as discussed in Chapter 2) is typically used by established firms. It can also be applied to the analysis of new ventures to assess the impact of industry and competitive forces. But you may ask: How does a new entrant evaluate the threat of other new entrants?

First, the new entrant needs to examine barriers to entry. If the barriers are too high, the potential entrant may decide not to enter or to gather more resources before attempting to do so. Compared to an older firm with an established reputation and available resources, the barriers to entry may be insurmountable for an entrepreneurial start-up. Therefore, understanding the force of these barriers is critical in making a decision to launch.

A second factor that may be especially important to a young venture is the threat of retaliation by incumbents. In many cases, entrepreneurial ventures *are* the new entrants that pose a threat to incumbent firms. Therefore, in applying the five-forces model to new ventures, the threat of retaliation by established firms needs to be considered.

Part of any decision about what opportunity to pursue is a consideration of how a new entrant will actually enter a new market. The concept of entry strategies provides a useful means of addressing the types of choices that new ventures have, and that is the subject we turn to next.

Entry Strategies

As suggested earlier, one of the most challenging aspects of launching a new venture is finding a way to begin doing business that generates cash flow, builds credibility, attracts good employees, and overcomes the liability of newness. One aspect of that effort is the initial decision about how to get a foothold in the market. The idea of an entry strategy or "entry wedge" describes several approaches that firms may take.[28] Several factors discussed earlier will affect this decision.

>LO3
Three types of entry strategies—pioneering, imitative, and adaptive—commonly used to launch a new venture.

- Does the venture founder prefer control or growth?
- Is the product/service high-tech or low-tech?
- What resources are available for the initial launch?
- What are the industry and competitive conditions?
- What is the overall market potential?

In some respects, any type of entry into a market for the first time may be considered entrepreneurial. But the entry strategy will vary depending on how risky and innovative the new business concept is.[29] New-entry strategies typically fall into one of three categories—pioneering new entry, imitative new entry, or adaptive new entry.

Pioneering New Entry

New entrants with a radical new product or highly innovative service may change the way business is conducted in an industry. This kind of breakthrough—creating new ways to solve old problems or meeting customer's needs in a unique new way—is referred to as a **pioneering new entry.** If the product or service is unique enough, a pioneering new entrant may actually have little direct competition. The first personal computer was a pioneering product; there had never been anything quite like it and it revolutionized computing. The first Internet browser provided a type of pioneering service. These breakthroughs created whole new industries and changed the competitive landscape. And breakthrough innovations continue to inspire pioneering entrepreneurial efforts. Consider the example of SkyTower Telecommunications, a year 2000 start-up that is hoping to take wireless communications to new heights:

pioneering new entry a firm's entry into an industry with a radical new product or highly innovative service that changes the way business is conducted.

> Wireless communications systems have only three ways to get to your cell phone or computer—radio towers that are often not tall enough, satellites that cost $50 million to $400 million to launch, and short-range Wi-Fi transmitters. SkyTower proposes a fourth alternative: unmanned, solar-powered airplanes that look like flying wings and send out Internet, mobile phone, and high-definition TV signals. The planes have already been successfully tested over Hawaii. They are able to fly at an altitude of 12 miles in a tight 2,000-foot-wide circle for six months at a time without landing. Designed as private communication systems for both businesses and consumers, they are able to deliver Internet service for about a third of the cost of DSL or cable. SkyTower has already received the backing of NASA and $80 million in investment capital. Its target customers are major Internet Service Providers (ISPs). The plan is not without problems, however. For one thing, the Federal Aviation Administration (FAA) currently prohibits the launch of unpiloted planes. Even so, SkyTower's flying wing satellite is a breakthrough technology that addresses the increasing demand for cost-effective wireless communications.[30]

The pitfalls associated with a pioneering new entry are numerous. For one thing, there is a strong risk that the product or service will not be accepted by consumers. The history of entrepreneurship is littered with new ideas that never got off the launching pad. Take, for example, Smell-O-Vision, an invention designed to pump odors into movie theatres from the projection room at preestablished moments in a film. It was tried only once (for the film *Scent of a Mystery*) before it was declared a major flop. Innovative? Definitely. But hardly a good idea at the time.[31]

A pioneering new entry is disruptive to the status quo of an industry. It is likely based on a technological breakthrough such as the one proposed by SkyTower. If it is successful, other competitors will rush in to copy it. This can create issues of sustainability for an entrepreneurial firm, especially if a larger company with greater resources introduces a similar product. For a new entrant to sustain its pioneering advantage, therefore, it may be necessary to protect its intellectual property, advertise heavily to build brand recognition, form alliances with businesses that will adopt its products or services, and offer exceptional customer service.

Imitative New Entry

Whereas pioneers are often inventors or tinkerers with new technology, imitators usually have a strong marketing orientation. They look for opportunities to capitalize on proven market successes. An **imitative new entry** strategy is used by entrepreneurs who see products or business concepts that have been successful in one market niche or physical locale and introduce the same basic product or service in another segment of the market.

imitative new entry a firm's entry into an industry with products or services that capitalize on proven market successes and that usually has a strong marketing orientation.

Sometimes the key to success with an imitative strategy is to fill a market space where the need had previously been filled inadequately. This was the approach used by Fixx Services, Inc., a restaurant and retail store maintenance service.

Maintenance and repairs is hardly a new business concept. But Mark Bucher found that restaurants and retail stores were poorly served. He provides a facility management service designed to alleviate the headaches associated with keeping everything running. "Customers want one number to call if their oven breaks or if someone throws a brick through their front window," says Bucher. Founded in 1999, home-based and self-funded for the first three years, Fixx Services now has 12 employees and annual sales of nearly $10 million.[32]

● Yoga's rising popularity has increased demand for related apparel and equipment. Both small players as well as multinational giants such as Nike and Reebok have entered the market.

Entrepreneurs are also prompted to be imitators when they realize that they have the resources or skills to do a job better than an existing competitor. This can actually be a serious problem for entrepreneurial start-ups if the imitator is an established company. Consider the example of Hugger Mugger Yoga Products, a Salt Lake City producer of yoga apparel and equipment such as yoga mats for practitioners of the ancient exercise art, with sales of $7.5 million annually.

> When founder Sara Chambers started the business in the mid-1980s, there was little competition. But once yoga went mainstream and became the subject of celebrity cover stories, other competitors saw an opportunity to imitate. Then Nike and Reebok jumped into the business with their own mats, clothes, and props. Hugger Mugger was a leading provider and had enjoyed 50 percent annual growth. But even after introducing a mass market line for stores such as Linens 'n' Things and hiring 50 independent sales reps, its growth rate has leveled off.[33]

Recall from Chapter 3 that the quality "difficult to imitate" was viewed as one of the keys to building sustainable advantages.[34] A strategy that can be imitated, therefore, seems like a poor way to build a business. In essence, this is true. But then consider the example of a franchise. Clearly, franchising is built on the idea of copying what another business has already done. If a business format is so easy to imitate, can it possibly have any competitive advantages? In the minds of many consumers of franchise products and services, the advantage is *because of* imitation. That is, consumers have confidence in franchises because they are familiar with them. "As time has gone by, the public has come to embrace franchising because they're familiar with the successful franchises and brand," claims Tony DeSio, founder of Mail Boxes Etc. "They know that, from one location to another, they can rely on product consistency." Thus, imitation is one of the central reasons why franchises are successful.

Adaptive New Entry   Most new entrants use a strategy somewhere between "pure" imitation and "pure" pioneering. That is, they offer a product or service that is somewhat new and sufficiently different to create new value for customers and capture market share. Such firms are adaptive in the sense that they are aware of marketplace conditions and conceive entry strategies to capitalize on current trends.

According to business creativity coach Tom Monahan, "Every new idea is merely a spin of an old idea. [Knowing that] takes the pressure off from thinking [you] have to be totally creative. You don't. Sometimes it's one slight twist to an old idea that makes all the difference."[35] Thus, an **adaptive new entry** approach does not involve "reinventing the wheel," nor is it merely imitative either. It involves taking an existing idea and adapting it to a particular situation. Let's look at the example of Under Armour:

adaptive new entry
a firm's entry into an industry by offering a product or service that is somewhat new and sufficiently different to create value for customers by capitalizing on current market trends.

> When Kevin Plank played football for the University of Maryland, it bothered him that the hard hitting game left him literally dripping wet. He knew that athletes such as competitive

AltiTunes: Success through Adaptation

"Darwin said it is not the strongest or fastest that survive but those that can adapt quickly," says Thomas Barry, chief investment officer at Bjurman, Barry & Associates. That's what Amy Nye Wolf learned when she launched her AltiTunes Partners LP business. She had been listening to the same music over and over during a six-week backpacking trip through Europe. At the end of the trip, she was elated to find a store selling music at London's Heathrow Airport. "I was so sick of the music I had, and I was just happy to see it."

About five years later, after finishing college and working as an investment banker, Wolf remembered her experience in the airport. She realized that selling CDs

was not an original idea but she thought there might be a need anyway. "I stole the idea," says Wolf, "and then did some serious adapting." Airports, she figured, constituted a unique market niche. She estimated that if she could sell just 30 CDs per day, she could keep the business afloat. Naming her business AltiTunes, Wolf took the plunge.

Today, AltiTunes sells 3,000 to 4,000 CDs per day at 27 stores in 20 airports and one train station. Sales of CDs and products such as portable stereos and computer games now exceed $15 million annually. And Wolf is still adapting. Her latest innovation is a gadget that lets shoppers roam around the store and sample any CD on the racks. It's a PDA-sized device developed by a company named MusiKube, LLC, that shoppers use by scanning a CD bar code to hear selections of music. It's just the latest improvement in Wolf's plan to stay cutting edge by continually adapting what she calls her "small format, extraordinary-location," music retailing business.

Sources: Barrett, A., & Foust, D. 2003. Hot growth companies. *Business-Week*, June 9: 74–77; Goldsmith, G. 2003. Retailers try new devices to make CD purchasing more enjoyable. *The Wall Street Journal*, June 12, www.wsj.com; Williams, G. 2002. Looks like rain. *Entrepreneur*, September: 104–111; and www.altitunes.com.

cyclists had started using moisture-wicking gear to stay drier. So Plank bought some sweat-wicking synthetic fabric and paid a tailor $460 to make seven shirts. When his teammates tried the shirts, they wanted their own. Plank had hundreds of samples made and began sending them to his football-playing friends. "I set out to build a better football undershirt," says Plank. By adapting a new fabric to an old problem, the Under Armour founder was on his way to building one of the hottest athletic apparel brands going. Between 2002 and 2005, the company grew an average of 78.3 percent per year, with 2005 sales of $310.6 million.[36]

There are several pitfalls that might limit the success of an adaptive new entrant. First, the value proposition set forth by the new entrant firm must be perceived as unique. Unless potential customers believe a new product or service does a superior job of meeting their needs, they will have little motivation to try it. Second, there is nothing to prevent a close competitor from mimicking the new firm's adaptation as a way to hold on to its customers. Third, once an adaptive entrant achieves initial success, the challenge is to keep the idea fresh. If the attractive features of the new business are copied, the entrepreneurial firm must find ways to adapt and improve the product or service offering. Strategy Spotlight 8.5 describes how adaptive new entrant Amy Nye Wolf has continually improved her venture to hold her customers' interest and grow her business.

Considering these choices, an entrepreneur or entrepreneurial team might ask, Which new entry strategy is best? As noted in Chapter 5, not one of the strategies is inherently more likely to succeed or generate profits than another. The choice depends on many competitive, financial, and marketplace considerations. Nevertheless, research indicates that the greatest opportunities may stem from being willing to enter new markets rather than seeking growth only in existing markets. A recent study found that companies that ventured into arenas that were new to the world or new to the company earned total profits of 61 percent for their efforts. In contrast, companies that made only incremental improvements, such as extending an existing product line, grew total profits by only 39 percent.[37]

These findings led W. Chan Kim and Renee Mauborgne in their new book *Blue Ocean Strategy* to conclude that companies that are willing to venture into market spaces where there is little or no competition—labeled "blue oceans"—will outperform those firms that limit growth to incremental improvements in competitively crowded industries—labeled "red oceans." Companies that identify and pursue blue ocean strategies follow somewhat different rules than those that are "bloodied" by the competitive practices in red oceans. Consider the following elements of a blue ocean strategy:

- *Create uncontested market space.* By seeking opportunities where they are not threatened by existing competitors, blue ocean firms can focus on customers rather than on competition.
- *Make the competition irrelevant.* Rather than using the competition as a benchmark, blue ocean firms cross industry boundaries to offer new and different products and services.
- *Create and capture new demand.* Rather than fighting over existing demand, blue ocean companies seek opportunities in uncharted territory.
- *Break the value/cost trade-off.* Blue ocean firms reject the idea that a trade-off between value and cost is inevitable and instead seek opportunities in areas that benefit both their cost structure and their value proposition to customers.
- *Pursue differentiation and low cost simultaneously.* By integrating the range of a firm's utility, price, and cost activities, blue ocean companies align their whole system to create sustainable strategies.

The essence of blue ocean strategy is not just to find an uncontested market, but to create one. Some blue oceans arise because new technologies create new possibilities, such as eBay's online auction business. Yet technological innovation is not a defining feature of a blue ocean strategy. Most blue oceans are created from within red oceans by companies that push beyond the existing industry boundaries. Thus, any of the new entry strategies described earlier could be used to pursue a blue ocean strategy. Strategy Spotlight 8.6 describes how Cirque du Soleil created a new market for circus entertainment by making traditional circus acts more like theatrical productions.

Once created, a blue ocean strategy is difficult to imitate. If customers flock to blue ocean creators, firms rapidly achieve economies of scale, learning advantages, and synergies across their organizational systems. Body Shop, for example chartered new territory by refusing to focus solely on beauty products. Traditional competitors such as Estee Lauder and L'Oreal, whose brands are based on promises of eternal youth and beauty, found it difficult to imitate this approach without repudiating their current images.

These factors suggest that blue ocean strategies provide an avenue by which firms can pursue an entrepreneurial new entry. Such strategies are not without risks, however. A new entrant must decide not only the best way to enter into business but also what type of strategic positioning will work best as the business goes forward. Those strategic choices can be informed by the guidelines suggested for the generic strategies. We turn to that subject next.

Generic Strategies

Typically, an entrepreneurial firm begins with a single business model that is equivalent in scope to a business-level strategy (Chapter 5). In this section we address how overall low cost, differentiation, and focus strategies can be used by new ventures to achieve competitive advantages.

Overall Cost Leadership　One of the ways entrepreneurial firms achieve success is by doing more with less. That is, by holding down costs or making more efficient use of resources than larger competitors, new ventures are often able to offer lower prices and still be profitable. Thus, under the right circumstances, a low-cost leader strategy is a viable

>LO4
How the generic strategies of overall cost leadership, differentiation, and focus are used by new ventures and small businesses.

Cirque du Soleil's Blue Ocean Strategy

The blue ocean strategy of Cirque du Soleil is a prime example of creating new market space within a declining industry. The promotional tagline that the Canadian-based circus company sometimes uses explains how they did it: "We reinvent the circus." By altering the industry boundaries that had traditionally defined the circus concept, Cirque has created a new type of circus experience that audiences have enthusiastically embraced. Since 1984, when it was founded by a group of street performers, Cirque du Soleil has staged a variety of different productions that have been seen by over 40 million people in some 90 cities around the world.

How did they do it? One of the keys to redefining the circus business was to challenge conventional thinking and create a new vision of circus entertainment. Since the days of Ringling Bros. and Barnum & Bailey, the circus had consisted of animal acts, star performers, and Bozo-like clowns. Cirque questioned this formula and sought to understand what its audiences really wanted. It found that interest in animal acts was declining in part because of public concerns over the treatment of circus animals. Since managing animals—and the celebrity trainers who performed with them—created a heavy economic burden, Cirque eliminated them.

Instead Cirque has focused on three elements of the classic circus tent event that still captivated audiences:

Sources: Kim, W. C., & Mauborgne, R. 2004. Blue ocean strategy. *Harvard Business Review*, 82(10): 76–84; and Tischler, L. 2005. Join the circus. *Fast Company*, 96: 52–58; and www.cirquedusoleil.com.

acrobatic acts, clowns, and the tent itself. Elegant acrobatics became a central feature of its performances, and clown humor became more sophisticated and less slapstick. Cirque also preserved the image of the tent by creating exotic facades that captured the symbolic elements of the traditional tent.

For Cirque to sail into a blue ocean, however, it had to make even bigger changes. It did so by introducing theatrical elements into its circus acts. Each production provides a range of features more commonly found in theatres than in circus tents—from using theatrical story lines to replacing hard benches with comfortable seating. Rather than displaying three different acts simultaneously, as in the classic three-ring circus, Cirque offers multiple productions giving audiences a reason to go to the circus more often. Each production has a different theme and its own original musical score.

As it has rolled out all of these changes, Cirque has kept its eye on the bottom line. In fact, a key motivator for many of its changes was to find ways to lower costs and increase revenues in the declining circus industry. Cutting the cost of animal acts and star performers as well as boosting revenues by offering a variety of productions has allowed it to achieve both low cost and differentiation advantages. Such a strategy creates value for both the company and its customers. The essence of its success, however, lies not in the extent to which it has outperformed competitors, but in how it has surpassed them by redefining the circus concept and becoming a prime mover in the market space it created.

alternative for some new ventures. The way most companies achieve low-cost leadership, however, is typically different for young or small firms.

Recall from Chapter 5 that three of the features of a low-cost approach included operating at a large enough scale to spread costs over many units of production (i.e., economies of scale), making substantial capital investments in order to increase scale economies, and using knowledge gained from experience to make cost-saving improvements. These elements of a cost-leadership strategy may be unavailable to new ventures. Because new ventures are typically small, they usually don't have high economies of scale relative to competitors. Because they are usually cash strapped, they can't make large capital investments to increase their scale advantages. And because many are young, they often don't have a wealth of accumulated experience to draw on to achieve cost reductions.

Given these constraints, how can new ventures successfully deploy cost-leader strategies? Compared to large firms, new ventures often have simple organizational structures that make decision making both easier and faster. The smaller size also helps young firms change more quickly when upgrades in technology or feedback from the marketplace indicate that improvements are needed. New ventures are also able to make decisions at the time they are founded that help them deal with the issue of controlling costs. For example, they may source materials from a supplier that provides them more cheaply or set up manufacturing facilities in another country where labor costs are especially low. Thus, new firms have several avenues for achieving low cost leadership.

Consider the example of UTStarcom, a fast-growing wireless phone service being marketed in mainland China:

> Taiwan-born founder Hong Liang Lu was an executive at Japan's Kyocera Corp. when he made his first visit to China in 1990. He found a population that badly needed decent phone service. "Before that trip, I hadn't really thought about doing business in China. Afterward, I felt it made no sense to do business anywhere else." Using Personal Access System (PAS), a technology that had never caught on in Japan, he created a low-cost service that uses existing copper networks as its backbone. The service costs only $100 per subscriber to deploy, about half the price of cellular-based systems. Customers pay nothing for incoming calls and outgoing ones are 25 percent of the cellular rate. Competing against the big telecom providers was difficult at first, but once they marketed the "Little Smart" as a low cost alternative to cellular, sales took off. Average annual revenues have grown 73 percent since 1999, and 2003 sales reached $1.96 billion. Says CEO Lu, "Our biggest problem is keeping up with demand."[38]

Whatever methods young firms use to achieve a low-cost advantage, this has always been a way that entrepreneurial firms take business away from incumbents—by offering a comparable product or service at a lower price.

Differentiation   Both pioneering and adaptive entry strategies involve some degree of differentiation. That is, the new entry is based on being able to offer a differentiated value proposition. Clearly, in the case of pioneers, the new venture is attempting to do something strikingly different, either by using a new technology or deploying resources in a way that radically alters the way business is conducted. Often, entrepreneurs do both.

Amazon founder Jeff Bezos set out to use Internet technology to revolutionize the way books are sold. He garnered the ire of other booksellers and the attention of the public by making bold claims about being the "earth's largest bookseller." As a bookseller, Bezos was not doing anything that had not been done before. But two key differentiating features—doing it on the Internet and offering extraordinary customer service—have made Amazon a differentiated success.

Even though the Internet and new technologies have provided many opportunities for entrepreneurs, differentiators don't have to be highly sophisticated to succeed. Consider the example of Spry Learning Co., a Portland, Oregon, start-up begun in 2000.

> Founders Sarah Chapman and Devin Williams believed that older people would benefit from using computers and surfing the Internet—if they only knew how. Working with gerontologists and instructional designers, they designed a computer-skills curriculum aimed at seniors. After piloting the program at two retirement communities, they successfully launched the differentiated service and, after just a few years, projected annual revenues over $4 million.[39]

There are several factors that make it more difficult for new ventures to be successful as differentiators. For one thing, the strategy is generally thought to be expensive to enact. For example, differentiation is often associated with strong brand identity, and establishing a brand is usually considered to be expensive because of the cost of advertising and promotion, paid endorsements, exceptional customer service, as well as other expenses typically associated with building brand. Differentiation successes are sometimes built on superior innovation or use of technology. These are also factors where it may be challenging for young firms to excel relative to established competitors.

Nevertheless all of these areas—innovation, technology, customer service, distinctive branding—are also arenas where new ventures have sometimes made a name for themselves even though they must operate with limited resources and experience. To be successful, according to Garry Ridge, CEO of the WD-40 Company, "You need to have a great product, make the end user aware of it, and make it easy to buy."[40] It sounds simple, but it is a difficult challenge for new ventures with differentiation strategies.

Strategic Focusing at Corporate Interns, Inc.

When Jason Engen was an undergraduate student at the University of St. Thomas in St. Paul, Minnesota, he learned the value of internships in which students worked for local companies. He wrote a business plan for one of his classes about forming an internship placement service in which he would screen students and match them with local companies. "[It's] a win–win situation." said Engen.

Sources: Torres, N. L. 2003. A perfect match. *Entrepreneur*, July: 112–114; and www.corporateinterns.com.

"The student gets the experience, and the company gets eager talent." The interest in his idea was great, and a week after graduation he started Corporate Interns, Inc.

It was difficult at first, however, because companies handle internships differently than other placement activities. But as Engen learned more, he realized this difference was an advantage: By positioning himself only in the college intern market, he avoided competing directly with large staffing companies. "Specialization is important," says Engen. "You have to stay focused on that niche." For Engen, that niche now generates $2 million in annual revenues.

Focus Focus strategies are often associated with small businesses because there is a natural fit between the narrow scope of the strategy and the small size of the firm. As we learned earlier, a focus strategy may include elements of differentiation and overall cost leadership, as well as combinations of these approaches. But to be successful within a market niche, the key strategic requirement is to stay focused. Here's why:

Despite all the attention given to fast-growing new industries, most start-ups enter industries that are mature.[41] In mature industries, growth in demand tends to be slow and there are often many competitors. Therefore, if a start-up wants to get a piece of the action, it often has to take business away from an existing competitor. If a start-up enters a market with a broad or aggressive strategy, it is likely to evoke retaliation from a more powerful competitor. Therefore, young firms can often succeed best by finding a market niche where they can get a foothold and make small advances that erode the position of existing competitors.[42] From this position, they can build a name for themselves and grow. Strategy Spotlight 8.7 considers the example of Corporate Interns, Inc.

As the Corporate Interns example indicates, many new ventures are very successful even though their share of the market is quite small. Giant companies such as Procter & Gamble and Ford are often described in terms of their market share—that is, their share of sales in a whole market. But many of the industries that small firms participate in have thousands of participants that are not direct competitors. For example, auto repair shops in California don't compete with those in Michigan or Georgia. These industries are considered "fragmented" because no single company is strong enough to have power over other competitors. Therefore, small firms focus on the market share only in their trade area. This may be defined as a geographical area or a small segment of a larger product group.

Consider, for example, the "Miniature Editions" line of books launched by Running Press, a small Philadelphia publisher. The books are palm-sized minibooks positioned at bookstore cash registers as point-of-sale impulse items costing about $4.95. Beginning with just 10 titles in 1993, Running Press grew rapidly and within 10 years had sold over 20 million copies. Even though these books represent just a tiny fraction of total sales in the $23 billion publishing industry, they have been a mainstay for Running Press.[43]

Although each of the three strategies holds promise, and pitfalls, for new ventures, firms that can make unique combinations of the generic approaches may have the greatest chances of success. It is that subject we address next.

Combination Strategies

One of the best ways for young and small businesses to achieve success is by pursuing combination strategies. By combining the best features of low-cost, differentiation, and focus strategies, new ventures can often achieve something truly distinctive.

Entrepreneurial firms are often in a strong position to offer a combination strategy because they have the flexibility to approach situations uniquely. For example, holding down expenses can be difficult for big firms because each layer of bureaucracy adds to the cost of doing business across the boundaries of a large organization. Consider how The Nartron Corporation manages this problem:

> To get a part made, or to outsource it, may be complicated and expensive for many large firms. By contrast, The Nartron Corporation, a small engineering firm whose innovations include the first keyless automobile entry system, solves that problem by building everything itself. By engineering its own products from its own designs, it not only saves money but also creates better parts. "Our parts look different from other people's because we keep adding functionality," says Nartron CEO Norman Rautiola. According to Rautiola, this capability allows the company to "run rings" around its competitors, which include Texas Instruments and Motorola.[44]

A similar argument could be made about entrepreneurial firms that differentiate. Large firms often find it difficult to offer highly specialized products or superior customer services. Entrepreneurial firms, by contrast, can often create high-value products and services through their unique differentiating efforts.

For nearly all new entrants, one of the major dangers is that a large firm with more resources will copy what they are doing. That is, well-established incumbents that observe the success of a new entrant's product or service will copy it and use their market power to overwhelm the smaller firm. Although this happens often, the threat may be lessened for firms that use combination strategies. Because of the flexibility of entrepreneurial firms, they can often enact combination strategies in ways that the large firms cannot copy. This makes the new entrant's strategies much more sustainable.

Perhaps more threatening than large competitors for many entrepreneurial firms are other firms that are close competitors. Because they have similar structural features that help them adjust quickly and be flexible in decision making, close competitors are often a danger to new ventures. Here again, a carefully crafted and executed combination strategy may be the best way for an entrepreneurial firm to thrive in a competitive environment. Nevertheless, competition among rivals is a key determinant of new venture success. To address this, we turn next to the topic of competitive dynamics.

Competitive Dynamics

New entry into markets, whether by start-ups or by incumbent firms, nearly always threatens existing competitors. This is true in part because, except in very new markets, nearly every market need is already being met, either directly or indirectly, by existing firms. As a result, the competitive actions of a new entrant are very likely to provoke a competitive response from companies that feel threatened. This, in turn, is likely to evoke a reaction to the response. As a result, a competitive dynamic—action and response—begins among the firms competing for the same customers in a given marketplace.

Competitive dynamics—intense rivalry among similar competitors—has the potential to alter a company's strategy. New entrants, for example, may be forced to change their strategies or develop new ones to survive competitive challenges by incumbent rivals. Indeed, new entry is among the most common reasons why a cycle of competitive actions and reactions gets started. But it's not the only reason. It might also occur because of threatening actions among existing competitors, such as aggressive cost cutting. Thus,

> **>LO5**
> How competitive actions, such as the entry of new competitors into a marketplace, may launch a cycle of actions and reactions among close competitors.

competitive dynamics intense rivalry, involving actions and responses, among similar competitors vying for the same customers in a marketplace.

Exhibit 8.6 Model of Competitive Dynamics

Sources: Adapted from Chen, M. J. 1996. Competitor analysis and interfirm rivalry: Toward a theoretical integration. *Academy of Management Review,* 21(1): 100–134; Ketchen, D. J., Snow, C. C., & Hoover, V. L. 2004. Research on competitive dynamics: Recent accomplishments and future challenges. *Journal of Management,* 30(6): 779–804; and Smith, K. G., Ferrier, W. J., & Grimm, C. M. 2001. King of the hill: Dethroning the industry leader. *Academy of Management Executive,* 15(2): 59–70.

>LO6

The components of competitive dynamics analysis—new competitive action, threat analysis, motivation and capability to respond, types of competitive actions, and likelihood of competitive reaction.

studying competitive dynamics helps explain why strategies evolve and reveals how, why, and when to respond to the actions of close competitors.

Exhibit 8.6 identifies the factors that competitors need to consider when determining how to respond to a competitive act. In the sections below, we will review the elements that contribute to a competitor's decision to launch a competitive attack.

New Competitive Action

Entry into a market by a new competitor is a good starting point to begin describing the cycle of actions and responses characteristic of a competitive dynamic process.[45] However, new entry is only one type of competitive action. Price cutting, imitating successful products, or expanding production capacity are other examples of competitive acts that might provoke competitors to react.

Why do companies launch new competitive actions? There are several reasons:

- Improve market position
- Capitalize on growing demand
- Expand production capacity
- Provide an innovative new solution
- Obtain first mover advantages

Underlying all of these reasons is a desire to strengthen financial outcomes, capture some of the extraordinary profits that industry leaders enjoy, and grow the business. Some companies are also motivated to launch competitive challenges because they want to build their reputation for innovativeness or efficiency. For example, Southwest Airlines, once an upstart airline with only a few routes, has become phenomenally successful and an industry leader. For years it went virtually unchallenged. But Southwest's costs have crept up, and now start-up airlines such as JetBlue are challenging the industry leader with their own low-cost strategies.[46] This is indicative of the competitive dynamic cycle. As former Intel Chairman Andy Grove stated, "Business success contains the seeds of its own destruction. The more successful you are, the more people want a chunk of your business and then another chunk and then another until there is nothing left."[47]

When a company enters into a market for the first time, it is like an attack on existing competitors. As indicated earlier in the chapter, any of the entry strategies can be used to take competitive action. But competitive attacks come from many sources besides new entrants. Some of the most intense competition is among incumbent rivals intent on gaining strategic advantages. "Winners in business play rough and don't apologize for it," according to Boston Consulting Group authors George Stalk, Jr. and Rob Lachenauer in their book *Hardball: Are You Playing to Play or Playing to Win.*[48] Exhibit 8.7 outlines their five strategies for improving competitive position and consolidating gains in preparation for another attack.

The likelihood that a competitor will launch an attack depends on many factors. In the remaining sections, we discuss factors such as competitor analysis, market conditions, types of strategic actions, and the resource endowments and capabilities companies need to take competitive action.

Threat Analysis

Prior to actually observing a competitive action, companies may need to become aware of potential competitive threats. That is, companies need to have a keen sense of who their closest competitors are and the kinds of competitive actions they might be planning.[49] This may require some environmental scanning and monitoring of the sort described in Chapter 2. Awareness of the threats posed by industry rivals allows a firm to understand what type of competitive response, if any, may be necessary.

For example, Netflix founder and CEO Reed Hastings has faced numerous competitive threats since launching the online movie rental company in 1997. According to Hastings, however, not all potential threats need to be taken seriously:

> We have to recognize that now there are tens and maybe hundreds of start-ups who think that they are going to eat Netflix's lunch. The challenge for a management team is to figure out which are real threats and which aren't. . . . It's conventional to say, "only the paranoid survive" but that's not true. The paranoid die because the paranoid take all threats as serious and get very distracted.
>
> There are markets that aren't going to get very big, and then there are markets that are going to get big, but they're not directly in our path. In the first camp we have small companies like Movielink—a well-run company but not an attractive model for consumers, sort of a $4-download to watch a movie. We correctly guessed when it launched four years ago that this was not a threat and didn't react to it.
>
> The other case I brought up is markets that are going to be very large markets, but we're just not the natural leader. Advertising supported online video, whether that's at CBS.com or You Tube—great market, kind of next door to us. But we don't do advertising-supported video, we do subscription, so it would be a huge competence expansion for us. And it's not a threat to movies."

Being aware of competitors and cognizant of whatever threats they might pose is the first step in assessing the level of competitive threat. Once a new competitive action becomes apparent, companies must determine how threatening it is to their business. Competitive dynamics are likely to be most intense among companies that are competing for the same customers or who have highly similar sets of resources.[50] Two factors are used to assess whether or not companies are close competitors:

- **Market commonality**—In other words, whether or not competitors are vying for the same customers and how many markets they share in common. For example, aircraft manufacturers Boeing and Airbus have a high degree of market commonality because they make very similar products and have many buyers in common.
- **Resource similarity**—In other words, the degree to which rivals draw on the same types of resources to compete. For example, the home pages of Google and Yahoo! may look very different but behind the scenes, they both rely on the talent pool of high-caliber software engineers to create the cutting-edge innovations that help them compete.

When any two firms have both a high degree of market commonality and highly similar resource bases, a stronger competitive threat is present. Such a threat, however, may not lead to competitive action. On the one hand, a market rival may be hesitant to attack a company that it shares a high degree of market commonality with because it could lead to an intense battle. On the other hand, once attacked, rivals with high market commonality will be much

market commonality the extent to which competitors are vying for the same customers in the same markets.

resource similarity the extent to which rivals draw from the same types of strategic resources.

Strategy	Description	Examples
Devastate rivals' profit sanctuaries	Not all business segments generate the same level of profits for a company. Through focused attacks on a rival's most profitable segments, a company can generate maximum leverage with relatively smaller-scale attacks. Recognize, however, that companies closely guard the information needed to determine just what their profit sanctuaries are.	In 2005, Wal-Mart began offering low-priced extended warranties on home electronics after learning that its rivals Best Buy and Circuit City derived most of their profits from extended warranties.
Plagiarize with pride	Just because a close competitor comes up with an idea first does not mean it cannot be successfully imitated. Second movers, in fact, can see how customers respond, make improvements, and launch a better version without all the market development costs. Successful imitation is harder than it may appear and requires the imitating firm to keep its ego in check.	Blockbuster copied the online DVD rental strategy of its rival Netflix. Not only does Blockbuster continue to struggle even after this imitation, but also Netflix sued Blockbuster for patent violations.
Deceive the competition	A good gambit sends the competition off in the wrong direction. This may cause the rivals to miss strategic shifts, spend money pursuing dead ends, or slow their responses. Any of these outcomes support the deceiving firms' competitive advantage. Companies must be sure to not cross ethical lines during these actions.	Boeing spent several years touting its plans for a new high-speed airliner. After it became clear the customer valued efficiency over speed, Boeing quietly shifted its focus. When Boeing announced its new 7e7 (now 787) Dreamliner, its competitor, Airbus Industries, was surprised and caught without an adequate response, which helped the 787 set new sales records.
Unleash massive and overwhelming force	While many hardball strategies are subtle and indirect, this one is not. This is a full-frontal attack where a firm commits significant resources to a major campaign to weaken rivals' positions in certain markets. Firms must be sure they have the mass and stamina required to win before they declare war against a rival.	Southwest Airlines took on US Airways in Baltimore and drove US Airway's market share from over 50 percent to 10 percent. Southwest recently began flying to Philadelphia and Pittsburgh as well— additional key markets for US Airways.
Raise competitors' costs	If a company has superior insight into the complex cost and profit structure of the industry, it can compete in a way that steers its rivals into relatively higher cost/lower profit arenas. This strategy uses deception to make the rivals think they are winning, when in fact they are not. Again, companies using this strategy must be confident that they understand the industry better than their rivals.	Ecolab, a company that sells cleaning supplies to businesses, encouraged a leading competitor, Diversity, to adopt a strategy to go after the low-volume, high-margin customers. What Ecolab knew that Diversity didn't is that the high servicing costs involved with this segment make the segment unprofitable—a situation Ecolab assured by bidding high enough to lose the contracts to Diversity but low enough to ensure the business lost money for Diversity.

Sources: Berner, R. 2005. Watch out, Best Buy and Circuit City. *BusinessWeek,* November 10; Halkias, M. 2006. Blockbuster strikes back at Netflix suit. *Dallas Morning News,* June 14; McCartney, S. 2007. Southwest makes inroads at hubs. *The Wall Street Journal,* May 1, page D3; Stalk, G. Jr. 2006. Curveball strategies to fool the competition. *Harvard Business Review,* 84(9): 114–121; and Stalk, Jr., G., & Lachenauer, R. 2004. *Hardball: Are you playing to play or playing to win?* Cambridge, MA: Harvard Business School Press. Reprinted by permission of Harvard Business School Press from G. Stalk, Jr. and R. Lachenauer. Copyright 2004 by the Harvard Business School Publishing Corporation; all rights reserved.

Exhibit 8.7 Five "Hardball" Strategies

AMD and Intel: Related Rivals

Few business battles are as intensely reported as the one between chipmakers Intel and Advanced Micro Devices (AMD). For years, Intel aggressively advertised its brand by pushing its "Intel Inside" logo to average consumers. In an effort to develop a stronger presence among consumers, AMD launched a successful initiative labeled internally, "War in the Store" to promote sales of AMD-based computers in retailers such as Best Buy and CompUSA. The effort prompted a retaliation by Intel that lowered the cost of chips enough to decrease PC prices $200. Meanwhile, AMD won a recent round when Dell announced it would start using AMD chips in its servers.

Why is the battle between the two companies so intense? Because they are so much alike. Both companies were founded in the late 1960s in Silicon Valley and were partners during their early history. But in 1986, Intel cancelled a key licensing agreement with AMD to manufacture microprocessors and refused to turn over technical details. AMD sued and, after years of litigation, the Supreme Court of California forced Intel to pay AMD over $1 billion in compensation for violations of the contract. The two companies have been battling ever since.

Consider how comparable the two companies are in terms of markets and resources.

Market Commonality

A key issue facing the two chipmakers is that to continue growing, they have had to enter each other's market space.

Sources: Edwards, C. 2006. AMD: Chipping away at Intel's lead. *Business-Week*, June 12: 72–73; Edwards, C. 2006. Intel sharpens its offensive game. *BusinessWeek*, July 31: 60. Gonsalves, A. 2007. AMD pays the price in awakening Intel Goliath. *InformationWeek*, www.informationweek.com, April 9; Gaudin, S. 2006. AMD cracks top 10 chip ranking, Intel sales slump. *InformationWeek*, www.informationweek.com, December 5; and www.wikipedia.org.

This is a major reason why the competition has become so heated. For example, Intel dominated that high-end server business in 2003. Now AMD holds 26 percent of the U.S. server chip business and supplies a 48 percent share of the multicore processors (which feature two or more chips on one slice of silicon). To maintain its status as the number one supplier, Intel launched a new family of processors called Core 2 Duo in 2007 that combines the performance of the Pentium 4 with the energy saving features of its notebook computer processors. "We intend to energetically compete for every single microprocessor opportunity," said Intel Executive Vice President Sean M. Maloney.

Resource Similarity

Intel is the world's number one supplier of semiconductors and is expected to have five manufacturing plants by the end of 2007. Because of new manufacturing techniques at three of its plants, it can squeeze more transistors onto a chip and its processors cost less to make than AMD's. By contrast, AMD has just two manufacturing plants but it has moved aggressively to match Intel's muscle. In 2005, it paid $5.4 billion to acquire graphics chipmaker ATI Technologies and has outsourced more manufacturing to Chartered Semiconductors. One result has been that AMD, now the number two maker of processors and graphic cards, increased semiconductor sales by 90 percent in 2006.

The battle between the two companies has been costly in recent years. When Intel retaliated for AMD's rapid gains, the result was slower sales for AMD and first quarter 2006 revenues of $1.23 billion rather than the $1.55 billion analysts expected. Meanwhile, Intel was hurt when Dell decided to begin installing AMD chips in its servers after years of using Intel exclusively. "The competitive dynamics have been more intense than we expected," commented Kevin B. Rollins, Dell's former CEO.

---

more motivated to launch a competitive response. This is especially true in cases where the shared market is an important part of a company's overall business.

How strong a response an attacked rival can mount will be determined by their strategic resource endowments. In general, the same set of conditions holds true with regard to resource similarity. That is, companies that have highly similar resource bases will be hesitant to launch an initial attack but pose a serious threat if required to mount a competitive response.[51] Greater strategic resources increase a firm's capability to respond.

In the next section, we look at the types of motivations and capabilities that a company needs to consider when evaluating its response to a competitive attack. First, Strategy Spotlight 8.8 addresses how the dynamics of market commonality and resource similarity have shaped the battle between chipmakers Intel and AMD and intensified their competitive rivalry.

Motivation and Capability to Respond

Once attacked, competitors are faced with deciding how to respond. Before deciding, however, they need to evaluate not only how they will respond, but also their reasons for responding and their capability to respond. Companies need to be clear about what problems a competitive response is expected to address and what types of problems it might create.[52] There are several factors to consider.

First, how serious is the impact of the competitive attack to which they are responding? For example, a large company with a strong reputation that is challenged by a small or unknown company may elect to simply keep an eye on the new competitor rather than quickly react or overreact. Part of the story of online retailer Amazon's early success is attributed to Barnes & Noble's over-reaction to Amazon's claim that it was "earth's biggest bookstore." Because Barnes & Noble was already using the phrase "world's largest bookstore," it sued Amazon, but lost. The confrontation made it to the front pages of *The Wall Street Journal* and Amazon was on its way to becoming a household name.[53]

Companies planning to respond to a competitive challenge must also understand their motivation for responding. What is the intent of the competitive response? Is it merely to blunt the attack of the competitor or is it an opportunity to enhance its competitive position?

Sometimes the most a company can hope for is to minimize the damage caused by a competitive action. Consider the recent price war among the top three U.S. automakers:

> When GM announced its "employee pricing" program in June, 2005, it had an immediate effect in terms of driving buyers into showrooms and increasing sales. Within days, Ford and Chrysler responded with their own incentive programs. In late summer, when GM extended its program until the end of September, so did Ford and Chrysler. All three automakers got a short-term payoff from the employee discount price war: the July 2005 sales of 1.8 million cars and light trucks was the biggest single month of sales in auto industry history. By late 2005, however, the reduced margins that the incentives caused led to lower profits and contributed to plans by GM and Ford to layoff 30,000 employees each. Early in 2007, DaimlerChrysler announced its Chrysler division was for sale.

A company that seeks to improve its competitive advantage may be motivated to launch an attack rather than merely respond to one. For example, Wal-Mart is known for its aggressive efforts to live up to its "everyday low prices" corporate motto. Strategy Spotlight 8.9 describes the retailer's recent assault on rivals Circuit City and Best Buy.

Another factor a company must consider when planning a competitive challenge involves assessing its capability to respond. What strategic resources can be deployed to fend off a competitive attack? Does the company have an array of internal strengths it can draw on, or is it operating from a position of weakness?

Consider, for example, the role of firm age and size in calculating a company's ability to respond. Most entrepreneurial new ventures start out small. The smaller size makes them more nimble compared to large firms so they can respond quickly to competitive attacks. Because they are not well-known, start-ups also have have the advantage of the element of surprise in how and when they attack. Innovative uses of technology, for example, allow small firms to deploy resources in unique ways.

Because they are young, however, start-ups may not have the financial resources needed to follow through with a competitive response. In contrast, older and larger firms may have more resources and a repertoire of competitive techniques they can use in a counterattack. Large firms, however, tend to be slower to respond. Older firms tend to be predictable in their responses because they often lose touch with the competitive environment and rely on strategies and actions that have worked in the past.

Other resources may also play a role in whether a company is equipped to retaliate. For example, one avenue of counterattack may be launching product enhancements or new product/service innovations. For that approach to be successful, it requires a company to

Wal-Mart's Cutthroat Pricing Schemes

Wal-Mart has a reputation as a relentless competitor in its pursuit of an overall cost leader strategy. Most of that reputation has come from its efforts to drive down costs in its dealings with suppliers. Wal-Mart sometimes goes on the offensive with rivals as well by driving down prices.

Recently, the retail giant took on Circuit City and Best Buy who it competes with head-on in the consumer electronics market. First Wal-Mart made big improvements in the electronics departments of 1,300 of its 3,100 U.S. stores by spiffing-up displays and adding high-end products such as Apple iPods, Toshiba laptops, and Sony liquid-crystal-display televisions. Then it delivered the two rivals a proverbial one-two punch—offering low-cost extended warranties and slashing prices on flat-panel TVs.

- **_Extended warranties._** These are the multiyear protection plans that salespeople offer at the close of a sale on items such as TVs and computers. For both Circuit City and Best Buy, they are one of the most profitable segments of their business accounting for

at least a third of their operating profits. In late 2005, Wal-Mart launched its own extended warranty program at prices nearly 50 percent lower than Best Buy and Circuit City.

- **_Flat-panel TVs._** This includes both liquid crystal display and big-screen plasma models that, until the 2006 holiday season, had never sold below $1,000. Wal-Mart broke that barrier by offering a 42-inch flat-panel TV for $998. The cuts were not limited to lesser-known brands such as Viore TV. Wal-Mart also lowered the 42-inch Panasonic high-definition TV by $500 to $1,294. The response was immediate. Circuit City lowered the price on the same Panasonic TV to $1,299 and Best Buy began offering a 42-inch Westinghouse LCD for $999.

Circuit City was among the hardest hit by this cutthroat competition. In early 2007, it closed 70 stores and laid off 3,400 employees. Best Buy, the largest electronic retailer, did a better job of absorbing the shock. Still, its stock fell 9 percent during the first quarter of 2007. Other retailers were also hit hard by the audacious pricing that has been labeled the "Wal-Mart effect" including CompUSA, which is shuttering 126 of its 229 stores, and Tweeter's, which is closing 49 of its 153 stores and laying off 650 workers.

Sources: Berner, R. 2005. Watch out, Best Buy and Circuit City. *BusinessWeek Online,* www.businessweek.com, November 10; and Gogoi, P. 2007. How Wal-Mart's TV prices crushed rivals. *BusinessWeek,* www.businessweek.com, April 27.

have both the intellectual capital to put forward viable innovations and the teamwork skills to prepare a new product or service and get it to market. Resources such as cross-functional teams and the social capital that makes teamwork production effective and efficient represent the type of human capital resources that enhance a company's capability to respond.

Types of Competitive Actions

Once an organization determines whether it is willing and able to launch a competitive action, it must determine what type of action is appropriate. Clearly, the actions taken will be determined by both its resource capabilities and its motivation for responding. There are also marketplace considerations. Managers must ask: What types of actions are likely to be most effective given a company's internal strengths and weaknesses as well as market conditions?

Two broadly defined types of competitive action include strategic actions and tactical actions. **Strategic actions** represent major commitments of distinctive and specific resources. Examples include launching a breakthrough innovation, building a new production facility, or merging with another company. Such actions require significant planning and resources and, once initiated, are difficult to reverse.

Tactical actions include refinements or extensions of strategies. Examples of tactical actions include cutting prices, improving gaps in service, or strengthening marketing efforts. Such actions typically draw on general resources and can be implemented quickly. Exhibit 8.8 identifies several types of strategic and tactical competitive actions.

Some competitive actions take the form of frontal assaults, that is, actions aimed directly at taking business from another company or capitalizing on industry weaknesses.

strategic actions major commitments of distinctive and specific resources to strategic initiatives.

tactical actions refinements or extensions of strategies usually involving minor resource commitments.

	Actions	Examples
Strategic Actions	• Entering new markets	• Make geographical expansions • Expand into neglected markets • Target rivals' markets • Target new demographics
	• New product introductions	• Imitate rivals' products • Address gaps in quality • Leverage new technologies • Leverage brand name with related products • Protect innovation with patents
	• Changing production capacity	• Create overcapacity • Tie up raw materials sources • Tie up preferred suppliers and distributors • Stimulate demand by limiting capacity
	• Mergers/Alliances	• Acquire/partner with competitors to reduce competition • Tie up key suppliers through alliances • Obtain new technology/intellectual property • Facilitate new market entry
Tactical Actions	• Price cutting (or increases)	• Maintain low price dominance • Offer discounts and rebates • Offer incentives (e.g., frequent flyer miles) • Enhance offering to move upscale
	• Product/service enhancements	• Address gaps in service • Expand warranties • Make incremetal product improvements
	• Increased marketing efforts	• Use guerilla marketing • Conduct selective attacks • Change product packaging • Use new marketing channels
	• New distribution channels	• Access suppliers directly • Access customers directly • Develop multiple points of contact with customers • Expand Internet presence

Sources: Chen, M. J. & Hambrick, D. 1995. Speed, stealth, and selective attack: How small firms differ from large firms in competitive behavior. *Academy of Management Journal,* 38: 453–482; Davies, M. 1992. Sales promotions as a competitive strategy. *Management Decision,* 30(7): 5–10; Ferrier, W., Smith, K., & Grimm, C. 1999. The role of competitive action in market share erosion and industry dethronement: A study of industry leaders and challengers. *Academy of Management Journal,* 42(4): 372–388; and Garda, R. A. 1991. Use tactical pricing to uncover hidden profits. *Journal of Business Strategy,* 12(5): 17–23.

Exhibit 8.8 Strategic and Tactical Competitive Actions

This can be especially effective when firms use a low-cost strategy. The airline industry provides a good example of this head-on approach. When Southwest Airlines began its no-frills, no-meals, no-reserved seating strategy in the late-1960s, it represented a direct assault on the major carriers of the day. Now Southwest is the target of bids by entrepreneurial airlines such as JetBlue to provide a low-cost alternative. In Europe, Ryanair has directly challenged the traditional carriers with an overall cost leadership strategy. Founded in 1985, Ryanair is one-seventh the size of British Airways in terms of revenues, but in 2006, due to cost-cutting measures that significantly improved operating margins, it had a higher market capitalization of $7.6 billion compared to BA's $7.3 billion.[54]

Guerilla offensives and selective attacks provide an alternative for firms with fewer resources.[55] These efforts are designed to draw attention to products or services by creating buzz or generating enough shock value to get some free publicity. For example, the open source software movement, which has been gaining momentum as major corporations become aware of its potential, still lacks the market power and omnipresence that software giant Microsoft enjoys.[56] Loyal users of open source software such as Linux stay connected and share software through online blogs. They also pull the occasional publicity stunt. Recently, users of Firefox, the open source browser developed by the Mozilla Corporation created a crop circle in Oregon based on the Firefox logo. The effort made the local news and garnered thousands of mentions on open source blogs and Internet news organizations.

Some companies limit their competitive response to defensive actions. Such actions rarely improve a company's competitive advantage, but a credible defensive action can lower the risk of being attacked and deter new entry. This may be especially effective during periods such as an industry shake-up, when pricing levels or future demand for a product line become highly uncertain. At such times, tactics such as lowering prices on products that are easily duplicated, buying up the available supply of goods or raw materials, or negotiating exclusive agreements with buyers and/or suppliers can insulate a company from a more serious attack.

Several of the factors discussed earlier in the chapter, such as types of entry strategies and the use of cost leadership versus differentiation strategies, can guide the decision about what types of competitive actions to take. Before launching a given strategy, however, assessing the likely response of competitors is a vital step.

Likelihood of Competitive Reaction

The final step before initiating a competitive response is to evaluate what a competitor's reaction is likely to be. Recall that the logic of competitive dynamics suggests that once competitive actions are initiated, it is likely they will be met with competitive responses.[57] Therefore, the last step before mounting an attack is to evaluate how competitors are likely to respond. Evaluating potential competitive reactions helps companies plan for future counterattacks. It may also lead to a decision to hold off—that is, not to take any competitive action at all because of the possibility that a misguided or poorly planned response will generate a devastating competitive reaction.

How a competitor is likely to respond will depend on three factors: market dependence, competitor's resources, and the reputation of the firm that initiates the action (actor's reputation). The implications of each of these is described briefly in the following sections.

Market Dependence   If a company has a high concentration of its business in a particular industry, it has more at stake because it must depend on that industry's market for its sales. Thus, single-industry businesses or those where one industry dominates its activities are more likely to mount a competitive response. Young and small firms, even though they may have a high degree of market dependence, may be limited in how they respond due to resource constraints. JetBlue, itself an aggressive competitor, is unable to match some of the perks its bigger rivals can offer, such as first-class seats or international travel benefits.

Competitor's Resources   Previously, we examined the internal resource endowments that a company must evaluate when assessing its capability to respond. Here, it is the competitor's resources that need to be considered. For example, a small firm may be unable to mount a serious attack due to lack of resources. As a result, it is more likely to react to tactical actions such as incentive pricing or enhanced service offerings because they are less costly to attack than large-scale strategic actions. In contrast, a firm with financial "deep pockets" may be able to mount and sustain a costly counterattack. As a way to combat these differences in market power, young firms can strengthen their resource positions by forming strategic alliances. Yahoo!, for example, pressed hard by its young but powerful rival Google, allied itself with a group of seven newspaper chains that publish a total of 176 U.S. daily papers in a content sharing arrangement. Both Yahoo! and the newspaper chains are trying to stay ahead of Google now that it is moving aggressively beyond ads on its search pages.

Actor's Reputation   Whether a company should respond to a competitive challenge will also depend on who launched the attack against it. In previous examples, we have noted that companies such as Wal-Mart and Intel are capable of bold offenses. These competitive actors also have the ability and motivation to mount overwhelming counterattacks. Compared to relatively smaller firms with less market power, competitors are more likely to respond to competitive moves by market leaders. Another consideration is how successful prior attacks have been. For example, price-cutting by the big automakers usually has the desired result—increased sales to price-sensitive buyers—at least in the short run. Given that history, when GM offers discounts or incentives, rivals Ford and Chrysler cannot afford to ignore the challenge and quickly follow suit.

Choosing Not to React: Forbearance and Co-opetition

The above discussion suggests that there may be many circumstances in which the best reaction is no reaction at all. This is known as forbearance—refraining from reacting at all as well as holding back from initiating an attack. For example, none of the Japanese automakers attempted to match the employee discount pricing war that cost the big U.S. automakers heavily in terms of lower profits and lost jobs. Yet, during the same period, Honda, Toyota and Nissan enjoyed substantial sales increases over the previous year. Exhibit 8.9 shows the U.S. sales performance of major automakers during a month when GM, Ford, and Chrysler were engaged in a major price war from which Honda, Toyota, and Nissan abstained. Thus, the Japanese rivals were able to enjoy higher margins.

Related to forbearance is the concept of "co-opetition." This is a term that was coined by network software company Novell's founder and former CEO Raymond Noorda to suggest that companies often benefit most from a combination of competing and co-operating.[58] Close competitors that differentiate themselves in the eyes of consumers may work together behind the scenes to achieve industrywide efficiencies.[59] For example, breweries in Sweden cooperate in recycling used bottles but still compete for customers on the basis of taste and variety. As long as the benefits of cooperating are enjoyed by all participants in a co-opetition system, the practice can aid companies in avoiding intense and damaging competition.[60]

Exhibit 8.9

U.S. Sales of Cars and Light Trucks in July 2005 and the Percentage Change from the Previous Year

Brand	Sales	Change	Employee Pricing
General Motors	524,218	15.2%	Yes
Ford Motor	365,329	28.5%	Yes
DaimlerChrysler	260,972	25.1%	Yes
Toyota Motor	216,417	8.1%	No
Honda	143,217	10.3%	No
Nissan	107,300	15.0%	No

Sources: Sender, I. 2006. Car incentives: More pain than gain? *BusinessWeek,* www.businessweek.com, June 29; and Woodyard, C. 2005. Employee pricing helps Big 3's July auto sales hit record. *USA Today,* www.usatoday.com, August 2.

XM, Sirius, and Satellite Radio's Uncertain Future

Satellitte radio providers XM and Sirius have been doing battle for years. Both new entrants have grown steadily as the pay-to-listen business model has gained acceptance. But their ongoing rounds of attacks and counterattacks may have cost them their future. Consider some of the key moves in the six years since satellite operations were launched:

- XM launches ahead of Sirius and gets a huge first mover advantage.
- Sirius outbids XM for a 7-year, $220 million deal to broadcast NFL football games.
- Sirius outbids XM again by signing radio shock jock Howard Stern to a five-year, $500 million contract.
- XM retaliates by signing Major League Baseball to an 11-year, $650 million deal to broadcast games.
- Sirius signs Martha Stewart, Jimmy Buffett, and Bruce Springsteen.
- XM signs the National Hockey League, Bob Dylan, and Oprah.

These high-profile signings have come at a high price. Instead of exercising a little forbearance, XM and Sirius

Sources: Kharif, O. 2007. Satellite static: The XM-Sirius merger. *Business-Week*, www.businessweek.com, February 21; Lowry, T., & Lehman, P. 2006. Grudge match. *BusinessWeek*, August 21/28: 86–87. Lowry, T., & Lehman, P. 2007. XM & Sirius: What a merger won't fix. *BusinessWeek*, www.business-week.com, March 5; and Rosenbush, S. 2007. New conditions may ease XM-Sirius merger. *BusinessWeek*, www.businessweek.com, February 28.

have spent themselve into the red. Both reported heavy losses in 2005, and their combined 2006 losses are expected to hit $1.7 billion. Subscriber rates were nearly 2 million fewer than projected at the end of 2006. More realistic forecasts, which could have been anticipated, might have curbed their enthusiasm for such a competitive spending spree.

To salvage the situation, the two rivals did an about face: They proposed a merger. The problem is that a merger would create a satellite radio monopoly. However, when the FCC first granted satellite radio licenses, it called for two competitive nationwide systems and clearly stated that any future merger of the two should be prohibited. The National Association of Broadcasters, which represents land-based radio stations, called on the FCC to block it.

To counter the appearance of collusion, the two companies argued that radiolike content is being delivered through many different media. The debate has turned to the role of MP3 players, Web radio, and multimedia wireless phones as competition for satellite radio. If these alternatives are truly rivals, it is curious that XM and Sirius did not take them more seriously earlier—it might have prevented them from spending so aggressively and overestimating subscriptions. Meanwhile, if the merger goes through, many analysts question the long-term viability of satellite radio. Their current satellites are expected to be obsolete in 10 to 15 years and alternatives such as high-definition terrestrial radio may bring this high-flying phenomen back down to earth.

Despite the potential benefits of co-opetition, companies need to guard against cooperating to such a great extent that their actions are perceived as collusion, a practice that has legal ramifications in the United States. Satellite radio competitors XM and Sirius faced several challenges recently related to whether it is better to cooperate or compete. Strategy Spotlight 8.10 describes the kinds of problems that can arise from too much co-opetition and too little forbearance.

Once a company has evaluated a competitor's likelihood of responding to a competitive challenge, it can decide what type of action is most appropriate. As we have seen, competitive actions can take many forms: the entry of a start-up into a market for the first time, an attack by a lower-ranked incumbent on an industry leader, or the launch of a breakthrough innovation that disrupts the industry structure. Such actions forever change the competitive dynamics of a marketplace. Thus, the cycle of actions and reactions that occur in business every day is a vital aspect of entrepreneurial strategy that leads to continual new value creation and the ongoing advancement of economic well-being.

Reflecting on Career Implications . . .

- **Opportunity Recognition:** What ideas for new business activities are actively discussed in your work environment? Could you apply the four characteristics of an opportunity to determine whether they are viable opportunities?
- **Entrepreneurial New Entry:** Are there opportunities to launch new products or services that might add value to the organization? What are the best ways for you to bring these opportunities to the attention of key managers? Or, might this provide an opportunity for you to launch your own entrepreneurial venture?
- **Entrepreneurial Strategy:** Does your organization face competition from new ventures? If so, how are those young firms competing: Low cost? Differentiation? Focus? What could you do to help your company to address those competitive challenges?
- **Competitive Dynamics:** Is your organization "on the offense" with its close competitors or "playing defense"? What types of strategic and/or tactical actions have been taken by your close rivals recently to gain competitive advantages?

Summary

New ventures and entrepreneurial firms that capitalize on marketplace opportunities make an important contribution to the U.S. economy. They are leaders in terms of implementing new technologies and introducing innovative products and services. Yet entrepreneurial firms face unique challenges if they are going to survive and grow.

To successfully launch new ventures or implement new technologies, three factors must be present: an entrepreneurial opportunity, the resources to pursue the opportunity, and an entrepreneur or entrepreneurial team willing and able to undertake the venture. Firms must develop a strong ability to recognize viable opportunities. Opportunity recognition is a process of determining which venture ideas are, in fact, promising business opportunities.

In addition to strong opportunities, entrepreneurial firms need resources and entrepreneurial leadership to thrive. The resources that start-ups need include financial resources as well as human and social capital. Many firms also benefit from government programs that support new venture development and growth. New ventures thrive best when they are led by founders or owners who have vision, drive and dedication, and a commitment to excellence.

Once the necessary opportunities, resources, and entrepreneur skills are in place, new ventures still face numerous strategic challenges. Decisions about the strategic positioning of new entrants can benefit from conducting strategic analyses and evaluating the requirements of niche markets. Entry strategies used by new ventures take several forms, including pioneering new entry, imitative new entry, and adaptive new entry. Entrepreneurial firms can benefit from using overall low cost, differentiation, and focus strategies although each of these approaches has pitfalls that are unique to young and small firms. Entrepreneurial firms are also in a strong position to benefit from combination strategies.

The entry of a new company into a competitive arena is like a competitive attack on incumbents in that arena. Such actions often provoke a competitive response, which may, in turn, trigger a reaction to the response. As a result, a competitive dynamic—action and response—begins among close competitors. In deciding whether to attack or counterattack, companies must analyze the seriousness of the competitive threat, their ability to mount a competitive response, and the type of action—strategic or tactical—that the situation requires. At times, competitors find it is better not to respond at all or to find avenues to cooperate with, rather than challenge, close competitors.

Summary Review Questions

1. Explain how the combination of opportunities, resources, and entrepreneurs helps determine the character and strategic direction of an entrepreneurial firm.
2. What is the difference between discovery and evaluation in the process of opportunity recognition? Give an example of each.
3. What are the differences between debt and equity sources of funding for entrepreneurial ventures?
4. Describe the three characteristics of entrepreneurial leadership: vision, dedication and drive, and commitment to excellence.

5. Briefly describe the three types of entrepreneurial entry strategies: pioneering, imitative, and adaptive.

6. Explain why entrepreneurial firms are often in a strong position to use combination strategies.

7. What does the term *competitive dynamics* mean?

8. Explain the difference between strategic actions and tactical actions and provide examples of each.

Key Terms

entrepreneurship, 267
opportunity recognition, 269
pioneering new entry, 278
imitative new entry, 278
adaptive new entry, 279

competitive dynamics, 285
market commonality, 287
resource similarity, 287
strategic actions, 291
tactical actions, 291

Applications Questions and Answers

1. E-Loan and Lending Tree are two young firms that offer lending services over the Internet. Evaluate the features of these two companies and, for each company:

a. Evaluate their characteristics and assess the extent to which they are comparable in terms of market commonality and resource similarity.

Company	Market Commonality	Resource Similarity
E-Loan		
Lending Tree		

b. Based on your analysis, what strategic and/or tactical actions might these companies take to improve their competitive position? Could E-Loan and Lending Tree improve their performance more through co-opetition rather than competition? Explain your rationale.

Company	Strategic Actions	Tactical Actions
E-Loan		
Lending Tree		

2. Using the Internet, research the Small Business Administration's Web site (www.sba.gov). What different types of financing are available to small firms? Besides financing, what other programs are available to support the growth and development of small businesses?

3. Think of an entrepreneurial firm that has been successfully launched in the last 10 years. What kind of entry strategy did it use—pioneering, imitative, or adaptive? Since the firm's initial entry, how has it used or combined overall low cost, differentiation and/or focus strategies?

4. Select an entrepreneurial firm you are familiar with in your local community. Research the company and discuss how it has positioned itself relative to its close competitors. Does it have a unique strategic advantage? Disadvantage? Explain.

Ethics Questions

1. Imitation strategies are based on the idea of copying another firm's idea and using it for your own purposes. Is this unethical or simply a smart business practice? Discuss the ethical implications of this practice (if any).

2. Intense competition such as price wars are an accepted practice in the United States, but cooperation between companies has legal ramifications because of antitrust laws. Should price wars that drive small businesses or new entrants out of business be illegal? What ethical considerations are raised (if any)?

References

1. The ESPN example is based on Lowry, T. 2006. ESPN's cell-phone fumble. *BusinessWeek,* October 30: 26; Medford, C. 2006. Final bell for Mobile ESPN. *Red Herring,* September 28, www.redherring.com; Seybold, A. M. 2006. Post-mortem of an MVNO. *Outlook 4Mobility,* www.outlook4mobility.com; and Zimmermann, K. 2006. ESPN Mobile failure: Bad news for mobile media in U.S. *Search Views,* September 28, www.searchviews.com.

2. Lowry, op. cit.

3. Medford, op. cit.

4. Seybold, op. cit.

5. Small Business Administration. 2004. *The small business economy* Washington, D.C.: U.S. Government Printing Office.

6. Timmons, J. A., & Spinelli, S. 2004. *New venture creation* (6th ed.). New York: McGraw-Hill/Irwin; and Bygrave, W. D. 1997. The entrepreneurial process. In W. D. Bygrave (Ed.), *The portable MBA in entrepreneurship* (2nd ed.). New York: Wiley.

7. Fromartz, S. 1998. How to get your first great idea. *Inc. Magazine,* April 1: 91–94; and, Vesper, K. H. 1990. *New venture strategies,* 2nd ed. Englewood Cliffs, NJ: Prentice-Hall.

8. For an interesting perspective on the nature of the opportunity recognition process, see Baron, R. A. 2006. Opportunity recognition as pattern recognition: How entrepreneurs 'connect the dots' to identify new business opportunities. *Academy of Management Perspectives,* February: 104–119.

9. Gaglio, C. M. 1997. Opportunity identification: Review, critique and suggested research directions. In J. A. Katz, ed. *Advances in entrepreneurship, firm emergence and growth,* vol. 3. Greenwich, CT: JAI Press: 139–202; Lumpkin, G. T., Hills, G. E., & Shrader, R. C. 2004. Opportunity recognition. In Harold L. Welsch, (Ed.), *Entrepreneurship: The Road Ahead,* pp. 73–90. London: Routledge; and, Long, W. & McMullan, W. E. 1984. Mapping the new venture opportunity identification process. *Frontiers of Entrepreneurship Research, 1984.* Wellesley, MA: Babson College: 567–90.

10. For an interesting discussion of different aspects of opportunity discovery, see Shepherd, D. A., & De Tienne, D. R. 2005. Prior knowledge, potential financial reward, and opportunity identification. *Entrepreneurship Theory & Practice,* 29(1): 91–112; and Gaglio, C. M. 2004. The role of mental simulations and counterfactual thinking in the opportunity identification process. *Entrepreneurship Theory & Practice,* 28(6): 533–552.

11. Stewart, T. A. 2002. How to think with your gut. *Business 2.0,* November: 99–104.

12. Timmons, J. A. 1997. Opportunity recognition. In W. D. Bygrave, ed. *The portable MBA in entrepreneurship,* 2nd ed. New York: John Wiley: 26–54.

13. Bhide, A. V. 2000. *The origin and evolution of new businesses.* New York: Oxford University Press.

14. Anonymous. 2001. Small Business 2001: Where are we now? *Inc. Magazine,* May 29: 18–19; and, Zacharakis, A. L., Bygrave, W. D., & Shepherd, D.A. 2000. *Global entrepreneurship monitor—National entrepreneurship assessment: United States of America 2000 Executive Report.* Kansas City, MO: Kauffman Center for Entrepreneurial Leadership.

15. Cooper, S. 2003. Cash cows. *Entrepreneur,* June: 36.

16. Bhide, op. cit.

17. Seglin, J. L. 1998. What angels want. *Inc. Magazine,* 20 (7): 43–44.

18. Torres, N.L. 2002. Playing an angel. *Entrepreneur,* May: 130–138.

19. For more on how different forms of organizing entrepreneurial firms as well as different stages of new firm growth and development affect financing, see Cassar, G. 2004. The financing of business start-ups. *Journal of Business Venturing,* 19(2): 261–283.

20. Eisenhardt, K. M., & Schoonhoven, C. B. 1990. Organizational growth: Linking founding team, strategy, environment, and growth among U.S. semiconductor ventures, 1978–1988. *Administrative Science Quarterly,* 35: 504–529.

21. Dubini, P., & Aldrich, H. 1991. Personal and extended networks are central to the entrepreneurship process. *Journal of Business Venturing,* 6(5): 305–333.

22. For more on the role of social contacts in helping young firms build legitimacy, see Chrisman, J. J., & McMullan, W. E. 2004. Outside assistance as a knowledge resource for new venture survival. *Journal of Small Business Management,* 42(3): 229–244.

23. Vogel, C. 2000. Janina Pawlowski. *Working Woman,* June: 70

24. For a recent perspective on entrepreneurship and strategic alliances, see Rothaermel, F. T., & Deeds, D. L. 2006. Alliance types, alliance experience and alliance management capability in high-technology ventures. *Journal of Business Venturing,* 21(4): 429–460; and Lu, J. W., & Beamish, P. W. 2006. Partnering strategies and performance of SMEs' international joint ventures. *Journal of Business Venturing,* 21(4): 461–486.

25. For more information, go to the Small Business Administration Web site at www.sba.gov.

26. Collins, J. 2001. *Good to great.* New York: HarperCollins.

27. Collins, op. cit.

28. The idea of entry wedges was discussed by Vesper, K. 1990. *New venture strategies* (2nd ed.). Englewood Cliffs, NJ: Prentice-Hall; and, Drucker, P. F. 1985. *Innovation and entrepreneurship.* New York: HarperBusiness.

29. See Dowell, G., & Swaminathan, A. 2006. Entry timing, exploration, and firm survival in the early U.S. bicycle industry. *Strategic Management Journal,* 27: 1159–1182, for a recent study of the timing of entrepreneurial new entry.

30. Frauenfelder, M. 2002. Look! Up in the sky! It's a flying cell phone tower! *Business 2.0,* November: 108–112.

31. Maiello, M. 2002. They almost changed the world. *Forbes,* December 22: 217–220.

32. Pedroza, G. M. 2003. Blanket statement. *Entrepreneur,* March: 92.

33. Gull, N. 2003. Just say om. *Inc. Magazine,* July: 42–44.

34. More on the role of imitation strategies is addressed in a recent article: Lieberman, M. B., & Asaba, S. 2006. Why do firms imitate each other? *Academy of Management Review,* 31(2): 366–385.

35. Williams, G. 2002. Looks like Rain. *Entrepreneur,* September: 104–111.

36. Carey, J. 2006. Perspiration inspiration. *BusinessWeek,* June 5: 64;

37. Pedroza, G. M. 2002. Tech tutors. *Entrepreneur,* September: 120.

38. Barrett, A. 2003. Hot growth companies. *BusinessWeek,* June 9: 74–77.

39. Dennis, Jr. W. J. 1997. *Business starts and stops.* Washington, DC: National Federation of Independent Business; and, Anonymous. 1992. *The state of small business: A report of the President, 1992.* Washington, DC: U.S. Government Printing Office: 65–90.

40. Romanelli, E. 1989. Environments and strategies of organization start-up: Effects on early survival. *Administrative Science Quarterly,* 34(3): 369–87.

41. Wallace, B. 2000. Brothers. *Philadelphia Magazine,* April: 66–75.

42. Buchanan, L. 2003. The innovation factor: A field guide to innovation. *Forbes,* April 21, www.forbes.com.

43. Kim, W. C., & Mauborgne, R. 2005. *Blue ocean strategy.* Boston: Harvard Business School Press.

44. Burrows, P. 2003. Ringing off the hook in China. *BusinessWeek,* June 9: 80–82.

45. Smith, K. G., Ferrier, W. J., & Grimm, C. M. 2001. King of the hill: Dethroning the industry leader. *Academy of Management Executive,* 15(2): 59–70.

46. Kumar, N. 2006. Strategies to fight low-cost rivals. *Harvard Business Review,* December: 104–112.

47. Grove, A. 1999. *Only the paranoid survive: How to exploit the crises points that challenge every company.* New York: Random House.

48. Stalk, Jr., G., & Lachenauer, R. 2004. *Hardball: Are you playing to play or playing to win?* Cambridge, MA: Harvard Business School Press.

49. Peteraf, M. A., & Bergen, M. A. 2003. Scanning competitive landscapes: A market-based and resource-based framework. *Strategic Management Journal,* 24: 1027–1045.

50. Chen, M. J. 1996. Competitor analysis and interfirm rivalry: Toward a theoretical integration. *Academy of Management Review,* 21(1): 100–134.

51. Chen, 1996, op.cit.

52. Chen, M. J., Su, K. H, & Tsai, W. 2007. Competitive tension: The awareness-motivation-capability perspective. *Academy of Management Journal,* 50(1): 101–118.

53. St. John, W. 1999. Barnes & Noble's Epiphany. *Wired,* www.wired.com, June.

54. Kumar 2006, op. cit.

55. Chen, M. J., & Hambrick, D. 1995. Speed, stealth, and selective attack: How small firms differ from large firms in competitive behavior. *Academy of Management Journal,* 38: 453–482.

56. Lyons, D. 2006. The cheap revolution. *Forbes,* September 18: 102–111.

57. Smith, K. G., Ferrier, W. J., & Ndofor, H. 2001. Competitive dynamics research: Critique and future directions. In M. A. Hitt, R. E. Freeman, & J. S. Harrison (Eds.), *The Blackwell handbook of strategic management,* pp. 315–361. Oxford, UK: Blackwell.

58. Gee, P. 2000. Co-opetition: The new market milieu. *Journal of Healthcare Management,* 45: 359–363.

59. Ketchen, D. J., Snow, C. C., & Hoover, V. L. 2004. Research on competitive dynamics: Recent accomplishments and future challenges. *Journal of Management,* 30(6): 779–804.

60. Khanna, T., Gulati, R., & Nohria, N. 2000. The economic modeling of strategy process: Clean models and dirty hands. *Strategic Management Journal,* 21: 781–790.

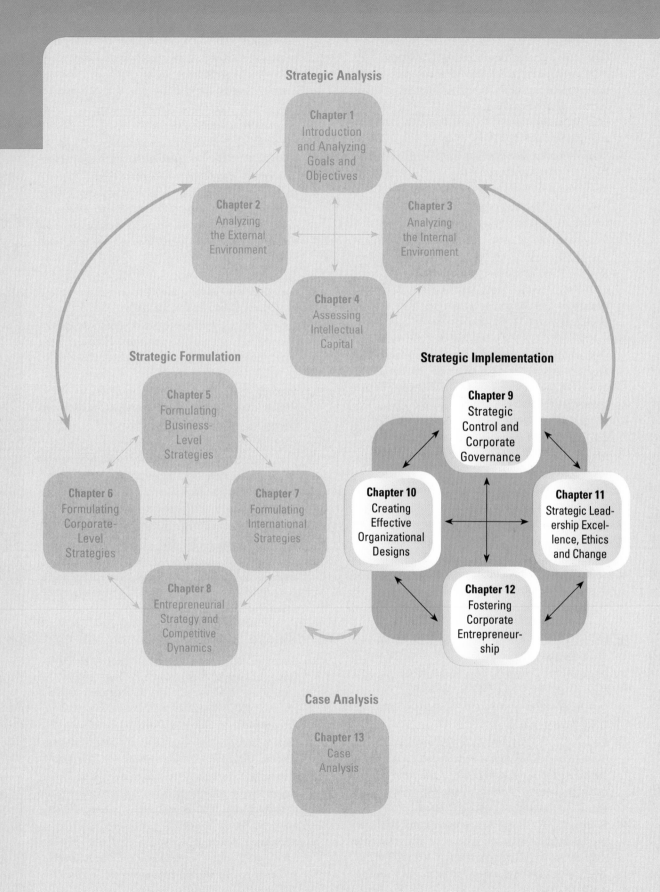

Strategic Analysis

Chapter 1
Introduction and Analyzing Goals and Objectives

Chapter 2
Analyzing the External Environment

Chapter 3
Analyzing the Internal Environment

Chapter 4
Assessing Intellectual Capital

Strategic Formulation

Chapter 5
Formulating Business-Level Strategies

Chapter 6
Formulating Corporate-Level Strategies

Chapter 7
Formulating International Strategies

Chapter 8
Entrepreneurial Strategy and Competitive Dynamics

Strategic Implementation

Chapter 9
Strategic Control and Corporate Governance

Chapter 10
Creating Effective Organizational Designs

Chapter 11
Strategic Leadership Excellence, Ethics and Change

Chapter 12
Fostering Corporate Entrepreneurship

Case Analysis

Chapter 13
Case Analysis

Strategic Implementation

chapter 9

Strategic Control and Corporate Governance

>learning objectives

After reading this chapter, you should have a good understanding of:

LO1 The value of effective strategic control systems in strategy implementation.

LO2 The key difference between "traditional" and "contemporary" control systems.

LO3 The imperative for "contemporary" control systems in today's complex and rapidly changing competitive and general environments.

LO4 The benefits of having the proper balance among the three levers of behavioral control: culture; rewards and incentives; and, boundaries.

LO5 The three key participants in corporate governance: shareholders, management (led by the CEO), and the board of directors.

LO6 The role of corporate governance mechanisms in ensuring that the interests of managers are aligned with those of shareholders from both the United States and international perspectives.

Organizations must have effective strategic controls if they are to successfully implement their strategies. This includes systems that exercise both informational control and behavioral control. In addition, a firm must promote sound corporate governance as well as have controls that are consistent with the strategy that the firm is following.

In the first section, we address the need to have effective informational control, contrasting two approaches to informational control. The first approach, which we call "traditional," is highly sequential. Goals and objectives are set, then implemented, and after a set period of time, performance is compared to the desired standards. In contrast, the second approach, termed "contemporary," is much more interactive. Here, the internal and external environments are continually monitored, and managers determine whether the strategy itself needs to be modified. Today the contemporary approach is required, given the rapidly changing conditions in virtually all industries.

Next, we discuss behavioral control. Here the firm must strive to maintain a proper balance between culture, rewards, and boundaries. We also argue that organizations that have strong, positive cultures and reward systems can rely less on boundaries, such as rules, regulations, and procedures. When individuals in the firm internalize goals and strategies, there is less need for monitoring behavior, and efforts are focused more on important organizational goals and objectives.

The third section addresses the role of corporate governance in ensuring that managerial and shareholder interests are aligned. We provide examples of both effective and ineffective corporate governance practices. We discuss three governance mechanisms for aligning managerial and shareholder interests: a committed and involved board of directors, shareholder activism, and effective managerial rewards and incentives. Public companies are also subject to external control. We discuss several external control mechanisms, such as the market for corporate control, auditors, banks and analysts, the media, and public activists. We close with a discussion of corporate governance from an international perspective.

Learning from Mistakes

Recently, the backdating of option grants has prompted the biggest corporate probe since the mid 1970s.[1] By March 2007, about 140 companies were under investigation by the U.S. government for backdating, including Cablevision, Barnes & Noble, and Broadcom. Over 75 of these firms plan to restate earnings to account for charges totaling more than $5 billion. Some 66 executives have lost their jobs, and several have been indicted.

What is backdating all about? Option grants give the recipient a right to buy a stock at a fixed "strike price." This price is generally set at the stock's market price the day of the grant. Typically, a company's board of directors or compensation committee must approve its options grants to executives.

Holders of these grants benefit if the stock rises above the strike price because it enables them to buy stock at the lower price. In the backdating scandal, companies have dated option grants to days when the stock was at a low, thus enhancing the potential payouts. Let's take a look at a particularly egregious case of backdating—Los Angeles–based KB Home:

> KB Home may be only the fifth largest home builder in the United States. However, it easily ranks number one when it comes to paying its chief executive. *[continued]*

Over the last three years, CEO Bruce Karatz made an astonishing $232.6 million in total compensation. That's nearly three times what the chief executives earned at Pulte Homes and Centex Corp.—two rivals that are much larger and more profitable.

Unfortunately, greed got the best of Mr. Karatz and he finds himself homeless (figuratively speaking!). On, November 12, 2006, he fell prey to the backdating scandal and retired under pressure. An internal investigation found that he and another executive handed out options backdated to days when the stock was cheap in order to make them more valuable. The moves cost the company $50 million in additional compensation over a seven-year period ending in 2005. Karatz agreed to pay back $13 million. However, Karatz won't go away empty handed. According to his employment contract, he could walk away with $175 million in severance pay, pension benefits, and stock options. Such a package has prompted fresh criticism from larger shareholder groups that claim that Karatz had been overpaid for years. And there's other bad news: On January 19, 2007, the Securities and Exchange Commission began a formal probe at KB Home because it believed that there was a violation of its rules, and it may subpoena documents and compel testimony.

What factors might explain Karatz's generous windfall at stockholders' expense? One factor sticks out: a very generous and friendly board of directors and compensation committee. The five-man compensation committee was headed by Occidental Chair and Chief Executive Ray Irani, who is no stranger to high pay. Occidental paid him an astonishing $461 million in 2006—much of it in the exercise of stock options! Two other chief executives were also on the committee: Leslie Mooves, of CBS Corporation, who earned $22.8 million in 2005, and J. Terrence Lanni, chairman and CEO of casino company MGM Mirage, who made $9.6 million and was granted options with a potential value of $35.5 million that year.

In response to such largess, Ed Durkin, director of corporate affairs at the United Brotherhood of Carpenters, which has a $40 billion pension fund asserts: "We are always leery when you have another company's CEO on a compensation committee. They don't want people to say no to them, so they are particularly generous."

A fourth member of the compensation committee is James A. Johnson. He has been dubbed a "problem director" by the AFL-CIO. Why? He served on the board of United Health Group Inc. (UHG) whose CEO, William W. McGuire, retired in 2006 in the wake of a stock-option scandal. (McGuire's options were worth an astounding $1.78 billion at some point; he'll get to keep around $1 billion after repricing them.) Johnson's experience with UHG was hardly what KB Home needed!

We now focus on how organizations can develop and use effective strategic control.[2] We first explore two central aspects of strategic control: (1) *informational control,* which is the ability to respond effectively to environmental change, and (2) *behavioral control,* which is the appropriate balance and alignment among a firm's culture, rewards, and boundaries. In the final section of this chapter, we focus on strategic control from a much broader perspective—what is referred to as *corporate governance.* Here, we direct our attention to the need for a firm's shareholders (the owners) and their elected representatives (the board of directors) to ensure that the firm's executives (the management team) strive to fulfill their fiduciary duty of maximizing long-term shareholder value. Clearly, corporate governance was not one of KB Home's noteworthy strengths.

Ensuring Informational Control: Responding Effectively to Environmental Change

>LO1
The value of effective strategic control systems in strategy implementation.

We discuss two broad types of control systems. The first one, labeled "traditional," is based on a feedback approach; that is, there is little or no action taken to revise strategies, goals, and objectives until the end of the time period in question, usually a quarter or a month.

Exhibit 9.1 Traditional Approach to Strategic Control

The second one, which we call "contemporary," emphasizes the importance of continually monitoring the environment (both internal and external) for trends and events that signal the need to make modifications to a firm's strategies, goals, and objectives. As both general and competitive environments become more unpredictable and complex, the need for contemporary systems increases.

A Traditional Approach to Strategic Control

The **traditional approach to strategic control** is sequential: (1) strategies are formulated and top management sets goals, (2) strategies are implemented, and (3) performance is measured against the predetermined goal set, as illustrated in Exhibit 9.1.

Control is based on a feedback loop from performance measurement to strategy formulation. This process typically involves lengthy time lags, often tied to a firm's annual planning cycle. Such traditional control systems, termed "single-loop" learning by Harvard's Chris Argyris simply compare actual performance to a predetermined goal.[3] They are most appropriate when the environment is stable and relatively simple, goals and objectives can be measured with a high level of certainty, and there is little need for complex measures of performance. Sales quotas, operating budgets, production schedules, and similar quantitative control mechanisms are typical. The appropriateness of the business strategy or standards of performance is seldom questioned.[4]

The idea that well-managed companies should move forward in accordance with detailed and precise plans has come under attack.[5] James Brian Quinn of Dartmouth College has argued that grand designs with precise and carefully integrated plans seldom work. Rather, most strategic change proceeds incrementally—one step at a time. Leaders should introduce some sense of direction, some logic in incremental steps.[6]

Similarly, McGill University's Henry Mintzberg has written about leaders "crafting" a strategy.[7] Drawing on the parallel between the potter at her wheel and the strategist, Mintzberg pointed out that the potter begins work with some general idea of the artifact she wishes to create, but the details of design—even possibilities for a different design— emerge as the work progresses. For businesses facing complex and turbulent business environments, the craftsperson's method seems more appropriate than that provided by the traditional, more rational, planner. The former helps us deal with the uncertainty about how a design will work out in practice and allows for a creative element.

Mintzberg's argument, like Quinn's, questions the value of rigid planning and goal-setting processes. Fixed strategic goals also become dysfunctional for firms competing in highly unpredictable competitive environments. Here, strategies need to change frequently and opportunistically. An inflexible commitment to predetermined goals and milestones can prevent the very adaptability that is required of a good strategy.

Even organizations that have been extremely successful in the past can become complacent or fail to adapt their goals and strategies to the new conditions. An example of such a firm is Cisco Systems, whose market value at one time approached an astonishing $600 billion, but as of mid 2007 was about $180 billion. Cisco has minimized the potential for such problems in the future by improving its informational control systems. Other firms such as Siebel Systems (now part of Oracle) have been more successful in anticipating

> **traditional approach to strategic control** a sequential method of organizational control in which (1) strategies are formulated and top management sets goals, (2) strategies are implemented, and (3) performance is measured against the predetermined goal set.

> **>LO2**
> The key difference between "traditional" and "contemporary" control systems.

When the Tech Bubble Burst

We can learn some lessons from fallen stars. Cisco Systems, Inc., once the invincible momentum stock adored by Wall Street, came crashing down just as we were beginning the 21st century. What went wrong?

Problems started when Cisco announced a $2.2 billion inventory write-off; Wall Street severely punished the stock as a result. With all of its experience, why didn't Cisco see the problems coming? Cisco made a common mistake: It projected the past into the future.

Past demand had been vigorous, but customers were requiring less and less of the firm's products. And financing was cheap—it was no problem for a company like Cisco to find capital to finance ongoing operations even when things didn't look so bright on the horizon. Overtaken

by its own success, Cisco failed to see the slowdown in customer demand. John Sterman at MIT sums up the situation: "If you were in the pasta business, you want to know how much pasta people are cooking and eating, not how much they're buying, and certainly not how much supermarkets and distributors are ordering from the factory." Consumers ultimately determine demand; Cisco missed this important point and inaccurately forecast new sales orders. When the orders didn't materialize, a stockpile of inventory sat on the shelves while Wall Street annulled the short-lived marriage between investors and their beloved Cisco.

In contrast, Siebel Systems, Inc., kept its eye on the future. The company rewarded its sales force for providing accurate information concerning future demand. Salespeople receive commissions not only for sales, but also for forecast information. Haim Mendelson at Stanford University remarked that this provides the company "with a deep understanding of what customers are going to do."

Sources: Weber, J. 2001. Management lessons from the bust. *BusinessWeek*, August 27: 104–112; Morrison, S. 2001. Positive sales news takes the sting out of Cisco revamp. *Financial Times Online*, August 26; Reuters. 2001. Siebel sees economic rebound late 2002: August 20.

change and have made proper corrections to their strategies. We discuss these firms in Strategy Spotlight 9.1.

Without doubt, the traditional "feedback" approach to strategic control has some important limitations. Is there another, better, way?

A Contemporary Approach to Strategic Control

>LO3

The imperative for "contemporary" control systems in today's complex and rapidly changing competitive and general environments.

Adapting to and anticipating both internal and external environmental change is an integral part of strategic control. The relationships between strategy formulation, implementation, and control are highly interactive, as suggested by Exhibit 9.2. It also illustrates two different types of strategic control: informational control and behavioral control. **Informational control** is primarily concerned with whether or not the organization is "doing the right things." **Behavioral control,** on the other hand, asks if the organization is "doing things right" in the implementation of its strategy. Both the informational and

informational control a method of organizational control in which a firm gathers and analyzes information from the internal and external environment in order to obtain the best fit between the organization's goals and strategies and the strategic environment.

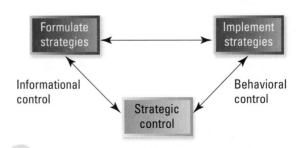

Exhibit 9.2 Contemporary Approach to Strategic Control

behavioral components of strategic control are necessary, but not sufficient, conditions for success. That is, what good is a well-conceived strategy that cannot be implemented? Or, alternatively, what use is an energetic and committed workforce if it is focused on the wrong strategic target?

behavioral control
a method of organizational control in which a firm influences the actions of employees through culture, rewards, and boundaries.

John Weston is the former CEO of ADP Corporation, the largest payroll and taxfiling processor in the world. He captures the essence of contemporary control systems.

> At ADP, 39 plus 1 adds up to more than 40 plus 0. The 40-plus-0 employee is the harried worker who at 40 hours a week just tries to keep up with what's in the "in" basket. He tries to do whatever he thinks he's supposed to do. Because he works with his head down, he takes zero hours to think about what he's doing, why he's doing it, and how he's doing it. Does he need to do it in the first place? On the other hand, the 39-plus-1 employee takes at least 1 of those 40 hours to think about what he's doing and why he's doing it. That's why the other 39 hours are far more productive.[8]

Informational control deals with the internal environment as well as the external strategic context. It addresses the assumptions and premises that provide the foundation for an organization's strategy. The key question becomes: Do the organization's goals and strategies still "fit" within the context of the current strategic environment? Depending on the type of business, such assumptions may relate to changes in technology, customer tastes, government regulation, and industry competition.

This involves two key issues. First, managers must scan and monitor the external environment, as we discussed in Chapter 2. Recall, for example, the failure of Coors to anticipate and act on the trend toward low-carb beer. Also, conditions can change in the internal environment of the firm, as we discussed in Chapter 3, requiring changes in the strategic direction of the firm. These may include, for example, the resignation of key executives or delays in the completion of major production facilities.

In the contemporary approach, information control is part of an ongoing process of organizational learning that continuously updates and challenges the assumptions that underlie the organization's strategy. In such "double-loop" learning, the organization's assumptions, premises, goals, and strategies are continuously monitored, tested, and reviewed. The benefits of continuous monitoring are evident—time lags are dramatically shortened, changes in the competitive environment are detected earlier, and the organization's ability to respond with speed and flexibility is enhanced.

A key question becomes: OK, but how is this done? Contemporary control systems must have four characteristics to be effective.[9]

1. They must focus on constantly changing information that top managers identify as having potential strategic importance.
2. The information is important enough to demand frequent and regular attention from operating managers at all levels of the organization.
3. The data and information generated by the control system are best interpreted and discussed in face-to-face meetings of superiors, subordinates, and peers.
4. The contemporary control system is a key catalyst for an ongoing debate about underlying data, assumptions, and action plans.

An executive's decision to use the control system interactively—in other words, to invest the time and attention to review and evaluate new information—sends a clear signal to the organization about what is important. The dialogue and debate that emerge from such an interactive process can often lead to new strategies and innovations. Strategy Spotlight 9.2 discusses how executives at *USA Today,* Gannett Co.'s daily newspaper, review information delivered each Friday.

Let's now turn our attention to behavioral control.

USA Today's Interactive Control System

Top managers at Gannett-owned *USA Today* meet each Friday to discuss ongoing strategy. Every week, they review information ranging from day-to-day operations to year-to-date data. This information enables top management to check the pulse of the industry on a frequent basis and minimizes the surprises that frequently beset other companies that don't keep close tabs on available information. Senior managers frequently meet with operations-level managers for intensive discussion to analyze the weekly information. The results of these high-level meetings on information control allow managers from the operating core of the newspaper to respond to industry trends and events on nearly a real-time basis.

By controlling information, *USA Today* managers:

- Compare projected advertising volume with actual volume.

Sources: Simons, R. 1995. Control in an age of empowerment. *Harvard Business Review*, 73(2): 80–88; Caney, D. 2001. Gannett, Knight Ridder walloped by ad slump. Reuters, July 17.

- Assess new advertising revenues by client type to better target client markets.
- Quickly discover revenue shortfalls before major problems arise.
- Become aware of unexpected successes that have often led to innovations.

These weekly meetings have returned significant rewards for *USA Today*. Innovations that have been implemented as a result of high information control include:

- A new market survey service targeted at the automobile industry (a potential source of high-volume advertising).
- The addition of fractional page color advertising (increasing the number of advertisers that use color, thereby increasing advertising revenue).
- Expanding the job function of circulation employees to include regional sales of advertising space.
- Developing a program of advertising inserts targeted toward specific customers and products.

>LO4

The benefits of having the proper balance among the three levers of behavioral control: culture, rewards and incentives, and boundaries.

Attaining Behavioral Control: Balancing Culture, Rewards, and Boundaries

Behavioral control is focused on implementation—doing things right. Effectively implementing strategy requires manipulating three key control "levers": culture, rewards, and boundaries. These three levers are illustrated in Exhibit 9.3. Furthermore, there are two compelling reasons for an increased emphasis on culture and rewards in implementing a system of behavioral controls.

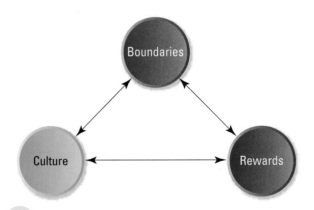

Exhibit 9.3 **Essential Elements of Behavioral Control**

First, the competitive environment is increasingly complex and unpredictable, demanding both flexibility and quick response to its challenges. As firms simultaneously downsize and face the need for increased coordination across organizational boundaries, a control system based primarily on rigid strategies and rules and regulations is dysfunctional. Thus, the use of rewards and culture to align individual and organizational goals becomes increasingly important.

Second, the implicit long-term contract between the organization and its key employees has been eroded.[10] Today's younger managers have been conditioned to see themselves as "free agents" and view a career as a series of opportunistic challenges. As managers are advised to "specialize, market yourself, and have work, if not a job," the importance of culture and rewards in building organizational loyalty claims greater importance. (We addressed this issue at length in Chapter 4.)

Each of the three levers—culture, rewards, and boundaries—must work in a balanced and consistent manner. Let's consider the role of each.

Building a Strong and Effective Culture

What is culture? Consistent with our discussion in Chapter 4, **organizational culture** is a system of shared values (what is important) and beliefs (how things work) that shape a company's people, organizational structures, and control systems to produce behavioral norms (the way we do things around here). How important is culture? Very. Over the years, numerous best sellers, such as *Theory Z, Corporate Cultures, In Search of Excellence*, and *Good to Great*,[11] have emphasized the powerful influence of culture on what goes on within organizations and how they perform.

Collins and Porras argued in *Built to Last* that the key factor in sustained exceptional performance is a cultlike culture.[12] You can't touch it, you can't write it down, but it's there, in every organization, and its influence is pervasive. It can work for you or against you.[13] Effective leaders understand its importance and strive to shape and use it as one of their important levers of strategic control.[14]

> **organizational culture** a system of shared values and beliefs that shape a company's people, organizational structures, and control systems to produce behavioral norms.

The Role of Culture   Culture wears many different hats, each woven from the fabric of those values that sustain the organization's primary source of competitive advantage. Some examples are:

- Federal Express and Southwest Airlines focus on customer service.
- Lexus (a division of Toyota) and Hewlett-Packard emphasize product quality.
- Newell Rubbermaid and 3M place a high value on innovation.
- Nucor (steel) and Emerson Electric are concerned, above all, with operational efficiency.

Culture sets implicit boundaries—that is, unwritten standards of acceptable behavior—in dress, ethical matters, and the way an organization conducts its business.[15] By creating a framework of shared values, culture encourages individual identification with the organization and its objectives. Thus, culture acts as a means of reducing monitoring costs.[16]

Sustaining an Effective Culture   Powerful organizational cultures just don't happen overnight, and they don't remain in place without a strong commitment—both in terms of words and deeds—by leaders throughout the organization. A viable and productive organizational culture can be strengthened and sustained. However, it cannot be "built" or "assembled"; instead, it must be cultivated, encouraged, and "fertilized."

Storytelling is one way effective cultures are maintained. Many are familiar with the story of how Art Fry's failure to develop a strong adhesive led to 3M's enormously successful Post-it Notes. Perhaps less familiar is the story of Francis G. Okie.[17] In 1922 Okie came up with the idea of selling sandpaper to men as a replacement for razor blades. The idea obviously didn't pan out, but Okie was allowed to remain at 3M. Interestingly, the technology developed by Okie led 3M to develop its first blockbuster product: a waterproof

● 3M is well known for its innovative culture. Above is a Yellow 3M Post-It Highlighter Package.

sandpaper that became a staple of the automobile industry. Such stories foster the importance of risk taking, experimentation, freedom to fail, and of course innovation—all vital elements of 3M's culture.

Rallies or "pep talks" by top executives also serve to reinforce a firm's culture. The late Sam Walton was well known for his pep rallies at local Wal-Mart stores. Four times a year, the founders of Home Depot—CEO Bernard Marcus and Arthur Blank—used to don orange aprons and stage Breakfast with Bernie and Arthur, a 6:30 a.m. pep rally, broadcast live over the firm's closed-circuit TV network to most of its 45,000 employees.[18]

Southwest Airlines' "Culture Committee" is a unique vehicle designed to perpetuate the company's highly successful culture. The following excerpt from an internal company publication describes its objectives:

The goal of the Committee is simple—to ensure that our unique Corporate Culture stays alive. . . . Culture Committee members represent all regions and departments across our system and they are selected based upon their exemplary display of the "Positively Outrageous Service" that won us the first-ever Triple Crown; their continual exhibition of the "Southwest Spirit" to our Customers and to their fellow workers; and their high energy level, boundless enthusiasm, unique creativity, and constant demonstration of teamwork and love for their fellow workers.[19]

Motivating with Rewards and Incentives

Reward and incentive systems represent a powerful means of influencing an organization's culture, focusing efforts on high-priority tasks, and motivating individual and collective task performance.[20] Just as culture deals with influencing beliefs, behaviors, and attitudes of people within an organization, the reward system—by specifying who gets rewarded and why—is an effective motivator and control mechanism.[21] Consider how John Thompson, CEO of $1 billion software security firm Symantec, distributes financial rewards based on contribution:[22]

When Thompson arrived at Symantec, any executive who was promoted to vice president automatically received a BMW. Senior management's bonuses were paid quarterly and were heavily skewed toward cash, not stock. Thompson says:

So if the stock didn't do well, they didn't care. We now have a stock option plan that is broad based but not universal. One of the things we recognized early on was that if we were going to grow at the rate that we were growing, we have to be more selective in who we gave options to so as not to dilute the value of our stock. And, the first thing we did was identify a range of employees who were valuable to the company but didn't need equity to come to work, and we focused their compensation around cash bonuses. Then we increased the equity we gave to the engineers and other people that were critical to our long term success.

By paying the two groups of people in a different manner, the new compensation scheme recognizes their distinctive importance.

The Potential Downside   Generally speaking, people in organizations act rationally, each motivated by their personal best interest.[23] However, the collective sum of individual behaviors of an organization's employees does not always result in what is best for the organization; that is, individual rationality is no guarantee of organizational rationality.

As corporations grow and evolve, they often develop different business units with multiple reward systems. They may differ based on industry contexts, business situations, stage of product life cycles, and so on. Thus, subcultures within organizations may reflect differences among an organization's functional areas, products, services, and divisions. To the extent that reward systems reinforce such behavioral norms, attitudes, and belief systems, cohesiveness is reduced; important information is hoarded rather than shared, individuals begin working at cross-purposes, and they lose sight of overall goals.

Such conflicts are commonplace in many organizations. For example, sales and marketing personnel promise unrealistically quick delivery times to bring in business, much to the dismay of operations and logistics; overengineering by R&D creates headaches for manufacturing; and so on. Conflicts also arise across divisions when divisional profits become a key compensation criterion. As ill will and anger escalate, personal relationships and performance may suffer.

Creating Effective Reward and Incentive Programs   To be effective, incentive and reward systems need to reinforce basic core values and enhance cohesion and commitment to goals and objectives. They also must not be at odds with the organization's overall mission and purpose.[24]

At General Mills, a manager's interest in the overall performance of his or her unit, half of a manager's annual bonus is linked to business-unit results and half to individual performance.[25] For example, if a manager simply matches a rival manufacturer's performance, his or her salary is roughly 5 percent lower. However, if a manager's product ranks in the industry's top 10 percent in earnings growth and return on capital, the manager's total pay can rise to nearly 30 percent beyond the industry norm.

Effective reward and incentive systems share a number of common characteristics. For example, the perception that a plan is "fair and equitable" is critically important. Similarly, the firm must have the flexibility to respond to changing requirements as its direction and objectives change. In recent years many companies have begun to place more emphasis on growth. Emerson Electric is one company that has shifted its emphasis from cost cutting to growth. To ensure that changes take hold, the management compensation formula has been changed from a largely bottom-line focus to one that emphasizes growth, new products, acquisitions, and international expansion. Discussions about profits are handled separately, and a culture of risk taking is encouraged.[26]

Exhibit 9.4 summarizes some of the attributes of effective reward and evaluation systems.

Setting Boundaries and Constraints

In an ideal world, a strong culture and effective rewards should be sufficient to ensure that all individuals and subunits work toward the common goals and objectives of the whole organization.[27] In practice, however, this is not usually the case. Counterproductive behavior can arise because of motivated self-interest, lack of a clear understanding of goals and

---

- Objectives are clear, well understood, and broadly accepted.
- Rewards are clearly linked to performance and desired behaviors.
- Performance measures are clear and highly visible.
- Feedback is prompt, clear, and unambiguous.
- The compensation "system" is perceived as fair and equitable.
- The structure is flexible; it can adapt to changing circumstances.

Exhibit 9.4

Characteristics of Effective Reward and Evaluation Systems

objectives, or outright malfeasance. Boundaries and constraints, when used properly, can serve many useful purposes for organizations, including:

- Focusing individual efforts on strategic priorities.
- Providing short-term objectives and action plans to channel efforts.
- Improving efficiency and effectiveness.
- Minimizing improper and unethical conduct.

Focusing Efforts on Strategic Priorities   Boundaries and constraints play a valuable role in focusing a company's strategic priorities. A well-known example of a strategic boundary is Jack Welch's (former CEO of General Electric) demand that any business in the corporate portfolio be ranked first or second in its industry. Similarly, Eli Lilly has reduced its research efforts to five broad areas of disease, down from eight or nine a decade ago.[28] This concentration of effort and resources provides the firm with greater strategic focus and the potential for stronger competitive advantages in the remaining areas.

Norman Augustine, Lockheed Martin's former chairman, provided four criteria for selecting candidates for diversification into "closely related" businesses.[29] They must (1) be high tech, (2) be systems-oriented, (3) deal with large customers (either corporations or government) as opposed to consumers, and (4) be in growth businesses. Augustine said, "We have found that if we can meet most of those standards, then we can move into adjacent markets and grow."

Boundaries also have a place in the nonprofit sector. For example, a British relief organization uses a system to monitor strategic boundaries by maintaining a list of companies whose contributions it will neither solicit nor accept. Such boundaries clearly go beyond simply taking the moral high road. Rather, they are essential for maintaining legitimacy with existing and potential benefactors.

Providing Short-Term Objectives and Action Plans   In Chapter 1 we discussed the importance of a firm having a vision, mission, and strategic objectives that are internally consistent and that provide strategic direction. In addition, short-term objectives and action plans provide similar benefits. That is, they represent boundaries that help to allocate resources in an optimal manner and to channel the efforts of employees at all levels throughout the organization.[30] To be effective, short-term objectives must have several attributes. They should:

- Be specific and measurable.
- Include a specific time horizon for their attainment.
- Be achievable, yet challenging enough to motivate managers who must strive to accomplish them.

Research has found that performance is enhanced when individuals are encouraged to attain specific, difficult, yet achievable, goals (as opposed to vague "do your best" goals).[31]

Short-term objectives must provide proper direction and at the same time provide enough flexibility for the firm to keep pace with and anticipate changes in the external environment. Such changes might include new government regulations, a competitor introducing a substitute product, or changes in consumer taste. Additionally, unexpected events within a firm may require a firm to make important adjustments in both strategic and short-term objectives. For example, the emergence of new industries can have a drastic effect on the demand for products and services in more traditional industries.

Along with short-term objectives, action plans are critical to the implementation of chosen strategies. Unless action plans are specific, there may be little assurance that managers have thought through all of the resource requirements for implementing their strategies. In addition, unless plans are specific, managers may not understand what needs to be implemented or have a clear time frame for completion. This is essential for the scheduling

Not all organizations place the same emphasis on each type of control.[39] For example, in high-technology firms engaged in basic research, members may work under high levels of autonomy. Here, an individual's performance is generally quite difficult to measure accurately because of the long lead times involved in research and development activities. Thus, internalized norms and values become very important.

When the measurement of an individual's output or performance is quite straightforward, control depends primarily on granting or withholding rewards. Frequently, a sales manager's compensation is in the form of a commission and bonus tied directly to his or her sales volume, which is relatively easy to determine. Here, behavior is influenced more strongly by the attractiveness of the compensation than by the norms and values implicit in the organization's culture. Furthermore, the measurability of output precludes the need for an elaborate system of rules to control behavior.

Control in bureaucratic organizations is dependent on members following a highly formalized set of rules and regulations. In such situations, most activities are routine and the desired behavior can be specified in a detailed manner because there is generally little need for innovative or creative activity. For example, managing an assembly plant requires strict adherence to many rules as well as exacting sequences of assembly operations. In the public sector, the Department of Motor Vehicles in most states must follow clearly prescribed procedures when issuing or renewing driver licenses.

Exhibit 9.6 provides alternate approaches to behavioral control and some of the situational factors associated with them.

Evolving from Boundaries to Rewards and Culture

In most environments, organizations should strive to provide a system of rewards and incentives, coupled with a culture strong enough that boundaries become internalized. This reduces the need for external controls such as rules and regulations. We suggest several ways to move in this direction.

First, hire the right people—individuals who already identify with the organization's dominant values and have attributes consistent with them. We addressed this issue in detail in Chapter 4; recall the "Bozo Filter" developed by Cooper Software. Microsoft's David Pritchard is well aware of the consequences of failing to hire properly.

> If I hire a bunch of bozos, it will hurt us, because it takes time to get rid of them. They start infiltrating the organization and then they themselves start hiring people of lower quality. At Microsoft, we are always looking for people who are better than we are.

Approach	Some Situational Factors
Culture: A system of unwritten rules that forms an internalized influence over behavior.	• Often found in professional organizations. • Associated with high autonomy. • Norms are the basis for behavior.
Rules: Written and explicit guidelines that provide external constraints on behavior.	• Associated with standardized output. • Tasks are generally repetitive and routine. • Little need for innovation or creative activity.
Rewards: The use of performance-based incentive systems to motivate.	• Measurement of output and performance is rather straightforward. • Most appropriate in organizations pursuing unrelated diversification strategies. • Rewards may be used to reinforce other means of control.

Exhibit 9.6

Organizational Control: Alternative Approaches

Second, training plays a key role. For example, in elite military units such as the Green Berets and Navy SEALs, the training regimen so thoroughly internalizes the culture that individuals, in effect, lose their identity. The group becomes the overriding concern and focal point of their energies. At firms such as FedEx, training not only builds skills, but also plays a significant role in building a strong culture on the foundation of each organization's dominant values.

Third, managerial role models are vital. Andy Grove at Intel doesn't need (or want) a large number of bureaucratic rules to determine who is responsible for what, who is supposed to talk to whom, and who gets to fly first class (no one does). He encourages openness by not having many of the trappings of success—he works in a cubicle like all the other professionals. Can you imagine any new manager asking whether or not he can fly first class? Grove's personal example eliminates such a need.

Fourth, reward systems must be clearly aligned with the organizational goals and objectives. Where do you think rules and regulations are more important in controlling behavior—Home Depot, with its generous bonus and stock option plan, or Wal-Mart, which does not provide the same level of rewards and incentives?

The Role of Corporate Governance

>LO5

The three key participants in corporate governance: shareholders, management (led by the CEO), and the board of directors.

We have addressed how management can exercise strategic control over the firm's overall operations through the use of informational and behavioral controls. Now we address the issue of strategic control in a broader perspective, typically referred to as "corporate governance." Here we focus on the need for both shareholders (the owners of the corporation) and their elected representatives, the board of directors, to actively ensure that management fulfills its overriding purpose of increasing long-term shareholder value.

Robert Monks and Nell Minow, two leading scholars in **corporate governance,** define it as "the relationship among various participants in determining the direction and performance of corporations. The primary participants are (1) the shareholders, (2) the management (led by the chief executive officer), and (3) the board of directors."* Consistent with Monks and Minow's definition, our discussion will center on how corporations can succeed (or fail) in aligning managerial motives with the interests of the shareholders and their elected representatives, the board of directors. As you will recall from Chapter 1, we discussed the important role of boards of directors and provided some examples of effective and ineffective boards.[40]

corporate governance the relationship among various participants in determining the direction and performance of corporations. The primary participants are (1) the shareholders, (2) the management, and (3) the board of directors.

There is little doubt that effective corporate governance can affect a firm's bottom line. Good corporate governance plays an important role in the investment decisions of major institutions, and a premium is often reflected in the price of securities of companies that practice it. The corporate governance premium is larger for firms in countries with sound corporate governance practices compared to countries with weaker corporate governance standards.[41] In addition, there is a strong correlation between strong corporate governance and superior financial performance. Strategy Spotlight 9.4 briefly summarizes two studies that provide support for this contention.

As indicated in our discussion above and in Strategy Spotlight 9.4, there is solid evidence linking good corporate governance with higher performance. At the same time, few topics in the business press are generating as much interest (and disdain!) as corporate governance.

---

* Management, of course, cannot ignore the demands of other important firm stakeholders such as creditors, suppliers, customers, employees, and government regulators. At times of financial duress, powerful creditors can exert strong and legitimate pressures on managerial decisions. In general, however, the attention to stakeholders other than the owners of the corporation must be addressed in a manner that is still consistent with maximizing long-term shareholder returns. For a seminal discussion on stakeholder management, refer to Freeman, R. E. 1984. *Strategic management: A stakeholder approach.* Boston: Pitman.

Good Corporate Governance and Performance: Research Evidence

Two studies found a positive relationship between the extent to which a firm practices good corporate governance and its performance outcomes. The results of these studies are summarized below.

1. *A strong correlation between corporate governance and price performance of large companies.* Over a recent three-year period, the average return of large capitalized firms with the best governance practices was more than five times higher than the performance of firms in the bottom corporate governance quartile.

2. *Across emerging markets.* In 10 of the 11 Asian and Latin American markets, companies in the top corporate governance quartile for their respective regions had a significantly higher (averaging 10 percentage points) return on capital employed (ROCE) than their market sample. In 12 of the emerging markets analyzed, companies in the lowest corporate governance quartile had a lower ROCE than the market average.

Sources: Gill, A. 2001. Credit Lyonnais Securities (Asia). *Corporate governance in emerging markets: Saints and sinners,* April; and Low, C. K. 2002. *Corporate governance: An Asia-Pacific critique.* Hong Kong: Sweet & Maxwell Asia.

Some recent notable examples of flawed corporate governance include:[42]

- Hewlett-Packard admitted that outside investigators, led by Chairman Patricia Dunn, used a potentially illegal tactic in which they impersonated directors, journalists, and two employees to obtain personal phone records. Dunn resigned as Chairman (September 12, 2006).

- Walter Forbes, former Chairman of Cendant Corp., a travel and real estate company (now known as Avis Budget Group, Inc.), was sentenced to 12 years in prison and ordered to pay $3.3 billion in one of America's biggest accounting scandals. Prosecutors said he oversaw a decade-long accounting scheme that overstated income. He was convicted on one count of conspiracy and two counts of false reporting (January 17, 2006).

- Board members of Nortel Networks meet with governance-minded investors to discuss possible changes to the board. This is after 10 executives and accounting officials are fired for artificially boosting the company's 2003 financial results (September 30, 2004).

- The Chairman of Boeing Company, Philip M. Condit, presides over a series of manipulations in accounting, acquisitions, and strategy. He conceals a $2.6 billion cost overrun from shareholders for months while his merger with McDonnell Douglas Corporation is completed, and as a result, he is forced to resign by the board (December 15, 2003).

- Royal Ahoud NV (owner of Stop and Shop), the world's third largest supermarket operator, fires its CEO and CFO for inappropriate accounting for discounts from suppliers. The company also reduces earnings for the prior two years by $500 million (February 25, 2003).

Clearly, because of the many lapses in corporate governance, we can see the benefits associated with effective practices. However, corporate managers may behave in their own self-interest, often to the detriment of shareholders. Next we address the implications of the separation of ownership and management in the modern corporation, and some mechanisms that can be used to ensure consistency (or alignment) between the interests of shareholders and those of the managers to minimize potential conflicts.

The Modern Corporation: The Separation of Owners (Shareholders) and Management

Some of the proposed definitions for a *corporation* include:

- "The business corporation is an instrument through which capital is assembled for the activities of producing and distributing goods and services and making investments. Accordingly, a basic premise of corporation law is that a business corporation should have as its objective the conduct of such activities with a view to enhancing the corporation's profit and the gains of the corporation's owners, that is, the shareholders." (Melvin Aron Eisenberg, *The Structure of Corporation Law*)
- "A body of persons granted a charter legally recognizing them as a separate entity having its own rights, privileges, and liabilities distinct from those of its members." (*American Heritage Dictionary*)
- "An ingenious device for obtaining individual profit without individual responsibility." (Ambrose Bierce, *The Devil's Dictionary*)[43]

All of these definitions have some validity and each one (including that from *The Devil's Dictionary!*) reflects a key feature of the corporate form of business organization—its ability to draw resources from a variety of groups and establish and maintain its own persona that is separate from all of them. As Henry Ford once said, "A great business is really too big to be human."

> **corporation** a mechanism created to allow different parties to contribute capital, expertise, and labor for the maximum benefit of each party.

Simply put, a **corporation** is a mechanism created to allow different parties to contribute capital, expertise, and labor for the maximum benefit of each party. The shareholders (investors) are able to participate in the profits of the enterprise without taking direct responsibility for the operations. The management can run the company without the responsibility of personally providing the funds. And, in order to make both of these possible, the shareholders have limited liability as well as rather limited involvement in the company's affairs. However, they reserve the right to elect directors who have the fiduciary obligation to protect their interests.

Over 70 years ago, Columbia University professors Adolf Berle and Gardiner C. Means addressed the divergence of the interests of the owners of the corporation from the professional managers who are hired to run it. They warned that widely dispersed ownership "released management from the overriding requirement that it serve stockholders." The separation of ownership from management has given rise to a set of ideas called "agency theory." Central to agency theory is the relationship between two primary players—the *principals* who are the owners of the firm (stockholders) and the *agents,* who are the people paid by principals to perform a job on their behalf (management). The stockholders elect and are represented by a board of directors that has a fiduciary responsibility to ensure that management acts in the best interests of stockholders to ensure long-term financial returns for the firm.

> **agency theory** a theory of the relationship between principals and their agents, with emphasis on two problems: (1) the conflicting goals of principals and agents, along with the difficulty of principals to monitor the agents, and (2) the different attitudes and preferences towards risk of principals and agents.

Agency theory is concerned with resolving two problems that can occur in agency relationships.[44] *The first is the agency problem that arises (1) when the goals of the principals and agents conflict, and (2) when it is difficult or expensive for the principal to verify what the agent is actually doing.* In a corporation, this means that the board of directors would be unable to confirm that the managers were actually acting in the shareholders' interests because, in most cases, managers are "insiders" with regard to the businesses they operate and thus are better informed than the principals. Thus, managers may act "opportunistically" in pursuing their own interests—to the detriment of the corporation.[45] Managers may, for example, spend corporate funds on expensive perquisites (e.g., company jets and expensive art), devote time and resources to pet projects (initiatives in which they have a personal interest but that have limited market potential), engage in power struggles (where they may fight over resources for their own betterment and to the detriment of the firm), and negate (or sabotage) attractive merger offers because they may result in increased employment risk.[46]

Crony Capitalism: Several Examples

When President George W. Bush signed the Sarbanes-Oxley Act into law on July 30, 2002, one of its goals was to prevent the kind of self-dealing and other conflicts of interest that had brought down Enron, WorldCom, Adelphia, and other corporate giants. Among other things, the Sarbanes-Oxley Act bans company loans to executives and prohibits extending the terms of existing loans.

Many companies, however, acted quickly *before* the bill was signed. For example, *one day* before the bill was signed, Crescent Real Estate Equities of Fort Worth, Texas, extended the payback deadline by 10 years on a loan of $26 million to its chief executive, John Goff. And Electronic Arts gave a $4 million loan to Warren Johnson, its chief financial officer, admitting in a filing that it was doing so a month prior to the "prohibition on loans to executive officers."

Despite legislation such as Sarbanes-Oxley and pressures from shareholders, related-party deals are quite common. According to the Corporate Library, a research group in Portland, Maine, 75 percent of 2,000 companies that were studied still engage in them. In essence, that means that companies must make embarrassing disclosures in their proxy statements about nepotism, property leased from top managers, corporate-owned apartments, and other forms of "insiderism."

Consider some examples:

- Two hundred companies have leased or bought airplanes from insiders. For example, Pilgrim's Pride of Pittsburgh, Texas, a chicken processor with $2.6 billion in annual sales has leased an airplane from its chief executive and founder Lonnie Pilgrim since 1985. Mr. Pilgrim made $656,000 in fiscal 2003 from this deal to go along with his $1.7 million in compensation. The company defends the pact as cost-efficient since its headquarters is located in a small town. Pilgrim also provides some bookkeeping services for his personal businesses, but he won't provide details.

- Micky M. Arison is chief executive of Carnival, the big cruise line. He is also chief executive and owner of the Miami Heat of the National Basketball Association. Carnival paid the Heat $675,000 in fiscal 2002 and 2003 for sponsorship and advertising as well as season tickets. Although that may be a rather small sum, given Carnival's $2.2 billion in net income for the period, we could still ask if the money would have been spent on something else if Arison didn't own the team.

- Alliance Semiconductor CEO N. Damodar Reddy has committed $20 million to Solar Ventures, a venture capital company run by his brother C. N. Reddy. Other unnamed insiders purchased undisclosed stakes in Solar. However, Alliance won't disclose whether its CEO is one of them. To date it has invested $12.5 million in Solar. Beth Young, senior research associate of the Corporate Library poses an interesting question: "Is Reddy using shareholder capital just to keep afloat his brother's fund and the insiders' investment?"

Source: MacDonald, E. 2004. Crony capitalism. *Forbes*, June 21: 140–146.

The second issue is the problem of risk sharing. This arises when the principal and the agent have different attitudes and preferences toward risk. For example, the executives in a firm may favor additional diversification initiatives because, by their very nature, they increase the size of the firm and thus the level of executive compensation. At the same time, such diversification initiatives may erode shareholder value because they fail to achieve some of the synergies that we discussed in Chapter 6 (e.g., building on core competencies, sharing activities, or enhancing market power). In effect, agents (executives) may have a stronger preference toward diversification than shareholders because it reduces their personal level of risk from potential loss of employment. In contrast, research has shown that executives who have large holdings of stock in their firms were more likely to have diversification strategies that were more consistent with shareholder interests—that is, increasing long-term returns.[47]

At times, top-level managers engage in actions that reflect their self-interest rather than the interests of shareholders. Some examples of such conflicts of interest are addressed in Strategy Spotlight 9.5.

Governance Mechanisms: Aligning the Interests of Owners and Managers

>LO6

The role of corporate governance mechanisms in ensuring that the interests of managers are aligned with those of shareholders from both the United States and international perspectives.

As noted above, a key characteristic of the modern corporation is the separation of ownership from control. To minimize the potential for managers to act in their own self-interest, or "opportunistically," the owners can implement some governance mechanisms.[48] We address three of these in the next sections. First, there are two primary means of monitoring the behavior of managers. These include (1) a committed and involved *board of directors* that acts in the best interests of the shareholders to create long-term value and (2) *shareholder activism,* wherein the owners view themselves as share*owners* instead of share*holders* and become actively engaged in the governance of the corporation. As we will see later in this section, shareholder activism has increased dramatically in recent years. Finally, there are managerial incentives, sometimes called "contract-based outcomes," which consist of *reward and compensation agreements.* Here the goal is to carefully craft managerial incentive packages to align the interests of management with those of the stockholders.

board of directors a group that has a fiduciary duty to ensure that the company is run consistently with the long-term interests of the owners, or shareholders, of a corporation and that acts as an intermediary between the shareholders and management.

A Committed and Involved Board of Directors   The **board of directors** acts as a fulcrum between the owners and controllers of a corporation. In effect, they are the intermediaries who provide a balance between a small group of key managers in the firm based at the corporate headquarters and a sometimes vast group of shareholders. In the United States, the law imposes on the board a strict and absolute fiduciary duty to ensure that a company is run consistent with the long-term interests of the owners—the shareholders. The reality, as we have seen, is somewhat more ambiguous.[49]

The Business Roundtable, representing the largest U.S. corporations, describes the duties of the board as follows:

1.   Select, regularly evaluate, and, if necessary, replace the chief executive officer. Determine management compensation. Review succession planning.
2.   Review and, where appropriate, approve the financial objectives, major strategies, and plans of the corporation.
3.   Provide advice and counsel to top management.
4.   Select and recommend to shareholders for election an appropriate slate of candidates for the board of directors; evaluate board processes and performance.
5.   Review the adequacy of the systems to comply with all applicable laws/regulations.[50]

Given these principles, what makes for a good board of directors? According to the Business Roundtable, the most important quality is a board of directors who are active, critical participants in determining a company's strategies.[51] That does not mean board members should micromanage or circumvent the CEO. Rather, they should provide strong oversight going beyond simply approving the CEO's plans. A board's primary responsibilities are to ensure that strategic plans undergo rigorous scrutiny, evaluate managers against high performance standards, and take control of the succession process.

Although boards in the past were often dismissed as CEO's rubber stamps, increasingly they are playing a more active role by forcing out CEOs who cannot deliver on performance. According to a recent study by the consulting firm Booz Allen Hamilton, the rate of CEO departures for performance reasons has more than tripled, from 1.3 percent to 4.2 percent, between 1995 and 2002.[52] And the trend has continued. In 2006, turnover among CEOs increased 30 percent over the previous year.[53] Well-known CEOs like Gerald M. Levin of AOL Time Warner and Jack M. Greenberg of McDonald's paid the price for poor financial performance by being forced to leave. Others, such as Bernard Ebbers of WorldCom, Inc., and Dennis Kozlowski of Tyco International, lost their jobs due to scandals. "Deliver or depart" is clearly the new message from the boards.

Another key component of top-ranked boards is director independence.[54] Governance experts believe that a majority of directors should be free of all ties to either the CEO or the company. That means a minimum of "insiders" (past or present members of the management team) should serve on the board, and that directors and their firms should be barred from doing consulting, legal, or other work for the company.[55] Interlocking directorships—in which CEOs and other top managers serve on each other's boards—are not desirable. But perhaps the best guarantee that directors act in the best interests of shareholders is the simplest: Most good companies now insist that directors own significant stock in the company they oversee.[56]

Such guidelines are not always followed. At times, the practices of the boards of directors are the antithesis of such guidelines. Consider the Walt Disney Co. Over a recent five-year period, Michael Eisner pocketed an astonishing $531 million. He likely had very little resistance from his board of directors:

> Many investors view the Disney board as an anachronism. Among Disney's 16 directors is Eisner's personal attorney—who for several years was chairman of the company's compensation committee! There was also the architect who designed Eisner's Aspen home and his parents' apartment. Joining them are the principal of an elementary school once attended by his children and the president of a university to which Eisner donated $1 million. The board also includes the actor Sidney Poitier, seven current and former Disney executives, and an attorney who does business with Disney. Moreover, most of the outside directors own little or no Disney stock. "It is an egregiously bad board—a train wreck waiting to happen," warns Michael L. Useem, a management professor at the University of Pennsylvania's Wharton School.[57]

This example also shows that "outside directors" are only beneficial to strong corporate governance if they are vigilant in carrying out their responsibilities.[58] As humorously suggested by Warren Buffett, founder and chairman of Berkshire Hathaway: "The ratcheting up of compensation has been obscene. . . . There is a tendency to put cocker spaniels on compensation committees, not Doberman pinschers."[59]

Many firms do have exemplary board practices. Below, for example, we list some of the excellent practices at Intel Corp., the world's largest semiconductor chip manufacturer, with $35 billion in revenues:[60]

- *Mix of inside and outside directors.* The board believes that there should be a majority of independent directors on the board. However, the board is willing to have members of management, in addition to the CEO, as directors.
- *Board presentations and access to employees.* The board encourages management to schedule managers to be present at meetings who: (1) can provide additional insight into the items being discussed because of personal involvement in these areas, or (2) have future potential that management believes should be given exposure to the board.
- *Formal evaluation of officers.* The Compensation Committee conducts, and reviews with the outside directors, an annual evaluation to help determine the salary and executive bonus of all officers, including the chief executive officer.

Exhibit 9.7 provides some suggestions for how boards of directors can improve their practices.

Shareholder Activism As a practical matter, there are so many owners of the largest American corporations that it makes little sense to refer to them as "owners" in the sense of individuals becoming informed and involved in corporate affairs. However, even an individual shareholder has several rights, including (1) the right to sell the stock, (2) the right to vote the proxy (which includes the election of board members), (3) the right to bring suit for damages if the corporation's directors or managers fail to meet their obligations, (4) the right to certain information from the company, and (5) certain residual rights following the company's liquidation (or its filing for reorganization under bankruptcy laws), once creditors and other claimants are paid off.[61]

Exhibit 9.7

Best Practice Ideas: The
New Rules for Directors

Issue	Suggestion
Pay	**Know the Math**
Companies will disclose full details of CEO payouts for the first time in their 2007 SEC filings. Activist investors are already drawing up hit lists of companies where CEO paychecks are out of line with performance.	Before okaying any financial package, directors must make sure they can explain the numbers. They need to adopt the mindset of an activist investor and ask: What's the harshest criticism someone could make about this package?
Strategy	**Make It a Priority**
Boards have been so focused on compliance that duties like strategy and leadership oversight too often get ignored. Only 59 percent of directors in a recent study rated their board favorably on setting strategy	To avoid spending too much time on compliance issues, move strategy up to the beginning of the meeting. Annual one-, two- or three-day offsite meetings on strategy alone are becoming standard for good boards.
Financials	**Put in the Time**
Although 95 percent of directors in the recent study said they were doing a good job of monitoring financials, the number of earnings restatements hit a new high in 2006, after breaking records in 2004 and 2005.	Even nonfinancial board members need to monitor the numbers and keep a close eye on cash flows. Audit committee members should prepare to spend 300 hours a year on committee responsibilities.
Crisis Management	**Dig in**
Some 120 companies are under scrutiny for options backdating, and the 100 largest companies have replaced 56 CEOs in the past five years—nearly double the terminations in the prior five years.	The increased scrutiny on boards means that a perfunctory review will not suffice if a scandal strikes. Directors can no longer afford to defer to management in a crisis. They must roll up their sleeves and move into watchdog mode.

Source: Byrnes, N., & Sassen, J. 2007. Board of hard knocks. *BusinessWeek.* January 22: 36–39.

Collectively, shareholders have the power to direct the course of corporations.[62] This may involve acts such as being party to shareholder action suits and demanding that key issues be brought up for proxy votes at annual board meetings.[63] In addition, the power of shareholders has intensified in recent years because of the increasing influence of large institutional investors such as mutual funds (e.g., T. Rowe Price and Fidelity Investments) and retirement systems such as TIAA-CREF (for university faculty members and school administrative staff).[64] Institutional investors hold approximately 50 percent of all listed corporate stock in the United States.

Shareholder activism refers to actions by large shareholders, both institutions and individuals, to protect their interests when they feel that managerial actions diverge from shareholder value maximization.

Many institutional investors are aggressive in protecting and enhancing their investments. In effect, they are shifting from traders to owners. They are assuming

shareholder activism actions by large shareholders to protect their interests when they feel that managerial actions of a corporation diverge from shareholder value maximization.

the role of permanent shareholders and rigorously analyzing issues of corporate governance. In the process they are reinventing systems of corporate monitoring and accountability.[65]

Consider the proactive behavior of CalPERS, the California Public Employees' Retirement System, which manages over $200 billion in assets and is the third largest pension fund in the world. Every year CalPERS reviews the performance of U.S. companies in its stock portfolio and identifies those that are among the lowest long-term relative performers and have governance structures that do not ensure full accountability to company owners. This generates a long list of companies, each of which may potentially be publicly identified as a CalPERS "Focus Company"—corporations to which CalPERS directs specific suggested governance reforms. CalPERS meets with the directors of each of these companies to discuss performance and governance issues. The CalPERS Focus List contains those companies that continue to merit public and market attention at the end of the process.

On April 19, 2006, CalPERS released its annual Focus List, which singled out six U.S. companies for poor financial and corporate governance.[66]

Firms on the list were: *Brocade Communications* of San Jose California; *Cardinal Health* of Dublin, Ohio; *Clear Channel Communications* of San Antonio Texas; *Mellon Financial* of Pittsburgh, Pennsylvania; *OfficeMax* of Itasca, Illinois; and *Sovereign Bancorp* of Philadelphia.

A few of CalPERS's concerns:

- Clear Channel Communications, a diversified media company that owns hundreds of radio stations, has excessive executive compensation and severance agreements, and lost 42 percent in stock value over the past five years compared with a 26 percent decline for industry peers.
- OfficeMax, a U.S. provider of office supplies, technology products and solutions, and furniture, has takeover defenses that are excessive, including an 80 percent supermajority requirement to amend bylaws. It performed well below its peer group for the past five years.

While appearing punitive to company management, such aggressive activism has paid significant returns for CalPERS (and other stockholders of the "Focused" companies). For example, a Wilshire Associates study of the "CalPERS Effect" of corporate governance examined the performance of 62 targets over a five-year period. The results indicated that, while the stock of these companies trailed the Standard & Poors Index by 89 percent in the five-year period before CalPERS acted, the same stocks outperformed the index by 23 percent in the following five years, adding approximately $150 million annually in additional returns to the fund.

Perhaps no discussion of shareholder activism would be complete without mention of Carl Icahn, a famed activist with a personal net worth of about $13 billion. As he forcefully points out:

> The bogeyman I am now chasing is the structure of American corporations, which permit managements and boards to rule arbitrarily and too often receive egregious compensation even after doing a subpar job. Yet they remain accountable to no one.[67]

Managerial Rewards and Incentives   As we discussed earlier in the chapter, incentive systems must be designed to help a company achieve its goals.[68] Similarly, from the perspective of governance, one of the most critical roles of the board of directors is to create incentives that align the interests of the CEO and top executives with the interests of owners of the corporation—long-term shareholder returns.[69] After all, shareholders rely on CEOs to adopt policies and strategies that maximize the value of their shares.[70] A combination of three basic policies may create the right monetary incentives for CEOs to maximize the value of their companies:

1. Boards can require that the CEOs become substantial owners of company stock.
2. Salaries, bonuses, and stock options can be structured so as to provide rewards for superior performance and penalties for poor performance.
3. Threat of dismissal for poor performance can be a realistic outcome.

In recent years the granting of stock options has enabled top executives of publicly held corporations to earn enormous levels of compensation. In 2005, the average CEO in the Standard & Poor's 500 stock index took home 369 times the pay of the average worker—up from 28 times the average in 1970. Needless to say, the counterargument, that the ratio is down from the 514 multiple in 2000, doesn't get much traction![71] And it has been estimated that there could be as many as 50 or more companies with CEO pay packages over $150 million.[72]

Many boards have awarded huge option grants despite poor executive performance, and others have made performance goals easier to reach. In 2002 nearly 200 companies swapped or repriced options—all to enrich wealthy executives who are already among the country's richest people. However, stock options can be a valuable governance mechanism to align the CEO's interests with those of the shareholders. The extraordinarily high level of compensation can, at times, be grounded in sound governance principles.[73] For example, Howard Solomon, CEO of Forest Laboratories, received a total compensation of $148.5 million in 2001.[74] This represented $823,000 in salary, $400,000 in bonus, and $147.3 million in stock options that were exercised. However, shareholders also did well, receiving gains of 40 percent. The firm has enjoyed spectacular growth over the past five years and Solomon has been CEO since 1977. Thus, huge income is attributed largely to gains that have built up over many years. As stated by compensation committee member Dan Goldwasser, "If a CEO is delivering substantial increases in shareholder value . . . it's only appropriate that he be rewarded for it."

However, the "pay for performance" principle doesn't always hold. In addition to the granting of stock options, boards of directors are often failing to fulfill their fiduciary responsibilities to shareholders when they lower the performance targets that executives need to meet in order to receive millions of dollars. At General Motors, for example, CEO G. Richard Wagoner, Jr., and other top executives were entitled to a special performance bonus if the company's net profit margin reached five percent by the end of 2003. However, the five percent target was later lowered.

TIAA-CREF has provided several principles of corporate governance with regard to executive compensation.[75] These include the importance of aligning the rewards of all employees—rank and file as well as executives—to the long-term performance of the corporation; general guidelines on the role of cash compensation, stock, and "fringe benefits"; and the mission of a corporation's compensation committee. Exhibit 9.8 addresses TIAA-CREF's principles on the role of stock in managerial compensation.

external governance control mechanisms methods that ensure that managerial actions lead to shareholder value maximization and do not harm other stakeholder groups and that are outside the control of the corporate governance system.

External Governance Control Mechanisms

Thus far, we've discussed internal governance mechanisms. Internal controls, however, are not always enough to ensure good governance. The separation of ownership and control that we discussed earlier requires multiple control mechanisms, some internal and some external, to ensure that managerial actions lead to shareholder value maximization. Further, society-at-large wants some assurance that this goal is met without harming other stakeholder groups. Now we discuss several **external governance control mechanisms** that have developed in most modern economies. These include the market for corporate

Exhibit 9.8
TIAA-CREF's Principles on the Role of Stock in Executive Compensation

Stock-based compensation plans are a critical element of most compensation programs and can provide opportunities for managers whose efforts contribute to the creation of shareholder wealth. In evaluating the suitability of these plans, considerations of reasonableness, scale, linkage to performance, and fairness to shareholders and all employees also apply. TIAA-CREF, the largest pension system in the world, has set forth the following guidelines for stock-based compensation. Proper stock-based plans should:

- Allow for creation of executive wealth that is reasonable in view of the creation of shareholder wealth. Management should not prosper through stock while shareholders suffer.
- Have measurable and predictable outcomes that are directly linked to the company's performance.
- Be market oriented, within levels of comparability for similar positions in companies of similar size and business focus.
- Be straightforward and clearly described so that investors and employees can understand them.
- Be fully disclosed to the investing public and be approved by shareholders.

Source: www.tiaa-cref.org/pubs.

control, auditors, governmental regulatory bodies, banks and analysts, media, and public activists.

The Market for Corporate Control   Let us assume for a moment that internal control mechanisms in a company are failing. This means that the board is ineffective in monitoring managers and is not exercising the oversight required of them and that shareholders are passive and are not taking any actions to monitor or discipline managers. Under these circumstances managers may behave opportunistically.[76] Opportunistic behavior can take many forms. First, they can *shirk* their responsibilities. Shirking means that managers fail to exert themselves fully, as is required of them. Second, they can engage in *on the job consumption.* Examples of on the job consumption include private jets, club memberships, expensive artwork in the offices, and so on. Each of these represents consumption by managers that does not in any way increase shareholder value. Instead, they actually diminish shareholder value. Third, managers may engage in *excessive product-market diversification.*[77] As we discussed in Chapter 6, such diversification serves to reduce only the employment risk of the managers rather than the financial risk of the shareholders, who can more cheaply diversify their risk by owning a portfolio of investments. Is there any external mechanism to stop managers from shirking, consumption on the job, and excessive diversification?

The **market for corporate control** is one such external mechanism that provides at least some partial solution to the problems described. If internal control mechanisms fail and the management is behaving opportunistically, the likely response of most shareholders will be to sell their stock rather than engage in activism.[78] As more and more stockholders vote with their feet, the value of the stock begins to decline. As the decline continues, at some point the market value of the firm becomes less than the book value. That is, a corporate raider can take over the company for a price less than the book value of the assets of the company. The first thing that the raider may do on assuming control over the company will be to fire the underperforming management. The risk of being acquired by a hostile raider

market for corporate control
an external control mechanism in which shareholders dissatisfied with a firm's management sell their shares.

takeover constraint
the risk to management of the firm being acquired by a hostile raider.

is often referred to as the **takeover constraint.** The takeover constraint deters management from engaging in opportunistic behavior.[79]

Although in theory the takeover constraint is supposed to limit managerial opportunism, in recent years its effectiveness has become diluted as a result of a number of defense tactics adopted by incumbent management (see Chapter 6). Foremost among them are poison pills, greenmail, and golden parachutes. Poison pills are provisions adopted by the company to reduce its worth to the acquirer. An example would be payment of a huge one-time dividend, typically financed by debt. Greenmail involves buying back the stock from the acquirer, usually at an attractive premium. Golden parachutes are employment contracts that cause the company to pay lucrative severance packages to top managers fired as a result of a takeover, often running to several million dollars.

Auditors   Even when there are stringent disclosure requirements, there is no guarantee that the information disclosed will be accurate. Managers may deliberately disclose false information or withhold negative financial information as well as use accounting methods that distort results based on highly subjective interpretations. Therefore, all accounting statements are required to be audited and certified to be accurate by external auditors. These auditing firms are independent organizations staffed by certified professionals who verify the firm's books of accounts. Audits can unearth financial irregularities and ensure that financial reporting by the firm conforms to standard accounting practices.

Recent developments leading to the bankruptcy of firms such as Enron and WorldCom and a spate of earnings restatements raise questions about the failure of the auditing firms to act as effective external control mechanisms. Why did an auditing firm like Arthur Andersen, with decades of good reputation in the auditing profession at stake, fail to raise red flags about accounting irregularities? First, auditors are appointed by the firm being audited. The desire to continue that business relationship sometimes makes them overlook financial irregularities. Second, most auditing firms also do consulting work and often have lucrative consulting contracts with the firms that they audit. Understandably, some of them tend not to ask too many difficult questions, because they fear jeopardizing the consulting business, which is often more profitable than the auditing work.

The recent restatement of earnings by Xerox is an example of the lack of independence of auditing firms. The SEC filed a lawsuit against KPMG, the world's third largest accounting firm, in January 2003 for allowing Xerox to inflate its revenues by $3 billion between 1997 and 2000. Of the $82 million that Xerox paid KPMG during those four years, only $26 million was for auditing. The rest was for consulting services. When one of the auditors objected to Xerox's practice of booking revenues for equipment leases earlier than it should have, Xerox asked KPMG to replace him. It did.[80]

Banks and Analysts   Commercial and investment banks have lent money to corporations and therefore have to ensure that the borrowing firm's finances are in order and that the loan covenants are being followed. Stock analysts conduct ongoing in-depth studies of the firms that they follow and make recommendations to their clients to buy, hold, or sell. Their rewards and reputation depend on the quality of these recommendations. Their access to information, knowledge of the industry and the firm, and the insights they gain from interactions with the management of the company enable them to alert the investing community of both positive and negative developments relating to a company.

It is generally observed that analyst recommendations are often more optimistic than warranted by facts. "Sell" recommendations tend to be exceptions rather than the norm. Many analysts seem to have failed to grasp the gravity of the problems surrounding failed companies such as Enron and Global Crossing till the very end. Part of the explanation may lie in the fact that most analysts work for firms that also have investment banking relationships with the companies they follow. Negative recommendations by analysts can displease the management, who may decide to take their investment banking business to a rival firm. Thus, otherwise independent and competent analysts may be pressured to overlook negative information or tone down their criticism. A recent settlement between the Securities and Exchange Commission and the New York State Attorney General with 10 banks requires them to pay $1.4 billion in penalties and to fund independent research for investors.[81]

Regulatory Bodies   All corporations are subject to some regulation by the government. The extent of regulation is often a function of the type of industry. Banks, utilities, and pharmaceuticals, for example, are subject to more regulatory oversight because of their importance to society. Public corporations are subject to more regulatory requirements than private corporations.

All public corporations are required to disclose a substantial amount of financial information by bodies such as the Securities and Exchange Commission. These include quarterly and annual filings of financial performance, stock trading by insiders, and details of executive compensation packages. There are two primary reasons behind such requirements. First, markets can operate efficiently only when the investing public has faith in the market system. In the absence of disclosure requirements, the average investor suffers from a lack of reliable information and therefore may completely stay away from the capital market. This will negatively impact an economy's ability to grow. Second, disclosure of information such as insider trading protects the small investor to some extent from the negative consequences of information asymmetry. That is, the insiders and large investors typically have more information than the small investor and can therefore use that information to buy or sell before the information becomes public knowledge.

The failure of a variety of external control mechanisms led the U.S. Congress to pass the Sarbanes-Oxley Act in 2002. This act calls for many stringent measures that would ensure better governance of U.S. corporations. Some of these measures include:[82]

- *Auditors* are barred from certain types of nonaudit work. They are not allowed to destroy records for five years. Lead partners auditing a client should be changed at least every five years.
- *CEOs* and *CFOs* must fully reveal off-balance-sheet finances and vouch for the accuracy of the information revealed.
- *Executives* must promptly reveal the sale of shares in firms they manage and are not allowed to sell when other employees cannot.
- *Corporate lawyers* must report to senior managers any violations of securities law lower down.

Strategy Spotlight 9.6 discusses some of the expenses that companies have incurred in complying with the Sarbanes-Oxley Act. There has been much debate as to whether the costs outweigh some of the benefits.

Media and Public Activists   The press is not usually recognized as an external control mechanism in the literature on corporate governance. There is, however, no denying that in all developed capitalist economies, the financial press and media play an important indirect role in monitoring the management of public corporations. In the United States, business magazines such as *BusinessWeek* and *Fortune,* financial newspapers such as *The Wall Street Journal* and *Investors Business Daily,* as well as television networks like Financial News Network and CNBC are constantly reporting on companies. Public perceptions about a company's financial prospects and the quality of its management are greatly influenced by the media. For example, Food Lion's reputation was sullied when ABC's *Prime Time Live*

Governance Reform: The Costs Add Up

In the aftermath of Enron and Worldcom and a spate of corporate scandals early in the decade, the U.S. Congress passed the Sarbanes-Oxley Act in 2002. It was an effort to restore investor confidence in the governance of corporations in general and financial reporting in particular. Three years later, a backlash seems to be developing among executives about the high compliance costs and some of the more draconian requirements.

The major source of resentment is the issue of cost. It is estimated that large corporations with revenues over $4 billion have to spend an average of $35 million a year to implement Sarbanes-Oxley. Medium-sized companies spend $3.1 million a year on average. Smaller companies find the cost of compliance particularly burdensome because they have a smaller revenue base. Some critics go to the extent of arguing that this amounts to a form of regressive taxation against small businesses. Many are even considering delisting to avoid compliance costs.

Costs are not the only problem that companies face. Meeting the requirements of Sarbanes-Oxley is very time consuming as well. For example, the law requires that financial numbers such as value of inventory and receivables are cross-checked. But it requires an army of additional people and significant additional costs to ensure this. Yellow Roadway Corporation, the nation's largest trucking firm, had to use 200 employees and $9 million to accomplish this in 2004. This was three percent of their total profits. And just think of the lost productivity!

Nasdaq officials say the Sarbanes-Oxley burden is heaviest on the smallest companies, and firms with less than $100 million in revenues make up half of Nasdaq's 3,000 listings. The regulatory costs average two percent of revenue at firms with revenue under $100 million, while they are only 0.1 percent for the biggest companies. Theodore Stebbins, chairman of investment banking at Canaccord Adams says, "Clearly, the low end of the Nasdaq is broken. We can no longer in good conscience recommend to our small clients that they go public on Nasdaq."

How much has Sarbanes-Oxley succeeded in improving governance and ensuring the accuracy and reliability of financial reporting? While it is too early to assess the impact, there is at least some anecdotal evidence that it is having some impact. Visteon Corp., an auto-parts supplier, reported that they uncovered problems with their accounts receivable while complying with the requirements of the act. Similarly, SunTrust Banks Inc. fired three officers after discovering errors in the calculation of loan allowances in their portfolios. Tough but fair regulations can improve governance, but the costs of compliance cannot be ignored.

Source: Brown, E. 2006. London calling. *Forbes,* May 8: 51–52; and Henry, D. 2005. Death, taxes & Sarbanes-Oxley? *BusinessWeek,* January 17: 28–31.

---

in 1992 charged the company with employee exploitation, false package dating, and unsanitary meat handling practices. Bethany McLean of *Fortune* magazine is often credited as the first to raise questions about Enron's long-term financial viability.[83]

Similarly, consumer groups and activist individuals often take a crusading role in exposing corporate malfeasance. Well-known examples include Ralph Nader and Erin Brockovich, who played important roles in bringing to light the safety issues related to GM's Corvair and environmental pollution issues concerning Pacific Gas and Electric Company, respectively. Ralph Nader has created over 30 watchdog groups including:[84]

- *Aviation Consumer Action Project.* Works to propose new rules to prevent flight delays, impose penalties for deceiving passengers about problems, and push for higher compensation for lost luggage.
- *Center for Auto Safety.* Helps consumers find plaintiff lawyers and agitate for vehicle recalls, increased highway safety standards, and lemon laws.
- *Center for Study of Responsive Law.* This is Nader's headquarters. Home of a consumer project on technology, this group sponsored seminars on Microsoft remedies and pushed for tougher Internet privacy rules. It also took on the drug industry over costs.

- **Pension Rights Center.** This center helped employees of IBM, General Electric, and other companies to organize themselves against cash-balance pension plans.

Corporate Governance: An International Perspective

As we have noted in this chapter (and in Chapter 1), the topic of corporate governance has long been dominated by agency theory and based on the explicit assumption of the separation of ownership and control.[85] The central conflicts are principal–agent conflicts between shareholders and management. However, such an underlying assumption seldom applies outside of the United States and the United Kingdom. This is particularly true in emerging economies and continental Europe. Here, there is often concentrated ownership, along with extensive family ownership and control, business group structures, and weak legal protection for minority shareholders. Thus, serious conflicts tend to exist between two classes of principals: controlling shareholders and minority shareholders. Such conflicts can be called **principal–principal (PP) conflicts** as opposed to *principal–agent* conflicts. Exhibits 9.9 and 9.10 address how principal–principal conflicts and principal–agent conflicts differ.

Strong family control is one of the leading indicators of concentrated ownership. For example, in East Asia (excluding China), approximately 57 percent of the corporations have board chairmen and CEOs from the controlling families. In continental Europe, this number is 68 percent. A very common practice is the appointment of family members as board chairman, CEOs, and other top executives. This happens because the families are controlling (not necessarily majority) shareholders. For example, in 2003, 30-year-old James Murdoch was appointed CEO of British Sky Broadcasting (BSkyB), Europe's largest satellite broadcaster. There was very vocal resistance by minority shareholders. Why was he appointed in the first place? James's father just happened to be Rupert Murdoch, who controlled 35 percent of BSkyB and chaired the board. Clearly, this is a case of a principal–principal conflict.

In general, three conditions must be met for PP conflicts to occur. There must be:

- A dominant owner or group of owners who have interests that are distinct from minority shareholders.
- Motivation for the controlling shareholders to exercise their dominant positions to their advantage.
- Few formal (such as legislation or regulatory bodies) or informal constraints that would discourage or prevent the controlling shareholders from exploiting their advantageous positions.

principal–principal conflicts conflicts between two classes of principals—controlling shareholders and minority shareholders—within the context of a corporate governance system.

● In Hong Kong, strong family control is characteristic of many corporations. At times, this has led to principal–principal (PP) conflicts. Above is Hong Kong's spectacular skyline, as seen from Victoria Point.

The result is often that family managers, who represent (or actually are) the controlling shareholders, engage in *expropriation* of minority shareholders, which is defined as activities that enrich the controlling shareholders at the expense of minority shareholders. What is their motive? After all, controlling shareholders have incentives to maintain firm value. But controlling shareholders may take actions that decrease aggregate firm performance if their personal gains from expropriation exceed their personal losses from their firm's lowered performance.

	Principal–Agent Conflicts	Principal–Principal Conflicts
Goal Incongruence	Between shareholders and professional managers who own a relatively small portion of the firm's equity.	Between controlling shareholders and minority shareholders.
Ownership Pattern	Dispersed—5%–20% is considered "concentrated ownership."	Concentrated—Often greater than 50% of equity is controlled by controlling shareholders.
Manifestations	Strategies that benefit entrenched managers at the expense of shareholders in general (e.g., shirking, pet projects, excessive compensation, and empire building).	Strategies that benefit controlling shareholders at the expense of minority shareholders (e.g., minority shareholder expropriation, nepotism, and cronyism).
Institutional Protection of Minority Shareholders	Formal constraints (e.g., judicial reviews and courts) set an upper boundary on potential expropriation by majority shareholders. Informal norms generally adhere to shareholder wealth maximization.	Formal institutional protection is often lacking, corrupted, or un-enforced. Informal norms are typically in favor of the interests of controlling shareholders ahead of those of minority investors.

Source: Adapted from Young, M., Peng, M. W., Ahlstrom, D., & Bruton, G. 2002. Governing the corporation in emerging economies: A principal–principal perspective. *Academy of Management Best Papers Proceedings,* Denver.

Exhibit 9.9 Traditional Principal–Agent Conflicts versus Principal–Principal Conflicts: How they Differ Along Dimensions

Exhibit 9.10 Principal–Agent Conflicts and Principal–Principal Conflicts: A Diagram

Source: Young, M. N., Peng, M. W., Ahlstrom, D., Bruton, G. D., Jiang, Y. forthcoming. Principal–principal conflicts in corporate governance (*Journal of Management Studies*); and Peng, M. V. 2006. *Global strategy.* Cincinnati: Thomson South-Western. We are very appreciative of the helpful comments of Mike Young of Hong Kong Baptist University and Mike Peng of the University of Texas at Dallas.

strategy spotlight

Effective and Ineffective Corporate Governance in Hong Kong

Finding examples of exemplary corporate governance in Hong Kong isn't easy due to the high incidence of family-controlled corporations and the lack of laws to protect minority shareholders. An exception is CLP, one of the largest electric utilities in Asia, which is 35 percent controlled by Chairman Michael Kadoorie and his family. Admirers say it is an example of how even a family-controlled company can move toward more transparency. The company's board has several independent directors, and its Web site gives comprehensive information on its corporate governance policy. Kadoorie says family shareholders are treated the same as others.

At the other end of the continuum is Henderson Land Development. The company is controlled by Lee Shau Kee, one of Hong Kong's wealthiest tycoons. In its latest corporate-governance snafu, Henderson attempted to buy 73 percent of its publicly listed subsidiary, Henderson Investment, for 30 percent below its reported net asset value. However, the related transaction was thwarted by minority shareholders, including the powerful Templeton Asset Management. At the time, Henderson Land Vice-Chairman Colin Lam insisted the dissenting investors had placed "a very, very high valuation on Henderson Investment," implying that this placed too high a value on its shares. Needless to say, the minority shareholders would hardly agree. However, it was perfectly legal in Hong Kong, and had it gone through, the minority shareholders would have been left holding the bag.

Had the Henderson Investment deal occurred in the United States, a shareholder lawsuit would have been launched. In Hong Kong, however, class-action lawsuits are not allowed. Consider the sentiment of Andrew Sheng, head of the Hong Kong Securities & Futures Commission, in the face of an action by another company taking advantage of minority shareholders: if the investors didn't like what was happening, they could simply sell their shares. Such a "buyer beware" attitude, even by regulatory bodies in one of the most developed emerging economies, causes firms to trade at a discount compared to firms in more mature economies.

Sources: Balfour, F., & Tashiro, H. 2004. A change in attitude. *BusinessWeek,* May 17: 48–50; Clifford, M. 2002. China Journal: Hong Kong's cautionary Christmas carol. *BusinessWeek* Online, August; and Young, M. N., Peng, M. W., Ahlstrom, D., Bruton, G. D., & Jiang, Y. forthcoming. Principal–principal conflicts in corporate governance. *Journal of Management Studies.*

Another ubiquitous feature of corporate life outside of the United States and Great Britain are *business groups* such as the keiretsus of Japan and the chaebols of South Korea. This is particularly dominant in emerging economies. A **business group** is "a set of firms that, though legally independent, are bound together by a constellation of formal and informal ties and are accustomed to taking coordinated action."[86] Business groups are especially common in emerging economies, and they are different from other organizational forms in that the groups are communities of firms without clear boundaries.

Business groups have many advantages that can enhance the value of a firm. For example, they often facilitate technology transfer or intergroup capital allocation that otherwise might be impossible because of inadequate institutional infrastructure such as excellent financial services firms. On the other hand, informal ties—such as cross-holdings, board interlocks, and coordinated actions—can often result in intragroup activities and transactions, often at very favorable terms to member firms. For example, expropriation can be legally done through *related transactions,* which can occur when controlling owners sell firm assets to another firm they own at below market prices or spin off the most profitable part of a public firm and merge it with another of their private firms.

Strategy Spotlight 9.7 provides examples from Hong Kong of effective corporate governance. It also shows how a firm attempted a related transaction that would have benefited controlling shareholders at the expense of minority shareholders.

business groups a set of firms that, though legally independent, are bound together by a constellation of formal and informal ties and are accustomed to taking coordinated action.

Reflecting on Career Implications . . .

- **Behavioral Control:** What sources of behavioral control does your organization employ? In general, too much emphasis on rules and regulations may stifle initiative and be detrimental to your career opportunities.
- **Rewards and Incentives:** Are your organization's reward structure fair and equitable? Does it effectively reward outstanding performance? If not, there may be a long-term erosion of morale which may have long-term adverse career implications for you.
- **Culture:** Consider the type of organization culture that would provide the best work environment for your career goals. How does your organization's culture deviate from this concept? Does your organization have a strong and effective culture? If so, professionals are more likely to develop strong "firm specific" ties, which further enhances collaboration.
- **Corporate Governance:** Does your organization practice effective corporate governance? Such practices will enhance a firm's culture and it will be easier to attract top talent. Operating within governance guidelines is usually a strong indicator of organizational citizenship which, in turn, should be good for your career prospects.

Summary

For firms to be successful, they must practice effective strategic control and corporate governance. Without such controls, the firm will not be able to achieve competitive advantages and outperform rivals in the marketplace.

We began the chapter with the key role of informational control. We contrasted two types of control systems: what we termed "traditional" and "contemporary" information control systems. Whereas traditional control systems may have their place in placid, simple competitive environments, there are fewer of those in today's economy. Instead, we advocated the contemporary approach wherein the internal and external environment are constantly monitored so that when surprises emerge, the firm can modify its strategies, goals, and objectives.

Behavioral controls are also a vital part of effective control systems. We argued that firms must develop the proper balance between culture, rewards and incentives, and boundaries and constraints. Where there are strong and positive cultures and rewards, employees tend to internalize the organization's strategies and objectives. This permits a firm to spend fewer resources on monitoring behavior, and assures the firm that the efforts and initiatives of employees are more consistent with the overall objectives of the organization.

In the final section of this chapter, we addressed corporate governance, which can be defined as the relationship between various participants in determining the direction and performance of the corporation. The primary participants include shareholders, management (led by the chief executive officer), and the board of directors. We reviewed studies that indicated a consistent relationship between effective corporate governance and financial performance. There are also several internal and external control mechanisms that can serve to align managerial interests and shareholder interests. The internal mechanisms include a committed and involved board of directors, shareholder activism, and effective managerial incentives and rewards. The external mechanisms include the market for corporate control, banks and analysts, regulators, the media, and public activists. We also addressed corporate governance from both a United States and an international perspective.

Summary Review Questions

1. Why are effective strategic control systems so important in today's economy?

2. What are the main advantages of "contemporary" control systems over "traditional" control systems? What are the main differences between these two systems?

3. Why is it important to have a balance between the three elements of behavioral control—culture; rewards and incentives; and, boundaries?

4. Discuss the relationship between types of organizations and their primary means of behavioral control.

5. Boundaries become less important as a firm develops a strong culture and reward system. Explain.

6. Why is it important to avoid a "one best way" mentality concerning control systems? What are the consequences of applying the same type of control system to all types of environments?

7. What is the role of effective corporate governance in improving a firm's performance? What are some of the key governance mechanisms that are used to ensure that managerial and shareholder interests are aligned?

8. Define principal–principal (PP) conflicts. What are the implications for corporate governance?

Key Terms

Experiential Exercise

McDonald's Corporation, the world's largest fast-food restaurant chain, with 2006 revenues of $22 billion, has recently been on a "roll." Its shareholder value has more than tripled between March 2003 and March 2007. Using the Internet or library sources, evaluate the quality of the corporation in terms of management, the board of directors, and shareholder activism. Are the issues you list favorable or unfavorable for sound corporate governance?

Application Questions Exercises

1. The problems of many firms may be attributed to a "traditional" control system that failed to continuously monitor the environment and make necessary changes in their strategy and objectives. What companies are you familiar with that responded appropriately (or inappropriately) to environmental change?

2. How can a strong, positive culture enhance a firm's competitive advantage? How can a weak, negative culture erode competitive advantages? Explain and provide examples.

3. Use the Internet to research a firm that has an excellent culture and/or reward and incentive system. What are this firm's main financial and nonfinancial benefits?

4. Using the Internet, go to the Web site of a large, publicly held corporation in which you are interested. What evidence do you see of effective (or ineffective) corporate governance?

Ethics Questions

1. Strong cultures can have powerful effects on employee behavior. How does this create inadvertent control mechanisms? That is, are strong cultures an ethical way to control behavior?

2. Rules and regulations can help reduce unethical behavior in organizations. To be effective, however, what other systems, mechanisms, and processes are necessary?

References

1. Burrows, P. 2007. A smaller options scandal? *Business-Week*, March 5: 28–31; Maurer, H. (Ed.). 2006. Options watch. *BusinessWeek*, October 30: 32; Anonymous. 2006. Exit of the week. *BusinessWeek*, November 27: 31; Anonymous. 2006. How KB Home CEO's pay went through the roof. www.hobb.org. December 17, np.; and Anonymous. 2006. Backdating. *Business-Week*. December 18: 108.

2. This chapter draws upon Picken, J. C., & Dess, G. G. 1997. *Mission critical.* Burr Ridge, IL: Irwin Professional Publishing.

3. Argyris, C. 1977. Double-loop learning in organizations. *Harvard Business Review*, 55: 115–125.

4. Simons, R. 1995. Control in an age of empowerment. *Harvard Business Review*, 73: 80–88. This chapter draws on this source in the discussion of informational control.

5. Goold, M., & Quinn, J. B. 1990. The paradox of strategic controls. *Strategic Management Journal*, 11: 43–57.

6. Quinn, J. B. 1980. *Strategies for change.* Homewood, IL: Richard D. Irwin.

7. Mintzberg, H. 1987. Crafting strategy. *Harvard Business Review*, 65: 66–75.

8. Weston, J. S. 1992. Soft stuff matters. *Financial Executive*, July–August: 52–53.

9. This discussion of control systems draws upon Simons, op. cit.

10. For an interesting perspective on this issue and how a downturn in the economy can reduce the tendency toward "free agency" by managers and professionals, refer to Morris, B. 2001. White collar blues. *Fortune*, July 23: 98–110.

11. Ouchi, W. 1981. *Theory Z.* Reading, MA: Addison-Wesley; Deal, T. E., & Kennedy, A. A. 1982. *Corporate cultures.* Reading, MA: Addison-Wesley; Peters, T. J., & Waterman, R. H. 1982. *In search of excellence.* New York: Random House; Collins, J. 2001. *Good to great.* New York: HarperCollins.

12. Collins, J. C., & Porras, J. I. 1994. *Built to last: Successful habits of visionary companies.* New York: Harper Business.

13. Lee, J., & Miller, D. 1999. People matter: Commitment to employees, strategy, and performance in Korean firms. *Strategic Management Journal,* 6: 579–594.

14. For an insightful discussion of IKEA's unique culture, see Kling, K., & Goteman, I. 2003. IKEA CEO Anders Dahlvig on international growth and IKEA's unique corporate culture and brand identity. *Academy of Management Executive,* 17(1): 31–37.

15. For a discussion of how professionals inculcate values, refer to Uhl-Bien, M., & Graen, G. B. 1998. Individual self-management: Analysis of professionals' self-managing activities in functional and cross-functional work teams. *Academy of Management Journal,* 41(3): 340–350.

16. A perspective on how antisocial behavior can erode a firm's culture can be found in Robinson, S. L., & O'Leary-Kelly, A. M. 1998. Monkey see, monkey do: The influence of work groups on the antisocial behavior of employees. *Academy of Management Journal,* 41(6): 658–672.

17. Mitchell, R. 1989. Masters of innovation. *Business-Week,* April 10: 58–63.

18. Sellers, P. 1993. Companies that serve you best. *Fortune,* May 31: 88.

19. Southwest Airlines Culture Committee. 1993. *Luv Lines* (company publication), March–April: 17–18; for an interesting perspective on the "downside" of strong "cultlike" organizational cultures, refer to Arnott, D. A. 2000. *Corporate cults.* New York: AMACOM.

20. Kerr, J., & Slocum, J. W., Jr. 1987. Managing corporate culture through reward systems. *Academy of Management Executive,* 1(2): 99–107.

21. For a unique perspective on leader challenges in managing wealthy professionals, refer to Wetlaufer, S. 2000. Who wants to manage a millionaire? *Harvard Business Review,* 78(4): 53–60.

22. Neilson, G. L., Pasternack, B. A., & Van Nuys, K. E. 2005. The passive-aggressive organization. *Harvard Business Review,* 83(10): 82–95.

23. These next two subsections draw upon Dess, G. G., & Picken, J. C. 1997. *Beyond Productivity.* New York: AMACOM.

24. For a discussion of the benefits of stock options as executive compensation, refer to Hall, B. J. 2000. What you need to know about stock options. *Harvard Business Review,* 78(2): 121–129.

25. Tully, S. 1993. Your paycheck gets exciting. *Fortune,* November 13: 89.

26. Zellner, W., Hof, R. D., Brandt, R., Baker, S., & Greising, D. 1995. Go-go goliaths. *BusinessWeek,* February 13: 64–70.

27. This section draws on Dess & Picken, op. cit.: chap. 5.

28. Simons, op. cit.

29. Davis, E. 1997. Interview: Norman Augustine. *Management Review,* November: 11.

30. This section draws upon Dess, G. G., & Miller, A. 1993. *Strategic management.* New York: McGraw-Hill.

31. For a good review of the goal-setting literature, refer to Locke, E. A., & Latham, G. P. 1990. *A theory of goal setting and task performance.* Englewood Cliffs, NJ: Prentice Hall.

32. For an interesting perspective on the use of rules and regulations that is counter to this industry's (software) norms, refer to Fryer, B. 2001. Tom Siebel of Siebel Systems: High tech the old fashioned way. *Harvard Business Review,* 79(3): 118–130.

33. Thompson, A. A., Jr., & Strickland, A. J., III. 1998. *Strategic management: Concepts and cases* (10th ed.): 313. New York: McGraw-Hill.

34. Ibid.

35. Teitelbaum, R. 1997. Tough guys finish first. *Fortune,* July 21: 82–84.

36. Weaver, G. R., Trevino, L. K., & Cochran, P. L. 1999. Corporate ethics programs as control systems: Influences of executive commitment and environmental factors. *Academy of Management Journal,* 42(1): 41–57.

37. Cadbury, S. A. 1987. Ethical managers make their own rules. *Harvard Business Review,* 65: 3, 69–73.

38. Weber, J. 2003. CFOs on the hot seat. *BusinessWeek,* March 17: 66–70.

39. William Ouchi has written extensively about the use of clan control (which is viewed as an alternate to bureaucratic or market control). Here, a powerful culture results in people aligning their individual interests with those of the firm. Refer to Ouchi, op. cit. This section also draws on Hall, R. H. 2002. *Organizations: Structures, processes, and outcomes* (8th ed.). Upper Saddle River, NJ: Prentice Hall.

40. Monks, R., & Minow, N. 2001. *Corporate governance* (2nd ed.). Malden, MA: Blackwell.

41. Pound, J. 1995. The promise of the governed corporation. *Harvard Business Review,* 73(2): 89–98.

42. Heinzl, M. 2004. Nortel's directors and investors discuss changes to the board. *The Wall Street Journal,* September 30: B4; Editorial. 2003. Pulling Boeing out of a tailspin. *BusinessWeek,* December 15: 136; and Zimmerman, A., Ball, D., & Veen, M. 2003. A global journal report: Supermarket giant Ahoud ousts CEO in big accounting scandal. *The Wall Street Journal,* February 25: A1; Ibid; and Maurer, H. 2006. Is this 'the HP way'? *BusinessWeek,* September 25: 34.

43. This discussion draws upon Monks & Minow, op. cit.

44. Eisenhardt, K. M. 1989. Agency theory: An assessment and review. *Academy of Management Review,* 14(1): 57–74. Some of the seminal contributions to agency theory include Jensen, M., & Meckling, W. 1976. Theory of the firm: Managerial behavior, agency costs, and ownership structure. *Journal of Financial Economics,* 3: 305–360; Fama, E., & Jensen, M. 1983. Separation of ownership and control. *Journal of Law and Economics,* 26: 301, 325; and Fama, E. 1980. Agency problems and the theory of the firm. *Journal of Political Economy,* 88: 288–307.

45. Managers may also engage in "shirking"—that is, reducing or withholding their efforts. See, for example, Kidwell, R. E., Jr., & Bennett, N. 1993. Employee propensity to withhold effort: A conceptual model to intersect three avenues of research. *Academy of Management Review,* 18(3): 429–456.

46. For an interesting perspective on agency and clarification of many related concepts and terms, visit the following Web site: www.encycogov.com.

47. Argawal, A., & Mandelker, G. 1987. Managerial incentives and corporate investment and financing decisions. *Journal of Finance,* 42: 823–837.

48. For an insightful, recent discussion of the academic research on corporate governance, and in particular the role of boards of directors, refer to Chatterjee, S., & Harrison, J. S. 2001. Corporate governance. In Hitt, M. A., Freeman, R. E., & Harrison, J. S. (Eds.). *Handbook of strategic management:* 543–563. Malden, MA: Blackwell.

49. This opening discussion draws on Monks & Minow, op. cit. 164, 169; see also Pound, op. cit.

50. Business Roundtable. 1990. *Corporate governance and American competitiveness,* March: 7.

51. Byrne, J. A., Grover, R., & Melcher, R. A. 1997. The best and worst boards. *BusinessWeek,* November 26: 35–47. The three key roles of boards of directors are monitoring the actions of executives, providing advice, and providing links to the external environment to provide resources. See Johnson, J. L., Daily, C. M., & Ellstrand, A. E. 1996. Boards of directors: A review and research agenda. *Academy of Management Review,* 37: 409–438.

52. McGeehan, P. 2003. More chief executives shown the door, study says. *New York Times,* May 12: C2.

53. Gerdes, L. 2007. Hello, goodbye. *BusinessWeek,* January 22: 16.

54. For an analysis of the effects of outside director's compensation on acquisition decisions, refer to Deutsch, T., Keil, T., & Laamanen, T. 2007. Decision making in acquisitions: The effect of outside directors' compensation on acquisition patterns. *Journal of Management,* 33(1): 30–56.

55. There are benefits, of course, to having some insiders on the board of directors. Inside directors would be more aware of the firm's strategies. Additionally, outsiders may rely too often on financial performance indicators because of information asymmetries. For an interesting discussion, see Baysinger, B. D., & Hoskisson, R. E. 1990. The composition of boards of directors and strategic control: Effects on corporate strategy. *Academy of Management Review,* 15: 72–87.

56. Hambrick, D. C., & Jackson, E. M. 2000. Outside directors with a stake: The linchpin in improving governance. *California Management Review,* 42(4): 108–127.

57. Ibid.

58. Disney has begun to make many changes to improve its corporate governance, such as assigning only independent directors to important board committees, restricting directors from serving on more than three boards, and appointing a lead director who can convene the board without approval by the CEO. In recent years, the Disney Co. has shown up on some "best" board lists. In addition Eisner has recently relinquished the chairman position.

59. Talk show. 2002. *BusinessWeek,* September 30: 14.

60. Ward, R. D. 2000. *Improving corporate boards.* New York: Wiley.

61. Monks and Minow, op. cit.: 93.

62. A discussion of the factors that lead to shareholder activism is found in Ryan, L. V., & Schneider, M. 2002. The antecedents of institutional investor activism. *Academy of Management Review,* 27(4): 554–573.

63. For an insightful discussion of investor activism, refer to David, P., Bloom, M., & Hillman, A. 2007. Investor activism, managerial responsiveness, and corporate social performance. *Strategic Management Journal,* 28(1): 91–100.

64. There is strong research support for the idea that the presence of large block shareholders is associated with value-maximizing decisions. For example, refer to Johnson, R. A., Hoskisson, R. E., & Hitt, M. A. 1993. Board of director involvement in restructuring: The effects of board versus managerial controls and characteristics. *Strategic Management Journal,* 14: 33–50.

65. For an interesting perspective on the impact of institutional ownership on a firm's innovation strategies, see Hoskisson, R. E., Hitt, M. A., Johnson, R. A., & Grossman, W. 2002. *Academy of Management Journal,* 45(4): 697–716.

66. www.calpers.ca.gov/index.jsp

67. Icahn, C. 2007. Icahn: On activist investors and private equity run wild. *BusinessWeek,* March 12: 21–22. For an interesting perspective on Carl Icahn's transition (?) from corporate raider to shareholder activist, read Grover, R. 2007. Just don't call him a raider. *BusinessWeek,* March 5: 68–69. The quote in the text is part of Icahn's response to the article by R. Grover.

68. For a study of the relationship between ownership and diversification, refer to Goranova, M., Alessandri, T. M., Brandes, P., & Dharwadkar, R. 2007. Managerial ownership and corporate diversification: A longitudinal view, *Strategic Management Journal,* 28(3): 211–226.

69. Jensen, M. C., & Murphy, K. J. 1990. CEO incentives—It's not how much you pay, but how. *Harvard Business Review,* 68(3): 138–149.

70. For a perspective on the relative advantages and disadvantages of "duality"—that is, one individual serving as both Chief Executive Office and Chairman of the Board, see Lorsch, J. W., & Zelleke, A. 2005. Should the CEO be the chairman? *MIT Sloan Management Review,* 46(2): 71–74.

71. Sasseen, J. 2007. A better look at the boss's pay. *BusinessWeek,* February 26: 44–45.

72. Byrnes, N., & Sasseen, J. 2007. Board of hard knocks. *BusinessWeek,* January 22: 36–39.

73. Research has found that executive compensation is more closely aligned with firm performance in companies with compensation committees and boards dominated by outside directors. See, for example, Conyon, M. J., & Peck, S. I. 1998. Board control, remuneration committees, and top management compensation. *Academy of Management Journal,* 41: 146–157.

74. Lavelle, L., Jespersen, F. F., & Arndt, M. 2002. Executive pay. *BusinessWeek,* April 15: 66–72.

75. www.tiaa-cref.org/pubs.

76. Such opportunistic behavior is common in all principal-agent relationships. For a description of agency problems, especially in the context of the relationship between shareholders and managers, see Jensen, M. C., & Meckling, W. H. 1976. Theory of the firm: Managerial behavior, agency costs, and ownership structure. *Journal of Financial Economics,* 3: 305–360.

77. Hoskisson, R. E., & Turk, T. A. 1990. Corporate restructuring: Governance and control limits of the internal market. *Academy of Management Review,* 15: 459–477.

78. For an insightful perspective on the market for corporate control and how it is influenced by knowledge intensity, see Coff, R. 2003. Bidding wars over R&D-intensive firms: Knowledge, opportunism, and the market for corporate control. *Academy of Management Journal,* 46(1): 74–85.

79. Walsh, J. P., & Kosnik, R. D. 1993. Corporate raiders and their disciplinary role in the market for corporate control. *Academy of Management Journal,* 36: 671–700.

80. Gunning for KPMG. 2003. *Economist,* February 1: 63.

81. Timmons, H. 2003. Investment banks: Who will foot their bill? *BusinessWeek,* March 3: 116.

82. Wishy-washy: The SEC pulls its punches on corporate-governance rules. 2003. *Economist,* February 1: 60.

83. McLean, B. 2001. Is Enron overpriced? *Fortune,* March 5: 122–125.

84. Bernstein, A. 2000. Too much corporate power. *BusinessWeek,* September 11: 35–37.

85. This section draws upon Young, M. N., Peng, M. W., Ahlstrom, D., Bruton, G. D., Jiang, Y. 2005. Principal–principal conflicts in corporate governance (unpublished manuscript); and, Peng, M. W. 2006. *Globalstrategy.* Cincinnati: Thomson South-Western. We are very appreciative of the helpful comments of Mike Young of Hong Kong Baptist University and Mike Peng of the University of Texas at Dallas.

86. Khanna, T., & Rivkin, J. 2001. Estimating the performance effects of business groups in emerging markets. *Strategic Management Journal*, 22: 45–74.

chapter 10

Creating Effective Organizational Designs

>learning objectives

After reading this chapter, you should have a good understanding of:

LO1 The importance of organizational structure and the concept of the "boundaryless" organization in implementing strategies.

LO2 The growth patterns of major corporations and the relationship between a firm's strategy and its structure.

LO3 Each of the traditional types of organizational structure: simple, functional, divisional, and matrix.

LO4 The relative advantages and disadvantages of traditional organizational structures.

LO5 The implications of a firm's international operations for organizational structure.

LO6 Why there is no "one best way" to design strategic reward and evaluation systems, and the important contingent roles of business- and corporate-level strategies.

LO7 The different types of boundaryless organizations—barrier-free, modular, and virtual—and their relative advantages and disadvantages.

LO8 The need for creating ambidextrous organizational designs that enable firms to explore new opportunities and effectively integrate existing operations.

_t_o implement strategies successfully, firms must have appropriate organizational structures. These include the processes and integrating mechanisms necessary to ensure that boundaries among internal activities and external parties, such as suppliers, customers, and alliance partners, are flexible and permeable. A firm's performance will suffer if its managers don't carefully consider both of these organizational design attributes.

In the first section, we begin by discussing the growth patterns of large corporations to address the important relationships between the strategy that a firm follows and its corresponding structure. For example, as firms diversify into related product-market areas, they change their structure from functional to divisional. We then address the different types of traditional structures—simple, functional, divisional, and matrix—and their relative advantages and disadvantages. We close with a discussion of the implications of a firm's international operations for the structure of its organization.

The second section takes the perspective that there is no "one best way" to design an organization's strategic reward and evaluation system. Here we address two important contingencies: business- and corporate-level strategy. For example, when strategies require a great deal of collaboration, as well as resource and information sharing, there must be incentives and cultures that encourage and reward such initiatives.

The third section discusses the concept of the "boundaryless" organization. We do _not_ argue that organizations should have no internal and external boundaries. Instead, we suggest that in rapidly changing and unpredictable environments, organizations must strive to make their internal and external boundaries both flexible and permeable. We suggest three different types of boundaryless organizations: barrier-free, modular, and virtual.

The fourth section focuses on the need for managers to recognize that they typically face two opposing challenges: (1) being proactive in taking advantage of new opportunities and (2) ensuring the effective coordination and integration of existing operations. This suggests the need for ambidextrous organizations; that is, firms that can both be efficient in how they manage existing assets and competencies and take advantage of opportunities in rapidly changing and unpredictable environments—conditions that are becoming more pronounced in today's global markets.

Learning from Mistakes

As 2007 began, Airbus' A380 double-decker jet was two years behind schedule, sending about $6 billion in potential profits down the drain.[1] However, the root of the problem may appear to be too simple to be true. Let's take a look.

> Airbus factories in Germany and France were using incompatible design software. Engineers in Hamburg were drawing on a two-dimensional computer program, while their counterparts in Toulouse were working in 3-D. Thus, wiring produced in Hamburg didn't fit properly into the plane on the assembly line in Toulouse. As noted by Hans Weber, CEO of San Diego–based consultant Tecop International, "The various Airbus locations had their own legacy software, methods, procedures, and Airbus never succeeded in unifying all those efforts." (There are 348 _miles_ of bundled wiring in each A380.)
>
> The A380 fiasco has become one of the costliest blunders in the history of commercial aviation and plunged Airbus into crisis. Chief Executive Christian Streiff quit in October, 2006 after only three months on the job. He clashed with Airbus' parent, European Aeronautic Defense & Space (EADS) Company, over how to sort out the mess. EADS will probably wind up taking a $6 billion hit to its **[continued]**

profit—measured by the expected loss in earnings from production delays over the next four years. Further, the resulting cash crunch could slow Airbus' plans to develop a new midsize wide-body plane to challenge Boeing's highly successful 787 Dreamliner. Through September 2006, Airbus fell far behind Boeing on total aircraft orders, logging only 226 versus 723 for its U.S. rival.

What Went Wrong?

The software debacle exposes a salient flaw in Airbus. Although it likes to project a seamless, pan-European image, Airbus is terribly balkanized. Its factories in Germany, France, Britain, and Spain cling to traditional operating methods and harbor cross-border jealousies. As Strieff told the French newspaper *Le Figaro* in an interview, "It is still, in part, a juxtaposition of four companies."

Each of those four companies comes, as one would expect, with a government attached. In essence, constant political meddling is the price Airbus must pay for the billions of dollars in low-interest government loans that have helped it launch new designs. Politicians have a powerful weapon with which to exert influence to spread work across Airbus's 16 European factories. As noted by *Washington Post* writer Steven Peaerlstein: ". . . it's about the pigheadedness of . . . partners who care less about how many planes Airbus sells than how the work is divided between the countries." Such attitudes sap efficiency and increase the risk of production glitches. Eric Chaney, Morgan Stanley's chief European economist asserts: "The fairy tale has turned into a nightmare that even the fiercest Euro-skeptics wouldn't have imagined possible."

There is, however, good news in all of this—for Boeing. The delays on the Airbus A380 have created a sort of virtuous cycle. First, they force air transport companies to switch freighter orders, as both International Lease Finance and FedEx did. Second, the delays in the passenger version of the A380 mean potential customers have to keep older planes, such as Boeing 747-400s, in passenger service longer, instead of converting them into cargo haulers—a much cheaper option than buying new. So fewer used jets lying around means more demand for the new cargo jets, which Boeing is happy to sell.

>LO1

The importance of organizational structure and the concept of the "boundaryless" organization in implementing strategies.

One of the central concepts in this chapter is the importance of boundaryless organizations. That is, successful organizations create permeable boundaries among the internal activities as well as between the organization and its external customers, suppliers, and alliance partners. We introduced this idea in Chapter 3 in our discussion of the value-chain concept, which consisted of several primary (e.g., inbound logistics, marketing and sales) and support activities (e.g., procurement, human resource management). Clearly, the underlying cause of Airbus' problem was its inability to establish close and effective working relationships between its various factories operating in four countries. Frequently, managers (and politicians) were seemingly more focused on national interests instead of what was best for Airbus' shareholders.

The most important implication of this chapter is that today's managers are faced with two ongoing and vital activities in structuring and designing their organizations. First, they must decide on the most appropriate type of organizational structure. Second, they need to assess what mechanisms, processes, and techniques are most helpful in enhancing the permeability of both internal and external boundaries.

Traditional Forms of Organizational Structure

Organizational structure refers to the formalized patterns of interactions that link a firm's tasks, technologies, and people.[2] Structures help to ensure that resources are used effectively in accomplishing an organization's mission. Structure provides a means of balancing two conflicting forces: a need for the division of tasks into meaningful groupings and the need to integrate such groupings in order to ensure efficiency and effectiveness. Structure identifies the executive, managerial, and administrative organization of a firm and indicates responsibilities and hierarchical relationships. It also influences the flow of information as well as the context and nature of human interactions.

Most organizations begin very small and either die or remain small. Those few that survive and prosper embark on strategies designed to increase the overall scope of operations and enable them to enter new product-market domains. Such growth places additional pressure on executives to control and coordinate the firm's increasing size and diversity. The most appropriate type of structure depends on the nature and magnitude of growth in a firm. Next, we address various types of structural forms, their advantages and disadvantages, and their relationships to the strategies that organizations undertake.

Patterns of Growth of Large Corporations: Strategy-Structure Relationships

A firm's strategy and structure change as it increases in size, diversifies into new product markets, and expands its geographic scope.[3] Exhibit 10.1 illustrates some of the common growth patterns that firms may follow.

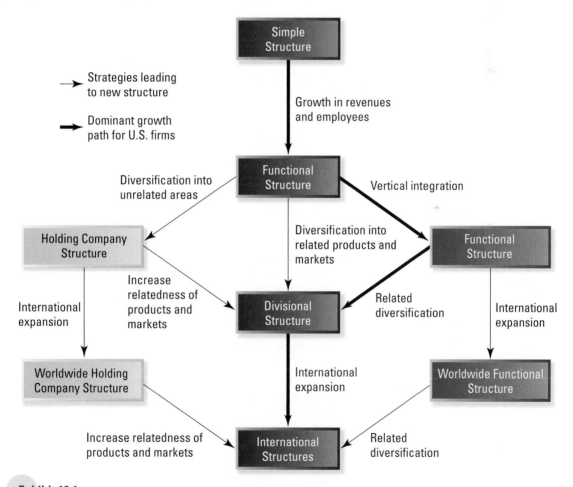

Exhibit 10.1 Dominant Growth Patterns of Large Corporations

Source: From *Strategy Implementation: Structure, Systems and Process,* 2nd edition by J. R. Galbraith and R. K. Kazanjian. Copyright © 1986. Reprinted with permission of South-Western, a division of Thomson Learning: www.thomsonrights.com. Fax: 800-730-2215.

A new firm with a *simple structure* typically increases its sales revenue and volume of outputs over time. It may also engage in some vertical integration to secure sources of supply (backward integration) as well as channels of distribution (forward integration). After a time, the simple-structure firm implements a *functional structure* to concentrate efforts on both increasing efficiency and enhancing its operations and products. This structure enables the firm to group its operations into either functions, departments, or geographic areas. As its initial markets mature, a firm looks beyond its present products and markets for possible expansion.

A strategy of related diversification requires a need to reorganize around product lines or geographic markets. This leads to a *divisional structure.* As the business expands in terms of sales revenues, and domestic growth opportunities become somewhat limited, a firm may seek opportunities in international markets. At this time, a firm has a wide variety of structures to choose from. These include *international division, geographic area, worldwide product division, worldwide functional,* and *worldwide matrix.* As we will see later in this section, deciding upon the most appropriate structure when a firm has international operations depends on three primary factors: the extent of international expansion, type of strategy (global, multidomestic, or transnational), and the degree of product diversity.[4]

There are some other common growth patterns. For example, some firms may find it advantageous to diversify into several product lines rather than focus their efforts on strengthening distributor and supplier relationships through vertical integration. Thus, they would organize themselves according to product lines by implementing a divisional structure. Also, some firms may choose to move into unrelated product areas, typically by acquiring existing businesses. Frequently, their rationale is that acquiring assets and competencies is more economical or expedient than developing them internally. Such an unrelated, or conglomerate, strategy requires relatively little integration across businesses and sharing of resources. Thus, a *holding company structure* becomes appropriate. As we would expect, there are many other growth patterns, but these are the most common.*

Now we will discuss some of the most common types of organizational structures—simple, functional, divisional (including two variants: *strategic business unit* and *holding company*), and matrix and their advantages and disadvantages. We will close the section with a discussion of the structural implications when a firm expands its operations into international markets.

Simple Structure

>LO3

Each of the traditional types of organizational structure: simple, functional, divisional, and matrix.

The **simple organizational structure** is the oldest, and most common, organizational form. After all, most organizations are very small and have a single or very narrow product line in which the owner-manager (or top executive) makes most of the decisions. In effect, the owner-manager controls all activities, and the staff serves as an extension of the top executive.

Advantages   The simple structure is highly informal and the coordination of tasks is accomplished by direct supervision. Decision making is highly centralized, there is little specialization of tasks, few rules and regulations, and an informal evaluation and reward system. Although the owner-manager is intimately involved in almost all phases of the business, a manager is often employed to oversee day-to-day operations.

simple organizational structure an organizational form in which the owner-manager makes most of the decisions and controls activities, and the staff serves as an extension of the top executive.

---

* The lowering of transaction costs and globalization have led to some changes in the common historical patterns that we have discussed. Some firms are, in effect, bypassing the vertical integration stage. Instead, they focus on core competencies and outsource other value-creation activities. Also, even relatively young firms are going global early in their history because of lower communication and transportation costs. For an interesting perspective on global start-ups, see McDougall, P. P., & Oviatt, B. M. 1996. New venture internationalization, strategic change and performance: A follow-up study. *Journal of Business Venturing,* 11: 23–40; and McDougall, P. P., & Oviatt, B. M. (Eds.). 2000. The special research forum on international entrepreneurship. *Academy of Management Journal,* October: 902–1003.

Exhibit 10.2 Functional Organizational Structure

Disadvantages A simple structure may often foster creativity and individualism since there are generally few rules and regulations. However, such "informality" may lead to problems. Employees may not clearly understand their responsibilities, which can lead to conflict and confusion. Employees also may take advantage of the lack of regulations and act in their own self-interest. Such actions can erode motivation and satisfaction as well as lead to the possible misuse of organizational resources. Further, small organizations have flat structures that limit opportunities for upward mobility. Without the potential for future advancement, recruiting and retaining talent may become very difficult.

Functional Structure

When an organization is small (15 employees or less), it is not necessary to have a variety of formal arrangements and groupings of activities. However, as firms grow, excessive demands may be placed on the owner-manager in order to obtain and process all of the information necessary to run the business. Chances are the owner will not be skilled in all specialties (e.g., accounting, engineering, production, marketing). Thus, he or she will need to hire specialists in the various functional areas. Such growth in the overall scope and complexity of the business necessitates a **functional organizational structure** wherein the major functions of the firm are grouped internally. The coordination and integration of the functional areas becomes one of the most important responsibilities of the chief executive of the firm. Exhibit 10.2 presents a diagram of a functional organizational structure.

functional organizational structure an organizational form in which the major functions of the firm, such as production, marketing, R&D, and accounting, are grouped internally.

Functional structures are generally found in organizations in which there is a single or closely related product or service, high production volume, and some vertical integration. Initially, firms tend to expand the overall scope of their operations by penetrating existing markets, introducing similar products in additional markets, or increasing the level of vertical integration. Such expansion activities clearly increase the scope and complexity of the operations. Fortunately, the functional structure provides for a high level of centralization that helps to ensure integration and control over the related product-market activities or multiple primary activities (from inbound logistics to operations to marketing, sales, and service) in the value chain (addressed in Chapters 3 and 4).

Strategy Spotlight 10.1 provides an example of an effective functional organization structure—Parkdale Mills.

Advantages As with any type of organizational structure, there are some relative advantages and disadvantages associated with the functional structure. By bringing together specialists into functional departments, a firm is able to enhance its coordination and control within each of the functional areas. The structure also ensures that decision making in the firm will be centralized at the top of the organization. This enhances the organizational-level (as opposed to functional area) perspective across the various functions in the organization. In addition, the functional structure provides for a more efficient use of managerial and

>LO4
The relative advantages and disadvantages of traditional organizational structures.

Parkdale Mills: A Successful Functional Organizational Structure

For more than 80 years, Parkdale Mills, with approximately $1 billion in revenues, has been the industry leader in the production of cotton and cotton blend yarns. Their expertise comes by concentrating on a single product line, perfecting processes, and welcoming innovation. According to CEO Andy Warlick, "I think we've probably spent more than any two competitors combined on new

Sources: Stewart, C. 2003. The perfect yarn. *The Manufacturer.com*, July 31; www.parkdalemills.com; Berman, P. 1987. The fast track isn't always the best track. *Forbes*, November 2: 60–64; and personal communication with Duke Kimbrell, March 11, 2005.

equipment and robotics. We do this because we have to compete in a global market where a lot of the competition has a lower wage structure and gets subsidies that we don't receive, so we really have to focus on consistency and cost control." Yarn making is generally considered to be a commodity business, and Parkdale is the industry's low-cost producer.

Tasks are highly standardized and authority is centralized with Duke Kimbrell, founder and chairman, and CEO Andy Warlick. The firm operates a bare-bones staff with a small staff of top executives. Kimbrell and Warlick are considered shrewd about the cotton market, technology, customer loyalty, and incentive pay.

---

technical talent since functional area expertise is pooled in a single department (e.g., marketing) instead of being spread across a variety of product-market areas. Finally, career paths and professional development in specialized areas are facilitated.

Disadvantages   There also are some significant disadvantages associated with the functional structure. First, the differences in values and orientations among functional areas may impede communication and coordination. Edgar Schein of MIT has argued that shared assumptions, often based on similar backgrounds and experiences of members, form around functional units in an organization. This leads to what are often called "stove pipes" or "silos," in which departments view themselves as isolated, self-contained units with little need for interaction and coordination with other departments. This erodes communication because functional groups may have not only different goals but also differing meanings of words and concepts. According to Schein:

> The word "marketing" will mean product development to the engineer, studying customers through market research to the product manager, merchandising to the salesperson, and constant change in design to the manufacturing manager. When they try to work together, they will often attribute disagreements to personalities and fail to notice the deeper, shared assumptions that color how each function thinks.[5]

Such narrow functional orientations also may lead to short-term thinking based largely upon what is best for the functional area, not the entire organization. For example, in a manufacturing firm, sales may want to offer a wide range of customized products to appeal to the firm's customers; research and development may overdesign products and components to achieve technical elegance; and manufacturing may favor no-frills products that can be produced at low cost by means of long production runs. In addition, functional structures may overburden the top executives in the firm because conflicts have a tendency to be "pushed up" to the top of the organization since there are no managers who are responsible for the specific product lines. Finally, functional structures make it difficult to establish uniform performance standards across the entire organization. Whereas it may be relatively easy to evaluate production managers on the basis of production volume and cost control, establishing performance measures for engineering, research and development, and accounting become more problematic.

Divisional Structure

The **divisional organizational structure** (sometimes called the multidivisional structure or M-Form) is organized around products, projects, or markets. Each of the divisions, in turn, includes its own functional specialists who are typically organized into departments. A divisional structure encompasses a set of relatively autonomous units governed by a central corporate office. The operating divisions are relatively independent and consist of products and services that are different from those of the other divisions. Operational decision making in a large business places excessive demands on the firm's top management. In order to attend to broader, longer-term organizational issues, top-level managers must delegate decision making to lower-level managers. Thus, divisional executives play a key role. In conjunction with corporate-level executives, they help to determine the product-market and financial objectives for the division as well as their division's contribution to overall corporate performance.[6] The rewards are based largely on measures of financial performance such as net income and revenue. Exhibit 10.3 illustrates a divisional structure.

General Motors was among the earliest firms to adopt the divisional organizational structure.[7] In the 1920s the company formed five major product divisions (Cadillac, Buick, Oldsmobile, Pontiac, and Chevrolet) as well as several industrial divisions. Since then, many firms have discovered that as they diversified into new product-market activities, functional structures—with their emphasis on single functional departments—were unable to manage the increased complexity of the entire business.

Advantages   There are many advantages associated with the divisional structure. By creating separate divisions to manage individual product markets, there is a separation of strategic and operating control. That is, divisional managers can focus their efforts on improving operations in the product markets for which they are responsible, and corporate officers can devote their time to overall strategic issues for the entire corporation. The focus on a division's products and markets—by the divisional executives—provides the corporation with an enhanced ability to respond quickly to important changes in the external environment. Since there are functional departments within each division of the corporation, the problems associated with sharing resources across functional departments are minimized.

> **divisional organizational structure** an organizational form in which products, projects, or product markets are grouped internally.

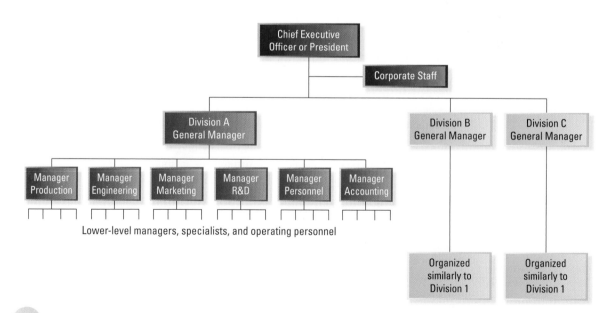

Exhibit 10.3 Divisional Organizational Structure

Brinker International Changes to a Divisional Organizational Structure

Although Brinker International had a traditional functional structure, changes in its competitive outlook forced management to take a closer look at the organizational design of the firm. The firm controls a variety of restaurant chains and bakeries, including Wildfire, Big Bowl, and Chili's.

With all these interests under one corporate roof, management of these disparate entities became difficult. The fragmented $330 billion restaurant and bakery industry caters to highly focused market niches. The original

Source: CEO interview: Ronald A. McDougall, Brinker International. 1999. *Wall Street Transcript,* January 20: 1–4.

functional design of the Brinker chain had some disadvantages as the company grew. With areas separated by function, it became hard to focus efforts on a single restaurant chain. The diverse markets served by the bakeries and restaurants began to lose their focus.

As a result, Brinker International changed to a divisional structure. This allowed the company to consolidate individuals who worked with a single restaurant or bakery chain into a separate division. Brinker referred to these as concept teams, with each concept team responsible for the operation of a single line of business. This focused effort streamlined the company's ability to concentrate on the market niche served by each of its restaurants and bakeries.

Finally, because there are multiple levels of general managers (that is, executives responsible for integrating and coordinating all functional areas), the development of general management talent is enhanced. Strategy Spotlight 10.2 discusses the rationale behind Brinker Corporation's change in structure from functional to divisional.

Disadvantages　　A divisional structure also has potential disadvantages. First, it can be very expensive; that is, there can be increased costs due to the duplication of personnel, operations, and investment since each division must staff multiple functional departments. There also can be dysfunctional competition among divisions since each division tends to become concerned solely about its own operations. Further, divisional managers are often evaluated on common measures such as return on assets and sales growth. Thus, if goals are conflicting, there can be a sense of a "zero-sum" game that would discourage sharing ideas and resources among the divisions for the common good of the corporation. Ghoshal and Bartlett, two leading strategy scholars, note:

> As their label clearly warns, divisions divide. The divisional model fragmented companies' resources; it created vertical communication channels that insulated business units and prevented them from sharing their strengths with one another. Consequently, the whole of the corporation was often less than the sum of its parts.[8]

Another potential disadvantage is that with many divisions providing different products and services, there is the chance that differences in image and quality may occur across divisions. For example, one division may offer no-frills products of lower quality that may erode the brand reputation of another division that has top quality, highly differentiated offerings. Finally, since each division is evaluated in terms of financial measures such as return on investment and revenue growth, there is often an urge to focus on short-term performance. For example, if corporate management uses quarterly profits as the key performance indicator, divisional management may tend to put significant emphasis on "making the numbers" and minimizing activities, such as advertising, maintenance, and capital investments, which would detract from short-term performance measures.

Before moving on, we'll discuss two variations of the divisional form of organizational structure: the strategic business unit (SBU) and holding company structures.

Strategic Business Unit (SBU) Structure   Highly diversified corporations such as ConAgra, a $12 billion food producer, may consist of dozens of different divisions.[9] If ConAgra were to use a purely divisional structure, it would be nearly impossible for the corporate office to plan and coordinate activities because the span of control would be too large. Instead, to attain synergies, ConAgra has put its diverse businesses into three primary SBUs: food service (restaurants), retail (grocery stores), and agricultural products.

With a **strategic business unit (SBU) structure,** divisions with similar products, markets, and/or technologies are grouped into homogenous units to achieve some synergies. These include those discussed in Chapter 6 for related diversification, such as leveraging core competencies, sharing infrastructures, and market power. Generally speaking, the more related businesses are within a corporation, the fewer SBUs will be required. Each of the SBUs in the corporation operates as a profit center.

> **strategic business unit (SBU) structure** an organizational form in which products, projects, or product market divisions are grouped into homogeneous units.

Advantages   The major advantage of the SBU structure is that it makes the task of planning and control by the corporate office more manageable. Also, with greater decentralization of authority, individual businesses can react more quickly to important changes in the environment than if all divisions had to report directly to the corporate office.

Disadvantages   There are also some disadvantages to the SBU structure. Since the divisions are grouped into SBUs, it may become difficult to achieve synergies across SBUs. That is, if divisions that are included in different SBUs have potential sources of synergy, it may become difficult for them to be realized. The additional level of management increases the number of personnel and overhead expenses, while the additional hierarchical level removes the corporate office further from the individual divisions. Thus, the corporate office may become unaware of key developments that could have a major impact on the corporation.

Holding Company Structure   The **holding company structure** (sometimes referred to as a *conglomerate*) is also a variation of the divisional structure. Whereas the SBU structure is often used when similarities exist between the individual businesses (or divisions), the holding company structure is appropriate when the businesses in a corporation's portfolio do not have much in common. Thus, the potential for synergies is limited.

> **holding company structure** an organizational form that is a variation of the divisional organizational structure in which the divisions have a high degree of autonomy both from other divisions and from corporate headquarters.

Holding company structures are most appropriate for firms with a strategy of unrelated diversification. Companies such as Hanson Trust, ITT, and the CP group of Thailand have used holding company structure to implement their unrelated diversification strategies. Since there are few similarities across the businesses, the corporate offices in these companies provide a great deal of autonomy to operating divisions and rely on financial controls and incentive programs to obtain high levels of performance from the individual businesses. Corporate staffs at these firms tend to be small because of their limited involvement in the overall operation of their various businesses.[10]

Advantages   An important advantage of the holding company structure is the cost savings associated with fewer personnel and the lower overhead resulting from a small corporate office and fewer hierarchical levels. In addition, the autonomy of the holding company structure increases the motivational level of divisional executives and enables them to respond quickly to market opportunities and threats.

Disadvantages   The primary disadvantage of the holding company structure is the inherent lack of control and dependence that corporate-level executives have on divisional executives. Major problems could arise if key divisional executives leave the firm, because the corporate office has very little "bench strength"—that is, additional managerial talent ready to quickly fill key positions. And, if problems arise in a division, it

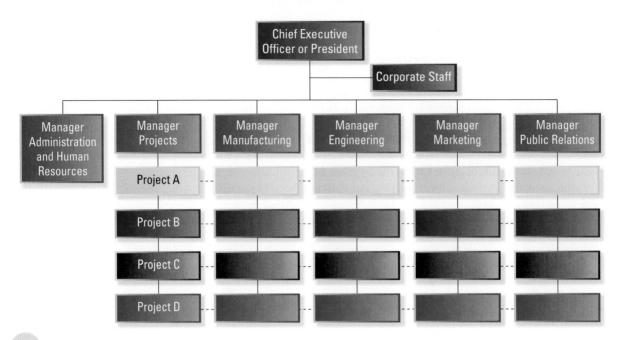

Exhibit 10.4 Matrix Organizational Structure

may become very difficult to turn around individual businesses because of limited staff support in the corporate office.

Matrix Structure

matrix organizational structure an organizational form in which there are multiple lines of authority and some individuals report to at least two managers.

At times, managers may find that none of the structures that we have described above fully meet their needs. One approach that tries to overcome the inadequacies inherent in the other structures is the **matrix organizational structure.** It is, in effect, a combination of the functional and divisional structures. Most commonly, functional departments are combined with product groups on a project basis. For example, a product group may want to develop a new addition to its line; for this project, it obtains personnel from functional departments such as marketing, production, and engineering. These personnel work under the manager of the product group for the duration of the project, which can vary from a few weeks to an open-ended period of time. The individuals who work in a matrix organization become responsible to two managers: the project manager and the manager of their functional area. Exhibit 10.4 illustrates a matrix structure.

In addition to the product-function matrix, other bases may be related in a matrix. Some large multinational corporations rely on a matrix structure to combine product groups and geographical units. Product managers have global responsibility for the development, manufacturing, and distribution of their own line, while managers of geographical regions have responsibility for the profitability of the businesses in their regions. In the mid-1990s, Caterpillar, Inc., implemented this type of structure.

Dell Computer relies on the matrix concept, with its dual reporting responsibility, to enhance accountability as well as develop general managers. According to former CEO Kevin Rollins:[11]

> . . . we're organized in a matrix of sales regions and product groups. Then we break each of those groups down to a pretty fine level of sub-products and sales sub-segments. Dell has more P&L managers, and smaller business units, than most companies its size. This not only increases accountability to the customer, it helps train general managers by moving them from smaller to larger businesses as their skills develop.

Our matrix organization has a third level—our business councils. For example, we have a small-business sales group in each country, along with product development people who become very familiar with what small-business customers buy. In addition, we have our worldwide small-business council made up of all our small-business GMs and product managers. Everyone in these councils sees everyone else's P&L, so it provides another set of checks and balances.

Advantages   A primary advantage of the matrix structure is that it facilitates the use of specialized personnel, equipment, and facilities. Instead of duplicating functions, as would be the case in a divisional structure based on products, the resources are shared. Individuals with high expertise can divide their time among multiple projects. Such resource sharing and collaboration enable a firm to use resources more efficiently and to respond more quickly and effectively to changes in the competitive environment. In addition, the flexibility inherent in a matrix structure provides professionals with a broader range of responsibility. Such experience enables them to develop their skills and competencies.

Disadvantages   Matrix structures have many potential disadvantages. The dual-reporting structures can result in uncertainty and lead to intense power struggles and conflict over the allocation of personnel and other resources. Additionally, working relationships become more complicated. This may result in excessive reliance on group processes and teamwork, along with a diffusion of responsibility, which in turn may erode timely decision making. Exhibit 10.5 briefly summarizes the advantages and disadvantages of the functional, divisional, and matrix organizational structures.

International Operations: Implications for Organizational Structure

Today's managers must maintain an international outlook on their firm's businesses and competitive strategies. To be successful in the global marketplace, managers must ensure consistency between their strategies (at the business, corporate, and international levels) and the structure of their organization. As firms expand into foreign markets, they generally follow a pattern of change in structure that parallels the changes in their strategies. Three major contingencies that influence the chosen structure are (1) the type of strategy that is driving a firm's foreign operations, (2) product diversity, and (3) the extent to which a firm is dependent on foreign sales.[12]

> **>LO5**
> The implications of a firm's international operations for organizational structure.

As international operations become an important part of a firm's overall operations, managers must make changes that are consistent with their firm's structure. The primary types of structures used to manage a firm's international operations are:[13]

- International division
- Geographic-area division
- Worldwide functional
- Worldwide product division
- Worldwide matrix

As we discussed in Chapter 7, multidomestic strategies are driven by political and cultural imperatives requiring managers within each country to respond to local conditions. The structures consistent with such a strategic orientation are the *international division* and *geographic-area division* structures. Here local managers are provided with a high level of autonomy to manage their operations within the constraints and demands of their geographic market. As a firm's foreign sales increase as a percentage of its total sales, it will likely change from an international division to a geographic-area division structure. And,

Functional Structure	
Advantages	**Disadvantages**
• Pooling of specialists enhances coordination and control. • Centralized decision making enhances an organizational perspective across functions. • Efficient use of managerial and technical talent. • Facilitates career paths and professional development in specialized areas.	• Differences in functional area orientation impede communication and coordination. • Tendency for specialists to develop short-term perspective and narrow functional orientation. • Functional area conflicts may overburden top-level decision makers. • Difficult to establish uniform performance standards.

Divisional Structure	
Advantages	**Disadvantages**
• Increases strategic and operational control, permitting corporate-level executives to address strategic issues. • Quick response to environmental changes. • Increases focus on products and markets. • Minimizes problems associated with sharing resources across functional areas. • Facilitates development of general managers.	• Increased costs incurred through duplication of personnel, operations, and investment. • Dysfunctional competition among divisions may detract from overall corporate performance. • Difficult to maintain uniform corporate image. • Overemphasis on short-term performance.

Matrix Structure	
Advantages	**Disadvantages**
• Increases market responsiveness through collaboration and synergies among professional colleagues. • Allows more efficient utilization of resources. • Improves flexibility, coordination, and communication. • Increases professional development through a broader range of responsibility.	• Dual-reporting relationships can result in uncertainty regarding accountability. • Intense power struggles may lead to increased levels of conflict. • Working relationships may be more complicated and human resources duplicated. • Excessive reliance on group processes and teamwork may impede timely decision making.

Exhibit 10.5   Functional, Divisional, and Matrix Organizational Structures: Advantages and Disadvantages

as a firm's product and/or market diversity becomes large, it is likely to benefit from a *worldwide matrix structure.*

Global strategies, on the other hand, are driven by economic pressures that require managers to view operations in different geographic areas to be managed for overall efficiency. The structures consistent with the efficiency perspective are the *worldwide functional* and *worldwide product division* structures. Here, division managers view the marketplace as homogeneous and devote relatively little attention to local market, political, and economic factors. The choice between these two types of structures is guided largely by the extent of product diversity. Firms with relatively low levels of product diversity may opt for a worldwide product division structure. However, if significant product–market diversity results from highly unrelated international acquisitions, a worldwide holding company structure should be implemented. Such firms have very little commonality among products, markets, or technologies, and have little need for integration.

Global Start-Ups: A New Phenomenon

Earlier, we suggested that international expansion occurs rather late for most corporations, typically after possibilities of domestic growth are exhausted. Increasingly, we are seeing two interrelated phenomena. First, many firms now expand internationally relatively early in their history. Second, some firms are "born global"—that is, from the very beginning, many start-ups are global in their activities. For example, Logitech Inc., the leading producer of the "mouse" that helps you use the personal computer, was global from day one. Founded in 1982 by a Swiss national and two Italians, the company was headquartered both in California and Switzerland. R&D and manufacturing were also conducted in both locations and, subsequently, in Taiwan and Ireland as well.[14]

The success of companies such as Logitech challenges the conventional wisdom that a company must first build up assets, internal processes, and experience before venturing into faraway lands. It also raises a number of questions: What exactly is a global start-up? Under what conditions should a company start out as a global start-up? What does it take to succeed as a global start-up?

A **global start-up** has been defined as a business organization that, from inception, seeks to derive significant competitive advantage from the use of resources and the sale of outputs in multiple countries. That is, right from the beginning, it uses inputs from around the world and sells its products and services to customers around the world. Geographical boundaries of nation-states are, by and large, irrelevant for a global start-up.

There is no reason for every start-up to be global. Being global necessarily involves higher communication, coordination, and transportation costs. Therefore, it is important to identify the circumstances under which going global from the beginning is advantageous.[15] First, if the required human resources are globally dispersed, going global may be the best way to access those resources. For example, Italians are masters in fine leather and Europeans in ergonomics. Second, in many cases foreign financing may be easier to obtain and more suitable. Traditionally, U.S. venture capitalists have shown greater willingness to bear risk, but they have shorter time horizons in their expectations for return. If a U.S. start-up is looking for patient capital, it may be better off looking overseas. Third, the target customers in many specialized industries are located in other parts of the world. Fourth, in many industries a gradual move from domestic markets to foreign markets is no longer possible because, if a product is successful, foreign competitors may immediately imitate it. Therefore, preemptive entry into foreign markets may be the only option. Finally, because of high up-front development costs, a global market is often necessary to recover the costs. This is particularly true for start-ups from smaller nations that do not have access to large domestic markets.

Successful management of a global start-up presents many challenges. Communication and coordination across time zones and cultures are always problematic. Since most global start-ups have far less resources than well-established corporations, one key for success is to internalize few activities and outsource the rest. It is absolutely important that managers of such firms have considerable prior international experience so that they can

global start-up a business organization that, from inception, seeks to derive significant advantage from the use of resources and the sale of outputs in multiple countries.

Israel: Home of Global Start-Ups

Israel may be a minor player in the world of international commerce, but surprisingly, the country has been the home base for a disproportionately large number of global start-ups. Blue chip venture capital firms and private equity firms from the United States funded as many as 111 start-ups in Israel in the fourth quarter of 2003.

Why is Israel home to so many global start-ups? First, being a small country of 6 million people, the home market is too small to support the growth of domestic companies. Second, the political uncertainties of the region encourage entrepreneurs to diversify their risk by establishing an international presence. Third, many younger generation Israelis have international networks of contacts either due to education or travel. More importantly, the country has an educated workforce with a work ethic second to none. No wonder, many international start-ups are blooming in this desert country! Here are three examples:

- Cash-U, founded by Gal Nachum and Amir Peleg, initially thought of developing games for cell phones but soon realized that it was difficult to come up with games that have universal appeal. Instead, they now supply a software platform that helps others develop games for cell phones. Once they created the product in their labs outside Tel Aviv,

they opened sales offices in London and Singapore. Today, their customers include firms such as Vodafone and Telefonica and their revenue growth is around 75 percent annually.

- Baradok Pridor, 38, and Yonatan Aumann, 42, founders of ClearForest, developed an innovative software product—a program that can analyze unstructured electronic data, such as a Web page or a video clip, as if it were already in a spreadsheet or database. Instead of waiting for customers to show up, right from the beginning, they started sending their engineers to make presentations to potential clients around the world. Today the company's customers include Dow Chemical, Thomson Financial, and the FBI itself! They have raised $33 million so far in three rounds of venture financing. Interestingly, the headquarters of the 83-person company is in Boston!

- HyperRoll, a company that makes software for analyzing massive databases, has raised $28 million in venture funding. Referring to their hiring practices, Yossi Matias, founder of HyperRoll, says, "We build the strongest team possible, unconstrained by locality, affinity, or culture. It requires every employee to accept and support a multicultural environment." Although essentially an Israeli start-up, he even banned the use of Hebrew in the office to facilitate greater integration between the American and Israeli employees!

Sources: Copeland, M. V. 2004. The start-up oasis. *Business 2.0*, August 46–48; and Brown, E. 2004. Global start-up. *Forbes*, November 29: 150–161.

---

successfully handle the inevitable communication problems and cultural conflicts. Another key for success is to keep the communication and coordination costs low. The only way to achieve this is by creating less costly administrative mechanisms. The boundaryless organizational designs that we discuss in the next section are particularly suitable for global start-ups because of their flexibility and low cost.

Strategy Spotlight 10.3 discusses two global start-ups that are based in Israel.

How an Organization's Structure Can Influence Strategy Formulation

Discussions of the relationship between strategy and structure usually strongly imply that structure follows strategy. That is, the strategy that a firm chooses (e.g., related diversification) dictates such structural elements as the division of tasks, the need for integration of activities, and authority relationships within the organization. However, an existing structure can influence strategy formulation. For example, once a firm's structure

strategy spotlight

How the Role of the Chief Diversity Officer (CDO) at Russell Athletic has Paid Off

Corporations have been adding "lighter" titles over the years such as Chief Yahoo, Chief Fun Office, and the like. In 1995, Denny's added a new "chief" title—Chief Diversity Officer. But this new title certainly wasn't done in an effort to inspire humor and lightheartedness. Rather, it was a direct result of their infamous class action discrimination lawsuit. In fact, Denny's Ray Hood-Phillips became the first Chief Diversify Officer in America. She claims, "I'm responsible for driving the cultural and structural change throughout the whole organization. And I take diversity and leverage it into a business advantage of the company."

In the corporate world, CDO's have been in vogue since Denny's initiative over 10 years ago. The more progressive companies are releasing CDOs from the confines of human resources and positioning them to work closely with the heads of product development, business development, marketing, and sales. *This change in reporting rela-*

Sources: Johansson, F. 2006. Masters of the multicultural. *Harvard Business Review,* 83(10): 18–19; Wells, J. 2003. Grandiose titles are proliferating in corporate boardrooms. www.msnbc.msn.com. August 12: np; and Young, N. 2006. Berkshire Hathaway to acquire Russell Corporation. *Press Release.* April 17.

tionships (a key component of organization structure) allows the CDO to more easily detect innovation opportunities throughout the organization. "Increasingly, CDOs report to the CEO, outside of HR," asserts Edie Fraser, founder and president of Diversity Best Practices, an organization that tracks diversity initiatives by corporations.

One company that has taken this approach is Russell Corporation, with $1.5 billion in revenues. The company (recently acquired by Berkshire Hathaway), founded in 1902, now has three business segments: apparel, sports equipment, and athletic shoes. At Russell, the human resources function handles the traditional diversity matters such as affirmative action, recruiting, and legal issues. However, CDO Kevin Clayton is busy turning a separate diversity department into a profit center. For example, Clayton's group discovered that a large number of Russell's employees had graduated from historically black colleges and universities. The group then used those graduates' ideas to create products for the black university market, resulting in an $8 million- to $10-million contract. Since then, Clayton has created several additional development groups that combine employees of different ethnicities and religions. Clayton is expecting to significantly increase revenues in the future.

---

is in place, it is very difficult and expensive to change.[16] Executives may not be able to modify their duties and responsibilities greatly, or may not welcome the disruption associated with a transfer to a new location. Further, there are costs associated with hiring, training, and replacing executive, managerial, and operating personnel. Thus, strategy cannot be formulated without considering structural elements.

The type of organizational structure can also strongly influence a firm's strategy, day-to-day operations, and performance.[17] We discussed Brinker International's move to a divisional structure in order to organize its restaurant groups into different units to focus on market niches. This new structure should enable the firm to adapt to change more rapidly and innovate more effectively with the various restaurant brands. Brinker's management did not feel that they were as effective with their previous functional organizational structure.

An organization's structure can also have an important influence on how it competes in the marketplace. Strategy Spotlight 10.4 discusses how a new role in many corporations, a Chief Diversity Officer (CDO), can promote diversity and spur innovation.

● Today's organizations need to be designed to draw on the strengths of a diversified workforce.

Linking Strategic Reward and Evaluation Systems to Business-Level and Corporate-Level Strategies

>LO6

Why there is no "one best way" to design strategic reward and evaluation systems, and the important contingent roles of business- and corporate-level strategies.

The effective use of reward and evaluation systems can play a critical role in motivating managers to conform to organizational strategies, achieve performance targets, and reduce the gap between organizational and individual goals. In contrast, reward systems, if improperly designed, can lead to behaviors that either are detrimental to organizational performance or can lower morale and cause employee dissatisfaction.

As we will see in this section, there is no "one best way" to design reward and evaluation systems. Instead, it is contingent on many factors. Two of the most important factors are a firm's business-level strategy (see Chapter 5) and its corporate-level strategy (see Chapter 6).

Business-Level Strategy: Reward and Evaluation Systems

In Chapter 5 we discussed two approaches that firms may take to secure competitive advantages: overall cost leadership and differentiation.[18] As we might expect, implementing these strategies requires fundamentally different organizational arrangements, approaches to control, and reward and incentive systems.

Overall Cost Leadership   This strategy requires that product lines remain rather stable and that innovations deal mostly with production processes. Given the emphasis on efficiency, costly changes even in production processes tend to be rare. Since products are quite standardized and change rather infrequently, procedures can be developed to divide work into its basic components—those that are routine, standardized, and ideal for semiskilled and unskilled employees. As such, firms competing on the basis of cost must implement tight cost controls, frequent and comprehensive reports to monitor the costs associated with outputs, and highly structured tasks and responsibilities. Incentives tend to be based on explicit financial targets since innovation and creativity are expensive and might tend to erode competitive advantages. Let's look at Nucor, a highly successful steel producer with $15 billion in revenues.

Nucor competes primarily on the basis of cost and, has a reward and incentive system that is largely based on financial outputs and financial measures.[19] Nucor uses four incentive compensation systems that correspond to the levels of management.

1. *Production incentive program.* Groups of 20 to 40 people are paid a weekly bonus based on either anticipated product time or tonnage produced. Each shift and production line is in a separate bonus group.
2. *Department managers.* Bonuses are based on divisional performance, primarily measured by return on assets.
3. *Employees not directly involved in production.* These include engineers, accountants, secretaries, receptionists, and others. Bonuses are based on two factors: divisional and corporate return on assets.
4. *Senior incentive programs.* Salaries are lower than comparable companies, but a significant portion of total compensation is based on return on stockholder equity. A portion of pretax earnings is placed in a pool and divided among officers as bonuses that are part cash and part stock.

The culture at Nucor reflects its reward and incentive system. Since incentive compensation can account for more than half of their paychecks, employees become nearly obsessed with productivity and apply a lot of pressure on each other. Ken Iverson, a former CEO, recalled an instance in which one employee arrived at work in sunglasses instead of safety glasses, preventing the team from doing any work. Furious, the other workers chased him around the plant with a piece of angle iron!

Differentiation   This strategy typically involves the development of innovative products and services that require using experts who can identify the crucial elements of intricate, creative designs and marketing decisions. Highly trained professionals such as scientists and engineers are essential for devising, assessing, implementing and continually changing complex product designs. New product design also requires extensive collaboration and cooperation among specialists and functional managers from different areas within a firm. Such individuals must, for example, evaluate and implement a new design, constantly bearing in mind marketing, financial, production, and engineering considerations.

Given the need for cooperation and coordination among professionals in many functional areas, it becomes quite difficult to evaluate individuals using set quantitative criteria. It also is difficult to measure specific outcomes of such efforts and attribute outcomes to specific individuals. Thus, more behavioral measures (such as how effectively employees collaborate and share information) and intangible incentives and rewards become necessary to support a strong culture and to motivate employees. Consider 3M, a highly innovative company whose core value is innovation.

> At 3M, rewards are tied closely to risk-taking and innovation-oriented behavior. Managers are not penalized for product failures. Instead, those same people are encouraged to work on another project that borrows from their shared experience and insight. A culture of creativity and "thinking out of the box" is reinforced by their well-known "15 percent rule," which permits employees to set aside 15 percent of their work time to pursue personal research interests. And a familiar 3M homily, "Thou shall not kill new ideas for products," is known as the 11th commandment. It is the source of countless stories, including one that tells how L. D. DeSimone (3M's former CEO) tried five times (and failed) to kill the project that yielded the 3M blockbuster product, Thinsulate.[20]

Corporate-Level Strategy: Strategic Reward and Evaluation Systems

In Chapter 6 we discussed two broad types of diversification strategies: related and unrelated. The type of diversification strategy that a firm follows has important implications for the type of reward and evaluation systems that it should use.

Sharp Corporation, a $25 billion Japanese consumer electronics giant follows a strategy of *related* diversification.[21] Its most successful technology has been liquid crystal displays (LCDs) that are critical components in nearly all of the firm's products. With their expertise in this area, they are moving into high-end displays for cellular telephones, hand-held computers, and digital computers.[22]

Given the need to leverage such technologies across multiple product lines, Sharp needs reward and evaluation systems that foster coordination and sharing. It must focus more on individuals' behavior rather than on short-term financial outcomes. For example, promotion is a powerful incentive, and it is generally based on seniority and subtle skills exhibited over time, such as teamwork and communication. It helps to ensure that the company's reward system will not reward short-term self-interested orientations.

Like many Japanese companies, Sharp's culture reinforces the view that the firm is a family or community whose members should cooperate for the greater good. In accordance with the policy of lifetime employment, turnover is low. This encourages employees to pursue what is best for the entire company. Such an outlook lessens the inevitable conflict over sharing important resources such as R&D knowledge.

In contrast to Sharp, firms such as Hanson PLC (a British conglomerate) followed a strategy of unrelated diversification for most of its history. At one time it owned as many as 150 operating companies in areas such as tobacco, footwear, building products, brewing, and food. There were limited product similarities across businesses and therefore little need for sharing of resources and knowledge across divisional boundaries. James Hanson and Gordon White, founders of the company, actually did not permit any sharing of resources between operating companies even if it was feasible!

Their reward and evaluation system placed such heavy emphasis on individual accountability that they viewed resource sharing, with its potential for mutual blaming, unacceptable. The operating managers had more than 60 percent of their compensation tied to annual financial performance of their subsidiaries. All decision making was decentralized so that subsidiary managers could be held responsible for the return on capital they employed. However, there was one area in which they had to obtain approval from the corporate office. No subsidiary manager was allowed to incur a capital expenditure greater than $3,000 without permission from the corporate office. Hanson managed to be successful with a very small corporate office because of its decentralized structure, tight financial controls, and an incentive system that motivated managers to meet financial goals. Gordon White was proud of claiming that he had never visited any of the operating companies that were part of the Hanson empire.[23]

To summarize, the key issue becomes the need for *in*dependence versus *inter*dependence. With cost leadership strategies and unrelated diversification, there tends to be less need for interdependence. Thus, the reward and evaluation systems focus more on the use of financial indicators because unit costs, profits, and revenues can be rather easily attributed to a given business unit or division.

In contrast, firms that follow differentiation or related diversification strategies have intense needs for tight interdependencies among the functional areas and business units. Here, sharing of resources, including raw materials, R&D knowledge, marketing information, and so on, is critical to organizational success. That is, it is more important to achieve synergies with value-creating activities and business units than with cost leadership or unrelated strategies. To facilitate sharing and collaboration, reward and evaluation systems tend to incorporate more behavioral indicators. Exhibit 10.6 summarizes our discussion of the relationship between strategies and control systems.

We must apply an important caveat. Although Exhibit 10.6 suggests guidelines on how an organization should match its strategies to its evaluation and reward systems, all organizations must have combinations of both financial and behavioral rewards. Both overall cost leadership and unrelated diversification strategies require a need for collaboration and the sharing of best practices across both value-creating activities and business units. General Electric, for example, has developed many integrating mechanisms to enhance sharing "best practices" across what would appear to be rather unrelated businesses such as jet engines, appliances, and network television. And, for both differentiation and related diversification strategies, financial indicators such as revenue growth and profitability should not be overlooked at both the business-unit and corporate levels.

Exhibit 10.6

Summary of Relationships between Reward and Evaluation Systems and Business-Level and Corporate-Level Strategies

Level of Strategy	Types of Strategy	Need for Interdependence	Primary Type of Reward and Evaluation System
Business-level	Overall cost leadership	Low	Financial
Business-level	Differentiation	High	Behavioral
Corporate-level	Related diversification	High	Behavioral
Corporate-level	Unrelated diversification	Low	Financial

Boundary Types

There are primarily four types of boundaries that place limits on organizations. In today's dynamic business environment, different types of boundaries are needed to foster high degrees of interaction with outside influences and varying levels of permeability.

1. *Vertical boundaries between levels in the organization's hierarchy.* SmithKline Beecham asks employees at different hierarchical levels to brainstorm ideas for managing clinical trial data. The ideas are incorporated into action plans that significantly cut the new product approval time of its breakthrough pharmaceuticals. This would not have been possible if the barriers between levels of individuals in the organization had been too high.

2. *Horizontal boundaries between functional areas.* Fidelity Investments makes the functional barriers more porous and flexible among divisions, such as marketing, operations, and customer service, in order to offer customers a more integrated experience when conducting business with the company. Customers can take their questions to one person, reducing the chance that customers will "get the runaround" from employees who feel customer service is not their responsibility. At Fidelity, customer service is everyone's business, regardless of functional area.

3. *External boundaries between the firm and its customers, suppliers, and regulators.* GE Lighting, by working closely with retailers, functions throughout the value chain as a single operation. This allows GE to track point-of-sale purchases, giving it better control over inventory management.

4. *Geographic boundaries between locations, cultures, and markets.* The global nature of today's business environment spurred PricewaterhouseCoopers to use a global groupware system. This allows the company to instantly connect to its 26 worldwide offices.

Source: Ashkenas, R. 1997. The organization's new clothes. In Hesselbein, F., Goldsmith, M., and Beckhard, R. (Eds.). *The organization of the future:* 104–106. San Francisco: Jossey Bass.

Boundaryless Organizational Designs

The term *boundaryless* may bring to mind a chaotic organizational reality in which "anything goes." This is not the case. As Jack Welch, GE's former CEO, has suggested, boundaryless does not imply that all internal and external boundaries vanish completely. Although boundaries may continue to exist in some form, they become more open and permeable.[24] Strategy Spotlight 10.5 discusses four types of boundaries and provides examples of how organizations have made them more permeable.

We are not suggesting that **boundaryless organizational designs** replace the traditional forms of organizational structure, but rather that they should complement them. For example, Sharp Corp. has implemented a functional structure to attain economies of scale with its applied research and manufacturing skills. However, to bring about this key objective, Sharp has relied on several integrating mechanisms and processes:

> To prevent functional groups from becoming vertical chimneys that obstruct product development, Sharp's product managers have responsibility—but not authority—for coordinating the entire set of value-chain activities. And the company convenes enormous numbers of cross-unit and corporate committees to ensure that shared activities, including the corporate R&D unit and sales forces, are optimally configured and allocated among the different product lines. Sharp invests in such time-intensive coordination to minimize the inevitable conflicts that arise when units share important activities.[25]

We will discuss three approaches to making boundaries more permeable. These approaches help to facilitate the widespread sharing of knowledge and information across both the internal and external boundaries of the organization. We'll begin with the *barrier-free*

>LO7

The different types of boundaryless organizations—barrier-free, modular, and virtual—and their relative advantages and disadvantages.

boundaryless organizational designs
organizations in which the boundaries, including vertical, horizontal, external, and geographic boundaries, are permeable.

type, which involves making all organizational boundaries—internal and external—more permeable. We'll place particular emphasis on team concepts, because teams as a central building block for implementing the boundaryless organization. In the next two sections, we will address the *modular* and *virtual* types of organizations. These forms focus on the need to create seamless relationships with external organizations such as customers or suppliers. While the modular type emphasizes the outsourcing of noncore activities, the virtual (or network) organization focuses on alliances among independent entities formed to exploit specific market opportunities.

The Barrier-Free Organization

The "boundary" mind-set is ingrained deeply into bureaucracies. It is evidenced by such clichés as "That's not my job," "I'm here from corporate to help," or endless battles over transfer pricing. In the traditional company, boundaries are clearly delineated in the design of an organization's structure. Their basic advantage is that the roles of managers and employees are simple, clear, well-defined, and long-lived. A major shortcoming was pointed out to the authors during an interview with a high-tech executive: "Structure tends to be divisive; it leads to territorial fights."

Today such structures are being replaced by fluid, ambiguous, and deliberately ill-defined tasks and roles. Just because work roles are no longer clearly defined, however, does not mean that differences in skills, authority, and talent disappear.

A **barrier-free organization** enables a firm to bridge real differences in culture, function, and goals to find common ground that facilitates information sharing and other forms of cooperative behavior. Eliminating the multiple boundaries that stifle productivity and innovation can enhance the potential of the entire organization.

Strategy Spotlight 10.6 describes how United Technologies Corporation used the boundaryless concept to develop a revolutionary product, PureCycle.

Creating Permeable Internal Boundaries   For barrier-free organizations to work effectively, the level of trust and shared interests among all parts of the organization must be raised. Similarly, the organization needs to develop among its employees the skill level needed to work in a more democratic organization. Barrier-free organizations also require a shift in the organization's philosophy from executive development to organizational development, and from investments in high-potential individuals to investments in leveraging the talents of all individuals.

Teams can be an important aspect of barrier-free structures.[26] Jeffrey Pfeffer, author of several insightful books, including *The Human Equation,* suggests that teams have three primary advantages.[27] First, teams substitute peer-based control for hierarchical control of work activities. In essence, employees control themselves, reducing the time and energy management needs to devote to control.

Second, teams frequently develop more creative solutions to problems because they encourage the sharing of the tacit knowledge held by individuals.[28] Brainstorming, or group problem solving, involves the pooling of ideas and expertise to enhance the chances that at least one group member will think of a way to solve the problems at hand.

Third, by substituting peer control for hierarchical control, teams permit the removal of layers of hierarchy and absorption of administrative tasks previously performed by specialists. This avoids the costs of having people whose sole job is to watch the people who watch other people do the work. As Norman Augustine humorously pointed out in *Augustine's Laws,* "If a sufficient number of management layers are superimposed on top of each other, it can be assured that disaster is not left to chance!"[29]

Effective barrier-free organizations must go beyond achieving close integration and coordination within divisions in a corporation. Research on multidivisional organizations

barrier-free organization an organizational design in which firms bridge real differences in culture, function, and goals to find common ground that facilitates information sharing and other forms of cooperative behavior.

strategy spotlight

10.6

United Technologies Corporation's PureCycle: An Effective Use of the Boundaryless Concept

United Technologies Corporation is a giant manufacturing conglomerate that has been on a roll. Revenues and profits for 2006 were $48 billion and $3.7 billion, respectively, which represents an annual increase of over 15 percent over the most recent four-year period.

Like many diversified firms, UTC faced a challenge in developing synergies across business units. UTC's wide variety of products include Carrier heating and air conditioning, Hamilton Sundstrand aerospace systems and industrial products, Otis elevators and escalators, Pratt & Whitney aircraft engines, Sikorsky helicopters, UTC Fire & Security systems, and UTC Power fuel cells. Overall, UTC spends a huge amount of money on research—about 3.5 percent of total revenues.

Historically, UTC's culture placed a high value on decentralized decision making, with each unit operating almost entirely independently of the others. Such an approach may have motivational benefits and helps each unit focus their efforts. However, it leads to "silo business units" and prevents the corporation from generating innovations in the white spaces between business units.

This approach to business troubled UTC senior vice president John Cassidy and Carl Nett, director of the firm's corporate research center, UTRC. The center is staffed with nearly 500 scientists, engineers, and staff who are charged with "bringing future technologies to the point of product insertion." They both believed that

Sources: www.utc.com; 2005 *UTC Annual Report;* Davidson, A. 2007. Conglomerates: United Technologies. *Forbes,* January 8: 96; and Cross, R., Liedtka, J., & Weiss, L. 2005. A practical guide to social networks. *Harvard Business Review,* 83(3): 92–101.

tremendous potential for growth existed in the junctures between the business units. However, such collaboration was not consistent with the history, work practices, and cultural norms at UTC. In fact, Cassidy felt that integrating expertise and talent across business units was an "unnatural act."

What did they do? In 2002, the two executives invited top technical talent from each unit to several brainstorming sessions. The goal was to bring together a diverse set of talented professionals to create and service new markets.

Early on, a potential winner emerged from the intersection of cooling, heating, and power. Engineers from Carrier, Pratt & Whitney, and UTRC recognized that using cooling and heating equipment could transform an innovative power generation concept into a revolutionary product. Called PureCycle, the product contained virtually no new components. However, it offered a breakthrough value proposition: Customers could convert waste heat to electricity at rates substantially below those of utilities. The product held great promise because U.S. industrial plants emit roughly as much waste heat as a 50-gigawatt power plant generates (enough to run most major U.S. cities).

In retrospect, engineers involved in the PureCycle project find it hard to believe that nobody had previously thought of the idea. Thierry Jomard, a former Carrier engineer who transferred to UTRC to head the effort explains, "Carrier people are trained to think in terms of using heat exchange to produce cold air—that's the output that counts: the compressor is just there to move the fluid. Pratt & Whitney engineers, on the other hand, are power people. The outcome they are about is power, and they use turbines to get it." It wasn't until they began their collaboration that anyone recognized the opportunities before them.

has stressed the importance of interdivisional coordination and resource sharing.[30] This requires interdivisional task forces and committees, reward and incentive systems that emphasize interdivisional cooperation, and common training programs.

Given the importance of collaboration and collective efforts, effective teams become critical. Frank Carruba (former head of Hewlett-Packard's labs) provides some interesting insights.[31] He found that the difference between mediocre teams and good teams was generally varying levels of motivation and talent. But what explained the difference between good teams and truly superior teams? Carruba found that the key difference—and this explained a 40 percent overall difference in performance—was the way members treated each other; that is, the degree to which they believed in one another and created an atmosphere of encouragement rather than competition. In other words, vision, talent, and motivation could carry a team only so far. What clearly stood out in the "super" teams were higher levels of authenticity and caring, which allowed the full synergy of their individual talents, motivation, and vision.

Developing Effective Relationships with External Constituencies   In barrier-free organizations, managers must also create flexible, porous organizational boundaries and establish communication flows and mutually beneficial relationships with internal (e.g., employees) and external (e.g., customers) constituencies. Michael Dell, founder and CEO of Dell Computer, is a strong believer in fostering close relationships with his customers. In an interview, he explained:

> We're not going to be just your PC vendor anymore. We're going to be your IT department for PCs. Boeing, for example, has 100,000 Dell PCs, and we have 30 people that live at Boeing, and if you look at the things we're doing for them or for other customers, we don't look like a supplier, we look more like Boeing's PC department. We become intimately involved in planning their PC needs and the configuration of their network.
>
> It's not that we make these decisions by ourselves. They're certainly using their own people to get the best answer for the company. But the people working on PCs together, from both Dell and Boeing, understand the needs in a very intimate way. They're right there living it and breathing it, as opposed to the typical vendor who says, "Here are your computers. See you later."[32]

Thus far, we have argued that barrier-free organizations create successful relationships between both internal and external constituencies. However, there is one additional constituency—competitors—with whom some organizations have benefited as they developed cooperative relationships.

For example, after years of seeing its empty trucks return from warehouses back to production facilities after deliveries, General Mills teamed up with 16 of its competitors. They formed an e-commerce business to help the firms to find carriers with empty cargo trailers to piggyback freight loads to distributors near the production facilities.[33] This increases revenue for all network members and reduces fuel costs.

Risks, Challenges, and Potential Downsides   Despite its potential benefits, many firms find that creating and managing a barrier-free organization can be frustrating.[34] For example, Puritan-Bennett Corporation, a Lenexa, Kansas, manufacturer of respiratory equipment, found that its product development time more than doubled after it adopted team management. Roger J. Dolida, director of R&D, attributed this failure to a lack of top management commitment, high turnover among team members, and infrequent meetings. Often, managers trained in rigid hierarchies find it difficult to make the transition to the more democratic, participative style that teamwork requires.

Christopher Barnes, now a consultant with PricewaterhouseCoopers in Atlanta, previously worked as an industrial engineer for Challenger Electrical Distribution (a subsidiary of Westinghouse, now part of CBS) at a plant in Jackson, Mississippi, which produced circuit-breaker boxes. His assignment was to lead a team of workers from the plant's troubled final-assembly operation with the mission: "Make things better." Not surprisingly, that vague notion set the team up for failure.

After a year of futility, the team was disbanded. In retrospect, Barnes identified several reasons for the debacle: (1) limited personal credibility—he was viewed as an "outsider"; (2) a lack of commitment to the team—everyone involved was forced to be on the team; (3) poor communications—nobody was told why the team was important; (4) limited autonomy—line managers refused to give up control over team members; and (5) misaligned incentives—the culture rewarded individual performance over team performance. Barnes's experience has implications for all types of teams, whether they are composed of

Exhibit 10.7
Pros and Cons of
Barrier-Free Structures

Pros	Cons
• Leverages the talents of all employees. • Enhances cooperation, coordination, and information sharing among functions, divisions, SBUs, and external constituencies. • Enables a quicker response to market changes through a single-goal focus. • Can lead to coordinated win–win initiatives with key suppliers, customers, and alliance partners.	• Difficult to overcome political and authority boundaries inside and outside the organization. • Lacks strong leadership and common vision, which can lead to coordination problems. • Time-consuming and difficult-to-manage democratic processes. • Lacks high levels of trust, which can impede performance.

managerial, professional, clerical, or production personnel.[35] The pros and cons of barrier-free structures are summarized in Exhibit 10.7.

The Modular Organization

As Charles Handy, author of *The Age of Unreason,* has noted:

> Organizations have realized that, while it may be convenient to have everyone around all the time, having all of your workforce's time at your command is an extravagant way of marshaling the necessary resources. It is cheaper to keep them outside the organization, employed by themselves or by specialist contractors, and to buy their services when you need them.[36]

Consistent with Handy's vision, the **modular organization** outsources nonvital functions, tapping into the knowledge and expertise of "best in class" suppliers, but retains strategic control. Outsiders may be used to manufacture parts, handle logistics, or perform accounting activities. As we discussed in Chapters 3 and 5, the value chain can be used to identify the key primary and support activities performed by a firm to create value. The key question becomes: Which activities do we keep "in-house" and which activities do we outsource to suppliers?[37] The organization becomes a central hub surrounded by networks of outside suppliers and specialists and, much like Lego blocks, parts can be added or taken away. Both manufacturing and service units may be modular.[38]

modular organization an organization in which nonvital functions are outsourced, which uses the knowledge and expertise of outside suppliers while retaining strategic control.

Apparel is an industry in which the modular type has been widely adopted. Nike and Reebok, for example, concentrate on their strengths: designing and marketing high-tech, fashionable footwear. Nike has few production facilities and Reebok owns no plants. These two companies contract virtually all their footwear production to suppliers in China, Vietnam, and other countries with low-cost labor. Avoiding large investments in fixed assets helps them derive large profits on minor sales increases. Thus, Nike and Reebok can keep pace with changing tastes in the marketplace because their suppliers have become expert at rapidly retooling to produce new products.

● Adidas is one of many athletic shoe companies that has outsourced most of its production to low-cost labor countries such as China and Vietnam.

In a modular company, outsourcing the noncore functions offers three advantages.

1. A firm can decrease overall costs, stimulate new product development by hiring suppliers whose talent may be superior to that of in-house personnel, avoid idle capacity, reduce inventories, and avoid being locked into a particular technology.
2. Outsourcing enables a company to focus scarce resources on the areas where it holds a competitive advantage. These benefits can translate into more funding for research and development, hiring the best engineers, and providing continuous training for sales and service staff.
3. By enabling an organization to tap into the knowledge and expertise of its specialized supply-chain partners, it adds critical skills and accelerates organizational learning.[39]

The modular type enables a company to leverage relatively small amounts of capital and a small management team to achieve seemingly unattainable strategic objectives.[40] Freed from the need to make big investments in fixed assets, the modular company can grow rapidly. Certain preconditions are necessary before the modular approach can be successful. First, the company must work closely with suppliers to ensure that the interests of each party are being fulfilled. Companies need to find loyal, reliable vendors who can be trusted with trade secrets. They also need assurances that suppliers will dedicate their financial, physical, and human resources to satisfy strategic objectives such as lowering costs or being first to market.

Second, the modular company must be sure that it selects the proper competencies to keep in-house. For Nike and Reebok, the core competencies are design and marketing, not shoe manufacturing; for Honda, the core competence is engine technology. These firms are unlikely to outsource any activity that involves their core competence. An organization must avoid outsourcing components that may compromise its long-term competitive advantages.

Strategic Risks of Outsourcing　While adopting the modular form clearly has some advantages, managers must also weigh associated risks. The main strategic concerns are (1) loss of critical skills or developing the wrong skills, (2) loss of cross-functional skills, and (3) loss of control over a supplier.[41]

Too much outsourcing can result in a firm "giving away" too much skill and control. Outsourcing relieves companies of the requirement to maintain skill levels needed to manufacture essential components. Over time, these skills that were once part of the knowledge base of the company disappear. At one time, semiconductor chips seemed like a simple technology to outsource. But now, they have become a critical component of a wide variety of products. Companies that have outsourced the manufacture of these chips run the risk of losing the ability to manufacture them as the technology escalates. Thus, they become more dependent upon their suppliers.

Cross-functional skills refer to the skills acquired through the interaction of individuals in various departments within a company. Often, such interaction assists a department in solving problems as employees interface with others across functional units. However, if a firm outsources key functional responsibilities, such as manufacturing, communication across departments can become more difficult. This is because a firm and its employees must now integrate their activities with a new, outside supplier. This typically brings about new challenges in the coordination of joint efforts.

Another drawback occurs when the outsourced products give suppliers too much power over the manufacturer. This happens when the manufacturer is dependent on a single supplier, or just a few suppliers, for critical components. Suppliers that are key to a manufacturer's success can, in essence, hold the manufacturer "hostage." Nike manages this potential problem by sending full-time "product expatriates" to work at the plants of its suppliers. Also, Nike often brings top members of supplier management and technical teams to its headquarters. This way, Nike keeps close tabs on the pulse of new developments, builds rapport and trust with suppliers, and develops long-term relationships with suppliers to prevent hostage situations.

Outsourcing for Talent: How Sony Develops Video Games

The convergence of Hollywood and Silicon Valley has led to the explosive growth of the worldwide video game industry, with revenues of $24.5 billion in 2004. Recently, it has overtaken the movie industry's box office receipts. The industry's sales are expected to soar to $55 billion by 2008, according to PricewaterhouseCoopers.

While broadcast TV audiences dwindle and moviegoing stagnates, gaming is emerging as the newest and perhaps strongest pillar in the media world. So it's no surprise that film studios, media giants, gamemakers, and Japanese electronics companies are all battling to win the "Games Wars." "This is a huge shift we're seeing, and nobody wants to be left behind," says Sony Entertainment Chairman, Michael Lynton.

In this sprawling market where controlling a broad portfolio of businesses is crucial, nobody is better positioned than Sony. Unlike other rivals, it has already assembled all of the pieces of a true video game empire. It sells hardware with its PlayStation consoles, and it has developed its handheld PlayStation Portable product. It also develops games such as the popular *Gran Turismo* racing and *EverQuest* online. And it owns Sony Pictures and MGM movie studios, whose Spider-Man and James Bond franchises have been mega hit games for Activision

and EA. This combination has enabled Sony to sell 80 million Play Station 2 (PS2) consoles worldwide.

The real payoff for Sony comes in game software sales. While Sony and other console makers sell their hardware for a loss, they typically make $5 to $10 in royalties for every game sold on their platform. PS2 has more than 2,000 software titles, with more than 775 million total game copies sold.

Central to Sony's strategy is how it has used outside developers to produce most of its games. It has even reached out to gamers themselves. "We didn't want outside developers to be peripheral to our business model," says Andrew House, an early PlayStation team member and executive vice president of Sony Computer Entertainment America. "We knew that the widest variety of content possible was the best way to build the largest consumer base possible."

Sony has searched high and low for talent. In 1997, it launched a developer kit aimed at hobbyists. "We sent it to budding college developers who wanted to try their hands," House says. Ideas from those amateurs made their way into commercial games in Japan. Meanwhile, externally developed titles like *Final Fantasy* and *Madden NFL Football* helped put Sony's second generation console, the PS2, at the top of the heap in 2001. Sony also launched a Linux developer kit for just $199 in 2002. "It's our way of feeding the market for the future. Some of the first great games were developed by people at home in their garages," say House. "If we're not getting people involved and looking for opportunities very early on, we really are missing out."

Sources: House, A. 2004. Sony. *Fast Company,* April: 65; and Grover, R. Edwards, C., Rowley, I., & Moon, I. 2005. Game wars. *BusinessWeek,* February 28: 35–40.

Strategy Spotlight 10.7 discusses how Sony outsources for talent to develop games for its highly successful video game business. Exhibit 10.8 summarizes the pros and cons of modular structures.[42]

The Virtual Organization

In contrast to the "self-reliant" thinking that guided traditional organizational designs, the strategic challenge today has become doing more with less and looking outside the firm for opportunities and solutions to problems. The virtual organization provides a new means of leveraging resources and exploiting opportunities.[43]

The **virtual organization** can be viewed as a continually evolving network of independent companies—suppliers, customers, even competitors—linked together to share skills, costs, and access to one another's markets.[44] The members of a virtual organization, by pooling and sharing the knowledge and expertise of each of the component organizations, simultaneously "know" more and can "do" more than any one member of the group could do alone. By working closely together, each gains in the long run from individual and organizational learning.[45] The term *virtual,* meaning "being in effect but not actually so," is commonly used in the computer industry. A computer's ability to appear to have

virtual organization
a continually evolving network of independent companies that are linked together to share skills, costs, and access to one another's markets.

Exhibit 10.8

Pros and Cons of Modular Structures

Pros	Cons
• Directs a firm's managerial and technical talent to the most critical activities.	• Inhibits common vision through reliance on outsiders.
• Maintains full strategic control over most critical activities—core competencies.	• Diminishes future competitive advantages if critical technologies or other competences are outsourced.
• Achieves "best in class" performance at each link in the value chain.	• Increases the difficulty of bringing back into the firm activities that now add value due to market shifts.
• Leverages core competencies by outsourcing with smaller capital commitment.	• Leads to an erosion of cross-functional skills.
• Encourages information sharing and accelerates organizational learning.	• Decreases operational control and potential loss of control over a supplier.

more storage capacity than it really possesses is called virtual memory. Similarly, by assembling resources from a variety of entities, a virtual organization may seem to have more capabilities than it really possesses.[46]

The virtual organization is a grouping of units from different organizations that have joined in an alliance to exploit complementary skills in pursuing common strategic objectives. A case in point is Lockheed Martin's use of specialized coalitions between and among three entities—the company, academia, and government—to enhance competitiveness. According to former CEO Norman Augustine:

> The underlying beauty of this approach is that it forces us to reach outward. No matter what your size, you have to look broadly for new ideas, new approaches, new products. Lockheed Martin used this approach in a surprising manner when it set out during the height of the Cold War to make stealth aircraft and missiles. The technical idea came from research done at the Institute of Radio Engineering in Moscow in the 1960s that was published, and publicized, quite openly in the academic media.
>
> Despite the great contrasts among government, academia and private business, we have found ways to work together that have produced very positive results, not the least of which is our ability to compete on a global scale.[47]

Virtual organizations need not be permanent and participating firms may be involved in multiple alliances. Virtual organizations may involve different firms performing complementary value activities, or different firms involved jointly in the same value activities, such as production, R&D, and distribution. The percentage of activities that are jointly performed with partners may vary significantly from alliance to alliance.[48]

How does the virtual type of structure differ from the modular type? Unlike the modular type, in which the focal firm maintains full strategic control, the virtual organization is characterized by participating firms that give up part of their control and accept interdependent destinies. Participating firms pursue a collective strategy that enables them to cope with uncertainty through cooperative efforts. The benefit is that, just as virtual memory increases storage capacity, the virtual organizations enhance the capacity or competitive advantage of participating firms. Strategy Spotlight 10.8 addresses the variety of collaborative relationships in the biotechnology industry.

Each company (as Strategy Spotlight 10.8 illustrates) that links up with others to create a virtual organization contributes only what it considers its core competencies. It will mix and match what it does best with the best of other firms by identifying its critical capabilities and the necessary links to other capabilities.[49]

Collaborative Relationships in Biotechnology

Collaboration in biotechnology has benefited a variety of firms. Amgen collaborates with a number of smaller firms including ARRIS, Environgen, Glycomex, and Interneuron, among others. The companies work on joint marketing projects and bring R&D scientists together to explore opportunities for new pharmaceutical product development. In exchange for the expertise of the scientists and marketers at the smaller companies, Amgen provides financial clout and technical assistance when new-product opportunities are identified.

Another biotech company that utilizes collaborative relationships with competitors is Biogen. This large pharmaceutical firm once outsourced clinical testing of its new drugs. But now, the company brings experts from other firms to Biogen laboratories to work with their scientists.

Chiron, one of the largest pharmaceutical firms, with over 7,500 employees, makes extensive use of collaborative efforts with its competitors. The company currently collaborates with over 1,400 companies, tapping into the knowledge base of R&D experts with a wide variety of skill and expertise in the field. Chiron considers this network one of its core competencies.

Source: Powell, W. W. 1998. Learning from collaboration: Knowledge and networks in the biotechnology and pharmaceutical industries. *California Management Review,* 40 (3): 228–240; Williams, E., & Langreth, R. 2001. "A biotech wonder grows up. *Forbes,* September 3: 118.

Challenges and Risks   Despite their many advantages, such alliances often fail to meet expectations. For example, the alliance between IBM and Microsoft soured in early 1991 when Microsoft began shipping Windows in direct competition to OS/2, which they jointly developed. The runaway success of Windows frustrated IBM's ability to set an industry standard. In retaliation, IBM entered into an alliance with Microsoft's archrival, Novell, to develop network software to compete with Microsoft's LAN Manager.

The virtual organization demands a unique set of managerial skills. Managers must build relationships with other companies, negotiate win–win deals for all parties involved, find the right partners with compatible goals and values, and provide the right balance of freedom and control. In addition, information systems must be designed and integrated to facilitate communication with current and potential partners.

Managers must be clear about the strategic objectives while forming alliances. Some objectives are time bound, and those alliances need to be dissolved once the objective is fulfilled. Some alliances may have relatively long-term objectives and will need to be clearly monitored and nurtured to produce mutual commitment and avoid bitter fights for control. The highly dynamic personal computer industry, for example, is characterized by multiple temporary alliances among hardware, operating systems, and software producers.[50] But alliances in the more stable automobile industry, such as those involving Nissan and Volkswagen as well as Mazda and Ford, have long-term objectives and tend to be relatively stable.

The virtual organization is a logical culmination of joint-venture strategies of the past. Shared risks, shared costs, and shared rewards are the facts of life in a virtual organization.[51] When virtual organizations are formed, they involve tremendous challenges for strategic planning. As with the modular corporation, it is essential to identify core competencies. However, for virtual structures to be successful, a strategic plan is also needed to determine the effectiveness of combining core competencies.

The strategic plan must address the diminished operational control and overwhelming need for trust and common vision among the partners. This new structure may be appropriate for firms whose strategies require merging technologies (e.g., computing and communication) or for firms exploiting shrinking product life cycles that require simultaneous entry into multiple geographical markets. Further, it may be effective for firms that desire to be quick to the

Exhibit 10.9

Pros and Cons of
Virtual Structures

Pros	Cons
• Enables the sharing of costs and skills.	• Harder to determine where one company ends and another begins, due to close interdependencies among players.
• Enhances access to global markets.	
• Increases market responsiveness.	• Leads to potential loss of operational control among partners.
• Creates a "best of everything" organization since each partner brings core competencies to the alliance.	• Results in loss of strategic control over emerging technology.
• Encourages both individual and organizational knowledge sharing and accelerates organizational learning.	• Requires new and difficult-to-acquire managerial skills.

Source: Miles, R. E., & Snow, C. C. 1986. Organizations: New concepts for new forms. *California Management Review,* Spring: 62–73; Miles & Snow. 1999. Causes of failure in network organizations. *California Management Review,* Summer: 53–72; and Bahrami, H. 1991. The emerging flexible organization: Perspectives from Silicon Valley. *California Management Review,* Summer: 33–52.

market with a new product or service. For example, the recent profusion of alliances among airlines was primarily motivated by the need to provide seamless travel demanded by the full-fare paying business traveler. Exhibit 10.9 summarizes the advantages and disadvantages of the virtual form.

Boundaryless Organizations: Making Them Work

Designing an organization that simultaneously supports the requirements of an organization's strategy, is consistent with the demands of the environment, and can be effectively implemented by the people around the manager is a tall order for any manager.[52] The most effective solution is usually a combination of organizational types. That is, a firm may outsource many parts of its value chain to reduce costs and increase quality, engage simultaneously in multiple alliances to take advantage of technological developments or penetrate new markets, and break down barriers within the organization to enhance flexibility. In Strategy Spotlight 10.9, we see how an innovative firm, Technical Computer Graphics, combines both barrier-free and virtual organizational forms.

When an organization faces external pressures, resource scarcity, and declining performance, it tends to become more internally focused, rather than directing its efforts toward managing and enhancing relationships with existing and potential external stakeholders. We believe that this may be the most opportune time for managers to carefully analyze their value-chain activities and evaluate the potential for adopting elements of modular, virtual, and barrier-free organizational types.

Regardless of the form of organization ultimately chosen, achieving the coordination and integration necessary to maximize the potential of an organization's human capital involves much more than just creating a new structure. Techniques and processes to ensure the coordination and integration of an organization's key value-chain activities are critical. Teams are key building blocks of the new organizational forms, and teamwork requires new and flexible approaches to coordination and integration.

Managers trained in rigid hierarchies may find it difficult to make the transition to the more democratic, participative style that teamwork requires. As Douglas K. Smith, co-author of *The Wisdom of Teams,* pointed out, "A completely diverse group must agree on a goal, put the notion of individual accountability aside and figure out how to work with each other. Most of all, they must learn that if the team fails, it's everyone's fault."[53] Within the framework of an appropriate organizational design, managers must select a mix and

Technical Computer Graphics' Boundaryless Organization

The Technical Computer Graphics (TCG) group manufactures items such as handheld bar code readers and scanning software. The company uses 13 "alliances," or small project teams, employing a total of 200 employees. Each team is responsible for either specific customers or specific products. Alliance teams share a common infrastructure, but they can develop new business opportunities without approval from upper management. Projects often emerge from listening to what customers need.

TCG uses a "triangulation approach"—alliances that include customers, suppliers, and other alliances. Suppliers and customers who provide funding are involved at the outset of the project. The alliances recognize that attaining the initial customer funding is crucial; it stimulates them to focus on what customers have to say. With an emphasis on speed, new products come to market quickly, providing the firm and its partners with tangible benefits. Sometimes another alliance acts as either the customer or the supplier and provides funding.

While each alliance is independent, it shares financial concern for other alliance teams. When a new business opportunity is discovered, an alliance draws on technical expertise from the other alliances. The purpose is not only to acquire additional knowledge, but also to share accumulated learning. There's no benefit to hoarding information: Learning gained from one software project might prove especially valuable to one under way in another alliance. This technological diffusion of information produces products that quickly reach the market.

TCG's formal structure is designed to ensure that such knowledge diffusion occurs. The company's culture is structured to encourage this as well. The TCG culture attracts both the entrepreneur and the team-oriented person at the same time. Working with multiple stakeholders through TCG's triangulation model forces employees to listen to the customers and respond quickly. Because the customer matters more than the functional title, teams lend expertise to each other in return for sharing the gains realized from supplying value to the customer.

Source: Snow, C. 1997. Twenty-first century organizations: Implications for a new marketing paradigm. *Journal of the Academy of Marketing Science,* Winter: 72–74; Allred, B. Snow, C. & Miles, R. 1996. Characteristics of managerial careers of the 21st century. *Academy of Management Executive,* November: 17–27; Herzog, V. L. 2001. Trust building on corporate collaborative teams. *Project Management Journal,* March: 28–41.

balance of tools and techniques to facilitate the effective coordination and integration of key activities. Some of the factors that must be considered include:

- Common culture and shared values.
- Horizontal organizational structures.
- Horizontal systems and processes.
- Communications and information technologies.
- Human resource practices.

Common Culture and Shared Values Shared goals, mutual objectives, and a high degree of trust are essential to the success of boundaryless organizations. It is neither feasible nor desirable to attempt to "control" suppliers, customers, or alliance partners in the traditional sense. In the fluid and flexible environments of the new organizational architectures, common cultures, shared values, and carefully aligned incentives are often less expensive to implement and are often a more effective means of strategic control than rules, boundaries, and formal procedures.

Horizontal Organizational Structures Horizontal organizational structures, which group similar or related business units under common management control, facilitate sharing resources and infrastructures to exploit synergies among operating units and help to create a sense of common purpose. Consistency in training and the development of similar structures across business units facilitates job rotation and cross training and enhances understanding of common problems and opportunities. Cross-functional teams and interdivisional committees and task groups represent important opportunities to improve understanding and foster cooperation among operating units.

Horizontal Systems and Processes   Organizational systems, policies, and procedures are the traditional mechanisms for achieving integration among functional units. Too often, however, existing policies and procedures do little more than institutionalize the barriers that exist from years of managing within the framework of the traditional model. The concept of business reengineering focuses primarily on these internal processes and procedures. Beginning with an understanding of basic business processes in the context of "a collection of activities that takes one or more kinds of input and creates an output that is of value to the customer," Michael Hammer and James Champy's 1993 best-selling *Reengineering the Corporation* outlined a methodology for redesigning internal systems and procedures that has been embraced, in its various forms, by many organizations.[54] Proponents claim that successful reengineering lowers costs, reduces inventories and cycle times, improves quality, speeds response times, and enhances organizational flexibility. Others advocate similar benefits through the reduction of cycle times, total quality management, and the like.

Communications and Information Technologies   Improved communications through the effective use of information technologies can play an important role in bridging gaps and breaking down barriers between organizations. Electronic mail and videoconferencing can improve lateral communications across long distances and multiple time zones and circumvent many of the barriers of the traditional model. Information technology can be a powerful ally in the redesign and streamlining of internal business processes and in improving coordination and integration between suppliers and customers. Internet technologies have eliminated the paperwork of purchase order and invoice documentation in many buyer–supplier relationships, enabling cooperating organizations to reduce inventories, shorten delivery cycles, and reduce operating costs. Today, information technology must be viewed more as a prime component of an organization's overall strategy than simply in terms of its more traditional role as administrative support. The close relationships that must exist between technology and other value-creating activities were addressed in Chapters 3, 4, and 5.

Human Resource Practices   Change, whether in structure, process, or procedure, always involves and impacts the human dimension of organizations. As we noted in Chapter 4, the attraction, development, and retention of human capital are vital to value creation. As boundaryless structures are implemented, processes are reengineered, and organizations become increasingly dependent on sophisticated information technologies, the skills of workers and managers alike must be upgraded to realize the full benefits.

Creating Ambidextrous Organizational Designs

>LO8

The need for creating ambidextrous organizational designs that enable firms to explore new opportunities and effectively integrate existing operations.

In Chapter 1, we introduced the concept of "ambidexterity," which incorporates two contradictory challenges faced by today's managers.[55] First, managers must explore new opportunities and adjust to volatile markets in order to avoid complacency. They must ensure that they maintain *adaptability* and remain proactive in expanding and/or modifying their product–market scope to anticipate and satisfy market conditions. Such competences are especially challenging when change is rapid and unpredictable—conditions that are becoming more pronounced in global markets.

Second, managers must also effectively exploit the value of their existing assets and competencies. They need to have *alignment,* which is a clear sense of how value is being created in the short term and how activities are integrated and properly coordinated. Firms that achieve both adaptability and alignment are considered *ambidextrous organizations*—aligned and efficient in how they manage today's business but flexible enough to changes in the environment so that they will prosper tomorrow.

As we would expect, handling such opposing demands is difficult because there will always be some degree of conflict. Such trade-offs can never really be entirely eliminated, and firms often suffer when they place too strong a priority on either adaptability or alignment. If it places too much focus on adaptability, the firm will suffer low profitability in the short term. On the other hand, if managers direct their efforts primarily at alignment, they will likely miss out on promising business opportunities.

Ambidextrous Organizations: Key Design Attributes

A recent study by Charles O'Reilly and Michael Tushman[56] provides some insights into how some firms were able to create successful **ambidextrous organizational designs.** They investigated companies that attempted to simultaneously pursue modest, incremental innovations as well as more dramatic, breakthrough innovations. In all, the team investigated 35 attempts to launch breakthrough innovations undertaken by 15 business units in nine different industries. They studied the organizational designs and the processes, systems, and cultures associated with the breakthrough projects as well as their impact on the operations and performance of the traditional businesses.

ambidextrous organizational designs organization designs that attempt to simultaneously pursue modest, incremental innovations as well as more dramatic, breakthrough innovations.

Companies structured their breakthrough projects in one of four primary ways:

- Seven were carried out within existing *functional organizational structures*. The projects were completely integrated into the regular organizational and management structure.
- Nine were organized as *cross-functional teams*. The groups operated within the established organization but outside of the existing management structure.
- Four were organized as *unsupported teams*. Here, they became independent units set up outside the established organization and management hierarchy.
- Fifteen were conducted within *ambidextrous organizations*. Here, the breakthrough efforts were organized within structurally independent units, each having its own processes, structures, and cultures. However, they were integrated into the existing senior management structure.

The performance results of the 35 initiatives were tracked along two dimensions:

- Their success in creating desired innovations was measured by either the actual commercial results of the new product or the application of practical market or technical learning.
- The performance of the existing business was evaluated.

The study found that the organizational structure and management practices employed had a direct and significant impact on the performance of both the breakthrough initiative and the traditional business. The ambidextrous organizational designs were more effective than the other three designs on both dimensions: launching breakthrough products or services (i.e., adaptation) and improving the performance of the existing business (i.e., alignment).

Why Was the Ambidextrous Organization the Most Effective Structure?

The study found that there were many factors. A clear and compelling vision, consistently communicated by the company's senior management team was critical in building the ambidextrous designs. The structure enabled cross-fertilization among business units while avoiding cross-contamination. The tight coordination and integration at the managerial levels enabled the newer units to share important resources from the traditional units such as cash, talent, expertise, and so on. Such sharing was encouraged and facilitated by effective reward systems that emphasized overall company goals. At the same time, the organizational separation ensured that the new units' distinctive processes, structures, and cultures were not overwhelmed by the forces of "business as usual." Furthermore, the established units were shielded from the distractions of launching new businesses, and they continued to focus all of their attention and energy on refining their operations, enhancing their products, and serving their customers.

- **Strategy–Structure:** Is there an effective "fit" between your organization's strategy and its structure? If not, there may be inconsistencies in how you are evaluated which often leads to role ambiguity and confusion. A poor fit could also affect communication among departments as well as across the organization's hierarchy.
- **Matrix Structure:** If your organization employs elements of a matrix structure (e.g., dual reporting relationships), are there effective structural supporting elements (e.g., culture and rewards)? If not, there could be a high level of dysfunctional conflict among managers.
- **The "Fit" Between Rewards and Incentives and "Levels of Strategy" (Business- and Corporate-Level):** What metrics are used to evaluate the performance of your work unit? Are there strictly financial measures of success or are you also rewarded for achieving competitive advantages (through effective innovation, organizational learning, or other activities that increase knowledge but may be costly in the short run)?
- **Boundaryless Organizational Designs:** Does your firm have structural mechanisms (e.g., culture, human resource practices) that facilitate sharing of information across boundaries? If so, you should be better able to enhance your human capital by leveraging your talents and competencies.

Summary

Successful organizations must ensure that they have the proper type of organizational structure. Furthermore, they must ensure that their firms incorporate the necessary integration and processes so that the internal and external boundaries of their firms are flexible and permeable. Such a need is increasingly important as the environments of firms become more complex, rapidly changing, and unpredictable.

In the first section of the chapter, we discussed the growth patterns of large corporations. Although most organizations remain small or die, some firms continue to grow in terms of revenues, vertical integration, and diversity of products and services. In addition, their geographical scope may increase to include international operations. We traced the dominant pattern of growth, which evolves from a simple structure to a functional structure as a firm grows in terms of size and increases its level of vertical integration. After a firm expands into related products and services, its structure changes from a functional to a divisional form of organization. Finally, when the firm enters international markets, its structure again changes to accommodate the change in strategy.

We also addressed the different types of organizational structure—simple, functional, divisional (including two variations—strategic business unit and holding company), and matrix—as well as their relative advantages and disadvantages. We closed the section with a discussion of the implications for structure when a firm enters international markets. The three primary factors to take into account when determining the appropriate structure are type of international strategy, product diversity, and the extent to which a firm is dependent on foreign sales.

In the second section, we took a contingency approach to the design of reward and evaluation systems. That is, we argued that there is no one best way to design such systems; rather, it is dependent on a variety of factors. The two that we discussed are business- and corporate-level strategies. With an overall cost leadership strategy and unrelated diversification, it is appropriate to rely primarily on cultures and reward systems that emphasize the production outcomes of the organization, because it is rather easy to quantify such indicators. In contrast, differentiation strategies and related diversification require cultures and incentive systems that encourage and reward creativity initiatives as well as the cooperation among professionals in many different functional areas. Here it becomes more difficult to measure accurately each individual's contribution, and more subjective indicators become essential.

The third section of the chapter introduced the concept of the boundaryless organization. We did not suggest that the concept of the boundaryless organization replaces the traditional forms of organizational structure. Rather, it should complement them. This is necessary to cope with the increasing complexity and change in the competitive environment. We addressed three types of boundaryless organizations. The barrier-free type focuses on the need for the internal and external boundaries of a firm to be more flexible and permeable. The modular type emphasizes the strategic outsourcing of noncore activities. The virtual type centers on the strategic benefits of alliances and the forming of network organizations. We discussed both the advantages and disadvantages of each type of boundaryless organization as well as suggested some techniques and processes that are necessary to successfully implement them. These are common culture and values, horizontal organizational structures, horizontal systems and processes, communications and information technologies, and human resource practices.

The final section addresses the need for managers to develop ambidextrous organizations. In today's rapidly changing global environment, managers must be responsive and proactive in order to take advantage of new opportunities. At the same time, they must effectively integrate and coordinate existing operations. Such requirements call for organizational designs that establish project teams that are structurally independent units, with each having its own processes, structures, and cultures. But, at the same time, each unit needs to be effectively integrated into the existing management hierarchy.

Summary Review Questions

1. Why is it important for managers to carefully consider the type of organizational structure that they use to implement their strategies?
2. Briefly trace the dominant growth pattern of major corporations from simple structure to functional structure to divisional structure. Discuss the relationship between a firm's strategy and its structure.

3. What are the relative advantages and disadvantages of the types of organizational structure—simple, functional, divisional, matrix—discussed in the chapter?
4. When a firm expands its operations into foreign markets, what are the three most important factors to take into account in deciding what type of structure is most appropriate? What are the types of international structures discussed in the text and what are the relationships between strategy and structure?
5. Briefly describe the three different types of boundaryless organizations: barrier-free, modular, and virtual.
6. What are some of the key attributes of effective groups? Ineffective groups?
7. What are the advantages and disadvantages of the three types of boundaryless organizations: barrier-free, modular, and virtual?
8. When are ambidextrous organizational designs necessary? What are some of their key attributes?

Key Terms

simple organizational structure, 342
functional organizational structure, 343
divisional organizational structure, 345
strategic business unit (SBU) structure, 347
holding company structure, 347

matrix organizational structure, 348
global start-up, 351
boundaryless organizational designs, 357
barrier-free organization, 358
modular organization, 361
virtual organization, 368
ambidextrous organizational designs, 369

Experiential Exercise

Many firms have recently moved toward a modular structure. For example, they have increasingly outsourced many of their information technology (IT) activities. Identify three such organizations. Using secondary sources, evaluate (1) the firm's rationale for IT outsourcing and (2) the implications for performance.

Firm	Rationale	Implication(s) for Performance
1.		
2.		
3.		

Application Questions Exercises

1. Select an organization that competes in an industry in which you are particularly interested. Go on the Internet and determine what type of organizational structure this organization has. In your view, is it consistent with the strategy that it has chosen to implement? Why? Why not?

2. Choose an article from *BusinessWeek, Fortune, Forbes, Fast Company,* or any other well-known publication that deals with a corporation that has undergone a significant change in its strategic direction. What are the implications for the structure of this organization?

3. Go on the Internet and look up some of the public statements or speeches of an executive in a major corporation about a significant initiative such as entering into a joint venture or launching a new product line. What do you feel are the implications for making the internal and external barriers of the firm more flexible and permeable? Does the executive discuss processes, procedures, integrating mechanisms, or cultural issues that should serve this purpose? Or are other issues discussed that enable a firm to become more boundaryless?

4. Look up a recent article in the publications listed in question 2 above that addresses a firm's involvement in outsourcing (modular organization) or in strategic alliance or network organizations (virtual organization). Was the firm successful or unsuccessful in this endeavor? Why? Why not?

Ethics Questions

1. If a firm has a divisional structure and places extreme pressures on its divisional executives to meet short-term profitability goals (e.g., quarterly income), could this raise some ethical considerations? Why? Why not?

2. If a firm enters into a strategic alliance but does not exercise appropriate behavioral control of its employees (in terms of culture, rewards and incentives, and boundaries—as discussed in Chapter 9) that are involved in the alliance, what ethical issues could arise? What could be the potential long-term and short-term downside for the firm?

References

1. Tomanio, J., Burke, D. & Morser, B. 2007. Missed connections. *Fortune,* March 5: 103–108; Schwartz, N. D. 2007. Big plane, big problems. *Fortune,* March 5: 95–98; Anonymous. 2007. Hard landing. *The Economist.* February 17: 68; Pearlstein, S. 2006. Political winds are pushing Airbus. www.washingtonpost.com. October 11: D01; Holmes, S. 2007. The secret weapon of Boeing. *BusinessWeek,* January 8: 34; Matlack, C. 2006. Wayward Airbus. *BusinessWeek,* October 23: 46–48; and Matlack, C. 2006. Airbus: First, blame the software. *BusinessWeek,* October 5, np.

2. This introductory discussion draws upon Hall, R. H. 2002. *Organizations: Structures, processes, and outcomes* (8th ed.). Upper Saddle River, NJ: Prentice Hall; and Duncan, R. E. 1979. What is the right organization structure? Decision-tree analysis provides the right answer. *Organizational Dynamics,* 7(3): 59–80. For an insightful discussion of strategy-structure relationships in the organization theory and strategic management literatures, refer to Keats, B., & O'Neill, H. M. 2001. Organization structure: Looking through a strategy lens. In Hitt, M. A., Freeman, R. E., & Harrison, J. S. 2001. *The Blackwell handbook of strategic management:* 520–542. Malden, MA: Blackwell.

3. This discussion draws upon Chandler, A. D. 1962. *Strategy and structure.* Cambridge, MA: MIT Press; Galbraith J. R., & Kazanjian, R. K. 1986. *Strategy implementation: The role of structure and process.* St. Paul, MN: West Publishing; and Scott, B. R. 1971. Stages of corporate development. Intercollegiate Case Clearing house, 9-371-294, BP 998. Harvard Business School.

4. Our discussion of the different types of organizational structures draws on a variety of sources, including Galbraith & Kazanjian, op. cit.; Hrebiniak, L. G., & Joyce, W. F. 1984. *Implementing strategy.* New York: Macmillan; Distelzweig, H. 2000. Organizational structure. In Helms, M. M. (Ed.). *Encyclopedia of management:* 692–699. Farmington Hills, MI: Gale; and Dess, G. G., & Miller, A. 1993. *Strategic management.* New York: McGraw-Hill.

5. Schein, E. H. 1996. Three cultures of management: The key to organizational learning. *Sloan Management Review,* 38(1): 9–20.

6. For a discussion of performance implications, refer to Hoskisson, R. E. 1987. Multidivisional structure and performance: The contingency of diversification strategy. *Academy of Management Journal,* 29: 625–644.

7. For a thorough and seminal discussion of the evolution toward the divisional form of organizational structure in the United States, refer to Chandler, op. cit. A rigorous empirical study of the strategy and structure relationship is found in Rumelt, R. P. 1974. *Strategy, structure, and economic performance.* Cambridge, MA: Harvard Business School Press.

8. Ghoshal, S., & Bartlett, C. A. 1995. Changing the role of management: Beyond structure to processes. *Harvard Business Review,* 73(1): 88.

9. Koppel, B. 2000. Synergy in ketchup? *Forbes,* February 7: 68–69; and Hitt, M. A., Ireland, R. D., & Hoskisson, R. E. 2001. *Strategic management: Competitiveness and globalization* (4th ed.). Cincinnati, OH: Southwestern Publishing.

10. Pitts, R. A. 1977. Strategies and structures for diversification. *Academy of Management Journal,* 20(2): 197–208.

11. Dell, M., & Rollins, K. 2005. Execution without excuses. *Harvard Business Review,* 83(3): 102–111.

12. Daniels, J. D., Pitts, R. A., & Tretter, M. J. 1984. Strategy and structure of U.S. multinationals: An exploratory study. *Academy of Management Journal,* 27(2): 292–307.

13. Habib, M. M., & Victor, B. 1991. Strategy, structure, and performance of U.S. manufacturing and service MNCs: A comparative analysis. *Strategic Management Journal,* 12(8): 589–606.

14. Our discussion of global start-ups draws from Oviatt, B. M., & McDougall, P. P. 2005. The internationalization of entrepreneurship. *Journal of International Business Studies,* 36(1): 2–8; Oviatt, B. M., & McDougall, P. P. 1994. Toward a theory of international new ventures. *Journal of International Business Studies,* 25(1): 45–64; and Oviatt, B. M., & McDougall, P. P. 1995. Global start-ups: Entrepreneurs on a worldwide stage. *Academy of Management Executive,* 9(2): 30–43.

15. Some useful guidelines for global start-ups are provided in Kuemmerle, W. 2005. The entrepreneur's path for global expansion. *MIT Sloan Management Review,* 46(2): 42–50.

16. See, for example, Miller, D., & Friesen, P. H. 1980. Momentum and revolution in organizational structure. *Administrative Science Quarterly,* 13: 65–91.

17. Many authors have argued that a firm's structure can influence a firm's strategy and performance. These include Amburgey, T. L., & Dacin, T. 1995. As the left foot follows the right? The dynamics of strategic and structural change. *Academy of Management Journal,* 37: 1427–1452; Dawn, K., & Amburgey, T. L. 1991. Organizational inertia and momentum: A dynamic model of strategic change. *Academy of Management Journal,* 34: 591–612; Fredrickson, J. W. 1986. The strategic decision process and organization structure. *Academy of Management Review,* 11: 280–297; Hall, D. J., & Saias, M. A. 1980. Strategy follows structure!

Strategic Management Journal, 1: 149–164; and Burgelman, R. A. 1983. A model of the interaction of strategic behavior, corporate context, and the concept of strategy. *Academy of Management Review,* 8: 61–70.

18. This discussion of generic strategies and their relationship to organizational control draws upon Porter, M. E. 1980. *Competitive strategy.* New York: Free Press; and Miller, D. 1988. Relating Porter's business strategies to environment and structure: Analysis and performance implications. *Academy of Management Journal,* 31(2): 280–308.

19. Rodengen, J. L. 1997. *The legend of Nucor Corporation.* Fort Lauderdale, FL: Write Stuff Enterprises.

20. The 3M example draws upon *Blueprints for service quality.* 1994. New York: American Management Association; personal communication with Katerine Hagmeier, program manager, external communications, 3M Corporation, March 26, 1998; Lei, D., Slocum, J. W., & Pitts, R. A. 1999. Designing organizations for competitive advantage: The power of unlearning and learning. *Organizational Dynamics,* 27(3): 24–38; and Graham, A. B., & Pizzo, V. G. 1996. A question of balance: Case studies in strategic knowledge management. *European Management Journal,* 14(4): 338–346.

21. The Sharp Corporation and Hanson plc examples are based on Collis, D. J., & Montgomery, C. A. 1998. Creating corporate advantage. *Harvard Business Review,* 76(3): 70–83.

22. Kunii, I. 2002. Japanese companies' survival skills. *BusinessWeek,* November 18: 18.

23. White, G. 1988. How I turned $3,000 into $10 billion. *Fortune,* November 7: 80–89. After the death of the founders, the Hanson plc conglomerate was found to be too unwieldy and was broken up into several separate, publicly traded corporations. For more on its more limited current scope of operations, see www.hansonplc.com.

24. An interesting discussion on how the Internet has affected the boundaries of firms can be found in Afuah, A. 2003. Redefining firm boundaries in the face of the Internet: Are firms really shrinking? *Academy of Management Review,* 28(1): 34–53.

25. Collis & Montgomery, op. cit.

26. For a discussion of the role of coaching on developing high performance teams, refer to Kets de Vries, M. F. R. 2005. Leadership group coaching in action: The zen of creating high performance teams. *Academy of Management Executive,* 19(1): 77–89.

27. Pfeffer, J. 1998. *The human equation: Building profits by putting people first.* Cambridge, MA: Harvard Business School Press.

28. For a discussion on how functional area diversity affects performance, see Bunderson, J. S., & Sutcliffe, K. M. 2002. *Academy of Management Journal,* 45(5): 875–893.

29. Augustine, N. R. 1983. *Augustine's laws.* New York: Viking Press.

30. See, for example, Hoskisson, R. E., Hill, C. W. L., & Kim, H. 1993. The multidivisional structure: Organizational fossil or source of value? *Journal of Management,* 19(2): 269–298.

31. Pottruck, D. A. 1997. Speech delivered by the co-CEO of Charles Schwab Co., Inc., to the Retail Leadership Meeting, San Francisco, CA, January 30; and Miller, W. 1999. Building the ultimate resource. *Management Review,* January: 42–45.

32. Magretta, J. 1998. The power of virtual integration: An interview with Dell Computer's Michael Dell. *Harvard Business Review,* 76(2): 75.

33. Forster, J. 2001. Networking for cash. *BusinessWeek,* January 8: 129.

34. Dess, G. G., Rasheed, A. M. A., McLaughlin, K. J., & Priem, R. 1995. The new corporate architecture. *Academy of Management Executive,* 9(3): 7–20.

35. Barnes, C. 1998. A fatal case. *Fast Company,* February–March: 173.

36. Handy, C. 1989. *The age of unreason.* Boston: Harvard Business School Press; Ramstead, E. 1997. APC maker's low-tech formula: Start with the box. *The Wall Street Journal,* December 29: B1; Mussberg, W. 1997. Thin screen PCs are looking good but still fall flat. *The Wall Street Journal,* January 2: 9; Brown, E. 1997. Monorail: Low cost PCs. *Fortune,* July 7: 106–108; and Young, M. 1996. Ex-Compaq executives start new company. *Computer Reseller News,* November 11: 181.

37. For a discussion of some of the downsides of outsourcing, refer to Rossetti, C., & Choi, T. Y. 2005. On the dark side of strategic sourcing: Experiences from the aerospace industry. *Academy of Management Executive,* 19(1): 46–60.

38. Tully, S. 1993. The modular corporation. *Fortune,* February 8: 196.

39. Quinn, J. B. 1992. *Intelligent enterprise: A knowledge and service based paradigm for industry.* New York: Free Press.

40. For an insightful perspective on outsourcing and its role in developing capabilities, read Gottfredson, M.,

Puryear, R., & Phillips, C. 2005. Strategic sourcing: From periphery to the core. *Harvard Business Review,* 83(4): 132–139.

41. This discussion draws upon Quinn, J. B., & Hilmer, F. C. 1994. Strategic outsourcing. *Sloan Management Review,* 35(4): 43–55.

42. See also Stuckey, J., & White, D. 1993. When and when not to vertically integrate. *Sloan Management Review,* Spring: 71–81; Harrar, G. 1993. Outsource tales. *Forbes ASAP,* June 7: 37–39, 42; and Davis, E. W. 1992. Global outsourcing: Have U.S. managers thrown the baby out with the bath water? *Business Horizons,* July–August: 58–64.

43. For a discussion of knowledge creation through alliances, refer to Inkpen, A. C. 1996. Creating knowledge through collaboration. *California Management Review,* 39(1): 123–140; and Mowery, D. C., Oxley, J. E., & Silverman, B. S. 1996. Strategic alliances and interfirm knowledge transfer. *Strategic Management Journal,* 17 (Special Issue, Winter): 77–92.

44. Doz, Y., & Hamel, G. 1998. *Alliance advantage: The art of creating value through partnering.* Boston: Harvard Business School Press.

45. DeSanctis, G., Glass, J. T., & Ensing, I. M. 2002. Organizational designs for R&D. *Academy of Management Executive,* 16(3): 55–66.

46. Barringer, B. R., & Harrison, J. S. 2000. Walking a tightrope: Creating value through interorganizational alliances. *Journal of Management,* 26: 367–403.

47. Davis, E. 1997. Interview: Norman Augustine. *Management Review,* November: 14.

48. One contemporary example of virtual organizations is R&D consortia. For an insightful discussion, refer to Sakaibara, M. 2002. Formation of R&D consortia: Industry and company effects. *Strategic Management Journal,* 23(11): 1033–1050.

49. Bartness, A., & Cerny, K. 1993. Building competitive advantage through a global network of capabilities. *California Management Review,* Winter: 78–103. For an insightful historical discussion of the usefulness of alliances in the computer industry, see Moore, J. F. 1993. Predators and prey: A new ecology of competition. *Harvard Business Review,* 71(3): 75–86.

50. See Lorange, P., & Roos, J. 1991. Why some strategic alliances succeed and others fail. *Journal of Business Strategy,* January–February: 25–30; and Slowinski, G. 1992. The human touch in strategic alliances. *Mergers and Acquisitions,* July–August: 44–47. A compelling argument for strategic alliances is provided by Ohmae, K. 1989. The global logic of

strategic alliances. *Harvard Business Review,* 67(2): 143–154.

51. Some of the downsides of alliances are discussed in Das, T. K., & Teng, B. S. 2000. Instabilities of strategic alliances: An internal tensions perspective. *Organization Science,* 11: 77–106.

52. This section draws upon Dess, G. G., & Picken, J. C. 1997. *Mission critical.* Burr Ridge, IL: Irwin Professional Publishing.

53. Katzenbach, J. R., & Smith, D. K. 1994. *The wisdom of teams: Creating the high performance organization.* New York: HarperBusiness.

54. Hammer, M., & Champy, J. 1993. *Reengineering the corporation: A manifesto for business revolution.* New York: HarperCollins.

55. This section draws on Birkinshaw, J., & Gibson, C. 2004. Building ambidexterity into an organization. *MIT Sloan Management Review,* 45(4): 47–55; and Gibson, C. B., & Birkinshaw, J. 2004. The antecedents, consequences, and mediating role of organizational ambidexterity. *Academy of Management Journal,* 47(2): 209–226. Robert Duncan is generally credited with being the first to coin the term "ambidextrous organizations" in his article entitled: Designing dual structures for innovation. In Kilmann, R. H., Pondy, L. R., & Slevin, D. (Eds.). 1976. *The management of organizations,* vol. 1: 167–188. For a seminal academic discussion of the concept of exploration and exploitation, which parallels adaptation and alignment, refer to: March, J. G. 1991. Exploration and exploitation in organizational learning. *Organization Science,* 2: 71–86.

56. This section is based on O'Reilly, C. A., & Tushman, M. L. 2004. The ambidextrous organization. *Harvard Business Review,* 82(4): 74–81.

chapter 11

Strategic Leadership:

Creating a Learning Organization and an Ethical Organization

>learning objectives

After reading this chapter, you should have a good understanding of:

LO1 The three key interdependent activities in which all successful leaders must be continually engaged.

LO2 The salience of power in overcoming resistance to change.

LO3 The crucial role of emotional intelligence (EI) in successful leadership as well as its potential drawbacks.

LO4 The value of creating and maintaining a "learning organization" in today's global marketplace.

LO5 The leader's role in establishing an ethical organization.

LO6 The difference between integrity-based and compliance-based approaches to organizational ethics.

LO7 Several key elements that organizations must have to become an ethical organization.

*t*o compete in the global marketplace, organizations need to have strong and effective leadership. This involves the active process of both creating and implementing proper strategies. In this chapter we address key activities in which leaders throughout the organization must be involved to be successful in creating and sustaining competitive advantages.

In the first section we provide a brief overview of the three key leadership activities. These are (1) setting a direction, (2) designing the organization, and (3) nurturing a culture committed to excellence and ethical behavior. Each of these activities is "necessary but not sufficient"; that is, to be effective, leaders must give proper attention to each of them. We also address the importance of a leader's effective use of power to overcome resistance to change.

The second section discusses the vital role of emotional intelligence (EI) in effective strategic leadership. EI refers to an individual's capacity for recognizing his or her emotions and those of others. It consists of five components: self-awareness, self-regulation, motivation, empathy, and social skills. We also address potential downsides or drawbacks that may result from the ineffective use of EI.

Next we address the important role of a leader in creating a "learning organization." Here, leaders must strive to harness the individual and collective talents of individuals throughout the entire organization. Creating a learning organization becomes particularly important in today's competitive environment, which is increasingly unpredictable, dynamic, and interdependent. Clearly, everyone must be involved in learning. It can't be only a few people at the top of the organization. The key elements of a learning organization are inspiring and motivating people with a mission or purpose, empowering employees at all levels, accumulating and sharing internal and external information, and challenging the status quo to enable creativity.

The final section discusses a leader's challenge in creating and maintaining an ethical organization. There are many benefits of having an ethical organization. In addition to financial benefits, it can enhance human capital and help to ensure positive relationships with suppliers, customers, society at large, and governmental agencies. On the other hand, the costs of ethical crises can be very expensive for many reasons. We address four key elements of an ethical organization: role models, corporate credos and codes of conduct, reward and evaluation systems, and policies and procedures.

Learning from Mistakes

Scott A. Livengood was fired as Chief Executive Officer (CEO) of Krispy Kreme on January 19, 2005.[1] He hasn't received very much good news lately. The firm's stock went up 10 percent the day of that announcement. And he received some rather dubious honors: he was recognized as one of *BusinessWeek*'s seven "Worst Managers" of 2004 and he was named 2004's "Worst CEO of the Year by Herb Greenberg of CBS MarketWatch.

What brought about the demise of Livengood, a 28-year veteran of the doughnut maker who had been CEO since 1998? Let's look at two of the central issues.

First, under his direction Krispy Kreme expanded far too rapidly. After its initial public offering in 2001, it continued to open stores at breakneck speed. Hoping to cash in on the nation's sweet tooth, the chain created media events in places like New York, San Francisco, and Boston. At times, cars would line up for blocks just to bring a box of the tasty confections to work. Unfortunately, while the craze faded, the costs of operating the franchises did not. By 2003, same-store sales had declined 16 percent, *[continued]* while the company's overhead continued to rise. In short, the brand quickly lost its novelty. Soon Krispy Kreme realized that many of its franchises would fail.

Recent financial results reflect the poor strategy. The once high-flying company posted a $3 million third-quarter loss in November 2004—its second losing quarter of the year. And in February 2005, the firm stated that it would restate earnings for the previous year, lowering previously reported income by as much as 8.6 percent.

Second, there are what *Fortune* has called "shady deals" surrounding how the firm conducted buybacks of some franchises owned by corporate insiders. For example, Krispy Kreme didn't disclose that a California franchise it repurchased in 2004 was partly owned by Livengood's ex-wife, whose stake was valued at $1.5 million. While executives aren't required to disclose transactions with former spouses, Livengood could be in trouble if the deal was made as part of a settlement or in lieu of alimony.

An even more troubling transaction is the 2003 deal in which the chain repurchased six stores in Dallas and Shreveport, Louisiana, that were partly owned by Krispy Kreme's former chairman and current director, Joseph McAleer. McAleer got a pretty good deal—$67 million (or $11 million per store). This comes to more than three times what the firm paid for many other shops! According to David Gourevitch, a former Securities and Exchange Commission (SEC) enforcement attorney, "At some point a transaction is not remotely reasonable, and it approximates a gift or payoff." Worst case scenario: The SEC could impose fines and require some officials to step down.

The SEC continues to investigate the firm and it upgraded its informal inquiry to a formal probe. Although customers may continue to enjoy Krispy Kreme's products, the investors have hardly had a pleasant experience. Krispy Kreme's stock price has continued to sink. By early 2007, it was at $12—less than one-fourth of the $50 peak that it reached in August 2003. This fall reflects a loss of market capitalization of $2 billion.

Clearly, many of the decisions and actions of Scott A. Livengood were not in the best interests of the firm and its shareholders. In contrast, effective leaders play an important and often pivotal role in creating and implementing strategies.

This chapter provides insights into how organizations can more effectively manage, change, and cope with increased environmental complexity and uncertainty. Below we will define leadership and introduce what are considered to be the three most important leadership activities as well as the important role of power. The second section focuses on a key trait—emotional intelligence—that has become increasingly recognized as critical to successful leadership. Then, the third major section, "Developing a Learning Organization," provides a useful framework for how leaders can help their firms learn and proactively adapt in the face of accelerating change. Central to this contemporary idea is the concept of empowerment, wherein employees and managers throughout the organization truly come to have a sense of self-determination, meaning, competence, and impact. The fourth section addresses the leader's role in building an ethical organization. Here, we address both the value of an ethical culture for a firm as well as the key elements that it encompasses.

Leadership: Three Interdependent Activities

In today's chaotic world, few would argue against the need for leadership, but how do we go about encouraging it? Let's focus on business organizations. Is it enough to merely keep the organization afloat, or is it essential to make steady progress toward some well-defined objective? We believe custodial management is not leadership. Rather, leadership is proactive, goal-oriented, and focused on the creation and implementation of a creative vision.

Leadership is the process of transforming organizations from what they are to what the leader would have them become. This definition implies a lot: *dissatisfaction* with the status quo, a *vision* of what should be, and a *process* for bringing about change. An insurance company executive recently shared the following insight on leadership, "I lead by the Noah Principle: It's all right to know when it's going to rain, but, by God, you had better build the ark."

Doing the right thing is becoming increasingly important. Many industries are declining; the global village is becoming increasingly complex, interconnected, and unpredictable; and product and market life cycles are becoming increasingly compressed. Recently, when asked to describe the life cycle of his company's products, the CEO of a supplier of computer components replied, "Seven months from cradle to grave—and that includes three months to design the product and get it into production!" Richard D'Aveni, author of *Hypercompetition,* went even further. He argued that in a world where all dimensions of competition appear to be compressed in time and heightened in complexity, *sustainable* competitive advantages are no longer possible.

Despite the importance of doing the "right thing," leaders must also be concerned about doing "things right." Charan and Colvin argued strongly that implementation (or execution) is also essential to success.

> Any way that you look at it, mastering execution turns out to be the odds-on best way for a CEO to keep his job. So what's the right way to think about that sexier obsession, strategy? It's vitally important—obviously. The problem is that our age's fascination feeds the mistaken belief that developing exactly the right strategy will enable a company to rocket past competitors. In reality, that's less than half the battle.[2]

Thus, leaders are change agents whose success is measured by how effectively they implement a strategic vision and mission.

Accordingly, many authors contend that successful leaders must recognize three interdependent activities that must be continually reassessed for organizations to succeed. As shown in Exhibit 11.1, these are: (1) determining a direction, (2) designing the organization, and (3) nurturing a culture dedicated to excellence and ethical behavior.[3]

The interdependent nature of these three activities is self-evident. Consider an organization with a great mission and a superb organizational structure and design, but a culture that implicitly encourages shirking and unethical behavior. Or a strong culture and organizational design but little direction and vision—in caricature, a highly ethical and efficient buggy whip manufacturer. Or one with a sound direction and strong culture, but counterproductive teams

Exhibit 11.1 Three Interdependent Activities of Leadership

and a "zero-sum" reward system that leads to the dysfunctional situation in which one party's gain is viewed as another party's loss, and collaboration and sharing are severely hampered.

Often, failure of today's organizations can be attributed to a lack of equal consideration of these three activities. The imagery of a three-legged stool is instructive: It will collapse if one leg is missing or broken. Let's briefly look at each of these activities.

Setting a Direction

A holistic understanding of an organization's stakeholders requires an ability to scan the environment to develop a knowledge of all of the company's stakeholders (e.g., customers, suppliers, shareholders) and other salient environmental trends and events. Managers must integrate this knowledge into a vision of what the organization could become. It necessitates the capacity to solve increasingly complex problems, become proactive in approach, and develop viable strategic options. As noted in Chapter 1, a strategic vision provides many benefits: a clear future direction; a framework for the organization's mission and goals; and enhanced employee communication, participation, and commitment.

At times the creative process involves what the CEO of Yokogawa, GE's Japanese partner in the Medical Systems business, called "bullet train" thinking.[4] That is, if you want to increase the speed by 10 miles per hour, you look for incremental advances. However, if you want to double the speed, you've got to think "out of the box" (e.g., widen the track, change the overall suspension system). In today's challenging times, leaders typically need more than just keeping the same train with a few minor tweaks. Instead, they must come up with more revolutionary visions.

Consider how Robert Tillman, CEO of Lowe's, dramatically revitalized his firm by setting a clear and compelling direction:

> He made Lowe's into a formidable competitor to Home Depot, Inc., the Goliath of the home-improvement and hardware retailing industry.[5] In his six years as CEO, Tillman has transformed the $43 billion chain, based in Wilkesboro, North Carolina. Its shares have more than doubled over the past four years, while Home Depot's have fallen about 20 percent.
>
> Tillman has redirected Lowe's strategy by responding effectively to research showing that women initiate 80 percent of home projects. While Home Depot has focused on the professionals and male customers, Tillman has redesigned Lowe's stores to give them a brighter appearance, stocked them with more appliances, and focused on higher-margin goods (including everything from Laura Ashley paints to high-end bathroom fixtures). And, like Wal-Mart, Lowe's has one of the best inventory systems in retailing. As a result, Lowe's profits are expected to continue to rise faster than Home Depot's.

Let's now turn to another key leadership activity: the design of the organization's structure, processes, and evaluation and control systems.

Designing the Organization

At times, almost all leaders have difficulty implementing their vision and strategies. Such problems—discussed in Chapter 10—may stem from a variety of sources, including:

- Lack of understanding of responsibility and accountability among managers.
- Reward systems that do not motivate individuals (or collectives such as groups and divisions) toward desired organizational goals.
- Inadequate or inappropriate budgeting and control systems.
- Insufficient mechanisms to integrate activities across the organization.

Successful leaders are actively involved in building structures, teams, systems, and organizational processes that facilitate the implementation of their vision and strategies. For example, we discussed the necessity for consistency between business-level and corporate-level strategies and organizational control in Chapter 9. For example, a firm would generally be unable to attain an overall low-cost advantage without closely monitoring its costs through detailed and formalized cost and financial control procedures. With regard to corporate-level strategy, in Chapter 9 we addressed how a related diversification strategy would necessitate reward systems that emphasize behavioral measures to promote sharing across divisions within a firm, whereas an unrelated strategy should rely more on financial (or objective) indicators of performance, such as revenue gains and profitability, since there is less need for collaboration across business units because they would have little in common.

Nurturing a Culture Dedicated to Excellence and Ethical Behavior

In Chapter 9 we discussed how organizational culture can be an effective means of organizational control. Leaders play a key role in developing and sustaining—as well as changing, when necessary—an organization's culture. Hector Ruiz is a good role model. After he became CEO of AMD, a $6 billion microprocessor producer, he dramatically improved his firm's competitive position vis-à-vis Intel—a firm six times as large. He says:[6]

> We have gotten larger and more complex. By definition that means we're going to make some mistakes. I'm much more comfortable in an environment when I know that's going to happen. That means we're learning. An aura of confidence begins to develop around people who can make mistakes and learn and go forward. At employee meetings I say, "Please, go get speeding tickets. I don't want you to get parking tickets."

In sharp contrast, leaders can also have a very detrimental effect on a firm's culture and ethics. Imagine the negative impact that Todd Berman's illegal activities have had on a firm that he cofounded—New York's private equity firm Chartwell Investments.[7] He recently began serving a five-year sentence in a Pennsylvania prison for stealing more than $3.6 million from the firm and its investors. Berman pleaded guilty to fraud charges brought by the Justice Department. For 18 months he misled Chartwell's investors concerning the financial condition of one of the firm's portfolio companies by falsely claiming it needed to borrow funds to meet operating expenses. Instead, Berman transferred the money to his personal bank account, along with fees paid by portfolio companies. Clearly, a leader's ethical behavior can make a strong impact on an organization—for good or for bad. Given the importance of this topic, we address it in detail in the last major section of this chapter.

Managers and top executives must also accept personal responsibility for developing and strengthening ethical behavior throughout the organization. They must consistently demonstrate that such behavior is central to the vision and mission of the organization. Several elements must be present and reinforced for a firm to become a highly ethical organization: role models, corporate credos and codes of conduct, reward and evaluation systems, and policies and procedures.

Strategy Spotlight 11.1 discusses how Nancy Snyder epitomizes the aforementioned three leadership activities. She was very effective in instilling a culture of innovation at Whirlpool Corporation.

Overcoming Barriers to Change and the Effective Use of Power

After discussing the three interdependent activities that leaders perform, we must address a key question: What are the **barriers to change** that leaders often encounter, and how can they use power to bring about organizational change? After all, people generally have some level of choice about how strongly they support or resist a leader's change initiatives. Why

barriers to change
characteristics of individuals and organizations that prevent a leader from transforming an organization.

>LO2
The salience of power in overcoming resistance to change.

Whirlpool: Becoming a Leader in Innovation

David R. Whitwam realized he had a major problem. The Chairman and CEO had helped build Whirlpool into the world's number one maker of big-ticket appliances, attaining unmatched economies of scale. He had also repeatedly cut costs by hundreds of millions of dollars. However, in 1999, everything—the stock price, profit margins, market share—had been about where it was a decade earlier. At the time, housing and sales of Whirlpool appliances were booming. Despite the strong demand, prices were falling by an average of 3.4 percent a year. The underlying problem was that its machines had been reduced to commodities. The solution was straightforward: Whirlpool had to come up with exciting new products that could command premium prices.

Whitman's goal of "innovation from everyone, everywhere" required major changes in the firm's management processes and culture, which had been designed to drive operational efficiency. He appointed Nancy Snyder, a corporate vice president to be Whirlpool's first "innovation czar." She rallied her colleagues around what was to become a five-year quest to reinvent the company's management processes. Key changes included:

- Making innovation a central topic in Whirlpool's leadership development programs.

- Setting aside $45 million from the capital budget for innovation in 2000 and doubling it in 2001 for projects that met a stringent standard of innovativeness.

- Requiring every product development plan to contain a sizable component of new-to-market innovation.

Sources: Arndt, M. 2006. Creativity overflowing. www.businessweek.com. May 8: np; Hamel, G. 2006. The why, what, and how of management innovation. *Harvard Business Review,* 84(2): 72–87; and, Salter, C. 2005. Whirlpool finds its cool. *Fast Company,* June: 73.

- Training more than 600 innovation mentors charged with encouraging a culture of innovation throughout the company.

- Setting up an intranet site that offered a do-it-yourself course on innovation and listing every project in the pipeline.

- Establishing innovation as a significant component of senior management's compensation program. If they failed to meet annual revenue and pipeline targets, they could lose 30 percent of their annual bonus.

- Setting aside time in quarterly business review meetings for an in-depth discussion of each unit's innovation performance.

Whirlpool's innovation efforts are paying off. The Duet, a matching washer and dryer introduced in 2001, has become a must-have appliance that seems to be selling like iPods. At $2,000, it is the company's most expensive washer-dryer set. With its stylish lines, portholelike door, and eye-catching colors, the Duet, says Chuck Jones, Whirlpool's Design Chief, "is like a Ferrari in your laundry room." That same year, Paris's Louvre Museum displayed Whirlpool's next generation concept products. And, in 2002, the Smithsonian Institution named Whirlpool the winner of its annual National Design Award in corporate achievement.

The bottom line results of Snyder's initiatives have been impressive. Since 2001, revenues from products that fit the company's definition of innovation have soared from $10 million to $760 million by 2005, or over five percent of the firm's record $14.3 billion revenue. Whirlpool's shares as of early 2007 were around $90—nearly double what they were five years ago. And prices are no longer eroding. Over the past three years, the average price of Whirlpool's appliances has risen five percent annually.

---

is there often so much resistance? There are many reasons why organizations at all levels are prone to inertia and are slow to learn, adapt, and change:

systemic barriers
barriers to change that stem from an organizational design that impedes the proper flow and evaluation of information.

1. Many people have **vested interests in the status quo.** People, in general, tend to be risk averse and resistant to change. Further, there is a broad stream of research on the subject of "escalation," wherein certain individuals continue to throw "good money at bad decisions" despite negative performance feedback.[8]

2. There are **systemic barriers.** Here, the design of the organization's structure, information processing, reporting relationships, and so forth impede the proper flow and evaluation of information. A bureaucratic structure with multiple layers, onerous requirements for documentation, and rigid rules and procedures will often "inoculate" the organization against change.

3. **Behavioral barriers** cause managers to look at issues from a biased or limited perspective. This can be attributed to their education, training, work experiences, and so forth. For example, consider an incident shared by David Lieberman, marketing director at GVO, an innovation consulting firm:

> A company's creative type had come up with a great idea for a new product. Nearly everybody loved it. However, it was shot down by a high-ranking manufacturing representative who exploded: "A new color? Do you have any idea of the spare-parts problem that it will create?" This was not a dimwit exasperated at having to build a few storage racks at the warehouse. He'd been hearing for years about cost cutting, lean inventories, and "focus." Lieberman's comment: "Good concepts, but not always good for innovation."

4. **Political barriers** refer to conflicts arising from power relationships. This can be the outcome of a myriad of symptoms such as vested interests (e.g., the aforementioned escalation problems), refusal to share information, conflicts over resources, conflicts between departments and divisions, and petty interpersonal differences.

5. **Personal time constraints** bring to mind the old saying about "not having enough time to drain the swamp when you are up to your neck in alligators." In effect, Gresham's law of planning states that operational decisions will drive out the time necessary for strategic thinking and reflection. This tendency is accentuated in organizations experiencing severe price competition or retrenchment wherein managers and employees are spread rather thin.

Successful leadership requires effective use of power in overcoming barriers to change.[9] As humorously noted by Mark Twain, "I'm all for progress. It's change I object to."

Power refers to a leader's ability to get things done in a way he or she wants them to be done. It is the ability to influence other people's behavior, to persuade them to do things that they otherwise would not do, and to overcome resistance and opposition to changing direction. Effective exercise of power is essential for successful leadership.[10]

A leader derives his or her power from several sources or bases. Numerous classifications of such sources or bases abound in the literature on power. However, the simplest way to understand the bases of power is by classifying them as organizational and personal, as shown in Exhibit 11.2.

behavioral barriers barriers to change associated with the tendency for managers to look at issues from a biased or limited perspective based on their prior education and experience.

political barriers barriers to change related to conflicts arising from power relationships.

power a leader's ability to get things done in a way he or she wants them to be done.

Exhibit 11.2 A Leader's Bases of Power

organizational bases of power power that stems from a leader's holding a formal management position.

Organizational bases of power refer to the power that a person wields because of holding a formal management position. These include legitimate power, reward power, coercive power, and information power. *Legitimate power* is derived from organizationally conferred decision-making authority and is exercised by virtue of a manager's position in the organization. *Reward power* depends on the ability of the leader or manager to confer rewards for positive behaviors or outcomes. *Coercive power* is the power a manager exercises over employees using fear of punishment for errors of omission or commission. *Information power* arises from a manager's access, control, and distribution of information that is not freely available to everyone in an organization.

Apart from the organizationally derived power, a leader might be able to influence subordinates because of his or her personality characteristics and behavior. These would be considered the **personal bases of power.** The personal bases of power are referent power and expert power. The source of *referent power* is a subordinate's identification with the leader. A leader's personal attributes or charisma might influence subordinates and make them devoted to that leader. On the other hand, the source of *expert power* is the leader's expertise and knowledge in a particular field. The leader is the expert on whom subordinates depend for information that they need to do their jobs successfully.

personal bases of power power that stems from a leader's personality characteristics and behavior.

Successful leaders use the different bases of power, and often a combination of them, as appropriate to meet the demands of a situation, such as the nature of the task, the personality characteristics of the subordinates, the urgency of the issue, and other factors. Leaders must recognize that persuasion and developing consensus are often essential, but so is pressing for action. Clearly, at some point stragglers must be prodded into line.[11] Peter Georgescu, who recently retired as CEO of Young & Rubicam (an advertising and media giant acquired by the UK-based WPP Group in 2000), summarized a leader's dilemma brilliantly (and humorously), "I have knee pads and a .45. I get down and beg a lot, but I shoot people too."[12]

Strategy Spotlight 11.2 addresses some of the subtleties of power. It focuses on William Bratton, Chief of the Los Angeles Police Department, who has enjoyed a very successful career in law enforcement.

Emotional Intelligence: A Key Leadership Trait

>LO3

The crucial role of emotional intelligence (EI) in successful leadership as well as its potential drawbacks.

In the previous section, we discussed three activities of strategic leadership. The focus was on "what leaders *do*." Now, the issue becomes "who leaders *are*," that is, what are the most important traits (or capabilities) of leaders. Clearly, these two issues are related, because successful leaders possess the valuable traits that enable them to perform effectively in order to create value for their organization.

There has been a vast amount of literature on the successful traits of leaders, including business leaders at the highest level.[13] These traits include integrity, maturity, energy, judgment, motivation, intelligence, expertise, and so on. However, for simplicity, these traits may be grouped into three broad sets of capabilities:

- Purely technical skills (like accounting or operations research).
- Cognitive abilities (like analytical reasoning or quantitative analysis).
- Emotional intelligence (which includes skills associated with self-management and managing relationships).

emotional intelligence (EI) an individual's capacity for recognizing his or her own emotions and those of others, including the five components of self awareness, self regulation, motivation, empathy, and social skills.

"Emotional intelligence (EI)" has become popular in both the literature and management practice in recent years.[14] Some evidence of this popularity is that *Harvard Business Review* articles published in 1998 and 2000 by psychologist/journalist Daniel Goleman, who is most closely associated with the concept, have become *HBR*'s most highly requested reprint articles. And two of Goleman's recent books, *Emotional Intelligence* and *Working with Emotional Intelligence,* were both on the *New York Times*'s best-seller lists. Goleman defines **emotional intelligence** as the capacity for recognizing one's own emotions and those of others.[15]

William Bratton: Using Multiple Bases of Power

William Bratton, Chief of the Los Angeles Police Department has an enviable track record in turning around police departments in crime-ridden cities. First, while running the police division of Massachusetts Bay Transit Authority (MBTA) in Boston, then as police commissioner of New York in the mid-1990s, and now in Los Angeles since 2002, Chief Bratton is credited with reducing crime and improving police morale in record time. An analysis of his success at each of these organizations reveals very similar patterns both in terms of the problems he faced and the many ways in which he used the different bases of power to engineer a rapid turnaround.

In Boston, New York, and Los Angeles, Chief Bratton faced similar hurdles: organizations wedded to the status quo, limited resources, demotivated staffs, and opposition from powerful vested interests. But he does not give up in the face of these seemingly insurmountable problems. He is persuasive in calls for change, capable of mobilizing the commitment of key players, silencing vocal naysayers, and building rapport with superiors and subordinates while building bridges with external constituencies.

Chief Bratton's persuasion tactics are unconventional, yet effective. When he was running the MBTA police, the Transit Authority decided to buy small squad cars, which are cheaper to buy and to run, but very inadequate for the police officer's task. Instead of arguing, Bratton invited the general manager for a tour of the city. He rode with the general manager in exactly the same type of car that was ordered for ordinary officers, and drove over every pothole on the road. He moved the seats forward so that the general manager could feel how little leg room was there. And he put on his belt, cuffs, and gun so that the general manager could understand how limited the space was. After two hours in the cramped car, the general manager was ready to change the order and get more suitable cars for the officers!

Another tactic Bratton used effectively was insisting on community meetings between police officers and citizens. This went against the long-standing practice of detachment between police and community to decrease the chances of corruption. The result was that his department had a better understanding of public concerns and rearranged their priorities, which in turn led to better community relations. For internal communications, he relied mainly on professionally produced videos instead of long, boring memos.

Chief Bratton also shows a remarkable talent for building political bridges and silencing naysayers. As he was introducing his zero-tolerance policing approach that aggressively targets "quality of life" crimes such as panhandling, drunkenness, and prostitution, opposition came from the city's courts which feared being inundated by a large number of small-crimes cases. Bratton enlisted the support of Rudolph Giuliani, the mayor of New York, who had considerable influence over the district attorneys, the courts, and the city jail. He also took the case to the *New York Times,* and managed to get the issue of zero-tolerance on the front pages of the newspaper. The courts were left with no alternative but to cooperate.

To a great extent, Bratton's success can be attributed to his understanding of the subtleties of power, including persuasion, motivation, coalition building, empathy for subordinates, and a focus on goals.

Sources: Chan Kim, W., & Renee Mauborgne, R. 2003. Tipping point leadership. *Harvard Business Review,* 81(4): 60–69; and McCarthy, T. 2004. The gang buster. *Time,* January 19: 56–58.

Recent studies of successful managers have found that effective leaders consistently have a high level of emotional intelligence.[16] Findings indicate that EI is a better predictor of life success (economic well-being, satisfaction with life, friendship, family life), including occupational attainments, than IQ. Such evidence has been extrapolated to the catchy phrase: "IQ gets you hired, but EQ (Emotional Quotient) gets you promoted." And surveys show that human resource managers believe this statement to be true, even for highly technical jobs such as those of scientists and engineers.

This is not to say that IQ and technical skills are irrelevant. Obviously, they do matter, but they become "threshold capabilities." That is, they are the necessary requirements for attaining higher-level managerial positions. EI, on the other hand, is essential for leadership success. Without it, Goleman claims, a manager can have excellent training, an incisive analytical mind, and many smart ideas but will still not be a great leader.

	Definition	Hallmarks
Self-management skills:		
Self-awareness	• The ability to recognize and understand your moods, emotions, and drives, as well as their effect on others.	• Self-confidence • Realistic self-assessment • Self-deprecating sense of humor
Self-regulation	• The ability to control or redirect disruptive impulses and moods. • The propensity to suspend judgment—to think before acting.	• Trustworthiness and integrity • Comfort with ambiguity • Openness to change
Motivation	• A passion to work for reasons that go beyond money or status. • A propensity to pursue goals with energy and persistence.	• Strong drive to achieve • Optimism, even in the face of failure • Organizational commitment
Managing relationships:		
Empathy	• The ability to understand the emotional makeup of other people. • Skill in treating people according to their emotional reactions.	• Expertise in building and retaining talent • Cross-cultural sensitivity • Service to clients and customers
Social skill	• Proficiency in managing relationships and building networks. • An ability to find common ground and build rapport.	• Effectiveness in leading change • Persuasiveness • Expertise in building and leading teams

Source: Adapted and reprinted by permission of *Harvard Business Review*. Exhibit from "What Makes a Leader," by D. Goleman, January 2004. Copyright © 2004 by the Harvard Business School Publishing Corporation; all rights reserved.

Exhibit 11.3 The Five Components of Emotional Intelligence at Work

There are five components of EI: self-awareness, self-regulation, motivation, empathy, and social skill. They are included in Exhibit 11.3. We now discuss each of them.

Self-Awareness

Self-awareness is the first component of EI and brings to mind that Delphic oracle who gave the advice "know thyself" thousands of years ago. Self-awareness involves a person having a deep understanding of his or her emotions, strengths, weaknesses, and drives. People with strong self-awareness are neither overly critical nor unrealistically optimistic. Instead, they are honest with themselves and others.

People generally admire and respect candor. Further, leaders are constantly required to make judgment calls that require a candid assessment of capabilities—their own and those of others. People who assess themselves honestly (i.e., self-aware people) are well suited to do the same for the organizations they run.

Self-Regulation

Biological impulses drive our emotions. Although we cannot do away with them, we can strive to manage them. Self-regulation, which is akin to an ongoing inner conversation, frees us from being prisoners of our feelings. People engaged in such conversation feel bad moods and emotional impulses just as everyone else does. However, they find ways to control them and even channel them in useful ways.

People who are in control of their feelings and impulses are able to create an environment of trust and fairness. In such an environment, political behavior and infighting are sharply reduced and productivity tends to be high. Further, people who have mastered their emotions are better able to bring about and implement change in an organization. When a new initiative is announced, they are less likely to panic; rather, they are able to suspend judgment, seek out information, and listen to executives explain the new program.

Motivation

Successful executives are driven to achieve beyond expectations—their own and everyone else's. They are driven to achieve. Although many people are driven by external factors, such as money and prestige, those with leadership potential are driven by a deeply embedded desire to achieve for the sake of achievement.

How can a person tell if he or she is motivated by a drive for achievement instead of external rewards? Look for a sign of passion for the work itself, such as seeking out creative challenges, a love of learning, and taking pride in a job well done. Also, motivated people have a high level of energy to do things better as well as a restlessness with the status quo. They are eager to explore new approaches to their work.

Empathy

Empathy is probably the most easily recognized component of EI. In a business setting, empathy means thoughtfully considering an employee's feelings, along with other factors, in the process of making intelligent decisions. Empathy is particularly important in today's business environment for at least three reasons: the increasing use of teams, the rapid pace of globalization, and the growing need to retain talent.[17]

When leading a team, a manager is often charged with arriving at a consensus—often in the face of a high level of emotions. Empathy enables a manager to sense and understand the viewpoints of everyone around the table.

Globalization typically involves cross-cultural dialogue that can easily lead to miscues. Empathetic people are attuned to the subtleties of body language; they can hear the message beneath the words being spoken. In a more general sense, they have a deep understanding of the existence and importance of cultural and ethnic differences.

Empathy also plays a key role in retaining talent. As we discussed in Chapter 4, human capital is particularly important to a firm in the knowledge economy when it comes to creating advantages that are sustainable. Leaders need empathy to develop and keep top talent. Today, that's even more important, because when high performers leave, they take their tacit knowledge with them.

At times, leaders in organizations can make blunders that exacerbate unfavorable situations—a time when effective leadership is essential. Astonishingly, Northwest Airlines sent a booklet entitled *101 Ways to Save Money* to a number of employees who were undergoing steep pay cuts or layoffs. "Helpful" suggestions included:

- (Tip #15) Get hand-me-down clothes and toys for your kids from family and friends.
- (Tip #18) Take shorter showers.
- (Tip #21) Make your own baby food.
- (Tip #39) Shop in thrift stores.
- (Tip #46) Don't be shy about pulling something you like out of the trash.

Would any of us want the manager(s) who came up with these ideas to be the one to comfort or counsel us during a personal misfortune or tragedy? We'd probably all agree that handing out this booklet would be the antithesis of empathy!

strategy spotlight

11.3

Emotional Intelligence: Cisco Systems' CEO John Chambers

John Chambers recently shared his insights on how he goes about performing his responsibilities as CEO of Cisco Systems. He exemplifies many of the concepts of emotional intelligence and, in his 15 years at Cisco Systems, has become one of the most respected high-tech executives in the world. Chambers' brief essay is one of a series in *Fortune* magazine on the topic of "How I Work."

> I started with the classic communications methods when I got here 15 years ago. I'd walk around and talk to small groups and larger groups. I'd see whose car is out in the parking lot. Then e-mail became very effective, because it gave me the ability to send a message to the whole group. But I'm a voice person. I communicate with emotion that way. I like to listen to emotion too. It's a lot easier to listen to a key customer if I hear how they're describing a problem to me. I'll leave 40 or 50 voicemails a day. I do them on the way to work and coming back from work. The newest thing for me is video on demand, which is my primary communication vehicle today. We have a small studio downstairs. We probably tape ten to fifteen videos a quarter. That way employees, and customers, can watch them when they want.
>
> As far as how I hear from employees, I host a monthly birthday breakfast. Anybody who has a birthday in that month gets to come and quiz me for an hour and 15 minutes. No directors or VPs in the room. It's how I keep my finger on the pulse of what's working and what's not. It's brutal, but it's my most enjoyable session.
>
> To be informed, I like summaries. Because of my dyslexia, I do very little novel reading or that type of activity. I love quick articles. Before every meeting and every panel I study briefing binders with all the information I need: What we're doing in a presentation, who we're meeting with, backgrounds on them, etc. It's two or three pages on each topic, and that is how I like to learn.
>
> I usually wrap up my day just before my wife, Elaine, and I go to bed. I review my critical accounts around the world and summarize a little bit. And then Elaine and I go to sleep talking. My wife has been my partner for 33 years, and we dated for seven years before that, so she understands my strengths and my limitations remarkably well. We make decisions together. My family is the most important thing in the world to me.

Source: Chambers, J. 2006. Lights! Camera! Cue From CEO! *Fortune,* August 21: 27. (Interviewed by Adam Lashinsky.) Copyright © 2006 Time, Inc. All rights reserved.

● The booklet *101 Ways to Save Money* sent out by Northwest Airlines' management was *not* well received by its employees.

Social Skill

While the first three components of emotional intelligence are all self-management skills, the last two—empathy and social skill—concern a person's ability to manage relationships with others. Social skill may be viewed as friendliness with a purpose: moving people in the direction you desire, whether that's agreement on a new marketing strategy or enthusiasm about a new product.

Socially skilled people tend to have a wide circle of acquaintances as well as a knack for finding common ground and building rapport. They recognize that nothing gets done alone, and they have a network in place when the time for action comes.

Social skill can be viewed as the culmination of the other dimensions of EI. People will be effective at managing relationships when they can understand and control their own emotions and empathize with others' feelings. Motivation also contributes to social skill. People who are driven to achieve tend to be optimistic, even when confronted with setbacks. And when people are upbeat, their "glow" is cast upon conversations and other social encounters. They are popular, and for good reason.

Strategy Spotlight 11.3 provides John Chambers' personal reflection on how he goes about his job as Chief Executive Officer of Cisco Systems, the $28 billion networking giant. This empathetic leader has become one of America's most respected high-tech executives.

Emotional Intelligence: Some Potential Drawbacks and Cautionary Notes

Many great leaders have been found to have great reserves of empathy, interpersonal astuteness, awareness of their own feelings, and an awareness of their impact on others.[18] And, more importantly, they apply these capabilities judiciously as best benefits the situation. In essence, the key to this is self-regulation; having some minimum level of these emotional intelligences will help a person be effective as a leader as long as they are channeled appropriately. However, if a person has a high level of these capabilities it may become "too much of a good thing" if they are allowed to drive inappropriate behaviors. Some additional potential drawbacks of EI can be gleaned from the flip side of the benefits from some of its essential components.

Effective Leaders Have Empathy for Others   However, they also must be able to make the "tough decisions." Leaders must be able to appeal to logic and reason and acknowledge others' feelings so that people feel the decisions are correct. However, it is easy to overidentify with others or confuse empathy with sympathy. This will make it more difficult to make the tough decisions.

Effective Leaders Are Astute Judges of People   A danger is that leaders may become judgmental and overly critical about the shortcomings they perceive in others. They are likely to dismiss other people's insights, making them feel undervalued.

Effective Leaders Are Passionate about What They Do, and They Show It   This doesn't mean that they are always cheerleaders. Rather, they may express their passion as persistence in pursuing an objective or a relentless focus on a valued principle. However, there is a fine line between being excited about something and letting your passion close your mind to other possibilities or cause you to ignore realities that others may see.

Effective Leaders Create Personal Connections with Their People   Most effective leaders take time to engage employees individually and in groups, listening to their ideas, suggestions and concerns, and responding in ways that make people feel that their ideas are respected and appreciated. However, the downside of such visibility is that if the leader makes too many unannounced visits, it may create a culture of fear and micromanagement. Clearly, striking a correct balance is essential.

Finally, from a moral standpoint, emotional leadership is neither good nor bad. Emotional leaders can be altruistic, focused on the general welfare of the company and its employees, and highly principled. On the other hand, they can be manipulative, selfish, and dishonest. For example, if a person is using leadership solely to gain formal or informal power, that is not leadership at all.[19] Rather, they are using their EI to grasp what people want and pander to those desires in order to gain authority and influence. After all, easy answers sell.

In the next section, we will discuss some guidelines for developing a "learning organization." In today's competitive environment, the old saying about "a chain is only as strong as the weakest link" applies more than ever before. People throughout organizations must become involved in leadership processes and play greater roles in the formulation and implementation of an organization's strategies and tactics. Put another way, to learn and adapt proactively, firms need "eyes, ears, and brains" throughout all parts of the organization. One person, or a small group of individuals, can no longer think and learn for the entire entity.

Developing a Learning Organization

Charles Handy, author of *The Age of Unreason* and *The Age of Paradox* and one of today's most respected business visionaries, shared an amusing story:

> The other day, a courier could not find my family's remote cottage. He called his base on his radio, and the base called us to ask directions. He was just around the corner, but his base managed to omit a vital part of the directions. So he called them again, and they called us again. Then the courier repeated the cycle a third time to ask whether we had a dangerous dog. When he eventually arrived, we asked whether it would not have been simpler and less aggravating to everyone if he had called us directly from the roadside telephone booth where he had been parked. "I can't do that," he said, "because they won't refund any money I spend." "But it's only pennies!" I exclaimed. "I know," he said, "but that only shows how little they trust us!"[20]

At first glance, it would appear that the story simply epitomizes the lack of empowerment and trust granted to the hapless courier: Don't ask questions, Do as you're told![21] However, implicit in this scenario is also the message that learning, information sharing, adaptation, decision making, and so on are *not* shared throughout the organization. In contrast to this admittedly rather extreme case, leading-edge organizations recognize the importance of having everyone involved in the process of actively learning and adapting. As noted by today's leading expert on learning organizations, MIT's Peter Senge, the days when Henry Ford, Alfred Sloan, and Tom Watson *"learned **for** the organization"* are gone.

> In an increasingly dynamic, interdependent, and unpredictable world, it is simply no longer possible for anyone to "figure it all out at the top." The old model, "the top thinks and the local acts," must now give way to integrating thinking and acting at all levels. While the challenge is great, so is the potential payoff. "The person who figures out how to harness the collective genius of the people in his or her organization," according to former Citibank CEO Walter Wriston, "is going to blow the competition away."[22]

Learning and change typically involve the ongoing questioning of an organization's status quo or method of procedure. This means that all individuals throughout the organization—not just those at the top—must reflect. Although this seems simple enough, it is easy to ignore. After all, many organizations get so caught up in carrying out their day-to-day work that they rarely, if ever, stop to think objectively about themselves and their businesses. They often fail to ask the probing questions that might lead them to call into question their basic assumptions, to refresh their strategies, or to reengineer their work processes. According to Michael Hammer and Steven Stanton, the pioneer consultants who touched off the reengineering movement:

> Reflection entails awareness of self, of competitors, of customers. It means thinking without preconception. It means questioning cherished assumptions and replacing them with new approaches. It is the only way in which a winning company can maintain its leadership position, by which a company with great assets can ensure that they continue to be well deployed.[23]

Successful **learning organizations** create a proactive, creative approach to the unknown, actively solicit the involvement of employees at all levels, and enable all employees to use their intelligence and apply their imagination. Higher-level skills are required of everyone, not just those at the top. A learning environment involves organizationwide commitment to change, an action orientation, and applicable tools and methods.[24] It must be viewed by everyone as a guiding philosophy and not simply as another change program that is often derisively labeled the new "flavor of the month."

A critical requirement of all learning organizations is that everyone feels and supports a compelling purpose. In the words of William O'Brien, CEO of Hanover Insurance, "Before there can be meaningful participation, people must share certain values and pictures about where we are trying to go. We discovered that people have a real need to feel that they're part of an enabling mission."[25]

learning organizations
organizations that create a proactive, creative approach to the unknown, characterized by (1) inspiring and motivating people with a mission and purpose, (2) empowering employees at all levels, (3) accumulating and sharing internal knowledge, (4) gathering and integrating external information, and (5) challenging the status quo and enabling creativity.

Inspiring and motivating people with a mission or purpose is a necessary but not sufficient condition for developing an organization that can learn and adapt to a rapidly changing, complex, and interconnected environment.

We briefly addressed the importance of articulating a mission or purpose. Exhibit 11.4 lists all five elements of a learning organization.

Empowering Employees at All Levels

"The great leader is a great servant," asserted Ken Melrose, CEO of Toro Company and author of *Making the Grass Greener on Your Side.*[26] A manager's role becomes one of creating an environment where employees can achieve their potential as they help move the organization toward its goals. Instead of viewing themselves as resource controllers and power brokers, leaders must envision themselves as flexible resources willing to assume numerous roles as coaches, information providers, teachers, decision makers, facilitators, supporters, or listeners, depending on the needs of their employees.

The central key to empowerment is effective leadership. Empowerment can't occur in a leadership vacuum. According to Melrose, "I came to understand that you best lead by serving the needs of your people. You don't do their jobs for them; you enable them to learn and progress on the job." Robert Quinn and Gretchen Spreitzer made an interesting point about two diametrically opposite perspectives on empowerment.[27] In the top-down perspective, empowerment is about delegation and accountability—senior management has developed a clear vision and has communicated specific plans to the rest of the organization. This strategy for empowerment encompasses the following:

- Start at the top.
- Clarify the organization's mission, vision, and values.
- Clearly specify the tasks, roles, and rewards for employees.
- Delegate responsibility.
- Hold people accountable for results.

By contrast, the bottom-up view looks at empowerment as concerned with risk taking, growth, and change. It involves trusting people to "do the right thing" and having a tolerance for failure. It encourages employees to act with a sense of ownership and typically "ask for forgiveness rather than permission." Here the salient elements of empowerment are:

- Start at the bottom by understanding the needs of employees.
- Teach employees self-management skills and model desired behavior.
- Build teams to encourage cooperative behavior.
- Encourage intelligent risk taking.
- Trust people to perform.

Clearly, these two perspectives draw a sharp contrast in assumptions that people make about trust and control. Interestingly, Quinn and Spreitzer recently shared these contrasting

strategy spotlight

Employee Empowerment at Chaparral Steel

Managers at Chaparral Steel, a steel minimill in Midlothian, Texas, are convinced that employee ownership empowers workers to act in the best interests of the company. They believe that ownership is not composed solely of the firm's equity but also of its knowledge. By sharing financial and knowledge resources with employees, Chaparral Steel is a model of employee empowerment—90 percent of its employees own company stock and everyone is salaried, wears the same white hard hats, drinks the same free coffee, and has access to the knowledge that goes into the innovative processes at the firm's manufacturing plants.

Sources: Johnson, D. 1998. Catching the third wave: How to succeed in business when it's changing at the speed of light. *Futurist,* March: 32–38; Petry, C. 1997. Chaparral poised on the brink of breakthrough: Chaparral Steel developing integrated automobile shredder-separation facility. *American Metal Market,* September 10: 18; Leonard-Barton, D. 1992. The factory as a learning laboratory. *Sloan Management Review,* 34: 23–38; and TXI Chaparral Steel Midlothian registered to ISO 2002. Chaparral Steel press release, July 8, 2001.

Rather than using managers as buffers between customers and line workers, Chaparral directly involves employees with customers. Customer concerns are routed directly to the line workers responsible for manufacturing a customer's specific products. "Everyone here is part of the sales department," president and CEO Gordon Forward said. "They carry their own business cards. If they visit a customer, we want them to come back and look at their own process differently. This helps employees from all levels to view operations from the customer's perspective." Forward believes that "if a melt shop crew understands why a customer needs a particular grade of steel, it will make sure the customer gets that exact grade."

This encourages employees to think beyond traditional functional boundaries and find ways to improve the organization's processes. By integrating the customer's perspective into their efforts, employees at Chaparral Steel become more than just salaried workers; they feel responsible to the firm as if each production process was their own creation and responsibility.

---

views of empowerment with a senior management team. After an initial heavy silence, someone from the first group voiced a concern about the second group's perspective, "We can't afford loose cannons around here." A person in the second group retorted, "When was the last time you saw a cannon of any kind around here?"

Many leading-edge organizations are moving in the direction of the second perspective— recognizing the need for trust, cultural control, and expertise (at all levels) instead of the extensive and cumbersome rules and regulations inherent in hierarchical control.[28] Some have argued that too often organizations fall prey to the "heroes-and-drones syndrome," wherein the value of those in powerful positions is exalted and the value of those who fail to achieve top rank is diminished. Such an attitude is implicit in phrases such as "Lead, follow, or get out of the way" or, even less appealing, "Unless you're the lead horse, the view never changes." Of course, few will ever reach the top hierarchical positions in organizations, but in the information economy, the strongest organizations are those that effectively use the talents of all the players on the team. Strategy Spotlight 11.4 illustrates how one company, Chaparral Steel, empowers its employees.

Accumulating and Sharing Internal Knowledge

Effective organizations must also *redistribute information, knowledge* (i.e., skills to act on the information), and *rewards.*[29] For example, a company might give frontline employees the power to act as "customer advocates," doing whatever is necessary to satisfy customers. Employees, however, also need to have the appropriate training. The company needs to disseminate information by sharing customer expectations and feedback as well as financial information. The employees must know about the goals of the business as well as how key value-creating activities in the organization are related to each other. Finally, organizations should allocate rewards on how effectively employees use information, knowledge, and power to improve customer service quality and the company's overall performance.

Jack Stack is the president and CEO of Springfield ReManufacturing Corporation (SRC) in Springfield, Missouri, and author of *The Great Game of Business*. He is generally considered the pioneer of "open book" management—an innovative way to gather and disseminate internal information. Implementing this system involves three core activities.[30] First, numbers are generated daily for each of the company's employees, reflecting his or her work performance and production costs. Second, this information is aggregated once a week and shared with all of the company's people from secretaries to top management. Third, employees receive extensive training in how to use and interpret the numbers—how to understand balance sheets as well as cash flows and income statements.

In explaining why SRC embraces open book management, Stack provided an insightful counterperspective to the old adage "Information is power."

> We are building a company in which everyone tells the truth every day—not because everyone is honest but because everyone has access to the same information: operating metrics, financial data, valuation estimates. The more people understand what's really going on in their company, the more eager they are to help solve its problems. Information isn't power. It's a burden. Share information, and you share the burdens of leadership as well.

Let's take a look at Whole Foods Market, Inc., the largest natural foods grocer in the United States.[31] An important benefit of the sharing of internal information at Whole Foods becomes the active process of *internal benchmarking*. Competition is intense at Whole Foods. Teams compete against their own goals for sales, growth, and productivity; they compete against different teams in their stores; and they compete against similar teams at different stores and regions. Similarly, there is an elaborate system of peer reviews through which teams benchmark each other. The "Store Tour" is the most intense. On a periodic schedule, each Whole Foods store is toured by a group of as many as 40 visitors from another region. Lateral learning—discovering what your colleagues are doing right and carrying those practices into your organization—has become a driving force at Whole Foods.

In addition to enhancing the sharing of company information both up and down as well as across the organization, leaders also have to develop means to tap into some of the more informal sources of internal information. In a recent survey of presidents, CEOs, board members, and top executives in a variety of nonprofit organizations, respondents were asked what differentiated the successful candidates for promotion. The consensus: The executive was seen as a person who listens. According to Peter Meyer, the author of the study, "The value of listening is clear: You cannot succeed in running a company if you do not hear what your people, customers, and suppliers are telling you. Poor listeners do not survive. Listening and understanding well are key to making good decisions."[32]

Strategy Spotlight 11.5 addresses a critical aspect of obtaining information from internal sources—listening skills. General Peter Pace, Chairman of the Joint Chiefs of Staff, shares his perspective on this topic. He is the highest-ranking military officer in the United States.

Gathering and Integrating External Information

Recognizing opportunities, as well as threats, in the external environment is vital to a firm's success. Focusing exclusively on the efficiency of internal operations may result in a firm becoming, in effect, the world's most efficient producer of manual typewriters or leisure suits—hardly an enviable position! As organizations *and* environments become more complex and evolve rapidly, it is far more critical for employees and managers to become more aware of environmental trends and events—both general and industry-specific—and more knowledgeable about their firm's competitors and customers. Next, we will discuss some ideas on how to do it.

First, the Internet has dramatically accelerated the speed with which anyone can track down useful information or locate people who might have useful information. Prior to the Net, locating someone who used to work at a company—always a good source of

strategy spotlight

11.5

Listening Skills: A Key to Obtaining Valuable Internal Information

"I don't want any yes-men around me," movie mogul Samuel Goldwyn once said. "I want them to tell me the truth, even if it costs them their jobs." We may laugh because it is often true. Organizations are usually not in the habit of rewarding people who speak uncomfortable truths—or, in the vernacular, "going against the company line." However, we need to hear from them.

According to General Peter Pace, "If you walk into a room as a senior person and innocently say, 'Here's what I'm thinking about this,' you have already skewed people's

thinking. His approach: "Start out with a question and don't voice an opinion."

Why? People can't support your position if they do not know where you stand on the issue. After all, supporting the boss is usually the politically expedient thing to do! Further, if you present subordinates with an intellectual challenge, they feel freer to offer their opinions without fear of offending somebody ranking higher in the organization. "If you are looking for answers, ask the question," suggests Pace, and "if you are looking for an honest critique, you ought to be the first person to self-critique." This is different from generals' metaphorically taking off their stars to ask for honest feedback. People know the stars will be back!

Source: Useem, M., & Useem, J. 2005. Great escapes. *Fortune,* June 27: 98, 100.

information—was quite a challenge. However, today people post their résumés on the Web; they participate in discussion groups and talk openly about where they work.

Marc Friedman, manager of market research at $1 billion Andrew Corporation, a fast-growing manufacturer of wireless communications products provides an example of effective Internet use.[33] One of Friedman's preferred sites to visit is Corptech's Web site, which provides information on 45,000 high-tech companies and more than 170,000 executives. One of his firm's product lines consisted of antennae for air-traffic control systems. He got a request to provide a country-by-country breakdown of upgrade plans for various airports. He knew nothing about air-traffic control at the time. However, he found a site on the Internet for the International Civil Aviation Organization. Fortunately, it had a great deal of useful data, including several research companies working in his area of interest.

Second, in addition to the Internet, company employees at all levels can use "garden variety" traditional sources to acquire external information. Much can be gleaned by reading trade and professional journals, books, and popular business magazines such as *BusinessWeek, Forbes, Fortune,* and *Fast Company.* Other venues for gathering external information include membership in professional or trade organizations and attendance at meetings and conventions. Networking among colleagues inside and outside of your industry is also very useful. Intel's Andy Grove, for example, gathers information from people like DreamWorks SKG's Steven Spielberg and Tele-Communications Inc.'s John Malone.[34] He believes that such interaction provides insights into how to make personal computers more entertaining and better at communicating. Internally, Grove spends time with the young "propeller-heads" who run Intel Architecture labs, an Oregon-based facility that Grove hopes will become the de facto R&D lab for the entire PC industry.

Third, benchmarking can be a useful means of employing external information. Here managers seek out the best examples of a particular practice as part of an ongoing effort to improve the corresponding practice in their own organization.[35] There are two primary types of benchmarking. *Competitive benchmarking* restricts the search for best practices to competitors, while *functional benchmarking* endeavors to determine best practices regardless of industry. Industry-specific standards (e.g., response times required to repair power outages in the electric utility industry) are typically best handled through competitive benchmarking, whereas more generic processes (e.g., answering 1-800 calls) lend themselves to functional benchmarking because the function is essentially the same in any industry.

Ford Motor Company used benchmarking to study Mazda's accounts payable operations.[36] Its initial goal of a 20 percent cut in its 500-employee accounts payable staff was ratcheted up to 75 percent—and met. Ford found that staff spent most of their time trying to match often conflicting data in a mass of paper, including purchase orders, invoices, and receipts. Following Mazda's example, Ford created an "invoiceless system" in which invoices no longer trigger payments to suppliers. The receipt does the job.

Fourth, focus directly on customers for information. For example, William McKnight, head of 3M's Chicago sales office, required that salesmen of abrasives products talk directly to the workers in the shop to find out what they needed, instead of calling on only front-office executives.[37] This was very innovative at the time—1909! But it illustrates the need to get to the end user of a product or service. (McKnight went on to become 3M's president from 1929 to 1949 and chairman from 1949 to 1969.) More recently, James Taylor, senior vice president for global marketing at Gateway 2000, discussed the value of customer input in reducing response time, a critical success factor in the PC industry.

> We talk to 100,000 people a day—people calling to order a computer, shopping around, looking for tech support. Our Web site gets 1.1 million hits per day. The time it takes for an idea to enter this organization, get processed, and then go to customers for feedback is down to minutes. We've designed the company around speed and feedback.[38]

Challenging the Status Quo and Enabling Creativity

Earlier in this chapter we discussed some of the barriers that leaders face when trying to bring about change in an organization. These included vested interests in the status quo, systemic barriers, behavioral barriers, political barriers, and personal time constraints. For a firm to become a "learning organization," it must overcome such barriers in order to foster creativity and enable it to permeate the firm. This becomes quite a challenge, of course, if the firm is entrenched in a status quo mentality.

Perhaps the best way to challenge the status quo is for the leader to forcefully create a sense of urgency. For example, Tom Kasten, vice president of Levi Strauss, has a direct approach to initiating change. He is charged with leading the campaign to transform the company for the 21st century.

> You create a compelling picture of the risks of *not* changing. We let our people hear directly from customers. We videotaped interviews with customers and played excerpts. One big customer said, "We trust many of your competitors implicitly. We sample their deliveries. We open *all* Levi's deliveries." Another said, "Your lead times are the worst. If you weren't Levi's, you'd be gone." It was powerful. I wish we had done more of it.[39]

Such initiative—if sincere and credible—establishes a shared mission and the need for major transformations. If effective, it can channel energies to bring about both change and creative endeavors.

Establishing a "culture of dissent" can be another effective means of questioning the status quo and serving as a spur toward creativity. Here norms are established whereby dissenters can openly question a superior's perspective without fear of retaliation or retribution. Consider the perspective of Steven Balmer, Microsoft's CEO.

> Bill [Gates] brings to the company the idea that conflict can be a good thing. . . . Bill knows it's important to avoid that gentle civility that keeps you from getting to the heart of an issue quickly. He likes it when anyone, even a junior employee, challenges him, and you know he respects you when he starts shouting back.[40]

Motorola has, in effect, gone a step further and institutionalized its culture of dissent.[41] By filing a "minority report," an employee can go above his or her immediate supervisor's head and officially lodge a different point of view on a business decision. According to former CEO George Fisher, "I'd call it a healthy spirit of discontent and a freedom by and large to express your discontent around here or to disagree with whoever it is in the company, me or anybody else."

It's innovation's great paradox: Success—that is, true breakthroughs—usually comes through failure. Here are some ideas on how to help your team get comfortable with taking risks and learning from mistakes:

- **Formalize Forums for Failure**
  To keep failures and the valuable lessons they offer from getting swept under the rug, *carve out time for reflection.* GE recently began sharing lessons from failures by bringing together managers whose "Imagination Breakthrough" efforts are put on the shelf.

- **Move the Goalposts**
  Innovation requires flexibility in meeting goals, since early predictions are often little more than educated guesses. Intuit's Scott Cook even suggests that teams developing new products ignore forecasts in the early days. "For every one of our failures, we had spreadsheets that looked awesome," he says.

- **Share Personal Stories**
  If employees hear leaders discussing their own failures, *they'll feel more comfortable talking about their own.* But it's not just the CEO's job. Front-line leaders are even more important, says Harvard Business School professor Amy Edmondson. "That person needs to be inviting, curious, and the first to say: 'I made a mistake'."

- **Bring in Outsiders**
  Outsiders can *help neutralize the emotions and biases that prop up a flop.* Customers can be the most valuable. After its DNA chip failed, Corning brought pharmaceutical companies in early to test its new drug-discovery technology, Epic.

- **Prove Yourself Wrong, Not Right**
  Development teams tend to look for supporting, rather than countervailing, evidence. "You have to reframe what you're seeking in the early days," says Innosight's Scott Anthony. *"You're not really seeking proof that you have the right answer.* It's more about testing to prove yourself wrong."

- **Celebrate Smart Failures**
  Managers should design performance-management systems that reward risk taking and foster a long-term view. But they should also *celebrate failures that teach something new,* energizing people to try again and offering them closure.

Source: McGregor, J. 2006. How failure breeds success. *BusinessWeek.* July10: 42–52.

Exhibit 11.5 Best Practices: Learning from Failures

Closely related to the culture of dissent is the fostering of a culture that encourages risk taking. "If you're not making mistakes, you're not taking risks, and that means you're not going anywhere," claimed John Holt, coauthor of *Celebrate Your Mistakes.*[42] "The key is to make errors faster than the competition, so you have more chances to learn and win."

Companies that cultivate cultures of experimentation and curiosity make sure that *failure* is not, in essence, an obscene word. People who stretch the envelope and ruffle feathers are protected. More importantly, they encourage mistakes as a key part of their competitive advantage. This philosophy was shared by Stan Shih, CEO of Acer, a Taiwan-based computer company. If a manager at Acer took an intelligent risk and made a mistake—even a costly one—Shih wrote off the loss as tuition payment for the manager's education. Such a culture must permeate the entire organization. As a high-tech executive told us during an interview: "Every person has a freedom to fail."

Exhibit 11.5 has insights on how organizations can both embrace risk and learn from failure.

ethics a system of right and wrong that assists individuals in deciding when an act is moral or immoral and/or socially desirable or not.

>LO5

The leader's role in establishing an ethical organization.

Creating an Ethical Organization

Ethics may be defined as a system of right and wrong.[43] Ethics assists individuals in deciding when an act is moral or immoral, socially desirable or not. The sources for an individual's ethics include religious beliefs, national and ethnic heritage, family practices, community standards, educational experiences, and friends and neighbors. Business ethics is the application of ethical standards to commercial enterprise.

Individual Ethics versus Organizational Ethics

Many leaders may think of ethics as a question of personal scruples, a confidential matter between employees and their consciences. Such leaders are quick to describe any wrongdoing as an isolated incident, the work of a rogue employee. They assume the company should not bear any responsibility for an individual's misdeeds. After all, in their view, ethics has nothing to do with leadership.

In fact, ethics has everything to do with leadership. Seldom does the character flaw of a lone actor completely explain corporate misconduct. Instead, unethical business practices typically involve the tacit, if not explicit, cooperation of others and reflect the values, attitudes, and behavior patterns that define an organization's operating culture. Ethics is as much an organizational as a personal issue. Leaders who fail to provide proper leadership to institute proper systems and controls that facilitate ethical conduct share responsibility with those who conceive, execute, and knowingly benefit from corporate misdeeds.

The ethical orientation of a leader is a key factor in promoting ethical behavior. Ethical leaders must take personal, ethical responsibility for their actions and decision making. Leaders who exhibit high ethical standards become role models for others and raise an organization's overall level of ethical behavior. In essence, ethical behavior must start with the leader before the employees can be expected to perform accordingly.

Over the last few decades, there has been a growing interest in corporate ethical performance. Perhaps some reasons for this trend may be the increasing lack of confidence regarding corporate activities, the growing emphasis on quality of life issues, and a spate of recent corporate scandals at such firms as Enron, Tyco, and others. Merely adhering to the minimum regulatory standards may not be enough to remain competitive in a world that is becoming more socially conscious.

Without a strong ethical culture, the chance of ethical crises occurring is enhanced. Ethical crises can be very expensive—both in terms of financial costs and in the erosion of human capital and overall firm reputation. Consider, for example, Texaco's class-action discrimination lawsuit.

> In 1994 a senior financial analyst, Bari-Ellen Roberts, and one of her co-workers, Sil Chambers, filed a class-action discrimination suit against Texaco after enduring racial slurs and being passed over for promotion on several occasions. The discrimination suit charged Texaco with using an "old boys network" to systematically discriminate against African Americans.
>
> Roberts remembers, "The hardest part of the suit was deciding to do it. I'd worked so hard to get where I was, and I had to risk all of that. Then I had to deal with loneliness and isolation. Even some of the other African Americans viewed me as a troublemaker. When you're standing up and calling for change, it makes people fear for their own security."
>
> Two years later, in 1996, Texaco settled the suit, paying $141 million to its African-American workers. This was followed with an additional $35 million to remove discriminatory practices.[44]

Please note that the financial cost alone of $176 million was certainly not the proverbial "drop in the bucket." This amount represented nearly 10 percent of Texaco Inc.'s entire net income for 1996.

As we are all aware, the past several years have been characterized by numerous examples of unethical and illegal behavior by many top-level corporate executives. These include executives of firms such as Enron, Tyco, Worldcom, Inc., Adelphia, and Healthsouth Corp., who were all forced to resign and are facing (or have been convicted of) criminal charges. And, recall the example of greed in the opening case of Chapter 9. Here KB Home's CEO Bruce Karatz made millions on options backdating. The resulting scandal eventually forced him to retire. And that's

Procter & Gamble: Using Ethics to "Build the Spirit of the Place"

John Pepper, former CEO and chairman of Procter & Gamble Company, shares his perspective on ethics.

Let me start by saying that while ethics may seem like a soft concept—not as hard, say, as strategy or budgeting or operations—it is, in fact, a very hard concept. It is tangible. It is crucial . . . it is good for business.

There are several reasons for this. First, a company's values have a tremendous impact on who is attracted to your company and who will stay with it. We only have one life to live. All of us want to live it as part of an institution committed to high goals and high-sighted means of reaching these goals. This is true everywhere I've been. In our most mature countries and our newest.

Strong corporate values greatly simplify decision making. It is important to know the things you won't even

think about doing. Diluting a product. Paying a bribe. Not being fair to a customer or an employee.

Strong values earn the respect of customers and suppliers and governments and other companies, too. This is absolutely crucial over the long term.

A company which pays bribes in a foreign market becomes an open target for more bribes when the word gets out. It never stops.

A company which is seen to be offering different trade terms to different customers based on how big they are or how hard they push will forever be beset by requests for special terms.

A company which is seen by a government as having weak or varying standards will not be respected by that government.

And more positively, governments and other companies really do want to deal with companies they feel are pursuing sound values because in many, if not most, cases, they believe it will be good for them.

One final but very fundamental reason for operating ethically is that strong values create trust and pride among employees. Simply put, they build the spirit of the place.

Source: Pepper, J. E. 1997. The boa principle: Operating ethically in today's business environment. Speech presented at Florida A&M University, Tallahassee, January 30.

just one example of what has taken place in more than 200 companies that have faced questions about backdating—in many cases leading to indictments and criminal penalties.

The ethical organization is characterized by a conception of ethical values and integrity as a driving force of the enterprise.[45] Ethical values shape the search for opportunities, the design of organizational systems, and the decision-making process used by individuals and groups. They provide a common frame of reference that serves as a unifying force across different functions, lines of business, and employee groups. Organizational ethics helps to define what a company is and what it stands for.

There are many potential benefits of an ethical organization, but they are often indirect. Research has found somewhat inconsistent results concerning the overall relationship between ethical performance and measures of financial performance.[46] However, positive relationships have generally been found between ethical performance and strong organizational culture, increased employee efforts, lower turnover, higher organizational commitment, and enhanced social responsibility.

Clearly, the advantages of a strong ethical orientation can have a positive effect on employee commitment and motivation to excel. This is particularly important in today's knowledge-intensive organizations, where human capital is critical in creating value and competitive advantages. As we discussed in Chapter 4, positive, constructive relationships among individuals (i.e., social capital) are vital in leveraging human capital and other resources in an organization. However, there are many other potential benefits as well. Drawing on the concept of stakeholder management that we discussed in Chapter 1, an ethically sound organization can also strengthen its bonds among its suppliers, customers, and governmental agencies. John E. Pepper, former chairman of Procter & Gamble, addresses such a perspective in Strategy Spotlight 11.6.

Integrity-Based versus Compliance-Based Approaches to Organizational Ethics

>LO6
The difference between integrity-based and compliance-based approaches to organizational ethics.

Before discussing the key elements of an ethical organization, one must understand the links between organizational integrity and the personal integrity of an organization's members.[47] There cannot be high-integrity organizations without high-integrity individuals. However, individual integrity is rarely self-sustaining. Even good people can lose their bearings when faced with pressures, temptations, and heightened performance expectations in the absence of organizational support systems and ethical boundaries. Organizational integrity, goes beyond personal integrity. It rests on a concept of purpose, responsibility, and ideals for an organization as a whole. An important responsibility of leadership in building organizational integrity is to create this ethical framework and develop the organizational capabilities to make it operational.

Lynn Paine, an ethics scholar at Harvard, identifies two approaches: the compliance-based approach and the integrity-based approach. (See Exhibit 11.6 for a comparison of compliance-based and integrity-based strategies.) Faced with the prospect of litigation, several organizations reactively implement **compliance-based ethics programs.** Such programs are typically designed by a corporate counsel with the goal of preventing, detecting, and punishing legal violations. But being ethical is much more than being legal, and an integrity-based approach addresses the issue of ethics in a more comprehensive manner.

Integrity-based ethics programs combine a concern for law with an emphasis on managerial responsibility for ethical behavior. It is broader, deeper, and more demanding than a legal compliance initiative. It is broader in that it seeks to enable responsible conduct. It is deeper in that it cuts to the ethos and operating systems of an organization and its members, their core guiding values, thoughts, and actions. And it is more demanding because it requires an active effort to define the responsibilities and aspirations that constitute an organization's ethical compass. Most importantly, in this approach, organizational ethics is seen as the work of management.

A corporate counsel may play a role in designing and implementing integrity strategies, but it is managers at all levels and across all functions that are involved in the process. Once integrated into the day-to-day operations, such strategies can prevent damaging ethical lapses, while tapping into powerful human impulses for moral thought and action. Ethics becomes the governing ethos of an organization and not burdensome

compliance-based ethics programs programs for building ethical organizations that have the goal of preventing, detecting, and punishing legal violations.

integrity-based ethics programs programs for building ethical organizations that combine a concern for law with an emphasis on managerial responsibility for ethical behavior, including (1) enabling ethical conduct; (2) examining the organization's and members' core guiding values, thoughts, and actions; and (3) defining the responsibilities and aspirations that constitute an organization's ethical compass.

Characteristics	Compliance-Based Approach	Integrity-Based Approach
Ethos	Conformity with externally imposed standards	Self-governance according to chosen standards
Objective	Prevent criminal misconduct	Enable responsible conduct
Leadership	Lawyer-driven	Management-driven with aid of lawyers, HR, and others
Methods	Education, reduced discretion, auditing and controls, penalties	Education, leadership, accountability, organizational systems and decision processes, auditing and controls, penalties
Behavioral Assumptions	Autonomous beings guided by material self-interest	Social beings guided by material self-interest, values, ideals, peers

Source: Reprinted by permission of *Harvard Business Review.* Exhibit from "Managing Organizational Integrity," by L. S. Paine. Copyright 1994 by the Harvard Business School Publishing Corporation; all rights reserved.

Exhibit 11.6 Approaches to Ethics Management

constraints. Here is an example of an organization that goes beyond mere compliance to laws in building an ethical organization:

> In teaching ethics to its employees, Texas Instruments, the $14 billion chip and electronics manufacturer, asks them to run an issue through the following steps: Is it legal? Is it consistent with the company's stated values? Will the employee feel bad doing it? What will the public think if the action is reported in the press? Does the employee think it is wrong? Further, if the employees are not sure of the ethicality of the issue, they are encouraged to ask someone until they are clear about it. In the process, employees can approach high-level personnel and even the company's lawyers. As can be clearly noted, at Texas Instruments, the question of ethics goes much beyond merely being legal. It is no surprise, therefore, that this company is a benchmark for corporate ethics and has been a recipient of three ethics awards: the David C. Lincoln Award for Ethics and Excellence in Business, American Business Ethics Award, and Bentley College Center for Business Ethics Award.[48]

>LO7
Several key elements that organizations must have to become an ethical organization.

To sum up, compliance-based approaches are externally motivated—that is, based on the fear of punishment for doing something unlawful. On the other hand, integrity-based approaches are driven by a personal and organizational commitment to ethical behavior.

A firm must have several key elements before it can become a highly ethical organization. The following elements must be both present and constantly reinforced:

- Role models.
- Corporate credos and codes of conduct.
- Reward and evaluation systems.
- Policies and procedures.

These elements are highly interrelated. For example, reward structures and policies will be useless if leaders are not sound role models. That is, leaders who implicitly say, "Do as I say, not as I do," will quickly have their credibility eroded and such actions will, in effect, sabotage other elements that are essential to building an ethical organization.

Role Models

For good or for bad, leaders are role models in their organizations. As we noted in Chapter 9, leaders must "walk the talk"; that is, they must be consistent in their words and deeds. The values as well as the character of leaders become transparent to an organization's employees through their behaviors. In addition, when leaders do not believe in the ethical standards that they are trying to inspire, they will not be effective as good role models. Being an effective leader often includes taking responsibility for ethical lapses within the organization—even though the executives themselves are not directly involved. Consider, for example, the perspective of Dennis Bakke, CEO of AES, the $12 billion global electricity company based in Arlington, Virginia.

> There was a major breach (in 1992) of the AES values. Nine members of the water treatment team in Oklahoma lied to the EPA about water quality at the plant. There was no environmental damage, but they lied about the test results. A new, young chemist at the plant discovered it, told a team leader, and we then were notified. Now, you could argue that the people who lied were responsible and were accountable, but the senior management team also took responsibility by taking pay cuts. My reduction was about 30 percent.[49]

Such action enhances the loyalty and commitment of employees throughout the organization. Many would believe that it would have been much easier (and personally less expensive!) for Bakke and his management team to merely take strong punitive action against the nine individuals who were acting contrary to the behavior expected in AES's ethical culture. However, by taking responsibility for the misdeeds, the top executives—through their highly visible action—made it very clear that responsibility and penalties for ethical lapses go well beyond the "guilty" parties. Such courageous behavior by leaders helps to strengthen an organization's ethical environment.

Corporate Credos and Codes of Conduct

Corporate credos or codes of conduct are mechanisms that provide a statement and guidelines for norms and beliefs as well as guidelines for decision making. They provide employees with a clear understanding of the organization's position regarding employee behavior. Such guidelines also provide the basis for employees to refuse to commit unethical acts and help to make them aware of issues before they are faced with the situation. For such codes to be truly effective, organization members must be aware of them and what behavioral guidelines they contain.[50]

Large corporations are not the only ones to develop and use codes of conduct. Consider the example of Wetherill Associates (WAI), a small, privately held supplier of electrical parts to the automotive market.

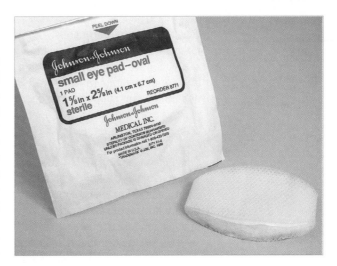

● Johnson & Johnson is well known for its credo, which stresses honesty, integrity, superior products, and putting people before profits. Above is one of its many products.

> Rather than a conventional code of conduct, WAI has a Quality Assurance Manual—a combination of philosophy text, conduct guide, technical manual, and company profile—that describes the company's commitment to honesty, ethical action, and integrity.
>
> Interestingly, WAI doesn't have a corporate ethics officer, because the company's corporate ethics officer is Marie Bothe, WAI's chief executive officer. She sees her main function as keeping the 350-employee company on the path of ethical behavior and looking for opportunities to help the community. She delegates the "technical" aspects of the business—marketing, finance, personnel, and operations—to other members of the organization.[51]

Perhaps the best-known credo, a statement describing a firm's commitment to certain standards, is that of Johnson & Johnson (J&J). It is reprinted in Exhibit 11.7. The credo stresses honesty, integrity, superior products, and putting people before profits. What distinguishes the J&J credo from those of other firms is the amount of energy the company's top managers devote to ensuring that employees live by its precepts:

> Over a three-year period, Johnson & Johnson undertook a massive effort to assure that its original credo, already decades old, was still valid. More than 1,200 managers attended two-day seminars in groups of 25, with explicit instructions to challenge the credo. The president or CEO of the firm presided over each session. In the end, the company came out of the process believing that its original document was still valid. However, the questioning process continues. Such "challenge meetings" are still replicated every other year for all new managers. These efforts force J&J to question, internalize, and then implement its credo. Such investments have paid off handsomely many times—most notably in 1982, when eight people died from swallowing capsules of Tylenol, one of its flagship products, that someone had laced with cyanide. Leaders such as James Burke, who without hesitation made an across-the-board recall of the product even though it affected only a limited number of untraceable units, send a strong message throughout the firm.

Reward and Evaluation Systems

It is entirely possible for a highly ethical leader to preside over an organization that commits several unethical acts. How? It may reflect a flaw in the organization's reward structure. A reward and evaluation system may inadvertently cause individuals to act in an inappropriate manner if rewards are seen as being distributed on the basis of outcomes instead of the means by which goals and objectives are achieved.[52]

Consider the example of Sears, Roebuck & Co.'s automotive operations. Here, unethical behavior, rooted in a faulty reward system, took place primarily at the operations level: its automobile repair facilities.[53]

Exhibit 11.7

Johnson & Johnson's
Credo

We believe our first responsibility is to the doctors, nurses and patients, to mothers and fathers and all others who use our products and services. In meeting their needs everything we do must be of high quality. We must constantly strive to reduce our costs in order to maintain reasonable prices. Customers' orders must be serviced promptly and accurately. Our suppliers and distributors must have an opportunity to make a fair profit.

We are responsible to our employees, the men and women who work with us throughout the world. Everyone must be considered as an individual. We must respect their dignity and recognize their merit. They must have a sense of security in their jobs. Compensation must be fair and adequate, and working conditions clean, orderly, and safe. We must be mindful of ways to help our employees fulfill their family responsibilities. Employees must feel free to make suggestions and complaints. There must be equal opportunity for employment, development, and advancement for those qualified. We must provide competent management, and their actions must be just and ethical.

We are responsible to the communities in which we live and work and to the world community as well. We must be good citizens—support good works and charities and bear our fair share of taxes. We must encourage civic improvements and better health and education. We must maintain in good order the property we are privileged to use, protecting the environment and natural resources.

Our final responsibility is to our stockholders. Business must make a sound profit. We must experiment with new ideas. Research must be carried on, innovative programs developed, and mistakes paid for. New equipment must be purchased, new facilities provided, and new products launched. Reserves must be created to provide for adverse times. When we operate according to these principles, the stockholders should realize a fair return.

Source: Reprinted with permission of Johnson & Johnson Co.

In 1992 Sears was flooded with complaints about its automotive service business. Consumers and attorneys general in more than 40 states accused the firm of misleading customers and selling them unnecessary parts and services, from brake jobs to front-end alignments. What were the causes?

In the face of declining revenues and eroding market share, Sears's management attempted to spur the performance of its auto centers by introducing new goals and incentives for mechanics. Automotive service advisers were given product-specific quotas for a variety of parts and repairs. Failure to meet the quotas could lead to transfers and reduced hours. Many employees spoke of "pressure, pressure, pressure" to bring in sales.

Not too surprisingly, the judgment of many employees suffered. In essence, employees were left to chart their own course, given the lack of management guidance and customer ignorance. The bottom line: In settling the spate of lawsuits, Sears offered coupons to customers who had purchased certain auto services over the most recent two-year period. The total cost of the settlement, including potential customer refunds, was estimated to be $60 million. The cost in terms of damaged reputation? Difficult to assess, but certainly not trivial.

This example makes two points. First, inappropriate reward systems may cause individuals at all levels throughout an organization to commit unethical acts that they might not otherwise commit. Second, the penalties in terms of damage to reputations, human capital erosion, and financial loss—in the short run and long run—are typically much higher than any gains that could be obtained through such unethical behavior.

Many companies have developed reward and evaluation systems that evaluate whether a manager is acting in an ethical manner. For example, Raytheon, a $20 billion defense contractor, incorporates the following items in its "Leadership Assessment Instrument":[54]

- Maintains unequivocal commitment to honesty, truth, and ethics in every facet of behavior.
- Conforms with the letter and intent of company policies while working to affect any necessary policy changes.

strategy spotlight

11.7

No More Whistleblowing Woes!

The landmark Sarbanes-Oxley Act of 2002 gives those who expose corporate misconduct strong legal protection. Henceforth, an executive who retaliates against the corporate whistleblower can be held criminally liable and imprisoned for up to 10 years. That's the same sentence a mafia don gets for threatening a witness. The Labor Department can order a company to rehire an employee without going to court. If the fired workers feel their case is moving too slowly, they can request a federal jury after six months.

Companies need to revisit their current policies, including nondisclosure pacts. They may no longer be able to enforce rules requiring employees to get permission to speak to the media or lawyers. Even layoffs should be planned in advance, lest they seem retaliatory.

Sources: www.sarbanes-oxley.com/pcaob.php/level=2&pub_id=Sarbanes-Oxley&chap_id=PCAOB11; Dwyer, P., Carney, D., Borrus, A., Woellert,L., & Palmeri, C. 2002. Year of the Whistle Blower. *BusinessWeek*, December 16: 107–109; and www.buchalter.com/FSL5CS/articles/articles204.asp.

Employees of publicly traded companies are now the most protected whistleblowers. Provisions coauthored by Senator Grassley in the Sarbanes-Oxley corporate-reform law:

- Make it unlawful to "discharge, demote, suspend or threaten, harass, or in any manner discriminate against" a whistleblower.
- Establish criminal penalties of up to 10 years in jail for executives who retaliate against whistleblowers.
- Require board audit committees to establish procedures for hearing whistleblower complaints.
- Allow the secretary of labor to order a company to rehire a terminated whistleblower with no court hearings whatsoever.
- Give a whistleblower a right to jury trial, bypassing months or years of cumbersome administrative hearings.

- Actions are consistent with words; follows through on commitments; readily admits mistakes.
- Is trusted and inspires others to be trusted.

As noted by Dan Burnham, Raytheon's former CEO: "What do we look for in a leadership candidate with respect to integrity? What we're really looking for are people who have developed an inner gyroscope of ethical principles. We look for people for whom ethical thinking is part of what they do—no different from 'strategic thinking' or 'tactical thinking.'"

Policies and Procedures

Many situations that a firm faces have regular, identifiable patterns. Typically, leaders tend to handle such routine by establishing a policy or procedure to be followed that can be applied uniformly to each occurrence. As noted in Chapter 9, such guidelines can be useful in specifying the proper relationships with a firm's customers and suppliers. For example, Levi Strauss has developed stringent global sourcing guidelines and Chemical Bank (part of J. P. Morgan Chase Bank) has a policy of forbidding any review that would determine if suppliers are Chemical customers when the bank awards contracts.

Carefully developed policies and procedures guide behavior so that all employees will be encouraged to behave in an ethical manner. However, it is not enough merely to have policies and procedures "on the books." Rather, they must be reinforced with effective communication, enforcement, and monitoring, as well as sound corporate governance practices. Strategy Spotlight 11.7 describes how the recently enacted Sarbanes-Oxley Act provides considerable legal protection to employees of publicly traded companies who report unethical or illegal practices.

We close our chapter on strategic leadership with a brief discussion of the Goolsby Leadership Model. It is addressed in Strategy Spotlight 11.8 and includes three dimensions: integrity, courage, and impact. The Goolsby Model synthesizes many of the ideas that we have addressed in this chapter and has important implications for career success.

The Goolsby Leadership Model: Integrity, Courage, and Impact

For many years there has been a focus in leadership research on inspirational styles that emphasize such traits as vision, charisma, and transformation. Some have criticized such approaches and have suggested that they may lead to unethical behavior. Why? They appeal to emotion rather than reason, lack checks and balances, and exploit followers to their detriment and to the benefit of the leader(s). Thus, some writers have begun to distinguish between authentic and inauthentic leaders. The Goolsby Leadership Model grows from the transformational leadership tradition and is anchored in the more recent emphasis on authentic leadership.

Clearly, most would agree that a healthy leader is at the heart of a healthy organization. Consider the alternative: The unhealthy leader has drawn attention to the damaging and debilitating effects—on both individuals and organizations—that result from such behaviors as excessive narcissism and toxic micromanagement. Also, recall the unethical and illegal activities in which some leaders participate that we addressed earlier in this chapter and in our discussion on corporate governance in Chapter 9. The Goolsby Leadership Model, in contrast, sets forth a healthy, positive model based on three core concepts: integrity, courage, and impact. It suggests that healthy leaders have integrity; act with courage and passion; and achieve high impact results for themselves, other individuals, and the organization. This model is shown in Exhibit 11.8. Next, we address each of the model's three dimensions.

Integrity

Integrity, a concept at the heart of good business practice, can be defined as consistency between word and deed as well as sound moral character. The four core questions of the Rotary Four-Way Test aim to test personal integrity. These questions evolved from a 100-word statement developed by Herbert J. Taylor during the economic challenges of the 1930s in the United States. Taylor was engineering a major business turnaround of Club Aluminum Corporation of America and the following questions were aimed at lifting his company above the competition and to giving them a competitive advantage:

1. Is it the truth?
2. Is it fair to all concerned?
3. Will it build goodwill and better friendships?
4. Will it be beneficial to all concerned?

In building on these questions, we suggest two key attributes of integrity in the healthy leader: authenticity and emotional competence. These two attributes, in part, draw on the concept of emotional intelligence (EI) that we addressed earlier in the chapter. As indicated in Exhibit 11.8, authenticity includes self-awareness, transparency, positive psychological states, and personal integrity. An authentic leader possesses good self-awareness, is transparent to others while being consistent, engenders positive psychological states within himself and his followers, and is widely known for having personal integrity. Essentially, authentic leaders are who they say they are; that is, there is a consistency between their values and intentions, their beliefs, their spoken words, and their actions and behaviors. In effect, the opposite of an authenticity is duplicity, which is a type of Jekyll-and-Hyde personality.

The second dimension of integrity is emotional competence, which involves the integration of thought and emotion, goes to the authentic characteristic of self-awareness, and is defined by its four dimensions shown in Exhibit 11.8: awareness of self, management of self, awareness of others, and management of others. Emotionally *(continued)*

Integrity

Authenticity
- Self-awareness
- Transparency
- Positive psychological states
- Personal integrity

Emotional competence
- Self-awareness
- Self-management
- Awareness of others
- Management of others

Courage

Purpose
- Goals
- Objectives

Energy
- Management
- Expenditure
- Renewal

Character
- Consistency
- Core Values

Impact

Individual health
- Vitality
- Productivity
- Flexibility

Organizational health
- Vitality
- Productivity
- Flexibility

Exhibit 11.8 The Goolsby Leadership Model

Source: Quick, J. C., Macik-Frey, M., & Cooper, C. L. 2007. *Journal of Management Studies*, 44(2):195. Reprinted with permission of Wiley-Blackwell Publishing Ltd.

(continued) competent leaders are aware of their own feelings and emotions and aware of the feelings and emotions in other people. In addition, the emotionally competent leader is able to act in ways that appropriately manage his own emotions while accommodating the emotions of others. Emotional competence helps the healthy leader to be hopeful, positive, and compassionate in his actions and behaviors.

Courage

Courage, the second element in the Goolsby Leadership Model as indicated in Exhibit 11.8, is defined as the capacity to act, even in the presence of adversity, fear, and danger. Courage involves purpose, energy, and character. Courage matters; it makes a difference in the course of human events. After conducting in-depth interviews with 28 senior executives, researchers recently found a wide variety of attributes and characteristics of great leaders. However, there was no variance along the dimension of purpose. Purpose is the heart of great leadership and the heart of character.

Energy and energy management are essential for healthy productivity and achievement. While many leaders may focus on time management, energy management becomes more important. Consider, for example, the personal leadership track at PepsiCo's, corporate leadership program in Purchase, New York. Here, consultants found that energy expenditure through full engagement is what leads to productive achievement and meaningful work accomplishment. The executive team at PepsiCo, agrees, and PepsiCo, as a corporation, has enjoyed an impressive

Source: This Strategy Spotlight draws upon Quick, J. C., Macik-Frey, M., & Cooper, C. L. 2007. Managerial dimensions of organizational health: The healthy leader at work. *Journal of Management Studies*, 44(2): 189–295.

12 percent annual growth in market valuation over the most recent four-year period. This is over twice the growth of its long-time rival, Coca Cola, whose corresponding figure is only 5 percent. Interestingly, to be most effective, the power of full engagement must be balanced with strategic disengagement through which leaders are able to achieve renewal based on the process of energy recovery. Rather than a marathon, good leadership may be viewed as a series of short runs punctuated by periods of rest and recovery.

A third dimension of courage is character, and it can be defined as who you are when no one is looking. Character has an important role because it leads to consistency in actions and behaviors based on core values and principles. It's been suggested that character can be measured and that strength and character is a powerful force that enables leaders to act with courage in the midst of business crises or disasters. Therefore, courageous leaders are purposeful, energetic, and possess strong character.

Impact

Strategic leadership is neither a philosophical nor contemplative activity. Great leaders have a strong impact on their followers and on the businesses they lead. Consider, for example, the impacts of such well-known leaders as Andy Grove at Intel, Richard Branson at Virgin, Inc., and Lou Gerstner at IBM. The Goolsby Leadership Model suggests that the important impacts of integrity and courage are individual and that organizational health and the characteristics of vitality, productivity, and flexibility are essential to effective organizations. When individuals and organizations function in a healthy manner, they get results and make a positive impact for a wide range of organizational stakeholders.

Reflecting on Career Implications . . .

- **Strategic Leadership:** Do managers in your firm effectively set the direction; design the organization; and, instill a culture committed to excellence and ethical behavior? If you are in a position of leadership, do you practice all of these three elements effectively?
- **Power:** What sources of power do managers in your organization use? For example, if there is an overemphasis on organizational sources of power (e.g., position power); there could be negative implications for creativity, morale and turnover among professionals. How much power do you have? What is the basis of it? How might it be used to both advance your career goals and benefit the firm?
- **Emotional Intelligence:** Do leaders of your firm have sufficient levels of EI? Alternatively, are there excessive levels of EI present that have negative implications for your organization? Is your level of EI sufficient to allow you to have effective interpersonal and judgment skills in order to enhance your career success?
- **Learning Organization:** Does your firm effectively practice all five elements of the learning organization? If one or more elements are absent, adaptability and change will be compromised. What can you do to enhance any of the elements that might be lacking?
- **Ethics:** Does your organization practice a compliance-based or integrity-based ethical culture? Integrity-based cultures can enhance your personal growth. In addition, such cultures foster greater loyalty and commitment among all employees.

Summary

Strategic leadership is vital in ensuring that strategies are formulated and implemented in an effective manner. Leaders must play a central role in performing three critical and interdependent activities: setting the direction, designing the organization, and nurturing a culture committed to excellence and ethical behavior. In the chapter we provided the imagery of these three activities as a "three-legged stool." If leaders ignore or are ineffective at performing any one of the three, the organization will not be very successful. Leaders must also use power effectively to overcome barriers to change.

For leaders to effectively fulfill their activities, emotional intelligence (EI) is very important. Five elements that contribute to EI are self-awareness, self-regulation, motivation, empathy, and social skill. The first three elements pertain to self-management skills, whereas the last two are associated with a person's ability to manage relationships with others. We also addressed some of the potential drawbacks from the ineffective use of EI. These include the dysfunctional use of power as well as a tendency to become overly empathetic, which may result in unreasonably lowered performance expectations.

Leaders must also play a central role in creating a learning organization. Gone are the days when the top-level managers "think" and everyone else in the organization "does." With the rapidly changing, unpredictable, and complex competitive environments that characterize most industries, leaders must engage everyone in the ideas and energies of people throughout the organization. Great ideas can come from anywhere in the organization—from the executive suite to the factory floor. The five elements that we discussed as central to a learning organization are inspiring and motivating people with a mission or purpose, empowering people at all levels throughout the organization, accumulating and sharing internal knowledge, gathering external information, and challenging the status quo to stimulate creativity.

In the final section of the chapter, we addressed a leader's central role in instilling ethical behavior in the organization. We discussed the enormous costs that firms face when ethical crises arise—costs in terms of financial and reputational loss as well as the erosion of human capital and relationships with suppliers, customers, society at large, and governmental agencies. And, as we would expect, the benefits of having a strong ethical organization are also numerous. We contrasted compliance-based and integrity-based approaches to organizational ethics. Compliance-based approaches are largely externally motivated; that is, they are motivated by the fear of punishment for doing something that is unlawful. Integrity-based approaches, on the other hand, are driven by a personal and organizational commitment to ethical behavior. We also addressed the four key elements of an ethical organization: role models, corporate credos and codes of conduct, reward and evaluation systems, and policies and procedures.

Key Terms

leadership, 379
barriers to change, 381
systemic barriers, 382
behavioral barriers, 383
political barriers, 383
power, 383
organizational bases of power, 384

personal bases of power, 384
emotional intelligence, 384
learning organizations, 390
ethics, 396
compliance-based ethics programs, 399
integrity-based ethics programs, 399

Summary Review Questions

1. Three key activities—setting a direction, designing the organization, and nurturing a culture and ethics—are all part of what effective leaders do on a regular basis. Explain how these three activities are interrelated.

2. Define emotional intelligence (EI). What are the key elements of EI? Why is EI so important to successful strategic leadership? Address potential "downsides."

3. The knowledge a firm possesses can be a source of competitive advantage. Describe ways that a firm can continuously learn to maintain its competitive position.

4. How can the five central elements of "learning organizations" be incorporated into global companies?

5. What are the benefits to firms and their shareholders of conducting business in an ethical manner?

6. Firms that fail to behave in an ethical manner can incur high costs. What are these costs and what is their source?

7. What are the most important differences between an "integrity organization" and a "compliance organization" in a firm's approach to organizational ethics?

8. What are some of the important mechanisms for promoting ethics in a firm?

Experiential Exercise

Select two well-known business leaders—one you admire and one you do not. Evaluate each of them on the five characteristics of emotional intelligence.

Emotional Intelligence Characteristics	Admired Leader	Leader Not Admired
Self-awareness		
Self-regulation		
Motivation		
Empathy		
Social skills		

Application Questions Exercises

1. Identify two CEOs whose leadership you admire. What is it about their skills, attributes, and effective use of power that causes you to admire them?

2. Founders have an important role in developing their organization's culture and values. At times, their influence persists for many years. Identify and describe two organizations in which the cultures and values established by the founder(s) continue to flourish. You may find research on the Internet helpful in answering these questions.

3. Some leaders place a great emphasis on developing superior human capital. In what ways does this help a firm to develop and sustain competitive advantages?

4. In this chapter we discussed the five elements of a "learning organization." Select a firm with which you are familiar and discuss whether or not it epitomizes some (or all) of these elements.

Ethics Questions

1. Sometimes organizations must go outside the firm to hire talent, thus bypassing employees already working for the firm. Are there conditions under which this might raise ethical considerations?

2. Ethical crises can occur in virtually any organization. Describe some of the systems, procedures, and processes that can help to prevent such crises.

References

1. Gagnier, M. 2005. Kremed again. *BusinessWeek*, January 17:40; Anonymous. 2005. Worst managers. *BusinessWeek*, January 10: 74–77; Stires, D. 2004. Krispy Kreme is in the hole—again. *Fortune*, November 11: 42–43; and, McGowan, W. P. 2005. Krispy Kreme: A recipe for business failure. *Canyon News*, 19: 23.

2. Charan, R., & Colvin, G. 1999. Why CEOs fail. *Fortune*, June 21: 68–78.

3. These three activities and our discussion draw from Kotter, J. P. 1990. What leaders really do. *Harvard Business Review*, 68(3): 103–111; Pearson, A. E. 1990. Six basics for general managers. *Harvard Business Review*, 67(4): 94–101; and Covey, S. R. 1996. Three roles of the leader in the new paradigm. In *The leader of the future:* 149–160. Hesselbein, F., Goldsmith, M., & Beckhard, R. (Eds.). San Francisco: Jossey-Bass. Some of the discussion of each of the three leadership activity concepts draws on Dess, G. G., & Miller, A. 1993. *Strategic management:* 320–325. New York: McGraw-Hill.

4. Day, C., Jr., & LaBarre, P. 1994. GE: Just your average everyday $60 billion family grocery store. *Industry Week,* May 2: 13–18.

5. The best (& worst) managers of the year. 2003. *BusinessWeek,* January 13: 63.

6. Kirkpatrick, D. 2006. Use humility as a weapon. *Fortune.* October 30: 118.

7. Anonymous. 2006. Looking out for number one. *BusinessWeek,* October 30: 66.

8. For insightful perspectives on escalation, refer to Brockner, J. 1992. The escalation of commitment to a failing course of action. *Academy of Management Review,* 17(1): 39–61; and Staw, B. M. 1976. Knee-deep in the big muddy: A study of commitment to a chosen course of action. *Organizational Behavior and Human Decision Processes,* 16: 27–44. The discussion of systemic, behavioral, and political barriers draws on Lorange, P., & Murphy, D. 1984. Considerations in implementing strategic control. *Journal of Business Strategy,* 5: 27–35. In a similar vein, Noel M. Tichy has addressed three types of resistance to change in the context of General Electric: technical resistance, political resistance, and cultural resistance. See Tichy, N. M. 1993. Revolutionalize your company. *Fortune,* December 13: 114–118. Examples draw from O'Reilly, B. 1997. The secrets of America's most admired corporations: New ideas and new products. *Fortune,* March 3: 60–64.

9. This section draws on Champoux, J. E. 2000. *Organizational behavior: Essential tenets for a new millennium.* London: South-Western; and The mature use of power in organizations. 2003. *RHR International-Executive Insights,* May 29, 12.19.168.197/execinsights/8-3.htm.

10. An insightful perspective on the role of power and politics in organizations is provided in Ciampa, K. 2005. Almost ready: How leaders move up. *Harvard Business Review,* 83(1): 46–53.

11. A discussion of the importance of persuasion in bringing about change can be found in Garvin, D. A., & Roberto, M. A. 2005. Change through persuasion. *Harvard Business Review,* 83(4): 104–113.

12. Lorsch, J. W., & Tierney, T. J. 2002. *Aligning the stars: How to succeed when professionals drive results.* Boston: Harvard Business School Press.

13. For a review of this literature, see Daft, R. 1999. *Leadership: Theory and practice.* Fort Worth, TX: Dryden Press.

14. This section draws on Luthans, F. 2002. Positive organizational behavior: Developing and managing psychological strengths. *Academy of Management Executive,* 16(1): 57–72; and Goleman, D. 1998. What makes a leader? *Harvard Business Review,* 76(6): 92–105.

15. EI has its roots in the concept of "social intelligence" that was first identified by E. L. Thorndike in 1920 (Intelligence and its uses. *Harper's Magazine,* 140: 227–235). Psychologists have been uncovering other intelligences for some time now and have grouped them into such clusters as abstract intelligence (the ability to understand and manipulate verbal and mathematical symbols), concrete intelligence (the ability to understand and manipulate objects), and social intelligence (the ability to understand and relate to people). See Ruisel, I. 1992. Social intelligence: Conception and methodological problems. *Studia Psychologica,* 34(4–5): 281–296. Refer to trochim.human. cornell.edu/gallery.

16. See, for example, Luthans, op. cit.; Mayer, J. D., Salvoney, P., & Caruso, D. 2000. Models of emotional intelligence. In Sternberg, R. J. (Ed.). *Handbook of intelligence.* Cambridge, UK: Cambridge University Press; and Cameron, K. 1999. Developing emotional intelligence at the Weatherhead School of Management. *Strategy: The Magazine of the Weatherhead School of Management,* Winter: 2–3.

17. An insightful perspective on leadership, which involves discovering, developing and celebrating what is unique about each individual, is found in Buckingham, M. 2005. What great managers do. *Harvard Business Review,* 83(3): 70–79.

18. This section draws upon Klemp. G. 2005. *Emotional intelligence and leadership: What really matters.* Cambria Consulting, Inc., www.cambriaconsulting.com.

19. Heifetz, R. 2004. Question authority. *Harvard Business Review,* 82(1): 37.

20. Handy, C. 1995. Trust and the virtual organization. *Harvard Business Review,* 73(3): 40–50.

21. This section draws upon Dess, G. G., & Picken, J. C. 1999. *Beyond productivity.* New York: AMACOM. The elements of the learning organization in this section are consistent with the work of Dorothy Leonard-Barton. See, for example, Leonard-Barton, D. 1992. The factory as a learning laboratory. *Sloan Management Review,* 11: 23–38.

22. Senge, P. M. 1990. The leader's new work: Building learning organizations. *Sloan Management Review,* 32(1): 7–23.

23. Hammer, M., & Stanton, S. A. 1997. The power of reflection. *Fortune,* November 24: 291–296.

24. For some guidance on how to effectively bring about change in organizations, refer to Wall, S. J. 2005. The protean organization: Learning to love change. *Organizational Dynamics,* 34(1): 37–46.

25. Covey, S. R. 1989. *The seven habits of highly effective people: Powerful lessons in personal change.* New York: Simon & Schuster.

26. Melrose, K. 1995. *Making the grass greener on your side: A CEO's journey to leading by servicing.* San Francisco: Barrett-Koehler.

27. Quinn, R. C., & Spreitzer, G. M. 1997. The road to empowerment: Seven questions every leader should consider. *Organizational Dynamics,* 25: 37–49.

28. Helgesen, S. 1996. Leading from the grass roots. In *Leader of the future:* 19–24 Hesselbein et al.

29. Bowen, D. E., & Lawler, E. E., III. 1995. Empowering service employees. *Sloan Management Review,* 37: 73–84.

30. Stack, J. 1992. *The great game of business.* New York: Doubleday/Currency.

31. Schafer, S. 1997. Battling a labor shortage? It's all in your imagination. *Inc.,* August: 24.

32. Meyer, P. 1998. So you want the president's job . . . *Business Horizons,* January–February: 2–8.

33. Imperato, G. 1998. Competitive intelligence: Get smart! *Fast Company,* May: 268–279.

34. Novicki, C. 1998. The best brains in business. *Fast Company,* April: 125.

35. The introductory discussion of benchmarking draws on Miller, A. 1998. *Strategic management:* 142–143. New York: McGraw-Hill.

36. Port, O., & Smith, G. 1992. Beg, borrow—and benchmark. *BusinessWeek,* November 30: 74–75.

37. Main, J. 1992. How to steal the best ideas around. *Fortune,* October 19: 102–106.

38. Taylor, J. T. 1997. What happens after what comes next? *Fast Company,* December–January: 84–85.

39. Sheff, D. 1996. Levi's changes everything. *Fast Company,* June–July: 65–74.

40. Isaacson, W. 1997. In search of the real Bill Gates. *Time,* January 13: 44–57.

41. Baatz, E. B. 1993. Motorola's secret weapon. *Electronic Business,* April: 51–53.

42. Holt, J. W. 1996. *Celebrate your mistakes.* New York: McGraw-Hill.

43. This opening discussion draws upon Conley, J. H. 2000. Ethics in business. In Helms, M. M. (Ed.). *Encyclopedia of management* (4th ed.): 281–285; Farmington Hills, MI: Gale Group; Paine, L. S. 1994. Managing for organizational integrity. *Harvard Business Review,* 72(2): 106–117; and Carlson, D. S., & Perrewe, P. L. 1995. Institutionalization of organizational ethics through transformational leadership. *Journal of Business Ethics,* 14: 829–838.

44. Kiger, P. J. 2001. Truth and consequences. *Working Woman,* May: 57–61.

45. Soule, E. 2002. Managerial moral strategies—in search of a few good principles. *Academy of Management Review,* 27(1): 114–124.

46. Carlson & Perrewe, op. cit.

47. This discussion is based upon Paine. Managing for organizational integrity; Paine, L. S. 1997. *Cases in leadership, ethics, and organizational integrity: A Strategic approach.* Burr Ridge, IL: Irwin; and Fontrodona, J. 2002. Business ethics across the Atlantic. Business Ethics Direct, www.ethicsa.org/BED_art_fontrodone.html.

48. www.ti.com/corp/docs/company/citizen/ethics/benchmark. shtml; and www.ti.com/corp/docs/company/citizen/ethics/quicktest.shtml.

49. Wetlaufer, S. 1999. Organizing for empowerment: An interview with AES's Roger Sant and Dennis Bakke. *Harvard Business Review,* 77(1): 110–126.

50. For an insightful, academic perspective on the impact of ethics codes on executive decision making, refer to Stevens, J. M., Steensma, H. K., Harrison, D. A., & Cochran, P. S. 2005. Symbolic or substantive document? The influence of ethics code on financial executives' decisions. *Strategic Management Journal,* 26(2): 181–195.

51. Paine. Managing for organizational integrity.

52. For a recent study on the effects of goal setting on unethical behavior, read Schweitzer, M. E., Ordonez, L., & Douma, B. 2004. Goal setting as a motivator of unethical behavior. *Academy of Management Journal,* 47(3): 422–432.

53. Paine. Managing for organizational integrity.

54. Fulmer, R. M. 2004. The challenge of ethical leadership. *Organizational Dynamics,* 33 (3): 307–317.

chapter 12

Managing Innovation and Fostering Corporate Entrepreneurship

>learning objectives

After reading this chapter, you should have a good understanding of:

LO1 The importance of implementing strategies and practices that foster innovation.

LO2 The challenges and pitfalls of managing corporate innovation processes.

LO3 How independent venture teams and business incubators are used to develop corporate ventures.

LO4 How corporations create an internal environment and culture that promote entrepreneurial development.

LO5 The role of product champions in internal corporate venturing.

LO6 How corporate entrepreneurship achieves both financial goals and strategic goals.

LO7 The benefits and potential drawbacks of real options analysis in making resource deployment decisions in corporate entrepreneurship contexts.

LO8 How an entrepreneurial orientation can enhance a firm's efforts to develop promising corporate venture initiatives.

*t*o remain competitive, established firms must continually seek out opportunities for growth and new methods for strategically renewing their performance. Changes in customer needs, new technologies, and shifts in the competitive landscape require that companies continually innovate and initiate corporate ventures in order to compete effectively. This chapter addresses how entrepreneurial activities can be an avenue for achieving competitive advantages.

In the first section, we address the importance of innovation in identifying venture opportunities and strategic renewal. Innovations can take many forms, including radical breakthrough innovations as well as incremental innovative improvements, and be used either to update products or renew organizational processes. We discuss how firms can successfully manage the innovation process. Impediments and challenges to effective innovation are discussed, and examples of good innovation practices are presented.

We discuss the unique role of corporate entrepreneurship in the strategic management process in the second section. Here we highlight two types of activities corporations use to remain competitive—focused and dispersed. New venture groups and business incubators are often used to focus a firm's entrepreneurial activities. In other corporations, the entrepreneurial spirit is dispersed throughout the organization and gives rise to product champions and other autonomous strategic behaviors that organizational members engage in to foster internal corporate venturing. We also discuss the benefits and potential drawbacks of real options analysis in making decisions about which venture activities merit additional investment and which should be abandoned.

In the final section we describe how a firm's entrepreneurial orientation can contribute to its growth and renewal as well as enhance the methods and processes strategic managers use to recognize opportunities and develop initiatives for internal growth and development. The chapter also evaluates the pitfalls that firms may encounter when implementing entrepreneurial strategies.

Learning from Mistakes

Companies often grow by commercializing new technologies. This is one of the most important paths to corporate entrepreneurship. But technologies change and yesterday's exciting innovation eventually becomes today's old news. Consider the case of Polaroid, a company that captivated the marketplace with its instant photography technology and grew to become a multibillion dollar enterprise on the strength of that innovation.[1]

Polaroid Corporation's founder, Edward Land, was a Harvard dropout. He was also a genius in optics, chemistry, and engineering who started his Cambridge, Massachusetts, company in 1937 to focus on sunglasses and other technologies that polarize light. During World War II, the company built infrared filters for gunsights and dark-adaptation goggles. It was after the war, however, that one of Land's innovations struck gold. In 1947 he introduced a single-step photographic process that would develop film in 60 seconds and launched the Land Camera. Over the next 30 years, the camera and its film evolved into the Polaroid One-Step, and sales surged to $1.4 billion by 1978.

In the process, Polaroid became one of the most admired companies and a best bet among stock pickers. It was a member of the "Nifty Fifty," a group of companies known for their innovative ideas whose stocks regularly traded at 40 or more times earnings. In 1991 it won a huge patent infringement lawsuit against rival Eastman Kodak, which had to pay Polaroid $925 million. The company also continued to launch new products using its instant film technology in a variety of different cameras with updated features. *[continued]*

● Polaroid's cameras were a stunning success when they were first introduced. However, the firm began to stumble in the 1990s after its founder, Edward Land, died.

On the surface, Polaroid seemed to be the picture of success. Land had been hailed as a new breed of corporate leader—both technically savvy and entrepreneurial. But by 1991, the year Land died, the company he built was unraveling. Instead of using the cash from the Kodak lawsuit to pay down its heavy debt, Polaroid spent the money to develop a new camera—the Captiva—which flopped in the marketplace. A few years later the I-Zone Pocket Camera, a product targeted at adolescents, had weak sales because the image quality was inconsistent and replacement film was considered too expensive for teens. Meanwhile, internally, Polaroid was spending 37 percent of its sales on administrative costs, compared to Kodak's 21 percent. Even though the company continued to sell millions of cameras each year—a record 13.1 million in 2000—its strength was deteriorating.

Polaroid's most serious problems began when it failed to get on the digital photography bandwagon. Rather than make the move into digital, Polaroid decided to stick with its proprietary technology. Once Polaroid realized the extent of the digital photography trend, it was too late. It eventually introduced digital cameras but they were often ranked low in consumer ratings. Polaroid even developed digital printing technologies, called Opal and Onyx, designed to deliver high resolution digital images. But because of its weakened financial state, it could not get the funding from investors to advertise and develop them. By 2001, it was in real trouble. Its debt was $950 million, it laid off 2,950 employees—35 percent of its workforce—and began missing interest payments to bondholders. In October 2001, it filed for Chapter 11 bankruptcy protection. Sale of its stock, which had traded as high as $60 in July 1997, was halted at 28 cents per share on the New York Stock Exchange.

The final blow to its reputation came in 2005 when it was announced, as part of a deal to sell Polaroid to a Minnesota-based conglomerate, that thousands of former Polaroid employees would have their pensions wiped out. Retirees and ex-employees, who also lost their health coverage and life insurance, received a total of just $47 for their years of service, while four former Polaroid executives split a $30 million dollar settlement among them![2]

What went wrong at Polaroid? Considered by many to be one of the first great research-based companies, Polaroid failed largely because it lost its ability to effectively innovate and launch new products. Many factors contributed to its downfall. Clearly, its failure to respond quickly to the digital photography phenomenon caused a serious setback. But the roots of the problem were deeper. As one writer put it, "They overestimated the value of their core business." That is, Polaroid's overconfidence in its early success prevented it from envisioning a purpose beyond its instant imaging capability. This phenomenon is sometimes referred to as "the innovator's dilemma"—firms become so preoccupied with meeting current needs that they fail to take steps to meet future needs.[3] This dilemma inhibited Polaroid's ability to change and affected every aspect of its business:

- Even though sales of its core products were strong, it lost touch with its customers. As a result, several of its innovations failed in the marketplace.
- It did not have a long-term strategy for financing growth. Because it relied heavily on investors to finance new product initiatives, when one failed, it created cash flow problems. To regain profitability, Polaroid would offer more shares and bonds to investors, which, in turn, devalued the stock and created even more indebtedness. Eventually, investors turned away. *[continued]*

- Buoyed by revenues that grew annually for over 30 years, it failed to control personnel costs and was weighed down by too many employees. Eventually these expenses overtook its sales.

In short, Polaroid stopped thinking and acting like an entrepreneurial firm. As a result of its lack of vision and failure to change, what had once been a leading innovator and top financial performer slowly fizzled out.[4]

Managing change, as we suggested in Chapter 11, is one of the most important functions performed by strategic leaders. What options are available to organizations that want to change and grow? This chapter addresses two major avenues through which companies can expand or improve their business—innovation and corporate entrepreneurship. These two activities go hand-in-hand because they both have similar aims. The first is strategic renewal. Innovations help an organization stay fresh and reinvent itself as conditions in the business environment change. This is why managing innovation is such an important strategic implementation issue. The second is the pursuit of venture opportunities. Innovative breakthroughs, as well as new product concepts, evolving technologies, and shifting demand, create opportunities for corporate venturing. In this chapter we will explore these topics—how change and innovation can stimulate strategic renewal and foster corporate entrepreneurship. First we turn to the challenge of managing innovation.

>LO1
The importance of implementing strategies and practices that foster innovation.

Managing Innovation

One of the most important sources of growth opportunities is innovation. **Innovation** involves using new knowledge to transform organizational processes or create commercially viable products and services. The sources of new knowledge may include the latest technology, the results of experiments, creative insights, or competitive information. However it comes about, innovation occurs when new combinations of ideas and information bring about positive change.

The emphasis on newness is a key point. For example, for a patent application to have any chance of success, one of the most important attributes it must possess is novelty. You can't patent an idea that has been copied. This is a central idea. In fact, the root of the word *innovation* is the Latin *novus,* which means new. Innovation involves introducing or changing to something new.[5]

Among the most important sources of new ideas is new technology. Technology creates new possibilities. Technology provides the raw material that firms use to make innovative new products and services. But technology is not the only source of innovations. There can be innovations in human resources, firm infrastructure, marketing, service, or in many other value-adding areas that have little to do with anything "high-tech." Strategy Spotlight 12.1 highlights a simple but effective innovation implemented by Target stores.

As the Target example suggests, innovation can take many forms. Next we will consider two frameworks that are often used to distinguish types of innovation.

innovation the use of new knowledge to transform organizational processes or create commercially viable products and services.

Types of Innovation

Although innovations are not always high-tech, changes in technology can be an important source of change and growth. When an innovation is based on a sweeping new technology, it often has a more far-reaching impact. However, sometimes even a small innovation can add value and create competitive advantages. Innovation can and should occur throughout an organization—in every department and all aspects of the value chain.

One way to view the impact of an innovation is in terms of its degree of innovativeness, which falls somewhere on a continuum that extends from incremental to radical.[6]

- *Radical innovations* produce fundamental changes by evoking major departures from existing practices. These breakthrough innovations usually occur because of

radical innovation an innovation that fundamentally changes existing practices.

Target's Low-Tech, High-Value Design Innovation

Sometimes a simple change can make a vast improvement. That's what Target discovered when it adopted a new design for the traditional amber-colored prescription pill bottle. The new design literally flips the old bottle on its head. The base of the bottle is a large cap that uses color-coded rings to help family members distinguish between different containers. The upper part includes a flat surface that holds wider and easier-to-read labels. "They're much easier to use, and it's a lot easier to read," says to Target customer Pat Howell.

Design student Deborah Adler came up with the new bottle after her grandmother Helen accidentally took her grandfather Herman's prescription. She noticed that the small lettering on the curved label of a traditional pill bottle was hard to read. Target, which commissioned a study that found that nearly 60 percent of prescription drugs are taken improperly, welcomed the design innovation. The new bottle, called the ClearRX, has won several design awards and improved Target's prescription drug sales by 14 percent—from $1.4 billion to $1.6 billion in a recent year.

Sources: Anonymous. 2005. Target turns old pill bottle design on its head. *MSNBC.com,* www.msnbc.com, April 26; Finn, B. 2006. Target ClearRX bottle. *Business 2.0,* April: 120; and www.target.com.

---

technological change. They tend to be highly disruptive and can transform a company or even revolutionize a whole industry. They may lead to products or processes that can be patented, giving a firm a strong competitive advantage. Examples include electricity, the telephone, the transistor, desktop computers, fiber optics, artificial intelligence, and genetically engineered drugs.

- ***Incremental innovations*** enhance existing practices or make small improvements in products and processes. They may represent evolutionary applications within existing paradigms of earlier, more radical innovations. Because they often sustain a company by extending or expanding its product line or manufacturing skills, incremental innovations can be a source of competitive advantage by providing new capabilities that minimize expenses or speed productivity. Examples include frozen food, sports drinks, steel-belted radial tires, electronic bookkeeping, shatterproof glass, and digital telephones.

incremental innovation an innovation that enhances existing practices or makes small improvements in products and processes.

Some innovations are highly radical; others are only slightly incremental. But most innovations fall somewhere between these two extremes. Exhibit 12.1 shows where several innovations fall along the radical–incremental continuum.

Another distinction that is often used when discussing innovation is between process innovation and product innovation.[7] *Product innovation* refers to efforts to create product designs and applications of technology to develop new products for end users. Recall from Chapter 5 how generic strategies were typically different depending on the stage of the industry life cycle. Product innovations tend to be more radical and are more common during the earlier stages of an industry's life cycle. As an industry matures, there are fewer opportunities for newness, so the innovations tend to be more incremental. Product innovations are also commonly associated with a differentiation strategy. Firms that differentiate by providing customers with new products or services that offer unique features or quality enhancements often engage in product innovation.

Process innovation, by contrast, is typically associated with improving the efficiency of an organizational process, especially manufacturing systems and operations. By drawing on new technologies and an organization's accumulated experience (Chapter 5), firms can often improve materials utilization, shorten cycle time, and increase quality. Process innovations are more likely to occur in the later stages of an industry's life cycle as companies seek ways to remain viable in markets where demand has flattened out and competition is more intense. As a result, process innovations are often associated with overall

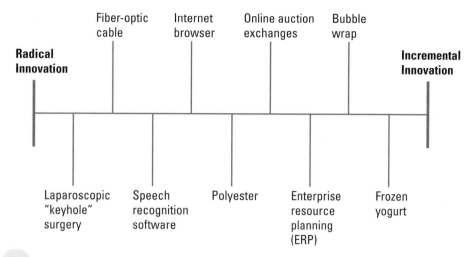

Exhibit 12.1 Continuum of Radical and Incremental Innovations

cost leader strategies, because the aim of many process improvements is to lower the costs of operations.

Innovation is a force in both the external environment (technology, competition) and also a factor affecting a firm's internal choices (generic strategy, value-adding activities). Nevertheless, innovation can be quite difficult for some firms to manage, especially those that have become comfortable with the status quo. Next, we turn to the challenges associated with successful innovation.

Challenges of Innovation

Innovation is essential to sustaining competitive advantages. Recall from Chapter 3 that one of the four elements of the Balanced Scorecard is the innovation and learning perspective. The extent and success of a company's innovation efforts are indicators of its overall performance. As management guru Peter Drucker warned, "An established company which, in an age demanding innovation, is not capable of innovation is doomed to decline and extinction."[8] To put it simply, in today's competitive environment, most firms have only one choice: "Innovate or die."

>LO2

The challenges and pitfalls of managing corporate innovation processes.

As with change, however, firms are often resistant to innovation. Only those companies that actively pursue innovation, even though it is often difficult and uncertain, will get a payoff from their innovation efforts. But managing innovation is challenging. As former Pfizer chairman and CEO William Steere puts it: "In some ways, managing innovation is analogous to breaking in a spirited horse. You are never sure of success until you achieve your goal. In the meantime, everyone takes a few lumps."[9]

What is it that makes innovation so difficult? Clearly the uncertainty about outcomes is one factor. Companies are often reluctant to invest time and resources into activities with an unknown future. Another factor is that the innovation process involves so many choices. These choices present five dilemmas that companies must wrestle with when pursuing innovation.[10]

- **Seeds versus Weeds.** Most companies have an abundance of innovative ideas. They must decide which of these is most likely to bear fruit—the "Seeds"—and which should be cast aside—the "Weeds." This is an ongoing dilemma that is often complicated by the fact that some innovation projects require a considerable level of investment before a firm can fully evaluate whether they are worth pursuing. As a result, firms need a mechanism with which they can choose among various innovation projects.
- **Experience versus Initiative.** Companies must decide who will lead an innovation project. Senior managers may have experience and credibility but tend to be more

risk averse. Midlevel employees, who may be the innovators themselves, may have more enthusiasm because they can see firsthand how an innovation would address specific problems. As a result, firms need to support and reward organizational members who bring new ideas to light.

- **Internal versus External Staffing.** Innovation projects need competent staffs to succeed. People drawn from inside the company may have greater social capital and know the organization's culture and routines. But this knowledge may actually inhibit them from thinking outside the box. Staffing innovation projects with external personnel requires that project managers justify the hiring and spend time recruiting, training, and relationship building. As a result, firms need to streamline and support the process of staffing innovation efforts.

- **Building Capabilities versus Collaborating.** Innovation projects often require new sets of skills. Firms can seek help from other departments and/or partner with other companies that bring resources and experience as well as share costs of development. However, such arrangements can create dependencies and inhibit internal skills development. Further, struggles over who contributed the most or how the benefits of the project are to be allocated may arise. As a result, firms need a mechanism for forging links with outside parties to the innovation process.

- **Incremental versus Preemptive Launch.** Companies must manage the timing and scale of new innovation projects. An incremental launch is less risky because it requires fewer resources and serves as a market test. But a launch that is too tentative can undermine the project's credibility. It also opens the door for a competitive response. A large-scale launch requires more resources, but it can effectively preempt a competitive response. As a result, firms need to make funding and management arrangements that allow for projects to hit the ground running and be responsive to market feedback.

These dilemmas highlight why the innovation process can be daunting even for highly successful firms. Strategy Spotlight 12.2 addresses the challenges and pitfalls that Microsoft faces in its efforts to be a strong innovator. How can companies successfully address these innovation challenges? Next, we consider four steps that firms can take to manage the innovation process.[11]

Defining the Scope of Innovation

Firms must have a means to focus their innovation efforts. By defining the "strategic envelope"—that is, the scope of a firm's innovation efforts—firms ensure that their innovation efforts are not wasted on projects that are outside the firm's domain of interest. Strategic enveloping defines the range of acceptable projects. As Alistair Corbett, an innovation expert who directs the Toronto office of the global consulting firm Bain & Company, recently said, "One man's radical innovation is another man's incremental innovation."[12] Thus, a strategic envelope creates a firm-specific view of innovation that defines how a firm can create new knowledge and learn from an innovation initiative even if the project fails. It also gives direction to a firm's innovation efforts, which helps separate seeds from weeds and builds internal capabilities.

One way to determine which projects to work on is to focus on a common technology. Then, innovation efforts across the firm can aim at developing skills and expertise in a given technical area. Another potential focus is on a market theme. Consider how DuPont responded to a growing concern for environmentally sensitive products:

> In the early 1990s, DuPont sought to use its knowledge of plastics to identify products to meet a growing market demand for biodegradable products. Over the next decade, it conducted numerous experiments with a biodegradable polyester resin it named Biomax. By trying different applications and formulations demanded by potential customers, the company was finally able to create a product that could be produced economically and had market appeal. Recently, Biomax was certified biodegradable and compostable by the Biodegradable Products Institute, an endorsement that should further boost sales.[13]

Microsoft's Innovation Challenges

You would think that Microsoft, the dominant software seller in the world with a $6.8 billion annual research and development budget, would be a major innovator. Instead, innovation seems to be Microsoft's Achilles' heel. From its earliest days, Microsoft has had far more success as an imitator than an innovator. Despite having well-funded research labs at its Redmond, Washington, headquarters, Microsoft has little to show for years of efforts to come up with the next big breakthrough innovation. Why is Microsoft is so innovation-challenged?

- **Innovation is hard.** There is no doubt that Microsoft is working hard at it. From 2000 to 2005, Microsoft acquired 2,188 patents to protect its researchers' work. But creating a commercially viable breakthrough innovation such as the Web browser (created by Netscape), the streaming media player (by RealNetworks) or interactive television (TiVo) is not easy. In many cases, it is more about luck and timing than money, dedication, and brilliance.

- **Bigger isn't better.** Large companies simply find it more difficult than smaller ones to sustain rapid growth through innovation. Good ideas are scarce

everywhere and most new innovations take a few years to get off the ground. Because of Microsoft's sheer size, the contribution that a new product can make is relatively small. For example, if Microsoft had matched Google's recent growth record, that business activity would have added only 4 percent to Microsoft's top line.

- **Defense is easier.** Most of Microsoft's research efforts go to helping it sustain its strong leadership in software products such as MS Office. Of every dollar it spends on research and development (R&D), "probably something on the order of 90 percent is directly in line, or in service of, the existing business groups," according to Craig Mundie, Microsoft's co-chief technology officer. In this respect, Microsoft is a victim of "the innovator's dilemma"—spending so much more time protecting its established lines of business and satisfying existing customers that it misses opportunities to make breakthroughs.

Microsoft continues to support innovation and its breakthrough product may come any day. But even its new project, the second generation videogame console known as XBox 360, lags far behind Sony's PlayStation2 in sales and market penetration. Microsoft may not be producing the next big thing, but as a fast follower of technology breakthroughs, it has been highly successful.

Sources: Grossman, L. 2005. Out of the Xbox. *Time*, May 23: 44–53; and Hawn, C. 2004. What money can't buy. *Fast Company*, 89: 68–73.

In defining a strategic envelope, companies must be clear not only about the kinds of innovation they are looking for but also the expected results. Therefore, each company needs to develop a set of questions to ask itself about its innovation efforts:

- How much will the innovation initiative cost?
- How likely is it to actually become commercially viable?
- How much value will it add; that is, what will it be worth if it works?
- What will be learned if it does not pan out?

In other words, however a firm envisions its innovation goals, it needs to develop a systematic approach to evaluating its results and learning from its innovation initiatives. Viewing innovation from this perspective helps firms manage the process.[14]

Managing the Pace of Innovation

Along with clarifying the scope of an innovation by defining a strategic envelope, firms also need to regulate the pace of innovation. An advantage of assessing the extent to which an innovation is radical or incremental is that it helps determine how long it will take for an innovation initiative to realistically come to fruition. The project time line of an incremental innovation may be 6 months to 2 years, whereas a more radical innovation is typically long term—10 years or more.[15] Thus, radical innovations often begin with a long period of exploration in which experimentation makes strict timelines unrealistic. In contrast, firms that are innovating incrementally in order to exploit a window of opportunity may use a milestone approach that is more stringently driven by goals and deadlines. This kind of sensitivity to realistic time frames helps companies separate dilemmas temporally so they are easier to manage.

The idea of time pacing can also be a source of competitive advantage, because it helps a company manage transitions and develop an internal rhythm.[16] Time pacing does not mean the company ignores the demands of market timing. Instead, it means that companies have a sense of their own internal clock in a way that allows them to thwart competitors by controlling the innovation process.

Not all innovation lends itself to speedy development, however. Radical innovation often involves open-ended experimentation and time-consuming mistakes. Further, the creative aspects of innovation are often difficult to time. When software maker Intuit's new CEO, Steve Bennett, began to turn around that troubled business, he required every department to implement Six Sigma, a quality control management technique that focuses on being responsive to customer needs. Everybody, that is, but the techies.

> "We're not GE, we're not a company where Jack says 'Do it,' and everyone salutes," says Bill Hensler, Intuit's vice president for process excellence. That's because software development, according to many, is more of an art than a science. At the Six Sigma Academy, president of operations Phil Samuel says even companies that have embraced Six Sigma across every other aspect of their organization usually maintain a hands-off policy when it comes to software developers. Techies, it turns out, like to go at their own pace.[17]

The example of software developers makes an important point about strategic pacing: some projects can't be rushed. Companies that hurry up their research efforts or go to market before they are ready can damage their ability to innovate—and their reputation. Thus, managing the pace of innovation can be an important factor in long-term success.

Staffing to Capture Value from Innovation

People are central to the processes of identifying, developing, and commercializing innovations effectively. Not only do they need broad sets of skills, but they also need experience—experience working with teams and experience working on successful innovation projects. To capture value from innovation activities, therefore, companies must provide strategic decision makers with staff members who make it possible to reap the benefits of innovative behavior.

This insight led strategy experts Rita Gunther McGrath and Thomas Keil to research the types of human resource management practices that effective firms use to capture value from their innovation efforts.[18] Four practices are especially important when creating staffs to engage in business venturing:

- Create innovation teams with experienced players who know what it is like to deal with uncertainty and can help new staff members learn venture management skills.
- Require that employees seeking to advance their career with the organization serve in the new venture group as part of their career climb.
- Once people have experience with the new venture group, transfer them to mainstream management positions where they can use their skills and knowledge to revitalize the company's core business.
- Separate the performance of individuals from the performance of the innovation. Otherwise, strong players may feel stigmatized if the innovation effort they worked on fails.

There are other staffing practices that may sound as if they would benefit a firm's innovation activities but may, in fact, be counterproductive. These include:

- Creating a staff that consists only of strong players whose primary experience is related to the company's core business. This provides too few people to deal with the uncertainty of innovation projects and may cause good ideas to be dismissed because they do not appear to fit with the core business.

Staffing for Innovation Success at Air Products

When it comes to implementing its innovation efforts, Air Products and Chemicals, Inc. (APCI) recognizes the importance of staffing for achieving success. Air Products is a global manufacturer of industrial gases, chemicals, and related equipment. Headquartered in Allentown, Pennsylvania, Air Products has annual sales of $5 billion, manufacturing facilities in over 30 countries, and 17,000 employees worldwide. The company has a strong reputation for effectively embedding innovation into its culture through its unique employee engagement processes.

Ron Pierantozzi, a 30-year veteran of the company and its director of innovation and new product development, says "Innovation is about discipline.... It requires a different

Sources: Chesbrough, H. 2007. Why bad things happen to good technology. *The Wall Street Journal:* April 28–29, R11; Leavitt, P. 2005. Delivering the difference: Business process management at APCI. *APQC,* www.apqc.com; McGrath, R. G., & Keil, T. 2007. The value captor's process: Getting the most out of your new business ventures. *Harvard Business Review,* May: 128–136; and www.apci.com.

type of training, different tools and new approaches to experimentation." To enact this philosophy, Pierantozzi begins with his people. He recruits people with diverse backgrounds and a wide range of expertise including engineers, entrepreneurs, and government officials. It is made clear to those on his innovation teams that they will return to mainstream operations after four years—a fact that most consider a plus since working in the innovation unit usually provides a career boost. He also assures players that there is no stigma associated with a failed venture because experimentation is highly valued.

Innovation teams are created to manage the company's intellectual assets and determine which technologies have the most potential value. A key benefit of this approach has been to more effectively leverage its human resources to achieve innovative outcomes without increasing its R&D expenses. These efforts resulted in an innovation award from APQC (formerly known as the American Productivity and Quality Center) which recognizes companies for exemplary practices that increase productivity.

- Creating a staff that consists only of volunteers who want to work on projects they find interesting. Such players are often overzealous about new technologies or overly attached to product concepts, which can lead to poor decisions about which projects to pursue or drop.
- Creating a climate where innovation team members are considered second-class citizens. In companies where achievements are rewarded, the brightest and most ambitious players may avoid innovation projects with uncertain outcomes.

Unless an organization can align its key players into effective new venture teams, it is unlikely to create any differentiating advantages from its innovation efforts.[19] An enlightened approach to staffing a company's innovation efforts provides one of the best ways to ensure that the challenges of innovation will be effectively met. Strategy Spotlight 12.3 describes the approach Air Products and Chemicals, Inc. is using to enhance its innovation efforts.

Collaborating with Innovation Partners

It is rare for any one organization to have all the information it needs to carry an innovation from concept to commercialization. Even a company that is highly competent with its current operations usually needs new capabilities to achieve new results. Innovation partners can provide the skills and insights that are often needed to make innovation projects succeed.

Innovation partners may come from many sources, including research universities and the federal government. Each year the federal government issues requests for proposals (RFPs) asking private companies for assistance in improving services or finding solutions to public problems. Universities are another type of innovation partner. Chip-maker Intel, for example, has benefited from underwriting substantial amounts of university research. Rather than hand universities a blank check, Intel bargains for rights to patents that emerge

InnoCentive's Collaborative Approach to Innovation

Eli Lilly's patent expired recently on its blockbuster drug Prozac, which accounted for 34 percent of Lilly's annual sales. Rather than launch a new drug, however, Lilly launched a new business: InnoCentive, LLC. InnoCentive, as the name implies, provides incentives for innovation. It does so by providing a platform for scientists from around the world to work in virtual communities to solve complex problems. The effort does not just benefit Lilly but provides a virtual, open source R&D organization that any member company can use.

Here's how it works: Drug companies, called "Seekers," put up "Wanted" posters describing problems that need addressing. Bounty-hunting scientists, labeled "Solvers," sign confidentiality agreements that gain them admission to a secure project room where they can access data and product specifications related to the problem. If they solve the problem, they get a reward of as much as $100,000 depending on

Sources: Breen, B. 2002. Lilly's R&D prescription. *Fast Company*, 57: 44; Chesbrough, H. *Open innovation: The new imperative for creating and profiting from technology.* 2003. Boston; Harvard Business School Press; Vencat, E. F. 2006. The power of we. *MSNBC/Newsweek International,* www.msnbc.msn.com, November 20; and www.innocentive.com.

the problem. Clients such as Procter & Gamble and Boeing have already benefited from this network approach to innovation. Procter & Gamble reports that a third of its new product concepts now originate outside the company.

Not only is InnoCentive a savvy application of digital technology, it is also an example of what Harvard Business Professor Henry Chesbrough calls "open innovation." The concept of open innovation builds on two other concepts seen in previous chapters—the importance of intellectual assets in today's economy (Chapter 4) and the use of boundaryless organizational arrangements to achieve strategic objectives (Chapter 10). Successful innovation, according to Chesbrough, involves collaborating and drawing on the knowledge and resources of competitors and other strategic partners. In other words, disclose your intellectual property (IP), cross organizational boundaries to achieve innovation goals, and let others share in the wealth. InnoCentive's collaborative model is on the cutting edge of this new approach to innovation. It remains to be seen whether other companies will adopt open innovation, but Chesbrough is convinced that the ones that are willing to seize this new approach will be the long-term winners.

---

from Intel-sponsored research. The university retains ownership of the patent, but Intel gets royalty-free use of it.[20]

Strategic partnering requires firms to identify their strengths and weaknesses and make choices about which capabilities to leverage, which need further development, and which are outside the firm's current or projected scope of operations. Consider Nextel in its decision to partner with RadioFrame Networks, a Seattle-based start-up.

> RadioFrame had developed an innovative radio transmitter that could be used inside buildings to make cell-phone signals clearer. Nextel, which did not have as much network capacity as some of its larger competitors, saw this as a way to increase bandwidth and add value to its existing set of services. Not only did the two firms form a partnership, but Nextel also became involved in the development process by providing senior engineers and funding to help build the system. "We really worked hand-in-hand with Nextel," says RadioFrame CEO Jeff Brown, "from user requirements to how to physically get the finished product into their distribution systems."[21]

To choose partners, firms need to ask what competencies they are looking for and what the innovation partner will contribute.[22] These contributions might include knowledge of markets, technology expertise, or contacts with key players in an industry. Innovation partnerships also typically need to specify how the rewards of the innovation will be shared and who will own the intellectual property that is developed.[23]

Innovation efforts that involve multiple partners and the speed and ease with which partners can network and collaborate are changing the way innovation is conducted. Strategy Spotlight 12.4 highlights the role of InnoCentive, which emphasizes collaboration and partnerships in a new approach to innovation labeled "open innovation."

Successful innovation involves a companywide commitment because the results of innovation affect every part of the organization. Innovation also requires an entrepreneurial spirit and skill set to be effective. Few companies have a more exemplary reputation than W. L. Gore Exhibit 12.2 highlights the policies that help make Gore an innovation leader. One of the most important ways that companies improve and grow is when innovation is put to the task of creating new corporate ventures. We will look at that topic next.

Exhibit 12.2

W. L. Gore's New Rules for Fostering Innovation

Rule	Implications
The power of small teams	Gore believes that small teams promote familiarity and autonomy. Even its manufacturing plants are capped at just 200 people. That way everyone can get to know one another on a first-name basis and work together with minimal rules. This also helps to cultivate "an environment where creativity can flourish," according to CEO Chuck Carroll.
No ranks, no titles, no bosses	Because Gore believes in maximizing individual potential, employees, dubbed "associates," decide for themselves what new commitments to take on. Associates have "sponsors," rather than bosses, and there are no standardized job descriptions or categories. Everyone is supposed to take on a unique role. Committees of co-workers evaluate each team member's contribution and decide on compensation.
Take the long view	Although impatient about the status quo, Gore exhibits great patience with the time—often years, sometimes decades—it takes to nurture and develop breakthrough products and bring them to market.
Make time for face time	Gore avoids the traditional hierarchical chain of command, opting instead for a team-based environment that fosters personal initiative. Gore also discourages memos and e-mail and promotes direct, person-to-person communication among all associates—anyone in the company can talk to anyone else.
Lead by leading	Associates are encouraged to spend about 10 percent of their time pursuing speculative new ideas. Anyone is free to champion products, as long as they have the passion and ideas to attract followers. Many of Gore's breakthroughs started with one person acting on his or her own initiative and developed as colleagues helped in their spare time.
Celebrate failure	When a project doesn't work out and the team decides to kill it, they celebrate just as they would if it had been a success—with some beer and maybe a glass of champagne. Rather than condemning failure, Gore figures that celebrating it encourages experimentation and risk taking.

Source: Deutschman, A. 2004. The fabric of creativity. *Fast Company*, 89: 54–62; Levering, R., & Moskowitz, M. 2006. The 100 best companies to work for. *Fortune*, www.fortune.com, January, and www.gore.com.

Corporate Entrepreneurship

corporate entrepreneurship
the creation of new value for a corporation, through investments that create either new sources of competitive advantage or renewal of the value proposition.

Corporate entrepreneurship (CE) has two primary aims: the pursuit of new venture opportunities and strategic renewal.[24] The innovation process keeps firms alert by exposing them to new technologies, making them aware of marketplace trends, and helping them evaluate new possibilities. Corporate entrepreneurship uses the fruits of the innovation process to help firms build new sources of competitive advantage and renew their value propositions. Just as the innovation process helps firms to make positive improvements, corporate entrepreneurship helps firms identify opportunities and launch new ventures.

Corporate new venture creation was labeled "intrapreneuring" by Gifford Pinchot because it refers to building entrepreneurial businesses within existing corporations.[25] However, to engage in corporate entrepreneurship that yields above-average returns and contributes to sustainable advantages, it must be done effectively. In this section we will examine the sources of entrepreneurial activity within established firms and the methods large corporations use to stimulate entrepreneurial behavior.

In a typical corporation, what determines how entrepreneurial projects will be pursued? That depends on many factors, including:

- Corporate culture.
- Leadership.
- Structural features that guide and constrain action.
- Organizational systems that foster learning and manage rewards.

In other words, all of the factors that influence the strategy implementation process will also shape how corporations engage in internal venturing.

Other factors will also affect how entrepreneurial ventures will be pursued.

- The use of teams in strategic decision making.
- Whether the company is product or service oriented.
- Whether its innovation efforts are aimed at product or process improvements.
- The extent to which it is high-tech or low-tech.

Because these factors are different in every organization, some companies may be more involved than others in identifying and developing new venture opportunities. These factors will also influence the nature of the CE process. In this section, we will address several avenues by which companies pursue growth and profit opportunities through entrepreneurial activities.

Successful corporate entrepreneurship typically requires firms to reach beyond their current operations and markets in the pursuit of new opportunities. In fact, it is often the breakthrough opportunities that provide the greatest returns. Such strategies are not without risks, however. In the sections that follow, we will address some of the strategic choice and implementation issues that influence the success or failure of CE activities. How various companies approach corporate venturing is a key factor.

Two distinct approaches to corporate venturing are found among firms that pursue entrepreneurial aims. The first is *focused* corporate venturing, in which CE activities are isolated from a firm's existing operations and worked on by independent work units. The second approach to CE is *dispersed*, in which all parts of the organization and every organization member are engaged in intrapreneurial activities. In the next two sections, we will address these approaches and provide examples of each.

Focused Approaches to Corporate Entrepreneurship

Firms using a focused approach typically separate the corporate venturing activity from the other ongoing operations of the firm. That is, corporate entrepreneurship is usually the domain of autonomous work groups that pursue entrepreneurial aims independent of the rest of the firm. The advantage of this approach is that it frees entrepreneurial team members to think and act without the constraints imposed by existing organizational norms and routines. This independence is often necessary for the kind of open-minded creativity that leads to strategic breakthroughs. The disadvantage is that, because of their isolation from the corporate mainstream, the work groups that concentrate on internal ventures may fail to obtain the resources or support needed to carry an entrepreneurial project through to completion. Two forms—new venture groups (NVGs) and business incubators—are among the most common types of focused approaches.

>LO3
How independent venture teams and business incubators are used to develop corporate ventures.

New Venture Groups (NVGs)   Corporations often form new venture groups whose goal is to identify, evaluate, and cultivate venture opportunities. These groups typically function as semi-autonomous units with little formal structure. The **new venture group** may simply be a committee that reports to the president on potential new ventures. Or it may be organized as a corporate division with its own staff and budget. The aims of the new venture group may be open-ended in terms of what ventures it may consider. Alternatively, some corporations use them to promote concentrated effort on a specific problem. In both cases, they usually have a substantial amount of freedom to take risks and a supply of resources to do it with.[26]

new venture group a group of individuals, or a division within a corporation, that identifies, evaluates, and cultivates venture opportunities.

New venture groups usually have a larger mandate than a typical R&D department. That is, their involvement extends beyond innovation and experimentation to coordinating with other corporate divisions, identifying potential venture partners, gathering resources, and, in some cases, actually launching the venture.

Firms that want to expand by way of new venture start-ups usually acquire existing ventures, as discussed in Chapter 6, or develop ventures internally. Strategy Spotlight 12.5 describes a third alternative for firms that want to be entrepreneurial but still maintain their autonomy: corporate venture funding.[27]

Business Incubators   The term *incubator* was originally used to describe a device in which eggs are hatched. **Business incubators** are designed to "hatch" new businesses. They are a type of corporate new venture group with a somewhat more specialized purpose—to support and nurture fledgling entrepreneurial ventures until they can thrive on their own as stand-alone businesses. Corporations use incubators as a way to grow businesses identified by the new venture group. Although they often receive support from many parts of the corporation, they still operate independently until they are strong enough to go it alone. Then, depending on the type of business, they are either integrated into an existing corporate division or continue to operate as a subsidiary of the parent firm. Additionally, the type of corporate venturing support reported in Strategy Spotlight 12.5 that external new ventures receive may also include allowing a young venture into the corporation's incubator.

business incubator a corporate new venture group that supports and nurtures fledgling entrepreneurial ventures until they can thrive on their own as stand-alone businesses.

Incubators typically provide some or all of the following five functions.[28]

- *Funding.* Usually includes capital investments but may also include in-kind investments and loans.
- *Physical space.* A common problem for new ventures; incubators in which several start-ups share space often provide fertile ground for new ideas and collaboration.
- *Business services.* Along with office space, young ventures need basic services and infrastructure; may include anything from phone systems and computer networks to public relations and personnel management.
- *Mentoring.* Senior executives and skilled technical personnel often provide coaching and experience-based advice.
- *Networking.* Contact with other parts of the firm and external resources such as suppliers, industry experts, and potential customers facilitates problem solving and knowledge sharing.

Corporate Venture Capital

What does a company do when it wants to enjoy the benefits of an entrepreneurial start-up but does not want to acquire a venture or take time to develop one internally? It finances one by providing venture capital.

Since the 1970s, major U.S. corporations such as Exxon Mobil have invested in externally generated business ideas in order to strengthen their innovation profile. Some firms invest in technologies that are similar to their core business or provide potential future synergies. Intel, for example, has invested in several e-business start-ups that are in a position to increase demand for Intel processors. With the high growth potential of industries such as information technology and biotechnology, the level of corporate venture capital is increasing. During the booming dot-com era, corporate venture unit investments jumped by a factor of five, from $1.4 billion to $7.8 billion. In 2000 alone, corporations worldwide invested nearly $17 billion in venture capital.

Several major corporations have launched venture financing efforts. In Germany alone there are over 20 corporate venture funds, including global players Siemens, Bertelsmann, and Deutsche Telekom. Even utilities are investing in emerging companies. AEP, a major U.S. electric power company, recently invested in PHPK, a cryogenics firm based in Columbus, Ohio. PHPK is poised to provide support of superconductivity applications, a rapidly growing energy niche that is seeking innovations. AEP prefers expansion-stage firms that need capital and guidance rather than earlier-stage firms. And AEP invests only in energy-related companies. PHPK has nearly doubled its business since AEP made its investment, which served as an immediate endorsement of PHPK's technology and capabilities.

The result? Intel, for one, has enjoyed tremendous returns. It has a portfolio of businesses worth $8 billion. But Intel's goal is not just to make money—it is looking for ways to cement ties early with promising start-ups. "Companies have discovered that it's a good way to do market development," according to Les Vadasz, head of Intel's venture program. "I do see it as a competitive weapon."

Louis Rajczi, managing partner at Siemens Venture Capital, agrees. Unlike traditional VCs which invest in businesses strictly for the financial returns, corporations invest in new ventures to advance their strategic vision and beat the competition. "If we get in on more good deals at an earlier stage than our competitors, we'll end up getting ahead," says Rajczi. "That will increase the value of the company and increase our returns."

Even so, corporate funding for external ventures dried up rapidly after the technology bubble burst in the early 2000s. In the first half of 2002, only $1.1 billion was invested, compared to $17 billion in 2000. Not only have new investments by corporations dropped dramatically, but also corporations such as Hewlett-Packard and Accenture have sold off large portions of their portfolios. Nevertheless, as a long-term strategy, corporate venture funding can benefit both new ventures and corporations and remains a viable alternative to internal corporate venturing.

Sources: Stein, T. 2002. Rip cord. *Red Herring,* November 28, www.redherring.com; Franzke, E. 2001. Four keys to corporate venturing success. *European Venture Capital Journal,* June 1: 36–37; Letzelter, J. 2000. The new venture capitalists: Utilities go shopping for deals. *Public Utilities Fortnightly,* December: 34–38; Rabinovitz, J. 2000. Venture capital, Inc. *Industry Standard,* April 17: 88–90; and, Worrell, D. 2003. The big guns. *Entrepreneur,* November, www.entrepreneur.com.

The risks associated with incubating ventures should not be overlooked. Companies have at times spent millions on new ideas with very little to show for it. Major corporations such as Lucent, British Airways, and Hewlett-Packard inactivated their incubators and scaled back new venture portfolios after experiencing major declines in value since the early 2000s.[29]

Thus, to encourage entrepreneurship, corporations sometimes need to do more than create independent work groups or venture incubators to generate new enterprises. In some firms, the entrepreneurial spirit is spread throughout the organization. It is this dispersed approach to corporate entrepreneurship that we turn to next.

Dispersed Approaches to Corporate Entrepreneurship

The second type of corporate entrepreneurship is dispersed. For some companies, a dedication to the principles and practices of entrepreneurship is spread throughout the organization. One advantage of this approach is that organizational members don't have to be reminded to think entrepreneurially or be willing to change. The ability to change is considered to be a core capability. This leads to a second advantage: Because of the firm's entrepreneurial reputation, stakeholders such as vendors, customers, or alliance partners can bring new ideas or venture opportunities to anyone in the organization and expect them to be well-received. Such opportunities make it possible for the firm to stay ahead of the competition. However, there are disadvantages as well. Firms that are overzealous about corporate entrepreneurship sometimes feel they must change for the sake of change, causing them to lose vital competencies or spend heavily on R&D and innovation to the detriment of the bottom line. Two related aspects of dispersed entrepreneurship include entrepreneurial cultures that have an overarching commitment to CE activities and the use of product champions in promoting entrepreneurial behaviors.

>LO4
How corporations create an internal environment and culture that promote entrepreneurial development.

Entrepreneurial Culture   In some large corporations, the corporate culture embodies the spirit of entrepreneurship. A culture of entrepreneurship is one in which the search for venture opportunities permeates every part of the organization. Recall from Chapter 3 that the key to creating value successfully is viewing every value-chain activity as a source of competitive advantage. In a similar way, the effect of corporate entrepreneurship on a firm's strategic success is strongest when it animates all parts of an organization. It is found in companies where the strategic leaders and the culture together generate a strong impetus to innovate, take risks, and seek out new venture opportunities.

In companies with an entrepreneurial culture, everyone in the organization is attuned to opportunities to help create new businesses. Many such firms use a top-down approach to stimulate entrepreneurial activity. That is, the top leaders of the organization support programs and incentives that foster a climate of entrepreneurship. Many of the best ideas for new corporate ventures, however, come from the bottom up. Here's what Martin Sorrell, CEO of the WPP Group, a London-based global communication services group, says about drawing on the talents of lower-level employees:

> The people at the so-called bottom of an organization know more about what's going on than the people at the top. The people in the trenches are the ones in the best position to make critical decisions. It's up to the leaders to give those people the freedom and the resources they need.[30]

Thus, an entrepreneurial culture is one in which change and renewal are on everybody's mind. Sony, 3M, Intel, and Cisco are among the corporations best known for their corporate venturing activities. Many fast-growing young corporations also attribute much of their success to an entrepreneurial culture. Best Buy's CEO Brad Anderson considers an entrepreneurial spirit to be essential for success in retailing. Strategy Spotlight 12.6 describes the kinds of activities that promote an entrepreneurial culture at Best Buy.

>LO5
The role of product champions in internal corporate venturing.

Product Champions   CE does not always involve making large investments in start-ups or establishing incubators to spawn new divisions. Often, innovative ideas emerge in the normal course of business and are brought forth and become part of the way of doing business. Entrepreneurial champions are often needed to take charge of internally generated ventures. **Product** (or project) **champions** are those individuals working within a corporation who bring entrepreneurial ideas forward, identify what kind of market exists for the product or service, find resources to support the venture, and promote the venture concept to upper management.[31]

When lower-level employees identify a product idea or novel solution, they will take it to their supervisor or someone in authority. Similarly, a new idea that is generated in a technology lab may be introduced to others by its inventor. If the idea has merit, it gains support and builds momentum across the organization.[32] Thus, even though the corporation may not be looking for new ideas or have a program for cultivating internal ventures, the independent behaviors of a few organizational members can have important strategic consequences.

product champion
an individual working within a corporation who brings entrepreneurial ideas forward, identifies what kind of market exists for the product or service, finds resources to support the venture, and promotes the venture concept to upper management.

Best Buy's Spirit of Innovation

Best Buy remains the number one electronics retailer despite intense competition from competitors such as Circuit City and Wal-Mart (see Strategy Spotlight 8.9). A major key to its success is the climate of innovation that permeates the company. According to Shari Ballard, Best Buy's vice president for human resources, "If you're going to turn on an innovation engine, a lot depends on whether managers listen for the brilliance in their employees' ideas." Here are a couple of Best Buy's recent innovation successes:

- Project manager Nate Omann noticed that a high number of flat-panel TVs were being damaged during home delivery. It was making customers angry and running up replacement costs. So Nate came up with the "TV taco"—a reusable device that fits around TVs to better protect them during transit. It is expected to save the company millions of dollars.

- *Sound and Vision Magazine* awarded Best Buy the Retail Innovation Award in 2005 for its Magnolia Home Theatre store-within-a-store concept. This innovation offers the kind of services usually found only at small specialty stores—quiet demo rooms, comfortable seating, a highly knowledgeable staff, and top quality brands.

More radical than its store innovations, Best Buy is also winning kudos for innovative human resources management. It implemented a program, called ROWE for "results-only work environment," designed to dramatically increase employee autonomy by focusing on output instead of hours worked. The program has been so successful, in fact, that Best Buy formed a subsidiary named CultureRx to implement similar programs at other companies. What it implements, however, is not the usual flextime, telecommuting program. ROWE co-founders Jody Thompson and Cali Ressler consider those programs, which still focus on hours worked, to be overly bureaucratic. ROWE employees, by contrast, are required to put in only as much time as it actually takes to do their work.

Is it working? In 2006, Best Buy's procurement department increased savings by 50 percent over the previous year after it entered the ROWE program. In the online ordering division, orders processed by people not working in the office were as much as 18 percent higher than those working in the office. Across the company, voluntary turnover has decreased significantly and ROWE participants report that they feel 35 percent more productive. As a result, Workforce Management gave Best Buy and CultureRx its 2007 Optimas Award for innovation.

Sources: Anonymous. 2006. 2005 Editor's Choice Awards: Best Buy. *Sound and Vision Magazine,* www.soundandvision.mag, February; Ballard, S. 2006. Fast talk: Best brains, *Fast Company,* November: 66; Conlin, M. 2006. Smashing the clock. *BusinessWeek,* www.businessweek.com, December 11; and Frauenheim, E. 2007. Best Buy & CultureRx: Optimas Award Winner for Innovation, *Workforce Management,* www.workforce.com, March 26.

No matter how an entrepreneurial idea comes to light, however, a new venture concept must pass through two critical stages or it may never get off the ground: project definition and project impetus:

1. ***Project definition.*** A promising opportunity has to be justified in terms of its attractiveness in the marketplace and how well it fits with the corporation's other strategic objectives.
2. ***Project impetus.*** For a project to gain impetus, its strategic and economic impact must be supported by senior managers who have experience with similar projects. The project then becomes an embryonic business with its own organization and budget.

For a project to advance through these stages of definition and impetus, a product champion is often needed to generate support and encouragement. Champions are especially important during the time after a new project has been defined but before it gains momentum. They form a link between the definition and impetus stages of internal development, which they do by procuring resources and stimulating interest for the product among potential customers.[33] Often, they must work quietly and alone. Consider the example of Ken Kutaragi, the Sony engineer who championed the PlayStation.

Even though Sony had made the processor that powered the first Nintendo video games, no one at Sony in the mid-1980s saw any future in such products. "It was a kind of snobbery," Kutaragi recalled. "For Sony people, the Nintendo product would have been very embarrassing to make because it was only a toy." But Kutaragi was convinced he could make a better product. He began working secretly on a video game. Kutaragi said, "I realized that if it was visible, it would be killed." He quietly began enlisting the support of senior executives, such as the head of R&D. He made a case that Sony could use his project to develop capabilities in digital technologies that would be important in the future. It was not until 1994, after years of "underground" development and quiet building of support, that Sony introduced the PlayStation. By the year 2000, Sony had sold 55 million of them, and Kutaragi became CEO of Sony Computer Entertainment. By 2005, Kutagari was Sony's Chief Operating Officer, and plans to launch the third generation version of the market-leading PlayStation (PS3) were well under way.[34]

● Sony's PlayStation is an exemplary example of successful product championing.

Thus, product champions play an important entrepreneurial role in a corporate setting by encouraging others to take a chance on promising new ideas.[35]

Measuring the Success of Corporate Entrepreneurship Activities

At this point in the discussion, it is reasonable to ask whether corporate entrepreneurship is successful. Corporate venturing, like the innovation process, usually requires a tremendous effort. Is it worth it? In this section we consider factors that corporations need to take into consideration when evaluating the success of CE programs. We also examine techniques that companies can use to limit the expense of venturing or to cut their losses when CE initiatives appear doomed.

Comparing Strategic and Financial CE Goals   Not all corporate venturing efforts are financially rewarding. In terms of financial performance, slightly more than 50 percent of corporate venturing efforts reach profitability (measured by ROI) within six years of their launch.[36] If this were the only criterion for measuring success, it would seem to be a rather poor return. On the one hand, these results should be expected, because CE is riskier than other investments such as expanding ongoing operations. On the other hand, corporations expect a higher return from corporate venturing projects than from normal operations. Thus, in terms of the risk–return trade-off, it seems that CE often falls short of expectations.[37]

>LO6
How corporate entrepreneurship achieves both financial goals and strategic goals.

There are several other important criteria, however, for judging the success of a corporate venture initiative. In addition to financial goals, most CE programs have strategic goals. The strategic reasons for undertaking a corporate venture include strengthening competitive position, entering into new markets, expanding capabilities by learning and acquiring new knowledge, and building the corporation's base of resources and experience. Three questions should be used to assess the effectiveness of a corporation's venturing initiatives:[38]

1. *Are the products or services offered by the venture accepted in the marketplace?* That is, is the venture considered to be a market success? If so, the financial returns are likely to be satisfactory. In addition, the venture may open doors into other markets and suggest avenues for other venture projects.

2. *Are the contributions of the venture to the corporation's internal competencies and experience valuable?* That is, does the venture add to the worth of the firm internally? If so, strategic goals such as leveraging existing assets, building new knowledge, and enhancing firm capabilities are likely to be met.

3. *Is the venture able to sustain its basis of competitive advantage?* That is, does the value proposition offered by the venture insulate it from competitive attack? If so, it is likely to place the corporation in a stronger position relative to competitors and provide a base from which to build other advantages.

As you can see, these criteria include both strategic and financial goals of CE. Another way to evaluate a corporate venture is in terms of the four criteria from the Balanced Scorecard (Chapter 3). In a successful venture, not only are financial and market acceptance (customer) goals met but so are the internal business and innovation and learning goals. Thus, when assessing the success of corporate venturing, it is important to look beyond simple financial returns and consider a well-rounded set of criteria.[39]

Next, we consider the role of "exit champions" in helping corporations limit their exposure to venture projects that are unlikely to succeed.

Exit Champions   Although a culture of championing venture projects is advantageous for stimulating an ongoing stream of entrepreneurial initiatives, many—in fact, most—of the ideas will not work out. At some point in the process, a majority of initiatives will be abandoned. Sometimes, however, companies wait too long to terminate a new venture and do so only after large sums of resources are used up or, worse, result in a marketplace failure. Motorola's costly global satellite telecom project known as Iridium provides a useful illustration. Even though problems with the project existed during the lengthy development process, Motorola refused to pull the plug. Only after investing $5 billion and years of effort was the project abandoned.[40]

How can companies avoid these costly and discouraging defeats? One way is to support a key role in the CE process: **exit champions.** In contrast to product champions and other entrepreneurial enthusiasts within the corporation, exit champions are willing to question the viability of a venture project.[41] By demanding hard evidence and challenging the belief system that is carrying an idea forward, exit champions hold the line on ventures that appear shaky.

Both product champions and exit champions must be willing to energetically stand up for what they believe. Both put their reputations on the line. But they also differ in important ways. Product champions deal in uncertainty and ambiguity. Exit champions reduce ambiguity by gathering hard data and developing a strong case for why a project should be killed. Product champions are often thought to be willing to violate procedures and operate outside normal channels. Exit champions, by contrast, often have to reinstate procedures and reassert the decision-making criteria that are supposed to guide venture decisions. Whereas product champions often emerge as heroes, exit champions run the risk of losing status by opposing popular projects.

Thus, the role of exit champion may seem unappealing. But it is one that could save a corporation both financially and in terms of its reputation in the marketplace. It is especially important because one measure of the success of a firm's CE efforts is the extent to which it knows when to cut its losses and move on. To address this, we turn to real options analysis, a useful tool in analyzing strategic decisions.

Real Options Analysis: A Useful Tool

One way firms can minimize failure and avoid losses from pursuing faulty ideas is to apply the logic of real options. **Real options analysis** (ROA) is an investment analysis tool from the field of finance. It has been slowly, but increasingly, adopted by consultants and executives to support strategic decision making in firms. What does real options analysis consist of and how can

exit champion an individual working within a corporation who is willing to question the viability of a venture project by demanding hard evidence of venture success and challenging the belief system that carries a venture forward.

real options analysis an investment analysis tool that looks at an investment or activity as a series of sequential steps, and for each step the investor has the option of (a) investing additional funds to grow or accelerate, (b) delaying, (c) shrinking the scale of, or (d) abandoning the activity.

it be appropriately applied to the investments required to initiate strategic decisions? To understand *real* options it is first necessary to have a basic understanding of what *options* are.

Options exist when the owner of the option has the right but not the obligation to engage in certain types of transactions. The most common are stock options. A stock option grants the holder the right to buy (call option) or sell (put option) shares of the stock at a fixed price (strike price) at some time in the future.[42] Another aspect of stock options important to note is that the investment to be made immediately is small, whereas the investment to be made in the future is generally larger. For example, an option to buy a rapidly rising stock currently priced at $50 might cost as little as $.50.[43] An important point to note is that owners of such a stock option have limited their losses to $.50 per share, while the upside potential is unlimited. This aspect of options is attractive because options offer the prospect of high gains with relatively small up-front investments that represent limited losses.

The phrase "real options" applies to situations where options theory and valuation techniques are applied to real assets or physical things as opposed to financial assets. Applied to entrepreneurship, real options suggest a path that companies can use to manage the uncertainty associated with launching new ventures. Some of the most common applications of real options are with property and insurance. A real estate option grants the holder the right to buy or sell a piece of property at an established price some time in the future. The actual market price of the property may rise above the established (or strike) price—or the market value may sink below the strike price. If the price of the property goes up, the owner of the option is likely to buy it. If the market value of the property drops below the strike price, the option holder is unlikely to execute the purchase. In the latter circumstance, the option holder has limited his or her loss to the cost of the option, but during the life of the option retains the right to participate in whatever the upside potential might be.

>LO7

The benefits and potential drawbacks of real options analysis in making resource deployment decisions in corporate entrepreneurship contexts.

Applications of Real Options Analysis to Strategic Decisions

The concept of options can also be applied to strategic decisions where management has flexibility; that is, the situation will permit management to decide whether to invest additional funds to grow or accelerate the activity, perhaps delay in order to learn more, shrink the scale of the activity, or even abandon it. Decisions to invest in new ventures or other business activities such as R&D, motion pictures, exploration and production of oil wells, and the opening and closing of copper mines often have this flexibility.[44] Important issues to note are the following:

- Real options analysis is appropriate to use when investments can be staged; in other words, a smaller investment up front can be followed by subsequent investments. In short, real options can be applied to an investment decision that gives the company the right, but not the obligation, to make follow-on investments.
- The strategic decision makers have "tollgates" or key points at which they can decide whether to continue, delay, or abandon the project. In short, the executives have the flexibility. There are opportunities to make other go or no-go decisions associated with each phase.
- It is expected that there will be increased knowledge about outcomes at the time of the next investment and that additional knowledge will help inform the decision makers about whether to make additional investments (i.e., whether the option is in the money or out of the money).

Many strategic decisions have the characteristic of containing a series of options. The phenomenon is called "embedded options," a series of investments in which at each stage of the investment there is a go/no–go decision. Consider the real options logic that Johnson Controls, a maker of car seats, instrument panels, and interior control systems uses to advance or eliminate entrepreneurial ideas.[45] Johnson options each new innovative idea by making a small investment in it. To decide whether to exercise an option, the idea must

Using Real Options Analysis to Evaluate a Pharmaceutical Venture

Pharmaceutical companies often use real options analysis in evaluating decisions about whether to invest in new R&D ventures. Developing new pharmaceutical products requires at least four stages of investments: basic research to yield new compounds and three FDA-mandated phases of clinical trials. Generally, each phase is more expensive to undertake than the previous phase. However, as each phase unfolds, management knows more about the underlying drug and its many sources of uncertainty, including the technical difficulties it faces and external market conditions that could affect sales. With this information, management can make the decision to invest more, speed up the process, delay the start of the next phase, or even abandon the R&D project.

Consider, for example, a privately held biotechnology firm that used real options analysis to evaluate whether to invest in a veterinary pharmaceutical product. The firm had developed a unique technology for introducing the coat protein of a particular virus into animal feedstocks. Ingesting the coat protein generated an immune response, thus protecting

the animal from the virus. The firm was at the beginning of the preclinical trials stage, the first of a series of tests required by FDA regulation and conducted through the FDA subagency called the Center for Veterinary Medicine.

The company expected the stage to take 18 months and cost $2 million. Long-standing experience indicated that 95 percent of new drug investigations are abandoned during this phase. Abandonment rates in subsequent stages would decrease somewhat, but costs would rise, with a total outflow from 2002 through its anticipated launch in 2007 of at least $18.5 million. The company's best estimate of the market from 2007 through 2017 was about $85 million per year. Still, there was a possibility the product would gain as much as a 50 percent market share. In short, there was huge potential, but in the interim there was a tremendous chance of failure (i.e., high risk), significant early outflows, and delayed inflows of revenue.

A traditional net present value (NPV) analysis (which sums revenues and costs for the life of the project and then discounts them using current interest rates) yielded a negative $2 million with an 11 percent risk-adjusted discount rate. However, viewing the investment as a multistage option and incorporating management's flexibility to alter its decision at least four times between 2002 and 2007 changes the valuation markedly. That is, a real options analysis demonstrated a present value of about $22 million. The question, then, was not whether to risk $18.5 million, but whether to invest $2 million today for the opportunity to earn $22 million at a future date.

Sources: Janney, J. J. &, Dess, G. G. 2004. Can real-options analysis improve decision making? Promises and pitfalls. *Academy of Management Executive,* 18(4): 60–75; Stockley, R. L., Jr., Curtis, S., Jafari, J., & Tibbs, K. 2003. The options value of an early-stage biotechnology investment. *Journal of Applied Finance,* 15(2): 44–55; and Triantis, A., et al. 2003. University of Maryland roundtable on real options and corporate practice. *Journal of Applied Corporate Finance,* 15(2): 8–23.

continue to prove itself at each stage of development. Here's how Jim Geschke, vice president and general manager of electronics integration at Johnson, describes the process:

> Think of Johnson as an innovation machine. The front end has a robust series of gates that each idea must pass through. Early on, we'll have many ideas and spend a little money on each of them. As they get more fleshed out, the ideas go through a gate where a go or no-go decision is made. A lot if ideas get filtered out, so there are far fewer items, and the spending on each goes up. . . . Several months later each idea will face another gate. If it passes, that means it's a serious idea that we are going to develop. Then the spending goes way up, and the number of ideas goes way down. By the time you reach the final gate, you need to have a credible business case in order to be accepted. At a certain point in the development process, we take our idea to customers and ask them what they think. Sometimes they say, "That's a terrible idea. Forget it." Other times they say, "That's fabulous. I want a million of them."

This process of evaluating ideas by separating winning ideas from losing ones in a way that keeps investments low has helped Johnson Controls grow its revenues to over $33 billion a year. Thus, using real options logic to advance the development process is a key way that firms reduce uncertainty and minimize innovation-related failures.[46]

Strategy Spotlight 12.7 provides an example of a pharmaceutical company that used ROA to guide its decision-making process.

Potential Pitfalls of Real Options Analysis

Despite the many benefits that can be gained from using real options analysis, managers must be aware of its potential limitations or pitfalls. Below we will address three major issues.[47]

Agency Theory and the Back-Solver Dilemma   Let's assume that companies adopting a real-options perspective invest heavily in training and that their people understand how to effectively estimate variance—that is, the amount of dispersion or range that is estimated for potential outcomes. Such training can help them use ROA. However, it does not solve another inherent problem: managers may have an incentive and the know-how to "game the system." Most electronic spreadsheets permit users to simply back-solve any formula; that is, you can type in the answer you want and ask what values are needed in a formula to get that answer. If managers know that a certain option value must be met in order for the proposal to get approved, they can back-solve the model to find a variance estimate needed to arrive at the answer that upper management desires. What would be the manager's motive to do this?

Agency problems are typically inherent in investment decisions. They may occur when the managers of a firm are separated from its owners—that is, when managers act as "agents" rather than "principals" (owners). Such problems could occur because a manager may have something to gain by not acting in the owner's best interests, or the interests of managers and owners are not co-aligned. Agency theory suggests that as managerial and owner interests diverge, managers will follow the path of their own self-interests. Sometimes this is to secure better compensation: Managers who propose projects may believe that if their projects are approved, they stand a much better chance of getting promoted. So while managers have an incentive to propose projects that *should* be successful, they also have an incentive to propose projects that *might* be successful. And because of the subjectivity involved in formally modeling a real option, managers may have an incentive to choose variance values that increase the likelihood of approval.

Managerial Conceit: Overconfidence and the Illusion of Control   Often, poor decisions are the result of such traps as biases, blind spots, and other human frailties. Much of this literature falls under the concept of *managerial conceit*.[48] Understanding how these traps affect decision makers can help to improve decision making.

First, managerial conceit occurs when decision makers who have made successful choices in the past come to believe that they possess superior expertise for managing uncertainty. They believe that their abilities can, therefore, reduce the risks inherent in decision making to a much greater extent than they actually can. Such managers are more likely to shift away from analysis to trusting their own judgment. In the case of real options, they can simply declare that any given decision is a real option and proceed as before. If asked to formally model their decision, they are more likely to employ variance estimates that support their viewpoint.

Second, employing the real-options perspective can encourage decision makers toward a bias for action. Such a bias may lead to carelessness. Managerial conceit is as much a problem (if not more so) for small decisions as for big ones. Why? The cost to write the first stage of an option is much smaller than the cost of full commitment, and managers pay less attention to small decisions than to large ones. Because real options are designed to minimize potential losses while preserving potential gains, any problems that arise are likely to be smaller at first, causing less concern for the manager. Managerial conceit could suggest that managers will assume that those problems are the easiest to solve and control—a concern referred to as the illusion of control. Managers may fail to respond appropriately because they overlook the problem or believe that since it is small, they can easily resolve it. Thus, managers may approach each real-option decision with less care and diligence than if they had made a full commitment to a larger investment.

Managerial Conceit: Irrational Escalation of Commitment A strength of a real options perspective is also one of its Achilles heels. Both real options and decisions involving escalation of commitment require specific environments with sequential decisions.[49] As the escalation-of-commitment literature indicates, simply separating a decision into multiple parts does not guarantee that decisions made will turn out well. This condition is potentially present whenever the exercise decision retains some uncertainty, which most still do. The decision to abandon also has strong psychological factors associated with it that affect the ability of managers to make correct exercise decisions.[50]

An option to exit requires reversing an initial decision made by someone in the organization (such as an exit champion). Organizations typically encourage managers to "own their decisions" in order to motivate them. One result is that as managers invest themselves in their decision, it proves harder for them to lose face by reversing course. In effect, for managers making the decision, it feels as if they made the wrong decision in the first place, even if it was initially a good decision. The more specific the manager's human capital becomes, the harder it is to transfer it to other organizations. Hence, there is a greater likelihood that managers will stick around and try to make an existing decision work. They are more likely to continue an existing project even if it should perhaps be ended.[51]

Despite the potential pitfalls of a real options approach, many of the strategic decisions that product champions and top managers must make are enhanced when decision makers have an entrepreneurial mind-set. In the next section, we look at the practices and characteristics associated with an entrepreneurial orientation.

Entrepreneurial Orientation

>LO8
How an entrepreneurial orientation can enhance a firm's efforts to develop promising corporate venture initiatives.

Firms that want to engage in successful corporate entrepreneurship need to have an entrepreneurial orientation (EO). EO refers to the strategy-making practices that businesses use in identifying and launching corporate ventures. It represents a frame of mind and a perspective toward entrepreneurship that is reflected in a firm's ongoing processes and corporate culture.[52]

An entrepreneurial orientation has five dimensions that permeate the decision-making styles and practices of the firm's members. These are autonomy, innovativeness, proactiveness, competitive aggressiveness, and risk taking. These factors can work together to enhance a firm's entrepreneurial performance. But even those firms that are strong in only a few aspects of EO can be very successful.[53] Exhibit 12.3 summarizes the dimensions of an **entrepreneurial orientation.** Below we discuss the five dimensions of entrepreneurial orientation and how they have been used to enhance internal venture development.

Autonomy

Autonomy refers to a willingness to act independently in order to carry forward an entrepreneurial vision or opportunity. It applies to both individuals and teams that operate outside an organization's existing norms and strategies. In the context of corporate entrepreneurship, autonomous work units are often used to leverage existing strengths in new arenas, identify opportunities that are beyond the organization's current capabilities, and encourage development of new ventures or improved business practices.[54]

The need for autonomy may apply to either dispersed or focused entrepreneurial efforts. Clearly, because of the emphasis on venture projects that are being developed outside of the normal flow of business, a focused approach suggests a working environment that is relatively autonomous. But autonomy may also be important in an organization where entrepreneurship is part of the corporate culture. Everything from the methods of group interaction to the firm's reward system must make organizational members feel as if they can think freely about venture opportunities, take time to investigate them, and act without fear of condemnation. This implies a respect for the autonomy of each individual

entrepreneurial orientation the strategy-making practices that businesses use in identifying and launching new ventures, consisting of autonomy, innovativeness, proactiveness, competitive aggressiveness, and risk taking.

autonomy independent action by an individual or team aimed at bringing forth a business concept or vision and carrying it through to completion.

Exhibit 12.3
Dimensions of
Entrepreneurial
Orientation

Dimension	Definition
Autonomy	Independent action by an individual or team aimed at bringing forth a business concept or vision and carrying it through to completion.
Innovativeness	A willingness to introduce novelty through experimentation and creative processes aimed at developing new products and services as well as new processes.
Proactiveness	A forward-looking perspective characteristic of a market-place leader that has the foresight to seize opportunities in anticipation of future demand.
Competitive aggressiveness	An intense effort to outperform industry rivals characterized by a combative posture or an aggressive response aimed at improving position or overcoming a threat in a competitive marketplace.
Risk taking	Making decisions and taking action without certain knowledge of probable outcomes; some undertakings may also involve making substantial resource commitments in the process of venturing forward.

Sources: Dess, G. G., & Lumpkin, G. T. 2005. The role of entrepreneurial orientation in stimulating effective corporate entrepreneurship. *Academy of Management Executive,* 19(1): 147–156; Covin, J. G., & Slevin, D. P. 1991. A conceptual model of entrepreneurship as firm behavior. *Entrepreneurship Theory & Practice,* Fall: 7–25; Lumpkin, G. T., and Dess, G. G. 1996. Clarifying the entrepreneurial orientation construct and linking it to performance. *Academy of Management Review,* 21: 135–172; Miller, D. 1983. The correlates of entrepreneurship in three types of firms. *Management Science,* 29: 770–791.

and an openness to the independent thinking that goes into championing a corporate venture idea. Thus, autonomy represents a type of empowerment (see Chapter 11) that is directed at identifying and leveraging entrepreneurial opportunities.

Exhibit 12.4 identifies two techniques that organizations often use to promote autonomy.

Creating autonomous work units and encouraging independent action may have pitfalls that can jeopardize their effectiveness. Autonomous teams, for example, often lack coordination. Excessive decentralization has a strong potential to create inefficiencies, such as duplication of effort and wasting resources on projects with questionable feasibility. For example, Chris Galvin, former CEO of Motorola, scrapped the skunkworks approach the company had been using to develop new wireless phones. Fifteen teams had created 128 different phones, which led to spiraling costs and overly complex operations.[55]

Thus, for autonomous work units and independent projects to be effective, such efforts have to be measured and monitored. This requires a delicate balance: companies must have the patience and budget to tolerate the explorations of autonomous groups and the strength to cut back efforts that are not bearing fruit. It must be undertaken with a clear sense of purpose—namely, to generate new sources of competitive advantage.

Innovativeness

Innovativeness refers to a firm's efforts to find new opportunities and novel solutions. In the beginning of this chapter we discussed innovation; here the focus is on innovativeness—that is, a firm's attitude toward innovation and willingness to innovate. It involves creativity and experimentation that result in new products, new services, or improved technological processes. Innovativeness is one of the major components of an entrepreneurial

innovativeness a willingness to introduce novelty through experimentation and creative processes aimed at developing new products and services as well as new processes.

Autonomy		
Technique	**Description/Purpose**	**Example**
Use skunkworks to foster entrepreneurial thinking	Skunkworks are independent work units, often physically separate from corporate headquarters. They allow employees to get out from under the pressures of their daily routines to engage in creative problem solving.	Overstock.com created a skunkworks to address the problem of returned merchandise. The solution was a business within-a-business: Overstock auctions. The unit has grown by selling products returned to Overstock and offers fees 30 percent lower than eBay's auction service.
Design organizational structures that support independent action	Established companies with traditional structures often need to break out of such old forms to compete more effectively.	Deloitte Consulting, a division of Deloitte Touche Tohmatsu, found it difficult to compete against young agile firms. So it broke the firm into small autonomous units called "chip-aways" that operate with the flexibility of a start-up. In its first year, revenues were $40 million—10 percent higher than its projections.

Sources: Conlin, M. 2006. Square feet. Oh how square! *BusinessWeek,* www.businessweek.com, July 3; Cross, K. 2001. Bang the drum quickly. *Business 2.0,* May: 28–30; Sweeney, J. 2004. A firm for all reasons. *Consulting Magazine,* www.consultingmag.com; and Wagner, M. 2005. Out of the skunkworks. *Internet Retailer,* January, www.internetretailer.com.

Exhibit 12.4

Autonomy Techniques

strategy. As indicated at the beginning of the chapter, however, the job of managing innovativeness can be very challenging.

Innovativeness requires that firms depart from existing technologies and practices and venture beyond the current state of the art. Inventions and new ideas need to be nurtured even when their benefits are unclear. However, in today's climate of rapid change, effectively producing, assimilating, and exploiting innovations can be an important avenue for achieving competitive advantages.

As our earlier discussion of CE indicated, many corporations owe their success to an active program of innovation-based corporate venturing.[56] Exhibit 12.5 highlights two of the methods companies can use to enhance their competitive position through innovativeness.

Innovativeness can be a source of great progress and strong corporate growth, but there are also major pitfalls for firms that invest in innovation. Expenditures on R&D aimed at identifying new products or processes can be a waste of resources if the effort does not yield results. Another danger is related to the competitive climate. Even if a company innovates a new capability or successfully applies a technological breakthrough, another company may develop a similar innovation or find a use for it that is more profitable. Finally, in many firms, R&D and other innovation efforts are among the first to be cut back during an economic downturn.

Therefore, even though innovativeness is an important means of internal corporate venturing, it also involves major risks because investments in innovations may not pay off. For strategic managers of entrepreneurial firms, however, successfully developing and adopting innovations can generate competitive advantages and provide a major source of growth for the firm.

Proactiveness

proactiveness a forward-looking perspective characteristic of a marketplace leader that has the foresight to seize opportunities in anticipation of future demand.

Proactiveness refers to a firm's efforts to seize new opportunities. Proactive organizations monitor trends, identify the future needs of existing customers, and anticipate changes in demand or emerging problems that can lead to new venture opportunities. Proactiveness involves not only

Innovativeness		
Technique	**Description/Purpose**	**Example**
Foster creativity and experimentation	Companies that support idea exploration and allow employees to express themselves creatively enhance innovation outcomes.	To tap into its reserves of innovative talent, Royal Dutch/Shell created "GameChanger" to help employees develop promising ideas. The process provides funding up to $600,000 for would-be entrepreneurs to pursue innovative projects and conduct experiments.
Invest in new technology, R&D, and continuous improvement	The latest technologies often provide sources of new competitive advantages. To extract value from a new technology, companies must invest in it.	Dell Computer Corporation's new OptiPlex manufacturing system revolutionized the traditional assembly line. Hundreds of custom-built computers can be made in an eight-hour shift using state of the art automation techniques that have increased productivity per person by 160 percent.

Sources: Breen, B. 2004. Living in Dell time. *Fast Company,* November: 88–92: Hammonds, K. H. 2002. Size is not a strategy. *Fast Company,* August: 78–83; Perman, S. 2001. Automate or die. eCompanyNow.com, July; Dell, M. 1999. *Direct from Dell.* New York: HarperBusiness; and Watson, R. 2006. Expand your innovation horizons. *Fast Company,* www.fastcompany.com, May.

Exhibit 12.5

Innovativeness Techniques

recognizing changes but also being willing to act on those insights ahead of the competition. Strategic managers who practice proactiveness have their eye on the future in a search for new possibilities for growth and development. Such a forward-looking perspective is important for companies that seek to be industry leaders. Many proactive firms seek out ways not only to be future oriented but also to change the very nature of competition in their industry.

Proactiveness is especially effective at creating competitive advantages, because it puts competitors in the position of having to respond to successful initiatives. The benefit gained by firms that are the first to enter new markets, establish brand identity, implement administrative techniques, or adopt new operating technologies in an industry is called first mover advantage.[57]

First movers usually have several advantages. First, industry pioneers, especially in new industries, often capture unusually high profits because there are no competitors to drive prices down. Second, first movers that establish brand recognition are usually able to retain their image and hold on to the market share gains they earned by being first. Sometimes these benefits also accrue to other early movers in an industry, but, generally speaking, first movers have an advantage that can be sustained until firms enter the maturity phase of an industry's life cycle.[58]

First movers are not always successful. The customers of companies that introduce novel products or embrace breakthrough technologies may be reluctant to commit to a new way of doing things. In his book *Crossing the Chasm,* Geoffrey A. Moore noted that most firms seek evolution, not revolution, in their operations. This makes it difficult for a first mover to sell promising new technologies.[59]

Even with these caveats, however, companies that are first movers can enhance their competitive position. Exhibit 12.6 illustrates two methods firms can use to act proactively.

Proactiveness		
Technique	Description/Purpose	Example
Introduce new products or technological capabilities ahead of the competition.	Being a first mover provides companies with an ability to shape the playing field and shift competitive advantages in their favor.	Sony's mission states, "We should always be the pioneers with our products—out front leading the market." This philosophy has made Sony technologically strong with industry-leading products such as the PlayStation and Vaio laptop computers.
Continuously seek out new product or service offerings.	Firms that provide new resources or sources of supply can benefit from a proactive stance.	Costco seized a chance to leverage its success as a warehouse club that sells premium brands when it introduced Costco Home Stores. The home stores are usually located near its warehouse stores and its rapid inventory turnover gives it a cost advantage of 15 to 25 percent over close competitors such as Bassett Furniture and the Bombay Company.

Sources: Bryce, D. J., & Dyer, J. H. 2007. Strategies to crack well-guarded markets. *Harvard Business Review,* May: 84–92; Collins, J. C., & Porras, J. I. 1997. *Built to last.* New York: HarperBusiness; Robinson, D. 2005. Sony pushes reliability in Vaio laptops. *IT Week,* www.itweek.co.uk, October 12; and www.sony.com

Exhibit 12.6

Proactiveness Techniques

Being an industry leader does not always lead to competitive advantages. Some firms that have launched pioneering new products or staked their reputation on new brands have failed to get the hoped-for payoff. Two major beverage companies—Coca-Cola and PepsiCo—invested $75 million to launch sodas that would capitalize on the low-carb diet trend. But with half the carbohydrates taken out, neither *C2,* Coke's entry, nor *Pepsi Edge* tasted very good. The two new brands combined never achieved more than one percent market share. PepsiCo announced in would halt production in 2006 and Coca-Cola was expected to follow suit.[60] Such missteps are indicative of the dangers of trying to proactively anticipate demand. Strategy Spotlight 12.8, in contrast, describes another type of proactiveness—how some organizations are using entrepreneurial thinking and practices to effectively promote corporate social responsibility.

Thus, careful monitoring and scanning of the environment, as well as extensive feasibility research, are needed for a proactive strategy to lead to competitive advantages. Firms that do it well usually have substantial growth and internal development to show for it. Many of them have been able to sustain the advantages of proactiveness for years.

Competitive Aggressiveness

competitive aggressiveness an intense effort to outperform industry rivals characterized by a combative posture or an aggressive response aimed at improving position or overcoming a threat in a competitive marketplace.

Competitive aggressiveness refers to a firm's efforts to outperform its industry rivals. Companies with an aggressive orientation are willing to "do battle" with competitors. They might slash prices and sacrifice profitability to gain market share or spend aggressively to obtain manufacturing capacity. As an avenue of firm development and growth, competitive aggressiveness may involve being very assertive in leveraging the results of other entrepreneurial activities such as innovativeness or proactiveness.

Unlike innovativeness and proactiveness, however, which tend to focus on market opportunities, competitive aggressiveness is directed toward competitors. The SWOT

Socially Responsible Corporate Entrepreneurship

One of the most important trends in U.S. business today is corporate social responsibility (CSR). Proactively oriented firms are seizing opportunities to take a leading role in issues such as the environment, product safety, and fair trade. Among the most interesting examples of this, as suggested in the Chapter 1 section on social innovation, are those firms that are taking an entrepreneurial approach to CSR. That is, they are using new technologies, environmentally friendly ventures, and entrepreneurial practices to advance their social responsibility goals. Following is a sample of three corporations that are taking a very entrepreneurial approach to corporate social responsibility.

Whirlpool Corporation—From efficiency to advocacy

> Whirlpool is perhaps best known for its "white boxes"—the refrigerators, freezers, and laundry appliances that account for over 60 percent of its $13 billion in annual sales. To explore what creates customer loyalty, Whirlpool conducted a global survey of its customers. "We discovered there is a strong correlation between a company's performance in appliance markets and their social response to issues such as energy efficiency and pollution," said Steve Willis, director of Whirlpool's global environment, health, and safety programs. One result has been its innovative Duet Series of washers and dryers that significantly reduces energy consumption. Recently, Whirlpool decided to take its environmental efforts a step farther: It joined The Natural Step, an entrepreneurial organization that is advancing the movement toward environmental sustainability by advocating the development of innovative products that meet high standards of ecological sustainability.

Interface, Inc.—Doing more with less

> In Chapter 1, we saw how some companies have changed their corporate missions to include socially responsible goals like protecting the environment. Carpet maker Interface Inc. has found a way not only to become more environmentally friendly but also to achieve a universal

entrepreneurial objective: Do more with less. By leasing rather than selling carpets, Georgia-based Interface is able to take back worn carpets and "remanufacture" them. As a result, it has cut its raw materials input costs by nearly 100 percent and its business customers get to deduct the cost of leasing. "Our costs are down, not up," according to chairman Ray Anderson. "Sustainability doesn't cost more, it saves." Recently, Interface instituted a program known as EcoSense to educate its employees about sustainability and reward them for making environmental improvements. These savings helped Interface survive the 40 percent decline in sales of office furnishings that followed the dot-com collapse and the September 11th terrorist attack. "We might not have made it if it were not for our EcoSense programs," says Anderson.

Green Mountain Coffee Roasters—Empowering local entrepreneurs

> As the name suggests, this NASDAQ-listed corporation (GMCR) is located in the Green Mountains of Vermont. But its reach is global. As a roaster and distributor of specialty coffees, GMCR has become a leading advocate for fair trade practices and providing financial support for local coffee growers. "Our president and CEO Robert Stiller visited places where coffee is grown and was struck by the levels of poverty. He wanted to do something about it," said Rick Peyser, director of public relations. As a result, GMCR now purchases coffee beans from small farm cooperatives in Peru, Mexico, and Sumatra. It also provides micro-loans to underwrite family businesses that are trying to create more diverse agricultural economies. Back home in its Waterbury, Vermont, roasting facility, GMCR uses a 95-kilowatt cogeneration system that captures waste heat from its propane-fired generator and recycles it for both coffee roasting and space heating.

Each of these companies has recently been named one of the 100 Best Corporate Citizens by *Business Ethics* magazine. However, major corporations still have their critics. In fact, companies that claim to be making progress in advancing CSR are often the most loudly criticized. For example, British Petroleum, which has endeavored to be an oil industry leader in supporting environmentally sensitive energy development, is often attacked by environmental groups despite initiatives such as investing $48 million to develop the world's largest solar energy project. Despite such criticism, it is encouraging to note that entrepreneurial activities can help companies achieve their social responsibility goals as well as their innovation and growth goals.

Sources: Asmus, P. 2005. 100 best corporate citizens for 2005. *Business Ethics,* www.business-ethics.com; Asmus, P. 2003. 100 best corporate citizens for 2003. *Business Ethics,* www.business-ethics.com; Baker, M. 2001. BP anounces world's largest solar project. *Business Respect,* 1: April 6; Hawken, P., Lovins, A., & Lovins, H. 2000. *Natural capitalism.* Boston: Back Bay Books; see also www.bp.com; www.domini.com; www.hoovers.com; and www.ifsia.com.

Competitive Aggressiveness		
Technique	**Description/Purpose**	**Example**
Enter markets with drastically lower prices.	Narrow operating margins make companies vulnerable to extended price competition.	Using open source software, California-based Zimbra, Inc. has become a leader in messaging and collaboration software. Its product costs about one-third less than its direct competitor Microsoft Exchange. Zimbra now has over 4 million users including 12,000 H&R Block tax preparers.
Find successful business models and copy them.	As long as a practice is not protected by intellectual property laws, it's probably okay to imitate it. Finding solutions to existing problems is generally quicker and cheaper than inventing them.	Best Practices, LLC is a North Carolina consulting group that seeks out best practices and then repackages and resells them. With annual revenues in excess of $8 million, Best Practices has become a leader in continuous improvement and benchmarking strategies.

Sources: Guth, R. A. 2006. Trolling the web for free labor, software upstarts are new force. *The Wall Street Journal,* November 12: 1; Mochari, I. 2001. Steal this strategy. *Inc.,* July: 62–67; www.best-in-class.com; and www.zimbra.com.

Exhibit 12.7

Competitive Aggressiveness Techniques

(strengths, weaknesses, opportunities, threats) analysis discussed in Chapters 2 and 3 provides a useful way to distinguish between these different approaches to corporate entrepreneurship. Proactiveness, as we saw in the last section, is a response to opportunities—the O in SWOT. Competitive aggressiveness, by contrast, is a response to threats—the T in SWOT. A competitively aggressive posture is important for firms that seek to enter new markets in the face of intense rivalry.

Strategic managers can use competitive aggressiveness to combat industry trends that threaten their survival or market position. Sometimes firms need to be forceful in defending the competitive position that has made them an industry leader. Firms often need to be aggressive to ensure their advantage by capitalizing on new technologies or serving new market needs. Exhibit 12.7 suggests two of the ways competitively aggressive firms enhance their entrepreneurial position.

Another practice companies use to overcome the competition is to make preannouncements of new products or technologies. This type of signaling is aimed not only at potential customers but also at competitors to see how they will react or to discourage them from launching similar initiatives. Sometimes the preannouncements are made just to scare off competitors, an action that has potential ethical implications.

Competitive aggressiveness may not always lead to competitive advantages. Some companies (or their CEOs) have severely damaged their reputations by being overly aggressive. Microsoft is a good example. Although it continues to be a dominant player, its highly aggressive profile makes it the subject of scorn by some businesses and individuals. Efforts to find viable replacements for the Microsoft products have helped fuel the open source software movement that threatens to erode Microsoft's leading role as a software provider.[61]

Therefore, competitive aggressiveness is a strategy that is best used in moderation. Companies that aggressively establish their competitive position and vigorously exploit opportunities to achieve profitability may, over the long run, be better able to sustain their competitive advantages if their goal is to defeat, rather than decimate, their competitors.

Risk Taking

Risk taking refers to a firm's willingness to seize a venture opportunity even though it does not know whether the venture will be successful—to act boldly without knowing the consequences. To be successful through corporate entrepreneurship, firms usually have to take on riskier alternatives, even if it means forgoing the methods or products that have worked in the past. To obtain high financial returns, firms take such risks as assuming high levels of debt, committing large amounts of firm resources, introducing new products into new markets, and investing in unexplored technologies.

In some ways, all of the approaches to internal development that we have discussed are potentially risky. Whether they are being aggressive, proactive, or innovative, firms on the path of corporate entrepreneurship must act without knowing how their actions will turn out. Before launching their strategies, corporate entrepreneurs must know their firm's appetite for risk. How far is it willing to go without knowing what the outcome will be?

Three types of risk that organizations and their executives face are business risk, financial risk, and personal risk:

- *Business risk taking* involves venturing into the unknown without knowing the probability of success. This is the risk associated with entering untested markets or committing to unproven technologies.
- *Financial risk taking* requires that a company borrow heavily or commit a large portion of its resources in order to grow. In this context, risk is used to refer to the risk/return trade-off that is familiar in financial analysis.
- *Personal risk taking* refers to the risks that an executive assumes in taking a stand in favor of a strategic course of action. Executives who take such risks stand to influence the course of their whole company, and their decisions also can have significant implications for their careers.

In many business situations, all three types of risk taking are present. Taking bold new actions rarely affects just one part of the organization. Consider the example of David D'Alessandro of John Hancock Financial Services, Inc.

> David D'Alessandro joined insurance giant John Hancock in 1984 as its vice president of corporate communications. At the time, Hancock's image was weak due in part to a series of forgettable TV ads that failed to distinguish it from other insurance carriers. D'Alessandro championed a new advertising campaign that featured "real life" images, such as a husband and wife arguing, and a lesbian couple adopting a Vietnamese baby. Although it was costly to produce and risky for the image of the traditional insurance carrier, sales surged 17 percent in the first year of the ad campaign. The risk also paid off for D'Alessandro personally: In May 2000 he was named the youngest chairman and CEO in John Hancock's history. (In 2004, John Hancock was acquired by Toronto-based Manulife Financial Corporation.)[62]

Even though risk taking involves taking chances, it is not gambling. The best-run companies investigate the consequences of various opportunities and create scenarios of likely outcomes. As we saw in the section on product champions, a key to managing entrepreneurial risks is to evaluate new venture opportunities thoroughly enough to reduce the uncertainty surrounding them. Exhibit 12.8 indicates two methods companies can use to strengthen their competitive position through risk taking.

Risk taking, by its nature, involves potential dangers and pitfalls. Only carefully managed risk is likely to lead to competitive advantages. Actions that are taken without sufficient forethought, research, and planning may prove to be very costly. Therefore, strategic managers must always remain mindful of potential risks. In his book *Innovation and Entrepreneurship,* Peter Drucker argued that successful entrepreneurs are typically not risk

risk taking making decisions and taking action without certain knowledge of probable outcomes. Some undertakings may also involve making substantial resource commitments in the process of venturing forward.

Risk Taking		
Technique	**Description/Purpose**	**Example**
Research and assess risk factors to minimize uncertainty	Companies that "do their homework"—that is, carefully evaluate the implications of bold actions—reduce the likelihood of failure.	Graybar Electric Co. took a risk when it invested $144 million to revamp its distribution system. It consolidated 231 small centers into 16 supply warehouses and installed the latest communications network. Graybar is now considered a leader in facility redesign and its sales have increased steadily since the consolidation, topping $4 billion in sales in a recent year.
Use techniques that have worked in other domains	Risky methods that other companies have tried may provide an avenue for advancing company goals.	Autobytel.com, one of the first companies to sell cars online, decided on an approach that worked well for others—advertising during the Super Bowl. It was the first dot-com ever to do so and its $1.2 million 30-second ad paid off well by generating weeks of free publicity and favorable business press.

Sources: Anonymous. 2006. Graybar offers data center redesign seminars. *Cabling Installation and Maintenance,* www.cim.pennnet.com, September 1; Keenan, F., & Mullaney, T. J. 2001. Clicking at Graybar. *BusinessWeek,* June 18: 132–34; Weintraub, A. 2001. Make or break for Autobytel. *BusinessWeek e.biz,* July 9: EB30-EB32; www.autobytel.com; and www.graybar.com.

Exhibit 12.8
Risk Taking Techniques

takers. Instead, they take steps to minimize risks by carefully understanding them. That is how they avoid focusing on risk and remain focused on opportunity.[63] Thus, risk taking is a good place to close this chapter on corporate entrepreneurship. Companies that choose to grow through internal corporate venturing must remember that entrepreneurship always involves embracing what is new and uncertain.

Reflecting on Career Implications . . .

- *Innovation:* Look around at the types of innovations being pursued by your company. Do they tend to be incremental or radical? Product-related or process-related? What new types of innovations might benefit your organization? How can you add value to such innovations?
- *Managing Innovation:* How might your organization's chances of a successful innovation increase through collaboration with innovation partners? Your ability to collaborate with individuals from other departments and firms will make you more receptive to and capable of innovation initiatives and enhance your career opportunities.
- *Corporate Entrepreneurship:* Do you consider the company you work for to be entrepreneurial? If not, what actions might you take to enhance its entrepreneurial spirit? If so, what have been the keys to its entrepreneurial success? Can these practices be repeated to achieve future successes?
- *Entrepreneurial Orientation:* Consider the five dimensions of entrepreneurial orientation. Is your organization especially strong at any of these? Especially weak? What are the career implications of your company's entrepreneurial strengths or weaknesses?

Summary

To remain competitive in today's economy, established firms must find new avenues for development and growth. This chapter has addressed how innovation and corporate entrepreneurship can be a means of internal venture creation and strategic renewal, and how an entrepreneurial orientation can help corporations enhance their competitive position.

Innovation is one of the primary means by which corporations grow and strengthen their strategic position. Innovations can take several forms, ranging from radical breakthrough innovations to incremental improvement innovations. Innovations are often used to update products and services or for improving organizational processes. Managing the innovation process is often challenging, because it involves a great deal of uncertainty and there are many choices to be made about the extent and type of innovations to pursue. By defining the scope of innovation, managing the pace of innovation, staffing to capture value from innovation, and collaborating with innovation partners, firms can more effectively manage the innovation process.

We also discussed the role of corporate entrepreneurship in venture development and strategic renewal. Corporations usually take either a focused or dispersed approach to corporate venturing. Firms with a focused approach usually separate the corporate venturing activity from the ongoing operations of the firm in order to foster independent thinking and encourage entrepreneurial team members to think and act without the constraints imposed by the corporation. In corporations where venturing activities are dispersed, a culture of entrepreneurship permeates all parts of the company in order to induce strategic behaviors by all organizational members. In measuring the success of corporate venturing activities, both financial and strategic objectives should be considered. Real options analysis is often used to make better quality decisions in uncertain entrepreneurial situations. However, a real options approach has potential drawbacks.

Most entrepreneurial firms need to have an entrepreneurial orientation: the methods, practices, and decision-making styles that strategic managers use to act entrepreneurially. Five dimensions of entrepreneurial orientation are found in firms that pursue corporate venture strategies. Autonomy, innovativeness, proactiveness, competitive aggressiveness, and risk taking each make a unique contribution to the pursuit of new opportunities. When deployed effectively, the methods and practices of an entrepreneurial orientation can be used to engage successfully in corporate entrepreneurship and new venture creation. However, strategic managers must remain mindful of the pitfalls associated with each of these approaches.

Summary Review Questions

1. What is meant by the concept of a continuum of radical and incremental innovations?
2. What are the dilemmas that organizations face when deciding what innovation projects to pursue? What steps can organizations take to effectively manage the innovation process?
3. What is the difference between focused and dispersed approaches to corporate entrepreneurship?
4. How are business incubators used to foster internal corporate venturing?
5. What is the role of the product champion in bringing a new product or service into existence in a corporation? How can companies use product champions to enhance their venture development efforts?
6. Explain the difference between proactiveness and competitive aggressiveness in terms of achieving and sustaining competitive advantage.
7. Describe how the entrepreneurial orientation (EO) dimensions of innovativeness, proactiveness, and risk taking can be combined to create competitive advantages for entrepreneurial firms.

Key Terms

innovation 413
radical innovation 413
incremental innovation 414
corporate
   entrepreneurship 422
new venture group 423
business incubator 423
product champion 425
exit champion 428

real options analysis 428
entrepreneurial
   orientation 432
autonomy 432
innovativeness 433
proactiveness 434
competitive
   aggressiveness 436
risk taking 439

Experiential Exercise

Select two different major corporations from two different industries (you might use Fortune 500 companies to make your selection). Compare and contrast these organizations in terms of their entrepreneurial orientation.

Entrepreneurial Orientation	Company A	Company B
Autonomy		
Innovativeness		
Proactiveness		
Competitive Aggressiveness		
Risk Taking		

Based on Your Comparison:

1. How is the corporation's entrepreneurial orientation reflected in its strategy?
2. Which corporation would you say has the stronger entrepreneurial orientation?
3. Is the corporation with the stronger entrepreneurial orientation also stronger in terms of financial performance?

Application Questions Exercises

1. Select a firm known for its corporate entrepreneurship activities. Research the company and discuss how it has positioned itself relative to its close competitors. Does it have a unique strategic advantage? Disadvantage? Explain.
2. Explain the difference between product innovations and process innovations. Provide examples of firms that have recently introduced each type of innovation. What are the types of innovations related to the strategies of each firm?
3. Using the Internet, select a company that is listed on the NASDAQ or New York Stock Exchange. Research the extent to which the company has an entrepreneurial culture. Does the company use product champions? Does it have a corporate venture capital fund? Do you believe its entrepreneurial efforts are sufficient to generate sustainable advantages?
4. How can an established firm use an entrepreneurial orientation to enhance its overall strategic position? Provide examples.

Ethics Questions

1. Innovation activities are often aimed at making a discovery or commercializing a technology ahead of the competition. What are some of the unethical practices that companies could engage in during the innovation process? What are the potential long-term consequences of such actions?
2. Discuss the ethical implications of using entrepreneurial policies and practices to pursue corporate social responsibility goals. Are these efforts authentic and genuine or just an attempt to attract more customers?

References

1. Sources for the Polaroid example include Charan, R., & Useem, J. 2002. Why companies fail. *Fortune,* May 15; Knox, N. 2001. Rivals push Polaroid toward Chapter 11. *USA Today,* October 11; McLaughlin, T. 2001. Harvard dropout made Polaroid an icon. *Toronto Star,* October 15; Pope, J. 2001. Polaroid's fortunes rose with Land, but fell under the burden of debt. *Daily Kent Stater* (OH), October 15; and www.polaroid.com.
2. Eagan, M. 2005. How did Polaroid's faithful ever land in this predicament? *Boston Herald,* April 28: 20; and St. Anthony, N. 2005. Petters wraps up Polaroid. *Star Tribune,* April 28: 1D.
3. Christensen, C. M. 1997. *The innovator's dilemma: When new technologies cause great firms to fail.* Cambridge, MA: Harvard Business School Press.

4. For a discussion about Polaroid, see Gavetti, G., & Levinthal, D. 2000. Looking forward and looking backward: Cognitive and experiential search. *Administrative Science Quarterly,* 45: 113–137.

5. For an interesting discussion, see Johannessen, J. A., Olsen, B., & Lumpkin, G. T. 2001. Innovation as newness: What is new, how new, and new to whom? *European Journal of Innovation Management,* 4(1): 20–31.

6. The discussion of radical and incremental innovations draws from Leifer, R., McDermott, C. M., Colarelli, G., O'Connor, G. C., Peters, L. S., Rice, M. P., & Veryzer, R. W. 2000. *Radical innovation: How mature companies can outsmart upstarts.* Boston: Harvard Business School Press; Damanpour, F. 1996. Organizational complexity and innovation: Developing and testing multiple contingency models. *Management Science,* 42(5): 693–716; and Hage, J. 1980. *Theories of organizations.* New York: Wiley.

7. The discussion of product and process innovation is based on Roberts, E. B. (Ed.). 2002. *Innovation: Driving product, process, and market change.* San Francisco: Jossey-Bass; Hayes, R., & Wheelwright, S. 1985. Competing through manufacturing. *Harvard Business Review,* 63(1): 99–109; and Hayes, R., & Wheelwright, S. 1979. Dynamics of product–process life cycles. *Harvard Business Review,* 57(2): 127–136.

8. Drucker, P. F. 1985. *Innovation and entrepreneurship:* 2000 New York: Harper & Row.

9. Steere, W. C., Jr., & Niblack, J. 1997. Pfizer, Inc. In Kanter, R. M., Kao, J., & Wiersema, F. (Eds.), *Innovation: Breakthrough thinking at 3M, DuPont, GE, Pfizer, and Rubbermaid:* 123–145. New York: HarperCollins.

10. Morrissey, C. A. 2000. Managing innovation through corporate venturing. *Graziadio Business Report,* Spring, gbr.pepperdine.edu; and Sharma, A. 1999. Central dilemmas of managing innovation in large firms. *California Management Review,* 41(3): 147–164.

11. Sharma, op. cit.

12. Canabou, C. 2003. Fast ideas for slow times. *Fast Company,* May: 52.

13. Biodegradable Products Institute. 2003. "Compostable Logo" of the Biodegradable Products Institute gains momentum with approval of DuPont™ Biomax® resin, www.bpiworld.org, June 12; Leifer et al., op. cit.

14. For more on defining the scope of innovation, see Valikangas, L., & Gibbert, M. 2005. Boundary-setting strategies for escaping innovation traps. *MIT Sloan Management Review,* 46(3): 58–65.

15. Leifer et al., op. cit.

16. Bhide, A. V. 2000. *The origin and evolution of new businesses.* New York: Oxford University Press; Brown, S. L., & Eisenhardt, K. M. 1998. *Competing on the edge: Strategy as structured chaos.* Cambridge, MA: Harvard Business School Press.

17. Caulfield, B. 2003. Why techies don't get Six Sigma. *Business 2.0,* June: 90.

18. McGrath, R. G., & Keil, T. 2007. The value captor's process: Getting the most out of your new business ventures. *Harvard Business Review,* May: 128–136.

19. For an interesting discussion of how sharing technology knowledge with different divisions in an organization can contribute to innovation processes, see Miller, D. J., Fern, M. J., & Cardinal, L. B. 2007. The use of knowledge for technological innovation within diversified firms. *Academy of Management Journal,* 50(2): 308–326.

20. Chesbrough, H. 2003. *Open innovation: The new imperative for creating and profiting from technology.* Boston: Harvard Business School Press.

21. Bick, J. 2003. Gold bond. *Entrepreneur,* March: 54–57.

22. For a recent study of what makes alliance partnerships successful, see Sampson, R. C. 2007. R&D alliances and firm performance: The impact of technological diversity and alliance organization on innovation. *Academy of Management Journal,* 50(2): 364–386.

23. For an interesting perspective on the role of collaboration among multinational corporations see Hansen, M. T., & Nohria, N. 2004. How to build collaborative advantage. *MIT Sloan Management Review,* 46(1): 22–30.

24. Guth, W. D., & Ginsberg, A. 1990. Guest editor's introduction: Corporate entrepreneurship. *Strategic Management Journal,* 11: 5–15.

25. Pinchot, G. 1985. *Intrapreneuring.* New York: Harper & Row.

26. Birkinshaw, J. 1997. Entrepreneurship in multinational corporations: The characteristics of subsidiary initiatives. *Strategic Management Journal,* 18(3): 207–229; and Kanter, R. M. 1985. *The change masters.* New York: Simon & Schuster.

27. For a closer look at how established firms can create value by investing in new ventures, see Dushnitsky, G., & Lenox, M. J. 2006. When does corporate venture capital investment create firm value? *Journal of Business Venturing,* 21: 753–772.

28. Hansen, M. T., Chesbrough, H. W., Nohria, N., & Sull, D. 2000. Networked incubators: Hothouses of the new economy. *Harvard Business Review,* 78(5): 74–84.

29. Stein, T. 2002. Corporate venture investors are bailing out. *Red Herring,* December: 74–75.

30. Is your company up to speed? 2003. *Fast Company,* June: 86.

31. For an interesting discussion, see Davenport, T. H., Prusak, L., & Wilson, H. J. 2003. Who's bringing you hot ideas and how are you responding? *Harvard Business Review,* 80(1): 58–64.

32. Howell, J. M. 2005. The right stuff. Identifying and developing effective champions of innovation. *Academy of Management Executive,* 19(2): 108–119. See also Greene, P., Brush, C., & Hart, M. 1999. The corporate venture champion: A resource-based approach to role and process. *Entrepreneurship Theory & Practice,* 23(3): 103–122; and Markham, S. K., & Aiman-Smith, L. 2001. Product champions: Truths, myths and management. *Research Technology Management,* May–June: 44–50.

33. Burgelman, R. A. 1983. A process model of internal corporate venturing in the diversified major firm. *Administrative Science Quarterly,* 28: 223–244.

34. Hamel, G. 2000. *Leading the revolution.* Boston: Harvard Business School Press.

35. Greene, Brush, & Hart, op. cit.; and Shane, S. 1994. Are champions different from non-champions? *Journal of Business Venturing,* 9(5): 397–421.

36. Block, Z., & MacMillan, I. C. 1993. *Corporate venturing—Creating new businesses with the firm.* Cambridge, MA: Harvard Business School Press.

37. For an interesting discussion of these trade-offs, see Stringer, R. 2000. How to manage radical innovation. *California Management Review,* 42(4): 70–88; and Gompers, P. A., & Lerner, J. 1999. *The venture capital cycle.* Cambridge, MA: MIT Press.

38. Albrinck, J., Hornery, J., Kletter, D., & Neilson, G. 2001. Adventures in corporate venturing. *Strategy + Business,* 22: 119–129; and McGrath, R. G., & MacMillan, I. C. 2000. *The entrepreneurial mind-set.* Cambridge, MA: Harvard Business School Press.

39. For an interesting discussion of how different outcome goals affect organizational learning and employee motivation, see Seijts, G. H., & Latham, G. P. 2005. Learning versus performance goals: When should each be used? *Academy of Management Executive,* 19(1): 124–131.

40. Crockett, R. O. 2001. Motorola. *BusinessWeek,* July 15: 72–78.

41. The ideas in this section are drawn from Royer, I. 2003. Why bad projects are so hard to kill. *Harvard Business Review,* 80(1): 48–56.

42. Hoskin, R. E. 1994. *Financial Accounting.* New York: Wiley.

43. We know stock options as derivative assets—that is, "an asset whose value depends on or is derived from the value of another, the underlying asset": Amram, M., & Kulatilaka, N. 1999. *Real options: Managing strategic investment in an uncertain world:* 34. Boston: Harvard Business School Press.

44. For an interesting discussion on why it is difficult to "kill options," refer to Royer, I. 2003. Why bad projects are so hard to kill. *Harvard Business Review,* 81(2): 48–57.

45. Slywotzky, A., & Wise, R. 2003. Double-digit growth in no-growth times. *Fast Company,* April: 66–72; www.hoovers.com; and www.johnsoncontrols.com.

46. For more on the role of real options in entrepreneurial decision making, see Folta, T. B., & O'Brien, J. P. 2004. Entry in the presence of dueling options. *Strategic Management Journal,* 25: 121–138.

47. This section draws on Janney, J. J., & Dess, G. G. 2004. Can real options analysis improve decision-making? Promises and pitfalls. *Academy of Management Executive,* 18(4): 60–75. For additional insights on pitfalls of real options, consider McGrath, R. G. 1997. A real options logic for initiating technology positioning investment. *Academy of Management Review,* 22(4): 974–994; Coff, R. W., & Laverty, K. J. 2001. Real options on knowledge assets: Panacea or Pandora's box. *Business Horizons,* 73: 79, McGrath, R. G. 1999. Falling forward: Real options reasoning and entrepreneurial failure. *Academy of Management Review,* 24(1): 13–30; and, Zardkoohi, A. 2004.

48. For an understanding of the differences between how managers say they approach decisions and how they actually do, March and Shapira's discussion is perhaps the best. March, J. G., & Shapira, Z. 1987. Managerial perspectives on risk and risk-taking. *Management Science,* 33(11): 1404–1418.

49. A discussion of some factors that may lead to escalation in decision making is included in Choo, C. W. 2005. Information failures and organizational disasters. *MIT Sloan Management Review,* 46(3): 8–10.

50. For an interesting discussion of the use of real options analysis in the application of wireless communications, which helped to lower the potential for escalation, refer to McGrath, R. G., Ferrier, W. J., &

Mendelow, A. L. 2004. Real options as engines of choice and heterogeneity. *Academy of Management Review,* 29(1): 86–101.

51. One very useful solution for reducing the effects of managerial conceit is to incorporate an "exit champion" into the decision process. Exit champions provide arguments for killing off the firm's commitment to a decision. For a very insightful discussion on exit champions, refer to Royer, I. 2003. Why bad projects are so hard to kill. *Harvard Business Review,* 81(2): 49–56.

52. Covin, J. G., & Slevin, D. P. 1991. A conceptual model of entrepreneurship as firm behavior. *Entrepreneurship Theory and Practice,* 16(1): 7–24; Lumpkin, G. T., & Dess, G. G. 1996. Clarifying the entrepreneurial orientation construct and linking it to performance. *Academy of Management Review,* 21(1): 135–172; and McGrath, R. G., & MacMillan, I. C. 2000. *The entrepreneurial mind-set.* Cambridge, MA: Harvard Business School Press.

53. Lumpkin, G. T., & Dess, G. G. 2001. Linking two dimensions of entrepreneurial orientation to firm performance: The moderating role of environment and life cycle. *Journal of Business Venturing,* 16: 429–451.

54. For an interesting discussion, see Day, J. D., Mang, P. Y., Richter, A., & Roberts, J. 2001. The innovative organization: Why new ventures need more than a room of their own, *McKinsey Quarterly,* 2: 21–31.

55. Crockett, R. O. 2001. Chris Galvin shakes things up—again. *BusinessWeek,* May 28: 38–39.

56. For an interesting discussion of the impact of innovativeness on organizational outcomes see Cho, H. J., & Pucik, V. 2005. Relationship between innovativeness, quality, growth, profitability, and market value. *Strategic Management Journal,* 26(6): 555–575.

57. Lieberman, M. B., & Montgomery, D. B. 1988. First mover advantages. *Strategic Management Journal,* 9 (Special Issue): 41–58.

58. The discussion of first mover advantages is based on several articles, including Lambkin, M. 1988. Order of entry and performance in new markets. Strategic Management Journal, 9: 127–140; Lieberman & Montgomery, op. cit.: 41–58; and Miller, A., & Camp, B. 1985. Exploring determinants of success in corporate ventures. Journal of Business Venturing, 1(2): 87–105.

59. Moore, G. A. 1999. Crossing the chasm (2nd ed.). New York: HarperBusiness.

60. Mallas, S. 2005. PepsiCo loses its Edge. The Motley *Fool,* June 1, www.fool.com.

61. Lyons, D. 2006. The cheap revolution. *Forbes,* September 18: 102–111.

62. Helman, C. 2001. Stand-up brand. *Forbes,* July 9: 27; and www.hoovers.com.

63. Drucker, op. cit., pp. 109–110.

Strategic Analysis

Chapter 1
Introduction and Analyzing Goals and Objectives

Chapter 2
Analyzing the External Environment

Chapter 3
Analyzing the Internal Environment

Chapter 4
Assessing Intellectual Capital

Strategic Formulation

Chapter 5
Formulating Business-Level Strategies

Chapter 6
Formulating Corporate-Level Strategies

Chapter 7
Formulating International Strategies

Chapter 8
Entrepreneurial Strategy and Competitive Dynamics

Strategic Implementation

Chapter 9
Strategic Control and Corporate Governance

Chapter 10
Creating Effective Organizational Designs

Chapter 11
Strategic Leadership Excellence, Ethics and Change

Chapter 12
Fostering Corporate Entrepreneurship

Case Analysis

Chapter 13
Case Analysis

part four 4

Case Analysis

13 Analyzing Strategic Management Cases

Cases

Analyzing Strategic Management Cases

>learning objectives

After reading this chapter, you should have a good understanding of:

LO1 How strategic case analysis is used to simulate real-world experiences.

LO2 How analyzing strategic management cases can help develop the ability to differentiate, speculate, and integrate when evaluating complex business problems.

LO3 The steps involved in conducting a strategic management case analysis.

LO4 How to get the most out of case analysis.

LO5 How conflict-inducing discussion techniques can lead to better decisions.

LO6 How to use the strategic insights and material from each of the 12 previous chapters in the text to analyze issues posed by strategic management cases.

Case analysis is one of the most effective ways to learn strategic management. It provides a complement to other methods of instruction by asking you to use the tools and techniques of strategic management to deal with an actual business situation. Strategy cases include detailed descriptions of management challenges faced by executives and business owners. By studying the background and analyzing the strategic predicaments posed by a case, you first see that the circumstances businesses confront are often difficult and complex. Then you are asked what decisions you would make to address the situation in the case and how the actions you recommend will affect the company. Thus, the processes of analysis, formulation, and implementation that have been addressed by this textbook can be applied in a real-life situation.

In this chapter we will discuss the role of case analysis as a learning tool in both the classroom and the real world. One of the benefits of strategic case analysis is to develop the ability to differentiate, speculate, and integrate. We will also describe how to conduct a case analysis and address techniques for deriving the greatest benefit from the process, including the effective use of conflict-inducing decision techniques. Finally, we will discuss how case analysis in a classroom setting can enhance the process of analyzing, making decisions, and taking action in real-world strategic situations.

Why Analyze Strategic Management Cases?

It is often said that the key to finding good answers is to ask good questions. Strategic managers and business leaders are required to evaluate options, make choices, and find solutions to the challenges they face every day. To do so, they must learn to ask the right questions. The study of strategic management poses the same challenge. The process of analyzing, decision making, and implementing strategic actions raises many good questions.

>LO1
How strategic case analysis is used to simulate real-world experiences.

- Why do some firms succeed and others fail?
- Why are some companies higher performers than others?
- What information is needed in the strategic planning process?
- How do competing values and beliefs affect strategic decision making?
- What skills and capabilities are needed to implement a strategy effectively?

How does a student of strategic management answer these questions? By strategic case analysis. **Case analysis** simulates the real-world experience that strategic managers and company leaders face as they try to determine how best to run their companies. It places students in the middle of an actual situation and challenges them to figure out what to do.[1]

Asking the right questions is just the beginning of case analysis. In the previous chapters we have discussed issues and challenges that managers face and provided analytical frameworks for understanding the situation. But once the analysis is complete, decisions have to be made. Case analysis forces you to choose among different options and set forth a plan of action based on your choices. But even then the job is not done. Strategic case analysis also requires that you address how you will implement the plan and the implications of choosing one course of action over another.

A strategic management case is a detailed description of a challenging situation faced by an organization.[2] It usually includes a chronology of events and extensive support materials, such as financial statements, product lists, and transcripts of interviews with employees. Although names or locations are sometimes changed to provide anonymity, cases usually report the facts of a situation as authentically as possible.

case analysis a method of learning complex strategic management concepts such as environmental analysis, the process of decision making, and implementing strategic actions through placing students in the middle of an actual situation and challenging them to figure out what to do.

One of the main reasons to analyze strategic management cases is to develop an ability to evaluate business situations critically. In case analysis, memorizing key terms and conceptual frameworks is not enough. To analyze a case, it is important that you go beyond textbook prescriptions and quick answers. It requires you to look deeply into the information that is provided and root out the essential issues and causes of a company's problems.

The types of skills that are required to prepare an effective strategic case analysis can benefit you in actual business situations. Case analysis adds to the overall learning experience by helping you acquire or improve skills that may not be taught in a typical lecture course. Three capabilities that can be learned by conducting case analysis are especially useful to strategic managers—the ability to differentiate, speculate, and integrate.[3] Here's how case analysis can enhance those skills.

>LO2

How analyzing strategic management cases can help develop the ability to differentiate, speculate, and integrate when evaluating complex business problems.

1. ***Differentiate.*** Effective strategic management requires that many different elements of a situation be evaluated at once. This is also true in case analysis. When analyzing cases, it is important to isolate critical facts, evaluate whether assumptions are useful or faulty, and distinguish between good and bad information. Differentiating between the factors that are influencing the situation presented by a case is necessary for making a good analysis. Strategic management also involves understanding that problems are often complex and multilayered. This applies to case analysis as well. Ask whether the case deals with operational, business-level, or corporate issues. Do the problems stem from weaknesses in the internal value chain or threats in the external environment? Dig deep. Being too quick to accept the easiest or least controversial answer will usually fail to get to the heart of the problem.

2. ***Speculate.*** Strategic managers need to be able to use their imagination to envision an explanation or solution that might not readily be apparent. The same is true with case analysis. Being able to imagine different scenarios or contemplate the outcome of a decision can aid the analysis. Managers also have to deal with uncertainty since most decisions are made without complete knowledge of the circumstances. This is also true in case analysis. Case materials often seem to be missing data or the information provided is contradictory. The ability to speculate about details that are unknown or the consequences of an action can be helpful.

3. ***Integrate.*** Strategy involves looking at the big picture and having an organization-wide perspective. Strategic case analysis is no different. Even though the chapters in this textbook divide the material into various topics that may apply to different parts of an organization, all of this information must be integrated into one set of recommendations that will affect the whole company. A strategic manager needs to comprehend how all the factors that influence the organization will interact. This also applies to case analysis. Changes made in one part of the organization affect other parts. Thus, a holistic perspective that integrates the impact of various decisions and environmental influences on all parts of the organization is needed.

In business, these three activities sometimes "compete" with each other for your attention. For example, some decision makers may have a natural ability to differentiate among elements of a problem but are not able to integrate them very well. Others have enough innate creativity to imagine solutions or fill in the blanks when information is missing. But they may have a difficult time when faced with hard numbers or cold facts. Even so, each of these skills is important. The mark of a good strategic manager is the ability to simultaneously make distinctions and envision the whole, and to imagine a future scenario while staying focused on the present. Thus, another reason to conduct case analysis is to help you develop and exercise your ability to differentiate, speculate, and integrate.

Case analysis takes the student through the whole cycle of activity that a manager would face. Beyond the textbook descriptions of concepts and examples, case analysis asks

Analysis, Decision Making, and Change at Sapient Health Network

Sapient Health Network (SHN) had gotten off to a good start. CEO Jim Kean and his two cofounders had raised $5 million in investor capital to launch their vision: an Internet-based health care information subscription service. The idea was to create an Internet community for people suffering from chronic diseases. It would provide members with expert information, resources, a message board, and chat rooms so that people suffering from the same ailments could provide each other with information and support. "Who would be more voracious consumers of information than people who are faced with life-changing, life-threatening illnesses?" thought Bill Kelly, one of SHN's cofounders. Initial market research and beta tests had supported that view.

During the beta tests, however, the service had been offered for free. The troubles began when SHN tried to convert its trial subscribers into paying ones. Fewer than 5 percent signed on, far less than the 15 percent the company had projected. Sapient hired a vice president of marketing who launched an aggressive promotion, but after three months of campaigning SHN still had only 500 members. SHN was now burning through $400,000 per month, with little revenue to show for it.

At that point, according to SHN board member Susan Clymer, "there was a lot of scrambling around trying to figure out how we could wring value out of what we'd already accomplished." One thing SHN had created was an expert software system which had two components: an "intelligent profile engine" (IPE) and an "intelligent query engine" (IQE). SHN used this system to collect detailed information from its subscribers.

SHN was sure that the expert system was its biggest selling point. But how could they use it? Then the founders remembered that the original business plan had suggested there might be a market for aggregate data about patient populations gathered from the Web site. Could they turn the business around by selling patient data? To analyze the possibility, Kean tried out the idea on the market research arm of a huge East Coast health care conglomerate. The officials were intrigued. SHN realized that its expert system could become a market research tool.

Once the analysis was completed, the founders made the decision: They would still create Internet communities for chronically ill patients, but the service would be free. And they would transform SHN from a company that processed subscriptions to one that sold market research.

Finally, they enacted the changes. Some of it was painful, including laying off 18 employees. Instead, SHN needed more health care industry expertise. It even hired an interim CEO, Craig Davenport, a 25-year veteran of the industry, to steer the company in its new direction. Finally, SHN had to communicate a new message to its members. It began by reimbursing the $10,000 of subscription fees they had paid.

All of this paid off dramatically in a matter of just two years. Revenues jumped to $1.9 million in 1998. Early in 1999 SHN was purchased by WebMD and less than a year later, WebMD merged with Healtheon. The combined company still operates a thriving office out of SHN's original location in Portland, Oregon.

Sources: Ferguson, S. 2007. Health care gets a better IT prescription. *Baseline,* www.baselinemag.com, May 24. Brenneman, K. 2000. Healtheon/WebMD's local office is thriving. *Business Journal of Portland,* June 2; Raths, D. 1998. Reversal of fortune. *Inc. Technology,* 2: 52–62.

you to "walk a mile in the shoes" of the strategic decision maker and learn to evaluate situations critically. Executives and owners must make decisions every day with limited information and a swirl of business activity going on around them. Consider the example of Sapient Health Networks, an Internet start-up that had to undergo some analysis and problem solving just to survive. Strategy Spotlight 13.1 describes how this company transformed itself after a serious self-examination during a time of crisis.

As you can see from the experience of Sapient Health Networks, businesses are often faced with immediate challenges that threaten their lives. The Sapient case illustrates how the strategic management process helped it survive. First, the company realistically assessed the environment, evaluated the marketplace, and analyzed its resources. Then it made tough decisions, which included shifting its market focus, hiring and firing, and redeploying its assets. Finally, it took action. The result was not only firm survival, but also a quick turnaround leading to rapid success.

How to Conduct a Case Analysis

The process of analyzing strategic management cases involves several steps. In this section we will review the mechanics of preparing a case analysis. Before beginning, there are two things to keep in mind that will clarify your understanding of the process and make the results of the process more meaningful.

First, unless you prepare for a case discussion, there is little you can gain from the discussion and even less that you can offer. Effective strategic managers don't enter into problem-solving situations without doing some homework—investigating the situation, analyzing and researching possible solutions, and sometimes gathering the advice of others. Good problem solving often requires that decision makers be immersed in the facts, options, and implications surrounding the problem. In case analysis, this means reading and thoroughly comprehending the case materials before trying to make an analysis.

The second point is related to the first. To get the most out of a case analysis you must place yourself "inside" the case—that is, think like an actual participant in the case situation. However, there are several positions you can take. These are discussed in the following paragraphs:

- *Strategic decision maker.* This is the position of the senior executive responsible for resolving the situation described in the case. It may be the CEO, the business owner, or a strategic manager in a key executive position.
- *Board of directors.* Since the board of directors represents the owners of a corporation, it has a responsibility to step in when a management crisis threatens the company. As a board member, you may be in a unique position to solve problems.
- *Outside consultant.* Either the board or top management may decide to bring in outsiders. Consultants often have an advantage because they can look at a situation objectively. But they also may be at a disadvantage since they have no power to enforce changes.

Before beginning the analysis, it may be helpful to envision yourself assuming one of these roles. Then, as you study and analyze the case materials, you can make a diagnosis and recommend solutions in a way that is consistent with your position. Try different perspectives. You may find that your view of the situation changes depending on the role you play. As an outside consultant, for example, it may be easy for you to conclude that certain individuals should be replaced in order to solve a problem presented in the case. However, if you take the role of the CEO who knows the individuals and the challenges they have been facing, you may be reluctant to fire them and will seek another solution instead.

The idea of assuming a particular role is similar to the real world in various ways. In your career, you may work in an organization where outside accountants, bankers, lawyers, or other professionals are advising you about how to resolve business situations or improve your practices. Their perspective will be different from yours but it is useful to understand things from their point of view. Conversely, you may work as a member of the audit team of an accounting firm or the loan committee of a bank. In those situations, it would be helpful if you understood the situation from the perspective of the business leader who must weigh your views against all the other advice that he or she receives. Case analysis can help develop an ability to appreciate such multiple perspectives.

One of the most challenging roles to play in business is as a business founder or owner. For small businesses or entrepreneurial start-ups, the founder may wear all hats at once—key decision maker, primary stockholder, and CEO. Hiring an outside consultant may not be an option. However, the issues faced by young firms and established firms are often not that different, especially when it comes to formulating a plan of action. Business plans that entrepreneurial firms use to raise money or propose a business expansion typically revolve around a

Using a Business Plan Framework to Analyze Strategic Cases

Established businesses often have to change what they are doing in order to improve their competitive position or sometimes simply to survive. To make the changes effectively, businesses usually need a plan. Business plans are no longer just for entrepreneurs. The kind of market analysis, decision making, and action planning that is considered standard practice among new ventures can also benefit going concerns that want to make changes, seize an opportunity, or head in a new direction.

The best business plans, however, are not those loaded with decades of month-by-month financial projections or that depend on rigid adherence to a schedule of events that is impossible to predict. The good ones are focused on four factors that are critical to new-venture success. These same factors are important in case analysis as well because they get to the heart of many of the problems found in strategic cases.

1. *The People.* "When I receive a business plan, I always read the résumé section first," says Harvard Professor William Sahlman. The people questions that are critically important to investors include: What are their skills? How much experience do they have? What is their reputation? Have they worked together as a team? These same questions also may be used in case analysis to evaluate the role of individuals in the strategic case.

2. *The Opportunity.* Business opportunities come in many forms. They are not limited to new ventures.

The chance to enter new markets, introduce new products, or merge with a competitor provide many of the challenges that are found in strategic management cases. What are the consequences of such actions? Will the proposed changes affect the firm's business concept? What factors might stand in the way of success? The same issues are also present in most strategic cases.

3. *The Context.* Things happen in contexts that cannot be controlled by a firm's managers. This is particularly true of the general environment where social trends, economic changes, or events such as the September 11, 2001, terrorist attacks can change business overnight. When evaluating strategic cases, ask: Is the company aware of the impact of context on the business? What will it do if the context changes? Can it influence the context in a way that favors the company?

4. *Risk and Reward.* With a new venture, the entrepreneurs and investors take the risks and get the rewards. In strategic cases, the risks and rewards often extend to many other stakeholders, such as employees, customers, and suppliers. When analyzing a case, ask: Are the managers making choices that will pay off in the future? Are the rewards evenly distributed? Will some stakeholders be put at risk if the situation in the case changes? What if the situation remains the same? Could that be even riskier?

Whether a business is growing or shrinking, large or small, industrial or service oriented, the issues of people, opportunities, context, and risks and rewards will have a large impact on its performance. Therefore, you should always consider these four factors when evaluating strategic management cases.

Sources: Wasserman, E. 2003. A simple plan. *MBA Jungle,* February: 50–55; DeKluyver, C. A. 2000. *Strategic thinking: An executive perspective.* Upper Saddle River, NJ: Prentice Hall; and Sahlman, W. A. 1997. How to write a great business plan. *Harvard Business Review,* 75(4): 98–108.

few key issues that must be addressed no matter what the size or age of the business. Strategy Spotlight 13.2 reviews business planning issues that are most important to consider when evaluating any case, especially from the perspective of the business founder or owner.

Next we will review five steps to follow when conducting a strategic management case analysis: becoming familiar with the material, identifying the problems, analyzing the strategic issues using the tools and insights of strategic management, proposing alternative solutions, and making recommendations.[4]

> **>LO3**
> The steps involved in conducting a strategic management case analysis.

Become Familiar with the Material

Written cases often include a lot of material. They may be complex and include detailed financials or long passages. Even so, to understand a case and its implications, you must become familiar with its content. Sometimes key information is not immediately apparent.

It may be contained in the footnotes to an exhibit or an interview with a lower-level employee. In other cases the important points may be difficult to grasp because the subject matter is so unfamiliar. When you approach a strategic case try the following technique to enhance comprehension:

- Read quickly through the case one time to get an overall sense of the material.
- Use the initial read-through to assess possible links to strategic concepts.
- Read through the case again, in depth. Make written notes as you read.
- Evaluate how strategic concepts might inform key decisions or suggest alternative solutions.
- After formulating an initial recommendation, thumb through the case again quickly to help assess the consequences of the actions you propose.

Identify Problems

When conducting case analysis, one of your most important tasks is to identify the problem. Earlier we noted that one of the main reasons to conduct case analysis was to find solutions. But you cannot find a solution unless you know the problem. Another saying you may have heard is, "A good diagnosis is half the cure." In other words, once you have determined what the problem is, you are well on your way to identifying a reasonable solution.

Some cases have more than one problem. But the problems are usually related. For a hypothetical example, consider the following: Company A was losing customers to a new competitor. Upon analysis, it was determined that the competitor had a 50 percent faster delivery time even though its product was of lower quality. The managers of company A could not understand why customers would settle for an inferior product. It turns out that no one was marketing to company A's customers that its product was superior. A second problem was that falling sales resulted in cuts in company A's sales force. Thus, there were two related problems: inferior delivery technology and insufficient sales effort.

When trying to determine the problem, avoid getting hung up on symptoms. Zero in on the problem. For example, in the company A example above, the symptom was losing customers. But the problems were an underfunded, understaffed sales force combined with an outdated delivery technology. Try to see beyond the immediate symptoms to the more fundamental problems.

Another tip when preparing a case analysis is to articulate the problem.[5] Writing down a problem statement gives you a reference point to turn to as you proceed through the case analysis. This is important because the process of formulating strategies or evaluating implementation methods may lead you away from the initial problem. Make sure your recommendation actually addresses the problems you have identified.

One more thing about identifying problems: Sometimes problems are not apparent until *after* you do the analysis. In some cases the problem will be presented plainly, perhaps in the opening paragraph or on the last page of the case. But in other cases the problem does not emerge until after the issues in the case have been analyzed. We turn next to the subject of strategic case analysis.

Conduct Strategic Analyses

This textbook has presented numerous analytical tools (e.g., five-forces analysis and value-chain analysis), contingency frameworks (e.g., when to use related rather than unrelated diversification strategies), and other techniques that can be used to evaluate strategic situations. The previous 12 chapters have addressed practices that are common in strategic management, but only so much can be learned by studying the practices and concepts. The best way to understand these methods is to apply them by conducting analyses of specific cases.

The first step is to determine which strategic issues are involved. Is there a problem in the company's competitive environment? Or is it an internal problem? If it is internal, does it have to do with organizational structure? Strategic controls? Uses of technology? Or perhaps the company has overworked its employees or underutilized its intellectual capital. Has the company mishandled a merger? Chosen the wrong diversification strategy? Botched a new product introduction? Each of these issues is linked to one or more of the concepts discussed earlier in the text. Determine what strategic issues are associated with the problems you have identified. Remember also that most real-life case situations involve issues that are highly interrelated. Even in cases where there is only one major problem, the strategic processes required to solve it may involve several parts of the organization.

Once you have identified the issues that apply to the case, conduct the analysis. For example, you may need to conduct a five-forces analysis or dissect the company's competitive strategy. Perhaps you need to evaluate whether its resources are rare, valuable, difficult to imitate, or difficult to substitute. Financial analysis may be needed to assess the company's economic prospects. Perhaps the international entry mode needs to be reevaluated because of changing conditions in the host country. Employee empowerment techniques may need to be improved to enhance organizational learning. Whatever the case, all the strategic concepts introduced in the text include insights for assessing their effectiveness. Determining how well a company is doing these things is central to the case analysis process.

Financial ratio analysis is one of the primary tools used to conduct case analysis. Appendix 1 to Chapter 13 includes a discussion and examples of the financial ratios that are often used to evaluate a company's performance and financial well-being. Exhibit 13.1 provides a summary of the financial ratios presented in Appendix 1 to this chapter.

In this part of the overall strategic analysis process, it is also important to test your own assumptions about the case.[6] First, what assumptions are you making about the case materials? It may be that you have interpreted the case content differently than your team members or classmates. Being clear about these assumptions will be important in determining how to analyze the case. Second, what assumptions have you made about the best way to resolve the problems? Ask yourself why you have chosen one type of analysis over another. This process of assumption checking can also help determine if you have gotten to the heart of the problem or are still just dealing with symptoms.

As mentioned earlier, sometimes the critical diagnosis in a case can only be made after the analysis is conducted. However, by the end of this stage in the process, you should know the problems and have completed a thorough analysis of them. You can now move to the next step: finding solutions.

> **financial ratio analysis** a method of evaluating a company's performance and financial well-being through ratios of accounting values, including short-term solvency, long-term solvency, asset utilization, profitability, and market value ratios.

Propose Alternative Solutions

It is important to remember that in strategic management case analysis, there is rarely one right answer or one best way. Even when members of a class or a team agree on what the problem is, they may not agree upon how to solve the problem. Therefore, it is helpful to consider several different solutions.

After conducting strategic analysis and identifying the problem, develop a list of options. What are the possible solutions? What are the alternatives? First, generate a list of all the options you can think of without prejudging any one of them. Remember that not all cases call for dramatic decisions or sweeping changes. Some companies just need to make small adjustments. In fact, "Do nothing" may be a reasonable alternative in some cases. Although that is rare, it might be useful to consider what will happen if the company does nothing. This point illustrates the purpose of developing alternatives: to evaluate what will happen if a company chooses one solution over another.

Thus, during this step of a case analysis, you will evaluate choices and the implications of those choices. One aspect of any business that is likely to be highlighted in this part of the analysis is strategy implementation. Ask how the choices made will be implemented. It may be that what seems like an obvious choice for solving a problem creates

Ratio	What It Measures
Short-term solvency, or liquidity, ratios:	
Current ratio	Ability to use assets to pay off liabilities.
Quick ratio	Ability to use liquid assets to pay off liabilities quickly.
Cash ratio	Ability to pay off liabilities with cash on hand.
Long-term solvency, or financial leverage, ratios:	
Total debt ratio	How much of a company's total assets are financed by debt.
Debt-equity ratio	Compares how much a company is financed by debt with how much it is financed by equity.
Equity multiplier	How much debt is being used to finance assets.
Times interest earned ratio	How well a company has its interest obligations covered.
Cash coverage ratio	A company's ability to generate cash from operations.
Asset utilization, or turnover, ratios:	
Inventory turnover	How many times each year a company sells its entire inventory.
Days' sales in inventory	How many days on average inventory is on hand before it is sold.
Receivables turnover	How frequently each year a company collects on its credit sales.
Days' sales in receivables	How many days on average it takes to collect on credit sales (average collection period).
Total asset turnover	How much of sales is generated for every dollar in assets.
Capital intensity	The dollar investment in assets needed to generate $1 in sales.
Profitability ratios:	
Profit margin	How much profit is generated by every dollar of sales.
Return on assets (ROA)	How effectively assets are being used to generate a return.
Return on equity (ROE)	How effectively amounts invested in the business by its owners are being used to generate a return.
Market value ratios:	
Price–earnings ratio	How much investors are willing to pay per dollar of current earnings.
Market-to-book ratio	Compares market value of the company's investments to the cost of those investments.

Exhibit 13.1 Summary of Financial Ratio Analysis Techniques

an even bigger problem when implemented. But remember also that no strategy or strategic "fix" is going to work if it cannot be implemented. Once a list of alternatives is generated, ask:

- Can the company afford it? How will it affect the bottom line?
- Is the solution likely to evoke a competitive response?
- Will employees throughout the company accept the changes? What impact will the solution have on morale?
- How will the decision affect other stakeholders? Will customers, suppliers, and others buy into it?

- How does this solution fit with the company's vison, mission, and objectives?
- Will the culture or values of the company be changed by the solution? Is it a positive change?

The point of this step in the case analysis process is to find a solution that both solves the problem and is realistic. A consideration of the implications of various alternative solutions will generally lead you to a final recommendation that is more thoughtful and complete.

Make Recommendations

The basic aim of case analysis is to find solutions. Your analysis is not complete until you have recommended a course of action. In this step the task is to make a set of recommendations that your analysis supports. Describe exactly what needs to be done. Explain why this course of action will solve the problem. The recommendation should also include suggestions for how best to implement the proposed solution because the recommended actions and their implications for the performance and future of the firm are interrelated.

Recall that the solution you propose must solve the problem you identified. This point cannot be overemphasized; too often students make recommendations that treat only symptoms or fail to tackle the central problems in the case. Make a logical argument that shows how the problem led to the analysis and the analysis led to the recommendations you are proposing. Remember, an analysis is not an end in itself; it is useful only if it leads to a solution.

The actions you propose should describe the very next steps that the company needs to take. Don't say, for example, "If the company does more market research, then I would recommend the following course of action. . . ." Instead, make conducting the research part of your recommendation. Taking the example a step further, if you also want to suggest subsequent actions that may be different *depending* on the outcome of the market research, that's OK. But don't make your initial recommendation conditional on actions the company may or may not take.

In summary, case analysis can be a very rewarding process but, as you might imagine, it can also be frustrating and challenging. If you will follow the steps described above, you will address the different elements of a thorough analysis. This approach can give your analysis a solid footing. Then, even if there are differences of opinion about how to interpret the facts, analyze the situation, or solve the problems, you can feel confident that you have not missed any important steps in finding the best course of action.

Students are often asked to prepare oral presentations of the information in a case and their analysis of the best remedies. This is frequently assigned as a group project. Or you may be called upon in class to present your ideas about the circumstances or solutions for a case the class is discussing. Exhibit 13.2 provides some tips for preparing an oral case presentation.

How to Get the Most from Case Analysis

One of the reasons case analysis is so enriching as a learning tool is that it draws on many resources and skills besides just what is in the textbook. This is especially true in the study of strategy. Why? Because strategic management itself is a highly integrative task that draws on many areas of specialization at several levels, from the individual to the whole of society. Therefore, to get the most out of case analysis, expand your horizons beyond the concepts in this text and seek insights from your own reservoir of knowledge. Here are some tips for how to do that.[7]

>LO4
How to get the most out of case analysis.

- ***Keep an open mind.*** Like any good discussion, a case analysis discussion often evokes strong opinions and high emotions. But it's the variety of perspectives that makes case analysis so valuable: Many viewpoints usually lead to a more complete analysis. Therefore, avoid letting an emotional response to another person's style or opinion keep you from hearing what he or she has to say. Once you evaluate what is said, you may

Rule	Description
Organize your thoughts.	Begin by becoming familiar with the material. If you are working with a team, compare notes about the key points of the case and share insights that other team members may have gleaned from tables and exhibits. Then make an outline. This is one of the best ways to organize the flow and content of the presentation.
Emphasize strategic analysis.	The purpose of case analysis is to diagnose problems and find solutions. In the process, you may need to unravel the case material as presented and reconfigure it in a fashion that can be more effectively analyzed. Present the material in a way that lends itself to analysis—don't simply restate what is in the case. This involves three major categories with the following emphasis: Background/Problem Statement 10–20% Strategic Analysis/Options 60–75% Recommendations/Action Plan 10–20% As you can see, the emphasis of your presentation should be on analysis. This will probably require you to reorganize the material so that the tools of strategic analysis can be applied.
Be logical and consistent.	A presentation that is rambling and hard to follow may confuse the listener and fail to evoke a good discussion. Present your arguments and explanations in a logical sequence. Support your claims with facts. Include financial analysis where appropriate. Be sure that the solutions you recommend address the problems you have identified.
Defend your position.	Usually an oral presentation is followed by a class discussion. Anticipate what others might disagree with and be prepared to defend your views. This means being aware of the choices you made and the implications of your recommendations. Be clear about your assumptions. Be able to expand on your analysis.
Share presentation responsibilities.	Strategic management case analyses are often conducted by teams. Each member of the team should have a clear role in the oral presentation, preferably a speaking role. It's also important to coordinate the different parts of the presentation into a logical, smooth-flowing whole. How well a team works together is usually very apparent during an oral presentation.

Exhibit 13.2 Preparing an Oral Case Presentation

disagree with it or dismiss it as faulty. But unless you keep an open mind in the first place, you may miss the importance of the other person's contribution. Also, people often place a higher value on the opinions of those they consider to be good listeners.

- *Take a stand for what you believe.* Although it is vital to keep an open mind, it is also important to state your views proactively. Don't try to figure out what your friends or the instructor wants to hear. Analyze the case from the perspective of your own background and belief system. For example, perhaps you feel that a decision is unethical or that the managers in a case have misinterpreted the facts. Don't be afraid to assert that in the discussion. For one thing, when a person takes a strong stand, it often encourages others to evaluate the issues more closely. This can lead to a more thorough investigation and a more meaningful class discussion.
- *Draw on your personal experience.* You may have experiences from work or as a customer that shed light on some of the issues in a case. Even though one of the purposes of

case analysis is to apply the analytical tools from this text, you may be able to add to the discussion by drawing on your outside experiences and background. Of course, you need to guard against carrying that to extremes. In other words, don't think that your perspective is the only viewpoint that matters! Simply recognize that firsthand experience usually represents a welcome contribution to the overall quality of case discussions.

- **Participate and persuade.** Have you heard the phrase, "Vote early . . . and often"? Among loyal members of certain political parties, it has become rather a joke. Why? Because a democratic system is built on the concept of one person, one vote. Even though some voters may want to vote often enough to get their candidate elected, it is against the law. Not so in a case discussion. People who are persuasive and speak their mind can often influence the views of others. But to do so, you have to be prepared and convincing. Being persuasive is more than being loud or long-winded. It involves understanding all sides of an argument and being able to overcome objections to your own point of view. These efforts can make a case discussion more lively. And they parallel what happens in the real world; in business, people frequently share their opinions and attempt to persuade others to see things their way.

- **Be concise and to the point.** In the previous point, we encouraged you to speak up and "sell" your ideas to others in a case discussion. But you must be clear about what you are selling. Make your arguments in a way that is explicit and direct. Zero in on the most important points. Be brief. Don't try to make a lot of points at once by jumping around between topics. Avoid trying to explain the whole case situation at once. Remember, other students usually resent classmates who go on and on, take up a lot of "airtime," or repeat themselves unnecessarily. The best way to avoid this is to stay focused and be specific.

- **Think out of the box.** It's OK to be a little provocative; sometimes that is the consequence of taking a stand on issues. But it may be equally important to be imaginative and creative when making a recommendation or determining how to implement a solution. Albert Einstein once stated, "Imagination is more important than knowledge." The reason is that managing strategically requires more than memorizing concepts. Strategic management insights must be applied to each case differently—just knowing the principles is not enough. Imagination and out-of-the-box thinking help to apply strategic knowledge in novel and unique ways.

- **Learn from the insights of others.** Before you make up your mind about a case, hear what other students have to say. Get a second opinion, and a third, and so forth. Of course, in a situation where you have to put your analysis in writing, you may not be able to learn from others ahead of time. But in a case discussion, observe how various students attack the issues and engage in problem solving. Such observation skills also may be a key to finding answers within the case. For example, people tend to believe authority figures, so they would place a higher value on what a company president says. In some cases, however, the statements of middle managers may represent a point of view that is even more helpful for finding a solution to the problems presented by the case.

- **Apply insights from other case analyses.** Throughout the text, we have used examples of actual businesses to illustrate strategy concepts. The aim has been to show you how firms think about and deal with business problems. During the course, you may be asked to conduct several case analyses as part of the learning experience. Once you have performed a few case analyses, you will see how the concepts from the text apply in real-life business situations. Incorporate the insights learned from the text examples and your own previous case discussions into each new case that you analyze.

- **Critically analyze your own performance.** Performance appraisals are a standard part of many workplace situations. They are used to determine promotions, raises, and work assignments. In some organizations, everyone from the top executive down is subject to such reviews. Even in situations where the owner or CEO is not evaluated by others, they often find it useful to ask themselves regularly, Am I being effective? The same can be applied to your performance in a case analysis situation. Ask yourself, Were my comments insightful? Did I make a good contribution? How might I improve next time? Use the same criteria on yourself that you use to evaluate others. What grade would you give yourself? This technique will not only make you more fair in your assessment of others but also will indicate how your own performance can improve.

- **Conduct outside research.** Many times, you can enhance your understanding of a case situation by investigating sources outside the case materials. For example, you may want to study an industry more closely or research a company's close competitors. Recent moves such as mergers and acquisitions or product introductions may be reported in the business press. The company itself may provide useful information on its Web site or in its annual reports. Such information can usually spur additional discussion and enrich the case analysis. (*Caution:* It is best to check with your instructor in advance to be sure this kind of additional research is encouraged. Bringing in outside research may conflict with the instructor's learning objectives.)

Several of the points suggested above for how to get the most out of case analysis apply only to an open discussion of a case, like that in a classroom setting. Exhibit 13.3 provides some additional guidelines for preparing a written case analysis.

Rule	Description
Be thorough.	Many of the ideas presented in Exhibit 13.2 about oral presentations also apply to written case analysis. However, a written analysis typically has to be more complete. This means writing out the problem statement and articulating assumptions. It is also important to provide support for your arguments and reference case materials or other facts more specifically.
Coordinate team efforts.	Written cases are often prepared by small groups. Within a group, just as in a class discussion, you may disagree about the diagnosis or the recommended plan of action. This can be healthy if it leads to a richer understanding of the case material. But before committing your ideas to writing, make sure you have coordinated your responses. Don't prepare a written analysis that appears contradictory or looks like a patchwork of disconnected thoughts.
Avoid restating the obvious.	There is no reason to restate material that everyone is familiar with already, namely, the case content. It is too easy for students to use up space in a written analysis with a recapitulation of the details of the case—this accomplishes very little. Stay focused on the key points. Only restate the information that is most central to your analysis.
Present information graphically.	Tables, graphs, and other exhibits are usually one of the best ways to present factual material that supports your arguments. For example, financial calculations such as break-even analysis, sensitivity analysis, or return on investment are best presented graphically. Even qualitative information such as product lists or rosters of employees can be summarized effectively and viewed quickly by using a table or graph.
Exercise quality control.	When presenting a case analysis in writing, it is especially important to use good grammar, avoid misspelling words, and eliminate typos and other visual distractions. Mistakes that can be glossed over in an oral presentation or class discussion are often highlighted when they appear in writing. Make your written presentation appear as professional as possible. Don't let the appearance of your written case keep the reader from recognizing the importance and quality of your analysis.

Exhibit 13.3 Preparing a Written Case Analysis

Using Conflict-Inducing Decision-Making Techniques in Case Analysis

Next we address some techniques often used to improve case analyses that involve the constructive use of conflict. In the classroom—as well as in the business world—you will frequently be analyzing cases or solving problems in groups. While the word *conflict* often has a negative connotation (e.g., rude behavior, personal affronts), it can be very helpful in arriving at better solutions to cases. It can provide an effective means for new insights as well as for rigorously questioning and analyzing assumptions and strategic alternatives. In fact, if you don't have constructive conflict, you may only get consensus. When this happens, decisions tend to be based on compromise rather than collaboration.

>LO5
How conflict-inducing discussion techniques can lead to better decisions.

In your organizational behavior classes, you probably learned the concept of "groupthink."[8] Groupthink, a term coined by Irving Janis after he conducted numerous studies on executive decision making, is a condition in which group members strive to reach agreement or consensus without realistically considering other viable alternatives. In effect, group norms bolster morale at the expense of critical thinking and decision making is impaired.[9]

Many of us have probably been "victims" of groupthink at one time or another in our life. We may be confronted with situations when social pressure, politics, or "not wanting to stand out" may prevent us from voicing our concerns about a chosen course of action. Nevertheless, decision making in groups is a common practice in the management of many businesses. Most companies, especially large ones, rely on input from various top managers to provide valuable information and experience from their specialty area as well as their unique perspectives. Chapter 11 emphasized the importance of empowering individuals at all levels to participate in decision-making processes. In terms of this course, case analysis involves a type of decision making that is often conducted in groups. Strategy Spotlight 13.3 provides guidelines for making team-based approaches to case analysis more effective.

Clearly, understanding how to work in groups and the potential problems associated with group decision processes can benefit the case analysis process. Therefore, let's first look at some of the symptoms of groupthink and suggest ways of preventing it. Then, we will suggest some conflict-inducing decision-making techniques—devil's advocacy and dialectical inquiry—that can help to prevent groupthink and lead to better decisions.

Symptoms of Groupthink and How to Prevent It

Irving Janis identified several symptoms of groupthink, including:

- *An illusion of invulnerability.* This reassures people about possible dangers and leads to overoptimism and failure to heed warnings of danger.
- *A belief in the inherent morality of the group.* Because individuals think that what they are doing is right, they tend to ignore ethical or moral consequences of their decisions.

● Effectively working in teams is a critical skill—both in the classroom and in business organizations.

Making Case Analysis Teams More Effective

Working in teams can be very challenging. Not all team members have the same skills, interests, or motivations. Some team members just want to get the work done. Others see teams as an opportunity to socialize. Occasionally, there are team members who think they should be in charge and make all the decisions; other teams have free-loaders—team members who don't want to do anything except get credit for the team's work.

One consequence of these various styles is that team meetings can become time wasters. Disagreements about how to proceed, how to share the work, or what to do at the next meeting tend to slow down teams and impede progress toward the goal. While the dynamics of case analysis teams are likely to always be challenging depending on the personalities involved, one thing nearly all members realize is that, ultimately, the team's work must be completed. Most team members also aim to do the highest quality work possible. The following guidelines provide some useful insights about how to get the work of a team done more effectively.

Spend More Time Together

One of the factors that prevents teams from doing a good job with case analysis is their failure to put in the necessary time. Unless teams really tackle the issues surrounding case analysis—both the issues in the case itself and organizing how the work is to be conducted—the end result will probably be lacking because decisions that are made too quickly are unlikely to get to the heart of the problem(s) in the case. "Meetings should be a precious resource, but they're treated like a necessary evil," says Kenneth Sole, a consultant who specializes in organizational behavior. As a result, teams that care more about finishing the analysis than getting the analysis right often make poor decisions.

Therefore, expect to have a few meetings that run long, especially at the beginning of the project when the work is being organized and the issues in the case are being sorted out, and again at the end when the team must coordinate the components of the case analysis that will be presented. Without spending this kind of time together, it is doubtful that the analysis will be comprehensive and the presentation is likely to be choppy and incomplete.

Make a Focused and Disciplined Agenda

To complete tasks and avoid wasting time, meetings need to have a clear purpose. To accomplish this at Roche, the Swiss drug and diagnostic product maker, CEO Franz Humer implemented a "decision agenda." The agenda focuses only on Roche's highest value issues and discussions are limited to these major topics. In terms of case analysis, the major topics include sorting out the issues of the case, linking elements of the case to the strategic issues presented in class or the text, and assigning roles to various team members. Such objectives help keep team members on track.

Agendas also can be used to address issues such as the time line for accomplishing work. Otherwise the purpose of meetings may only be to manage the "crisis" of getting the case analysis finished on time. One solution is to assign a team member to manage the agenda. That person could make sure the team stays focused on the tasks at hand and remains mindful of time constraints. Another role could be to link the team's efforts to the steps presented in Exhibits 13.2 and 13.3 on how to prepare a case analysis.

Pay More Attention to Strategy

Teams often waste time by focusing on unimportant aspects of a case. These may include details that are interesting but irrelevant or operational issues rather than strategic issues. It is true that useful clues to the issues in the case are sometimes embedded in the conversations of key managers or the trends evident in a financial statement. But once such insights are discovered, teams need to focus on the underlying strategic problems in the case. To solve such problems, major corporations such as Cadbury Schweppes and Boeing hold meetings just to generate strategic alternatives for solving their problems. This gives managers time to consider the implications of various courses of action. Separate meetings are held to evaluate alternatives, make strategic decisions, and approve an action plan.

Once the strategic solutions or "course corrections" are identified—as is common in most cases assigned—the operational implications and details of implementation will flow from the strategic decisions that companies make. Therefore, focusing primarily on strategic issues will provide teams with insights for making recommendations that are based on a deeper understanding of the issues in the case.

Produce Real Decisions

Too often, meetings are about discussing rather than deciding. Teams often spend a lot of time talking without reaching any conclusions. As Raymond Sanchez, CEO of Florida-based Security Mortgage Group, says, meetings are often used to "rehash the hash that's already been hashed." To be efficient and productive, team meetings need to be about more than just information sharing and group input. For example, an initial meeting may result in the team realizing that it needs to study the case in greater depth and examine links to strategic issues   *(continued)*

(continued) more carefully. Once more analysis is conducted, the team needs to reach a consensus so that the decisions that are made will last once the meeting is over. Lasting decisions are more actionable because it frees team members to take the next steps.

One technique for making progress in this way is recapping each meeting with a five-minute synthesis report. According to Pamela Schindler, director of the Center for Applied Management at Wittenberg University, it's important to think through the implications of the meeting before

Sources: Mankins, M. C. 2004. Stop wasting valuable time. *Harvard Business Review*, September: 58–65; and Sauer, P. J. 2004. Escape from meeting hell. *Inc. Magazine*, May, www.inc.com.

ending it. "The real joy of synthesis," says Schindler, "is realizing how many meetings you won't need."

Not only are these guidelines useful for helping teams finish their work, but they can also help resolve some of the difficulties that teams often face. By involving every team member, using a meeting agenda, and focusing on the strategic issues that are critical to nearly every case, the discussion is limited and the criteria for making decisions become clearer. This allows the task to dominate rather than any one personality. And if the team finishes its work faster, this frees up time to focus on other projects or put the finishing touches on a case analysis presentation.

- *Stereotyped views of members of opposing groups.* Members of other groups are viewed as weak or not intelligent.
- *The application of pressure to members who express doubts about the group's shared illusions or question the validity of arguments proposed.*
- *The practice of self-censorship.* Members keep silent about their opposing views and downplay to themselves the value of their perspectives.
- *An illusion of unanimity.* People assume that judgments expressed by members are shared by all.
- *The appointment of mindguards.* People sometimes appoint themselves as mindguards to protect the group from adverse information that might break the climate of consensus (or agreement).

Clearly, groupthink is an undesirable and negative phenomenon that can lead to poor decisions. Irving Janis considers it to be a key contributor to such faulty decisions as the failure to prepare for the attack on Pearl Harbor, the escalation of the Vietnam conflict, and the failure to prepare for the consequences of the Iraqi invasion. Many of the same sorts of flawed decision making occur in business organizations—as we discussed above with the EDS example. Janis has provided several suggestions for preventing groupthink that can be used as valuable guides in decision making and problem solving:

- Leaders must encourage group members to address their concerns and objectives.
- When higher-level managers assign a problem for a group to solve, they should adopt an impartial stance and not mention their preferences.
- Before a group reaches its final decision, the leader should encourage members to discuss their deliberations with trusted associates and then report the perspectives back to the group.
- The group should invite outside experts and encourage them to challenge the group's viewpoints and positions.
- The group should divide into subgroups, meet at various times under different chairpersons, and then get together to resolve differences.
- After reaching a preliminary agreement, the group should hold a "second chance" meeting which provides members a forum to express any remaining concerns and rethink the issue prior to making a final decision.

Using Conflict to Improve Decision Making

In addition to the above suggestions, the effective use of conflict can be a means of improving decision making. Although conflict can have negative outcomes, such as ill will, anger, tension, and lowered motivation, both leaders and group members must strive to assure that it is managed properly and used in a constructive manner.

Two conflict-inducing decision-making approaches that have become quite popular are *devil's advocacy* and *dialectical inquiry*. Both approaches incorporate conflict into the decision-making process through formalized debate. A group charged with making a decision or solving a problem is divided into two subgroups and each will be involved in the analysis and solution.

Devil's Advocacy   With the devil's advocate approach, one of the groups (or individuals) acts as a critic to the plan. The devil's advocate tries to come up with problems with the proposed alternative and suggest reasons why it should not be adopted. The role of the devil's advocate is to create dissonance. This ensures that the group will take a hard look at its original proposal or alternative. By having a group (or individual) assigned the role of devil's advocate, it becomes clear that such an adversarial stance is legitimized. It brings out criticisms that might otherwise not be made.

Some authors have suggested that the use of a devil's advocate can be very helpful in helping boards of directors to ensure that decisions are addressed comprehensively and to avoid groupthink.[10] And Charles Elson, a director of Sunbeam Corporation, has argued that:

> Devil's advocates are terrific in any situation because they help you to figure a decision's numerous implications. . . . The better you think out the implications prior to making the decision, the better the decision ultimately turns out to be. That's why a devil's advocate is always a great person, irritating sometimes, but a great person.

As one might expect, there can be some potential problems with using the devil's advocate approach. If one's views are constantly criticized, one may become demoralized. Thus, that person may come up with "safe solutions" in order to minimize embarrassment or personal risk and become less subject to criticism. Additionally, even if the devil's advocate is successful with finding problems with the proposed course of action, there may be no new ideas or counterproposals to take its place. Thus, the approach sometimes may simply focus on what is wrong without suggesting other ideas.

Dialectical Inquiry   Dialectical inquiry attempts to accomplish the goals of the devil's advocate in a more constructive manner. It is a technique whereby a problem is approached from two alternative points of view. The idea is that out of a critique of the opposing perspectives—a thesis and an antithesis—a creative synthesis will occur. Dialectical inquiry involves the following steps:

1. Identify a proposal and the information that was used to derive it.
2. State the underlying assumptions of the proposal.
3. Identify a counterplan (antithesis) that is believed to be feasible, politically viable, and generally credible. However, it rests on assumptions that are opposite to the original proposal.
4. Engage in a debate in which individuals favoring each plan provide their arguments and support.
5. Identify a synthesis which, hopefully, includes the best components of each alternative.

There are some potential downsides associated with dialectical inquiry. It can be quite time consuming and involve a good deal of training. Further, it may result in a series of compromises between the initial proposal and the counterplan. In cases where the original proposal was the best approach, this would be unfortunate.

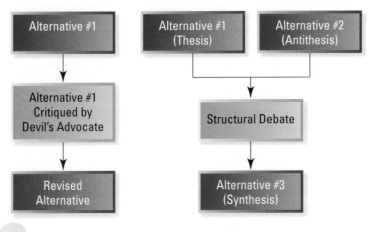

Exhibit 13.4 Two Conflict-Inducing Decision-Making Processes

Despite some possible limitations associated with these conflict-inducing decision-making techniques, they have many benefits. Both techniques force debate about underlying assumptions, data, and recommendations between subgroups. Such debate tends to prevent the uncritical acceptance of a plan that may seem to be satisfactory after a cursory analysis. The approach serves to tap the knowledge and perspectives of group members and continues until group members agree on both assumptions and recommended actions. Given that both approaches serve to use, rather than minimize or suppress, conflict, higher quality decisions should result. Exhibit 13.4 briefly summarizes these techniques.

Following the Analysis-Decision-Action Cycle in Case Analysis

In Chapter 1 we defined strategic management as the analysis, decisions, and actions that organizations undertake to create and sustain competitive advantages. It is no accident that we chose that sequence of words because it corresponds to the sequence of events that typically occurs in the strategic management process. In case analysis, as in the real world, this cycle of events can provide a useful framework. First, an analysis of the case in terms of the business environment and current events is needed. To make such an analysis, the case background must be considered. Next, based on that analysis, decisions must be made. This may involve formulating a strategy, choosing between difficult options, moving forward aggressively, or retreating from a bad situation. There are many possible decisions, depending on the case situation. Finally, action is required. Once decisions are made and plans are set, the action begins. The recommended action steps and the consequences of implementing these actions are the final stage.

Each of the previous 12 chapters of this book includes techniques and information that may be useful in a case analysis. However, not all of the issues presented will be important in every case. As noted earlier, one of the challenges of case analysis is to identify the most critical points and sort through material that may be ambiguous or unimportant.

In this section we draw on the material presented in each of the 12 chapters to show how it informs the case analysis process. The ideas are linked sequentially and in terms of an overarching strategic perspective. One of your jobs when conducting case analysis is to see how the parts of a case fit together and how the insights from the study of strategy can help you understand the case situation.

>LO6

How to use the strategic insights and material from each of the 12 previous chapters in the text to analyze issues posed by strategic management cases.

1. *Analyzing organizational goals and objectives.* A company's vision, mission, and objectives keep organization members focused on a common purpose. They also influence how an organization deploys its resources, relates to its stakeholders, and matches its short-term objectives with its long-term goals. The goals may even impact how a company formulates and implements strategies. When exploring issues of goals and objectives, you might ask:

   - Has the company developed short-term objectives that are inconsistent with its long-term mission? If so, how can management realign its vision, mission, and objectives?
   - Has the company considered all of its stakeholders equally in making critical decisions? If not, should the views of all stakeholders be treated the same or are some stakeholders more important than others?
   - Is the company being faced with an issue that conflicts with one of its long-standing policies? If so, how should it compare its existing policies to the potential new situation?

2. *Analyzing the external environment.* The business environment has two components. The general environment consists of demographic, sociocultural, political/legal, technological, economic, and global conditions. The competitive environment includes rivals, suppliers, customers, and other factors that may directly affect a company's success. Strategic managers must monitor the environment to identify opportunities and threats that may have an impact on performance. When investigating a firm's external environment, you might ask:

   - Does the company follow trends and events in the general environment? If not, how can these influences be made part of the company's strategic analysis process?
   - Is the company effectively scanning and monitoring the competitive environment? If so, how is it using the competitive intelligence it is gathering to enhance its competitive advantage?
   - Has the company correctly analyzed the impact of the competitive forces in its industry on profitability? If so, how can it improve its competitive position relative to these forces?

3. *Analyzing the internal environment.* A firm's internal environment consists of its resources and other value-adding capabilities. Value-chain analysis and a resource-based approach to analysis can be used to identify a company's strengths and weaknesses and determine how they are contributing to its competitive advantages. Evaluating firm performance can also help make meaningful comparisons with competitors. When researching a company's internal analysis, you might ask:

   - Does the company know how the various components of its value chain are adding value to the firm? If not, what internal analysis is needed to determine its strengths and weakness?
   - Has the company accurately analyzed the source and vitality of its resources? If so, is it deploying its resources in a way that contributes to competitive advantages?
   - Is the company's financial performance as good as or better than that of its close competitors? If so, has it balanced its financial success with the performance criteria of other stakeholders such as customers and employees?

4. *Assessing a firm's intellectual assets.* Human capital is a major resource in today's knowledge economy. As a result, attracting, developing, and retaining talented workers is a key strategic challenge. Other assets such as patents and trademarks are also critical. How companies leverage their intellectual assets through social networks and strategic alliances, and how technology is used to manage knowledge may be a major

influence on a firm's competitive advantage. When analyzing a firm's intellectual assets, you might ask:

- Does the company have underutilized human capital? If so, what steps are needed to develop and leverage its intellectual assets?
- Is the company missing opportunities to forge strategic alliances? If so, how can it use its social capital to network more effectively?
- Has the company developed knowledge-management systems that capture what it learns? If not, what technologies can it employ to retain new knowledge?

5. *Formulating business-level strategies.* Firms use the competitive strategies of differentiation, focus, and overall cost leadership as a basis for overcoming the five competitive forces and developing sustainable competitive advantages. Combinations of these strategies may work best in some competitive environments. Additionally, an industry's life cycle is an important contingency that may affect a company's choice of business-level strategies. When assessing business-level strategies, you might ask:

- Has the company chosen the correct competitive strategy given its industry environment and competitive situation? If not, how should it use its strengths and resources to improve its performance?
- Does the company use combination strategies effectively? If so, what capabilities can it cultivate to further enhance profitability?
- Is the company using a strategy that is appropriate for the industry life cycle in which it is competing? If not, how can it realign itself to match its efforts to the current stage of industry growth?

6. *Formulating corporate-level strategies.* Large firms often own and manage portfolios of businesses. Corporate strategies address methods for achieving synergies among these businesses. Related and unrelated diversification techniques are alternative approaches to deciding which business should be added to or removed from a portfolio. Companies can diversify by means of mergers, acquisitions, joint ventures, strategic alliances, and internal development. When analyzing corporate-level strategies, you might ask:

- Is the company competing in the right businesses given the opportunities and threats that are present in the environment? If not, how can it realign its diversification strategy to achieve competitive advantages?
- Is the corporation managing its portfolio of businesses in a way that creates synergies among the businesses? If so, what additional business should it consider adding to its portfolio?
- Are the motives of the top corporate executives who are pushing diversification strategies appropriate? If not, what action can be taken to curb their activities or align them with the best interests of all stakeholders?

7. *Formulating international-level strategies.* Foreign markets provide both opportunities and potential dangers for companies that want to expand globally. To decide which entry strategy is most appropriate, companies have to evaluate the trade-offs between two factors that firms face when entering foreign markets: cost reduction and local adaptation. To achieve competitive advantages, firms will typically choose one of three strategies: global, multidomestic, or transnational. When evaluating international-level strategies, you might ask:

- Is the company's entry into an international marketplace threatened by the actions of local competitors? If so, how can cultural differences be minimized to give the firm a better chance of succeeding?
- Has the company made the appropriate choices between cost reduction and local adaptation to foreign markets? If not, how can it adjust its strategy to achieve competitive advantages?

- Can the company improve its effectiveness by embracing one international strategy over another? If so, how should it choose between a global, multidomestic, or transnational strategy?

8. ***Formulating entrepreneurial strategies.*** New ventures add jobs and create new wealth. To do so, they must identify opportunities that will be viable in the marketplace as well as gather resources and assemble an entrepreneurial team to enact the opportunity. New entrants often evoke a strong competitive response from incumbent firms in a given marketplace. When examining the role of strategic thinking on the success of entrepreneurial ventures and the role of competitive dynamics, you might ask:
    - Is the company engaged in an ongoing process of opportunity recognition? If not, how can it enhance its ability to recognize opportunities?
    - Do the entrepreneurs who are launching new ventures have vision, dedication and drive, and a commitment to excellence? If so, how have these affected the performance and dedication of other employees involved in the venture?
    - Have strategic principles been used in the process of developing strategies to pursue the entrepreneurial opportunity? If not, how can the venture apply tools such as five-forces analysis and value-chain analysis to improve its competitive position and performance?

9. ***Achieving effective strategic control.*** Strategic controls enable a firm to implement strategies effectively. Informational controls involve comparing performance to stated goals and scanning, monitoring, and being responsive to the environment. Behavioral controls emerge from a company's culture, reward systems, and organizational boundaries. When assessing the impact of strategic controls on implementation, you might ask:
    - Is the company employing the appropriate informational control systems? If not, how can it implement a more interactive approach to enhance learning and minimize response times?
    - Does the company have a strong and effective culture? If not, what steps can it take to align its values and rewards system with its goals and objectives?
    - Has the company implemented control systems that match its strategies? If so, what additional steps can be taken to improve performance?

10. ***Creating effective organizational designs.*** Organizational designs that align with competitive strategies can enhance performance. As companies grow and change, their structures must also evolve to meet new demands. In today's economy, firm boundaries must be flexible and permeable to facilitate smoother interactions with external parties such as customers, suppliers, and alliance partners. New forms of organizing are becoming more common. When evaluating the role of organizational structure on strategy implementation, you might ask:
    - Has the company implemented organizational structures that are suited to the type of business it is in? If not, how can it alter the design in ways that enhance its competitiveness?
    - Is the company employing boundaryless organizational designs where appropriate? If so, how are senior managers maintaining control of lower-level employees?
    - Does the company use outsourcing to achieve the best possible results? If not, what criteria should it use to decide which functions can be outsourced?

11. ***Creating a learning organization and an ethical organization.*** Strong leadership is essential for achieving competitive advantages. Two leadership roles are especially important. The first is creating a learning organization by harnessing talent and encouraging the development of new knowledge. Second, leaders play a vital role in

motivating employees to excellence and inspiring ethical behavior. When exploring the impact of effective strategic leadership, you might ask:

- Do company leaders promote excellence as part of the overall culture? If so, how has this influenced the performance of the firm and the individuals in it?
- Is the company committed to being a learning organization? If not, what can it do to capitalize on the individual and collective talents of organizational members?
- Have company leaders exhibited an ethical attitude in their own behavior? If not, how has their behavior influenced the actions of other employees?

12. ***Fostering corporate entrepreneurship.*** Many firms continually seek new growth opportunities and avenues for strategic renewal. In some corporations, autonomous work units such as business incubators and new-venture groups are used to focus corporate venturing activities. In other corporate settings, product champions and other firm members provide companies with the impetus to expand into new areas. When investigating the impact of entrepreneurship on strategic effectiveness, you might ask:

- Has the company resolved the dilemmas associated with managing innovation? If so, is it effectively defining and pacing its innovation efforts?
- Has the company developed autonomous work units that have the freedom to bring forth new product ideas? If so, has it used product champions to implement new venture initiatives?
- Does the company have an entrepreneurial orientation? If not, what can it do to encourage entrepreneurial attitudes in the strategic behavior of its organizational members?

Summary

Strategic management case analysis provides an effective method of learning how companies analyze problems, make decisions, and resolve challenges. Strategic cases include detailed accounts of actual business situations. The purpose of analyzing such cases is to gain exposure to a wide variety of organizational and managerial situations. By putting yourself in the place of a strategic decision maker, you can gain an appreciation of the difficulty and complexity of many strategic situations. In the process you can learn how to ask good strategic questions and enhance your analytical skills. Presenting case analyses can also help develop oral and written communication skills.

In this chapter we have discussed the importance of strategic case analysis and described the five steps involved in conducting a case analysis: becoming familiar with the material, identifying problems, analyzing strategic issues, proposing alternative solutions, and making recommendations. We have also discussed how to get the most from case analysis. Finally, we have described how the case analysis process follows the analysis-decision-action cycle of strategic management and outlined issues and questions that are associated with each of the previous 12 chapters of the text.

Key Terms

case analysis 449

financial ratio analysis 455

References

1. The material in this chapter is based on several sources, including Barnes, L. A., Nelson, A. J., & Christensen, C. R. 1994. *Teaching and the case method: Text, cases and readings.* Boston: Harvard Business School Press: Guth, W. D. 1985. Central concepts of business unit and corporate strategy. In W. D. Guth (Ed.). *Handbook of business strategy:* 1–9. Boston: Warren, Gorham & Lamont; Lundberg,

C. C., & Enz, C. 1993. A framework for student case preparation. *Case Research Journal,* 13 (Summer): 129–140; and Ronstadt, R. 1980. *The art of case analysis: A guide to the diagnosis of business situations.* Dover, MA: Lord Publishing.

2. Edge, A. G., & Coleman, D. R. 1986. *The guide to case analysis and reporting* (3rd ed.). Honolulu, HI: System Logistics.

3. Morris, E. 1987. Vision and strategy: A focus for the future. *Journal of Business Strategy* 8: 51–58.

4. This section is based on Lundberg & Enz, op. cit., and Ronstadt, op. cit.

5. The importance of problem definition was emphasized in Mintzberg, H., Raisinghani, D., & Theoret, A. 1976. The structure of "unstructured" decision processes. *Administrative Science Quarterly,* 21(2): 246–275.

6. Drucker, P. F. 1994. The theory of the business. *Harvard Business Review,* 72(5): 95–104.

7. This section draws on Edge & Coleman, op. cit.

8. Irving Janis is credited with coining the term *groupthink,* and he applied it primarily to fiascos in government (such as the Bay of Pigs incident in 1961). Refer to Janis, I. L. 1982. *Victims of groupthink* (2nd ed.). Boston: Houghton Mifflin.

9. Much of our discussion is based upon Finkelstein, S., & Mooney, A. C. 2003. Not the usual suspects: How to use board process to make boards better. *Academy of Management Executive,* 17(2): 101–113; Schweiger, D. M., Sandberg, W. R., & Rechner, P. L. 1989. Experiential effects of dialectical inquiry, devil's advocacy, and consensus approaches to strategic decision making. *Academy of Management Journal,* 32(4): 745–772; and Aldag, R. J., & Stearns, T. M. 1987. *Management.* Cincinnati: South-Western Publishing.

10. Finkelstein and Mooney, op. cit.

Appendix 1 to Chapter 13

Financial Ratio Analysis

Standard Financial Statements

One obvious thing we might want to do with a company's financial statements is to compare them to those of other, similar companies. We would immediately have a problem, however. It's almost impossible to directly compare the financial statements for two companies because of differences in size.

For example, Oracle and IBM are obviously serious rivals in the computer software market, but IBM is much larger (in terms of assets), so it is difficult to compare them directly. For that matter, it's difficult to even compare financial statements from different points in time for the same company if the company's size has changed. The size problem is compounded if we try to compare IBM and, say, SAP (of Germany). If SAP's financial statements are denominated in German marks, then we have a size *and* a currency difference.

To start making comparisons, one obvious thing we might try to do is to somehow standardize the financial statements. One very common and useful way of doing this is to work with percentages instead of total dollars. The resulting financial statements are called *common-size statements.* We consider these next.

Common-Size Balance Sheets

For easy reference, Prufrock Corporation's 2006 and 2007 balance sheets are provided in Exhibit 13A.1. Using these, we construct common-size balance sheets by expressing each item as a percentage of total assets. Prufrock's 2006 and 2007 common-size balance sheets are shown in Exhibit 13A.2.

Notice that some of the totals don't check exactly because of rounding errors. Also notice that the total change has to be zero since the beginning and ending numbers must add up to 100 percent.

In this form, financial statements are relatively easy to read and compare. For example, just looking at the two balance sheets for Prufrock, we see that current assets were 19.7 percent of total assets

Source: Adapted from Rows, S. A., Westerfield, R. W., & Jordan, B. D. 1999. *Essentials of Corporate Finance* (2nd ed.). chap. 3. New York: McGraw-Hill, 1999.

	2006	2007
Assets		
Current assets		
Cash	$ 84	$ 98
Accounts receivable	165	188
Inventory	393	422
Total	$ 642	$ 708
Fixed assets		
Net plant and equipment	$2,731	$2,880
Total assets	$3,373	$3,588
Liabilities and Owners' Equity		
Current liabilities		
Accounts payable	$ 312	$ 344
Notes payable	231	196
Total	$ 543	$ 540
Long-term debt	$ 531	$ 457
Owners' equity		
Common stock and paid-in surplus	$ 500	$ 550
Retained earnings	1,799	2,041
Total	$2,299	$2,591
Total liabilities and owners' equity	$3,373	$3,588

Exhibit 13A.1

Prufrock Corporation
Balance Sheets as of December 31, 2006 and 2007 ($ in millions)

in 2006, up from 19.1 percent in 2007. Current liabilities declined from 16.0 percent to 15.1 percent of total liabilities and equity over that same time. Similarly, total equity rose from 68.1 percent of total liabilities and equity to 72.2 percent.

Overall, Prufrock's liquidity, as measured by current assets compared to current liabilities, increased over the year. Simultaneously, Prufrock's indebtedness diminished as a percentage of total assets. We might be tempted to conclude that the balance sheet has grown "stronger."

Common-Size Income Statements

A useful way of standardizing the income statement, shown in Exhibit 13A.3, is to express each item as a percentage of total sales, as illustrated for Prufrock in Exhibit 13A.4.

This income statement tells us what happens to each dollar in sales. For Prufrock, interest expense eats up $.061 out of every sales dollar and taxes take another $.081. When all is said and done, $.157 of each dollar flows through to the bottom line (net income), and that amount is split into $.105 retained in the business and $.052 paid out in dividends.

These percentages are very useful in comparisons. For example, a relevant figure is the cost percentage. For Prufrock, $.582 of each $1.00 in sales goes to pay for goods sold. It would be interesting to compute the same percentage for Prufrock's main competitors to see how Prufrock stacks up in terms of cost control.

Ratio Analysis

Another way of avoiding the problems involved in comparing companies of different sizes is to calculate and compare *financial ratios*. Such ratios are ways of comparing and investigating the relationships

Exhibit 13A.2

Prufrock Corporation

Common-Size Balance Sheets as of December 31, 2006 and 2007 (%)

	2006	2007	Change
Assets			
Current assets			
Cash	2.5%	2.7%	+ .2%
Accounts receivable	4.9	5.2	+ .3
Inventory	11.7	11.8	+ .1
Total	19.1	19.7	+ .6
Fixed assets			
Net plant and equipment	80.9	80.3	− .6
Total assets	100.0%	100.0%	.0%
Liabilities and Owners' Equity			
Current liabilities			
Accounts payable	9.2%	9.6%	+ .4%
Notes payable	6.8	5.5	−1.3
Total	16.0	15.1	− .9
Long-term debt	15.7	12.7	−3.0
Owners' equity			
Common stock and paid-in surplus	14.8	15.3	+ .5
Retained earnings	53.3	56.9	+3.6
Total	68.1	72.2	+4.1
Total liabilities and owners' equities	100.0%	100.0%	.0%

Note: Numbers may not add up to 100.0% due to rounding.

Exhibit 13A.3

Prufrock Corporation

2007 Income Statement ($ in millions)

Sales		$2,311
Cost of goods sold		1,344
Depreciation		276
Earnings before interest and taxes		$ 691
Interest paid		141
Taxable income		$ 550
Taxes (34%)		187
Net income		$ 363
Dividends	$121	
Addition to retained earnings	242	

between different pieces of financial information. We cover some of the more common ratios next, but there are many others that we don't touch on.

One problem with ratios is that different people and different sources frequently don't compute them in exactly the same way, and this leads to much confusion. The specific definitions we use here

Sales	100.0%
Cost of goods sold	58.2
Depreciation	11.9
Earnings before interest and taxes	29.9
Interest paid	6.1
Taxable income	23.8
Taxes (34%)	8.1
Net income	15.7%
Dividends	5.2%
Addition to retained earnings	10.5

may or may not be the same as others you have seen or will see elsewhere. If you ever use ratios as a tool for analysis, you should be careful to document how you calculate each one, and, if you are comparing your numbers to those of another source, be sure you know how its numbers are computed.

For each of the ratios we discuss, several questions come to mind:

1. How is it computed?
2. What is it intended to measure, and why might we be interested?
3. What is the unit of measurement?
4. What might a high or low value be telling us? How might such values be misleading?
5. How could this measure be improved?

Financial ratios are traditionally grouped into the following categories:

1. Short-term solvency, or liquidity, ratios.
2. Long-term solvency, or financial leverage, ratios.
3. Asset management, or turnover, ratios.
4. Profitability ratios.
5. Market value ratios.

We will consider each of these in turn. In calculating these numbers for Prufrock, we will use the ending balance sheet (2007) figures unless we explicitly say otherwise. The numbers for the various ratios come from the income statement and the balance sheet.

Short-Term Solvency, or Liquidity, Measures

As the name suggests, short-term solvency ratios as a group are intended to provide information about a firm's liquidity, and these ratios are sometimes called *liquidity measures.* The primary concern is the firm's ability to pay its bills over the short run without undue stress. Consequently, these ratios focus on current assets and current liabilities.

For obvious reasons, liquidity ratios are particularly interesting to short-term creditors. Since financial managers are constantly working with banks and other short-term lenders, an understanding of these ratios is essential.

One advantage of looking at current assets and liabilities is that their book values and market values are likely to be similar. Often (though not always), these assets and liabilities just don't live long enough for the two to get seriously out of step. On the other hand, like any type of near cash, current assets and liabilities can and do change fairly rapidly, so today's amounts may not be a reliable guide to the future.

Current Ratio   One of the best-known and most widely used ratios is the *current ratio.* As you might guess, the current ratio is defined as:

$$\text{Current ratio} = \frac{\text{Current assets}}{\text{Current liabilities}}$$

For Prufrock, the 2007 current ratio is:

$$\text{Current ratio} = \frac{\$708}{\$540} = 1.31 \text{ times}$$

Because current assets and liabilities are, in principle, converted to cash over the following 12 months, the current ratio is a measure of short-term liquidity. The unit of measurement is either dollars or times. So, we could say Prufrock has $1.31 in current assets for every $1 in current liabilities, or we could say Prufrock has its current liabilities covered 1.31 times over.

To a creditor, particularly a short-term creditor such as a supplier, the higher the current ratio, the better. To the firm, a high current ratio indicates liquidity, but it also may indicate an inefficient use of cash and other short-term assets. Absent some extraordinary circumstances, we would expect to see a current ratio of at least 1, because a current ratio of less than 1 would mean that net working capital (current assets less current liabilities) is negative. This would be unusual in a healthy firm, at least for most types of businesses.

The current ratio, like any ratio, is affected by various types of transactions. For example, suppose the firm borrows over the long term to raise money. The short-run effect would be an increase in cash from the issue proceeds and an increase in long-term debt. Current liabilities would not be affected, so the current ratio would rise.

Finally, note that an apparently low current ratio may not be a bad sign for a company with a large reserve of untapped borrowing power.

Quick (or Acid-Test) Ratio   Inventory is often the least liquid current asset. It's also the one for which the book values are least reliable as measures of market value, since the quality of the inventory isn't considered. Some of the inventory may later turn out to be damaged, obsolete, or lost.

More to the point, relatively large inventories are often a sign of short-term trouble. The firm may have overestimated sales and overbought or overproduced as a result. In this case, the firm may have a substantial portion of its liquidity tied up in slow-moving inventory.

To further evaluate liquidity, the *quick,* or *acid-test, ratio* is computed just like the current ratio, except inventory is omitted:

$$\text{Quick ratio} = \frac{\text{Current assets} - \text{Inventory}}{\text{Current liabilities}}$$

Notice that using cash to buy inventory does not affect the current ratio, but it reduces the quick ratio. Again, the idea is that inventory is relatively illiquid compared to cash.

For Prufrock, this ratio in 2007 was:

$$\text{Quick ratio} = \frac{\$708 - 422}{\$540} = .53 \text{ times}$$

The quick ratio here tells a somewhat different story than the current ratio, because inventory accounts for more than half of Prufrock's current assets. To exaggerate the point, if this inventory consisted of, say, unsold nuclear power plants, then this would be a cause for concern.

Cash Ratio   A very short-term creditor might be interested in the *cash ratio:*

$$\text{Cash ratio} = \frac{\text{Cash}}{\text{Current liabilities}}$$

You can verify that this works out to be .18 times for Prufrock.

Long-Term Solvency Measures

Long-term solvency ratios are intended to address the firm's long-run ability to meet its obligations, or, more generally, its financial leverage. These ratios are sometimes called *financial leverage ratios* or just *leverage ratios.* We consider three commonly used measures and some variations.

Total Debt Ratio   The *total debt ratio* takes into account all debts of all maturities to all creditors. It can be defined in several ways, the easiest of which is:

$$\text{Total debt ratio} = \frac{\text{Total assets} - \text{Total equity}}{\text{Total assets}}$$

$$= \frac{\$3,588 - 2,591}{\$3,588} = .28 \text{ times}$$

In this case, an analyst might say that Prufrock uses 28 percent debt.[1] Whether this is high or low or whether it even makes any difference depends on whether or not capital structure matters.

Prufrock has $.28 in debt for every $1 in assets. Therefore, there is $.72 in equity ($1 − .28) for every $.28 in debt. With this in mind, we can define two useful variations on the total debt ratio, the *debt-equity ratio* and the *equity multiplier:*

$$\text{Debt-equity ratio} = \text{Total debt/Total equity}$$

$$= \$.28/\$.72 = .39 \text{ times}$$

$$\text{Equity multiplier} = \text{Total assets/Total equity}$$

$$= \$1/\$.72 = 1.39 \text{ times}$$

The fact that the equity multiplier is 1 plus the debt-equity ratio is not a coincidence:

$$\text{Equity multiplier} = \text{Total assets/Total equity} = \$1/\$.72 = 1.39$$

$$= (\text{Total equity} + \text{Total debt})/\text{Total equity}$$

$$= 1 + \text{Debt-equity ratio} = 1.39 \text{ times}$$

The thing to notice here is that given any one of these three ratios, you can immediately calculate the other two, so they all say exactly the same thing.

Times Interest Earned   Another common measure of long-term solvency is the *times interest earned* (TIE) *ratio.* Once again, there are several possible (and common) definitions, but we'll stick with the most traditional:

$$\text{Times interest earned ratio} = \frac{\text{EBIT}}{\text{Interest}}$$

$$= \frac{\$691}{\$141} = 4.9 \text{ times}$$

As the name suggests, this ratio measures how well a company has its interest obligations covered, and it is often called the interest coverage ratio. For Prufrock, the interest bill is covered 4.9 times over.

Cash Coverage   A problem with the TIE ratio is that it is based on earnings before interest and taxes (EBIT), which is not really a measure of cash available to pay interest. The reason is that depreciation, a noncash expense, has been deducted. Since interest is most definitely a cash outflow (to creditors), one way to define the *cash coverage ratio* is:

$$\text{Cash coverage ratio} = \frac{\text{EBIT} + \text{Depreciation}}{\text{Interest}}$$

$$= \frac{\$691 + 276}{\$141} = \frac{\$967}{\$141} = 6.9 \text{ times}$$

The numerator here, EBIT plus depreciation, is often abbreviated EBDIT (earnings before depreciation, interest, and taxes). It is a basic measure of the firm's ability to generate cash from operations, and it is frequently used as a measure of cash flow available to meet financial obligations.

[1]Total equity here includes preferred stock, if there is any. An equivalent numerator in this ratio would be (Current liabilities + Long-term debt).

Asset Management, or Turnover, Measures

We next turn our attention to the efficiency with which Prufrock uses its assets. The measures in this section are sometimes called *asset utilization ratios.* The specific ratios we discuss can all be interpreted as measures of turnover. What they are intended to describe is how efficiently, or intensively, a firm uses its assets to generate sales. We first look at two important current assets: inventory and receivables.

Inventory Turnover and Days' Sales in Inventory   During the year, Prufrock had a cost of goods sold of $1,344. Inventory at the end of the year was $422. With these numbers, *inventory turnover* can be calculated as:

$$\text{Inventory turnover} = \frac{\text{Cost of goods sold}}{\text{Inventory}}$$

$$= \frac{\$1,344}{\$422} = 3.2 \text{ times}$$

In a sense, we sold off, or turned over, the entire inventory 3.2 times. As long as we are not running out of stock and thereby forgoing sales, the higher this ratio is, the more efficiently we are managing inventory.

If we know that we turned our inventory over 3.2 times during the year, then we can immediately figure out how long it took us to turn it over on average. The result is the average *days' sales in inventory:*

$$\text{Days's sales in inventory} = \frac{365 \text{ days}}{\text{Inventory turnover}}$$

$$= \frac{365}{3.2} = 114 \text{ days}$$

This tells us that, on average, inventory sits 114 days before it is sold. Alternatively, assuming we used the most recent inventory and cost figures, it will take about 114 days to work off our current inventory.

For example, we frequently hear things like "Majestic Motors has a 60 days' supply of cars." This means that, at current daily sales, it would take 60 days to deplete the available inventory. We could also say that Majestic has 60 days of sales in inventory.

Receivables Turnover and Days' Sales in Receivables   Our inventory measures give some indication of how fast we can sell products. We now look at how fast we collect on those sales. The *receivables turnover* is defined in the same way as inventory turnover:

$$\text{Receivables turnover} = \frac{\text{Sales}}{\text{Accounts receivable}}$$

$$= \frac{\$2,311}{\$188} = 12.3 \text{ times}$$

Loosely speaking, we collected our outstanding credit accounts and reloaned the money 12.3 times during the year.[2]

This ratio makes more sense if we convert it to days, so the *days' sales in receivables* is:

$$\text{Days' sales in receivables} = \frac{365 \text{ days}}{\text{Receivables turnover}}$$

$$= \frac{365}{12.3} = 30 \text{ days}$$

Therefore, on average, we collect on our credit sales in 30 days. For obvious reasons, this ratio is very frequently called the *average collection period* (ACP).

Also note that if we are using the most recent figures, we can also say that we have 30 days' worth of sales currently uncollected.

---

[2]Here we have implicitly assumed that all sales are credit sales. If they were not, then we would simply use total credit sales in these calculations, not total sales.

Total Asset Turnover   Moving away from specific accounts like inventory or receivables, we can consider an important "big picture" ratio, the *total asset turnover ratio*. As the name suggests, total asset turnover is:

$$\text{Total asset turnover} = \frac{\text{Sales}}{\text{Total assets}}$$

$$= \frac{\$2,311}{\$3,588} = .64 \text{ times}$$

In other words, for every dollar in assets, we generated $.64 in sales.

A closely related ratio, the *capital intensity ratio,* is simply the reciprocal of (i.e., 1 divided by) total asset turnover. It can be interpreted as the dollar investment in assets needed to generate $1 in sales. High values correspond to capital intensive industries (e.g., public utilities). For Prufrock, total asset turnover is .64, so, if we flip this over, we get that capital intensity is $1/.64 = $1.56. That is, it takes Prufrock $1.56 in assets to create $1 in sales.

Profitability Measures

The three measures we discuss in this section are probably the best known and most widely used of all financial ratios. In one form or another, they are intended to measure how efficiently the firm uses its assets and how efficiently the firm manages its operations. The focus in this group is on the bottom line, net income.

Profit Margin   Companies pay a great deal of attention to their *profit margin:*

$$\text{Profit margin} = \frac{\text{Net income}}{\text{Sales}}$$

$$= \frac{\$363}{\$2,311} = 15.7\%$$

This tells us that Prufrock, in an accounting sense, generates a little less than 16 cents in profit for every dollar in sales.

All other things being equal, a relatively high profit margin is obviously desirable. This situation corresponds to low expense ratios relative to sales. However, we hasten to add that other things are often not equal.

For example, lowering our sales price will usually increase unit volume, but will normally cause profit margins to shrink. Total profit (or, more importantly, operating cash flow) may go up or down; so the fact that margins are smaller isn't necessarily bad. After all, isn't it possible that, as the saying goes, "Our prices are so low that we lose money on everything we sell, but we make it up in volume!"[3]

Return on Assets   *Return on assets* (ROA) is a measure of profit per dollar of assets. It can be defined several ways, but the most common is:

$$\text{Return on assets} = \frac{\text{Net income}}{\text{Total assets}}$$

$$= \frac{\$363}{\$3,588} = 10.12\%$$

Return on Equity   *Return on equity* (ROE) is a measure of how the stockholders fared during the year. Since benefiting shareholders is our goal, ROE is, in an accounting sense, the true bottom-line measure of performance. ROE is usually measured as:

$$\text{Return on equity} = \frac{\text{Net income}}{\text{Total equity}}$$

$$= \frac{\$363}{\$2,591} = 14\%$$

[3]No, it's not; margins can be small, but they do need to be positive!

For every dollar in equity, therefore, Prufrock generated 14 cents in profit, but, again, this is only correct in accounting terms.

Because ROA and ROE are such commonly cited numbers, we stress that it is important to remember they are accounting rates of return. For this reason, these measures should properly be called *return on book assets* and *return on book equity*. In addition, ROE is sometimes called *return on net worth*. Whatever it's called, it would be inappropriate to compare the results to, for example, an interest rate observed in the financial markets.

The fact that ROE exceeds ROA reflects Prufrock's use of financial leverage. We will examine the relationship between these two measures in more detail below.

Market Value Measures

Our final group of measures is based, in part, on information not necessarily contained in financial statements—the market price per share of the stock. Obviously, these measures can only be calculated directly for publicly traded companies.

We assume that Prufrock has 33 million shares outstanding and the stock sold for $88 per share at the end of the year. If we recall that Prufrock's net income was $363 million, then we can calculate that its earnings per share were:

$$EPS = \frac{\text{Net income}}{\text{Shares outstanding}} = \frac{\$363}{33} = \$11$$

Price-Earnings Ratio   The first of our market value measures, the *price-earnings,* or PE, *ratio* (or multiple), is defined as:

$$PE \text{ ratio} = \frac{\text{Price per share}}{\text{Earnings per share}}$$

$$= \frac{\$85}{\$11} = 8 \text{ times}$$

In the vernacular, we would say that Prufrock shares sell for eight times earnings, or we might say that Prufrock shares have, or "carry," a PE multiple of 8.

Since the PE ratio measures how much investors are willing to pay per dollar of current earnings, higher PEs are often taken to mean that the firm has significant prospects for future growth. Of course, if a firm had no or almost no earnings, its PE would probably be quite large; so, as always, be careful when interpreting this ratio.

Market-to-Book Ratio   A second commonly quoted measure is the *market-to-book ratio:*

$$\text{Market-to-book ratio} = \frac{\text{Market value per share}}{\text{Book value per share}}$$

$$= \frac{\$88}{(\$2,591/33)} = \frac{\$88}{\$78.5} = 1.12 \text{ times}$$

Notice that book value per share is total equity (not just common stock) divided by the number of shares outstanding.

Since book value per share is an accounting number, it reflects historical costs. In a loose sense, the market-to-book ratio therefore compares the market value of the firm's investments to their cost. A value less than 1 could mean that the firm has not been successful overall in creating value for its stockholders.

Conclusion

This completes our definition of some common ratios. Exhibit 13A.5 summarizes the ratios we've discussed.

I. Short-term solvency, or liquidity, ratios

$$\text{Current ratio} = \frac{\text{Current assets}}{\text{Current liabilities}}$$

$$\text{Quick ratio} = \frac{\text{Current assets} - \text{Inventory}}{\text{Current liabilities}}$$

$$\text{Cash ratio} = \frac{\text{Cash}}{\text{Current liabilities}}$$

II. Long-term solvency, or financial leverage, ratios

$$\text{Total debt ratio} = \frac{\text{Total assets} - \text{Total equity}}{\text{Total assets}}$$

$$\text{Debt-equity ratio} = \text{Total debt/Total equity}$$

$$\text{Equity multiplier} = \text{Total assets/Total equity}$$

$$\text{Times interest earned ratio} = \frac{\text{EBIT}}{\text{Interest}}$$

$$\text{Cash coverage ratio} = \frac{\text{EBIT} + \text{Depreciation}}{\text{Interest}}$$

III. Asset utilization, or turnover, ratios

$$\text{Inventory turnover} = \frac{\text{Cost of goods sold}}{\text{Inventory}}$$

$$\text{Days' sales in inventory} = \frac{365 \text{ days}}{\text{Inventory turnover}}$$

$$\text{Receivables turnover} = \frac{\text{Sales}}{\text{Accounts receivable}}$$

$$\text{Days' sales in receivables} = \frac{365 \text{ days}}{\text{Receivables turnover}}$$

$$\text{Total asset turnover} = \frac{\text{Sales}}{\text{Total assets}}$$

$$\text{Capital intensity} = \frac{\text{Total assets}}{\text{Sales}}$$

IV. Profitability ratios

$$\text{Profit margin} = \frac{\text{Net income}}{\text{Sales}}$$

$$\text{Return on assets (ROA)} = \frac{\text{Net income}}{\text{Total assets}}$$

$$\text{Return on equity (ROE)} = \frac{\text{Net income}}{\text{Total equity}}$$

$$\text{ROE} = \frac{\text{Net income}}{\text{Sales}} \times \frac{\text{Sales}}{\text{Assets}} \times \frac{\text{Assets}}{\text{Equity}}$$

V. Market value ratios

$$\text{Price-earnings ratio} = \frac{\text{Price per share}}{\text{Earnings per share}}$$

$$\text{Market-to-book ratio} = \frac{\text{Market value per share}}{\text{Book value per share}}$$

Exhibit 13A.5 A Summary of Five Types of Financial Ratios

Appendix 2 to Chapter 13

Sources of Company and Industry Information*

For business executives to make the best decisions when developing corporate and/or business strategies, it is critical for them to be knowledgeable about their competitors and about the industries in which they compete. The process used by corporations to learn as much as possible about competitors is called "competitive intelligence." This appendix provides an overview of important and widely available sources of information that may be useful in conducting basic competitive intelligence. Much information of this nature is available in libraries, article databases, business reference books, and on Web sites. This list provides a variety of recommendations. Ask a librarian for assistance because library collections and resources vary.

The information sources are organized into 10 categories: Competitive Intelligence; Public or Private, Subsidiary or Division, U.S. or Foreign?; Annual Report Collections—Public Companies; Guides and Tutorials; SEC Filings/EDGAR—Company Disclosure Reports; Company Rankings; Business Metasites and Portals; Strategic and Competitive Analysis—Information Sources; Sources for Industry Research and Analysis; and Search Engines.

Competitive Intelligence

Students and other researchers who want to learn more about the value and process of competitive intelligence should see four recent books on this subject.

*This information was compiled by Ruthie Brock and Carol Byrne, Business Librarians at The University of Texas at Arlington. We greatly appreciate their valuable contribution.

Craig Fleisher and Babette Bensoussan. *Business and Competitive Analysis: Effective Application of New and Classic Methods.* Philadelphia, PA: Wharton School, 2007.

Leonard M. Fuld. *The Secret Language of Competitive Intelligence.* New York: Crown Business, 2006.

David L. Blenkhorn and Craig S. Fleisher, eds. *Competitive Intelligence and Global Business.* Westport, CT: Praeger Publishers, 2005.

Benjamin Gilad. *Early Warning: Using Competitive Intelligence to Anticipate Market Shifts, Control Risk, and Create Powerful Strategies.* New York: American Management Association, 2004.

Public or Private, Subsidiary or Division, U.S. or Foreign?

Companies traded on stock exchanges in the United States are required to file a variety of reports that disclose information about the company. This begins the process that produces a wealth of data on public companies and at the same time distinguishes them from private companies, which often lack available data. Similarly, financial data of subsidiaries and divisions are typically filed in a consolidated financial statement by the parent company instead of being treated independently, thus limiting the kind of data available on them. On the other hand, foreign companies that trade on U.S. stock exchanges are required to file 20F reports, similar to the 10-K for U.S. companies—the most comprehensive of the required reports—although the number of foreign companies doing so is relatively small.

Corporate Directory of U.S. Public Companies. San Mateo, CA: Walker's Research, LLC, 2007.
The Corporate Directory provides company profiles of more than 9,000 publicly traded companies in the United States, including foreign companies trading on the U.S. exchanges (American depository receipts or ADRs). Some libraries may subscribe to an alternative online version at http://www.walkersresearch.com.

Corporate Affiliations. New Providence, NJ: A LexisNexis Group, 2006.
This directory features brief profiles of major U.S. and foreign corporations, both public and private, as well as their subsidiaries, divisions, and affiliates. The directory also indicates hierarchy of corporate relationships. An online version of the directory allows retrieval of a list of companies that meet specific criteria. Results can be downloaded to a spreadsheet. The online version requires a subscription.

ReferenceUSA. Omaha, NE: infoUSA, 2007
ReferenceUSA is an online directory of more than 14 million businesses located in the United States. One of its unique features is that it includes public and private companies, both large and small. Also, results can be analyzed using the data summary feature, which allows for a snapshot of how the industry breaks down by size, geographic location, etc. Library subscriptions may vary.

Ward's Business Directory of U.S. Private and Public Companies. Detroit, MI: Thomson Gale, 2007. 8 volumes.
Ward's Business Directory lists brief profiles on more than 110,000 public and private companies and indicates whether they are public or private and a subsidiary or division. Two volumes of the set are arranged using the Standard Industrial Classifications (SIC) and the North American Industry Classification System (NAICS) and feature company rankings within industries.

Annual Report Collections—Public Companies

Most companies have their Annual Report to Shareholders and other financial reports available on their corporate Web site. A few "aggregators" also conveniently provide an accumulation of links to many reports of U.S. and international corporations or include a PDF document as part of their database.

AnnualReports.com. IR Solutions. Weston, FL.
This Web site contains annual reports in HTML or PDF format. Reports can be retrieved by company name, ticker symbol, exchange, industry, or sector.
http://www.annualreports.com

Company Annual Reports Online (CAROL). Carol Ltd. London, UK.
This Web site is based in the United Kingdom, so many reports are European. Links are also provided for companies in Asia and the United States. A pull-down menu allows selection of companies within an industry. Access is free, but registration is required.
http://www.carol.co.uk/

Public Register's Online Annual Report Service. Baytact Corp. Woodstock Valley, CT.
Visitors to this Web site may choose from more than 4,500 company annual reports and 10-K filings to view online or order a paper copy. Access is free, but registration is required.
www.annualreportservice.com/

Mergent Online. Mergent, Inc. New York, NY.
Mergent Online provides company financial data for public companies headquartered in the United States, as well as those headquartered in other countries, including a large collection of corporate annual reports in PDF format. For industry ratios, Mergent Online offers an advanced search option. Industry reports are available as a subscription add-on. Library subscriptions to Mergent Online may vary.

Guides and Tutorials

Researching Companies Online. Debbie Flanagan. Fort Lauderdale, FL.
This site provides a step-by-step process for finding free company & industry information on the Web.
www.learnwebskills.com/company/

Annual Reports and Financial Statements: An Introduction. IBM. Armonk, NY.
These educational guides, located on IBM's Web site, provide basic information on how to read financial statements and other information in annual reports.
http://www.ibm.com/investor/tools/annualreportsAnatomy.phtml
http://www.ibm.com/investor/tools/financials.phtml

EDGAR Full-Text Search Frequently Asked Questions (FAQ). U.S. Securities and Exchange Commission. Washington D.C.
The capability to search full-text SEC filings (popularly known as EDGAR filings) was vastly improved when the SEC launched its new search form in late 2006. Features are explained at the FAQ page.
http://www.sec.gov/edgar/searchedgar/edgarfulltextfaq.htm

Locating Company Information. Tutorial. William and Joan Schreyer Business Library. Penn State University. University Park, PA.
Created by librarians at Penn State, this outstanding tutorial provides suggestions for online and print resources for company information. Click on "how to" links for each item to view a brief instruction vignette.
http://www.libraries.psu.edu/instruction/business/information/companyi.htm Lo

Locating Industry Information. Tutorial. William and Joan Schreyer Business Library. Penn State University. University Park, PA.
Created by librarians at Penn State, this outstanding tutorial provides suggestions for online and print resources for industry information. Click on "how to" links for each item to view a brief instruction vignette.
http://www.libraries.psu.edu/instruction/business/information/industryi.htm

Ten Steps to Industry Intelligence. Industry Tutorial. George A. Smathers Libraries. University of Florida. Gainesville, FL
A step by step approach is provided for finding information about industries, with embedded links to recommended sources.
http://web.uflib.ufl.edu/cm/business/tutors/indtutor.htm

SEC Filings/EDGAR—Company Disclosure Reports

SEC Filings are the various reports that publicly traded companies must file with the Securities Exchange Commission to disclose information about their corporation. These are often referred to as "EDGAR" filings, an acronym for the Electronic Data Gathering, Analysis and Retrieval System. Some Web sites and commercial databases improve access to these reports by offering additional retrieval features not available on the official (www.sec.gov) Web site.

EDGAR Database Full-Text Search. U.S. Securities and Exchange Commission (SEC). Washington D.C.
The 10-K reports, and other corporate documents, are made available in the EDGAR database within 24 hours after being filed. Annual reports, on the other hand, are typically sent directly to

shareholders and are not required as part of EDGAR by the SEC, although some companies voluntarily include them. Both 10-Ks and shareholder's annual reports are considered basic sources of company research. In late 2006, the SEC launched their new and improved search interface for full-text searching of the content and exhibits of EDGAR SEC filings. The advanced search can be used to locate "hard to find" information within documents filed by corporations and their competitors. Searches for specific types of reports or certain industries can also be performed. http://searchwww.sec.gov/EDGARFSClient/jsp/EDGAR_MainAccess.jsp

EdgarScan—An Interface to the SEC EDGAR Database. PricewaterhouseCoopers. New York, NY. Using filings from the SEC's servers, EdgarScan's intelligent interface parses the data automatically into a common format that is comparable across companies. A small Java applet called the "Benchmarking Assistant" performs graphical financial benchmarking interactively. Extracted financial data from the 10-K includes ratios with links to indicate where the data were derived and how it was computed. Tables showing company comparisons can be downloaded as Excel charts. http://edgarscan.pwcglobal.com/servlets/edgarscan

LexisNexis Academic—SEC Filings & Reports. LexisNexis. Bethesda, MD. EDGAR filings and reports are available through the "Business" option of LexisNexis Academic. These reports and filings can be retrieved by company name, industry code (SIC), or ticker symbol for a particular time period or by a specific report. Proxy, prospectus and registration filings are also available.

Mergent Online—EDGAR. Mergent, Inc. New York, NY. From the "EDGAR Search" tab within Mergent Online, EDGAR SEC filings and reports can be searched by company name or ticker symbol, filing date range and file type (10-K, 8-K, ARS). The reports are available in HTML or Word format. Using the "Find in Page" option from the browser provides the capability of jumping to specific sections of an SEC report.

Company Rankings

Fortune 500. Time Inc. New York, NY. The Fortune 500 list and other company rankings are published in the printed edition of *Fortune* magazine, and are also available online. http://money.cnn.com/magazines/fortune/fortune500/index.html

Hoover's Handbook of American Business. Austin, TX: Hoovers, Inc., 2007. This two-volume set gives a company overview, a list of competitors, and basic financial information for large U.S. companies. A special feature is a section called "The List Lovers' Companion," which includes a variety of lists with company rankings, some that include companies listed in Hoover's Handbooks; others reprinted from *Fortune, Forbes,* and other publications. In addition to the American edition, Hoover's handbooks are available for private companies, emerging companies, and companies headquartered outside of the United States.

Ward's Business Directory of U.S. Private and Public Companies. Detroit, MI: Thomson Gale, 2006. 8 volumes. *Ward's Business Directory* is one of the few directories to rank both public and private companies together by sales within an industry, using both the Standard Industrial Classification system (in Volume 5 only) and the North American Industry Classification System (in Volume 8 only). With this information, it is easy to spot who the big players are in a particular product or industry category. Market share within an industry group can be calculated by determining what percentage a company's sales figure is of the total given by Ward's for that industry group.

Business Metasites and Portals

Yahoo Finance. Sunnyvale, CA: Yahoo! Inc. This metasite links to information on U.S. markets, world markets, data sources, finance references, investment editorials, financial news, and other helpful websites. http://finance.yahoo.com

Hoover's Online. Hoover's, Inc., Dun & Bradstreet Corporation. Short Hills, NJ. Hoover's Online includes a limited amount of free information on companies, industries, and executives. The subscribers' edition provides more in-depth information, especially for competitors and industries. http://www.hoovers.com/free

VIBES—Virtual International Business & Economic Sources
VIBES provides over 3,000 links to Internet sources of international business and economic information in English and available free of charge. Links include full-text articles, research reports, statistical tables, and portals linking to other sources.
http://library.uncc.edu/vibes/

Strategic and Competitive Analysis—Information Sources

Analyzing a company can take the form of examining its internal and external environment. In the process, it is useful to identify the company's strengths, weaknesses, opportunities, and threats (SWOT). Sources for this kind of analysis are varied, but perhaps the best would be to locate articles from *The Wall Street Journal,* business magazines, and industry trade publications. Publications such as these can be found in the following databases available at many public and academic libraries. When using a database that is structured to allow it, try searching the company name combined with one or more key words, such as "IBM and competition" or "Microsoft and lawsuits" or "AMR and fuel costs," to retrieve articles relating to the external environment.

ABI/Inform Complete. Ann Arbor, MI: ProQuest–CSA LLC, 2007.
ABI/Inform Complete provides abstracts and full text articles covering management, law, taxation, human resources, and company and industry information from more than 4,000 business and management journals. It also includes market condition reports, corporate strategies, case studies, executive profiles, and global industry conditions.

Business & Company Resource Center. Detroit, MI: Thomson Gale.
Business & Company Resource Center provides company and industry intelligence for a selection of public and private companies. Company profiles include parent–subsidiary relationships, industry rankings, products and brands, investment reports, industry statistics, and financial ratios. A selection of full-text investment reports from Investext Plus is also available.

Business Source Complete. Ipswich, MA: EBSCO Publishing.
Business Source Complete is a full text database with over 3,800 scholarly business journals covering management, economics, finance, accounting, international business, and more. The database also includes detailed company profiles of the world's 10,000 largest companies as well as selected country economic reports provided by the Economist Intelligence Unit (EIU). The database includes case studies, investment and market research reports, SWOT analyses, and more. Business Source Complete contains over 1,100 peer-reviewed business journals.

Investext Plus. Detroit, MI: Thomson Gale.
Investext Plus offers full-text analytical reports on more than 47,000 public companies and 54 industries. The reports are excellent sources for strategic and financial profiles of a company, its competitors, and industry trends. Developed by a global roster of brokerage, investment banking, and research firms, these full-text investment reports include a wealth of current and historical information useful for evaluating a company or industry over time.

International Directory of Company Histories. Detroit, MI: St. James Press, 1988 to present. 84 volumes to date.
This directory covers more than 4,500 multinational companies and the series is still adding volumes. Each company history is approximately three to five pages in length and provides a summary of the company's mission, goals, and ideals, followed by company milestones, principal subsidiaries, and competitors. Strategic decisions made by the company are usually noted. This series covers public and private companies and nonprofit entities. Entry information includes a company's legal name, headquarters information, URL, incorporation date, ticker symbol, stock exchange, sales figures, and the primary North American Industry Classification System (NAICS) code. Further reading selections complete the entry information.

LexisNexis Academic. Bethesda, MD: LexisNexis.
The "Business" category in *LexisNexis Academic* provides access to timely business articles from newspapers, magazines, journals, wires, and broadcast transcripts. Other information available in this section includes detailed company financials, company comparisons, and industry and market information for over 25 industries.

LexisNexis Statistical. Bethesda, MD: LexisNexis.

LexisNexis Statistical provides access to a variety of statistical publications indexed in the American Statistics Index (ASI), Statistical Reference Index (SRI) and the Index to International Statistics (IIS). Use the PowerTables search to locate historical trends, future projections, and industry or demographic information. LexisNexis Statistical provides links to originating government Web sites when available.

The Wall Street Journal. New York: Dow Jones & Company.

This respected business newspaper is available in searchable full text from 1984 to present in the Factiva database. The "News Pages" link provides access to current articles and issues of *The Wall Street Journal.* Dow Jones, publisher of the print version of *The Wall Street Journal,* also has an online subscription available at wsj.com.

Sources for Industry Research and Analysis

Factiva. New York: Dow Jones & Company.

The Factiva database has several options for researching an industry. One is to search the database for articles in the business magazines and industry trade publications. The second option is to search in the Companies/Markets category for company/industry comparison reports.

Mergent Online. New York, Mergent Inc.

Mergent Online is a searchable database of over 10,000 U.S. public companies and more than 18,000 international public companies. The database offer worldwide industry reports, U.S. and global competitors, and executive biographical information. Mergent's enhanced Basic Search option features searching by primary industry codes (either SIC or NAICS). Once the search is executed, companies in that industry should be listed. A comparison or standard peer group analysis can be created to analyze companies in the same industry on various criteria. The improved Advanced Search allows the user to search a wider range of financial and textual information. Results, including ratios for a company and its competitors, can be downloaded to a spreadsheet.

North American Industry Classification (NAICS)

The North American Industry Classification System has officially replaced the Standard Industrial Classification (SIC) as a numerical structure used to define and analyze industries, although some publications and databases offer both classification systems. The NAICS codes are used in Canada, the United States, and Mexico. In the United States, the NAICS codes are used to conduct an Economic Census every five years, providing a snapshot of the U.S. economy at a given moment in time.

NAICS—http://www.census.gov/epcd/www/naics.html
Economic Census—http://www.census.gov/econ/census02/

NetAdvantage. New York: Standard & Poor's.

The database includes company, financial and investment information as well as the well-known publication *Industry Surveys*. Each industry report includes information on the current environment, industry trends, key industry ratios and statistics, and comparative company financial analysis. It is available in HTML, PDF, or Excel formats.

Search Engines

Google. Mountain View, CA: Google, Inc. Recognized for its advanced technology, quality of results and simplicity, the search engine Google is highly recommended by librarians and other expert Web "surfers."

http://www.google.com

Clusty. Pittsburgh, PA: Vivisimo, Inc. This search engine not only finds relevant results, but organizes it in logical subcategories.

http://www.clusty.com

Cases

Case 1   Robin Hood*

It was in the spring of the second year of his insurrection against the High Sheriff of Nottingham that Robin Hood took a walk in Sherwood Forest. As he walked he pondered the progress of the campaign, the disposition of his forces, the Sheriff's recent moves, and the options that confronted him.

The revolt against the Sheriff had begun as a personal crusade, erupting out of Robin's conflict with the Sheriff and his administration. Alone, however, Robin Hood could do little. He therefore sought allies, men with grievances and a deep sense of justice. Later he welcomed all who came, asking few questions, and only demanding a willingness to serve. Strength, he believed, lay in numbers.

He spent the first year forging the group into a disciplined band, united in enmity against the Sheriff, and willing to live outside the law. The band's organization was simple. Robin ruled supreme, making all important decisions. He delegated specific tasks to his lieutenants. Will Scarlett was in charge of intelligence and scouting. His main job was to shadow the Sheriff and his men, always alert to their next move. He also collected information on the travel plans of rich merchants and tax collectors. Little John kept discipline among the men, and saw to it that their archery was at the high peak that their profession demanded. Scarlock took care of the finances, converting loot into cash, paying shares of the take, and finding suitable hiding places for the surplus. Finally, Much the Miller's son had the difficult task of provisioning the ever-increasing band of Merrymen.

The increasing size of the band was a source of satisfaction for Robin, but also a source of concern. The fame of his Merrymen was spreading, and new recruits poured in from every corner of England. As the band grew larger, their small bivouac became a major encampment. Between raids the men milled about, talking and playing games. Vigilance was in decline, and discipline was becoming harder to enforce. "Why," Robin reflected, "I don't know half the men I run into these days."

The growing band was also beginning to exceed the food capacity of the forest. Game was becoming scarce, and supplies had to be obtained from outlying villages. The cost of buying food was beginning to drain the band's financial reserves at the very moment when revenues were in decline. Travelers, especially those with the most to lose, were now giving the forest a wide berth. This was costly and inconvenient to them, but it was preferable to having all their goods confiscated.

Robin believed that the time had come for the Merrymen to change their policy of outright confiscation of goods to one of a fixed transit tax. His lieutenants strongly resisted this idea. They were proud of the Merrymen's famous motto: "Rob the rich and give to the poor." "The farmers and the townspeople," they argued, "are our most important allies. How can we tax them, and still hope for their help in our fight against the Sheriff?"

Robin wondered how long the Merrymen could keep to the ways and methods of their early days. The Sheriff was growing stronger and better organized. He now had the money and the men, and was beginning to harass the band, probing for its weaknesses.

The tide of events was beginning to turn against the Merrymen. Robin felt that the campaign must be decisively concluded before the Sheriff had a chance to deliver a mortal blow. "But how," he wondered, "could this be done?"

Robin had often entertained the possibility of killing the Sheriff, but the chances for this seemed increasingly remote. Besides, while killing the Sheriff might satisfy his personal thirst for revenge, it would not improve the situation. Robin had hoped that the perpetual state of unrest, and the Sheriff's failure to collect taxes, would lead to his removal from office. Instead, the Sheriff used his political connections to obtain reinforcement. He had powerful friends at court, and was well regarded by the regent, Prince John.

Prince John was vicious and volatile. He was consumed by his unpopularity among the people, who wanted the imprisoned King Richard back. He also lived in constant fear of the barons, who had first given him the regency, but were now beginning to dispute his claim to the throne. Several of these barons had set out to collect the ransom that would release King Richard the Lionheart from his jail in Austria. Robin was invited to join the conspiracy in return for future amnesty. It was a dangerous proposition. Provincial banditry was one thing, court intrigue another. Prince John's spies were everywhere. If the plan failed, the pursuit would be relentless and retribution swift.

The sound of the supper horn startled Robin from his thoughts. There was the smell of roasting venison in the air. Nothing was resolved or settled. Robin headed for camp promising himself that he would give these problems his utmost attention after tomorrow's raid.

* Prepared by Joseph Lampel, City University, London. Copyright Joseph Lampel © 1985, Revised 1991. Reprinted with permission.

Case 2   Edward Marshall Boehm, Inc.*

Edward Marshall Boehm—a farmer, veterinarian, and nature lover living near New York City—was convinced by his wife and friends to translate some of his clay animal sculptures into pieces for possible sale to the gift and art markets. Boehm recognized that porcelain was the best medium for portraying his creations because of its translucent beauty, permanence, and fidelity of color as well as form. But the finest of the porcelains, hard paste porcelain, was largely a secret art about which little technical literature existed. Boehm studied this art relentlessly, absorbing whatever knowledge artbooks, museums, and the few U.S. ceramic factories offered. Then, after months of experimentation in a dingy Trenton, New Jersey, basement, Boehm and some chemist friends developed a porcelain clay equal to the finest in the world.

Next Boehm had to master the complex art of porcelain manufacture. Each piece of porcelain sculpture is a technical as well as artistic challenge. A 52-step process is required to convert a plasticine sculpture into a completed porcelain piece. For example, one major creation took 509 mold sections to make 151 parts, and consumed 8 tons of plaster in the molds. Sculptural detail included 60,000 individually carved feather barbs. Each creation had to be kiln-fired to 2400° where heat could change a graceful detail into a twisted mass. Then it had to be painted, often in successive layers, and perhaps fired repeatedly to anneal delicate colors. No American had excelled in hard paste porcelains. And when Boehm's creations first appeared no one understood the quality of the porcelain or even believed it was hard paste porcelain.

But Boehm began to create in porcelain what he knew and loved best—nature, particularly the more delicate forms of animals, birds, and flowers. In his art Boehm tried "to capture that special moment and setting which conveys the character, charm, and loveliness of a bird or animal in its natural habitat." After selling his early creations for several years during her lunch hours, his talented wife, Helen, left an outstanding opthalmic marketing career to "peddle" Boehm's porcelains full time. Soon Mrs. Boehm's extraordinary merchandising skills, promotional touch, and sense for the art market began to pay off. People liked Boehm's horses and dogs, but bought his birds. And Boehm agreeably complied, striving for ever greater perfection on ever more exotic and natural bird creations.

By 1968 some Boehm porcelains (especially birds) had become recognized as collector's items. An extremely complex piece like "Fondo Marino" might sell for $28,500 at retail, and might command much more upon resale. Edward Marshall Boehm, then 55—though flattered by his products' commercial success—considered his art primarily an expression of his love for nature. He felt the ornithological importance of portraying vanishing species like U.S. prairie chickens with fidelity and traveled to remote areas to bring back live samples of rare tropical birds for study and later rendering into porcelain. A single company, Minton China, was the exclusive distributor of Boehm products to some 175 retail outlets in the United States. Boehm's line included (1) its "Fledgling" series of smaller, somewhat simpler pieces, usually selling for less than $100, (2) its profitable middle series of complex sculptures like the "Snowy Owl" selling from $800 to $5,000, and (3) its special artistic pieces (like "Fondo Marino" or "Ivory Billed Woodpeckers") which might sell initially for over $20,000.

Individual Boehm porcelains were increasingly being recognized as outstanding artistic creations and sought by some sophisticated collectors. Production of such designs might be sold out for years in advance, but it was difficult to anticipate which pieces might achieve this distinction. Many of the company's past policies no longer seemed appropriate. And the Boehms wanted to further position the company for the long run. When asked what they wanted from the company, they would respond, "to make the world aware of Mr. Boehm's artistic talent, to help world wildlife causes by creating appreciation and protection for threatened species, and to build a continuing business that could make them comfortably wealthy, perhaps millionaires." No one goal had great precedence over the others.

---

* Republished with permission from H. Mintzberg and J. B. Quinn, *The Strategy Process*, Prentice Hall, New York, 1996.

Case 3 The Skeleton in the Corporate Closet*

"David," Donna Cooper exclaimed. "You won't believe it, but these look like love letters! And look, they're from when he was in the service!"

David Fisher, the corporate archivist for GPC Incorporated, hastened toward the young woman sprawled on his dusty floor but cheerily holding aloft a packet of yellowed envelopes. Unaccustomed to so much commotion in this room, he was still trying to process what had just happened. A moment ago, he'd been giving Miss Cooper, the writer hired to pen GPC's 75th anniversary book, a tour of his admittedly cluttered storeroom. Following at some distance, she'd chosen another path through the debris, only to reach an impasse. He'd glanced back just in time to see her give a shove to—of all things—the founder's writing desk. The brittle wooden legs, now in their 100th year at least, could hardly have been expected to scoot across the rough cement swirls of the basement floor. One had snapped immediately, the desk had toppled, and Miss Cooper had followed the whole wreck down.

Which was when, even through the air of the old storeroom, semiopaque with suspended dust, and even despite the early-stage cataract in his left eye, David spotted something that made his historian's heart leap. The back of the desk, now splintered, had mysteriously yielded a drawer, one he had never discovered in his years of puttering around it. Visible inside were some papers. Following his wondering gaze, the infuriating, wonderful Miss Cooper had spied, and snatched out, the treasure.

A Bittersweet Discovery

She was right, of course. They were letters composed to a sweetheart by Hudson Parker after he'd shipped out with Company K, the 137th U.S. Infantry unit made up of recruits from Kansas and Missouri. The first was dated August 6, 1917—a full decade before he'd founded General Parkelite Company. David took quick note of the addressee: Mary Beatrice White. Not a name he'd heard before. Clearly this romance preceded Virginia, the woman Hud had married. David was faintly scandalized to realize that old Hud had squirreled away these letters, no doubt unbeknownst to his wife. At the same time, he was touched at the thought of an unforgotten first love. And although his first instinct would usually have been to don cotton gloves and carry the letters into better light, he instead cleared a bit of floor space near Miss Cooper and sat. There was an undeniable charm in having this young woman eagerly extract letters from envelopes and read them aloud.

* *Harvard Business Review*'s cases, which are fictional, present common managerial dilemmas and offer concrete solutions from experts.

Reprinted by permission of *Harvard Business Review*. "The Skeleton in the Corporate Closet" by Julia Kirby, June 2002. Copyright © 2002 by the Harvard Business School Publishing Corporation; all rights reserved.

"My dearest Mary," she recited. "It began raining here this morning, and it is still at it. No drill today, so I will have time to write a letter or two." Impatient to find something juicier, she scanned the rest of the letter before handing it over. "Oh, look, David, how he signs it: 'With best of love to my own little girl.'" David accepted the letter and pushed his glasses down on his nose to peer over them. As always, he took a moment to appreciate the superior penmanship of an earlier age. Then his trained eye went to work on the page, drilling for facts that could be cataloged and cross-referenced with other accounts of the founder's war years. Donna, meanwhile, merrily called out other quaint snippets.

A half-hour passed in this way before David's joints, chilled by the bare floor, started to protest, and he suggested a change of venue. "Yeah," said Donna. "It's pretty musty in here, isn't it?" But as David took a moment to prop up the damaged desk and replace its drawer, Donna pulled another paper from an envelope. "Oh, this is the kind of thing you'll like," she noted, unfolding what looked, curiously, like drafting paper. She thrust it toward him and promptly launched into the accompanying letter. "You will recall from my last letter that we expect to see action this week, Mary darling. Enclosed is a document I hardly expect you to find interesting but entreat you to keep safe till my return." Indeed, it didn't interest Donna, so she rose to her feet and briskly dusted her skirt. "Honestly, David, I don't know how you work in here. My eyes are beginning to burn." But when she turned toward him, she was dismayed to see him staring at the paper he was clutching, his own eyes filling with tears.

Our Founder, a Thief?

A day passed before David appeared at the door of Jill Pierce, the communications VP who was his boss, and asked for a meeting at her convenience. Masking her surprise (in her seven years as his superior, she couldn't recall his ever initiating contact), she invited him in on the spot. Soon she was holding the letter herself and listening to David explain its import. Shockingly, it proved that the formula for Parkelite—the miracle plastic that was the company's first patent and its bread and butter for two full decades—had been someone else's innovation, not Hud Parker's. Not to put too fine a point on it, GPC's revered founder was a thief.

David filled in the parts of the story she didn't know. Of course, she needed no reminder of what Parkelite was. Although it had long since been superseded by better materials, it had been a huge technological advance in its day. A dense synthetic polymer, it could be molded or extruded and had the advantage of not changing shape after being mixed and heated. Most important, it wasn't flammable like earlier celluloid plastics. Manufacturers had used it to make things like engine parts, radio boxes, switches—even costume jewelry and inexpensive dinnerware. At the height of its popularity, General Parkelite was producing some 200,000 tons of the stuff per year.

What Jill had never heard was that in 1938, a lawsuit had been brought against Hud Parker and General Parkelite by the father of Karl Gintz, claiming that his son had been the true, sole inventor of Parkelite. Hud and Karl had studied chemistry together at Princeton, David explained, and had been star pupils who had egged each other on. But as well as being competitors, they were close friends, even to the extent that when war broke out in Europe, they enlisted together. Both dreamed of becoming pilots in the Army's Signal Corps, and both easily made the grade. They were transferred to the 94th Pursuit Group and posted to France. But in August 1918—just a week, Jill noted with a shiver, prior to the postmark on the envelope she held—Karl had been killed in maneuvers when the wing of his French-built trainer had collapsed. David pointed out that the formulas and diagrams neatly lettered on the graph paper were clearly the genesis of Parkelite, which Hud Parker had patented in 1920. Just as clearly, they were the work of Karl Gintz. "This is the document," David concluded, "that would have allowed the Gintz family to win its case."

Unprepared for the Worst

Jill had kept her composure while David was in her office, but as soon as he left, she opened her desk drawer, fished out a bottle of liquid antacid, and took a slug. David's chief concern seemed to be who would tell Hap—that is, Hudson Parker III, GPC's longtime CEO and the grandson of the founder. But that was the least of her worries. Clearly, this was a potential PR disaster, and her mind raced through the various ways it might play out. In honor of GPC's 75th anniversary, she'd introduced a heavy dose of nostalgia into this year's advertising. Hud Parker's image was splashed everywhere, along with the tag line, "He started it all." More like he *stole* it all, Jill thought bitterly, then felt guilty that such a remark would even occur to her. What a contrast to the pride she'd felt last summer when some focus groups she'd observed had come up with words like "trusted," "straight shooting," and "dependable" to describe the GPC brand. This was a catastrophe. And with all the extra planning that the special anniversary promotions required, she was already working flat out.

On her way to the CEO's office that afternoon, she lost her nerve at least three times. The fourth time, she even had Hap's doorway in sight, only to detour to the elevator lobby instead. She had a sudden determination to go down to the archives and urge David to destroy the incriminating paper and forget about it. But the fantasy died quickly as she recalled his haggard look in her office that morning. He'd already struggled with whether he could do that, she now realized, and decided he couldn't. She stopped short of hitting the down button and turned back toward the corner office.

History in the Remaking

Three days later, it was Hap Parker who was deciding what to do with the unwelcome news and 80-year-old graph paper now in his possession.

He'd been shocked, of course, and indeed had lost an entire weekend working through the implications on a purely personal level. On Saturday morning, he'd driven the two hours to the lakeside cottage where he'd spent summer days with his grandfather half a century before. He sat cross-legged on the dock, looked across the glittering water, then put his face in his hands and wept. First for his grandfather, who regardless of this incident didn't deserve to be impugned. The Parkelite patent, after all, was only a formula. It still took a great man to build a great company—and he had. And he had hardly coasted on that initial success. Instead, he'd infused the whole organization with the importance and excitement of constant innovation. It was his continuing attention to R&D that had led to General Parkelite's next generation of products, which, along with those of competitors, had made Parkelite obsolete. He'd won the respect of business leaders—indeed, of his country. He was a World War I ace, for God's sake! And a fair-dealing businessman, philanthropist, and community leader. A compassionate employer, certainly. And a dear grandfather, revered no less by his grandchildren for his tendency to dote on them.

This line of thought led Hap directly to self-pity. For neither did he, who had always held himself to the highest standard—with his grandfather's example as his North Star—deserve to have his name smeared. What was that line from Exodus about the sins of the fathers? He struggled to retrieve a long-forgotten catechism. Something about being visited on even the third and fourth generations. And now a fresh horror occurred to him: How much would Chip suffer, and even little Teddy, if this became known?

If. Had he really allowed himself to think "if"? He meant "when."

Reputation—or Reparation?

By Monday, Hap's thoughts were back with GPC and its employees, shareholders, and customers. He was listening to Newland Lowell, GPC's legal counsel, weigh in on the matter. No doubt about it, Newland was sharp. He'd come up with angles on this thing Hap hadn't anticipated.

As soon as he'd pressed the door shut behind him, in fact, Newland had broken into an improbable grin. "I know you're upset, Hap, so I'm going to get to the bottom line first," he said. "We haven't been able to turn up an heir to Karl Gintz." When he got no reaction, he hastened to pull out his other notes. "So. Let's take this from the top."

Newland first outlined a carefully reasoned argument that the letter, had it been introduced at trial long ago, would not necessarily have changed the verdict. The jury, he managed to persuade Hap, was fundamentally sympathetic to Hud Parker and not a little suspicious of Gintz's family. "If there's one thing I've learned," Newland said, "it's that jurors vote with their hearts and then find the legal hook to hang their emotions on." Besides, there would have been no proof that Karl hadn't meant to give the intellectual property to his friend and fellow soldier. "After all, no one else in his family was a chemist. They wouldn't have been able to make heads or tails of his notes. How do we know it wasn't his intent to let your grandfather take it forward? Maybe they were collaborating on it."

"But, Newland," Hap interjected. "If that had been the case, why wouldn't Hud have simply said so?"

"We're talking about a court case," Lowell reminded him. "His legal counsel would never have let him say that."

Hap fell silent again and let Newland continue to lay out his next argument: that there was no way of knowing when the letters Hud had sent to Mary Beatrice White had come back into his possession. It could have been years after the court case. "Not to mention," Newland added, "that if he needed this paper to fudge his own documentation for the patent, then why was it still in that envelope? Isn't it conceivable that the innovation was essentially your grandfather's but that Karl had taken careful notes on it to study and perhaps improve upon?"

Believing his arguments were carrying the day, Newland finally plunged into his last set of notes. These were legal strategies for "containing the discovery"—in essence placing a gag order on the few people in the organization who knew the truth. But Hap had already begun to chafe at what were sounding increasingly like elaborate rationalizations, and this was a bridge too far. He stood up from his desk and nodded to Newland. "Thank you, that's as much as I care to hear this afternoon."

Newland Lowell had known Hap Parker long enough not to mistake his tone, courteous though it might have seemed to others. He sighed as he swept his files back into his briefcase and rose from his chair. "Look, Hap. I'll be straight with you. I know you have a strong sense of what's ethical here. But you also have an organization to take care of. Your employees will be better off, not to mention your shareholders—hell, the *world* is better off

if Hud Parker remains a hero. Don't be overly fastidious about this."

Doing the Right Thing

Packing up for the day, Hap had made up his mind. It was absurd that a company whose culture was all about honesty and integrity would tolerate a lie at its core. Maybe there was no one deserving of reparations out there, but surely the company deserved to pay some. He'd find some heir, somewhere.

He wasn't 20 yards down the hall, though, before he encountered a group of three GPC managers, two of them quite new to the company and the other a veteran. As he approached, he overheard the veteran, whose back was to Hap, saying patiently to one of the others, "Well, but, of course, Kevin, that just wouldn't be right." Then, catching sight of Hap, he fell into step with him, hoping to sound out the boss on some other matter.

Just out of earshot, Hap tilted his head back toward where the three had been standing and asked, "What was that about?" The manager explained that Kevin had proposed a marketing idea that seemed a little, well, not exactly underhanded, but. . . . The kid had come to GPC from a competitor with a certain industry reputation. "You know, people there learn to work all the angles and do a lot of things with a wink," he shrugged. "Don't worry, though. He wasn't comfortable there—that's why we got him."

"So you think he's got the potential to be a GPC'er?" Hap pressed.

"Well, that's the great thing about a strong culture, isn't it, Hap? It rubs off. He'll soon pick up on how things are done around here."

The unintended irony of those words made Hap queasy. Suddenly, he couldn't imagine damaging the strong belief in GPC held by this decent man and his 8,000 coworkers. Maybe Newland was right, he thought, and he was being too narrow in his ethics—even self-indulgent.

Was it possible for the right thing to be a lie?

Case 4   The Best-Laid Incentive Plans*

Hiram Phillips finished tying his bow tie and glanced in the mirror. Frowning, he tugged on the left side, then caught sight of his watch in the mirror. Time to get going. Moments later, he was down the stairs, whistling cheerfully and heading toward the coffeemaker.

"You're in a good mood," his wife said, looking up from the newspaper and smiling. "What's that tune? 'Accentuate the Positive'?"

"Well done!" Hiram called out. "You know, I do believe you're picking up some pop culture in spite of yourself." It was a running joke with them. She was a classically trained cellist and on the board of the local symphony. He was the one with the Sinatra and Bing Crosby albums and the taste for standards. "You're getting better at naming that tune."

"Or else you're getting better at whistling." She looked over her reading glasses and met his eye. They let a beat pass before they said in unison: "Naaah." Then, with a wink, Hiram shrugged on his trench coat, grabbed his travel mug, and went out the door.

Fat and Happy

It was true. Hiram Phillips, CFO and chief administrative officer of Rainbarrel Products, a diversified consumer-durables manufacturer, was in a particularly good mood. He was heading into a breakfast meeting that would bring nothing but good news. Sally Hamilton and Frank Ormondy from Felding & Company would no doubt already be at the office when he arrived and would have with them the all-important numbers—the statistics that would demonstrate the positive results of the performance management system he'd put in place a year ago. Hiram had already seen many of the figures in bits and pieces. He'd retained the consultants to establish baselines on the metrics he wanted to watch and had seen various interim reports from them since. But today's meeting would be the impressive summation capping off a year's worth of effort. Merging into the congestion of Route 45, he thought about the upbeat presentation he would spend the rest of the morning preparing for tomorrow's meeting of the corporate executive council.

It was obvious enough what his introduction should be. He would start at the beginning—or, anyway, his own beginning at Rainbarrel Products a year ago. At the time, the company had just come off a couple of awful quarters. It wasn't alone. The sudden slowdown in consumer spending,

after a decade-long boom, had taken the whole industry by surprise. But what had quickly become clear was that Rainbarrel was adjusting to the new reality far less rapidly than its biggest competitors.

Keith Randall, CEO of Rainbarrel, was known for being an inspiring leader who focused on innovation. Even outside the industry, he had a name as a marketing visionary. But over the course of the ten-year economic boom, he had allowed his organization to become a little lax.

Take corporate budgeting. Hiram still smiled when he recalled his first day of interviews with Rainbarrel's executives. It immediately became obvious that the place had no budget integrity whatsoever. One unit head had said outright, "Look, none of us fights very hard at budget time, because after three or four months, nobody looks at the budget anyway." Barely concealing his shock, Hiram asked how that could be; what did they look at, then? The answer was that they operated according to one simple rule: "If it's a good idea, we say yes to it. If it's a bad idea, we say no."

"And what happens," Hiram had pressed, "when you run out of money halfway through the year?" The fellow rubbed his chin and took a moment to think before answering. "I guess we've always run out of good ideas before we've run out of money." Unbelievable!

"Fat and happy" was how Hiram characterized Rainbarrel in a conversation with the headhunter who had recruited him. Of course, he wouldn't use those words in the CEC meeting. That would sound too disparaging. In fact, he'd quickly fallen in love with Rainbarrel and the opportunities it presented. Here was a company that had the potential for greatness but that was held back by a lack of discipline. It was like a racehorse that had the potential to be a Secretariat but lacked a structured training regimen. Or a Ferrari engine that needed the touch of an expert mechanic to get it back in trim. In other words, the only thing Rainbarrel was missing was what someone like Hiram Phillips could bring to the table. The allure was irresistible; this was the assignment that would define his career. And now, a year later, he was ready to declare a turnaround.

Lean and Mean

Sure enough, as Hiram steered toward the entrance to the parking garage, he saw Sally and Frank in a visitor parking space, pulling their bulky file bags out of the trunk of Sally's sedan. He caught up to them at the security checkpoint in the lobby and took a heavy satchel from Sally's hand.

Moments later, they were at a conference table, each of them poring over a copy of the consultants' spiral-bound report. "This is great," Hiram said. "I can hand this out just as it is. But what I want to do while you're here is to really nail down what the highlights are. I have the floor for 40 minutes, but I guess I'd better leave ten for questions. There's no way I can plow through all of this."

Harvard Business Review's cases, which are fictional, present common managerial dilemmas and offer concrete solutions from experts.

* Steven Kerr is the chief learning officer at Goldman Sachs in New York. Prior to joining Goldman Sachs in 2001, he spent seven years as the chief learning officer and head of leadership development at General Electric. He was responsible for GE's leadership development center at Crotonville.

"If I were you," Sally advised, "I would lead off with the best numbers. I mean, none of them are bad. You hit practically every target. But some of these, where you even exceeded the stretch goal. . . ."

Hiram glanced at the line Sally was underscoring with her fingernail. It was an impressive achievement: a reduction in labor costs. This had been one of the first moves he'd made, and he'd tried to do it gently. He'd come up with the idea of identifying the bottom quartile of performers throughout the company and offering them fairly generous buyout packages. But when that hadn't attracted enough takers, he'd gone the surer route. He'd imposed an across-the-board headcount reduction of 10% on all the units. In that round, the affected people were given no financial assistance beyond the normal severance.

"It made a big difference," he nodded. "But it wasn't exactly the world's most popular move." Hiram was well aware that a certain segment of the Rainbarrel workforce currently referred to him as "Fire 'em." He pointed to another number on the spreadsheet. "Now, that one tells a happier story: lower costs as a result of higher productivity."

"And better customer service to boot," Frank chimed in. They were talking about the transformation of Rainbarrel's call center—where phone representatives took orders and handled questions and complaints from both trade and retail customers. The spreadsheet indicated a dramatic uptick in productivity: The number of calls each service rep was handling per day had gone up 50%. A year earlier, reps were spending up to six minutes per call, whereas now the average was less than four minutes. "I guess you decided to go for that new automated switching system?" Frank asked.

"No!" Hiram answered. "That's the beauty of it. We got that improvement without any capital investment. You know what we did? We just announced the new targets, let everyone know we were going to monitor them, and put the names of the worst offenders on a great big 'wall of shame' right outside the cafeteria. Never underestimate the power of peer pressure!"

Sally, meanwhile, was already circling another banner achievement: an increase in on-time shipments. "You should talk about this, given that it's something that wasn't even being watched before you came."

It was true. As much as Rainbarrel liked to emphasize customer service in its values and mission statement, no reliable metric had been in place to track it. And getting a metric in place hadn't been as straightforward as it might've seemed—people had haggled about what constituted "on time" and even what constituted "shipped." Finally, Hiram had put his foot down and insisted on the most objective of measures. On time meant when the goods were promised to ship. And nothing was counted as shipped till it left company property. Period. "And once again," Hiram announced, "not a dollar of capital expenditure. I simply let people know that, from now on, if they made commitments and didn't keep them, we'd have their number."

"Seems to have done the trick," Sally observed. "The percentage of goods shipped by promise date has gone up steadily for the last six months. It's now at 92%."

Scanning the report, Hiram noticed another huge percentage gain, but he couldn't recall what the acronym stood for. "What's this? Looks like a good one: a 50% cost reduction?"

Sally studied the item. "Oh, that. It's a pretty small change, actually. Remember we separated out the commissions on sales to employees?" It came back to Hiram immediately. Rainbarrel had a policy that allowed current and retired employees to buy products at a substantial discount. But the salespeople who served them earned commissions based on the full retail value, not the actual price paid. So, in effect, employee purchases were jacking up the commission expenses. Hiram had created a new policy in which the commission reflected the actual purchase price. On its own, the change didn't amount to a lot, but it reminded Hiram of a larger point he wanted to make in his presentation: the importance of straightforward rules—and rewards—in driving superior performance.

"I know you guys don't have impact data for me, but I'm definitely going to talk about the changes to the commission structure and sales incentives. There's no question they must be making a difference."

"Right," Sally nodded. "A classic case of 'keep it simple,' isn't it?" She turned to Frank to explain. "The old way they calculated commissions was by using this really complicated formula that factored in, I can't remember, at least five different things."

"Including sales, I hope?" Frank smirked.

"I'm still not sure!" Hiram answered. "No, seriously, sales were the most important single variable, but they also mixed in all kinds of targets around mentoring, prospecting new clients, even keeping the account information current. It was all way too subjective, and salespeople were getting very mixed signals. I just clarified the message so they don't have to wonder what they're getting paid for. Same with the sales contests. It's simple now: If you sell the most product in a given quarter, you win."

With Sally and Frank nodding enthusiastically, Hiram again looked down at the report. Row after row of numbers attested to Rainbarrel's improved performance. It wouldn't be easy to choose the rest of the highlights, but what a problem to have! He invited the consultants to weigh in again and leaned back to bask in the superlatives. And his smile grew wider.

Cause for Concern

The next morning, a well-rested Hiram Phillips strode into the building, flashed his ID badge at Charlie, the guard, and joined the throng in the lobby. In the crowd waiting for the elevator, he recognized two young women from Rainbarrel, lattes in hand and headphones around their necks. One was grimacing melodramatically as she turned to her friend. "I'm so dreading getting to my desk," she said. "Right when I was leaving last night, an e-mail showed up from the buyer at Sullivan. I just know it's going to be some big, hairy problem to sort out. I couldn't bring myself to open it, with the day I'd had. But I'm going to be sweating it today trying to respond by five o'clock. I can't rack up any more late responses, or my bonus is seriously history."

Her friend had slung her backpack onto the floor and was rooting through it, barely listening. But she glanced up to set her friend straight in the most casual way. "No, see, all they check is whether you responded to an e-mail within 24 hours of opening it. So that's the key. Just don't open it. You know, till you've got time to deal with it."

Then a belltone announced the arrival of the elevator, and they were gone.

More Cause for Concern

An hour later, Keith Randall was calling to order the quarterly meeting of the corporate executive council. First, he said, the group would hear the results of the annual employee survey, courtesy of human resources VP Lew Hart. Next would come a demonstration by the chief marketing officer of a practice the CEO hoped to incorporate into all future meetings. It was a "quick market intelligence," or QMI, scan, engaging a few of Rainbarrel's valued customers in a prearranged—but not predigested—conference call, to collect raw data on customer service concerns and ideas. "And finally," Keith concluded, "Hiram's going to give us some very good news about cost reductions and operating efficiencies, all due to the changes he's designed and implemented this past year."

Hiram nodded to acknowledge the compliment. He heard little of the next ten minutes' proceedings, thinking instead about how he should phrase certain points for maximum effect. Lew Hart had lost him in the first moments of his presentation on the "people survey" by beginning with an overview of "purpose, methodology, and historical trends." Deadly.

It was the phrase "mindlessly counting patents" that finally turned Hiram's attention back to his colleague. Lew, it seemed, was now into the "findings" section of his remarks. Hiram pieced together that he was reporting on an unprecedented level of negativity in the responses from Rainbarrel's R&D department and was quoting the complaints people had scribbled on their surveys. "Another one put it this way," Lew said. "We're now highly focused on who's getting the most patents, who's getting the most copyrights, who's submitting the most grant proposals, etc. But are we more creative? It's not that simple."

"You know," Rainbarrel's chief counsel noted, "I have thought lately that we're filing for a lot of patents for products that will never be commercially viable."

"But the thing that's really got these guys frustrated seems to be their 'Innovation X' project," Lew continued. "They're all saying it's the best thing since sliced bread, a generational leap on the product line, but they're getting no uptake."

Eyes in the room turned to the products division president, who promptly threw up his hands. "What can I say,

gang? We never expected that breakthrough to happen in this fiscal year. It's not in the budget to bring it to market."

Lew Hart silenced the rising voices, reminding the group he had more findings to share. Unfortunately, it didn't get much better. Both current and retired employees were complaining about being treated poorly by sales personnel when they sought to place orders or obtain information about company products. There was a lot of residual unhappiness about the layoffs, and not simply because those who remained had more work to do. Some people had noted that, because the reduction was based on headcount, not costs, managers had tended to fire low-level people, crippling the company without saving much money. And because the reduction was across the board, the highest performing departments had been forced to lay off some of the company's best employees. Others had heard about inequities in the severance deals: "As far as I can tell, we gave our lowest performers a better package than our good ones," he quoted one employee as saying.

And then there was a chorus of complaints from the sales organization. "No role models." "No mentoring." "No chance to pick the veterans' brains." "No knowledge sharing about accounts." More than ever, salespeople were dissatisfied with their territories and clamoring for the more affluent, high-volume districts. "It didn't help that all the sales-contest winners this year were from places like Scarsdale, Shaker Heights, and Beverly Hills," a salesperson was quoted as saying. Lew concluded with a promise to look further into the apparent decline in morale to determine whether it was an aberration.

The Ugly Truth

But if the group thought the mood would improve in the meeting's next segment—the QMI chat with the folks at longtime customer Brenton Brothers—they soon found out otherwise. Booming out of the speakerphone in the middle of the table came the Southern-tinged voices of Billy Brenton and three of his employees representing various parts of his organization.

"What's up with your shipping department?" Billy called out. "My people are telling me it's taking forever to get the stock replenished."

Hiram sat up straight, then leaned toward the speakerphone. "Excuse me, Mr. Brenton. This is Hiram Phillips—I don't believe we've met. But are you saying we are not shipping by our promise date?"

A cough—or was it a guffaw?—came back across the wire. "Well, son. Let me tell you about that. First of all, what y'all promise is not always what we are saying we require—and what we believe we deserve. Annie, isn't that right?"

"Yes, Mr. Brenton," said the buyer. "In some cases, I've been told to take a late date or otherwise forgo the purchase. That becomes the promise date, I guess, but it's not the date I asked for."

"And second," Billy continued, "I can't figure out how you fellas define 'shipped.' We were told last Tuesday an order had been shipped, and come to find out, the stuff was sitting on a railroad siding across the street from your plant."

"That's an important order for us," another Brenton voice piped up. "I sent an e-mail to try to sort it out, but I haven't heard back about it." Hiram winced, recalling the conversation in the lobby that morning. The voice persisted: "I thought that might be the better way to contact your service people these days? They always seem in such an all-fired hurry to get off the phone when I call. Sometimes it takes two or three calls to get something squared away."

The call didn't end there—a few more shortcomings were discussed. Then Keith Randall, to his credit, pulled the conversation onto more positive ground by reaffirming the great regard Rainbarrel had for Brenton Brothers and the mutual value of that enduring relationship. Promises were made and hearty thanks extended for the frank feedback. Meanwhile, Hiram felt the eyes of his colleagues on him. Finally, the call ended and the CEO announced that he, for one, needed a break before the last agenda item.

Dazed and Confused

Hiram considered following his boss out of the room and asking him to table the whole discussion of the new metrics and incentives. The climate was suddenly bad for the news he had looked forward to sharing. But he knew that delaying the discussion would be weak and wrong. After all, he had plenty of evidence to show he was on the right track. The problems the group had just been hearing about were side effects, but surely they didn't outweigh the cure.

He moved to the side table and poured a glass of ice water, then leaned against the wall to collect his thoughts. Perhaps he should reframe his opening comments in light of the employee and customer feedback. As he considered how he might do so, Keith Randall appeared at his side.

"Looks like we have our work cut out for us, eh, Hiram?" he said quietly—and charitably enough. "Some of those metrics taking hold, um, a little too strongly?" Hiram started to object but saw the seriousness in his boss's eyes.

He lifted the stack of reports Felding & Company had prepared for him and turned to the conference table. "Well, I guess that's something for the group to talk about."

Should Rainbarrel revisit its approach to performance management?

Case 5   Growing for Broke*

Look, you've *got* to grow. It's what our economy is all about. Hey, it's what our country is all about! Certainly, it's what drives me. My father, Constantine Anaptyxi, came to America from Greece because he saw big opportunities here. He worked hard, took a few risks, and realized his dreams. I came to this company as CEO five years ago—giving up a senior VP position at a Fortune 500 manufacturer—because I saw big potential for Paragon Tool, then a small maker of machine tools. I didn't make the move so that I could oversee the company's *down*sizing! I didn't intend to create value—for our customers, for our employees, for our shareholders—by thinking small!! I didn't intend to *shrink* to greatness, for God's sake!!!

Okay, so I'm getting a little worked up over this. Maybe I'm just trying to overcome my own second thoughts about our company's growth plans. I know it isn't just about growth; it's about *profitable* growth, as my CFO, William Littlefield, is always happy to remind me. "Nicky," he'll say, "people always talk about getting to the top when they should be focusing on the bottom . . . line, that is." Quite a comedian, that Littlefield. But lame as the quip is, it tells you a lot about Littlefield and what, in my opinion, is his limited view of business. Sometimes you've got to sacrifice profits up front to make *real* profits down the line.

To me, acquiring MonitoRobotics holds just that kind of promise. The company uses sensor technology and communications software to monitor and report real-time information on the functioning of robotics equipment. By adapting this technology for use on our machine tools, we could offer customers a rapid-response troubleshooting service—what consultants these days like to call a "solutions" business. Over time, I'd hope we could apply the technology and software to other kinds of machine tools and even to other kinds of manufacturing equipment. That would make us less dependent on our slow-growing and cyclical machine-tool manufacturing operation and hopefully give us a strong position in a technology market with terrific growth potential. It would also nearly double our current annual revenue of around $400 million—and force Wall Street to pay some attention to us.

What does Littlefield say to this? Oh, he gives a thumbs-down to the acquisition, of course—too risky. But get this: He also thinks we should sell off our existing services division—a "drag on profits," he says. With the help of some outside consultants, the senior management team has spent the last few months analyzing both our services business and the pros and cons of a MonitoRobotics acquisition. Tomorrow, I need to tell Littlefield whether we should go ahead and put together a presentation on the proposed acquisition

for next week's board meeting. If we do move forward on this, I have a hunch a certain CFO might start returning those headhunter calls. And I'd hate to lose him. Whatever our differences, there's no denying that he's capable and smart—in fact, a lot smarter than I am in some areas. On this issue, though, I just don't think he gets it.

Mom and Apple Pie

In 1946, when my father was 21, he left the Greek island of Tinos and came to New York City with his new bride. He worked at a cousin's dry-cleaning store in Astoria, Queens, then started his own on the other side of town. When I was seven, he took his savings and bought a commercial laundry in Brooklyn. Over the next several years, he scooped up one laundry after another, usually borrowing from the bank, sometimes taking another mortgage on the three-family home in Bensonhurst where we had moved. By the time I was a teenager, he was sitting on a million-dollar business that did the linens for all kinds of hotels and hospitals around greater New York. "Nikolas, growth is as American as Mom and apple pie," my father would say to me—he loved using all-American expressions like that. "You gotta get bigger to get better."

My mom was somewhat less expansive in her outlook. She kept my father's accounts, having studied bookkeeping in night school as soon as her English was good enough. And she had her own saying, one that deftly, if inadvertently, bolted together two other platitudes of American slang. "Keep your shirt on," she would say to my father when, arms waving, he would enthusiastically describe some new expansion plan for his business. "Or else you might lose it." My father was the genius behind his company's growth, but I have no doubt that my mother was the one responsible for its profits.

When I was 15, we moved to a nice suburb in Jersey. I never quite fit in: too small for sports, a little too ethnic for the social set, only a middling student. I worked hard, though, and went to Rutgers, where I majored in economics and then stayed on to get an MBA. Something clicked in business school. I seemed to have a knack for solving the real-world problems of the case studies. And I flourished in an environment where the emphasis was on figuring out what you *can* do instead of what you *can't*, on envisioning how things could go right instead of trying to anticipate how they could go wrong. (Thank God I didn't follow my uncle's advice and become a corporate lawyer!)

When I graduated, I got a job at WRT, the Cleveland-based industrial conglomerate where I'd interned the summer before. Over the next 15 years or so, I moved up through the ranks, mainly because of my ability to spot new market opportunities. And by the time I was 45, I was heading up the machine-tool division, a $2.3 billion business. Both revenues and profits surged in the three years I was there, it's true. But I still found my job frustrating. Every proposed acquisition or new initiative of any substance had to be approved by people at headquarters who were far removed from our business. And whenever corporate profits flagged, the response was mindless across-the-board cost cutting that took little account of individual divisions' performance.

So when I was offered the opportunity to head up a small but profitable machine-tool maker in southern Ohio, I jumped at the chance.

Sunflower Tableau

I still remember driving to work my first day at Paragon Tool five years ago. Winding through the Ohio countryside, I saw a stand of sunflowers growing in a rocky patch of soil next to a barn. "Now *there's* a symbol for us," I thought, "a commonplace but hardy plant that quickly grows above its neighbors, often in fairly tough conditions." I was confident that Paragon—a solid, unexceptional business operating in an extremely difficult industry and economic environment—had the potential to grow with similarly glorious results.

For one thing, Paragon was relatively healthy. The company was built around a line of high-end machines—used by manufacturers of aerospace engines, among others—that continued to enjoy fairly good margins, despite the battering that the machine-tool industry as a whole had taken over the previous decade and a half. Still, the market for our product was essentially stagnant. Foreign competition was beginning to take its toll. And we continued to face brutal cyclical economic swings.

I quickly launched a number of initiatives designed to spur revenue growth. With some aggressive pricing, we increased sales and gained share in our core market, driving out a number of our new foreign rivals. We expanded our product line and our customer base by modifying our flagship product for use in a number of other industries. We also made a string of acquisitions in the industrial signage and electronic-labeling field, aiming to leverage the relationships we had with our machine-tool customers. No question, these moves put real pressure on our margins. Along with the price cuts and the debt we took on to make the acquisitions, we had to invest in new manufacturing equipment and a larger sales force. But we were laying the foundation for what I hoped would be a highly profitable future. The board and the senior management team, including Littlefield, seemed to share my view.

Indeed, the CFO and I had developed a rapport, despite our differing business instincts. Early on in our working relationship, this sixth-generation Yankee started in with the kidding about my alma mater. "Is that how they taught you to think about it at Rutgers?" he'd say if I was brainstorming and came up with some crazy idea. "Because at *Wharton,* they taught us. . . ." I'd just laugh and then tell whoever else was in the room how proud we were that Littlefield had been a cheerleader for the Penn football team—like that was his biggest scholarly accomplishment. One time he "let it slip" that in fact he was Phi Beta Kappa,

and we all just groaned. I said, "Give it up, Littlefield. You may have been Phi Beta Kappa, but, despite those letters on your gold pin, you'll never out-*Greek* me." To tell the truth, our skills are complementary, and between us we manage to do a pretty good job for the company.

As Paragon grew, so did the sense of excitement and urgency among our managers—indeed, among the entire workforce. People who once had been merely content to work at Paragon now couldn't wait to tackle the next challenge. And that excitement spread throughout the small Ohio town where we are based. When I'd go with my wife to a party or speak at the local Rotary Club or even stop to buy gas, people would show a genuine interest in the company and our latest doings—it helped that we always mentioned the job-creation impact when announcing new initiatives. There's no doubt it stoked my ego to be one of the bigger fish in the local pond. But even more important for me was the sense that this was business at its best, providing people with a justified sense of well-being about the present and confidence in the future.

Anyway, my point here is that we've grown fast since I arrived, but we still have a long way to go. I've come to think that the real key to our future is in the company's services division. We currently offer our customers the option to buy a standard service contract, under which we provide periodic machine maintenance and respond to service calls. But we've been developing technology and software, similar to MonitoRobotics', that would allow us to respond immediately if a machine at a customer's site goes down. The division currently accounts for less than 10% of our revenue and, because of the cost of developing the new technology, it's struggling to turn a profit.

But I can see in the services division the seeds of a business that will ultimately transform us from a manufacturing company into a high-tech company. Such a transformation, requiring an overhaul of our culture and capabilities, won't be easy. And it will surely require significant additional investments. But the potential upside is huge, with the promise of sales and profit growth that could make our current single-digit gains seem trivial by comparison. Besides, what choice do we have? A number of our competitors have already spotted these opportunities and have begun moving ahead with them. If we don't ramp up quickly, we might well miss out on the action altogether.

A Company in Play

Just over a month ago, I was sitting at my desk preparing a presentation for the handful of analysts who cover our company. Until recently, most of them have had only good things to say about all our growth moves. But last quarter, when we again reported a year-on-year drop in earnings, a few of them started asking pointed questions about our investments and when they could be expected to bear fruit. As I was giving some thought to how I'd answer their questions in the upcoming meeting, the phone rang. It was our investment banker, Jed Nixon.

"Nicky, I think we should talk," he said. I could tell from the sound of his voice he was on to something big, and then he told me what it was: "MonitoRobotics is in play."

We both did some calendar juggling and managed to get together for lunch the very next day at Jed's office in Cincinnati. The rumor was that one of our direct competitors, Bellows & Samson, was about to launch a hostile takeover bid for MonitoRobotics. As it happened, we had just started a conversation with MonitoRobotics' management a few months before, about collaborating on remote servicing technology for machine tools. But Jed's call had had its intended effect, changing my thinking about the company: Why not acquire it ourselves?

Although MonitoRobotics' technology was designed to detect and report operating failures in robotics equipment, managers there had told us when we met that adapting it for use on other industrial machinery was feasible. Indeed, MonitoRobotics had recently licensed the technology to a company that planned to modify it for use on complex assembly lines that experienced frequent breakdowns. Our engineers had confirmed that a version could be developed for our machines—though in their initial assessment they hadn't been exactly sure how long this would take.

Still, the potential benefits of acquiring MonitoRobotics seemed numerous. It would give us a powerful presence in a fast-growing business while preempting a competitor from staking a claim there. Whatever the time lag in adapting MonitoRobotics' technology for use with our products, we would almost certainly be able to offer our customers this valuable troubleshooting service more quickly than if we continued to develop the technology ourselves. And though our products were different, MonitoRobotics and Paragon potentially served many of the same manufacturing customers. "Think of the cross-selling opportunities," Jed said, as he took a bite of his sandwich. The greatest opportunity, though, lay in the possibility that MonitoRobotics' software technology would become the standard means for machine tools—and ultimately a variety of industrial machines—to communicate their service needs to the people who serviced them and to other machines that might be affected by their shutdown.

This was a fairly speculative train of thought. But a MonitoRobotics acquisition had for me the earmarks of a breakthrough opportunity for Paragon. And our earlier conversations with its management team had been cordial, suggesting the company might welcome a friendly offer from us to counter Bellows & Samson's hostile bid. Of course, even if we were able to get MonitoRobotics at a fair price, an acquisition of this size would further delay our return to the margins and profit growth we had known in the past. And that, I knew, wouldn't sit well with everyone.

Management Dissension

The day after my meeting with Jed, I called together members of our senior management team. There was a barely suppressed gasp when I mentioned the potential acquisition, particularly given its size. "Boy, that would be a lot to digest with everything we've got on our plate right now," said Joe McCollum, our senior VP of marketing. "It also might represent the chance of a lifetime," countered Rosemary Witkowski, head of the services division. Then Littlefield spoke up. His skepticism wasn't surprising.

"I was just running a few simple numbers on what the MonitoRobotics acquisition might mean to our bottom line," he said. "Besides the costs associated with the acquisition itself, we'd be looking at some significant expenses in the near term, including accelerated software research, hiring and training, and even brand development." He pointed out that these costs would put further pressure on our earnings, just as our profits were struggling to recover from earlier growth-related investments.

Littlefield did concede that a bold acquisition like this might be just the sort of growth move that would appeal to some of our analysts—and might even prompt a few more securities firms to cover us. But he insisted that if our earnings didn't start bouncing back soon, Wall Street was going to pillory us. Then he dropped his bombshell: "I frankly think this is an opportunity to consider getting out of the services business altogether. Eliminating the continued losses that we've been experiencing there would allow us to begin realizing the profit growth that we can expect from the investments we've made in our still-healthy machine-tool business."

Littlefield argued that, whether we acquired MonitoRobotics or not, it wasn't clear we'd be able to dominate the machine-tool services market because a number of our competitors were already flocking there. Furthermore, the market might not be worth fighting over: Many of our customers were struggling with profitability themselves and might not be willing or able to buy our add-on services. "Last one in, turn out the lights" was the phrase Littlefield used to describe the rush to dominate a profitless market.

As soon as she had a chance, Rosemary shot back in defense of her operation. "This is the one area we're in that has significant growth potential," she said. "And we've already sunk an incredible amount of money into developing this software. I can't believe you'd throw all of that investment out the window." But a number of heads nodded when Littlefield argued that we'd recoup much of that investment if we sold the money-losing business.

Several days later, I polled the members of the senior management team and found them split on the issue of the acquisition. And, to be honest, I was beginning to doubt myself on this. I respected Littlefield's financial savvy. And no one had yet raised the issue of whether Paragon, a traditional manufacturing company, had the management capabilities to run what was essentially a software start-up. We decided to hire two highly regarded consulting firms to do quick analyses of the proposed MonitoRobotics acquisition.

The Sunflowers' Successor

Today, the consultants came back to us with conflicting reports. One highlighted the market potential of MonitoRobotics' technology, noting that we might be too far behind to develop similar technology on our own. The other focused on the difficulties both of integrating the company's technology with ours and of adapting it to equipment beyond the robotics field.

So as I drove home tonight, the dilemma seemed no closer to being resolved. In many ways, I am persuaded by the cautionary message of Littlefield's number crunching. At the same time, I firmly believe the pros and cons of such a complex decision can't be precisely quantified; sometimes you just have to go with your instincts—which in my case favor growth. As I turned the issue over in my head, I looked out the car window, half-consciously seeking inspired insight. Sure enough, there was the barn where the sunflowers had been growing five years before. But the bright yellow blossoms, highlighted by the red timbers of the barn, were gone. Instead, a carpet of green kudzu was growing up the side of the increasingly dilapidated building. This fast-growing vine, which already had ravaged much of the South, was now spreading, uncontrolled and unproductive, into southern Ohio.

My mind started to drift and the image of kudzu—a more sinister symbol of growth than the sunflower—began to merge with thoughts of my father, who had died of lung cancer two years before, and my mother, who these days spends most of her time managing her investments. Suddenly, my parents' favorite phrases came to mind. It occurred to me that kudzu was now becoming as American as Mom and apple pie. Even so, its dense foliage certainly seemed like a place where, if you weren't careful, you could easily misplace your shirt.

Should Paragon Tool further its growth ambitions by trying to acquire MonitoRobotics?

Case 6   Crown Cork & Seal in 1989*

John F. Connelly, Crown Cork & Seal's ailing octogenarian chairman, stepped down and appointed his long-time disciple, William J. Avery, chief executive officer of the Philadelphia can manufacturer in May 1989. Avery had been president of Crown Cork & Seal since 1981, but had spent the duration of his career in Connelly's shadow. As Crown's new CEO, Avery planned to review Connelly's long-followed strategy in light of the changing industry outlook.

The metal container industry had changed considerably since Connelly took over Crown's reins in 1957. American National had just been acquired by France's state-owned Pechiney International, making it the world's largest beverage can producer. Continental Can, another long-standing rival, was now owned by Peter Kiewit Sons, a privately held construction firm. In 1989, all or part of Continental's can-making operations appeared to be for sale. Reynolds Metals, a traditional supplier of aluminum to can makers, was now also a formidable competitor in cans. The moves by both suppliers and customers of can makers to integrate into can manufacturing themselves had profoundly redefined the metal can industry since John Connelly's arrival.

Reflecting on these dramatic changes, Avery wondered whether Crown, with $1.8 billion in sales, should consider bidding for all or part of Continental Can. Avery also wondered whether Crown should break with tradition and expand its product line beyond the manufacture of metal cans and closures. For 30 years Crown had stuck to its core business, metal can making, but analysts saw little growth potential for metal cans in the 1990s. Industry observers forecast plastics as the growth segment for containers. As Avery mulled over his options, he asked: Was it finally time for a change?

The Metal Container Industry

The metal container industry, representing 61% of all packaged products in the United States in 1989, produced metal cans, crowns (bottle caps), and closures (screw caps, bottle lids) to hold or seal an almost endless variety of consumer and industrial goods. Glass and plastic containers split the balance of the container market with shares of 21% and 18%, respectively. Metal cans served the beverage, food, and general packaging industries.

* Professor Stephen P. Bradley and Research Associate Sheila M. Cavanaugh prepared this case. Harvard Business School cases are developed solely as the basis for class discussion. Cases are not intended to serve as endorsements, sources of primary data, or illustrations of effective or ineffective management.

9-793-305

Metal cans were made of aluminum, steel, or a combination of both. Three-piece cans were formed by rolling a sheet of metal, soldering it, cutting it to size, and attaching two ends, thereby creating a three-piece, seamed can. Steel was the primary raw material of three-piece cans, which were most popular in the food and general packaging industries. Two-piece cans, developed in the 1960s, were formed by pushing a flat blank of metal into a deep cup, eliminating a separate bottom, a molding process termed "drawn and ironed." While aluminum companies developed the original technology for the two-piece can, steel companies ultimately followed suit with a thin-walled steel version. By 1983, two-piece cans dominated the beverage industry where they were the can of choice for beer and soft drink makers. Of the 120 billion cans produced in 1989, 80% were two-piece cans.

Throughout the decade of the 1980s, the number of metal cans shipped grew by an annual average of 3.7%. Aluminum can growth averaged 8% annually, while steel can shipments fell by an average of 3.1% per year. The number of aluminum cans produced increased by almost 200% during the period 1980–1989, reaching a high of 85 billion, while steel can production dropped by 22% to 35 billion for the same period (see Exhibit 1).

Industry Structure   Five firms dominated the $12.2 billion U.S. metal can industry in 1989, with an aggregate 61% market share. The country's largest manufacturer—American National Can—held a 25% market share. The four firms trailing American National in sales were Continental Can (18% market share), Reynolds Metals (7%), Crown Cork & Seal (7%), and Ball Corporation (4%). Approximately 100 firms served the balance of the market.

Pricing   Pricing in the can industry was very competitive. To lower costs, managers sought long runs of standard items, which increased capacity utilization and reduced the need for costly changeovers. As a result, most companies offered volume discounts to encourage large orders. Despite persistent metal can demand, industry operating margins fell approximately 7% to roughly 4% between 1986 and 1989. Industry analysts attributed the drop in operating margins to (1) a 15% increase in aluminum can sheet prices at a time when most can makers had guaranteed volume prices that did not incorporate substantial cost increases; (2) a 7% increase in beverage can production capacity between 1987 and 1989; (3) an increasing number of the nation's major brewers producing containers in house; and (4) the consolidation of soft drink bottlers throughout the decade. Forced to economize following costly battles for market share, soft drink bottlers used their leverage to obtain packaging price discounts.[1] Overcapacity and a shrinking customer base contributed to an unprecedented squeeze on manufacturers' margins, and the can manufacturers themselves contributed to the margin

Exhibit 1 Metal Can Shipments by Market and Product, 1981–1989 (millions of cans)

	1981	%	1983	%	1985	%	1987	%	(Est.) 1989	%
Total Metal Cans Shipped	88,810		92,394		101,899		109,214		120,795	
By Market										
For sale:	59,433	67	61,907	67	69,810	69	81,204	74	91,305	76
Beverage	42,192		45,167		52,017		62,002		69,218	
Food	13,094		12,914		13,974		15,214		18,162	
General packaging	4,147		3,826		3,819		3,988		3,925	
For own use:	29,377	33	31,039	33	32,089	31	28,010	26	29,490	24
Beverage	14,134		16,289		18,160		14,771		17,477	
Food	15,054		14,579		13,870		13,167		11,944	
General packaging	189		171		59		72		69	
By Product										
Beverage:	56,326	63	61,456	67	70,177	69	76,773	70	86,695	72
Beer	30,901		33,135		35,614		36,480		37,276	
Soft drinks	25,425		28,321		34,563		40,293		49,419	
Food:	28,148	32	26,941	29	27,844	27	28,381	26	30,106	25
Dairy products	854		927		1,246		1,188		1,304	
Juices	13,494		11,954		11,385		11,565		12,557	
Meat, poultry, seafood	2,804		3,019		3,373		3,530		3,456	
Pet food	3,663		3,571		4,069		4,543		5,130	
Other	7,333		7,470		7,771		7,555		7,659	
General packaging:	4,336	5	3,997	4	3,878	4	4,060	4	3,994	3
Aerosol	2,059		2,144		2,277		2,508		2,716	
Paint: varnish	813		817		830		842		710	
Automotive products	601		229		168		128		65	
Other nonfoods	863		807		603		582		503	
By Materials Used										
Steel	45,386	52	40,116	45	34,316	37	34,559	34	35,318	29
Aluminum	42,561	48	48,694	55	58,078	63	67,340	66	85,477	71

Source: Can Shipment Report, Can Manufacturers Institute, 1981–1989.

deterioration by aggressively discounting to protect market share. As one manufacturer confessed, "When you look at the beverage can industry, it's no secret that we are selling at a lower price today than we were 10 years ago."

Customers Among the industry's largest users were the Coca-Cola Company, Anheuser-Busch Companies, Inc., Pepsico Inc., and Coca-Cola Enterprises Inc. (see Exhibit 2). Consolidation within the soft drink segment of the bottling industry reduced the number of bottlers from approximately 8,000 in 1980 to about 800 in 1989 and placed a significant amount of beverage volume in the hands of a few large companies.[2] Since the can constituted about 45% of the total cost of a packaged beverage, soft drink bottlers and brewers usually maintained relationships with more than one can supplier. Poor service and uncompetitive prices could be punished by cuts in order size.

Distribution Due to the bulky nature of cans, manufacturers located their plants close to customers to minimize transportation costs. The primary cost components of the metal can included (1) raw materials at 65%; (2) direct labor at 12%; and (3) transportation at roughly 7.5%. Various estimates placed the radius of economical distribution for a plant at between 150 and 300 miles. Beverage can producers preferred aluminum to steel because of aluminum's lighter weight and lower shipping costs. In 1988, steel cans weighed more than twice as much as aluminum.[3] The costs incurred in transporting cans to overseas markets made international trade uneconomical.

Exhibit 2   Top U.S. Users of Containers, 1989

Rank	Company	Soft Drink/Beverage Sales ($000)	Principal Product Categories
1	The Coca-Cola Company[a] (Atlanta, GA)	$8,965,800	Soft drinks, citrus juices, fruit drinks
2	Anheuser-Busch Companies, Inc.[b] (St. Louis, MO)	7,550,000	Beer, beer imports
3	PepsiCo Inc. (Purchase, NY)	5,777,000	Soft drinks, bottled water
4	The Seagram Company, Ltd. (Montreal, Quebec, Canada)	5,581,779	Distilled spirits, wine coolers, mixers, juices
5	Coca-Cola Enterprises, Inc.[a] (Atlanta, GA)	3,881,947	Soft drinks
6	Philip Morris Companies, Inc. (New York, NY)	3,435,000	Beer
7	The Molson Companies, Ltd. (Toronto, Ontario, Canada)	1,871,394	Beer, coolers, beer imports
8	John Labatt, Ltd. (London, Ontario, Canada)	1,818,100	Beer, wine
9	The Stroh Brewery Company[c] (Detroit, MI)	1,500,000	Beer, coolers, soft drinks
10	Adolph Coors Company[d] (Golden, CO)	1,366,108	Beer, bottled water

Source: Beverage World, 1990–1991 Databank.

[a]The Coca-Cola Company and Coca-Cola Enterprises purchased (versus in-house manufacture) all of its cans in 1989. Coca-Cola owned 49% of Coca-Cola Enterprises—the largest Coca-Cola bottler in the United States.

[b]In addition to in-house manufacturing at its wholly owned subsidiary (Metal Container Corporation), Anheuser-Busch Companies purchased its cans from four manufacturers. The percentage of cans manufactured by Anheuser-Busch was not publicly disclosed.

[c]Of the 4 to 5 billion cans used by The Stroh Brewery in 1989, 39% were purchased and 61% were manufactured in-house.

[d]Adolph Coors Company manufactured all of its cans, producing approximately 10 to 12 million cans per day, five days per week.

Foreign markets were served by joint ventures, foreign subsidiaries, affiliates of U.S. can manufacturers, and local overseas firms.

Manufacturing   Two-piece can lines cost approximately $16 million, and the investment in peripheral equipment raised the per-line cost to $20–$25 million. The minimum efficient plant size was one line and installations ranged from one to five lines. While two-piece can lines achieved quick and persistent popularity, they did not completely replace their antecedents—the three-piece can lines. The food and general packaging segment—representing 28% of the metal container industry in 1989—continued using three-piece cans throughout the 1980s. The beverage segment, however, had made a complete switch from three-piece to two-piece cans by 1983.

A typical three-piece can production line cost between $1.5 and $2 million and required expensive seaming, end-making, and finishing equipment. Since each finishing line could handle the output of three or four can-forming lines, the minimum efficient plant required at least $7 million in basic equipment. Most plants had 12 to 15 lines for the increased flexibility of handling more than one type of can at once. However, any more than 15 lines became unwieldy because of the need for duplication of set-up crews, maintenance, and supervision. The beverage industry's switch from three- to two-piece lines prompted many manufacturers to sell complete, fully operational three-piece lines "as is" for $175,000 to $200,000. Some firms shipped their old lines overseas to their foreign operations where growth potential was great, there were few entrenched firms, and canning technology was not well understood.

Exhibit 3   Comparative Performance of Major Aluminum Suppliers, 1988 (dollars in millions)

	Sales	Net Income	Net Profit Margin %	Long-Term Debt	Net Worth	Earnings Per Share
Alcan Aluminum						
1988	$8,529.0	$931.0	10.9%	$1,199.0	$4,320.0	$3.85
1987	6,797.0	445.0	6.5	1,336.0	3,970.0	1.73
1986	5,956.0	177.0	3.0	1,366.0	3,116.0	.79
1985	5,718.0	25.8	0.5	1,600.0	2,746.0	.12
1984	5,467.0	221.0	4.0	1,350.0	2,916.0	1.00
Alcoa						
1988	9,795.3	861.4	8.8	1,524.7	4,635.5	9.74
1987	7,767.0	365.8	4.7	2,457.6	3,910.7	4.14
1986	4,667.2	125.0	2.7	1,325.6	3,721.6	1.45
1985	5,162.7	107.4	2.1	1,553.5	3,307.9	1.32
1984	5,750.8	278.7	4.8	1,586.5	3,343.6	3.41
Reynolds Metals[a]						
1988	5,567.1	482.0	8.7	1,280.0	2,040.1	9.01
1987	4,283.8	200.7	4.7	1,567.7	1,599.6	3.95
1986	3,638.9	50.3	1.4	1,190.8	1,342.0	.86
1985	3,415.6	24.5	0.7	1,215.0	1,151.7	.46
1984	3,728.3	133.3	3.6	1,146.1	1,341.1	3.09

Source: *Value Line.*

[a]Reynolds Metals Company was the second-largest aluminum producer in the United States. The company was also the third-largest manufacturer of metal cans with a 7% market share.

Suppliers   Since the invention of the aluminum can in 1958, steel had fought a losing battle against aluminum. In 1970, steel accounted for 88% of metal cans, but by 1989 had dropped to 29%. In addition to being lighter, of higher, more consistent quality, and more economical to recycle, aluminum was also friendlier to the taste and offered superior lithography qualities. By 1989, aluminum accounted for 99% of the beer and 94% of the soft drink metal container businesses, respectively.

The country's three largest aluminum producers supplied the metal can industry. Alcoa, the world's largest aluminum producer with 1988 sales of $9.8 billion, and Alcan, the world's largest marketer of primary aluminum, with 1988 sales of $8.5 billion, supplied over 65% of the domestic can sheet requirements. Reynolds Metals, the second-largest aluminum producer in the United States, with 1988 sales of $5.6 billion, supplied aluminum sheet to the industry and also produced about 11 billion cans itself.[4] Reynolds Metals was the only aluminum company in the United States that produced cans (see Exhibit 3).

Steel's consistent advantage over aluminum was price. According to The American Iron and Steel Institute in 1988, steel represented a savings of from $5 to $7 for every thousand cans produced, or an estimated savings of $500 million a year for can manufacturers. In 1988, aluminum prices increased an estimated 15%, while the lower steel prices increased by only 5% to 7%. According to a representative of Alcoa, the decision on behalf of the firm to limit aluminum price increases was attributed to the threat of possible inroads by steel.[5]

Industry Trends   The major trends characterizing the metal container industry during the 1980s included (1) the continuing threat of in-house manufacture; (2) the emergence of plastics as a viable packaging material; (3) the steady competition from glass as a substitute for aluminum in the beer market; (4) the emergence of the soft drink industry as the largest end-user of packaging, with aluminum as the primary beneficiary; and (5) the diversification of, and consolidation among, packaging producers.

In-House Manufacture Production of cans at "captive" plants—those producing cans for their own company use—accounted for approximately 25% of the total can output in 1989. Much of the expansion in in-house manufactured cans, which persisted throughout the 1980s, occurred at plants owned by the nation's major food producers and brewers. Many large brewers moved to hold can costs down by developing their own manufacturing capability. Brewers found it advantageous to invest in captive manufacture because of high-volume, single-label production runs. Adolph Coors took this to the extreme by producing all their cans in-house and supplying almost all of their own aluminum requirements from their 130-million-pound sheet rolling mill in San Antonio, Texas.[6] By the end of the 1980s, the beer industry had the capacity to supply about 55% of its beverage can needs.[7]

Captive manufacturing was not widespread in the soft drink industry, where many small bottlers and franchise operations were generally more dispersed geographically compared with the brewing industry. Soft drink bottlers were also geared to low-volume, multilabel output, which was not as economically suitable for the in-house can manufacturing process.

Plastics Throughout the 1980s, plastics was the growth leader in the container industry with its share growing from 9% in 1980 to 18% in 1989. Plastic bottle sales in the United States were estimated to reach $3.5 billion in 1989, with food and beverage—buoyed by soft drinks sales—accounting for 50% of the total. Plastic bottles accounted for 11% of domestic soft drink sales, with most of its penetration coming at the expense of glass. Plastic's light weight and convenient handling contributed to widespread consumer acceptance. The greatest challenge facing plastics, however, was the need to produce a material that simultaneously retained carbonation and prevented infiltration of oxygen. The plastic bottle often allowed carbonation to escape in less than 4 months, while aluminum cans held carbonation for more than 16 months. Anheuser-Busch claimed that U.S. brewers expected beer containers to have at least a 90-day shelf-life, a requirement that had not been met by any plastic can or bottle.[8] Additionally, standard production lines that filled 2,400 beer cans per minute required containers with perfectly flat bottoms, a feature difficult to achieve using plastic.[9] Since 1987, the growth of plastics had slowed somewhat apparently due to the impact on the environment of plastic packaging. Unlike glass and aluminum, plastics recycling was not a "closed loop" system.[10]

There were many small players producing plastic containers in 1988, often specializing by end-use or geographic region. However, only seven companies had sales of over $100 million. Owens-Illinois, the largest producer of plastic containers, specialized in custom-made bottles and closures for food, health and beauty, and pharmaceutical products. It was the leading supplier of prescription containers, sold primarily to drug wholesalers, major drug chains, and the government. Constar, the second-largest domestic producer of plastic containers, acquired its plastic bottle operation from Owens-Illinois, and relied on plastic soft drink bottles for about two-thirds of its sales. Johnson Controls produced bottles for the soft drink industry from 17 U.S. plants and six non-U.S. plants, and was the largest producer of plastic bottles for water and liquor. American National and Continental Can both produced plastic bottles for food, beverages, and other products such as tennis balls (see Exhibit 4 for information on competitors).

Exhibit 4 Major U.S. Producers of Blow-Molded Plastic Bottles, 1989 (dollars in millions)

Company	Total Sales	Net Income	Plastic Sales	Product Code	Major Market
Owens-Illinois	$3,280	$ (57)	$754	1,3,4,6	Food, health and beauty, pharmaceutical
American National	4,336	52	566	1,2,3,6	Beverage, household, personal care, pharmaceutical
Constar	544	12	544	1,2,3,4,6	Soft drink, milk, food
Johnson Controls	3,100	104	465	2	Soft drink, beverages
Continental Can	3,332	18	353	1,2,3,4,5,6	Food, beverage, household, industrial
Silgan Plastics	415	96	100	1,2,3,4,6	Food, beverage, household, pharmaceutical, personal care
Sonoco Products Co.	1,600	96	N/A	1,3,4,6	Motor oil, industrial

Source: *The Rauch Guide to the U.S. Plastics Industry*. 1991; company annual reports.
Product code: (1) HDPE; (2) PET; (3) PP; (4) PVC; (5) PC; (6) multilayer.

Glass Glass bottles accounted for only 14% of domestic soft drink sales, trailing metal cans at 75%. The cost advantage that glass once had relative to plastic in the popular 16-ounce bottle size disappeared by the mid-1980s because of consistently declining resin prices. Moreover, soft drink bottlers preferred the metal can to glass because of a variety of logistical and economic benefits: faster filling speeds, lighter weight, compactness for inventory, and transportation efficiency. In 1989, the delivered cost (including closure and label) of a 12-ounce can (the most popular size) was about 15% less than that of glass or plastic 16-ounce bottles (the most popular size).[11] The area in which glass continued to outperform metal, however, was the beer category where consumers seemed to have a love affair with the "long neck" bottle that would work to its advantage in the coming years.[12]

Soft Drinks and Aluminum Cans Throughout the 1980s, the soft drink industry emerged as the largest end-user of packaging. In 1989, soft drinks captured more than 50% of the total beverage market. The soft drink industry accounted for 42% of metal cans shipped in 1989—up from 29% in 1980. The major beneficiary of this trend was the aluminum can. In addition to the industry's continued commitment to advanced technology and innovation, aluminum's penetration could be traced to several factors: (1) aluminum's weight advantage over glass and steel; (2) aluminum's ease of handling; (3) a wider variety of graphics options provided by multipack can containers; and (4) consumer preference.[13] Aluminum's growth was also supported by the vending machine market, which was built around cans and dispensed approximately 20% of all soft drinks in 1989. An estimated 60% of Coca-Cola's and 50% of Pepsi's beverages were packaged in metal cans. Coca-Cola Enterprises and Pepsi Cola Bottling Group together accounted for 22% of all soft drink cans shipped in 1989.[14] In 1980, the industry shipped 15.9 billion aluminum soft drink cans. By 1989, that figure had increased to 49.2 billion cans. This increase, representing a 12% average annual growth rate, was achieved during a decade that experienced a 3.6% average annual increase in total gallons of soft drinks consumed.

Diversification and Consolidation Low profit margins, excess capacity, and rising material and labor costs prompted a number of corporate diversifications and subsequent consolidations throughout the 1970s and 1980s. While many can manufacturers diversified across the spectrum of rigid containers to supply all major end-use markets (food, beverages, and general packaging), others diversified into nonpackaging businesses such as energy (oil and gas) and financial services.

Over a 20-year period, for example, American Can reduced its dependence on domestic can manufacturing, moving into totally unrelated fields, such as insurance. Between 1981 and 1986 the company invested $940 million to acquire all or part of six insurance companies. Ultimately, the packaging businesses of American Can were acquired by Triangle Industries in 1986, while the financial

services businesses re-emerged as Primerica. Similarly, Continental Can broadly diversified its holdings, changing its name to Continental Group in 1976 when can sales dropped to 38% of total sales. In the 1980s, Continental Group invested heavily in energy exploration, research, and transportation, but profits were weak and they were ultimately taken over by Peter Kiewit Sons in 1984.

While National Can stuck broadly to containers, it diversified through acquisition into glass containers, food canning, pet foods, bottle closures, and plastic containers. However, instead of generating future growth opportunities, the expansion into food products proved a drag on company earnings.

Under the leadership of John W. Fisher, Ball Corporation, a leading glass bottle and can maker, expanded into the high-technology market and by 1987 had procured $180 million in defense contracts. Fisher directed Ball into such fields as petroleum engineering equipment, and photo-engraving and plastics, and established the company as a leading manufacturer of computer components.

Major Competitors in 1989 For over 30 years, three of the current five top competitors in can manufacturing dominated the metal can industry. Since the early 1950s, American Can, Continental Can, Crown Cork & Seal, and National Can held the top four rankings in can manufacturing. A series of dramatic mergers and acquisitions among several of the country's leading manufacturers throughout the 1980s served to shift as well as consolidate power at the top. Management at fourth-ranked Crown Cork & Seal viewed the following four firms as constituting its primary competition in 1989: American National Can, Continental Can, Reynolds Metals, and Ball Corporation. Two smaller companies—Van Dorn Company and Heekin Can—were strong competitors regionally (see Exhibit 5).

American National Can Representing the merger of two former, long-established competitors, American National—a wholly-owned subsidiary of the Pechiney International Group—generated sales revenues of $4.4 billion in 1988. In 1985, Triangle Industries, a New Jersey–based maker of video games, vending machines, and jukeboxes, bought National Can for $421 million. In 1986, Triangle bought the U.S. packaging businesses of American Can for $550 million. In 1988, Triangle sold American National Can (ANC) to Pechiney, SA, the French state-owned industrial concern, for $3.5 billion. Pechiney was the world's third-largest producer of aluminum and, through its Cebal Group, a major European manufacturer of packaging. A member of the Pechiney International Group, ANC was the largest beverage can maker in the world—producing more than 30 billion cans annually. With more than 100 facilities in 12 countries, ANC's product line of aluminum and steel cans, glass containers, and caps and closures served the major beverage, food, pharmaceuticals, and cosmetics markets.

Continental Can Continental Can had long been a financially stable container company; its revenues increased

Exhibit 5   Comparative Performance of Major Metal Can Manufacturers (dollars in millions)

Company[a]	Net Sales	SG&A as a % of Sales	Gross Margin	Operating Income	Net Profit	Return on Sales	Return on Average Assets	Return on Average Equity
Ball Corporation								
1988	$1,073.0	8.1%	$161.7	$113.0	$47.7	4.4%	5.7%	11.6%
1987	1,054.1	8.5	195.4	147.6	59.8	5.7	7.8	15.7
1986	1,060.1	8.2	168.0	150.5	52.8	5.0	7.6	15.2
1985	1,106.2	7.5	140.7	140.5	51.2	4.6	8.1	16.4
1984	1,050.7	7.9	174.1	123.9	46.3	4.4	7.8	16.6
1983	909.5	8.2	158.2	114.6	39.0	4.3	7.3	15.6
1982	889.1	8.4	147.4	100.5	34.5	3.9	6.9	15.8
Crown Cork & Seal								
1988	1,834.1	2.8	264.6	212.7	93.4	5.1	8.6	14.5
1987	1,717.9	2.9	261.3	223.3	88.3	5.1	8.7	14.5
1986	1,618.9	2.9	235.3	202.4	79.4	4.9	8.8	14.3
1985	1,487.1	2.9	216.4	184.4	71.7	4.8	8.6	13.9
1984	1,370.0	3.1	186.6	154.8	59.5	4.4	7.3	11.4
1983	1,298.0	3.3	182.0	138.9	51.5	4.0	6.2	9.3
1982	1,351.8	3.3	176.2	132.5	44.7	3.3	5.2	7.9
Heekin Can, Inc.								
1988	275.8	3.7	38.9	36.4	9.6	3.5	4.8	22.6
1987	230.4	4.0	33.6	30.2	8.8	3.8	5.8	26.3
1986	207.6	4.1	31.1	28.0	7.0	3.4	5.4	27.5
1985	221.8	3.2	31.8	29.0	6.8	3.1	5.2	42.5
1984	215.4	2.7	28.4	26.5	5.5	2.6	4.3	79.7
1983	181.6	3.2	24.4	22.8	3.8	2.1	3.3	102.7
1982[b]	—							
Van Dorn Company								
1988	333.5	16.5	75.3	26.7	11.7	3.5	6.6	12.2
1987	330.0	15.7	73.6	28.4	12.3	3.7	7.7	12.7
1986	305.1	16.3	70.4	26.5	11.7	3.8	7.7	12.9
1985	314.3	15.1	75.6	33.6	15.4	4.9	10.6	19.0
1984	296.4	14.7	74.9	36.5	16.8	5.7	12.9	24.9
1983	225.9	14.8	48.5	20.1	7.4	3.3	6.8	12.8
1982	184.3	16.1	37.7	12.7	3.6	2.0	3.5	6.6
American Can Company[c]								
1985	2,854.9	22.6	813.4	1670.0	149.1	5.2	5.2	10.9
1984	3,177.9	18.0	740.8	168.3	132.4	4.2	4.9	11.2

(continued)

Exhibit 5   *(Continued)*

Company[a]	Net Sales	SG&A as a % of Sales	Gross Margin	Operating Income	Net Profit	Return on Sales	Return on Average Assets	Return on Average Equity
American Can Company (cont.)								
1983	$3,346.4	15.0%	$625.4	$123.6	$94.9	2.8%	3.5%	9.7%
1982	4,063.4	16.1	766.3	113.4	23.0	0.6	0.8	2.4
1981	4,836.4	15.0	949.6	223.0	76.7	1.2	2.7	7.2
1980	4,812.2	15.8	919.5	128.1	85.7	1.8	3.1	8.0
National Can Company[d]								
1983	1,647.5	5.1	215.3	93.5	22.1	1.3	2.7	6.3
1982	1,541.5	4.6	206.3	100.7	34.1	2.2	4.4	10.0
1981	1,533.9	4.6	191.7	86.3	24.7	1.6	3.1	7.5
1980	1,550.9	5.4	233.7	55.0	50.6	3.3	6.4	16.7
The Continental Group, Inc.[e]								
1983	4,942.0	6.3	568.0	157.0	173.5	3.5	4.4	9.4
1982	5,089.0	6.4	662.0	217.0	180.2	3.5	4.3	9.6
1981	5,291.0	7.2	747.0	261.0	242.2	4.6	5.9	13.6
1980	5,171.0	7.2	700.0	201.0	224.8	4.3	5.5	13.7
1979	4,544.0	6.5	573.0	171.0	189.2	4.2	5.3	13.1

Source: *Value Line* and company annual reports (for SGA, COGS, and Asset figures).

[a]Refer to Exhibit 3 for Reynolds Metals Company.

[b]Figures not disclosed for 1982.

[c]In 1985, packaging made up 60% of total sales at American Can, with the remainder in specialty retailing. In 1986 Triangle Industries purchased the U.S. packaging business of American Can. In 1987, American National Can was formed through the merger of American Can Packaging and National Can Corporation. In 1989, Triangle sold American National Can to Pechiney, SA.

[d]In 1985, Triangle Industries bought National Can.

[e]In 1984, Peter Kiewit Sons purchased The Continental Group. SG&A as a percentage of sales for Continental Can hovered around 6.5% through the late 1980s.

every year without interruption from 1923 through the mid-1980s. By the 1970s, Continental had surpassed American Can as the largest container company in the United States. The year 1984, however, represented a turning point in Continental's history when the company became an attractive takeover target. Peter Kiewit Sons Inc., a private construction firm in Omaha, Nebraska, purchased Continental Group for $2.75 billion in 1984. Under the direction of Vice Chairman Donald Strum, Kiewit dismantled Continental Group in an effort to make the operation more profitable. Within a year, Strum had sold $1.6 billion worth of insurance, gas pipelines, and oil and gas reserves. Staff at Continental's Connecticut headquarters was reduced from 500 to 40. Continental Can generated sales revenues of $3.3 billion in 1988, ranking it second behind American National. By the late 1980s, management at Kiewit considered divesting—in whole or in part—Continental Can's packaging operations, which included Continental Can USA, Europe, and Canada, as well as metal packaging operations in Latin America, Asia, and the Middle East.

Reynolds Metals   Based in Richmond, Virginia, Reynolds Metals was the only domestic company integrated from aluminum ingot through aluminum cans. With 1988 sales revenues of $5.6 billion and net income of $482 million, Reynolds served the following principal markets: packaging and containers; distributors and fabricators; building and construction; aircraft and automotive; and electrical. Reynolds' packaging and container revenue amounted to $2.4 billion in 1988. As one of the industry's leading can makers, Reynolds was instrumental in establishing new uses for the aluminum can and was a world leader in can-making technology. Reynolds' developments included high-speed can-forming machinery with capabilities in excess of 400 cans per minute, faster inspection equipment (operating at speeds of up to 2,000 cans per minute), and spun aluminum tops which contained less material. The company's next generation of can end-making technology was scheduled for installation in the early 1990s.

Ball Corporation   Founded in 1880 in Muncie, Indiana, Ball Corporation generated operating income of $113 million on sales revenues of $1 billion in 1988. Considered one of the industry's low-cost producers, Ball was the fifth-largest manufacturer of metal containers as well as the third-largest glass container manufacturer in the United States. Ball's packaging businesses accounted for 82.5% of total sales and 77.6% of consolidated operating earnings in 1988. Ball's can-making technology and manufacturing flexibility allowed the company to make shorter runs in the production of customized, higher-margin products designed to meet customers' specifications and needs. In 1988, beverage can sales accounted for 62% of total sales. Anheuser-Busch, Ball's largest customer, accounted for 14% of sales that year. In 1989, Ball was rumored to be planning to purchase the balance of its 50%-owned joint venture, Ball Packaging Products Canada, Inc. The acquisition would make Ball the number two producer of metal beverage and food containers in the Canadian market.

Van Dorn Company   The industry's next two largest competitors, with a combined market share of 3%, were Van Dorn Company and Heekin Can, Inc. Founded in 1872 in Cleveland, Ohio, Van Dorn manufactured two product lines: containers and plastic injection molding equipment. Van Dorn was one of the world's largest producers of drawn aluminum containers for processed foods, and a major manufacturer of metal, plastic, and composite containers for the paint, petroleum, chemical, automotive, food, and pharmaceutical industries. Van Dorn was also a leading manufacturer of injection molding equipment for the plastics industry. The company's Davies Can Division, founded in 1922, was a regional manufacturer of metal and plastic containers. In 1988, Davies planned to build two new can manufacturing plants at a cost of about $20 million each. These facilities would each produce about 40 million cans annually. Van Dorn's consolidated can sales of $334 million in 1988 ranked it sixth overall among the country's leading can manufacturers.

Heekin Can   James Heekin, a Cincinnati coffee merchant, founded Heekin Can in 1901 as a way to package his own products. The company experienced rapid growth and soon contained one of the country's largest metal lithography plants under one roof. Three generations of the Heekin family built Heekin into a strong regional force in the packaging industry. The family sold the business to Diamond International Corporation, a large, diversified publicly held company, in 1965. Diamond operated Heekin as a subsidiary until 1982 when it was sold to its operating management and a group of private investors. Heekin went public in 1985. With 1988 sales revenues of $275.8 million, seventh-ranked Heekin primarily manufactured steel cans for processors, packagers, and distributors of food

and pet food. Heekin represented the country's largest regional can maker.

Crown Cork & Seal Company

Company History   In August 1891, a foreman in a Baltimore machine shop hit upon an idea for a better bottle cap—a piece of tin-coated steel with a flanged edge and an insert of natural cork. Soon this crown-cork cap became the hit product of a new venture, Crown Cork & Seal Company. When the patents ran out, however, competition became severe and nearly bankrupted the company in the 1920s. The faltering Crown was bought in 1927 by a competitor, Charles McManus.[15]

Under the paternalistic leadership of McManus, Crown prospered in the 1930s, selling more than half of the United States and world supply of bottle caps. He then correctly anticipated the success of the beer can and diversified into can making, building one of the world's largest plants in Philadelphia. However, at one million square feet and containing as many as 52 lines, it was a nightmare of inefficiency and experienced substantial losses. Although McManus was an energetic leader, he engaged in nepotism and never developed an organization that could run without him. Following his death in 1946, the company ran on momentum, maintaining dividends at the expense of investment in new plants. Following a disastrous attempt to expand into plastics and a ludicrous diversification into metal bird cages, Crown reorganized along the lines of the much larger Continental Can, incurring additional personnel and expense that again brought the company near to bankruptcy.

At the time, John Connelly was just a fellow on the outside, looking to Crown as a prospective customer and getting nowhere. The son of a Philadelphia blacksmith, Connelly had begun in a paperbox factory at 15 and worked his way up to become eastern sales manager of the Container Corporation of America. When he founded his own company, Connelly Containers, Inc., in 1946, Crown promised him some business. That promise was forgotten by the post-McManus regime, which loftily refused to "take a chance" on a small supplier like Connelly. By 1955, when Crown's distress became evident, Connelly began buying stock and in November 1956 was asked to be an outside director—a desperate move by the ailing company.[16]

In April 1957, Crown Cork & Seal teetered on the verge of bankruptcy. Bankers Trust Company withdrew Crown's line of credit; it seemed that all that was left was to write the company's obituary when John Connelly took over the presidency. His rescue plan was simple—as he called it, "just common sense." Connelly's first move was to pare down the organization. Paternalism ended in a blizzard of pink slips. Connelly moved quickly to cut headquarters staff by half to reach a lean force of 80. The company returned to a simple functional organization. In 20 months Crown had eliminated 1,647 jobs or 24% of the payroll. As part of the company's reorganization, Connelly discarded divisional accounting practices; at the same time he eliminated the divisional line and staff concept. Except for one accountant maintained at each plant location, all accounting and cost control was performed at the corporate level; the corporate accounting staff occupied one-half the space used by the headquarters group. In addition, Connelly disbanded Crown's central research and development facility.

The second step was to institute the concept of accountability. Connelly aimed to instill a deep-rooted pride of workmanship throughout the company by establishing Crown managers as "owner-operators" of their individual businesses. Connelly gave each plant manager responsibility for plant profitability, including any allocated costs. (All company overhead, estimated at 5% of sales, was allocated to the plant level.) Previously, plant managers had been responsible only for controllable expenses at the plant level. Although the plant managers' compensation was not tied to profit performance, one senior executive pointed out that the managers were "certainly rewarded on the basis of that figure." Connelly also held plant managers responsible for quality and customer service.

The next step was to slow production to a halt and liquidate $7 million in inventory. By mid-July Crown paid off the banks. Connelly introduced sales forecasting dovetailed with new production and inventory controls. This move put pressure on the plant managers, who were no longer able to avoid layoffs by dumping excess products into inventory.

By the end of 1957, Crown had, in one observer's words, "climbed out of the coffin and was sprinting." Between 1956 and 1961, sales increased from $115 million to $176 million and profits soared. Throughout the 1960s, the company averaged an annual 15.5% increase in sales and 14% in profits. Connelly, not satisfied simply with short-term reorganizations of the existing company, developed a strategy that would become its hallmark for the next three decades.

Connelly's Strategy

According to William Avery, "From his first day on the job, Mr. Connelly structured the company to be successful. He took control of costs and did a wonderful job taking us in the direction of becoming owner-operators." But what truly separated Connelly from his counterparts, Avery explained, was that while he was continually looking for new ways of controlling costs, he was equally hell-bent on improving quality. Connelly, described by *Forbes* as an individual with a "scrooge-like aversion to fanfare and overhead," emphasized cost efficiency, quality, and customer service as the essential ingredients for Crown's strategy in the decades ahead.

Products and Markets   Recognizing Crown's position as a small producer in an industry dominated by American Can and Continental Can, Connelly sought to develop a product line built around Crown's traditional strengths in metal forming and fabrication. He chose to emphasize the areas Crown knew best—tin-plated cans and crowns—and to concentrate on specialized uses and international markets.

A dramatic illustration of Connelly's commitment to this strategy occurred in the early 1960s. In 1960, Crown held over 50% of the market for motor oil cans. In 1962, R. C. Can and Anaconda Aluminum jointly developed fiber-foil cans for motor oil, which were approximately 20% lighter and 15% cheaper than the metal cans then in use. Despite the loss of sales, management decided that it had other more profitable opportunities and that new materials, such as fiber-foil, provided too great a threat in the motor oil can business. Crown's management decided to exit from the oil can market.

In the early 1960s Connelly singled out two specific applications in the domestic market: beverage cans and the growing aerosol market. These applications were called "hard to hold" because cans required special characteristics to either contain the product under pressure or to avoid affecting taste. Connelly led Crown directly from a soldered can into the manufacture of two-piece steel cans in the 1960s. Recognizing the enormous potential of the soft drink business, Crown began designing its equipment specifically to meet the needs of soft drink producers, with innovations such as two printers in one line and conversion printers that allowed for rapid design changeover to accommodate just-in-time delivery.[17] After producing exclusively steel cans through the late 1970s, Connelly spearheaded Crown's conversion from steel to aluminum cans in the early 1980s.

In addition to the specialized product line, Connelly's strategy was based on two geographic thrusts: expand to national distribution in the United States and invest heavily abroad. Connelly linked domestic expansion to Crown's manufacturing reorganization; plants were spread out across the country to reduce transportation costs and to be nearer customers. Crown was unusual in that it did not set up plants to service a single customer. Instead, Crown concentrated on providing products for a number of customers near their plants. In international markets, Crown invested heavily in developing nations, first with crowns and then with cans as packaged foods became more widely accepted. Metal containers generated 65% of Crown's $1.8 billion 1988 sales, while closures generated 30% and packaging equipment 5%.

Manufacturing   When Connelly took over in 1957, Crown had perhaps the most outmoded and inefficient production facilities in the industry. Dividends had taken precedence over new investment, and old machinery combined with the cumbersome Philadelphia plant had generated very high production and transportation costs. Soon after he gained control, Connelly took drastic action, closing down the Philadelphia facility and investing heavily in new and geographically dispersed plants. From 1958 to 1963, the company spent almost $82 million on relocation and new facilities. From 1976 through 1989, Crown had 26 domestic plant locations versus 9 in 1955. The plants were small (usually 2 to 3 lines for two-piece cans) and were located close to the customer rather than the raw material source. Crown operated its plants 24 hours a day with unique 12-hour shifts. Employees had two days on followed by two days off and then three days on followed by three days off.

Crown emphasized quality, flexibility, and quick response to customer needs. One officer claimed that the key to the can industry was "the fact that nobody stores cans" and when customers need them "they want them in a hurry and on time. . . . Fast answers get customers." To accommodate customer demands, some of Crown's plants kept more than a month's inventory on hand. Crown also instituted a total quality improvement process to refine its manufacturing processes and gain greater control. According to a Crown spokesperson, "The objective of this quality improvement process is to make the best possible can at the lowest possible cost. You lower the cost of doing business not by the wholesale elimination of people, but by reducing mistakes in order to improve efficiency. And you do that by making everybody in the company accountable."

Recycling In 1970, Crown formed Nationwide Recyclers, Inc., as a wholly owned subsidiary. By 1989, Crown believed Nationwide was one of the top four or five aluminum can recyclers in the country. While Nationwide was only marginally profitable, Crown had invested in the neighborhood of $10 million in its recycling arm.

Research and Development (R&D) Crown's technology strategy focused on enhancing the existing product line. As one executive noted, "We are not truly pioneers. Our philosophy is not to spend a great deal of money for basic research. However, we do have tremendous skills in die forming and metal fabrication, and we can move to adapt to the customer's needs faster than anyone else in the industry."[18] For instance, Crown worked closely with large breweries in the development of the two-piece drawn-and-ironed cans for the beverage industry. Crown also made an explicit decision to stay away from basic research. According to one executive, Crown was not interested in "all the frills of an R&D section of high-class, ivory-towered scientists. . . . There is a tremendous asset inherent in being second, especially in the face of the ever-changing state of flux you find in this industry. You try to let others take the risks and make the mistakes. . . ."

This philosophy did not mean that Crown never innovated. For instance, Crown was able to beat its competitors into two-piece can production. Approximately $120 million in new equipment was installed from 1972 through 1975, and by 1976 Crown had 22 two-piece lines in production—more than any other competitor.[19] Crown's research teams also worked closely with customers on specific customer requests. For example, a study of the most efficient plant layout for a food packer or the redesign of a dust cap for the aerosol packager were not unusual projects.

Marketing and Customer Service The cornerstone of Crown's marketing strategy was, in John Connelly's words, the philosophy that "you can't just increase efficiency to succeed; you must at the same time improve quality." In conjunction with its R&D strategy, the company's sales force maintained close ties with customers and emphasized Crown's ability to provide technical assistance and specific problem solving at the customer's plant. Crown's manufacturing emphasis on flexibility and quick response to customers' needs supported its marketing emphasis on putting the customer first. Michael J. McKenna, president of Crown's North American Division, insisted, "We have always been and always will be extremely customer driven."[20]

Competing cans were made of identical materials to identical specifications on practically identical machinery, and sold at almost identical prices in a given market. At Crown, all customers' gripes went to John Connelly, who was the company's best salesman. A visitor recalled being in his office when a complaint came through from the manager of a Florida citrus-packing plant. Connelly assured him the problem would be taken care of immediately, then casually remarked that he would be in Florida the next day. Would the plant manager join him for dinner? He would indeed. As Crown's president put the telephone down, his visitor said that he hadn't realized Connelly was planning to go to Florida. "Neither did I," confessed Connelly, "until I began talking."[21]

Financing After he took over in 1957, Connelly applied the first receipts from the sale of inventory to get out from under Crown's short-term bank obligations. He then steadily reduced the debt/equity ratio from 42% in 1956 to 18.2% in 1976 and 5% in 1986. By the end of 1988, Crown's debt represented less than 2% of total capital. Connelly discontinued cash dividends in 1956, and in 1970 repurchased the last of the preferred stock, eliminating preferred dividends as a cash drain. From 1970 forward, management applied excess cash to the repurchase of stock. Connelly set ambitious earnings goals and most years he achieved them. In the 1976 annual report he wrote, "A long time ago we made a prediction that some day our sales would exceed $1 billion and profits of $60.00 per share. Since then, the stock has been split 20-for-1 so this means $3.00 per share." Crown Cork & Seal's revenues reached $1 billion in 1977 and earnings per share reached $3.46. Earnings per share reached $10.11 in 1988 adjusted for a 3-for-1 stock split in September 1988.

International A significant dimension of Connelly's strategy focused on international growth, particularly in developing countries. Between 1955 and 1960, Crown received what were called "pioneer rights" from many foreign governments aiming to build up the industrial sectors of their countries. These "rights" gave Crown first chance at any new can or closure business introduced into these developing countries. Mark W. Hartman, president of Crown's International Division, described Connelly as "a Johnny Appleseed with respect to the international marketplace. When the new countries of Africa were emerging, for example, John was there offering crown-making capabilities to help them in their industrialization, while at the same time getting a foothold for Crown. John's true love was international business."[22] By 1988, Crown's 62 foreign plants generated 44% of sales and 54% of operating profits. John Connelly visited each of Crown's overseas plants. (See Exhibit 6 for map of plant locations.)

Exhibit 6 Crown Cork & Seal Facilities, 1989

Crown emphasized national management wherever possible. Local people, Crown asserted, understood the local marketplace: the suppliers, the customers, and the unique conditions that drove supply and demand. Crown's overseas investment also offered opportunities to recycle equipment that was, by U.S. standards, less sophisticated. Because can manufacturing was new to many regions of the world, Crown's older equipment met the needs of what was still a developing industry overseas.

Performance Connelly's strategy met with substantial success throughout his tenure at Crown. With stock splits and price appreciation, $100 invested in Crown stock in 1957 would be worth approximately $30,000 in 1989. After restructuring the company in his first three years, revenues grew at 12.2% per year while income grew at 14.0% over the next two decades (see Exhibit 7). Return on equity averaged 15.8% for much of the 1970s, while Continental Can and American Can lagged far behind at 10.3% and 7.1%, respectively. Over the period 1968–1978 Crown's total return to shareholders ranked 114 out of the Fortune 500, well ahead of IBM (183) and Xerox (374).

In the early 1980s, flat industry sales, combined with an increasingly strong dollar overseas, unrelenting penetration by plastics, and overcapacity in can manufacturing at home, led to declining sales revenues at Crown. Crown's sales dropped from $1.46 billion in 1980 to $1.37 billion by 1984. However, by 1985 Crown had rebounded and annual sales growth averaged 7.6% from 1984 through 1988 while profit growth averaged 12% (see Exhibits 8 and 9). Over the period 1978–1988 Crown's total return to shareholders was 18.6% per year, ranking 146 out of the Fortune 500. In 1988, *Business-Week* noted that Connelly—earning a total of only $663,000 in the three years ending in 1987—garnered shareholders the best returns for the least executive pay in the United States. As an industry analyst observed, "Crown's strategy is a no-nonsense, back-to-basics strategy—except they never left the basics."[23]

John Connelly's Contribution to Success

Customers, employees, competitors, and Wall Street analysts attributed Crown's sustained success to the unique leadership of John Connelly. He arrived at Crown as it headed into bankruptcy in 1957, achieved a 1,646% increase in profits on a relatively insignificant sales increase by 1961, and proceeded to outperform the industry's giants throughout the next three decades. A young employee expressed the loyalty created by Connelly: "If John told me to jump out the window, I'd jump—and be sure he'd catch me at the bottom with a stock option in his hand."

Yet Connelly was not an easy man to please. Crown's employees had to get used to Connelly's tough, straight-line management. *Fortune* credited Crown's success to Connelly, "whose genial Irish grin masks a sober salesman executive who believes in the eighty-hour week and in traveling while competitors sleep." He went to meetings uninvited, and expected the same devotion to Crown of his employees as he demanded of himself. As one observer remembered:

> The Saturday morning meeting is standard operating procedure. Crown's executives travel and confer only at night and on weekends. William D. Wallace, vice president for operations, travels 100,000 miles a year, often in the company plane. But Connelly sets the pace. An associate recalls driving to his home in the predawn blackness to pick him up for a flight to a distant plant. The Connelly house was dark, but he spotted a figure sitting on the curb under a street light, engrossed in a loose-leaf book. Connelly's greeting, as he jumped into the car: "I want to talk to you about last month's variances."[24]

Avery's Challenge in 1989

Avery thought long and hard about the options available to him in 1989. He considered the growing opportunities in plastic closures and containers, as well as glass containers. With growth slowing in metal containers, plastics was the only container segment that held much promise. However, the possibility of diversifying beyond the manufacture of containers altogether had some appeal, although the appropriate opportunity was not at hand. While Crown's competitors had aggressively expanded in a variety of directions, Connelly had been cautious, and had prospered. Avery wondered if now was the time for a change at Crown.

Within the traditional metal can business, Avery had to decide whether or not to get involved in the bidding for Continental Can. The acquisition of Continental Can Canada (CCC)—with sales of roughly $400 million—would make Canada Crown's largest single presence outside of the United States. Continental's USA business—with estimated revenues of $1.3 billion in 1989—would double the size of Crown's domestic operations. Continental's Latin American, Asian, and Middle Eastern operations were rumored to be priced in the range of $100 million to $150 million. Continental's European operations generated estimated sales of $1.5 billion in 1989 and included a work force of 10,000 at 30 production sites. Potential bidders for all, or part of Continental's operations, included many of Crown's U.S. rivals in addition to European competition: Pechiney International of France, Metal Box of Great Britain (which had recently acquired Carnaud SA), and VIAG AG, a German trading group, among others.

Avery knew that most mergers in this industry had not worked out well. He also thought about the challenge of taking two companies that come from completely different cultures and bringing them together. There would be inevitable emotional and attitudinal changes, particularly for Continental's salaried managers and Crown's "owner-operators." Avery also knew that the merger of American Can and National Can had its difficulties. That consolidation was taking longer than expected and, according to one observer, "American Can would be literally wiped out in the end."

Avery found himself challenging Crown's traditional strategies and thought seriously of drafting a new blueprint for the future.

Exhibit 7 Crown Cork & Seal Company Consolidated Statement of Income (dollars in millions, year-end December 31)

	1956	1961	1966	1971	1973	1975	1977	1979
Net Sales	$115.1	$177.0	$279.8	$448.4	$571.8	$825.0	$1,049.1	$1,402.4
Costs, Expenses and Other Income:								
Cost of products sold	95.8	139.1	217.2	350.9	459.2	683.7	874.1	1,179.3
Sales and administration	13.5	15.8	18.4	21.1	23.4	30.1	34.8	43.9
Depreciation	2.6	4.6	9.4	17.0	20.9	25.4	5.6	16.4
Net interest expense	1.2	1.3	4.6	5.1	4.4	7.4	31.7	40.1
Provision for taxes on income	.1	7.6	12.7	24.6	26.7	34.9	48.7	51.8
Net income	.3	6.7	16.7	28.5	34.3	41.6	53.8	70.2
Earnings per common share (actual)	(6.01)	.28	.80	1.41	1.81	2.24	3.46	4.65
Selected Financial Statistics								
Return on average equity	0.55%	9.66%	16.44%	14.05%	14.46%	15.20%	15.88%	15.57%
Return on sales	0.24	3.76	5.99	6.35	6.00	5.04	5.13	5.00
Return on average assets	0.32	6.00	6.76	7.25	8.00	7.69	9.13	8.93
Gross profit margin	16.76	21.43	22.37	21.76	19.69	17.13	16.68	15.90
Cost of goods sold/sales	83.24	78.57	77.63	78.24	80.31	82.87	83.32	84.29
SGA/sales	11.73	8.65	6.56	4.70	4.09	3.65	3.32	3.13

Crown Cork & Seal Company Consolidated Statement of Financial Position (dollars in millions, year-end December 31)								
	1956	1961	1966	1971	1973	1975	1977	1979
Total current assets	$50.2	$ 66.3	$109.4	$172.3	$223.4	$265.0	$340.7	$463.3
Total assets	86.5	129.2	269.5	398.1	457.5	539.0	631.1	828.2
Total current liabilities	15.8	24.8	75.3	110.2	139.6	170.0	210.8	287.1
Total long-term debt	20.2	17.7	57.9	41.7	37.9	29.7	12.8	12.2
Shareholders' equity	50.3	77.5	110.8	211.8	243.9	292.7	361.8	481.0
Selected Financial Statistics								
Debt/equity	0.40	0.23	0.52	0.20	0.16	0.10	0.04	0.03
Capital expenditures	1.9	11.8	32.7	33.1	40.4	49.0	58.9	55.9
Book value per share of common stock	1.57	2.74	5.19	10.62	13.13	16.64	23.54	31.84

Source: Adapted from Annual Reports.

Exhibit 8   Crown Cork & Seal Company Consolidated Statement of Income (dollars in millions except earnings per share, year-end December 31)

	1981	1982	1983	1984	1985	1986	1987	1988
Net Sales	$1,373.9	$1,351.9	$1,298.0	$1,369.6	$1,487.1	$1,618.9	$1,717.9	$1,834.1
Costs, Expenses, and Other Income:								
Cost of products sold	1,170.4	1,175.6	1,116.0	1,172.5	1,260.3	1,370.2	1,456.6	1,569.5
Sales and administrative	45.3	44.2	42.9	42.1	43.0	46.7	49.6	50.9
Depreciation	38.0	39.9	38.4	40.2	43.7	47.2	56.9	57.2
Interest expense	12.3	9.0	9.0	8.9	12.2	6.2	8.9	10.0
Interest income	—	—	—	—	—	—	(15.2)	(14.8)
Total Expenses	1,266.1	1,268.6	1,206.2	1,263.6	1,359.2	1,470.3	1,556.8	1,672.9
Income before taxes	107.8	83.2	91.8	105.9	127.9	148.6	161.1	161.2
Provision for taxes on income	43.0	38.5	40.2	46.4	56.2	69.2	72.7	67.8
Net income	64.8	44.7	51.5	59.5	71.7	79.4	88.3	93.4
Earnings per common share	1.48	1.05	1.27	1.59	2.17	2.48	2.86	3.37

Note: Earnings per common share have been restated to reflect a 3-for-1 stock split on September 12, 1988

Selected Financial Statistics

	1981	1982	1983	1984	1985	1986	1987	1988
Return on Average Equity (%):	11.72%	7.94%	9.34%	11.42%	13.94%	14.34%	14.46%	14.45%
Return on sales	4.72	3.31	3.97	4.35	4.82	4.91	5.14	5.09
Return on average assets	7.38	5.19	6.20	7.31	8.58	8.80	8.67	8.61
Gross profit margin	14.81	13.04	14.03	14.39	15.25	15.36	15.21	14.42
Cost of goods sold/sales	85.19	86.96	85.97	85.61	84.75	84.64	84.79	85.58
SGA/sales	3.30	3.27	3.30	3.07	2.89	2.88	2.89	2.78
Net Sales ($):								
United States	775.0	781.0	749.9	844.5	945.3	1,010.3	985.5	1,062.5
Europe	324.0	304.4	298.7	283.0	282.8	365.6	415.6	444.2
All others	283.6	273.1	259.1	261.3	269.3	269.0	342.5	368.6
Operating Profit ($):								
United States	62.8	58.9	55.0	67.1	88.9	92.8	95.4	70.6
Europe	20.6	19.0	24.0	17.2	17.0	21.9	22.4	33.4
All others	40.0	37.3	33.1	38.3	40.6	39.6	64.9	66.1
Operating Ratio (%):								
United States	8.1	7.5	7.3	7.9	9.4	9.7	9.6	6.6
Europe	6.3	6.2	8.0	6.0	6.0	5.9	5.4	7.5
All others	14.1	13.6	12.7	14.6	15.0	14.7	18.9	17.9

Source: Adapted from Annual Reports.
Note: The above sales figures are before the deduction of intracompany sales.

Exhibit 9 Crown Cork & Seal Company Consolidated Statement of Financial Position (dollars in millions, year-end December 31)

	1981	1982	1983	1984	1985	1986	1987	1988
Current Assets:								
Cash	$ 21.5	$ 15.8	$ 21.0	$ 7.0	$ 14.8	$ 16.5	$ 27.6	$ 18.0
Accounts receivable	262.8	257.1	240.6	237.6	279.0	270.4	280.7	248.1
Inventory	206.2	184.4	170.2	174.6	171.9	190.1	228.1	237.6
Total Current Assets	490.6	457.3	431.7	419.2	465.6	477.0	536.4	503.8
Investments	12.4	14.6	26.7	28.8	41.5	43.7	NA	NA
Goodwill	11.2	10.8	9.6	10.3	11.8	14.1	16.7	16.5
Property, plant and equipment	368.4	357.8	353.7	348.0	346.9	404.0	465.7	495.9
Other noncurrent assets	NA	NA	NA	NA	NA	NA	79.1	57.0
Total Assets	882.6	840.6	821.7	806.4	865.8	938.8	1,097.9	1,073.2
Current Liabilities:								
Short-term debt	22.7	21.6	24.4	42.0	16.3	17.2	44.0	20.2
Accounts payable	193.0	165.6	163.1	177.9	197.1	220.1	265.9	277.6
U.S. and foreign taxes	17.3	4.7	11.4	6.0	11.4	11.3	28.4	23.3
Total Current Liabilities	233.0	191.9	198.8	225.8	224.8	248.5	338.2	321.2
Long-term debt	5.8	5.6	2.8	2.7	2.2	1.4	19.7	9.4
Other	14.5	18.5	12.8	15.8	31.2	29.3	0.0	0.0
Total Long-term Debt	20.3	24.1	15.6	18.5	33.5	30.7	19.7	9.4
Deferred income taxes	55.5	57.7	57.8	60.7	71.3	79.2	89.4	93.7
Minority equity in subsidiaries	7.2	7.2	5.2	3.7	4.7	3.8	5.0	0.9
Shareholders' equity	566.7	559.8	544.3	497.8	531.5	576.6	645.6	648.0
Liability and owners' equity	882.6	840.6	821.7	806.4	865.8	938.8	1,097.9	1,073.2

	Selected Financial Statistics							

	1981	1982	1983	1984	1985	1986	1987	1988
Debt/equity	1.02%	0.99%	0.51%	0.54%	0.42%	0.24%	3.06%	1.45%
Debt/(debt + equity)	3.5%	4.1%	2.7%	3.5%	6.0%	5.0%	3.0%	1.4%
Shares outstanding at year end (M)	14.5	14.0	13.2	11.5	10.5	10.0	9.5	27.0
Capital expenditures ($M)	$ 63.8	$ 50.3	$ 55.5	$ 53.8	$ 50.9	$ 94.0	$ 99.5	$ 102.6
Shares repurchased (000)	75.4	528.3	863.1	1,694.5	1,006.0	677.1	638.7	2,242.9
Stock price: High[a]	$ 12.00	$ 10.00	$ 13.00	$ 15.75	$ 29.62	$ 38.25	$ 46.87	$ 46.72
Stock price: Low[a]	$ 8.00	$ 7.00	$ 10.00	$ 11.75	$ 15.12	$ 25.25	$ 28.00	$ 30.00

Source: Adapted from Annual Reports.
[a]Restated for 9/1988 stock split.

Endnotes

1. Salomon Brothers. 1990. *Beverage Cans Industry Report*, March 1.

2. Davis T. 1990. Can do: A metal container update. *Beverage World,* June: 34.

3. Sheehan J. J. 1988. Nothing succeeds like success. *Beverage World,* November: 82.

4. Until 1985, aluminum cans were restricted to carbonated beverages because it was the carbonation that prevented the can from collapsing. Reynolds discovered that by adding liquid nitrogen to the can's contents, aluminum containers could hold noncarbonated beverages and still retain their shape. The liquid nitrogen made it possible for Reynolds to make cans for liquor, chocolate drinks, and fruit juices.

5. Sly, J. 1988. A "can-do crusade" by steel industry. *Chicago Tribune,* July 3: 1.

6. Merrill Lynch Capital Markets. 1991. *Containers and Packaging Industry Report*. March 21, 1991.

7. Salomon Brothers Inc. 1991. *Containers/Packaging: Beverage Cans Industry Report,* April 3.

8. Agoos, A. 1985. Aluminum girds for the plastic can bid. *Chemical Week,* January 16: 18.

9. Oman, B. 1990. A clear choice? *Beverage World*, June: 78.

10. In response to public concern, the container industry developed highly efficient "closed loop" recycling systems. Containers flowed from the manufacturer, through the wholesaler/distributor, to the retailer, to the consumer, and back to the manufacturer or material supplier for recycling. Aluminum's high recycling value permitted can manufacturers to sell cans at a lower cost to beverage producers. The reclamation of steel cans lagged that of aluminum because collection and recycling did not result in significant energy or material cost advantages.

11. Lang, N. 1990. A touch of glass. *Beverage World,* June: 36.

12. Ibid.

13. U.S. Industrial Outlook, 1984–1990.

14. The First Boston Corporation. 1990. *Packaging Industry Report,* April 4.

15. Whalen, R. J. 1962. The unoriginal ideas that rebuilt Crown Cork. *Fortune,* October.

16. Ibid.: 156.

17. In the mid-1960s, growth in demand for soft drink and beer cans was more than triple that for traditional food cans.

18. Hamermesh, R. G., Anderson, M. J. Jr., and Harris, J. E. 1978. Strategies for low market share business. *Harvard Business Review,* May–June: 99.

19. In 1976, there were 47 two-piece tinplate and 130 two-piece aluminum lines in the United States.

20. *One Hundred Years.* Crown Cork & Seal Company, Inc.

21. Whalen, The unoriginal ideas that rebuilt Crown Cork.

22. *One Hundred Years.* Crown Cork & Seal Company, Inc.

23. *BusinessWeek.* 1987. These penny-pinchers deliver a big bang for their bucks. May 4.

24. Whalen, The unoriginal ideas that rebuilt Crown Cork.

Case 7 Sun Life Financial: Entering China*

Introduction

In early 2000, Dikran Ohannessian, Sun Life Financial's vice president, China, was flipping through piles of consultants' reports on the plane from Toronto, Canada, to Beijing, China.

As Ohannessian got up to stretch, he thought about what had been achieved: a representative office in Beijing, valuable contacts with the Chinese government and businesspeople, and an agreement to partner with a well-established Chinese financial services group. He knew there were many major milestones ahead, such as forming an entry strategy, choosing the geographical market area in which to operate, while keeping an eye on the financial viability as well as all the necessary hurdles to obtain a business license in China.

History of Sun Life Financial

Sun Life Financial of Canada began in 1865, in Montreal, selling insurance policies to Canadians in the process of the country's creation. By the 1890s, Sun Life Financial had begun an internationalization process, by expanding into Nicaragua, Ecuador, Peru, and Chile and later into Asia, including Japan, India, and China. At the turn of the century, Sun Life Financial looked to diversify its investments and began expanding through growing industries, such as electric utilities, gas, telephone, and transport. Sun Life Financial maintained private ownership and staved off a take-over attempt by a U.S. firm in the 1950s, allowing it to strengthen its roots within Canada.

In 1999, Sun Life Financial posted revenues of $14.7 billion,[1] of which $3.3 billion was life insurance premiums, $1.2 billion was health insurance, $3.5 billion was annuities, $4.1 billion was net investment income, and $2.6 billion was fee income. Sun Life Financial's net income was $164 million in 1999, up from $54 million realized on revenues of $12.9 billion in 1998. Net income in 1998 and 1999 had been negatively impacted by the costs associated with pensions sales practices reviews and increased reserves for guaranteed annuity rates in the U.K. business, as well as a significant increase in reserves in the discontinued accident and health reinsurance business. By early 2000, Sun Life Financial was a month away from a $2.1 billion initial public offering (IPO) in Toronto, New York, London, and the Philippines. Although there was pent-up demand for Sun Life Financial's shares in the Canadian marketplace, executives of Sun Life Financial and their advisers (RBC Dominion Securities and Morgan Stanley) had two tensions to balance—not letting the stock rise too quickly for those policy holders who had decided to take cash instead of becoming shareholders, while giving the investment community and those policy holders who were to become shareholders a strong initial stock price increase. The IPO would be the fifth in a string of Canadian life insurance companies that had gone public since the summer of 1999.[2]

Sun Life Financial had a six-pronged approach to its strategy:

1. Aggressively expand the wealth management business
2. Strategically grow higher return protection business lines
3. Achieve superior shareholder returns while maintaining financial discipline
4. Leverage strong brands across multiple product offerings
5. Capitalize on distribution strengths
6. Pursue expansion in key strategic markets

Exhibit 1 shows Sun Life Financial's sales by country. By early 2000, the majority of sales for Sun Life Financial were generated by sales in Canada and the United States. Although Sun Life Financial was not profitable in every country in which it operated, the company was not committed to any business that was not able to meet 15 percent after-tax return on equity in the future.[3] This low return on equity was the case in the country's U.K. operations, which some industry observers believed Sun Life Financial would sell off. Sun Life Financial believed that it would drive revenue growth through its 80 percent ownership of the Boston-based MFS wealth management business and, in the longer term, its foray into China.

Product and Services

Sun Life Financial's two principal businesses were wealth management and protection. Wealth management included all asset management, mutual funds, pensions, annuities, trusts, and banking operations. The wealth management business primarily was based in Canada, the United States and the United Kingdom and made up 52 percent of the company's revenues with $7.7 billion and 89 percent of its assets ($268.9 billion) in 1999. The complete wealth management business served 2.9 million individual investors and 7,000 institutional investors around the world. Almost all of the company's wealth management products (97 percent) were sold through independent third parties.

* Ken Mark and Jordan Mitchell prepared this case under the supervision of Professor Paul W. Beamish solely to provide material for class discussion. The authors do not intend to illustrate either effective or ineffective handling of a managerial situation. The authors may have disguised certain names and other identifying information to protect confidentiality.

Revenue by Business 1999

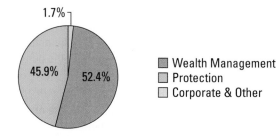

- Wealth Management
- Protection
- Corporate & Other

Revenue by Geography 1999

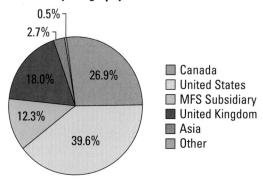

- Canada
- United States
- MFS Subsidiary
- United Kingdom
- Asia
- Other

Exhibit 1 **Sun Life Financial Revenue by Business and Geography**

Source: Sun Life Financial Initial Public Offering Booklet, Introduction, March 23, 2000.

The protection business included Sun Life Financial's insurance products, including individual insurance, group life insurance, and health insurance, making up 46 percent or $6.8 billion of the company's revenues in 1999. Principally, the group life and health insurance was based in Canada, the United States, and the United Kingdom, whereas the individual insurance business was in all the company's markets. Sun Life Financial was ranked second for group and health insurance in Canada and third in the United Kingdom. For individuals, Sun Life Financial offered whole life, term life, universal life, unit-linked life, and corporate-owned life insurance products. For groups, life, health, and disability insurance were available. Exhibit 2 shows definitions of insurance terms.

Sun Life Financial believed it had a winning formula in its protection business, due to its wide range of products backed by the company's financial strength and the effectiveness of it customer service and underwriting ability. In North America, Sun Life Financial was competing in a mature industry; however, the company needed to respond to the mounting pressures from banks that had entered the insurance industry, often undercutting prices. Due to deregulation in the marketplace, direct marketers and telemarketers were becoming more common in insurance sales. With greater emphasis on retirement planning in the mature markets, traditional life insurance products were losing ground against universal life in Canada and the United States and

unit-linked life insurance in the United Kingdom. This trend was not necessarily the case in Asia or South America, where traditional life insurance products were still popular.

Sun Life Financial's focus in the United States was on high net worth individuals with tailored packages for executive benefit plans. The company had restructured its United States sales force in 1997 by moving away from a career agency sales force to general agents selling a wide variety of products. In 1999, 65 percent of U.S. insurance sales were through general agents, and 35 percent were through third parties, such as banks and investment advisers. The general shift of sales approach caused a decrease in the number of policies, but through focusing on the high net worth segment, Sun Life Financial was able to increase total premium revenues.

In Canada, Sun Life Financial believed that it had expertise in selling group life and health insurance to large businesses as it had more than 7,000 policies representing more than 3 million individuals. Sun Life Financial marketed and distributed its group life and health insurance through its own sales representatives and career agents, independent brokers and consultants, Canadian associations, such as professional and alumni organizations, and through the Internet.

For individual life insurance, Sun Life Financial had 627,000 individual life insurance policies in force with 450,000 policyholders. Sun Life Financial had experienced an increase in premium income, despite a decreasing number of policies, due to success in selling through independent agents who tended to focus on high net worth individuals, increasing the average size of the policy. Although Sun Life Financial increasingly sold through independent life insurance brokers, such as financial planners and investment dealers, it still distributed a large portion through career agents, meaning that costs of distributing the insurance were moving from fixed to variable costs. Four years prior, in 1996, third-party distributors accounted for seven percent of sales for new individual life insurance, whereas in 1999, 30 percent were created through independents. In March 1999, Sun Life Financial formed a distribution alliance with Great-West Life, London Life, and Investors Group, where each organization could sell each other's universal life and term life insurance products.

History of Sun Life Financial's Involvement in China

In 1992, China opened two geographical market areas in the country to foreign investment—Shanghai and Guangzhou. To create a presence in China, a country that Sun Life Financial had operated in nearly a century earlier, Sun Life Financial opened a representative office in Beijing. (By 1920, Sun Life Financial had grown to be the largest foreign insurance company, but like all other foreign-owned insurance firms, it was forced to leave China in 1949, when the Communist party took power.)[4] The purpose of the office was to establish a presence, provide information to the Canadian headquarters, stay

Exhibit 2   Definitions of Insurance Types

Actuary

A person professionally trained in the technical aspects of pensions, insurance, and related fields. The actuary estimates how much money must be contributed to an insurance or pension fund in order to support the benefits that will become payable in the future.

Life Insurance

Insurance providing for payment of a specified amount on the insured's death, either to his or her estate or to a designated beneficiary; or in the case of an endowment policy, to the policy holder at a specified date.

Premium

The sum paid by a policyholder to keep an insurance policy in force.

Nonparticipating Policy

One that does not provide for the payment of a dividend.

Participating Policy

One under which the policy owner is entitled to receive shares of the divisible surplus of the insurer. Such shares are commonly called dividends.

Reinsurance

The purchase of insurance by an insurance company from another insurance company (reinsurer) to provide it protection against large losses on cases it has already insured.

Term Insurance

Life or health insurance protection during a limited number of years but expiring without value if the insured survives the stated period.

Unit-linked Life Insurance

An insurance product linked to a particular investment fund in which the policy holder would combine tax advantages with protection. Common in Europe and the United Kingdom.

Universal Life Insurance

A flexible premium life insurance policy under which the policyholder may change the death benefit from time to time (with satisfactory evidence of insurability for increases) and vary the amount or timing of premium payments. Premiums (less expense charges) are credited to a policy account from which mortality charges are deducted and to which interest is credited at a rate that may change from time to time.

Source: www.haskayne.ucalgary.ca/rmin/rmin_glossary_a.html, accessed December 16, 2003.

abreast of Chinese regulatory policies and lobby the local and national governments to acquire a license. In May 1999, the Chinese government granted the right for Sun Life Financial to apply for a license. Seven months later, Sun Life Financial signed a memorandum of understanding for a joint venture with China Everbright Group. Joint venture agreements were required by the Chinese government to maintain domestic involvement in business expansion within the country.

Sun Life Financial's strategy was to partner with a respected and prestigious firm that had clout with the national and local authorities. The company wanted to create an entity that was "Chinese in operation in spirit with Western business practices, management and technology." Sun Life Financial aimed to enter into the "strategically higher return protection business lines," followed by plans to enter the wealth management business. This plan would mean creating a mutual fund and starting a fee-based asset

management business. In the future, Sun Life Financial felt that the pensions business would be attractive. However, both wealth management and pensions domains were not yet open to foreign companies.[5]

China Everbright Group and the Joint Venture Agreement   China Everbright Group was founded in 1983, as part of China's open economic policy. It was a state-owned entity with direct control coming from the State Council. The group's primary business was financial services with several divisions, including Everbright Bank (the sixth largest bank on a national level) and Everbright Securities, considered to be the premier brokerage company in the country. China Everbright Group controlled $40 billion in assets and posted profits of $675 million in 1999.

In making the decision to partner with Everbright, Sun Life Financial had to consider other alternatives. An executive from the insurance company Winterthur gave his opinion between one alternative and Everbright:

> Given a choice, I would prefer the alternative to Everbright. We know [the alternative] well and have done business with them for many years. We like them very much. They are very sophisticated and professional—and that is hard to find in China. Of course, [they] have on-going business in financial services that may compete with you later, and given [their] high-level political relations, you have to go forward assuming confidentiality is impossible. But, those high-level political relations could be very useful.[6]

An executive with AXA believed Everbright to be a better choice:

> Everbright is the best partner, bar none. Its management is tops, and even this recent blip with the chairman [his removal] does not change that. They want to be in the insurance business, and they want a foreign partner to manage. They are aggressive, and not as bureaucratic as [some others]. Also not as arrogant. They are easier to deal with. AXA, in my view, made a serious mistake going with Minmetals. . . .[7]

The decision to partner with Everbright was made and a memorandum of understanding with China Everbright was signed in December 1999. The working name for the joint venture was Guang Da Yong Ming, or Sun Life Everbright in English. The agreement called for both sides to own 50 percent, with each partner contributing $18 million as an initial capital start-up. In year four, it was predicted that each partner would need to contribute an additional $3 million. Each side split decision-making duties, with four board members being appointed from each partner. All board-level decisions required their parent partners to give the nod. Everbright had the right to appoint the first chairman, with partners making the decision on an alternating three-year basis.

For the first five years of the venture, Sun Life Financial was responsible for the day-to-day operations. The foreign partner under Chinese regulations was required to provide its technology knowledge for free during the start-up period. Sun Life Financial had planned on providing insurance software for free, negotiating for the new entity to cover the costs of non-insurance software and hardware outlays. In addition to technology, Sun Life Financial was poised to provide management direction and the sales agent training. In doing so, any expatriate costs over the cost of a comparable local Chinese employee were required to be covered outside of the partnership by the foreign partner. Everbright was expected to share its distribution network and its management's local expertise and ability to deal with the governments in seeking approvals.

Sun Life Financial projected that the operation would show a profit in seven years. In the circumstance that profits were 10 percent lower than expected, both sides would need to provide an additional $1.5 million in capital, with the first profit year being pushed back one year.

China[8]

China was geographically the fourth largest country with 9.6 million square kilometres across 23 provinces and had the largest population in the world with 1.3 billion people. The average age was 31.7 years, and the population comprised 23.1 percent aged zero to 14 years, 69.5 percent aged 15 to 64 years, and 7.4 percent aged 65 years and older. On average, the country's residents were expected to live to 72.2 years, with the average life expectancy being 70.33 years for men and 74.28 years for women. The total fertility rate was estimated at 1.7 children born per woman. The population growth rate was estimated at 0.6 percent.

China's communist system had been put in place under Mao Zedong in 1949, and it placed tight controls on the country through political, social, and economic policies. Eventually, some of the economic policies were relaxed in the late 1970s, allowing for some decentralized economic decision making and greater foreign trade. China was seen as a market with untapped potential due to its population size and underdeveloped business in some industries. Although its gross domestic product (GDP) per capita was wedged between Ukraine and Swaziland, ranked at 129th at US$4,400, the country was considered to be second to the United States on purchasing power parity basis. Ten percent of the population was considered to be living below the poverty line.

China had quadrupled its GDP since 1978, driven through industry and construction (51.2 percent of GDP), agriculture (15.2 percent of GDP), and services (33.6 percent of GDP) gains, some of which were attributed to the involvement of foreign enterprises helping to increase domestic goods and exports. The current GDP was estimated at more than $5 trillion, second to the United States, and growing at approximately eight percent. The exchange rate for China's currency, the yuan or reminibi (RMB), was pegged at 8.28 to US $1, and inflation was slightly negative at −0.8 percent. China was criticized for its bureaucracy as well as the growing disparity in income, due to the influx of new business. The government was seen to periodically loosen and retighten its controls, making for uneven operating conditions. The government had made progress but was not always successful at reducing corruption in business or keeping its state-owned enterprises in check. Missing payments or not providing full pension amounts were not uncommon. Approximately 80 million to 120 million rural workers were considered to be surplus, moving freely between small towns and large cities, and this movement was seen to add to problems of maintaining the country's living standards. While unemployment in urban areas was estimated to be 10 percent, unemployment rates of migrant or rural workers was seen to be much higher. It was estimated that the workforce was 744 million people of whom 50 percent worked in agriculture, 22 percent in industry, and 28 percent in services.

Risks of Doing Business in China Due to the country's population size and growing economy, management of many foreign firms were excited about the possibilities

Exhibit 3 China: Premium Income 1990 to 1999 (US$ millions)

	Life Growth			Nonlife Growth			Total Growth		Penetration (%)		
	Premium	%	% of Total	Premium	%	% of Total	Premium	%	Life	General	Total
1990	1,088.8		32.0	2,311.3		68.0	3,400.1		0.3	0.7	1.0
1991	1,316.1	25.8	30.0	3,069.1	38.2	70.0	4,385.3	34.2	0.3	1.2	1.6
1992	1,829.6	47.1	27.9	4,734.5	63.3	72.1	6,564.1	58.4	0.4	1.1	1.5
1993	1,721.6	(5.1)	19.0	7,338.6	56.3	81.0	9,060.1	39.2	0.3	1.2	1.5
1994	2,802.9	137.1	38.0	4,572.3	(9.3)	62.0	7,375.2	18.5	0.5	0.8	1.3
1995	3,086.1	8.4	35.0	5,730.8	23.4	65.0	8,816.9	17.7	0.4	0.8	1.3
1996	4,319.0	39.8	42.0	5,965.1	4.0	58.0	10,284.1	16.5	0.5	0.7	1.3
1997	7,332.1	69.4	56.0	5,760.5	(3.6)	44.0	13,092.7	27.0	0.8	0.6	1.5
1998	9,037.4	22.8	60.0	6,025.0	4.2	40.0	15,062.4	14.6	0.9	0.6	1.6
1999	10,538.1	16.6	62.6	6,296.3	4.5	37.4	16,834.3	11.8	1.1	0.6	1.7

Source: Global Insurers in China, Nomura, April 3, 2003, p. 4.

of benefiting from a largely untapped marketplace. However, many foreign business people were critical of China for the level of bureaucracy in obtaining the appropriate licenses and being heavily restricted as to the types of products and services allowed to be offered for sale. Corruption and piracy still existed as well.

China's Pending WTO Membership As of early 2000, China was not yet a member of the World Trade Organization (WTO). The WTO comprised 145 countries, with the responsibility to set up standards for international trade and commerce. Through its pending membership, expected to take place in 2001, observers felt that China would be further opened up, where potential growth could

be harnessed. However, the membership also meant pressure on the country's tight political controls.

Chinese Life Insurance Market

China's life insurance market was widely considered to have one of the largest growth rates over the next 10 years, due to low penetration (an estimated 1.69 percent of the population had life insurance, and general insurance was 0.63 percent).[9] China was valued at US$16.8 billion per year in premium income in 1999. Exhibit 3 shows growth and penetration rates of both life and nonlife insurance in China, and Exhibit 4 shows comparative data for six cities. Industry analysts believed that low insurance penetration coupled with economic growth could produce annual compounded

Exhibit 4 Comparative Data—Six Cities

City	Population (in millions)	Number of Households (millions)	Total GDP (RMB billions/ US$ billions)	GDP % Increase over Previous Year	GDP per Capita (RMB '000s/ US$ 000s)
Chongqing (+ region)	30	2.9	143.5/17.3	8.5	4.8/0.6
Shanghai	14	4.6	368.8/44.3	10.1	26.3/2.5
Tianjin	9	2.8	134.1/16.2	9.3	14.9/1.8
Guangzhou	6.6	1.9	184.4/21.1	13	28.0/3.8
Dalian	5.4	1.7	93.5/11.3	12.2	17.3/2.1
Shenzhen	3.8	0.3	128.9/15.5	14.5	34.0/4.1
Average	11.5	2.4	175.5/21.1	11.3	20.8/2.5

growth of 15 percent over a 10-year period.[10] Within Asia, China was the fourth largest market in premium revenues behind Japan (US$279 billion), Korea (US$56 billion) and Taiwan (US$28 billion).

The Chinese insurance market was divided into life insurance and general insurance. Under life insurance, options were open to group insurance or individual. Group insurance was open to domestic firms only, while individual insurance was open to both foreign and domestic companies. Thus far, foreign firms were only permitted to operate in Shanghai (China's largest city with a population of 14 million), with the exception being American International Assurance (AIA), which was licensed to do business in Guangzhou as well. Foreign enterprises were able to open representative offices to investigate, research, and make contacts with government officials. It was expected in early 2000 that, in addition to Shanghai and Guangzhou, four more cities would open: Tianjin, Shenzhen, Dalian and Chongqing. However, if no foreign company showed interest in opening up an office in those markets, the government was not likely to open it up. Furthermore, if a foreign insurer could make a strong case to open up in a particular city, it could enlist the help of the municipal government with a possibility that it would be granted a license.

China's entry into the World Trade Organization (WTO) called for the government to completely open up the market by 2005, permitting foreign companies to operate in any city or province. Some speculators believed that the Chinese government would ultimately control that decision, even after 2005. Domestic competitors were permitted to operate in 14 cities, other than the state-owned People's Insurance Company of China (PICC), which was not restricted. An industry analyst talked about the WTO and the benefits for local firms:

> We believe existing insurance companies will benefit from the WTO. We do see foreign companies introducing a dose of competition, but, actually, quite a mild one. There are five significant national domestic insurance groups and around 25 foreign insurers in operation in China. Despite the competition, the five national players have a near-complete lock on market share, at about 98 percent of the market. Foreign insurers still face restriction expansions. Nonetheless, their entry to the market should boost local standards.[11]

The insurance regulator was the People's Bank of China until November 1998, when the CIRC (China Insurance Regulatory Commission) was established. The aim of the CIRC was to approve new regulations and police insurance activity within the country. With just over one year of being in operation, the CIRC was still formulating its identity. One foreign insurance representative was complimentary of the new organization:

> The CIRC is receptive to new ideas. They may like the concept of limiting agency force and using the Internet to distribute products—if you show them how you are going to create jobs for Chinese.[12]

Another foreign insurance representative had a different view:

> I was chief representative in Beijing for more than five years, and in that time, China's regulators have not changed. No, maybe they have gotten worse, more bureaucratic. The new regulators just say "no" to requests, especially if they are about something that PICC does not want to change. [Note: the CIRC is led by former PICC officials.] That said, I think the CIRC wants to implement regulation "by the book" but PICC does not want that if it encourages competition. Our strongest competitor is PICC.[13]

Foreign firms participating in life insurance sales were permitted to own up to a maximum of 50 percent of the venture, forcing them to seek a partnership with a domestic organization. In the general insurance category, foreign enterprises would be allowed to own up to 100 percent in 2004.[14]

Chinese Consumers for Insurance Generally, as a country's GDP per capita increases, a broader base of its population is more likely to have insurance.[15] China's consumers in the US$1,000 to US$10,000 GDP per capita bracket did not have enough to take a risk in the equity market, but they still had disposable income, making China a ripe ground for insurance. By avoiding risk in playing the equity markets, Chinese consumers would typically increase savings in deposits or guaranteed return instruments (usually at 2.5 percent). Although sometimes offering lower returns, insurance offered an alternative to these vehicles through greater protection to its policy holders.[16] Throughout the mid-1990s, the composition of an average Chinese household's financial assets were: savings deposits 67 percent to 77 percent, securities 9 percent to 11 percent, cash 12 percent to 21 percent, and insurance less than 1 percent.[17]

The other major change that was occurring was the decreasing dependence on lifelong security through state-operated organizations. Known as the "iron rice bowl," this security was fading fast from the employer and moving into the direction of private enterprise. A study performed in Shanghai by Watson Wyatt in 1996 showed that 84 percent of respondents purchased insurance for reasons of protection, 10 percent purchased it for savings, 5 percent because it was trendy, and 1 percent for other reasons.[18]

Types of Insurance Products There were six general classifications for insurance products in China: personal life, property, liability, agricultural, reinsurance, and foreign insurance (to cover persons or objects outside of China). The types of insurance products sold varied greatly depending on the area within the country. For example, Shanghai sold extensive individual life insurance, while group life made up less than 10 percent of the total life insurance market there. In contrast, Guangzhou's group life policies represented more than 60 percent of its total life insurance market.[19]

Competition

There were several hungry foreign firms that had signed agreements with Chinese domestic firms or were looking

Company	Foreign Country Involved	License	Premiums US$ million	Number of Agents
AIA	U.S.	Shanghai, 1992 Guangzhou, 1995	170.0	4,850
Manulife Sinochem	Canada	Shanghai, 1996	33.0	3,089
China Pacific-Aetna	U.S.	Shanghai, 1997	25.0	5,168
Allianz Dazhong	Germany	Shanghai, 1998	6.6	934
AXA-minmetal	France	Shanghai, 1999	7.7	1,334
China Life Colonial Mutual	Australia	Expected in 2000		
John Hancock—Tian An	U.S.	Rep Office		
Prudential CITIC	U.K.	Rep Office		
Sun Life Financial Everbright	Canada	Rep Office		

for partnerships to enter the insurance market. One of the differentiating factors would be the channel of distribution—the method of sale of insurance products via door-to-door sales, force, telephone sales, or through companies.

There were two distinct camps in the Chinese insurance market: domestic firms or joint-ownership between domestic and foreign companies. All the market leaders in life insurance in 1999 were domestic firms. PICC had 68.63 percent of market share followed by Ping An with 20.24 percent, China Pacific with 7.48 percent, New China Life with 1.20 percent, and Tai Kang with 0.71 percent. PICC was the oldest insurance firm in the country (established in 1949), was government-owned and provided its policy owners with the perception of stability and history. Its closest competitor, Ping An, was regarded to have strong business practices, a good asset base (30 percent in cash and deposits), and was able to retain the right to offer financial services and insurance services, a feat that few other insurance firms were able to achieve. It was also the first Chinese insurance company to comply with international accounting standards. Although it was considered to be a domestic firm, Morgan Stanley and Goldman Sachs each owned six percent of Ping An. China Pacific was attempting to prepare for international competition by signing a joint-venture agreement with Aetna for life insurance, as well as developing a specialty in insurance for large-scale projects.

Out of the five major established foreign firms, the estimated combined market share was under two percent. The most established foreign life insurance firm was American International Assurance (AIA), founded in 1992, with 4,850 sales agents and RMB 1,406 million in premium revenues. The above table depicts the other foreign firms operating joint ventures or companies with representative offices.

With licenses taking several years, the process of establishing an insurance business for a foreign firm was arduous. Companies needed to also engage in the difficult task of contracting qualified individuals, as the insurance market in China was less than 20 years old. As such, com-panies were enacting training programs to attract strong agents. Actuary work could be outsourced, but selling insurance was seen to be a combination of understanding the products and having the personal ability to sell with the appropriate cultural manner.

As an employee from Aetna stated, "Under the current environment, Aetna may never make money for 20 years—but it does not matter because Aetna is limiting costs and waiting for change, and anyway, Aetna is really in China for the chairman's ego."[20] Opinions from the French firm, AXA, were not much different: "There is no profit to be made in China for decades or more, unless the regulations change."[21]

What Do the Consultants Think Sun Life Financial Should Do?

A consultant's report dated in September 1999 talked about the business opportunity for Sun Life Financial in China:

> Our starting hypothesis was that market constraints and other environmental factors make China a significant challenge to success for Sun Life Financial [as] the main business is currently the type we want to exit, market access and freedom of action are largely restricted, short-term rewards and economic success are illusionary and operating risks are high and difficult to control. While we believe that by and large our hypothesis still holds true today, in particular with respect to timing, signs of sustained and favourable change are evident:
>
> - continued attempts to break the regulatory product gauntlet with indications that the product licensing approach may be abandoned within the coming two years
> - two large and distinct segment markets are growing rapidly and offer opportunities in almost every location
> - large-scale social asymmetry and lack of long-term security are propelling selectively the health and pension businesses

- distribution alternatives are being recognized by a number of players supported by solid growth in Internet users

We still have to recognize that the industry as a whole [is developing], but governmental and business pressure indicate a move towards better trained, qualified, and rational participants. This trend does favorably support a player like Sun Life Financial with its ethical business approach.

In the same consultant's report, three different strategies were outlined for Sun Life Financial's entry into China: the "Minimalist" approach, the "Full Speed" development or the "Model Citizen." The minimalist approach called for the selection of a less advanced city, focusing on traditional insurance products and containing the capital investment. The idea with this approach was to maintain a presence and "shift gears" when restrictions were dropped and the marketplace became more favorable. The full speed strategy involved selecting a high-growth city, building a large agency force and developing a full portfolio of products in the eventuality that regulations would change. The model citizen plan called for selecting a city based more on co-operation, with a focus on building government relations. This option also called for capital containment and the slow development of new insurance products beginning with the traditional portfolio.

City Selection There were six cities about to be opened for foreign insurers: Guangzhou, Shenzhen, Tianjin, Dalian, Shanghai, and Chongqing. Exhibit 5 shows comparisons of some of the cities. A consultant's report defined each market in terms of the foreign companies currently involved on the following grid:[22]

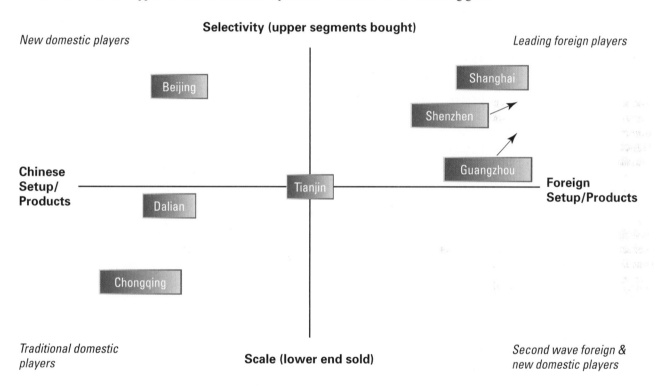

Selectivity (upper segments bought)

New domestic players   *Leading foreign players*

Beijing

Shanghai

Shenzhen

Chinese Setup/ Products   Tianjin   **Foreign Setup/Products**

Dalian

Guangzhou

Chongqing

Traditional domestic players   **Scale (lower end sold)**   *Second wave foreign & new domestic players*

Based on government relations and market attractiveness, Sun Life Financial narrowed its options down to Shanghai, Guangzhou, and Tianjin in order to start its insurance sales operations. The city selection was seen to be important for several reasons. Once the market opened, the Chinese government required that insurers have a minimum of RMB 100 million (US$12 million) in premium revenues in its entry city before applying for a second license. Also, if the insurer was not successful in its city of choice, it would risk disappointing its partner, the municipal government, and its headquarters. A poor city selection would also put the company further behind in its break-even targets.

Sun Life Financial had hired another consulting company to do a complete investigation of Shanghai, Gaungzhou, and Tianjin. Along with the consultants, Sun Life Financial had established the criteria of the city, based on market size, purchasing potential, market growth, and market development. The consultants gave a greater weighting to market size and purchasing potential as they believed that a bigger market would provide a greater opportunity to carve out a niche. Shanghai had the largest market and strong market growth. Along with Gaungzhou, both were estimated to lead China's economic growth, while Tianjin would be in line with the national average. Shanghai and Guangzhou were equal in

Target Population by Age Segment

Life Insurance Density 1987 to 1998 (in RMB per head)

Exhibit 5 Comparative Data—Three Cities

terms of market development, and Guangzhou was the clear leader for purchasing potential.

With the results of the findings, the consultants' report suggested that Sun Life Financial enter into the Shanghai market with the following explanations:

Shanghai appears to enjoy significantly higher political support from the central government than does Guangzhou: Their closely knit group of senior advisors includes many former bureaucrats in the Shanghai Municipal Government. Shanghai's cosmopolitanism should not be underrated. The city was Asia's financial services centre before WWII, and governments and consumers clearly intend for Shanghai to regain that stature. This desire manifests itself in a much more cosmopolitan attitude in Shanghai, which

translates into a greater willingness to experiment with foreign products and services.

We also believe that a market presence in Shanghai is more replicable in other cities than if Sun Life Financial began in Guangzhou. Cultural differences are greater than those between Shanghai and other provinces: Key staff trained in a Shanghai operation are more likely to be able to hit the ground running in other cities in the future. While there is far greater competition in the insurance industry in Shanghai, this could prove to be a benefit for the company. Competition focuses business strategy, promotes innovation, increases efficiencies, leads to greater tolerance of risk, and potentially leverages higher returns.

There is no major cost differential between Shanghai and Guangzhou: Rents in both cities for Grade A office space are US$40 to $60/m2/day, operating costs are about the same, local business taxes (eight percent), and salary costs (US$300 to US$500 for administrative staff, $600 to $1,200 for department managers, and $1,000 to $2,000/month for senior managers) are also likely to be at par.

The same report assessed Tianjin, the lower cost alternative:

We do not believe that Tianjin is a suitable point for market entry into China. Market conditions, under-investment, and structural economic problems will continue to drag the urban and regional economy of Tianjin with serious unemployment looming as a major challenge. In such a context, we do not believe that a significant number of consumers will divert comparatively lower discretionary incomes to purchase of insurance products. While establishment and operational costs will certainly be lower than in Shanghai or Guangzhou, we suggest that, ultimately, the purchasing power of regional markets should dictate the selection of market entry point. In establishing in Tianjin, Sun Life Financial would admittedly have a low-cost operation in a city with little competition; this is fully understandable given the inherent weakness in the Tianjin market.

Another consultant's report had a different view of the attractiveness of each market:

From a supply side point of view, there is ample opportunity for a new player to gain market share in either city although the large incumbent agency base in Shanghai reduces the outlook for a new entrant. Under almost any growth scenario Tianjin quickly outpaces Shanghai in attractiveness. This can be explained by Tianjin still being on the "steep" part of the development curve while Shanghai is already on the "flatter" part. Guangzhou is a distant third given the Hong Kong offshore market factor. Even without a privileged position, Tianjin becomes the first choice under a balanced growth scenario.

Because Tianjin was on the "steep" part of the development curve, the consultant's report above argued that Tianjin's life insurance market would grow at a much faster rate than Shanghai's or Guangzhou's. The other part of the equation was the growth of GDP per capita, which was calculated based on historical figures for the next five years: Shanghai 15 percent, Guangzhou 23 percent, and Tianjin 12 percent. Exhibit 6 shows comparative data for the three cities.

	Average Salary (RMB)	Life Insurance Premium Spending (RMB)	Retail Sales Consumer Goods (RMB)	% of Salary Spent on Life Premiums	% of Salary Spent on Retail Sales
Shanghai	11,425	478	1,325	4%	12%
Tianjin	8,238	188	535	2%	6%
Guangzhou	13,118	384	803	3%	6%

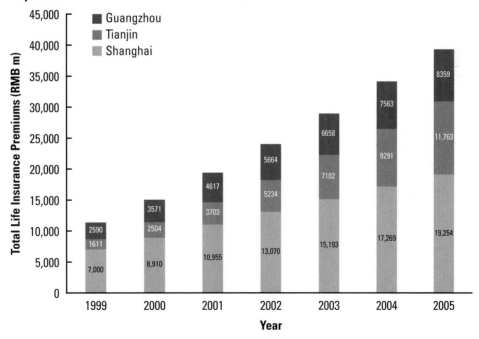

Exhibit 6 **Comparative Data—Three Cities**

Conclusion

Now in a taxi amongst the hectic Beijing traffic, Ohannessian had a lot of information to digest about the Chinese market and the opportunity to sell life insurance products. He wondered about the best way to organize his company's entry into the country, the first city to choose, and the strategy that would provide long-term viability while not exhausting Sun Life Financial's or Everbright's resources.

Endnotes

1. All monies in Cdn$ unless otherwise specified.
2. Andrew Willis, "Tension surrounds Sun Life Financial IPO," *Report on Business,* March 24, 2000.
3. John Patridge, "Sun Life Financial IPO Shines Brightly in TSE Trading," *Report on Business,* March 24, 2000.
4. August Chow et al., *A Guide to the China Insurance Market,* 1st ed., Watson Wyatt Worldwide, Hong Kong, 1996, p. 5.
5. "Board of Directors' Meeting," Sun Life Financial Company documents, April 13, 2000, pp. 3–6.
6. *Creating a Winning Vision,* Riddell Tseng, September 9, 1999, p. 62.
7. Ibid.
8. *CIA Factbook,* available at www.cia.org, accessed November 15, 2003.
9. "Global Insurers in China," Global Equity Research, Nomura, April 1, 2003, p. 4.
10. Ibid., p. 5.
11. Ibid., p. 14.
12. "Creating a Winning Vision," Riddell Tseng, September 9, 1999, p. 48.
13. Ibid.
14. Ibid., p. 14.
15. Ibid., p. 6.
16. Ibid.
17. *Creating a Winning Vision,* Riddell Tseng, September 9, 1999, p. 11.
18. August Chow et al., *A Guide to the China Insurance Market,* 1st ed., Watson Wyatt Worldwide, Hong Kong, 1996, p. 175.
19. *Creating a Winning Vision,* Riddell Tseng, September 9, 1999, p. 13.
20. China Insurance Yearbook 1998.
21. Ibid.
22. *Creating a Winning Vision,* Riddell Tseng, September 9, 1999, p. 14.

Case 8 Automation Consulting Services

As they had been doing twice a year for the past six years, the three founding partners of Automation Consulting Services (ACS) convened at Cliff Reed's summer home in Cape Cod in August 2000 to spend a weekend assessing the status of their consulting firm and planning its future. Not surprisingly, they each had come away from their recent tour of ACS' four offices with a long list of questions, concerns, and ideas for change.

Over the years, the semi-annual practice of visiting each office and holding formal meetings with its partners and principals had been an effective way for the three founding partners to identify major problems and new opportunities. This year, however, the three founders sensed that the magnitude of the issues that needed their direct attention had grown out of control. They worried that two days of brainstorming would not be an adequate response to the current challenges and those projected for the next decade.

Company Background

Clifford Reed, Jack Leland, and Angela Goldberg had founded ACS in 1993 as a technical consulting firm specializing in factory automation for industrial manufacturing firms. ACS advised clients on the development of automation strategy and long-term facilities planning and also provided guidance in the design and implementation of specific automation projects.

From its home base in Boston, ACS had expanded into three additional locations. Offices had been opened in Philadelphia and Detroit in 1995 and 1996, respectively, and ACS had acquired a local partnership in San Jose, California in 1998. By 2000, ACS had a professional staff of 83 consultants and revenues of nearly $52 million. The ACS partnership had tentative plans to open an office in Europe in the near future.

When Reed, Leland, and Goldberg had first formed their partnership in 1993, demand for automation expertise was growing steadily and their market research indicated that the trend would continue through the 2000s. From the outset, the founders had agreed that revenue growth would be a top priority. They had considered rapid growth an imperative for three main reasons. First, most of their clients

Hilary A. Weston prepared this case under the supervision of Professor Robert Simons as the basis for class discussion rather than to illustrate either effective or ineffective handling of an administrative situation.

HARVARD | BUSINESS | SCHOOL

9-190-053

and likely prospects were relatively large corporations, often with multiple manufacturing sites; these firms preferred hiring technical consulting firms that could provide the depth and breadth of expertise and geographical coverage to meet all their automation needs. Second, the founders wanted to establish as many client relationships as possible while the market was still young and fragmented in an attempt to build client exit barriers. Third, without a high growth rate, the partnership would not be able to attract, motivate, and retain ambitious junior consultants with the promise of a fast-paced promotion policy and potentially rapid career development. As of the summer of 2000, ACS management had surpassed its aggressive growth goals by doubling revenues in each year of operation, and its founders had no plans to let up the pressure for growth in the near future.

ACS' phenomenal success was attributable, in part, to the mix of talent and experience embodied in its founders. Cliff Reed was a 10-year veteran engineer from a "Big Three" auto manufacturer, where he had specialized in factory automation. Jack Leland, also an engineer, was a graduate of MIT with eight years of practical experience in manufacturing operations at a high-tech firm before founding ACS. Angela Goldberg was a Harvard MBA, with ten years of experience marketing computers and related equipment to industrial clients.

The three founders—who constituted the Executive Committee—were the only partners with firm-wide responsibilities; all other partners focused only on their own offices. Each of the four offices was headed by a managing partner who was responsible for his or her office's revenues, recruiting efforts, staffing, and client development. The offices varied substantially in size. Each office had 3 to 6 partners as well as from 8 to 31 non-partner professionals. (See Exhibit 1 for an organizational chart.)

In keeping with the Executive Committee's emphasis on revenue growth, each office was managed as a revenue center, with the partnership as a whole treated as the sole profit center. Each partner's compensation consisted of a share of the firm's total profits in proportion to his share of total revenue generation. (The founders and other managing partners received an additional bonus tied to firm-wide and office-specific revenue growth, respectively.) Expenses were accumulated and monitored on a consolidated firm-wide basis. In addition, each ACS office monitored total hours billed and utilization[1] as proxies for office profitability. Revenues, utilization, and other performance measures for 1999 are reported, by office, in Exhibit 2.

---

[1] Utilization refers to the percentage of the professional staff's compensated working time that is charged out to clients—i.e., time that is spent on revenue-generating activities.

	Boston	Philadelphia	Detroit	San Jose
	Managing Partners (2) A. Goldberg C. Reed	Managing Partner J. Leland	Managing Partner S. Margolies	Managing Partner K. Ross
Number of:				
– Partners (including managing partners)	6	3	3	3
– Principals	8	5	4	4
– Senior Associates and Associates	23	12	8	4
Total Professional Staff	37[a]	20[b]	15	11

[a]Boston headcount includes Cliff Reed and Angela Goldberg.
[b]Philadelphia headcount includes Jack Leland.

Exhibit 1 Automation Consulting Services Organization Chart (June 2000)

August 2000: The Executive Committee Retreat

Cliff, Jack, and Angela had not prepared a formal agenda in advance of their two-day retreat. Instead, they began as they had in the past: by discussing their thoughts and concerns, one office at a time, based on their recent tour as well as their individual interactions with the consultants of each office. During this discussion, they kept a running list of priority problems and opportunities, which would serve as the agenda for the second day of their retreat. The following sections highlight the major issues raised on Saturday, August 19.

The San Jose Office

The Executive Committee was particularly concerned with the operations of the San Jose office, because it was the only office they had acquired rather than built and molded themselves. The acquisition had been completed less than a year ago. Consequently, the combining of management styles, practices, and personalities was still sorting itself out. To date, all three partners were generally pleased with the acquired staff's skills, experience, and performance.

A recent incident, however, seemed cause for concern. Angela had discovered that one of the San Jose partners, Douglas Crowley, had employed a client billing practice of

Exhibit 2   FY 1999 Summary Statistics—By Office

	Boston	Philadelphia	Detroit	San Jose
Revenues	$23,021,120	$12,481,820	$8,602,200	$7,416,000
Utilization[a] (annual average)	80%	78%	91%	82%
No. of projects completed during FY	52	24	8	15
No. of clients served during FY	29	12	5	11

[a]Utilization = (Professional hours billed to clients) ÷ (Total available professional work hours).

which she did not approve. Crowley had just completed a project for Powerhouse Inc., a client that needed help in expanding and automating its production capabilities. The project had involved space and equipment planning, mechanical and electrical machine design, and the development of a master plan for increasing production. As was common in ACS' work, Crowley's original proposal and the subsequent contract had stated a price range for the job with a guaranteed price ceiling, rather than a fixed price. As with all clients, Crowley billed Powerhouse monthly. Angela was outraged, however, when she learned from a principal on the project that Crowley had boosted his final bill to Powerhouse to "subsidize" another job that was running over budget.

The principal who informed Angela apparently did not consider Crowley's action a problem. In fact, before seeing Angela's reaction, he told her that "cross-subsidizing" occurred regularly, with Managing Partner Kyle Ross' approval, whenever the costs of a particular job were significantly below the contract price ceiling. "As long as a client's total bill is below the ceiling," the principal claimed, "no one was exploited by cross-subsidizing, and ACS met its revenue target." Angela saw things differently. She wanted to fire Crowley and any others who had engaged in cross-subsidizing. She was particularly angry because Powerhouse, the overcharged client, was a subsidiary of one of her oldest Boston-based clients.

Cliff and Jack agreed with Angela that Crowley's action was clearly not in line with their objective of building long-term client relationships. The founders, however, had never articulated guidelines for partners, in terms of either general business conduct or selling and billing practices. Every partner managed his clients according to his own style and strategy and that of his managing partner. The Executive Committee had never before encountered a major conflict for two reasons: first, at least one of the three founders had been on the team of most of the projects, particularly in the early years; and second, nearly all of the partners except for the three in San Jose had risen through the ACS ranks, and tended to share the same billing practices and client philosophy used by the founders.

The three realized that some type of explicit action or directive might be needed in order to prevent future departures from what they deemed acceptable billing practices. They did not, however, want to overreact and kill the entrepreneurial spirit that had allowed the firm to flourish. An aggressive managing partner like Kyle Ross was the key to ACS' revenue growth. The unwritten rule at ACS had always been local autonomy. The founders believed that this made good business sense, and their managing partners had come to expect substantial independence.

As a result of the California incident, however, Reed, Leland, and Goldberg now questioned the merit of their hands-off management style and wondered what sort of guidance they should provide for the partners and how they should communicate and enforce new policies. They worried that any action that appeared too authoritative could threaten the good working relationships they had with all of the partners. Failure to provide some guidance, however, might expose the firm to serious risks as their operations expanded both in size and geographic reach. In addition to devising appropriate preventive measures, the founders had to decide what, if any, disciplinary action to take with the San Jose consultants directly and indirectly involved in cross-subsidizing. Finally, they also had to decide whether to reveal the billing error to Powerhouse (and other mischarged clients) and whether to return to them a portion of their fees. In principle, all three partners felt they should return the fees, but they did not yet know how many dollars would be involved and they were not sure what explanation to provide to the clients.

The Detroit Office

The Detroit office was on the verge of an unforeseen crisis. Within two months, fifty percent of its current client work would be completed and almost no new projects were definitively lined up to fill the void. Nearly half of the office's professional staff would have no billable work. Meanwhile, revenues, profits, and cash flow would dwindle.

ACS had never before faced such a situation because demand for their services had always exceeded supply. The Detroit office relied on a small number of large clients and lacked the client breadth that had developed at the larger, older offices. Instead of compensating for this vulnerability with a business development plan, the Detroit partners had been focusing their attention almost exclusively on three very large existing projects. Two of the three were scheduled to end in the fall of 2000. The anticipated "Phase Two's" had not materialized on either project.

While in the Detroit office the previous week, the Executive Committee had launched a three-point crisis plan: (1) They made arrangements for several Detroit consultants to be assigned temporarily to projects based at the other three offices; (2) they designed a marketing plan to solicit work from existing and new clients; and (3) they transferred a partner with particularly strong selling skills from Boston to Detroit.

The Executive Committee realized that their crisis plan was merely a band-aid. They discussed the client prospecting system that they had tried to install two years earlier. The system, which Angela had heard about from a business school friend in a large consulting firm, was designed to monitor prospecting activity and the probable volume of upcoming work. The system worked as follows:

Each managing partner would use a chart to keep track of the staffing requirements of all existing and prospective projects. A six-month time line, starting with the current week, would run across the top. Down the left side the partner would list projects grouped into four categories: Ongoing, Sold-but-not-Started, Submitted Proposals, and Prospects. He would then fill in the boxes with the number of junior and senior consultants each project demanded or would demand per week and then sum each column. For bids not yet won, the managing partner would calculate expected staff utilization by applying to each contract an estimated percentage probability of winning it. He could then monitor total projected utilization for each week on the chart and use the chart to run weekly staffing meetings with the other partners. The chart would allow staff meetings to focus on how to hit a particular utilization target and where the pressure points were for new client work. The chart could also provide useful information to top management on the activity at individual offices.

In 1997, when the founders had explained the monitoring system to the rest of the partnership, most of the partners had strongly opposed its adoption. The managing partners, whose acceptance was critical, were particularly negative. They had considered the proposed system a time-consuming, bureaucratic activity that would intrude on their freedom to manage their offices autonomously. They had persuaded the founders to abandon the idea based on two arguments:

1. We have always been a decentralized partnership, in our philosophy and in our practices, and there is no evidence in our financial performance that the current arrangements are inadequate; and
2. There is no need for a detailed monitoring system to manage utilization levels since we already have the right financial incentive in place for all partners. Managing partners worry about prospecting and utilization daily—as do all partners—because the size of their paychecks depends on their annual revenue contribution.

The three founders now discussed how best to revisit the issue with the entire partnership:

Cliff: This Detroit problem has convinced me that our financial incentives alone are not a foolproof way to control utilization.

Jack: I agree. But you know that some partners will say the incentive system is just fine, as long as partners apply good judgment. Some of them will point the finger at Margolies [Detroit managing partner] and say he screwed up despite the incentive system.

Angela: Let's try to put aside the issue of blame for now. We need to install some preventative measures so this doesn't happen again. We have to persuade the managing partners to adopt some sort of monitoring system. We may have to agree to let them run it on a decentralized basis to get their cooperation.

Cliff: But I think the system has to be centralized. Those staffing charts would provide extremely useful information to the three of us. We need to know what sort of prospecting activity is occurring at each office to help us with resource

planning for the whole firm. Where should our next office be? What skills should we be recruiting? What sorts of bids are we losing out on? What are our competitors doing? A centralized view of the prospecting charts would also help us to better serve our large multi-site clients—the ones we work with, or could work with, out of more than one office.

Jack: You're right. But in my opinion, a more basic reason to insist that some form of the reports reaches our desks is that if we don't insist, we have no way of ensuring that everyone is adhering to the system and updating their forecasts on a regular basis.

The discussion then focused on problems of implementation. All three wondered where to begin and how to get the partners to use it. How sophisticated should the tracking system be? Should the system be maintained by partners or should new staff specialists be hired to implement and run the system? How frequently should it be updated? How often should reports be sent to the Executive Committee? Finally, the discussion returned to whether centralized monitoring would really be necessary as long as they had good managers using the data in each office.

Boston

Like the two offices discussed above, the Boston office was also confronted by a dilemma that the Executive Committee believed could become a company wide concern. Alan Shapiro, a Boston partner, had recently won a bid to oversee the automation of a university library cataloging and ordering system. ACS had never before served a client in a non-manufacturing business, and one month into the project, ACS' inexperience was revealing itself. Not only was the project running over budget and behind schedule (that had happened before), but it looked like the project team would have to bring in an outside specialist in database management to complete the work promised to the client. ACS had never before "subcontracted" work.

When the proposal for the job had initially been prepared, Angela and Cliff, who jointly managed the Boston office, had been wary about ACS' ability to meet the prospective client's needs. They had decided, however, to let Shapiro make the decision himself as to whether to bid for the job.

Angela identified two issues that the founders had to address—apart from dealing with the specific project. In her words, "First, we must figure out how to guide the firm's strategic direction and expertise so that we are not working on an ad hoc basis, relying on individual partners' decisions to bid for one-time projects. And second, if we are to articulate a strategic direction for the firm, we must determine what it should be with respect to manufacturing versus service sector clients. The service sector is growing rapidly and dramatically increasing its use of technology. But the most effective way to employ the firm's existing

Exhibit 3 Automation Consulting Services Fiscal Year 1999 Summary Profit and Loss Statement

	Boston		Philadelphia		Detroit		San Jose		Total
Revenues:	$ 23,021,120		$ 12,481,820		$ 8,602,200		$ 7,416,000		$ 51,521,140
Expenses:									
Salary and benefits[a]	7,712,076	50%	4,874,150	55%	3,078,788	57%	2,789,900	57%	18,454,914
Rent and utilities[b]	2,313,622	15%	886,210	10%	540,138	10%	636,292	13%	4,376,262
Supplies and equipment[c]	2,622,106	17%	1,417,934	16%	1,026,262	19%	783,130	16%	5,849,432
Other[d]	2,776,348	18%	1,683,798	19%	756,194	14%	685,238	14%	5,901,578
Total	15,424,152	100%	8,862,092	100%	5,401,382	100%	4,894,560	100%	34,582,186
Income (pretax)	$ 7,596,968		$ 3,619,728		$ 3,200,818		$ 2,521,440		$ 16,938,954
Profit Margin (pretax)	33%		29%		37%		34%		33%

[a]Includes salary, wages, and all benefits of professional and nonexempt staff; excludes distribution of profits to partners.

[b]Includes office space, heat and electricity, and telecommunications.

[c]Includes stationary, office supplies, computers and leased copiers.

[d]Includes graphics services, temp employees, travel and entertainment, subscriptions, on-line databases, library, recruiting support, training materials, and miscellaneous.

skill base—given the sorts of people we have already hired and developed—is to focus on manufacturing."

In addressing the strategy-setting process, Jack commented, "The three of us have always considered ACS to be a consulting firm exclusively for manufacturers, and I think that we have assumed that the partnership both understands and agrees with this focus. Maybe we've been lucky that the firm has maintained its strategic focus as long as it has. It's time we bring the whole partnership together to discuss and draft a long-term plan. The partnership should develop a set of criteria that defines our strategic focus and then each partner would be required to use the criteria as a check list in determining whether a prospective job fit within our core business. If it doesn't, he walks away from the project."

Cliff and Angela agreed with Jack that it was time to think about a longer-term strategy and put it down on paper, but they were wary about getting into formal planning and strategic checklists. Cliff also worried, "What if we cannot reach consensus, or if we do not agree with the general consensus among the rest of the partnership? A discussion among all partners could be very time-consuming, especially if we feel our strategy should be reviewed annually. I wonder if this decision as to our future strategy isn't a call we should make ourselves and then just communicate to the other partners?"

Philadelphia

Jack Leland, who managed the Philadelphia office, sensed a problem at his office that he suspected ran through the whole firm. He was concerned that the focus on revenues, at the exclusion of expenses, had allowed various expense categories at the office level to creep up and get out of control. (See Exhibit 3 for firm-wide income statement.)

Jack explained his concern:

As revenue centers, the offices are not given explicit line-by-line budgets for expenses. So, although the managing partners are given overall expense budgets, they do not really worry about the level of specific expense categories. The number of dollars being spent on recruiting events, office equipment, training, and other "supporting" activities has been creeping up, but we don't have the detailed expense information to react. The limited itemization of costs on the P&L may have been adequate a few years ago, but now there are a lot more things buried in that 15% to 20% called "Other Expenses" that we ought to be monitoring.

The founders discussed the ramifications of converting each office to a profit center so that partners would have incentives to manage costs more closely. Despite the benefits of greater control over costs and profitability, they had concerns about converting ACS offices to profit centers. First, there were the challenges of implementation. They would have to negotiate profit targets with each managing partner. Would the local partners resent this interference with the way they ran their practices? And how much time would the process take?

The switch to office profit centers would also require changes in their incentive plan, which currently rewarded partners based primarily on firm-wide growth and profitability rather than office-specific profits. With compensation tied solely to individual office performance, would partners still be motivated to help other offices and maintain a unified, firm-wide image?

Lastly, as Cliff noted, "It is somewhat of a Catch-22. On the one hand, we don't want to send out new signals that conflict with our basic goal of revenue growth; but on the other hand, as our growth rate inevitably slows down, cost control becomes increasingly important. It will become more difficult to absorb cost increases."

Day One Wrap-Up

On Saturday evening, the three founders spent an hour reviewing their notes and jointly summarizing the major issues raised during the day's discussions. Sunday would be spent attempting to develop solutions for these issues. Exhibit 4 reproduces the outline they developed Saturday evening.

Exhibit 4   Executive Committee Retreat

AUTOMATION CONSULTING SERVICES

AUGUST 19, 2000

DAY ONE SUMMARY—Prepared by Cliff Reed

- AS OUR FIRM'S SIZE AND EXPERIENCE BASE CONTINUE TO GROW, THE SET OF OPPORTUNITIES THAT WE CAN PURSUE GROWS EXPONENTIALLY. WE NEED MORE FORMAL MANAGEMENT SYSTEMS AND PROCEDURES THROUGHOUT THE PRACTICE IN ORDER TO:

    1) IDENTIFY AND MAINTAIN A UNIFIED COMPANY STRATEGY AND IMAGE
    2) MAINTAIN A HIGH AND PROFITABLE GROWTH RATE
    3) COMMUNICATE GOALS AND RESPONSIBILITIES TO EMPLOYEES
    4) EFFECTIVELY MOTIVATE AND MONITOR PERFORMANCE
    5) FACILITATE THE SHARING OF KNOWLEDGE AND IDEAS AMONG OFFICES

- THE EXECUTIVE COMMITTEE AND ACTIVE PARTNERS ALREADY HAVE MORE THAN ENOUGH RESPONSIBILITIES. WE MUST FIND A WAY TO LIMIT THE AMOUNT OF TIME THAT WE DEVOTE TO NEW MANAGEMENT SYSTEMS AND PROCEDURES.

- A SPIRIT OF ENTREPRENEURSHIP AND CREATIVITY IS OUR STRENGTH AND WE MUST MAINTAIN THAT SPIRIT IN THE FUTURE.

    ANY NEW MANAGEMENT SYSTEMS MUST BE CONSISTENT WITH THE FIRM'S CULTURE AND OVERALL STRATEGY IN THE SIGNALS THEY SEND TO OUR EMPLOYEES.

Case 9   The Kmart–Sears Merger*

"Unless this new retail giant proves that it's capable of creating stronger customer connections, there will be no real value to this merger."

        —William J. McEwen, Gallup Management Journal

"As a retailer, we really have not grown at all for the last 35 years."

        —Alan Lacy, Vice Chairman of SHC,
        Ex-Chairman of Sears

"The idea is to form 'one great culture.'"

        —Edward Lampert, Chairman of SHC,
        Ex-Chairman of Kmart

The Merger

In late 2004, two giant U.S. retail corporations—Sears, Roebuck and Co. and Kmart Holding Corporation—announced that they would merge operations to form the Sears Holding Company (SHC). In terms of how the new entity's name was selected, the Sears name was apparently held in higher esteem by consumers than the Kmart name. Based on a survey of 1,050 U.S. adults conducted by Rivkin & Associates, Opinion Research Corp., 75 percent of Americans preferred the "Sears" name over "Kmart."

Under the terms of the merger, SHC became the third largest retailer in the United States with approximately $55 billion in annual revenues and 2,350 full-line and off-mall stores and 1,100 specialty retail stores in the United States. Kmart shareholders received one share of SHC common stock for each Kmart share. Sears shareholders had the right to elect $50 in cash or 0.5 of a share of SHC for each share of Sears's common stock. At the time of the merger, it was estimated that the former shareholders of Kmart would have an approximate 63 percent interest in SHC and former shareholders of Sears would hold a 37 percent interest in SHC. On the morning of March 24, 2005, the merger approval date, Sears shares fell $6.06 (about 11 percent) to $50.74 (NYSE) and Kmart shares rose $1.19 (about 1 percent) to $126.02 (NASDAQ).

Twelve teams—composed of members from both companies—were created to ease the merger process. According to Alan Lacy, former president and chief executive officer of Sears and new vice chairman of SHC, one post-merger goal is that "Kmart will benefit from the planned cost sharing of several of Sears leading proprietary brands" as well as present opportunities "to capture significant revenue and cost synergies, including merchandise and non-merchandise purchasing, distribution and

other SG&A expenses." Ultimately, the goal of the merger, according to Edward S. Lampert, former chairman of Kmart and new chairman of SHC, was to "seek to leverage the combined strengths of Sears and Kmart to obtain greater long-term value than either could have generated on a stand-alone basis. SHC plans to offer customers a new, more compelling experience with a differentiated and expanded product range."[1]

These changes are the first of many for these historic and somewhat disparate companies, both of which were founded in the late 1800s and are woven in American culture. The newly merged entity—SHC—will face challenges of marrying two distinct retail entities in terms of their unique cultures to create requisite synergies to keep pace with (or surpass) the competition. Before looking on to the future, it is important to look at the historical evolution of Sears and Kmart to better understand the respective organizations' strategies and cultures.

Background of Companies

Sears, Roebuck & Co.   Richard W. Sears found the R.W. Sears Watch Co. in 1886. The early days of the organization were filled with changes in structure and partnership—moving to Chicago, taking on Alvah Roebuck (an Indiana watchmaker) as a partner, and publishing the company's first mail-order catalog (which contained 80 pages) in 1888. The watch business was sold in 1889, and by 1891, Sears had developed the nation's first mail-order business. In 1893, the company's name changed to Sears, Roebuck and Co. At that time, the company's sales had exceeded $400,000. By 1895, the 532-page Sears catalog offered a variety of merchandise, including apparel, shoes, china, saddles, musical instruments, firearms, buggies, wagons, fishing tackle, watches, and jewelry.

In 1911, when banks did not lend to consumers, Sears opted to offer credit services to its customers. Around this time, Sears also established a research lab to ensure product standards and conduct merchandise quality-control checks. In February 1925, Sears opened its first retail store. In terms of retail history making, Richard Sears is credited with creating the modern department store; he also came up with the idea of the "unconditional money back guarantee."

Like most other U.S. companies, Sears struggled during the great depression. After the depression, the company continued its growth in terms of number of retail locations, business line diversification (e.g., Sears introduced a line of tires, "Allstate," which was ultimately expanded into an automobile insurance and life insurance company), international expansion (e.g., early expansions included Cuba in 1942 and Mexico in 1947), acquisitions of several other organizations (e.g., Simpsons Ltd. of Canada and Coldwell Banker Co.), and the erection of the Sears Tower in Chicago in the 1970s (at the time, the tallest building in the world). By 1963, Sears was the number

* This case was prepared by Professor Noushi Rahman, Professor Alan B. Eisner, and Graduate student Pamela Monastero of Pace University as a basis for class discussion rather than to illustrate either effective or ineffective handling of an administrative situation. Copyright © 2005 Noushi Rahman and Alan B. Eisner.

one retailer in the United States and one in five consumers shopped at Sears regularly.

Early success ultimately made Sears complacent. By the 1970s, competition became stiff, and other discounters (e.g., S. S. Kresge Co., which later became Kmart) started cutting into Sears' profits. In 1974 alone, Sears experienced a $170 million drop in profits. In an effort to continue its growth, Sears attempted to further diversify its businesses. Despite diversification in the 1980s (e.g., purchase of Coldwell Banker, then the nation's largest real estate broker; Dean Witter Reynolds, a securities firm; the launch of Prodigy, an online service with IBM and CBS; the launch of the Discover Card; and ultimately the transformation of Sears into a collection of specialty stores), profits continued to decline through the 1990s. In 1992, Sears slashed jobs and suffered a year-end loss of almost $2.3 billion. This outcome prompted Sears to sell off several of its businesses (e.g., Coldwell Banker and Dean Witter Reynolds).

As a strategic response to declining revenue in the 1990s, Sears made an effort to target female consumers, introducing the "softer side of Sears." To support this strategy, Sears restructured its stores by moving appliances, hardware, and furniture from mall stores to their own free-standing retail outlets. By 1995, profits hit $1 billion again, and in 1997, Sears stock reached an all-time high of $65.25 per share. By 1998, however, Sears again saw downturns in business, and many executives, including the chief executive officer, departed. In October 2000, current President Alan Lacy took the reins and created "The Great Indoors" store concept. Another strategic move made by Lacy was to transfer Sears account holders to MasterCard,

as Sears had come to rely too heavily on its credit card financing operations. This move resulted in many consumer defaults because of the higher interest rates. Sears in-store sales also continued to falter. In 2003 sales were slumping and staff layoffs were instituted again. In addition, the credit card business was sold for $3 billion to Citigroup. The "softer side of Sears" was ultimately considered to be "too soft" as witnessed by the eleven consecutive months of declining sales seen in 2004 (see Exhibits 1 and 2 for Sears' revenues and net income).

In general, Sears' retail business had been weak, consistent with its declining store sales. Sears' in-mall locations had been a major impediment to its sales of home-related categories because the majority of home goods are sold in off-mall locations. Indeed, Sears was able to retain some of its charisma in small-town America where its off-mall stores were located.

Kmart Holding Corporation   Kmart was founded as S. S. Kresge Co. in 1899 by Sebastian Spering Kresge as a five-and-dime retail store in downtown Detroit. It then expanded into chain stores, similar to Woolworth, and ultimately acquired Mount Clemens Pottery, which manufactured inexpensive, popular dinnerware sold in the stores. By 1912, Kresge stores were the second largest five-and-dime chain in the United States with 85 stores and annual sales of over $10 million. By 1924, there were 257 stores with annual sales of $90 million.

Similar to Sears, Kresge stores struggled through the Great Depression. Unlike Sears, Kresge stores did not offer credit to its customers in the early years. Although

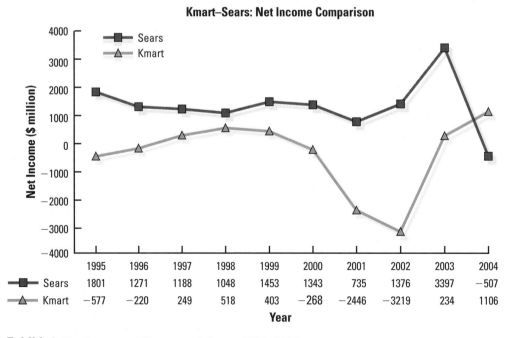

Kmart–Sears: Net Income Comparison

Year	1995	1996	1997	1998	1999	2000	2001	2002	2003	2004
Sears	1801	1271	1188	1048	1453	1343	735	1376	3397	−507
Kmart	−577	−220	249	518	403	−268	−2446	−3219	234	1106

Exhibit 1 Net Income of Kmart and Sears, 1995–2004

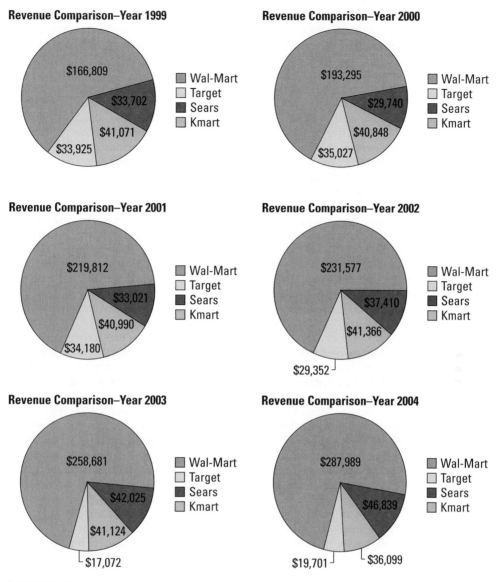

Exhibit 2 Revenue Comparison ($ millions)

Kresge offered layaway payment plans, this approach hurt the company because customers were more attracted to credit offerings.

In the late 1950s, food grew into the single largest department in Kresge stores and in-store luncheonettes were created. Consequently, Kresge acquired various food companies (e.g., Furr's Cafeterias and Bishop Buffets), created a fast food drive-through called Kmart Chef, and ultimately entered grocery retailing in the 1970s. Kmart Chef was discontinued in 1974.

In 1962, Kresge's president, Harry Cunningham, conducted a research study on discounters and competition. Cunningham found that discount stores were the main competition for Kresge stores. As a strategic response, Kmart was born in Garden City, Michigan.

Kmart's first year sales reached $483 million and plans were made to open 32 additional Kmart locations that were geographically isolated from the competition. Through the 1960s, Kmart and Kresge continued to evolve and older Kresge stores were converted to Jupiter Discount. By 1976, Kmart became the second largest general merchandise retailer in the United States with annual sales of $8.4 billion. The corporation controlled the stock, holding 1,206 out of 1,647 shares, and maintained 271 stores. The S. S. Kresge name was officially changed to Kmart Corp. in 1977.

In the mid-1970s, Kmart expanded internationally into Australia. However, Kmart sold its stake in the Australian Kmart in 1978. In the 1980s, Kmart expanded into Mexico, where the stores were operated by a prominent Mexican retailer; the company also formed a joint venture with Japan's top retailer.

By 1981, Kmart had 2,000 worldwide stores and continued expanding through acquisitions of Penske Auto, Walden Books, and Home Centers America (renamed Builders Square). By 1987, sales were up to $25.6 billion. To continue its growth, from 1980 through the 1990s, Kmart Corp. acquired Sports Authority, OfficeMax, and Borders Inc.; merged with PayLess Drug Stores; launched the Jaclyn Smith Collection; and opened Super Kmart Centers (1,200 sites by 1997). During this time, Kmart also enjoyed the growth of its apparel business, which was the store's fastest growing business.

In 1994, Kmart streamlined operations in response to shareholder displeasure. The company closed 110 stores, laying off 6,000 staff members and managers. It also sold off several of its previously acquired businesses, including OfficeMax, Borders/Walden bookstores, PayLess Drugs, Penske Auto, and Sports Authority.

Facing tremendous competition from other major retailers (mainly Wal-Mart and Target), Kmart continued to change throughout the 1990s by selling its stake in the Rite Aid Corp.; partnering with Salton/Maxim Housewares, giving Kmart exclusive distribution rights to Salton/Maxim's small electrical appliances, consumer electronics, kitchen housewares, and personal care pro ducts and other White Westinghouse brands; introducing the highly successful Martha Stewart line of home fashion products that neared $1 billion in sales; creating BlueLight.com, an independent e-commerce company formed in 1999; and entering the food retailing segment. However, all this shuffling proved futile, as Kmart continued to lose market share (see again Exhibits 1 and 2 for Kmart's revenues and net income). Kmart Corp. filed for Chapter 11 bankruptcy protection in January 2002.

Edward Lampert, former chairman of Kmart, turned around Kmart from bankruptcy in less than two years. By the end of 2004, Kmart reported three consecutive profitable quarters and operated 1,511 Kmart discount stores and SuperCenters. Such expedited recovery sent Kmart's stock price above $100 per share in late 2004. Despite the turnaround orchestrated by Lampert, Kmart's market share continued to shrink. Some suggested that Lampert pumped Kmart to generate cash rather than to build the business.[2]

The New Entity: Sears Holdings Corporation

As indicated in the comparison chart (see Exhibit 3), there is common territory among the products offered by the Sears and Kmart stores, with the primary overlaps being in the home goods and apparel arenas. Some major differences

in product offerings exist too. Sears sells lawn, garden, tools, large appliances, automotive, hardware and window/siding products, which are not offered by Kmart. Kmart's retail food line and pharmacy operations are not common to Sears. Differences in product lines need to be exploited by SHC, as the new entity "will feature a powerful home appliance franchise with strong positions in tools, lawn and garden, home electronics and auto repair and maintenance." The new company expects that these product lines, in addition to the combined strengths of the apparel lines previously offered by both Sears and Kmart, the strength of the Martha Stewart Home line, and the predicted extra traffic generated by the retail food line, will result in a realization of approximately $200 million in incremental gross margin from revenue synergies capitalized by these cross-selling opportunities and by the conversion of off-mall Kmart stores to Sears. According to an SHC Press Release, "The company expects to achieve annual costs savings of $300 million principally through improved merchandising and non-merchandising purchasing scale as well as improved supply chain, administrative and other operational efficiencies."[3]

Lampert believes that the anticipated $200 million in additional revenue, the $300 million in cost savings, and Kmart's $3.8 billion in tax credits, which will shield profits for a number of years, will help SHC's per share price to rise. As a result, SHC should be able to accumulate cash and be in a strong market position. His vision for SHC is to build a broader customer base and to increase sales to achieve profits of 10 percent EBITDA-to-sales ratio, similar to successful retailers like The Gap and Home Depot. This will be accomplished using several strategies.

First, SHC will convert Kmart stores to the Sears name in markets where existing Kmart stores better fit Sears' demographic of slightly higher-income shoppers. Second, given its huge real estate portfolio, SHC will benefit from the flexibility of switching stores between chains and selling stores as necessary, although this can be limited by mall owners, because 74 percent of mall owners followed by Merrill Lynch have a Sears store.

Third, SHC will expand on the Sears Grand concept (off-mall stores which carry consumables) to counter the "loss of consumers to savvier rivals." Plans are already in place to open 60 Sears Grand stores by 2006. Sears Grand expectations should benefit from Kmart's experience in the consumables and apparel markets. Consumables are viewed by the SHC as "traffic builders."

Fourth, SHC will expand the Sears Essentials stores (relatively smaller convenience-driven stores) by converting approximately 400 existing Kmart locations. Sears Essentials will offer products such as appliances, lawn and garden tools, home electronics, apparel and home fashions as well as convenience goods such as health and beauty aids, a pharmacy, pantry items, household products, paper products, pet supplies, and toys.

These stores will benefit from Kmart's position as one of the nation's largest pharmacy and health care retailers with 1,150 in-store pharmacies, 2,400 staff pharmacists, and significant expertise in disease management. The Kmart stores slated for conversion are located in key urban and high-density suburban markets with customer demographics and income levels matching those of the typical Sears shopper. The first 25 Sears Essential stores will open in Spring 2005.

Fifth, SHC will cross-sell products by having Kmart and Sears carry each other's lines. For example, Kmart will carry Kenmore appliances, Craftsman tools, and DieHard batteries, while Sears will carry some of Kmart's brands in the future.

Lastly, SHC will be able to emphasize apparel labels that appeal to a multicultural audience. Latinos and African Americans make up a significant share of Sears' shoppers and this group also represents a large share of the shoppers at Kmart's inner-city locations.

Overall, management's strategy for the restructuring is aimed at better supporting existing Sears stores, although both stores will continue to operate separately under their respective names for quite some time after the merger. The new structure creates eight regions that cover 110 districts, each composed of six to nine stores. There will be a new position entitled "director of stores" to manage each district. This position will report to a regional vice president. Since SHC will operate under at least six different formats, a challenge for the new leadership will be to determine how the retail formats would fit in each market and how they should be named (e.g., Sears Grand, Sears Essentials, etc.). Therefore, to avoid the inherent confusion that will result among stakeholders (e.g., consumers, SHC employees, shareholders, and analysts), it will be critical for the leadership of SHC to clearly define the organization's identity, image, and direction. This is even more important because, historically, both Sears and Kmart were accused of having an ill-defined media image caused by frequently changing strategies. Both firms were also deficient in strategy execution and employee training. Because of this, the new SHC executive staff, in particular Aylwin Lewis, the former president and CEO of Kmart, is focused on team building and staff training.[4]

Equally important in terms of strategy is retaining and building customer loyalty. A former Kmart executive, Gary Ruffing, who now serves as senior director of retail consulting for BBK, Ltd, has advice for the SHC management team: "You can fix a lot of things, but if you can't get the customer back, it doesn't matter. . . . My advice to the new CEO is to listen to the customer and keep the team focused on four or five critical points of the shopping experience . . . the keys are the in-stock position, the touch points at checkout, the friendly service and keeping the pricing within the value range." Ruffing also underscored the importance of strategically placing Aylwin Lewis.

[H]is ability to understand and bring brands and positions together to drive the success of Sears Holding Co. and Kmart's ability to fit outside of discounting . . . where they fit has always been an issue. . . . [E]ventual success could lie in the chains' combining of product lines rather than that of the retail brands. Many people say the retailers are two losers. The brand equity is not the Sears or Kmart name . . . brands are brands . . . you have to understand who they are and put together a marketing program and the ambient features that go with that. You need somebody who has done that.

Aylwin Lewis is credited with the successful transformation of Kentucky Fried Chicken from a sleepy Southern brand touted by an aged colonel to the hip and urban KFC.[5]

In terms of changes for stakeholders as a result of the merger, one glaring difference will be the loss of dividend payments to former Sears shareholders. Another change, which will directly affect employees, is the reduction by SHC of the number of employees eligible for stock options (Sears had already reduced the number from 17,000 to 2,000 in early 2004 and further reductions are expected). In addition, there will be the inherent management changes and organizational policy changes. According to a March 14, 2005, article in *Home Textiles Today,* "there will be seismic shifts among senior executives and middle managers immediately following the merger." Importantly, in April 2005 SHC announced the first of a series of staff layoffs (which will directly affect employees and management at the Sears Chicago headquarters) as well as salary and benefits changes to take effect in 2006.

Management   The new Board of Directors consists of seven directors from the former Kmart Board and three directors from the former Sears Board. The executive team is also a blend of former Kmart and Sears staff members, as follows:

- Edward S. Lampert, chairman (formerly chairman of Kmart)
- Alan J. Lacy, vice chairman (formerly chairman of Sears)
- Aylwin B. Lewis, president of Sears Holdings and CEO of Sears Retail (formerly president and CEO of Kmart)

In addition, two other previous Sears executives and five Kmart executives were appointed to SHC.

Retail Industry and Competition

Retail Industry   The retail industry is the second largest industry in the United States when ranked by number of establishments (20 percent of all establishments) and number of employees (18.3 percent of all employment covered

Exhibit 3 Premerger Operations and Financial Comparisons of Sears and Kmart (data as of 1/1/05)

Item	Sears	Kmart
1/1/05 Revenue	$36,099,000,000	$17,072,000,000
Full-time employees	247,000	158,000
Number of shares outstanding	253,824,000	89,629,000
Dividends per share	$0.92	$0
Earnings per share	$1.53	$2.52
Price per share	52 Week High: $50.49 52 Week Low: $49.81	52 Week High: $99.64 52 Week Low: $97.35
Stockholder's equity	$6,092,000,000	$2,192,000,000
Long-term debt	$3,473,000,000	$477,000,000
Total assets	$22,474,000,000	$6,084,000,000
Total liabilities	$16,382,000,000	$3,892,000,000
Return on equity	5.45%	11.31%
Return on assets	1.48%	4.08%
Return on investment	(1.36)	106.77
Net profit margin	(1.40%)	1.45
Total debt to equity ratio	0.57	0.22
Fortune 2005 "America's Most Admired Companies" —General Merchandisers	Overall score: 6.67; ranked third behind Wal-Mart (7.86) and Kohl's (6.71) and moved from fourth to third place from last year	Overall score: 4.22; ranked tenth following Wal-Mart, Kohl's, Sears, JC Penney, Federated Dept. Stores, Target, Dollar General, May Dept. Stores, and Dillard's and moved from eleventh to tenth place from last year
Number of stores in United States	873 full-line department stores, 1,307 specialty-format stores (auto, neighborhood hardware) and 15 Lands' End retail stores	1,511 (includes Puerto Rico, Guam and the U.S. Virgin Islands) and 60 Kmart Supercenters
Fortune 500	Ranked 32 in 2004; was 30 in 2003.	Ranked 67 in 2004; was 39 in 2003.
Analysis	*In 2004*, total revenue decreased 12.2% from 2003 (attributable to the decline in credit and financial products revenues as a result of the sale of the domestic Credit and Financial Products business). *In 2003*, total revenue decreased 0.6% from 2002.	*In 2004*, Kmart did not have a 10K filing. In 2003, Kmart was in the midst of reorganizing from its 2002 Chapter 11 filing, which resulted in the closing of 284 stores and the elimination of 22,000 jobs and a charge of more than $1 billion. *In 2003*, total revenue decreased 15.4% from 2002.
Business Description	*Home group:* Includes appliances, electronics, home fashions, home improvement products (e.g., tools, fitness equipment, lawn and garden equipment), and the Kenmore, Craftsman and WeatherBeater brands. *Apparel/Accessories:* Includes apparel and footwear, jewelry and accessories, and the Lands' End, Covington, Canyon River Blues, Apostrophe, and TKS Basics brands.	*Home group:* Includes appliances, electronics, home fashions, fitness and sports equipment, and the Martha Stewart Everyday brand. *Apparel/Accessories:* Includes apparel and footwear, jewelry and accessories, and the Disney, Jaclyn Smith, Joe Boxer, Route 66, Thalia Sodi, Sesame Street, and Kathy Ireland brands.

	Sears	Kmart
	Sears Auto Centers: Includes automotive services and sales of tires and batteries, including the DieHard brand. Has 1,000 specialty stores in off-mall locations, an Internet retail site (sears.com), 792 dealer stores (which are primarily independently owned), 245 hardware stores (Sears Hardware and Orchard Supply Hardware), 18 The Great Indoors stores (specializing in home decorating and remodeling interiors), and 45 Sears Outlet stores (carrying overstocks and discount merchandise).	*Kmart Supercenters:* 60 stores that combine a grocery, deli, and bakery along with general merchandise.
Significant International Presence	*Sears Canada:* Similar to U.S. operations with 122 department stores, 42 furniture and appliance stores, 144 dealer stores, 14 outlet stores, 53 floor covering stores, 49 automotive centers, 110 travel offices, and 2,200 catalog pick-up locations. Sells brands similar to those sold in the United States.	No significant presence outside the United States.
Motto and Business Model	*Motto:* "Satisfaction guaranteed or your money back." Their vision is to be the preferred and most trusted resource for products and services that enhance their customers' home and family life. *Business Model:* To offer a compelling customer value proposition through the combination of high-quality products and services at competitive prices. This is affected by low pricing and promotional activities and minimization of product and service costs. This is achieved through economies of scale, centralized overhead expense structure, reinvestment of operating cash flows into capital projects, and quality improvements in proprietary brands. The goal is to return profits to shareholders, issue dividends, repurchase shares, and increase share price. *Differentiation:* To offer high-quality national brands as well as Sears proprietary brands, which enjoy high levels of consumer awareness, trust, and integrity (Kenmore, Craftsman, DieHard, and Land's End brands are offered exclusively at Sears stores) and retail-related services such as delivery, installation, product repair, product warranty, and protection services. *Premerger challenges:* Consumers do not prefer retail stores within a mall-based format. Sears has been challenged by competitors that specialize in certain types of consumer goods and has focused on being the lowest cost provider in those categories.	*Motto:* Unclear. No reference of a formal motto can be traced. *Business Model:* The historical core competency of Kmart is in designing and sourcing apparel and in its merchandising and marketing approach on quality brand names. *Differentiation:* To design and source its apparel. *Premerger challenges:* Kmart has been challenged by competitors like Wal-Mart and Target and was forced to close stores, eliminate jobs, and declare Chapter 11 bankruptcy in 2002 due to a rapid decline in liquidity which resulted from below-plan sales and earnings performance in the fourth quarter of fiscal 2001, the evaporation of the surety bond market, erosion of supplier confidence, intense competition, unsuccessful sales and marketing initiatives, and the continuing recession and capital market volatility. After emerging as Kmart Holding Corp., the focus was to generate profitable sales, control costs, streamline overhead, increase asset productivity, and improve customer service.

by unemployment insurance). The retail industry expanded at unprecedented rates from the late 1990s to 2000, before the recession resulted in a manufacturing slowdown, job losses, high consumer debt, and retail bankruptcies. The industry was further plagued by the dot-com bust, uncertainty following the September 11, 2001 terrorist attacks, and global unrest. The rise of Wal-Mart and other big box discount retailers (or "mass merchandisers") and the economic recovery in the mid-2000s changed the retail landscape. Retailers responded to these market pressures by restructuring stores, reorganizing internal operations, and marketing patterns and by taking advantage of technology to assist with e-commerce, inventory issues, point-of-sale systems, and data analysis. In 2004 (which is considered by analysts to be the most "stable" retail year in quite some time), the top 10 U.S. general merchandise retailers based on 2004 sales figures were: (1) Wal-Mart ($285 billion), (2) Sears Holding Corp. (recently merged with a combined $55 billion), (3) Target ($48 billion), (4) Federated/May (recently merged with a combined $30 billion), (5) JCPenney ($18 billion), (6) Gap Inc. ($16 billion), (7) TJX Cos. ($15 billion), (8) Limited Brands ($9 billion), (9) Dillard's ($8 billion), and (10) Saks ($6 billion). Home Depot, the number two retailer in the United States, is not considered a department store. While retail sales were strong in the luxury and discount sector in 2004, department stores and other retailers struggled to make their numbers. In early 2005, the gross domestic product (GDP) had risen 4.4 percent, which was the fastest pace in five years, and was led by consumer and capital spending.[6]

The architecture of the retail industry has drastically changed from the introduction of catalogs and general trading stores, to department stores, to the rise of indoor malls, to the growth of discounters and big box stores, to Internet-based selling, to changing demographics (more single parent households, double income households, geographic shifts and increased catalog sales due to busy lifestyles). In addition, catalogs and e-commerce have globalized the retail market.

Several other notable changes are taking place in the 2000s. For example, as enclosed malls are falling out of favor with consumers, new open-air "lifestyle centers" are becoming increasingly popular. These centers have plenty of outdoor space—fountains, plazas, and walking paths—designed to attract customers and keep them there for longer periods of time. Because retailers generally pay less rent for these open air arenas, profits are higher. In addition, consumers can park very close to the store entrance, unlike traditional mall setups.[7]

More mega-mergers (such as the Sears–Kmart combination and Federated–May stores) will result in the closing of more stores, which in turn will propel even more mergers and acquisitions in retail and closely related industries. Because of this activity, suppliers may be forced to merge to survive the huge bargaining clout created by these mega-mergers. Suppliers potentially face fewer orders, higher pressure for markdowns, discounts, and promotions from the shrinkage wave following these mergers. Ultimately, smaller suppliers will be swallowed up by larger, healthier entities as they will be unable "to meet the demands and prices of the newly emerging retail behemoths."[8]

Another recent trend is that clothing vendors, such as Ralph Lauren, are opening their own stores, which has created somewhat of a backlash on major retailers. In retaliation, chain operators like Federated are opening a series of ministores (mini-Macys, mini-Bloomingdales and other specialty ministores such as Charter Club and INC.) throughout the country to accommodate consumers' varied tastes.[9]

In the current retail economy, consumer trends lean toward value and frugality, leading to a movement away from department stores and to the rise of discount retailers warehouse and wholesale clubs such as Costco and Sam's Club. Warehouse shopping outlets are currently growing at a rate of 10 percent per year—twice as fast as the rest of the retail industry. The long-term forecast for department stores in the United States suggests a continued slow growth rate into the next century as the industry continues to battle online retailing, direct marketing, and home shopping networks.

Competition Wal-Mart was established in 1962 in Arkansas and is currently the largest retailer in the United States and in the world. Wal-Mart is also considered to be the low-price leader. The company went public in 1970 and has 4,800 stores worldwide with 75 percent of those located in the United States. Annual sales in the United States in 2004 were $256.3 billion, and their sales were higher than the combined total of the nine second-largest stores (Target, Sears, Kmart, JCPenney, Federated, Mays, TJX, Kohl's, and Dillards). Wal-Mart is planning to open 500 new stores by the end of 2005, which will result in an 8 percent expansion of total square footage to 55 million square feet. Wal-Mart also has entered the grocery market, which has been strategic to its growth in recent years. In 2005, Wal-Mart will add 240 to 250 Supercenters (stores that sell both general merchandise and groceries), 30 to 40 Sam's Clubs (large warehouse stores), and 25 to 30 Neighborhood Markets (smaller grocery-store formats designed to accommodate zoning in metropolitan areas).

Wal-Mart has significant power over its suppliers and has been accused of unfair labor practices for years (they maintain a strict anti-union position). It has a 44 percent turnover rate in its hourly workforce and, in 2001, the average Wal-Mart employee's salary was below the poverty level. Wal-Mart is also accused of putting many small town department stores and individual establishments out of business and has been criticized for limiting the public's choices by catering to conservative special interest groups. Wal-Mart accounts for 2.3 percent of the gross national product (GNP). By comparison, General Motors contributed 3 percent to the GNP in 1955, and U.S. Steel contributed 2.8 percent in 1917 at their respective peaks. In 2003, Wal-Mart was plagued by class-action employment suits (sexual discrimination against women, with nearly 1.5 million potential plaintiffs, and employees forced to work off-the-clock to avoid overtime payments) and use of illegal immigrants in cleaning companies.

Target is now the fourth-largest retailer in the United States (due to the Sears–Kmart merger, Target moved from third to fourth place) with 1,275 stores and 2004 annual U.S. sales of $48.16 billion. Target has its roots in the J.L. Hudson company, which was established in 1881 in Michigan and was the largest retailer of men's clothing by 1891. They opened their first Target store in 1962. Target is considered an upscale discounter with better brands and is very attractive to chic, hip, young consumers.

JCPenney is ranked fifth in the retail category for 2004 with total revenues of $18 billion. JCPenney stands to suffer from the Sears–Kmart merger because the move gives SHC an opportunity to increase its off-mall locations at a rapid pace. Although it appears that SHC may be positioned more as a discount retailer, which would not directly compete with JCPenney, which is known for its value fashions for moderate consumers, the indirect result for JCPenney could be problematic if SHC pulls their stores out of malls (the absence of Sears mall anchor stores would reduce foot traffic to malls which could ultimately hurt JCPenney's bottom line).[10]

Clearly, there is no shortage of retail competition between Wal-Mart, Target, Federated–May Department Stores, JCPenney, and others. If SHC were to focus exclusively on the strength of the Sears brand lines of Kenmore, Craftsman, DieHard, and other home services, then their competitors would include Home Depot and Lowe's. At the moment, however, it appears that SHC may be aiming to become more of a mass merchandiser by cross-selling both hard and soft product lines in various formats such as Sears Grand, Sears Essentials and mall/off-mall locations. In this category, Wal-Mart is the undisputed leader. Competing head-on with Wal-Mart will prove to be a daunting task as noted by Howard Davidowitz, chairman of consulting and investment banking firm Davidowitz & Associates: "All the dead retailers had grandiose plans . . . there's been more than 100 casualties. Nobody has ever taken on Wal-Mart and lived."

The Future of the Sears Holding Company To be successful, SHC's business strategy must specifically address the issues of competition, culture, and synergy in a very focused way. "Four out of five companies that have attempted to change business strategies have failed to meet the new strategy's objectives,"[11] and "employees resisting change may make implementing a strategic change difficult or impossible."[12] In terms of competition, the mere combination of the Sears and Kmart retail empires does not propose any significant threat to competitors (e.g., Wal-Mart, Target, Home Depot, etc.), because their consumer messages are more consistent and they continue to grow by building market share. With regard to culture, both organizations come from distinct, historic, and proud pasts, and it will be a challenge to combine these disparate entities to form one unique forward-driven culture. And, finally, while there are countless opportunities to combine brands, product lines, operations, and systems, corporate history books are filled with failed mergers (e.g., AOL–Time Warner) that underscore the difficulty of creating synergies on such a large scale.[13]

It should be noted that 70 percent of mergers fall short when it comes to achieving their targets for revenue synergies, while 40 percent lead to cost-synergy disappointment. Other mergers are "dis-synergy disasters," such as the aforementioned AOL–Time Warner merger, which resulted in $99 billion in write-downs by January 2003.

Miscalculations of revenue synergies can be attributed to unexpectedly high consumer defection levels, poor assumptions about market growth and competitive realities, and overly optimistic prospects for cross-selling opportunities in a deal's wake. It is also important to make efforts to retain employees from both companies. Bad assumptions, such as overly optimistic projections, simplistic predictions and assumptions, and poor time projections, "will lead to substantial over-estimates of synergy net present value by making cash flow accretion and other deal metrics look unrealistically positive."[14]

The question looming over the top management of Sears Holding Company is whether they can create a distinct brand image and identity to outperform fierce competitors like Wal-Mart and Target. To take on the competition successfully, key goals will be to create a culture of success among the disparate organizations of Sears and Kmart, to generate consumer loyalty, and to appropriately position SHC based on its identity in the general merchandise market.

Analyst Reviews

Analysts' reviews of the merger are mixed, ranging from optimism and faith in the leadership and vision of Lampert to ultimate failure of SHC (see Exhibit 4). There is, however, much speculation among analysts about whether Lampert can successfully accomplish the stated goals without selling off real estate. Hailed by *BusinessWeek* as the next Warren Buffet, Lampert closely mirrors Buffet's strategy of investing in cash-rich, old-line companies, and he stands to benefit enormously from the merger via his private investment fund and ESL Investments, which held 52.6 percent of Kmart and 14.6 percent of Sears premerger. As of March 2005, many industry analysts and insiders remained skeptical as to Lampert's motives—whether they would build a successful retail empire or merely generate cash.

Exhibit 4 Analysts' Reviews

Date	Positive Reviews	Negative Reviews	Source
November 18, 2004		There are "two threats immediately for the merged firms: debt will be more expensive because bond-rating firms are downgrading Sears' credit-worthiness, and the power and growth of Web shopping are weak areas for both firms . . . neither Sears nor Kmart have strong Internet sales . . . Walmart.com and Target.com have seen significant growth in sales but this merger is not likely to improve the Internet presence for Kmart or Sears." —Cynthia Jeffrey, Associate Professor, Iowa State College of Business	*Ascribe Newswire.* Iowa State sources offer expertise, perspective on Sears/Kmart merger
November 22, 2004	They will provide a compelling power brand statement in both fashion and home categories that will drive shoppers to the stores. If they pool their war chest of brand names and become one, they may solve the "brand image" problem that has eluded both. Sears Grand expectations should benefit from Kmart's experience in the consumables market.		*Retail Merchandiser.* Consultants question success of Sears/Kmart merger
November 22, 2004	Sears has long offered ethnic-specific programs . . . Kmart has just begun to "officially" target Hispanics . . . . Perhaps bringing the benefits of big box retailing combined with these power brands to inner city, lower income, ethnic shoppers will provide the right niche for a still underserved audience.		*Retail Merchandiser.* Consultants question success of Sears/Kmart merger
November 22, 2004	"Long-term, the combined entity's success will hinge on execution, where neither company had a particularly good track record. . . . In our view, neither management team brings a significant track record of operating success to the transaction. . . . Still, better real estate locations will give them access to greater customer traffic, so we think it would be rash to discount the deal entirely." —Danielle Fox, Merrill Lynch analyst		*Business and Industry, HFN,* "The big deal: S-Mart?" by Barbara Thau, p. 1, ISSN: 1082–3010

Date	Quote	Source
November 22, 2004	"We do not believe that adding Sears appliances to Kmarts or Joe Boxer apparel to Sears will turn either company around." —George Strachan, Goldman Sachs analyst	*Business and Industry, HFN,* "The big deal: S-Mart?" by Barbara Thau, p. 1, ISSN: 1082–3010
November 29, 2004	Overall, Kmart brings stronger soft home goods to the merger . . . the Martha Stewart brand will be re-energized and become the focus private-label brand for the merged chain.	*Business and Industry, HFN.* Battle of the brands for Kmart and Sears, p. 4
November 30, 2004	Most analysts are skeptical the combination of two struggling retail brands that will continue to operate separately will thrive in a sector dominated by Wal-Mart.	*Retail Merchandiser.* How Kmart–Sears merger affects suppliers
February 10, 2005	"You have two retailers who are doing badly right now. . . . It's hard to fathom how combining them is suddenly going to produce a new entity that will do better." —Stephen Hoch, The Wharton School	*Gallup Management Journal.* Merger myopia: Two retail giants join forces. But how will the customer benefit? by William J. McEwen
March 24, 2005	"It's about profitability, not about sales. It may get smaller, but . . . it's going to be more profitable, more stable, with a better strategy. And it'll be more competitive with Wal-Mart and Target." —Richard Hastings, independent retail analyst	*The Associated Press.* Kmart buyout of Sears gets final approval; changes loom, by Dave Carpenter
March 24, 2005	"For the short term, it's very exciting. But for the long term, watch out." Davidoff forecasts a "bleak outlook" for Sears unless the move away from malls is successful. —Howard Davidoff, Davidoff and Associates	*The Associated Press.* Kmart buyout of Sears gets final approval; changes loom, by Dave Carpenter

Endnotes

1. SHC press release, March 24, 2005, www.searsholdings.com.
2. Garbato, Debby. 2004. Team Grit. *Retail Merchandiser,* February 1; *BusinessWeek,* November 2004; Thau, Barbara. 2004. The Big Deal: S-mart? *Business and Industry, HFN,* November 22: 1.
3. SHC press release, November 17, 2004, www.searsholdings.com.
4. Guy, Sandra. 2005. Brands a key in success of merger. *Chicago Sun-Times,* March 22; Berner, Robert, & Weber, Joseph. 2004. Eddie's master stroke. *BusinessWeek,* November 29: 34.
5. Clark, Ken. 2004. Kmart orders out. *Chain Store Age,* December, 80(12): 39.
6. Sway, Roxanne, & Mussleman, Faye. 2005. 2004, a very good year. *Display & Design Ideas,* March, 17(3): 34.
7. Kennedy, Kim. 2005. Retailing changes create opportunities. *FDM,* March, 77(3):18.
8. Ostroff, Jim. 2005. Store mergers to roil suppliers. *Kiplinger Business Forecasts,* March 8.
9. Ibid.
10. *DSN Retailing Today.* 2004. J. C. Penney merchandised itself better than Sears. December 13: 3.
11. Porter, Michael E. 1996. What is strategy? *Harvard Business Review,* 74(6): 61.
12. Lewin, Kurt. 1952. Group decision and social change. In Swanson, G. E., Newcombe, T. M., & Harley, E. L. *Readings in Social Psychology, 2nd ed.,* pp. 459–473. New York: Holt.
13. Sway & Musselman. 2004, a very good year.
14. Frieswick, Kris. 2005. Acquirers seeking synergies would do well to shrink their expectations. *CFO Magazine,* February.

Case 10   Enron: On the Side of the Angels*

"We're on the side of angels. We're taking on the entrenched monopolies. In every business we've been in, we're the good guys."

—Jeffrey Skilling, President and CEO,
Enron Corporation

On the day he was elected CEO, Enron's president, Jeffrey Skilling, was pictured on the front cover of the February 12, 2001 edition of *BusinessWeek* dressed in a black turtleneck and holding an electrified orb in his right hand, appearing more sorcerer than executive. Enron was charging into the deregulated energy markets. Skilling defended Enron's activities, saying;

> We're on the side of angels. We're taking on the entrenched monopolies. In every business we're in, we're the good guys.[1]

By August 2001, the charge would be over and Skilling would resign after only six months as CEO. In September 2000, Enron's stock price was in the $85 to $90 region; by November 2001 it had declined to less than a dollar. In January 2002, John Clifford Baxter, an Enron executive, died, an apparent suicide. Timothy Belden, an Enron trader in the California markets, would plead guilty to conspiracy to manipulate markets in the California energy market[2] and another, John Forney, would be arrested for conspiracy and wire fraud in the same California market.[3] The angels, it seems, had come back to earth.

From Pipelines to Commodity Trader

In June 1984, the board of Houston Natural Gas (HNG), a natural gas distribution firm, hired Kenneth Lay as Chair and CEO. His first task was to defend HNG from a takeover bid by refocusing HNG on its core business. In a 1990 speech, Lay characterized his leadership:

> In carrying out that assignment, between June 1984 and January 1985, $632 million of non-natural gas operations were sold and $1.2 billion of natural gas operations were purchased. As one director was heard to quip at the time, the Board gave me unlimited authority, and I exceeded it.[4]

Lay created Enron, a natural gas and oil company, in 1986, through the merger of HNG with InterNorth, a natural gas pipeline company and other acquisitions.[5] Lay, the merger's architect and Enron's first CEO, appeared to be one of the few individuals who recognized the opportunities of deregulation in the U.S. and privatization abroad. By the early 1990s, Enron owned an interest in a 4,100 mile pipeline in Argentina, and commenced its power marketing business worldwide.

In 1994, *Fortune* ranked Enron first in a new category, pipelines, and 39th overall as one of "America's Most Admired Companies." By 1996 Enron had climbed to 22nd overall. In the 1990s, Enron busily expanded its business structure into other areas, such as energy generation, broadband, and financial markets. Yet Enron maintained its dominance of the pipeline industry's ranking and was ranked in the top 20 firms overall through February 2001. In that year, *Fortune* named Enron the most innovative firm in the U.S. for the second consecutive year. It first won the category in 1997. From 1994 to 2001 the firm steadily climbed in *Fortune*'s "America's Most Admired Company" list. Its stock price rose as dramatically: on December 31, 1996, Enron's stock listed at $21\frac{7}{16}$ (adjusted for a 1999 split), and on December 31, 2000, its price was $83\frac{1}{8}$. In the entry foyer, a huge banner was placed, reading, "World's Leading Company."[6] Skilling's license plate, which had once read "WLEC" (World's Leading Energy Company) changed to "WMM" (We Make Markets).[7]

Throughout 2001, as Enron's stock declined, its rankings dropped from first to last in its industry. Enron was ranked 523 (of 530) in wise use of corporate assets and quality of management and 521 in fiscal soundness.

"Get It Done. Get It Done Now. Reap the Rewards."

Lay built a management team, not of gas and energy people, but primarily of MBAs. Rebecca Mark, an energy professional who rose from part-time trader to president of Enron International and Azurix Water, characterized Enron employees as ex-military, Harvard Business School, and ex-entrepreneurship types. A *Fortune* article described the employees as "aggressive, well-compensated traders."[8] Enron had developed from an oil and gas exploration and pipeline company to a derivatives trading company. In its office tower, the executive offices on the seventh floor overlooked the sixth floor, an expansive derivatives trading operation.[9]

Enron's management saw creativity and human capital as the real resource behind its future growth. In the 1999 Annual Report Letter to Shareholders, Lay wrote:

> Creativity is a fragile commodity. Put a creative person in a bureaucratic atmosphere, and the creative output will die. We support employees with the most innovative culture possible, where people are measured not by how many mistakes they make, but how often they try.[10]

---

* This case was prepared from published materials by Professors Donald Schepers and Naomi A. Gardberg from Baruch College, City University of New York, to provide a basis for class discussion. Copyright © 2003 by the *Journal of Business and Applied Management.* Reprinted with permission of the *Journal of Business and Applied Management.* Readers may find the two Appendices at the end of the case helpful in reading the case. Appendix A is a timeline of major events in this case. Appendix B is a glossary of various financial terms used in the case.

Every employee received a copy of the *Code of Ethics,* and with it a memo from Lay dated July 1, 2000 that read in part:

> As officers and employees of Enron Corp. . . . we are responsible for conducting the business affairs of the Company in accordance with all applicable laws and in a moral and honest manner. . . . An employee shall not conduct himself or herself in a manner, which directly or indirectly would be detrimental to the best interests of the Company or in a manner which would bring the employee financial gain separately derived as a direct consequence of his or her employment with the Company. . . . We want to be proud of Enron and to know that it enjoys a reputation for fairness and honesty that is respected. . . . **Let's keep that reputation high.**[6]

In April 2002 Lay described Enron's culture:

> One of our greatest successes at Enron was creating a culture, an environment, where people could try to achieve their God-given potential. But certainly I wanted it to be a highly moral and highly ethical environment. I have done the best job I can of following that everywhere I have been.[11]

Skilling put his own mark on Enron's culture. Extravagance was celebrated. At one meeting, Mark rode onto the stage with another executive on a Harley. At another, an adult elephant was brought in. One executive arrived at an employee gathering with a tractor-trailer full of expensive sports cars. The floors of the parking garage were marked by words to remind employees of valued attributes: bold, innovative, smart, united, ambitious, accomplished, resourceful, creative, confident, adventurous, adaptable, and undaunted.[6]

Two realities of life existed at Enron: stock price and the Peer Review Committee (PRC).[12] Nothing else mattered. Michael J. Miller, a manager in Enron's failed high-speed Internet service venture described the atmosphere as "Get it done. Get it done now. Reap the rewards." An acrylic paperweight from the legal department stated its mission as "To provide prompt and first-rate legal service to Enron on a proactive and cost-effective basis."[13] Below that was "Translation: We do big, complex, and risky deals without blowing up Enron." Employees were rewarded for earnings that could be quickly booked, regardless of the long-term consequences. Two of the Enron executives who closed the deal on the doomed Dabhol power project in India received bonuses in the range of $50 million just for closing the deal.[14]

Like many dot-coms in the 1990s, Enron had a high reward structure. More than 2000 Enron employees were millionaires. Employees received free laptops and handheld devices, expensive ergonomic chairs and lunches at Houston's finest restaurants. Enron's Board of Directors was also well compensated. Chosen by management, Enron directors received cash and stock worth $300,000 a year.[14]

Recruitment took place both in long, intense interviews and visits to topless bars and strip clubs.[6] Once past an initial interview, candidates were invited to a "Super Saturday" session of 8, 50-minute interviews. Offers would go out within a few days, and candidates that declined would be offered signing bonuses or other financial inducements.[12]

Central to Enron's human resource policy was Skilling's PRC, or what became known as the "rank and yank" process.[6] Every six months, each person would choose five individuals (four plus the immediate supervisor) to provide feedback on his or her performance. This feedback went to the PRC's ratings meeting where employees were rated on a scale from 1 (excellent) to 5 (worst performing). The PRC took place behind closed doors, but in plain sight, since interior walls on the trading floors were glass. The picture of the individual being discussed would appear on a slide show, visible to all on the floor, while management discussed the evaluations. The PRC was a forced ranking system, where 15% of those reviewed had to receive 5s. These would then be "redeployed," meaning they had to search for a job in the organization or find themselves unemployed.

On the trading floor, men rated women as potential calendar models. When one of the "candidates" would walk onto the floor, someone would yell the name of the month to alert others of her presence.[6] Gambling was also prevalent. One year, the NCAA basketball pool supposedly reached almost $90,000.[15]

This culture spilled out of the doors and into Enron's relationships with others. On one occasion, Andy Fastow, the Chief Financial Officer (CFO), was asked by a Citigroup banker if he understood the equations on the whiteboard in the conference room next to his office. Fastow replied, "I pulled them out of a book to intimidate people."[16]

Analysts who listened to the quarterly earnings report conference calls would be derided if they had questions about the details. During the April 17, 2001, conference call, Skilling had finished presenting the numbers and was responding to questions when Richard Grubman, a managing director of Highlands Capital Management, asked about Enron's balance sheet and cash-flow statement after earnings. Enron had failed to provide either. When Grubman commented that Enron was the only financial institution that never provided such statements for these calls, Skilling shot back, "Well, thank you very much. We appreciate that, [expletive]."[6]

Enron and the Capital Markets

Prior to his employment at Enron, Skilling served as consultant to Enron for McKinsey & Co. In 1989, Enron launched GasBank at Skilling's urging for the purpose of hedging risk for natural gas producers and wholesale suppliers.[12] Both parties could arrange forward contracts (contracts to purchase or sell commodities at a future date) at set prices, and Enron would sell financial derivative contracts to sell the risk of the forward contracts to other interested investors. In 1990, Enron became a market maker, a financial clearinghouse, for natural gas, selling swaps and futures on the New York Mercantile Exchange. In that same year, Lay hired Skilling as CEO of Enron Gas Services (EGS), and Skilling hired Fastow as CFO. EGS was ultimately renamed Enron Capital and Trade Resources (ECT).

ECT provided financial and risk management services for Enron and its trading partners. The process, asset securitization, involves selling the rights to future cash flow streams. Corporations, such as mortgage companies, would take their risky investments and sell them to another financial institution, such as an investment bank. The investment bank, in turn, would bundle a number of such investments together, separate the cash flows by level of risk, and put the result into securities they would then sell. In the case of mortgage-backed securities, investment banks might offer two securities, one based on the principal and the second on the interest payments. Each would have a different yield, based on the level of risk. Asset securitization is attractive to the originating corporation on two counts: it transfers risk of default to the investment bank and lowers cost of capital by providing immediate cash inflow.

ECT fulfilled two functions. First, it provided asset securitization services for Enron's natural gas and oil entities, making those entities much more profitable. Second, it moved Enron further toward Lay's vision of the company as a market maker for a variety of commodities. With the attainment of risk management and capital flow-through, Enron could in principle trade anything. Through the 1990s, Enron was rapidly becoming a commodities market based in Houston. Even weather risk was commoditized and traded.[6] This was supplemented with what Skilling would term "asset-lite": the hard assets Enron originally controlled in such deals would be sold, in many cases to special-purpose entities (SPEs) that were created by Enron.

Two Critical Elements: Mark-to-Market and the SPEs Enron funded its growth as a financial services firm using very sophisticated financial practices, mark-to-market accounting, and SPEs. Originally termed mark-to-model, the mark-to-market accounting method was intended to assist investors in obtaining some reference point in valuing a security. A model was constructed using a number of assumptions, and the security was then valued using that model. In reality, these prices were generated by computers, not by market process. Enron relied on this procedure to establish prices (sometimes unrealistically high) in its new commodities (for example, weather) where there were no reference prices.[9]

The second mechanism Enron used was the creation of special-purpose entities. SPEs are financial devices designed to give companies greater flexibility in finance and risk management. There are two requirements for SPEs to be legitimate: first, there must be a 3 percent outside equity position; and second, the outside capital must clearly be at risk.

Fastow set up a number of SPEs for Enron. Among the more famous were partnerships named Chewco, JEDI, LJM1, and LJM2, and four investments named Raptors. In 1993, Joint Energy Development Investment (JEDI), a $500 million partnership between Enron and the California Public Employees Retirement System (CalPERS), was the first SPE created. This partnership would continue until 1997, when CalPERS sold its position to Chewco, another SPE created specifically by Enron to purchase the CalPERS shares in JEDI. Enron hoped that this buyout would then encourage CalPERS to invest in JEDI II, a proposed $1 billion venture.

SPEs would be used to solve Enron's financial problems. Enron not only brokered commodities contracts, but actually bought and sold natural gas. High default risk on Enron's part would ruin the swap business. SPEs provided Enron the opportunity to continually move debt from its balance sheet, keeping its high credit rating and its swap business.

As Enron expanded the use of SPEs, new investors were required to satisfy the SEC requirement of 3 percent outside equity investment. Fastow and Michael Kopper (managing director, Enron Global Finance, and a direct report to Fastow) established the "Friends of Enron." These "friends" were actually relatives or friends of Enron's executives. Fastow and Kopper funneled monies through these people to finance the "outside equity" in the SPEs.

Enron's need for a high credit rating drove the creation of over 3,000 SPEs to keep debt off the balance sheet.[9] Maturing markets meant decreasing profits, but profits were necessary to continue Enron's trading mechanism. The only way to create more profits was to open new commodity markets, exploit them quickly, and then create newer markets. The SPEs were critical to this strategy, keeping debt from the books and providing capital. Enron's stock price soared dramatically, unburdened by the debt that was accumulating in the SPEs.

The SPEs presented Enron with the opportunity to disguise debt and loss as revenue, but did not necessarily result in cash flow.[9] Enron would establish an SPE by issuing Enron stock to collateralize the SPE, and then engage other entities such as banks to invest in the SPE. Enron would then "sell" the SPE deal that it had set up to handle in return for either cash or a promissory note, which Enron would then book as revenue. In one case, it was a forward contract on shares of an Internet company in which Enron had invested. Another case was "dark fiber"; that is, fiber optic cable that was already laid but as yet unusable. In both cases, Enron had a "make whole" contract with the SPE, insuring that the SPE would not lose money. However, even as the dot-com bubble burst, the shares in the Internet company declined, and the value of the dark fiber likewise dropped, Enron was able to shield its balance sheet from these losses.

Constructed on Enron stock, these SPE arrangements contained triggers, that is, valuation points where these deals would need infusions of either more Enron stock or other collateral. For example, in an SPE named Osprey, if Enron's stock fell below $59.78, Enron was obligated to either issue new stock or provide cash sufficient to bring the value of Osprey up to cover its debt obligations.[17] In another instance, Enron's stock price decline forced restructuring of four SPEs named Raptor I, II, III, and IV in December 2000, and then requiring an additional infusion of stock in the first quarter of 2001 to shore up their falling credit capacity. By the end of the restructuring, Raptors II and IV owed an additional $260 million to Enron.[18]

The Investment Bank Connection Enron's need for a high credit rating influenced its relationships with investment banks as well. In return for its business, Enron sought short-term deals that allowed it to disguise loans as sales revenue, and in turn unload (for brief periods of time) unprofitable entities from Enron's balance sheet. Between 1992 and 2001, Enron borrowed $8 billion from Citigroup and J.P. Morgan Chase & Co. in transactions that had the appearance of gas trades rather than loans, understating Enron's debt by $4 billion, and overstating its $3.2 billion cash flow from operations by 50 percent.[19] An independent bank examiner, Neal Batson, found that Enron had recorded profit of $1.4 billion through similar transactions with six investment banks.[20]

The Enron Control System

> Our philosophy is not to stand in the way of our employees, so we don't insist on hierarchical approval. We do, however, keep a keen eye on how prudent they are, and rigorously evaluate and control the risk involved in each of our activities.[10]

The Enron culture was not without its system of checks and balances, particularly in the financial dealings. The Board turned to those checks and balances when approving the deals with the SPEs, as well as Fastow's role in the various SPEs. It was the task of Risk Assessment and Control (RAC) to examine each deal and perform due diligence. RAC had the responsibility to oversee and approve all deals in which Enron engaged, over 400 each year. Each deal was accompanied by a Deal Approval Sheet (DASH) assembled by the business unit responsible for the deal. Each DASH had a description of the deal, origination information, economic data, a cash-flow model, risk components, financial approval sheet, and authorization page.[6] Corporate policy required approval from the relevant business unit, legal department, RAC, and senior management. Many of the DASH forms for SPEs had incomplete authorizations. In particular, Skilling's signature is blank on many of the DASH forms associated with the LJM deals.[18]

As the number of deals with LJM increased, a separate LJM approval sheet was added as a control procedure. This approval sheet was printed with check marks already in the boxes. No third-party documentation was required to substantiate claims made on the document. Conclusions were used as questions ("Was this transaction done strictly on an arm's-length basis?"), while others revealed low standards ("Was Enron advised by any third party that this transaction was not fair, from a financial perspective, to Enron?").[18]

Enron formed 20 deals with LJM1 and LJM2. In setting up the LJM entities, the Board had waived Enron's Code of Ethics and allowed Fastow to be named general partner, with a $1 million investment in LJM1 alone. When Fastow presented the option of creating the LJM entities to the Board, he portrayed them as alternative purchasers for Enron assets, providing perhaps better valuations for assets Enron was in the process of selling. In fact, there were no alternative buyers for most of what was sold to the SPEs.

The Board made two critical assumptions. First, it assumed that, since the operational results of each division were at stake, each division would therefore aggressively market assets. Second, it assumed that Andersen's counsel on the LJM deals would be independent. The Board relied on the reviews by Richard Causey (Chief Accounting Officer) and Richard Buy (Chief Risk Officer) as a first level of control. In addition, the Board's Audit and Finance committees were assigned the task of reviewing all the previous year's transactions. The Board also required Skilling to review and approve all LJM transactions, as well as to review Fastow's economic interest in Enron and LJM.

Skilling, as COO and later CEO, did not sign many of the DASH forms for the LJM transactions. No evidence exists that Skilling knew how much money Fastow was making through LJM. Skilling, in one note, simply said that Fastow's first duty was to Enron because he received more compensation through salary and options than he might be making through LJM.

Neither stockholders nor analysts found it easy to monitor Enron's overall performance. Information on the financial dealings, particularly those with the SPEs, was difficult to find. The information on the SPE deals was disclosed either through proxy statements or in footnotes on the 10-Ks and 10-Qs. At one level, accounting standards required adequate information for management to assert the related-party transactions were at least comparable with those that would have taken place with unrelated parties. Second, details were often omitted. In the 2000 10-K, Enron stated, "Enron paid $123 million to purchase share-settled options from the [Raptor] entities on 21.7 million shares of Enron common stock." What Enron had actually purchased were put options, thereby betting that its stock would decline.[18]

Three International Deals

Rebecca Mark served as president of Enron Development Corporation. The power plant at Dabhol, India, was one of her achievements, though its overall value to Enron faded over time. Mark finalized the $3 billion deal in 1995, partnering Enron with General Electric and Bechtel (Enron's share was 65 percent; GE and Bechtel each owned 10 percent). The remaining 15 percent was owned by the state of Maharashtra electric utility. In addition to the partners, four lenders (the Industrial Development Bank of India, Citibank, Bank of America, and the Overseas Private Investment Corporation, a U.S. government agency) lent $2 billion.[21]

The Dabhol plant was troubled from the beginning with local and state authorities. The Clinton administration, at Lay's request, sent Ron Brown, secretary of commerce, to India in 1995 to keep the deal afloat. During construction, there were reports of human rights violations by guards.[22] Enron distanced itself from such instances, noting that it was only leasing the property, though it also paid the guards.

There were local benefits. Roads were constructed, and the local economy benefited both from increasing levels of employment and consumption. But when the plant opened in 1999, opposition exploded as energy bills rose as much as 400 percent. Maharashtra annulled its contract, and the plant was shuttered.

Mark also negotiated the Cuiaba project in Brazil. Enron had a 65 percent share in a gas-fired power generating plant and its associated pipelines. Construction exceeded the budget by over $120 million and showed no signs of profit. In 1999, LJM1 bought a 13 percent interest in the project for $11.3 million, enabling Enron to shield the associated debts from its balance sheet. In addition, the sale allowed Enron to mark to market a related power supply contract. With the sale and recognition of this contract, Enron booked a total of $65 million profit in the last half of 1999. Enron had a secret agreement with LJM1 to buy the interest back, should it be necessary for LJM1's profit. This buyback occurred in 2001, for $13.725 million.[23]

Azurix was a 1998 spin-off from Enron. Mark was named chair and CEO, with the mandate to create deals in the water supply industry. Enron's strategy was to assert itself as an international market maker in water. With Azurix divorced from Enron, these deals could be done under Enron oversight without the debt accruing to the balance sheet. Azurix went public in 1999, amassing $695 million in capital in the process.[12]

In 1999, Azurix acquired Wessex Water in the UK for $2.4 billion in cash and $482 million in debt.[24] Following that, Azurix bought the rights to an Argentinian water utility. These two acquisitions quickly undid Azurix, Mark, and any remaining Enron strategy involving hard assets. The Argentinian utility was plagued with contaminated water and labor union issues. The British government re-

duced the price Wessex could charge for its water. Mark was forced to resign in the summer of 2000, and she left Enron. Wessex Water was sold in 2002 to YTL Power International, a Malaysian firm, for $777 million in cash, with YTL also assuming $991 million in Wessex debt.[24]

It Comes Undone   Six months after taking the reins as CEO on February 12, 2001, Skilling abruptly resigned effective August 14, 2001. His 15 years at Enron were over, but Enron would haunt him long after. Skilling cited "personal reasons" as the cause, but there was widespread speculation that more was behind it.

Exhibit 1 provides a quick glance at Enron's profit and loss from 1998 to 2000. The declining gross margin indicates that Enron's nonderivatives business was losing money. Any profitability was coming from derivatives. In fact, Enron's derivative profits were roughly equivalent to Goldman Sachs, Inc.'s annual net revenue.[9]

In the Raptor restructurings from late 2000 to early 2001, a series of promissory notes from the Raptors had been recorded as increases in shareholders' equity, eventually totaling $1 billion. In August 2001, Andersen accountants declared that Raptors I, II, and IV were improperly accounted for, and revisions were required. On November 8, 2001, Lay announced a $1.2 billion reduction to shareholders' equity, with the additional $200 million write-down resulting from a difference in contracts between the Raptors and Enron. In addition to the $1.2 billion write-down in shareholders' equity, Enron consolidated the SPEs back to 1997. Hence, the balance sheets of Chewco, JEDI, and LJM were now part of Enron's balance sheet. These adjustments reduced Enron's income by $591 million, and increased its debt by just less than $2.6 billion. And some feared that the restatements were insufficient.

In the midst of this restructuring, Milberg Weiss Bershad Hynes & Lerach, LLP filed a class-action suit on behalf of Enron shareholders on October 22, 2001. As part of its filing the lawsuit disclosed the names and amounts of stock sold by Enron insiders, both senior management and directors (see Exhibit 2).[6]

Exhibit 1   Enron Corp. and Subsidiaries 2000 Consolidated Income Statement (in $ millions)

	2000	1999	1998
Nonderivative revenues	$93,557	$34,774	$27,215
Nonderivative expenses	94,517	34,761	26,381
Nonderivatives gross margin	(960)	13	834
Gain (loss) from derivatives	7,232	5,338	4,045
Other expenses	(4,319)	(4,549)	(3,501)
Operating income	1,953	802	1,378

Source: Testimony of Frank Partnoy in Hearings before the United States Senate Committee on Governmental Affairs, January 24, 2002.

Exhibit 2 Senior Management and Board of Director Members Accused of Insider Trading

Senior Management and Board Members	Proceeds from Enron Stock Traded between October 1998 and November 2001
J. Clifford Baxter[a]	$ 34,734,854
Robert A. Belfer[b]	$111,941,200
Norman P. Blake Jr.[b]	$ 1,705,328
Richard B. Buy[a]	$ 10,656,595
Richard A. Causey[a]	$ 13,386,896
James V. Derrick Jr.[a]	$ 12,563,928
John H. Duncan[b]	$ 2,009,700
Andrew S. Fastow[a]	$ 33,675,004
Mark A. Frevert[a]	$ 54,831,220
Wendy L. Gramm[b]	$ 278,892
Kevin P. Hannon[a]	"Unknown but substantial"
Ken L. Harrison[a]	$ 75,416,636
Joseph M. Hirko[a]	$ 35,168,721
Stanley C. Horton[a]	$ 47,371,361
Robert K. Jaedicke[b]	$ 841,438
Steven J. Kean[a]	$ 5,166,414
Mark E. Koenig[a]	$ 9,110,466
Kenneth L. Lay[a,b]	$184,494,426
Rebecca P. Mark[a,b]	$ 82,536,737
Michael S. McConnell[a]	$ 2,506,311
Jeffrey McMahon[a]	$ 2,739,226
Cindy K. Olson[a]	$ 6,505,870
Lou L. Pai[a]	$270,276,065
Kenneth D. Rice[a]	$ 76,825,145
Jeffrey K. Skilling[a,b]	$ 70,687,199
Joseph W. Sutton[a]	$ 42,231,283
Lawrence Greg Whalley[a]	"Unknown but substantial"

[a]Employee, Enron Corp.

[b]Member, Enron Board of Directors

Source: Cruver, B. 2002. *Anatomy of greed: The unshredded truth from an Enron insider.* New York: Carroll and Graf Publishers: 132–133.

During this time, Enron's one hope was a proposed merger with Dynegy, a corporation once viewed by Enron employees as an insignificant competitor. This merger also died of the same problems that had plagued Enron: fear of what was not disclosed. The merger was announced on November 9, the day after the restatements. On November 28, Standard & Poor's downgraded Enron debt to junk status, Dynegy declared the merger dead, and Enron's share price dropped from $3.69 at opening to $0.61 at close. On December 2, 2001, Enron filed for Chapter 11 bankruptcy protection. Jeff McMahon (Executive Vice President, Finance, and Treasurer, Enron Corp.) was named president and CEO following Ken Lay's resignation on January 23, 2002. McMahon would in turn resign in April 2002.

The Aftershocks

Criminal Actions In addition to a number of Congressional hearings, the Enron bankruptcy also brought criminal actions by the government. David Duncan, Arthur Andersen's lead auditor for Enron, pleaded guilty to obstruction of justice in April 2002 for document shredding in connection with the Enron account. Kopper pleaded guilty in August 2002 to conspiracy to commit wire fraud and money laundering, losing almost approximately $12 million that he admitted he had improperly acquired through various SPE deals. Fastow was indicted in October 2002 on 78 counts for his role at Enron and in the various SPEs, and his accounts were frozen. On January 13, 2004, Fastow pled guilty to two counts, one for covering up financial problems and one for defrauding the company, and was sentenced to 10 years in a federal prison.[25] His wife, Lea, pled guilty to one count of tax fraud and received a 1-year sentence. On February 21, 2004, Jeff Skilling and Rick Causey were indicted for their roles, and on July 7, 2004,[26] Ken Lay was indicted for his.[25]

The Retirement Vanishes Enron had been a significant holding in many large funds, particularly pension funds that sought to invest by industry segment. Enron employees' 401(k)s were primarily Enron, and they were barred from selling their shares until they turned 55. Many were solely invested in Enron. As late as the summer of 2001, Ken Lay was predicting that Enron would regain much of its loss in stock price. His e-mail announcing the resignation of Skilling as CEO, and his own resumption of that post, ends with this:

> Our performance has never been stronger; our business model has never been more robust; our growth has never been more certain; and most importantly, we have never had a better nor deeper pool of talent throughout the company. We have the finest organization in American business today. Together, we will make Enron the world's leading company.[12]

At the same time, however, Lay was busy selling much of his Enron stock. During 2001, Lay is reported to have sold $70 million in Enron shares. For almost an entire year, he was selling between 3,000 and 4,000 shares each workday.[27] He sold some shares back to the company to repay a loan from Enron. By doing so, he not only disposed of the stock, but also circumvented disclosure laws that would have required him to report insider stock sales.

The pension funds of every state were invested, to some extent, in Enron stock. The estimated loss to these funds was $1.5 billion. Florida lost $328 million, California $142 million, and Georgia $122 million.[28]

The Accounting Profession Fallout spread throughout the accounting profession as well, as reports of inadequate oversight continued throughout the fall of Enron. In the fall of 2001, the Houston office of Arthur Andersen shredded documents associated with the Enron account. Nancy Temple, a lawyer associated with Arthur Andersen's Chicago offices, e-mailed David Duncan, the lead Enron auditor for Andersen, a reminder of the corporate policy on memo retention leading to massive document shredding efforts at Andersen's Houston offices. Duncan later pleaded guilty to criminal obstruction of justice, and Temple was named by a grand jury as one of four or five "corrupt persuaders" who encouraged the destruction of documents.[29] Andersen itself was stripped of its license to audit public corporations in the U.S. and ceased to do business.

A major feature of the Sarbanes-Oxley Act was aimed at the conflicts that some thought brought about Enron: the mix of consulting and audit business. Andersen had both audit and consulting relationships with Enron, earning $52 million in 2001, split almost equally between consulting and audit fees. Enron was Andersen's largest client.[9] Audit firms would no longer be allowed to offer consulting services to audit clients. In addition, a number of other services were also proscribed, such as actuarial services, expert witnessing, and investment banking services, to name a few. In short, many of the services rendered by audit firms in attempts to generate extra revenue are now banned.

The Charity Fallout Enron and its executives were very generous to not only their hometown of Houston but to educational institutions nationwide and the favorite causes of its board members. Initiatives included sponsorship of Enron Field (home to the Houston Astros), college scholarships, United Way, and university endowments.

Enron also generously contributed to the causes of several of its directors.[30] For instance, when the president of M.D. Andersen Cancer Center, John Mendelsohn, became an Enron director and member of its audit committee, Enron and Lay donated $332,150 to the center. Of $60,000 donated to a think tank at George Mason University, $45,000 was contributed after Wendy Lee Gramm (wife of then Senator Phil Gramm, R-TX, and an associate of the center), became an Enron board member. Concerned with an appearance of conflict of interest and a threat to independence, the U.S. House of Representatives passed a bill dubbed the "Enron Bill" to require disclosure of certain contributions and noncash gifts to organizations associated with board members.

Conclusion This case is still writing its own ending. Many of the stakeholders will never recover from their losses. Criminal actions have resulted in some going to jail, and others being indicted and waiting for trial. Two of the investment banks, Citigroup and J.P. Morgan Chase, have settled investor lawsuits for $2.575 billion and $2.2 billion, respectively. Other investment banks still face civil actions.[31] And federal lawmakers are debating the cost of some provisions of the Sarbanes-Oxley Act. This case will evolve for years to come.

Appendix A   Enron Timeline

1984	Ken Lay becomes CEO of Houston Natural Gas (HNG).
1985	HNG merges with Internorth. Lay becomes CEO of the new company.
1986	Company changes name to Enron, and moves to Lay's hometown, Houston.
1990	Skilling leaves McKinsey & Co. to join Enron as executive officer of Enron Gas Services. Skilling hires Andrew Fastow from banking industry.
1991	Enron adopts mark-to-market accounting strategy, reporting income and value of assets at their replacement cost. Fastow forms first legitimate SPEs.
1993	Deregulation of worldwide energy markets. Enron begins marketing power and forms first SPE, JEDI, with CalPERS to invest in natural gas projects.
1994	As deregulation in the U.S. grows, Enron begins trading electricity.
1996	Enron commences construction of the Dabhol power plant in India. Lay promotes Skilling to Enron's president and COO.
1997	Enron buys first electric utility, Portland General Electric. Fastow promoted to head new finance department. Enron applies energy-trading model to new commodities markets such as weather derivatives, coal, pulp and paper, and bandwidth capacity. Chewco (another SPE) created to purchase CalPERS' shares of JEDI1 so that CalPERS could participate in a larger partnership, JEDI2. Chewco never meets the 3 percent outside ownership and is never a legitimate SPE.
1998	Fastow named CFO. Enron begins power trading in Argentina, becoming first power marketer, and gains control of Brazilian utility. Enron acquires UK utility Wessex Water and forms Azurix, a global water business. It then takes Azurix public, retaining a 69 percent stake. Enron trades most of Enron Oil & Gas for cash and its properties in India and China.
1999	New Houston Astros baseball stadium named Enron Field. Skilling and Fastow present LJM partnerships to board of directors.
2000	
February	*Fortune* names Enron "the most innovative company in America" for the fifth consecutive year.
April	Enron creates the first Raptor SPE.
August	Rebecca Mark resigns due to poor results at Azurix and tension with Skilling. Stock hits all-time high of $90 and revenue surpasses $100 billion making it the seventh largest company in the Fortune 500.
2001	
February	Lay steps down as CEO. President and COO Skilling replaces Lay as CEO.
August	Skilling resigns and Lay becomes CEO again. Sherron Watkins, an Enron accountant, sends anonymous memo to Lay warning of potential accounting scandal.
September	Arthur Andersen compels Enron to change an aggressive accounting action, causing a $1.2 billion reduction in Enron's equity.
October	SEC launches investigation of Enron's off-balance-sheet partnerships. Enron changes its 401(k) pension plan administrator, preventing employees from selling Enron stock for 30 days. Fastow is put on leave. Enron establishes special committee to investigate third-party transactions to be known as the Powers Report. Enron's stock drops to $11.
November	Enron strikes deal with Dynegy, its largest energy-industry rival. Dynegy backs out of the deal once more details of Enron's finances are available. Enron trades at less than $1 per share.
December	Enron files for Chapter 11 bankruptcy protection and lays off 4,000 employees.

(continued)

2002

January	Watkin's memo leaked to Congress. U.S. Justice Department launches a criminal investigation into Enron's fall. Enron fires Arthur Andersen LLP. Enron sells its energy trading business to UBS's investment banking unit. Sells Wessex Water to a Malaysian firm, and shuts down its broadband unit. Lay resigns, and McMahon becomes CEO. Former Enron Vice Chairman Cliff Baxter is found dead as government investigation deepens.
February	Skilling testifies before Congress. Lay pleads the Fifth Amendment. Watkins testifies before Congress about her memo to Lay.
April	Andersen lays off 7,000 employees. McMahon resigns as of June 1.
August	Kopper pleads guilty to money laundering and wire-fraud conspiracy. Cooperates with authorities.
October	Fastow indicted on 78 counts of federal fraud, conspiracy, and money laundering.

2003

May	Federal prosecutors file new charges against Fastow and two others. Indicted Fastow's wife and seven other former Enron officials for fraud and other criminal charges.

2004

January	Fastow pleads guilty on two counts and receives 10 years in federal prison. Lea Fastow pleads guilty to one count of tax fraud and receives a 1-year sentence.
February	Skilling and Causey indicted on 42 counts, including securities fraud, wire fraud, and insider trading.
July	Lay indicted on 11 counts, including wire and bank fraud, as well as making false statements.

Appendix B   Glossary of Terms

Adjustments	A deduction made to financial statements to charge off a loss, as with a bad debt.
Asset-lite	Enron jargon for short-term or noncapital-intensive assets.
CalPERS	California Public Employees Retirement System
DASH	Deal Approval Sheet
Derivative	A financial instrument whose characteristics and value depend upon the characteristics and value of an underlier, typically a commodity, bond, equity or currency.
Downgrade	A negative change in an analyst's ratings for a security.
Hedge	An investment made in order to reduce the risk of adverse price movements in a security, by taking an offsetting position in a related security.
Insider stock sales	Selling of a company's stock by individual directors, executives or other employees.
JEDI	Joint Energy Development Investment—an Enron SPE
Mark-to-Market	Recording the price or value of a security, portfolio, or account on a daily basis to calculate profits and losses or to confirm that margin requirements are being met.
Off-balance sheet	Financing from sources other than debt and equity offerings, such as joint ventures, R&D partnerships, and operating leases.
Options	The right, but not the obligation, to buy (for a call option) or sell (for a put option) a specific amount of a given stock, commodity, currency, index, or debt, at a specified price (the strike price) during a specified period of time.
Premium	The amount by which a bond or stock sells above its par value.

Privatization	The process of moving from a government-controlled system to a privately run, for-profit system.
Put options	An option contract that gives the holder the right to sell a certain quantity of an underlying security to the writer of the option, at a specified price (strike price) up to a specified date (expiration date); also called *put*.
RAC	Risk Assessment & Control, an Enron department.
Rank and Yank	Employee jargon for Enron's employee review process.
Securitization	The process of aggregating similar instruments, such as loans or mortgages, into a negotiable security.
SPEs	Special Purpose Entities
Write-down	Make a downward adjustment in the accounting value of an asset.
Yields	The annual rate of return on an investment, expressed as a percentage.

Endnotes

1. BusinessWeek Online, February 12, 2001.
2. Eichenwald, K. 2002. A powerful, flawed witness against Enron. *New York Times,* October 21: C1.
3. Eichenwald, K. 2003. Ex-trader at Enron is charged in California power case. *New York Times,* June 4: C6.
4. Lay, K. 1990. The Enron story. Speech delivered on October 9, 1990 in New York to Newcomen Society of the United States.
5. A more detailed history of the origin of Enron can be found at www.hoovers.com.
6. Cruver, B. 2002. *Anatomy of greed: The unshredded truth from an Enron insider.* New York: Carroll & Graf Publishers.
7. Preston, R., & Koller, M. 2000. *Enron feels the power.* Internetweekonline: October 30.
8. O'Reilly, B. 1997. The secrets of America's most admired corporations: New ideas, new products. *Fortune,* 135(4): 60–64.
9. Testimony of Frank Partnoy in Hearings before the United States Senate Committee on Governmental Affairs, January 24, 2002.
10. 1999 Annual Report, Enron Corp.
11. Grulye, B., & Smith, R. 2002. Anatomy of a fall: Keys to success left Kenneth Lay open to disaster—From rural Missouri to helm of Enron to ignominy—Trust and willful optimism— "The American dream is alive." *The Wall Street Journal,* April 26: A1.
12. Fusaro, P. C., & Miller, R. M. 2002. *What went wrong at Enron: Everyone's guide to the largest bankruptcy in U.S. History.* Hoboken, NJ: John Wiley & Sons.
13. Schwartz, J. 2002. As Enron purged its ranks, dissent was swept away. *New York Times,* February 4.
14. Levin, C. 2002. After Enron: Government's role and corporate cultures. *Mid-American Journal of Business,* 17(2): 7–10.
15. Banerjee, N., Berboza, D., & Warren, A. 2002. Enron's many strands: Corporate culture; at Enron, lavish excess often came before success. *New York Times,* February 26: C1.
16. Raghavan, A., Kranhold, K., & Barriounuevo, A. 2002. Full speed ahead: How Enron bosses created a culture of pushing limits—Fastow and others challenged staff, badgered bankers; Porsches, Ferraris were big—A chart to "intimidate people." *The Wall Street Journal,* August 26: A1
17. Note 8, Q3 SEC filing, 2001.
18. Report of Investigation by the Special Investigative Committee of the Board of Directors of Enron Corp. (the Powers Report).
19. Reason, CFO.com, 2002.
20. Berger, E., & Fowler, T. 2002. The fall of Enron; Enron masked loans as sales, report says; deals inflated bottom line by $1.4 billion. *Houston Chronicle,* September 22: A1.
21. Rai, S. 2002. Seeking ways to sell Enron's plant in India. *New York Times,* April 11: W1.
22. Kolker, C., & Fowler, T. 2002. The fall of Enron; roots of discontent; dead Enron power plant affecting environment, economy and livelihoods in India. *Houston Chronicle,* August 4: B1.
23. Criminal Complaint, United States Securities and Exchange Commission v. Andrew S. Fastow, October 1, 2002, #s 15–22.
24. Goldberg, L. 2002. Enron's Azurix to well Wessex Water at a loss. *Houston Chronicle,* March 26: B4.
25. Eichenwald, K. 2004. Enron ex-chief indicted by U.S. in fraud case. *New York Times,* July 8: A1.
26. Carr, R. 2004. Former Enron chief indicted. *Atlanta Constitution,* February 20: 1A.
27. Flood, M., & Fowler, T. 2002. The fall of Enron; grand jurors eye Lay; $70 million in stock sales focus of probe. *Houston Chronicle,* October 24: A1.
28. Healy, B. 2002. Shared pain: Bay State isn't alone in taking a hit from Enron. *Boston Globe,* September 10: C1.
29. Fowler, T. 2002. Andersen attorney may be next. *Houston Chronicle,* June 27: B1.
30. Weber, J., & McNamee, M. 2002. Boardroom charity: Reforms don't go far enough. *BusinessWeek,* June 10: 128.
31. Creswell, J. 2005. J.P. Morgan Chase to pay Enron investors $2.2 billion. *New York Times,* June 15: C1.

Case 11   American Red Cross*

As Marsha "Marty" Johnson Evans took the helm of the American Red Cross on August 5, 2002, she was faced with the challenge of restoring the public's faith in the organization. During the past 24 months, there had been a barrage of negative publicity regarding the American Red Cross. In June 2000 Red Cross workers went on strike. The organization was hit by a lawsuit filed by HemaCare Corporation and Coral Blood Services in January 2001. The plaintiffs alleged that the American Red Cross engaged in unfair trade practices in the pricing of blood. The Better Business Bureau made false public statements about the ability of the American Red Cross to meet their standards for charitable solicitations. Then on September 11, 2001, Americans watched in horror as terrorists flew two planes into the World Trade Center buildings and a third into the Pentagon in Washington. In the aftermath of this tragedy, donations poured into the American Red Cross, and a special fund—the Liberty Disaster Relief Fund—was established by the then-president of the Red Cross, Dr. Bernadine Healy. When it was announced that not all donations would be used for victims of the 9/11 disaster, there was a huge public outcry from donors. Healy was forced to retire, and interim president and CEO Harold Decker announced that all donations to the Liberty Disaster Relief Fund would be used in the organization's 9/11 relief efforts. Finally, on March 10, 2002, *60 Minutes,* a CBS news show, ran a misleading and inaccurate story about the American Red Cross.

On June 27, 2002, Marsha Johnson Evans was named the new CEO and president of the American Red Cross. At the time of this announcement, Evans stated:

> This is a time of great challenge for many charitable organizations including the American Red Cross. On the one hand, we need to motivate Americans to donate their time and their treasure, which is never easy, but always comes down to whether they trust an organization and believe in their work. On the other hand, we face a host of challenges including the need to better prepare this nation for disasters both natural and man-made; as well as the rigors of furnishing a safe and available blood supply with all the costs and complexity this involves.[1]

History and Operations of the American Red Cross

Henry Dunant set forth the idea of the Red Cross in 1859 when he saw wounded and dying soldiers on the battlefield in Solferino, Italy. He organized local people to bind the soldiers' wounds and to feed and care for them. Henry Dunant called for the creation of a national relief society and this pointed the way to the future Geneva Convention. Four years later, in 1863, the International Red Cross was created in Geneva, Switzerland, with the purpose of providing nonpartisan care in time of war. The Red Cross emblem was adopted as a symbol of neutrality although today the Red Crescent is also a recognized symbol. Today the Red Cross incorporates the International Committee of the Red Cross and the International Federation of Red Cross and Red Crescent Societies as well as national societies in 175 countries. The fundamental principles of the International Red Cross are listed in Exhibit 1. Clara Barton successfully organized the first lasting Red Cross Society in America in Washington, D.C., on May 21, 1881. The American Red Cross provided services beyond those of the International Red Cross by providing disaster relief in addition to battlefield assistance. Clara Barton served as the organization's president through 1904.[2]

As stated in its 2000–2001 Annual Report, "the American Red Cross is a humanitarian organization, led by volunteers, whose mission is to provide relief to victims of disasters and help people prevent, prepare for, and respond to emergencies." The vision of the American Red Cross is "the American Red Cross . . . always there . . . touching more lives, in new ways . . . under the same trusted symbol." Since its founding, the American Red Cross has symbolized the nobility of the human spirit by representing service and goodwill across America. Its purpose, or intent, is to "prevent and relieve human suffering." Each year March is proclaimed as American Red Cross month. To support the fundamental principles of the International Red Cross, the American Red Cross has adopted a set of values (see Exhibit 2).

The American Red Cross is governed by a Board of Governors that formulates policy and delegates authority to the volunteer boards of its 1,000 local chapters. Decentralization allows the Red Cross to provide immediate, effective, and efficient assistance to those in need.[3] Annually, the American Red Cross helps victims of more than 63,000 natural and man-made disasters. The worst disaster ever dealt with by the American Red Cross was the hurricane that killed an estimated 6,000 people in Galveston, Texas, in 1900.

The American Red Cross helps victims through a wide range of services:[4]

- Armed Forces Emergency Services. Provides military families with emergency communication services, financial assistance, counseling, and so forth.
- Biomedical Services. Blood, tissue, and plasma services; research; and national testing labs. In fiscal year 2001 more than 3.8 million volunteers donated

Exhibit 1 Principles of International Red Cross

- **Humanity:** The International Red Cross and Red Crescent Movement, born of a desire to bring assistance without discrimination to the wounded on the battlefield, endeavors, in its international and national capacity, to prevent and alleviate human suffering where it may be found. Its purpose is to protect life and health and to ensure respect for the human being. It promotes mutual understanding, friendship, cooperation, and lasting peace amongst all peoples.
- **Impartiality:** It makes no discrimination as to nationality, race, religious beliefs, class, or political opinions. It endeavors to relieve the suffering of individuals, being guided solely by their needs, and to give priority to the most urgent cases of distress.
- **Neutrality:** In order to continue to enjoy the confidence of all, the Movement may not take sides in hostilities or engage at any time in controversies of a political, racial, religious, or ideological nature.
- **Independence:** The Movement is independent. The National Societies, while auxiliaries in the humanitarian services of their governments and subject to the laws of their respective countries, must always maintain their autonomy so that they may be able at all times to act in accordance with the principles of the Movement.
- **Voluntary Service:** It is a voluntary relief movement not prompted in any manner by desire for gain.
- **Unity:** There can be only one Red Cross or one Red Crescent Society in any one country. It must be open to all. It must carry on its humanitarian work throughout its territory.
- **Universality:** The International Red Cross and Red Crescent Movement, in which all Societies have equal status and share equal responsibilities and duties in helping each other, is worldwide.

Source: American Red Cross, www.redcross.org.

Exhibit 2 Values of the American Red Cross

- **Humanitarianism:** We exist to serve others in need, independently, and without discrimination, providing relief for victims of disasters and helping people prevent, prepare for, and respond to emergencies.
- **Stewardship:** We act responsibly, effectively, and efficiently with resources entrusted to us, always seeking to improve.
- **Helping Others:** We are attentive and responsive to those we serve, always listening to their needs and looking for ways to serve through existing or new initiatives.
- **Respect:** We acknowledge, respect, and support the rights and diversity of each person in our organization and in the communities we serve.
- **Voluntary Spirit:** As a family of donors, volunteers, and staff we search for ways to provide hope to those we serve while demonstrating compassion, generosity, and appreciation.
- **Continuous Learning:** We seek, collectively and individually, to identify, obtain, and maintain competencies and the awareness required for exceptional service.
- **Integrity:** We act with honesty, demonstrate courage and accountability under pressure, and openly share ideas and information with each other.

Source: www.redcross.org.

in excess of 6 million pints of blood. The American Red Cross supplies 3,000 hospitals with about half of the blood used in the United States.
- Community Services. Help for the homeless, seniors, and youth; food and nutrition information; transportation; and so forth.
- Disaster Services. Educational services to prepare for disasters. Each year 83,000 volunteers help disaster victims by providing food, shelter, financial assistance, mental health counseling, and so on.
- Health and Safety Services. Swimming and lifeguard classes, HIV/AIDS education, living well programs,

and so forth. Each year more than 12 million Americans take advantage of lifesaving courses offered by the Red Cross.

- International Services. Emergency disaster response, feeding programs, primary health care programs, Geneva Conventions, and so on. The Red Cross is able to provide long-term aid and education to those in need. Also, Red Cross delegates help local citizens rebuild infrastructure, strengthen public health, and improve response time to local disasters.
- Nursing. Student nurses, Jane Delano Society, and so forth.
- Youth Involvement. Helping kids, teens, and young adults.
- Volunteering. Recruiting and organizing volunteers.

Financial Overview

In fiscal year 2001–2002 the American Red Cross had operating revenues of $4.117 billion. Total operating revenues for fiscal year 2000–2001 were $2.743 billion. Three main funding sources for the American Red Cross were:[5]

- Contributions: Fund-raising efforts by the United Way & Combined Federal Campaign, legacies, grants, other monetary and in-kind contributions.
- Products and services: Fees for products, materials, and courses; fees from collecting, testing, and distributing blood and tissue.
- Investment income and other income: Investment income from endowments and reserve funds and income from contracts to provide various programs.

Total operating expenses for the 2000–2001 fiscal year were $2.712 billion, and major expenses included:[6]

- Disaster costs: Assistance to victims.
- Funding disaster services: Expenses to solicit donations, administer funds; staff expenses at disaster sites; and so on.
- Biomedical services: Facility maintenance; expenses in blood, plasma, and tissue services.

Total operating expenses for the fiscal year 2001–2002 were $3.570 billion (see Exhibits 3, 4, and 5).[7]

Technology and Operations

Technology has helped the American Red Cross better coordinate its efforts among its 1,400 chapters and to expand its reach across America. In 2000 it launched "iGiveLife," a service that enables blood drive sponsors to use their intranets to recruit donors and allows hospital customers to order blood products online.[8]

The Internet provides information about nonprofit organizations and can provide "click-to-donate" sites for those individuals who are willing to help out with contributions while they are online. These "click" sites appeal to a newer and often younger audience for the nonprofits. For Cindee Archer, online media manager for the American Red Cross in Washington, D.C., the Internet serves as a vital source of information to the American public and as a new way to collect donations. Archer stated, "The Internet has definitely changed how the whole organization thinks. You feel this sense of urgency whenever there's a disaster—you want that information up as quickly as you can get it."[9] Archer worked on developing a Web site where visitors could enter a zip code and quickly find information. The Web site helps visitors locate local Red Cross shelters, find relatives in a disaster area, keep up with breaking news, and obtain information about donating and volunteering. Cindy Archer also believed that "more and more people are coming online—this isn't going to go away, it's only going to get more pervasive."[10] However, there were costs associated with a Web site that many nonprofit groups did not realize. Russ Finkelstein, director of outreach at Action Without Borders has stated, "Some of them think this is going to be a kind of panacea for doing fund-raising, and it's not necessarily that."[11]

About 12 million Americans enroll in Red Cross courses each year. It is now possible to make these courses available online. The Red Cross has routinely published the latest public health information, and the use of new technology will make this information available online. Wireless communication allows the American Red Cross to make faster damage assessment at the scene. The communication network allows it to locate family members during crises more efficiently. In the near future, it may be possible for the American Red Cross to offer an online shopping network to generate additional resources.[12]

Strategic Alliances

The American Red Cross has established a number of alliances with other organizations. It works with the World Health Organization to alleviate malnutrition, lack of pure water, and diarrhea in poor countries and to support primary health care. A donation to the World Hemophilia Foundation of plasma product is used to treat hemophilia. In 1999 the American Red Cross joined the Federal Emergency Management Agency for "TOPOFF," a nationwide disaster simulation to help prepare for acts of terrorism. As a result of recent research and development, Massachusetts General Hospital and the American Red Cross jointly own a patent for a protein associated with the underlying cause of Alzheimer's disease. In addition, the American Red Cross supplies over 3,000 hospitals with blood donations.[13]

In February 2001 the American Red Cross teamed up with Coinstar, Inc., to collect Red Cross donations for disaster relief efforts. Consumers could drop loose change into the Coinstar machines located in local supermarkets. Coinstar machines were located within two miles of 130 million Americans. John Clizbe, vice president of Disaster Services at the American Red Cross, indicated that "If every American near a Coinstar machine would donate a handful

Exhibit 3 Consolidated Statement of Financial Position, June 30, 2002 (with summarized information as of June 30, 2001) (in thousands)

Assets	Unrestricted	Temporarily Restricted	Permanently Restricted	Totals 2002	Totals 2001
Current assets:					
Cash and cash equivalents	$146,247	$439,569	$ 1,386	$ 587,202	$ 177,492
Investments	309,913	11,050	12,514	333,477	355,090
Receivables, net of allowance for doubtful accounts of $19,604 in 2002 and $19,301 in 2001:					
Trade	304,543	15,258	—	319,801	317,767
Contributions, current portion	16,411	110,103	56	126,570	133,183
Other	—	—	15,825	15,825	9,302
Inventories, net of allowance for obsolescence of $7,750 in 2002 and $6,784 in 2001	197,252	6,402	—	203,654	190,272
Other assets	12,547	3,162	183	15,892	23,289
Total current assets	986,913	585,544	29,964	1,602,421	1,206,395
Investments	548,633	155,674	325,238	1,029,545	1,120,773
Contributions receivable	4,209	28,374	2,243	34,826	39,339
Prepaid pension costs	—	—	—	—	11,858
Land, buildings, and other property, net	823,541	—	—	823,541	733,177
Other assets	11,089	1,500	22,704	35,293	26,171
Total assets	2,374,385	771,092	380,149	3,525,626	3,137,713

Liabilities and Net Assets

	Unrestricted	Temporarily Restricted	Permanently Restricted	Totals 2002	Totals 2001
Current liabilities:					
Accounts payable and accrued expenses	287,209	9,453	—	296,662	293,476
Current portion of debt and capital leases	39,894	—	—	39,894	89,372
Postretirement benefits	18,924	—	—	18,924	16,807
Other current liabilities	20,653	2,840	63	23,556	18,068
Total current liabilities	366,680	12,293	63	379,036	417,723
Debt and capital leases	357,453	—	—	357,453	360,870
Pension and postretirement benefits	120,042	—	—	120,042	108,339
Other liabilities	92,623	1,180	20	93,823	86,644
Total liabilities	936,798	13,473	83	950,354	973,576
Net assets	1,437,587	757,619	380,066	2,575,272	2,164,137
Commitments and contingencies					
Total liabilities and net assets	$2,374,385	$771,092	$380,149	$3,525,626	$3,137,713

Source: American Red Cross. 2002. Annual Report.

Exhibit 4 Consolidated Statement of Activities, Year ended June 30, 2002 (with summarized information for the year ended June 30, 2001) (in thousands)

	Unrestricted	Temporarily Restricted	Permanently Restricted	Totals 2002	Totals 2001
Operating revenues and gains					
Public Support:					
United Way and other federated	$ 65,616	$ 122,452	$ —	$ 188,068	$ 205,549
Disaster relief	—	133,376	—	133,376	84,601
Liberty disaster relief—Sept. 11 response	—	989,060	—	989,060	—
Legacies and bequests	67,118	6,745	22,022	95,885	115,594
Services and materials	22,034	96,222	—	118,256	49,728
Grants	21,236	67,175	—	88,411	76,351
Other contributions	213,289	36,915	705	250,909	230,845
Products and services:					
Biomedical	1,924,077	—	—	1,924,077	1,686,090
Program materials	136,582	906	—	137,488	121,724
Contracts	58,171	—	—	58,171	50,175
Investment income	81,394	1,069	—	82,463	81,405
Other revenues	49,089	2,008	—	51,097	40,844
Net assets released from restrictions	1,035,410	(1,035,410)	—	—	—
Total operating revenues and gains	3,674,016	420,518	22,727	4,117,261	2,742,906
Operating expenses					
Program services:					
Armed Forces Emergency Services	61,513	—	—	61,513	65,756
Disaster services	308,156	—	—	308,156	284,822
Liberty disaster relief—Sept. 11 response	617,960	—	—	617,960	—
Biomedical services	1,872,967	—	—	1,872,967	1,699,978
Health and safety services	213,614	—	—	213,614	203,058
Community services	152,902	—	—	152,902	150,108
International services	32,736	—	—	32,736	45,238
Total program services	3,259,848	—	—	3,259,848	2,448,960
Supporting services:					
Fund raising	136,901	—	—	136,901	108,616
Management and general	174,182	—	—	174,182	154,726
Total supporting services	311,083	—	—	311,083	263,342
Total operating expenses	3,570,931	—	—	3,570,931	2,712,302
Change in net assets from operations	103,085	420,518	22,727	546,330	30,604
Nonoperating gains (losses)	(131,900)	(548)	(2,747)	(135,195)	(63,876)
Cumulative effect of accounting change	—	—	—	—	2,201
Change in net assets	(28,815)	419,970	19,980	411,135	(31,071)
Net assets, beginning of year	1,466,402	337,649	360,086	2,164,137	2,195,208
Net assets, end of year	$1,437,587	$ 757,619	$380,066	$2,575,272	$2,164,137

Source: American Red Cross. 2002. Annual Report.

Exhibit 5 Consolidated Statement of Functional Expenses, Year ended June 30, 2002 (with summarized information for the year ended June 30, 2001)(in thousands)

				Program Services				
	Armed Forces Emergency Services	Disaster Services	Liberty Disaster Relief—Sept. 11 Response	Biomedical Services	Health and Safety Services	Community Services	International Services	Total Program Services
Salaries and wages	$35,329	$ 76,450	$ 4,966	$ 749,046	$100,866	$ 66,654	$ 8,340	$1,041,651
Employee benefits	6,701	16,758	773	165,697	19,894	13,698	1,706	225,227
Subtotal	42,030	93,208	5,739	914,743	120,760	80,352	10,046	1,266,878
Travel and maintenance	1,673	20,479	32,601	35,515	5,068	4,111	1,826	101,273
Equipment maintenance and rental	1,173	11,105	11,387	62,322	5,005	5,950	515	97,457
Supplies and materials	3,394	25,095	10,416	417,349	44,001	21,937	849	523,041
Contractual services	8,252	42,887	61,479	379,081	27,643	20,859	1,788	541,989
Financial and material assistance	2,803	106,406	496,338	14,132	3,528	13,811	17,236	654,254
Depreciation and amortization	2,188	8,976	—	49,825	7,609	5,882	476	74,956
Total expenses	$61,513	$308,156	$617,960	$1,872,967	$213,614	$152,902	$32,736	$3,259,848

	Supporting Services			Total Operating Expenses	
	Fund Raising	Management and General	Total Supporting Services	2002	2001
Salaries and wages	$ 42,260	$ 81,174	$123,434	$1,165,085	$1,046,171
Employee benefits	8,436	16,145	24,581	249,808	199,204
Subtotal	50,696	97,319	148,015	1,414,893	1,245,375
Travel and maintenance	3,708	6,466	10,174	111,447	78,208
Equipment maintenance and rental	1,902	5,260	7,162	104,619	84,227
Supplies and materials	35,167	6,494	41,661	564,702	477,547
Contractual services	41,147	44,991	86,138	628,127	563,436
Financial and material assistance	1,713	4,285	5,998	660,252	175,994
Depreciation and amortization	2,568	9,367	11,935	86,891	87,515
Total expenses	$136,901	$174,182	$311,083	$3,570,931	$2,712,302

Source: American Red Cross. 2002. Annual Report.

of change on their next supermarket visit, the Red Cross would be that much better prepared to respond to disaster immediately." Rich Stillman, COO of Coinstar, said, "You no longer need a credit card or checkbook to provide financial support to those in need. If all Americans donate the change in their wallet or pocket, those handfuls will make a huge difference in our capacity to help others this year."[14]

Masterfoods USA, a Mars Incorporated Company, created a special package of red, white, and blue M&Ms specifically to benefit the Red Cross. The national campaign theme used for this promotion was "Taking Care of America Everyday." "Through appearances on television, radio and newspapers, and creative displays in stores across the country, the new M&Ms' captured the heart of America," stated Skip Seitz, senior vice president, American Red Cross Growth and Integrated Development.[15] One hundred percent of all profits from the sales of these M&Ms were donated to the American Red Cross Disaster Relief Fund. In January 2002 Masterfoods USA presented a check to the Red Cross in the amount of $3.5 million.

In August 2001 the American Red Cross and the American Society of Association Executives (ASAE) signed an agreement under which the two organizations will share data regarding disasters, declarations, and changes in legislation, and will explore efforts in joint training exercises. The ASAE provides the Red Cross with demographic information about associations and assistance with identifying organizations they wish to contact during times of need.[16]

Recent Problems

Events between 2000 and 2002 provided the American Red Cross with a number of challenges.

Worker Strike   In June 2000 Red Cross workers who collected blood donations and delivered them to hospitals went on strike after rejecting a contract offer by the American Red Cross. The workers were unhappy about long hours, frequent schedule changes, and increasing health benefit costs.[17]

Unfair Trade Practices Lawsuit   The Red Cross derived 60 percent of its revenues from the sale of blood. In providing more than half the nation's blood, the Red Cross had annual sales of more than $1.3 billion.[18] In January 2001 a California blood supplier filed an antitrust suit against the American Red Cross claiming the organization used its clout to eliminate competitors. HemaCare Corp. and Coral Blood Services alleged the Red Cross had cost them more than $25 million in lost business. They further alleged that the American Red Cross priced some blood products (e.g., platelets) below production costs to drive out competitors while it charged higher prices for the same products in markets where there is no competition. In the lawsuit, the plaintiffs alleged the Red Cross violated Section 2 of the Sherman Antitrust Act, which prohibits monopolization. The lawsuit also charged tortuous interference, unfair trade practices, and

unfair competition under the California Business and Professional Code. William Nicely, HemaCare's chief executive officer, stated, "We believe that's unfair and illegal. The Red Cross is a fine organization. We just want them to play by the rules that are reasonable and fair and compete on a level playing field."[19] Blythe Kubina, a Red Cross spokeswoman, said in a written statement, "We believe the American Red Cross has done nothing inappropriate regarding HemaCare's claims to unfair business practices and we were surprised by this lawsuit. We have been in full compliance with the law, and we will vigorously defend this lawsuit."[20]

Liberty Disaster Relief Fund   After the terrorist attacks on September 11, the American Red Cross rose to the challenge of providing the most extensive relief operation in its 120-year history. In response to the tragedy, the Red Cross set up family assistance centers to provide counseling, child care, food, financial assistance, and other services to victims' families and others affected. Respite centers were set up in New York City, Somerset County, Pennsylvania, and at the Pentagon to provide meals, sleeping quarters, and other items to relief workers and volunteers. Funds were used for travel, lodging, and meals for volunteers and staff working on-site. Financial assistance, counseling, and transportation were provided to families of missing foreign nationals.

Millions of dollars, thousands of blood donations, and help from a myriad of volunteers contributed to Red Cross efforts to provide aid to survivors, victims' families, and relief workers. Because of the large dollar amount of donations from the American people, the Red Cross created the Liberty Disaster Relief Fund to be used exclusively to meet the needs of people directly affected by the September 11 tragedy.

Within 15 days of the September 11, 2001, attack, the Red Cross had collected $202 million in donations. Deborah Goldburg, a Red Cross spokesperson, stated, "Everything is happening at such a fast pace. Right now we are just trying to keep up with responses."[21] Goldburg stated that the entire amount raised by the Red Cross since the disaster would go into the newly created Liberty Fund. She indicated that organization officials earmarked $100 million from the fund to provide short-term financial assistance to families of victims. Bernadine Healy, MD, the president and chief executive officer of the Red Cross, said in a written statement, "What has taken place is extraordinary, and we must respond in an extraordinary way. The American Red Cross has a heavy burden—to live up to the inspiration and memory of those lost. It is with great humility and pride that we carry out this noble obligation."[22]

On October 12, 2001, the American Red Cross released a spending plan for the first $300 million in the Liberty Fund. Less than 50 percent of the money raised was targeted for victims, their families, or rescue workers. The remainder was earmarked to help the Red Cross improve its own organization and expand into new aid programs that might be needed in the event of future terrorist attacks.[23] This planned distribution of funds, based on Healy's policy of using donations for a "long period of uncertainty and recovery," caused a huge uproar.[24] The donors blasted Healy because they expected their donations to be helping September 11 disaster victims now. The attorney general of New York State threatened legal action.[25] Healy finally responded with her announcement of retirement. "I had no choice," she said, claiming that the organization's board had pushed her out.[26]

On November 14, 2001, interim CEO and president of the Red Cross, Harold Decker, announced changes adopted by the American Red Cross Board of Governors to meet the immediate and long-term needs of people affected by the September 11 terrorist attacks. The Red Cross would provide increased financial support to families, participate in a database to be shared among relief agencies, hire an additional 200 caseworkers, and extend the use of toll-free telephone lines. David T. McLaughlin, chairman of the American Red Cross Board of Governors, stated, "The people of this country have given the Red Cross their hard-earned dollars, their trust, and very clear direction for our September 11 relief effort. Regrettably, it took us too long to hear their message."[27] In an article in *U.S. News & World Report,* David McLaughlin stated, "If we don't subject ourselves to public scrutiny, we will never have public trust."[28]

In addition to donating money, the American public donated blood for the disaster victims. These donations were given in response to Healy's "Together, we can save a life" public service announcement. Experts questioned the wisdom of calling for blood donations when there were very few blood recipients. By November 2001 about 10 percent of the red blood cells collected on September 11 and 12 had expired.[29] In a congressional hearing, Healy was confronted with allegations of "panicking the public into wasteful donations of blood." *The Lancet* reported, "Donors charged the organization with abuse of their good intentions."[30]

On March 7, 2002, the American Red Cross saluted the staff and volunteers who provided assistance to the more than 54,500 families affected by the attacks. David McLaughlin stated, "Today we are recognizing the work of our staff, volunteers, and donors who responded to September 11th." Harold Decker, interim president, announced that the American Red Cross received $930 million in contributions and this money was used to provide the following:[31]

	$ millions
Direct assistance to 3,266 families of deceased and seriously injured	$169
Assistance to 51,000 families of displaced workers and disaster workers	270
Provision for 14 million meals, mental health services for 232,000 people, and health services for 129,000 people	94

BBB Wise Giving Alliance   On February 16, 2002, the Better Business Bureau Wise Giving Alliance removed the American Red Cross from its "give.org" Web site, allegedly because the American Red Cross did not provide a timely report to the alliance. In addition, H. Art Taylor, president of the alliance, made some unsupported public statements regarding the Red Cross that were reported in the *Philadelphia Inquirer.* A letter from Harold Decker to the Wise Giving Alliance explained that a request by the alliance for an updated report from the Red Cross was received in January 2002. Given the recent activities of the American Red Cross, it was determined that such a report could not be provided by the due date. Jack Campbell, CFO of the Red Cross, and Bennett Weiner, COO of the alliance, agreed to a March 30 deadline for the updated report. In his letter Decker requested a public retraction of Taylor's statements and that the Better Business Bureau's current report on the Red Cross be restored to the give.org Web site.[32]

60 Minutes Program   Another onslaught of negative publicity for the American Red Cross occurred March 10, 2002, on the CBS news show *60 Minutes.* It appears to have contained some inaccuracies concerning floods, fires, and the financial accountability of Red Cross chapters. Deborah Daley, a spokesperson for the Red Cross, sent a letter to CBS News indicating the errors and an explanation:[33]

1. In a comment about advertising practices, Mike Wallace reported, "They also decided to put a disclaimer in their ads saying that donations will be used for this and other disasters. The trouble is, it's in small print."

    In response, Deborah Daley reported, "In the West Virginia flood ad, the "this and other disasters" language appears in the same font and size as the rest of the body copy appealing for support.

2. Wallace reported, "Outside audits of local Red Cross chapters are rare. In fact, there is so little accountability that local chapters—and there are more than one thousand of them—aren't even required to submit financial reports to Red Cross headquarters in Washington."

    Deborah Daley responded that chapters are accountable in a number of ways. All chapters must have an independent annual review. Chapters that have over $100,000 in annual expenses must have an external audit conducted by an independent CPA. The largest 126 chapters must send quarterly financial reports to the national Red Cross. The Red Cross does regular audits of chapters. Chapters must meet specific national guidelines to maintain their charters. She stated that Wallace's claim that chapters "are not even required to submit financial reports" is completely false.

3. As for the Alpine fire in Southern California, Wallace reported, "As of last week, 14 months after the fire,

San Diego was still waiting for a full accounting of how the money donated for the fire victims has been and will be spent."

Deborah Daley responded that the chapter has provided up-to-date financial information on its response to the Alpine fire three times since November.

Looking to the Future

After a five-month search, Marsha Johnson Evans was named president and CEO of the American Red Cross on June 27, 2002. Evans has served as national executive director of the Girl Scouts of the USA for the past four years, prior to which she had a 29-year career in the U.S. Navy, where she earned the rank of rear admiral. In his announcement, David McLaughlin, chairman of the Board of Governors of the American Red Cross, said, "Marty's unique style of leadership along with her experience as established administrator will bring new vigor to the American Red Cross. With great insight into our mission, she is well poised to guide our organization as we continue to provide vital services in a world faced by new challenges."[34] Evans remarked that:

> In the midst of responding to the extraordinary demands of 9/11 and a lot of criticism about these efforts, my observation is that the Red Cross never lost sight of its responsibility to every community and every victim of the other disasters that occurred, some 45,000 in the months since last September. The timely and capable response day-in and day-out to these disasters speaks volumes about the character of the volunteers and staff, their talent, and most especially their dedication.[35]

As she begins to guide the organization, Marsha Johnson Evans must confront the many issues faced by the American Red Cross. How should she proceed?

Endnotes

1. American Red Cross. 2002. Press release, June 27.
2. American Red Cross. www.redcross.org.
3. American Red Cross. 2002. Press release, February 1.
4. American Red Cross. 2000–2001. Annual Reports.
5. American Red Cross. 2001–2002. Annual Reports.
6. Ibid.
7. Ibid.
8. American Red Cross. 2000. Annual Report.
9. Sanborn, Stephanie. 2000. Nonprofits reap rewards of the Web—Internet proves to be a great fund-raising tool for charities, but there are costs. *Infoworld,* 22(25): 37.
10. Ibid.
11. Ibid.
12. American Red Cross. 2000. Annual Report.
13. Ibid.
14. *US Newswire.* 2001. American Red Cross and Coinstar to launch new fundraising technology to prepare for disasters. February 12.
15. American Red Cross. 2002. Press release, February 1.
16. *Association Management.* 2001. ASAE and American Red Cross formalize partnership agreement. 53(8): 12.
17. *Fund Raising Management.* 2000. Red Cross workers on strike. 31(4): 33.
18. Greenberg, Daniel S. 2001. Blood, politics, and the American Red Cross. *Lancet,* November 24: 1789; Taylor, Mark. 2001. Red Cross faces antitrust lawsuit. *Modern Healthcare* 31, January 1: 20.
19. Taylor, Red Cross faces antitrust lawsuit.
20. Ibid.
21. Becker, Cinda. 2001. A torrent of donations; charities wrestle with how best to spend money pouring in since attacks. *Modern Healthcare* 31, October 1: 8.
22. Ibid.
23. Tyrangiel, Josh. 2001. The charity olympics: After weeks of record giving, Americans want to know: Is that money helping? *Time,* November 5: 75.
24. *PR Newswire.* 2001. Newsweek: Former Red Cross head says her fundraising message was clear. . . . December 9.
25. Greenberg, Blood, politics, and the American Red Cross.
26. Tyrangiel, Charity olympics.
27. *US Newswire.* 2001. Red Cross announces major changes in Liberty Fund: Fund solely used for people affected by September 11 tragedy. November 14.
28. Levine, Samantha. 2001. Red Crossroads. *U.S. News & World Report,* November 19.
29. Tyrangiel, Charity olympics.
30. Greenberg, Blood, politics, and the American Red Cross.
31. American Red Cross. 2002. Press release, March 7.
32. *PR Newswire.* 2002. American Red Cross letter to Better Business Bureau's Wise Giving Alliance. February 16.
33. Red Cross announces major changes in Liberty Fund.
34. American Red Cross. 2002. Press release, June 27.
35. Ibid.

Case 12 Whole Foods Market 2007: Will There Be Enough Organic Food to Satisfy the Growing Demand?*

Reflecting back over his three decades of experience in the grocery business, John Mackey smiled to himself over his previous successes. His entrepreneurial history began with a single store that he has now grown to the nation's leading natural food chain. While proud of the past, John had concerns about the future direction the Whole Foods Market® chain should head. Whole Foods Market was an early entrant into the organic food market, and it has used its early-mover advantage to solidify its position and continue its steady growth.

In 2005 Whole Foods Market acquired the Wild Oats Food chain. Wild Oats operates 100 full service stores in 24 states and Canada. With the changing economy and a more competitive industry landscape, John Mackey is uncertain about how to meet the company's aggressive growth targets. Whole Foods Markets objective is to reach $12 billion in revenue with 300+ stores by 2010 without sacrificing quality and its current reputation. This is not an easy task, and John is unsure of the best way to proceed.

Company Background

Whole Foods carries both natural and organic food, offering customers a wide variety of products. "Natural" refers to food that is free of growth hormones or antibiotics, whereas "certificated organic" food conforms to the standards defined by the U.S. Department of Agriculture in October 2002.[1] Whole Foods Market is the world's leading retailer of natural and organic foods, with 193 stores in 31 states, Canada, and the United Kingdom. John Mackey, current president and cofounder of Whole Foods, opened Safer Way natural grocery store in 1978. The store had limited success because it was a small location that allowed only a limited selection, focusing entirely on vegetarian foods.[2] John joined forces with Craig Weller and Mark Skiles, founders of Clarsville Natural Grocery (founded in 1979), to create Whole Foods Market.[3] This joint venture took place in Austin, Texas, in 1980 and resulted in a new company—a single natural food market with a staff of 19.

In addition to the supermarkets, Whole Foods owns and operates several subsidiaries. Allegro Coffee Company was formed in 1977 and purchased by Whole Foods Market in 1997, and it now acts as their coffee roasting and distribution center. Pigeon Cove is Whole Foods' seafood processing facility, which was founded in 1985 and known as M&S Seafood until 1990. Whole Foods purchased Pigeon Cove, located in Gloucester, MA in 1996. The company is now the only supermarket to own and operate a waterfront seafood facility.[4] The last two subsidiaries are Produce Field Inspection Office and Select Fish, which is Whole Foods' West Coast seafood processing facility acquired in 2003.[5] In addition to the above, the company has eight distribution centers, seven regional bake houses, and four commissaries.[6]

"Whole Foods Market remains uniquely mission driven: The company is highly selective about what they sell, dedicated to stringent quality standards, and committed to sustainable agriculture. They believe in a virtuous circle entwining the food chain, human beings and Mother Earth: each is reliant upon the others through a beautiful and delicate symbiosis."[7] The message of preservation and sustainability are followed while providing high quality goods to customers and high profits to investors.

Whole Foods has grown over the years through mergers, acquisitions, and several new store openings.[8] Today, Whole Foods Market is the largest natural food supermarket in the United States.[9] The company consists of 32,000 employees operating 193 stores in the United States, Canada, and the United Kingdom with an average store size of 32,000 square feet.[10] While the majority of Whole Foods locations are in United States, the company has made acquisitions expanding its presence in the UK. European expansion provides enormous potential growth due to the large population and it holds "a more sophisticated organic-foods market than the United States in terms of suppliers and acceptance by the public."[11] Whole Foods targets its locations specifically by an area's demographics. The company targets locations where 40% or more of the residents have a college degree, as they are more likely to be aware of nutritional issues.[12]

Whole Foods Market's Philosophy

Its corporate Web site defines the company philosophy as follows, "Whole Foods Market's vision of a sustainable future means our children and grandchildren will be living in a world that values human creativity, diversity, and individual choice. Businesses will harness human and material resources without devaluing the integrity of the individual or the planet's ecosystems. Companies, governments, and institutions will be held accountable for their actions. People will better understand that all actions have repercussions and that planning and foresight coupled with hard work and flexibility can overcome almost any problem encountered. It will be a world that values education and a free exchange of ideas by an informed citizenry; where people are encouraged to discover, nurture, and share their life's passions."[13]

While Whole Foods recognizes it is only a supermarket, it is working toward fulfilling its vision within the context of its industry. In addition to leading by example, it strives to conduct business in a manner consistent with its mission and vision. By offering minimally processed, high-quality food; engaging in ethical business practices; and providing

* By Patricia Harasta and Alan N. Hoffman, Bentley College. The authors would like to thank Ann Hoffman, Christopher Ferrari, Robert Marshall, Julie Giles, Jennifer Powers and Gretchen Alper for their research and contributions to this case. Please address all correspondence to Dr. Alan N. Hoffman, AGC 320, Department of Management, Bentley College, 175 Forest Street, Waltham, MA 02452-4705, voice (781) 891-2287, ahoffman@bentley.edu, fax (781) 459-0335. Printed by permission of Dr. Alan N. Hoffman, Bentley College.

a motivational, respectful work environment, the company believes it is on the path to a sustainable future.[14]

Whole Foods incorporates the best practices of each location back into the chain.[15] This can be seen in the company's store product expansion from dry goods to perishable produce, including meats, fish, and prepared foods. The lessons learned at one location are absorbed by all, enabling the chain to maximize effectiveness and efficiency while offering a product line customers love. Whole Foods carries only natural and organic products. The best tasting and most nutritious food available is found in its purest state—unadulterated by artificial additives, sweeteners, colorings, and preservatives.[16]

Whole Foods continually improves customer offerings, catering to its specific locations. Unlike business models for traditional grocery stores, Whole Foods products differ by geographic regions and local farm specialties.

Employee and Customer Relations

Whole Foods encourages a team-based environment allowing each store to make independent decisions regarding its operations. Teams consist of up to 11 employees and a team leader. The team leaders typically head up one department. Each store employs anywhere from 72 to 391 team members.[17] The manager is referred to as the "store team leader." The store team leader is compensated by an Economic Value Added (EVA) bonus and is also eligible to receive stock options.[18]

Whole Foods tries to instill a sense of purpose among its employees and has been named one of the 100 Best Companies to Work for in America by *Fortune* magazine for the past six years. In employee surveys, 90 percent of its team members stated that they always or frequently enjoy their job.[19]

The company strives to take care of its customers, realizing they are the "lifeblood of our business," and the two are "interdependent on each other."[20] Whole Foods' primary objective goes beyond 100 percent customer satisfaction with the goal to "delight" customers in every interaction.

Competitive Environment

Natural Products Sales Top $45 Billion in 2004

American shoppers spent nearly $45.8 billion on natural and organic products in 2004, according to research published in the "24th Annual Market Overview" in the June issue of *The Natural Foods Merchandiser*. In 2004, natural products sales increased 6.9 percent across all sales channels, including supermarkets, mass marketers, direct marketers, and the Internet. Sales of organic products rose 14.6 percent in natural products stores. As interest in low-carb diets waned, sales of organic baked goods rose 35 percent. Other fast-growing organic categories included meat, poultry, and seafood—up 120 percent; coffee and cocoa—up 64 percent; and cookies—up 63 percent.

At the time of Whole Foods' inception, there was almost no competition, with fewer than six other natural food stores in the United States. Today, the organic foods industry is growing, and Whole Foods' finds itself competing hard to maintain its elite presence. As the population has become increasingly concerned about its eating habits, natural foods stores, such as Whole Foods, are flourishing. Other successful natural food grocery chains today include Trader Joe's Co. and Wild Oats Market (see Exhibit 1).[21]

Trader Joe's, originally known as Pronto Markets was founded in 1958 in Los Angeles by Joe Coulombe. By expanding its presence and product offerings while maintaining high quality at low prices, the company has found its competitive niche.[22] The company has 215 stores,

Exhibit 1 Sales

	Sales (in Millions)						
Company	2000	2001	% Growth	2002	% Growth	2003	% Growth
Whole Foods Market[a]	$1,838.60	$2,272.20	23.60%	$2,690.50	18.40%	$3,148.60	17.00%
Trader Joe's Company[b]	$1,670.00	$1,900.00	13.80%	$2,200.00	15.80%	$2,500.00	13.60%
Wild Oats Market[c]	$838.10	$893.20	6.60%	$919.10	2.90%	$969.20	5.50%

[a]Hoovers Online: http://www.hoovers.com/whole-foods/–ID_10952–/free-co-factsheet.xhtml: December 1, 2004.

[b]Hoovers Online: http://www.hoovers.com/trader-joe's-co/–ID-47619–/free-co-factsheet.xhtm: December 1, 2004.

[c]Hoovers Online: http://www.hoovers.com/wild-oats-markets/–ID_41717–/free-co-factsheet.xhtml: December 1, 2004.

primarily on the west and east coasts of the United States. The company "offers upscale grocery fare such as health foods, prepared meals, organic produce and nutritional supplements."[23] A low-cost structure allows Trader Joe's to offer competitive prices while still maintaining its margins. Trader Joe's stores have no service department and average just 10,000 square feet in store size. A privately held company, Trader Joe's enjoyed sales of $2.5 million in 2003—a 13.6 percent increase from 2002.[24]

Additional competition has arisen from grocery stores such as Stop 'N Shop and Shaw's, which now incorporate natural foods sections in their conventional stores, placing them in direct competition with Whole Foods. Because larger grocery chains have more flexibility in their product offerings, they are more likely to promote products through sales—a strategy Whole Foods rarely practices.

Despite being in a highly competitive industry, Whole Foods maintains its reputation as the world's number one natural foods chain.[25] As the demand for natural and organic food continues to grow, pressure on suppliers will increase. Only 3 percent of U.S. farmland is organic, so there is limited output.[26] The increased demand for these products may further elevate prices or result in goods being out of stock, with possible price wars looming.

The Changing Grocery Industry

Before the emergence of the supermarket, the public was largely dependent upon specialty shops or street vendors for dairy products, meats, produce, and other household items. In the 1920s, chain stores began to threaten independent retailers by offering convenience and lower prices by procuring larger quantities of products. Appel explains that the emergence of the supermarkets in the 1930s was a result of three major changes in society:

1. The shift in population from rural to urban areas
2. An increase in disposable income
3. Increased mobility through ownership of automobiles[27]

Perhaps the earliest example of the supermarket as we know it today is King Kullen, America's first supermarket, which was founded by Michael Cullen in 1930. "The essential key to his plan was volume, and he attained this through heavy advertising of low prices on nationally advertised merchandise," Appel states. As the success of Cullen's strategy became evident, other stores such as Safeway, A&P, and Kroger adopted it as well. By the time the United States entered World War II, 9,000 supermarkets accounted for 25 percent of industry sales.[28]

Low prices and convenience continue to be the dominant factors driving consumers to supermarkets today. The industry is characterized by low margins and continuous downward pressure on prices made evident by coupons, weekly specials, and rewards cards. Over the years firms have introduced subtle changes to the business model by providing additional conveniences, such as the inclusion of bakeries, banks, pharmacies, and even coffee houses co-located within the supermarket. Throughout their existence, supermarkets have also tried to cater to the changing tastes and preferences of society by providing healthier diets such as the Atkins diet and low carbohydrate foods. The moderate changes to strategy within supermarkets have been imitated by competitors, that are returning the industry to a state of price competition. Supermarkets themselves now face additional competition from wholesalers such as Costco, BJ's, and Sam's Club.

A Different Shopping Experience

The setup of the organic grocery store is a key component to Whole Foods' success. The store's setup and its products are carefully researched to ensure that they are meeting the demands of the local community. Locations are primarily in cities and are chosen for their large space and heavy foot traffic. According to Whole Foods' 10K, "approximately 88 percent of our existing stores are located in the top 50 statistical metropolitan areas."[29] The company uses a specific formula to choose its store sites that is based upon several metrics, which include but are not limited to income levels, education, and population density.

Upon entering a Whole Foods supermarket, it becomes clear that the company attempts to sell the consumer on the entire experience. Team members (employees) are well trained and the stores themselves are immaculate. There are in-store chefs to help with recipes, wine tasting and food sampling. There are Take Action food centers[30] where customers can access information on the issues that affect their food, such as legislation and environmental factors. Some stores offer extra services such as home delivery, cooking classes, massages, and valet parking.[31] Whole Foods goes out of its way to appeal to the above-average income earner.

Whole Foods uses price as a marketing tool in a few select areas, as demonstrated by the 365 Whole Foods brand name products that are priced less than similar organic products carried within the store. However, the company does not use price to differentiate itself from competitors.[32] Rather, Whole Foods focuses on quality and service as a means of standing out from the competition.

Whole Foods only spent 0.5 percent [33] of its total sales from fiscal year 2004 on advertising; it relies on other means to promote its stores. The company relies heavily on word-of-mouth advertising from its customers to help market itself in the local community. It is also promoted in several health-conscious magazines, and each store budgets for in-store advertising each fiscal year.

Whole Foods also gains recognition via charitable contributions and the awareness that it brings to the treatment of animals. The company donates 5 percent of its after-tax profits to not-for-profit charities.[34] The company is also very active in establishing systems to make sure that the animals used in its products are treated humanely.

The Aging Baby Boomers

The aging of the Baby Boomer generation will expand the senior demographic over the next decade as their children grow up and leave the nest. Urban singles are another group that has extra disposable income due to their lack of dependants. These two groups present an opportunity for growth for Whole Foods. Americans spent 7.2 percent of their total expenditures on food in 2001, making it the seventh highest category on which consumers spend their money.[35] Additionally, U.S. households with incomes of more than $100,000 per annum represent 22 percent of aggregate income today compared with 18 percent a decade ago.[36]

This shift in demographics has created an expansion in the luxury store group, while slowing growth in the discount retail market.[37] To that end, there is a gap in supermarket retailing between consumers who can only afford to shop at low-cost providers like Wal-Mart, and the population of consumers who prefer gourmet food and are willing to pay a premium for perceived higher quality.[38] "The Baby Boomers are driving demand for organic food in general because they're health-conscious and can afford to pay higher prices," says Professor Steven G. Sapp, a sociologist at Iowa State University who studies consumer food behavior.[39]

The perception that imported, delicatessen, exotic, and organic foods are of higher quality, and therefore should command higher prices, continues to bode well for Whole Foods Market. As John Mackey, explains "we're changing the [grocery-shopping] experience so that people enjoy it. . . . It's a richer, [more fun], more enjoyable experience. People don't shop our stores because we have low prices."[40] The consumer focus on a healthy diet is not limited to food. More new diet plans emerged in America in the last half of the 20th century than in any other country. This trend has also increased the demand for nutritional supplements and vitamins.[41]

In recent years, consumers have made a gradual move toward the use of fresher, healthier foods in their everyday diets. Consumption of fresh fruits and vegetables, pasta, and other grain-based products has increased.[42] This is evidenced by the aggressive expansion by consumer products companies into healthy food and natural and organic products.[43] "Natural and organic products have crossed the chasm to mainstream America."[44] The growing market can be attributed to the acceptance and widespread expansion of organic product offerings beyond milk and dairy.[45] Mainstream acceptance of the Whole Foods offering can be attributed to this shift in consumer food preferences as consumers continue to cite taste as the number one motivator for purchasing organic foods.[46]

With a growing percentage of women working out of the home, the traditional role of home-cooked meals prepared from scratch has waned. As fewer women have the time to devote to cooking, consumers are giving way to the trend of convenience through prepared foods. Sales of ready-to-eat meals have grown significantly. "The result is that grocers are starting to specialize in quasi-restaurant food."[47] Just as women entering the workforce has propelled the sale of prepared foods, it has also increased consumer awareness of the need for the one-stop shopping experience. Hypermarkets such as Wal-Mart, that offer nonfood items and more mainstream product lines, allow consumers to conduct more shopping in one place rather than moving from store to store.

The growth in sales of natural foods is expected to continue at the rate of 8 to 10 percent annually, according to the National Nutritional Foods Association. The sale of organic food has largely outpaced traditional grocery products due to consumer perception that organic food is healthier.[48] The purchase of organic food is perceived to be beneficial to consumer health by 61 percent of consumers, according to a Food Marketing Institute (FMI)/*Prevention* magazine study. Americans believe organic food can help improve fitness and increase their longevity.[49] Much of this perception has grown out of fear of how nonorganic foods are treated with pesticides for growth and then preserved for sale. Therefore, an opportunity exists for Whole Foods to contribute to consumer awareness by funding nonprofit organizations that focus on educating the public on the benefits of organic lifestyles.

Operations

Whole Foods purchases most of their products from regional and national suppliers. This allows the company to leverage its size to receive deep discounts and favorable terms with its vendors. The company still permits stores to purchase from local producers to keep the stores aligned with local food trends and to be seen as supporting the community. The company owns two procurement centers and handles the majority of procurement and distribution itself. Whole Foods also owns several regional bake houses that distribute products to their stores. The largest independent vendor is United Natural Foods, which accounted for 20 percent of Whole Foods' total purchases for fiscal year 2004.[50] Product categories at Whole Foods include, but are not limited to:

- Produce
- Seafood
- Grocery
- Meat and poultry
- Bakery
- Prepared foods and catering
- Specialty (Beer, Wine and Cheese)
- Whole body (nutritional supplements, vitamins, body care, and educational products such as books)
- Floral
- Pet products
- Household products[51]

While Whole Foods carries all the items that one would expect to find in a grocery store (and plenty that one would not), their ". . . heavy emphasis on perishable foods is designed to appeal to both natural foods and gourmet shoppers."[52] Perishable foods accounted for 67 percent of its retail sales in 2004 and are the core of Whole Foods' success.[53] This is demonstrated by its statement that, "We believe it is our strength of execution in perishables that has attracted many of our most loyal shoppers."[54]

Whole Foods also provides fully cooked frozen meal options through their private label Whole Kitchen to satisfy the demands of working families. For example, the Whole Foods Market located in Woodland Hills, California, that has redesigned its prepared foods section more than three times[55] in response to a 40 percent growth in prepared foods sales.[56]

Whole Foods doesn't take just any product and put it on its shelves. In order to make it into the Whole Foods grocery store, products have to undergo a strict test to determine if they are "Whole Foods material." The quality standards that all potential Whole Foods products must meet include:

- Foods that are free of preservatives and other additives
- Foods that are fresh, wholesome, and safe to eat
- Organically grown foods
- Foods and products that promote a healthy life[57]

Meat and poultry products must adhere to a higher standard:

- No antibiotics or added growth hormones
- An affidavit from each producer that outlines the whole production process and how the animals are treated
- An annual inspection of all producers by Whole Foods Market
- Successful completion of a third-party audit to attest to these findings[58]

Also, due to the lack of available nutritional brands with a national identity, Whole Foods decided to enter into the private-label product business. They currently have three private-label products and are considering a fourth program, called Authentic Food Artisan, that promotes distinctive products that are certified organic. The three private-label products are: (1) 365 Everyday Value—a well-recognized and trusted brand that meets the standards of Whole Foods and is less expensive than the regular product lines, (2) Whole Kids Organic—Healthy items that are directed at children, and (3) 365 Organic Everyday Value—all the benefits of organic food at reduced prices.[59]

When opening a new store, Whole Foods stocks it with almost $700,000 worth of initial inventory, which their vendors partially finance.[60] Like most conventional grocery stores, the majority of Whole Foods' inventory is turned over fairly quickly; this is especially true of produce. Fresh organic produce is central to Whole Foods' existence and turns over on a faster basis than other products.

Financial Operations

Whole Foods Market focuses on earning a profit while providing job security to its workforce to lay the foundation for future growth. The company is determined not to let profits deter it from providing excellent service to its customers and a quality work environment for its staff. Their mission statement defines their recipe for financial success.

> Whole Foods, Whole People, Whole Planet emphasizes that our vision reaches far beyond just being a food retailer. Our success in fulfilling our vision is measured by customer satisfaction, Team Member excellence and happiness, return on capital investment, improvement in the state of the environment, and local and larger community support.[61]

Whole Foods also caps the salary of its executives at no more than 14 times that of the average annual salary of a Whole Foods worker; this includes wages and incentive bonuses as well. The company also donates 5 percent of its after-tax profits to nonprofit organizations.[62]

Over a five-year period from 2000 through 2004, the company experienced an 87 percent growth in sales, reaching $3.86 billion in 2004. Annual sales increases during that period were equally dramatic—24% in 2001, 18% in 2002, 17% in 2003, and 22% in 2004 (see Exhibits 2 and 3).[63] The company achieved $5.6 billion in sales in 2006 which was up from $4.7 billion in 2005, resulting in a yearly increase of 19.2 percent. On average, the company's sales have grown 19.4 percent over the past five years. In fiscal 2006, Whole Foods achieved 11 percent comparable-store sales growth (CSSG),* which is well above the industry average. This growth is perhaps more impressive given the relatively negative economic environment and recession in the United States.

Whole Foods' strategy of expansion and acquisition has fueled growth in net income since the company's inception. This is particularly evident when looking at the net income growth in 2002 (24.47 percent), 2003 (22.72 percent), and 2004 (27.94 percent).[64] In 2006, the company earned $204 million—a 50 percent increase from the $136 million it earned in 2005.

The ticker for Whole Foods, Inc. is WFMI. In reviewing the performance history of Whole Foods stock since its initial public offering reveals a mostly upward trend. The 10-year price trend shows the company increasing from under $10 per share to a high of over $100 per share, reflecting an increase of over 1,000 percent.[65] In 2007, the stock has been on a downward trend due to slowing same-store sales. The current price of $47 with 140 million shares outstanding gives the company a market valuation of $6.7 billion (Apr, 2007).[66] As of 2006, Whole Foods had only $8.6 million in long-term debt, while having $256.2 million in cash and cash equivalent balances (see Exhibit 4).

---

* Comparable-store sales growth (CSSG) is a key industry metric for measuring sales. Stores are considered comparable after 53 weeks of operation.

Exhibit 2 Whole Foods Market, Inc. Unaudited Five-Year Historical Data[1]

	Average Weekly Sales	Sales (000)	YOY Increase[2]	Comparable Store Sales Growth	2-Year Comps[3]	Identical Store Sales Growth	2-Year Idents[3]	Ending Square Footage	YOY Increase	Weighted Average YOY Increase[4]	Number of New Stores	Acquired Stores	Relocated/ Closed Stores	Ending Store Count	Gross Margin	Store Contribution[5]
1Q02	$376,335	$ 780,799	21.3%	9.4%	16.7%	7.5%	14.0%	3,841,559	16.4%	18%	2	3	3	128	33.9%	8.6%
2Q02	$395,062	$ 622,789	20.5%	10.1%	19.7%	9.1%	17.3%	3,974,266	16.8%	16%	3	0	0	131	35.0%	10.3%
3Q02	$406,019	$ 648,763	21.1%	10.5%	20.7%	9.5%	18.2%	4,040,492	16.5%	17%	4	0	2	133	34.9%	10.0%
4Q02	$395,831	$ 638,124	19.9%	10.5%	20.7%	9.6%	18.4%	4,098,492	13.9%	16%	2	0	0	135	35.1%	9.6%
FY02	$392,837	$2,690,475	20.7%	10.0%	19.2%	8.7%	16.8%	4,098,492	13.9%	17%	11	3	5	135	34.6%	9.5%
1Q03	$414,571	$ 923,760	18.3%	10.5%	19.9%	10.1%	17.6%	4,287,368	11.6%	11%	5	0	0	140	34.0%	8.6%
2Q03	$422,554	$ 725,139	16.4%	7.0%	17.1%	6.4%	15.5%	4,423,052	11.3%	12%	3	0	0	143	34.4%	9.4%
3Q03	$432,906	$ 749,042	15.5%	7.6%	18.1%	7.0%	16.5%	4,463,883	10.5%	11%	1	0	0	144	34.5%	9.4%
4Q03	$429,020	$ 750,651	17.6%	8.8%	19.3%	8.3%	17.9%	4,545,433	10.9%	10%	3	0	2	145	34.2%	8.7%
FY03	$424,095	$3,148,593	17.0%	8.6%	18.6%	8.1%	16.8%	4,545,433	10.9%	11%	12	0	2	145	34.2%	9.0%
1Q04[6]	$478,666	$1,118,148	21.0%	14.7%	25.2%	14.3%	24.4%	4,578,933	6.8%	8%	1	0	0	146	34.4%	9.1%
2Q04[6]	$488,908	$ 902,140	24.4%	17.1%	24.1%	17.0%	23.4%	4,759,050	7.6%	7%	3	7	0	156	35.4%	9.9%
3Q04	$483,560	$ 917,355	22.5%	14.1%	21.7%	13.7%	20.7%	5,004,963	12.1%	9%	5	0	1	160	34.5%	9.1%
4Q04	$478,165	$ 927,306	23.5%	14.0%	22.8%	13.3%	21.6%	5,145,261	12.1%	13%	3	0	0	163	34.6%	8.6%
FY04	$482,061	$1,864,950	22.8%	14.9%	23.5%	14.5%	22.6%	5,145,261	12.1%	9%	12	7	1	163	34.7%	9.2%

1Q05	$516,277	$1,368,328	22.4%	11.4%	26.1%	10.7%	25.0%	5,258,601	14.8%	15%	3	0	0	166	34.6%	9.1%
2Q05	$539,003	$1,085,158	20.3%	11.6%	28.7%	10.2%	27.2%	5,399,604	13.5%	13%	4	0	2	168	35.7%	10.2%
3Q05	$556,912	$1,132,736	23.5%	15.2%	29.3%	13.2%	26.9%	5,536,424	10.6%	13%	3	0	1	170	35.2%	10.0%
4Q05	$541,987	$1,115,067	20.2%	13.4%	27.4%	11.9%	25.2%	5,819,413	13.1%	12%	5	0	0	175	35.3%	7.2%
FY05	$536,986	$4,701,289	21.6%	12.8%	27.8%	11.5%	26.0%	5,819,413	13.1%	13%	15	0	3	175	35.1%	9.1%
1Q06	$584,554	$1,666,953	21.8%	13.0%	24.4%	12.0%	22.7%	6,056,121	15.2%	15%	5	0	0	180	34.5%	9.0%
2Q06	$601,908	$1,311,520	20.9%	11.9%	23.6%	10.9%	21.1%	6,172,105	14.3%	14%	3	1	1	183	35.3%	10.1%
3Q06	$605,365	$1,337,885	18.1%	9.9%	25.1%	9.6%	22.8%	6,225,756	12.5%	14%	1	0	1	183	35.3%	10.2%
4Q06	$584,498	$1,291,017	15.8%	8.6%	22.0%	8.4%	20.3%	6,376,817	9.6%	11%	4	0	1	186	34.8%	9.2%
FY06	$593,439	$5,607,376	19.3%	11.0%	23.8%	10.3%	21.8%	6,376,817	9.6%	13%	13	1	3	186	35.0%	9.6%
1Q07	$619,966	$1,870,731	12.2%	7.0%	20.0%	6.2%	18.2%	6,581,347	8.7%	8%	4	0	1	189	34.3%	8.4%

[1]FY03–FY05 gross margins and store contribution are restated.

[2]Excludes extra week in FY01.

[3]Sum of two years of comparable and identical store sales increases.

[4]Defined as increase in current year weighted average square footage over prior year weighted average square footage.

[5]Defined as gross profit minus direct store expenses.

[6]Results positively impacted by strikes at conventional grocery stores in Southern California for majority of Q1 and half of Q2.

Note: Sales of a store are deemed to be "comparable" commencing in the 53rd full week after the store was opened or acquired. Identical store sales exclude sales from remodels with expansions of square footage greater than 20 percent and relocations. Stores closed for seven or more days due to unusual events such as fires, snowstorms, or hurricanes are excluded from the comparable and identical store base in the first week of closure until re-opened for a full fiscal week.

Exhibit 3 Whole Foods Market, Inc. Consolidated Quarterly Statements of Operations (in thousands, except per share amounts)

Fiscal Year 2006	1st Quarter January 15, 2006	2nd Quarter April 09, 2006	3rd Quarter July 02, 2006	4th Quarter September 24, 2006	YTD September 24, 2006
Sales	$1,666,953	$1,311,520	$1,337,886	$1,291,017	$5,607,376
Cost of goods sold and occupancy costs	1,092,018	848,020	866,260	841,436	3,647,734
Gross profit	574,935	463,500	471,626	449,581	1,959,642
Direct store expenses	424,438	330,470	335,555	331,505	1,421,968
Store contribution	150,497	133,030	136,071	118,076	537,674
General and administrative expenses	50,889	43,421	43,955	42,979	181,244
Operating income before pre-opening	99,608	89,609	92,116	75,097	356,430
Pre-opening expenses	7,823	5,696	6,604	11,935	32,058
Relocation costs	668	1,628	1,256	1,811	5,363
Operating income	91,117	82,285	84,256	61,351	319,009
Other income (expense):					
Interest expense	(3)	—	(8)	(21)	(32)
Investment and other income	6,082	4,068	5,581	5,005	20,736
Income before income taxes	97,196	86,353	89,829	66,335	339,713
Provision for income taxes	38,878	34,542	35,931	26,534	135,885
Net income	$ 58,318	$ 51,811	$ 53,898	$ 39,801	$ 203,828
Basic earnings per share	$ 0.42	$ 0.37	$ 0.38	$ 0.28	$ 1.46
Weighted average shares outstanding	137,532	139,450	140,712	140,215	139,328
Diluted earnings per share	$ 0.40	$ 0.36	$ 0.37	$ 0.28	$ 1.41
Weighted average shares outstanding, diluted basis	145,317	145,546	145,925	143,462	145,082
Dividends per share	$ 2.15	$ 0.15	$ 0.15	$ —	$ 2.45

Exhibit 4   Whole Foods Market, Inc. Consolidated Balance Sheets (in thousands) September 24, 2006 and September 25, 2005

Assets	2006	2005
Current assets:		
Cash and cash equivalents	$ 2,252	$ 308,524
Short-term investments—available-for-sale securities	193,847	—
Restricted cash	60,065	36,922
Trade accounts receivable	82,137	66,682
Merchandise inventories	203,727	174,848
Prepaid expenses and other current assets	33,804	45,965
Deferred income taxes	48,149	39,588
Total current assets:	623,981	672,529
Property and equipment, net of accumulated depreciation and amortization	1,236,133	1,054,605
Goodwill	113,494	112,476
Intangible assets, net of accumulated amortization	34,767	21,990
Deferred income taxes	29,412	22,452
Other assets	5,209	5,244
Total assets	$2,042,996	$1,889,296

Liabilities and Shareholders' Equity	2006	2005
Current liabilities:		
Current installments of long-term debt and capital lease obligations	$ 49	$ 5,932
Trade accounts payable	121,857	103,348
Accrued payroll, bonus and other benefits due team members	153,014	126,981
Dividends payable	—	17,208
Other current liabilities	234,850	164,914
Total current liabilities:	509,770	418,383
Long-term debt and capital lease obligations, less current installments	8,606	12,932
Deferred rent liability	120,421	91,775
Other long-term liabilities	56	530
Total liabilities	638,853	523,620
Shareholder's equity:		
Common stock no par value, 300,000 shares authorized; 142,198 and 136,017 shares issued 139,607 and 135,908 shares outstanding in 2006 and 2005, respectively	1,147,872	874,972
Common stock in treasury, at cost	(99,964)	—
Accumulated other comprehensive income	6,975	4,405
Retained earnings	349,260	486,299
Total shareholder's equity	1,404,143	1,365,676
Commitments and contingencies		
Total liabilities and shareholders' equity	$2,042,996	$1,889,296

The Code of Conduct

From its inception, the company has sought to be different from conventional grocery stores, with a heavy focus on ethics. Besides an emphasis on organic foods, the company has also established a contract of animal rights, which states the company will only do business with companies that treat their animals humanely. While they realize that animal products are vital to their business, they oppose animal cruelty.[67]

The company has a unique 14-page Code of Conduct document that addresses the expected and desired behavior for its employees. The code is broken down into the following four sections:

- Potential conflicts of interest
- Transactions or situations that should never occur
- Situations where you may need the authorization of the Ethics Committee before proceeding
- Times when certain actions must be taken by executives of the company or team leaders of individual stores.[68]

This Code of Conduct covers, in detail, the most likely scenarios that the manager of a store might encounter. It includes several checklists that are to be filled out on a regular, or at least an annual, basis by team leaders and store managers. After completion, the checklists must be signed and submitted to corporate headquarters and copies retained on file in the store.[69] They ensure that everyone at Whole Foods is following the company's ethical standards. The ethical efforts of Whole Foods didn't go unrecognized; they ranked number 70 out of the 100 Best Corporate Citizens.[70]

Possible Scarce Resources: Prime Locations and the Supply of Organic Foods

Prime store locations and the supply of organic foods are potential scarce resources and could be problematic for Whole Foods Market in the future.

Whole Foods likes to establish a presence in highly affluent cities where their target market resides. The majority of Whole Foods customers are well-educated and have high salaries that enable them to afford the company's higher prices. Whole Foods is particular when deciding on new locations, as location is extremely important for top- and bottom-line growth. However, there are a limited number of communities where 40 percent of the residents have college degrees.

Organic food is another possible scarce resource. Organic crops yield a lower quantity of output and are rarer, accounting for only 3 percent of U.S. farmland usage.[71] Strict government requirements must be satisfied, and these are incredibly time consuming, more effort intensive, and more costly to adhere to. With increased demands from mainstream supermarkets also carrying organics, the demand for such products could outreach the limited supply.

The market for organic foods grew from $2.9 billion in 2001 to $5.3 billion in 2004—an 80.5 percent increase in the three-year period.[72] Currently, there are about 10,000 American farmers on about 2.3 million acres of land. Many companies have already started to look for resources outside of the United States to meet their growing customer demands. As organics become more mainstream, people are worried that standards will be lowered and farmers and businesses might resort to questionable farming practices. The Organic Trade Association estimates that the organic foods industry makes up about 2.5 percent of total U.S. food sales.[73] This figure is up from 0.8 percent in 1997 and represents annual sales increases of between 15 and 21 percent, compared to total U.S. food sales of approximately 2 to 4 percent.

In 2005, consumer sales of organic foods totaled $13.8 billion. Whole Foods is the largest natural foods chain and, with its acquisition of Wild Oats, it now represents $3.2 billion of total organic food dollars. Together these two companies represent 47 percent of the U.S. organic foods market. Roughly 46 percent of total organic food dollar volume was sold through the mass-market channel, which includes supermarkets/grocery stores, mass merchandisers, and club stores. The remaining 7 percent was made up of farmer's markets, food service, and other nonretail sales. Whole Foods recognizes that the increased demand for organic foods may adversely affect their earnings and has informed their investors of this. In a publication entitled *Changes in the Availability of Quality Natural and Organic Products Could Impact Our Business,* whole foods tells its investors. "There is no assurance that quality natural and organic products will be available to meet our future needs. If conventional supermarkets increase their natural and organic product offerings or if new laws require the reformulation of certain products to meet tougher standards, the supply of these products may be constrained. Any significant disruption in the supply of quality natural and organic products could have a material impact on our overall sales and cost of goods."[74]

Endnotes

1. http://www.organicconsumers.org/organic/most071904.cfm.
2. Boorstin, J. 2003. No preservatives, no unions, lots of dough. *Fortune,* September 15: 127.
3. Whole Foods. http://www.wholefoods.com/company/timeline.html November 4, 2004.
4. Boorstin, J. 2003. No preservatives, no unions, lots of dough. *Fortune,* September 15: 127.
5. Whole Foods. http://www.wholefoods.com/company/facts.html November 5, 2004.
6. Whole Foods. http://www.wholefoods.com/issues/org_commentsstandards0498.html November 5, 2004.
7. Whole Foods. http://www.wholefoods.com/company/index.html. November 5, 2004.
8. Whole Foods. http://www.wholefoods.com/company/history.html. November 5, 2004.
9. 2002 The natural: Whole Foods founder John Mackey builds an empire on organic eating. *Time.*

10. Whole Foods http://www.wholefoods.com/company/facts. html (November 11, 2004.

11. "Whole Foods Buying chain of stores based in London: $38 million deal marks U.S. health-food retailer's initial thrust into overseas market" Robert Elder Jr. January 17, 2004.

12. Jones, J. L. 2004. Whole Foods is bagging locations. *Puget Sound Business Journal,* August 13:1.

13. Whole Foods. http://www.wholefoodsmarket.com/company/ sustainablefuture.html. November 5, 2004.

14. Whole Foods. http://www.wholefoodsmarket.com/company/ sustainablefuture.html. November 5, 2004.

15. Boorstin, J. 2003. No preservatives, no unions, lots of dough. *Fortune,* September 15: 127.

16. http://www.wholefoodsmarket.com/products/index.html. July 25, 2005.

17. Whole Foods 10K-Q 2003 (page 7). November 11, 2004. http://www.wholefoodsmarket.com/investor/10K-Q/ 2003_10K.pdf.

18. Whole Foods 10K-Q 2003 (page 7). November 11, 2004. http://www.wholefoodsmarket.com/investor/10K-Q/2003_ 10K.pdf.

19. Whole Foods 10K-Q 2004 (page 10). August 15, 2005. http://www.wholefoodsmarket.com/investor/10K-Q/ 2004_10KA.pdf.

20. http://www.wholefoodsmarket.com/company/declaration. html. July 29, 2005.

21. Hoovers Online. http://www.hoovers.com/whole-foods/–ID_ 10952–/free-co-factsheet.xhtml. November 8, 2004.

22. Trader Joe's Company. www.traderjoes.com. November 8, 2004.

23. Hoovers Online. lhttp://www.hoovers.com/trader-joe's-co/ –ID-47619–/free-co-factsheet.xhtm. November 8, 2004.

24. Hoovers Online. lhttp://www.hoovers.com/trader-joe's-co/ –ID-47619–/free-co-factsheet.xhtm. November 8, 2004.

25. Hoovers Online. http://www.hoovers.com/whole-foods/ –ID_10952–/free-co-factsheet.xhtml. November 8, 2004.

26. Grimaldi, P. Providence, RI, grocery targets new approach to pricing. *Knight Ridder Tribune Business News.* September 28, 2004: 1.

27. Appel, D. 1972. The supermarket: Early development of an institutional innovation. *Journal of Retailing.* 48 (1): 40.

28. Appel, D. 1972. The supermarket: Early development of an institutional innovation. *Journal of Retailing.* 48 (1): 40. (Appel, 47)

29. Whole Foods 10K-Q for 2003 (page 8). November 11, 2004. http://www.wholefoodsmarket.com/investor/10K-Q/ 2003_10K.pdf.

30. Whole Foods 10K-Q 2003 (page 8). November 11, 2004. http://www.wholefoodsmarket.com/investor/10K-Q/ 2003_10K.pdf.

31. Whole Foods 10K-Q 2003 (page 8). November 11, 2004. http://www.wholefoodsmarket.com/investor/10K-Q/ 2003_10K.pdf.

32. Whole Foods. (page 10) November 12, 2004. http:// www.wholefoodsmarket.com/investor/10K-Q/2003_10K.pdf.

33. Whole Foods 10K-Q 2004 (page 10). August 15, 2005. http://www.wholefoodsmarket.com/investor/10K-Q/ 2004_10KA.pdf.

34. Whole Foods 10K-Q 2003 (page 9). November 11, 2004. http://www.wholefoodsmarket.com/investor/10K-Q/ 2003_10K.pdf.

35. Consumer Lifestyles in the United States (May 2003). 12.2 Expenditure on Food. *Euromonitor.* Solomon Smith Baker Library, Bentley College, Waltham, MA. November 1, 2004.

36. Gapper, J. 2004. Organic food stores are on a natural high. *The Financial Times,* September.

37. Gapper, J. 2004. Organic food stores are on a natural high. *The Financial Times,* September.

38. Gapper, J. 2004. Organic food stores are on a natural high. *The Financial Times,* September.

39. Murphy McGill, R. 2004. Truth or Scare. *American Demographics.* 26(2): 26.

40. Sechler, B. 2004. Whole Foods picks up the pace of its expansion. *The Wall Street Journal* (Eastern edition), September 29: 1.

41. Consumer Lifestyles in The United States (May 2003). 12.7 What Americans Eat. *Euromonitor.* Solomon Smith Baker Library, Bentley College, Waltham, MA. November 1, 2004.

42. Consumer Lifestyles in The United States (May 2003). 12.4 Popular Foods. *Euromonitor.* Solomon Smith Baker Library, Bentley College, Waltham, MA. November 1, 2004.

43. "Profile in B2B Strategy: Supermarket news sidles into natural, organic trend with new quarterly" *Business Customer-Wire.* Regional Business News. October 25, 2004.

44. "Profile in B2B Strategy: Supermarket news sidles into natural, organic trend with new quarterly" *Business Customer-Wire.* Regional Business News. October 25, 2004.

45. The World Market for Dairy Products (January 2004). 4.5 Organic Foods. 4.5.1 Global Market Trends in Organic Foods. *Euromonitor.* Solomon Smith Baker Library, Bentley College, Waltham, MA. November 1, 2004.

46. The World Market for Dairy Products (January 2004). 4.5 Organic Foods. 4.5.1 Global Market Trends in Organic Foods. *Euromonitor.* Solomon Smith Baker Library, Bentley College, Waltham, MA. November 1, 2004.

47. Supermarkets' prepared meals save families time. *Los Angeles Daily News* September 13, 2004.

48. Packaged Food in the United States (January 2004). 3.4 Organic Food. *Euromonitor.* Solomon Smith Baker Library, Bentley College, Waltham, MA. November 1, 2004.

49. Packaged Food in the United States (January 2004). 3.4 Organic Food. *Euromonitor.* Solomon Smith Baker Library, Bentley College, Waltham, MA. November 1, 2004.

50. Found on 10K-Q for 2004 (page 10). August 15, 2005. http://www.wholefoodsmarket.com/investor/10K-Q/ 2004_10KA.pdf. Found on 10K-Q for 2003 (page 8) November 11, 2004.

51. Whole Foods 10K-Q for 2003 (page 6). November 13, 2004.

52. Whole Foods 10K-Q 2003 (page 5). November 13, 2004. http://www.wholefoodsmarket.com/investor/10K-Q/ 2003_10K.pdf.

53. Whole Foods 10K-Q 2004 (page 14). August 15, 2005. http://www.wholefoodsmarket.com/investor/10K-Q/ 2004_10KA.pdf.

54. Whole Foods 10K-Q 2003 (page 6). November 13, 2004. http://www.wholefoodsmarket.com/investor/10K-Q/ 2003_10K.pdf.

55. Supermarkets' prepared meals save families time. *Los Angeles Daily News,* September 13, 2004.

56. Supermarkets' prepared meals save families time. *Los Angeles Daily News,* September 13, 2004.

57. Whole Foods 10K-Q 2003 (page 5). November 13, 2004. http://www.wholefoodsmarket.com/investor/10K-Q/2003_10K.pdf.

58. Whole Foods 10K-Q 2003 (page 6). November 13, 2004. http://www.wholefoodsmarket.com/investor/10K-Q/2003_10K.pdf.

59. Found on 10K-Q for 2003 (page 7). November 11, 2004. http://www.wholefoodsmarket.com/investor/10K-Q/2003_10K.pdf.

60. Whole Foods 10K-Q for 2003 (page 8). November 7, 2004. http://www.wholefoodsmarket.com/investor/10K-Q/2003_10K.pdf.

61. Whole Foods. November 7, 2004. www.wholefoodsmarket.com/company/declaration.html.

62. Whole Foods. November 7, 2004. www.wholefoodsmarket.com/company/declaration.html.

63. Whole Foods 10K-Q 2003. November 7, 2004. www.wholefoodsmarket.com/investor/10k-Q/2003_10k.pdf.

64. Whole Foods 10K-Q 2003. November 7, 2004. www.wholefoodsmarket.com/investor/10k-Q/2003_10k.pdf.

65. Nasdaq.com Market Symbol for Whole Foods is WFMI. http://quotes.nasdaq.com/quote.dll?page=charting&mode=basics&intraday=off&timeframe=10y&charttype=ohlc&splits=off&earnings=off&movingaverage=None&lowerstudy=volume&comparison=off&index=&drilldown=off&symbol=WFMI&selected=WFM November 11, 2004.I.

66. Nasdaq.com Market Symbol for Whole Foods is WFMI. http://quotes.nasdaq.com/Quote.dll?mode=stock&symbol=wfmi&symbol=&symbol=&symbol=&symbol=&symbol=&symbol=&symbol=&symbol=&symbol=&multi.x=31&multi.y=6 November 11, 2004.

67. Whole Foods. (Page 6) November 11, 2004. http://www.wholefoodsmarket.com/investor/10K-Q/2003_10K.pdf.

68. Whole Foods Code of Conduct found at company Web site: http://www.wholefoodsmarket.com/investor/codeofconduct.pdf (page 11). November 11, 2004.

69. Whole Foods Code of Conduct found at company Web site: http://www.wholefoodsmarket.com/investor/codeofconduct.pdf (page 11). November 11, 2004.

70. 100 Best companies to work for *Business Ethics.* November 12, 2004. http://www.business-ethics.com/100best.htm.

71. Grimaldi, P. *Knight Ridder Tribune Business News.* Providence, RI, grocery targets new approach to pricing, September 28, 2004: 1.

72. http://www.preparedfoods.com/PF/FILES/HTML/Mintel_Reports/Mintel_PDF/Summaries/sum-OrganicFoodBeverages-Aug2004.pdf

73. OTA's 2006 Manufacturer Survey. March 2006. http://www.ota.com/pics/documents/short%20overview%20MMS.pdf.

74. Whole Foods 10K (page 14). http://www.wholefoodsmarket.com/investor/10K-Q/2004_10KA.pdf.

Case 13   QVC*

On March 22, 2007, QVC, one of the world's largest multi-media retailers, shipped its billionth package in the United States. It was shipped to Mary Pew in Canton, Michigan, who received a 24-hour shopping spree and a $10,000 gift card from QVC for being its billionth customer. The firm also offered special prices with free shipping and handling on selected products that were featured each hour on its television home shopping channel throughout the day. "This is our chance to acknowledge the millions of loyal customers who have made this milestone possible," said the firm's new president and CEO Mike George.[1]

Since it was launched in 1986, QVC has rapidly grown to become the largest television shopping network. Although it entered the market a couple of years after rival Home Shopping Network, the channel has managed to build a leading position. By 2006, its reach had extended to over 95 percent of all U.S. cable homes as well as over 25 million satellite homes. It shipped over 140 million packages during 2006 to customers around the world, resulting in almost $7.1 billion in sales and an over $1 billion operating profit (see Exhibits 1 and 2). Its sales were made to over 10 million customers, who watched its shows across the United States, the UK, Germany, and Japan (see Exhibit 3). Almost a fifth of these represented new customers who had shopped with QVC for the first time.

The success of QVC is largely driven by its popular television home shopping shows that feature a wide variety of eye-catching products, many of which are unique to the channel. It organizes product searches in cities all over the United States to continuously find new offerings that can be pitched to customers. During these events, the firm has to screen hundreds of products to select those that it will offer. In one of its recent searches, QVC had to evaluate the appeal of products such as nail clippers that catch clippings, bicycle seats built for bigger bottoms, and novelty items shaped like coffins.

Exhibit 1   Sales Growth

2006	$7.1 billion
2004	5.7 billion
2001	3.8 billion
1998	2.4 billion
1995	1.6 billion
1992	0.9 billion
1989	0.2 billion

Source: QVC, Liberty Media.

* This case was developed by Professor Jamal Shamsie, Michigan State University with the assistance of Professor Alan B. Eisner, Pace University. Material has been drawn from published sources to be used for class discussion. © 2007 Jamal Shamsie & Alan B. Eisner.

Exhibit 2   Income Statement

	Years Ended December 31		
	2006	2005	2004
	(Amounts in $ Millions)		
Net Revenue	$7,074	6,501	5,687
Cost of Sales	(4,426)	(4,112)	(3,594)
Gross Profit	2,648	2,389	2,093
Operating Expenses*	(579)	(570)	(497)
S, G, & A Expenses	(413)	(397)	(366)
Operating Cash Flow	1,656	1,422	1,230
Stock Compensation	(50)	(52)	(33)
Depreciation & Amortization**	(476)	(449)	(437)
Operating Income	$1,130	$ 921	$760

*Operating expenses consist of commissions and license fees, order processing and customer service, credit card processing fees, and provision for doubtful accounts.

**Depreciation & amortization includes amortization of intangible assets recorded in connection with the purchase of QVC by Liberty Media.

Source: Liberty Media, QVC.

Thousands of entrepreneurs have used QVC's product searches over the years to try to sell their products on the popular home shopping channel. A chance to display their offerings to QVC's national TV audience can transform a one-person operation into a multibillion-dollar business. "The vendors who are our success stories for this past decade have done over $1 billion in sales on QVC over the past ten years," said Marilyn Montross, the channel's director of vendor relations.[2]

Early in 2007, QVC partnered with Oprah Winfrey on a Search for the Next Big Idea. Oprah invited hopeful entrepreneurs to pitch their creative products during one of three national trade shows that QVC was sponsoring in Chicago, Los Angeles, and Philadelphia during March 2007. Up to 10 finalists from these events would get the opportunity to present their invention on *The Oprah Winfrey Show* and the studio audience would vote for their favorite. The winning invention would eventually be featured on QVC's home shopping network. A QVC publicist remarked about the use of such stunts to find products: "It's the *American Idol* of retailing."[3]

Pursuing a Leading Position

QVC was founded by Joseph Segel in June 1986 and began broadcasting by November of the same year. In early 1986, Segel had tuned into the Home Shopping Network, which

Exhibit 3 Geographical Revenue Breakdown

	Years Ended December 31		
	2006	2005	2004
	(Amounts in $ Millions)		
U.S.	$4,983	4,640	4,141
UK	612	554	487
Germany	848	781	643
Japan	631	526	416
HOMES			
	Years Ended December 31		
	2006	2005	2004
	(Amounts in Millions)		
U.S.	90.7	90.0	88.4
UK	19.4	17.8	15.6
Germany	37.9	37.4	35.7
Japan	18.7	16.7	14.7

Source: Liberty Media, QVC.

had been launched just two years earlier. He had not been particularly impressed with the crude programming and the down-market products of the firm. But Segel was convinced that another televised shopping network would have the potential to attract a large enough client base. He also felt that such an enterprise should be able to produce significant profits because the operating expenses for a shopping network could be kept relatively low.

Over the next few months, Segel raised $30 million in start-up capital, hired several seasoned television executives, and launched his own shopping network. Operating out of headquarters that were located in West Chester, Pennsylvania, QVC offered 24-hour-a-day, seven-day-a-week television home shopping to consumers. By the end of its first year of operation, QVC had managed to extend its reach to 13 million homes by satellite and cable systems. 700,000 viewers had already become customers, resulting in the shipping of 3 million orders. Its sales had already topped $100 million, and the firm was actually able to show a small profit.

Segel attributed the instant success of his company to the potential offered by television shopping. "Television's combination of sight, sound and motion is the best way to sell a product. It is more effective than presenting a product in print or just putting the product on a store shelf," he stated. "The cost-efficiency comes from the cable distribu-

tion system. It is far more economical than direct mail, print advertising, or traditional retail store distribution."[4]

In the fall of 1988, Segel acquired the manufacturing facilities, proprietary technology, and trademark rights of the Diamonique Corporation, which produced a wide range of simulated gemstones and jewelry that could be sold on QVC's shows. Over the next couple of years, Segel expanded QVC by acquiring its competitors such as the Cable Value Network Shopping channel.

By 1993, QVC had overtaken Home Shopping Network to become the leading televised shopping channel in terms of sales and profits. Its reach extended to over 80 percent of all cable homes and to 3 million satellite dishes. Segel retired during the same year, passing control of the company to Barry Diller. Since then, QVC's sales have continued to grow at a substantial rate. As a result, it has consistently widened the gap between its sales and those of Home Shopping Network, which has remained its closest competitor.

Achieving Efficiency in Operations

Over the years, QVC had managed to establish itself as the world's preeminent virtual shopping mall that never closes. Its televised shopping channel has become a place where customers around the world can, and do, shop at any hour at the rate of more than five customers per second. It sells a wide variety of products, using a combination of description and demonstration by live program hosts. Each of the products is presented by QVC in a format where it is attractively modeled and carefully explained by the hosts of the show and by representatives from the vendor. QVC works hard to develop descriptions for each of their offerings that have been carefully crafted to resonate with its viewing audience. If necessary, complete on-air instructions are also provided for the use of every product that it sells.

In addition, most of the products are offered on regularly scheduled shows, each of which is focused on a particular type of product and a well-defined market (see Exhibit 4). Each of these shows typically lasts for one hour and is based on a theme such as "Now You're Cooking" or "Cleaning Solutions." QVC has enticed celebrities such as clothing designers or book authors to appear live on special program segments to sell their own products. On some occasions, customers are able to call in and have on-air conversations with program hosts and visiting celebrities.

Over the past year, QVC has been trying to capitalize on the growing success of reality-based television shows. It has begun to incorporate some of the concepts from these popular shows into its shopping programs. In one of its recently introduced shows, *Room for Improvement,* the shopping channel has carried out an extensive renovation of a bedroom and a kitchen for a family. Products that were featured on the show sold well. In another show, Finola Hughes, who sells jewelry on QVC, plans to focus on the elaborate makeover of an individual participant.

QVC's themed programs are telecast live 24 hours a day, seven days a week, to over 90 million households in

Exhibit 4 QVC Programming Typical Weekly Schedule

Eastern Standard Time	Monday	Tuesday	Wednesday	Thursday	Friday	Saturday	Sunday
7–8 AM	The QVC MORNING SHOW	THE QVC MORNING SHOW	THE QVC MORNING SHOW	THE QVC MORNING SHOW	THE QVC MORNING SHOW FASHION FRIDAY	Select Comfort Sleep Number	AM STYLE
8–9 AM						AM STYLE	
9–10 AM	PATRICIA WEXLER, MD DERMATOLOGY	SPRING SPOTLIGHT	NutriSystem Nourish Weight-Loss Program	SUSAN GRAVER STYLE	SLEEP SOLUTIONS		
10–11 AM	CITIKNITS	BATH SHOP	FINE JEWELRY COLLECTION	ORGANIZE IT ALL	TRAVELING WITH KIDS	CREATING KEEPSAKES MAGAZINE PAPER CRAFTING	
11 AM–12 PM	HOME STYLE	DENIM & CO	ELLIOTT LUCCA HANDBAGS	WHITE MOUNTAIN FOOTWEAR	IMPERIAL GOLD		MODERN SOUL KNITWEAR
12–1 PM	BEAUTY BEAT	NOW YOU'RE COOKING	14K GOLD JEWELRY	EATING SMART		BY POPULAR DEMAND	DIALOGUES THE NEW LANGUAGE OF STYLE
1–2 PM	LINEN CLOSET	LINEA BY LOUIS DELL'OLIO	B.O.C. FOOTWEAR	BY POPULAR DEMAND	THE FAMILY ROOM	PATIO & GARDEN	LINEA BY LOUIS DELL'OLIO
2–3 PM	OUTDOOR ENTERTAINING		QON ASLETT'S CLEANING SECRETS	NINA LEONARD COLLECTION FASHION	BIRKENSTOCK COLLECTIONS	SMASHBOX COSMETICS	SUMMER FUN FASHION
3–4 PM	DENIM & CO	EPIPHANY PLATINUM CLAD SILVER & DIAMONIQUE JEWELRY	PROACTIV SOLUTION SKIN CARE		INSTANT FLOWER GARDEN	ANNA GRIFFIN ELEGANT CRAFTING	CITIKNITS
4–5 PM	QVC SAMPLER		In-Home Care	AUTO SHOP	AROUND THE HOUSE	CREATING KEEPSAKES MAGAZINE–PAPER CRAFTING	STATEMENTS ON STYLE
5–6 PM	ETIENNE AIGNER	FOCUS ON FASHION	JEWELRY SHOWCASE	PATRICIA WANG JADE STUDIO		SCRAPBOOKING DAY CELEBRATION	DENIM & CO
6–7 PM	HOME STYLE	KITCHEN IDEAS	NutriSystem Nourish Weight-Loss Program	QVC SAMPLER	KITCHEN IDEAS	Select Comfort Sleep Number	
7–8 PM	PATRICIA WEXLER, MD DERMATOLOGY	LINEA BY LOUIS DELL'OLIO	KEEP IT CLEAN	MADE FOR iPOD	ELECTRONICS TODAY	SATURDAY NIGHT BEAUTY	SUSAN GRAVER STYLE

Source: QVC.

the United States and 160 million homes worldwide. The shopping channel transmits its programming live from its central production facilities in Pennsylvania through uplinks to a satellite. Of all the orders placed with QVC, more than 90 percent are shipped within 48 hours from one of their distribution centers. Paul Day, a logistics manager for QVC, explained how they can ensure the fast delivery to their customers: "The whole supply chain has to be working, from how the buyers buy and set up dates on their or-

ders to how we receive the orders."[5] The distribution centers have a combined floor space of 4.6 million square feet, which is equivalent to the size of 103 football fields.

In order to make it easier for viewers to purchase products that they may see on their home shopping channel, QVC also provides a credit program to allow customers to pay for goods over a period of several months. Everything it sells is also backed by a 30-day unconditional money-back guarantee. Furthermore, QVC does not impose any hidden charges, such as a restocking fee, for any returned merchandise. These policies help the home shopping channel to attract customers for products that they can view but are not able to either touch or feel.

Searching for Profitable Products

More than 100 experienced, informed buyers comb the world on a regular basis to search for new products to launch on QVC. The shopping channel concentrates on unique products that can be demonstrated on live television. Furthermore, the price of these products must be high enough for viewers to justify the additional shipping and handling charge. Over the course of a typical year, QVC carries more than 50,000 products. Almost 1,700 items are typically offered in any given week, of which about 15 percent, or 250, are new products for the network. QVC's suppliers range from some of the world's biggest companies to small entrepreneurial enterprises.

All new products must, however, pass through stringent tests that are carried out by QVC's in-house Quality Assurance Lab. In many cases, this inspection process is carried out manually by the firm's employees. Only 15 percent of the products pass the firm's rigorous quality inspection on the first try and as many as a third are never offered to the public because they fail altogether. Everyone at QVC works hard to make sure that every item works as it should before it is shipped and that its packaging will protect it during the shipping process. "Nothing ships unless it is quality-inspected first," said Day. "Since our product is going business-to-consumer, there's no way to fix or change a product-related problem."[6]

About a third of QVC's sales come from broadly available national brands. The firm has been able to build trust among its customers in large part through the offering of these well-known brands. QVC also relies upon promotional campaigns with a variety of existing firms for another third of its sales. It has made deals with firms ranging from Dell, Target, and Bath & Body Works for special limited time promotional offerings. But QVC has been most successful with products that are exclusively sold on QVC or not readily available through other distribution channels. Although such products account for another third of its sales, the firm has been able to earn higher margins with these proprietary products, many of which come from firms that are either start-ups or new entrants into the U.S. market.

Apart from searching for exclusive products, QVC has also been trying to move away from some product categories, such as home appliances and electronic gadgets, which offer lower margins. It has been gradually expanding into many new product categories that have higher margins such as cosmetics, apparel, food, and toys. Several of these new categories have also displayed the strongest rates of growth in sales for the shopping channel over the past couple of years.

The shopping channel has been turning to products by various fashion designers such as Arnold Scassi, Heidi Klum, and Dana Buchman. Many designers have been attracted to QVC because of its access to a much broader market. More recently, the firm has been offering apparel, jewelry, and accessories by exclusive designers that have been specifically created for the mass market. In late 2004, QVC contracted with Marc Bouwer to develop an M collection to be sold exclusively on its home shopping channel. Bouwer's initial products included a $50 kimono blouse, $50 matte jersey pants with side slits, and a $149 silk dress with a ruffled front. "Where else can you sell thousands of units in virtually minutes?" Bouwer asked.[7]

Expanding on the Customer Base

By 2005, QVC's shopping channel had penetrated almost all of the cable television and broadcast satellite homes in the United States. The firm was still trying to increase sales by making it easier for customers to buy its products by adding features such as an interactive service that would allow them to purchase whatever it is offering on its shopping channel with the single click of a remote. QVC is also relying on the reasonably strong reputation that surveys have indicated it has established among a large majority of its current consumers. By its initials alone, QVC had promised that it would deliver quality, value, and convenience to its viewers. More than three-quarters of the shopping channel's customers have given it a score of seven out of seven for trustworthiness. This has led most of its customers to demonstrate a strong tendency to purchase often from the channel and to recommend it to their friends.

QVC has also been trying to enter new markets by offering its shopping channel to customers outside North America. Over the last decade, QVC has expanded to the UK, Germany, and Japan, giving it access to almost 70 million new households in these three countries. Partly as a result of this expansion into new markets, a large part of the shopping network's strong growth in sales over the past few years has come from the regular addition of new customers. In a typical month, QVC can gain as many as 200,000 new customers worldwide, and many of them stay on to become repeat customers. The firm's total customer base is approaching 45 million customers who are spread over a few different countries.

QVC has also benefited from the growing percentage of women entering the workforce, resulting in a significant increase in dual-income families. Although the firm's current customer base does span several socioeconomic groups, it is led by young professional families who have above average disposable income. They also enjoy various forms of thrill-seeking activities and rank shopping relatively high as a leisure activity when compared to the typical consumer.

In 1995, QVC launched its own retail Web site to complement its television home shopping channel. Called iQVC, the 24-hour service has provided the firm access to more than 100 million households in the United States that have Internet connections. The Web site has also allowed the firm to perform well with some product categories that have not done as well on the television channel. For example, its Books, Movies and Music link offers more than 500,000 books, 100,000 movies, and 150,000 compact discs. During 2006, QVC was able to generate $1 billion of sales on its Internet operations.

Recently, QVC has also been adding branded video-on-demand channels through a partnership with AOL. This includes the AOL Video portal's first live streaming channel. The live stream of QVC's broadcast will carry the shopping channel's live 24/7 format. Another QVC On Demand channel will include more than 400 clips of video content from various daily shows and events that will be updated continuously. "QVC is looking for new ways to be everywhere consumers want to shop," said Bob Myears, Senior Vice President of QVC.com. "Launching streaming video on AOL will allow more e-commerce consumers to experience QVC and our innovative product offerings."[8]

Positioning for Future Growth

Over the last year, QVC has been deploying aggressive marketing campaigns to create more publicity for the firm. Jeff Charney, its newly appointed marketing director challenged employees to a competition in which the individual that attracted the most attention while wearing a QVC T-shirt would win $10,000. Before the contest ended in September 2006, the firm had 725 entries, with employees who wore the T-shirt engaging in activities ranging from forming an aerial Q while skydiving to recording a musical that drew 5,000 viewers on YouTube.

During 2003, John Malone placed a value of $14.1 billion on QVC when he purchased the firm. It was clear that Malone felt that the home shopping network would continue to grow in spite of the development of competing forms of home shopping. Over the years, QVC's sales have actually grown to match that of Internet giant Amazon.com. But while the Internet firm has been struggling to show strong profits, QVC has been generating tons of cash. Furthermore, QVC certainly looks like it is well positioned with its shopping channel, its Web site, and streaming videos for continued growth in sales from a vast assortment of merchandise.

In fact, since the launching of its Web site, QVC has taken steps to become an innovative practitioner of electronic retailing. Its Web site has moved well beyond its initial capabilities, when it simply offered supplementary information on the products that were featured on the television shopping channel. The recent introduction of the interactive service for the shopping channel represents one of the first launches of on-screen interactivity, the kind in which viewers can interact with television content simply through the remote control. Looking towards the future, QVC is already focusing on new avenues for growth, such as those that might be offered through retailing on the mobile telephone.

Regular technological developments may, in fact, allow QVC to continue to offer much higher margin products to both existing and new markets. Doug Rose, the vice president of merchandising brand development, claims that interactivity in all aspects of the firm's business, including its television shopping channel, will only become more pronounced in the future, making it easier for customers to act on what they see. QVC believes that it still has a lot of room to grow, since only about 2 percent to 3 percent of its television viewers currently purchase at any given time.

"I was at an anniversary for employees last month, and they were showing clips of what QVC looked like 10 years ago," Rose said. "I was just stunned at how, by my reckoning, it looked so primitive. I fully expect that in 10 years, I'll be looking at clips of what we are doing now and think, 'How primitive.' So much has changed here, and yet we are taking baby steps. We're very much in our infancy."[9]

Endnotes

1. QVC. Talk about a special delivery: QVC ships its billionth package. Press Release, March 22, 2007.
2. Feldstein, M. J. 2005. Investors, entrepreneurs vie for QVC appearance. *Knight Ridder Tribune Business News,* February 11:1.
3. Kilgannon, C. 2006. Oh, to be discovered by the folks at QVC. *New York Times,* November 15: 9.
4. QVC Annual Report, 1987–1988.
5. Gilligan, E. 2004. The show must go on. *Journal of Commerce,* April 12: 1.
6. *Journal of Commerce,* April 12, 2004, p. 1.
7. Feitelberg, R. 2004. Bouwer prime for QVC. *WWD,* November 23: 8.
8. QVC, AOL, and QVC launch first live streaming channel on AOL video. Press Release, January 17, 2007.
9. Duff, M. 2005. QVC Turns up the volume. *DSN Retailing Today,* March 14: 2.

Case 14   Will the Real Ann Taylor Please Dress Up?*

In 2007, Key Krill, president and CEO of Ann Taylor Stores Corporation (ANN), finally felt she had positioned women's specialty clothing retailer Ann Taylor as "the premier destination for updated classic, yet stylish, professional and special occasion dressing."[1] ANN, a publicly traded company, had experienced erratic performance since 2000, and Krill had faced a challenge. Krill had been appointed president of ANN in late 2004, and succeeded to President/CEO in late 2005 when previous CEO J. Patrick Spainhour retired after eight years in charge. At the time, there had been concern among commentators and customers that the Ann Taylor look was getting "stodgy," and the question was how to "re-establish Ann Taylor as the preeminent brand for beautiful, elegant, and sophisticated occasion dressing."[2] In order to do that, Kay Krill had acknowledged the important of the consumer, since for Ann Taylor to succeed long term, "enough women still need to dress up for work."[3]

Her challenge was based on the ANN legacy. Ann Taylor was founded in 1954 as a wardrobe source for busy socially upscale women, and the classic basic black dress and woman's power suit with pearls were Ann Taylor staples for years. In 1995 Ann Taylor LOFT was launched to appeal to a younger more casual and cost-conscious but still professional consumer. Starting in the late 1990s, under the leadership of Ms. Krill, LOFT began to outperform its big sister. After the Ann Taylor division's 50th anniversary collection missed the mark with consumers in the fall of 2004, a wholesale management shift at ANN occurred, leading to Ms. Krill's promotion in October of 2005.

Kay Krill was faced with the challenge of rebuilding the Ann Taylor brand, meeting the "wardrobing needs of the updated classic consumer"[4] while maintaining the image and market share of Ann Taylor LOFT. Ann Taylor became "one of a growing number of specialty retailers wrestling with how to keep a founding brand fresh without cannibalizing a newcomer."[5] What strategy could Ms. Krill utilize to keep moving forward?

Although ANN was consistently profitable, and consistently in the *Women's Wear Daily* "Top 10" list for dresses, suits and eveningwear[6] and the "Top 20" list of publicly traded specialty retailers,[7] ANN's Ann Taylor division (AT) had lost ground during 2003 and 2004 to Ann Taylor LOFT (LOFT). In the third quarter of 2004, for the first time, LOFT outsold AT.[8] At 2004 fiscal year end, LOFT had increased sales by 40 percent over 2003, while AT declined by 1.5 percent.

In a conference call, CEO Krill stated her goals as "improving profitability while enhancing both brands, restoring performance at the Ann Taylor division and restoring the momentum at LOFT" (see Exhibit 1).[9] In February of 2005 CEO Kay Krill announced that LOFT had reached $1 billion dollars in sales, stating, "This is an important milestone for our Company. In an intensely competitive and fragmented apparel market, Ann Taylor LOFT has

*This case was prepared by Professor Pauline Assenza of Manhattanville College, Professor Alan B. Eisner of Pace University and Professor Jerome C. Kuperman of Minnesota State University–Moorhead. This case was solely based upon library research and was developed for class discussion rather than to illustrate either effective or ineffective handling of an administrative situation. Copyright © 2007 Pauline Assenza and Alan B. Eisner.

Exhibit 1   AT vs. LOFT Financial Performance 2003–2007

	Fiscal Years Ended				
	February 3 2007	January 28 2006	January 29 2005	January 31 2004	February 1 2003
Net Sales (in thousands)					
Total Company	$2,342,900	$2,073,146	$1,853,583	$1,587,708	$1,380,966
Ann Taylor	753,800	873,886	854,865	867,855	828,913
Ann Taylor LOFT	471,500	991,940	826,556	588,801	439,789
Other*	283,683	207,320	172,162	131,052	112,264
Comparable Store Sales Percentage Increase (decrease)					
Total Company	2.8%	0.1%	3.6%	5.3%	(3.9)%
Ann Taylor	3.1%	0.6%	(2.7)%	3.2%	(5.3)%
Ann Taylor LOFT	1.9%	(0.3)%	12.8%	9.4%	(1.0)%

Source: Company financials.

*Includes Ann Taylor Factory Store and Internet Business.

Exhibit 2 ANN Stock Price 2003–2007

Source: Market Data from Yahoo Finance.

been one of the industry's most successful and fastest-growing apparel retail concepts since its launch in 1998. LOFT brings a relaxed and versatile sensibility to fashionable, updated classics for every occasion and features regular and petite sizes, accessories and footwear—all at surprising prices. LOFT's success reaffirms the importance of maintaining a strong connection with our client and evolving with her wardrobe needs over time."[10]

By the end of fiscal year 2006 that momentum was rolling; net sales for ANN were a record $2.3 billion. Total comparable store sales for the fiscal year increased 2.8 percent compared to a 0.1 percent increase in 2005. Outlook for fiscal year 2007 was positive, including continued plans for expansion and related capital expenditure. The stock market approved, sending the stock to near year highs, and analysts were mainly supportive, and, although wary of gross margin trends, cited "confidence in the retailer's strong management team, improving store products, and conservative inventory management" (see Exhibits 2–6).[11]

ANN celebrated with the opening of the 10,000 square foot flagship LOFT store in Times Square Manhattan in November, 2006. Kay Krill commented, "We definitely have to keep the music pumped up. . . . This is a great branding experience."[12] It appeared that the Ann Taylor brand, at least according to LOFT customers, still had its historic appeal, although in the highly competitive retail environment the future always involved risks and uncertainties, including the fate of the Ann Taylor division and ANN's overall "ability to predict accurately client fashion preferences."[13] The end of 2006 was perhaps proof that fashion is a risky business; as ANN's net income fell more than 21 percent for the fourth quarter. Krill said that "At Loft, we had much success in the first half with the brand-appropriate product

offering that our clients loved, however, in the second half we did not offer the appropriate balance of updated classics versus fashion."[14] While ANN was up for the year on the heels of a strong first half of the year and improved inventory management, fashion is a business that is always changing.

Industry and Competitor Overview

In 2007, the state of the apparel industry was fragmented, consumer confidence was lacking and the consumer's desire was to spend their money elsewhere, perhaps in electronics. As such, the industry was forced to try and think of ways to retain customers. "The pendulum to and from spending on fashion used to swing more slowly," observed Marshal Cohen, chief industry analyst of The NPD Group. "Now it has been accelerated. . . . Now (consumers are spending on) electronics and this will all eat into apparel's wallet share. . . . In the past three years, electronics has gained 4 percent of consumers' spending, and apparel has lost."[15]

As a result of this fragmentation, trying to be the brand for everyone had become a recipe for disaster in the apparel industry. Contrary to other businesses, apparel's future seemed to be in narrowly targeted niches. For example, Abercrombie & Fitch had four distinct lines that targeted four distinct groups of customers: men and women between the ages of 18 to 22, boys and girls between the ages of 10 to 14. A&F's Hollister Co. targeted high school boys and girls, and the Ruehl division targeted post-collegiate men and women between the ages of 22 to 35.

This strategy of creating niche stores through brand extensions could be risky. In January 2007, Gap, Inc., the big player in the retail apparel sector, with the three major brands Gap, Old Navy and Banana Republic, closed its 19 Forth & Towne stores. Opened in 2005 in an attempt to

Exhibit 3   Income Statements

	02/03/2007	01/28/2006	01/29/2005	01/31/2004	02/01/2003
			(in thousands)		
Net sales	2,342,907	2,073,146	1,853,583	1,587,708	1,380,966
Cost of sales	1,085,897	1,017,122	906,035	721,463	633,473
Gross margin	1,257,010	1,056,024	947,548	866,245	747,493
Selling, general, & administrative expenses	1,033,173	924,998	842,590	694,590	612,479
Operating income (loss)	223,837	131,026	104,958	171,655	135,014
Interest income	17,174	9,318	5,037	3,298	3,279
Interest expense	2,230	2,083	3,641	6,665	6,886
Income (loss) before income taxes	238,781	138,261	106,354	168,288	131,407
Current federal income tax provision (benefit)	80,923	58,024	36,654	48,595	32,959
Deferred federal income tax provision (benefit)	(8,565)	(13,632)	(3,469)	4,947	10,467
Total federal income tax provision (benefit)	72,358	44,392	33,185	53,542	43,426
Current state income tax provision (benefit)	20,268	12,661	9,821	14,291	5,726
Deferred state income tax provision (benefit)	(2,115)	(1,731)	(1,472)	(1,100)	1,569
Total state income tax provision (benefit)	18,153	10,930	8,349	13,191	7,295
Current foreign income tax provision (benefit)	5,417	1,075	1,632	690	577
Deferred foreign income tax provision (benefit)	(129)	(8)	(88)	(77)	(49)
Total foreign income tax provision (benefit)	5,288	1,067	1,544	613	528
Income tax provision (benefit)	95,799	56,389	43,078	67,346	51,249
Net income (loss)	142,982	81,872	63,276	100,942	80,158
Weighted average shares outstanding–basic	70,993	71,554	69,607	66,613.5	66,372
Weighted average shares outstanding–diluted	72,107	72,270	72,933	73,144.5	72,451.5
Year end shares outstanding	69,373.074	72,491.287	70,632.448	68,067	67,322.832
Net earnings (loss) per share–basic	2.01	1.14	0.91	1.513	1.207
Net earnings (loss) per share–diluted	1.98	1.13	0.88	1.42	1.147

Source: Company Data accessed from MergentOnline.com.

develop a specialty channel catering to women 35 and older, Forth & Towne was an attempt to increase Gap's share of this market, but analysts said the brand never gained "much traction" and became a "big distraction" for Gap during a time when the flagship stores were also seeing falling same-store sales: the brand expansion "never made much sense, given Gap's troubles connecting with shoppers of all ages." As one analyst said, "the landscape is so competitive that each retailer has to have a clear reason to be in existence, and Forth & Towne never had that."[16]

In the world of retail, apparel was unique because it was the one sector that called for "more niche concepts, trying to link products with more specific shoppers." Some companies in the industry in 2005 were trying to take that stand via mergers and acquisitions. Activity had increased due to "$120 billion of hedge fund money on the side-lines, strategic players flush with cash and ongoing market consolidation."[17]

Several large strategic moves had occurred, including the acquisition of Barneys New York, Inc. by Jones Apparel Group Inc. and Federated's acquisition of May Company.

Exhibit 4 Balance Sheets

	02/03/2007	01/28/2006	01/29/2005	01/31/2004	02/01/2003
			(in $ thousands)		
Cash & cash equivalents	360,560	380,654	62,412	337,087	212,821
Short-term investments	—	—	192,400	—	—
Accounts receivable, net	16,489	17,091	12,573	12,476	10,367
Merchandise inventories	233,606	204,503	229,218	172,058	185,484
Prepaid expenses & other current assets	79,950	73,964	90,711	55,747	46,599
Total current assets	690,605	676,212	587,314	577,368	455,271
Land & buildings	10,436	10,419	10,040	10,040	10,040
Leasehold improvements	579,821	516,727	412,920	194,737	171,404
Furniture & fixtures	—	—	361,856	318,228	277,917
Furniture, fixtures, equipment, & software	482,669	422,228	—	—	—
Construction in progress	32,314	46,523	68,954	19,444	19,134
Property & equipment, gross	1,105,240	995,897	853,770	542,449	478,495
Less accumulated depreciation & amortization	541,132	483,132	419,442	276,880	231,380
Property & equipment, net	564,108	512,765	434,328	265,569	247,115
Goodwill, net	286,579	286,579	286,579	286,579	286,579
Deferred financing costs, net	652	1,017	1,382	4,886	4,170
Other assets	26,559	16,333	17,735	17,471	17,691
Total assets	1,568,503	1,492,906	1,327,338	1,151,873	1,010,826
Accounts payable	106,519	97,398	88,340	52,170	57,058
Accrued salaries & bonus	28,304	8,633	21,617	23,714	27,567
Accrued tenancy	45,024	44,036	32,264	11,185	10,808
Gift certificates & merchandise credits redeemed	52,989	45,916	38,892	32,120	25,637
Accrued expenses	66,582	61,603	62,633	42,431	30,125
Total current liabilities	299,418	257,586	243,746	161,620	151,195
Convertible debentures, net	—	—	—	125,152	121,652
Long-term debt, including current portion	—	—	—	125,152	121,652
Long-term debt, net	—	—	—	125,152	121,652
Deferred lease costs	214,466	198,714	—	—	—
Other liabilities	4,708	2,124	—	—	—
Deferred lease costs & other liabilities	—	—	156,848	34,465	23,561
Common stock	559	558	545	336	332
Additional paid-in capital	753,030	723,230	669,128	516,824	500,061
Retained earnings (accumulated deficit)	670,307	527,325	445,410	393,926	296,113
Accumulated other comprehensive income (loss)	(5,373)	—	—	—	—
Deferred compensation on restricted stock	—	12,006	11,746	6,148	3,968
Total stockholders' equity before treasury stock	1,418,523	1,239,107	1,103,337	904,938	792,538
Treasury stock, at cost	368,612	204,625	176,593	74,302	78,120
Total stockholders' equity	1,049,911	1,034,482	926,744	830,636	714,418

Source: Company Data accessed from MergentOnline.com.

Exhibit 5   **Statement of Annual Cash Flows**

	02/03/2007	01/28/2006	01/29/2005	01/31/2004	02/01/2003
			(in $ thousands)		
Net income (loss)	142,982	81,872	63,276	100,942	80,158
Deferred income taxes	(10,809)	(15,421)	(5,022)	3,771	12,008
Depreciation & amortization	105,890	93,786	78,657	51,825	47,687
Loss (gain) on disposition & write-down of property & equipment	7,896	3,497	1,301	1,085	1,384
Non-cash compensation expense	24,722	770	5,350	—	—
Non-cash interest	483	789	1,858	4,320	4,261
Tax benefit from exercise of stock options	8,189	12,566	7,262	4,050	3,548
Amortization of stock awards	—	10,400	7,392	3,678	5,931
Loss (gain) on sale of proprietary cred card	—	—	—	—	(2,095)
Accounts receivable	602	(5,024)	56	(1,909)	(475)
Merchandise inventories	(29,103)	24,715	(57,159)	10,926	(5,367)
Prepaid expenses & other current assets	(13,543)	24,678	(28,621)	(8,570)	(898)
Other non-current assets & liabilities, net	21,042	50,510	32,713	6,775	(4,272)
Accounts payable & accrued expenses	37,580	28,185	62,196	12,725	17,177
Net cash flows from operating activities	295,931	311,323	169,259	189,618	159,047
Purchases of available-for-sale securities	—	(20,600)	(414,150)	—	—
Sales of available-for-sale securities	—	213,000	532,125	—	—
Proceeds from sale of proprietary credit card	—	—	—	—	57,800
Purchases of property & equipment	(165,926)	(187,613)	(152,483)	(71,364)	(45,450)
Net cash flows from investing activities	(165,926)	4,787	(34,508)	(71,364)	12,350
Issuance of common stock pursuant to ADSPP	3,295	3,006	2,950	—	2,359
Common stock activity relative to stock-based compensation program	—	—	—	20,329	—
Proceeds from exercise of stock options	26,743	47,279	19,872	—	10,293
Excess tax benefits from stock-based compensation	4,992	—	—	—	—
Payment of financing costs	—	—	(22)	(1,536)	(15)
Repurchases of common & restricted stock	(185,129)	(48,153)	(121,698)	—	—
Repurchase of common stock	—	—	—	(12,781)	—
Payments of mortgage	—	—	—	—	(1,250)
Net cash flows from financing activities	(150,099)	2,132	(98,898)	6,012	11,387
Net increase (decrease) in cash	(20,094)	318,242	35,853	124,266	182,784
Cash & cash equivalents, beginning of year	380,564	62,412	26,559	212,821	30,037
Cash & cash equivalents, end of year	360,560	380,654	62,412	337,087	212,821
Cash paid during the year for interest	1,769	1,293	1,770	2,202	1,307
Cash paid during the year for income taxes	94,723	47,030	58,226	56,147	40,088

Source: Company Data accessed from MergentOnline.com.

Exhibit 6 Stores, Employees, Inventory Turns

Stores	FY 2006	FY 2005	FY 2004	FY 2003
Total Company	869	824	738	648
Ann Taylor	348	357	359	354
Ann Taylor LOFT	464	416	343	268
Ann Taylor Factory	57	51	36	26
Employees	17,700	16,900	14,900	13,000
Inventory Turns	5.0	4.7	4.5	4.1

Source: Company Reports.

There was speculation that the Federated–May merger "could set off a seemingly endless scenario of bigger fish-swallows-littler fish until there are only a handful of large retailers and vendors left in the U.S." One analyst suggested "vendors just need to be big enough to create need for their brands." However some of the major vendors may "have to start making acquisitions to continue on their growth tracks with larger bases."[18] Regarding Ann Taylor Stores Corporation, there had been rumors since 2000 about a possible acquisition of ANN by Liz Claiborne, Inc. but neither company had recently commented on the matter.[19]

Another analyst said "there's a lot of money around and both the retail companies and the supporting apparel companies realize that there are economies of scale that are brought into bear through size, and that it's imperative for them to continue to be competitive. . . . No deal should be driven by anything other than economic factors, competitive advantage, control of marketplace, ability to source, ability to pick up market share—otherwise a transaction will be a disaster."[20]

Volatility in the apparel industry was nothing new. In 1992 analysts were saying, "the party is over for the specialty retailers," noting "a growing polarization that increasingly favors the low-margin, mass-volume retailers on one end and high-price haute-service boutiques offering one-of-a-kind or unusual items on the other," where shoppers who once bought at Gap or Victoria's Secret had moved downmarket to Wal-Mart, Kmart, and Target. The challenge for women's specialty stores like Ann Taylor was to provide something new and different to these customers.[21] In 1995, the retailing industry was characterized as "treacherous," with analysts pointing to the demise of Caldor and Bradlees, and cautioning that specialty houses such as ANN needed to carefully monitor their financials.[22]

By 2005, the apparel industry's model seemed to be one of continual re-evaluation and quest for differentiation even in the midst of consolidation. As one reporter commented, citing differences in resource utilization of design sourcing, manufacturing expertise, and supply chain management, "It never ceases to amaze me how apparel companies can operate so very differently from one to another, even when they are serving the same markets with similar products."[23] (For information on the top 20 specialty retailers based on 2005 year end numbers, see Exhibit 7.)

In 2006, the hot demographic appeared to be the evolving tastes of women over 35, especially those 45 and older, with American Eagle and Abercrombie & Fitch opening brand extension stores for this market, in addition to Gap's failed extension—more competition for the niche marketers such as Talbots, Coldwater Creek, Chico's, and Ann Taylor.[24] Even given the potential for market segmentation, the industry expected to see more acquisitions by apparel makers that were "scouting for niche brands and products to add to their already-sizable offerings."[25] As an example of niches, in 2006 ANN concentrated their focus on "the occasion," and, similar to Jos A. Banks in the men's wear area, tried to be "the first place people think of when they're going to a wedding".[26] In 2006, Talbots purchased J. Jill, in a quest for the woman customer over 45, creating a women's specialty chain potentially large enough to overtake ANN, and with Talbots celebrating its 60th year in business in 2007, this retailer continued to be a driving force.[27]

As an example of the kind of success possible with a clearly developed branding message, Chico's FAS Inc., started in 1983 as a store selling Mexican folk art and cotton sweaters, had had an extended run of top performance, outperforming nearly everyone in women's apparel. The original brand developed embellished private label comfortable and colorful styles aimed at baby-boomer women, with a unique sizing system (a scale from 0 to 3 rather than 4 to 16) that appealed to their aging customers. Through creative marketing and merchandising, Chico's had some of the best margins in the retail sector, and, starting in 2004, developed three other brands to extend their reach to younger women, intimate apparel, and active wear markets.

Exhibit 7 *Women's Wear Daily* **High Volume Specialists in 2005**

Store	Fiscal 2005 Dollar Volume (billions)	Percent Change— Volume	Last Year's Rank	Comments
Gap (GPS)	$16.02	−1.0	1	Includes Old Navy. 2004 was highest income growth in Gap's 36 year history, but 2005 saw slumping sales.
Limited Brands, Inc. (LTD)	$9.7	+3.0	2	Includes Victoria's Secret and Bath & Body Works, both up. Apparel chains Express and Limited are struggling.
Abercrombie & Fitch Co. (ANE)	$2.78	+38.0	4	Considering overseas expansion to London.
Charming Shoppes, (CHRS)	$2.76	+18.0	3	Plus-size retailer: Lane Bryant, FashionInc. Bug, Catherines. Bought catalogue firm Crosstown Traders. Planning move into lifestyle merchandise bath/beauty prods.
American Eagle Outfitters (AEOS)	$2.3	+23.0	5	Sells internationally via Web site. Opened new concept store for 25–40 yrs old.
Ann Taylor Stores Corp. (ANN)	$2.07	+12.0	6	AT, LOFT, AT Factory—"in the midst of a turnaround" (per Krill)?
Talbots Inc. (TLB)	$1.81	+7.0	7	Customer niche: professional, college-educated women +35 years old. Now includes J. Jill. Plus Size and Talbots Kids were strong.
The Children's Place (PLCE)	$1.67	+44.0	Not ranked	Also owns Disney Stores. Designs & manufactures clothes for kids up to age 10.
Chico's FAS Inc. (CHS)	$1.4	+32.0	12	Private label women's retailer. Looking to sustain 25% growth.
Pacific Sunwear of California, Inc. (PSUN)	$1.39	+13.0	10	Trendy casual apparel for young men & women—hip-hop inspired. Launched One Thousand Steps shoe store in 2006.
Claire's Stores Inc. (CLE)	$1.37	+7.0	8	Sells value-priced accessories, jewelry, cosmetics to young adults. Sales in Europe keep climbing.
Aeropostale, Inc. (ARO)	$1.2	+25.0	13	Young men & women ages 11–20. Planning to open 70 stores in 2006.
New York & Company (NWY)	$1.13	+9.0	11	Moderately priced women's apparel, age range 25–45.
Urban Outfitters, Inc. (URBN)	$1.09	+32.0	14	Includes Anthropologie, Urban Outfitters, Free People
The Dress Barn (DBRN)	$1.0	+33.0	Not ranked	Purchased Maurice's, small town stores, in 2005.
Guess, Inc. (GES)	$0.936	+28.0	19	Opened Marciano, more expensive clothing line. Now also sells eyeglasses, fragrances.

(continued)

Exhibit 7 *Women's Wear Daily* **High Volume Specialists in 2005** *(concluded)*

Store	Fiscal 2005 Dollar Volume (billions)	Percent Change— Volume	Last Year's Rank	Comments
The Cato Corp.	$0.836	+6.0	15	Juniors/Misses/Plus Sizes. Privately owned.
Coldwater Creek, Inc. (CWTR)	$0.780	+32.0	18	Targeting women ages 35–60. Opened Day Spas in 2005.
Tween Brands, Inc. (TWB)	$0.758	+12.0	16	Formerly Too, Inc, serves ages 7–12, also includes Limited Too, Justice stores.
Hot Topic (HOTT)	$0.725	+10.0	17	Music video inspired: teens ages 12–22.

Source: Adapted from Gustke, Constance, High Volume Specialists: Top 20 publicly traded specialty retailers ranked by most recent annual volume, *Women's Wear Daily*, July 20, 2006, Vol. 192, Iss. 12, p. 12.

However, in 2006, Chico's shares fell more than 50 percent when the company reported sales and earnings below analysts' expectations (see Exhibits 8 and 9). The company was undeniably still profitable, but apparently analysts were worried that it had been so successful that "the concept may be hitting a saturation point . . . and there may not be many new customers left to attract."[28]

Ann Taylor Background

Ann Taylor Stores Corporation, retailer of fashionable clothing for professional women, had three store formats: Ann Taylor for upscale suits and special occasion dresses and accessories; Ann Taylor LOFT for mid-priced casual; Ann Taylor Factory originally for clearance of Ann Taylor and Ann Taylor LOFT merchandise but transitioned in 2005–2006 to highlight merchandise specifically designed and made to carry the Ann Taylor Factory label within the outlet environment. The company had traded on the New York Stock Exchange since 1991 under the symbol ANN.

Starting out in 1954 on Chapel Street in New Haven, CT, founder Robert Liebeskind had established a clothing store that would provide clothing to suit the lifestyles of

Exhibit 8 **5-Year Stock Comparison Ann Taylor (ANN) versus Chico's (CHS) versus Retail Apparel Industry (SEC 5371)**

Source: Market Data from Yahoo Finance http://finance.yahoo.com.

Exhibit 9   Competitor and Related Businesses, Key Statistics

	2006 Revenue	2006 Gross Profit	2006 Profit Margin	2006 Operating Margin	2005 Revenue	2005 Gross Profit	2004 Revenue	2004 Gross Profit	2006 # Stores	
Ann Taylor Inc. (ANN)	$2,073,146	$1,056,024	6.45%	10.53%	$1,853,583	$947,548	$1,587,708	$866,245	828	
Talbots, Inc. (TLB)	$1,808,606	$654,872	2.47%	5.5%	$1,697,842	$604,820	$1,624,339	$622,655	1,086 / 205	Talbot / J. Jill
Chico's FAS Inc. (CHS)	$1,404,575	$857,043	12.24%	18.56%	$1,066,882	$654,974	$768,499	$471,022	799	
Coldwater Creek, Inc. (CWTR)	$971,980	$355,190	5.75%	8.9%	$590,310	$255,942	$518,844	$202,818	175	
Jos A. Banks (JOSB).	$516,100	$287,630	7.14%	12.37%	$464,633	$287,627	$372,500	$224,826	328	

Ann Taylor Inc. (ANN)—Specialty retailer of women's apparel, shoes and accessories, including career and casual separates and dress wear, sold through retail and Internet. Brands include Ann Taylor, Ann Taylor LOFT, and Ann Taylor Factory.

Talbots, Inc. (TLB)—Retailer of women's, children's, and men's classic apparel, accessories, and shoes, including classic sportswear, casual and dress wear, sold through retail and Internet. Brands include Talbots and J. Jill.

Chico's FAS Inc. (CHS)—Retailer of private label, casual-to-dressy clothing, intimates, complementary accessories, and non-clothing gift items to women 25 and older, sold through retail, catalog, Internet, and a small franchise network. Brands include Chico's, White House/Black Market, Soma by Chico's and Fitigues. Clothing is made from natural fabrics and synthetic blends.

Coldwater Creek, Inc. (CWTR)—Specialty retailer of women's apparel, accessories, jewelry, and gift items sold through catalog, Internet, retail, resort, and outlet stores. Also operates a spa near Portland, OR offering spa treatments, and a line of cosmetics and personal care products.

Jos A. Banks (JOSB)—Men's tailored and casual clothing and accessories, including tuxedos, suits, shirts, vests, ties, sport coats, pants, sportswear, overcoats, sweaters, belts and braces, socks and underwear, branded shoes, and other items sold through retail stores, catalog, Internet, as well as through franchisees.

Source: Data from http://finance.yahoo.com as of 2/2007. All dollars in thousands. Financials provided by Edgar Online.

women in the area. When Liebeskind's father, Richard Liebeskind, Sr., a designer himself, gave his son exclusive rights to one of his best selling dresses, "Ann Taylor," as a good luck gesture, the company name was established. Ann Taylor was never a real person, but her persona lived on in the profile of the consumer.

According to Hoovers online, the stores proliferated in New England. In 1977 Liebeskind sold out to Garfinckel,

Brooks Brothers, and Miller & Rhodes, which in 1981 was bought by Allied Stores. Under Allied, Ann Taylor was the top performer, guided by Sally Frame Kasaks, who was president from 1983 to 1985.

Campeau Corporation made a hostile takeover of Allied in 1985. Heavily in debt, Campeau sold Ann Taylor in 1989 for $420 million to private investors and the division's management. Ann Taylor had suffered from lack of attention and image drift under Campeau, and its new management failed to put more focus on the company's target career-woman customer; in addition, the chain was slow to see the trend toward more casual career dressing.

In 1991 AnnTaylor went public, but it had a high debt load and was struggling to fix quality problems with both clothes and designs. Kasaks returned as CEO in 1992, after stints at the head of Talbots and then Abercrombie & Fitch, and began a short lived joint venture with Cygne Design, a private label apparel company that contracted mainly with overseas manufacturers.[29] She also added a catalog business, a fragrance line, and free-standing shoe stores in 1994 and continued the aggressive store expansion started under Campeau.[30] A lower-priced apparel concept, Ann Taylor LOFT, originally located in factory outlet centers, was launched in 1995, and Kazaks incorporated more casual clothing, petite sizes, denims, and accessories in an attempt to create a one-stop shopping environment.[31] The mail order catalog attempt ended in late 1995, the company's fashion sense became a problem again—cropped T-shirts didn't fit in with the workplace attire—and Ann Taylor suffered another loss in fiscal 1996. Kasaks left that year. (As an example of the recycling of management talent in retail, Kasaks was asked in the fall of 2006 to serve as interim CEO of youth retailer Pacific Sunwear upon the sudden resignation of its CEO.)

New ANN CEO Patrick Spainhour, former CFO at Donna Karen with previous experience at Gap, and new president Patricia DeRosa, also from Gap's Old Navy division, closed the shoe stores in 1997 and ended the relationship with Cygne Designs. New in-house designers refocused the company's line, and a new supplier, DoDo Fashion Ltd. of Hong Kong, improved the clothes' quality.[32] The company opened 29 Ann Taylor LOFT stores in 1999 in accelerated pursuit of the younger, more cost-conscious consumers.

Ann Taylor attempted a cosmetic line in 2000, which it discontinued in 2001. In 2000, the Online Store at www.anntaylor.com was launched to great fanfare, only to be cut back in late 2001 when projected cash flow goals were not met. In early 2001 DeRosa left the company. Spainhour then restructured management reporting relationships, creating new President positions for both Ann Taylor and Ann Taylor LOFT divisions, subsequently promoting Kay Krill from executive vice-president to president of LOFT.[33]

In 2003 Spainhour brought in designer Jerome Jessup from Gap to modernize the Ann Taylor look. After a costly campaign to celebrate Ann Taylor's 50th anniversary failed to revitalize sales, Jessup resigned in early 2005. Kay Krill was promoted once again to president of ANN in late 2004, bringing both Ann Taylor and LOFT under her control.[34] LOFT began testing sleepwear and swimwear, and experimented with children's wear, to see if a separate retail operation might be possible.

In June 2005 the company completed a move to its new headquarters in Times Square Tower in New York City. In August ANN announced it had entered into a trademark licensing agreement with China's Guangzhou Pan Yu San Yuet Fashion Manufactory Ltd. that owns rights to use the Ann Taylor name in China. In the Fall of 2005, Chairman and CEO J. Patrick Spainhour retired and was succeeded as CEO by the company's President Kay Krill. Ronald W. Hovsepian, a director of the company since 1998, became chairman.[35]

Operational Information

As the end of fiscal year 2005, ANN had 824 stores in 46 states, the District of Columbia and Puerto Rico: 357 Ann Taylor, 416 Ann Taylor LOFT, and 51 Ann Taylor Factory stores, with flagship locations in New York, Chicago, and San Francisco. With an online presence since 2000, sales were also conducted at www.anntaylor.com and www.anntaylorLOFT.com.

According to the ANN 2005 Annual Report, the Ann Taylor client base consisted of fashion conscious women from the ages of 25 to 55. The Ann Taylor concept was designed to appeal to professional women with limited time to shop, who were attracted to Ann Taylor by its focused merchandising and total wardrobing strategy, personalized client service, efficient store layouts, and continual flow of new merchandise. The Ann Taylor LOFT concept appealed to women with a more relaxed lifestyle and work environment, who appreciated the Ann Taylor style and compelling value. Certain clients of Ann Taylor and Ann Taylor LOFT cross-shopped both brands. The Ann Taylor Factory concept served not only as a clearance vehicle, but also made available an increasing percentage of merchandise specifically designed to carry the Ann Taylor Factory label.

Substantially all merchandise offered in ANN's stores was developed by the Company's in-house product design and development teams, which designed merchandise exclusively for the Company. ANN sourced merchandise from approximately 285 manufacturers and vendors, none of which accounted for more than 4 percent of the Company's merchandise purchases in Fiscal 2005. Merchandise was manufactured in over 25 countries, including China, Hong Kong, and the Philippines.

ANN's planning departments analyzed each store's size, location, demographics, sales, and inventory history to determine the quantity of merchandise to be purchased for and allocated to the stores. Merchandise was typically sold at its original marked price for several weeks, with the length of time varying by item. Markdowns were used if inventory exceeded client demand for reasons of design, seasonal adaptation, or changes in client preference, or if it was determined that the inventory would not sell at its currently marked price. Some marked-down items remaining unsold were moved periodically to the Company's Ann Taylor Factory stores, where additional markdowns were taken. The Company used a centralized distribution system under which nearly all merchandise was sent to stores through the center located in Louisville, Kentucky.

An important aspect of ANN's business strategy was a real estate expansion program designed to reach new clients through the opening of new stores in markets with a sufficient concentration of target clients, or expansion of the size of existing stores as market conditions warranted and sites became available. Store locations were determined on the basis of various factors, including geographic location, demographic studies, anchor tenants in a mall location, other specialty stores in a mall or specialty center location or in the vicinity of a village location, and the proximity to professional offices in a downtown or village location.

Stores opened in factory outlet centers were located in factory outlet malls in which co-tenants generally included a significant number of outlet or discount stores operated under nationally recognized upscale brand names. The average Ann Taylor store was approximately 5,200 square feet in size, with Ann Taylor LOFT averaging approximately 5,900 square feet and Ann Taylor Factory Stores 8,400 square feet.

ANN provided private label credit card services to its customers. Investments in information services and technology in 2005 allowed it to continue to support and enhance design, merchandising, sourcing, logistics and finance operations, as well as measure store associates performance against learning and productivity goals. ANN had approximately 16,900 non-unionized employees as of January 28, 2006. ANN's risks and uncertainties regarding forward-looking statements included "our ability to anticipate and respond to changing client preferences and fashion trends in a timely manner" and respond to "the effect of competitive pressures from other retailers."[36]

Problems for the Ann Taylor Division

Created in 1995, LOFT was meant to be the division selling clothing that provided a "relaxed and versatile sensibility." Originally, LOFT stores were only found in outlet centers but then in 1998 the stores in the outlet mills were transitioned to Ann Taylor Factory while LOFT brand stores were opened in more prestigious regional malls and shopping centers. By 1999 LOFT clothes were a distinct line of more casual, yet business tailored, fun, feminine, and about 30 percent less expensive than the merchandise at AT.[37] In the second quarter of 2004 LOFT opened its 300th store, surpassing the Ann Taylor division in total square footage. This division had been a success for the company to the extent that some analysts in 2004 credited LOFT for keeping ANN afloat.[38]

Created in 1995, LOFT was meant to be the division selling clothing that provided a "relaxed and versatile sensibility." By 2004 LOFT sales had surpassed AT. Due to its success, and with the hope of bringing that success over to AT, ANN had made various changes, starting with upper management. In the fall of 2005, Kay Krill, former president of LOFT, took over the role of CEO and President of the Ann Taylor Stores Corporation, replacing J. Patrick Spainhour who had been the CEO and President of the company since 1996. Analysts believed this was a positive move because Krill was a proven retailing talent, as witnessed by her success at LOFT, and she could use that talent to turn AT around. Spainhour had always been on the operations side of the business and analysts had suspected that this was a major problem for the AT business.[39]

The AT division seemed to have lost its way in the retail world during the late 1990s. Customers had grown to expect a professional and polished look from the retailer and they were willing to pay higher prices for the clothes. However, during this era, customers encountered closer fitting, lower quality, trendier clothing, with too-short skirts and color palettes that did not suit their lifestyles. Ann Taylor appeared to have strayed from the career professional focus.[40]

The Ann Taylor brand, with its historically loyal following, was ripe for brand extension when it went public in 1991. At one point, ANN had Ann Taylor, Ann Taylor's Studio Shoes, Ann Taylor LOFT, Ann Taylor Petites, and Ann Taylor Factory, and they were experimenting with a make-up line and children's clothes. By 2005, the company had closed the shoe stores, reduced the amount of accessories that they would carry, and eliminated the makeup line. However, they were still offering petites and experimenting with children's clothes and sleepwear through LOFT division.

Since 1999 analysts had commented that ANN needed to be wary of cannibalization within the brands: would customers turn away from Ann Taylor in order to buy at LOFT? ANN had always tried to respond to the customer with "wardrobing," a philosophy of "outfitting from head to toe," combining relaxed everyday wear with more dressy pieces.[41] Since LOFT sold more relaxed but still tailored items at a lower price than AT, it was possible that some of AT's customers shopped at LOFT for things that they previously would have bought at AT. As one analyst said, "It's not clear that the Ann Taylor customer will continue paying $88 for a silk cardigan sweater when she knows she can pick up a similar cardigan for $39 less than a few block away at LOFT."[42]

During the late 1990s, AT also had problems maintaining clothing quality and did not lower prices when quality declined. This discouraged customers from buying because they were not willing to pay AT prices for subpar quality. With the inventory building, AT had to resort to markdowns to clear the racks. Therefore, waiting for sales was something that AT clients were used to doing, and there was no guarantee that customers would be willing to pay the regular prices at AT even for improved merchandise. Customers were heard to say, "I feel stupid if I pay full price" since "it seems like they're planning to mark things down." The concern with possible cannibalism continued. Even though the industry was used to brand extensions, such as Gap's Old Navy chain, the Ann Taylor LOFT used the main store in its name, reinforcing customer perception that they could get the same brand for less.[43]

Finally, another struggle at ANN had been turnover, especially within its upper management ranks. Since 1991, ANN had seen Sally Kasaks named CEO of the company in 1994, Patrick J. Spainhour named Chairman and CEO of the company in 1996 following Kasaks' departure, and finally Kay Krill promoted from LOFT to CEO in 2005. Kazaks implemented an ill-fated diversification strategy that included opening shoes boutiques, starting a catalog and cosmetic line, and adjusting the basic look of the professional clothing at AT to try to appeal to a younger audience.

Under Spainhour, managers' key suppliers were replaced, in-house designers were hired, and the brand was narrowed. President Patricia DeRosa, brought in by Spainhour, left in 2001. In 2003, he hired Jerome Jessup, head designer for Gap, in an attempt to modernize Ann Taylor's look. Jessup created the 2004 50th anniversary campaign, featuring a version of the original "Ann Taylor" shirtdress, to signal a return to sportswear classics. However, customers had difficulty reconciling his colorful, rather impractical styles with the classic Ann Taylor image, and the drop in sales lead to Jessup's resignation in January of 2005. Spainhour's revolving door activity had made other potential managers reluctant to work for him, prompting yet another reorganization.[44]

Kay Krill's Revitalization Strategy

When Kay Krill took over as CEO of the company upon Spainhour's retirement in the fall of 2005, she was faced with the challenge of rebuilding the Ann Taylor brand, meeting the "wardrobing needs of the updated classic consumer"[45] while maintaining the image and market share of Ann Taylor LOFT. As one reporter said, Ann Taylor is "one of a growing number of specialty retailers wrestling with how to keep a founding brand fresh without cannibalizing a newcomer."[46]

One of Krill's first actions was to recruit Laura Weil to a new position as COO. Weil came from American Eagle Outfitters where she had focused on financial issues involving real estate, pricing, sourcing, and logistics and had to handle the divestiture of underperforming assets. In her role as COO at ANN she would be expected to focus on inventory management and merchandise planning, information systems, and supply chain operations, allowing Krill to focus on merchandising and marketing.[47]

In addition to Weil, four other staff changes were made, reconfiguring the top management structure. Instead of separate divisional leaders, Krill created the COO, EVP of planning and allocation and EVP/chief marketing officer to coordinate activities at both AT and LOFT, allowing her to "lead both divisions in a more hands-on way." AT and LOFT would continue to have separate EVPs for merchandising and design, and SVPs for divisional marketing, design, sourcing, and store direction.[48]

Focused attention was put on improving merchandise, especially at AT, and in the "fit" of accessory lines, better inventory management, reducing cost through improved processes and technology, looking at sourcing efficiency and supply chain speed, providing more appropriate initial retail pricing with less merchandise sold at markdown, streamlining promotional activities, spending capital investment dollars on store facelifts to upgrade the AT real estate, and generally putting a greater emphasis on teamwork across the entire organization. In addition, plans put in place during 2006, to be operational in 2007, were to transition the Ann Taylor Factory Store to a stand-alone concept, revamp the ANN Web site and begin to reach out more to international customers, and explore a fourth store concept for children's wear under the Little Loft label.[49]

New inventory management strategies reduced inventory per square foot by 22 percent in fiscal 2005, with inventory refreshed every two to three weeks, and new "quick sourcing" software reducing lead-times; a real estate reinvestment strategy enhanced the look and feel of 43 stores in 2005 in a move toward the "store of the future."[50] This emphasis on improved inventory turnover and more "full-price selling," due to a strategy of offering only a limited quantity of even hot fashions, encouraged shoppers to "buy it while it's there."[51] This momentum resulted in fewer markdowns and higher margins at ANN, with a 2006 gross profit of 50.64 percent, well over the WWD industry 2006 gross margin rate for specialty retailers of 39.49 percent.[52]

The focus on inventory management and store design improvements were credited for improving the investor's outlook for long-term performance at ANN, but concerns surfaced based on the extent of the company's investment in remodeling and store expansion. According to company announcements in the second quarter of 2006, ANN planned to update 52 Ann Taylor stores and build 60 LOFT stores in 2006, with 50 more scheduled in 2007 (see Exhibit 6: Stores Growth & Inventory Levels; # Employees, Inventory Turns). With the increased emphasis on supply chain efficiency, ANN's Sole distribution center in Louisville, Kentucky, had made upgrades as well, with incremental improvements through automation and software integration. However in 2006 John Singleton, SVP of Logistics, noted that the distribution center had sufficient capacity to supply 1,050 stores, but after that the building footprint would have to be expanded.[53]

This potential additional real estate investment, along with the over 800 existing stores' planned expansion and upgrades, meant a considerable lease expense, one which certain analysts questioned. If the growth in sales was fueled in part by store expansion, the long-term lease obligation meant that ANN had to be careful about its cost of capital, and whether projected earnings would cover this. One analyst in 2006 warned, "Store expansion is a risk for all apparel retailers. Gap Inc., for example, spent massively to add stores in the 1990s and . . . the stores became a big cost overhead once Gap's clothes stopped selling well." In the face of these concerns, Krill continued to stress that AT was "managing its growth."[54]

Regarding merchandising, one of Krill's first areas of focus was the development of "brand books" or profiles of the typical Ann Taylor and LOFT clients. The "Ann," focus was a married 36-year-old working mother of two children with a household income of $150K. She would lead a busy, sophisticated life. When giving a presentation to a client, she'd wear a formal suit with a blouse, not a camisole, underneath, and her idea of dressing down at work might be a velvet jacket with jeans.

The Ann Taylor LOFT client was married, in her 30s with children, worked in a laid-back, less-corporate environment, and had a household income between $75K and $100K. She would call her style "casual chic" and might wear pants and a floral top with ruffled sleeves to work, while on the weekend she would wear a printed shoulder-baring halter top with cropped jeans. To illustrate the difference between the older and younger brands, a recent catalog photo shoot had Ann Taylor fashions highlighted by the upscale Breaker's Hotel in Palm Springs, Florida, and had LOFT catalog shot on a beach in Jamaica.[55]

One marketer was concerned that the two personas were too stereotypical, and perhaps ignored those professional women who were unmarried and childless, stating that she had worn Ann Taylor when she was younger and trying to impress, but now that she was older she didn't get dressed up that often, and preferred Ann Taylor LOFT, so she was the exact opposite of their personas.[56]

Regarding the cannibalization risk, Krill felt there was "a pretty clear differentiation," with "special occasion and work primarily being the focus" at AT, and "more relaxed, separates and fashion" at LOFT.[57] Upon being named CEO in 2005, Krill made differentiation a top priority. She had previously commented, "as women's wardrobes have evolved over the years, we have not evolved with them. We need a good balance in our offerings, including wear-to-work clothes, separates and casual, and special occasion wear. We disappointed the customer with the work and casual component. Our first order of business is getting the suit business up on its feet."[58]

The Company also expanded its focus on special events with the introduction of its Celebrations Collection—a line of classic, elegant dresses and coordinating accessories for special occasion, such as weddings and engagement parties—in August 2005.[59] Ann Taylor had been quietly serving brides and bridesmaids for decades and the brand saw the potential to expand upon this opportunity with a dedicated offering and more personalized service. Of particular interest to long-term ANN customers was the introduction of dye-to-match sashes and accessories for bridesmaids in 2006, with fully coordinated jewelry and shoe styles, offered in petite as well as regular sizes.[60] The expansion of the selection in petite sizes, especially online, was seen as a great opportunity, since some department stores had reduced their petite offerings.[61]

Restructuring, Refocusing Worries Continue

In the spring of 2006 Krill embarked on further restructuring after the rather abrupt departure of Laura Weil, who left with no explanation. Analysts wondered if the job was too broad for Weil's primarily financial background, since at ANN Weil had responsibility for merchandise planning; information systems; all supply chain operations including sourcing, logistics, and distribution; real estate; construction and facilities; and purchasing in addition to finance, accounting, and investor relations.[62] Krill decided not to replace Weil, moving up Jim Smith, CFO, and Tony Romano, now Supply Chain Executive Vice President, to report directly to her. In addition, Krill hired Michael Kingston away from Coach to become Chief Information Officer, reporting to Romano. This move underscored the importance of technology and information systems to improving efficiencies. In addition to the departure of Weil, Chief Marketing Officer Muriel Gonzalez left to join Macy's.

In June of 2006, Krill made more personnel changes by promoting long-time ANN employees Adrienne Lazarus and Donna Noce to President of Ann Taylor and Ann Taylor LOFT, respectively. Brian Lynch was promoted to Executive Vice President of Ann Taylor Factory Stores, and Elaine Boltz was promoted to Executive Vice President/Chief Marketing Officer. All had played important roles in the performance revitalization since Krill took control. This now gave each ANN division an experienced leader who understood ANN's environment and culture from working within. Consultants and analysts were pleased. As one said, "Ann Taylor has had mixed results from hiring outside. This is a refreshing and potentially positive change."[63]

Regardless of these structural changes, performance still affected personnel. In January, 2007, Donna Noce, the 10-year ANN employee who had been recently promoted to President of LOFT, left the company. Speculation was that problems with same store sales declines at LOFT since August, presumably due to poor merchandising/fashion choices, led to Noce's departure[64] Kay Krill assumed leadership of LOFT again, playing a dual role while searching for a new divisional president.

Krill commented, "I believe that building a winning team is critical to fully realizing our company's full potential."[65] In January of 2007 it appeared that the eagerly anticipated revitalization was taking longer than anticipated. When interviewed in September of 2006 Krill had shared that she still oversaw "all aspects" of building the product lines at both AT and LOFT, that she was the one "racing back and forth" to make sure each brand was distinct.[66] Although the "brand books" seemed to have helped "hit the right balance," one source wondered about the pressure on Krill, especially since she didn't have a "strong operating partner" to help with merchandising and other creative decisions.[67]

When it became obvious to commentators in the late 1990s that LOFT had emerged as a more affordable version of AT, and, a such, was confusing to customers. Krill admitted it "was a near disaster" and, as of 2007, had taken "about five years to reverse the damage."[68] However, retail strategists warned that "before you can declare victory, you've got to have pretty much two years of positive performance on different financial indices," including store-for-store sales, gross margin improvement, and net profit, so that there "has to be a sense of a growing customer base, and not just a temporary turnaround by doing expedient things. . . . A solid turnaround is at least two years in the making, or maybe more, depending on the complexity of the problems the company was encountering."[69] Some believed that the "truer test of whether there is a genuine revival of the brand" at Ann Taylor would come in 2007.[70]

The 2006 Annual Report commented further on the respective performances of AT and LOFT. In the CEO's letter to shareholders, Kay Krill noted, as it related specially to the Ann Taylor brand,

> Our Ann Taylor division continued the turnaround begun in 2005 to deliver a very stronger year in 2006. Among the most important accomplishments of the year was our success in reestablishing Ann Taylor as *the* premier destination for updated classic, yet stylish, professional and special occasion dressing…."

AT's business had been strong and healthy going into 2007, while LOFT was in a transitional stage. As the first quarter of 2007 ended, Krill said,

> our Ann Taylor division continued to offer compelling product assortments that resonated with our clients and drove increased full-price selling, while our Loft division continued to be challenged with a product assortment that was not balanced and did not offer enough updated classics or color."[71]

It appeared that AT was doing well, but now LOFT was suffering. Would Krill's ongoing strategy by adequate for helping both divisions to do well, in the same year?

Endnotes

1. Krill, K. As quoted in Q3 2005 Ann Taylor Stores Earnings Conference Call—Final. *Fair Disclosure Wire,* December 2, 2005.
2. Merrick, A. 2005. Parent Trap: Once a bellwether, Ann Taylor fights its stodgy image." *The Wall Street Journal (Eastern Edition),* July 12, 2005, p. A.1.
3. Ibid.
4. Feitelberg, R. 2005. "Dominating in the mid-range," *Women's Wear Daily,* July 2005, vol. 190, p. 55.
5. Merrick, 2005, op. cit.
6. Feitelberg, 2005, op. cit.
7. Hall, C. & Derby, M. 2005. Leaders of the pack, *Women's Wear Daily,* 189 (101):12.
8. ANN commentators were careful to note that there was no apparent cause and effect relationship between ANN's losses and LOFT's gains. Personal communication, Beth Warner, Director Corporate Communications, Ann Taylor Stores Corporation, July 2007.
9. Krill. 2005, op. cit.
10. Ann Taylor announces LOFT division reaches $1 billion in sales', February 12, 2005, from http://investor.anntaylor.com/news/20060213-187405.cfm?t=n.
11. Ann Taylor stores jumps on strong earnings. Associated Press; March 10, 2006, from http://news.moneycentral.msn.com/ticker/article.asp?Feed=AP&Date=20060310&ID=5570346&Symbol=US:ANN.
12. Moin, D. 2006. Lofty Times for Ann Taylor. *Women's Wear Daily,* 192 (107):11.
13. Ann Taylor Announces January 2007 and Fiscal Year 2006 Sales Results. February 8, 2007, from http://investor.anntaylor.com/news/20070208-229019.cfm?t=n.
14. Moin, D. 2007. Ann Taylor profits fall 21.5% in 4th quarter. *Women's Wear Daily,* March 19: 2.
15. The squeeze on Apparel's sweet spots 2005. *Women's Wear Daily,* February 9: 24.
16. Liedtke, M. 2007. Gap to close Forth & Towne Chain. *AP Business,* February 26.
17. Young, V. M., & Moin, D. 2005. The speculation game: Mergers, sales, buys have retail world abuzz. *Women's Wear Daily,* 189 (30): 1–19.
18. Clark, E. 2005. Building new titans: More mergers seen in the chase for scale. *Women's Wear Daily,* 189 (44): 1–11.
19. Curan, op. cit.
20. Young & Moin, op. cit.
21. Morgenson, G. 1992. Here come the cross-shoppers. *Forbes,* 150 (13): 90.
22. Pulliam, S., & Agins, T. 1995. Heard on the street: For Ann Taylor, the short-term crisis eases, but underlying problems won't disappear. *The Wall Street Journal* (Eastern Edition), October 6: C2.
23. DesMarteau, K. 2005. Eyes wide open. *Apparel,* 47 (3): 1.
24. Chandler, M. 2006. Clothing chain seeks the right fit. *Mercury News,* March 11, from http://www.mercurynews.com/mld/mercurynews/business/14074847.htm.
25. Apparel firms gird for possible merger wave. June 16, 2005. http://www.WSJ.com.
26. Moin, D. 2006. Rebound at Ann Taylor: CEO Kay Krill fashions retailer's new career. *Women's Wear Daily,* 191 (134): 1.
27. Retailers tailor style to suit older women. *The Boston Globe,* March 10, 2006, from *International Herald Tribune,* http://www.iht.com/articles/2006/03/10/yourmoney/mbrf1.php.
28. Merrick, A. 2006. Chico's falls out of fashion. post-gazette.com: A service of the *Pittsburgh Post-Gazette,* 7/28/2006, from http://www.post-gazette.com/pg/pp/06209/709279.stm.
29. Agins, T. Retailing: Ann Taylor aims to resew torn image. *The Wall Street Journal* (Eastern Edition), New York, September 14, 1992, pg. B1.
30. Book, E.W. 1994. The treachery of success. *Forbes,* 54 (6): 88.
31. Wilson, M. 1995. Reinventing Ann Taylor. *Chain Store Age Executive with Shopping Center Age,* 71 (1): 26.
32. Leder, M. 1998. Ann Taylor's material improvements. *Crain's New York Business,* 14 (37): 1.
33. Ann Taylor announces January sales results, revised fourth quarter 2000 earnings estimate and organizational changes. February 8, 2001, from http://investor.anntaylor.com/news/20010208-34534.cfm?t=n.
34. Moin, D. 2004. "Ann Taylor elevates Krill. *Women's Wear Daily,* 188 (100): 12.
35. The above section is partly adapted from http://premium.hoovers.com, History.
36. From http://investor.anntaylor.com/downloads/2005AnnualReport.pdf.

37. Summers, M. 1999. New outfit. *Forbes,* 164 (15): 88.
38. Tucker, R. 2004. LOFT continues to pace Ann Taylor. *Womens' Wear Daily,* 188 (21): 12.
39. Curan, C. 2001. Ann Taylor LOFTs expansion plans right into a storm. *Crain's New York Business,* 17 (18): 4.
40. Summers, op. cit.
41. Kennedy, K. 2000. This is not your momma's clothing store—not by a longshot. *Apparel Industry Magazine,* 61 (12): 22–25.
42. Curan, C. 1999. Ann Taylor aims for LOFT-y goal with new stores. *Crain's New York Business,* 15 (13): 1.
43. Curan, C. 2000. Ann Taylor comes undone, again. *Crain's New York Business,* 16 (10): 3.
44. Ann Taylor chain seeks COO to help new chief mend company. *Crain's New York Business,* April 11, 2005: 12.
45. Feitelberg, R. 2005, op. cit.
46. Merrick, A. 2005, op. cit.
47. Derby, M. 2005. Wall Street bullish on Ann Taylor's Weil. *Women's Wear Daily* 190 (71): 20.
48. Moin, D. 2005. Ann Taylor stores taps two to fill out executive ranks. *Women's Wear Daily,* 189 (45): 3.
49. Q3 2005 Ann Taylor Stores earnings conference call—final. *Fair Disclosure Wire,* December 2, 2005.
50. From http://investor.anntaylor.com/downloads/2005AnnualReport.pdf, p. 6.
51. O'Donnell, J. 2006. Retailers try to train shoppers to buy now; limited supplies, fewer sales could get consumers to stop waiting for discounts. *USA TODAY,* September 26: B3.
52. Gustke, C. 2006. High profit makers; top publicly traded specialty retailers, ranked by most recent annual gross margins. *Women's Wear Daily,* 192 (61): 28.
53. Ann Taylor: Upgrade with style. *Modern Material Handling* (Warehousing Management Edition), March 2006: 38.
54. Jones, S. D. 2006. Moving the market—tracking the numbers/outside audit: Ann Taylor's data draw a big critic; research firm questions retailer's earnings quality amid high costs of capital. *The Wall Street Journal* (Eastern Edition), August 17: C3.
55. Merrick, op. cit.
56. Buchanan, H. 2005. Ann Taylor persona. July 27. http://marketingtowomenonline.typepad.com/blog/2005/07/ann_taylor_pers.html.
57. Q3 2005 Ann Taylor stores earnings conference call—final. *Fair Disclosure Wire,* December 2.
58. Derby, M., & Edelson, S. 2005. Kay Krill named CEO at Ann Taylor. *Women's Wear Daily,* 189 (57): 2.
59. Greenberg, J. 2005. Ann Taylor dresses up its offerings. *Women's Wear Daily,* 190 (86): 14.
60. Ann Taylor introduces fall 2006 "celebrations," an exclusive collection of signature elegance for life's finest moments. August 29 from http://investor.anntaylor.com/news/20060829-209201.cfm?t=n.
61. Ann Taylor and Ann Taylor LOFT—the specialty resource for petites. August 23, 2006, from http://investor.anntaylor.com/news/20060823-208165.cfm?t=n.
62. Moin, D. 2006. Laura Weil exits Ann Taylor. *Women's Wear Daily,* 191 (97): 2.
63. Butler, E. 2006. Corporate ladder: Donna Noce, Adrienne Lazarus, stylish sibling rivalry. *Crain's New York Business,* 22 (29): 29.
64. Edelson, S. 2007. Noce steps down as Ann Taylor LOFT president. *Women's Wear Daily,* 193 (15): 15.
65. ANN 2005 Annual Report, page 6, at http://investor.anntaylor.com/annual.cfm.
66. Merrick, A. 2006. Boss talk: Asking "What would Ann do?" In Turning around Ann Taylor, CEO Kay Krill got to know her customers, "Ann" and "Loft." *The Wall Street Journal* (Eastern Edition), 9/15/2006, p. B1.
67. Moin, D. 2006. Rebound at Ann Taylor: CEO Kay Krill fashions retailer's new career. *Women's Wear Daily,* 191 (134): 1.
68. Felgner, B. 2007. New challenges in branding. *Home Textiles Today,* 2/5/2007, 28(5): 1–31.
69. Moin, D. 2006. Experts seeks sustained performance. *Women's Wear Daily,* 191 (134): 9.
70. Moin. 2006. Rebound at Ann Taylor, op. cit.
71. Young, V.M. 2007. "Aeropostale leads specialty retailers," *Women's Wear Daily,* 5/25/2007, Vol. 193(113): 3.

Case 15   United Way of America*

United Way of America and United Way International provided support for member organizations worldwide: over 1,300 local United Ways in the United States and 3,000 United Way organizations operating in 45 countries relied on their respective parents for resources such as leadership education, public policy advocacy, marketing support, and standards for ethical governance and financial reporting. United Ways worldwide were part of a federation of non-profits formed by caring people to serve the needs of their communities. They raised and distributed funds to the most effective local service providers, built alliances and coordinated volunteer support among charities, businesses and other entities, and acted as best practice models of management and financial accountability—which was where problems had arisen. With three high profile ethical scandals since 1995 at both the national and local level, the United Way brand had to combat an erosion of trust, as well as deal with an increasingly competitive and changing environment for charitable contributors.

Even after over 120 years of solid financial performance and steady growth, since the year 2000 United Way had seemingly reached a plateau of fundraising in the United States. Certainly there were options for growth from international members, and from the energy and direction of nationwide objectives stated by United Way of America (education about and implementation of the national 2-1-1 phone network; early childhood educational initiatives Success by 6 and Born Learning; encouraging nationwide voluntarism through the Lend a Hand public service announcements funded by a donation from the NFL; and the Assets for Family Success economic self-sufficiency program for working families), but charitable donations still had not topped the inflation-adjusted peak year campaign of 1989.[1]

In addition, in 2007 veteran fund raisers on all fronts were citing challenges such as competition for donations, difficulty recruiting and keeping qualified fund raisers, difficulty raising money for general operating costs, and a growing focus on large gifts from very wealthy individuals, which, when publicized, could reduce the motivation for smaller donors to contribute (the donor thought: "If someone like Bill Gates was providing funds, why would they need my dollars?").[2] From the donors' perspective, the opportunities for both individuals and businesses to engage in charitable giving had expanded, with over 40 percent of new nonprofits appearing since 2000.[3] Many of these, especially those supporting disaster relief in the wake of 9/11 and Hurricane Katrina, had a single-issue focus that had the potential for creating a close bond with the donor. This meant that some individuals might have bypassed organizations such as the United Way, believing these to have support targets that were too broad, preferring instead to specify exactly where donations should go (the donor thought: "If I'm giving, I want to make sure my money is going where I want it to go, to the cause I want to support").

Even prior to 9/11 American donors had expressed concern about their ability to access information regarding how their donations were going to be used, what percent of the charity's spending went toward actual current programs, how their privacy was going to be protected when giving via the Internet, and whether the charity met voluntary standards of conduct.[4] It didn't help that many nonprofits, including United Way of America, suffered widely publicized scandals over misappropriation of funds. Organizations that serve community or broader social needs must continually be perceived as legitimate, as acting in an appropriate and desirable way within "some socially constructed set of norms, values, beliefs and definitions"[5] in order to receive needed donations. It was especially difficult for nonprofits like United Way to maintain trust since their products and services did not easily lend themselves to traditional quality assessment and performance review, and once that trust was broken it was very difficult to get it back.

United Way of America's CEO Brian Gallagher formally initiated a shift in strategy. Responding to the environment, Gallagher, established new membership standards to enhance the level of accountability and transparency in United Way affiliates' operations, re-branded United Way as doing "what matters" in the communities it served, and updated the "standards of excellence," providing a description of benchmark standards and best practices to better reflect the organization's strategic shift from its traditional role as strictly a fundraiser to a new mission focused on identifying and addressing the long-term needs of communities.

These initiatives required that the United Way affiliates buy into the change effort, since the power of the parent organization was limited to removing the affiliate from United Way membership if it didn't comply. It was imperative for a nonprofit organization to get the necessary support at the local level in order to achieve stated organizational goals. Would Gallagher's various strategies be successfully implemented? Was the shift in strategy sufficient to ensure the continued viability of the United Way, or was its very mission perhaps no longer relevant?

Overview and History of the United Way of America

United Way was founded in 1887 as the Charity Organizations Society of Denver, raising $21,700 for 22 local agencies in its second year of operation. In 1913 this model was

* By Professor Pauline Assenza of Manhattanville College, Professor Alan B. Eisner of Pace University, and graduate student Luz Barrera of Pace University. This case is based upon public documents, and was developed for class discussion rather than to illustrate either effective or ineffective handling of the situation. This research was supported in part by the Wilson Center for Social Entrepreneurship, Pace University. Copyright © 2007 Pauline Assenza & Alan B. Eisner.

expanded to become a "Community Chest" in Cleveland, and in 1918 12 fund-raising federations met in Chicago to form the American Association for Community Organizations. From 1919 to 1929, over 350 Community Chests were created, and by 1948 more than 1,000 communities had these United Way Community Chests in operation. In 1973 the partnership between United Way and the National Football League began, with the goal to increase public awareness of social service issues facing the country. In addition to public service announcements in which volunteer NFL players, coaches, and owners appeared, NFL players supported their local United Ways through personal appearances, special programs, and by sitting on United Way governing boards.

In 1974 United Ways in America and Canada raised $1,038,995,000, marking the first time in history that an annual campaign of a single organization raised more than $1 billion. In that same year, United Way International was formed to help nations around the world create United Way–type organizations. The 1981–1985 and 1997–1998 campaigns became the time frames with the greatest percentage increase in revenues. Amounts raised since 1999 had generally failed to keep up with the rate of inflation, although a $10.5 million gift from Bill and Melinda Gates and a $50 million donation by Bank of America in 1999 made that year a good one (see Exhibit 1).[6]

The United Way was essentially a financial intermediary, providing fund-raising activities, primarily through donor organizations' employee payroll deductions, distributing those funds to agencies that could actually deliver services to clients in the target community. The parent organizations, United Way of America and United Way International, serviced the local United Way chapters, who performed the bulk of the fund-raising. Although other sources of revenue included individual donations and government grants, still around 70 percent of donations came from employees in local businesses, the majority of which (75 percent) were considered unrestricted dollars that the local United Ways could put to use to address critical needs in their respective communities.

The parent organization United Way of America (UWA) was supported primarily by local United Way member organizations that paid annual membership fees based on an agreed upon formula, 1 percent of their communitywide campaign contributions. Trademark members, United Way member organizations raising less than $100,000, paid a fee of 0.3 percent of their total contributions. In addition to membership support and individual and corporate sponsorship and federal grants, other sources for funds for the national umbrella organization were from conferences, program service fees, promotional material sales, investment income, rental, and service income (see Exhibits 2 and 3).

United Way was a system that operated as a federation—a network of local affiliates that shared a mission, a brand and a program model, but were legally independent from one another, and from the national office. Histori-cally, United Way had been the loosest of federations, with almost all power residing at the local level. Each United Way chapter member was not only independent, but also separately incorporated and governed by a local volunteer board. Through communitywide campaigns, each local United Way raised funds to support a great variety of health and human services organizations, utilizing a network of local volunteers.

Over the years, as United Way's local chapters had grown bigger and more prosperous, they had begun to consider themselves more autonomous—gatekeepers, allocators and managers of the local public trust—and had begun to question whether the seal of approval bestowed by United Way affiliation was worth it in light of the declining financial rewards. Therefore, some United Way agencies had considered forming their own member-oriented, self-governing federations.

Current Competition and Challenges

By 2007 the charitable giving industry had fragmented into tiny, possible fraudulent, single-focus agencies that could be both competitors and recipients of United Way programs. In addition, since United Way's traditional function had been parceling out the contribution it received to local charities, donors had begun to question the need for an organization that essentially just processed money—donors asked themselves, "Why not just give directly to the charity of my choice?" The perception was that the administrative function of United Way and other blanket charities just added an additional level of overhead to organizational costs, with a smaller portion of the original donation actually reaching the intended target.

In addition, donors were increasingly supporting specific causes, and therefore were more attracted to alternative recipient organizations, those possibly more responsive to the idea of community based on gender, race, or sexual orientation, among other socially driven issues.[7] A spokesperson for the American Cancer Society remarked, "Today a person might have an interest in prostate cancer, because his father died of it, or breast cancer, because it is a social issue as well as a health issue. We have to remember that an organization's mission is at least as important to supporters as its integrity." This meant that "donor-advised funds, which allow people to create grant-making accounts and recommend which charities get the money" were becoming increasingly popular.[8] This did not mean that the traditional and venerable organizations like United Way, Red Cross, the Salvation Army, and Goodwill Industries were necessarily in trouble, just perhaps in need of some strategic adjustment (see Exhibits 4a and 4b).

The partnership between United Way and the disaster relief organizations such as the Red Cross, the Salvation Army, Boys & Girls Clubs, and Catholic Charities was still a strong and viable one, but increasingly all these national charities needed to understand the need for a diversified revenue stream. In a video interview with UWA's Brian

Exhibit 1   United Way Campaign History

	Amount Raised in Current $			Average Annual CPI* (1982–1984 100)	Inflation Rate %	Amount Raised in Constant $		
Year	(In Billions)	Change (In Millions)	%			(In Billions)	Change (In Millions)	%
1971	0.813		3.3	40.5	4.4	2.0072		−1.0
1972	0.858	45.2	5.6	41.8	3.2	2.0529	45.7	2.3
1973	0.916	58.3	6.8	44.4	6.2	2.0640	11.1	0.5
1974	0.979	62.4	6.8	49.3	11.0	1.9854	−78.6	−3.8
1975	1.023	44.1	4.5	53.8	9.1	1.9013	−84.1	−4.2
1976	1.104	81.4	8.0	56.9	5.8	1.9408	39.5	2.1
1977	1.205	100.5	9.1	60.6	6.5	1.9881	47.3	2.4
1978	1.318	112.9	9.4	65.2	7.6	2.0210	32.9	1.7
1979	1.424	105.8	8.0	72.6	11.3	1.9607	−60.3	−3.0
1980	1.526	102.5	7.2	82.4	13.5	1.8519	−108.8	−5.5
1981	1.680	154.0	10.1	90.9	10.3	1.8482	−3.8	−0.2
1982	1.780	100.0	6.0	96.5	6.2	1.8446	−3.6	−0.2
1983	1.950	170.0	9.6	99.6	3.2	1.9578	113.3	6.1
1984	2.145	195.0	10.0	103.9	4.3	2.0645	106.7	5.4
1985	2.330	185.0	8.6	107.6	3.6	2.1654	100.9	4.9
1986	2.440	110.0	4.7	109.6	1.9	2.2263	60.8	2.8
1987	2.600	160.0	6.6	113.6	3.6	2.2887	62.5	2.8
1988	2.780	180.0	6.9	118.3	4.1	2.3500	61.2	2.7
1989	2.980	200.0	7.2	124.0	4.8	2.4032	53.3	2.3
1990	3.110	130.0	4.4	130.7	5.4	2.3795	−23.7	−1.0
1991	3.170	60.0	1.9	136.2	4.2	2.3275	−52.0	−2.2
1992	3.040	−130.0	−4.1	140.3	3.0	2.1668	−160.7	−6.9
1993	3.047	7.0	0.2	144.5	3.0	2.1087	−58.1	−2.7
1994	3.078	31.0	1.0	148.2	2.6	2.0769	−31.7	−1.5
1995	3.148	70.0	2.3	152.4	2.8	2.0656	−11.3	−0.5
1996	3.248	100.0	3.2	156.9	3.0	2.0701	4.5	0.2
1997	3.402	154.0	4.7	160.5	2.3	2.1196	49.5	2.4
1998	3.577	175.0	5.1	163.0	1.6	2.1945	74.9	3.5
1999	3.769	192.0	5.4	166.6	2.2	2.2623	67.8	3.1
2000	3.912	143.0	3.8	172.2	3.4	2.2718	9.5	0.4
2001	3.949	37.0	0.9	177.1	2.8	2.2298	−42.0	−1.8
2002	3.709	−240.0	−6.1	179.9	1.6	2.0617	−168.1	−7.5
2003	3.591	−118.0	−3.2	184.0	2.3	1.9516	−110.1	−5.3
2004	3.606	15.0	0.4	188.9	2.7	1.9089	−42.7	−2.2

*CPI is annualized rate for a calendar year

Source: United Way of America, Research Services. August 2005

Exhibit 2 Give.org Charity Report for United Way America 2006

Governance:

Chief Executive: Brian A. Gallagher, President and CEO

Compensation: $632,423*

Chair of the Board: Rodney E. Slater

Chair's Profession/Business Affiliation: Partner, Patton Boggs LLP

Board Size: 26

Paid Staff Size: 180

Uses of Funds as a % of Total Expenses for Year Ended December 31, 2006:

Fund Raising: 0.78%

Administrative: 13.50%

Programs: 85.72%

2006

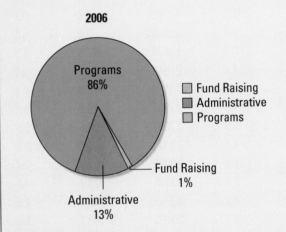

*2005 compensation includes annual salary and, if applicable, benefit plans, expense accounts, and other allowances. UWA indicates that Mr. Gallagher's total salary represents $405,000 in salary, $52,500 in incentive pay, and $174,923 in deferred compensation.

Source: BBB Wise Giving Alliance at Give.org

Gallagher, *Forbes* asked about what had changed in 2006. Gallagher noted that 55 percent of donations still came from employees in the workplace and corporate contributions from companies such as UPS, Microsoft, and IBM, and that the relationship with the NFL was still a powerful one, with 50 percent of volunteers being recruited through the NFL campaign. He mentioned that online participation was growing, and that individual donations averaged $200 per year per individual, with contributions coming increasingly from women and people of color, representing $75 million from all United Way chapters in 2005.[9]

Entering 2007 with the donor community becoming increasingly diverse and the societal problems increasingly challenging, charitable nonprofits needed to engage in ongoing assessment of the relevance of their respective missions. This was not a new problem. In 1999 Michael Porter and Mark Kramer considered the strategic challenges facing nonprofits. Noting that the number of charitable foundations in the United States had doubled in the two decades since the 1970s, they also believed that these philanthropic organizations were not devoting enough effort to measuring their results and to figuring out how to create the most value for society with the resources they had at their disposal. This value could have been created by selecting the appropriate grantees, signaling other donors of appropriately chosen charities, improving the performance of grant recipients, and advancing the state of knowledge and practice, however many philanthropic organizations lacked a strategic focus, with resources scattered across too many fields and with staff spread to thin, servicing too many small grants. One suggestion was to engage in more performance assessment and unique positioning with unique activities aimed specifically at creating value, however this would require most nonprofits to also assess the effectiveness of their governance systems.[10]

Scandals and Governance

The year 2002 was bad for corporate scandals: Enron, ImClone, WorldCom, and Tyco all hit the headlines with examples of corporate greed and misappropriation of both funds and public trust. Given these types of wrongdoings in publicly held organizations, the tolerance of the general population for similar activities in nonprofits was increasingly eroded, especially given the nature of the relationship—one based on donor trust.

The first major scandal at United Way had occurred 10 years earlier, in 1992, when William Aramony, president and CEO of United Way of America (UWA), and two other UWA executives were convicted of fraud, conspiracy, and money laundering in a scheme that siphoned around $1 million from the organization. This event was perceived as a turning point in public perceptions of charitable organizations, and was blamed for the first drop in United Way donations since World War II.[11]

In 2001, the United Way of the National Capital Area, the Washington DC chapter and the second largest local United Way member in the country in donations, was in the news, again because of fraud. CEO Oral Suer took over $500,000 from the charity to pay for personal expenses, annual leave and an early pension payout he was not entitled to. Other employees took additional money for personal use, with the total fraud amounting to $1.6 million. Then in 2002, new United Way National Capital Area CEO Norman O. Taylor was asked to resign over misstated revenues, and questionable overhead and credit card charges. In 2003 the CFO of the Michigan Capital Area United Way, Jacqueline Allen-MacGregor, was imprisoned for the theft

Exhibit 3 United Way of America Consolidated Financial Statements

For Year Ended	Dec. 31, 2006	Dec. 31, 2005	Dec. 31, 2004
Source of Funds			
Contributions	$15,477,000	$30,439,000	$9,772,000
Membership support (net)	28,978,000	29,231,000	23,015.000
Campaign efforts (net)	7,717,000	—	—
Promotional material sales	6,575,000	6,514,000	7,525,000
Transaction fees	3,307,000	2,979,000	1,234,000
Conferences	2,622,000	1,892,000	1,447,000
Program service fees	942,000	1,228,000	775,000
Investment income	1,667,000	1,055,000	319,000
Rental and service income	405,000	646,000	408,000
Miscellaneous and other	425,000	241,000	147,000
Total Income	**$68,115,000**	**$74,225,000**	**$44,642,000**
Program Expenses			
Field leadership	—	—	3,683,000
Brand leadership	$7,880,000	$8,872,000	6,156,000
Community impact leadership	5,031,000	6,008,000	9,051,000
Investor relations	6,639,000	5,944,000	5,446,000
Center for Community Leadership	6,519,000	5,622,000	4,972,000
Funds distribution	6,056,000	5,042,000	5,157,000
Cost of goods sold	3,266,000	3,226,000	2,940,000
Enterprise services	2,281,000	2,190,000	2,927,000
Campaign public relations	388,000	—	—
Selling expenses	325,000	1,448,000	1,123,000
Public policy	24,715,000	14,531,000	2,258,000
Total Program Expenses:	**$63,100,000**	**$52,883,000**	**$43,713,000**
Total income	$68,115,000	$74,225,000	$44,642,000
Program expenses	63,100,000	52,883,000	43,713,000
Fund-raising expenses	577,000	616,000	78,000
Administrative expenses	9,934,000	6,504,000	4,489,000
Total expenses	$73,611,000	$60,003,000	$48,280,000
Income in excess of expenses	(5,496,000)	14,222,000	(3,638,000)
Beginning net assets	25,968,000	11,087,000	15,973,000
Changes in net assets	(5,076,000)	14,881,000	(4,886,000)
Ending net assets	$20,892,000	$25,968,000	$11,087,000
Total liabilities	$76,624,000	$52,626,000	$46,364,000
Total assets	$97,516,000	$78,594,000	$57,451,000

Source: United Way of America, http://national.unitedway.org/about/form990.cfm.

Exhibit 4a *Forbes* 2006 25 Largest U.S. Charities

Name	Total Revenue ($ millions)	Total Expenses ($ millions)	Surplus/Loss ($ millions)	Net Assets ($ millions)
Mayo Clinic	6,118	5,606	512	3,546
Salvation Army	5,300	2,748	2,516	9,334
YMCAs in the United States	5,104	4,468	363	NA
United Way	4,175	4,175	0	NA
Cleveland Clinic Foundation	4,004	3,702	302	1,770
American National Red Cross	3,842	3,397	445	2,646
Catholic Charities USA	3,385	3,318	67	NA
New York Presbyterian Hospital	2,858	2,566	293	3,053
Goodwill Industries International	2,653	2,511	143	1,542
The Arc of the United States	2,211	2,149	62	714
Memorial Sloan-Kettering Cancer Center	1,973	1,605	368	3,553
Mount Sinai	1,927	1,864	63	828
Children's Hospital of Philadelphia	1,623	1,470	154	1,271
Cedars-Sinai Medical Center	1,566	1,472	94	919
Henry Ford Health System	1,535	1,440	96	321
Boys & Girls Clubs of America	1,329	1,180	149	2,436
AmeriCares	1,320	1,076	244	328
Habitat for Humanity International	1,022	801	220	1,442
Beth Israel Deaconess Medical Center	995	946	70	407
American Cancer Society	938	866	71	1,304
Nature Conservancy	936	602	334	3,852
World Vision	905	870	35	169
Planned Parenthood Federation of America	902	847	55	839
Children's Hospital	888	775	113	698
Gifts in Kind International	860	866	−6	67

Source: Forbes.com, http://www.forbes.com/lists/2006/14/pf_phil_06charities_The-200-Largest-U.S.-Charities_TotalRev.html.

of $1.9 million from the charity, which she had used to purchase race horses for her personal farm. Also in 2003, Pipeline, Inc., a spin-off from the California Bay Area United Way created to collect contributions, was investigated for losing $18 million when the financial records did not accurately reflect the amount owed the charity.[12] In 2006, a former CEO of the United Way of New York City was investigated for diverting organizational assets valued at $227,000 for his own personal use.[13]

To be fair, United Way was not the only high-profile charity to experience these kinds of problems since 2002. After 9-11 and Katrina, the American Red Cross had come under scrutiny for misdirection of disaster funds. In addition, the bookkeeper at Easter Seals of Iowa had stolen $230,000, the former president and seven others at Goodwill Industries of California embezzled $26 million, the financial administrator of the American Heart Association of New Jersey was convicted of a theft of $186,000, and an executive at Goodwill Industries of Michigan was found guilty of stealing $750,000 from the agency over a 23-year period.[14] What could be done to curtail this disturbing trend?

The United Way of America's board during the Aramony scandal contained many Fortune 500 CEOs who were, according to Aramony, fully informed about his

Exhibit 4b *Forbes* 2006 10 Largest Charities by Revenue

Name	Total Revenue ($ millions)	Total Expenses ($ millions)	Charitable Commitment[1]	Fundraising Efficiency[2]	Donor Dependency[3]
Mayo Clinic	6,118	5,606	94% —	91% ▲	−92% ▲
Salvation Army	5,300	2,748	83% —	96% ▲	30% ▼
YMCAs in the United States	5,104	4,468	81% ▼	89% ▼	64% ▲
United Way	4,175	4,716	82% ▼	91% —	100% —
Cleveland Clinic Foundation	4,004	3,702	90% ▼	93% ▼	−154% ▲
American National Red Cross	3,842	3,397	92% ▲	91% ▲	66% ▼
Catholic Charities USA	3,385	3,318	89% ▼	94% ▲	90% ▲
New York Presbyterian Hospital	2,858	2,566	77% ▼	93% ▼	−116% ▼
Goodwill Industries International	2,653	2,511	83% ▼	97% ▲	66% ▼
The Arc of the United States	2,211	2,149	89% ★	77% ★	30% ★

[1]Charitable services as percent of total expenses.

[2]Percent of private support tremaining after fundraising expenses.

[3]Percent of private support remaining after surplus.

A negative number indicates private support exceeded surplus.

▲Ratio increase from previous reported period.

▼Ratio decrease from previous reported period.

—Same as previously reported period.

★No comparable

Sources: *Forbes.com*, http://www.forbes.com/lists/2006/14/largest-american-charities-pf-philo_cz_wb_1122charities_land.html.

compensation and perquisites.[15] Yet it appeared they still failed to exercise appropriate oversight, as did the boards at the DC and Michigan chapters. Finding committed and knowledgeable board members was critical to United Way's continued success. Given the federation model, each local chapter had its own board, recruited from community members who had not only fund-raising skills, but also relationships with local leaders, politicians, or even regulators. Many local United Ways wanted to distance themselves from the scandals at UWA and other high-profile chapters, and therefore tried to stress local leadership and board autonomy. Serving on such a board required a commitment to the community and to the goals of the local United Way, and, regardless of the degree of well-intentioned communication and disclosure, sometimes the goals of board members could have been in conflict.

A 2004 survey by McKinsey & Company of executives and directors at 32 of *Worth* magazine's top 100 nonprofit performers found that many nonprofit boards had recurring problems, one of which was consensus over mission and goals: "Only 46 percent of the directors we surveyed thought that other directors on their boards could both summarize the mission of the organizations they serve and present a vision of where those organizations hope to be in five years' time."

In addition, for an organization such as the United Way, the goals of the diverse stakeholders, both donors and recipients, may have differed widely. This lack of consensus, coupled with the difficulty of measuring and evaluating performance, meant that nonprofit boards in general needed to practice serious self-scrutiny: "The time when nonprofit boards were populated by wealthy do-gooders who just raised money, hired CEO's, and reaffirmed board policy is over."[16]

In 2006, more than 1.8 million nonprofit organizations in the United States controlled upward of $2.5 trillion in assets, received revenues of $1.25 trillion, and were increasingly relied upon to help address both gaps in federal, state, and local governments' support after natural and manmade disasters, and the lingering affects of society's general ills. Given the degree to which the public trust had been violated after nonprofits were found to be acting irresponsibly, the Senate Finance Committee was considering "tax-exempt reform containing provisions similar to those found in the Sarbanes-Oxley Act."[17]

This demand for greater accountability was not new. Nonprofits had been sometimes notoriously ineffective at accomplishing their social missions; inefficient at getting maximum return on the money they raised due to high administration costs; willing to take

Exhibit 5   Watchdog Agencies—Information Resources for Nonprofits

- AICPA Audit Committee Nonprofit Toolkit
  http://www.aicpa.org/audcommctr/toolkitsnpo/
  homepage.htm
- American Institute of Philanthropy
  http://www.charitywatch.org
- Governance Matters
  http://www.governancematters.com
- Better Business Bureau Wise Giving Alliance
  http://www.give.org
- Board Source
  http://www.boardsource.org
- Charity Navigator
  http://www.charitynavigator.org
- Guidestar
  http://www.guidestar.com
- Independent Sector
  http://www.independentsector.org
- IRS Exempt Organizations
  http://www.irs.gov/charities

- Internet Nonprofit Center
  http://www.nonprofits.org
- National Association of Attorneys General
  http://www.naag.org
- National Association of State Charity Officials
  http://www.nasconet.org
- National Council for Nonprofit Organizations
  http://www.ncna.org
- New York State Attorney General
  http://www.oag.state.ny.us/charities/charities.html
- Nonprofit Financial Center
  http://www.nfconline.orgn
- OMB Watch
  http://www.ombwatch.org
- Philanthropy Foundation
  http://ephilanthropy.org
- Standards for Excellence Institute
  http://www.standardsforexcellenceinstitute.org

on too much risk, either through inexperience or ignorance; and, sometimes because of lax oversight procedures, those individuals in control of the nonprofits were willing to engage in outright fraud, acquiring excessive benefits for themselves. These problems were enhanced due to nonprofits' failure to provide extensive analysis, disclosure, and dissemination of relevant performance information, and due to the lack of sanctions.[18] If nonprofit organizations would not police themselves, watchdog agencies would create external standards and provide public feedback, sometimes to the detriment of the organization under scrutiny (see Exhibit 5).[19]

Gallagher's Strategic Response

In 2006 then United Way of America CEO Brian Gallagher was invited back by the U.S. Senate Finance Committee to participate in a roundtable discussion on needed reforms in nonprofit boards and governance. He was prepared to provide specific commentary. Since accepting the CEO position in 2001, Gallagher had been working to promote a change in the United Way strategy, including a change in mission, the creation of standards of performance excellence, and a requirement that local members certify their adherence to the membership standards.

Regarding the mission of United Way, Gallagher had worked to change the focus from fundraising to community impact—from "how much money did we raise?" to "how much impact did we have on our community?" In his initial statement to the Senate Committee at their first meeting in 2005, Gallagher said:

> The ultimate measure of success is whether family violence rates have gone down and whether there is more affordable housing. And fundraising is [just] part of making that happen. When you are asking people to contribute, you're asking for an investment in your mission. And like a for profit business, you are then accountable to your investors, not just for keeping good books, but for creating value and offering a concrete return. For those of us in human development, that means efforts that lead to measurable improvements in people's lives. In other words, the organizations that produce the greatest results should grow and be rewarded. Those that do not should be forced to change or go out of business. The American public doesn't give us money just because our operations are clean. Why they really give us money is because they want to make a difference.[20]

As a result of the new mission, UWA required local affiliates to provide the national headquarters with annual financial reports, and to embrace the revised standards of excellence developed by more than 200 United Way employees, volunteers, and consultants. Of interest is the fact that these standards were not mandatory but were presented as guidelines, giving chapters suggestions for how they might revise their local strategies. These standards urged the affiliates to identify community problems, raise money

Exhibit 6   United Way New Standards of Excellence

In March 2005, United Way of America unveiled new Standards of Excellence, a comprehensive description of benchmark standards and best practices. Developed in conjunction United Way executives, staff, and volunteers throughout the country, the standards are designed to enhance the effectiveness of the 1,350 United Way affiliates.

- **Introduction to the Standards of Excellence**—Spanning more than 100 pages, the new standards provide highly detailed descriptions regarding five key areas of operation.

- **Community Engagement and Vision**—Working with formal and informal leaders to develop a shared vision and goals for a community, including the identification of priority issues affecting the overall well-being of its citizens.

- **Impact Strategies, Resources, and Results**—Creating "impact strategies" that address the root causes and barriers of a community's priority issues; mobilizing essential assets such as people, knowledge, relationships, technology, and money; effectively implementing impact strategies; and evaluating the effectiveness of impact strategies in fostering continuous improvement.

- **Relationship Building and Brand Management**—Developing, maintaining, and growing relationships with individuals and organizations in order to attract and sustain essential assets.

- **Organizational Leadership and Governance**—Garnering trust, legitimacy, and support of the United Way in local communities through leadership and overall management.

- **Operations**—Providing efficient and cost-effective systems, policies, and processes that enable the fulfillment of the United Way's mission, while ensuring the highest levels of transparency and accountability.

Source: United Way of America Web site, http://national.unitedway.org/soe.

to solve them, and demonstrate measurable progress toward their goals by adopting a code of ethics that included an annual independent financial audit. The hope was that by adopting these guidelines, the chapters would be able to provide tangible proof to donors, especially wealthy contributors, that the United Ways and the charities they support were making a difference (see Exhibit 6).[21]

Local United Ways faced a continual challenge, with inevitable tension between the diverse constituencies they served: were their primary "customers" the donors who contribute needed funds or the agencies who were the recipients of these charitable donations? Or should the local United Way act as a networking institution, providing mechanisms for discussion of local problems and community service needs; or even going further to act as an activist organization, leading the way with comprehensive community planning, advocating major public policy, and redistributing resources as needed? Kirsten Gronbjerg, of the Center on Philanthropy, Indiana University, stated, "The activist role is very difficult for United Ways to play because they need to satisfy diverse constituency groups and therefore avoid conflict. As they become more donor driven institutions, they will be less able to take an activist approach just when such an approach is sorely needed."[22]

In addition, the local United Ways needed to maintain their internal consensus, providing a coherent and inspiring vision for their mainly volunteer workforce, while managing potential conflicts and sharing resources with other United Ways in their geographical areas. This problem of potentially scarce resources and corporate headquarters of traditional donor organizations either consolidating their physical operations or leaving an area meant the traditional broad base of business and industry was shrinking. This and other factors prompted the consolidation of several United Ways into more regional organizations. This movement meant potential savings and operational efficiencies from sharing marketing, financial management, and information technology functions,[23] however it also meant a possible diffusion of mission over a larger community, with a potential loss of focus, and more challenges for communicating this mission and marketing services to a more diverse donor and recipient base.

The ongoing issues faced by United Way in its 120-year history had remained constant. Consider this: during the holiday season, "When local United Way drives take place almost everywhere, likely as not questions will arise about what United Way is up to, how well it is doing what it claims to do, and for that matter, whether United Way is the best way for you to do your charitable giving."[24] This statement was written in 1977, yet could still apply in 2007. Concerns about United Way seemed timeless, and Brian Gallagher was only one in a long line of CEOs determined to answer the critics once and for all.

Endnotes

1. Barrett, W. P. 2006. United Way's new way. Forbes.com, 1/16/2006, retrieved from http://www.forbes.com/2006/01/12/united-way-philanthropy-cz_wb_0117unitedway.htr.

2. Barton, N. & Hall, H. 2006. A year of big gains. *The Chronicle of Philanthropy*, 10/26/2006, retrieved from http://philanthropy.com/free/articles/v19/i02/02000601.htm.

3. Barrett, op. cit.

4. Executive Summary of the Donor Expectations Survey, conducted by Princeton Survey Research Associates in the Spring of 2001, as reported by Give.org BBB Wise Giving Alliance, retrieved from http://www.give.org/news/survey1.asp.

5. Suchman, M. 1995. Managing legitimacy: Strategic and institutional approaches. *Academy of Management Review, 20,* 571–610.

6. From the United Way Web site, http://national.unitedway.org.

7. Contesting community: The transformation of workplace charity. Report on the book by Emily Barman, published by Stanford University Press, 2006, *Philanthropy News Digest,* posted 2/28/07 at http://foundationcenter.org/pnd/offtheshelf/ots_print.jhtml?id=171600045.

8. Barton & Hall, op. cit.

9. Charitable giving diversifies. *Forbes* Video Report, 12/13/2006, from http://www.forbes.com/video/?video=frn/business/ab_charity121306.

10. Porter, M. E., & Kramer, M. R. 1999. Philanthropy's new agenda; Creating value. *Harvard Business Review,* 77 (6): 121–130.

11. United Way ex-head sentenced to 7 years in prison for fraud. *The New York Times,* June 23, 1995, p. B2.

12. Gibelman, M., & Gelman, S. R. 2004. A loss of credibility: Patterns of wrongdoing among nongovernmental organizations. *International Journal of Voluntary and Nonprofit Organizations,* 15 (4): 355–381. This article provides a content analysis of worldwide NGO scandals from 2001–2004. Although the United States is overrepresented, it is certainly not alone in the world for incidents of wrongdoing.

13. Investigation finds former United Way of NYC CEO improperly diverted funds. *Philanthropy News Digest,* posted April 17, 2006 at http://foundationcenter.org/pnd/news/story_print.jhtml?id=140000004.

14. Gibelman & Gelman, op. cit.

15. Sinclair, M. 2002. William Aramony is back on the streets. *The NonProfit Times,* March 1.

16. Jansen, P., & Kilpatrick, A. 2004. The dynamic nonprofit board. *McKinsey Quarterly,* 2: 72–81.

17. Kelley, C., & Anderson, S. 2006. Advising nonprofit organizations. *CPA Journal,* 76 (8): 20–26.

18. Herzlinger, R. 1996. Can public trust in nonprofits and governments be restored? *Harvard Business Review,* March–April: 97–107.

19. Gibelman, & Gelman, op. cit.

20. Statement of Brian A. Gallagher, President and CEO United Way of America before United States Senate Committee on Finance, April 5, 2005, p. 1. Retrieved from http://national.unitedway.org.

21. Blum, D. E. 2005. Held to a new standard. *Chronicle of Philanthropy,* 17 (13).

22. United Way system at the crossroads: Valuable lessons from the United Way of Chicago. 2002. *Snapshots: Research Highlights from the Nonprofit Sector Research Fund,* The Aspen Institute, Nov/Dec, no. 26.

23. Gosier, C. 2007. 3 Chapters of United Way to combine. *Knight Ridder Tribune Business News,* February 23.

24. United Way: Are the criticisms fair? *Changing Times,* October 1977: 29.

Case 16 JetBlue Airlines: Is the Blue Fading?*

No other airline bore the brunt of bad weather as JetBlue did during Valentine's Day 2007. With hundreds of passengers stranded in the airports for more than 10½ hours, about half of its 500 daily flights canceled due to snow and ice, and over another 1,100 flights canceled due to the snowball effect of the Valentine's Day disaster, the otherwise dream airline company—JetBlue—is being called into question with respect to its operational efficacy (see Exhibit 1). In a major effort to protect its brand image and public relations, the company spent about $14 million for refunds and chartering other airplanes to fly its passengers and earmarked another $16 million in future free flights for the affected customers. David Neeleman, the CEO of JetBlue, apologized publicly and promised that such an event would not repeat ever again.[1]

Within a week's time, Morgan Stanley and others had downgraded JetBlue shares citing an estimated cost of $25 million to $30 million in pretax profits. William Greene, a Morgan Stanley analyst wrote in a research report that the stock is "dead money for now"(see Exhibit 2 for stock performance). In embarking on the repair measures, David

* This case study was prepared by Naga Lakshmi Damaraju of The Ohio State University, Alan B. Eisner, Pace University, and Gregory G. Dess of the University of Texas at Dallas. This case study has been developed purely from secondary sources. The purpose of the case is to stimulate class discussion rather than illustrating effective or ineffective handling of a business situation. Copyright © 2007 Damaraju, Eisner, & Dess.

Neeleman announced a Customer Bill of Rights. The bill included promises such as notifying customers about delays and cancellations, as well as deplaning passengers from flights ground-delayed for five hours. "This is a big wake-up call for JetBlue," said Neeleman adding "If there's a silver lining, it is the fact that our airline is going to be stronger and even better prepared to serve our customers."

However, the wake-up call seems to have come otherwise. Within less than three months from the meltdown, Neeleman was pushed out from being the CEO in May 2007. Dave Barger, the chief operating officer and an airline veteran, took his place. Neeleman has been the chief executive since 1998, but now will continue as the chairman. Some experts opine that JetBlue was already heading towards a leadership change even before the operations meltdown in February 2007. "That might have been the final straw but they were moving in that direction already," said Neidl, who downgraded his recommendation to neutral after its April 2007 earnings report. "JetBlue has reached a certain size where they need tough, experienced managers." Neeleman said he agreed with the decision to make a management change. "When you're a founder and an entrepreneur and you get mired in the operation, it's not good for anybody. This is a much better structure for us going forward. That was the board's recommendation, and I said, 'Great, let's do it'." So is a change in management going to fix the problems at JetBlue? Or is the problem deeper?[2]

	Cancellations	As share of airline's total flights
American	914	13.4%
United	865	17.1
US Airways	728	19.6
JetBlue	634	39.6
Continental	119	3.7

Exhibit 1 Flight cancellations Feb. 13–15, 2007 due to severe weather
Source: FlightStats

Exhibit 2 JetBlue's Stock Performance vs. Southwest vs. S&P 500

Source: http://finance.yahoo.com/.

The U.S. Airline Industry[3]

Deregulation of the U.S. airline industry in 1978 ushered in competition in the previously protected industry. Several low-cost, low-fare operators entered the competitive landscape that Southwest pioneered. In 1971 Southwest initiated service as a regional carrier, but by 1990 it became a major airline when its revenues crossed the $1 billion mark.[4] The Southwest model was based on operating a single-type aircraft fleet with high utilization, a simplified fare structure with single-class seating, and high productivity from its human and physical assets. On the other hand, the "hub-and-spoke" system, increased labor costs, and increases in multitype aircraft fleets bloated the cost structure of the major airlines. There are three primary segments in the airline industry: major airlines, regional airlines, and low-fare airlines. Major U.S. airlines, as defined by the Department of Transportation, are those with annual revenues of over $1 billion. Eleven passenger airlines belong to this category, the largest of which include American Airlines, Continental Airlines, Delta Air Lines, Northwest Airlines, and United Airlines. These airlines offer scheduled flights to most large cities within the United States and abroad and also serve numerous smaller cities. Most major airlines adopted the hub-and-spoke route system. In this system, the operations are concentrated in a limited number of hub cities while other destinations are served by providing one-stop or connecting service through the hub. As of the beginning of 2007, there are 16 major airlines. Regional airlines typically operate smaller aircraft on lower-volume routes than major airlines. Unlike the low-fare airlines, the regional airlines do not have an independent route system. They typically enter into relationships with major airlines and carry their passengers on the "spoke"—that is, between a hub or larger city and a smaller city. There are five regional major U.S. airlines as of 2007. The low-fare airlines, on the other hand, operate from "point to point" and have their own route system. The target segment of low-fare airlines is fare-conscious leisure and business travelers who might otherwise have used alternative forms of transportation or not traveled at all. Low-fare airlines stimulated demand in this segment and also have been successful in weaning business travelers from the major airlines. There are four major low-cost U.S. airlines. The main bases of competition in the airline industry are fare pricing, customer service, routes served, flight schedules, types of aircraft, safety record and reputation, code-sharing relationships, in-flight entertainment systems, and frequent flyer programs.

The economic downturn in the late 1990s and the terrorist attacks on the World Trade Center and the Pentagon on September 11, 2001, severely affected the airline industry. The demand for air travel dropped significantly and led to a reduction in traffic and revenue. Security concerns, security costs, and liquidity concerns increased. Lower fares and also increased capacity of the low-cost airlines created a very unprofitable environment for traditional network. Most of the traditional network airlines, since 2001, have filed for bankruptcy or undergone financial restructuring, mergers and/or consolidations. With these restructurings, many of them are able to significantly reduce labor costs, restructure debt, and have generally gained a more competitive cost structure. The major airlines are able to provide innovative offerings similar to those of low-cost airlines while still maintaining their alliances, frequent flier programs, and expansive route networks. The gap between low-cost airlines and traditional network airlines has been diminishing quite drastically. In 2005 and 2006, the industry experienced further consolidation and this could result in further rationalized route structures and lower operating costs, which could lead to aggressive competition in the future.[5]

Neeleman and JetBlue[6]

Born in São Paulo, Brazil, and brought up in Salt Lake City, David Neeleman dropped out of the University of Utah after his freshman year to move back to Brazil and become a missionary. After two years of missionary work, he made his modest beginning in establishing his own business by renting out condominiums in Hawaii. He then established his own travel agency and began chartering flights from Salt Lake City to the islands to bring in prospective clients for his rental services. Neeleman's sales prowess caught the attention of June Morris, who owned one of Utah's largest corporate travel agencies. Soon after, in 1984, Neeleman and Morris launched the Utah-based "Morris Air," a charter operation. Morris Air was closely modeled after Southwest Airlines, the legendary discount airlines in the United States. Neeleman considered Herb Kelleher, Southwest's founder, his idol. He studied everything Kelleher accomplished and tried to do it better, which meant keeping costs low and turning planes around quickly, among a host of other operational and strategic activities/choices. While following the Southwest model, Neeleman brought his own innovations into the business. He pioneered the use of "at-home reservation agents"—routing calls to agents' homes to save money on office rent and infrastructure expense. He also developed the first electronic ticketing system in the airline industry. By 1992 Morris Air had grown into a regularly scheduled airline and was ready for an initial public offering (IPO) when Southwest, impressed by Morris's low costs and high revenue, bought the company for $129 million. Neeleman became the executive vice president of Southwest. However, Neeleman could not adjust to Southwest's pace of doing things. By 1994, he was at odds with the top executives and left after signing a five-year noncompete agreement. In the interim between leaving Southwest and establishing JetBlue, Neeleman developed the electronic ticketing system he initiated at Morris Air into one of the world's simplest airline reservation systems: Open Skies. He sold Open Skies to Hewlett-Packard in 1999. During the same period, he was also a consultant to a low-fare Canadian start-up airline, WestJet Airlines.[7] After the completion of the noncompete agreement with Southwest Airlines in 1999, Neeleman launched his own airline. He raised about $130 million of capital in a span of two weeks, an unprecedented amount for a start-up airline.[8] Weston Presidio Capital and Chase Capital, venture capital firms that backed Neeleman's prior ventures, were return investors, and financier George Soros was also brought into the deal. "David's a winner; I knew anything David touched would turn to gold," said Michael Lazarus of Weston Presidio Capital, which had earlier funded Morris Air. "We were intrigued with his ideas about a low-cost airline."[9] With such strong support from venture capitalists, JetBlue began as the highest funded start-up airline in U.S. aviation history.

JetBlue commenced operations in August 2000, with John F. Kennedy International Airport (JFK) as its primary base of operations. In 2001 JetBlue extended its operations to the West Coast from its base at Long Beach Municipal Airport, which served the Los Angeles area. In 2002 the company went public and was listed on the Nasdaq as JBLU. JetBlue had expected to sell 5.5 million shares at about $24 to $26 in its initial public offering. Instead, it sold 5.87 million shares at $27 per share through its lead underwriters Morgan Stanley and Merrill Lynch. The shares closed at $47, up by $18, on the first day of trading. Jet Blue's stock offering was one of the hottest IPOs of the year.[10] Jet Blue was established with the goal of being a leading low-fare passenger airline that offered customers a differentiated product and high-quality customer service. It was positioned as a low-cost, low-fare airline providing quality customer service on point-to-point routes. JetBlue had a geographically diversified flight schedule that included both short-haul and long-haul routes. The mission of the company, according to David Neeleman, was "to bring humanity back to air travel." The airline focused on underserved markets and large metropolitan areas that had high average fares in order to stimulate demand. The "JetBlue effect" aspired to create fares going down, traffic going up, and JetBlue ending up with a big chunk of business (Exhibit 3).

JetBlue was committed to keeping its costs low. To achieve this objective, the company originally operated a single-type aircraft fleet comprising Airbus A320 planes as opposed to the more popular but costly Boeing 737. The

Exhibit 3 The JetBlue Effect

Route	Increase in Daily Passengers %	Decrease in Average Fare %	JetBlue's Share of Local Traffic %
New York to Miami/Ft. Lauderdale	14%	17% (to $121.50)	23.1%
New York to Los Angeles Basin	2	26 (to $219.31)	18.0
New York to Buffalo	94	40 (to $86.09)	61.2

Figures as of second quarter, 2003.

Source: Data from Back Aviation Solutions: adapted from W. Zellner. 2004. Is JetBlue's flight plan flawed? *BusinessWeek*, February 16.

Exhibit 4 JetBlue's Growth

| Year | Destinations | Employees | Operating Aircraft | | |
			Owned	Leased	Total
2000	12	1,174	4	6	10
2001	18	2,361	9	12	21
2002	20	4,011	21	16	37
2003	21	5,433	29	24	53
2004	30	7,211	44	25	69
2005	33	9,021	61	31	92
2006	49	10,377	70	49	119

Source: JetBlue SEC filings 2006.

A320s had 162 seats compared to 132 seats in the Boeing 737. According to JetBlue, the A320 was thus cheaper to maintain and also was more fuel-efficient. Since all of Jet-Blue's planes were new, the costs of maintenance were also lower. In addition, the single type of aircraft kept training costs low and increased manpower utilization. JetBlue was the first to introduce the "paperless cockpit" in which pilots, equipped with laptops, had ready access to flight manuals that were constantly updated at headquarters. As a result, pilots could quickly calculate the weight and balance and take-off performance of the aircraft instead of having to download and print the manuals for making the calculations. The paperless cockpit thus ensured faster take-offs by reducing paperwork and helped in achieving quicker turnarounds and higher aircraft utilization.[11] There were no meals served on the planes, and pilots even had to be ready, if need be, to do the cleanup work on the plane to keep the time the aircraft was on the ground as short as possible. This was further helped by the airline's choice of less congested airports.[12] Innovation was everywhere; for example, there were no paper tickets to lose and no mileage statements to mail to frequent fliers. With friendly, customer service-oriented employees, new aircraft, roomy leather seats with 36 channels of free LiveTV, 100 channels of free XM satellite radio and movie channel offerings from FOX-Inflight, and wider legroom (one row of seats was removed from its A320 aircraft to create additional space), JetBlue promises its customers a distincitive flying experience, the "JetBlue Experience." With virtually no incidences of passengers being denied boarding; high completion factors (99.6 percent as compared to other major airlines which are at 98.3 percent); lowest incidence of delayed, mishandled or lost bags; and third lowest customer complaints, the company was indeed setting standards for low-cost operations in the industry. The company was voted the best domestic airline in the Conde Nast Traveler's Readers' Choice Awards for the fifth consecutive year and was rated the

World's Best Domestic Airline by readers of *Travel + Leisure Magazine* in 2006. In addition, it also earned the Passenger Service Award from *Air Transport World*.[13]

Expansion and Growth

Within a span of seven years of its existence, JetBlue grew to serve more than 50 destinations in 21 states, Puerto Rico, Mexico, and the Carribean. Service to about 17 new destinations began in 2006 (see Exhibit 4). In March 2007, JetBlue added services from White Plains, New York to Florida and in April 2007, it expanded services from Boston to San Diego and the Caribbean Island of Aruba. Also in summer 2007, it plans to double its services from Salt Lake City and to launch new services from this destination to San Diego and San Francisco.[14]

On the other hand, the clear divergence from its original model can be seen. From operating a single aircraft type, which was the basis of having low training costs, flexibility in manpower management, etc., the airline moved to include a second type of aircraft, the Embraer 190. The company is still not comfortable operating this type of plane. Also, JetBlue acquired LiveTV, LLC, in 2002 for $41 million in cash and the retirement of $39 million of LiveTV debt.[15] Further, the company is embarking on other paths where it does not necessarily have prior experience. On February 6, 2007, *USA Today* announced that JetBlue plans to enter into an alliance with Aer Lingus, an Irish flag carrier. The alliance is expected to facilitate easy transfers to both airlines' customers but will not allow either airline to sell seats on the other airline, unlike traditional codeshare alliances, meaning customers must make individual reservations with both carriers.[16] On February 14, 2007, the first codeshare agreement with Cape Air was announced. Under this agreement, JetBlue passengers from Boston's Logan Airport will be carried to Cape Air's destinations throughout Cape Cod and the surrounding islands. Under

Exhibit 5 Statements of Operations Data[19]

Statements of Operations Data (in $ millions, except per share data)	Year Ended December 31				
	2006	2005	2004	2003	2002
Operating revenues	2,363	1,701	1,265	998	635
Operating expenses					
Salaries, wages, and benefits	553	428	337	267	162
Aircraft fuel	752	488	255	147	76
Landing fees and other rents	158	112	92	70	44
Depreciation and amortization	151	115	77	51	27
Aircraft rent	103	74	70	60	41
Sales and marketing	104	81	63	54	44
Maintenance materials and repairs	87	64	45	23	9
Other operating expenses	328	291	215	159	127
Total operating expenses	2,236	1,653	1,154	831	530
Operating income	127	48	111	167	105
Government compensation	—	—	—	23	—
Other income (expense)	−118	−72	−36	−16	−10
Income (loss) before income taxes	9	−24	75	174	95
Income tax expense (benefit)	10	−4	29	71	40
Net income (loss)	−1	−20	46	103	55
Earnings (loss) per common share					
Basic	—	−0.13	0.3	0.71	0.49
Diluted	—	−0.13	0.28	0.64	0.37
Other Financial Data					
Operating margin %	5.4	2.8	8.8	16.8	16.5
Pre-tax margin %	0.4	−1.4	5.9	17.4	15
Ratio of earnings to fixed charges	—	—	1.6	3.1	2.7
Net cash provided by operating activities	274	170	199	287	217
Net cash used in investing activities	−1,307	−1,276	−720	−987	−880
Net cash provided by financing activities	1,037	1,093	437	789	657

this agreement, customers on both airlines will be able to purchase seats on both airlines under one reservation.

On the other hand, high fuel prices, the competitive pricing environment, and other cost increases, are making it increasingly difficult to fund JetBlue's growth profitability. The airline suffered its first ever losses after its IPO in 2005. It posted net loss of $1 million and $20 million for the years ending December 31, 2006 and 2005, respectively, with the primary reasons being rising fuel costs (see Exhibit 5 and Exhibit 6). In 2006, the company modified its growth plans by reducing the number of Airbus A320 aircraft and Embraer 190 aircraft to be delivered through 2010 and by selling five Airbus A320 aircraft. In its 10-k for 2006, the company also stated it will reduce its future growth plans from previously announced levels. As much touted as its unique culture is, in 2006, the IAM (International Association of Machinists) attempted to unionize JetBlue's ramp service workers. Though the union organizing petition was dismissed by the National Mediation Board because fewer than 35 percent of eligible employees

Exhibit 6   Operating Statistics (Unaudited)[20]

Operating Statistics (Unaudited)*					
	Year Ended December 31				
	2006	2005	2004	2003	2002
Revenue passengers ($ thousands)	18,565	14,729	11,783	9,012	5,752
Revenue passenger miles ($ millions)	23,320	20,200	15,730	11,527	6,836
Available seat miles (ASMs) ($ millions)	28,594	23,703	18,911	13,639	8,240
Load factor %	81.6	85.2	83.2	84.5	83
Breakeven load factor (%)*	81.4	86.1	77.9	72.6	71.5
Aircraft utilization (hours per day)	12.7	13.4	13.4	13	12.9
Average fare ($)	119.73	110.03	103.49	107.09	106.95
Yield per passenger mile (cents)	9.53	8.02	7.75	8.37	9
Passenger revenue per ASM (cents)	7.77	6.84	6.45	7.08	7.47
Operating revenue per ASM (cents)	8.26	7.18	6.69	7.32	7.71
Operating expense per ASM (cents)	7.82	6.98	6.1	6.09	6.43
Operating expense per ASM, excluding fuel (cents)	5.19	4.92	4.75	5.01	5.51
Airline operating expense per ASM (cents)*	7.76	6.91	6.04	6.08	6.43
Departures	159,152	112,009	90,532	66,920	44,144
Average stage length (miles)	1,186	1,358	1,339	1,272	1,152
Average number of operating aircraft during period	106.5	77.5	60.6	44	27
Average fuel cost per gallon ($)	1.99	1.61	1.06	0.85	0.72
Fuel gallons consumed (millions)	377	303	241	173	106
Percent of sales through jetblue.com during period	79.1	77.5	75.4	73	63
Full-time equivalent employees at period end*	9,265	8,326	6,413	4,892	3,572

*This excludes results of employees and operations of LiveTV LLC that are unrelated to the airline operations.

Note: See Case Appendix for a glossary of terms used.

supported an election, unionization is a possibility going forward.[17] What all this means to JetBlue's cultural fabric remains yet to be seen.

The Operations Meltdown and Beyond[18]

Valentine's Day 2007 is perhaps the nightmare in JetBlue's hitherto glorious history for more than one reason. The event not only destroyed JetBlue's reputation for customer friendliness and cost Neeleman his job, but it also exposed the critical weaknesses in the systems at the airline that keep the operations going.

There was trouble in the Midwest for several days before the Valentine's Day storm reached the East Coast. Unlike the blowing snow and frigid temperatures that were occurring in cities like Chicago, the storm turned into freezing rain and sleet, slamming the mid-Atlantic region,

causing havoc on major highways, and virtually shutting down airports. Most other airlines cancelled dozens of flights in preparation for the storm. However, JetBlue management opted to wait it out. With its policy to do whatever it can to ensure a flight is completed, even if it means waiting for several hours, the airline sent outbound flights to the runway at John F. Kennedy airport in New York at about 8 a.m. This was to ensure that they were ready to take off as soon as the weather let up. But instead of letting up, the weather only deteriorated further. The federal aviation guidelines do not allow planes to take off in ice pellet conditions, and so soon planes and equipment were literally freezing to the tarmac. By about 3 p.m., with no hope of getting planes off the ground, the airline began calling in buses to bring passengers back to the terminal. However, the damage was done by then. Airport terminals, more so in the JFK hub, were filled with passengers still expecting to get on flights, and compounding the problem, they were now being joined by hundreds of infuriated passengers getting off planes. "Things spiraled out of control. We did a horrible job," said Neeleman in a conference call early the next week. "We got ourselves into a situation where we were doing rolling cancellations instead of a massive cancellation. Communications broke down, we weren't able to reach out to passengers and they continued to arrive at the airports . . . it had a cascading effect." The chaotic situation could not be brought under control for another week.

A number of shortcomings in the company's information systems were responsible for this debacle, according to Charles Mees, the new CIO who joined the company a few months before the event. The reservation system, for example, was not expanded enough to meet the extreme customer call volume. As the seriousness of the Valentine's Day situation became apparent, managers with JetBlue's Salt Lake City–based reservation office began calling in off-duty agents to assist with the expected high volume of calls. These agents otherwise primarily work from their homes, using an Internet-based communications system to tap into the company's Navitaire Open Skies reservation system (headquarted in Minneapolis, Navitaire hosts the reservation system for JetBlue and about another dozen discount airlines). The passengers who were bumped off or arrived at JFK and other East Coast airports to find their JetBlue flights had been cancelled had only one option to rebook their flights: call the JetBlue reservation office. JetBlue customers did not have an option to rebook their flights via its Web site using airport kiosks. The company has been working on the online rebooking issue since December 2006 but the new feature was not yet ready to be rolled out by February 2007. As a result, the Salt Lake City reservation agents were suddenly flooded with calls from irate passengers looking to get on another flight or to find out compensation possibilities. With Mees's emergency call to Navitaire, the system could be boosted to accommodate up to 950 agents at one time (up 300 from the original 650), but then it hit a wall. Even with the boosted capacity, there was difficulty finding enough bodies to staff the phones. Off-duty crews and airport personnel volunteered for the task, but they were not trained in how to use the system.

Also in a mess was the baggage-handling mechanism. As passengers struggled through to get reservations, their bags piled up in huge mounds at airports. Very interestingly, JetBlue did not have a computerized system in place for recording and tracking lost bags. Since the airline hardly ever cancelled flights, if there were bags left over at the end of a flight, airport personnel figured out ownership by looking up a passenger's record. However, such a process became totally unmanageable with massive cancellations happening. The airline had entered into an agreement earlier with Lufthansa in 2003 to purchase a system called BagScan, but the system was never implemented. Mees admits, "We didn't prioritize it—probably because it is so

focused on the SAP Project." JetBlue was growing fast and needed increased capabilities in the SAP ERP system to handle its human resources functions.

There were other systems headaches to deal with. JetBlue uses several applications from Sabre Airline solutions of Southlake, Texas, as part of its core operations infrastructure. This is in addition to the Navitaire reservation system. The application, Sabre Flight Control Suite, provides the airline utilities to manage, schedule, and track its planes and crews, while Sabre's Dispatch Manager is used to develop actual flight plans. Another application, Flite Trac, within the Flight Control Suite, interfaces with the Navitaire reservation system. This application provides real-time information to managers on factors such as flight status; fuel information; passenger lists; and the original, revised, estimated, and actual arrival times. Sabre CrewTrac is another application that tracks crew assignments, ensures legal requirements are met, and provides pilots and flight attendants with access to their schedules via a secure Web portal. During this disastrous event, there was a glitch between these Sabre applications and Navitaire's SkySolver that JetBlue uses to figure out the best way to emerge from flight disruptions.

Neeleman said, "We had so many people in the company who wanted to help who weren't trained to help. We had an emergency control center full of people who didn't know what to do. I had flight attendants sitting in hotel rooms for three days who couldn't get a hold of us. I had pilots e-mailing me saying, 'I'm available, what do I do?'" Mees says he does not have an idea why the information could not be transferred or why the system incompatibility could not be discovered beforehand. He, of course, added that there were other day-to-day priorities to manage. "In the heat of battle at any rapidly growing company, you're always trying to address your most immediate needs," Mees said. "But you've got to continually remind yourself that you have to take a step back and look at the things that aren't right in front of you—find out what the tipping points are—before they can impact you."

Southwest by contrast handled the Valentine's Day weather disaster with ease by simply canceling most services during this period. It looked as if JetBlue had completely missed out on this obvious solution (see Exhibit 7 for direct competitor comparison).

The airline's reputation was hitting rock-bottom. Apart from announcing huge compensations to customers as refunds and future flights, which were to cost the airline about $30 million, Neeleman quickly announced the new Customer Bill of Rights. This Customer Bill of Rights basically outlined self-imposed penalties for JetBlue and major rewards for its passengers if the airline experienced operational problems and could not adjust to weather-related cancellations within a "reasonable" amount of time. For example, the bill contained provisions for notifying customers of delays prior to scheduled departure, cancellations and diversions, and their causes. It also promises that the airline will take necessary action to deplane customers if an aircraft is ground-delayed for five hours. Further, if a flight landed and was unable to taxi in to a gate

Exhibit 7　Direct Competitor Comparison

	JetBlue	AMR Corp	Southwest	UAL Corp	Delta Airlines	Major Airlines
Market Capitalization (billions)	$ 1.89	$ 6.22	$ 11.16	$ 3.76	$ 3.60	$ 3.81
Employees	8,393	86,600	32,664	55,000	51,300	49.96K
Quarterly Revenue Growth (yoy)	24.10%	1.60%	8.90%	−2.10%	11.40%	8.90%
Revenue (billions)	$ 2.48	$ 22.65	$ 9.27	$ 19.25	$ 17.60	$ 17.60
Gross Margin	30.88%	28.13%	62.99%	15.06%	18.14%	28.13%
EBITDA (millions)	$ 311	$ 2,570	$ 1,360	$ 1,530	$ 1,980	$ 1,530
Operating Margins	5.12%	5.27%	8.28%	2.43%	4.04%	4.38%
Net Income (millions)	$ 9	404	531	86	−4.260	275
EPS	0.051	1.5	0.652	0.738	−21.606	1.5
P/E	208.04	17.24	21.92	45.18	N/A	15.3

Source: http://finance.yahoo.com/ as of May, 2007.

right away, customers were to receive compensation between $25 to the full-amount of their one-way fare (in vouchers redeemable towards a future JetBlue flight), depending on the extent of delay.

All these announcements and even a public apology could, of course, not restore things to normalcy. Neeleman was pushed out as CEO on May 10, 2007. While this move is being framed as having been an already impending management change in view of JetBlue outgrowing being an entrepreneurial venture, is JetBlue standing on thinner ice than was thought earlier?

Endnotes

1. Bachman, J. 2007. JetBlue's fiasco could improve flying. *BusinessWeek* Online Edition, http://www.businessweek.com/bwdaily/dnflash/content/feb2007/db20070221_957314_page_2.htm.
2. http://money.cnn.com/2007/05/10/news/companies/jetblue/index.htm.
3. This section draws heavily from the SEC filings of JetBlue for the year 2007. Other sources include: Zellner, W. 2003. Look who's buzzing the discounters. *BusinessWeek,* November 24; Zellner, W. 2004. Folks are finally packing their bags. *BusinessWeek,* January 12; and a joint study by Kearney, A. T., & the Society of British Aerospace Companies, The emerging airline industry; www.atkearney.com/shared_res/pdf/Emerging_Airline_Industry_S.pdf.
4. www.southwest.com/about_swa/airborne.html.
5. JetBlue SEC filings, 2006.
6. This section draws heavily from Gajilan, A. T. 2004. The amazing JetBlue. Fortune Small Business, www.fortune/smallbusiness/articles/0.15114,444298-2,00.html.
7. Brazilian-American Chamber of Commerce of Florida. 2004. *Chamber News,* 2004 Excellence Award, www.brazilchamber.org/news/chambernews/ExcellenceAward2004.htm.
8. JetBlue Airways Corporation, *International directory of company histories;* http://galenet.galegroup.com.
9. Gajilan, 2004. Op. cit. DiCarlo, L. 2001. Management and trends, Jet Blue skies. Forbes.com, January 31, www.forbes.com/2001/01/31/0131jetblue.html.
10. JetBlue IPO soars. 2002. *CNNmoney,* April 12, http://money.cnn.com/2002/04/12/markets/ipo/jetblue/.
11. WEBSMART50. 2003. *BusinessWeek,* November 24: 92.
12. Interview with David Neeleman by Willow Bay of CNN Business Unusual. 2002. Aired June 23; www.cnn.com/TRANSCRIPTS/0206/23/bun.00.html.
13. JetBlue SEC filings, 2006.
14. From the company's press releases, www.jetblue.com.
15. From the company's press releases, www.jetblue.com.
16. JetBlue, Aer Lingus to forge world's first international discount alliance. www.usatoday.com. February 6, 2007.
17. Schlangenstein, M. 2006. No union vote for JetBlue. *Bloomberg News.* July 19. http://findarticles.com/p/articles/mi_qn4188/is_20060719/ai_n16541848.
18. This section draws heavily from the following sources: Bartholomew, D., & Duvall, M. 2007. What really happened at JetBlue?, http://www.baselinemag.com/article2/0,1397,2111614,00.asp; Bailey, J. 2007. Long delays hurt image of JetBlue. *The New York Times*, p. 1.
19. JetBlue SEC filings, 2006.
20. JetBlue SEC filings, 2006.

Appendix

aircraft utilization—The average number of block hours operated per day per aircraft for the total fleet of aircraft.

available seat miles—The number of seats available for passengers multiplied by the number of miles the seats are flown.

average fare—The average one-way fare paid per flight segment by a revenue passenger.

average stage length—Average number of miles flown per flight.

breakeven load factor—The passenger load factor that will result in operating revenues being equal to operating expenses, assuming constant revenue per passenger mile and expenses.

load factor—The percentage of aircraft seating capacity that is actually utilized (revenue passenger miles divided by available seat miles).

operating expense per available seat mile—Operating expenses divided by available seat miles.

operating revenue per available seat mile—Operating revenues divided by available seat miles.

passenger revenue per available seat mile—Passenger revenue divided by available seat miles.

revenue passenger miles—The number of miles flown by revenue passengers.

revenue passengers—The total number of paying passengers flown on all flight segments.

yield per passenger mile—The average amount one passenger pays to fly one mile.

Source: JetBlue. SEC filings, 2006.

Case 17   Panera Bread Co. in 2007*

Fuel and energy costs are at an all-time high. Interest rates are increasing. Wages aren't keeping pace with increasing costs, resulting in decreasing disposable incomes, and the restaurant industry is suffering. Casual dining restaurants saw a decline in sales during the summer of 2006. However, one segment of the restaurant industry is thriving as a result of consumers trading casual dining experiences for fast-casual meals. With over 100,000 quick-casual concept restaurants in the United States, there are plenty of choices for diners.[1]

When Panera's management team began building the artisan bread tradition over 14 years ago, they hoped to build Panera Bread into a place where people could slow down to enjoy "real food you crave and trust" with friends and family. They wanted to serve the best bread in America. Has Panera Bread achieved this? In 2006 in a survey conducted by Sandelman & Associates, Panera Bread was rated "Excellent" by 58 percent of the 76,000 consumers participating in the survey. The company has also been named "best bakery" and "best bread" by numerous magazines and newspapers throughout the country.[2] Can Panera continue this trend of providing a great customer experience in such a dynamic, competitive industry?

The Restaurant Industry

The National Restaurant Association reports there are 935,000 restaurant locations in the U.S. that are expected to serve over 70 billion meals and snacks in 2007. Sales in 2007 are predicted to be $537 billion. Restaurant industry sales are expected to grow 5 percent in 2007, which will equal 4 percent of the U.S. gross domestic product. The industry employs a total of 12.8 million people, which represents 9 percent of all people employed in the United States The restaurant industry is the largest employer in the United States outside of the government. For every additional $1 million in restaurant sales there are 37 jobs added in the industry. It is predicted that 2 million jobs will be added in the restaurant industry in the next 10 years, and by 2017, there will be 14.8 million people employed by restaurants. In 2005, the average household expenditure for food away from home was $2,634, or $1,054 per person.[3]

In the past, the restaurant industry has defined three main sectors: fast food (price ranges from $5 to $6), casual dining (prices ranges $10 to $12), and fine dining (price ranges over $20). According to Paul G. Fetscher, president of Great American Brokerage, "Fast-casual really hit the radar over the last three to four years. There was a gap in the [restaurant] market. People were spending $4 to $5 at [fast-food] restaurants or $10 at sit-down places."[4]

This gap in pricing and type of food has allowed the quick-casual segment to develop and grow. A common definition of quick-casual includes: a $7 to $10 price range, a five- to eight-minute order time, made-to-order food preparation, nice ambience and décor, and a system where customers place orders at a counter and the food is brought to the table. The quick-casual segment had $11 billion in sales in 2006, which accounted for about 9 percent of total industry sales. The segment is expected to grow 10.8 percent to 12.5 percent each year through 2009. Although 18- to 34-year-olds tend to buy the most fast-food, they now represent 37 percent of the quick-casual consumers.[5]

There are approximately 100,000 quick-casual concept restaurants in the United States. Competitors in this sector include: Panera Bread, Chipotle Mexican Grill, Café Express, New World Restaurants, Starbucks, Kahala Corp., Bear Rock Salads, Buffalo Wild Wings Grill and Bar, Noodles & Company, Camille's Café, and Atlanta Bread Company. Some restaurant companies have invested in multiple types of restaurants. Wendy's International owns Baja Fresh Mexican Grill, Café Express, and Pasta Pomodoro; McDonald's has ownership in Boston Market; Jack in the Box owns Qdoba Mexican Grill; and Raving Brands owns Moe's Southwest Grill, Plant Smoothie, Mama Fu's Asian House, and Doc Green's Gourmet Salads.

Revenues and sales growth information for the top fast-casual restaurants are shown in Exhibit 1.

Exhibit 1   **Restaurant Sales**

Restaurant	Revenue— 1 Year (millions), May 2007	1-Year Revenue Growth as of May 2007	3-Year Revenue Growth as of May 2007
Starbuck's	$3,578.3	22.3%	24.1%
P.F. Changs	$ 973.4	15.9%	20.2%
Panera Bread	$ 874.7	29.5%	31.6%
Chipotle, Inc.	$ 822.9	31.1%	37.7%
Krispy Kreme Donuts	$ 461.2	−15.1%	−10.8%
New World Restaurants	$ 390.9	0.2%	0.6%
Buffalo Wild Wings	$ 278.2	32.7%	30.0%
Kahala	$ 5.6	−42.1%	26.6%

Source: Reuters.com, May 2007.

There are a number of trends and events that are influencing the restaurant industry:

- Today's customer is demanding better quality food, better service, and better food safety and restaurateurs must meet these demands with innovative food preparation and service.[6]

* This case was prepared by Debora J. Gilliard, Ph.D. and Rajendra Khandekar, Ph.D. of Metropolitan State College–Denver as a basis for class discussion rather than to illustrate either effective or ineffective handling of an administrative situation. Copyright © 2007 by Debora J. Gilliard & Rajendra Khandekar.

- Companies will enter the industry using one-product concepts. Cereality serves only cereal with a number of toppings and milk choices. Peanut Butter and Co. is a sandwich shop that offers only varieties of peanut butter sandwiches. Franktitude is a gourmet hot dog chain that allows customers to customize hot dogs by choosing from a range of toppings and franks.[7]
- Consumers are requesting healthier menu options. Restaurants are offering trans fat-free foods, organic ingredients, and locally grown products.[8] Menu options will include wraps, chicken dishes, and energy drinks. Consumers will like menu flexibility.[9]
- Success in the quick-casual sector is forcing fast-food restaurants to change and upgrade their menus.[10]
- Increases in state and federal minimum wages will increase labor costs in the industry. Quick casual restaurants may try to continue their operations with lower levels of labor. The Senate Finance Committee is considering legislation that includes tax relief for restaurants in jurisdictions that are facing voter-mandated increases in minimum wages.[11]
- In the quick-casual segment there are four food flavors that will see growth: authentic Mexican, Pan Asian, Middle Eastern, and Mediterranean. Vamonos restaurant represents a trend away from Tex-Mex toward authentic Mexican; Pei Wei (a smaller version of P.F. Changs) and Mama Fu's offer Pan Asian foods; and Taverna Opa is a fast growing Greek restaurant chain.[12]
- Wine continues to grow in popularity and it is expected that quick-casual restaurants will add wine to their drink menus. Wine bars will continue to grow through 2007.[13]
- There will continue to be growth in the industry as many regional restaurant chains expand. Most prominent will be West Coast restaurant chains opening stores in the Southeast regions.

Restaurant Institutions reports that in the rapidly changing restaurant environment it is imperative for restaurants to engage in brand reengineering. Restaurants do this by changing their name to reflect changes in concepts, changes in menus, new signage, and new décor. Lee Peterson, executive director of the design group at WD Partners, a firm that works with chain restaurants, indicates that restaurants do not have set shelf lives, but they do have life cycles. He further indicates that concepts are destined to die out, but they do require refurbishing to survive. Peterson states, "Birth of the fast-casual segment made the quick-service industry realize it was aging. But that is healthy because it spurs reflection and improvement."[14] Mature brands will need to reinvent themselves in 2007. National chains will reposition themselves in 2007, and luxury brands will flourish. Restaurant concepts will develop smaller store formats and marketing practices will shift from mass media outlets to nontraditional outlets such as local store marketing, four-walls marketing, and public relations.[15]

Over the past three years the quick services restaurants have responded to trends by refreshing their menus and expanding into fast-casual concepts. The Hale Group[16] reports the McDonald's and Jack in the Box have introduced premium salads, Burger King has "fire-grilled" burgers, Arby's has had success with its Market Fresh Sandwiches, Subway is repositioning itself as a provider of healthy foods, and Schlotzsky's has introduced a healthy menu.

Panera Bread Company[17]

History[18]   Ron Shaich co-founded Au Bon Pain Co. in 1981 when three bakery-cafes and one cookie store were opened. The company continued to grow throughout the 1980s and 1990s. By the end of 1997, the company had 160 bakery-cafes in the United States mostly located on the East Coast, and 96 bakery-cafes internationally in Chile, the Philippines, Indonesia, Thailand, Brazil, and the United Kingdom. The company had bakery-cafes located in 9 domestic airports and 14 DoubleTree Hotels.

Twenty-five years ago Ken Rosenthal first tasted the sourdough bread that would become a vital part of Panera Bread. He was so taken by the bread's texture and flavor that he persuaded the family to sell him the sourdough starter. In October 1987, Ken packed the starter in a cooler and brought it back to St. Louis and he started the St. Louis Bread Co. The handcrafted bread became a favorite among local citizens of St. Louis and the concept soon evolved to include other breads, bagels, pastries, sandwiches, salads, and espresso beverages.

On December 22, 1993, the Au Bon Pain Co. purchased the St. Louis Bread Co. At the time, the St. Louis Bread Co. consisted of 19 company-owned and one franchised bakery-cafes that were located primarily in the St. Louis area, and Au Bon Pain Co. consisted of over 300 quick-service bakeries in the East. In 1998, Au Bon Pain Co.'s CEO, Ron Shaich, decided to build St. Louis Bread Co. into a national brand under the name Panera Bread. Panera means "time of bread" and the name change reflected the vision and focus of expanding the company: "The time of bread was dawning in America." In May 1999, Au Bon Pain Co., Inc. sold the Au Bon Pain bakery-cafe business unit and officially changed the corporate name to Panera Bread Company. In 2006, the company reported company bakery-cafe sales of $0.7 billion and franchise bakery sales of $1.2 billion. As of December 2006, the company had over 1,027 bakery-cafes in 38 states.

Company Concept and Strategy[19]

The company brings the tradition of freshly baked bread to neighborhoods. Only the highest quality ingredients are used and the bread is baked fresh every day—only fresh dough is used and no preservatives. Panera Bread is known for its handcrafted, fresh-baked, artisan bread

Exhibit 2 Panera Bread/St. Louis Bread Co. Bakery-Cafes

Sale	Company-Owned Bakery-Cafes	Franchise-Operated Bakery-Cafes	Total Bakery-Cafes
Alabama	10	—	10
Arkansas	—	3	3
California	17	32	49
Colorado	—	22	22
Connecticut	8	9	17
Delaware		3	3
Florida	20	58	78
Georgia	10	14	24
Iowa	2	15	17
Illinois	54	41	95
Indiana	29	—	29
Kansas	—	18	18
Kentucky	11	2	13
Massachusetts	2	29	31
Maryland	—	34	34
Maine	—	4	4
Michigan	39	13	52
Minnesota	—	25	25
Missouri	44	18	62
North Carolina	9	25	34
Nebraska	10	—	10
Nevada	—	4	4
New Hampshire	—	8	8
New Jersey	—	42	42
New York	26	20	46
Ohio	8	74	82
Oklahoma	—	17	17
Oregon	1	—	1
Pennsylvania	18	37	55
Rhode Island	—	5	5
South Carolina	7	4	11
South Dakota	1	—	1
Tennessee	9	12	21
Texas	9	17	26
Virginia	40	6	46
Washington	7	—	7
West Virginia	—	5	5
Wisconsin	—	20	20
Totals	**391**	**636**	**1,027**

and the company's mission is to put "a loaf of bread in every arm." Guests can relax in a warm atmosphere with free Internet access through a managed WiFi network as they enjoy wholesome and flavorful food. Managers at Panera Bread believe the distinctive menu offerings, quality of the bakery-cafe operations, the cafe design, and locations of the cafes are key to the company's success.

The menu, operating system, design, and real estate strategy allow Panera Bread to operate in several successful dayparts: breakfast, lunch, PM daytime "chill out," and dinner or the evening daypart. The company sells bread to take-home, provides on-premises sales, and sales through Via Panera® catering. In an effort to increase sales during the evening daypart (dinner), the company added a new product to the menu—the Crispani® a hand-crafted pizza.

The bakery-cafes are primarily located in suburban, strip mall and regional mall locations. As of December 26, 2006, the company operated 636 franchise-operated bakery-cafes and 391 company-owned bakery-cafes in 38 states as can be seen in Exhibit 2.

Panera Bread has received many awards over the years and has won "best of" awards in nearly every market in the 38 states it operates in.

In 1992, the company established Operation Dough-Nation® as a program that ensures Panera Bread contributes back into the community. The company donated over $1 million in 2006 to charities such as: local food banks and pantries, Meals On Wheels, Make a Wish Foundation, American Cancer Society, Special Olympics, and Habitat for Humanity. Through the Day-End Dough-Nation program, unsold loaves of bread and bakery items are taken to local food banks and charities. In 2006, the company donated over $12 million worth of bread products to nonprofits served by America's Second Harvest. The company has also developed a Dough For Funds® program that allows nonprofit groups to sell special coupons for Panera Bread products and keep half of the proceeds for their causes. Panera Bread has also entered into a partnership with the Scrip fundraising program that allows nonprofit organizations to pre-purchase $10 Panera Cards® at a 9 percent discounted rate and then resell the Panera Cards at full price.

Management The management team at Panera Bread Company is filled with individuals with a great deal of food service experience. Ron Shaich was the co-founder of Au Bon Pain Co. in 1981 and has been in the bakery-cafe business since that time. Today he is the Chairman and Chief Executive Officer of Panera Bread Co. He received his Bachelor of Arts degree in 1976 and a Master's Degree in Business Administration from Harvard Business School in 1978. Shaich was a national finalist for the 2004 Ernst & Young Entrepreneur of the Year award, received the Gold Plate Award from the International Foodservice Manufacturers Association in 2005, and in 2004 was honored as a Golden Chain Recipient by the Multi-Unit Foodservice Operators. Neal Yanofsky currently serves as President. He joined Panera Bread in June 2003 as Executive Vice President and Chief Administrative and Corporate Staff Officer. He worked as an independent business consultant specializing in strategy development for high growth firms. Panera Bread was one of his clients. He is a graduate of Harvard College and Harvard Business School, and was a postgraduate research fellow at London School of Economics. John Maguire serves as Executive Vice President. Prior to joining Panera Bread in 1994 he held various positions with Au Bon Pain Co. The top management team also includes: Mark Borland, Senior V.P. & Chief Supply Chain Officer; Scott G. Davis, Senior V.P. and Chief Concept Officer; Rebecca Fine, Senior V.P. & Chief People Officer; Patricia Gray, Senior V.P. & Chief Legal Officer; Jeffrey Kip, Senior V.P. and CFO; Thomas Kish, Senior V.P. and CIO; Michael Kupstas, Senior V.P. and Chief Franchise Officer; Michael Markowitz, Senior V.P. and Chief Brand Officer; and Michael Nolan, Senior V.P. and Chief Development Officer.

Company Operations

Menu The menu groups at Panera Bread include fresh baked goods, made-to-order sandwiches, Crispani pizzas, soups, salads, and cafe beverages. Company personnel are continually monitoring and revising menu offerings in order to satisfy customers. New menu items are developed in test kitchens and then tested in a few bakery-cafes to attain customer response and verify that the preparation procedures will meet high quality standards. During 2006, the company introduced Crispani, Panera Kids,™ four new sandwiches, six new soups, one new Panini, and one new salad.

Marketing The company competes not only on price but also by offering an entire experience for customers. Extensive market research, including the use of focus groups, is done to determine customer preferences. Sales in each location are increased through menu development, product merchandising, promotions, and sponsoring local charitable events.

Numerous local/regional advertising associations have been established to promote and advertise bakery-cafes in specific geographic regions. In 2006, the company used a portion of its national advertising fund to market the evening daypart and the introduction of the Crispani.

Site Selection and Bakery-Cafe Design Prior to building a new Panera Bread bakery-cafe, the management team studies the surrounding trade area, the demographics of the area, and competitors. Then using predictive analysis software, the expected sales and return on investment can be determined. If parameters are met, the site is considered appropriate for the addition of a new bakery-cafe.

Each bakery-cafe is designed to be complementary to the local neighborhood and may include a fireplace, seating areas, outdoor seating areas, and the WiFi network. Each bakery-cafe is approximately 4,600 square feet. All facilities are leased for 10 years with renewal options.

Management Information Systems The cash registers at each bakery-cafe collect point-of-sale transaction data that is used to generate marketing information, product mix, and average check amount. The in-store system is designed to assist managers in labor scheduling, food cost management, providing access to retail data, and allowing for online ordering. The sales, bank deposit, and variance data for each bakery-cafe are submitted to the company's accounting department daily and information is then used to generate weekly reports and monthly financial data. Information from bakery-cafes, such as the average check, customer count, product mix, and other sales trends are monitored. The eLearning system allows online training for retail associates and provides online baking instructions for bakers. Most bakery-cafes offer customers free Internet access, which is provided through a managed WiFi network. As a result, Panera Bread hosts one of the largest free public WiFi networks in the country.

Franchise Operations Panera Bread began its franchising program in 1996. The company tends to establish area development agreements (ADAs) rather than individual franchises. The ADA requires a franchisee to develop a specified number of bakery-cafes on or before specific dates as designated in each agreement. Franchisee-owned bakery-cafes must meet the same standards for product quality, menu, site selection and construction as do company-owned bakery-cafes. Franchisees are required to purchase all dough products from company-approved sources and the company's commissary supplies all fresh dough products. The franchise fee is $35,000, and the total investment for a bakery-cafe ranges from $1,003,000 to $2,235,175. A 4 percent to 5 percent royalty fee on gross sales is payable each week. As of December 26, 2007, the company was working with 41 franchisee groups and had 636 franchised bakery-cafes open and commitments to open 359 additional franchised bakery-cafes. Managers and the head baker are required to attend Panera Bread's training program. The Management Training course classroom portion lasts for five days and the in-store training portion lasts four to six weeks. During the training program topics discussed include area and shift management, administration, customer service, quality assurance, company history, safety procedures, and human resources.

Bakery Supply Chain All bakery-cafes use fresh dough, which is supplied daily by a company regional commissary, for the sourdough bread, artisan breads, Crispani, and bagels. As of December 26, 2007, the company had 19 regional fresh dough facilities. Although the distribution system requires a major commitment of capital, it provides cost efficiencies and assures consistent

Exhibit 3 Balance Sheets

Panera Bread Company
Consolidated Balance Sheets
(in thousands except share and per share information)

	December 26 2006	December 27 2005
Assets		
Current assets:		
Cash and cash equivalents	$ 52,097	$ 24,451
Investments in government securities	20,025	36,200
Trade accounts receivable, net	19,041	18,229
Other accounts receivable	11,878	6,929
Inventories	8,714	7,358
Prepaid expenses	12,036	5,736
Deferred income taxes	3,827	3,871
Total current assets	127,618	102,774
Property and equipment, net	345,977	268,809
Other assets:		
Investments in government securities	—	10,108
Goodwill	57,192	48,540
Other intangible assets, net	6,604	3,219
Deposits and other	5,218	4,217
Total other assets	69,014	66,084
Total assets	$542,609	$437,667
Liabilities and Stockholders' Equity		
Current liabilities:		
Accounts payable	$ 5,800	$ 4,422
Accrued expenses	102,718	81,559
Deferred revenue	1,092	884
Total current liabilities	109,610	86,865
Deferred income taxes	—	5,022
Deferred rent	27,684	23,935
Other long-learn liabilities	7,649	4,867
Total liabilities	144,943	120,689
Commitments and contingencies		
Stockholders' equity:		
Common stock. $.0001 par value:		
Class A. 75,000,000 shares authorized: 30,453,157 issued and 30,344,157 outstanding in 2006: and 29,957,297 issued and 29,848,297 outstanding in 2005	3	3
Class B. 10,000,000 shares authorized: 1,400,031 issued and outstanding in 2006 and 1,400.621 in 2005	—	—
Treasury stock, carried at cost	(900)	(900)
Additional paid-in capital	176,241	154,402
Retained earnings	222,322	163,473
Total stockholders' equity	397,666	316,978
Total liabilities and stockholders' equity	$542,609	$437,667

Exhibit 4 Income Statements

Panera Bread Company Consolidated Statements of Operations (in thousands, except per share information)			
	For the Fiscal Year Ended		
	December 26 2006	December 27 2005	December 25 2004
Revenues:			
Bakery-cafe sales	$666,141	$499,422	$362,121
Franchise royalties and fees	61,531	54,309	44,449
Fresh dough sales to franchisees	101,299	86,544	72,569
Total revenue	828,971	640,275	479,139
Costs and expenses:			
Bakery-cafe expenses:			
Cost of food and paper products	197,182	142,675	101,832
Labor	204,956	151,524	110,790
Occupancy	48,602	35,558	25,040
Other operating expenses	92,176	70,003	51,044
Total bakery-cafe expenses	542,916	399,760	288,706
Fresh dough cost of sales to franchisees	85,618	75,036	65,627
Depreciation and amortization	44,166	33,011	25,298
General and administrative expenses	59,306	46,301	33,338
Pre-opening expenses	6,173	5,072	4,332
Total costs and expenses	738,179	559,180	417,301
Operating profit:	90,792	81,095	61,838
Interest expense	92	50	18
Other (income) expense, net	(1,976)	(1,133)	1,065
Income before income taxes	92,676	82,178	60,755
Income taxes	33,827	29,995	22,175
Net income	$ 58,849	$ 52,183	$ 38,580
Per share data:			
Net income per share			
Basic	$ 1.88	$ 1.69	$ 1.28
Diluted	$ 1.84	$ 1.65	$ 1.25
Weighted average shares of common and common equivalent shares outstanding			
Basic	31,313	30,871	30,154
Diluted	32,044	31,651	30,768

Exhibit 5 Key Statistics for Panera Bread and Competitors. (12 Months Ended December 26, 2006)

Key Numbers	Panera Bread	Chipotle	Starbucks	Industry Median
Annual Sales ($ mil.)	829.0	822.9	7,786.9	
Gross Profit Margin	24.20%	20.90%	58.8%	23.3%
Net Profit Margin	7.10%	5.0%	7.2%	3.40%
Return on Equity	16.5%	10.6%	25.5%	10.4%
Return on Assets	12.0%	8.3%	14.4%	5.3%
Return on Invested Capital	15.0%	9.3%	21.1%	6.2%
Price/Earnings Ratio	29.86	50.84	40.59	25.15
Days of Sales Outstanding	15.30	6.47	14.43	10.22
Inventory Turnover	78.2	212.3	6.8	51.3
Current Ratio	1.16	2.92	.79	.82
Leverage Ratio	—	—	.08	0.25
Total Debt/Equity	—	—	0.15	0.47
12-Month Revenue Growth	29.5%	31.1%	22.3%	8.3%
12-Month Net Income Growth	12.8%	9.9%	13.6%	8.1%
36-Month Revenue Growth	132.9%	160.8%	88.6%	30.7%
36-Month Net Income Growth	93.5%	0.0%	98.9%	40.5%

Source: Hoovers Online, May 2007.

quality and a supply of dough to the bakery-cafes that gives Panera Bread a competitive advantage. The product consistency enhances the brand identity. The company distributes the dough using a leased fleet of temperature-controlled trucks. The optimal distribution limit is within 300 miles of the commissary and the average distribution route delivers dough to seven bakery-cafes. Although the company may contract for needed ingredients with only one supplier, there are numerous product suppliers making it easy for the company to switch to another supplier if necessary.

The company has signed an agreement with Dawn Food Products, Inc. to provide sweet goods for the period 2003 to 2008. Independent distributors deliver the sweet good products, tuna, and other materials to the bakery-cafes. Only the fresh dough products and most of the cream cheese are supplied by the fresh dough facilities. All other food products and supplies (paper goods, coffee, etc.) are contracted by the company and delivered by the vendors to the bakery-cafes.

Employees As of December 26, 2006, the company employed 7,200 full-time associates—those employees who average 25 hours or more per week. Approximately 400 are employed in administrative functions, 900 employed in the

fresh dough facilities, and 5,900 employed in the bakery-cafes. The company employs about 10,200 part-time hourly associates. The company provides employees with medical and life insurance, a 401(k) plan with company match, an employee stock purchase plan, a section 125 flexible spending account, paid vacations, competitive salaries, and product discounts.

During fiscal year 2006, Panera Bread's stock price ranged from a high of $74.59 achieved May 5, 2006, to a low of $46.25 on August 10, 2006. The company achieved systemwide comparable bakery-cafe sales growth of 4.1 percent, systemwide average weekly sales increased 2.2 percent to $39,150, and 155 new bakery-cafes were opened. Earnings per share for 2006 was $1.84, which places Panera Bread as one of the highest growth companies in the restaurant industry.

A number of exciting events occurred during 2006: Panera Bread increased its presence in the evening daypart with the introduction of the Crispani hand-crafted pizza. The fresh catering business, Via Panera,® continued to grow during the year. The company launched the Panera Kids menu, which features artisan white whole grain bread especially made for kids.

Panera's growth strategy includes developing new markets and continuing to penetrate existing markets. The company will continue to use franchising as a method to open new bakery-cafes. Today, approximately 62 percent of the bakery-cafes are operated by franchisees. Expanding into foreign markets is expected to occur in 2007. The company plans to open bakery-cafes in the Canadian market in 2007, primarily through franchise agreements.

On February 1, 2007, Panera Bread purchased 51% of the outstanding shares of Paradise Bakery and Café, a franchisor of 23 locations that includes 22 bakery-cafes, of which 17 are in the Phoenix market. Panera Bread has the right to purchase the remaining 49 percent of outstanding stock after January 1, 2009.

During first quarter 2007, 31 new bakery-cafes were opened, 4 bakery-cafes were acquired from a franchisee, and 1 company-owned bakery-cafe was closed. Revenue for the first quarter increased 24 percent to $240 million, up from $194 million for first quarter 2006 (see Exhibits 3 and 4).

Panera Bread continues to perform very well and achieves better financial returns than the industry average (see Exhibit 5). Can Panera Bread continue its success in such a dynamic, competitive market? Competition comes from specialty food, casual dining restaurants, and other quick services restaurants. Competitors may be national, regional, or locally owned. There are more than 400 brands of quick casual restaurants in the United States and new brands are opening every day as they find food niches or geographic niches that are underserved. Competitors can be corporate firms such as Raving Brands of Atlanta that offers three quick casual brands with two more brands in development or a company as simple as Tossed (which offers tossed-to-order green-leaf salads) that started as one restaurant in 1997 and by 2006 has plans to open 200 restaurants within five years.

In addition to high levels of competition, Panera Bread must contend with fast-changing customer preferences. In 2004, consumers were interested in low-carb foods, having comfort foods on the menu, and looking to chicken entrees for healthy food choices. By 2007, consumers are demanding higher quality food, healthier menu options, and they have more interest in ethnic foods.

What should Panera Bread do in order to maintain its leadership position in the quick casual restaurant segment?

Endnotes

1. Bilsky, C. 2007. Feasting on fast-casual. *Commercial Investment Real Estate Magazine,* (online), January–February, www.ciremagazine.com/article.
2. Panera Bread Company. 2006 Annual Report.
3. National Restaurant Industry. 2007. *Restaurant Industry Facts* (online), www.restuarant.org/research/industry_glance.
4. Bilsky, C. 2007. Feasting on fast-casual, *Commercial Investment Real Estate Magazine,* (online), January–February, www.ciremagazine.com/article.
5. Ibid.
6. Hamaker, S. S., & Panitz, B. 2002. In vogue: What's hot in the restaurant industry: *Restaurants USA* (online), May, www.restaurant.org/rusa/magArticle.
7. Quantified Marketing Group. (2007). *2007 Restaurant Trends Forecast* (online), www.quantifiedmarketing.com/learning_center.
8. Heller, L. 2007. Casual dining increase could rub off on packaged goods. Food Navigator USA.com (online), www.foodnavigator-usa.com/news/printNewsBis.
9. Quantified Marketing Group. (2007). *2007 Restaurant Trends Forecast* (online), www.quantifiedmarketing.com/learning_center.
10. Strong, M. 2007. Operating on the fast track: Success quick-casual brands sparked a race to upgrade in other segments but now find themselves playing the same catch-up game. *LookSmart* (online), http://findarticles.com.
11. Ibid.
12. Quantified Marketing Group. 2007. *2007 Restaurant Trends Forecast* (online), www.quantifiedmarketing.com/learning_center.
13. Ibid.
14. Hume, S. 2004. Reinventing the wheels impact of fast casual. *Restaurant Institutions* (online), April, www.keepmedia.com.
15. Quantified Marketing Group. 2007. *2007 Restaurant Trends Forecast* (online), www.quantifiedmarketing.com/learning_center.
16. Rothstein, K. 2003. Fast casual sends a strategic signal. *Strategic Initiative* (online) (18)3, www.halegroup.com.
17. Panera Bread (December 2006) Annual Report.
18. www.panerabread.com, 2007. Company Web site.
19. Panera Bread (December 2006) Annual Report.

Case 18   Southwest Airlines: From Simple to Complex "LUV"?*

Southwest Airlines emerged as a larger carrier of domestic customers than any other U.S. airline by the end of January 2007, according to the U.S. Department of Transportation's Bureau of Transportation Statistics. By April 2007, the airline flew 5.9 billion revenue passenger miles (RPMs), a 3.3 percent increase from the 5.7 billion RPMs flown in April 2006.[1] With a $499 million in recorded profit for the year ended 2006, an increase of $15 million or 3.1 percent, compared to its $484 million net income in 2005, Southwest Airlines continues to be the most profitable in the U.S. airline industry. It is the 63rd consecutive quarter or rather, the 34th consecutive year of profitability for the company, which is unmatched in this cut-throat, long-time bleeding industry. For the 11th year in a row, the airline was recognized by *Fortune* magazine in its annual survey of corporate reputations. Among all industries in 2006, Southwest Airlines was listed as number five among America's top ten most admired corporations. With an extraordinarily charismatic chairman and co-founder, Herb Kelleher, a cultlike culture and hoards of loyal followers, a Wal-Martian devotion to cost control and emphasis on efficiency, Southwest made a miracle happen, and for quite a long while.[2]

However, now every airline wants to play Southwest's game. With the majors having gone through drastic restructuring and cost slashing of primarily wages and pensions, with upstarts such as JetBlue and AirTran having copied Southwest's model and added further frills, it is not clear how long Southwest will sustain its advantage. Indeed, Gary Kelly, its erstwhile CFO and the current CEO, said, "Hey, I can admit it, our competitors are getting better. Sure, we have an enormous cost advantage. Sure, we're the most efficient. The problem is, I just don't see how that can be indefinitely sustained without some sacrifice." Indeed, in the last couple of years, Southwest has been doing things that it was vehemently opposed to all through its existence. The airline now serves congested hub airports, links with rivals through code-sharing (e.g., ATA), hunts the big boys on their own turf—much like its competitors from whom it always wanted to be different.[3]

Background and Growth

The inconvenience and expense of ground travel by bus or automobile between the cities of Houston, Dallas, and San Antonio—the Golden Triangle that was experiencing rapid economic and population growth during the late 1960s—offered an opportunity for an intrastate airline. The idea

was suggested by Rollin King, a San Antonio entrepreneur who owned a small commuter air service, when his banker, John Parker, complained about the issue. King then talked to Herb Kelleher—a New Jersey–born, New York University Law School graduate who moved to San Antonio in 1967 to practice law. They soon pooled the seed money to start Southwest Airlines. The infant Southwest Airlines (SWA) fought long-drawn legal battles, primarily engineered by the major airline carriers, for over four years before it got its first flight off the ground in 1971. Later on, the company had to work around a regulation intended to penalize SWA's decision to operate out of Dallas Love Field instead of moving to the new Dallas–Fort Worth (DFW) airport. With Herb's brilliant legal expertise and extensive lobbying with the House of Representatives, the issue was settled and SWA was allowed to operate out of Love Field in 1979. The struggle for existence in the initial years worked to the advantage of the company as it created the esprit de corps for which it became so well known. The employees were caught up in fighting for the "SWA cause" that created "the warrior mentality, the very fight to survive," according to Colleen Barrett, who became the president and chief operating officer of SWA in 2001. (She now is the President and Secretary.)[4]

Kelleher, however, was not the first chief executive officer of Southwest. Lamar Muse, an airline veteran who worked earlier with Trans Texas, Central, and Universal Airlines was brought in to get the company off to a good start. That was followed by the brief tenure of Howard Putnam, another airline veteran hired from United Airlines, where he worked from 1978 to 1982. Herb Kelleher served as the chairman of the board during that period, then he took the CEO position in 1982 and championed Southwest's expansion (at that time the company had only 27 planes, $270 million in revenues, and flew to only 14 cities).[5] SWA was one of a kind right from its beginning. It was the pioneer of the "low-cost strategy." It flew planes point-to-point—short-haul flights bypassing the expensive hub-and-spoke operations. It chose less popular, less congested airports to achieve quicker turnarounds.

SWA offered airfares so low that it gave the bus and car travel companies a run for their money. It served no meals on its airlines and provided only a snack of peanuts. That saved plenty of money and manpower. There was no assigned seating, which reduced boarding times and helped planes turn around faster. The average turnaround time for planes was around 25 minutes. Faster turnaround times and higher aircraft utilization also meant a reduced number of aircraft and gate facilities than would otherwise have been necessary. SWA's attractive flight attendants in hot pants were a source of live entertainment on flights (e.g., the flight attendants made funny presentations of the otherwise routine and boring safety instructions or performed preflight tricks such as popping out of overhead bins).[6] It was the first major airline that introduced ticketless travel and one of the first to

* This case study was prepared by Ms. Naga Lakshmi Damaraju of The Ohio State University, Professor Alan B. Eisner at Pace University, and Professor Gregory G. Dess at University of Texas at Dallas. The purpose of the case is to stimulate class discussion rather than to illustrate effective or ineffective handling of a business situation. The authors thank Professor Michael Oliff at the University of Texas at Dallas, for his valuable comments on an earlier version of this case. Several parts of the case are from an earlier version. Copyright © 2007 Damaraju, Eisner, & Dess.

put up a Web site and offer online booking.[7] It operated a single aircraft type, Boeing 737, that kept its training costs low and manpower utilization high as it offered great flexibility in manpower deployment. Starting with three Boeing 737s in 1971, the company fleet grew to 481 Boeing 737 aircraft providing service to 63 cities in 32 states throughout the United States, with 397 city pairs being served nonstop, by the beginning of 2007 (see Exhibits 1, 2, and 3).[8]

Exhibit 1 Financial and Operating Data for Southwest Airlines 2002–2006

Financial Data					
Years Ended December 31 (in millions, except per share amounts)	**2006**	**2005**	**2004**	**2003**	**2002**
Operating revenues	$9,086	$7,584	$6,530	$5,937	$5,522
Operating expenses	$8,152	$6,859	$6,126	$5,558	$5,181
Operating income	$934	$725	$404	$379	$341
Other expenses (income) net	$144	$(54.00)	$65	$(225.00)	$24
Income before income taxes	$790	$779	$339	$604	$317
Provision for income taxes	$291	$295	$124	$232	$129
Net income	$499	$484	$215	$372	$188
Net income per share, basic	$0.63	$0.61	$0.27	$0.48	$0.24
Net income per share, diluted	$0.61	$0.6	$0.27	$0.46	$0.23
Cash dividends per common share	$0.018	$0.018	$0.018	$0.018	$0.018
Total assets at period end	$13,460	$14,003	$11,137	$9,693	$8,766
Long-term obligations at period end	$1,567	$1,394	$1,700	$1,332	$1,553
Stockholders' equity at period end	$6,449	$6,675	$5,527	$5,029	$4,374
Operating Data					
Revenue passengers carried	83,814,823	77,693,875	70,902,773	65,673,945	63,045,988
Enplaned passengers	96,276,907	88,379,900	81,066,038	74,719,340	72,462,123
Revenue passenger miles (RPMs) (000s)	67,691,289	60,223,100	53,418,353	47,943,066	45,391,903
Available seat miles (ASMs) (000s)	92,663,023	85,172,795	76,861,296	71,790,425	68,886,546
Load factor	73.1%	70.7%	69.5%	66.8%	65.9%
Average length of passenger haul (miles)	808	775	753	730	720
Average stage length (miles)	622	607	576	558	537
Trips flown	1,092,331	1,028,639	981,591	949,882	947,331
Average passenger fare	$104.4	$93.68	$88.57	$87.42	$84.72
Passenger revenue yield per RPM	12.93¢	12.09¢	11.76¢	11.97¢	11.77¢
Operating revenue yield per ASM	9.81¢	8.9¢	8.5¢	8.27¢	8.02¢
Operating expenses per ASM	8.8¢	8.05¢	7.97¢	7.74¢	7.52¢
Operating expenses per ASM, excluding fuel	6.49¢	6.48¢	6.67¢	6.59¢	6.41¢
Fuel cost per gallon (average)	$1.53	$1.03	$0.83	$0.72	$0.68
Number of Employees at year-end	32,664	31,729	31,011	32,847	33,705
Size of fleet at year end	481	445	417	388	375

*Refer to appendix for a list of terms used in the airline industry.

Source: Southwest Airlines, SEC filings, Form 10-k, www.sec.gov/.

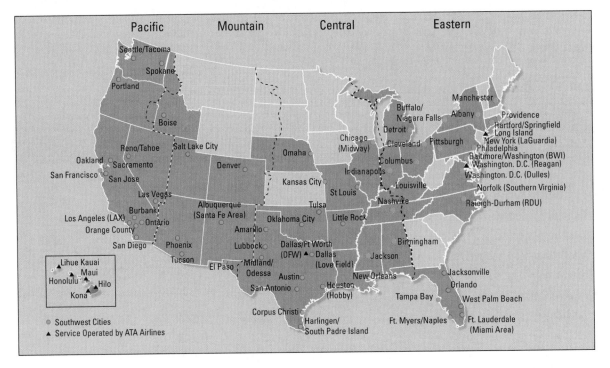

Exhibit 2 Cities Served by Southwest Airlines

*Service to Kona, HI begins June 14, 2007 (operated by ATA Airlines); service to Lihue Kauai, HI begins June 15, 2007 (operated by ATA Airlines); service to San Francisco, CA begins August 26, 2007.

Source: Printed with permission from company, http://www.southwest.com/about_swa/routemap.html.

Exhibit 3 Growth in the Number of Cities Served by Southwest Airlines 1994–2006

Year Ended	Number of Cities Served
1994	44
1995	45
1996	49
1997	51
1998	52
1999	56
2000	57
2001	58
2002	58
2003	58
2004	58
2005	61
2006	63

Source: Southwest Airlines, Forms 10-k filed with SEC.

The SWA Leadership and Culture

There are many stories about Herb Kelleher's flamboyant style as CEO. He smoked cigars, loved Wild Turkey whiskey, was often seen dressed up as Elvis Presley, and publicly arm-wrestled and won over a rival company CEO to settle a dispute over an advertisement slogan.[9] Kelleher truly believed that business could and should be fun—at too many companies, people put on masks when they came to the office. At work, people were not themselves and would be overly serious, which explained why most business encounters were bland and impersonal. Therefore, SWA tried not to hire people who were humorless, self-centered, or complacent. Not surprisingly, there was no human resources department but rather a People Department at Southwest. The guiding principle for recruitment at SWA was "Hire for attitude and train for skills." Herb believed that to be the most important principle. When an employee from the People Department said to him, "Herb, I'm getting a little embarrassed because I've interviewed 34 people for a ramp agent position in Amarillo," Herb replied, "If you have to interview 134 people to find the appropriate person to be a ramp agent in Amarillo, do it. Because the most important thing is to get the right people, and if you get the wrong ones they start poisoning everybody else."[10]

Kelleher's penchant for laughter and fun became a part of Southwest's culture. Prospective employees were asked how humor helped them out of a difficult situation. Prospective pilots were sometimes asked to pull on shorts and the ones who saw fun in it passed the interview. All people at the company were to be treated with dignity and respect and Herb did not believe in hierarchical barriers. When a vice-president complained to the CEO that customers, gate agents, pilots, and baggage handlers had more access to him than he did, Kelleher said to him, "Let me explain this: They're more important than you are." Herb recognized the key to satisfied customers was having satisfied employees. So employees came first and that orientation was embodied in the mission statement (Exhibit 4).

The culture was put into operation through a number of policies and programs. The casual dress policy reinforced the company's desire that people be themselves on the job. Celebrations such as spirit parties, culture parties, and weekly deck parties were organized at headquarters regularly to bring employees together. Activities at the events included gong shows, talent shows, dance contests, limbo contests, and famous person look-alike themes. The culture committee at SWA welcomed new employees with a "New Hire Welcome Kit" that included a bag, T-shirt, badge holder, pen, and a welcome letter. To build solidarity across all departments, there was an employee recognition program in which employees recognized each other's achievements. Such a practice helped community building within and across departments. For example, one work group committee recognized flight attendants 10 times a year with "Hokey Days," named for the broom apparatus used by flight attendants to sweep the cabin after the flights. Committee members chose two locations at which to honor flight attendants, greeted each arriving plane, waited until passengers got off, and then boarded with goodies. Flight

attendants were asked to relax while the committee members cleaned the plane for them. There were similar programs to honor other departments as well.[11] There was also a "Walk a Mile Program" designed to foster problem solving and cooperation, in which an employee could do somebody else's job for a day (while operations people obviously could not fly the airplanes, pilots could do the work as operations agents).[12] Further, the company had the "Star of the Month"—outstanding employees who were chosen to appear in *Spirit,* Southwest's in-flight magazine—which recognized the distinct contributions of employees toward excellence in customer service.[13]

The company also expressed warmth toward its employees by other means. At Southwest's headquarters in Dallas, the walls were covered with more than 10,000 picture frames that contained photos of employees' pets, of stewardesses in miniskirts, of Southwest planes gnawing on competitor's aircraft. Also there were teddy bears, jars of pickled hot peppers, and pink flamingos. There was cigarette smoking and lots of chuckling. "To me, it's comfortable," said Colleen Barrett, who was most responsible for nurturing Southwest culture from its early days. "This is an open scrapbook. We aren't uptight. We celebrate everything. It's like a fraternity, a sorority, a reunion. We are having a party!" she said. Barrett also regularly traveled to meet the employees and personally sent them birthday cards, not so much to win their loyalty as to communicate the true spirit of a family. The company celebrated with its employees when good things happened and grieved with them when they had devastating experiences.[14] She said, "What we do is very simple, but it's not simplistic. We really do everything with passion. We scream at each other and we hug each other."[15]

Cost consciousness was another important part of the culture. "Yes, our culture is almost like a religion," said Gary Kelly, the erstwhile CFO and the present CEO of Southwest. "But it's a dichotomy. In many ways we are conservative. Financially, for instance," he added.[16] According to Herb Kelleher, close attention to costs had produced the kind of financial success Southwest had seen. He said, "Even in the best of times, we kept our costs low and questioned every expenditure. For years, I used to approve every expenditure over $1,000. Why? To encourage a cost-conscious culture. I couldn't look at all of them, of course. But I would question them selectively, and that kept people paying attention."[17]

Treating employees well at Southwest did not mean that they were paid high salaries. By creating value through intangibles, the company kept wages lower than those of competitors. Officers at Southwest were paid about 30 percent less, on average, than their counterparts at other airlines. But the airline made stock options widely available, so all employees—not just executives—could share in the company's financial success. Southwest even had a policy that its officers received pay increases that were no larger, proportionally, than what other employees received. But employees were also expected to take pay reductions when times were not good. Job security was ensured, however, with a "no-furlough policy" and Southwest did not lay off

Exhibit 4   The Mission of Southwest Airlines

The mission of Southwest Airlines is dedication to the highest quality of Customer Service delivered with a sense of warmth, friendliness, individual pride, and Company Spirit.

To Our Employees

We are committed to provide our Employees a stable work environment with equal opportunity for learning and personal growth. Creativity and innovation are encouraged for improving the effectiveness of Southwest Airlines. Above all, Employees will be provided the same concern, respect, and caring attitude within the organization that they are expected to share externally with every Southwest Customer.

Source: Southwest Airlines http://www.southwest.com/about_swa/mission.html.

a single employee during the economic downturn after the terrorist attacks on September 11, 2001, while many of its competitors did.[18] Caring for employee happiness showed positive results. Southwest had less employee turnover than its competitors. For years, Southwest enjoyed the loyalty of its employees despite the high level of employee unionization. "Once labor leaders realize that you're trying to take care of your people, most of the edge [in contract negotiations] is gone," said Kelleher.[19]

Southwest's employees worked more hours than their counterparts at other airlines. Southwest pilots flew nearly 80 hours a month compared to United's 50 hours. Southwest pilots were paid by trip, not per hour, which created a strong interest in keeping flights on schedule. Also, pilots tended to be cost conscious because a big part of their compensation came from stock options. On some occasions, pilots even pitched in to help ground crews move luggage to ensure on-time flights—something virtually unheard of at Southwest's bigger rivals. Flight attendants at Southwest worked about 150 hours a month, compared with 80 hours at many other airlines, according to union president Thom McDaniel. Southwest attendants were required by contract to make a reasonable effort to tidy the airplane between flights, a job performed by maintenance personnel at rival airlines. According to an airline labor expert, senior flight attendants at United got as many as 52 vacation days a year (compared with 35 days for veterans at Southwest) and they never had to clean up after the passengers.[20]

Maintaining focus on the core business was another element for both cost control and pursuing a niche strategy. Kelleher consciously ensured that the company did not diverge into allied businesses such as car rentals or reservations. Most of Southwest's growth had been organic, that is, by adding more flights on its existing routes and by connecting more dots (adding cities). The airline started complementing its short-haul flights with long-haul flights and began transcontinental services. According to Kelleher, the airline did not plan for international flights as that would mean a total change in the way it operated and would involve training its 35,000 employees to handle that change.[21]

The cost consciousness and employee commitment translated into operational excellence and increased profitability. Southwest's planes flew about 10.9 hours per day, much more than any other airline except for that of JetBlue, which flew close to 13.0 hours per day. Southwest could offer lower fares—as much as 50 percent lower than its major rivals—and still remain profitable. With such low costs, it created what was called the "Southwest effect," an explosion in the traffic and nabbing of customers who would have driven before.[22] The term "Southwest effect" was coined by the U.S. Department of Transportation to refer to the consistent phenomenon of a decrease in average fares and stimulation of demand that occurred when Southwest Airlines entered any market.[23]

In May 1988 Southwest became the first airline to win the coveted "Triple Crown" for a month: Best On-Time Record, Best Baggage Handling, and Fewest Customer Complaints. Since then, Southwest has won it more than 30 times, as well as five annual Triple Crowns for 1992, 1993, 1994, 1995, and 1996. Southwest crossed its $1 billion revenue mark in 1990 to become a major airline and topped the monthly domestic originating passenger rankings for the first time in May 2003. It was also the largest carrier based on scheduled domestic departures. Stories circulated of Southwest employees providing excellent customer service abound, and Southwest even set up a direct TV to show how its employees treated customers.[24]

The Changing Times and Challenges

Southwest Airlines had a change in leadership in August 2001 when Herb Kelleher relinquished power to two of his close aides. Colleen C. Barrett, vice-president for customers, became the president and chief operating officer; and James F. Parker, general counsel, became the chief executive officer. Barrett and Parker had each worked together for over 22 years and both had worked with Kelleher for much longer—from the time he was a lawyer. In contrast to Kelleher's obtrusive personality, Parker was a quiet diplomat. He had been the company's lead labor negotiator for years, and his opponents said he pursued the company line quite forcefully, if politely, in talks. "He will surprise you because he doesn't look like he's tough, but he doesn't give anything away," said a former vice president of the airline's pilot association.[25] Unlike Kelleher, Parker was not as fond of celebrations because he didn't see them as contributing to productivity. But he came to realize that the party preparations were a model of teamwork and employee bonding and he started participating in the celebrations in 2002.[26]

Barrett, on the other hand, had been the culture keeper of Southwest since the earliest days of the company. However, she was a reluctant public speaker. Thus, she let Parker take the lead with Wall Street and the media. Whether the lieutenants could replaced the "rock star" personality of Kelleher, who exuded warmth to his employees, was too early to guess. Kelleher remained chairman of the board and focused on long-range strategy and government affairs. He maintained control of schedule planning and aircraft acquisitions, the backbone of Southwest's strategy during the period of transition.[27] Whether things would be the same after Kelleher left the scene completely was another important question facing Southwest.

The growth of the company and the consequent increase in the number of employees also posed challenges to keeping the culture intact. The distance between the rank-and-file and top management was growing. While Colleen Barrett could reach all the employees through personally signed birthday cards when the company was small, such a task was becoming increasingly unrealistic. Even though she continued to do so, she could reach only a fraction of Southwest's 35,000 employees dispersed over different cities. Keeping in close touch with employees was becoming an increasingly challenging task. In earlier times of difficulty, Herb Kelleher personally addressed and rallied his troops, but such an exercise was no longer easy.

In addition, the otherwise warm employee relations at Southwest seemed to chill over time. Unions were becoming more aggressive in expressing their frustration, in contrast to earlier days when disputes were resolved more amicably and peacefully. In the summer of 2001, ramp workers picketed near company headquarters with signs that read, "Record Profits Empty Pockets." They complained that staff shortages, combined with Southwest's record passenger loads, and a drive to improve on-time performance, meant they had to lift more bags and had to do so more quickly which put them at risk of injury.[28] And, for the first time in company history, in July 2002 Southwest's mechanics union asked federal mediators to intervene to break a contract deadlock over pay. While the company was nowhere near a strike, the incident clearly signaled the strains appearing in employee relations.[29]

Since 2002 the company was also engaged without much success in a contract renegotiation with flight attendants. In July 2003 a group of flight attendants staged a demonstration at the headquarters with signs "Spread the LUV" and handed out cards to travelers reading "Give our flight attendants a break." The move was an expression of frustration toward management's idea of increasing their work hours. Also, workers who had been working hard to boost the productivity of the company were not seeing much return from profit sharing and a pummeled stock. After years of hard work, some long-time employees felt that they had no more to give. Karen Amos, a 26-year Southwest veteran, said, "We have been there for them. There comes a time when it becomes too much."[30] The company had to drop the move to increase work hours, but still could not get a deal made with the flight attendants. Some workers perceived that the company had been fairer in its negotiations in past years.

In November 2003, after 11 rounds of talks without success, the flight attendants threw a Thanksgiving party at Salt Lake City International Airport, primarily as a means of putting pressure on management to accept their demands for holiday pay and better working conditions. Kevin Onstead, a Southwest negotiator and flight attendant, said, "We are concerned about the culture of the airline. We are fighting for the recognition of our contribution to that culture. We've been key in Southwest Airlines' success. Flight attendants are prepared to strike as a last resort. We are willing to do whatever it takes to get a fair contract."[31] The negotiations had not borne fruit by early 2004. Thom McDaniel, president of the TWU, said that flight attendants were willing to return to the negotiating table. However, he made the point that the latest management offer fell short of their expectations. "We feel that our culture is at risk because of the actions taken by Southwest's management during these negotiations."[32] Many of the employee groups started feeling that Southwest Airlines was no longer the underdog and that their pay should match the profitability of the company. Love (LUV) alone no longer seemed to be enough. That meant a twin challenge in terms of culture and costs.

In July of 2004 James Parker abruptly resigned as CEO of Southwest amid strained labor negotiations with flight attendants. Some people said that Parker had spent too much time in the back offices of Southwest and was never really cut out for a job in the limelight.[33] Herb Kelleher stepped into the negotiations, and the flight attendants walked away smiling with a 31 percent pay raise.[34]

Gary C. Kelly, former chief financial officer of Southwest, took the helm. Kelly appears to have some of the aggressiveness and flamboyance of Kelleher. Kelly is certainly energetic, showing up at the office Halloween party in 2004 dressed as Gene Simmons, leader of the rock group Kiss.[35] He, of course, decided later that he was better off being Kelly than someone else. Kelly audaciously acquired six gates at Chicago's Midway Airport from bankrupt carrier ATA and signed Southwest's first ever code-share agreement with ATA, primarily in response to AirTran eyeing a move into Chicago. This is so different from their original model where they preferred simplicity and wanted to avoid complications of code-sharing and connecting flights. Some argue that the airline is creating a hub in Chicago.

Southwest was already experiencing cost increases per average seat mile (ASM), a key metric used to measure performance in the industry, primarily due to increases in fuel costs and wages. The cost per ASM went up from 7.07 cents in 1995 to 8.8 cents in 2006, with fuel costs, wages, and benefits as the major contributors (Exhibit 5). Southwest's cost per average seat mile, however, remained below that of the big carriers. The company was already working hard on controlling costs. With more of its customers making reservations online (about 71.2 percent by the end of first quarter 2007), and the labor cost advantage narrowing between major airlines after restructuring, further cost squeezing appeared to be a difficult proposition. Though Kelly does not concede it openly, he understands that further cost reductions are hard to come by without modest fare increases and possible employee layoffs—something that is totally against Southwest's culture.[36]

Intensifying competition in the low-fare segment was another factor that had become difficult to ignore. While the newly launched competitors such as JetBlue and AirTran, were not direct threats to Southwest on its existing routes, further expansion of those carriers could bring them head-on with Southwest. These new airlines offered far more attractive services such as leather seats and in-flight entertainment systems, for almost the same fare. Therefore, these rivals could make the no-frills approach of Southwest pale before them. Whether Southwest's loyal customers would still stick with the airline when they could get more value for their money elsewhere was another significant question. Southwest's investments to automate and significantly streamline the ticketing and boarding process with computer-generated bag tags, automated boarding passes, and self-service boarding pass kiosks, and its investments to increase the functionality of its Web site, along with its moves to enhance aircraft interiors with leather seats, can hardly be

Exhibit 5   Southwest Airline's Operating Expenses per Average Seat Mile, 2000–2006

Category	2006	2005	2004	2003	2002	2001	2000
Salaries, wages, and benefits ¢	3.29	3.27	3.18	3.10	2.89	2.84	2.81
Fuel and oil	2.31	1.58	1.30	1.16	1.11	1.18	1.34
Maintenance materials and repairs	0.51	0.52	0.60	0.60	0.57	0.61	0.63
Aircraft rentals	0.17	0.19	0.23	0.25	0.27	0.29	0.33
Landing fees and other rentals	0.53	0.53	0.53	0.52	0.50	0.48	0.44
Depreciation and amortization	0.56	0.55	0.56	0.53	0.52	0.49	0.47
Other	1.43	1.41	1.37	1.37	1.47	1.49	1.44
	8.8	8.05	7.77	7.53	7.33	7.38	7.46

Source: Southwest Airlines, Forms 10-k filed with SEC 2000–2006.

described as *not* motivated by competition.[37] That JetBlue caught Southwest's attention was clear by the comment that Southwest was studying the possibility of introducing an in-flight entertainment system, although at the moment it was too costly to adopt. Thus, matching amenities with the newly emerging competition could pose additional challenges to the low-cost strategy. Kelleher's reaction to the emerging competition was simple—he had seen that movie before.

Meanwhile, Southwest entered the Philadelphia market, a stronghold of US Air, in May of 2004. The Philadelphia market was one of the most overpriced and underserved. Southwest aimed at capturing the market with its tried and tested low-cost, no frills formula albeit, with leather seats on some of its newer planes. US Air responded, "We will be a vigorous competitor to Southwest in Philadelphia on every route they fly."[38]

In addition to the ATA codeshare for Chicago's Midway,[39] Kelly added Phoenix to the codeshare in April of 2005.[40] Then, Kelly directed the entry into Pittsburgh in May of 2005 announcing, "The Pittsburgh International Airport will be a great addition to our system."[41] In October of 2005 Southwest started new service out of Southwest Florida International Airport in Fort Myers, making it the 61st Southwest city.[42] Robert M. Ball, Executive Director of Florida's Lee County Port Authority said after courting Southwest for nearly a decade, "We have been working closely with Southwest for many years and are pleased they have selected Southwest Florida as their newest destination."[43] Gary Kelly, Southwest's Chief Executive Officer was on hand to wave the banner and said, "Now, our Southwest Florida customers have to look no further than their own backyard for Southwest's legendary low fares and great customer service." Denver, Colorado, and Washington Dulles International Airport were added to the list in 2006. Service to San Francisco is expected to commence by the end of August 2007, and that raises the number of cities served to 64.[44]

In the in-flight entertainment arena, Southwest still shuns expensive in-flight video systems. However, they struck a deal with online movie rental company, Movielink LLC, to allow passengers to "rent" movies by downloading them over the Internet to their laptop computers for viewing in-flight. Southwest customers will receive a voucher for their first movie free and a 20 percent discount thereafter on Movielink movie rentals.[45]

Wright Amendment and Beyond   With legacy carriers achieving significant labor restructuring agreements eroding SWA's once considerable wage-rate advantage, overcapacity in the East pushing down passenger yields lower than SWA would prefer, and other low-cost carriers such as JetBlue and AirTran carving their niches and reducing the "underserved and overpriced markets" that form the heart of the airline's commercial strategy, further growth and even cost reductions are difficult to come by.[46] No wonder, Kelly pushed for the repeal of the Wright amendment.[47] Southwest entered into an agreement with the City of Dallas, the City of Forth Worth, American Airlines Inc., (American has its hub at Dallas–Fort Worth airport), and the DFW International Airport Board following which, these five parties sought enactment of legislation to amend the original Wright Amendment. Congress responded with a reform act that substantially reduced earlier restrictions. It now works to Southwest's advantage because it can fly to many more destinations from Love Field than earlier, provided those flights first stop in a state within the Wright perimeter. This includes, New Mexico, Oklahoma, Missouri, Arkansas, Louisiana, Mississippi, Kansas, and Alabama along with Texas.[48] Southwest controls about 90 percent of the Love Field market, there are more than 130 daily departures out of Love Field, and its customers can fly 58 out of the 63 destinations from Dallas. Southwest's passenger traffic at Love Field has risen by about 18 percent since the Wright restrictions were loosened in October 2006. This, of course, has a price war brewing between

American and Southwest.[49] Southwest continued its march ahead with 5.9 billion RPMs flown in April 2007, a 3.3 percent increase from the 5.7 billion RPMs flown in April 2006. In terms of available seat miles, it increased 9.6 percent to 8.2 billion from the April 2006 level of 7.5 billion. The load factor for the month was 72.3 percent, compared to 76.7 percent for the same period in 2006. None of the members of the senior management would concede that Southwest is becoming a different creature. This is primarily because of the huge psychic investment they have in being the "underdog." "We're bigger, let's put it that way," says Kelleher. "I think the airline business is fundamentally an opportunistic business. . . . We suddenly have some opportunities materializing that are new to us." However, the more critical question is whether Southwest can continue to play its own game, as effectively, as it goes on the offensive?[50]

Endnotes

1. http://www.southwest.com/about_swa/press/factsheet.html.
2. Southwest's SEC filings 2006 and company's Web site.
3. Gimbel, B. 2005. Southwest's new flight plan. http://money.cnn.com/magazines/fortune/fortune_archive/2005/05/16/8260158/index.htm.
4. Freiberg, K., & Freiberg, J. 1996. Nuts! Southwest Airlines' crazy recipe for personal and business success. Austin, TX: Bard Press: 20–27, http://archives.californiaaviation.org/airport/msg15249.html.
5. Ibid.
6. Freiberg, & Freiberg. 1996. Nuts! Southwest Airlines crazy recipe: 6.
7. Greylock Associates, 2003, Herb Kelleher, chairman, CEO and president, Southwest Airlines.
8. Southwest Airlines, 10-k filings 2003, 2006.
9. McConnell, B. 2001. The wild, flying turkey with wings: Creating customer evangelists—A profile of Herb Kelleher, www.creatingcustomerevangelists.com/resources/evangelists/herb_kelleher.asp.
10. Kelleher, Herb. 2003. Interview with Mark Morrison of BusinessWeek at Texas McComb's School of Business, December 23, www.businessweek.com.
11. Southwest Airlines. 2003. Great Place to Work Institute—Innovation Awards; www.greatplacetowork.com/education/innovate/honoree-2003-southwest.htm.
12. Kelleher, Herb. 1997. Leader to Leader, No. 4, www.pfdf.org/leaderbooks/L2L/spring97/kelleher.html.
13. Southwest Airlines, www.southwest.com/careers/stars/stars.html.
14. Shinn, S. 2003. LUV, Colleen. BizEd., March–April.
15. Serwer. 2004. Southwest Airlines: The hottest thing in the sky.
16. Ibid.
17. What makes Southwest Airlines fly? http://knowledge.wharton.upenn.edu/articles.cfm?catid=2&articleid=753.
18. Ibid.; Kelleher. 1997. Leader to Leader; Freedman, M. 2002. Non-stop growth? ABCNews.com, July 2.
19. What makes Southwest Airlines fly?
20. Donnelly, S. B. 2002. One airline's magic. Time. October 28: 45–47.
21. Kelleher. 2003. Interview with Mark Morrison; McConnell. 2001. The wild, flying turkey with wings.
22. Zellner, W. 2001. Southwest: After Kelleher, more blue skies. BusinessWeek, April 2: 45.
23. Southwest Airlines, www.southwest.com/swatakeoff/southwest_effect.html.
24. www.southwest.com; Serwer. 2004. Southwest Airlines: The hottest thing in the sky: 88–106.
25. Freedman. 2002. Non-stop growth?
26. Trotman, M. 2003. Inside Southwest Airlines, storied culture feels strains. Wall Street Journal Online, July 11, http://online.wsj.com.
27. Zellner. 2001. Southwest: After Kelleher, more blue skies; Zellner, W., & Arndt, M. 2003. Holding steady. BusinessWeek, February 3: 66–68.
28. Trotman. 2003. Inside Southwest Airlines.
29. Roman. 2002. Southwest Air's family feud, 48.
30. Trotman. 2003. Inside Southwest Airlines.
31. Warchol, G., 2003, Southwest crews rally for their cause. Salt Lake Tribune, November 26, www.sltrib.com/2003/Nov/11262003/Business/Business.asp.
32. Southwest flight attendants may resume contract talks. 2004. AIRwise News, February 18, www.airwise.com/news/airlines/southwest.html.
33. Economist.com/Global Agenda. London: July 16, 2004: 1, www.economist.com.
34. Gimbel, Barney. 2005. Southwest's new flight plan. Fortune, May 16, 151(10):93–97.
35. Zellner, Wendy. 2005. Dressed to kill . . . competitors. BusinessWeek, February 21, 39(21): 60.
36. Gimbel, B. Southwest's new flight plan. Fortune, May 16.
37. Southwest Airlines, SEC filings of Form 10-k.
38. Serwer, 2004, Southwest Airlines: The hottest thing in the sky. Fortune, March 8, 2004, pp. 88–106.
39. Zellner, Wendy. 2005. Dressed to kill . . . competitors. BusinessWeek, February 21, 39(21): 60.
40. Southwest Airlines, press releases, March 7, 2005 and June 28, 2005.
41. Southwest Airlines, press release, May 4, 2005.
42. Southwest Airlines, press release, July 14, 2005
43. Southwest Airlines, press release June 27, 2005.
44. Southwest Airlines, press release, May 11, 2007.
45. Johnson, Avery. 2005. Travel watch. The Wall Street Journal. (Eastern edition), February 2005: D.4.
46. Flint, P. 2005. Southwest keeps it simple. Air Transport World, April 2005, p. 26.
47. The Federal law that limited airlines operating at Dallas Love Field to serving destinations in Texas and seven nearby states primarily with an intention to protect the then new Dallas–Fort Worth international airport. Southwest was not initially a part of the agreement and therefore its original quest for existence led to its 'underdog' mentality.
48. SEC filing 2006.
49. Mutzabaugh, B. 2007. Southwest soars at Dallas Love following relaxed Wright rules. USAToday, March 23, 2007. http://blogs.usatoday.com/sky/wright_amendment/index.html.
50. Gimbel, B. Southwest's new flight plan. Fortune, May 16.

Appendix   Key Terms Used

Aircraft utilization. The average number of block hours operated per day per aircraft for the total fleet of aircraft.

Available seat miles. The number of seats available for passengers multiplied by the number of miles the seats are flown.

Average fare. The average one-way fare paid per flight segment by a revenue passenger.

Average stage length. The average number of miles flown per flight.

Breakeven load factor. The passenger load factor that will result in operating revenues being equal to operating expenses, assuming constant revenue per passenger mile and expenses.

Load factor. The percentage of aircraft seating capacity actually utilized (revenue passenger miles divided by available seat miles).

Operating expense per available seat mile. Operating expenses divided by available seat miles.

Operating revenue per available seat mile. Operating revenues divided by available seat miles.

Revenue passenger miles. The number of miles flown by revenue passengers.

Revenue passengers. The total number of paying passengers flown on all flight segments.

Yield per passenger mile. The average amount one passenger pays to fly one mile.

Case 19   Johnson & Johnson*

On April 17, 2007, health care products maker Johnson & Johnson projected that its sales and profits for the current year would not be significantly affected by the decline in sales over safety concerns about its drug-coated stents. But the firm's growth in earnings has begun to fall over the last couple of years, after it had managed to deliver well over 10 percent growth each year for the previous two decades. In response to this slower growth rate, J&J's stock struggled to maintain its value, a sharp contrast to the spark that had driven its value up twentyfold since the mid-1980s.

Most of the growth for J&J has clearly been driven by the acquisitions that it has made over the years, mostly of small firms that were working on promising new products. Over the past decade, the firm made more than 60 acquisitions with a combined value that exceeds $30 billion. But the firm recently lost out to Boston Scientific in its long struggle to acquire Guidant Corporation. The acquisition would have been the largest that the firm would have made in its 120-year-old history, giving J&J a strong presence in the fast growing market for devices that stabilize heart rhythms.

William C. Weldon, chairman and chief executive officer, realizes that it is getting much harder for J&J to maintain its growth rate through a reliance on acquisitions. During 2006, the firm's biggest acquisition was the $16.6 billion purchase of consumer products from Pfizer. Although these products show greater consistency in sales growth, they provide much lower margins. But it has become increasingly difficult to spot smaller firms with promising drugs and to avoid running up against other firms that are looking to make the same kinds of deals. "You get to a point where finding acquisitions that fit the mold and make a contribution becomes increasingly difficult," warned UBS Warburg analyst David Lothson.[1]

Weldon recently told investors that his firm would search for other avenues for growth: "We'll come at it from a variety of different ways, to accelerate top- and bottom-line growth."[2] In particular, he has been trying to squeeze out more growth from J&J's existing businesses. Weldon also wants to decrease his firm's reliance on pharmaceuticals, which have consistently accounted for almost half of the firm's revenues and operating profits. Like the rest of the pharmaceutical industry, J&J has been looking at declining revenues from its best-selling drugs because of expiring patents and growing competition.

Given the scope of the businesses that J&J manages, Weldon has felt that the best opportunities may come from increased collaboration between its different units. The firm has the ability to develop new products by combining its strengths across pharmaceutical products, medical devices and diagnostics, and consumer products. But Weldon is also aware that the success of J&J has been based on the relative autonomy and independence that it has accorded its various business units. Any push for greater collaboration must build upon the entrepreneurial spirit that has been built over the years through this type of organization.

Creating Autonomous Business Units

As it has grown, J&J has developed into an astonishingly complex enterprise, made up of over 200 different businesses organized into three different divisions. The most widely known of these is the division that makes consumer products such as Band-Aid adhesive strips, Aveeno skin-care lotions and various baby products. But most of J&J's recent growth has come from its pharmaceutical products and from its medical devices and diagnostics. With revenues exceeding $50 billion, J&J has already become one of the largest health care companies in the United States (see Exhibits 1 and 2). Its competitors in this field are well aware of J&J's rare combination of scientific expertise and marketing savvy that have helped it to gain a leading position.

To a large extent, however, J&J's success across its three divisions and many different businesses has hinged on its unique structure and culture. Each of its far-flung business units has operated pretty much as an independent enterprise (see Exhibit 3). The firm has been able to turn itself into a powerhouse precisely because each of the businesses that it either buys or starts has always been granted near-total autonomy. That independence has fostered an entrepreneurial attitude that has kept J&J intensely competitive as others around it have faltered. The relative autonomy that is accorded to the business units provides the firm with the ability to respond swiftly to emerging opportunities.

In other words, the business units have been given considerable freedom to set their own strategies. Besides developing their strategies, these units are allowed to plan for their own resources. Many of the businesses even have their own finance and human resources departments. While this degree of decentralization makes for relatively high overhead costs, none of the executives that have run J&J, Weldon included, has ever thought that this was too high a price to pay. "The company really operates more like a mutual fund than anything else," commented Pat Dorsey, director of equity research at Morningstar.[3]

* This case was developed by Professor Jamal Shamsie, Michigan State University with the assistance of Professor Alan B. Eisner, Pace University. Material has been drawn from published sources to be used for class discussion. Copyright © 2007 Jamal Shamsie & Alan B. Eisner.

In spite of the benefits that J&J has derived from giving its various enterprises considerable autonomy, there is a growing feeling that they can no longer operate in near isolation. Weldon has begun to realize, as do most others in the industry, that some of the most important breakthroughs in 21st century medicine are likely to come from the ability to apply scientific advances in one discipline to another. J&J should therefore be in a strong position to exploit new opportunities by drawing on the diverse skills of its various business units across the three divisions.

Pushing for Synergies

Weldon strongly believes that J&J is perfectly positioned to profit from this shift toward combining drugs, devices, and diagnostics, since few companies can to match its reach and strength in these basic areas. According to Weldon, "There is a convergence that will allow us to do things we haven't done before."[4] Indeed, J&J has top-notch products in each of those categories (see Exhibit 4). It has been boosting its research and development budget by more than 10 percent annually for the past few years, which puts it among the top spenders. It now spends about 13 percent of its sales, or $6.5 billion, on over 9,000 scientists working in research laboratories around the world.

Weldon believes, however, that J&J can profit from this convergence by finding ways to make its fiercely independent businesses work together. Through pushing these units to pool their resources, Weldon believes that the firm could become one of the few that may actually be able to attain that often-promised, rarely delivered idea of synergy. Some of the firm's new products, such as the new Cyper drug-coated stent, have clearly resulted from the collaborative efforts and sharing of ideas between its various far-flung divisions (see Exhibit 5).

Weldon's vision for the new J&J may well have emerged from the steps that he took to reshape the pharmaceutical operation shortly after he took it over in 1998. At the time, J&J's drug business had been making solid gains as a result of popular products such as the anemia drug Procrit and the anti-psychotic medication Risperdal. But Weldon did expect that regulatory hurdles and competitive challenges would cut into the revenues and profits that his firm could derive from pharmaceuticals.

Consequently, Weldon felt that J&J should try to increase its efforts to develop new drugs that might become blockbusters. Towards this end, he created a new post to oversee all of the pharmaceutical division's R&D efforts. He also formed a divisional committee that brought together executives from R&D with those from sales and marketing to decide which projects to greenlight. Up until then, the R&D group had made these critical decisions on their own without the involvement of any other departments.

But Weldon felt that his firm could further increase its new product development and reduce its dependence

upon drugs through interaction between the business units that lie across its pharmaceutical, medical devices, and consumer products divisions. Such a push for communication and coordination would allow J&J to develop the synergy that Weldon was seeking. But any effort to get the different business units to collaborate must not quash the entrepreneurial spirit that has spearheaded most of the growth of the firm to date. Jerry Caccott, managing director of consulting firm Strategic Decisions Group, emphasized that cultivating those alliances "would be challenging in any organization, but particularly in an organization that has been so successful because of its decentralized culture."[5]

Shifting the Company Culture

Weldon, like every other leader in the company's history, has worked his way up through the ranks. His long tenure within the firm has turned him into a true believer in the J&J system. He certainly does not want to undermine the entrepreneurial spirit that has resulted from the autonomy that has been given to each of the businesses. Consequently, even though Weldon may talk incessantly about synergy and convergence, he has been cautious in the actual steps he has taken to push J&J's units to collaborate with each other.

For the most part, Weldon has confined himself to the development of new systems to foster better communication and more frequent collaboration among J&J's disparate operations. Among other things, he has worked with James T. Lenehan, vice-chairman and president of J&J, to set up groups that draw people from across the firm to focus their efforts on specific diseases. Each of the groups is expected to report every six months on potential strategies and projects.

Although most of the changes that Weldon has instituted at J&J are not likely to yield real results for some time, there is already some evidence that this new collaboration is working. Perhaps the most promising result of this approach has been J&J's drug-coated stent, called Cypher. The highly successful new addition to the firm's lineup was a result of the efforts of teams that combined people from the drug business with others from the device business. They collaborated on manufacturing the stent, which props open arteries after angioplasty. Weldon claims that if J&J had not been able to bring together people with different types of expertise, it could not have developed the stent without getting assistance from outside the firm.

Even the company's fabled consumer brands have been starting to show growth as a result of increased collaboration between the consumer products and pharmaceutical divisions. Its new liquid Band-Aid is based on a material used in a wound-closing product sold by one of J&J's hospital-supply businesses. And J&J has used its prescription antifungal treatment, Nizoral, to develop a dandruff shampoo. In fact, products that have developed in large part

Exhibit 1 Income Statements

Annual Income Statement	12/31/2006	01/01/2006	01/02/2005	12/28/2003	12/29/2002
			(in $ Millions)		
Sales to customers	53,324	50,514	47,348	41,862	36,298
Cost of products sold	15,057	13,954	13,422	12,176	10,447
Gross profit	38,267	36,560	33,926	29,686	25,851
Selling, marketing, & administrative expenses	17,433	16,877	15,860	14,131	12,216
Research expense	7,125	6,312	5,203	4,684	3,957
Purchased in-process research & development expenses	559	362	18	918	189
Interest income	829	487	195	177	256
Interest expense, net of portion capitalized	63	54	187	207	160
Other income (expense), net	671	214	(15)	385	(294)
Total income (expenses), net	23,680	22,904	21,088	19,378	16,560
Earnings before taxes—U.S.	8,110	7,381	7,895	—	—
Earnings before taxes—international	6,477	6,275	4,943	—	—
Earnings before provision for taxes on income	14,587	13,656	12,838	10,308	9,291
U.S. taxes–current	3,625	2,181	3,654	2,934	2,042
International taxes–current	1,077	1,110	1,173	897	726
Total current taxes	4,702	3,291	4,827	3,831	2,768
U.S. taxes (benefit)–deferred	(726)	228	(70)	(409)	20
International taxes (benefit)–deferred	(442)	(274)	(428)	(311)	(94)
Total deferred taxes (benefit)	(1,168)	(46)	(498)	(720)	(74)
Provision for taxes on income	3,534	3,245	4,329	3,111	2,694
Net earnings	11,053	10,411	8,509	7,197	6,597
Weighted average shares outstanding–basic	2,936.4	2,973.9	2,968.4	2,968.1	2,998.3
Weighted average shares outstanding–diluted	2,961	3,012.5	3,003.5	3,008.1	3,054.1
Year-end shares outstanding	2,893.23	2,974.478	2,971.023	2,967.973	2,968.295
Net earnings per share–basic	3.76	3.5	2.87	2.42	2.2
Net earnings per share–diluted	3.73	3.46	2.84	2.4	2.16
Dividends per common share	1.455	1.275	1.095	0.925	0.795
Total number of employees	122,200	115,600	109,900	110,600	108,300
Number of common stockholders	176,808	181,031	187,840	187,708	—

Source: J&J, Mergentonline.com.

Exhibit 2 Balance Sheets

	12/31/2006	01/01/2006	01/02/2005	12/28/2003	12/29/2002
			(in $ Millions)		
Cash & cash equivalents	4,083	16,055	9,203	5,377	2,894
Marketable securities	1	83	3,681	4,146	4,581
Accounts receivable, trade, gross	8,872	7,174	7,037	6,766	5,590
Less: allowance for doubtful accounts	160	164	206	192	191
Accounts receivable, trade, net	8,712	7,010	6,831	6,574	5,399
Raw materials & supplies	980	931	964	966	835
Goods in process	1,253	1,073	1,113	981	803
Finished goods	2,656	1,955	1,667	1,641	1,665
Inventories	4,889	3,959	3,744	3,588	3,303
Deferred taxes on income	2,094	1,845	1,737	1,526	1,419
Prepaid expenses & other receivables	3,196	2,442	2,124	1,784	1,670
Total current assets	22,975	31,394	27,320	22,995	19,266
Marketable securities, noncurrent	16	20	46	84	121
Land & land improvements	611	502	515	594	472
Buildings & building equipment	7,347	5,875	5,907	5,219	4,364
Machinery & equipment	13,108	10,835	10,455	9,558	7,869
Construction in progress	2,962	2,504	1,787	1,681	1,609
Property, plant & equipment, cost	24,028	19,716	18,664	17,052	14,314
Less: accumulated depreciation	10,984	8,886	8,228	7,206	5,604
Property, plant & equipment, net	13,044	10,830	10,436	9,846	8,710
Intangible assets, net	15,348	6,185	11,842	11,539	9,246
Goodwill, net	13,340	5,990	—	—	—
Deferred taxes on income	3,210	385	551	692	236
Other assets	2,623	3,221	3,122	3,107	2,977
Total assets	70,556	58,025	53,317	48,263	40,556
Loans & notes payable	4,579	668	280	1,139	2,117
Accounts payable	5,691	4,315	5,227	4,966	3,621
Accrued liabilities	4,587	3,529	3,523	2,639	3,820
Accrued rebates, returns, & promotions	2,189	2,017	2,297	2,308	—
Accrued salaries, wages, & commissions	1,391	1,166	1,094	1,452	1,181
Accrued taxes on income	724	940	1,506	944	710
Total current liabilities	19,161	12,635	13,927	13,448	11,449
Convertible subordinated debentures	182	202	737	—	—
Debentures	1,250	1,250	1,250	—	1733
Notes	591	578	596	—	166

(continued)

Exhibit 2   **Balance Sheets** *(continued)*

	12/31/2006	01/01/2006	01/02/2005	12/28/2003	12/29/2002
			(in $ Millions)		
Long-term debt	2,023	2,030	2,583	—	2,099
Less: current portion	9	13	18	—	77
Total long-term debt	2,014	2,017	2,565	2,955	2,022
Deferred tax on income	1,319	211	403	780	643
Pension benefits	2,380	1,264	1,109	—	643
Postretirement benefits	2,009	1,157	1,071	—	907
Postemployment benefits	781	322	244	—	193
Deferred compensation	631	511	397	—	335
Employee-related obligations	5,584	3,065	2,631	2,262	1,967
Other liabilities	3,160	2,226	1,978	1,949	1,778
Total liabilities	31,238	20,154	21,504	—	—
Common stock	3,120	3,120	3,120	3,120	3,120
Note receivable from employee stock ownership	—	—	(11)	(18)	(25)
Foreign currency translations	(158)	(520)	(105)	(373)	—
Unrealized gains (losses) on securities	61	70	86	27	—
Pension liability adjustments	(2,030)	(320)	(346)	(64)	—
Gains (losses) on derivative hedging	9	15	(150)	(180)	—
Accumulated other comprehensive income (loss)	(2,118)	(755)	(515)	(590)	(842)
Retained earnings (accumulated deficit)	49,290	41,471	35,223	30,503	26,571
Total equity before treasury stock	50,292	43,836	37,817	33,015	28,824
Less: common stock held in treasury, at cost	10,974	5,965	6,004	6,146	6,127
Total shareholders' equity (deficit)	39,318	37,871	31,813	26,869	22,697

Source: J&J, Mergentonline.com.

out of such a form of cross-fertilization have allowed the firm's consumer business to grow by 2 to 3 percent per year over the last four years.

Some of the projects that J&J is currently working on could produce even more significant results. Researchers working on genomic studies in the firm's labs were building a massive database using gene patterns that correlate to a certain disease or to someone's likely response to a particular drug. Weldon encouraged them to share this data with the various business units. As a result, the diagnostics team has been working on a test that the researchers in the pharmaceutical division could use to predict which patients would benefit from an experimental cancer therapy.

Maintaining the Pressure

Even as Weldon moves carefully to encourage collaboration between the business units, he has continued to push for the highest possible levels of performance. Those who know him well would say that he is compulsively competitive. As Weldon has been known to state on more than one occasion, "It's no fun to be second."[6] He is such an intense athlete that he was just a sprint away from ruining

Exhibit 3 Segment Information

Johnson & Johnson is made up of over 200 different companies, many of which it has acquired over the years. These individual companies have been assigned to three different divisions:

Pharmaceuticals

Share of Firm's 2006 Sales: 44%

Share of Firm's 2001 Sales: 46%

Share of Firm's 2006 Operating Profits: 46%

Share of Firm's 2001 Operating Profits: 63%

Medical Devices

Share of Firm's 2006 Sales: 38%

Share of Firm's 2001 Sales: 35%

Share of Firm's 2006 Operating Profits: 43%

Share of Firm's 2001 Operating Profits: 25%

Consumer Products

Share of Firm's 2006 Sales: 18%

Share of Firm's 2001 Sales: 20%

Share of Firm's 2006 Operating Profits: 11%

Share of Firm's 2001 Operating Profits: 12%

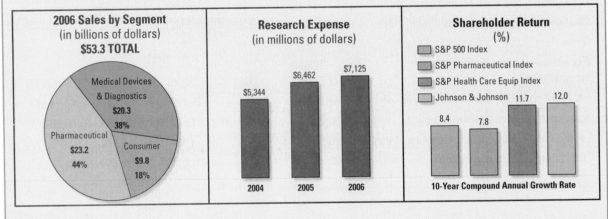

Source: J&J.

his knee altogether when he finally decided to give up playing basketball.

Weldon is not discouraged by setbacks, such as J&J has been facing in its pharmaceutical business. At this point, several of J&J's important drugs are under assault from competitors. The recent expiry of the patent on the firms' blockbuster pain drug, Duragesic, has resulted in a significant drop in its sales. Its well-known anemia drug Procit has been dealing with rising competition and with growing safety concerns. Furthermore, a new anti-psychosis drug, called Invega, recently launched to replace a best-selling older drug, Risperdal, has shown lackluster sales in its first few months. Attempts to launch other new drugs have run into regulatory hurdles with the Food and Drug Administration. "We are seeing increasing risk aversion among regulators, influenced by growing political sentiment for risk-free medicine," explained Weldon.[7]

Weldon is confident that the various divisions will find ways to deal with the challenges that they face.

Exhibit 4   **Key Brands**

Pharmaceuticals

Risperdal for schizophrenia

Procrit for anemia

Remicade for rheumatoid arthritis

Topamix for epilepsy

Medical Devices

Depuy orthopedic joint reconstruction products

Cordis Cypher stents

Ethicon endo surgery products

Lifescan diabetic testing products

Medical Devices & Diagnostics Segment Sales
Sales by Major Franchise
2006 Sales: $20,283 million   Growth Rate: 6.2%
(in millions of dollars)

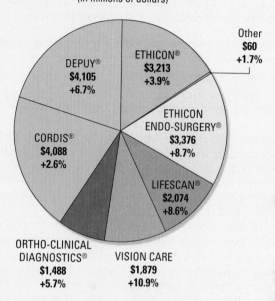

Pharmaceutical Segment Sales
Sales by Major Product
2006 Sales: $23,267 million   Growth Rate: 4.2%
(in millions of dollars)

Consumer Segment Sales
Sales by Major Franchise
2006 Sales: $9,774 million   Growth Rate: 7.5%
(in millions of dollars)

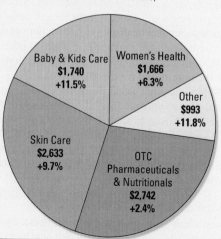

Consumer Products

Tylenol pain killers

Splenda sweetners

Johnson & Johnson baby care products

Stay Free women's health products

Source: J&J 2006 Annual Report.

Exhibit 5   Synergies at J&J

Improved Drugs

J&J's pharmaceutical operation is working with the company's drug-delivery operation, Alza, to come up with a new formulation of the epilepsy drug Topamax. The drug has been shown to also promote weight loss, and this would make it a more tolerable obesity treatment.

New Medical Tests

A new diagnostic unit is working with data generated by drug researchers; they could, for example, develop a gene-based test to identify patients most likely to respond to experimental cancer treatments.

Cutting-edge Consumer Products

In 2002, J&J rolled out the new Band-Aid Brand Liquid Bandage, a liquid coating that is applied to cuts on hard-to-cover areas like fingers and knuckles. The product is based on a material used in a wound-closing product sold by J&J's hospital-products company, Ethicon.

Source: *BusinessWeek.* Barrett, Amy, "Staying on Top," Business Week, May 5, 2003, p. 60.

According to Vice Chairman Christine A. Poon, who leads the firm's pharmaceutical group, "We'll deal with these external challenges as we have always."[8] In fact, sales of schizophrenia drug Risperdal and rheumatoid-arthritis drug Remicade have continued to show growth, even as their patents are set to expire and they are facing growing competition. And despite a drop in sales arising out of safety concerns, J&J's Cypher drug stent continues to be a market leader.

For the most part, Weldon is also letting his managers make their own decisions on the teams where they are working with each other on various projects. He usually does like to get briefed once a month on the progress that is being made on these projects. Beyond that, Weldon claims that he likes to trust his people. "They are the experts who know the marketplace, know the hospitals, and know the cardiologists," Weldon said about the team that has been working on the Cypher stent. "I have the utmost confidence in them."[9]

Even as Weldon tries to let his managers handle their own affairs, he clearly expects them to seek results with the same tenacity that he displayed in his climb to the top. As he rose through the ranks at J&J, Weldon became famous for setting near-impossible goals for his people and holding them to it. And for those executives who may fall short, Weldon does not usually have any difficulty in making it clear that he does not like to be disappointed. When a new J&J drug business, Centocor Incorporated, failed to meet the aggressive sales goals it was set for 2000, Weldon was at its headquarters before the week was out. Everyone at the firm knew they could not allow their performance to fall below the targeted level for the next year.

Is There a Cure Ahead?

Weldon realizes that J&J may face a few challenges over the next couple of years as it tries to find new blockbusters to replace those that are likely to show less growth potential. In both its medical devices and its pharmaceuticals businesses, the firm is confronting growing safety concerns, higher levels of competition and greater pricing uncertainty. Consequently, the firm may have to accept lower growth rates over the short term. "We don't commit to double-digit growth every single year, but we do have this goal of delivering that kind of growth over long periods of time," said Poon.[10]

J&J is in the final stages of acquiring the consumer health care unit of Pfizer, which will result in the addition of more familiar brands such as Listerine mouthwash and Visine eye drops. The purchase of Pfizer's brands will continue to reduce the firm's dependence on the volatile pharmaceuticals business and boost the share of consumer products to almost 25 percent of total sales. Commenting on the acquisition, Weldon explained: "It took some risk out because it doesn't have the volatility of others, but it also just enhances our opportunities as we go further into the future."[11]

But it is becoming much more difficult to find promising acquisitions that do not command a high price. Without reliance on acquisitions for its growth, Weldon will need to draw on all of his competitive spirit to maintain J&J's growth trajectory. He recently announced that the firm has at least 10 new drugs in the late stages of development, some of which could become blockbusters. These would compete for a share of promising markets such as for thinning blood and for treating hepatitis. Above all, Weldon has high hopes for more products that will be developed as a result of his efforts to get different business units across different divisions of J&J to work together. Cross-divisional teams have been working on possible new treatments for diabetes and for stroke.

But it is clear that as Weldon searches for various avenues to maintain J&J's growth record, he must find ways to encourage its businesses to work more closely together than they have ever done in the past. The firm can tap into many more opportunities when it tries to bring together the various skills that it has managed to develop across different divisions. At the same time, he is acutely aware that much of the firm's success has resulted from the relative autonomy that it has granted to each of its business units. Weldon knows that even as he strives to push for more collaborative effort, he does not want to threaten the entrepreneurial spirit that has served J&J so well.

Endnotes

1. Barrett, A. 2003. Staying on top. *BusinessWeek,* May 5: 61
2. Bowe, C. 2006. J&J reveals its guidant motive. *Financial Times,* January 25: 17.
3. Preston, H. H. 2005. Drug giant provides a model of consistency. *Herald Tribune,* March 12–13: 12.
4. *BusinessWeek.* 2003. May 5: 62.
5. *BusinessWeek.* 2003. May 5: 62.
6. *BusinessWeek.* 2003. May 5: 62.
7. Hensley, S. 2006 J&J's Drug sales hurt revenue. *The Wall Street Journal,* January 25: A3.
8. Barrett, A. 2004. Toughing out the drought. *BusinessWeek,* January 26: 85.
9. *BusinessWeek.* 2003. May 5: 66.
10. Weintraub, A. 2007. Under the weather at J&J. *BusinessWeek,* April 23: 82.
11. Johnson, J&J's consumer play paces growth. *The Wall Street Journal,* January 24: A3.

Case 20   Yahoo!*

Terry Semel, who had headed Yahoo! since 2001, resigned from his position as CEO after shareholders expressed dissatisfaction with his performance at the annual shareholders meeting on June 12, 2007. In particular, shareholders complained about the $71.7 million that the former Hollywood mogul received in 2006, putting him at the top of the list of highest-paid CEOs among Standard & Poor's 500 companies. Semel's compensation drew a strong reaction from shareholders because the shares of Yahoo! have dropped 10 percent over the last year, and its revenue growth has fallen in each of the last four quarters (see Exhibits 1 and 2).

* This case was developed by Professor Jamal Shamsie, Michigan State University with the assistance of Professor Alan B. Eisner, Pace University. Material has been drawn from published sources to be used for class discussion. Copyright © 2007 Jamal Shamsie & Alan B. Eisner.

Exhibit 1   Income Statements

	2006	2005	2004	2003	2002
	(in $ millions)				
Revenue	6,425.68	5,257.67	3,574.52	1,625.1	953.07
Total Revenue	6,425.68	5,257.67	3,574.52	1,625.1	953.07
Total Cost of Revenue	2,669.1	2,096.2	1,342.34	370.09	162.88
Gross Profit	3,756.58	3,161.47	2,232.18	1,255.01	790.19
Selling/General/Administrative Expenses, Total	2,002.49	1,397.41	1,072.92	709.67	539.05
Research & Development	688.34	547.14	368.76	207.29	141.77
Depreciation/Amortization	124.79	109.2	101.92	42.39	21.19
Operating Income	940.97	1,107.73	688.58	295.67	88.19
Interest Income (Expense)	139.78	1,092.45	475.96	45.98	87.69
Gain (Loss) on Sale of Assets	15.16	337.97	0.0	0.0	0.0
Other	2.09	5.44	20.49	1.53	2.35
Income Before Tax	1,098.0	2,543.58	1,185.02	343.17	178.23
Income Tax	458.01	767.82	437.97	147.02	71.29
Income After Tax	639.99	1,775.77	747.06	196.15	106.94
Minority Interest	−0.71	−7.78	−2.5	−5.92	0.0
Equity In Affiliates	112.11	128.24	94.99	47.65	0.0
U.S. GAAP Adjustment	0.0	0.0	0.0	0.0	0.0
Net Income Before Extra Items	751.39	1,896.23	839.55	237.88	106.94
Total Extraordinary Items	0.0	0.0	0.0	0.0	−64.12
Accounting Change	0.0	0.0	0.0	0.0	−64.12
Net Income	751.39	1,896.23	839.55	237.88	42.82

Source: Yahoo!

Exhibit 2   Balance Sheets

	2006	2005	2004	2003	2002
			(in $ millions)		
Assets					
Cash and Short-Term Investments	2,601.4	2,560.83	3,511.98	1,309.52	774.18
Cash & Equivalents	1,569.87	1,429.69	823.72	415.89	310.97
Short-Term Investments	1,031.53	1,131.14	2,688.25	893.63	463.2
Total Receivables, Net	930.96	721.72	479.99	282.42	113.61
Accounts Receivable—Trade, Net	930.96	721.72	479.99	282.42	113.61
Accounts Receivable—Trade, Gross	969.16	763.58	514.21	314.38	137.46
Provision for Doubtful Accounts	−38.2	−41.86	−34.22	−31.96	−23.85
Prepaid Expenses	68.81	70.71	72.62	50.99	82.22
Total Other Current Assets	148.97	96.27	25.89	78.79	0.0
Total Current Assets	**3,750.14**	**3,449.53**	**4,090.48**	**1,721.71**	**970.0**
Total Property/Plant/Equipment	955.3	648.9	531.7	449.51	371.27
Goodwill	2,968.56	2,895.56	2,550.96	1,805.56	415.23
Intangibles	405.82	534.62	480.67	445.64	96.25
Long-Term Investments	2,873.12	3,200.34	1,295.37	1,447.63	763.41
Total Other Long-Term Assets	560.67	102.9	229.04	61.6	174.02
Total Assets	**11,513.61**	**10,831.83**	**9,178.2**	**5,931.65**	**2,790.18**
Liabilities and Shareholders' Equity					
Accounts Payable	109.13	70.29	48.21	31.89	18.74
Accrued Expenses	1,035.12	826.64	657.2	483.63	257.58
Total Other Current Liabilities	329.74	307.13	475.3	192.28	135.5
Total Current Liabilities	**1,473.99**	**1,204.05**	**1,180.71**	**707.8**	**411.81**
Total Long Term Debt	749.92	750.0	750.0	750.0	0.0
Long-Term Debt	749.92	750.0	750.0	750.0	0.0
Deferred Income Tax	19.2	243.58	35.77	72.37	0.0
Minority Interest	8.06	0.0	44.27	37.48	31.56
Total Other Liabilities	101.83	67.8	66.01	0.52	84.54
Total Liabilities	**2,353.0**	**2,265.42**	**2,076.76**	**1,568.16**	**527.91**
Common Stock	1.49	1.47	1.42	1.35	0.61
Additional Paid-In Capital	8,615.92	6,417.86	5,682.88	4,340.51	2,430.22
Retained Earnings (Accumulated Deficit)	3,717.56	2,966.17	1,069.94	230.39	−7.49
Treasury Stock–Common	−3,324.86	−547.72	−159.99	−159.99	−159.99
Total Other Equity	150.51	−271.36	507.2	−48.78	−1.08
Total Equity	**9,160.61**	**8,566.42**	**7,101.45**	**4,363.49**	**2,262.27**
Total Liabilities & Shareholders' Equity	**11,513.61**	**10,831.83**	**9,178.2**	**5,931.65**	**2,790.18**
Total Common Shares Outstanding	1,360.25	1,430.16	1,383.58	1,321.41	1,189.72

Source: Yahoo!

Yahoo! has trailed Google in revenues and profits largely because it has not been able to match its rival in crucial areas of Web search and related advertising. Semel had shaken up his firm's management in December and launched its much-delayed search advertising system known as Project Panama in February. The new system had promised to deliver more targeted ads with search results, an area in which Google's technology holds a big edge. "Our goal is to create an advertising platform that takes advantage of Yahoo!, which has the largest network of both users and content in the world," said CEO Terry S. Semel.[1]

The eagerly awaited Panama, on which the firm has been working for the past 18 months, was expected to allow Yahoo! to close the gap with Google in the search for search advertising dollars. But Tim Cadogan, vice president for Yahoo! Search Marketing had been worried about high expectations. "Panama is a foundation for us to start sewing together all our advertising assets," he said. "I don't think it gets us ahead. It gets us to a place where we can compete more effectively."[2]

Semel was persuaded by Yahoo! cofounder Jerry Yang to come out of retirement in 2001 to take over the floundering firm. Advertising revenues at the Internet icon had been plummeting, leading to a precipitous decline in its stock value. When he took over, Semel articulated a basic strategy to build the Yahoo! Web site into a digital form of Disneyland, a souped-up theme park for the Internet Age. His goal has been to build the Yahoo! site into a self-contained world of irresistible offerings that would grab and keep surfers glued to it for hours at a time. By imposing such a strong sense of direction, he managed to craft one of the most remarkable revivals of a beleaguered dot-com.

In spite of his significant accomplishments, Semel had been under considerable pressure to build on opportunities for the future growth of Yahoo!. He had failed to clinch some crucial deals, including one with Facebook, one of the hottest social-networking Web sites. Morale among the firm's employees had begun to sag as some of the top talent had been defecting to the developing competition. More critically, Yahoo! had begun to show slower growth in display advertising, which had long represented one of its key strengths. All of these developments had led Ellen Siminoff, a former Yahoo! executive to state, "Panama is very important to Yahoo!, but it is not the only thing they need to focus on."[3]

Remaking the Culture

Like many other Internet firms, Yahoo! began by attracting visitors by developing a site that would offer a variety of services for free. Those who logged on were able to obtain, among other things, the latest stock quotes and news headlines. The firm relied on online advertising for as much as 90 percent of its revenue. Yahoo! founders Koogle and Yang were confident that advertisers would continue to pay in order to reach its younger and technologically savy surfers. In fact, the firm had made little effort to reach out to clients or to try and build any long-term relationships with them.

By the spring of 2001, Yahoo!'s advertising revenue was falling precipitously, its stock was losing most of its value, and some observers were questioning the firm's business model. With the collapse of the dot-com advertisers, the firm's revenue was down by almost a third from the previous year. Its stock had fallen below an all-time low of $15, having lost more than two-thirds of its value from just two years earlier. Semel was asked to help turn Yahoo! around, but he agreed to take on the task only after the firm's admired cofounder Timothy Koogle had agreed to step down as chairman.

When Semel took over, the changes that he set about making may not have been evident to the casual observer. Visitors to Yahoo!'s headquarters could still see the purple cow in the lobby, be confronted with acres of cubicles, and meet workers clad in jeans. But Semel's style was in stark contrast to the relaxed, laid back approach of Koogle. He immediately started to work on replacing Yahoo!'s freewheeling culture with a much more deliberate sense of order. Semel moved swiftly to chop down the 44 business units he inherited to 5, stripping many executives of pet projects. He did not care much for the firm's "cubicles only" policy, finally locating his own office into a cube adjacent to a conference room so he could make phone calls in private.

Semel even changed Yahoo!'s old freewheeling approach to decision making. When Koogle was in charge, executives would brainstorm for hours, often following hunches with new initiatives. Under Semel, managers have been required to make formal presentations to bring up their new ideas in weekly meetings of a group called the Product Council. Championed by Semel and his chief operating officer, Daniel Rosensweig, the Product Council has typically included nine managers from all corners of the company. The group sizes up business plans to make sure all new projects bring benefits to Yahoo!'s existing businesses.

"We need to work within a framework," said Semel. "If it's a free-for-all . . . we won't take advantage of the strengths of our company."[4] With the focus and discipline that he imposed on the firm, Semel made some progress in getting Yahoo! to grow again. Most of the employees, who had been anxious to see the value of their stock rise again, began to support Semel in his efforts to remake Yahoo!. "People don't always agree with the direction they're getting, but they're happy the direction is there," said a Yahoo! manager who requested anonymity.[5]

Rethinking the Business Model

Semel began turning Yahoo! around by wooing traditional advertisers, making gestures to advertising agencies that it had angered with its arrogance during the boom. He tried to attract back the business of big advertisers by using technology that allowed the Web site to move beyond static banner advertising, offering eye-catching animation, videos,

Exhibit 3   Breakdown of Revenues (in $ millions)

	Advertising	Fees
2006	5,627	798
2005	4,594	664
2004	3,127	447
2003	1,322	303
	U.S.	Foreign
2006	4,366	2,060
2005	3,668	1,590
2004	2,653	921
2003	1,355	270

Source: Yahoo!

and other rich-media formats. As a result of these efforts, Yahoo! was able to show a significant increase in its advertising revenues benefiting in part from the gradual resurgence in online advertising (see Exhibit 3).

Semel also used the deal-making skills that made him a legend in the movie business to land crucial acquisitions and partnerships that would be allow Yahoo! to tap into new sources of advertising revenue (see Exhibit 4). His

Exhibit 4   Significant Acquisitions

2006	Flickr
	Photo sharing
	Del.icio.us
	Social book marking
2005	Verdisoft
	Software development
2004	Musicmatch
	Personalized music
	Kelkoo
	Online consumer shopping
2003	Overture
	Search advertising
	Inktomi
	Search

Source: Yahoo!

biggest was a $1.8 billion deal for Overture Services, whose "pay per click" lets advertisers buy placement next to search results. The move allowed Yahoo! to move away from its reliance on Google for search capabilities, which Semel saw a growing rival. It was also expected to provide Yahoo! with a substantial new stream of revenue from a new form of search-related advertising.

But Semel did not want Yahoo! to rely primarily on advertising revenues. He has been trying to add services that consumers would be willing to pay for. The strategy has been slow to put into place. When Semel took over, he was shocked to find out that Yahoo! did not have the technology in place to handle surging demand for paid services such as online personals, say two former executives. He had to crack down on the firm to whip it into shape to handle the addition of such premium services.

With the capabilities in place, Semel also began making acquisitions that would allow Yahoo! to offer more premium services. One of the first of these was the buyout of HotJobs.com in 2002, which moved the firm into the online job-hunting business. Semel followed up with the acquisition of online music service Musicmatch Inc., hoping to bring more subscribers into the Yahoo! fold. Over the last year, the firm has acquired more promising firms such as Flickr, a photo-sharing site, and Del.icio.us, a bookmark-sharing site (see Exhibit 5 for key Yahoo! offerings).

By making such smart deals, Semel built Yahoo! into a site that can offer surfers many different services, with several of them requiring the customer to pay a small fee. The idea has been to coax Web surfers to spend hard cash on everything from digital music and online games to job listings and premium e-mail accounts with loads of extra storage. Semel hopes that the contribution from such paid services will continue to rise over the next few years, allowing the firm to rely less heavily on advertising. He talked about the opportunities that will be provided by premium services: "We planted a lot of seeds . . . and some are beginning to grow."[6]

Building a Theme Park

In order to build upon the foundation that he has already laid, Semel envisions building Yahoo! into a digital Disneyland, a souped-up theme park for the Internet Age. The idea was that Web surfers logging on to Yahoo!'s site, like customers squeezing through the turnstiles in Anaheim, should find themselves in a self-contained world full of irresistible offerings. Instead of Yahoo! being an impartial tour guide to the Web, it should be able to entice surfers to stay inside its walls as long as possible.

This vision for Yahoo! represents a drastic change from the model that had been developed by its original founders. Koogle had let his executives develop various offerings that operated relatively independently. Managers had built up their own niches around the main Yahoo! site. No one had thought about developing the portal as a whole, much less how the various bits and pieces could work together. "Managers would beg, borrow, and steal from the

Exhibit 5 Key Yahoo! Offerings

Search
Yahoo! Search
Yahoo! Local
Yahoo! Yellow Pages
Yahoo! Maps

Marketplace
Yahoo! Shopping
Yahoo! Real Estate
Yahoo! Travel
Yahoo! Personals
Yahoo! HotJobs

Information & Entertainment
My Yahoo!
Yahoo! News
Yahoo! Finance
Yahoo! Sports
Yahoo! Music
Yahoo! Movies
Yahoo! Games

Communications
Yahoo! Mail
Yahoo! Messanger
Yahoo! Photos
Yahoo! Mobile

Source: Yahoo!

have any new offerings tied in with what was already being offered on Yahoo! He claimed this made them easier for customers to find, increasing their chances of success. Although many different ideas are always under consideration, only a few are eventually offered by Yahoo!.

A key element of Semel's strategy to build Yahoo! into a digital theme park also rested on his ability to push customers into broadband. Lots of the services that he was banked on, such as music and interactive games, are data hogs that appeal mostly to surfers who have high-speed links. Furthermore, since broadband is always on, many of Yahoo!'s customers are more likely to be be lingering in Semel's theme park for hours on end, day after day. "The more time you spend on Yahoo!, the more apt you are to sample both free and paid services," he says.[8]

Searching for a Focus

In spite of Semel's efforts to tightly control the growth of Yahoo! into new areas, the push to develop a digital theme park has led some analysts to question whether the firm has spread itself too thin (see Exhibit 6). Few people inside Yahoo! question its goal of providing a broad range of services that can attract an audience that can be sold to advertisers. But Brad Garlinghouse, a senior Yahoo! vice president, who once shaved a "Y" in the back of his head, has argued that the firm needs to focus on a few areas. This would allow the Web site to make heavier investments in activities in which it thinks it can excel and move away from others that it does not regard as essential.

In particular, there has been some concern about Yahoo!'s lack of relative success in new areas that are likely to fuel future growth. The firm ran into problems with its move into video programming. It recruited some talent from Hollywood to develop new video-focused Web sites, but dropped the idea because of considerable internal resistance. Subsequently, the media group and the search

network to help their own properties," said Greg Coleman, Yahoo!'s executive vice-president for media and sales.[7]

Semel pushed to stitch it all together. He demanded that Yahoo!'s myriad offerings from e-mail accounts to stock quotes to job listings interact with each other. Semel calls this concept "network optimization" and regards this as a key goal for the firm. To make this concept work, every initiative should not only make money but also feed Yahoo!'s other businesses. Most of the focus of the Product Council meetings has been on the painstaking job of establishing these interconnections between the various services that are offered on the site.

With these constraints, it has become much harder for new projects to get approved. Semel was determined to

Exhibit 6 Top US Search Providers

July 2007 Share of U.S. Search Audience	
Google	53.3%
Yahoo!	20.1%
MSN	13.6%
AOL	5.2%
Ask Jeeves	1.8%
All Others	6.0%

Source: Nielsen/NetRatings.

group fought with each other to offer a service for users to upload their own video clips. The delay allowed YouTube, a start-up, to dominate the market.

Yahoo! took the early lead in social networking with the 2005 acquisition of Flickr, a popular photo-sharing site. Since then, however, its efforts have been overshadowed by the acquisition of MySpace by News Corporation and YouTube by Google. Rob Norman, a WPP Group executive, claimed that these represented opportunities that Semel failed to pursue: "Yahoo! had every single asset you would have needed to do those bigger, faster, and sooner than anyone else."[9] Meanwhile, Yahoo! has failed to make much headway with Yahoo! 360, its own social networking site. Semel then began looking at a deal to buy Facebook, a social networking site that is popular among college students.

Semel recently acknowledged that Yahoo! needed to sharpen its focus on key areas. "We've got to get back to basics and again zero in on a few key priorities," he recently stated. "I am not satisfied with our current financial performance and we intend to improve it."[10] The areas that Yahoo! expects to focus on include search and display advertising, video clips, and social media. It is expected that services for individuals such as online dating and services for small businesses such as Web hosting are likely to be dropped.

Garlinghouse believes that efforts to focus the firm would result in more focused responsibilities and speedier decision making. Yahoo!'s attempts to offer a wide variety of services have led to a proliferation of new executive hires, which have contributed to a growth of conflict between various business units. There was a push to create managerial positions to take charge of each of the areas that the firm wanted to develop. He was considering replacing the current "matrix" structure that involved many executives with the appointment of managers who would take responsibility for bottom-line results in their respective areas.

Back to the Future?

Although Semel resigned from his position as chief executive, he did agree to stay on as nonexecutive chairman of the board. This allowed the firm to deal with the shareholder concerns about his hefty compensation. But many analysts believed that Semel did deserve to be rewarded for pulling off a stunning revival of a floundering firm by cutting costs, imposing discipline, and making deals. At the same time, Yahoo!'s growth in revenues and profits has fallen further and further behind those of Google. Semel had argued that Yahoo! is more of an all-round media company that competes in searches with Google, in e-mail with Microsoft, in instant messaging with AOL, in news with CNN, and in social working with MySpace.

Above all, Semel had been well aware that Yahoo! was not the only player with aspirations to becoming a digital theme park. Given the scope of its ambitions, critics have argued that Semel should have moved more aggressively to close the deals that are necessary to make sure that Yahoo! holds on to its status as the world's most popular Web site. "When you become Yahoo!'s size, you become a little complacent, a little fat and happy," said Youssef H. Squali, an analyst for Jefferies and Company.[11] An outside advisor to the firm believes that the firm had fallen behind because it took too much time to make decisions as a result of Semel's low-risk, nonconfrontational nature. At the same time, some people who are close to the company have argued that its decision not to buy high-flying start-up businesses such as MySpace or YouTube represented sound financial management that is likely to pay off in the long run.

With Semel's departure, Jerry Yang, one of the two founders who had continued to serve on the board, took over the job on a temporary basis. Unlike his predecessor, Yang may be able to use his technical background to turn around the morale, which has been dropping as a result of the departure of some of the firm's top talent. He may also be much better at challenging the engineers and bringing in new ones. Yang may also be better at clinching deals with some of the entrepreneurial start-ups that Yahoo! needs to acquire in order to keep growing.

In spite of the slower growth, few observers would question the ability of Yahoo! to survive and grow even in a more intensely competitive environment. They believe that Semel has already managed to build Yahoo! into a brand that will be able to hold its own against formidable rivals. It is expected that under Yang, the firm will be able to move on to tackle the other challenges that it faces. "We are a healthy paranoid company," said Dan Rosenweig, the firm's chief operating officer. "We are appropriately focused on the fact that this is a fluid market, but we're a company born out of competition."[12]

Exhibit 7 **Direct Competitor Comparison (in $ millions)**

	Yahoo!	Google
Market Cap:	$ 38,510	$155,380
Employees:	11,400	10,674
Quarterly Revenue Growth:	6.70%	62.60%
Revenue:	$ 6,530	$ 12,020
Gross Margin:	60.01%	60.29%
EBITDA:	$ 2,050	$ 5,230
Operating Margins:	13.92%	33.62%
Net Income:	$ 734	$ 3,490

Source: Yahoo! Finance.

Endnotes

1. Chmielewski, D. C. 2007. Yahoo's ad system is almost ready. *Los Angeles Times,* January 24: C1.
2. Helft, M. 2007. A long-delayed ad system has Yahoo crossing its fingers. *New York Times,* February 5: C3.
3. *New York Times,* February 5, 2007: C3.
4. Elgin, B., & Grover R. 2003. Yahoo!: Act two. *Business-Week,* June 2: 74.
5. *BusinessWeek,* June 2, 2003: 74.
6. *BusinessWeek,* June 2, 2003: 72.
7. *BusinessWeek,* June 2, 2003: 74.
8. *BusinessWeek,* June 2, 2003: 72.
9. Delaney, K. J. 2006. As Yahoo falters, executive's memo calls for overhaul. *The Wall Street Journal,* November 18–19: A7.
10. *The Wall Street Journal,* November 18–19, 2006: A7.
11. Hansell, S. 2006. At Yahoo, all is not well. *New York Times,* October 11: C7.
12. Zeller, T. Jr., 2005. Yahoo's profit soars in quarter on ad spending and investments. *New York Times,* January 19: C5.

Case 21   Heineken*

In January 2007, 10 months after Heineken had launched an assault on the highly profitable U.S. market for light beer, the Dutch brewer estimated that it had sold a half billion barrels of its new Heineken Premium Light beer during 2006, almost 50 percent more than it had originally projected. The firm tried 20 different versions over 15 months in order to find a taste that would appeal to the light drinker's palate without losing the brand's European cachet. "We've been able to deliver a beer that plays in the light beer sandbox but is true to the Heineken brand," proclaimed Andy Thomas, the head of Heineken USA.[1]

Heineken spent $50 million on the launch of Premium Light, the first time the brewer has produced an extension of its flagship brand and the most it has spent on any launch. But one of the firm's best moves may be the green bottle with a short neck that it designed for Premium Light. Its slimmer, taller silhouette has been used to heavily promote the new entry in billboards and in advertising, a departure from the sophomoric humor or sexy women that are typically used to attract young males who consume the bulk of light beers. "It's like a pretty girl you coveted," says Harry Schumacher of *Beer Business Daily,* "a little treasure you want in your refrigerator."[2]

Heineken executives are especially pleased to find that Premium Light has managed to attract customers without cannibalizing sales from its original brew. In fact, the growing popularity of Premium Light could help the firm revitalize its flagship Heineken brand, which lost its status several years ago as the leading imported beer in the United States to Mexico's Corona. Success with its new light beer also could allow Heineken to maintain double-digit growth rate that it has shown over the last year, which came after three years of sluggish growth (see Exhibits 1 to 3).

The decision to launch a light beer was part of a series of changes that the Dutch brewer has been making to raise its stature in the U.S. market and to respond to changes that are occurring in the global market for beer. Beer consumption has been declining in key markets as a result of tougher drunk-driving laws and a growing appreciation for wine. At the same time, the beer markets around the world have become ever more competitive, as the largest brewers have been expanding across the globe through acquisitions of smaller regional and national players.

The need for change was clearly reflected in the appointment in October 2005 of Jean-Francois van Boxmeer as Heineken's first non-Dutch CEO. He was brought in to replace Thorny Ruys, who had decided to resign 18 months ahead of schedule because of his failure to show much improvement in performance. Prior to the appointment of Ruys in 2002, Heineken had been run by three generations of Heineken ancestors, whose portraits still adorn the dark paneled office of the CEO in its Amsterdam headquarters. Like Ruys, van Boxmeer faces the challenge of preserving the firm's family-driven traditions, while trying to deal with threats that have never been faced before.

Confronting a Globalizing Industry

Heineken was one of the pioneers of an international strategy, using cross-border deals to expand its distribution of Heineken, Amstel or 170 other beer brands in more than 150 countries around the globe (see Exhibits 4 and 5). For years, it has been picking up small brewers from several countries to add more brands and to get better access to new markets. From its roots on the outskirts of Amsterdam, the firm has evolved into one of the world's largest brewers, claiming a little more than 8 percent of the worldwide market for beer.

In fact, the firm's flagship Heineken brand ranked second only to Budweiser in a global brand survey jointly undertaken by *BusinessWeek* and *Interbrand* a couple of years ago. The premier brand has achieved worldwide recognition according to Kevin Baker, director of alcoholic beverages at British market researcher Canadean Ltd. A U.S. wholesaler recently asked a group of marketing students to identify an assortment of beer bottles that had been stripped of their labels. The stubby green Heineken container was the only one that incited instant recognition among the group. However, research from Impact Databank and Euromonitor showed that Heineken, while well recognized was the number five choice among beer drinkers worldwide by 2006. Bud Lite and Budweiser from Anheuser-Busch were the number one and two brands, followed by Skol from InBev (Brazil) and Corona from Grupo Moledo (Mexico).

But the beer industry has been undergoing significant change due to a furious wave of consolidation. Most of the bigger brewers have begun to acquire or merge with their competitors in foreign markets in order to become global players. Over the past six years, South African Breweries Plc acquired U.S. based Miller Brewing to become one of the world's largest global brewers. In 2004, Belguim's Interbrew combined with Brazil's AmBev, eventually rising to the position of the largest global brewer with operations across most of the continents. U.S.-based Coors linked with Canadian-based Molson in 2005, with their combined operations allowing it to rise to a leading position among the world's biggest brewers.

Many brewers have also expanded their operations without the use of such acquisitions. For example, Anheuser-Busch has brought equity stakes and struck partnership deals with Mexico's Grupo Modelo, China's Tsingtao, and Chile's CCU. Such cross-border deals have provided significant benefits to the brewing giants. To begin with, it has

*This case was developed by Professor Jamal Shamsie, Michigan State University wit the assistance of Professor Alan B. Eisner, Pace University. Material has been drawn from published sources to be used for class discussion. Copyright © 2007 Jamal Shamsie & Alan B. Eisner.

Exhibit 1   Income Statements

(in EUs millions)	Consolidated Income Statement For the year ended 31 December	
	2006	2005
Revenue	11,829	10,796
Other income	379	63
Raw materials, consumables, and services	7,376	6,657
Personnel expenses	2,241	2,180
Amortization, depreciation, and impairments	786	768
Total expenses	**10,403**	**9,605**
Results from operating activities	**1,805**	**1,254**
Interest income	52	60
Interest expenses	(185)	(199)
Other net finance income	11	25
Net finance expenses	**(122)**	**(114)**
Share of profit of associates	27	29
Profit before income tax	**1,710**	**1,169**
Income tax expense	(365)	(300)
Profit	**1,345**	**869**
Attributable to:		
Equity holders of the company (net profit)	1,211	761
Minority interest	134	108
Profit	**1,345**	**869**
Weighted average number of share—basic	489,712,594	489,974,594
Weighted average number of shares—diluted	489,974,594	489,974,594
Basic earnings per share	2.47	1.55
Diluted earnings per share	2.47	1.55

Source: Heineken.

given them ownership of local brands that has propelled them into a dominant position in various markets around the world. Beyond this, acquisitions of foreign brewers can provide the firm with the manufacturing and distribution capabilities that they could use to develop a few global brands. "The era of global brands is coming," said Alan Clark, Budapest-based managing director of SABMiller Europe.[3]

InBev, the combination of Interbrew and AmBev have been pushing to develop Stella Artois, Brahma, and Becks as their three global flagship brands. Each of these three brands originated in different locations, with Stella Artois coming from Belgium, Brahma from Brazil, and Becks from Germany. Similarly, the newly formed SAB Miller

has been attempting to develop the Czech brand Pilsner Urquell into a global brand. Exports of this pilsner have doubled since SAB acquired it in 1999. John Brock, the CEO of InBev, commented; "Global brands sell at significantly higher prices, and the margins are much better than with local beers."[4]

Wrestling with Change

Although the management of Heineken has moved to non-family members for the first time, they have been well aware of the long-standing and well-established family traditions that would be difficult to change. Even with the appointment of nonfamily members to manage the firm, a

Exhibit 2 Balance sheet

Consolidated Balance Sheet As at 31 December		
(in EUs millions)	2006	2005
Assets		
Property, plant, & equipment	4,944	5,067
Intangible assets	2,449	2,380
Investments in associates	186	172
Other investments	786	646
Deferred tax assets	395	286
Total noncurrent assets	**8,760**	**8,551**
Inventories	893	883
Other investments	12	23
Trade and other receivables	1,917	1,787
Cash and cash equivalents	1,374	585
Assets classified as held for sale	41	—
Total current assets	**4,237**	**3,278**
Total assets	**12,997**	**11,829**
Equity		
Share capital	784	784
Reserves	666	568
Retained earnings	3,559	2,617
Equity attributable to equity holders of the company	5,009	3,969
Minority interests	511	545
Total equity	**5,520**	**4,514**
Liabilities		
Loans and borrowings	2,091	2,233
Employee benefits	665	664
Provisions	242	273
Deferred tax liabilities	471	393
Total noncurrent liabilities	**3,469**	**3,563**
Bank overdraft	747	351
Loans and borrowings	494	709
Trade and other payables	2,496	2,451
Tax liabilities	149	141
Provisions	122	100
Total current liabilities	**4,008**	**3,752**
Total liabilities	**7,477**	**7,315**
Total equity and liabilities	**12,997**	**11,829**

Source: Heineken.

Exhibit 3 Statement of Cash Flows

Consolidated Statement of Cash Flows For the year ended 31 December		
(in millions of EUs)	2006	2005
Operating activities		
Profit	1,345	869
Adjustments for:		
Depreciation, amortization, and impairments	786	768
Net interest expenses	133	139
Gain on safe of property, plant & equipment, intangible assets and subsidiaries, joint ventures, and associates	(379)	(63)
Investment income and share of profit of associates	(40)	(42)
Income tax expense	365	300
Other noncash items	285	368
Cash flow from operations before changes in working capital and provisions	**2,495**	**2,339**
Change in inventories	(50)	(18)
Change in trade and other receivables	46	(76)
Change in trade and other payables	102	208
Total change in working capital	**98**	**114**
Change in provisions and employee benefits	(211)	(240)
Cash flow from operations	**2,382**	**2,213**
Interest paid & received	(138)	(141)
Dividend received	13	20
Income taxes paid	(408)	(220)
Cash flow used for interest, dividend, and income tax	**(533)**	**(341)**
Cash flow from operating activities	**1,849**	**1,872**
Investing activities		
Proceeds from sale of property, plant & equipment, and intangible assets	182	161
Purchase of property, plant, & equipment	(844)	(853)
Purchase of intangible assets	(33)	(21)
Loans and advances issued to customers and other investments	(166)	(152)
Repayment on loans and advances to customers	134	131
Cash flow used in operational investing activities	**(727)**	**(734)**
Acquisition of subsidiaries, joint ventures, minority interests, and associates, net of cash acquired	(113)	(730)
Disposal of subsidiaries, joint ventures, minority interests, and associates, net of cash disposed	41	270
Cash flow used for acquisitions and disposals	**(72)**	**(460)**
Cash flow used in investing activities	**(799)**	**(1,194)**
Financing activities		
Proceeds from long-term borrowings	262	363
Repayment of long-term borrowings	(578)	(700)
Dividends paid	(294)	(271)
Purchase own shares	(14)	—
Other	(25)	16
Cash flows used in financing activities	**(649)**	**(592)**
Net Cash Flow	**401**	**86**
Cash and cash equivalents at 1 January	234	161
Effect of movements in exchange rates	(8)	(13)
Cash and cash equivalents at 31 December	**627**	**234**

Source: Heineken.

Exhibit 4 Geographical Breakdown of Revenues

Geographical Breakdown (in EUs millions)		
	2006	2005
Western Europe	5,351	5,226
Central & Eastern Europe	3,359	2,796
Americas	1,975	1,733
Africa & Middle East	1,182	1,052
Asia Pacific	560	502

Source: Heineken

little over half of the shares of Heineken are still owned by a holding company which is controlled by the family. With the death of Freddy Heineken, the last family member to head the Dutch brewer, control has passed to his only child and heir, Charlene de Carvalho, who has insisted on having a say in all of the major decisions.

Exhibit 5 Heineken Brands

Significant Heineken Brands in Various Markets	
U.S.	Heineken, Amstel Light, Paulaner,[1] Moretti
Netherlands	Heineken, Amstel, Kylian, Lingen's Blond, Murphy's Irish Red
France	Heineken, Amstel, Buckler,[2] Desperados[3]
Germany	Paulaner,[1] Kulmbacher, Thurn und Taxis
Italy	Heineken, Amstel, Birra Moretti
Poland	Heineken, Zywiec
China	Tiger, Reeb*
Singapore	Heineken, Tiger
Kazakhstan	Tian Shan, Amstel
Egypt	Fayrouz[2]
Israel	Maccabee, Gold Star*
Nigeria	Amstel Malta, Maltina
Panama	Soberana, Panama

*Minority Interest

[1]Wheat Beer

[2]Nonalcoholic Beer

[3]Tequila-Flavored Beer

But the family members were behind some of changes that were announced at the time of van Boxmeer's appointment that would support its next phase of growth as a global organization. As part of the plan, dubbed Fit 2 Fight, the Executive Board was cut down from five members to three, all of whom are younger than 50. Along with van Boxmeer, the board is made up of the firm's Chief Operating Officer and Chief Financial Officer. The change is expected to assist the firm in thinking about the steps that it needs to take to win over younger customers across different markets whose tastes are still developing.

Heineken has also created management positions that would be responsible for five different operating regions and nine different functional areas. These positions were created to more clearly define different spheres of responsibility. Van Boxmeer argues that the new structure also provides incentives for people to be accountable for their performance: "There is more pressure for results, for achievement."[5] He claims the new structure has already encouraged more risk taking and boosted the level of energy within the firm.

The management group of Heineken was also cut down from 36 to 13 members in order to speed up the decision-making process. Besides the three members of the Executive Board, the management group consists of the managers who are responsible for the five different operating regions and five of the key functional areas. Van Boxmeer hopes that the reduction in the size of this group will allow the firm to combat the cumbersome consensus culture that has made it difficult for Heineken to respond swiftly to various challenges even as its industry has been experiencing considerable change.

Finally, the restructuring program has also set a an ambitious goal of cutting costs in order to produce an annual savings of 200m euros by 2008. Heineken has always been known for its efficiencies and it has considerably reduced its costs for producing beer over the last 10 years. But the firm is seeking to cut costs further by closing some breweries and make cuts in its 64,000-person workforce.

Maintaining a Premium Position

For decades, Heineken has been able to rely upon the success of its flagship Heineken brand, which has enjoyed a leading position among premium beers in many markets around the world. It had been the best-selling imported beer in the United States for several decades, giving it a steady source of revenues and profits from the world's biggest market. But by the late 1990s, Heineken had lost its 65-year-old leadership among imported beers in the United States to Group Modelo's Corona. The Mexican beer has been able to reach out to the growing population of Hispanic Americans who represent one of the fastest growing segments of beer drinkers.

Furthermore, the firm was also concerned that Heineken was being perceived as an obsolete brand by many young drinkers. John A. Quelch, a professor at Harvard Business School who has studied the beer industry said of Heineken,

Leading Beer Brands

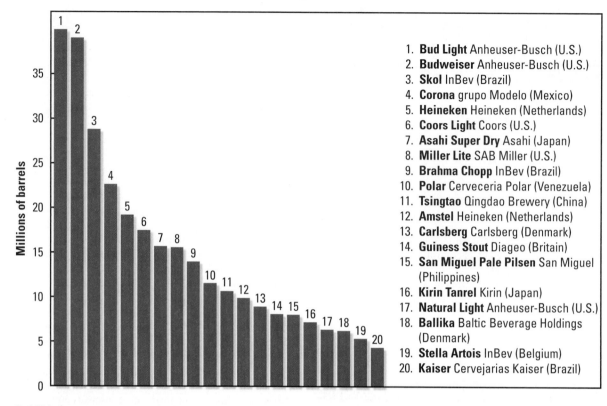

1. **Bud Light** Anheuser-Busch (U.S.)
2. **Budweiser** Anheuser-Busch (U.S.)
3. **Skol** InBev (Brazil)
4. **Corona** grupo Modelo (Mexico)
5. **Heineken** Heineken (Netherlands)
6. **Coors Light** Coors (U.S.)
7. **Asahi Super Dry** Asahi (Japan)
8. **Miller Lite** SAB Miller (U.S.)
9. **Brahma Chopp** InBev (Brazil)
10. **Polar** Cerveceria Polar (Venezuela)
11. **Tsingtao** Qingdao Brewery (China)
12. **Amstel** Heineken (Netherlands)
13. **Carlsberg** Carlsberg (Denmark)
14. **Guiness Stout** Diageo (Britain)
15. **San Miguel Pale Pilsen** San Miguel (Philippines)
16. **Kirin Tanrel** Kirin (Japan)
17. **Natural Light** Anheuser-Busch (U.S.)
18. **Ballika** Baltic Beverage Holdings (Denmark)
19. **Stella Artois** InBev (Belgium)
20. **Kaiser** Cervejarias Kaiser (Brazil)

Exhibit 6 Leading Beer Brands

Source: Impact Databank.

"It's in danger of becoming a tired, reliable, but unexciting brand."[6] The firm has, therefore, been working hard to increase awareness of their flagship brand by spending much more on marketing the brand, particularly among younger drinkers. The average age of the Heineken drinker has been reduced from about 40 in the mid-1990s to about 30 over the past couple of years.

At the same time, Heineken has also been pushing on other brands that would reduce its reliance on its core Heineken brand. It has already achieved considerable success with Amstel Light, which has become the leading imported light beer in the United States and has been selling well in many other countries. But many of the other brands that it carries are strong local brands that it has added through its string of acquisitions of smaller breweries around the globe. It has managed to develop a relatively small but loyal base of consumers by promoting some of these as specialty brands, such as Murphy's Irish Red and Moretti.

Finally, Heineken has been stepping up its marketing to Hispanics, who account for one-quarter of U.S. sales. It concluded a deal in 2004 with a leading Mexican brewer to market and distribute its five popular brands which include Tecate and Dos Equis within the United States. Benj Steinman, publisher and editor of the *Beer Marketer's Insight* newsletter claims that the deal will give a tremendous boost to Heineken. "This gives Heineken a commanding share of the U.S. import business and . . . gives them a bigger presence in the Southwest . . . and better access to Hispanic consumers," he stated.[7]

Above all, Heineken wants to maintain its leadership in the premium beer industry, which represents the most profitable segment of the beer business. In this category, the firm's brands face competition from domestic beers such as Anheuser's Budweiser Select and imported beers such as InBev's Stella Artois. Although premium brews often have slightly higher alcohol content than standard beers, they are developed through a more exclusive positioning of the brand. This allows the firm to charge a higher price for these brands. A six-pack of Heineken, for example, costs $10, versus around $7 for a six-pack of Budweiser.

Heineken's interest in the premium segment is also driven by the prospects for future growth in this category. Its success with Premium Light is significant, because even though light beers account for half of U.S. beer sales, few premium beers have been introduced in this important category. Furthermore, while Heineken expects overall global beer consumption to grow at a rate of just 2 percent over the next couple of years, the premium market is expected to grow at twice that rate. Just-drinks.com, a London-based online research service, estimates that the market for premium beer will expand by 84 percent, to $230 billion, by 2012, from $125 billion in 2004.

Building a Global Stature

Van Boxmeer is well aware of the need for Heineken to use its brands to build upon its existing stature across global markets. In spite of its formidable presence in markets around the world, Heineken has failed to match the recent moves of formidable competitors such as Belgium's InBev and U.K.'s SABMiller, which have grown significantly through mega-acquisitions. In large part, it is assumed that the firm has been reluctant to make such acquisitions because of the dilution of family control.

For the most part, therefore, Heineken has limited itself to snapping up small national brewers, such as Italy's Moretti and Spain's Cruzcampo, that have provided it with small, but profitable avenues for growth. In 1996, for example, Heineken had acquired Fischer, a small French brewer, whose Desperados brand has been quite successful in niche markets. Similarly, Paulaner, a wheat beer that the firm picked up in Germany a few years ago, has been making inroads into the U.S. market.

But as other brewers have been reaching out to make acquisitions from all over the globe, Heineken runs the risk of falling behind its more aggressive rivals. To deal with this growing challenge, the firm has broken out of its play-it-safe corporate culture to make a few big deals. In 2003, Heineken spent $2.1 billion to acquire BBAG, a family-owned company based in Linz, Austria. Because of BBAG's extensive presence in Central Europe, Heineken has become the biggest beer maker in seven countries across Eastern Europe.

At the same time, Heineken has been making an aggressive push into Russia with the acquisition of mid-sized brewing concerns. Through seven acquisitions since 2002, Russia has become Heineken's largest market by volume, with 10 breweries producing around 6 million barrels of beer a year. Heineken now ranks as the third-largest brewer in Russia, behind Sweden's Baltic Beverages Holding and InBev.

Rene Hooft Graafland, the company's Chief Financial Officer, has stated that Heineken will continue to participate in the consolidation of the $437 billion global retail beer industry by targeting many different markets around the world. During the last three years, the firm has also added several labels to Heineken's shelf, pouncing on brewers in far flung places like Panama, Egypt, and Kazakhstan. In Egypt, Ruys bought a majority stake in Al Ahram Beverages Company and hopes to use the Cairo-based brewer's fruit-flavored, nonalcoholic malts as an avenue into other Muslim countries.

A Break from the Past?

When Mr van Boxmeer took over the helm of Heineken, he announced that he would have to work on the company's culture in order to accelerate the speed of decision making. This led many people both inside and outside the firm to expect that the new management would try to break loose from the conservative style that has resulted from the family's tight control. Instead, the affable 44-year-old Belgian suggested that he would adhere even more closely to the firm's existing culture than his predecessors.

Van Boxmeer's devotion to the firm is quite evident. Heineken's first non-Dutch CEO spent 20 years working his way up within the firm. Even his cufflinks are silver miniatures of a Heineken bottle top and opener. "We are in the logical flow of history," he recently explained. "Every time you have a new leader you have a new kind of vision. It is not radically different, because you are defined by what your company is and what your brands are."[8]

Furthermore, van Boxmeer seems quite comfortable working with the family-controlled structure. "Since 1952 history has proved it is the right concept," he stated about the current ownership structure. "The whole business about family restraint on us is absolutely untrue. Without its spirit and guidance, the company would not have been able to build a world leader. Your long-term strategy does not change because you have a few less successful years."[9]

Most analysts believe that van Boxmeer and his team will manage to build Heineken into a powerful global competitor even as he continues to adhere to its powerful family traditions. Rene Hooft Graafland, the firm's CFO, hesitates to provide specific figures, but he made it clear that the new management's initiatives were designed to drive long-term growth. In his own words, "We are positive that the momentum in the company and trends will continue."[10]

Endnotes

1. Carter, A. 2007. A shining light for Heineken. *BusinessWeek*, January 15: 48.
2. *BusinessWeek*, January 15, 2007: 48.
3. Ewing, J., & Khermouch, G. 2003. Waking up Heineken. *BusinessWeek*, September 8: 68.
4. Tomlinson, R. 2004. The new king of beers. *Fortune*, October 18: 238.
5. Bickerton, I., & Wiggins, J. 2006. Change is brewing at Heineken. *Financial Times*, May 9: 12.
6. *BusinessWeek*, September 8, 2003: 69.
7. Kaplan, A. 2004. Border crossings. *Beverage World*, July 15: 6.
8. *Financial Times*, May 9, 2006: 12.
9. *Financial Times*, May 9, 2006: 12.
10. Williams, C. C. 2006. Heineken seeing green. *Barron's*, September 18: 19.

Case 22 Rocky Mountain Chocolate Factory, Inc.*

The gourmet chocolate segment is the fastest growing segment in the chocolate industry and accounts for 10 percent of overall chocolate sales. Gourmet chocolate sales were $1.3 billion in 2005 and are expected to reach $1.8 billion in 2010, which reflects a 6.4 percent growth rate. Two main reasons contribute to this growth: the health benefits from the antioxidants in chocolate and the placement of products in mass-market channels. Don Montouri, publisher of *Packaged Facts* states, "Gourmet chocolates have come out of the closet and are showing some muscle in the mass market arena with exceptional branding that is making gourmet indulgence a household phenomenon. Higher cocoa content, the health benefits associated with chocolate, the introduction of organics, "single origin chocolates," and exotic flavors such as grapefruit and habaneros are having a major impact on the industry, helping it grow more quickly than standard chocolate."[1]

On May 10, 2007, managers at the Rocky Mountain Chocolate Factory announced record earnings for the fiscal year ended February 28, 2007. Bryan Merryman, COO and CFO of the company, stated, "We are very pleased to report another year of impressive net income growth with diluted earnings per share increasing 23 percent to a record $0.75 in Fiscal 2007. Our revenues rose over 12 percent to a record $31.6 million, while total systemwide sales of our franchised and company-owned stores increased 9 percent to $108.9 million, compared with $99.7 million in the previous fiscal year."[2]

While Rocky Mountain Chocolate Factory was growing nicely, the question on the minds of CEO Frank Crail and his management team had to be whether they could maintain this level of growth in the years to come in the highly competitive, fragmented chocolate and confections industry.

Company Operations[3]

History   In 1981, Frank Crail had a dream of raising his family in a quiet, small-town environment. Upon the family's arrival in Durango, Colorado, Frank did not have a plan to support his family so he surveyed the town's local residents and merchants. Frank recalls, "It came down to either a car wash or a chocolate shop. I think I made the right choice."[4] The original shop is still located on Main Street and the smell of chocolate lures the tourists and local citizens into the store. The company offers 300 chocolate candies and other confectionary products and during the Christmas, Easter, and Valentine's Day holidays the company will offer an additional 100 products. As of March 31, 2007, there are 5 company-owned and 316 franchised store locations in 38 states, Canada, the

United Arab Emirates, and Guam. The company employs about 235 people.

The philosophy at Rocky Mountain Chocolate Factory is to use only the finest, highest quality ingredients and no artificial preservatives. Its marketing motto is "the Peak of Perfection in Handmade Chocolates."[5] The Rocky Mountain Chocolate Factory brand name is well known and company managers believe this, along with its reputation for quality, variety, and taste of products, special ambiance of the stores, store site selection criteria, expertise in the manufacture and merchandising of chocolate candy products, and good customer service, provide the company with a competitive advantage.

The company board of directors has adopted a code of ethics that all employees, officers, and directors must follow. The code covers such topics as compliance with laws, conflicts of interest, confidential information, intellectual property, public disclosures, records management, fair dealing, insider trading, and discrimination and sexual harassment.

In June 2005, it was announced that Rocky Mountain Chocolate Factory was included on *Fortune*'s list of America's 100 fastest-growing small public companies. Frank Crail commented, "We are proud that *Fortune* magazine has selected Rocky Mountain Chocolate Factory as one of the 100 fastest-growing small public companies in America. Our goal is to build Rocky Mountain Chocolate Factory into the premier retail chocolatier in the United States, and our 16 percent increase in revenues and 43 percent increase in earnings during the most recent fiscal year clearly illustrate our progress towards this goal. This recognition by *Fortune* magazine is consistent with the visibility our Company has achieved within the investment community in recent years."[6]

Products   In order to maintain high quality levels and provide the best taste experience to customers, only the finest chocolates and ingredients are used. The proprietary recipes have been developed by the master candy maker. Each store offers at least 100 types of chocolate candies at any one time and during special holidays a store may offer as many as 200 products, many of which are in specially designed packages for the holiday season. Stores may offer more than 15 types of fudge and over 30 varieties of caramel-covered apples. The fudge is made fresh in the store each day and is shaped into a 22 pound loaf. One company signature piece of candy is the "Bear"™ which is a paw-sized mixture of caramel, roasted nuts, and chocolate. Other favorite candies that are offered include nut clusters, butter creams, exotic flavored truffles, toffee, and a large peanut butter cup (called the "Bucket"). The company also dips a variety of fruits, nuts, pretzels, and cookies in milk, dark, or white chocolates. Recently introduced is a line of sugar-free and no-sugar-added candies.

*This case was prepared by Debora J. Gilliard, Ph.D. Metropolitan State College–Denver as a basis for class discussion rather than to illustrate either effective or ineffective handling of an administrative situation. Copyright © 2007 by Debora J. Gilliard.

One trademark of the company is the large portions of chocolate. Frank Crail reports that ". . . this was a fortunate mistake. In the early days, my partners and I did not know how to make chocolate and had to literally learn on a ping pong table. From the start we made the candy centers too big, not compensating for the added size and weight when coating the pieces in chocolate. And if they didn't look quite right we would dip them again."[7] The oversized pieces were a hit with customers and have become a Rocky Mountain benchmark.

Working with Lucie and Desi Arnaz to develop a licensing agreement, the Rocky Mountain Chocolate Factory has created a trademarked I Love Lucy® line of candies. Some of the products in this line include bags of almond toffee (Lucy's favorite candies), chocolate bars, assorted chocolates, lollipops, and a Lucy's Chocolate Factory Heart Tin. Lucie Arnaz has stated, "To put Lucy together with chocolate and create a lasting tribute to my parents and *I Love Lucy,* their legendary television show, has been a dream of mine for over a decade. My brother, Desi, and I are confident that we have found just that in Rocky Mountain Chocolate Factory."[8]

In 2000, managers hired a nationally recognized packaging design firm to completely redesign the packaging that is featured in the retail stores. The project was completed in 2002 and the design is very contemporary and highlights a coordinated line of packaged products that conveys the Rocky Mountain Chocolate Factory store experience of freshness, fun, and excitement.

Stores and Distribution   Company managers are very careful about selecting sites for new stores. When identifying possible sites, managers review and consider tenant mix, visibility, attractiveness, accessibility, foot traffic, and costs. Locations of stores are in factory outlet malls, tourist environments, regional malls, street fronts, airports, and other entertainment-oriented sites.

There are 110 factory outlet malls in the United States and by February 28, 2007, Rocky Mountain Chocolate Factory had stores in 65 of these malls in 25 states. The company has about 45 stores in locations considered tourist environments or entertainment-oriented sites. These locations include Fisherman's Wharf in San Francisco and the Riverwalk in San Antonio. There are about 1,400 regional malls in the United States and the company has stores in about 100 of the malls. Regional mall locations include the Mall of America in Minnesota and Fort Collins, Colorado. Other sites that company managers consider appropriate locations include airports and sports arenas. Rocky Mountain Chocolate Factory has nine stores in airports: two at Denver International Airport; one at Charlotte International Airport; one at Minneapolis International Airport; one in Phoenix Sky Harbor Airport; one at Salt Lake City International Airport; and three in Canada at Edmonton International Airport, Toronto Pearson Airport, and Vancouver International Airport.

The stores are designed to establish an inviting atmosphere to customers. Products such as fudge, barks, and caramel apples are made in the store. Approximately 50 percent of store sales are from products made on site. This concept conveys freshness and homemade quality to customers, and in-store preparation is fun and entertaining as customers watch the candy being made. In 2000, managers hired a design firm to evaluate existing store design. A new design was developed and implementation began in 2002. By March 2007, 159 stores incorporating the new design had been opened. The pre-2002 design was a country Victorian décor that included wood cabinets, copper and brass accents, and etched mirrors. The post-2002 design is more modern and designed specifically for the high-traffic mall locations. The average store size is 1,000 square feet with 650 square feet of selling space.

In 2002, the company opened its first full service retail kiosk. The kiosk is used when the retail environment is not suitable for a larger store, such as when space is unavailable or when build-out costs or rent does not meet company criteria. The kiosk, which is between 150 and 250 square feet, still includes the cooking area where caramel apples and fudge are prepared in front of customers and core products are available for sale. As of March 2007, 24 kiosks were in operation.

In addition to its stores, the company also sells product through wholesaling, fundraising, corporate sales, mail order, and the Internet.

Manufacturing Operations   Rocky Mountain Chocolate Factory candy products are made at the factory located in Durango, Colorado. The manufacturing process involves cooking or preparing the candy centers, which include nuts, caramel, peanut butter, creams, and jellies, and then coating them with chocolate and other toppings. Temperature ranges are carefully controlled and quality control measures exist at every step of the manufacturing process. Both manual and automated processes are employed. When it becomes cost effective, the company will move a manual operation to an automated process, but they are careful to not compromise product quality or appearance when changing to an automated process.

In order to maintain fresh product, stores do not carry high levels of inventory. Store managers are encouraged to only order the amount of product that can be expected to be sold within two to four weeks.

Chocolate, nuts, sugar, corn syrup, cream, and butter are the main ingredients used in candy products. Shipments of ingredients arrive at the factory daily in order to ensure freshness. The company buys ingredients from a limited number of reliable suppliers and often enters into purchase contracts of between 6 and 18 months in order to ensure a constant supply of ingredients, especially chocolate and nuts. At least one alternative source is maintained for all essential ingredients so that the loss of a supplier would not have a substantial effect on the operations of the company. A limited amount of candy is purchased from third parties and is sold in stores as a private label product.

A large portion of product is shipped from the factory to stores via the eight company-owned trucks so that product arrives at stores quickly and cost-efficiently. Ingredients, supplies, and products from third parties are back-hauled on return trips in order to maintain low costs for the trucking operations.

Controlling costs and continuing to find ways to increase efficiencies is important to company managers. In recent years the company has purchased additional automated factory equipment; implemented a comprehensive MRP II system that includes forecasting, planning, scheduling, and reporting; and installed an enhanced point-of-sale system in all company-owned stores and 162 of the franchised stores.

Marketing

In-store promotions and point-of-purchase materials are the primary means of marketing used by Rocky Mountain Chocolate Factory. Local store marketing is important to the company so advertisements, coupons, flyers, and mail order catalogs are customized for each store by the in-house Creative Services Department. The company participates in local and regional events, sponsorships, and charitable causes as a means to attain low-cost but high return publicity.

Franchising

In 2002, most company-owned stores were sold and in March 2007, the company had 316 franchised stores. The company began franchising stores in 1982. The initial investment is between $129,000 and $435,515 and the franchise fee is $24,500. Rocky Mountain Chocolate Factory has been ranked the number one franchise opportunity in the candy category by *Entrepreneur Magazine*.

Most new franchises are awarded to people who have been referred by current franchisees, customers who have visited Rocky Mountain Chocolate Factory stores and are interested in owning one, and to existing franchisees. The company does advertise for new franchises in national and regional newspapers in areas where suitable potential store locations have been identified. Franchisees are selected based on net worth and liquidity, work ethic, and a personality that is compatible with the company's operating philosophy. Because of the emphasis on excellent customer service, the company looks for high levels of motivation and energy when hiring employees or evaluating franchisees. In 1992, the company entered into a franchising development agreement with Immaculate Confections, Ltd. of Vancouver, British Columbia to develop stores in Canada. By March 2007 there were 35 stores operating in the Canadian market. In 2000, the company entered into a franchise development agreement covering the Gulf Cooperation Council States and the Al Muhairy Group purchased the exclusive right to develop the franchise. In March 2007, 3 stores were operated under this agreement.

Rocky Mountain Chocolate Factory provides a comprehensive seven-day training program to franchisees at its training center in Durango. Franchisees learn about store operations and management at the full size replica store. Topics covered during the training program include company philosophy, customer service, merchandising, pricing, cooking, inventory and cost control, quality standards, record keeping, labor scheduling, and personnel management. During the program, trainees are completely oriented to company operations by working in key factory operational areas and by meeting senior managers. Operating standards are stated in operating manuals provided to trainees.

Franchisees are continually supported by company field consultants who regularly visit franchise store sites and talk with franchisees via phone. Field consultants review and discuss operating results and provide advice and guidance to franchisees on improving profitability and implementing marketing and merchandising programs. A handbook containing a prepackaged local store marketing plan is provided to all franchisees.

Franchisees must pay the initial franchise fee, royalties based on monthly gross sales, and a marketing fee based on monthly gross sales. Franchisees are granted an exclusive area of operation. Chocolate and candy products that are not made on-site must be purchased from the company factory or from approved suppliers.

Finances

Rocky Mountain Chocolate Factory derives income from three sources: (1) sales of chocolates and confectionary products to franchisees, (2) sales of product at company-owned stores, and (3) initial franchise fees and royalties from franchisees. At fiscal year end February 28, 2007, 72 percent of revenues were from sales of products to franchisees, 8 percent from company-owned store sales, and 20 percent from franchise and royalties fees.

Company sales vary seasonally with the most sales occurring during the Christmas holiday and summer vacation season.

Revenues increased 12.5 percent from fiscal 2006 to fiscal 2007, operating income increased 17.1 percent, and net income increased 16.7 percent. Exhibit 1 contains a breakdown of amounts received from the revenue sources.

The increase in revenue is primarily due to the increased number of franchise stores that were in operation during the year. In fiscal year 2007, 37 new franchised operations were opened. In fiscal year 2008, the company expects franchisees

Exhibit 1   Revenues[9]

	(in $ thousands)		
	2007	2006	% Change
Factory Sales	$22,709	$19,297	17.7%
Retail Sales	2,626	3,046	−13.8%
Royalty & marketing fees	5,604	5,048	11.0%
Franchise fees	634	683	−7.1%
TOTAL	$31,573	$28,074	12.5%

to open between 35 and 40 new stores, and the company expects net income to increase 15 to 20 percent. In May 2006, the board of directors authorized the repurchase of up to $2 million in common stock. On May 3, 2007, this repurchase was completed and the board of directors authorized the repurchase of an additional $5 million, or up to 350,000 shares, of common stock.

For the 12 months ending May 2007, the stock price ranged from a high of $15.49 per share to a low of $11.67 per share. The P/E ratio for Rocky Mountain Chocolate Factory is 20.14 compared to an industry average of 21.68 (see Exhibits 2 to 4).

Frank Crail summed up Rocky Mountain Chocolate Factory's growth and performance over the years when he

Exhibit 2   Income Statements

Rocky Mountain Chocolate Factory, Inc. Statements of Income			
	For the Years Ended February 28		
	2007	**2006**	**2005**
Revenues			
Sales	$25,335,739	$22,343,209	$19,380,861
Franchise and royalty fees	6,237,594	5,730,403	5,142,758
Total revenues	31,573,333	28,073,612	24,523,619
Costs and Expenses			
Cost of sales, exclusive or depreciation and amortization expense of $412,546, $391,141, and $359,633	15,988,620	13,956,550	11,741,205
Franchise costs	1,570,026	1,466,322	1,411,901
Sales and marketing	1,538,476	1,320,979	1,294,702
General and administrative	2,538,667	2,239,109	2,497,718
Retail operating	1,502,134	1,755,738	1,453,740
Depreciation and amortization	873,988	875,940	785,083
Total costs and expenses	24,011,911	21,614,638	19,184,349
Operating Income	7,561,422	6,458,974	5,339,270
Other Income (Expense)			
Interest expense	—	(19,652)	(99,988)
Interest income	67,071	95,360	92,938
Other	67,071	75,708	(7,050)
Income Before Income Taxes	7,628,493	6,534,682	5,332,220
Income Tax Expense	2,883,575	2,470,110	2,015,580
Net Income	$ 4,744,918	$ 4,064,572	$ 3,316,640
Basic Earnings per Common Share	$ .77	$ .65	$ .55
Diluted Earnings per Common Share	$ .75	$ .61	$ .51
Weighted Average Common Shares Outstanding	6,125,831	6,268,202	6,006,882
Dilutive Effect of Employee Stock Options	216,524	407,411	474,499
Weighted Average Common Shares Outstanding, Assuming Dilution	6,342,355	6,675,613	6,481,382

Source: Company 10-K report.

Exhibit 3   Balance Sheets

Rocky Mountain Chocolate Factory, Inc. Balance Sheets		
	As of February 28	
	2007	2006
Assets		
Current Assets		
Cash and cash equivalents	$ 2,830,175	$ 3,489,750
Accounts receivable, less allowance for doubtful accounts or $187,519 and $46,920	3,756,212	3,296,690
Notes receivable	50,600	116,997
Inventories, less reserve for slow moving inventory of $147,700 and $61,032	3,482, 139	2,938,234
Deferred income taxes	272,871	117,715
Other	367,420	481,091
Total current assets	10,759,417	10,440,477
Property and Equipment	5,754,122	6,698,604
Other Assets		
Notes receivable, less valuation allowance of $0 and $52,005	310,453	278,741
Goodwill	939.074	1,133,751
Intangible assets	349,359	402,469
Other	343,745	103,438
Total other assets	1,942,630	1,918,399
Total assets	$18,456,169	$19,057,480
Liabilities and Stockholders' Equity		
Current Liabilities		
Accounts payable	$ 898,794	$ 1,145,410
Accrued salaries and wages	931,614	507,480
Other accrued expenses	585,402	750,733
Dividend payable	551,733	504,150
Deferred income	288,500	—
Total current liabilities	$ 3,256,043	$ 2,907,773
Deferred Income Taxes	685,613	663,889
Commitments and Contingencies		
Stockholders' Equity		
Common stock, $ .03 par value; 100,000,000 shares authorized; 100,000,000 and 6,113,243, 6,281,920 shares issued and outstanding	183,397	188,458
Additional paid-in capital	6,996,728	10,372,530
Retained earnings	7,334,388	4,924,930
Total stockholders' equity	14,514,513	15,485,818
Total liabilities and stockholders' equity	$18,456,169	$19,057,480

Source: Company 10-K report.

Exhibit 4 Cash Flow Statements

Rocky Mountain Chocolate Factory, Inc.
Statements of Cash Flows

	For the Years Ended February 28		
	2007	**2006**	**2005**
Cash Flows from Operating Activities:			
Net Income	$ 4,744,918	$ 4,064,572	$ 3,316,640
Adjustments to reconcile net income to net cash provided by operating activities			
Depreciation and amortization	873,988	875,940	785,083
Provision for loss on accounts and notes receivable and related foreclosure costs	70,000	—	25,000
Provision for inventory loss	70,000	45,000	90,000
Loss on sale of assets	101	37,411	44,789
Expense recorded for stock options	201,269	—	—
Deferred income taxes	(133,432)	4,195	135,716
Changes in operating assets and liabilities			
Accounts receivable	(711,456)	(445,921)	(453,255)
Refundable income taxes	—	364,630	(364,630)
Inventories	(613,905)	(461,207)	(136,402)
Other assets	104,843	(236,640)	89,661
Accounts payable	(246,616)	56,934	135,934
Income taxes payable	(33,729)	(824,860)	(121,403)
Accrued liabilities	452,255	602,187	23,726
Deferred Income	5,000	—	—
Net cash provided by operating activities	4,783,236	4,082,241	3,570,859
Cash Flows from Investing Activities:			
Additions to notes receivable	(124,452)	—	(236,142)
Proceeds received on notes receivable	211,143	345,442	172,776
Proceeds (expense) from sale or distribution of assets	434,335	(4,395)	23,834
Decrease in other assets	(134,221)	15,748	451
Purchase of property and equipment	(201,037)	(1,300,314)	(1,406,698)
Net cash provided by (used in) investing activities	185,768	(943,519)	(1,445,779)
Cash Flows from Financing Activities:			
Payments on long-term debt	—	(1,665,084)	(1,401,490)
Costs of stock split or dividend	—	(8,902)	(15,638)
Issuance of common stock	623,206	1,072,729	591,126
Tax benefit or stock option exercise	159,930	1,182,830	531,360
Repurchase and redemption of common stock	(4,381,090)	(2,958,441)	(844,206)
Dividends paid	(2,030,625)	(1,710,980)	(1,099.639)
Net cash used in financing activities	(5,628,579)	(4,087,848)	(2,238,487)
Net Decrease in Cash and Cash Equivalents	(659,575)	(949,126)	(113,407)
Cash and Cash Equivalents at Beginning of Year	3,489,750	4,438,876	4,552,283
Cash and Cash Equivalents at End of Year	$ 2,830,175	$ 3,489,750	$ 4,438,876

Source: Company 10-K report.

stated, "Fiscal 2007 represented another year of progress towards our goal of building Rocky Mountain Chocolate Factory into the premier retail chocolatier in the United States with systemwide sales breaking the $100 million mark for the first time in the Company's history."[10]

Analyst David Lee Smith writes, "I must admit that I'm intrigued by Rocky Mountain Chocolate Factory. While the company's clearly not a Hershey in scope, and despite its share price having been essentially flat over the past year, I would venture that its debt-free balance sheet and its earnings growth will stand it in good stead going forward. Further, as one who appreciates sound communication almost as much as I relish good stocks, I find management's obvious enthusiasm for the company to be refreshing."[11]

The Chocolate and Confections Industry

The National Confectioners Association (NCA) estimates that 2006 retail confectionary sales reached $28.9 billion, a 2.8 percent increase over 2005. Retail chocolate sales reached $16.3 billion for the year ended December 2006. Per capita consumption of chocolate was over 13 pounds in 2004. Gourmet chocolates account for about 10 percent of the chocolate industry with sales of $1.3 billion in 2005 and expectations that sales will reach $1.8 billion by 2010, a 6.4 percent growth rate. One major reason for this growth rate in the gourmet chocolate segment is the expansion of distribution through food, drug, and mass market channels. Exhibit 5 contains a listing of major competitors in the U.S gourmet chocolate industry.[12]

Exhibit 6 contains the The National Confectioners Association reports of confectionary sales for 2006.[13]

Confectionery products are sold through multiple convenience stores as shown in Exhibit 7.[14]

The National Confectioners Association also reports seasonal trends in Exhibit 8.[15]

The NCA predicts Valentine's and Christmas sales will be up in 2007 and Easter and Halloween sales will be comparable to 2006.

What new products and trends from chocolate and confectionery manufacturers can consumers expect to see in the future? Dark chocolate is still a consumer favorite. It appeals to the older demographic and it is being touted for

its health benefits. Dark chocolate sales increased 49 percent from 2003 to 2006. Marcia Mogelonsky, a senior analyst with Mintel International states, "Companies have been working hard to introduce people to different ranges of dark chocolate, from 45 percent to 75 percent cacao."[16] New products from Hershey's include the Extra Dark line; Pure Dark with cranberries, blueberries, and almonds; and Pure Dark with macadamia nuts and cranberries. Nestle's has Dark Chocolate Raisinets, Treasures, and Turtles.[17] Ghirardelli will introduce Intense Dark Gourmet Chocolate Bars and Botticelli® will introduce Choco-Omeg (which

Exhibit 5 Gourmet Chocolate Marketers

Company	Brand Names
See's Candies	
MasterFoods USA	Dove, Dove Promises
Lindt & Sprungli A.G.	Lindt, Lindt Lindor, Ghirardelli
Ferrero USA Inc.	Confetteria Raffaello, Ferroro Rocher, Mon Cheri
Hersheys	Joseph Schmidt Confections, Scharffen Berger
Nestlé USA Inc.	Nestlé, After Eight, Perugina
Campbell Soup Co.	Godiva Chocolatier
Kraft Foods, Inc.	Terrys, Toblerone chocolate
Maxfield Candy Co.	Mrs. Field, Maxfield's, Hallmark
Alfred Ritter Gmbh & Co.	Ritter Sport
Droste BV	Droste

Exhibit 6 2006 Confectionery Sales

	(in billions of dollars)		
Category	Retail Sales	Manufacturer Sales	% Change
Total	$28.9	$18.8	+2.8%
Chocolate	$16.3	$10.5	+3.1%
Non-Chocolate	$8.9	$5.8	+1.7%
Gum	$3.7	$2.5	+3.6%

Exhibit 7　Convenience Store Sales Lead Growth

Channel	2006 Sales	Confectionery Growth
	(in billions of dollars)	
Supermarkets	$4.3	+0.19%
Wal-Mart*	$3.2	+6.7%
Mass Excluding Wal-Mart	$1.3	+1.5%
Convenience Stores	$4.2	+9.4%
Drug Stores	$2.4	+4.6%
Warehouse Clubs*	$3.1	−0.3%
Dollar Stores*	$0.8	−0.3%
Vending	$1.2	+0.5%

*Estimates.

comes in 3 formulas: the cardio bar with omega-3s, the calcium bar with calcium and omega-3s, and the memory bar with choline and omega-3s).[18,19] Consumers will see more high-end chocolates with the introduction of Chocolate Bows Dark Almond Chocolates and Sweet Candy Company Gourmet Taffy twists. Fortified candies that have vitamins and skin-enhancing ingredients that are being introduced by N.I. Corporation. Pure Beauty Strips and Jelly Belly Sport Beans™ come in fruit punch and berry blue. Sugar-free and healthy sweets products will be introduced with Simply Lite Foods' Sunkist fruit gummies with Vitamin C, Hershey Sticks that are 60-calorie chocolate treats, and a sugar-free Dove Dark. Russell Stover is beginning to sell its No Added Sugar products in the UK. Sugar-free sales account for 7 percent of the UK confectionery market, 58 percent of Spain's confectionery market, and 32 percent of France's market.[20] In 2005, 2,767 new confectionery products were introduced to consumers and studies have found that 23 percent of candy sales can be attributed to new products.[21]

Other trends in the industry have been predicted by NCA:[22]

- Product placement, in-store promotions, candy displays, and signage will become more important to gourmet chocolate manufacturers as they try to achieve product differentiation. Retail space allocated to candy products has not changed much in the past 10 years. In 1993, retailers allocated 21.7 linear feet to candy, on average, and in 2004 retailers devoted about 22.2 linear feet. However, average store size has increased by 33 percent, thus the percentage of linear feet allocated to candy has decreased.[23]
- More national retailers are offering candy, gum, and mints at cash registers. Home Depot, Dick's Sporting Goods, Circuit City stores, and Staples are a few of the national retailers carrying candy products. Sales through these nontraditional outlets have doubled over the last several years.[24]
- Snacking occasions are seeing growth in Europe and the value of super-premium snacking will go from $12.3 billion in 2004 to $15 billion in 2009. In the United States, the market will go from $8 billion in 2004 to $10.7 billion in 2009. Chocolate's share of the U.S. market is expected to increase by 5 percent from $670 million in 2004 to $855 million in 2009.
- Artisan chocolates created by small manufacturers are creating a niche market. These chocolate makers are experimenting with exotic flavors and ingredients mixes.
- As consumers become more ethically aware, it is expected there will be growth and new introductions in the organic, natural, and varietal chocolates. Consumers have indicated that they would purchase more fair trade items if they were available. In the confectionery industry, Fair Trade Certification indicates that cacao farmers are paid fair prices.
- Demographic changes are also affecting the industry. Asians are the prime consumers of gourmet/premium chocolates. Younger adults who are not married, are college graduates, and rent or are condo/co-op dwellers will consume above average amounts of gourmet and premium chocolates. Premium chocolate consumers

Exhibit 8　Seasonal Confectionery Trends

Season	2006	2005	2004	2003
Valentine's Day	+0.1%	−4.0%	−3.0%	−7.6%
Easter	+7.0%	−7.6%	+5.5%	+2.2%
Halloween	+2.8%	+2.3%	+2.4%	−0.4%
Christmas	+1.0%	+2.4%	−3.5%	−3.0%

are not correlated to high income groups. The following industry opinion of the most important consumer group to target with higher-quality products: 10 percent indicated 10- to 17-years-olds, 36 percent indicated 18- to 24-year-olds, 18 percent indicated 25- to 34-year-olds, 50 percent indicated 35- to 49-year-olds, and no one indicated seniors aged 50 and over.

• Manufacturers may create new opportunities for consumers to purchase candy by focusing on nontraditional candy holidays (such as July 4th) or by cross selling products such as candy and greeting cards or chocolates and wine.[25]

• Obesity is becoming a major concern in the United States. In 1986, the Centers for Disease Control reported that just eight states had 10 to14 percent of the residents obese. In 2002, every state reported at least 15 to 19 percent of its residents were obese. Today, it is more socially acceptable to be overweight than at any time in the past. NCA speakers at the 2006 conference indicate that the amount of sweets an individual consumes does not materially affect an individual's weight and that sweets represent 4.1 percent of total calorie intake for adults with optimal Body Mass Index. Sweets account for 4 percent of total calorie intake for overweight adults and 4.3 percent for obese adults.

• The confectionery industry has many strengths that manufacturers can take advantage of; including impulse consumption, expandable snacking occasions, affordability, superior pricing power, responsiveness to innovation, and rational competitive dynamics. Purchases can be increased through promotion and product innovations; 79 percent of snacks sold in a retail establishment cost less than $1; there are many opportunities for distribution such as supermarkets, drug stores, mass merchandisers, convenience stores, kiosks, and vending machines; and confections is the largest segment of the $65 billion snacking market accounting for about 38 percent of sales.[26]

The chocolate and confectionery industry must comply with numerous regulations that cover health, sanitation, safety, and franchise operations (relating to registration and disclosure of information). Product labels must comply with the Nutrition Labeling and Education Act of 1990 and the Food Allergen Labeling and Consumer Protection Act of 2004.[27] During 2005, the NCA was actively involved in supporting or fighting numerous legislative proposals. Vending machine restrictions were proposed in New Jersey, California, and Connecticut. Candy taxes were proposed in Pennsylvania, North Carolina, Nebraska, and West Virginia. Legislation concerning the levels of lead in candy was introduced in California, Texas, New York, and Maryland. The NCA supported the Central American Free Trade Agreement (CAFTA) that provided for an increase in sugar imports to the United States. CAFTA was signed by President Bush in August 2005.[28] During 2006, the

NCA was instrumental in defeating the candy tax bill in West Virgina, the aspartame ban bill in New Mexico, and vending machine restriction bills in many states. The NCA lobbied for national uniform food safety standards and against bills regarding lead in candy. In 2007, the organization will fight sugar reform that is being discussed in the Farm Bill in efforts to minimize the impact the bill will have on sugar prices.[29]

The prices of chocolates and nuts can vary significantly in the commodities market due to monetary fluctuations and economic, political, and weather conditions in the countries where products are grown. It was reported in June 2006, that the black pod, frosty pod, and witches' broom diseases could adversely affect the cacao beans if these plant diseases are not controlled. There are 4 million metric tons of beans valued at $4 billion produced each year.[30] Cocoa is produced mainly in developing countries. Eight countries produce 90 percent of the world's production of cocoa (see Exhibit 9).

Major cocoa consuming countries are the United States, Germany, France, the United Kingdom, Russian Federation, Japan, Italy, Brazil, Spain, Mexico, Canada, Poland, and Belgium.

The ripe fruit of the cocoa tree is harvested by farmers with machetes. Once the raw cocoa bean is fermented and dried, it is taken to the processing factory where the inner part of the kernel, the nib, is heat treated. After the roasting process, the color and taste of the cocoa mass determines if it is an intermediate or semifinished product. Fat is pressed out of the cocoa mass and once this cocoa butter is filtered it goes to the manufacturer either in liquid form in tankers or in solid form in cardboard boxes. What remains after the butter has been removed is pressed into cocoa cakes. These cakes are broken up and ground into fine cocoa powder. Chocolate is made from cocoa mass, sugar, cocoa butter, and, optionally, milk may be added. [32] Today, the World Cocoa Foundation (established in 2000) helps to strengthen

Exhibit 9 Coca Producing Countries 2006[31]

Country	Production
Ivory Coast	38%
Ghana	21%
Indonesia	13%
Nigeria	5%
Cameroon	5%
Brazil	4%
Ecuador	3%
Malaysia	1%
Others	10%

the partnership between the industry and the cocoa farmers by educating farmers on safe labor practices and helping them earn more money for their cocoa crops. The International Cocoa Initiative (established in 2002) actively promotes responsible labor practices on the cocoa farms.[33]

The retail sales of confectionery products are very competitive and the candy market is maturing, with expected 4 percent annual growth rates. Close competitors of Rocky Mountain Chocolate Factory are Godiva Chocolatier, with annual sales of $825 million; Russell Stover, with annual sales of $450 million; and See's Candies, with annual sales of $325 million. Today, it is not uncommon to read about a new chocolatier opening a store or a major manufacturer introducing a new chocolate product. How will Rocky Mountain Chocolate Factory continue to compete in this fast-paced industry?

Endnotes

1. Moran, M. 2006. *The Gourmet Retailer,* June 1, www.gourmetretailer.com.
2. Rocky Mountain Chocolate Factory, news release, May 10, 2007, www.rmcf.com.
3. SEC 10-K report for fiscal year ending February 28, 2007 and company Web site, www.rmcf.com.
4. Rocky Mountain Chocolate Factory, Web site, www.rmcf.com.
5. SEC 10-K report for Fiscal Year ending February 28, 2007, www.rmcf.com.
6. Rocky Mountain Chocolate Factory, Web site, www.rmcf.com.
7. Rocky Mountain Chocolate Factory, Web site, www.rmcf.com.
8. Ibid.
9. SEC 10-K report for fiscal year end February 28, 2007.
10. Rocky Mountain Chocolate Factory press release, May 2007, www.rmcf.com/corp.
11. Smith, D. L. 2007. Rocky Mountain's sweet results. *Motley Fool,* May 14, www.fool.com.
12. Moran, M. 2006. Category analysis: Chocolate: Quality satisfies American sweet tooth. *The Gourmet Retailer,* June www.gourmetretailer.com.
13. 2006 NCA's Year in Review. 2007, www.candyusa.com.
14. Ibid.
15. Ibid.
16. Das, A. 2007. U.S. dark chocolate sales soar on health benefits, *Reuters,* May 4.
17. Angrisani, C. 2006. Dark future seen for chocolate sales. *Supermarket News,* Web site, www.0-premium.hoovers.com.
18. Show offers something healthy for your sweet tooth. *Chicago Sun Times,* June 7, 2006, www.0-premium.hoovers.com.
19. All candy expo forecasts new candy trends. *PR Newswire,* June 6, 2006, www.0-premium.hoovers.com.
20. Sugar-free U.S. sweets for UK. *The Grocer,* May 10, 2006, www.0-premium.hoovers.com.
21. Ibid.
22. Moran, M. 2006. Category analysis: Chocolate: Quality satisfies American sweet tooth. *The Gourmet Retailer,* June 1 www.gourmetretailer.com.
23. Kuhn, M. E. 2006. NCA State of the Industry Conference Report, www.candyindustry.com.
24. Candy moves up front. *The Gourmet Retailer,* December 12, 2006, www.gourmetretailer.com.
25. Kuhn, M. E. 2006. NCA State of the Industry Conference Report, www.candyindustry.com.
26. Confectioners face broad range of challenges in expanding sweets universe. *CandyNews,* 2006, www.candyindustry.com.
27. SEC 10-K report for fiscal year end February 28, 2007.
28. 2006 NCA's Year in Review. 2006, www.candyusa.com.
29. 2006 NCA Year in Review. 2007, www.candyusa.com.
30. Chocolates could succumb to plant disease! *Hindustan Times,* June 7, 2006, www.0-premium.hoovers.com.
31. UNCTAD, (accessed May 2007), Cocoa Market, *Info Comm,* http://r0.unctad.org/inforcomm
32. Cocoa story: The production process—from cocoa beans to semi-finished product. European Cocoa Association (accessed May 2007), www.eurococoa.com.
33. Help children on cocoa farms. World Cocoa Foundation, April 20, 2007, www.worldcocoafoundation.org.

Case 23   World Wrestling Entertainment*

On Sunday, April 1, 2007, 80,103 people from 24 countries and all 50 states packed the cavernous Ford Field stadium in Detroit for WrestleMania, the annual pop culture spectacular that is hosted by World Wrestling Entertainment (WWE). Among the attractions was a marquee matchup pitting Bobby Lashley, fighting on behalf of Donald Trump, against Umaga, fighting on behalf of WWE co-founder and Chairman Vince McMahon, in the Battle of the Billionaires. Fans packed the venue from ringside to the rafters, even as the show was being delivered by satellite to millions more in over 110 countries. Kurt Schneider, Executive Vice President of Marketing proclaimed, "Ford Field shook to the very core of its foundation with the thunderous noise from the record setting crowd."[1]

The drawing power of the annual event indicated that WWE had clearly moved out of a slump that it had to endure between 2001 and 2005. During the 1990s, WWE's potent mix of shaved, pierced, and pumped-up muscled hunks; buxom, scantily clad, and sometimes cosmetically enhanced beauties; and body-bashing clashes of good versus evil had resulted in an empire that claimed over 35 million fans. Furthermore, the vast majority of these fans were males between the ages of 12 and 34, the demographic segment that makes most advertisers drool. And these guys had driven up WWE's revenues by their insatiable appetite for tickets, broadcasts, and merchandise.

By the end of 1999, the husband-and-wife team of Vince and Linda McMahon used WWE's surge in popularity to raise $170 million through an initial public offering. But the firm's failure with a football league, which folded after just one season, was followed by a drop in revenues from its core wrestling businesses. Its attendance began to drop off at its live shows, and advertising revenues for its television shows started to decline. WWE struggled with its efforts to build new wrestling stars and to introduce new characters into its shows.

Since 2005, however, things finally seem to be turning around for WWE (see Exhibits 1 and 2). Vince and Linda have turned pro wrestling into a perpetual traveling road show that makes more than 2 million fans pass through turnstiles worldwide. Its wrestling shows attract more than 15 million television viewers every week, making them a fixture among the top-rated cable programs. WWE sold more than 4 million DVDs during the last year and signed pacts with 100 different licensees to sell merchandise such as video games, toys, and trading cards (see Exhibits 3 to 5).

WWE was also drawing on its wrestling roots to build up a stronger ad-supported Internet presence, selling merchandise and offering video programming. Even bolder was the firm's expansion into feature film production with its wrestling superstars. "We continue to see the distribution of our creative content through various emerging channels," stated WWE's President and CEO Linda McMahon.[2] According to a recent ranking of popular Web searches, WWE was drawing considerable attention. It had the fourth most online buzz, trailing only top television hits such as *American Idol* and *Dancing with the Stars*.

Developing a Wrestling Empire

Most of the success of the WWE can be attributed to the persistent efforts of Vince McMahon. He was a self-described juvenile delinquent who went to military school as a teenager to avoid being sent to a reformatory institution. Around 1970, Vince joined his father's wrestling company, Capital Wrestling Corporation. He did on-air commentary, developed scripts, and otherwise promoted wrestling matches. Vince bought Capital Wrestling from his father in 1982, eventually renaming it World Wrestling Federation (WWF). At that time, wrestling was managed by regional fiefdoms where everyone avoided encroaching on anyone else's territory. Vince began to change all that by paying local television stations around the country to broadcast his matches. His aggressive pursuit of audiences across the country gradually squeezed out most of the other rivals. "I banked on the fact that they were behind the times, and they were," said McMahon.[3]

Soon after, Vince broke another taboo by admitting to the public that wrestling matches were scripted. Although he had made this admission in order to avoid the scrutiny of state athletic commissions, wrestling fans appreciated the honesty. The WWF began to draw in more fans through the elaborate story lines and the captivating characters of its wrestling matches. The firm turned wrestlers such as Hulk Hogan and Andre the Giant into mainstream icons of pop culture. By the late 1980s, the WWF's *Raw is War* had become a top-rated show on cable and the firm had also begun to offer pay-per-view shows.

Vince faced his most formidable competition after 1988, when Ted Turner brought out World Championship Wrestling (WCW), one of the few major rivals that was still operating. He spent millions luring away WWF stars such as Hulk Hogan and Macho Man Randy Savage. He used these stars to launch a show on his own TNT channel to go up against WWF's major show, *Raw is War*. Although Turner's new show caused a temporary dip in the ratings for WWF's shows, Vince fought back with pumped-up scripts, mouthy muscle-men, and lyca-clad women. "Ted Turner decided to come after me and all of my talent," growled Vince, "and now he's where he should be. . . ."[4]

In 2001, Vince was finally able to acquire WCW from Turner's parent firm AOL Time Warner for a bargain price of $5 million. Because of the manner in which he eliminated most of his rivals, Vince has earned a reputation for being as

* This case was developed by Professor Jamal Shamsie, Michigan State University with the assistance of Professor Alan B. Eisner, Pace University. Material has been drawn from published sources to be used for class discussion. Copyright © 2007 Jamal Shamsie & Alan B. Eisner.

Exhibit 1 Income Statements

	12/31/2006	04/30/2006	04/30/2005
	(in $ thousands)		
Net revenues	262,937	400,051	366,431
Cost of revenues	157,094	227,172	213,289
Selling, general, & administrative expenses	61,043	87,173	86,874
Depreciation & amortization	5,557	10,472	11,874
Stock compensation costs	—	4,694	4,101
Operating income (loss)	39,243	70,540	50,293
Investment income	6,440	7,390	5,362
Interest expense	421	587	642
Other income (loss)	884	553	1,346
Income before income taxes	46,146	77,896	56,359
Current federal income taxes	11,514	22,595	10,443
Current state & local income taxes	278	7,232	1,623
Current foreign income taxes	295	2,718	5,325
Deferred federal income taxes	2,167	(2,139)	2,183
Deferred state & local income taxes	275	478	(993)
Provision for income taxes	14,529	30,884	18,581
Income (loss) from continuing operations	31,617	47,012	37,778
Income (loss) from discontinued operations	—	35	1,369
Net income (loss)	31,617	47,047	39,147
Year end shares outstanding	70,997.479	70,556.998	68,880.655
Dividend per share	0.36	0.72	0.36
Total number of employees	560	460	433
Number of class A common stockholders	11,794	11,374	11,282
Number of class B common stockholders	3	3	3

Source: Mergentonline.com.

aggressive and ambitious as any character in the ring. Paul MacArthur, publisher of *Wrestling Perspective*, an industry newsletter praised his accomplishments: "McMahon understands the wrestling business better than anyone else. He's considered by most in the business to be brilliant."[5]

In 2002, WWF was also hit by a ruling from a British court that stated that their original WWF acronym belonged to the World Wildlife Fund. The firm had to undergo a major branding transition, changing its well-known name and triple logo from WWF back to WWE. Although the change in name was costly, it did not seem to have hurt

the firm in the long run. "Their product is really the entertainment. It's the stars. It's the bodies," said Larry McNaughton, managing director and principal of CoreBrand, a branding consultancy.[6] Linda stated that the new name might have actually been beneficial for the firm. "Our new name puts the emphasis on the 'E' for entertainment," she commented.[7]

Creating a Script for Success

Since taking over the firm, Vince began to change the entire focus of the wrestling shows. He looked to television soap operas for enhancing the entertainment value of his

Exhibit 2 Balance Sheets

	12/31/2006	04/30/2006	04/30/2005
	(in $ thousands)		
Cash & cash equivalents	86,267	175,203	56,568
Short-term investments	161,889	105,655	201,487
Accounts receivable	—	71,515	65,188
Allowance for doubtful accounts	—	3,740	3,287
Accounts receivable, net	52,113	67,775	61,901
Inventory	3,049	1,788	1,057
Prepaid expenses & other current assets	13,334	11,140	15,191
Assets of discontinued operations	469	457	544
Total current assets	317,121	362,018	336,748
Land, buildings, & improvements	56,084	55,957	51,958
Equipment	45,752	44,788	42,511
Corporate aircraft	20,829	20,710	20,710
Vehicles	634	518	542
Gross property & equipment	123,299	121,973	115,721
Less: accumulated depreciation & amortization	55,327	54,403	49,083
Net property & equipment	67,972	67,570	66,638
Feature film production assets	53,560	36,094	28,771
Gross intangible assets	11,012	—	—
Less: accumulated amortization—intangible assets	7,684	—	—
Net intangible assets	3,328	1,461	2,608
Other assets	11,304	12,247	6,640
Total assets	453,285	479,390	441,405
Current portion of long-term debt	862	817	756
Accounts payable	14,909	19,826	15,669
Accrued pay-per-view event costs	5,228	7,500	5,691
Accrued income taxes	—	7,418	—
Accrued talent royalties	—	714	368
Accrued payroll related costs	5,403	9,176	6,038
Accrued television costs	—	1,487	1,958
Accrued legal & professional fees	2,051	3,254	1,007
Accrued home video production & distribution	5,144	3,121	2,013
Accrued publishing print & distribution	—	625	580
Accrued other expenses	7,709	2,722	3,496
Accrued expenses & other current liabilities	25,535	36,017	21,151
Deferred income	20,166	19,874	20,843
Liabilities of discontinued operations	302	294	254
Total current liabilities	61,774	76,828	58,673
Long-term debt	5,800	6,381	7,198
Class A common stock	233	227	210
Class B common stock	477	479	479
Additional paid-in capital	286,985	277,693	254,716
Accumulated other comprehensive income (loss)	666	355	(908)
Retained earnings (accumulated deficit)	97,350	117,427	121,037
Total stockholders' equity	385,711	396,181	375,534

Source: Mergentonline.com.

Exhibit 3   Breakdown of Net Revenues

	December 31, 2006	April 30, 2006	April 30, 2005
	(in $ millions)		
Live & televised entertainment	183.0	290.8	299.5
Consumer products	59.2	86.4	53.9
Digital media	20.7	22.9	13.0
WWE films	—	—	—
Total	262.9	400.1	366.4

Source: WWE.

Exhibit 4   Breakdown of Operating Income

	December 31, 2006	April 30, 2006	April 30, 2005
	(in $ millions)		
Live & televised entertainment	57.0	93.9	100.6
Consumer products	26.9	46.4	26.9
Digital media	3.8	2.9	1.2
WWE films	(1.1)	(1.3)	(1.0)

Source: WWE.

Exhibit 5   Percentage Breakdown of Net Revenues

	December 31, 2006	April 30, 2006	April 30, 2005
Live & televised entertainment			
Live events	20%	19%	22%
Venue merchandise sales	5%	4%	3%
Television	22%	20%	21%
Pay per view	20%	24%	23%
Video on demand	1%	—	—
Consumer products			
Licensing	6%	8%	6%
Home video	13%	11%	6%
Magazine publishing	3%	3%	3%
Digital media	3%	2%	2%
WWE films	—	—	—

Source: WWE.

live events. Vince reduced the amount of actual wrestling and replaced it with wacky, yet somewhat compelling, story lines. He began to develop interesting characters and create compelling story lines by employing techniques that were quite similar to those being used by many successful television shows. There was a great deal of reliance on the "good versus evil" or the "settling the score" themes in the development of the plots for his wrestling matches. The plots and subplots ended up providing viewers with a mix of romance, sex, sports, comedy, and violence against a backdrop of pyrotechnics.

Over time, the scripts for the matches became tighter, with increasingly intricate story lines, plots, and dialogue. All the details of every match were worked out well in advance, leaving the wrestlers themselves to decide only the manner in which they would dispatch their opponents to the mat. Vince's use of characters was well thought out and he began to refer to his wrestlers as "athletic performers" who were selected on the basis of their acting ability in addition to their physical stamina. Vince also ensured that his firm owned the rights to the characters that were played by his wrestlers. This would allow him to continue to exploit the characters that he developed for his television shows, even after the wrestler that played that character had left his firm.

By the late 1990s Vince had two weekly shows on television. Besides *Raw,* the original flagship program on the USA cable channel, WWE had added a *Smackdown!* show on the UPN broadcast channel. He developed a continuous storyline using the same characters so that his audience would be driven to both the shows. But the acquisition of the WCW resulted in a significant increase in the number of wrestling stars under contract. Trying to incorporate more than 150 characters into the story lines for WWE's shows proved to be a challenging task. At the same time, the move of *Raw* to Spike TV channel resulted in a loss of viewers.

In October 2005, WWE signed a new agreement with NBC that moved *Raw* back to the USA channel and gave the firm a new show called *ECW: Extreme Championship Wrestling* on the SCI FI channel. Because of the greater coverage of these cable channels, the firm has seen a significant rise in viewers. Its other show, *Smackdown* is now carried by the new expanded CW channel, which resulted from the recent combination of the UPN network with the WB network. The shows are also attracting new viewers because of the growth in popularity of a new breed of characters such as John Cena and Chris Benoit.

Managing a Road Show

A typical work week for the WWE can be grueling for the McMahons, for the talent and for the crew. The organization is now putting on more than 300 live shows a year requiring everyone to be on the road most days of the week. The touring crew includes over 200 crew members, including stage hands. All of WWE's live events, including those that are used for its two longstanding weekly shows *Raw*

and *Smackdown!* as well as the newer ones, are held in different cities. Consequently, the crew is always packing up a dozen 18-wheelers and driving hundreds of miles to get from one performance to the next. Since there are no repeats of any WWE shows, the live performances must be held all year round.

In fact, the live shows form the core of all of WWE's businesses (see Exhibit 6). They give the firm a big advantage in the entertainment world. Most of the crowd shows up wearing WWE merchandise and screams throughout the show. Vince and his crew pay special attention to the response of the audience to different parts of the show. They claim that these live events provide them with a real-time assessment of the popularity of their storylines and characters. The script for each performance is not set until the day of the show and sometimes changes are made even in the middle of a show. Vince boasted: "We're in contact with the public more than any entertainment company in the world."[8]

Although the live shows usually fill up, the attendance fee—running on average around $35—barely covers the cost of the production. But these live performances provide content for nine hours of original television programming as well as for the growing list of pay-per-view offerings. Much of the footage from these live shows is also being used on the WWE Web site, which is the growth engine for its new digital media business. Finally, the shows create strong demand for WWE merchandise ranging from home videos and magazines to video games and toys.

The whole endeavor is managed not only by Vince, but by all of his family. Vince's efforts notwithstanding, the development of the WWE has turned into a family affair. While the slick and highly toned Vince could be regarded as the creative muscle behind the growing sports entertainment empire, his wife Linda began to quietly manage its day-to-day operation. Throughout its existence, she helped to balance the books, do the deals, and handle the details that were necessary for the growth and development of the WWE franchise.

One of Vince and Linda's greatest pleasures has been to see their kids also move into the business. Their son, Shane, heads wwe.com, the firm's streaming-media site and their daughter Stephanie, has been part of the creative writing team. "This business is my heart and soul and passion and always has been," Stephanie commented.[9] The family's devotion lies behind much of the success of WWE. "If they are out there giving 110 percent, it's a lot easier to get it from everyone else," said wrestler Steve Blackman.[10]

Pursuing New Opportunities

In 1999, shortly after going public, WWF (as it was called then) launched an eight-team football league called the XFL. Promising full competitive sport unlike the heavily-scripted wrestling matches, Vince tried to make the XFL a faster-paced, more fan-friendly form of football than the NFL's brand. Vince was able to partner with NBC, which was looking for a lower priced alternative to the NFL televised games. The XFL kicked off with great fanfare in February 2001. Although the games drew good attendance,

Exhibit 6   **Wrestlemania's Five Best Bouts**

Andre the Giant vs. Hulk Hogan

WrestleMania III, March 29, 1987

- **The Lowdown:** A record crowd of 93,173 witnessed Andre the Giant, undefeated for 15 years, versus Hulk Hogan, wrestling's golden boy.
- **The Payoff:** Hogan body-slammed the 500-pound Giant, becoming the sport's biggest star and jump-starting wrestling's first big boom.

The Rock vs. Stone Cold Steve Austin

WrestleMania X-7, April 1, 2001

- **The Lowdown:** The two biggest stars of wrestling's modern era went toe-to-toe in the culmination of a two-year-long feud.
- **The Payoff:** Good-guy Austin aligned with "evil" WWE owner Vince McMahon and decimated the Rock to win the title in front of a shocked crowd.

Hulk Hogan vs. The Ultimate Warrior

WrestleMania VI, April 1, 1990

- **The Lowdown:** The most divisive feud ever—fan favorite Hulk Hogan defended his title against up-and-coming phenom the Ultimate Warrior.
- **The Payoff:** Half the crowd went into cardiac arrest (the other half were in tears) when Hogan missed his patented leg drop and the Warrior won.

Bret Hart. vs. Shawn Michaels

WrestleMania XII, March 31, 1996

- **The Lowdown:** Two men who didn't like each other outside the ring locked up in a 60-minute Iron Man match for the title.
- **The Payoff:** After an hour, neither man had scored a pinfall. Finally, Michaels, aka the Heartbreak Kid, pinned Hart in overtime to win the belt.

Kurt Angle vs. Brock Lesnar

WrestleMania XIX, March 30, 2003

- **The Lowdown:** Olympic medalist Angle squared off against former NCAA wrestling champ Lesnar in a punishing bout.
- **The Payoff:** The 295-pound Lesnar landed on his head after attempting a high-flying attack. But he recovered to pin Angle and capture the championship.

Source: *TV Guide.* 2004. March 13.

television ratings dropped steeply after the first week. The football venture folded after just one season, resulting in a $57 million loss for WWF. Both Vince and Linda insist that the venture could have paid off if it had been given enough time. Vince commented; "I think our pals at the NFL went out of their way to make sure this was not a successful venture."[11]

Since then, the firm has tried to seek out growth opportunities that are driven by its core wrestling business. With more characters at their disposal and different characters being used in each of their shows, WWE has been ramping up the number of live shows, including more in overseas locations. During 2006, the firm staged over 40 live events outside the United States in far-flung locations such as the U.K., Spain, Panama, the Philippines, and New Zealand. An increase in the number of shows around the globe is also helping to boost the worldwide revenues that the firm is able to generate from its merchandise.

There has also been considerable excitement generated by the launch of WWE 24/7, a subscriber video on-demand service. The new service allows the firm to distribute for a fee about 40 hours of content each month consisting of highlights from old shows as well as exclusive new programming. The service is being expanded to various cable companies reaching a growing number of VOD enabled homes. Within a year of its launch, WWE 24/7 has shown considerable growth, generating over $1.5 million in revenue.

WWE is also pushing into a new area of digital media, building an e-commerce site that offers the widest range of the firm's merchandise. The site also offers a wide range of content, including live broadcasts, transactional video footage, and original programming. In a recent tally, WWE.com was attracting more than 16 million unique users each month. The firm has barely tapped into the online ad market, with digital media revenue accounting for less than 10 percent of its total revenue. "The real value creation and growth will come from monetizing the presence on the Internet, where the company has a fanatic and loyal fan base," said Bobby Melnick, general partner with Terrier Partners, a New York money management firm that owns WWE stock.[12]

Finally, WWE has also become involved with movie production using its wrestling stars, releasing two films during 2006. *See No Evil,* a horror thriller starring Kane was released by Lions Gate, and John Cena's action adventure *The Marine* was released by Twentieth Century Fox. Though the films generated a small revenue in theaters, Linda believes that their movies will earn a small profit from home video markets, distribution on premium channels, and offerings on pay-per-view. In fact, *The Marine* debuted in January 2007 as the top DVD rental.

Poised for a Resurgence?

In spite of the growth of WWE in many directions, WrestleMania remains the pinnacle. An annual event that began at New York's Madison Square Garden in 1985, WrestleMania is now an almost weeklong celebration of everything wrestling. No wrestler becomes a true star until their performance is featured at WrestleMania, and any true fan must make the pilgrimage at least once in his life.

Besides the hoopla that is created through each of the stagings of WrestleMania, Vince and his crew have been using the new WWE name to try to recreate the buzz that had surrounded his firm during the 1990s before it hit some serious bumps. The firm has used a new advertising campaign with the message "Get the 'F' out." Linda rejects any suggestion that the fortunes of WWE may be driven by a fad that is unlikely to last. She maintains that the interest in their shows will survive in spite of growing competition from newer sources of entertainment such as reality-based television shows.

Furthermore, Vince and Linda McMahon claim that their attempts to diversify were never meant to convey any loss of interests in wrestling. In fact, they believed that it was their experience with staging wrestling shows over the years that had provided them with the foundation to move into other areas of entertainment. After all, it was their ability to use wrestling to create a form of mass entertainment that had made the WWE such a phenomenal success. In response to critics who question the value of wrestling matches whose outcomes are rigged, James F. Byrne, senior vice president for marketing, had stated: "Wrestling is 100 percent entertainment. There's no such thing as fake entertainment."[13]

Although WWE stock has failed to show much appreciation, the firm has boosted its dividend three times in the past five years. Analysts have noted that the firm has little debt and considerable cash flow, making it a relatively good investment over the longer term. "For long term investors, WWE is very interesting," remarked Michael Kelman, an analyst with Susquehanna Financial Group.[14] "We make money when we are not hot," explained Vince. "When we are hot, its off the charts."[15]

"Those who understand don't need an explanation. Those who need an explanation will never understand."

—**Marty,** a 19-year-old wrestling addict quoted in *Fortune,* October 6, 2000.

Endnotes

1. WWE. Wrestlemania blows away attendance record at Ford Field. Press Release, April 1, 2007.
2. WWE. World Wrestling Entertainment, Inc. Reports Q3 Results. Press Release, February 23, 2005.
3. McLean, B. 2000. Inside the world's weirdest family business. *Fortune,* October 16: 298.
4. Bradley, D. 2000. Wrestling's real grudge match. *BusinessWeek,* January 24: 164.
5. Mooradian, D. 2001. WWF gets a grip after acquisition. *Amusement Business,* June 4: 20.
6. Oestricher, D., & Steinberg, B. 2002. WW . . . E it is, after fight for F nets new name. *The Wall Street Journal,* May 7: B2.
7. Finnigan, D. 2002. Down but not out, WWE is using a rebranding effort to gain strength. *Brandweek,* June 3: 12.
8. *Fortune,* October 16, 2000: 304.
9. *Fortune,* October 16, 2000: 302.
10. *Fortune,* October 16, 2000: 302.
11. Bradley, D. 2004. Rousing itself off the mat? *BusinessWeek,* February 2: 73.
12. La Monica, P. R. 2007. Wrestling's "Trump" card. CNN Money.com, March 30, 2007.
13. Wyatt, E. 1999. Pro wrestling tries to pin down a share value. *New York Times,* August 4: c11.
14. CNN Money.com, March 30, 2007.
15. *BusinessWeek,* February 2, 2004: 74.

Case 24 Procter & Gamble*

Procter & Gamble announced on January 30, 2007 that its revenues and profits had risen substantially as a result of its integration of the Gillette Company, the shaving products company that it had purchased in 2005 for about $57 billion in stock. The merger had created the world's largest consumer products conglomerate, combining some of the world's best-known billion-dollar brands like Tide, Crest, and Pampers with Gillette, Right Guard, and Duracell. The expanded firm was able to benefit from the successful launch of products ranging from Tide Simple Pleasures detergent to Gillette Fusion five-blade razors.

The acquisition represented part of an ongoing effort by Alan G. "A.G." Lafley, a 23-year veteran, to help P&G reclaim its previous status as the premier consumer goods firm. He believed that his firm would derive substantial benefits from its merger with another company operating in similar markets and using complementary skills. "The combination of these two recognizes the pressures from strengthening retail customers, variety-seeking consumers, and the investment necessary to build scale in the developing market," said Ann Gillin-Lefever, an equity analyst for Lehman Brothers who follows both P&G and Gillette.[1]

Lafley had begun to restructure P&G even before he took over the helm in June 2000. He was asked to take over from Durk I. Jaeger, whose attempts to revive the firm during his 17-month tenure had failed to stop the firm's decline. Like many of its competitors, the firm was being squeezed by slowing sales, growing costs, and waning pricing power. P&G had become saddled with old and tired brands, as the Swiffer dust mop represented the only successful new brand that it has managed to develop over the previous 15 years. At the same time, big-box retail chains such as Wal-Mart, Costco, and Carefour have begun to use their growing clout with consumers to negotiate for better pricing deals from their suppliers.

Under Lafley, P&G has begun to strip away much of the bureaucracy in order to speed up its product development and build upon on its well-known brands. By divesting its weaker brands, the firm has been investing in extending the reach of brands that exhibit greater potential. Lafley wants to focus the firm on building a small number of "superbrands," each with annual sales of over $1 billion. The purchase of Gillette would allow P&G to increase the number of such brands from 16 to 21 (see Exhibit 1). According to Clayton C. Daley Jr., the firm's chief financial officer; "We will have more $1 billion brands, more opportunities to bring product innovation to the market because that's what retailers want."[2]

But Lafley has many more ideas about how to make P&G relevant in the 21st century, as speed and agility become necessary for competitive advantage. Even as president of North American operations, he had spoken with CEO Jager about the need to remake the company. Now that he has taken charge, Lafley has been pushing for the most sweeping transformation of the company since it was founded by William Procter and James Gamble in 1837 as a maker of soap and candles.

Exhibit 1 Product Information

Beauty Care

Key Product Segments: Cosmetics, Deodorants, Feminine Care, Hair Care, Personal Cleansing, Skin Care

Billion Dollar Brands: Always, Head & Shoulders, Olay, Pantene, Wella

Fabric & Home Care

Key Product Segments: Fabric Care, Air Care, Dish Care, Surface Care

Billion Dollar Brands: Ariel, Dawn, Downey, Tide

Baby & Family Care

Key Product Segments: Diapers, Baby Wipes, Bath Tissue, Kitchen Towels

Billion Dollar Brands: Bounty, Charmin, Pampers

Health Care

Key Product Segments: Oral Care, Pharmaceuticals, Personal Health Care

Billion Dollar Brands: Actonel, Crest, Oral B

Pet Health, Snacks, & Coffee

Key Product Segments: Pet Health, Snacks, Coffee

Billion Dollar Brands: Folgers, Iams, Pringles

Blades & Razors

Key Product Segments: Men's & Women's Blades & Razors

Billion Dollar Brands: Gillette, Mach 3

Duracell & Braun

Key Product Segments: Batteries, Electric Razors, Small Appliances

Billion Dollar Brands: Braun, Duracell

Source: P&G.

* This case was developed by Professor Jamal Shamsie, Michigan State University with the assistance of Professor Alan B. Eisner, Pace University. Material has been drawn from published sources to be used for class discussion. Copyright © 2007 Jamal Shamsie & Alan B. Eisner.

An Attempted Turnaround

For most of its long history, P&G has been one of America's preeminent companies. The firm has developed several well-known brands such as Tide, one of the pioneers in laundry detergents, which was launched in 1946, and Pampers, the first disposable diaper, which was introduced in 1961. P&G built its brands through its innovative marketing techniques. In the 1880s, it was one of the first companies to advertise nationally. Later on, P&G invented the soap opera by sponsoring *Ma Perkins* when radio caught on and *Guiding Light* when television took hold. In the 1930s, P&G was the first firm to develop the idea of brand management, setting up marketing teams for each brand and urging them to compete against each other.

But by the 1990s, P&G was in danger of becoming another Eastman Kodak or Xerox, a once-great company that might have lost its way. Sales on most of its 18 top brands were slowing as it was being outhustled by more focused rivals such as Kimberly-Clark and Colgate-Palmolive. The only way P&G kept profits growing was by cutting costs, which would hardly work as a strategy for the long term. At the same time, the dynamics of the industry were changing as power shifted from manufacturers to massive retailers. Retailers such as Wal-Mart were starting to use their size to try and get better deals from P&G, further squeezing its profits.

In 1999, P&G decided to bring in Durk I. Jaeger to try and make the big changes that were obviously needed to get P&G back on track. But the moves that he made generally misfired, sinking the firm into deeper trouble. He introduced expensive new products that never caught on while letting existing brands drift. He also put in place a companywide reorganization that left many employees perplexed and preoccupied. During the fiscal year when he was in charge, earnings per share showed an anemic rise of just 3.5 percent, much lower than in previous years. And during that time, the share price slid 52 percent, cutting P&G's total market capitalization by $85 billion. The effects were widely felt within the firm, where employees and retirees hold about 20 percent of the stock (see Exhibits 2 to 5).

But Jager's greatest failing was his scorn for the family. Jager, a Dutchman who had joined P&G overseas and worked his way to corporate headquarters, pitted himself against the P&G culture. Susan E. Arnold, president of P&G's beauty and feminine care division, said that Jager tried to make the employees turn against the prevailing culture, contending that it was burdensome and insufferable. Some go-ahead employees even wore buttons that read "Old World/New World" to express disdain for P&G's past.

Exhibit 2 Income Statements

	06/30/2006	06/30/2005	06/30/2004	06/30/2003	06/30/2002
	(in $ millions)				
Net sales	68,222	56,741	51,407	43,377	40,238
Cost of products sold	33,125	27,804	25,076	22,141	20,989
Marketing, research, administrative expenses	21,848	18,010	16,504	13,383	12,571
Operating income	13,249	10,927	9,827	7,853	6,678
Interest expense	1,119	834	629	561	603
Other nonoperating income	283	346	152	238	308
Earnings before income taxes	12,413	10,439	9,350	7,530	6,383
Current provision for income taxes	3,841	2,532	2,454	2,281	—
Deferred income tax provisions (credits)	(112)	650	415	63	—
Income taxes	3,729	3,182	2,869	2,344	2,031
Net earnings	8,684	7,257	6,481	5,186	4,352
Preferred dividends	—	—	—	—	124
Net earnings to common shares	—	—	—	—	4,228
Year end shares outstanding	3,178.841	2,472.9	2,543.8	2,594.4	2,601.6
Dividends per common share	1.15	1.03	0.93	0.82	0.76
Total number of employees	138,000	110,000	110,000	98,000	102,000

Source: Mergentonline.com.

Exhibit 3 Balance Sheets

	06/30/2006	06/30/2005	06/30/2004	06/30/2003	06/30/2002
			(in $ millions)		
Cash & cash equivalents	6,693	6,389	5,469	5,912	3,427
Investment securities	1,133	1,744	423	300	196
Accounts receivable	5,725	4,185	4,062	3,038	3,090
Materials & supplies	1,537	1,424	1,191	1,095	1,031
Work in process	623	350	340	291	323
Finished goods	4,131	3,232	2,869	2,254	2,102
Total inventories	6,291	5,006	4,400	3,640	3,456
Deferred income taxes	1,611	1,081	958	843	521
Prepaid expenses & other receivables	2,876	1,924	1,803	1,487	1,476
Total current assets	24,329	20,329	17,115	15,220	12,166
Buildings	5,871	5,292	5,206	4,729	4,532
Machinery & equipment	25,140	20,397	19,456	18,222	17,963
Land	870	636	642	591	575
Property, plant & equipment, at cost	31,881	26,325	25,304	23,542	23,070
Less: accumulated depreciation	13,111	11,993	11,196	10,438	9,721
Net property, plant & equipment	18,770	14,332	14,108	13,104	13,349
Goodwill	55,306	19,816	19,610	11,132	10,966
Trademark & other intangible assets	33,721	4,347	4,290	2,375	2,464
Net goodwill & other intangible assets	89,027	24,163	23,900	13,507	13,430
Other noncurrent assets	3,569	2,703	1,925	1,875	1,831
Total assets	135,695	61,527	57,048	43,706	40,776
Accounts payable	4,910	3,802	3,617	2,795	2,205
Marketing & promotion	2,357	1,912	1,876	1,802	—
Liability under Wella Domination Agreement	207	1,087	1,106	—	—
Compensation expenses	1,471	1,045	1,049	804	—
Accrued Gillette exit costs	929	—	—	—	—
Other accrued & other liabilities	4,623	3,487	3,658	2,906	—
Accrued & other liabilities	9,587	7,531	7,689	5,512	5,330
Taxes payable	3,360	2,265	2,554	1,879	1,438
Current portion of long-term debt	1,930	2,606	—	—	—
Commercial paper	—	5,531	—	—	—
Bridge credit facility	—	3,010	—	—	—
Other short-term debt	198	294	—	—	—
Debt due within one year	2,128	11,441	8,287	2,172	3,731
Total current liabilities	19,985	25,039	22,147	12,358	12,704

(continued)

Exhibit 3 Balance Sheets (*continued*)

	06/30/2006	06/30/2005	06/30/2004	06/30/2003	06/30/2002
	(in $ millions)				
Notes	10,309	13,253	11,412	9,027	—
Bank credit facility	21,412	—	—	—	—
Debentures	1,000	1,000	1,000	1,000	—
All other long-term debt	5,185	1,240	1,660	2,541	—
Current portion of long-term debt	1,930	2,606	1,518	1,093	—
Long-term debt	35,976	12,887	12,554	11,475	11,201
Deferred income taxes	12,354	2,894	2,261	1,396	1,077
Pension benefits	2,550	2,096	—	—	—
Other noncurrent liabilities	1,922	1,034	2,808	2,291	2,088
Total other noncurrent liabilities	4,472	3,230	—	—	—
Total liabilities	72,787	44,050	39,770	27,520	27,070
Convertible class A preferred stock	1,451	1,483	1,526	1,580	1,634
Common stock	3,976	2,473	2,544	1,297	1,301
Additional paid-in capital	57,856	3,142	2,425	2,931	2,490
Reserve for ESOP debt retirement	1,288	1,259	1,283	1,308	1,339
Accumulated other comprehensive (loss)	(518)	(1,566)	(1,545)	(2,006)	(2,360)
Treasury stock, at cost	34,235	—	—	—	—
Retained earnings	35,666	13,204	13,611	13,692	11,980
Total shareholders' equity	62,908	17,477	17,278	16,186	13,706

Source: Mergentonline.com.

A New Style of Leadership

On June 6, 2000, the day of his 30th wedding anniversary, Alan G. Lafley received a call from John Pepper, a former CEO who was now a board member. He was asked to take over the reins of P&G from Jager, representing a boardroom coup unprecedented in the firm's history. In a sense, Lafley had been preparing for this job his entire adult life. He never hid the fact that he wanted to run P&G one day. Recruited as a brand assistant for Joy dish detergent in 1977, Lafley rose quickly to head P&G's soap and detergent business, where he introduced Liquid Tide in 1984. A decade later, he moved to Kobe, Japan to head the Asian division. Lafley returned to Cincinnati in 1998 to run the company's entire North American operations.

By the time he had taken charge of P&G, Lafley had developed a reputation as a boss who steps back to give his staff plenty of responsibility and who helps shape decisions by asking a series of keen questions. As CEO, Lafley has refrained from making any grand pronouncements on the future of P&G. Instead, he has been spending an inordinate amount of time patiently communicating to his employees about the types of changes that he would like to see at P&G.

Lafley did begin this tenure by breaking down the walls between management and the employees. Since the 1950s, all of the senior executives at P&G used to be located on the eleventh floor at the firm's corporate headquarters. Lafley changed this setup, moving all five division presidents to the same floors as their staff. Then he turned some of the emptied space into a leadership training center. On the rest of the floor, he knocked down the walls so that the remaining executives, including himself, would share open offices.

Lafley chose to place his office next to the two people he talks to the most, which, in true P&G style, was officially established by a flow study. They are the head of Human Resources, Ricard L. Antoine, and the Vice-Chairman, Bruce Byrnes. In fact, Lafley has established a tradition of meeting with Antoine every Sunday evening to review the performance of the firm's 200 most senior executives. This reflects Lafley's determination to make sure the best people rise to the top. And Byrnes, whom Lafley refers to as "Yoda,"

Exhibit 4 Financial Breakdown

Beauty Care

	Net Sales:		Net Earnings:	
	2006: $21.1 billion		2006: $3.1 billion
	2005: $19.7 billion		2005: $2.8 billion
	2004: $17.3 billion		2004: $2.3 billion

Fabric & Home Care

	Net Sales:		Net Earnings:	
	2006: $17.1 billion		2006: $2.4 billion
	2005: $15.8 billion		2005: $2.1 billion
	2004: $14.4 billion		2004: $2.2 billion

Baby & Family Care

	Net Sales:		Net Earnings:	
	2006: $12.0 billion		2006: $1.3 billion
	2005: $11.7 billion		2005: $1.2 billion
	2004: $10.5 billion		2004: $0.9 billion

Health Care

	Net Sales:		Net Earnings:	
	2006: $7.9 billion		2006: $1.2 billion
	2005: $6.1 billion		2005: $0.8 billion
	2004: $5.4 billion		2004: $0.7 billion

Pet Health, Snacks & Coffee

	Net Sales:		Net Earnings:	
	2006: $4.4 billion		2006: $0.4 billion
	2005: $4.3 billion		2005: $0.5 billion
	2004: $4.0 billion		2004: $0.4 billion

Blades & Razors

	Net Sales:		Net Earnings:	
	2006: $3.5 billion		2006: $0.8 billion

Duracell & Braun

	Net Sales:		Net Earnings:	
	2006: $2.9 billion		2006: $0.3 billion

Source: P&G.

the sagelike Star Wars character, gets a lot of face time because of his marketing expertise. As Lafley says, "The assets at P&G are what? Our people and our brands."[3]

Lafley's leadership style has been particularly visible in P&G's new conference room, where he and the firm's 12 other top executives meet every Monday at 8 a.m. to review results, plan strategy, and set the drumbeat for the week. The table is now round instead of rectangular. Instead of sitting where they were told, the executives now sit where they like. True to his character, Lafley maintains a low profile at most of these meetings. He occasionally joins in the discussion, but most of the time the executives talk as much to each other as to Lafley.

Indeed, Lafley's charm offensive has so disarmed most P&G staffers that he has been able to make drastic changes within the company. He has replaced more than half of the company's top 30 officers, more than any P&G boss in

memory, and trimmed its workforce by as many as 9,600 jobs. And he has moved more women into senior positions. In fact, Lafley skipped over 78 general managers with more seniority to name 42-year-old Deborah A. Henretta to head P&G's then-troubled North American baby care division. "The speed at which A.G. has gotten results is five years ahead of the time I expected," said Scott Cook, founder of software maker Intuit Incorporated, who joined P&G's board shortly after Lafley's appointment.[4]

A New Strategic Focus

Lafley is intent on shifting the focus of P&G back to its consumers. At every opportunity that he gets, he has tried to drill his managers and employees to not lose sight of the consumer. He feels that P&G has often let technology dictate its new products rather than consumer needs. He would like to see the firm work more closely with retailers, the

Price History—Procter & Gamble (Jan 2002–Jun 2007)

Exhibit 5 **Stock Chart**

Source: Data from MSN.com.

place where consumers first see the product on the shelf. And he would like to see much more concern with the consumer's experience at home. At the end of a three-day leadership seminar, Lafley was thrilled when he heard the young marketing managers declare, "We are the voice of the consumer within P&G, and they are the heart of all we do."[5]

In order to better focus on serving the needs of its consumers, Lafley is putting a tremendous amount of emphasis on the firm's brands. When he describes the P&G of the future, he said, "We're in the business of creating and building brands."[6] Since Lafley has taken over P&G, the firm has updated all of its 200 brands by adding innovative new products. It has begun to offer devices that build on its core brands, such as Tide StainBrush, a battery powered brush for removing stains and Mr. Clean AutoDry, a water pressure powered car cleaning system that dries without streaking. "We are growing market share in 70 percent of our businesses," commented Clayton Daley, the firm's chief financial officer. "That doesn't happen unless you have strong innovation."[7]

Lafley has fostered this innovative spirit by pushing everyone at P&G to approach its brands more creatively.

Crest, for example, which used to be marketed as a toothpaste brand, is now defined an oral care brand. The firm now sells Crest-branded toothbrushes and tooth whiteners. There's even an electric toothbrush, SpinBrush, which was added to the Crest line after P&G acquired it in January, 2001. The cheap, fun-to-use brush has created a new and positive vibe around the whole Crest brand. "People remember experiences," Lafley explained. "They don't remember attributes."[8]

A key element of Lafley's strategy has also been to move P&G away from basic consumer products such as laundry detergents, which can be knocked off by private labels, to higher-margin products. This has led him to focus more strongly on the firm's beauty care business. Under Lafley, P&G has made some of its costly acquisitions to complement its Cover Girl and Oil of Olay brands. He purchased Clairol in 2001 for $5 billion, and followed this up by acquiring German beauty firm Wella in 2003 for $6.9 billion. With the acquisition of Gillette, Lafley is trying to move P&G into the men's market for personal care products.

P&G is also willing to work with other firms to develop its products and get them to the marketplace. The firm has been partnering with appliance makers who make hardware to support its unique products. Applica Inc. recently launched the Home Café, a one-cup coffee maker that uses distinctive Folgers and Millstone coffee pads from P&G. It joined with Clorox Company, maker of Glad Bags, last October to share a food-wrap technology it had developed. It was unprecedented for P&G to work with a competitor, says licensing head Jeffrey Weedman. The overall effect is undeniable. "Lafley has made P&G far more flexible," said Banc of America's William H. Steele.[9]

A Revolution Still in the Making

Although Lafley has managed to give a tremendous push to P&G to rethink is business model, it is quite clear he has more revolutionary changes in mind. A confidential memo was circulated among P&G's top brass in late 2001 that even drew a sharp response from some of its board members. It argued that P&G could be cut to 25,000 employees, less than a quarter of its current size. Lafley admitted that the memo had drawn a strong reaction: "It terrified our organization."[10]

Even though Lafley did not write this infamous memo, it did reflect the central tenet of his vision that P&G should do only what it does best and nothing more. He clearly wants a more outwardly focused, flexible company. This means that P&G does not have to do everything in house. If there are no clear benefits that stem from doing something within the firm, it should be contracted out. Such a philosophy has serious implications for every facet of P&G's operations from R&D to manufacturing.

Lafley has clearly challenged the supremacy of P&G's research and development operations. He has confronted head-on the stubbornly held notion that everything must be invented within P&G, asserting that half of its new products should come from the outside. Under his tenure, the firm has begun to get about 20 percent of its new product ideas from outside the firm. This is double the 10 percent figure that existed at P&G when he took over.

A variety of other activities are also being driven out of the firm. In April 2003, Lafley turned over all bar-soap manufacturing, including Ivory, P&G's oldest surviving brand, to a Canadian contractor. One month later, he outsourced P&G's information-technology operation to Hewlett-Packard Company. While Lafley shies away from saying just how much of P&G's factory and back-office operations he may hand over to someone else, he does admit that facing up to the realities of the marketplace may force some hardships on its employees.

Lafley is well aware that nearly one-half of the firm's 102,000 employees work in its plants. So far, he has taken concrete steps to ease the hardships that may be caused by cutting back on P&G's operations. At the bar-soap operations, based entirely in Cincinnati, 200 of the 250 employees went to work for the Canadian contractor. Similarly, all 2,000 of the information-technology workers were moved over to HP. "Lafley has deftly handled the outsourcing deals, which has lessened fear within P&G," said Roger Martin, a close adviser of Lafley's who is dean of the University of Toronto's Joseph L. Rotman School of Management.[11]

Such moves to outsource some of the activities may also create more flexibility for the firm over the longer term. It could decide how much it wants to invest in particular brands, products, or even lines of businesses. No one would dispute that these moves are clearly revolutionary for a firm such as P&G. "He's absolutely breaking many well-set molds at P&G," said eBay's CEO, Margaret C. "Meg" Whitman, whom Lafley had recently appointed to the board.[12]

Daunting Challenges

Despite the recent performance improvements, Lafley remains under enormous pressure to restore P&G to a company that is admired, imitated, and uncommonly profitable. Nowhere are those expectations more apparent than on the second floor of headquarters, where three of its former chief executives are still active. John Pepper, a popular former boss who returned briefly as chairman when Jager left has stated, "It's now clear to me that A.G. is going to be one of the great CEOs in this company's history."[13]

In order to find new avenues for growth, Lafley has been pushing the firm to build on its most promising brands, partly by creating new product forms and even new forms of devices such as the Tide StainBrush and Mr. Clean AutoDry. It is still unclear whether these new introductions can generate sustained demand that will allow P&G to maintain its higher margins. Sales of the firm's Dawn Power Dish Brush, for example, have eased considerably since its launch in 2003. P&G's managers are also worried about the quality of these devices, which can ultimately hurt the overall brand. The firm recently recalled its Swiffer Vac because of electrical problems. Lafely has acknowledged that they have to be careful with their new devices: "We have to be careful we don't push it too far."[14]

The reliance on external sources for new products can also be problematic. As any scientist will attest, decisions to purchase a new product idea often tend to be extremely hard to make. The process of picking winners from other labs is likely to be both difficult and expensive. P&G already missed a big opportunity by passing up the chance to buy water-soluble strips that contain mouthwash. Listerine managed to grab the product and has profited handsomely from the deal.

But finding new avenues to grow could be the only way to balance P&G's growing reliance on Wal-Mart. Former and current P&G employees say the discounter could account for one-third of P&G's global sales by the end of the decade. Meanwhile, the pressure from consumers and competitors to keep prices low will only increase. "P&G has improved its ability to take on those challenges, but those challenges are still there," said Lehman analyst Ann Gillin.[15]

The biggest risk, though, is that Lafley will lose the people at P&G. The firm's insular culture has been famously resistant to new ideas. Employees form a tightly knit family because most of them start out and grow up together at P&G, which only promotes from within. Over the years, these people have gradually adopted the culture of the firm and come to believe in it. Lafley is well aware of his predicament. He recently admitted, "I am worried that I will ask the organization to change ahead of its understanding, capability, and commitment."[16]

Endnotes

1. Dash, E. 2005. A merger in search of a home. Yours. *New York Times,* January 29: B3.
2. Grant, J. 2005. P&G starts on integration plan. *Financial Times,* January 31: 17.
3. Berner, R. 2003. P&G: New and improved. *BusinessWeek,* July 7: 62.
4. *BusinessWeek,* July 7, 2003: 55.
5. *BusinessWeek,* July 7, 2003: 62.
6. *BusinessWeek,* July 7, 2003: 63.
7. Berner, R. Byrnes N., & Zellner, W. 2004. P&G has rivals in a wringer. *BusinessWeek,* October 4: 74.
8. Berner, R. & Symonds, W.C. 2005. Welcome to Procter & gadget. *BusinessWeek,* February 7: 77.
9. *BusinessWeek,* July 7, 2003: 63.
10. *BusinessWeek,* July 7, 2003: 55.
11. *BusinessWeek,* July 7, 2003: 63.
12. *BusinessWeek,* July 7, 2003: 58.
13. *BusinessWeek,* July 7, 2003: 55.
14. *BusinessWeek,* February 7, 2005: 77.
15. *BusinessWeek,* July 7, 2003: 63.
16. *BusinessWeek,* July 7, 2003: 58.

Case 25 The Casino Industry*

Driven by the steady growth in gaming revenues, Las Vegas is experiencing another building boom as construction cranes share air space with towering casino resorts. Ever since the mobster Bugsy Siegel opened the first of the modern day casinos in 1946, firms have competed against each other by building more expensive and extravagant casino resorts. But even Las Vegas has never witnessed the kind of expansion that is clearly evident in the spring of 2007. "This is the most outrageous, over-the-top expansion," said legendry casino mogul Steve Wynn.[1] His Wynn Resort represented the one of the most expensive casino resorts ever built when it was launched in 2005.

Topping the list of new projects is the City Center, being built at an expense of more than $7 billion by MGM Mirage, which owns the neighboring Bellagio along with several other well-known casinos in Las Vegas. The project is already becoming known as the most expensive privately financed project in American history. Even competitors marvel at the scope of this minicity bordering the Las Vegas Strip, which will feature six towering buildings that will reach as high as 61 stories. Covering 67 acres, City Center will include a 4,000 room hotel, 2,700 condominium units, a sprawling convention center, and a half million square feet of retail space. "We think it will be the hub of Las Vegas," said MGM Mirage CEO Terry Lanni.[2]

Furthermore, progress on the City Center is being matched by the gradual rise of several other glamorous new resorts all over Las Vegas. Boyd Gaming has started to develop a casino called Echelon Place on the former site of Stardust, which was demolished in March 2007. At $4.4 billion, the 5,000-room Echelon Place will be far more expensive than the previous record for a single casino, which was set when Wynn built his $2.7 billion resort. Other casinos are also building expensive additions to their properties. Las Vegas Sands is completing a 3,025-room resort called the Palazzo adjacent to its Venetian casino. And Steve Wynn is constructing Encore at Wynn Las Vegas, next to his recently opened resort.

Fueling this construction frenzy is the high occupancy rates at most of the Las Vegas casino resorts, as the city attracted just under 39 million visitors in 2006—an 86 percent increase over the 21 million who visited the city in 1990 (see Exhibit 1). The growth has occurred even as American Indian casinos and other gambling outposts have mushroomed across more than 30 states. With the growth in the acceptance and popularity of various forms of gaming, Las Vegas continues to attract people who want to enjoy the experience that it offers (see Exhibit 2).

With more hotel rooms than any other city in the United States, there is much speculation about the number

* This case was developed by Professor Jamal Shamsie, Michigan State University with the assistance of Professor Alan B. Eisner, Pace University. Material has been drawn from published sources to be used for class discussion. Copyright © 2007 Jamal Shamsie & Alan B. Eisner.

Exhibit 1 Las Vegas Visitors

	(in $ millions)
2006	39.0
2005	38.6
2004	37.4
2003	35.5
2002	35.1
2001	35.0
2000	35.8
1999	33.8
1998	30.6
1997	30.5
1996	29.6
1995	29.0

Source: Las Vegas Convention & Visitors Authority.

of casinos that Las Vegas can keep adding. But David G. Schwartz, director of the Center for Gambling Research at the University of Nevada–Las Vegas, shrugs off these questions. "People have been predicting dating back to 1955 that Las Vegas will reach a saturation point. But me, I wouldn't bet against casino growth."[3]

Riding the Growth Wave

Although some form of gambling can be traced back to colonial times, the recent advent of casinos can be traced back to the legalization of gaming in Nevada in 1931. For many years, this was the only state in which casinos were allowed. As a result, Nevada still retains its status as the state with the highest revenues from casinos, with gambling revenues rising to almost $12 billion in 2006. After New Jersey passed laws in 1976 to allow gambling in Atlantic City, this allowed the large population on the East Coast easier access to casinos. However, the further growth of casinos has only been possible since 1988, as more and more states have begun to legalize the operation of casinos because of their ability to help generate more commercial activity and create more jobs, in large part through the growth of tourism.

The greatest growth has come in the form of waterborne casinos operating in six states that have allowed casinos to develop at waterfronts such as rivers and lakes. As of 2006, about 70 such casinos generated almost $11 billion in revenues. Several of the casinos along the Gulf Coast were destroyed or severely damaged by Hurricane Katrina.

Exhibit 2 U.S. Casino Industry Gaming Revenues*

	2006	2005	2004	2003	2002	2001	2000
	Revenues (in $ millions)						
Nevada, total	12,622	11,649	10,562	9,625	9,447	9,469	9,600
Las Vegas Strip	6,688	6,034	5,334	4,760	4,654	4,704	4,806
Atlantic City, total	5,218	5,018	4,807	4,489	4,382	4,303	4,301
Western towns, total	867	839	804	768	786	735	685
Deadwood, SD	85	84	78	70	66	58	53
Colorado	782	755	726	698	720	677	632
Other land-based, total	1,641	1,458	1,509	1,412	1,400	1,257	989
New Orleans	338	229	320	282	275	250	245
Detroit	1,303	1,229	1,189	1,130	1,125	1,007	744
Riverboats, total	11,237	10,640	10,626	10,232	10,156	9,714	9,038
Iowa	814	747	727	694	656	615	598
Illinois	1,924	1,799	1,717	1,710	1,832	1,784	1,658
Mississippi	2,570	2,472	2,777	2,700	2,717	2,701	2,649
Louisiana	1,853	1,676	1,562	1,566	1,610	1,633	1,447
Missouri	1,592	1,532	1,473	1,332	1,279	1,138	997
Indiana	2,484	2,414	2,370	2,230	2,062	1,843	1,689
Native American casinos	25,700	22,600	16,700	15,055	13,290	11,400	9,700
Total	57,285	52,204	45,008	41,581	39,461	36,877	34,313

Sources: Casino Journal's National Gaming Summary; Standard & Poor's estimates.

*Gaming revenues include the amount of money won by casinos from various gaming activities such as slot machines, table games, and sports betting.

To encourage casinos to rebuild, Mississippi lawmakers passed a law in 2005 allowing casinos to operate up to 800 feet from the shore, which gives them a stronger foundation to withstand future hurricanes. Most of the damaged casinos in the area had reopened by early 2007.

As casinos have spread to more states, there has also been a growing tendency to regard casino gambling as an acceptable form of entertainment for a night out. Although casinos have tended to draw players from all demographic segments, a recent national survey found that their median age was 47 and their median household income was around $50,000. On the whole, casino gamblers tended to be better educated and more affluent than those who bought lottery tickets. In fact, the bigger casinos attracted a high-roller segment, which could stake millions of dollars and included players from all over the world. Many of the casinos work hard to obtain the business of this market segment, despite the risk that the sustained winning streak of a single player could significantly weaken the earnings for a particular quarter.

The growth of casino gambling has also been driven by the significantly better payouts that they give players compared with other forms of gambling. Based on industry estimates, casinos typically keep less than $5 of every $100 that is wagered. This compares favorably with racetrack betting which holds back over $20 of every $100 that is wagered and with state-run lotteries that usually keep about $45 of every $100 that is spent on tickets. Such comparisons can be somewhat misleading, however, because winnings are put back into play in casinos much faster than they are in other forms of gaming. This provides a casino with more opportunities to win from a customer, largely offsetting its lower retention rate.

Finally, most of the growth in casino revenues has come from the growing popularity of slot machines. Coin-operated slot machines typically account for more than 60 percent of all casino gaming revenues. A major reason for their popularity is that it is easier for prospective gamblers to feed a slot machine than to learn the nuances of various table games. New slot machines tend to be based on familiar games such as Monopoly or TV shows such as *Star Trek, The Munsters,* or *Wheel of Fortune.* With the advent of new technology, these slot machines are being replaced by electronic gaming devices that have video screens instead of spinning wheels, buttons to push instead of handles to pull, and use prepaid tickets rather than coins for payment.

Betting on a Few Locations

Although casinos have spread across much of the country, two cities have dominated the casino business. Both Las Vegas and Atlantic City have seen a spectacular growth in casino gaming revenues over the years (see Exhibit 3). Although Las Vegas has far more hotel casinos, each of the dozen casinos in Atlantic City typically generate much higher revenues. By 2006, these two locations accounted for almost a quarter of the total revenues generated by all forms of casinos throughout the United States.

Las Vegas clearly acts a magnet for the overnight casino gamblers, offering more than 150,000 hotel rooms and many choices for fine dining, great shopping, and top-notch entertainment. It is linked by air to many major cities both in the United States and around the world. During the 1990s, Las Vegas tried to become more receptive to families, with attractions such as circus performances, animal reserves, and pirate battles. But the city has been very successful with its recent return to its sinful roots with a stronger focus on topless shows, hot night clubs, and other adult offerings that have been highlighted by the new advertising slogan "What happens in Vegas, stays in Vegas." Paul Cappelli, who creates advertising messages, believes that Las Vegas lost its way with the effort to become family friendly. "People don't see Vegas as Jellystone Park. They don't want to go there with a picnic basket," he explained.[4]

For the most part, Las Vegas has continued to show a consistent pattern of visitor growth. "We still compete with Orlando and New York," said Terry Jicinsky, head of

marketing for the Las Vegas Convention and Visitors Authority. "But based on overnight visitors, we're the top destination in North America."[5] In order to accommodate this growth, several of the major resorts such as Bellagio and Mandalay Bay did add new wings during 2003 and 2004, leading to the opening of Steve Wynn's brand new casino resort in the spring of 2005. Even some of the older properties have been remodeled. Caesars Palace has been given an expensive renovation and expanded to include a new Colosseum and a new Roman Plaza. According to Tom Graves, stock analyst at Standard & Poor's, "There's a perception among gamblers that Las Vegas is still the foremost gaming market."[6]

By comparison, Atlantic City cannot compete with Las Vegas in terms of the broad range of dining, shopping, and entertainment choices. It does, however, offer a beach and a boardwalk along which its dozen large casino hotels are lined. Atlantic City attracts gamblers from various cities in the Northeast, many of whom arrive by charter bus and stay for less than a day. Atlantic City officials point out that one-quarter of the nation's population lives sufficiently close so that they can drive there on just one tank of gas.

The opening of the much-ballyhooed Borgata Hotel Casino in 2003 has started a drive to make Atlantic City much more competitive with Las Vegas. As the first new casino to open in the city in 13 years, the Borgata is at the center of a $2 billion makeover of Atlantic City that might make it a hotter destination. "There's no question that this is a Las Vegas–style megaresort," said Bob Boughner, the CEO of the Borgata.[7] Two of the town's older casinos are adding expensive new wings to accommodate more overnight visitors. Other casino hotels such as Caesars, Trump Plaza, and Hilton have also added outdoor bars on the beach that have helped to turn the waterfront into one big party zone. "Bogata is the catalyst for a new Atlantic City," said Mike Epifanio, the editor of *Atlantic City Weekly.* "There's been a major change of thinking in town."[8]

Raising the Stakes

The gradual rise in the number of casinos, including those on riverboats, has led each of them to compete more heavily with each other to entice gamblers. Casinos have had to continuously strive to offer more in order to stand out and gain attention. This is most evident in Las Vegas and Atlantic City, the two destinations where most of the largest casinos are located next to each other. Potential gamblers have more choices when they visit either of these cities than they have anywhere else.

In Las Vegas, each of the casinos has tried to deal with this competition by differentiating itself in several different ways. A large number of them have tried to differentiate on the basis of a special theme that characterizes their casino, such as a medieval castle, a pirate ship, or a movie studio. Others have tried to incorporate into their casinos the look and feel of specific foreign destinations. Luxor's pyramids and columns evoke ancient Egypt, Mandalay Bay borrows looks from the Pacific Rim, and the Venetian's plazas and canals recreate the Italian resort.

Exhibit 3   Comparitive Statistics

	Las Vegas	Atlantic City
Gambling legalized	1931	1976
Annual visitors	39 million	34 million
Average stay	3.4 days	1.5 days
Number of casinos	190	12
Casino revenue	$6.2 billion	$5.3 billion
Hotel rooms	133,000	16,000
Largest hotel	MGM Grand	Borgata
	5,035 rooms	2,002 rooms

Sources: Nevada Casino Control Board, Las Vegas News Bureau, New Jersey Casino Control Commission, Atlantic City Convention & Visitors Bureau.

Aside from ramping up the appeal of their particular properties, most casinos must also offer incentives to keep their customers from moving over to competing casinos. These incentives can be particularly helpful in retaining those high rollers who come often and spend large amounts of money. Casinos try to maintain their business by providing complimentary rooms, food, beverages, shows, and other perks each year that are worth billions of dollars. Gamblers can also earn various types of rewards through the loyalty programs that the casinos offer, with the specific rewards being tied to the amount that they bet on the slot machines and at the tables.

Some of the larger casinos in Las Vegas are also trying to fend off competition by growing through mergers and acquisitions. In 2004, Harrah's announced that it was buying casino rival Caesars, allowing it to become the nation's leading operator of casinos, with several properties in both Las Vegas and Atlantic City. This deal came just a month after MGM Mirage had stated that it was buying the Mandalay Resort Group, allowing it to double the number of casinos it held on the Las Vegas Strip. Firms that own several casinos can also pitch each of their properties to a different market and allow all of their customers to earn rewards on the firm's loyalty program by gambling at any of these properties (see Exhibit 4).

Such a trend toward consolidation, however, does not seem to make a serious dent in smaller firms that operate just one or two resorts that appeal to particular types of customers. Wynn's new casino hotel is expected to attract up to 8 million customers each year, which represents about 60 percent of the annual attendance of Disneyland. Las Vegas Sands has also been drawing hordes of visitors to the luxury suites that it offers in its opulent Venetian Resort. In fact, the recently opened 455-room Palms Hotel Casino has already become one of the hottest and most profitable properties in Las Vegas. "There will always be a market for a person who doesn't feel comfortable in a big casino setting," said George Maloof, a co-owner of the Palms Resort.[9]

Responding to Growing Threats

Even though the traditional casinos have been working hard to maintain and build upon their sizable market, they are facing growing competition from a variety of sources. Foremost among these is the rise in the number of Native American casinos. The Indian Gaming and Recreation Act of 1988 authorized Native Americans to offer gaming on tribal lands as a way to encourage their self-sufficiency. Of the approximately 550 Native American tribes in the United States, more than 200 have negotiated agreements with states to allow gaming on tribal land. Native American casinos are exempt from federal regulations and are not required to pay any taxes on their revenues, but they generally pay a percentage of their winnings to the state in which they are located.

Estimates from the National Indian Gaming Commission indicate that in fiscal 2006, Native American casinos generated over $19 billion in gaming revenues, representing almost 60 percent of the total gaming revenues that were generated outside Nevada and Atlantic City. At two high-volume casinos in southern Connecticut, one owned by the Mashantucket Pequot tribe and the other by the Mohegan tribe, total gaming revenues were expected to exceed $2.5 billion in 2006. About 70 percent of the growth in U.S. gaming revenues over the past five years has come from all Native American casinos.

The impact of Native American casinos over the traditional casino industry is likely to increase over the next few years. Several states are reaching agreements to allow the introduction or expansion of Native American casinos because of the additional revenues that they can provide. This has created fears that the growth of these Native American casinos is likely to draw gamblers away from the other types of casinos. In particular, the growth of these casinos in states such as California and New York may reduce the number of gamblers that make trips to gambling destinations such as Las Vegas and Atlantic City.

The casino industry is also facing growing competition as a result of the move to introduce gaming machines at racetracks. Several states are passing legislation that would allow racetracks to raise their revenues by providing slot machines to their visitors. The introduction of gaming machines at racetracks—sometimes referred to as "racinos"—has being growing in popularity in the six states where they are presently allowed. According to the American Gaming Association, gaming activity at these racetracks has shown considerable growth over the last five years.

Finally, all casinos are closely observing the growth of gambling on the Internet. Although the United States has introduced legislation to ban Internet gambling, some 2,000 offshore sites generated about $12 billion in revenue in 2005. Electronic payment systems have made it possible for gamblers in the United States to make bets on these sites without cash, checks, or credit cards. Most casino operators believe that Internet gambling could represent both a threat and an opportunity for them. Placing bets through home computers offers convenience for prospective gamblers and a potentially low-cost business model for firms that already operate casinos. It is widely believed that gambling on the Internet might eventually be legalized, regulated, and taxed. "We frankly find attempts at prohibition to be very shortsighted," said Alan Feldman, senior vice-president of MGM Mirage in Las Vegas.[10]

Gambling on the Future

Even as the competition from both rivals and substitutes continues to grow, all of the firms in the casino industry have little choice but to keep spending in order to survive and grow. In many cases, the heavy spending can burden the firm with large amounts of debt that must be serviced through profits from the casino. The debt can be harder to manage if demand for casino gambling does not stay strong and even show some growth. A few casinos in Las Vegas and Atlantic City have run into financial problems, forcing

Exhibit 4 Leading Casino Operators

Harrah's Entertainment

2006 Revenue: $9.67 billion

2006 Income: $535.8 million

Was purchased by a private equity firm in early 2007. Operates 36 casinos across the United States, including 12 riverboats. Also operates 4 casinos on Indian reservations. Runs several upscale casinos such as Bellagio, Caesars Palace, Ballys, Paris, Flamingo, Harrah's, and Rio in Las Vegas. Also planning overseas expansion into Spain and Bahamas.

MGM Mirage

2006 Revenue: $7.18 billion

2006 Income: $648.3 million

Operates 19 casinos throughout the country. Most of its casinos in Las Vegas, such as MGM Grand, Bellagio, New York New York, Mirage, Treasure Island, Luxor, and Monte Carlo, cater to the high end of the market. Developing the City Center project in Las Vegas. Also operates casinos on the Gulf coast and in Detroit. Overseas, is developing MGM Grand Macau.

Boyd Gaming

2006 Revenues: $2.28 billion

2006 Income: $116.8 million

Operates 16 casinos in various states around the United States. Las Vegas properties that target the middle income segment include Barbary Coast, Orleans, and Sam's Town. Is developing a higher end casino Echelon Place in Las Vegas. Runs the newly opened Borgata in Atlantic City.

Las Vegas Sands

2006 Revenues: $2.24 billion

2006 Income: $442 million

Operates the Venetian and will open the sister casino Palazzo in Las Vegas. Also developing several casinos in Macau, spearheaded by the Venetian Macau and developing a casino in Singapore.

Penn National Gaming

2006 Revenues: $2.24 billion

2004 Income: $327.1 million

In 2005, merged with Argosy Gaming. Operates 11 mid-priced casinos spread across the United States, including 5 riverboats spread over different states. No properties in Las Vegas or Atlantic City. Also operates several racetracks.

Wynn Resorts

2006 Revenues: $1.43 billion

2006 Income: $628.7 million

Operates the higher end Wynn Resort and will shortly open sister Encore casino, both in Las Vegas. Also expanding overseas with the Wynn Macau.

Station Casinos

2006 Revenues: $1.34 billion

2006 Income: $110.2 million

Operates 9 mid-priced casinos in Las Vegas area. Leading casinos are Palace Station, Sunset Station, and Boulder Station.

Aztar Corporation

2006 Revenues: $1.10 billion*

2006 Income: $225 million*

Was acquired by private equity firm in early 2007. Operates 13 mid-market casinos including 2 riverboats. Runs the Tropicana in both Las Vegas and Atlantic City.

Trump Entertainment Resorts

2006 Revenues: $1.03 billion

2006 Income: $(18.5) million

Operates 3 casinos in Atlantic City, a riverboat in Indiana and an overseas casino. Atlantic City properties consist of Trump Taj Mahal, Trump Plaza, and Trump Marina.

Ameristar Casinos

2006 Revenues: $1.00 billion

2006 Income: $59.6 million

Operates 7 mid-priced casinos across the United States including a couple of riverboats. No properties in Las Vegas or Atlantic City.

Isle of Capri Casinos

2006 Revenues: $988 million

2006 Income: $19 million

Operates 13 riverboat casinos across the United States.

*Estimated figures.

some of them to close. Most recently, Alladin, one of the recent additions to the Las Vegas Strip, was sold off to a partnership of Planet Hollywood and Starwood Resorts.

Most of the gaming firms nevertheless believe that the industry is certain to grow well into the future. Their optimism is based on the growing number of aging boomers who are entering the empty-nest phase of their free-spending lives. Las Vegas has shifted its image away from being family-friendly and is catering to this lucrative segment that is likely to spend more of their money on gambling. But it is still not clear how gaming revenues might be affected by any significant increases in gas prices, which will make travel more expensive and reduce disposable income.

Furthermore, there are questions about the possible impact of the proliferation of casinos around the country and the availability of Internet gambling on the revenue growth of gaming centers such as Las Vegas and Atlantic City. Some observers believe that the spread of gaming has created a bigger market for the casino resorts in these locations. People who gain a taste for gambling will eventually want to visit Las Vegas or Atlantic City in order to get a feel of the real thing. "I suppose one day Las Vegas will reach its limit," said Anthony Curtis, president of LasVegasAdvisor.com, a local travel site. "But that day is nowhere in sight."[11]

Endnotes

1. Rivlan, G. 2007. Too many hotels aren't enough. *New York Times,* April 24: C1.
2. Woodyard, C. 2004. MGM Mirage plans hotel-condo complex that would be Las Vegas "hub." *USA Today,* November 11: B3.
3. *New York Times,* April 24, 2007: C10.
4. McCarthy, M. 2005. Vegas goes back to naughty roots; ads trumpet return to adult playground. *USA Today,* April 11: B6.
5. *USA Today,* April 11, 2005: B6.
6. Chris Woodyard, C., & Krantz, M. 2004. Latest Vegas marriage: Harrah's, Caesars tie knot; $5 billion deal marks strategy to reach more gamblers. *USA Today,* July 16: B1.
7. Sloan, G. 2003. Atlantic City bets on glitz: Down-at-the-heels resort rolls the dice, wagering a cool $2 billion that it will one day rival Las Vegas. *USA Today,* August 29: D1.
8. *USA Today,* August 29, 2003: D1.
9. Palmeri, C. 2004. Little guys with big plans for Vegas. *BusinessWeek,* August 2: 49.
10. Woellert, L. 2004. Can online betting change its luck? *BusinessWeek,* December 20: 67.
11. *New York Times,* April 24, 2007: C10.

Case 26 Samsung Electronics*

On April 13, 2007, Samsung Electronics reported a 15 percent drop in profits for the first quarter, driven largely by lower prices for its memory chips and flat panel screens. But the firm's performance was expected to show improvement by the end of the year. "I think the results hit the bottom in the first quarter and they will get better from the second quarter, with visible improvement in the second half," said James Song at Goodmorning Shinhan Securities.[1] In fact, the market value of Samsung had risen above $100 billion just one year ago, making it one of only four Asian companies to move above that mark. Based in Suwon, South Korea, the firm has moved past well-known rivals such as Sony, Nokia, and Motorola on the basis of its revolutionary products.

Such a level of achievement clearly indicates that Samsung has come a long way from its brush with bankruptcy just eight years ago (see Exhibits 1 and 2). For years, it had squeezed out profits by producing cheap television sets and microwave ovens based on technology that had been developed by other firms. Since then, Samsung has transformed itself into a much more innovative firm, creating cutting-edge technology across a spectrum of product lines (see Exhibit 3). Its feature-jammed gadgets have been racking up design awards, and the company has been rapidly muscling its way to the top of consumer-brand awareness surveys.

In the process, Samsung has grown to become a global leader in several different products ranging from flash memory chips to big LCD screens to CDMA mobile phones (see Exhibit 4). The firm's goal is to become the leader in twice as many product categories by 2010. Samsung's dramatic rise in value can also be attributed in large part to its decision to focus on niches that

command higher prices and fatter margins. For example, the firm's seventh-generation LCD factory is producing high-definition screens the size of a king-size bed.

Based on its success with a wide range of technologies that drive the development of its product line, the global consulting firm Interbrand recently declared Samsung to be the world's fastest-growing brand, setting its brand value at a staggering $15 billion. "Samsung continues to operate on a scale that few in the world can match, so I can't picture many companies trying to replicate it," said Brad Aham, a fund manager at State Street Global Advisors in Boston. "Its challenge now is to identify the areas that will allow them to grow earnings off the already high base they've reached."[2]

But Samsung continues to be hounded by many doubts about the sustainability of its business model. Most industry observers insist that high technology firms must focus upon developing proprietary content in order to maintain higher margins and hold off competition. Yet Samsung has defiantly stuck with its focus on hardware, choosing to partner with software firms. Furthermore, it insists on developing and manufacturing all of the components—ranging from chips to displays—that are used in its own products.

*This case was developed by Professor Jamal Shamsie, Michigan State University with the assistance of Professor Alan B. Eisner, Pace University. Material has been drawn from published sources to be used for class discussion. Copyright © 2007 Jamal Shamsie & Alan B. Eisner.

Exhibit 2 Balance Sheet

Years Ending December 31 (in Trillions of Korean Won)			
	2006	2005	2004
Total Assets	57,086	49,890	43,254
Total Liabilities	12,392	10,743	9,256
Total Shareholders' Equity	44,695	39,148	33,998

Source: Samsung.

Exhibit 1 Income Statement

Years Ending December 31 (in Trillions of Korean Won)					
	2006	2005	2004	2003	2002
Net Sales	58,236	56,720	56,893	36,409	33,261
Gross Profit	16,405	17,078	20,091	11,749	11,249
Operating Profit	6,847	7,956	11,862	6,009	6,247
Net Income	7,827	7,542	10,648	4,978	5,981

Source: Samsung.

Exhibit 3   Revenue Breakdown

Years Ending December 31 (in Trillions of Korean Won)		Sales	Profits
Semiconductors Including DRAMS, SRAMS, & NAND Flash Chips	2006	22.3	5.5
	2005	19.9	5.3
	2004	21.3	7.6
	2003	13.9	3.6
Telecommunications Includes Digital Phones & Handsets	2006	21.8	2.1
	2005	20.6	2.4
	2004	20.4	3.0
	2003	15.0	2.8
Digital Media Includes Plasma & Projection Displays & Televisions	2006	22.3	0.6
	2005	17.3	0.3
	2004	17.3	0.4
	2003	15.6	(0.6)
LCD Displays Includes panels for desktop & laptop computers	2006	11.8	0.9
	2005	8.5	0.6
	2004	8.9	1.8
	2003	4.3	0.9
Digital Appliances Includes "Intelligent" Refrigerators, Microwave Ovens, Air Conditioners	2006	6.0	(0.02)
	2005	5.5	(0.03)
	2004	5.3	0.02
	2003	4.8	(0.05)

Source: Samsung.

"If we get out of manufacturing," said CEO and Vice Chairman Jong-Yong Yun, "we will lose."[3]

Discarding a Failing Strategy

The transformation of Samsung into a premier brand has been the result of the ceaseless efforts of Jong-Yong Yun, who was appointed to the position of president and CEO in 1996. When Yun took charge, Samsung was still making most of its profits from lower-priced appliances that consumers were likely to pick up if they could not afford a higher-priced brand such as Sony or Mitsubishi. It had also become an established low-cost supplier of various components to larger and better-known manufacturers around the world.

Although the firm was making profits, Yun was concerned about the future prospects of a firm that was relying on a strategy of competing on price with products that were based

on technologies that had been developed by other firms. The success of this strategy was tied to the Samsung's ability to continually scout for locations that would allow it to keep its manufacturing costs down. At the same time, it would need to keep generating sufficient orders to maintain a high volume of production. In particular, Yun was concerned about the growing competition that the firm was likely to face from the many low-cost producers that were springing up in other countries such as China.

Yun's concerns were well founded. Within a year of his takeover, Samsung was facing serious financial problems that threatened its very survival. The company was left with huge debt as an economic crisis engulfed most of Asia in 1997, leading to a drop in demand and a crash in the prices of many electronic goods (see timeline, Exhibit 5). In the face of such a deteriorating environment, Samsung continued to push for maintaining its production and sales

Exhibit 4   Global Market Ranking

2005	
Product Category	**Market Rank**
Memory chips	1
Computer monitors	1
LCD displays	1
Big screen TVs*	1
DVD-VCR combos	1
Projection TVs	2
DVD players	2
MP3 players	2
Laser printers	2
Mobile phones	3
Microwave ovens	3
Plasma TVs	4
Camcorders	4

*Priced at $3,000 and above.

Source: Samsung.

records even as much of its output was ending up unsold in warehouses.

By July 1998, Samsung Electronics was losing millions of dollars each month. "If we continued, we would have gone belly-up within three or four years" Yun recalled.[4] He knew that he had to make some drastic moves in order to turn things around. Yun locked himself in a hotel room for a whole day with nine other senior managers to try and find a way out. They all wrote resignation letters and pledged to resign if they failed.

After much deliberation, Yun and his management team decided to take several steps to try and push Samsung out of its precarious financial position. To begin with, they decided to lay off about 30,000 employees, representing well over a third of its entire workforce. They also closed down many of Samsung's factories for two months so that they could get rid of its large inventory. Finally, they sold off about $2 billion worth of businesses like pagers and electric coffeemakers that were perceived to be of marginal significance for the firm's future.

Developing a Premium Brand

Having managed to stem the losses, Yun wanted to move Samsung away from its strategy of competition based largely on the lower price of its offerings. Consequently, he began to push the firm to develop its own products rather than to copy those that other firms had developed. In

Exhibit 5   Samsung Milestones

1969	Samsung Electronics established as maker of televisions with technology borrowed from Sanyo.
1977	Samsung introduces its first color television.
1981	Samsung begins to focus on undercutting Japanese rivals with me-too products, with little emphasis on design.
1988	Samsung launches first mobile phone.
1993	Chairman Lee Kun Hee tells Samsung executives to reinvent the firm through design.
1994	Samsung hires design consultancy IDEO to help develop computer monitors.
1995	Samsung sets up in-house design school, the Innovative Design Lab of Samsung.
1996	Lee declares "Year of Design Revolution," stressing that designers should lead in product planning.
1998	Asian financial crisis dents Samsung's ambitions, forcing it to cut design staff by 28 percent.
2000	Samsung once again focuses on design and CEO Yun Jong Yong calls for design-led management.
2001	Yun initiates quarterly design meetings for top executives and opens design labs in Los Angeles and London.
2002	Samsung's "usability laboratory" inaugurated in downtown Seoul.
2003	Samsung wins a total of 33 awards at top design contests in the United States, Europe, and Asia.
2006	Market value of Samsung rises above $100 billion, making it one of only four Asian firms to move above this mark.

Source: Samsung.

particular, Yun placed considerable emphasis on the development of products that would impress consumers with their attractive designs and their advanced technology. By focusing on such products, Yun hoped that he could develop Samsung into a premium brand that would allow him to charge higher prices.

In order to achieve this, Yun had to reorient the firm and help it to develop new capabilities. He recruited new managers and engineers, many of whom had developed considerable experience in the United States. Once they had been recruited, Yun got them into shape by putting them through a four-week boot camp that consisted of martial arts drills at the crack of dawn and mountain hikes that would last all day. To create incentives for this new talent, Yun discarded Samsung's rigid seniority-based system and replaced it with a merit-based system for advancement.

As a result of these efforts, Samsung began to start launching an array of products that were designed to make a big impression on consumers. These included the largest flat-panel televisions, cell phones with a variety of features such as cameras and PDAs, ever-thinner notebook computers, and speedier and richer semiconductors. The firm calls them "wow products" and they are designed to elevate Samsung in the same way the Trinitron television and the Walkman had helped to plant Sony in the minds of consumers

A large part of the success of Samsung's products can be attributed to their efforts to focus on the specific needs of prospective customers. Mike Linton, executive vice-president of Best Buy stated that Samsung regularly gets information from retailers about the new features that customers want to see in their electronic devices. This close link with retailers has helped Samsung to come up with two of their recent best-selling products: a combined DVD/VCR player and a cellular phone that also works as a PDA. According to Graeme Bateman, head of research for Japanese investment bank Nomura Securities, "Samsung is no longer making poor equivalents of Sony products. It is making things people want."[5]

Finally, to help Samsung change its image among consumers, Yun hired a marketing whiz, Eric Kim, who has worked hard to create a more upscale image of the firm and its products. Kim moved Samsung's advertising away from 55 different advertising agencies around the world and placed them with one firm, Madison Avenues's Foote, Cone & Belding Worldwide, in order to create a consistent global brand image for its products. He has also begun to pull Samsung out of big discount chains like Wal-Mart and Kmart and place more of its products into more upscale specialty stores such as Best Buy and Circuit City.

Pushing for New Products

Yun has taken many steps to speed up Samsung's new product development process. He is well aware that he will only be able to maintain the higher margins as long as his firm is able to keep introducing new products into the market well ahead of its established rivals. Samsung managers who have worked for big competitors say they have to go through far fewer layers of bureaucracy than they had to in the past to win approval for new products, budgets, and marketing plans, speeding up their ability to seize opportunities.

Apart from reducing the bureaucratic obstacles, Yun made heavy investments into key technologies ranging from semiconductors to LCD displays that could allow it to push out a wide variety of revolutionary digital products. Samsung has continually invested more than any of its rivals on its research and development, rising during the past couple of years to almost 9 percent of its revenue. It has a large and growing force of designers and engineers working in 17 research centers located all around the world (see Exhibit 6). Yun has also forced Samsung's own units to compete with outsiders in order to speed up the process for developing innovative new products. In the liquid-crystal-display business, Samsung buys half of its color filters from Sumitomo Chemical Company of Japan and sources the other half internally, pitting the two teams against each other. "They really press these departments to compete," said Sumitomo President Hiromasa Yonekura.[6]

As a result of these steps, Samsung claims that it has been able to reduce the time that it takes to go from new product concept to rollout to as little as six months, compared to over a year that it used to take the firm just six years ago. In large part, this has resulted from the effort of the firm's top managers, engineers, and designers who work relentlessly in the five-story VIP center nestled amid the firm's industrial complex in Suwon. They work day and night in the center, which includes dormitories and showers for brief rests to work out any problems that may hold back a product launch.

The progress that is made by teams that pursue new product designs in the VIP center allows Samsung to reduce complexity in the early stages of the design cycle. This allows the firm to get its products to manufacturing quickly with minimal problems and at the lowest possible cost. In turn, this can lead to a faster market launch of a product that is more likely to be more innovative than all others. Kyunghan Jung, a senior manager of the center explained, "Seventy to eighty percent of quality, cost and delivery time is determined in the initial stages of product development."[7] Such an emphasis on early design issues

Exhibit 6 **Designers Employed**

2006	550
2004	470
2002	310
2000	210
1998	170
Source: Samsung.	

allowed Samsung to figure out how the D600, one of its latest music-playing camera phones could be assembled in as little as eight seconds.

The speedier development process has allowed Samsung to introduce the first voice-activated phones, handsets with MP3 players, and digital camera phones that send photos over a global system for mobile communications networks. The firm has been just as fast in digital televisions, becoming the first to market projection TVs using new chips from Texas Instruments that employed digital-light processing. DLP chips contain 1.3 million micromirrors that flip at high speeds to create a sharper picture. Texas Instruments had given Japanese companies the technology early in 1999, but they never figured out how to make the sets economically. "They'll get a product to market a lot faster than their counterparts," said George Danko, Best Buy's senior vice-president for consumer electronics.[8]

Designing for the Digital Home

Yun is hoping that Samsung's advances in digital technologies will increase its chances of dominating the digital home. He believes that his firm is in a better position to benefit from the day when all home appliances, from handheld computers to intelligent refrigerators, will be linked to each other and adapt to the personal needs of consumers. In particular, Samsung appears to be well placed to take advantage of its capabilities to design and manufacture a wide array of products that straddle traditional technology categories. "We have to combine computers, consumer electronics and communications as Koreans mix their rice with vegetables and meats," said Dae Je Chin, the head of Samsung's digital media division.[9]

Yun has worked closely with Chin to summon engineers and designers from across the firm to mix wireless, semiconductor, and computer expertise in order to pursue its vision of domination of the digital home. One such product from the firm has been NEXiO, a combined cell phone and handheld computer. The device has a five-inch screen that is large enough for a user to run a spreadsheet or to browse the Web. Another new offering is a refrigerator called Zipel that has a 15-inch flat screen panel touch screen tucked into the door. The display can be used to surf the Internet and to send or receive e-mail.

In developing these products, Samsung has begun to place a lot of emphasis on the role of design in making its products irresistible in an increasingly competitive marketplace. Since 2000, the firm has opened or expanded design centers in San Francisco, London, Tokyo, Los Angeles, and Shanghai. Inside these centers, designers observe the way that consumers actually use various products. They may watch from behind a two-way mirror how consumers stuff a refrigerator with bagfuls of groceries. Samsung has also begun to send its growing group of designers to various locations to spend a few months at fashion houses, furniture designers, and cosmetic specialists to stay current with trends in other industries.

Samsung has also created the post of chief design officer to make sure that designers can get their ideas to top managers. A successful rear-projection television was developed by a designer who pitched it to one of the heads of television production. Engineers are pushed to find ways to work with the designs that are presented to them. As a result of these efforts, Samsung has earned a total of more than 100 citations at top design contests in the United States, Europe, and Asia. Commenting on this achievement, Yun stated, "We want to be the Mercedes of home electronics."[10]

Samsung is relying on the attractiveness of its products to make them the centerpiece of a digital home. It has been displaying its version of such a networked home in Seoul's Tower Palace apartment complex, where 2,400 families could operate appliances from washing machines to air conditioners by tapping on a wireless "Web pad" device, which doubles as a portable flat-screen TV. It may sound a bit futuristic, but when the digital home does become more realistic, Samsung has a chance. "They've got the products, a growing reputation as the innovator, and production lines to back that up," said In-Stat/MDR consumer-electronics analyst Cindy Wolf.[11]

Creating a Sustainable Model?

Yun's strategy to focus on higher-end products has clearly enhanced the firm's brand image and led to a sharp increase in its revenues and profits. In fact, many executives in the U.S. retail market said they have been astounded by the firm's ability to generate a superior brand image. The firm's revenues and profits have more than doubled over the past seven years. "Samsung is going to be the first Korean company to create a true global brand," according to the firm's marketing head, Eric Kim.[12]

These results have failed to address serious questions about Samsung's ability to rely exclusively on its hardware to continue to generate high margins. The life cycle of most electronics products can be brutally short, with prices tending to drop sharply over time. The profitability of a hardware firm rests on its ability to keep addressing new opportunities such as those offered by Microsoft's launch of the new Windows Vista operating systems. At the same time, it must keep seeking ways to reduce its costs in order to be competitive with lower margin products.

Yun appears to be well aware of the challenges that lie ahead for Samsung. He understands that his firm must keep investing heavily into R&D and keep developing new factories in locations that offer lower costs. Despite its achievements, Samsung is still searching for a product that would be comparable to Apple's iPod or Sony's Walkman. But Yun remains convinced that Samsung will maintain its leadership in digital technology, allowing it to keep turning out advanced products with desirable features that will continue to fetch higher margins.

Several industry experts doubt that Samsung can sustain its success without having to branch out into software and content. However, Yun has refused to consider branching out like Sony or Apple into music, movies, and games. He has decided against such a move in spite of growing evidence that subscription-to-content can provide a firm with a more lucrative source of revenue. Instead, Yun has chosen to collaborate with various content and software providers such as Microsoft and Time Warner.

By choosing to focus on hardware, Yun has placed his faith in Samsung's ability to stay at the forefront of core technologies and to master its manufacturing capabilities. "Everyone can get the same technology now," he recently commented. "But that doesn't mean they can make an advanced product."[13] In effect, Yun is betting Samsung's future on an unwavering commitment to its ability to keep putting out exceptional products. In his own words: "We stand at the crossroads to becoming a world leader or a major failure."[14]

Endnotes

1. Song, J. A. 2007. Samsung looks to second half as profit falls 15%. *Financial Times,* April 14: 9.
2. Cho, Y. S. 2006. Samsung market value surpasses $100 billion. *International Herald Tribune,* January 5: 15.
3. Edwards, C., Ihlwan, M., & Engardio, P. 2003. The Samsung way, *BusinessWeek,* June 16: 58.
4. Holstein, W. J. 2002. Samsung's golden touch. *Fortune,* April 1: 32.
5. Gibney, F., Jr. 2002. Samsung moves upmarket. *Time.* March 25: 49.
6. *BusinessWeek,* June 16, 2003: 60.
7. Lewis, P. 2005. A perpetual crisis machine. *Fortune,* September 19: 65.
8. *BusinessWeek,* June 16, 2003: 61.
9. Stone, B. 2002. Samsung in bloom. *Newsweek,* July 15: 34.
10. Rocks, D., & Ihlwan, M. Samsung design. *BusinessWeek,* December 6, 2004: 90.
11. *BusinessWeek,* June 16, 2003: 61, 64.
12. Solomon, J. 2002. Seoul survivors: Back from the brink. *The Wall Street Journal,* June 13: A1.
13. *BusinessWeek,* June 16, 2003: 64.
14. *Fortune,* September 19, 2005: 66.

Case 27   Claire's Stores: Competing Betwixt and Between*

In the fall of 2006, Marla and Bonnie Schaefer, co-chairwomen and co-CEOs of Claire's Stores, Inc. (CLE), faced several challenges. Since their promotion to coleadership of the company after their father's stroke and subsequent retirement in 2002, they had done well, nearly doubling profits in the first two years of their tenure,[1] but analysts were beginning to wonder whether this growth could be sustained. In 2005, when net income increases began to slow, Marla Schaefer, considered the more visionary of the two sisters, responded, "You can post double-digit increases when you are building a business but at some point you mature and level off. Our goal is to keep the business healthy, keep inventories in line and keep moving forward. We always want to be ready for the next hot item. We don't run the business for Wall Street. We run it for our shareholders and employees and customers."[2]

Claire's Stores had been enviable because of its unique niche in the specialty retail sector. With no direct competitors for its "tween" and teen shoppers, ages 7 to 17, who were looking for low-price but trendy jewelry, hair ornaments, cosmetics, and fashion accessories, Claire's was able to grow steadily, albeit cautiously, both in the United States and abroad. With low overhead and high margins, partly due to an efficient distribution system, the real key to success seemed to be effective merchandising—both anticipating and creating trends and keeping inventories fluid, updated, and well priced. The average selling price hadn't varied much from the $4.00 level in almost 10 years. As one market researcher said in 2005, "Claire's has carved out a niche that does not have much to do with economic times. It's about merchandising, and they've got the merchandise that teens want."[3]

However, in retail it was never good to get complacent. Discounters such as Wal-Mart and Target were devoting increasingly more square footage to accessories,[4] and were debuting celebrity merchandise by Mary Kate and Ashley Olsen and Hillary Duff, among others, who were of major appeal to Claire's Stores' main demographic.[5] Claire's was also able to sign these teen designers to deals for jewelry, cosmetics, and signature accessories, but the celebrity draw was traditionally short-lived. In addition, the big-box players such as Target could use their size and "fashion-forward" merchandising to further appeal to Claire's target market, but with lower price points.[6] When asked about competition from other teen-targeted retailers like Abercrombie & Fitch, Marla bluntly replied, "We have always had competition,

and we always will have competition. In fact, I call it stealth competition because it seems to come from all sides. Even malls love to open accessory kiosks right in front of our stores. But we do it bigger and better."[7]

Claire's Stores had steadily increased its store presence in malls across the United States, growing from a total of 1,167 U.S. stores in 1995 to 2,106 in 2006, but there wasn't much room for real estate growth, with available mall space in short supply, and it was possible the core stores had reached market saturation. At that point, retailers usually considered brand extension, with spin-offs targeting slightly different demographics to retain growth. Claire's had acquired the Afterthoughts chain from Woolworth's in 1999 and revamped it, calling it Icing by Claire's, as a way to reach out beyond the teen market to customers aged 17 to 27, but, as of 2006, sales per square foot had not met expectations, and planned expansion had been slow, partly out of fear that the concept might cannibalize Claire's Stores sales.[8]

In addition, the older consumer, especially women from 25 to 40, a potential market for Claire's, expected a certain level of service and store design that might have required more experimentation before Claire's could get it right. As one market researcher said, "A woman will know within the first 7 to 12 seconds of entering a store whether she will buy or not. She is a very visual consumer who makes up her mind quickly. She's driven by a combination of factors: the look of the product, how it's displayed, will it be easy for her to make a purchase decision, and somehow a lot of things resonate within her before she buys."[9] If Claire's decided to try to reach out to this market with the Icing concept, further differentiation of Icing by Claire's from Claire's Stores might require a different look and feel to the store shopping experience.

As Claire's Stores had steadily increased its presence in malls across the United States and in Puerto Rico, it had also embarked on a steady international expansion. Starting in late 1994, Claire's had entered into a joint venture in Japan with AEON, Co. Ltd., and then, in 1995, opened 45 new stores in Canada. Claire's continued to expand into the U.K. by acquiring 48 Bows & Bangles stores in 1996. In 1998, Claire's acquired Bijoux One, a 53-store chain covering Switzerland, Austria, and Germany, and in 2000 acquired Cleopatre's 42 stores in France. Additional stores were opened in Belgium, Holland, and Spain. In 2000, Claire's also made its first venture into franchising, in Kuwait, the United Arab Emirates, and Saudi Arabia, followed in 2004 with merchandising agreements in South Africa (see Exhibit 1). Entering the fall season of 2006, Claire's Stores, Inc. had continued to post growth numbers worldwide (see Exhibits 2A, 2B, 2C and 3).

With the European stores about half the size of the average 1,200 square foot ones in the United States, yet sales per square foot almost twice as much, international

* This case was prepared by Professor Pauline Assenza of Manhattanville College, Professor Alan B. Eisner of Pace University and Professor Ron Heimler, LIM—The College for the Business of Fashion. This case was primarily based upon library research as well as interviews and was developed for class discussion rather than to illustrate either effective or ineffective handling of an administrative situation. Copyright © 2007 Pauline Assenza, Alan B. Eisner, and Ron Heimler.

Exhibit 1 Claire's Store Growth 1992–2006

Claire's Stores Consolidated Store Growth Fiscal 1992–2006*					
FYE	**Number of Stores****	**Sales per Square Foot**	**Sales per Store**	**Inventory Turns**	**Return on Sales**
2006	3,050	477	$475,000	2.9	12.60%
2005	2,984	476	$468,000	2.9	11.40%
2004	2,935	413	$415,000	3	10.20%
2003	2,912	370	$357,000	3	7.80%
2002	2,875	339	$326,000	2.9	4.53%
2001	2,873	347	$332,000	2.5	7.22%
2000	2,887	379	$365,000	3.4	12.27%
1999	1,941	348	$340,000	2.6	11.36%
1998	1,725	328	$314,000	2.9	11.70%
1997	1,560	320	$301,000	3	10.31%
1996	1,359	296	$273,000	3.1	8.70%
1995	1,232	294	$263,000	3.2	7.70%
1994	1,087	293	$265,000	3.3	8.40%
1993	1,038	269	$244,000	3.1	5.90%
1992	995	279	$248,000	2.3	2.20%

*From continuing operations.

**Excludes franchised stores.

FY 2006 Store Locations*			
North America	2,106	Holland	10
Austria	28	Japan	172
Belgium	1	Spain	15
France	201	Switzerland	53
Germany	17	U.K./Ireland	447

*In addition, 84 Claire's Stores operate under various licensing and merchandising agreements throughout the Middle East in Kuwait and Saudia Arabia with seven located in South Africa.

Source: Claire's Stores.

expansion appeared to be the best strategy. However, the Schaefer sisters seemed to be cautious. As Bonnie Schaefer said, "We like to be methodical, and we don't want to go into any venture recklessly with our own company or others. We do take a modest approach, and it has worked well for us so far."[10] With overall revenue growth slowing for Claire's in 2006, and same-store September sales up only 1 percent compared to 8 percent in 2005, analysts were getting frustrated. In 2006 one said, "The whole issue in the U.S. is there is no unit growth for Icing or Claire's. The company has played around with a number of new concepts, but to really have a super premium or superior model, you need a growth vehicle, and they don't have one queued up. That's the big negative here."[11]

For a specialty retailer targeting an age demographic, paying attention to trends and adjusting store concepts accordingly was crucial. According to Philadelphia-based marketing consultancy Twentysomething Inc., there were 38 million young people between the ages of 11 and 19 in the United States at the beginning of 2006, with an estimated buying power of almost $2,000 per capita per year. As one retailer said, "Where are all these folks going to go when

Exhibit 2   Claire's Stores Financials

2A Claire's Stores, Inc. Annual Balance Sheet (in U.S. $ millions)					
Period Ended	**1/28/2006**	**1/29/2005**	**1/31/2004**	**2/1/2003**	**2/2/2002**
Assets					
Cash	431.12	191.01	224.63	195.48	99.91
Marketable Securities	—	134.61	—	—	1.56
Receivables	10.33	—	—	—	—
Total Inventories	118.52	110.07	92.5	88.33	78.6
Raw Materials	5.11	—	—	—	—
Finished Goods	113.41	110.07	92.5	88.33	78.6
Other Current Assets	38.05	57.64	42.9	37.79	34.35
Total Current Assets	**598.01**	**493.33**	**360.02**	**321.61**	**214.42**
Net Property, Plant & Equipment	222.72	204.53	187.4	174.48	163.97
Property, Plant & Equipment	509.31	467.89	432.19	385.81	341.97
Accumulated Depreciation	286.6	263.37	244.79	211.33	178
Interest and Advance to Subsidiaries	5.1	3.2	—	—	—
Intangibles	254.81	253.54	242.15	227.45	211.37
Deposits & Other Assets	10.06	11.54	16.35	14.59	21.81
Total Assets	**1,090.70**	**966.13**	**805.92**	**738.13**	**611.58**
Liabilities					
Accounts Payable	50.24	41.99	48.94	43.19	30.87
Current Long-Term Debt	—	—	—	40.92	21.04
Accrued Expense	74.44	94.34	65.24	43.76	25.82
Income Taxes	36.71	30.6	29.15	13.15	4.8
Other Current Liabilities	18.06	—	—	—	—
Total Current Liabilities	**179.45**	**166.94**	**143.33**	**141.01**	**82.54**
Deferred Charges	42.94	43.5	30.15	25.87	14.75
Long-Term Debt	—	—	—	70	110.1
Total Liabilities	**222.38**	**210.44**	**173.47**	**236.88**	**207.39**
Shareholder Equity					
Common Stock	4.97	4.95	4.95	2.44	2.44
Capital Surplus	63.32	50.48	49.39	32.83	29.87
Retained Earnings	781.68	672.22	558	458.76	389.04
Treasury Stock	—	—	—	—	0.45
Total Shareholders' Equity	**868.32**	**755.69**	**632.45**	**501.25**	**404.19**
Total Liabilities & Shareholders' Equity	**1,090.70**	**966.13**	**805.92**	**738.13**	**611.58**

Source: Data Provided by Thomson Financial.

(*continued*)

Exhibit 2   Claire's Stores Financials (*continued*)

2B Claire's Stores, Inc. Annual Income Statement
(in U.S. $ millions of U.S. Dollars except for per share items)

Period Ended	1/28/2006	1/29/2005	1/31/2004	2/1/2003	2/2/2002
Net Sales	1,369.75	1,279.41	1,132.83	1,001.54	918.74
Cost of Goods Sold	625.87	587.69	524.46	486.86	473.79
Gross Profit	**743.89**	**691.72**	**608.38**	**514.68**	**444.95**
SG & A Expense	498.46	475.75	385.45	351.39	328.79
Non-Operating Income	14.24	5.86	−45.94	−38.73	−41.15
Interest Expense	—	0.19	2.56	4.44	10.42
Income Before Taxes	**259.67**	**221.64**	**174.42**	**120.12**	**64.6**
Provision for Income Taxes	87.33	75.38	59.38	42.14	23.47
Extra Items & Discount Operations	—	−3.14	—	−0.24	−21.54
Net Income	**172.34**	**143.12**	**115.04**	**77.74**	**19.58**

Source: Data Provided by Thomson Financial.

2C Claire's Stores, Inc. Annual Cash Flow
(in U.S. $ millions)

Period Ended	1/28/2006	1/29/2005	1/31/2004	2/1/2003	2/2/2002
Net Income (Loss)	172.34	146.26	115.04	77.98	41.13
Depreciation/Amortization	50.13	46.01	42.66	38.62	43.78
Net Increase (Decrease) in Assets/Liabilities	16.09	−0.89	37.08	56.74	8.62
Cash Flow from Discount Operations	—	—	—	0.35	20.58
Other Adjustments—Net	4.29	7.91	9.63	−6.45	−5.11
Net Cash Flow from Operating	**242.86**	**199.29**	**204.41**	**167.24**	**108.99**
Increase (Decrease) in Property Plant & Equipment	−73.44	−63.57	−50.09	−45.5	−45.06
Increase (Decrease) in Securities Invest.	134.61	−134.61	—	1.56	−1.56
Other Cash Flow from Investing	−9.06	−7.46	−8.62	−7.19	−11.11
Net Cash Flow from Investing	**52.11**	**−205.64**	**−58.71**	**−51.12**	**−57.73**
Issue (Repayment) of Debt	—	—	−85.93	−20.23	−51.49
Increase (Decrease) in Borrowing	—	—	−25	—	—
Dividends, Other Distribution	−62.89	−28.91	−13.34	−7.58	−7.57
Net Cash Flow from Financing	**−58**	**−28.14**	**−113.98**	**−24.83**	**−59.02**
Effect of Exchange Rate on Cash	3.14	0.86	−2.57	4.29	−4.2
Cash or Equivalents at Year Start	191.01	224.63	195.48	—	—
Cash or Equivalents at Year End	431.12	191.01	224.63	—	—
Net Change in Cash or Equivalent	**240.12**	**−33.62**	**29.15**	**95.57**	**−11.95**

Source: Claire's Stores.
Data Provided by Thomson Financial.

Exhibit 3   Claire's Stores Key Historical Statistics (in $ millions of U.S. dollars except unit prices)

	1995	1998	2006
Store Profile			
Average Square Feet	900	960	1,150 U.S./600 Int'l
Total Stores	1,214	1,752	3,050
U.S. & Puerto Rico	1,167	1,495	2,106
Canada	45	102	Included in U.S.
Japan*	2	54	172
Other International	0	101[†]	772**
Net Income	$23.9	$58.2	$172.3
Gross Profit	53.9%	53.3%	54.3%
Total Sales	$301.4	$500.2	$1,370
U.S. Sales	—	$445.2	$964[††]
International Sales	—	$10.8	$405.7
Average Unit Selling Price	$4.00	$4.00	$4.40
Accessories Sales[‡]	35%	51.6%	42% U.S./55% Int'l
Jewelry Sales	65%	48.4%	58% U.S./45% Int'l

*Japanese stores are operated under a joint venture arrangement with Jusco Co., Ltd.

**Includes 84 stores licensed in the Middle East under an agreement with Al Shaya Co., Ltd., a Kuwaiti company, and 7 stores in South Africa licensed to the House of Busby Limited.

[†]England

[††]Includes Canada

[‡]Accessories sales include hair ornaments, totes and bags, trend gifts, and apparel. Jewelry sales include ear-piercing services.

Source: Claire's Stores.

they get tired of shopping in teenage land?" To make matters more complicated, reconfiguring to chase the twentysomething market may not have been a good long-term strategy because there was a smaller generation behind it—only about 27.6 million 6- to 12-year-olds in the United States as of 2006.[12] The number of Americans ages 25 to 34 was expected to rise to 5.2 percent of the population by 2010, but those ages 12 to 18 were forecasted to fall by 3.3 percent.[13]

Based on these numbers, Claire's Stores' major target market was shrinking. Other specialty retailers of apparel such as Abercrombie & Fitch, Aeropostale, and American Eagle Outfitters were creating new stores as brand extensions to try to capture the 18- to 40-year-olds. Given this trend, the success of Icing by Claire seemed increasingly important for long-term growth. With the shortage of desirable U.S. real estate, an option for Claire's might have been acquisition of a related concept retailer, as when it bought Afterthoughts, but this had not always worked well in the past. The boys and men's apparel store Mr. Rags, acquired in 1998, never performed for Claire's, and was sold off in 2002. When asked in 2005 about this potential strategy, Marla Schaefer said, "Over the course of 30 years

we have made acquisitions that have not been in our core capabilities, and we have learned lessons from that, which is stick to your knitting, do what you do best, and excel at it. That's what we intend to continue doing."[14]

In 2005 Claire's tested a concept, Claire's Club, targeted at children age 0 to 6, but results had not been up to expectations, and the idea was not expanded. This young target demographic caused Claire's problems for another reason. In 2006 a Minneapolis 4-year-old died of lead poisoning from swallowing a piece of a charm bracelet (not from Claire's). This prompted Maryland and California to take action requiring U.S. retailers and distributors to dramatically reduce the levels of lead in costume jewelry, particularly when sold to children.[15] The Baltimore health department found a ring sold at Claire's Stores to contain more than 100 times the level of lead acceptable under federal regulations, and Claire's removed the ring from Baltimore stores, but kept it for sale in stores elsewhere, pending in-house testing. Marisa Jacobs, Claire's Corporate Communications VP, stated that the chance of the jewelry injuring a child was a "remote possibility." Wal-Mart, notified of problems with one of their items, also a ring, pulled the product from its stores nationwide. The Baltimore Health Commissioner said that Wal-Mart's response was exactly right, and that "it is a mistake" for Claire's not to pull all its products off the shelves right away.[16]

One other larger issue that affected Claire's Stores' potential growth was the scarcity of retail talent "in the wings." Given the consolidation of retailing since 1995, training programs had been cut, and executives tended to cycle from one related company to another.[17] Given the uncertainty preceding the Schaefer sisters' promotion at Claire's, succession planning was a concern. Both Marla and Bonnie appeared resistant to any outsider, and had said someone "would need at least a year to learn the business" in order to succeed in an executive role at Claire's.[18] This might have been expected, given that their father had run the business for over 40 years. Rowland Schaefer had not been able to relinquish control easily, going through five Claire's Presidents from 1991 to 2000.[19] If the company was to remain a family firm, Marla and Bonnie had to work to keep the business in the family long enough for Marla's two daughters, teenagers in 2006, to have the same experience, should they be interested.

In the Annual Report for the fiscal year ending January 28, 2006, Marla and Bonnie Schaefer had laid out a "strategic roadmap" for the next five years. In it they mentioned the need for international expansion into new countries, continued astute merchandising, upgrading and enhancement of operational and information technology, more reliance on data mining for market research and management decision making, and depth of management. In the closing remarks they said, "We will be expanding our talent pool to ensure that we are appropriately staffed at all levels of the organization. Depth of management is critically important as Claire's continues to move into new forms of business and expands its global reach."[20]

In 2005, when asked why investors should be interested in Claire's Stores, Marla Schaefer responded, "I think it's a great concept with enormous expansion possibilities throughout much of the world. We have a healthy balance sheet. We generate an enormous amount of cash. We have a great demographic with disposable income who also loves to shop. We've got enormous brand name recognition, and we are steady. We've been in business over 30 years, and we have not yet had a year that was not profitable. So I think that says it all."[21] Merriam-Webster's Online Dictionary defines "betwixt and between" as "neither one thing nor the other."[22] Claire's Stores was not the normal specialty retailer, nor did it have the normal management structure. It had successfully captured the attention of the "tweens," and was "betwixt" the apparel and the high-end accessories retailers. Were these strengths or weaknesses? Were the Schaefer sisters too sure of themselves, would their formula for success falter due to caution or complacency? What would it take to keep the business growing?

In early December 2006, Claire's Stores announced it was putting itself up for sale, but with no guarantee it could find a buyer. Like other publicly-traded firms in this time frame, CLE had reached out to private equity firms for some relief from public scrutiny in a tightening sales market. Sales through November 2006 had slowed to an average of 2.6 percent, down from the 6 percent in the same period in 2005. Profit was also lower than previously, partly because of currency factors and lower demand in Europe and a shift of sales from jewelry to accessories, with accompanying lower margins. Claire's did have a healthy balance sheet, as Marla had said, with no debt, and a working capital at the end of Fiscal 2006 of $418.6 million, which made it attractive to potential buyers. As of December 2006, between Marla and Bonnie Schaefer and their father, they held 9.3 percent of the company's common shares, and controlled 32 percent of the votes.[23]

Industry Overview

The specialty retail industry had traditionally been volatile. Specialty retailers offered products within a single category, often to a specifically segmented target market. Unlike department stores that sold many different types of products for a one-stop shopping experience, specialty retailers could focus on one type of item and offer many varieties of that item. Wal-Mart and JC Penney were examples of the department store. Gap, Best-Buy, Barnes & Noble, and Toys-R-Us were examples of retailers who specialized in one general product category, sometimes offered to only one market segment: Gap offered clothing, Best-Buy offered electronics, Barnes & Noble offered books, and Toys "R" Us offered toys and gifts specifically for children. At the extreme end of the specialty market were the mall kiosks and carts, sometimes only seasonal, which often offered a way for entrepreneurs to test a narrowly focused concept prior to a more extensive sales and marketing investment.

The major advantage for any specialty retailer was the reduced cost in merchandising and distribution, sometimes using only one or two suppliers, and the associated ability to change inventory quickly with little to no adaptation needed in the physical layout of the selling space. The major disadvantage was that the single product category required the retailer to keep on top of trends in the category, since lost sales in one area could not be recouped by a shift of interest to another entirely different product area in the store. As a comparison, at Wal-Mart or JC Penney, if interest in apparel, for instance, was down in any particular sales cycle, new housewares or toys offerings may have been able to offset the temporary loss.

Within the specialty environment, companies might also do specialty branding to a more closely focused target market. For instance, as of 2006, Gap had created Forth & Towne to appeal to a more upscale, sophisticated female customer, augmenting Gap's existing apparel brands of Banana Republic, Old Navy, and the online shoe store Piperlime, launched in 2006. Another major player, Limited Brands (formerly known as The Limited, Inc.), as of 2006 operated Victoria's Secret (lingerie), Express (contemporary clothing for men and women), Bath & Body Works (fragrances, bath items), The Limited (general apparel), C.O. Bigelow (a specialty pharmacy), The White Barn Candle Co. (home fragrances), and Henri Bendel (upscale women's apparel). More focused specialty retailers in 2006 included the Charming Shoppes holding company, operating women's clothing stores for niche sizes such as Lane Bryant, Fashion Bug, Catherine's (all three for plus-sizes), and Petit Sophisticates. A major international presence in the United States since 2000, H&M (Hennes & Mauritz, AB, a Swedish public company) expanded significantly worldwide into Dubai, Kuwait, and China in 2006. H&M, known for inexpensive yet fashionable men's and women's clothing, bought out the Gap's German holdings in 2004 and had been aggressively marketing itself, fairly successfully, in North America.

Both acquisitions and spin-offs were common in this apparel, accessories, and home fashion specialty retail category. Well-known names such as Abercrombie & Fitch, Lane Bryant, Lerner New York, and The Limited Too all had changed hands over the years, sometimes in order to capitalize on the ability to concentrate merchandising and marketing on a specific category and market segment (see Exhibit 4).

As of 2007, the top specialty retailers targeting teenagers included apparel, gifts and accessories brands Limited Too and Justice (owned by Tween Brands, Inc.), and Club Libby Lu, an "experience-based" store for girls aged 6 to 12, a wholly owned subsidiary of Saks, Inc. Where Limited Too and Justice sold mainly apparel, Club Libby Lu sold cosmetics, bath products, and ear piercing, all supporting a palette of pinks and purples, accented by glitter and sparkle, and provided a clublike environment where girls could purchase a "makeover" kit used to create pretend characters such as a rock star or princess, create their own spa package

to use to hold home parties, or select a furry stuffed "pooch" companion to take home in a couture carrier. Their celebrity tween cosmetic line, "Pink Twinkle," is the creation of Ashley Tisdale, Disney actress and pop star.[24]

Club Libby Lu was created by former Claire's Stores executive Mary Drolet in 2000 and was acquired by Saks, Inc. in 2003. The store held group activities like birthday parties in its predominately pink interior and offered membership in the VIP ("Very Important Princess") club. Responding to this very specific targeting, one reporter commented, "Besides encouraging kids to be egotistical brats, Libby Lu and other kiddie stores like Monkey Dooz reinforce annoying stereotypes—as opposed to legitimate sexual differences—and transform children into tiny grotesques destined for an adulthood as gender-polarized as their parents'. Do all little girls long to be pretty in pink?"[25]

Regardless of the effect of this kind of specialty targeting, the tween market (children between ages 8 to 12) was large and potentially lucrative. As industry research revealed, "Children 11 and older don't consider themselves children any more . . . by treating pre-adolescents as independent, mature consumers, marketers have been very successful in removing the gatekeepers (parents) from the picture."[26] Data showed that 86 percent of the time the choice of brand was made by the tween rather than the parent, even though in most instances, the parent paid.[27] Cosmetics was one of the areas predicted to grow, and Target had created a brand, "Dottie

Exhibit 4 Specialty Retailers Changing Hands as of 2006

Brand Name	First Established	Formerly Owned/ Acquired By	Now Owned By	Fiscal 2005 Total Sales (in $ billions)	Comments
Abercrombie & Fitch	1892	The Limited, Inc, in 1988	Abercrombie & Fitch Co., as of 1996	$2.78	"Casual luxury" preppy image
Lane Bryant	1904	The Limited, Inc., in 1982	Charming Shoppes, as of 2001	$2.76	Number one in women's plus-size apparel
Lerner New York	1918	The Limited, Inc. in 1985	New York & Company, as of 2002	$1.13	Moderately priced women's apparel
Limited Too	1987 as a younger girls/infants version of The Limited	The Limited, Inc. in 1987	Tween Brands, Inc. 2006, also operates Justice, girl's sportswear	$0.758	Apparel & lifestyle products to girls 7–14

Note: In Fiscal 2005, Gap had total sales of $16.02B; Limited Brands, Inc. had total sales of $9.7B. Gap, Limited Brands, Abercrombie & Fitch, and Charming Shoppes were numbers one through four on the *Woman's Wear Daily* list of the Top 20 publicly traded specialty retailers in 2005. Claire's was number 11. (From Gustke, C. 2006. High volume specialists: Top 20 publicly traded specialty retailers ranked by most recent annual volume. *Women's Wear Daily*, 192 (12): 12.

Loves," in 2005 that included accessories, apparel, glittery cosmetics, and pink costumes, but the line was quickly discontinued by 2006, highlighting the fleeting nature of this type of specific merchandising. For those continuing to target these tweens, at least one analyst in late 2006 believed that Tween Brands, Inc., with its Limited Too and Justice apparel brands, had "no direct specialty retail competitor" and had "the ability to become the category killer in the tween market across all income brackets," with opportunities during 2007 "to increase its operating margin to 15% or more."[28]

Claire's Background

The profile of Claire's Stores, Inc. in 2007 was almost certainly due to the vision of Rowland Schaefer, who bought Harry Camp & Co. in 1960 and subsequently turned that firm, a seller of wigs, handbags, and accessories from leased department store counters, into Fashion Tress, Inc., a manufacturer of wigs and accessories distributed worldwide. Fashion Tress went public in over-the-counter trading in 1961, and in 1973 Schaefer renamed it FT Industries, Inc. after he purchased Claire's Boutiques, Inc., a small specialty chain with 60 stores in the Chicago area. After realizing that the Claire's name had some brand significance, Schaefer changed the company name to Claire's Stores, Inc. in 1983, and the common stock was listed on the New York Stock Exchange in 1985.

Starting in 1994, Claire's embarked on expansion outside North America, with the initiation of a joint venture with Japan's Jusco Co., Ltd., a member of the AEON Group. The first store opened in Tokyo in November 1994 and by 2006 included 172 locations. In 1995, Claire's purchased Bow Bangles Holding, Ltd., a Birmingham, England–based chain of 71 accessories stores, eventually rebranding them as Claire's Accessories. Further major European expansion continued. In 1998, Claire's acquired Bijoux One, a 53-store chain covering Switzerland, Austria, and Germany, and in 2000 acquired 42 Cleopatre stores in France.

Starting in 1993, Rowland Schaeffer had steadily bought up rival small accessories businesses, including Topkapi, Dara Michelle, L'cessory, Accessory Place, and The Icings, a major acquisition in 1996. Various forays into related businesses included "trend gift" stores such as Arcadio; Art Explorion; E. 57th, which sold T-shirts, unframed posters, calendars and stationery products, and a mail-order apparel and accessories catalog operation under the trade name "just nikki." Starting in 1995, the "trend gift" stores were either closed or converted into accessory stores, and the catalog business was allowed to close. In 1998, Claire's acquired a unisex teenage apparel chain operating under the trade name Mr. Rags from Lux Corporation. The concept never really worked for Claire's, and Mr. Rags was sold off in 2002. Claire's had acquired the Afterthoughts chain of 768 stores from Woolworth's in 1999, incorporating that into the existing Icing stores, renaming this Icing by Claire's as a brand extension targeting older teens and young women.

Operational Information

Claire's Stores experienced the traditional retail seasonal sales cycle, with peak periods during Christmas, Easter, and back-to-school time frames. Stores were predominately located in enclosed shopping malls using company-designed displays in such a way that merchandise could be adjusted and rotated easily, and allowed presentation of a wide variety of items in a relatively small space. The low square footage combined with the normally small merchandise size allowed for high sales per square foot, even at an average unit retail price of $4.40 in 2006.

Merchandise was sourced from importers primarily located in Asia and was distributed from the central warehouse in Illinois for North America and Puerto Rico and from Birmingham, England, for stores in the U.K., Ireland, France, Holland, and Belgium. Additional distribution facilities in Zurich, Switzerland, and Vienna, Austria, served stores in Switzerland, Austria, Germany, and Spain. Merchandise was typically delivered to stores three to five times a week. Over the years, Claire's had been able to use its increasing buying power to negotiate lower prices from vendors, resulting in correspondingly higher mark-ups and resulting margins, especially on jewelry items.

To a large extent, similar to most specialty retail operations, Claire's success was dependent on merchandising—anticipating the fashion trends and being able to respond to changes and switch out merchandise without having to take inventory loss. Active management of merchandising was accomplished through constant product testing and assessment of the effectiveness of store displays. Significant investment in management information systems, begun in earnest in 1997 and continuing through 2006, allowed for efficient decision making and effective utilization of inventory distribution systems. The emphasis in 2007 was on conversion of all international information systems to a single, unified platform so merchandise decisions could be made with centralized control.

Claire's had always been known for astute money management—significant cash on hand and the ability to generate cash flow from operations and available funds under its credit line. Under the Schaefers, Claire's also was able to keep debt to a minimum and in 2006 had no debt at all.

Imperatives and Challenges

At Claire's Stores, Inc., Marla Schaefer, located in New York City, identified herself as the visionary, and had a background in merchandising. Bonnie Schaefer, located at the company's headquarters in Pembroke Pines, Florida, was the operations and real estate expert and international strategist. They said they worked well together, and although at least one consultant believed that manager-duos can be a key to success, some worried whether the Schaefer sisters would be able to continue to balance each other's strengths and weaknesses, especially if the company was going to grow under their leadership.[29] If their strategic vision was just a hold-over from their father, they risked being replaced.

The Schaefer sisters' task may have been made easier because they had no real direct competitors as of 2007. Even the competitors selected by financial analysts didn't consistently measure up to Claire's operational numbers (see Exhibits 5 & 6). However, Claire's continued to be under

Exhibit 5   Claire's Stores Direct Competitor Comparison as of 2006 (dollar figures in $ millions)

	Claire's Stores	Forever 21*	Tween Brands, Inc.	Wet Seal, Inc.	Industry**
Market Cap:	$2,660	—	$1,290	$467.84	$1.830
Employees:	7,560	—	2,800	1,735	5,060
Quarterly Revenue Growth (yoy):	7.4%	—	19.90%	2.50%	14.10%
Revenue (ttm):	$1,400	$640.00	$819.53	$525.35	$1.940
Gross Margin (ttm):	53.65%	—	38.14%	45.25%	46.24%
EBITDA (ttm):	$299.20	—	$123.12	$73.81	$255.94
Oper Margins (ttm):	17.36%	—	11.10%	13.58%	10.42%
Net Income (ttm):	$172.85	—	$60.68	$(18.55)	$94.57
EPS (ttm):	1.743	—	1.808	−0.312	1.51
P/E (ttm):	16.04	—	21.69	—	20.92
PEG (5 yr expected):	1.08	—	0.81	0.39	1.07
P/S (ttm):	1.92	—	1.59	0.89	1.37

*Privately held

**Apparel Stores

Source: Yahoo! Finance. From http://finance.yahoo.com/q/co?s=CLE as of 2006.

Tween Brands, Inc., founded in 1987, operates as specialty retailer for tween girls in the United States. It primarily operates two specialty retailing concepts under Limited Too and Justice brand names. The company's product portfolio comprises apparel, such as jeanswear and bottoms, knit tops and T-shirts, graphic T-shirts, dresses, and outerwear; accessories, including jewelry, hair ornaments, hats, key chains, wallets, backpacks, purses, watches, and legwear; footwear, such as slippers, sandals, boots, and shoes; lifestyle products comprising bedroom furnishings, music, small electronics, stationary, candy, and party favors; personal care products, which include cosmetics and toiletries; and add-ons, such as underwear, sleepwear, and swimwear for girls aged 7 to 14 years. It also offers these products through its Web site, www.limitedtoo.com As of July 10, 2006, the company operated 565 Limited Too stores in 46 states and Puerto Rico and 111 Justice stores in the United States. The company also licenses approximately 19 Limited Too stores in the Kingdom of Saudi Arabia, Kuwait, the United Arab Emirates, and Qatar.

The Wet Seal, Inc. and its subsidiaries operate as a specialty retailer of apparel and accessory items designed for female consumers in the United States. The company operates two mall-based chains of retail stores under the names Wet Seal and Arden B. The Wet Seal targets the fashion-conscious junior customer by providing brand name and company-developed apparel and accessories. The Arden B. stores delivers a feminine, contemporary, sophisticated wardrobe of branded fashion separates and accessories. The company also provides Wet Seal online, a Web-based store located at www.wetseal.com, as well as at www.ardenb.com, which offers Arden B. apparel and accessories. As of April 10, 2006, it operated 400 retail stores in 46 states, Puerto Rico, and Washington DC, including 308 Wet Seal stores and 92 Arden B. stores. The company, formerly known as Lorne's, was founded in 1962 by Lorne Huycke and is headquartered in Foothill Ranch, California.

You don't have to be over 21 to shop at **Forever 21**'s stores—you just need your wallet. The company operates about 390 mainly mall-based U.S. stores in the United States and Canada under the Forever 21, Forever XXI, and For Love 21 banners. The stores offer cheap and chic fashions and accessories for women and junior girls. Its trendy clothes are priced 2 percent lower than its competitors. Most of the retailer's apparel is private label and is made in Southern California. Forever XXI stores are larger than classic Forever 21 shops and offer men's and women's fashions, as well as lingerie, footwear, cosmetic items, and other accessories. Owner and CEO Don Chang and his wife founded the company as Fashion 21 in 1984.

Exhibit 6 Claire's Stores (CLE) Stock Price vs. Tween Brands (TWB) (Competitor)

the scrutiny of the public investment community. Certainly there were demographic, technological, economic, and social trends that would be important to address going forward from 2007, both in the United States and internationally.

Regarding management depth in Claire's upper ranks, changing demographics in 2006 predicted a future shortage of entry-level retail employees. In retail, managers tended to rotate from retailer to retailer, recycling talent within the industry. Since Claire's preferred to "grow their own," they had to create relationships with prospective employees. Claire's Stores was a member of the DECA Association of Marketing Students National Advisory Board, offered scholarships to DECA students employed in its stores, and created internships in various retail-related career tracks.[30] The Annual Report of 2006 seemed to indicate this was a strategy that would take time to mature.

Well developed over 40 years, Claire's operational mechanisms seemed to be a major source of their strength. The Schaefer sisters were emphasizing the upgrading of management information systems and appeared to give the same level of attention to their marketing and sales. Marla said she believed Claire's had "practically 100 percent name recognition" among its core demographic, and that anyone "who has female children knows exactly what Claire's is."[31] Claire's appeared to be continuing to utilize a strategy that might be sustainable over time, although not at the growth levels of the past, but this strategy assumed no direct pressure from creative players like Target, Abercrombie & Fitch, or the combined might of Limited Brands. Claire's corporate strategy seemed to be, as Marla said, to "stick to the knitting." Unlike many of their fellow specialty retailers, they didn't pursue more diversification, seeming content to know that Rowland Schaefer had already tested those waters, for instance with the Mr. Rags apparel line. Limited Brands, however, with its diversified holdings, received positive marks going into the holiday shopping season of

2006, especially after seeing its first quarter earnings increase by 56 percent.[32]

International expansion seemed to be of primary importance for Claire's Stores going into 2007, with their revised franchising and merchandising strategies. Bonnie Schaefer seemed to prefer building new stores rather than acquiring existing ones and seemed to believe in importing North American "best practices" to the stores abroad, to gain operational efficiencies.[33] Sometimes this didn't translate well to other cultures. In their 2006 10K Filing, the Schaefer's identified their strategy as one of organic growth—entering into agreements with "unaffiliated third parties who are familiar with the local retail environment and have sufficient retail experience to operate stores in accordance with our business model."[34] Analysts were cautious to see if Claire's entry and operational strategies would be appropriate for their new chosen foreign markets. For reaching beyond the physical store front, Claire's Stores had a consumer Web site at www.claires.com, but it was not a shopping site.

Given that Claire's Stores was a publicly traded family firm with ownership in 2006 still heavily in family hands and most investors of the institutional variety, Claire's might have to make sure they have succession planning systems that allow top nonfamily executives to move forward. Although Claire's had a good "corporate governance quotient," better than 61 percent of other retailers,[35] governance of family businesses was always troublesome during transitions (see Exhibit 7).[36] If the Schaefer sisters modeled themselves after their father, it would have been hard for them to relinquish control, yet as they expanded into more international locations and considered implications of U.S. stagnation, they had to have considered different possible operational configurations. As always, challenges remained regarding how to spur new growth during 2007 and beyond, especially if the company was taken private in a leveraged buyout.

Exhibit 7   Claire's Stores Management Structure, 2006

Claire's Stores Inc.	
Co-Chairman, Co-CEO	Marla L. Schaefer
Co-Chairman, Co-CEO	E. Bonnie Schaefer
SVP, CFO	Ira D. Kaplan
VP Finance	William H. Girard III
VP Finance–International Operations	Mary Fitzwilliam
VP Taxation	David G. Ovis
Corporate Treasurer	Michael L. Winer
SVP, Corporate General Counsel	Rebecca Orand, Esq.
SVP, Chief Information Officer	E. Keith Pickens
VP Corporate Communications, Investor Relations	Marisa F. Jacobs, Esq.
Claire's North America	
President, COO (reports to co-CEOs)	Nancy Rich
Chief Administrative Officer	Joseph A. DeFalco
SVP of Store Operations (reports to N.A. COO)	Colleen Collins
6 Territorial Vice Presidents	
21 Regional Managers	
221 District Managers—each responsible for 10 stores	
Claire's U.K. (including Ireland, Holland, & Belgium)	
President, (reports to N.A. COO)	Roger Esdon
Claire's France, Switzerland, Austria, Germany, & Spain	
S.A.G. Group President (reports to Co-CEOs)	Lisa LaFosse
1 Territorial Vice President	
7 Regional Managers	
82 District Managers	

Source: Claire Stores.

Endnotes

1. Foust, D. 2006. A sister act that's wowing them. *BusinessWeek Online,* 3/13/2006, from http://www.businessweek.com.
2. LeClaire, J. 2005. Sitting pretty: Claire's Stores is raking in a pretty penny with value-priced fashion jewelry. Can the company keep up with Wall Street's expectations? *South Florida CEO,* July, from http://www.findarticles.com/p/articles/mi_m0OQD/is_6_9/ai_n14841842.
3. LeClaire, op. cit.
4. Little, M. 2006. Fashionably profitable: With an estimated $30 spent annually on women's fashion accessories, stores are taking notice. *Knight Ridder Tribune Business News,* June 4: 1.
5. Celebrity merchandising aims at the young; the Olsen twins' success led other stars to try to cash in on the teen and preteen market. *Los Angeles Times* (Home Edition), 7/11/2006: C8.
6. Owen, E. 2006. Claire's Stores reaps big market in accessories for young shoppers. *The Wall Street Journal* (Eastern Edition), April 12.
7. LeClaire, op. cit.
8. Owen, op. cit.
9. Baker, S. 2006. The apparel industry's top seven mega-trends: Management briefing: Smart retailers and brands give consumers more options, more often. *Just–Style,* October: 6.
10. Owen, op. cit.

11. Owen, op. cit.

12. Kang, S. 2006. Chasing Generation Y: Retailers scramble to serve a glut of twentysomethings. *The Wall Street Journal* (Eastern Edition), September 1: A11.

13. Barbaro, M. 2006. New clothing chain caters to the 25-to-40 buyer. *New York Times* (Late Edition–East Coast), September 5: C1.

14. CEO interview: Marla Schaefer—Claire's Stores Inc. *The Wall Street Transcript Corporation,* March 14: 1.

15. Attorney General Lockyer announces court approves settlement with Wal-Mart to reduce lead in costume jewelry. *U.S. Fed News Service,* Including U.S. State News (Dateline Sacramento, CA), 4/20/2006.

16. Emery, C. 2006. City plans to ban tainted jewelry: U.S. fails to protect children from lead, health chief says. *Knight Ridder Tribune Business News,* August 15: 1.

17. Gustke, C., & Poggi, J. 2006. Biggest earners; the top 20 apparel retail executives of publicly held U.S. companies with the highest compensation packages from 2005. *Woman's Wear Daily,* 192 (39): 12.

18. Foust, op. cit.

19. Fakler, J. T. 2000. Claire's Stores ring up sales but lose another president. *Business Journal,* 21 (6): A27.

20. Claire's Stores, Inc. Annual Report Fiscal Year Ended January 28, 2006, from http://www.clairestores.com/ phoenix.zhtml?c=68915&p=irol-report2006.

21. *The Wall Street Transcript Corporation,* op. cit.

22. http://www.m-w.com.

23. Cimilluca, D. 2006. Claire's hires Goldman, contacts potential buyers, people say. *Bloomberg News,* 12/1/06, http://www.bloomberg.com/apps/news?pid=20601103&sid =ajMDL8B_NEvI&refer=news.

24. "High School Musical" star Ashley Tisdale adds panache to new tween cosmetic line from Club Libby Lu. July 13, 2006, from http://www.cllublibbylu.com/news.aspx?cat1=7.

25. Chonin, N. 2006. Nothin' but a Tween thang. *San Francisco Chronicle,* July 23, from http://66.35.240.8/cgi-bin/article. cgi?file=/chronicle/archive/2006/07/23/PKGDOILVQU1. DTL&type=printable.

26. Special issues for tweens and teens, retrieved 12/9/06 from http://www.media-awareness.ca/english/parents/marketing/ issues_teens_marketing.cfm.

27. Clack, E. 2004. What a tween wants . . . now, *Children's Business,* 4/01/04, http://www.reachadvisors.com/ childrensbusinessarticle2.html.

28. RTTNews, 2006. Management reshuffles—weekly recap. November 24, from *Quote.com,* http://new.quote.com/news/ story.action?id=RTT611241030000462.

29. Pounds, M. H. 2006. *South Florida Sun-Sentinel* Business Strategies column. *Knight Ridder Tribune Business News,* March 1: 1.

30. From http://www.clairestores.com/phoenix.zhtml?c= 68915&p=irol-commitment.

31. *The Wall Street Transcript Corporation,* op. cit.

32. Halpern, S. 2006. Stock picking pros favor specialty retail and apparel. *MarketWatch: The Stock Advisors.com,* December 4, http://www.marketwatch.com/News/Story/ Story.aspx?guid=%7B9F8A2608-3D44-4775-88B6-42A68 F71D7FB%7D&siteid=yhoo&dist=.

33. Q2 2007 Claire's Stores, Inc. earnings conference call. *Fair Disclosure Wire,* 8/17/2006.

34. Claire's Stores 10K Filing, 4/12/06, p. 12, from http://www. clairestores.com/phoenix.zhtml?c=68915&p=irol-sec&secCat01v1_rs=31&secCat01v1_rc=10.

35. From http://finance.yahoo.com/q/pr?s=CLE.

36. Loyalka, M. D. 2006. Family-biz circle: The boomer handoff. *BusinessWeek Online,* February 14, http://www.businessweek. com/smallbiz/content/feb2006/sb20060213_147073. htm?chan=careers_careers_career+information.

Case 28   Caribou Coffee, Inc.*

In celebration of the first full year as a public company listed on the NASDAQ, Michael Coles, Chairman, CEO, and President of Caribou Coffee, opened the exchange on Tuesday January 9, 2007, by ringing the opening bell. Although celebration was warranted given this milestone for Caribou, Coles faced serious issues veiled under the cover of significant growth. The bottom line net loss for Caribou was increasing as the historic growth model, via company owned and operated stores, became increasingly incompatible with projected future growth (see Exhibits 1 to 6). The serious issues brewing included net losses increasing at an growing rate (in thousands)—($937) in 2003,

Exhibit 1   Net Income Impacted by Infrastructure Growth, Expenses, Depreciation, & Amortization

Net Income Impacted by Infrastructure Growth						
	2001	2002	2003	2004	2005	2006
	(in $ millions)					
General & Administrative Expense	($9.6)	($10.3)	($12.3)	($15.5)	($22.7)	($25.9)
Adjusted EBITDA[1]	$11.3	$11.8	$11.6	$14.4	$15.9	$15.0
Depreciation & Amortization	($7.0)	($8.1)	($11.8)	($15.3)	($19.4)	($23.6)
Net Income/(Loss)	$3.2	$3.1	($0.9)	($2.1)	($4.9)	($9.1)
Capital Expenditures	$15.3	$12.2	$20.7	$32.4	$43.2	$34.3
Total Coffeehouses[3]	185	203	251	306	395	464

[1]See the Company's 2005 10-K at www.cariboucoffee.com for a reconciliation of fiscal year 2001 through 2005 net loss to Adjusted EBITDA. See the Company's 10-K filed April 2, 2007 at www.cariboucoffee.com for a reconciliation of the fiscal 2006 net loss to adjusted EBITDA.

[2]Includes one time nonrecurring expenses excluded from adjusted EBITDA.

[3]Company owned and franchised coffeehouses opened at end of period.

Source: www.cariboucoffee.com Investor Relations Presentations 2007.

Annual Revenue Trends

CAGR:	2001–2003	2003–2006
	+10.7%	+24.1%

Exhibit 2 Caribou Annual Sales

Source: www.cariboucoffee.com Investor Relations Presentations 2007.

* This case was prepared by Graduate Student Keith F. Moody and Professor Alan B. Eisner of Pace University as a basis for class discussion rather than to illustrate either effective or ineffective handling of an administrative situation. Copyright © 2007 Keith F. Moody and Alan B. Eisner.

Exhibit 3 Price and Sales per Caribou Store

Average Investment (in $ thousands)	
Capital Expenditures (net of tenant improvements allowances)	$365–$415
Initial Inventory	$10
Total	$375–$425
Comparable Coffeehouse Sales Range	
Year 1 (months 13th–24th)	Mid-Teens
Year 2 (months 25th–36th)	Mid-Single Digits
Mature Store Performance— (New stores open at −80 percent of a mature store level)	
Sales	$500–$700
Store-level cash flow margin	17%–20%
Year 3 contribution	$85–$140
Year 3 cash-on-cash ROI	**−30%**
Average Store Payback	**4–5 Years**

Source: www.cariboucoffee.com Investor Relations Presentations 2007.

($2,074) in 2004, ($4,905) in 2005, and ($9,059) in fiscal year ending 12/31/06,[1] a stock price that had decreased from the IPO of $14 per share on 9/29/05 down to $7.29 per share on 4/13/06, and the potential for a class-action lawsuit by Caribou store managers seeking overtime pay.[2] In addition to these issues at Caribou, the competitive environment appeared to be perking up. In October 2006, Starbucks had announced increasing its long-term store goal to 40,000 from its prior target of 30,000. In light of the management issues and the environment, Coles and his management team concluded that a balanced and diversified growth strategy for Caribou was critical to minimize capital requirements, grow EBITDA, and, most importantly, achieve positive net income.[3]

"To lure latte drinkers from Starbucks, specialty coffee competitors have differentiated themselves using everything from atmosphere to product mix to regional specialization. Coffee is the second largest U.S. import, and the specialty coffee market is estimated to be worth $11 billion annually."[4] The retail segment of the gourmet coffee industry remains highly fragmented and, with the exception of Starbucks Corporation (Starbucks), contains few companies with strong brands. As of April 2007, no high-quality alternative to Starbucks has emerged with a national presence. Competition within the segment includes Starbucks; regional or local market coffeehouses;

numerous convenience stores, restaurants, coffee shops, street vendors; and, to a degree, quick service restaurants such as Dunkin' Donuts and McDonalds.

Specialty coffee sales continued to grow in the United States and abroad. Specialty coffee consumption grew over 48 percent in the United States from 2001 to 2006, and coffeehouses accounted for 69 percent of specialty coffee sales.[5]

The next step in this industry's development was taking place, as specialty coffee continued to grow in popularity and develop a major presence; it had begun to consolidate into a few major corporate brands (Starbucks purchased Seattle's Best in 2003 and Diedrich Coffee in September 2006). Many regional companies were looking to expand and the market was looking to see what firm would become number two to Starbucks.[6]

Developing during a time of uncertain affluence, specialty coffee had been part of a larger trend that includes such developments as microbrewed beer, single malt scotches, and organic foods. In each case, a consumer product had been recast as something more authentic, more traditional, diverse, flavorful, and healthful than the mass-produced product it supplants. In each case, the new "specialty" product was hyped as the original, traditional item that had been debased by mass production and corporatism.

The U.S. per capita consumption of coffee was estimated to be 424 servings, which includes in-home and out-of-home roast and ground, instant, and ready-to-drink (bottled/canned) coffee.[7] The total coffee market in 2003 was estimated to be 1.8 billion pounds or $19.3 billion.[8]

The "Specialty Coffee" Industry

Specialty coffee is coffee roasted using mainly high-quality Arabica beans. The Arabica bean is widely considered superior to its counterpart, the Robusta, which is used mainly in nonspecialty coffee. High-quality Arabica beans usually grow at high elevations, absorb little moisture, and mature slowly. These factors result in beans with a mild aroma and a bright, pleasing flavor that is suitable for specialty coffee.

The specialty coffee industry consists of two distinct business segments: whole bean, including ground, coffee sales (for home, office, and restaurant consumption) and coffee beverage sales. One major thrust behind the specialty coffee growth is the increase in the number of specialty coffeehouses, which grew from 500 units in 1991 to over 24,000 units in 2006, as reported by the Specialty Coffee Association of America (SCAA) (see Exhibit 7). The SCAA predicts that approximately 5,000 new coffee bars will open every year in the United States and that this industry will not peak until the year 2015. The National Coffee Association's (NCA) 2000 National Coffee Drinking Trends survey discovered that 79 percent of adults 18 years or older consumed coffee over the past year, compared to 78 percent in 1999 and 75 percent in 1997. Daily consumption in 2000 was 54 percent, or 110 million Americans, an increase of 1 million new daily drinkers over 1999. Factors contributing

Exhibit 4   Caribou Income Statements

Fiscal Year	2006	2005	2004	2003	2002
	(in $ thousands)				
Coffeehouse sales	225,649.269	191,309.555	157,534.501	121,812.018	103,290.888
Other sales	10,579.467	6,682.277	3,336.047	1,923.804	4,662.846
Total net sales	236,228.736	197,991.832	160,870.548	123,735.822	107,953.734
Cost of sales & related occupancy costs	98,655.629	80,242.163	65,319.899	50,640.931	44,882.647
Operating expenses	97,319.754	80,025.542	65,029.4	49,363.795	40,064.314
Opening expenses	1,737.637	2,095.945	1,201.829	822.165	439.356
Depreciation & amortization expense	21,548.195	16,375.704	13,381.562	10,452.583	7,430.665
General & administrative expenses	25,943.045	22,742.13	15,534.987	12,343.113	10,295.502
Closing expense & disposal of assets	510.461	571.985	1,034.422	166.577	917.126
Operating income (loss)	(9,485.985)	(4,061.637)	(631.551)	(53.342)	3,924.124
Other income	1,059.936	1,336.081	—	—	—
Interest income	553.767	265.977	5.583	8.902	29.168
Interest expense	695.323	1,602.529	963.356	511.002	495.926
Income (loss) before provision for income taxes	(8,567.605)	(4,062.108)	(1,589.324)	(555.442)	3,457.366
Current income taxes–U.S. federal	80.158	35.44	667.187	(205.117)	172.218
Current income taxes–state	189.444	44.124	306.653	201.124	178.54
Current income taxes–foreign	43.725	—	—	—	—
Total current income taxes	313.327	79.564	973.84	(3.993)	350.758
Deferred income taxes–U.S. federal	—	—	(667.187)	205.117	(172.218)
Deferred income taxes–state	—	—	(87.323)	26.846	(22.54)
Total deferred income taxes	—	—	(754.51)	231.963	(194.758)
Provision for income taxes	313.327	79.564	219.33	227.97	156
Income (loss) before minority interest & accounting changes	(8,880.932)	(4,141.672)	(1,808.654)	(783.412)	3,301.366
Minority interest	178.158	318.943	265.163	153.415	187.937
Income (loss) before effect of accounting changes	(9,059.09)	(4,460.615)	—	—	—
Cumulative effect of accounting changes, net	—	(444.861)	—	—	—
Net income (loss)	(9,059.09)	(4,905.476)	(2,073.817)	(936.827)	3,113.429
Weighted average shares outstanding–basic	19,281.74	15,254.761	13,798.347	13,347.571	13,293.824
Weighted average shares outstanding–diluted	19,281.74	15,254.761	13,798.347	13,347.571	13,296.304
Year-end shares outstanding	19,286.425	19,269.133	13,801.436	13,794.369	13,293.824
Earnings (loss) per share before cumulative effect	(0.47)	(0.29)	—	—	—
Earnings (loss) per share–cumulative effect office	—	(0.03)	—	—	—
Net income (loss) per share–basic	(0.47)	(0.32)	(0.15)	(0.07)	0.23
Earnings (loss) per share before cumulative effect	(0.47)	(0.29)	—	—	—
Earnings (loss) per share–cumulative effect office	—	(0.03)	—	—	—
Net income (loss) per share–diluted	(0.47)	(0.32)	(0.15)	(0.07)	0.23
Total number of employees	6,698	5,745	4,933	—	—
Number of common stockholders	92	8,012	58	—	—

Source: Company 10-Ks, Mergentonline.com.

Exhibit 5 Caribou Balance Sheets

Fiscal Year	2006	2005	2004	2003
	(in $ thousands)			
Operating funds	12,184.408	7,602.905	—	—
Operating funds & interest-bearing deposits	—	—	7,617.351	4,778.211
Money market funds	—	—	1.119	1.106
Money market funds/short-term investments	2,567.861	26,243.206	—	—
Cash & cash equivalents	14,752.269	33,846.111	7,618.47	4,779.317
Accounts receivable, gross	1,675.832	1,374.715	892.592	581.731
Allowance for doubtful accounts	12.693	237.595	34.9	34.9
Accounts receivable, net	1,663.139	1,137.12	857.692	546.831
Other receivables	1,769.256	2,260.254	1,093.675	1,391.723
Income tax receivable	—	135.75	451.168	100
Coffee	3,879.079	5,048.815	2,579.718	1,696.607
Merchandise held for sale	3,627.035	3,311.014	1,086.611	890.966
Supplies	2,788.379	2,822.683	2,038.111	1,584.033
Inventories	10,294.493	11,182.512	5,704.44	4,171.606
Prepaid expenses & other current assets	1,339.596	1,251.555	441.014	783.329
Total current assets	29,818.753	49,813.302	16,166.459	11,772.806
Leasehold improvements	95,044.683	87,516.286	64,519.192	49,267.663
Furniture, fixtures, & equipment	103,580.625	80,531.306	60,265.603	44,902.619
Property & equipment, gross	198,625.308	168,047.592	124,784.795	94,170.282
Less accumulated depreciation & amortization	93,870.423	72,024.872	57,145.063	44,722.317
Property & equipment, net of accumulated deprecation	104,754.885	96,022.72	67,639.732	49,447.965
Notes receivable–related party	48.413	64.531	80.649	96.705
Restricted cash	286.005	321.03	539.983	539.983
Other assets	1,399.542	1,738.717	1,780.105	152.065
Total assets	136,307.598	147,960.3	86,206.928	62,009.524
Accounts payable	9,681.879	14,553.743	5,311.686	3,627.894
Accrued compensation	5,676.449	5,462.657	4,707.242	2,750.675
Accrued expenses	7,860.487	8,504.552	5,469.931	3,674.07
Deferred revenue	9,002.588	8,165.26	5,308.713	3,439.533
Current portion of deferred compensation	—	—	—	165.781
Current portion of note payable & revolving credit	—	—	—	717.494
Total current liabilities	32,221.403	36,686.212	20,797.572	14,375.447
Revolving credit facility	—	—	19,923.93	6,050.1
Note payable to a landlord	—	—	—	0.981
Total note payable & revolving credit	—	—	19,923.93	6,051.081
Less current portion	—	—	—	717.494
Note payable & revolving credit facility	—	—	19,923.93	5,333.587
Asset retirement liability	872.184	760.997	—	—
Deferred rent liability	11,733.473	10,485.177	8,420.509	6,246.729
Deferred revenue	2,919	2,964	3,055	—
Minority interests in affiliates	159.05	138.159	217.206	236.542
Total long-term liabilities	15,683.707	14,348.333	31,616.645	11,816.858
Common stock	192.864	192.699	138.014	137.944
Treasury stock	—	9.011	—	—
Additional paid-in capital	122,153.502	121,626.855	53,634.009	53,584.77
Retained earnings (accumulated deficit)	(33,943.878)	(24,884.788)	(19,979.312)	(17,905.495)
Total shareholders' equity	88,402.488	96,925.755	33,792.711	35,817.219

Source: Company 10-Ks, Mergentonline.com.

Exhibit 6   Caribou Coffeehouses

	Fiscal Year Ended				
	2006	2005	2004	2003	2002
	(in $ thousands, except per share and operating data)				
Non-GAAP Financial Measures:					
EBITDA	$15,040	$14,796	$13,893	$11,561	$11,786
Adjusted EBITDA	15,040	15,911	14,393	11,561	11,786
Operating Data:					
Percentage change in comparable	(1)%	6%	8%	3%	(2)%
Company-Owned:					
Coffeehouses open at beginning of year	386	304	251	203	185
Coffeehouses opened during the year	60	86	57	50	24
Coffeehouses closed during the year	(6)	(4)	(4)	(2)	(6)
Coffeehouses open at end of year:					
Total Company-Owned	440	386	304	251	203
Franchised:					
Coffeehouses open at beginning of year	9	2	—	—	—
Coffeehouses opened during the year	20	7	2	—	—
Coffeehouses closed during the year	(5)	—	—	—	—
Coffeehouses open at end of year:					
Total Franchised	24	9	2	—	—
Total coffeehouses open at end of year	464	395	306	251	203

Source: Company financials, 10-K report.

Exhibit 7   Number of U.S. Specialty Coffeehouse Chain Units by Brand

U.S. Specialty Coffeehouse Chain Unit by Brand							
Year	Starbucks	Dunkin' Donuts	Caribou	Coffee Beanery	Peet's	Coffee Bean & Tea Leaf	Other	Total
2006	8,896	5,027	464	137	136	280	14,087	24,000
2005	7,353	4,345	395	142	111	213	13,186	21,400
2004	6,177	4,076	306	159	92	210	11,656	18,600
2003	5,239	3,864	251	149	76	200	11,485	17,400

Sources: SEC 10K Starbucks, SEC 10K Peet's, Entrepreneur.com 5/11/07, Coffee Beanery, & Dunkin' Donuts, Dunkin' Donuts Talk 6/23/06 Business Wire, Total—Specialty Coffee Association of America (SCAA).

to this increase include development of new quality beverages, an expanding coffee menu, and a new public place for coffee's social consumption: the gourmet coffee house.

Daily consumption in the gourmet coffee sector had grown from less than three percent of the adult population in 1995 to nine percent in 2000. Occasional consumption in the gourmet coffee sector has increased from 35 percent of the population in 1997 to 53 percent in 2000, while 52 percent of the American adult population (age 18+) drinks some type of coffee beverage on a daily basis, averaging about 3.2 cups per day.

Consumers have a strong interest in purchasing whole bean specialty coffee for home consumption. The sale of whole bean coffee has grown in popularity because the increasingly sophisticated consumer grinds the beans at home and brews the freshly ground coffee. According to the 1999 Gallup Survey on Coffee Consumption, nearly 36 percent of all coffee drinkers purchased specialty whole bean coffee for home consumption over the past three-month period. Consumers favor the supermarket or grocery store for the purchase of whole bean specialty coffee. According to the Gallup Survey, 61 percent of those consumers who had purchased such products did so most frequently in a supermarket or grocery store. Other important purchase locations included specialty coffee stores (14 percent), mail order catalogs or clubs (4 percent), and gourmet food stores (2 percent).

The "by the cup" (BTC) specialty coffee segment remained highly fragmented. Organizations competing in the BTC segment include Green Mountain Coffee Roasters (GMCR), Coffee Bean & Tea Leaf, Costa Coffee, Peet's Coffee and Tea, Caribou Coffee, and Starbucks, in addition to an estimated 500 smaller and regional brands.

The specialty coffee market was highly competitive. In the Office Coffee Service (OCS), convenience store, and food service areas, Sara Lee, Kraft, Procter & Gamble, and New England Coffee are competitors. In addition, retail coffee chains offering, but not limited to, specialty coffee include Dunkin' Donuts, Tim Hortons, and Krispy Kreme Doughnuts & Coffee. In the supermarket channel, Starbucks has a significant presence nationwide. Additionally, specialty coffee companies compete with commercial coffee roasters, to the extent that they try to "upsell" consumers to the specialty coffee segment.

Caribou Coffee Caribou Coffee was the second largest company-owned gourmet coffeehouse operator in the United States based on the number of coffeehouses operated. As of April 1, 2007, Caribou Coffee had 475 coffeehouses, including 8 franchised coffeehouses in the United States and 25 international franchise coffeehouses. Caribou Coffee's coffeehouses were located in 17 states and the District of Columbia. Caribou Coffee focuses on creating a unique experience for their customers through the combination of high-quality products, a distinctive coffeehouse environment, and customer service. To maintain product quality, Caribou sources the highest grades of Arabica beans, craft roasts beans in small batches to achieve optimal flavor profiles, and enforces strict packaging and brewing standards. Caribou focused on offering their customers high-quality gourmet coffee and espresso-based beverages and offers specialty teas, baked goods, whole bean coffee, branded merchandise, and related products. In addition, Caribou sold their products to grocery stores and mass merchandisers, office coffee providers, airlines, hotels, sports and entertainment venues, college campuses, and other commercial customers.

Founded in Minnesota in 1992, Caribou Coffee had been in a period of accelerated growth since the arrival of their Chief Executive Officer and President, Michael J. Coles, in January 2003 (see Exhibit 8). Under the

Exhibit 8 **Depth and Breadth of Executive Experience at Caribou Coffee**

Executive	Position		Years of Experience	Years at Caribou
Michael Coles	CEO	40+	Great American Cookies, Charter Bank & Trust	4
Roz Mallet	President & COO	30	la Madeleine	<1
George Mileusnic	CFO	29	Burger King, Coleman	6
Amy O'Neil	SVP, Store Operations	13	Caribou Coffee	13
Henry Stein	VP, Business Development & Commercial Sales	25	Coca-Cola	3
Kathy Hollenhorst	VP, Marketing	20	Carlson Companies, Inc.	2
Chris Rich	VP, Franchising	20	T.G.I. Friday's	<2

Source: www.cariboucoffee.com Investor Relations Presentations 2007.

direction of Mr. Coles, Caribou has implemented a series of strategic initiatives to improve their operations, including:

1. Enhancing their focus on customer service
2. Improving their selection and training of coffeehouse personnel
3. Strengthening their site selection strategy
4. Increasing coffeehouse openings
5. Developing new products and strategic partnerships

1) Customer Service Delivering excellent customer service was a key element of the Caribou Coffee culture. Caribou believes the personal interaction of their employees with customers is an important differentiating factor for Caribou. They also believed that their selective hiring practices, extensive training program, and lower employee turnover, compared to industry turnover, led to a superior customer experience. Caribou encouraged their employees to know customers' names and their preferred drink or other menu items, stimulating customer loyalty through familiarity and further differentiating Caribou from their competition.

Caribou was guided by a pay-for-performance philosophy that allowed them to identify and reward team members who meet high performance standards. Caribou provided incentive bonuses to coffeehouse managers and district managers. Bonuses for coffeehouse and district managers were based on coffeehouse sales, profit, and customer service standards. Because of Caribou's strong commitment to customer service, if a coffeehouse or district manager's score in customer service was below the required minimum, no bonus was given regardless of the score in other areas. To aid them in evaluating service standards in their coffeehouses, Caribou arranged for unannounced visits by "mystery shoppers" from a third-party service provider who supplied feedback on the customer service, products, coffeehouse appearance, and overall experience they encounter in the coffeehouses they visit.

Caribou Coffee believed that excellence was a product of hard work, and that life was too short for anything else. This vision served as a guide as Caribou Coffee strived to create a special experience for their customers. The mission at Caribou Coffee was to provide an experience that made the day better.[9]

2) Selection and Training of Coffeehouse Personnel Caribou strove for operational excellence by recruiting, training, and supporting high-quality managers and coffeehouse employees, whom they refered to as "team members." Caribou recognized two categories of in-store team membership:

- **Team Members** were dubbed the "vice presidents of smiles and service." They're the ones in charge of first impressions—either as a coffee-drink maker, a sales ringer, a merchandise stocker, or as a conversationalist with Caribou's guests.

- **Shift Supervisors** were second-in-command after the manager, making sure all systems run smoothly and efficiently. When the manager was absent, they were officially in charge. Additionally, they often took on many of the same roles as the Team Members. Caribou built its store teams' confidence, knowledge, and sales with official trainers.

- **Certified Instructor Trainers** were the in-store gurus of Caribou's core value, "excellent, not average," when it came to guest service and drink presentation. CITs conducted New Team Member certifications and served as trainers for Caribou College classes.

   Each Caribou coffeehouse was managed by a coffeehouse manager who oversaw an average of 15 team members. Each coffeehouse manager was responsible for the day-to-day operations of that coffeehouse, including hiring, training, and developing of personnel and local coffeehouse marketing and operating results.

- **Caribou Coffee Managers** acted as business owners of their stores, with built-in structure and support from Caribou. They command high standards of themselves, working for the greater good of the company; focused on meeting and exceeding sales goals; grow sales by delivering top-quality products through timely and friendly service in clean, pleasant surroundings; recruit and hire Team Members; train and develop the Team to deliver excellent guest service— providing regular feedback and coaching; lead by example, dividing time equally among employees and guests; channel successful sales and marketing efforts with local communities; develop and maintain relationships with vendors; work 55 hours per week, including nights and weekends; commit to three years in a Store Manager role and; make a positive influence on their communities.

Caribou also employed district managers who were responsible for overseeing the operations of approximately 10 coffeehouses, and directors of operations, who were each responsible for overseeing approximately 10 district managers and the operations of approximately 100 coffeehouses. As of January 1, 2006, Caribou had 40 district managers and four directors of operations. Caribou Coffee employed managers who cared about people. Caribou believed that this call-to-service was their trump card for success, and when managers fostered a true sense of collegiality among Team Members and guests and took full ownership and responsibility for their stores, there were personal and professional rewards. Caribou Coffee's investment in management included all of the elements that went with the position: helping to generate a top-notch staff to support store goals, ongoing professional training, enforcing high performance standards, and recognizing outstanding service and results.

Caribou Headquarters—Brooklyn Center, Minnesota USA At Caribou Headquarters, an innovative staff supported over 450 stores in 18 states. This mission of headquarters was to support the Caribou stores, either directly or indirectly. This fact was the reason Caribou commonly refered to their headquarters as the Support Center.

Organizational Culture—"Where the Entrepreneurial Spirit Roams Free"

At Caribou, there was significant flexibility in most departments. Because the organization was not overly structured, employees at Caribou got to work on a variety of projects and take on a wide range of responsibilities. At Caribou, promotion from within was ingrained in their culture. Caribou's dress code was business casual, and they tended to communicate in person, rather than sending impersonal e-mails or memos.

Training

Caribou believed that the training and development of their employees was key to fulfilling their mission of creating "an experience that makes the day better" for every guest on every visit. Caribou instilled a sense of purpose in all of their training practices to create a strong sense of commitment in their employees to deliver excellent service. Caribou had specific training and certification requirements for all new team members, including a combination of in-store training, classroom training, a training video, and drink certification. In addition to requiring that all new team members be "drink certified," Caribou also required ongoing drink re-certifications for team members.

This rigorous process helped to ensure that all employees were executing Caribou's beverage recipes and standards accurately and consistently. To ensure a consistency of experience, Caribou required their licensees to undergo training at one of their facilities prior to opening their first coffeehouse and to provide ongoing classroom and in-store training for their employees. Employees at licensed locations also went through the same certification process as team members at company-operated coffeehouses.

3) Site Selection Strategy, Design, and Atmosphere

The site selection for Caribou coffeehouses was integral to the successful execution of their growth strategy. Caribou evaluated potential locations using a statistical model, which compared the demographics of a particular location as well as site attributes, such as the type of venue, the potential for signage, and whether the location would have a drive through, to the demographics and attributes of their existing coffeehouse base. This process allowed Caribou to develop revenue forecasts and a financial plan for a potential location, which resulted in site selection most likely to produce successful and profitable coffeehouses. Caribou attempted to find geographic areas of expansion, within their existing marketing areas and new markets, in which they believed significant demand for Caribou Coffee could be shifted from competition and grown organically. Specifically,

Caribou's target market areas had a residential population of 20,000 or a daytime population of 60,000 people within a three-mile radius who meet certain demographic criteria regarding income, education, and occupation. To source competitive leases, field real estate managers at Caribou worked with local brokers. Field managers at Caribou had knowledge of the real estate markets in the regions they covered and had historically been able to negotiate favorable lease terms. After identifying a potential site, Caribou developed a site plan, space plan, and project budget that were reviewed and approved by senior management, coffeehouse operations, and real estate personnel.

Caribou had an experienced in-house construction team that is dedicated to budgeting and overseeing the construction of each coffeehouse through its opening. Experienced outside architects assisted Caribou's design and construction team with site plan approvals and building permits. By utilizing its own dedicated design and construction group, Caribou believed it was able to maximize flexibility in the design process and retain control over the cost and timing of the construction process.

Coffeehouse Design and Atmosphere Caribou coffeehouses were designed to look and feel like a mountain lodge, providing a strong point of differentiation. A casual and inviting atmosphere was created with earth tone fabrics and paints and comfortable seating, including leather sofas, chairs, and large tables. Most Caribou coffeehouses had a fireplace that added to the warm, relaxed atmosphere. The coffeehouses also featured exposed wooden beams and are decorated with lodge fixtures.[10] One of the primary attributes of the Caribou coffeehouse layout was that it provides quick and convenient access to facilitate take-out business, while simultaneously encouraging customers to gather and relax. Caribou coffeehouses featured two defined areas to meet customers' different needs. The service order and pick-up area facilitated maximum efficiency during busy times, while large tables and comfortable lounge sofas and chairs were located in a separate seating area where customers could read, socialize with friends, or have informal business meetings. Most locations offered wireless Internet access as well as a kids' corner with toys, games, and special seating for children. The lodge concept and design was flexible and could be successfully implemented in a variety of coffeehouse locations, configurations, and sizes. The prototypical Caribou coffeehouse was approximately 1,200 to 1,600 square feet, a size that allowed Caribou to satisfy both the rushed and the relaxed customer.

4) Coffeehouse Openings From 2002 to 2006, the net sales at Caribou had grown at a compounded annual rate of 21.6 percent. Their comparable coffeehouse sales had grown 3 percent in 2003, 8 percent in 2004, and 6 percent in 2005. From December 29, 2002 to April 1, 2007, Caribou expanded from 203 to 442 coffeehouses, including 8 licensed locations. During this time period, they also expanded geographically, increasing the number of Caribou

Limited Footprint Provides Growth Opportunity

442 company-owned coffeehouses and 8 franchised coffeehouses in 18 states and the District of Columbia*

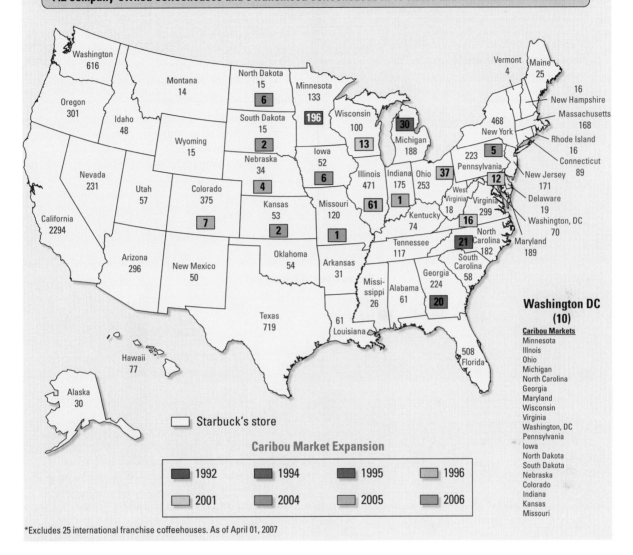

Washington 616
Montana 14
North Dakota 15 **6**
Minnesota 133 **196**
Vermont 4
Maine 25
Oregon 301
Idaho 48
South Dakota 15 **2**
Wisconsin 100 **13**
Michigan 188 **30**
New York 468
223 Pennsylvania **5**
New Hampshire 16
Massachusetts 168
Rhode Island 16
Connecticut 89
Wyoming 15
Nebraska 34 **4**
Iowa 52 **6**
Illinois 471 **61**
Indiana 175 **1**
Ohio 253 **37**
12
New Jersey 171
West Virginia 18
Virginia 299
Delaware 19
Washington, DC 70
Nevada 231
Utah 57
Colorado 375 **7**
Kansas 53 **2**
Missouri 120 **1**
Kentucky 74
16
North Carolina 182 **21**
Maryland 189
California 2294
Arizona 296
New Mexico 50
Oklahoma 54
Arkansas 31
Tennessee 117
South Carolina 58
Georgia 224 **20**
Texas 719
Missi-ssippi 26
Alabama 61
Louisiana 61
Florida 508
Hawaii 77
Alaska 30

☐ Starbuck's store

Caribou Market Expansion

■ 1992	■ 1994	■ 1995	☐ 1996
☐ 2001	■ 2004	☐ 2005	☐ 2006

*Excludes 25 international franchise coffeehouses. As of April 01, 2007

Washington DC (10)

Caribou Markets
Minnesota
Illnois
Ohio
Michigan
North Carolina
Georgia
Maryland
Wisconsin
Virginia
Washington, DC
Pennsylvania
Iowa
North Dakota
South Dakota
Nebraska
Colorado
Indiana
Kansas
Missouri

Exhibit 9 Caribou and Starbucks Locations

Source: www.cariboucoffee.com and starbucks.com

coffeehouses outside of Minnesota from 105 to 246, including 8 franchised coffeehouses (see Exhibit 9).

Michael Coles, Caribou's Chief Executive Officer commented, "We plan to aggressively grow the business and we see domestic licensing as a means to capitalize on the large growth potential in the U.S." Mr. Coles added, "Licensing coffeehouses will enable us to expand beyond our existing geographical footprint more efficiently than we could by opening only company-owned stores."[11]

The plan was to seek well-qualified area developers who had the necessary financial resources and local market

expertise to successfully open and operate Caribou coffeehouses in new U.S. markets (see Exhibits 10 and 11).

5) Developing New Products and Strategic Partnerships
In a news release dated November 30, 2006, Caribou Coffee and Coca-Cola North America (CCNA) announced a plan to launch a new line of premium ready-to-drink iced coffees in the United States during the summer of 2007. This launch marked the sixth new product initiative announced by CCNA in the fast-growing coffee, tea, and indulgent beverage segments in

Exhibit 10 Caribou Unit Expansion

Disciplined market roll-out strategy 20%–25% per year	**Coffeehouse Franchise Opportunity**
Desirable tenant for major landlords	Management Expertise
Match specific demographic criteria	• Michael Coles
	• 21 years of franchising experience
• High population density	• Chris Rich—VP Global Store Licensing
• Above average household income	• 13 years with TGIF
• High traffic patterns—drive thru's	• Negotiated agreements covering 50 countries
Strict site selection process	Domestic Area Developers
Significant License Opportunities	• Well qualified
	• Financial resources
• International, domestic and nontraditional locations	• Market expertise
	• Proven successful operators
Filed UFOC August 2006	International Opportunities
Long-term opportunity of 2,500+ units	• Middle East
	• South Korea

Source: www.cariboucoffee.com Investor Relations Presentations 2007.

Stores Open at Period End

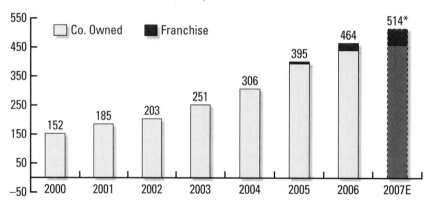

Exhibit 11 Caribou Coffeehouse Growth (Number of Stores) 2000 to 2007

Source: www.cariboucoffee.com Investor Relations Presentation 2007.

Exhibit 12 Caribou's Strategic Partners 2006 to 2007

2006. The ready-to-drink iced coffee launch with Coca-Cola North America was the third brand licensing arrangement for Caribou Coffee. In the second quarter of 2006, Caribou formed a strategic partnership with General Mills to launch a line of Caribou Coffee snack bars and with Kemps to launch a Caribou Coffee premium ice cream (see Exhibit 12).

CEO Michael Coles stated, "Our partnership with Coca-Cola North America (CCNA) will extend our great premium coffee taste experience into the ready-to-drink category and allow us to take advantage of CCNA's world-class distribution system." "Volume in the ready-to-drink

Strategic Partners—Product Licensing

Nationwide Launch (July 2006): General Mills, Caribou Coffee snack bars

Midwest Launch (March 2006): Kemps, Caribou Coffee ice cream

Nationwide Launch (Summer 2007): Coca-Cola, ready-to-drink coffee

Nationwide Launch (Spring 2007): Keuring, single serving brew pods

Source: www.cariboucoffee.com Investor Relations Presentations 2007.

coffee category has grown 17 percent in the last four years, and revenues are up 24 percent," said J. A. M. "Sandy" Douglas, president, CCNA. "Caribou's expertise, involvement and focus in brewing the perfect coffee will allow us to create a wonderful ready-to-drink coffee."[12]

Caribou's strategy was to expand its concept into a nationally recognized brand in the United States while adding select international locations through licensing. The intent of licensing Caribou branded products through strategic partners was to:

• Enable Caribou to progress their strategic initiatives
• Replicate the success that strategic partnerships have provided for Starbucks, with Pepsi distributing Frappuccino (annual sales > $400 million) and KRAFT Foods distributing Starbucks Coffee to the grocery and supermarket channel
• Grow EBITDA with a lower capital requirement than the historic coffeehouse strategy
• Progress toward a positive net income.

Keurig, Incorporated, a leader in gourmet single cup brewing, and Caribou Coffee announced a partnership on January 8, 2007, to market Caribou's gourmet coffees in Keurig K-Cup® portion packs. Keurig offered eight Caribou coffee varieties to choose from both at home and in the office. "We are proud to welcome Caribou to the Keurig family," stated Nick Lazaris, President of Keurig. "Caribou is an exceptionally strong brand with a loyal following among gourmet coffee lovers. Our office and home Keurig users will be delighted with Caribou in K-Cups."[13]

Caribou CEO Coles stated, "We've partnered with Keurig because their technology ensures our coffees will deliver a gourmet coffee experience at home or in the office that Caribou customers love in our coffeehouses." Under the terms of the arrangement, Caribou Coffee blended and sold its gourmet coffee beans to Keurig. Keurig packaged the coffee into K-Cups in accordance with Caribou Coffee's specifications. Under license from Caribou Coffee, Keurig also served as the wholesale distributor and a direct retailer for all Caribou Coffee K-Cups. Caribou Coffee K-Cups began to be available in Q2 of 2007 online at www.keurig.com. In addition, Keurig expected many of its premium retail partners to add Caribou Coffee K-Cups to the wide selection of K-Cups they already carried in 6,700 stores coast to coast. For the office coffee channel, Caribou Coffee K-Cups were offered through Keurig's Authorized Distributors for marketing to offices where Keurig brewers were installed. Over time, Caribou intended to market both Caribou Coffee K-Cups and Keurig brewers in many of its coffeehouses. Keurig, Inc., a wholly owned subsidiary of Green Mountain Coffee Roasters, was a pioneer and leading manufacturer of single-cup brewing systems. Keurig's proprietary brewing system combined a pressurized hot water brewer with multiple varieties of K-Cups, which feature a patented design that preserves the freshness of gourmet coffee. Through licensing agreements, Keurig offered more than 100 varieties of premium branded coffees and teas in K-Cups. More than 1 billion cups of Keurig brewed coffee and tea had been enjoyed since 1998.[14]

The success experienced with Keurig K-Cups by competitor Green Mountain Coffee Roasters had been well documented in GMCR's annual report, "Overall, sales of our coffee and Celestial Seasonings® Teas in K-Cups increased 40 percent in fiscal 2005."[15] Coke and Caribou were also forming a strategic partnership to take on Starbucks in providing iced coffee drinks. The new ready-to-drink coffee beverage would be available in either a can or a bottle. This was to be a straight-up coffee offering, not to be confused with Coke Blak, coffee-cola hybrid. Starbucks was way ahead of the game with Coke's arch-rival Pepsi who provided bottled Starbucks Frappuccino. The Starbucks and Pepsi strategic partnership has landed Starbuck's Frappuccino on supermarket shelves and in convenience stores. The deal with Coke was an aggressive move to get the Caribou brand in front of more and more people. It would not be an easy task to take on Starbucks, even with a powerful ally like Coke. Starbucks captured loyal customers with its coffee offerings and was able to become the "it" brand in premium coffee. Once a company manages to make its brand the entrenched one, it's hard to knock it off its pedestal.[16]

Pursuing an exclusive wholesale strategy within the specialty coffee industry has resulted in growth and profitability for Green Mountain Coffee Roasters as revealed in Exhibit 13.

Caribou Coffee, the only "excellent coffee" in the ratings, was complex and well-balanced. The quality of Caribou's already ground coffee was too varied for *Consumer Reports* (CR) to rate. Ratings were based on blind taste tests by two coffee experts. In measuring coffee, CR followed manufacturer's instructions. When instructions allowed, CR made adjustments to improve flavor. CR ground whole bean coffee in identical grinders for 15 seconds. Desirable flavors include floral, like the scent of a mixed flower arrangement, and earthy, like the scent of clean, moist soil. Darker roast was as judged by testers. Done right, dark roasting caramelized the beans and tones down the coffee acidity. Astringent coffees might make your mouth pucker. Burnt coffee tasted of charred beans. Cost per pound was based on the approximate retail price (see Exhibit 14).[17]

The Industry Leader In October 2006, Starbucks reported that sales for September at stores open at least 13 months rose 6 percent and raised its long-term store opening goal to 40,000 from its prior target of 30,000. For the fiscal year 2006, Starbucks said consolidated net revenues were $7.8 billion, up 22 percent from the year-ago period (see Exhibit 15). Same-store sales increased 7 percent for the fiscal year, marking its 15th consecutive year of 5 percent or greater same-store sales growth. "As we look at the markets in which Starbucks operates and the unique ways, in which we are able to leverage real-estate opportunities, we have determined that the long-term growth opportunity is greater

Exhibit 13 Green Mountain Coffee Roasters Income Statement

Green Mountain Coffee Roasters, Inc. Consolidated Statement of Operations (in $ thousands except per share data)	53 weeks ended September 30, 2006	52 weeks ended September 24, 2005	52 weeks ended September 25, 2004
Net sales	$ 225,323	$ 161,536	$ 137,444
Cost of sales	143,289	104,561	83,360
Gross profit	82,034	56,975	54,084
Selling and operating expenses	46,808	31,517	29,738
General and administrative expenses	17,112	9,554	9,493
Operating income	18,114	15,904	14,853
Other income	202	163	61
Interest expense	(2,261)	(498)	(282)
Income before income taxes	16,055	15,569	14,632
Income tax expense	(6,649)	(6,121)	(5,731)
Income before equity in losses of Keurig, Incorporated, net of tax benefit	9,406	9,448	8,901
Equity in losses of Keurig, Incorporated, net of tax benefit	(963)	(492)	(1,076)
Net income	$ 8,443	$ 8,956	$ 7,825
Basic income per share:			
Weighted average shares outstanding	7,505,567	7,192,431	7,004,605
Net income	$ 1.12	$ 1.25	$ 1.12
Diluted income per share			
Weighted average shares outstanding	7,909,116	7,666,832	7,409,426
Net income	$ 1.07	$ 1.17	$ 1.06

Source: Company financials, 10-K report.

Exhibit 14 Blind Taste Tests by Consumer Reports

			Attributes				
Poduct	Style	Cost per lb	Floral	Earthy	Darker Roast	Astringent	Burnt
1 Caribou "Excellent"	bean	$11.25	✓	✓	✓		
11 Starbucks "Very Good"	bean	$10.45		✓	✓	✓	✓

Source: *Consumer Reports* December 2004 page 47–49.

Exhibit 15 Starbucks Income Statement

Starbucks Consolidated Statement of Earnings 52 Weeks Ending	FY06	FY05	% Change	% of Total Net Revenue	% of Total Net Revenue
Net Revenues:					
Company-Operated Retail	$6,583,098	$5,391,927	22.1%	84.5%	84.7%
Specialty:					
Licensing	$ 860,676	$ 673,015	27.9%	11.1%	10.5%
Food service and other	$ 343,168	$ 304,358	12.8%	4.4%	4.8%
Total Specialty	$1,203,844	$ 977,373	23.2%	15.5%	15.3%
Total Net Revenues	$7,786,942	$6,369,300	22.3%	100%	100%
Net Earnings	$ 564,259	$ 494,370	14.1%	7.2%	7.8%

Source: Company financials, 10-K report.

than we previously thought," Starbucks President and Chief Executive James Donald said in a statement. "Starbucks is truly in the early stages of growth." Starbucks plans to grow its Specialty Operations and pursue other opportunities to leverage the brand through the introduction of new products and the development of new channels of distribution.[18]

Starbucks operates more than 12,000 retail locations in North America, Latin America, Europe, the Middle East, and the Pacific Rim. Starbucks produces and sells bottled Starbucks Frappuccino® coffee drinks, Starbucks DoubleShot® espresso drinks, and Starbucks® super-premium ice creams through its joint-venture partnerships and Starbucks™ Coffee and Cream Liqueurs through a marketing and distribution agreement in other convenient locations outside its retail operations.

Channel Scope

Starbucks sells whole bean and ground coffee to several types of wholesale accounts, including office coffee distributors, hotels, airlines, retailers, and restaurants as well as institutional food service companies that serve business, industry, education, and healthcare accounts. The Starbucks' efforts to increase its sphere of strategic interest via its joint venture with PepsiCo and Dreyer's, and its move to sell coffee in supermarkets, represents an ongoing drive to continually reinvent the way Starbucks does business. Gerry Lopez, president of Global Consumer Products Group, announced that, through its joint venture with PepsiCo, Starbucks aims to transform coffee vending with its plans to offer superior hot latte and cocoa beverages through the Starbucks hot vending initiative. Through this initiative, Starbucks aims to transform the hot coffee vending experience by creating a new, high-quality hot drink segment within the estimated $900 million ready-to-drink beverage category in the United States. Unlike other coffee

vending experiences in the market, the Starbucks vending platform utilizes proprietary heat-on-demand technology, developed by PepsiCo, which will offer customers another convenient way to enjoy Starbucks on-the-go.

On the grocery store front, Starbucks announced the expansion of its relationship with Kraft to distribute Starbucks coffee to a wide variety of retail channels across Canada and the United Kingdom. In grocery and warehouse club stores throughout the United States, Starbucks sells a selection of Starbucks whole bean and ground coffees, as well as Seattle's Best Coffee®, Torrefazione Italia® branded coffees, and a selection of premium Tazo® teas through a licensing relationship with Kraft Foods Inc. By the end of fiscal 2006, the company's coffees and teas were available in approximately 31,900 grocery and warehouse club stores, with 30,000 in the United States and 1,900 in International markets. Revenue from this category comprised 24 percent of specialty revenues in fiscal 2006.[19]

Starbucks strategy for expanding its specialty operations is to reach customers where they work, travel, shop, and dine by establishing relationships with prominent third parties who share Starbucks values. These relationships take various forms, including retail store licensing agreements, wholesale accounts, grocery channel licensing agreements, and joint ventures.

The Starbucks Experience and Company-Operated Retail Stores Starbucks' retail goal is to become the leading retailer and brand of coffee in each of its target markets by selling the finest quality coffee and related products and by providing a unique Starbucks Experience. The Starbucks Experience, or third-place experience, after home and work, is built on superior customer service as well as clean and well-maintained company-operated retail stores that reflect the personalities

Exhibit 16 Caribou versus Starbucks Customer Experience

An Experience that Makes the Day Better		
	Caribou Coffee	Starbucks Coffee
Taste/Flavor	30%	24%
Service/Atmosphere	29%	14%
Selection/Variety	20%	20%
Convenience	19%	40%

*Preference of customers who have visited both in last 12 months.

Source: www.cariboucoffee.com 10/1/06—2004 AAU Study for all markets in which both Starbucks and Caribou have coffeehouses.

of the communities in which they operate (see Exhibit 16). Starbucks' strategy for expanding its retail business is to increase its market share in existing markets primarily by opening additional stores and opening stores in new markets where the opportunity exists to become the leading specialty coffee retailer. Starbucks Company-operated retail stores accounted for 85 percent of total net revenue during fiscal 2006.

The average Starbucks' company-operated store sales in the United States has demonstrated continuous sales (in $ thousands) growth per year per store from $671 for new stores and $812 for total average in 2002 to $920 for new stores and $1,045 for total average in 2006.[20]

"For Starbucks, our ambitious long-term goal is to become an enduring great company with the most recognized and respected brand in the world, known for inspiring and nurturing the human spirit. The Starbucks of today falls short of these aspirations. We make a lot of mistakes," said Starbucks' Chairman Howard Schultz.[21]

The Future for Caribou In light of Starbucks announcement in October 2006 to raise its long-term store goal to 40,000, Caribou faced increased pressure as they assessed the competitive environment and their strategy to compete with the industry leader. As of March 2007, Starbucks was grappling with two lackluster quarters, apparently due to competition in the coffee category from rivals. A leaked memo from Starbucks Chairman Howard Schultz raised concerns about the company's swift growth rate, commoditization of the brand, and a "watering-down of the Starbucks experience." Margins have also been under pressure, and wage increases for employees at Starbucks will crimp profits in the short term according to Angela Moore of MarketWatch 3/16/07.

As conveyed at the SunTrust 36th Annual Institutional Conference in April 2007, although Caribou's balance sheet supports growth, with $14.8 million in cash and a $60 million credit facility, the past reliance on company-owned and operated stores may constrain profitable growth. Chairman and CFO Michael Coles was under pressure from shareholders to turn the stock performance around and from store managers demanding overtime pay. Significant opportunities existed to improve store level comparable sales and margins. A balanced and diversified growth strategy should incorporate these opportunities and leverage the franchise option for store growth, an option currently unavailable to Starbucks in the United States.

As Michael Coles savored the final sip of his Turtle Mocha, he pondered the future of Caribou. Coles questioned whether as a "runner-up" to an industry giant, if Caribou can and/or should try to compete with Starbucks. After all, at one time Dunkin' Donuts was the giant of the retail coffee industry, yet Starbucks was able to move beyond the competition.

Endnotes

1. www.cariboucoffee.com, 4/13/07.
2. United Press International, 4/3/07.
3. SunTrust 36th Annual Institutional Conference, 4/11/07.
4. *Business 2.0,* October 2006: 62.
5. Specialty Coffee Association and the National Coffee Association.
6. Peel, C., 1997. Los Angeles, a microcosm of the country. *Tea and Coffee Trade Journal,* 169(4): 16–28.
7. Nestlé S.A.
8. Datamonitor.
9. www.cariboucoffee.com, 10/1/06.
10. www.cariboucoffee.com, 10/1/06.
11. www.cariboucoffee.com, 10/1/06.
12. www.cariboucoffee.com, 12/5/06.
13. *Business Wire,* 1/8/07.
14. Press Releases, 4/14/07, www.cariboucoffee.com.
15. Green Mountain Coffee Roasters 2005 Annual Report.
16. Lomax, A. 2006. Caribou and Coke crank up the caffine. December 4, www.fool.com.
17. *Consumer Reports,* December 2004.
18. Form 10-K Starbucks Corporation For Fiscal Year Ended October 2, 2005.
19. Form 10-K Starbucks Corporation for Fiscal year Ending October 1, 2006.
20. JP Morgan Gaming, Lodging, and Restaurant Conference, 3/22/07.
21. Schultz, H., & Yang, D. J. 1997. Pour your heart into it. *Hyperion.*

Case 29 eBay: Expanding into Asia*

On December 19, 2006 eBay announced it will shut down its existing site in China and buy 49 percent of a joint venture with Biejing-based Tom Online. Tom Online, which primarily sells cell phone add-on services such as ring tones and text messaging, will run the renovated auction business with eBay's help. The move is expected to give eBay some of the local expertise it desperately needs to compete with China's top auction site, Taobao. Despite Meg Whitman, CEO of eBay, calling the deal an evolution of the company's China strategy and not a failure, analysts view it as an indication that U.S. Web players are still struggling with their strategy in Asia.[1] With Asia's population exceeding 3.7 billion, more than half the world's population, and Internet usage in the region skyrocketing at 248 percent, eBay must develop a strategy that will successfully adapt to Asian local markets and compete with Taobao and other major local competitors.

eBay

On January 24, 2007 eBay.inc announced its fourth quarter and full year financial results for 2006. According to Meg Whitman, CEO of eBay, "All three of the company's business units delivered impressive results, including record earnings and payment volumes in several areas." Since its inception in 1995, the company has enjoyed strong revenue growth and is a dominant player in the online auction industry. Between 2004 and 2006, the company's net revenues grew between 30 and 59 percent per quarter. By 2006, the company reached revenues of $5.9 billion, up from $3.2 billion in 2004. eBay expects consolidated net revenues for 2007 to be in the range of $7 to $7.3 billion.

eBay's founder, Pierre Omidyar, envisioned a community built on commerce, sustained by trust, and inspired by opportunity. The company's mission is to "enable individual self-empowerment on a global scale" and employ "business as a tool for social good." Omidyar cites "trust between strangers" as the social impact tied to eBay's ability to remain profitable. The company's unique business model, which unites buyers and sellers in an online marketplace, has attracted over 221 million registered users. eBay enables ecommerce at multiple levels (local, national, and international) through an array of Web sites, including eBay Marketplaces, Paypal, Skype, Rent.com and Shopping.com. The company's range of products and services has also evolved from collectibles to household products, customer services, automobiles, and so on. The variety of products attracts a range of users that includes students, small businesses, independent sellers, major corporations, and government agencies.

Despite eBay's outstanding growth performance, the company still faces a number of challenges in both domestic and international markets. The low entry barriers in the

online marketplace have attracted a number of large dot-com competitors that include Amazon, Yahoo, uBid, and Overstock. Historically the company acquired other online competitors, such as Stubhub (tickets), but established players such as Yahoo and Amazon pose a major threat to eBay's market share and ability to sustain profitability. Still, Whitman feels the company will end up as a specialty business suggesting little threat from these major competitors:

We have specialized in e-commerce, payment and voice communication. Google stands for search, Yahoo largely stands for content—so I think we may on the fringe compete, but I suspect that over time the businesses will become more specialized.

—**Meg Whitman,** February 8, 2006

The company has no plans for further big acquisitions but intends to expand and identify synergies within existing business lines.

eBay also acknowledges its inability to grow and compete in certain international markets. The company has localized sites in 24 countries and a presence in Latin America through its investment in MercadoLibre.com. However, eBay's numerous attempts to penetrate the Asia Pacific market, specifically China and Japan, have ended in failure, with the company pulling out of Japan and buying out Chinese startup Eachnet, essentially cancelling years of invested work. According to many analysts, the company's recent joint venture with Beijing-based Tom Online is further indication that the company can't compete in these countries. To remain successful and enjoy the same financial performance as the past, eBay must develop an effective strategy to compete in major Asian markets and mitigate the risk of existing local competitors.

Evolution of Auctions

Traditional Auctions According to Greek scribes, the first known auctions occurred in Babylon in 500 B.C. During this period, women were sold on the condition of marriage and it was considered illegal for daughters to be sold outside auctions. Auctions evolved during the French Revolution and through the American Civil War, where colonels auctioned goods that were seized by armies.[2] Although there are various types of auctions, they all provide a forum where sellers can find buyers or hobbyists who are looking to purchase rare items and collectibles. Auctions are considered one of the purest markets since buyers pay what they are willing to spend for an item, determining the true market value of the item. Over time auction formats continued to evolve and through technological advances and improved communication, they found a new home—the Internet.

Online Auctions The primary difference between traditional and online auctions is that the auction process occurs over the Internet as opposed to a specific location

* This case was prepared by Professor Alan B. Eisner and graduate student David J. Morates of Pace University. This case was solely based upon library research and was developed for class discussion rather than to illustrate either effective or ineffective handling of an administrative situation. Copyright © 2007 Alan B. Eisner.

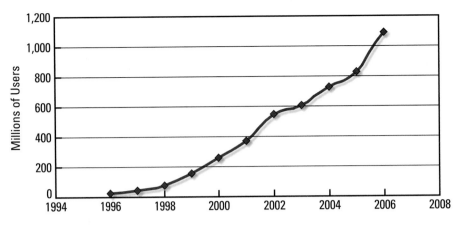

Exhibit 1 Internet Usage Growth

Source: Internet World Stats—Global Village Online, 2007.

where both buyers and sellers are present. Online auctions offer strategic advantages to both parties that are not typically available in traditional auctions. Buyers can select from millions of products and engage in multiple auctions simultaneously. Given the massive inventory of an online auction market, items are usually available in multiple auctions, allowing buyers to compare starting bid prices and search for better prices. On the other hand, sellers are exposed to millions of buyers since more users have access to the Internet and feel comfortable making purchases online. The net impact is increased price competition since there are more buyers who are willing to purchase items at a higher price. In both instances, the Internet gives buyers and users access to a marketplace that spans worldwide.

Online auctions also offer the following strategic advantages:

1. No time constraints since bid can be placed at any time.
2. No geographic constraints since sellers and buyers can participate from any location with Internet access.
3. Network economies—the large number of bidders attracts more sellers, which attracts more bidders, and so on. This creates a large system that has more value for both parties.

Online auctions also allow businesses to easily sell off excess inventory or discontinued items. This is done through either business-to-business (B2B) or business-to-consumer (B2C) auctions. Offering products and services in an online auction helps small businesses build their brand and reputation, by establishing a devoted customer base. Finally, some businesses use the online marketplace as an inexpensive yet effective way to test market for upcoming products.

E-commerce

Although Vannevar Bush originally conceived the idea of the Internet in 1945, it wasn't until the 1990s that it became overwhelmingly popular. According to Internet World Stats, in December 2006 there were over 1 billion Internet users in over 150 countries. Exhibit 1 shows Internet usage growth between 1996 and 2006.

As of March 19, 2007, North America was considered the region most penetrated by the Internet, with approximately 69.7 percent of the population already online. However, Internet usage growth between 2000 and 2007 was considerably less in North America than in other regions. The regions with the highest Internet usage growth were in developing countries where penetration was low, such as Africa, Asia, Latin America, and the Middle East. Considering close to 80 percent of the world's population resides in these areas, it is inevitable that Internet usage growth will continue to increase dramatically in these regions. Exhibit 2 shows the world Internet usage and population as of March 2007.

Although Asia comprises approximately 57 percent of the world's population, its penetration rate is only 10.7 percent. When comparing Asia to other regions with high usage growth rates such as Africa and the Middle East, Asia has invested more in its technology infrastructure and contains by far the most current Internet users, making it a more attractive market. Exhibit 3 provides more detail on how Asia stacks against the rest of the world in terms of Internet usage.

As the usage growth of the Internet increased, so did the popularity of e-commerce. E-commerce, which stands for electronic commerce, is the concept of conducting business transactions over the Internet. As in the case with online auctions, e-commerce eliminates boundaries such as time and geography, allowing businesses and customers to interact with one another constantly. As more users are exposed to the Internet, they become comfortable with the idea of conducting transactions online. In correlation with Internet growth usage, revenue generated through e-commerce has increased dramatically since the 1990s. Exhibit 4 shows U.S. online retail revenues generated through e-commerce over the past 7 years:

Exhibit 2 World Internet Usage and Population Statistics

World Regions	Population*	Population %	Internet Usage*	% Penetrated	Usage % of World	Usage Growth 2000–2007
Africa	933.4	14.2%	33.3	3.6%	3.0%	638.4%
Asia	3,712.5	56.5%	398.7	10.7%	35.8%	248.8%
Europe	809.6	12.3%	314.8	38.9%	28.3%	199.5%
Middle East	193.4	2.9%	19.4	10.0%	1.7%	491.4%
North America	334.5	5.1%	233.2	69.7%	20.9%	115.7%
Latin America	556.6	8.5%	96.4	17.3%	8.7%	433.4%
Australia	34.4	0.5%	18.4	53.5%	1.7%	142.0%
Total	**6,574.7**	**100.0%**	**1,114.2**	**16.9%**	**100.0%**	**208.7%**

*in millions

Source: Internet World Stats—Usage and Population Statistics, 2006.

Exhibit 3 Internet Usage in Asia

Region	Population*	Population %	Internet Users*	% Penetrated	Usage % of World	Usage Growth 2000–2007
Asia	3,712.5	56.5%	398.7	10.7%	35.8%	248.8%
Rest of World	2,862.2	43.5%	715.6	25.0%	64.2%	190.1%
Total	**6,574.7**	**100.0%**	**1,114.3**	**16.9%**	**100.0%**	**208.7%**

*in millions

Source: Internet World Stats—Usage and Population Statistics, 2006.

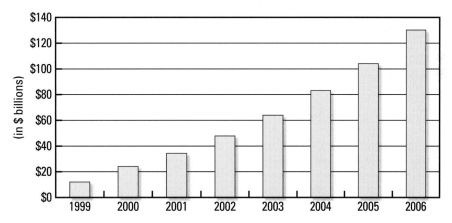

Exhibit 4 U.S. Online Retail Revenues

Source: Internet World Stats—E-Commerce Market Size and Trends, 2006.

E-commerce has grown rapidly in other regions as well, especially in Asia since China's admission into the World Trade Organization (WTO) on December 11, 2001. Induction in the WTO allows China to conduct business with other nations more freely by reducing tariffs and eliminating market and government impediments.

Company Background

Computer programmer Pierre Omidyar founded the online auction Web site in San Jose, California on September 3, 1995. Pierre was born in Paris, France and moved to Maryland with his family when his father took on a residency at Johns Hopkins University Medical Center. Pierre became fascinated with computers and later graduated from Tufts University with a degree in computer science. While living and working in the San Francisco Bay area, Pierre met his current wife Pamela Wesley, a management consultant, who later became a driving force in launching the site. The couple's vision was to establish an online marketplace where people can share the same passion and interest as Pamela's hobby.[3] Omidyar also envisioned an online auction format that would create a fair and open marketplace, where the market truly determined an item's value. To ensure trust in the open forum, Omidyar based the site on five main values:

1. People are basically good.
2. Everyone has something to contribute.
3. An honest, open environment can bring out the best in people.
4. Everyone deserves recognition and respect as a unique individual.
5. You should treat others the way you wanted to be treated.

On Labor Day weekend in 1995, Omidyar launched Auction Web, an online trading platform. After the business exploded, Omidyar decided to dedicate more attention to his new enterprise and work as a consultant under the name Echo Bay Technology Group. When he tried to register a Web site for his company, Omidyar discovered Echo Bay was unavailable so he decided to use the abbreviated version eBay, which also stood for electronic bay area. The company's name was also selected to attract San Francisco residents to the site and prompt them to buy and sell items.

Initially, the company did not charge fees to either buyers or sellers, but as traffic grew rapidly Omidyar was forced to charge buyers a listing fee to cover Internet service provider costs. When Omidyar noticed the fees had no impact on the level of bids, he then realized the potential for profitability of his business. To handle and manage the company's day-to-day operations, Omidyar hired Jeffrey Skoll (B.A.Sc. University of Toronto, MBA Stanford University). Jeffrey was hired as the company's first president and wrote the business plan that eBay later followed from its emergence as a start-up to a financial success. The two worked out of Skoll's living room and various Silicon Valley facilities until they eventually settled in the company's current location in San Jose, California.

By the middle of 1997, less than a year under the name eBay, the company was hosting nearly 800,000 auctions a day.[4] Although the rapid expansion of eBay's traffic caused the company to suffer a number of service interruptions, the site remained successful and continued to gain the confidence of its strong customer base. Skoll remained president until early 1998 when the company hired current President and CEO Meg Whitman. At the time, the company only had 30 employees and was solely located in the United States; it now has over 11,000 employees. In

Exhibit 5   eBay Growth (millions)

	2004	2005	2006
Confirmed Registered Users[1]	135.5	180.6	221.6
Active Users[2]	56.1	71.8	81.8
Number of Store Listings[3]	72.7	187.2	369.2
Gross Merchandise Volume[4]	$34,168	$44,299	$52,473
eBay Stores[5]	254,000	383,000	593,000

[1]Cumulative total of all users who have completed the registration process on one of eBay's trading platforms
[2]All users, excluding users of Half.com, Internet Auction, Rent.com, Shopping.com, and our classified Web sites, who bid on, bought, or listed an item with the previous 12-month period
[3]All listings on eBay's trading platforms, regardless of whether listing subsequently closed successfully
[4]Total value of all successfully closed items between users on eBay's trading platform in millions of dollars
[5]Primarily, GMV related to eBay's "Buy it Now" feature on eBay's trading platform

Source: eBay Unaudited Supplemental Operating Data, December 2006.

September 1998, eBay launched a successful public offering, making both Omidyar and Skoll instant billionaires. By the time eBay went public, less than 3 years after Omidyar created eBay, the site had more than a million registered users. The company grew exponentially in the late 1990s and, based on current performance, indicates no sign of stopping. Exhibit 5 highlights the company's recent growth performance in the marketplace segment.

Platforms   eBay's overall strategy is comprised of three primary components: products, sense of community, and aggressive expansion. All three components evolved around the various geographic and specialty platforms the company introduces.

Product Categories   eBay has an array of product categories and trading platforms that offer a range of pricing formats, such as fixed-pricing. Relatively new for the company, establishing a fixed-price format allows eBay to compete directly with major competitors such as Amazon.com and penetrate new market space. Prior to fixed pricing, selling prices were solely determined by the highest auction bid, which took days or weeks depending on the length of the auction. eBay's different trading platforms also offer distinct services and target specific market niches, which allow eBay to broaden its customer base. The platforms include:

- *Paypal*—Founded in 1998 and acquired by eBay in 2002, PayPal enables individuals to securely send payments quickly and easily online. PayPal is considered the global leader in online payments with tens of millions of registered users.

- **Rent.com**—Acquired by eBay in February 2005, Rent.com is the most visited online apartment listing service in the United States, with more than 20,000 properties listed.
- **Skype**—Acquired by eBay in October 2005, Skype is the world's fastest-growing online communication solution, allowing free video and audio communication between users of Skype software.
- **Shopping.com**—With thousands of merchants and millions of products and reviews, Shopping.com empowers consumers to make informed choices, which drive value for merchants. The company was acquired by eBay in August 2005.
- **Stubhub.com**—Recently acquired by eBay in January 2007, StubHub is an online marketplace for selling and purchasing tickets for sports, concerts, and other live entertainment events.

eBay's acquisition of Skype was expected to enhance the customer experience by improving communication between buyers and sellers. According to Meg Whitman, "Communications is at the heart of e-commerce and community. By combining the two leading e-commerce franchises, eBay and Paypal, with the leader in Internet voice communications, we will create an extraordinary powerful environment for business on the Net."

However, some analysts were confused by the hefty $2.6 billion acquisition and cited the move as being defensive and trying to acquire as much online traffic as possible. Still, eBay feels Skype will increase trade velocity in the marketplace, which is critical for categories that require more involved communications.

The use of product categories such as eBay Express and eBay Motors provides further depth in eBay's product offerings and enables the company to target a broader market.

- **eBay Express**—Introduced in April 2006, eBay Express behaves like a standard Internet shopping site but gives sellers access to over 200 million buyers worldwide. Sellers can design both product categories within minutes and buyers can purchase from multiple sellers by using a single shopping cart.
- **eBay Motors**—This specialty site is considered the largest marketplace for automobile buyers and sellers. Buyers can purchase anything from automobile parts to new or antique vehicles.

Sense of Community The underlying key to all eBay sites and trading platforms is creating trust between sellers and buyers. The company creates "community values," which is why eBay users are willing to send money to strangers across the country. The Feedback Forum was created in February 1996 and encourages users to post comments about trading partners. Originally, Omidyar handled disputes between buyers and sellers via e-mail by putting the disputing parties in touch with each other to resolve the issue themselves. He soon realized that an open forum where users can post opinions and feedback about one another would create the trust and sense of community the site required. Buyers and sellers are encouraged to post comments (positive, negative, or neutral) about each other at the completion of each transaction. The individual feedback is recorded and amended to a user profile, which ultimately establishes a rating and reputation for each buyer and seller. eBay users can view this information prior to engaging in a transaction. The company believes the feedback forum was critical for creating initial user acceptance for purchasing and selling over the Internet and contributed more than anything else to eBay's success.

Aggressive Expansion To compete effectively and create a global trading platform, the company continued to develop in U.S. and international markets that utilized the Internet. With intense competition in the online auction industry, eBay looked to increase market share and revenue through acquisitions and partnerships in related and unrelated businesses that include but are not limited to:

- In June 2000 eBay acquired Half.com for $318 million.
- In August 2001, eBay acquired MercadoLibre, Lokau, and iBazar, Latin American auction sites.
- On August 13, 2004, eBay took a 25 percent stake in Craigslist, an online central network of urban communities.
- In September 2005, eBay invested $2 million in the Meetup social networking site.
- In August 2006, eBay announced international cooperation with Google.
- In January 2007, eBay acquired online ticket marketplace Stubhub for $310 million.

During this timeframe, eBay also made a number of acquisitions and investments into international markets. In mid-2006, eBay also announced an agreement to share services, such as advertising and online payments, with Yahoo in an attempt to minimize the intense competition of rival search engine giant Google.[5]

Company Business Model

eBay's business model is based on a person-to-person marketplace on the Internet where sellers conveniently list items for sale and interested buyers bid on these items. The objective is to create a forum that allows buyers and sellers to come together in an efficient and effective manner. The business model overcomes the inefficiencies of traditional fragmented marketplaces, which tend to offer a limited variety of goods. According to Meg Whitman, the company started with commerce and what grew out of that was a community, essentially creating a community–commerce model.[6] The company's success primarily relies on establishing a trustworthy environment that attracts a large number of buyers and sellers. As eBay's reputation grew, so did the number of buyers and sellers, keeping the company in line with Omidyar's original vision. However, as new competitors entered the online auction business and the popularity of the Internet increased, eBay tweaked its business model to accommodate the changes in the fast-paced environment.

The company is aggressively expanding globally and looking to offer new products and services to customers. It is also looking closely at the kind of merchants who sell on eBay. In the beginning, eBay focused on a consumer-to-consumer business model but since some of the individuals became small dealers, the model changed to a mix of consumer-to-consumer and business-to-consumer. The sellers look to maintain their business on eBay since it's their most profitable distribution channel. eBay looks for new ways to generate revenue as a result of more small dealers and businesses selling their products through the company's Web site.

eBay generates revenue through three main channels: marketplaces, payments, and most recently, communications. Marketplaces, which generates revenue by charging sellers a fee for every item they sell, generates over 70 percent of the company's revenue. As of December 2006, marketplace revenue was approximately $4.3 billion of the company's $5.9 billon total revenue. Another 24 percent of the company's revenue comes from fees charged through electronic payments made through the company Web site, primarily PayPal. In December 2006, the company's revenue generated through payments was $1.4 billion, with the international share at 40 percent. Payment revenue also experienced strong growth between 2004 and 2006 by more than doubling during that timeframe. The newest source of revenue for eBay is communications (Skype), which is comprised of the smallest percentage of the company's revenue at 3 percent or $194 million. Although free, eBay's communication software, generates revenue through its premium offerings such as making and receiving calls to and from landline and mobile phones, as well as voicemail, ring tones, and call forwarding. Despite its small percentage of eBay's total revenue, the product is new and has experienced the strongest growth between 2005 and 2006, with 85 percent of the revenue generated in international markets in December 2006. Exhibit 6 shows the company's recent revenue performance by type.

In addition to the primary revenue sources, there are specific elements of eBay's business model that made the company a success. eBay's dominance of the online auction market and the large number of buyers, sellers, and listed items are primary reasons for eBay's tremendous growth. The trust and safety programs, such as the Feedback Forum, continue to attract and retain new and current eBay users. The cost-effective and convenient trading, coupled with the strong sense of community, adds further value to the company's business model. However, as the company continues to grow and new trends evolve, eBay must continue to adjust its model to remain competitive. Exhibit 7 presents the company's recent income statement.

International Expansion

As competition intensified in the online auction industry, eBay expanded its international presence in an effort to create an online global marketplace. Currently, eBay has localized sites in the following countries:

- **Asia Pacific**—Australia, China, Hong Kong, India, Malaysia, New Zealand, Philippines, Singapore, South Korea, and Taiwan
- **Europe**—Austria, Belgium, France, Germany, Ireland, Italy, Netherlands, Poland, Spain, Sweden, Switzerland, and the United Kingdom
- **North America**—Canada and the United States

Exhibit 6   Net Revenues by Type ($ thousands)

	2004	2005	2006
Marketplaces	$2,496,187	$3,402,301	$4,203,340
Payments (Paypal)	680,813	1,001,915	1,401,824
Communications (Skype)	—	24,809	192,756
Total Net Transaction Revenues	3,177,000	4,429,025	5,797,920
Advertising and other nontransaction revenues	94,309	123,376	171,821
Total Net Revenues	**$3,271,309**	**$4,552,401**	**$5,969,741**
International Net Revenues	$1,381,373	$2,081,128	$2,860,755
% of revenue that is international	42.2%	45.7%	47.9%

Source: eBay.

Exhibit 7   Income Statement ($ thousands)

	2004	2005	2006
Net Revenues	$3,271,309	$4,552,401	$5,969,741
Cost of Net Revenues	614,415	818,104	1,256,792
Gross Profit	2,656,894	3,734,297	4,712,949
Operating Expenses	1,597,652	2,292,590	3,289,993
Income from Operations	1,059,242	1,441,707	1,422,956
Interest and Other Income, Net	77,867	111,148	130,021
Interest Expense	(8,879)	(3,478)	(5,916)
Income Before Taxes and Minority Interest	1,128,230	1,549,377	1,547,061
Provision for Income Taxes	(343,885)	(467,285)	(421,418)
Minority Interest	(6,122)	(49)	(4)
Net Income	**$ 778,223**	**$1,082,043**	**$1,125,639**
Net Income Per Basic Share	$ 0.59	$ 0.79	$ 0.80
Net Income Per Diluted Share	$ 0.57	$ 0.78	$ 0.79
Weighted Average Shares:			
Basic	$1,319,458	$1,361,708	$1,399,251
Diluted	$1,367,720	$1,393,875	$1,425,472
Operating Margin	32%	32%	24%

Source: eBay.

In many of the international Web sites, eBay provides local language and currency options to gain popularity and ensure the sense of community feeling. In most cases, eBay expanded its business by either acquiring or forming a partnership with a local company. This strategy helped eBay better understand local cultures and ensure the company was meeting specific local needs. This approach proved successful with the company's equity investment in MercadoLibre.com, which targeted Argentina, Brazil, Chile, Colombia, Costa Rica, Dominican Republic, Ecuador, Mexico, Panama, Peru, Uruguay, and Venezuela. At the end of 2006, MercadoLibre.com reported 18 million registered users that performed 15.8 million transactions worth $1.1 billion.[7] Other notable international growth acquisitions include:

Asia Pacific:

- July 2003—Acquired China–based Eachnet for approximately $150 million. eBay's failure to manage the company resulted in its most recent partnership with communications company Tom Online.
- June 2004—Acquired all outstanding shares of India's Baazee.com, which later became eBay India.

- September 2004—Acquired Korean rival Internet Auction Co. by purchasing nearly 3 million shares. Acquisition has not proven successful due to intense competition from top Korean auction site GMarket.

Europe:

- 1999—Acquired Alando auction house for $43 million, which later changed to eBay Germany. Alando was previously considered Germany's leading online trading company. Germany is now eBay's second largest market accounting for 21% of the company's total listings.
- November 2004—Acquired Dutch competitor Marktplaats.nl, which had 80 percent of the Netherlands market share.
- April 2006—Acquired Sweden's leading online auction Tradera.com for $48 million.

For the most part, eBay was successful in expanding in Europe and Latin America, where it was able to quickly adapt to local needs through its partners. The company was also successful in countries it expanded to from the ground up, such as Canada and the United Kingdom. Today, the

United Kingdom accounts for 15.5 percent of eBay's total listings. By engaging the local community in these countries, eBay customized its sites to meet specific local needs while providing access to the online global community.

eBay is considered the leader in each of its markets with the exception of Japan and China, in which they have struggled repeatedly to gain market share. In 2002, eBay was forced to pull out of Japan due to rising costs and intense competition by rival Yahoo Japan. eBay also faced fierce competition in Korea, where GMarket, another investment of Yahoo, dominated the market.

Despite its lack of success in local Asian markets, eBay continues its attempts to expand into the region, recognizing the tremendous growth potential that's available. In June 2006, eBay formed a joint venture with PChome Online in Taiwan. PChome Online is an Internet service provider in Taiwan with more than 10 million members.[8] The company offers services such as Internet portal, e-commerce platform, and telecommunications. The move is expected to provide eBay with the local e-commerce expertise to launch a new trading Web site that caters to the needs of Taiwan's Internet users.

Most recently, eBay's CEO Meg Whitman emphasized her commitment to the Chinese e-commerce market by announcing a new joint venture with Beijing-based Internet Company Tom Online Inc. Tom Online, which primarily sells cell phone add-on services, such as ringtones and avatars, put in $20 million for 51 percent share and management control of eBay's online China site Eachnet.[9] In 2002, eBay purchased a 30 percent stake in Eachnet and within a year bought out local investors. Central management control of Eachnet was maintained in eBay's San Jose, California location. Many believe the move is a result of eBay's failure to adapt to local needs and successfully compete with China's online auction market leader Taobao, which controls approximately 70 percent of the market. Jack Ma, the chief executive of Alibaba.com, Taobao's parent company, believes eBay's failure in Japan was due to an ability to build a community effect in the country, which according to Ma begins with customer satisfaction. Ma also feels that since eBay must adhere to a global platform, meeting specific local needs is difficult since changes at a global level must be approved in the United States, which further limits the company's ability to produce a Web site tailored to the Chinese market.[10] In an Interview with *Internetnews* in 2005, Ma states eBay's lack of success in China is predominantly due to the company's quickness to replace local management with foreigners and the mind-set to control the market through spending rather than building it from the ground up.[11]

Competitors

As eBay's product offerings and pricing formats evolved so did its range of competitors. Originally, the company faced competition from alternative auctions or other venues for collectors, such as flea markets and garage sales. However, as the company grew and introduced fixed pricing, the range

of competitors included large companies like Wal-Mart and Kmart that also had retail Web sites. eBay's product platforms, like eBay Motors, put the company in direct competition with auto dealers and other online auto sites such as Autobytes. Still, eBay faces the harshest competition from major online companies that include Yahoo and Amazon, which also have online auctions that rival eBay's.

Yahoo!   eBay's larger online competitor is Yahoo!, which also has a strong global presence, particularly in Asian markets. Yahoo! originally started as a search engine and quickly evolved to add additional products and services such as Yahoo! Mail, Yahoo! Maps, and Yahoo! Messenger. The company also offers e-commerce services through Yahoo! Shopping, Yahoo! Autos, Yahoo! Auctions, and Yahoo! Travel. Like eBay, Yahoo's e-commerce sites allow users to obtain relevant information and make transactions and purchases online. However, Yahoo's business model primarily focuses on generating revenue through search advertising. In the United States and in response to potential threats from Web giant Google, Yahoo! and eBay formed an alliance in which Yahoo! utilizes eBay's payment system, PayPal, and eBay gains additional advertising through Yahoo! searches. Still Yahoo! poses a major competitive threat in foreign markets, particularly Asia Pacific, through its partnerships with GMarket and Taobao.

GMarket   Yahoo's stake in Korean auction site GMarket has proven successful, with more than 17.2 million unique visitors. Founded in 2000, GMarket is a Korean online auction and shopping mall Web site that generates its revenue by charging a fee based on selling price.[12] Like Taobao, GMarket offers fixed prices and provides an option to negotiate prices with sellers on an exclusive basis. This allows buyers to conduct deals instantly instead of waiting until bids are completed. GMarket offers cheaper listings and fixed prices with an option to negotiate with a seller exclusively. These options along with constant new features allow GMarket to dominate the Korea online auction industry.[13] GMarket frequently introduces new marketing initiatives to provide sellers with various options to attract new customers. GMarket grew financially powerful in 2006 when the company launched its IPO and Yahoo purchased a 9 percent stake in the company.

Taobao   In 2005, Yahoo! entered a strategic partnership with Alibaba.com, Taobao's parent company, which created an instant threat in the Chinese market. The move created one of the largest Internet companies in China, with a leading position in business-to-business e-commerce, consumer e-commerce, and online payments. Today, Taobao is eBay's largest competitor in China, controlling over 70 percent of the Chinese online auction market. Like GMarket, Taobao offers buyers and sellers quick and convenient ways to conduct business. Its instant messaging and fixed price arrangements allow transactions to be conducted quickly. Most recently, the company partnered with Intel to offer customers a wireless platform. This will further improve communication and the convenience when conducting transactions.

Amazon Despite not having a huge presence in the online auction industry, Amazon is still considered a fierce online global competitor. Amazon started as Earth's biggest bookstore and rapidly evolved to selling everything, including toys, electronics, home furnishings, apparel, health and beauty aids, groceries and so on. Still, books, CDs and DVDs account for more than 65 percent of the firm's sales. Although Amazon has a large international presence, the company's linkage to brick-and-mortar shops in the United States makes it a greater threat locally than in foreign markets. Amazon's international local sites include Canada, United Kingdom, Germany, Japan, France, and China. Despite its large online presence Amazon has scaled back its online auction business by cutting staff and shutting down Livebid as part of an overall corporate restructuring.

The Future of eBay

eBay has a number of opportunities in which they've already taken action. In 2005, eBay made a number of strategic acquisitions that include Rent.com, international classified Web sites, Shopping.com, and Skype. These acquisitions add and complement eBay's product offering and further diversify the company's targeted market. With increased competition from Google and other major online companies, eBay must continue to diversify and provide depth in its product offering to remain competitive. Creating options and targeting distinct market niches will enable eBay to distinguish it from other competitors. This is particularly important because as e-commerce and Internet usage rates continue to grow, so will the market opportunity for eBay. Because of its market leading brand, eBay is in a unique position to capture a significant share of this market at an early stage.

eBay can also expand its existing products and services, such as PayPal and Skype. Both products are relatively new and have the potential to grow and attract new customers, especially in international markets. Expanding PayPal into international markets enables eBay to provide a simple way to conduct transactions across market borders. Considering the growth potential in developing markets like in Africa, Asia, and the Middle East, expanding PayPal will attract many new customers, thus increasing eBay's revenue base. In line with e-commerce growth, as more customers feel comfortable with conducting transactions online, PayPal has the potential to be the preferred form of payment over the Internet.

However, for eBay to capitalize on these opportunities, the company must overcome the challenges of expanding into large foreign markets such as China and Japan. With almost 70 percent of the North American population using the Internet and only 10.7 percent using it in Asia Pacific, eBay has a tremendous opportunity to expand and gain new customers. Considering the Asia Pacific region has more than 50 percent of the world's population and is experiencing some of the largest online usage growth percentages in the world, tapping into this market is critical for eBay to expand.

Endnotes

1. Balfour, F. 2006. Tom Online: eBay's last China card. *BusinessWeek Online.* December 19.
2. The history of auction method of marketing. National Auctions Association. 2005. www.onlyatauction.com.
3. Pierre Omidyar—The man behind eBay. Internet Based Moms, April 2007.
4. Biography—Pierre Omidyar. Academy of Achievement, www.achievement.org. November 9, 2005.
5. Hoover's Company Records. In-depth records. eBay, Inc, February 13, 2007.
6. Q&A with eBay's Meg Whitman. *BusinessWeek Online,* May 31, 1999.
7. Argentina: MercadoLibre has 18mil registered users. *IT Digest,* January 25, 2007, www.infobae.com.
8. eBay and PChome Online to Form Joint Venture in Taiwan. eBay Press Release, www.ebay.com.
9. Market spotlight: Asia Internet strategy. LexisNexis. December 21, 2006.
10. Alibaba CEO says Taobao will dominate China online auctions. May 2005, Forbes.com.
11. Kuchinskas, S. 2004. October 22. *Internetnews,* www.internetnews.com.
12. Ihlwan, M. 2006. Gmarket eclipses eBay in Asia. *BusinessWeek Online,* June 28, 2006.
13. Out-eBaying eBay in Korea. *BusinessWeek Online*, July 17, 2006.

Case 30 Apple Inc.: Taking a Bite Out of the Competition*

Apple Computer, Inc., incorporated in 1977, sold the first computer with a graphical user interface (communicating with the user via icons on the screen),[1] and had continued to innovate both in hardware and software, particularly when led by cofounder and charismatic visionary Steve Jobs. By 2006, after 30 years of carving a niche for itself as the premier provider of technology solutions for graphic artists, Web designers and educators, Apple appeared to be reinventing itself as a digital entertainment company, moving beyond the personal computer industry. Even though, by many reports, Apple had "the highest brand and repurchase loyalty of any computer manufacturer,"[2] it had consistently ceded market share to lower-priced Windows-based machines. In 1980, according to Gartner, a research firm that tracks computer market share, Apple had 15.8 percent of the personal computer market. In 1996 Apple's worldwide share was figured at between 4.6 and 5.1 percent, and by 2005 it was hovering around 2 percent. Even though Apple had been profitable since 2002, with profit margins in 2005 exceeding industry averages and overall sales more than doubling since 2001, it was still a distant fifth in the U.S. computer market. In its computer business, although recognized for being innovative, Apple was still considered to have niche status (see Exhibits 1 and 2).[3]

As an example of innovation, the iPod portable digital music player introduced by Apple in 2001 became one of its most famous products and provided a needed financial boost. The iPod in its subsequent many variations was linked to the success of Apple's iTunes Music Store, established in 2003 for purchasing music downloadable to the iPod via both the Macintosh and Windows-based personal computers. In 2005 Steve Jobs, Apple's CEO, announced that the company's Macintosh personal computer line would transition to an Intel microprocessor, subsequently paving the way in April 2006 for the announcement of BootCamp software, making it possible to run Windows applications on the Mac. Apple's personal computers, known for their stylish design, ease-of-use, seamless integration of peripherals, and high performance, had never been able to capture significant market share while competing with Windows-based machines, partly because of the proliferation of Windows software in the business computer consumer environment. Now that one of the major switching barriers was removed, could Apple gain market share and sustain its profitability in the very competitive computer industry space, while simultaneously extending its reach into multimedia software and personal digital entertainment devices? The announcement in 2007 of the iPhone, a product incorporating a wireless phone, a music and video player, and a mobile Internet browsing device, meant Apple was also competing in the cell phone/Smartphone industry. Could Apple continue taking bites out of the competition on all fronts?

Company Background

Founder Steve Jobs Apple Computer was founded in Mountain View, California, on April 1, 1976, by Steve Jobs and Steve Wozniak. Jobs was the visionary and marketer, Wozniak was the technical genius, and A. C. "Mike" Markkula, Jr., who joined the team several months later, was the businessman. Jobs set the mission of empowering individuals, one person–one computer, and doing so with elegance of design and fierce attention to detail. In 1977 the first version of the Apple II became the first computer ordinary people could use right out of the box, and its instant success in the home market caused a computing revolution, essentially creating the personal computer industry. By 1980 Apple was the industry leader and went public in December of that year.

IBM entered the personal computer business in 1981 and initiated a major challenge to Apple's business model. IBM made the decision to use the Microsoft DOS operating system with an open-architecture hardware standard that others could copy based on an Intel microprocessor. The updated Apple III introduced in 1983 to compete with IBM and others had design flaws and subsequent quality problems that discouraged customers, opening the door further to IBM competition.

Also in 1983, although not achieving commercial success, innovation was evident in the Lisa, the first Apple computer to use a graphical user interface (GUI) and a point-and-click mouse. Lisa allowed several applications to run at the same time, in the first Windows-type environment but was incompatible with other computers, including the Apple II & III, and was priced at $10,000, making it difficult to sell.

In 1983, Wozniak left the firm and Jobs hired John Sculley away from PepsiCo to take the role of CEO at Apple, citing the need for someone to spearhead marketing and operations while Jobs worked on technology. The result of Jobs' creative focus on developing a cheaper yet even more advanced version of Lisa was the Macintosh. Introduced in 1984, with the now famous Super Bowl television ad based on George Orwell's novel, the Macintosh was a breakthrough in terms of elegant design and ease of use. Its ability to handle large graphic files quickly made it a favorite with graphic designers, but it had slow performance and limited compatible software was available, so the product was unable to significantly help Apple's failing bottom line. In addition, Jobs had given Bill Gates at Microsoft some Macintosh prototypes to use to develop software, and in 1985 Microsoft subsequently came out with the Windows operating system, a version of GUI for use on IBM PCs.

* This case was prepared by Professor Alan B. Eisner of Pace University and Professor Pauline Assenza of Manhattanville College. This case was solely based upon library research and was developed for class discussion rather than to illustrate either effective or ineffective handling of an administrative situation. Copyright © 2007 Alan B. Eisner and Pauline Assenza.

Exhibit 1   Apple Inc. 2006 Competitive Landscape—Top Competitors

Key Numbers FY2006	Apple	Dell	Hewlett-Packard	Microsoft	
Annual Sales (in $ million)	19,315.0	55,908.0	91,658.0	44,282.0	
Employees	18,000	66,100	156,000	71,000	
Market Cap (in $ million)	102,379.7	62,244.0	123,320.5	292,807.5	

Profitability	Apple	Dell	Hewlett-Packard	Microsoft	Industry[1]
Gross Profit Margin	31.50%	17.50%	24.60%	80.70%	34.80%
Pre-Tax Profit Margin	18.40%	7.60%	8.10%	40.50%	4.80%
Net Profit Margin	12.90%	6.00%	6.90%	28.00%	3.90%
Return on Equity	26.6%	75.6%	17.7%	36.0%	12.5%
Return on Assets	17.1%	14.9%	8.4%	21.2%	4.4%
Return on Invested Capital	24.6%	45.8%	13.6%	30.5%	6.9%

Valuation	Apple	Dell	Hewlett-Packard	Microsoft	Industry[1]
Price/Sales Ratio	4.74	1.09	1.30	5.91	1.45
Price/Earnings Ratio	36.43	18.96	19.33	21.85	20.35
Price/Book Ratio	8.35	18.38	3.22	8.37	2.75
Price/Cash Flow Ratio	22.22	13.28	12.93	17.55	18.18

Operations	Apple	Dell	Hewlett-Packard	Microsoft	Industry[1]
Days of Sales Outstanding	39.01	37.20	50.10	76.77	68.89
Inventory Turnover	71.8	83.7	9.4	6.7	4.7
Days Cost of Goods Sold in Inventory	5	4	39	55	78
Asset Turnover	1.3	2.5	1.2	0.8	1.1
Net Receivables Turnover Flow	11.9	11.3	7.8	5.1	5.5
Effective Tax Rate	29.7%	21.7%	14.5%	31.0%	26.5%

Financial	Apple	Dell	Hewlett-Packard	Microsoft	Industry[1]
Current Ratio	2.92	1.07	1.21	1.98	2.03
Quick Ratio	2.9	1.0	1.0	1.9	1.4
Leverage Ratio	—	—	0.07	—	0.21
Total Debt/Equity	—	—	0.15	—	0.44
Interest Coverage	—	156.00	31.63	—	12.47

Growth	Apple	Dell	Hewlett-Packard	Microsoft	Industry[1]
12-Month Revenue Growth	24.7%	11.1%	7.0%	16.2%	13.2%
12-Month Net Income Growth	61.6%	4.7%	143.0%	2.9%	29.1%
12-Month EPS Growth	55.5%	10.8%	152.1%	10.2%	25.4%
36-Month Revenue Growth	200.9%	53.9%	25.9%	39.2%	47.1%
36-Month Net Income Growth	1,520.9%	50.2%	136.7%	87.3%	77.9%
36-Month EPS Growth	1,283.0%	65.5%	163.3%	211.1%	69.5%

[1]Public companies trading on the New York Stock Exchange, the American Stock Exchange, and the NASDAQ National Market.

Sources: Hoover's North America, data provided from EDGAR Online.

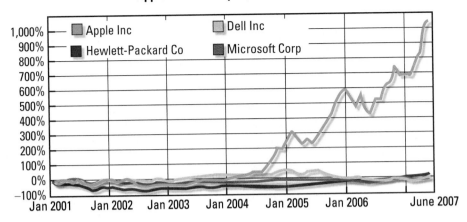

Apple Price History—(1/1/2001–6/8/2007)

Exhibit 2 Stock Price History, Percent Change over Time Since 2001: Apple vs. Microsoft, Dell, and Hewlett-Packard

Source: MSN Money, http://moneycentral.msn.com

Steve Jobs' famous volatility lead to his resignation from Apple in 1985. Jobs then founded NeXT Computer, however the NeXT Cube computer proved too costly for this business to become commercially profitable, but its technological contributions could not be ignored. In 1997, then Apple CEO Gilbert Amelio bought out NeXT, hoping to use its Rhapsody, a version of the NeXTStep operating system, to jump start the Mac OS development, and Jobs was brought back as a part-time advisor.

Under CEO's Sculley, Spindler, and Amelio John Sculley moved to try to take advantage of Apple's unique capabilities. In 1986 he introduced the Macintosh Plus, with much expanded memory, and the LaserWriter printers. Encouraged by the hardware, software developers such as Aldus (later Adobe) began writing powerful desktop publishing programs for the Macintosh, contributing to the Mac's growing reputation with graphic artists, and turning Apple into a worldwide brand.

By 1990, Apple still did all design in-house and manufactured most of its own products except the microprocessor and some applications software. The operating system and most peripherals, including printers, were proprietary to the Macintosh. Because of this, Macintosh computers were easy to use, with seamless integration (the original plug-and-play) and reliable performance. This premium performance meant Apple could charge a premium price. However, with the price of IBM compatibles dropping, and Apple's costs, especially R&D, way above industry averages (in 1990 Apple spent 9 percent of sales on R&D compared to 5 percent at Compaq and 1 percent for many manufacturers of IBM clones),[4] this was not a sustainable scenario.

In 1991, Apple introduced one of the first truly portable (small and reliable) notebook computers, the Powerbook 100, to rave reviews. In a further attempt to innovate around the Microsoft and IBM-compatible threat, Sculley formed an alliance with IBM and Motorola, intending to use this joint venture to develop a new operating system based around IBM's new PowerPC chip. In 1992 Sculley also secretly authorized Apple designers to create a way for the Mac OS to run on an Intel-based computer.

All Sculley's innovative efforts were not enough to substantially improve Apple's bottom line, and he was replaced as CEO in 1993 by company President Michael Spindler. Spindler continued a focus on innovation, producing the PowerMac based on the PowerPC microprocessor in 1994. Even though this combination produced a significant price-performance edge over both previous Macs and Intel-based machines, the IBM clones continued to undercut Apple's prices. Spindler's response was to allow other companies to manufacture Mac clones, a strategy that ultimately led to clones stealing 20 percent of Macintosh unit sales and was cancelled by Steve Jobs in 1998. Continued operational and quality problems as well as financial losses lead to Spindler's removal in early 1996.

Gilbert Amelio, an Apple director and former semiconductor turnaround expert, was asked to reverse the company's financial direction. Amelio intended to reposition Apple as a premium brand, but his extensive reorganizations and cost-cutting strategies couldn't prevent Apple's stock price slipping to a new low. However, Amelio's decision to stop work on a brand new operating system and try to jump start this development by using NeXTStep brought Steve Jobs back to Apple in 1997.

Steve Jobs' Return One of Jobs' first strategies upon his return was to strengthen the relationships with third-party software developers, including Microsoft. In 1997, Jobs announced an alliance with Microsoft that would allow for the creation of a Mac version of the popular Microsoft Office software. He also made a concerted effort to woo other developers, such as Adobe, to continue to produce Mac-compatible programs. Then in 1998, one year after Jobs' return to Apple, under his leadership, the Apple design team unveiled the iMac. This personal computer, with its translucent plastic case available in many cool colors, was considered a hallmark of industrial design[5] and became phenomenally successful, selling 800,000 units in 1998.

From 1999 to 2001, Apple began acquiring software companies and creating entertainment software products such as Final Cut Pro and DVD Studio Pro video editing programs to complement their reputation as a professional digital imaging destination. They also developed PowerSchool, a Web-based software information management system for K–12 school administrators. Applications such as these continued to cement relationships with these key customer bases. In 1999, Apple began selling built-to-order computer systems online and also introduced the iBook laptop. Shortly thereafter, Jobs unveiled Apple's new Internet software application, iTools. The G4 Cube personal computer, introduced in 2000, did not get the anticipated acceptance in the market. Priced at a premium, it failed to appeal to a new audience, one of the few missteps of this period.

In 2001, Apple introduced Mac OS X, the operating system based on NeXTStep and incorporating Unix stability, reliability, and security. Although not fully backward compatible with previous Mac programs, Apple provided dual operating system environments on each new computer to ease the transition. Also in 2001, Apple announced the opening of retail stores in major U.S. markets. These stores were designed to allow knowledgeable Apple salespeople to influence customers' switch to the Apple environment, and to overcome competition with other brands sold via third-party resellers.

Although 2001 was a year with a net loss for Apple, their new strategy was to position the Mac as a digital hub. One of those applications was iTunes, a proprietary digital media player application. Launched in January of 2001, it was intended to play and organize digital music and video files on the Mac personal computer. It was Apple's hope that the new digital lifestyle would revitalize Apple's sales and guarantee the long-term security of the company, however existing digital music players were of poor quality, so Jobs challenged his engineers to develop one.

In late October of 2001, Apple released its first major noncomputer product, the iPod. This device was an MP3 music player that packed up to 1,000 CD-quality songs into an ultra-portable, 6.5 ounce design: "With iPod, Apple has invented a whole new category of digital music player that lets you put your entire music collection in your pocket and listen to it wherever you go," said Steve Jobs. "With iPod, listening to music will never be the same again."[6]

This prediction became even truer in 2002 when Apple introduced an iPod that would download from Windows, creating its first product that didn't require a Macintosh computer and opened up the Apple "magic" to everyone. In 2003 all iPod products sold with a Windows version of iTunes, making it even easier to use the device regardless of computer platform.

In January 2002, Apple reinvented the consumer desktop again when it released its flat panel iMac. It also announced iPhoto, a new software package designed to improve the digital camera users' experience. Three weeks after it was introduced, Apple received a record-breaking 150,000 pre-orders for the new iMac. Designed to be the center of the emerging digital lifestyle and run Apple's award-winning suite of software for digital photography, music, and video, all new iMac models included iMovie 2, video editing software, and iTunes 2—the digital music software that let users put their entire music collection on their Mac, burn custom CDs, and seamlessly sync to Apple's iPod portable digital music player.

"Apple is the Mount Washington of the computer industry, generating a weather system all its own. No matter how sunny the outlook for the rest of the computer industry, it will rain on Mount Apple if the company fails to produce innovative products," said Charles Haddad in *BusinessWeek,* "The reason? Apple has not one but four hot products: the iBook, the new iMac, the Titanium Power Book, and iPod MP3 player."[7] At that time in 2002 Apple had 4 percent market share in computers.

In 2003 the new Power Book sold well, and the sales of flat panel iMacs remained steady. IBM was developing a new set of chips to replace the aging Motorola processors used in Apple's G4 line, and in June the PowerMac G5 was released based on IBM's Power4 chip. Meanwhile, the iPod was beginning to generate considerable sales interest. In April of 2003, Apple opened the online iTunes Music Store, which sold individual songs through the iTunes application, for 99 cents each. When announced, the iTunes Music Store already had the backing of five major record labels and a catalog of 200,000 songs. Later that year, iTunes Music Store was selling roughly 500,000 songs a day. The iPod was the only portable digital player that could play music purchased from iTunes, and this intended exclusivity helped both products become dominant.

In 2003 Apple sold 939,000 of the iPod devices, bringing in $345 million in revenues. In addition, improved orders from schools, 203 percent increase in sales of the slick PowerBook portables and higher demand for the apple's powerful new G5 Power Mac, created overall gross margins of 27.5 percent for a profit of $69 million (see Exhibit 3).

Once again timing, luck and innovation put Apple ahead of the curve. In January 2004, Apple released the iPod mini. It was selling so fast that Apple had trouble keeping up with demand. One year since iTunes was opened, the store had sold 70 million digital songs, exceeding the company's "wildest expectations." According to Jobs, Apple held a 40 percent market share in digital music players and a 70 percent share of the paid music-download market (the United States, Japan, and Western Europe).[8] By the end of the year, iPod had become a must-have Christmas present, and Apple released a black and stylish iPod U2 special edition and iPod Photo. Worldwide sales reached the 10 million mark, and iTunes sold over 200 million tracks.

In January 2005, Apple released the new MacMini computer module and iShuffle, a flash memory-based digital music player. Also, Apple introduced Mac OSX version Tiger, billed as the world's most advanced operating system.

Exhibit 3   Apple Inc. Sales by Operating Segment and Product

	FY 2006	Change	FY 2005	Change	FY 2004	Change	FY 2003	FY 2002	FY 2001
	(net sales in $ millions, units in thousands)								
Net Sales by Operating Segment:									
Americas net sales	$ 9,307	41%	$ 6,590	64%	$4,019	26%	$3,181		
Europe net sales	$ 4,094	33%	$ 3,073	371%	$1,799	37%	$1,309		
Japan net sales	$ 1,208	31%	$920	36%	$ 677	−3%	$ 698		
Retail net sales	$ 3,359	45%	$ 2,350	98%	$1,185	91%	$ 621		
Other Segments net sales (a)	$ 1,347	35%	$998	67%	$ 599	51%	$ 398		
Total net sales	**$19,315**	**39%**	**$13,931**	**68%**	**$8,279**	**33%**	**$6,207**	**$5,742**	**$5,363**
Unit Sales by Operating Segment:									
Americas Macintosh unit sales	$ 2,432	11%	$ 2,184	30%	$1,682	4%	$1,620		
Europe Macintosh net sales	$ 1,346	18%	$ 1,138	47%	$ 773	13%	$ 684		
Japan Macintosh net sales	$ 304	−3%	$ 313	8%	$ 291	−14%	$ 339		
Retail Macintosh unit sales	$ 886	45%	$ 609	94%	$ 341	68%	$ 187		
Other Segments Macintosh unit sales (a)	$ 335	16%	$ 290	26%	$ 230	26%	$ 182		
Total Macintosh unit sales	**$ 5,303**	**17%**	**$ 4,534**	**38%**	**$3,290**	**9%**	**$3,012**		
Net Sales by Product:									
Desktops (b)	$ 3,319	−3%	$ 3,436	45%	$2,373	−4%	$2,475		
Portables (c)	$ 4,056	43%	$ 2,839	11%	$2,550	26%	$2,016		
Total Macintosh net sales	**$ 7,375**	**18%**	**$ 6,275**	**27%**	**$4,923**	**10%**	**$4,491**		
iPod	$ 7,676	69%	$ 4,540	248%	$1,306	279%	$ 345		
Other music-related products and services (d)	$ 1,885	110%	$ 899	223%	$ 278	672%	$ 36		
Peripherals and other hardware (e)	$ 1,100	−2%	$ 1,126	18%	$ 951	38%	$ 691		
Software, service, and other sales (f)	$ 1,279	17%	$ 1,091	33%	$ 821	27%	$ 644		
Total net sales	**$19,315**	**39%**	**$13,931**	**68%**	**$8,279**	**33%**	**$6,207**		
Unit Sales by Product:									
Desktops (b)	2434	−3%	2520	55%	1625	−8%	1761		
Portables (c)	2869	42%	2014	21%	1665	33%	1251		
Total Macintosh unit sales	5303	17%	4534	38%	3290	9%	3012		
Net sales per Macintosh unit sold (g)	$ 1,391	1%	$ 1,384	−7%	$4,196	0%	$1,491		
iPod unit sales	39409	75%	22497	409%	4416	370%	939		
Net sales per iPod unit sold (h)	$ 195	−3%	$ 202	−32%	$ 296	−19%	$ 367		
Cost of Sales	**$13,717**		**$ 9,888**		**$6,020**		**$4,499**	**$4,139**	**$4,128**

(continued)

Exhibit 3   Apple Inc. Sales by Operating Segment and Product *(continued)*

	FY 2006	Change	FY 2005	Change	FY 2004	Change	FY 2003	FY 2002	FY 2001
					(net sales in $ millions, units in thousands)				
Gross Margin (i)	$5,598		$4,042		$2,259		$1,708		
Gross Margin percentage	29.0%		29.0%		27.3%		27.5%		
Research and Development	$ 712		$ 534		$ 489		$ 471		
Percentage of net sales	4%		4%		6%		8%		
Selling, general and administrative expenses	$2,433		$1,859		$1,421		$1,212		
Percentage of net sales	13%		13%		17%		20%		
Restructuring Costs	—		—		$23		$ 26		
Total Operating Expenses	$3,145		$2,393		$1,910		$1,709	$1,586	$1,579
Net Income (Loss) (j)	$1,989		$1,335		$ 276		$ 69	$ 65	$ (25)

(a) Other segments include Asia Pacific and FileMaker

(b) Includes iMac, eMac, Mac mini, Power Mac and Xserve product lines

(c) Includes iBook and PowerBook product lines

(d) Consists of iTunes Music Store sales, iPod services, and Apple-branded and third-party iPod accessories

(e) Includes sales of Apple-branded and third-party displays, wireless connectivity and networking solutions, and other hardware accessories

(f) Includes sales of Apple-branded operating system, application software, third-party software, AppleCare and Internet services

(g) Derived by dividing total Macintosh net sales by total Macintosh unit sales

(h) Derived by dividing total iPod net sales by total iPod unit sales

(i) Comments: in general, gross margins and margins on individual products, including iPods, will remain under significant downward pressure due to a variety of factors, including continued industrywide global pricing pressures, increased competition, compressed product life cycles, potential increases in the cost and availability of raw material and outside manufacturing services, and potential changes to the Company's product mix, including higher unit sales of consumer products with lower average selling prices and lower sales margins

(j) Calculated as total net sales minus cost of sales minus total operating expenses. Includes the effect of interest and other income or expense, and provision or benefit for income taxes.ir.net/media_files/ird/10/107357/reports/10k_FY2005.pdf

From Apple Computer Inc. Annual Reports, 2005 and 2006

Apple announced a free recycle program for iPod. Beginning in June, customers could bring an iPod they no longer wanted to any of company's retail stores in the United States for free environmentally friendly disposal, and receive a 10 percent discount on the purchase of a new iPod that day. Also, the company settled a lawsuit, and agreed to give $50 vouchers and extended warranties to customers who had problems with the lifespan of their iPod batteries.

On June 6, 2005 Apple announced the switch to Intel chips in their personal computers. "Our goal is to provide our customers with the best personal computers in the world, and looking ahead Intel has the strongest processor roadmap by far," Jobs said. "It's been ten years since our transition to the Power PC, and we think Intel's technology will help us create the best personal computers for the next ten years."[9]

The move came with risk. "Since its inception, Apple has profited hugely from a customer base whose dedication often bordered on religious devotion," wrote Charles King, an analyst with Pund-IT Research. "Many members of that group tend to deeply distrust the concept of computing promoted by and its long-time partner Microsoft."[10] In addition, for existing Mac users, Apple software developers needed to create programs that ran on both PowerPC and Intel, since the transition would not be completed until 2007. During the uncertainty period, these existing Mac consumers needed to upgrade their programs to work with the new models.

Apple's Businesses

The Personal Computer Market   At the beginning of 2007, Dell was the number one in the U.S. market because of its significant competitive advantage in supply chain execution, followed by Hewlett-Packard, Gateway, IBM, and Apple. Dell was also on the top of the chart worldwide (see Exhibit 4).

Apple Computer had long been considered a niche player. In 2006 Apple's market shares were nearly 2.6 percent worldwide and nearly 6.1 percent in the United States. Whether this share was considered good or bad may have been a matter of perspective. "Apple's market share is bigger than BMW's or Mercedes' or Porsche's in the

Exhibit 4   PC Market Share 2006, Top Five Manufacturers

U.S. Personal Computer Manufacturers	Percent Share	Worldwide Personal Computer Manufacturers*	Percent Share
Dell	32.1	HP	16.3
HP	23.0	Dell	16.1
Gateway	6.4	Lenovo	7.5
Apple	6.1	Acer	5.9
Toshiba	5.1	Toshiba	4.3

*Apple worldwide share was 2.6 percent

Sources: Gartner, Inc. as reported by Marsal, K., Jade, K. "Apple's share of U.S. PC market jumps to 6.1 percent," *Apple Insider*, October 18, 2006.

automotive market. What's wrong with being BMW or Mercedes?" said Steve Jobs.[11]

Apple believed that their retail stores could service the customer better than third-party retailers. While still using multichannel distribution, including resellers, by 2006 Apple had opened on average 30 stores a year, and in May of 2006 opened their flagship store in Manhattan at 767 Fifth Avenue. Open 24 hours a day, 365 days a year, this underground location was an innovative design, with the entrance a glass cube, allowing light to filter down onto the entire 20,000-square-foot space. One analyst reported that the Fifth Avenue store was seeing 12,000 people a day during its first month of operation.[12] Citing a belief in the importance of face-to-face customer service, in 2006 Apple's stores averaged over $4,000 per square foot in sales; even more than luxury store Tiffany & Co.'s $2,666.[13] In the second quarter of 2007, Apple had an average of 172 stores open, with average store revenue of about $5 million, and 10,000 customers per store per week. This retail business generated $32 million in profit for the quarter. Apple was also expanding internationally, with Apple stores scheduled to open in late 2007 in Scotland and Australia, as well as expanding third-party retailing through a unique merchandising agreement with Best Buy.[14]

The PC market in the United States in 2007 appeared saturated. Although innovations in computing technology were always occurring, users needed reasons to replace their hardware. Could it be faster, more reliable, more portable or more productive? Could it be cheaper? In many cases, software, such as the new Microsoft operating system, Vista, required more powerful computing capability to run. Software might become the reason customers decided to upgrade or switch hardware.

This created an opportunity for Apple, and the popularity of the iPod provided an easy introduction to Apple's product line. Regarding a head-to-head competition against Dell, Steve Jobs was quick to point out that market share wasn't everything. If Dell's dominance was partly because of its efficient supply chain management, Apple had outperformed Dell in inventory metrics since 2001.[15]

Apple had also always refused to compete on price, relying on its reliability, design elegance, ease of use and integrated features to win customers. Some analysts believed Apple had the opportunity to steal PC market share as long as the system was compatible, and no longer exclusively proprietary, and offered upgrades at a reasonable cost.[16] Apple also offered a variety of computer accessories such as the iSight video conferencing camera, the AirPort wireless networking products, and Apple Cinema HD display as well as computer displays, wireless mice and keyboards, and the Apple USB modem. But the real opportunity for increased market share was the Intel-based iMac desktop and the MacBook/MacBook Pro portable, both using an Intel Core Duo processor introduced in 2005. The only part of the computer system not designed and manufactured by Apple was this processor and the memory.

With a Windows-based PC available at around $500 with rebates, an Intel-based iMac was retailing for over $1,200 in 2007, while the top-of-the-line MacBook Pro was over $2,000. However, Apple's Mac Mini, without a display, keyboard, or mouse, was offered as a second computer or entry-level machine for $600 (see Exhibit 5 and Figure 1).

With Apple's release of the Boot Camp software allowing these Macs to run both Apple's OS X and Windows XP, customers would have the elegance and reliability of Apple while being able to run their legacy Windows applications. Customers would have to purchase a new copy of Windows XP, and Apple would not support this Microsoft software, but benchmark tests demonstrated that the Apple machines running XP, especially the MacBook Pro, came very close to outperforming Dell, HP, and HP Compaq on all tests (see Exhibit 6). With a level playing field, it appeared that Apple's claims that 50 percent of people buying Macs in Apple retail stores in early 2006 were new to the Mac and might have been switching over from Windows machines were legitimate indications of Apple's potential market growth.[17]

By June 2006, Charles Wolf of Needham and Co. was projecting that Apple could "end up with a global PC market

Exhibit 5   **Mac to PC Comparisons**

Personal Computer Comparison as of 6/2006 (from *PCWorld* and *CNET*)		
	Apple iMac Desktop	**Dell Dimension 5150C**
Processor	Intel Core Duo 2 ghz	Intel Core Duo 2.8ghz
Memory	512 MB	512 MB
Hard Drive	250 GB	250 GB
Graphics Card	ATI Radeon 128MB	ATI Radeon 128MB
Media Drive	8X DVD/CD RW	8X DVD/CD RW
Networking	Ethernet 10/100/1000	Ethernet 10/100
Connection	Wireless	Wireless
Display	20"	20"
Operating System	OS X/Windows XP	Windows XP Media
Software	iLife,* Quicken	Corel WordPerfect
Price	$1,699	$1,428
PC Mag Reviews	very good (4.5 out of 5)	very good (4 out of 5)
Extras	built-in camera all-in-one (no tower)	Yahoo MusicMatch
	Apple MacBook Pro	**Toshiba Qosmio G35-AV650**
Processor	Intel Core Duo 2.16 ghz	Intel Core Duo 2.0 ghz
Memory	1 GB	1 GB
Hard Drive	120 GB	200 GB
Graphics Card	ATI Radeon 256 MB	GeForce 256MB
Media Drive	8x DVD/CD RW	8x DVD/CD RW
Networking	Ethernet 10/100/1000	Ethernet 10/100/1000
Connection	Wireless	Wireless
Display	17"	17"
Operating System	OS X/Windows XP	Windows XP Media
Software	iLife,* Quick Books	Microsoft Works, Quicken
Price	$2,799	$2,999
PC Mag Reviews	very good (4 out of 5)	very good (4.5 out of 5)
Extras	built-in camera remote presentation	TV Tuner
	Mac Mini	
Processor	Intel Core Duo 1.66 ghz	
Memory	512 MB	
Hard Drive	80 GB	
Graphics Card	integrated 64MB	
Media Drive	8x DVD/CD RW	
Networking	Ethernet 10/100/1000	
Connection	Wireless	
Display	none	
Operating System	OS X/Windows XP	
Software	iLife,* Quicken	
Price	$799	
PC Mag Reviews	very good (4 out of 5)	
Extras	no keyboard or mouse 6.5" square, 2" tall	

*iLife includes iTunes, iPhoto, iMovie HD, iDVD, iWeb, GarageBand

Sources: *PCWorld* and *CNET*.

Figure 1 **Apple Computer Products: iMac and Mac Mini**

share north of 5 percent by 2011," based on a Harris Interactive poll of 2,400 people. Asked about their intentions to purchase a Mac, 8% of respondents said they would switch to a Mac if it could run Windows, and 20% of respondents who already owned an iPod said they'd switch even if the Mac couldn't run Windows applications. Wolf stressed that he "bent over backwards" to interpret the survey results conservatively. His projection of future sales was based on forecasts of future PC sales growth from market research firm Interactive Data.[18]

Confirming these estimates, market research firm IDC reported that Apple's share of the worldwide PC market rose during the first quarter of 2007 to 2.6 percent, despite the launch during this same timeframe of Vista, Microsoft's first major operating system upgrade in over five years. An analyst with Piper Jaffray predicted that Apple would continue to see strong performance throughout 2007, especially because of its "dominance in the portable sector" and the continued popularity of Apple's media management via iTunes and other software. The move to the Intel-based processor had already had an effect. "Since coming out of the Intel transition Mac market share has seen year-over-year

Exhibit 6 XP on Mac Benchmarks—Windows XP Testing

Test System	Processor	WorldBench 5 Score	Mulititasking Test	Windows Media Encoder 9	Roxio VideoWave	Adobe Photoshop 7.0.1	Microsoft Office 2002 S
Apple iMac	2.0 GHz Core Duo T2500	96	423	294	267	320	54
Apple MacBook Pro	2.16 GHz Core Duo T2600	98	**419**	280	**259**	**305**	53
Dell Inspiron E1705 (portable)	2.0 GHz Core Duo T2500	97	498	305	271	325	54
HP Compaq nx9420 (portable)	2.16 GHz Core Duo T2600	**101**	444	**279**	**259**	311	57
HP Pavilion a1250n Media Center Desktop PC	2.0 GHz Athlon 64 X2 3800+	94	521	321	290	367	56
		>Better	<Better	<Better	<Better	<Better	<Better

Best results in bold. All individual test results in seconds.

All systems had 1 GB RAM. Macs used Apple's Boot Camp beta to install Windows.

Source: Galbraith, James and Jung, Jerry. http://www.macworld.com/2006/04/firstlooks/xpbenchmarks/index.php?pf=1.

increases, and year-over-year unit sales growth of about 30 percent, which have been about three times the industry average of about 10 percent."[19] In the second quarter of 2007, Apple reported that "demand for MacBooks and MacBook Pros during the quarter was exceptional," with notebook sales growing 70 percent year over year.[20]

Further confirming this, at least for the U.S. market, according to Gartner, Inc., Mac computer sales grew faster than any other major PC manufacturer during 2006, contributing to a U.S. market share of 6.1 percent. This result moved Apple up to the number four spot in the U.S. overall PC market.[21] As another indication of the strong growth of the Mac OS, Internet search data showed that the machines browsing the net using the Mac operating system, both the old Mac and the new "MacIntel" processor bases, had seen a remarkable increase, from a 3.64 percent share in 2005 to a 6.27 percent share in 2007 (see Exhibit 7).[22]

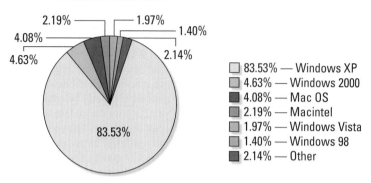

OS Market Share 2007

- 83.53% — Windows XP
- 4.63% — Windows 2000
- 4.08% — Mac OS
- 2.19% — Macintel
- 1.97% — Windows Vista
- 1.40% — Windows 98
- 2.14% — Other

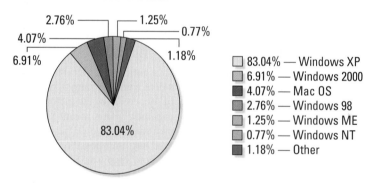

OS Market Share 2006

- 83.04% — Windows XP
- 6.91% — Windows 2000
- 4.07% — Mac OS
- 2.76% — Windows 98
- 1.25% — Windows ME
- 0.77% — Windows NT
- 1.18% — Other

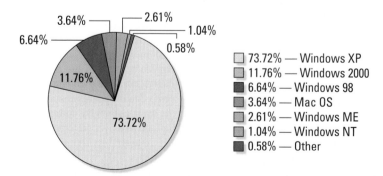

OS Market Share 2005

- 73.72% — Windows XP
- 11.76% — Windows 2000
- 6.64% — Windows 98
- 3.64% — Mac OS
- 2.61% — Windows ME
- 1.04% — Windows NT
- 0.58% — Other

Exhibit 7 **Computer Operating Systems Market Share 2005–2007**

Source: marketshare.hitslink.com.

One further comment on the concept of share of the consumer market involved the distinction between market share, the vendor's percentage of sales in a market over a specific period of time, and the installed base, or the total number of units sold and in use for that vendor's platform. Partly due to the increasing pace of operating system upgrades from Microsoft that demanded hardware upgrades as well, PCs running a Windows OS had a useful life span of about two years, compared to a Mac's five-year life. Apple had always supported older Mac operating systems for longer than Microsoft did theirs, and Apple operating systems did not have the history of Windows virus infections, prompting Apple customers to keep a Mac in active use almost twice as long as a Windows-based PC. One technical analyst noted that this had implications for Microsoft, since "every new Mac sold to a former PC user means that at least two Windows PCs will go unsold: the initial PC and its mid-life crisis, second string replacement."[23]

The Personal Digital Entertainment Devices/ Consumer Electronics Market: iPod

One of the most popular personal digital entertainment products since 2005, outside of gaming devices and mobile phones, has been the portable media player. Originally known as the MP3 player, named for the most popular file format for digitizing audio files, these devices originally provided a way to store audio media and play back music while on the go. These products had evolved into multiple function devices, allowing playback of music, video, and audiobooks as well as storage and viewing of photos, game playing, access to FM radio, and voice or line-in recording in multiple formats with varying ability to produce high-quality output, both through ear plugs or via a hook-up to TV, stereo, camcorder, or CD player.

Two basic form factors were available: (1) internal hard disks, allowing for storage of various data such as an address book, calendar, clock functions, or simple spreadsheet and word processing files, some with memory card slots for swapping of data between portable devices and PCs and (2) fixed memory flash-based players, which were much simpler and smaller devices. Due to the multitude of possible audio and video file formats and copyright protection software, not all players were able to access all digital content. The customer had to make trade-offs.

The digital music player market was ambitious and treacherous. Between 2004 and 2005 new hard drive and flash music players were repeatedly launched from Dell, Creative Labs, Archos, iRiver, Cowon, Samsung, and SanDisk. The venerable Rio player line was terminated in August of 2005. Produced by Digital Networks North America, a subsidiary of D&M Holdings, Inc. of Tokyo, maker of audiophile brands Denon, Marantz, and others, Rio products were among the first to pioneer the digital music player in the late 1990s and subsequently capture market share, only to lose it rapidly when Apple entered with the iPod product line.[24]

In 2004, ReignCom's president announced new portable media player products in an attempt to "restore Korea's reputation as the global MP3 player powerhouse,"[25] yet in 2005, even while holding 50 percent of the Korean market, iRiver posted quarterly losses of 84.5 percent.[26] By 2007 iRiver, a subsidiary of Korea's ReignCom, was still making competitive products and gaining excellent reviews.

Niche producers such as France-based Archos and Korea-based Cowon, concentrated on high-quality, high-priced products for audiophiles, and both saw good sales in 2005.[27] Creative Labs, the Singapore-based creator of SoundBlaster PC sound cards and PC audio speaker systems, as well as a solid line of MP3 players, was also highly regarded for innovation and quality yet posted a $31.9 million loss in the third quarter of 2005. This was in spite of the fact that Creative portable digital media devices held a 20 percent market share in 2005, making them number two in the world, behind Apple, which held over 60 percent.[28]

While Apple still dominated digital music players it was considered by some unwise to expect the iPod to be the revenue machine it had been. For several reasons, technical and marketing experts believed MP3 devices could become extinct. Serious music fans tended to stay away from iPods and other digital music players because of the poor-quality sound. Just as the CD format pushed out vinyl and tape delivery systems, CD-quality sound delivered to home-based PCs, possibly via wireless systems, was the goal of many users, and the MP3 player couldn't fill that bill.[29] Also, the Yankee Group did a study in 2006 that estimated 30.3 million users would switch from digital music players to mobile music phones and believed that connectivity via wireless and Bluetooth would be the new standard for content acquisition, not the PC.

This meant that Apple and other competitors would have to anticipate a major shake-out. Apple appeared to have anticipated at least some of this, especially by making a deal with Samsung to get a deep discount and dedication of 40 percent of the factory's flash memory manufacturing capacity.[30] This meant rivals who did not produce their own memory would be at a disadvantage. Only Samsung, SanDisk, and possibly Sony were capable of surviving a memory chip war. Since these components were the most expensive part of the flash-based digital player, declining profit margins would force out all others.

When the iPod Nano came on the market in late 2005, market research firm iSuppli took the $199 2-gigabyte version and deconstructed it. They determined that Apple spent $90.18 in materials and $8 for assembly, leaving a 50 percent profit margin before marketing and distribution costs. Since flash memory is the largest component of material cost, and Apple, because of the Samsung deal, was paying an estimated $54 for 2-gigabyte's worth, this gave Apple a 40 percent edge over other manufacturers who had to pay $90 for the same chip.[31] By comparison, iRiver's 20-gigabyte H320 hard drive player material costs were estimated at $119 plus $16 in assembly. That device retailed for $299 for a similar margin in 2005, but prices had fluctuated and memory inventories were costly to carry, perhaps leading in part to iRiver's financial troubles in 2006.[32]

A comparison of Apple's iPod products to equivalent and popular alternatives as of June 2006 showed that the iPod did not have the features, the price points or, in some cases, the quality of its competitors (see Exhibit 8 and Figure 2). However, the iPod product line had undeniably captured the imagination of the consumer. As of early 2007, there were over 4,000 accessories made specifically for the iPod, and more than 70 percent of 2007 model U.S. automobiles

Exhibit 8 **Digital Music Player Comparison**

Digital Music Player Comparison as of 6/2006		
	iPod	**Creative Zen Vision**
Capacity	30 GB/60 GB	30 GB
Type	hard drive	hard drive
Battery Life	20 hours	13 hours
Plays	audio/photos/video	audio/photos/video
Extras	plays on TV via dock Apple remote	FM radio, voice recorder compact flash card slot
	$299/$399	$299
Other Issues	no FM radio	
PC Mag Reviews	very good (4 out of 5)	very good (4 out of 5)
CNET reviews	excellent (8 out of 10)	excellent (8 out of 10)
	iPod Nano	**iRiver Clix (U10)**
Capacity	1 GB/2 GB/4 GB	2 GB
Type	flash	flash
Battery Life	14 hours	27 hours
Plays	audio/photos	audio/photos/video
Extras		FM radio, voice recorder docking available
	$149/$199/$249	$195
Other Issues		no Audible.com support WMP11 + URGE ready
PC Mag Reviews	very good (4.5 out of 5)	very good (4 out of 5)
CNET reviews	excellent (8.3 out of 10)	excellent (8.7 out of 10)
	iPod Shuffle	**Samsung YP-U2**
Capacity	512 MB/1 GB	512 MB
Type	flash	flash
Battery Life	12 hours	14 hours
Plays	audio	audio
Extras		FM radio, voice recorder
	$69/$99	$70
Other Issues	direct plug-into usb	direct plug-into usb
PC Mag Reviews	very good (4 out of 5)	good (3.5 out of 5)—U1
CNET reviews	good (6.7 out of 10)	very good (7.7 out of 10)

Sources: PC World and CNET.

iPod shuffle: Smaller than a pack of gum and much more fun.

Figure 2 Apple Digital Music Players: iPod, iPod Nano, iPod Shuffle

offered iPod connectivity. On April 9, 2007, Apple announced the sale of the 100 millionth iPod, a remarkable journey from its introduction five and a half years previously.[33]

Whether due to elegant and pleasing design or creative marketing, the iPod had made a significant impact on the world. A report on "podcasting," the audio recording equivalent of a blog that can be created and listened to by anyone with a computer or portable digital audio player, explained that the word derived from "broadcasting" and "iPod," even though any player can be used, not just the Apple device. The iPod had become the agent of the "podification" of society.[34]

In 2006 it was reported that Apple's operating system rival Microsoft was partnering with Japanese companies such as mobile handset manufacturer NTT DoCoMo, Toshiba Cor, and Napster Japan to create an "iPod killer."[35] This product, the Zune, debuted in November 2006 at a price of $249 and was a 30-GB player intended to draw customers from the high-end iPod market. Utilizing a variation of the Windows CE operating system and a modified version of Windows Media Player 11, Zune played music and video, displayed images, received FM radio and, on a limited basis, shared files wirelessly with other Zunes and via USB with Xbox 360s. Zune software allowed users to manage files, copy audio CDs, and buy songs from the online Zune Marketplace. Both the player and the marketplace used Windows Media DRM, incompatible with other DRM systems and not part of Microsoft's original playsforsure platform.[36]

Although early adopters of Zune gave Microsoft a market share boost during the 2006 holiday season, there was a "rapid freefall" of Zune sales after its debut week.[37] NPD Group noted a drop in Zune share of the high-end hard disk player market from 10.2 percent in December of 2006 to 8.7 percent in February 2007.[38] Reviews of the Microsoft product were "less than stellar," prompting

analysts to comment, "Zune does not appear to be any threat to iPod at this time."[39]

In early 2006, analysts calculated that Apple had 69 percent of unit sales share in the entire music player space. The only other manufacturer in the top 10 was a Sandisk product with only 512 MB of space that retailed for under $100 (see Exhibit 9).[40] Even when Apple had distribution trouble at Christmas and the Shuffle sold out at the online store, Morgan Stanley analyst Rebecca Runckle did an informal survey and discovered that only 4 percent of customers would buy an alternative player if the iPod was not available.[41] As of January of 2007, NPD Group estimated that the iPod had 72.7 percent of the worldwide retail music player sales (see Exhibit 10).[42] In the second quarter of 2007, Apple itself reported a 70 percent share of the U.S. market; 60 percent share in Australia and Canada; over 50 percent share in Japan and Hong Kong; over 40 percent share in the UK, Switzerland, and Denmark; and about a 28 percent share in Germany.[43]

Speculation in late 2007 over the next generation of the iPod included the possibility of moving away from the 1.8-inch hard disk drive to a flash drive player with an approximate 32-GB capacity, paving the way for a significant increase in battery life and a slimmer design. Apple's long-term supplier agreements and price declines in flash memory pricing gave Apple a financial advantage yet again. One of the challenges for the iPod was the degree of video capability, not because of technology limitations, but because of the possibility of a conflict with the iPhone and Apple TV: a widescreen video option for the iPod would have made it difficult to differentiate between the products, especially since the projected price points were similar.[44]

iPhone In 2007, further competition came from the blurring of lines between the digital music player and other consumer electronic devices: The telecom players

Exhibit 9 **MP3 Player Market Share, 2006**

Music Player	Company	Ranking	Unit Share (%)	Dollar Share (%)
30-GB Black Video iPod	Apple	1	12.3	19.5
512-MB iPod shuffle	Apple	2	10.1	5.3
2-GB Black iPod Nano	Apple	3	9.8	10.4
30-GB White Video iPod	Apple	4	8.1	12.8
2-GB White iPod Nano	Apple	5	7.1	7.5
512-MB Sensa m230	Sandisk	6	4.4	2.0
4-GB Black iPod Nano	Apple	7	4.0	5.3
60-GB Black iPod w/Video	Apple	8	3.3	6.9
4-GB White iPod Nano	Apple	9	2.9	3.8
60-GB White iPod w/Video	Apple	10	2.4	5.0
Others			35.6	21.5

Source: NPD Group/NPD Techworld, as reported in *BusinessWeek Online*, February 9, 2006, http://www.businessweek.com/technology/tech_stats/mp3s060209.htm.

wanted to join the digital music market. While Apple and others may have seen the computer as central to the future of digital music, the telecom companies thought the mobile phone could become a center of this emerging world. One example of this was the emergence of Samsung as a strong participant in several arenas. Samsung already had entries in the portable media player space and in 2006 introduced several phone plus dedicated MP3 music playback capability products.

$225,000,000 of Retail Music Player Sales January 2007, NPD Group

iPod 72.7%
SanDisk 8.9%
Zune 3.2%
Creative 2.9%
Other 10.3%
Samsung 2.0%

Exhibit 10 Music Player Sales, January 2007

Source: NPD Group.

In May of 2006 there were rumors that Apple had initiated an agreement with Softbank, Japan's third-largest cellular carrier to develop cell phones that could play songs downloaded via iTunes. This would have allowed market share growth in Asia.[45] With product scheduled to ship in June of 2007, this device combined an Internet-enabled smartphone and video iPod. The iPhone allowed users to access all iPod content and play music and video content purchased from iTunes. Apple made an exclusive arrangement with AT&T's Cingular Wireless network to provide cellular service.

Although some commentators were skeptical about Apple's ability to compete with the well entrenched cell phone and smartphone manufacturers such as Nokia, Motorola, Samsung, Sony Ericsson, LG, Research in Motion's Blackberry, and Palm's Treo, there was also praise for the iPhone's "multitouch" user interface, considered by some to be "the first major step toward the third-generation PC user interface" (see Figure 3).[46]

The iPhone debuted with a 4-GB model for $499 and an 8-GB model for $599, and estimates from component manufacturers suggested it would cost between $230 and $265 to make, yielding Apple's preferred gross margin of about 50 percent.[47] This would allow room for price adjustments based on component or customer demand. The smartphone market in 2007 was estimated at 10 percent of all mobile phone sales, or 100 million devices a year. Steve Jobs said he "would like to see the iPhone represent 1 percent of all mobile phone sales by the end of 2008."[48]

Apple TV Further expanding Apple's reach into digital entertainment was the Apple TV set-top box. Also introduced in 2007 at a retail price of $299, this 40-GB hard

Figure 3 Apple iPhone, Samsung Mobile Phone/
Digital Portable Media Player SCH a930

drive unit was about eight inches square and one inch high. Plugged into a wide-screen digital TV and set up on a wired or wireless network, Apple TV allowed the user to move movies and TV shows from the computer to be shown on the wide screen. Digital video content could be purchased from iTunes, downloaded to the computer and then viewed via Apple TV. Steve Jobs had introduced the device by saying, "Apple TV is like a DVD player for the 21st century—you connect it to your entertainment system just like a DVD player, but it plays digital content you get from the Internet rather than DVDs you get from a physical store."[49]

Although this seemed like a good idea, one analyst said, "The worst thing about Apple TV is that it tries to do for video what the iPod has done for music. . . . Apple's laudable effort to simplify video downloads by running everything through iTunes leaves too much good content out in the cold."[50] This reference was to the confusion around digital video formats. With so many different options available, there was as yet no standardized delivery format that provided consistent high quality.

The Creative/Entertainment Software Market

Although Apple had always created innovative hardware, software development was also an important goal, with implications for long-term sales growth. Software was increasingly becoming Apple's core strength.[51] Steve Jobs commented on what appeared to be Apple's move into the consumer electronics and software market:

> I've always wanted to own and control the primary technology in everything we do. Take audio. For years, the primary technology was the marking mechanism inside a CD or DVD player. But we became convinced that software was going to be the primary technology, and we're a pretty good software company. So we developed iTunes. We're a good hardware company, too, but we're really good at software. So that led us to believe that we had a chance to reinvent the music business, and we did.[52]

The premier piece of Apple software was the operating system. OS X allowed Apple to develop software applications such as Final Cut Pro, a video-editing program for professionals' digital camcorders, and the simplified version for regular consumers, called iMovie. In 2005, iLife, bundled for free on every Mac or purchased separately for around $79, provided five integrated applications allowing the computer to become a home studio. Those applications included iMovie; iDVD for recording photos, movies, and music onto DVDs; iPhoto for touching up digital photos; GarageBand for making and mixing personally created music; and the iTunes digital music jukebox. Also available was iWork, containing a PowerPoint–type program called Keynote and a word-processor/page-layout program called Pages.

iTunes was a free downloadable software for consumers running either newer Mac or Windows operating systems. It was bundled with all Mac computers and iPods and connected with the iTunes Music Store for purchase of digital music and movie files that could be played by iPods and by iTunes on PCs.

Music purchased from iTunes Music Store was copy protected with Apple's FairPlay digital rights management (DRM) system, and Steve Jobs had negotiated a deal with the Big Five record companies (Sony Music Entertainment, BMG, EMI, Universal, and Warner) to sell these protected songs on iTunes. Other digital music services had similar arrangements but had to use Microsoft copy protection, which meant downloaded songs could not be played on the iPod. In 2007 Jobs made a request of the music labels to stop requiring digital music distributors like iTunes to use copyright protection such as FairPlay. By taking the lead in this, Apple could potentially come out ahead of the game again, since then iTunes songs could be played on non-iPod music players, and music purchased on other services could be played on the iPod. In what might have been perceived as a PR ploy, Jobs said that allowing music to be sold online without digital rights management technology would "create a truly interoperable music marketplace—one that Apple would embrace "wholeheartedly."[53]

The iTunes Music Store began offering music videos and content from TV shows including ABC's *Lost* and *Desperate Housewives* in 2005. Offerings were expanded throughout 2006 to include more TV shows and movie clips, and in May of 2007 Apple launched iTunes U, providing access to free educational content such as course lectures, language lessons, lab demonstrations, sports highlights, and campus tours provided by top U.S. colleges and universities. The Provost of Stanford University, John Etchemendy said, "Our partnership with Apple and iTunes U provides a creative and innovative way to engage millions of people with our teaching, learning and research and share the experience of intellectual exploration and discovery that defines our university."[54]

In April of 2007, over 2.5 billion songs, 50 million TV shows, and over 1.3 million movies had been downloaded since the Windows-plus-Mac version of the service first became available in April of 2003. Although the volume was there, iTunes had not necessarily been a profitable venture. Out of the 99 cents Apple charged for a song, about 65 cents went to the music label; 25 cents went for distribution costs, including credit card charges, servers, and bandwidth; and the balance went to marketing, promotion, and the amortized cost of developing the iTunes software. Because of this, the iTunes music store made a small profit for the first time in the first quarter of 2004.[55]

Several competitors were trying to compete with the iTunes service. iTunes Music Store in 2006 had accounted for 75 percent of all music download sales on the Web and 83 percent of all legally downloaded music in the month of December 2005.[56] RealNetworks' Rhapsody subscription service, Yahoo MusicMatch, Napster, eMusic, BuyMusic.com, Wal-Mart, Sony, and AOL music downloads all had tried to compete for the remaining market share, using the potentially buggy Microsoft Windows Media format.[57]

In 2006, MTV and Microsoft announced a new on-line music store called URGE as part of a new release of Windows Media Player 11. iRiver's 2006 Clix flash device came WMP11 and URGE ready. This service would not be compatible with the Mac or the iPod, but, according to MTV spokesman Jason Hirschhorn, was an attempt to talk to "the 95 percent of people that aren't buying online music yet."[58]

However, when Microsoft launched Zune in late 2006, it did not use the playsforsure DRM technology, preferring instead to create a Windows Media DRM that was incompatible with other DRM systems and not part of the playsforsure program, meaning that music previously purchased from Microsoft's own MSN Music service, and possibly downloaded onto Samsung, SanDisk or Creative music players, could not be played on a Zune.[59]

Making it potentially worse for Apple's competitors, the music artists were overwhelmingly supportive of Apple, since, as Jobs reported, "Almost every song and CD is made on a Mac, it's recorded on a Mac, its mixed on a Mac. The artwork's done on a Mac. Almost every artist I've met has an iPod, and most of the music execs now have iPods. And one of the reasons Apple was able to do what we did was because we are perceived by the music industry as the most creative technology company."[60]

Operating Systems   Further opportunity came from the Mac's new ability to run Windows. Third-party software developers such as Adobe had always had to make a sometimes risky decision to create Mac OS versions of their popular products. Now that the Macs were using Intel duo core chips, much more versatility and cross-platform compatibility made it more profitable to design and develop for this new market.

Apple's largest competitor in this software arena was Microsoft, but in 2006 Microsoft was facing a loss of confidence with its shareholders. Revenues and earnings in the Windows operating system and Office productivity

suite product groups had only grown by single digits. Since these products traditionally dominated the bottom line, the news in 2006 that the new Vista and Office 2007 would be delayed, and that the market for Office might erode further as customers wondered why they needed to upgrade with open source software and Apple iWorks software now more available, all made Microsoft's future more uncertain.[61] In response, Microsoft announced it would be spending more money on trying to find new technology growth areas. This would involve hardware as well as software. In addition to the Xbox gaming console, Microsoft was putting effort into its portable music player, Zune.

This announcement of a potential new direction for Microsoft coincided with Bill Gates' planned phase-out as Chief Architect for development and replacement by Ray Ozzie, prompting one analyst to question:

> Whether Microsoft under its new leadership can match the performance of its halcyon years under Gates going forward into a new era of consumer computing remains to be seen. Notably, Microsoft's biggest rival in this space is Apple, a company which is once again ruled by the man who did a lot to popularize consumer computing, Steve Jobs. An Ozzie versus Jobs match up should be interesting to watch. Some may speculate that Ozzie is punching above his weight, and that Microsoft needs a Gates to drive the company's direction, just as Apple needed Jobs to get it back on track.[62]

The Future of Apple

Although Steve Jobs had been credited with Apple's ability to innovate and to appeal especially to a certain type of consumer (Jobs estimated Apple's market share in the creative-professional marketplace as over 50 percent[63]), Jobs himself would credit his people:

> We hire people who want to make the best things in the world . . . our primary goal is to make the world's best PCs—not to be the biggest or the richest. We have a second goal, which is to always make a profit—both to make some money but also so we can keep making those great products. . . . [regarding the systemization of innovation] the system is that there is no system. That doesn't mean we don't have process. Apple is a very disciplined company, and we have great processes. But that's not what it's about. Process makes you more efficient . . . but innovation . . . comes from saying no to 1,000 things to make sure we don't get on the wrong track or try to do too much. We're always thinking about new markets we could enter, but it's only by saying no that you can concentrate on the things that are really important.[64]

Some analysts believed Apple had "changed the rules of the game for three industries—PCs, consumer electronics, and music . . . and appears to have nothing to fear from major rivals."[65] The iPod sales were not slowing appreciably, the Mac computers, especially the Intel-equipped portable computers, were attracting new consumers, and the software improvements would only accelerate this trend. It was possible that Apple could see a doubling of its personal computer market share over the next few years and, with cash reserves sufficient to continue to fund R&D, could continue to innovate and grow in other areas. In 2007, Apple continued to hold the number one spot in the *Business Week*–Boston Consulting Group's list of the World's Most Innovative Companies for the third year in a row.[66]

Steve Jobs announced on January 9, 2007, that Apple Computer would become Apple Inc. This name change confirmed for many commentators that Apple had made the shift from computers to become an integrated digital consumer electronics company. Jobs said, "Apple's name change doesn't have any direct impact on the business, but it does accomplish the following—it signals to employees the company's long-term strategy, it clarifies the marketing message and it prods investors to compare Apple to consumer electronics firms rather than just computer makers." It also meant that Apple was now "much more diversified, so you don't compare it by peer group as much as by product line."[67]

While surgery was successful, Jobs bout with pancreatic cancer hasn't been forgotten. Even though Jobs reportedly was secure in his confidence with his chief operations officer, Tim Cook, many analysts worried that Apple might not survive Jobs' departure a second time. Although Cook "is a respected operations wonk, he lacks Job's charisma, leadership, and gut for tech trends."[68]

Another uncertainty continuing on into 2007 was the issue of option backdating. Apple was being investigated by the Securities & Exchange Commission as part of a wide probe of over 200 public companies that may have granted employee stock options dated prior to the date that the company actually granted the options without providing proper disclosure to stockholders.[69] Although Steve Jobs had gotten the support of Apple's Board of Directors (including former Vice-President Al Gore and Google's CEO Dr. Eric Schmidt, among others), some commentators were still skeptical about his role. Others, however, pointed out that even if it was proven that Jobs intended to deceive shareholders, having him resign might cause more damage to Apple's investors, customers, and business partners than the backdating did: "Steve Jobs is a national treasure, and Apple has to do everything it can to keep him actively engaged. If Martha Stewart can stay at her company, there should be no issue—even in the worst case—in designing a structure that keeps Steve Jobs at Apple."[70]

Endnotes

1. Apple was the first firm to have commercial success selling GUI systems, but Xerox developed the first systems in 1973. Xerox PARC researchers built a single user computer called the Alto that featured a bit-mapped display and a mouse and the world's first What-You-See-Is-What-You-Get (WYSIWYG) editor. http://www.parc.xerox.com/about/history/default.html, retrieved on 5/07/2007.
2. From User Culture in Apple Computer at Wikipedia, http://en.wikipedia.org retrieved 3/12/2006.
3. Langberg, M. Low market share is a badge of honor, as far as Mac faithful are concerned. SiliconValley.com, 3/26/2006, http://www.siliconvalley.com/mld/siliconvalley/business/columnists/mike_langberg/14191452.htm.
4. See Mank, D. A., & Nystrom, H. E. 2000. The relationship between R&D spending and shareholder returns in the computer industry. *Engineering Management Society, Proceedings of the 2000 IEEE,* p. 501–504.
5. From Wikipedia, Apple Computer, 1998 to 2005—New beginnings, http://en.wikipedia.org.
6. Ultra-portable MP3 music player puts 1,000 songs in your pocket. October 23, 2001, http://www.apple.com/pr/library/2001/oct/23ipod.html.
7. Haddad, C. 2002. Apple harvests the fruits of innovation. *BusinessWeek Online,* May 1, http://www.businessweek.com/technology/content/apr2002/tc2002051_3757.htm?chan=search.
8. Salkever, A. 2004. It's time for an iPod IPO. *BusinessWeek Online,* May 5, http://www.businessweek.com/technology/content/may2004/tc2004055_8689_tc056.htm?chan=search.
9. Apple to use Intel microprocessors beginning in 2006. Apple Worldwide Developer Conference, June 6, 2005, http://www.apple.com/pr/library/2005/jun/06intel.html.
10. Burrows, P. 2005. Apple hits the Intel switch. *BusinessWeek Online,* June 7, http://www.businessweek.com/technology/content/jun2005/tc2005067_6674_tc024.htm.
11. Snell, J. 2004. Steve Jobs on Mac's 20th anniversary. Exclusive Interview. *Macworld.* February 1, http://www.macworld.com/2004/02/features/themacturns20jobs/.
12. Hesseldahl, A. 2006. Apple's growing bite of the market. *BusinessWeek Online,* June 15, http://www.businessweek.com/technology/content/jun2006/tc20060615_080175.htm.
13. Martin, S. 2006. How Apple stores beat Tiffany. December 19, http://www.redherring.com/Article.aspx?a=20332&hed=How+Apple+Stores+Beat+Tiffany.
14. Notes of interest from Apple's Q207 quarterly conference call. *Apple Insider,* April 25, 2007, http://www.appleinsider.com/articles/07/04/25/notes_of_interest_from_apples_q207_quarterly_conference_call.html.
15. Burrows, P. 2004. The seed of Apple's innovation. *BusinessWeek Online,* October 12, http://www.businessweek.com/bwdaily/dnflash/oct2004/nf20041012_4018_db083.htm?chan=search.
16. Growing market share—Branding in the computer industry 2006, http://www.stealingshare.com/content/1137644625875.htm.
17. Hesseldahl, A. 2006. Apple's switch-hit homer. *BusinessWeek Online,* April 20, http://www.businessweek.com/technology/content/apr2006/tc20060420_719591.htm.
18. Hesseldahl, ibid.
19. Marsal, K. 2007. Apple's Mac share inches upwards during first quarter. *Apple Insider,* April 30, http://www.appleinsider.com/articles/07/04/30/apples_mac_share_inches_upwards_during_first_quarter.html.
20. *Apple Insider* Staff. Notes of interest from Apple's Q207 quarterly conference call. April 25, 2007, http://www.appleinsider.com/articles/07/04/25/notes_of_interest_from_apples_q207_quarterly_conference_call.html.

21. Marsal, K., & Jade, K. 2006. Apple's share of U.S. PC market jumps to 6.1 percent. *Apple Insider,* October 18, http://www.appleinsider.com/articles/06/10/18/apples_share_of_us_pc_market_jumps_to_61_percent.html.

22. Data from *Market Share by Net Applications,* http://marketshare.hitslink.com/report.aspx?qprid=2&qpmr=15&qpdt=1&qpct=3&qpcal=1&qptimeframe=Y&qpsp=2007.

23. Dilger, D. E. 2007. Market share vs. installed base: iPod vs. Zune, Mac vs PC. *RoughlyDrafted Magazine,* March 18, http://www.roughlydrafted.com/RD/RDM.Tech.Q1.07/9E601E8E-2ACC-4866-A91B-3371D1688E00.html.

24. Burrows, P. 2005. Steve Job's tiny but sure bet. *BusinessWeek Online,* September 9, http://www.businessweek.com/technology/content/sep2005/tc2005099_1930_tc119.htm.

25. Via *Korea Times,* December 16, 2004, posted on http://www.dapreview.net/comment.php?comment.news.799.

26. "iRiver shows heavy quarterly losses. October 28, 2005, http://digitalmusicnews.com/stories/102805iriver/?searchterm=iRiver%20posted%20loss%202005.

27. Archos posts record sales, moves into black. February 7, 2006, http://digitalmusicnews.com/stories/020706archos/?searchterm=archos%202005; "South Korea pushes digital music ubiquity," November 15, 2004, http://digitalmusicnews.com/stories/111504korea/?searchterm=cowon%202005.

28. Creative suffers disappointing quarter, iPod drags earnings. August 16, 2005, http://digitalmusicnews.com/stories/081105creative/?searchterm=creative%20Labs%20loss%20first%20quarter%202005; "Creative numbers challenge iPod market share data," December 13, 2005, http://digitalmusicnews.com/stories/121305creative/?searchterm=creative%20market%20share%202005.

29. Sandoval, G. 2006. Syncing high-def music with digital generation. *CNET News.com,* May 15, 2006, http://news.com.com/Syncing+high+def+music+with+digital+generation/2100-1027_3-6072028.html.

30. Hesseldahl, A. 2005. A memorable deal for Apple and Samsung? *BusinessWeek Online,* August 26, 2005, http://www.businessweek.com/technology/content/aug2005/tc20050826_8564_tc024.htm

31. Hesseldahl, A. 2005. Unpeeling Apple's Nano. *BusinessWeek Online,* September 22, http://www.businessweek.com/technology/content/sep2005/tc20050921_4557.htm.

32. How much does an MP3 player cost to make? September 12, 2005, http://www.anythingbutipod.com/archives/industry.

33. 100 million iPods sold. April 9, 2007, http://www.apple.com/pr/library/2007/04/09ipod.html.

34. Podcasting power for the people. February 23, 2005, http://www.pbs.org/newshour/extra/features/jan-june05/podcasting_2-23.html; "Apple's iPod a technological, cultural phenomenon," May 15, 2006, http://www.pbs.org/newshour/bb/media/jan-june06/ipod_05-15.html.

35. Beer, S. 2006. Microsoft poised to launch iPod and iTunes rivals. *ITWire,* June 17, http://www.itwire.com.au/content/view/4660/.

36. See Zune, http://en.wikipedia.org/wiki/Zune.

37. Dilger, D. E. 2006. iPod vs Zune: Microsoft's slippery Astroturf. *RoughlyDrafted Magazine,* December 1, http://www.roughlydrafted.com/RD/Q4.06/D0BC712B-7DBA-46CA-AA44-19376E64FBA6.html.

38. Zune, from http://en.wikipedia.org/wiki/Zune.

39. Montalbano, E. 2006. Microsoft's Zune player not challenging iPod sales. *PC World,* November 26, http://www.pcworld.com/article/id,128032/article.html.

40. Sandisk surprise, February 9, 2006, http://www.businessweek.com/technology/tech_stats/mp3s060209.htm.

41. *Apple Insider* Staff. 2005. Morgan Stanley: Consumers seek more iPods than cell phones this holiday. *Apple Insider,* December 16, http://www.appleinsider.com/articles/05/12/16/morgan_stanley_consumers_seek_more_ipods_than_cell_phones_this_holiday.html.

42. Dilger, D. E. 2007. Market Share Myth 2007: iPod vs. Zune and Mac vs. PC. *Roughly Drafted Magazine,* March 16, http://www.roughlydrafted.com/RD/RDM.Tech.Q1.07/FFE4A8E2-9816-4344-9FB0-61BED246674C.html.

43. *Apple Insider* Staff. Notes of interest from Apple's Q207 quarterly conference call. April 25, 2007, http://www.appleinsider.com/articles/07/04/25/notes_of_interest_from_apples_q207_quarterly_conference_call.html.

44. Jade, K., & McLean, P. 2007. Next-gen video iPod still a ways out, sources say. *Apple Insider,* March 2, http://www.appleinsider.com/articles/07/03/02/next_gen_video_ipod_still_a_ways_out_sources_say.html.

45. Williams, M. 2006. Reports: Apple, Softbank plan iPod cell phone. *CIO Tech Informer,* May 15, http://www.cio.com/blog_view?CID=21085.

46. Elgan, M. 2007. Why the iPhone will change the (PC) world. *Computerworld,* February 16, http://www.computerworld.com/action/article.do?command=viewArticleBasic&articleId=9011412.

47. Hesseldahl, A. 2007. What the iPhone will cost to make. *BusinessWeek Online,* January 18, http://www.computerworld.com/action/article.do?command=viewArticleBasic&articleId=9011412.

48. Zemen, E. 2007. Ballmer says iPhone won't succeed. Has Windows mobile? *Information Week,* Over the Air, May 1, http://www.informationweek.com/blog/main/archives/2007/05/ballmer_says_ip.html.

49. "Apple TV coming to your living room," January 9, 2007, http://www.apple.com/pr/library/2007/01/09appletv.html.

50. Wildstrom, S. H. 2007. "Apple TV's blurry future," *BusinessWeek.com, Technology & You,* March 21, 2007, http://www.businessweek.com/technology/content/mar2007/tc20070321_959989.htm

51. Schlender, B. 2005. How big can Apple get? *Fortune,* February 21, http://money.cnn.com/magazines/fortune/fortune_archive/2005/02/21/8251769/index.htm

52. Burrows, op. cit.

53. Hesseldahl, A. 2007. Steve Jobs' music manifesto. *BusinessWeek Online,* February 7, http://www.businessweek.com/technology/content/feb2007/tc20070206_576721.htm?chan=search.

54. Apple announces iTunes U on the iTunes store. May 30, 2007, http://www.apple.com/pr/library/2007/05/30itunesu.html.

55. Cherry, S. 2004. Selling music for a song. *Spectrum Online,* December, http://www.spectrum.ieee.org/dec04/3857.

56. McLean, P., & Jade, K. 2006. Notes of interest from Apple's Q1 2006 conference call. *Apple Insider,* January 18,

http://www.appleinsider.com/articles/06/01/18/notes_of_interest_from_apples_q1_2006_conference_call.html.

57. Leonard, D. 2006. The player. *Fortune,* March 8, http://money.cnn.com/magazines/fortune/fortune_archive/2006/03/20/8371750/index.htm.

58. Dalrymple, J. 2006. MTV, Microsoft launch URGE music service this week. *Playlist,* May 15, http://playlistmag.com/news/2006/05/15/urge/index.php?/ssrc=mwtoprss.

59. Zune, http://en.wikipedia.org/wiki/Zune

60. Goodell, J. 2003. Steve Jobs: The *Rolling Stone* interview. *Rolling Stone,* December 3, http://www.rollingstone.com/news/story/5939600/steve_jobs_the_rolling_stone_interview.

61. Beer, S. 2006. Microsoft knows Windows and Office can't deliver growth. *ITWire,* April 29, http://www.itwire.com.au/content/view/4077/106/.

62. Beer, S. 2006. Microsoft poised to launch iPod and iTunes rivals. *ITWire,* June 17, http://www.itwire.com.au/content/view/4660/.

63. Goodell, op. cit.

64. Burrows, op cit.

65. Schlender, op. cit.

66. The world's 50 most innovative companies. *BusinessWeek Online,* May 4, 2007, http://www.businessweek.com/innovate/content/may2007/id20070504_051674.htm?chan=innovation_special+report+–+2007+most+innovative+companies_2007+most+innovative+companies.

67. What's in a name? For Apple, a focus on the digital living room. *Knowledge@Wharton,* January 24, 2007, http://knowledge.wharton.upenn.edu/article.cfm?articleid=1641.

68. Burrows, P. 2007. Is Steve Jobs untouchable? *BusinessWeek Online,* January 4, http://www.businessweek.com/technology/content/jan2007/tc20070104_659422.htm

69. See http://en.wikipedia.org/wiki/Options_backdating for an overview.

70. Burrows, op. cit.

Case 31 Wal-Mart: The Challenges of Dominance*

By the turn of the century, Wal-Mart had been named Retailer of the Century by *Discount Store News,* made *Fortune* magazine's lists of the Most Admired Companies in America and the 100 Best Companies to Work For, and was ranked on the *Financial Times'* list of the Most Respected Companies in the World. In 2002 Wal-Mart became number one on the Fortune 500 list and was presented with the Ron Brown Award for Corporate Leadership, a presidential award that recognizes companies for outstanding achievement in employee and community relations.

By the end of 2003, Wal-Mart was the world's largest corporation with a market valuation of more than $400 billion, 1.4 million employees, and 4,700 store locations in the United States and abroad (see Appendixes 1A, 1B, and 2A starting on page C271). By the end of 2006, Wal-Mart's valuation had slipped to $200 billion. It had 1.9 million employees and 6,779 store locations in the United States and abroad. Operating the world's biggest private satellite communications system, the firm tracked sales, replenished inventory, processed payments, and regulated individual store temperatures in real-time. Wal-Mart's Retail Link-System was the largest civilian database in the world, slightly smaller than that of the Pentagon, and three times the size of the Internal Revenue Service's database.

The company's combined annual growth rate during 1999 to 2006 was 13.5 percent in revenue and 12.7 percent in earnings before interest and taxes (EBIT). Similar growth rates over the next decade, if sustained, would result in a $1 trillion business generating well over $50 billion EBIT with a workforce in excess of 4 million people (see Appendix 2B). Virtually everybody—industry experts, market analysts, consumers, special interest groups, competitors, and suppliers—questioned not only the sustainability, but also the desirability of such current or projected growth rates and consequent dominance. Global 24-hour visibility and exposure were two things that Sam Walton had strived to avoid. His legacy could no longer hope to escape these.

Wal-Mart's leadership was primarily concerned with sustainability. How do you maintain a projected $40 billion growth in revenue and $20 billion growth in EBIT per year? Aware that the past did not always predict the future reliably, top management must have wondered if the firm's formula for success and its current resource allocation strategy would be sufficient to ensure such astronomical growth. How many more Super Centers could be built in the Americas? Could Wal-Mart build a distinctive competency in international operations to fuel growth when neither it nor any other major retailer had yet succeeded in doing so? Could it transport its distinctive competency in logistics to Europe and China

along with its corporate culture? With its increased global presence, the firm was being attacked from all sides. Human resource practices, supplier relationships, and purchasing practices, along with community relations were increasingly being targeted. A small group of old-timers in Bentonville, Arkansas (the company's headquarters), reminisced over simpler times when Sam would have just advised them to "Manage one store at a time, respect the individual, and create value with our customers."

Company History—Sam Walton's Era, 1962–1992[1]

With previous retailing experience and expertise, Sam Walton and his brother Bud Walton opened their first Wal-Mart Discount City store in 1962 (the same year that Kmart and Target were founded) in Rogers, Arkansas. They opened 15 department-sized stores in small rural towns throughout the Midwest by the end of the 1960s (see Appendix 3).

While Wal-Mart's huge stores and variety of branded merchandising resembled Kmart and other competitors, Sam's "every day low price" (EDLP) and limited promotional budgets proved unique in the industry. A hub-and-spoke distribution system with wholly owned warehousing and transportation together propelled Wal-Mart to *Forbes*'s number one ranking among U.S. discounters in 1977 (the ranking was based on return on equity, return on capital, sales growth, and earnings growth).

Sam Walton's Four Basic Beliefs and Three Pricing Philosophies[2]   At the heart of Sam Walton's philosophy and Wal-Mart's corporate culture were four basic beliefs: excellence in the workplace, respect for the individual, customer service, and always having the lowest prices. The company had stayed true to these principles since 1962. Sam envisioned customers who trusted Wal-Mart's pricing philosophy and the ability to find the lowest prices with the best possible customer service. Years ago, Sam Walton challenged associates to practice what he called "aggressive hospitality." He said "Let's be the most friendly—offer a smile of welcome and beyond what our customers expect. Why not? You can do it and do it better than any other retailing company in the world . . . exceed your customers' expectations and they'll come back over and over again."

Perhaps the most unique belief Walton had was that each store should reflect the values of its customers and support the vision they hold for their community. As a result, Wal-Mart's community outreach programs were guided by local associates who grew up in the area and understood its needs. Sam's initial pricing policies permeated the Wal-Mart culture. His every day low price (EDLP) strategy flew in the face of another competitor's "blue-light specials." Not considered as a "sale," an ongoing process at Wal-Mart would ensure EDLP. Another strategy, the "special buy," resulted from the continuous pressure on costs and the global search for merchandise of exceptional value.

* This case was prepared by Professor Michael D. Oliff with the support of research assistants Isil Kosdere and Mahrukh Jangda as the basis for class discussion. It was developed within the scope of Enterprise 2020, a development program conducted with global enterprises. The School of Management, University of Texas, Dallas, Copyright © 2007.

Growth and Increased Visibility Sam's Clubs, established in 1983, marked the entrance into the cash-and-carry discount membership market. It also led to expansion into cities and population centers. Within eight years, 150 clubs would be opened in the United States. Format innovations continued as Sam experimented with France's hypermarket concept—stadium-sized stores with groceries, general merchandise, and a host of satellite services. These ultimately gave way to Wal-Mart Super Centers (a 150,000-square-foot format with foods, more items, and more accessible merchandise) with hundreds built in the 1990s.

Wal-Mart enjoyed a 12-year stretch of 35 percent annual profit growth through 1987. Its internal reengineering of the supply chain did not come without external consequences. The firm's buying and distribution practices and general competitive impact on small, independent businesses repeatedly came under fire. Vendor-direct purchasing led to an "uprising" of more than 100,000 independent sales representatives in 1987. Wal-Mart was accused of "excluding them from the selling process." In towns where it had operated for eight or more years, small businesses—drugstores, hardware, clothing, sporting goods—found it virtually impossible to compete with the firm's economies of scale.

In a public relations effort motivated by good business sense, Wal-Mart sent an open letter to U.S. manufacturers in March 1985, inviting them to take part in a "Buy American" program. The company offered to work with them in producing products that could compete against imports. "Our American suppliers must commit to improving their facilities and machinery, remain financially conservative, and work to fill our requirements and, most importantly, strive to improve employee productivity," Walton told American Business in April 1988.

During the same period, Wal-Mart developed a record for community service that began with awarding $1,000 scholarships to high school students in each community it served. At the same time, the company's refusal to stock dozens of widely circulated adult and teen magazines had some critics claiming that Wal-Mart was willfully narrowing the choices of the buying public and in essence bowing to pressure from conservative special interest groups.

Purchases of upstream businesses—Western Merchandise and the McLane Company—increased economies of scale. The merger of the Wholesale Club (adding 28 stores to the Sam's Clubs) and the introduction of Sam's American Choice, the company's own brand of products, signaled the firm's aggressive posture with regard to both current competitors and suppliers.

In 1991 Wal-Mart expanded outside the United States for the first time when it entered into a joint venture with Mexico's largest retailer, Cifra. The venture developed a price club called Club Aurrera, a store that required an annual membership fee of $25. Shoppers could choose from 3,500 products ranging from frozen vegetables to fur coats.

Founder Sam Walton died of bone cancer on April 5, 1992. At the time of his death, he was the second richest man in the world, after the sultan of Brunei, having built a personal fortune in 30 years based solely on creating value with customers. David Glass, CEO, handpicked as Sam's successor, had led a smooth management transition since 1988 and now began to focus on the decade of challenges ahead.

Wal-Mart after Sam

Glass and his management team accelerated growth immediately. From 1992 to 1993, Wal-Mart opened 161 stores, and closed only one. Another 48 Sam's Clubs and 51 Bud's Warehouse Outlets were also opened with expansions or relocations at 170 existing Wal-Mart stores and 40 Sam's Clubs (the company's 2,138 stores included 34 Wal-Mart Super Centers and 256 Sam's Clubs with a net addition of 34.5 million square feet of retail space).

In January 1993 Wal-Mart's reputation was assaulted when NBC-TV's *Dateline* news reported on child laborers in Bangladesh producing merchandise for Wal-Mart stores. The program showed children working for pennies per hour in a country that lacked child labor laws. The program further alleged that items made outside the United States were being sold under "Made in USA" labels as part of the company's "Buy American" campaign started in 1985. Glass appeared on the program saying that he did not know of any child exploitation by the company, but he apologized for some of the incorrect signage.

In April 1993 Wal-Mart expanded further upstream and introduced its private-label "Great Value," which included a line of 350 packaged food items. In the same year Wal-Mart purchased 91 Pace Membership Warehouse clubs from Kmart and converted the new units into Sam's Clubs. Concurrently, the formation of PriceCostco Inc., later renamed Costco Cos., signaled the emergence of Sam's Clubs' only viable rival—a competitor that would challenge the firm's dominance in the cash-and-carry market over the next decade.

Slowdown in the Mid-1990s Wal-Mart's double-digit comparable store sales rates began falling in 1994 and varied between 4 and 7 percent, which was closer to the retail industry average. The Wal-Mart discount store chain, which reached a peak of 1,995 units in 1996, was reduced to 1,921 units by 1998. Instead, the company staked its domestic future on the Wal-Mart Super Center chain, expanded from 34 units in 1993 to 441 units in 1998. Most of the new Super Centers—377 in total—were converted Wal-Mart discount stores, as the company sought the additional per store revenue that could be gleaned from selling groceries. Meanwhile, the Sam's Club chain was struggling and not as profitable as the company overall. As it attempted to turn this business around, Wal-Mart curtailed its expansion in the United States; only 17 more Sam's Clubs were opened between 1995 and 1998.

Wal-Mart's International Growth[3]

International sales accounted for approximately 22.3 percent of total company sales in fiscal year 2006. During 2006 Wal-Mart International opened 576 units in 12 countries and Puerto Rico. The international segment included several different retail formats and restaurants, including discount stores, super centers, and Sam's Clubs that operate outside the United States. Starting from scratch 14 years before, Wal-Mart International had grown into a $63 billion business. It was the fastest-growing part of Wal-Mart. Even subtracting one-time gains from acquisitions, it grew at nearly 12 percent, double the rate of Wal-Mart's American stores.

Overall, however, the international division's profitability lagged well behind that of domestic operations. The retail giant had struggled in countries including South Korea and Japan and had discovered that its formula for success—low prices, zealous inventory control and a large array of merchandise—did not translate directly to markets with their own discount chains and shoppers with different habits.

Wal-Mart's other international expansion targets also presented unique challenges. India did not permit foreign companies to set up stores there unless they sold only one brand. China's state-run union had tried to force Wal-Mart to set up unions at its 60 stores. In addition, China drafted rules to regulate large-scale shopping outlets, which impeded the expansion plans of foreign retailers.

Having already sold off loss-making operations in South Korea and Germany in 2006 and 2007, Wal-Mart's ambitions in Japan were also under scrutiny. Some of Wal-Mart's problems stemmed from hubris, a uniquely powerful American enterprise trying to impose its values around the world. Wal-Mart had worked diligently to overcome cultural problems and earn acceptable returns on its investments. The Wal-Mart brand carried less weight in foreign markets—70 percent of Wal-Mart's international sales come from outlets with names like Asda in Britain, Seiyu in Japan, or Bompreco in Brazil.

Wal-Mart's global ambitions now focused on Asia and Latin America. It sees India and China as the most promising markets to try to replicate the rapid growth it witnessed in the U.S. It has been opening stores in China, and recently received approval to open a liaison office in Bangalore, India.

Wal-Mart is also trying to integrate acquisitions with more sensitivity—a process that involves issues like deciding whether to consolidate multiple foreign headquarters and how aggressively to impose Wal-Mart's corporate culture on non-American employees.

Faced with lagging domestic sales, an aggressive international expansion ensued. Following its 1991 move into Mexico, Wal-Mart entered into the other North American Free Trade Agreement (NAFTA) market, Canada, three years later, when it purchased 122 Woolco stores from Woolworth Corporation. Over the next six years, Wal-Mart became the largest retailer in both Mexico and Canada and made additional entries into Puerto Rico, Argentina, and Brazil.

Brazil In Brazil, Wal-Mart opened only 25 stores in its first decade and struggled to compete against bigger local rivals. Then, in 2004, it bought Bompreco, giving it a presence in the country's poor, but fast-growing, northeast. Wal-Mart did not change the names of the stores from neighborhood grocers to large American-style hypermar-

kets. But with 295 stores in Brazil, in 2006, they ranked third in the market, after Carrefour of France and the market leader, CompanhiaBrasileira de Distribucao.

Japan The firm ventured into Japan and Korea in the late 1990s. Since taking a stake in Seiyu in 2002, the chain's struggling Japanese operations lost well over $1 billion. Just as worrying, sluggish sales suggest that Japanese shoppers, like their Korean and German counterparts, hadn't warmed up to the Wal-Mart way.

Korea In South Korea, Wal-Mart had only 16 stores—a small presence that contributed to its decision in 2006 to sell to a Korean discount chain. Many Koreans had never heard of Wal-Mart. In Seoul, a sprawling area of 10 million, there was only a single store. This lack of scale caused another problem that afflicted Wal-Mart in several countries—its inability to compete with established discounters, like the Aldi chain in Germany and E-Mart in Korea. In Korea, Wal-Mart's stores originally had taller racks than those of local rivals, forcing shoppers to use ladders or stretch for items on high shelves. Wal-Mart's utilitarian design—ceilings with exposed pipes—put off shoppers used to the decorated ceilings in E-Mart stores.

China Wal-Mart entered China in August 1996 with the opening of its first Super Center and Sam's Club in Shenzhen, near Hong Kong. As a harbinger of China's economic reform and the fastest-growing coastal city in China, Shenzhen proved to be the best location for Wal-Mart's investment. Four years later Wal-Mart had 28 stores and employed more than 15,000 associates in Shenzhen. Wal-Mart subsequently opened 26 additional joint venture stores including 21 Super Centers and 5 Sam's Club units in China's coastal cities.

Britain ASDA, Britain's best-value food and clothing superstore, became part of the Wal-Mart family in July 1999. The company had 247 stores and 21 depots across the United Kingdom employing 125,000 associates. The Wal-Mart name appeared on a U.K. store for the first time in 2000, when the first ASDA–Wal-Mart Super Center opened in Bristol. ASDA–Wal-Mart Super Centers brought a unique shopping experience to British customers, offering the best products of both organizations. By 2007 the company operated 23 ASDA–Wal-Mart Super Centers and 291 supermarkets throughout the U.K. ASDA accounting for 43 percent of Wal-Mart's international revenue.

Germany and Wal-Mart's First International "War"[4]

By the second millennium, Germany accounted for 15 percent of Europe's $2 trillion-a-year retail market. Yet it suffered from a shrinking percentage of consumer spending. In conditions of near oligopoly, the top five German retailers alone accounted for over 60 percent of market share. With average profits of 0.8 percent of sales, this was the least profitable retail market in the industrial world. Such lackluster profitability could be attributed in part to the family ownership of a majority of German retailers; zoning regulations that imposed severe limits on the construction of large-scale stores; the euro conversion on January 1, 2002, and subsequent confusion among consumers; and the apparent preponderance of price/value versus service/quality expectations held by much of the population.

The acquisition of the 21-unit Wertkauf hypermarket chain in Germany in December 1997 marked not only Wal-Mart's entry into Europe but also into the most competitive retail battleground in the world. The German chain had annual sales of $1.4 billion and was the eighth largest hypermarket operator in the country. The takeover of Spar and its 74 domestic locations (revenues: $1.1 billion) marked the second wave of Wal-Mart's attack. By many accounts, Wal-Mart Germany was not a success from its inception until the beginning of 2004. Pundits argued that the firm chose wisely with the Wertkauf acquisition but poorly with Spar. The latter, considered by Germans to be the weakest player in the market, posed significant brand and quality challenges from the beginning.[5] Knorr and Arndt claimed Wal-Mart Germany's operations had also suffered from:[6]

- A "hubris and clash of cultures" approach by management to labor relations.
- A failure to deliver on its legendary "we sell for less—always," "every day low prices," and "excellent service" value proposition.
- Bad publicity from its repeated infringement of some important German laws and regulations.
- Wal-Mart never established comfortable relations with its German labor unions.

After nine years of struggle, in summer of 2006, Wal-Mart sold its 85 stores to German rival Metro. After nearly a decade, Wal-Mart could not crack the deutsche market—failing to become the all-in-one shopping destination for Germans that it was for so many millions of Americans. The company took a $1 billion loss as Metro paid $100 million less for the Wal-Mart stores than the value of the real estate, unsold merchandise, and other physical assets. Family-owned discount retailers offered very low prices. German shoppers were frugal and demanding and regulations restricted store hours and other retailing basics. Wal-Mart's biggest global competitor, Carrefour SA of France, operated in 29 countries, but had steered clear of Germany.

Wal-Mart's failure in Germany was attributed to several missteps. Perhaps its most glaring was misjudging the German consumer and business culture. For instance, German Wal-Marts adopted the U.S. custom of bagging groceries, which many German consumers found distasteful because they didn't like strangers handling their food. Wal-Mart also imported its U.S.–style company ethic, which included strongly discouraging interoffice romances. Many employees found the code intrusive. The company also had repeated clashes with unions.

Just as important was Wal-Mart's apparent underestimation of the competition and its naivety in the market. They were the king of low prices in the United States, but were often undercut in Germany by local rivals such as Aldi and Lidl.

Wal-Mart also spent many years renovating the few stores it did have and adjusting its business model to Germany. In the end, to work efficiently, Wal-Mart would have had to invest massively to acquire more sites. Wal-Mart's decision to get out of Germany left its plans for Europe unclear. It owned the 315-store Asda chain in the United Kingdom. If Wal-Mart had amassed scale in Germany, it would have gained muscle to negotiate with European suppliers and gained a gateway into Eastern Europe.

The Global Retail Industry

The globalization of modern retail continues to accelerate. Since 2001, more than 49 retailers had entered 90 new markets. In 2005 alone, more than 30 "wave 2" companies—those that follow the primary entrants such as supermarkets—including do-it-yourself and apparel retailers, entered new markets. But acceleration does not equal success: Retailers left 17 markets in 2005.

Retailing is the second largest industry in the United States, comprising more than 530,000 companies, excluding new, used, and recreational motor vehicle parts dealers. According to the U.S. Census Bureau, these corporations produced around $3.8 trillion or $11,690 per capita in sales annually, making the U.S. retailing sector one of the largest in the world.

Retailing, the second largest industry in the United States, both in the number of establishments and number of employees, was also one of the largest worldwide. In 2005 the retail industry employed over 23 million Americans and generated more than $3 trillion in sales annually. Single-store businesses accounted for over 95 percent of all U.S. retailers, but generated less than 50 percent of all retail store sales. Wal-Mart was by far the largest retailing entity not only in the United States but also in the world, equaling the combined sales of the next four largest global players (see Exhibit 1). An unstable business environment, weak economic growth, and nervous consumers contributed to minimal growth among the world's 100 largest retailers.

The average growth rate for the top 100 retailers from 2001 to 2002 dropped to less than 4 percent, with both the "largest" and "smallest" operators struggling to replicate prior-year growth.[7] While Wal-Mart had held the top spot since 1990, there was significant movement among other leading players—both up and down the list—as tough competitive, political, and economic factors took their toll. Further, unlike in prior years, retailers in the U.K., not the United States, were the strongest performers overall.[8] Metro, Carrefour, and Royal Ahold were all focused on new store sales and continued expansion internationally while grappling with growth in existing markets.

As of January 2007, the retail industry was still fragmented globally with no single player yet able to prove it could dominate across several continents. Industry experts agreed retailers that could successfully develop China, Southeast Asia, and the former Soviet Republics (in that

Exhibit 1 Top 10 Retail Companies in the World, 2006

Rank 2005	Company	Country of Origin	Sales 2005 (in US $ millions)
1	Wal-Mart	United States	285,222
2	Carrefour	France	113,356
3	Home Depot	United States	81,511
4	Metro	Germany	67,908
5	Tesco	UK	67,883
6	Kroger	United States	56,434
7	Target	United States	51,271
8	Costco	United States	51,862
9	Sears Holdings	United States	49,124
10	Schwarz	Germany	1341

order) would reap long-term benefits for decades to come. It was also clear that traditional internationalization strategies that relied on "exports" (of products, processes, or services) across borders had not fared well in an environment characterized by small, immobile, and uninformed consumers. To succeed internationally, Wal-Mart would have to pick its way carefully. What vehicles—joint ventures, strategic alliances, franchising, shareholdings in local retailers, mergers, or acquisitions—and capabilities would it invest in?

The North American Retail Industry

U.S. retailing comprised more than 530,000 companies, excluding new, used, and recreational motor vehicle parts dealers. Consumer spending was the key component of the retail industry, accounting for more than two-thirds of the nation's economic activity. As a result, retail sales were an important factor in determining the strength of the economy. Target Corporation, the number two discounter in the United States, had carved out a niche by offering more upscale, fashionable merchandise than rivals Wal-Mart and struggling Kmart. Target had distinguished itself by employing a strategy that relied on exclusive private-label offerings from big name designers. The nation's number two discounter was number one when it came to corporate giving. Target topped the *Forbes* list of America's Most Philanthropic Companies in 2001, donating 2.5 percent of its 2000 income (nearly $86 million). By comparison, Wal-Mart gave away $116.5 million in 2001, less than 1 percent of its income in 2000.

In 2003 Kroger was the number one pure grocery chain in the United States. The grocery chain planned to spend $120 million by the end of 2004 to open as many as nine new stores and remodel older ones in Tennessee, where Wal-Mart was introducing its Neighborhood Market stores. Also in response to intense competition from Wal-Mart Super Centers, which captured 13.0 percent of

the U.S. grocery market in 2002 compared to Kroger's 7.2 percent share, Kroger had been cutting prices to hang onto customers. Wal-Mart operated Super Centers in more than half of Kroger's markets. Lured by the growing popularity of dollar stores, Kroger was experimenting with the concept in two of its Houston supermarkets.

During the same period, Sears was developing a freestanding off-mall format—Sears Grand—to compete directly with the big discounter chains by selling consumables, health and beauty aids, housewares, and toys, among other offerings. The first store (twice the size of an average Sears store) opened in Utah in September 2003. The second Sears Grand shop was set to open in Chicago in the spring of 2004, followed by a third in Las Vegas in the fall. (See Exhibit 2 for a financial comparison of these three North American competitors.)

The Wal-Mart Culture and Distinctive Competencies

As Wal-Mart continued to grow into new areas and develop new formats, much of its success was attributed to its corporate culture and distinctive competencies (see Appendix 4). Walton wanted all his managers and workers to have a hands-on approach to their jobs and to be totally committed to Wal-Mart's main goal, which he defined as total customer satisfaction. To motivate his employees, Walton created a strategic control system that gave employees at all levels continuous feedback about their performance and the company's.[9]

The culture pushed decision-making authority down to store managers, department managers, and individual employees. Wal-Mart was renowned for treating its employees well, but at the same time demanding commitment and excellent performance. This culture was backed up with profit-sharing and stock ownership plans for all employees,

Exhibit 2 The North American Competitors (in $ millions) 2005–2007

		2007	2006	2005
Target	Total revenue	59,490	52,620	46,839
	Net income	2,787	2,408	3,198
Sears	Total revenue	53,012	49,124	19,701
	Net income	1,490	858	1,106
Kroger	Total revenue	66,111	60,553	56,434
	Net income	1,115	958	−100

including associates, to make every employee "think and behave like an owner of the company." No wonder Wal-Mart had higher employee productivity, less shrinkage (employee theft), and lower costs than industry rivals.

The Wal-Mart Distinctive Competencies

As the number of stores grew, Wal-Mart pioneered the development of a hub-and-spoke distribution system, where central distribution warehouses were strategically located to serve clusters of stores. This system allowed Wal-Mart to rapidly replenish stock in its stores and to keep the amount of unproductive space to a minimum.

The results included higher sales per square foot and more rapid inventory turnover. This combination helped to increase store sales and drive down inventory and logistics costs (see Exhibit 3). The firm was also one of the first to utilize computer-based information systems to track in-store sales and transmit this information to suppliers. This information was used to determine pricing and stocking strategies that optimized inventory management. The combination of state-of-the art information systems and the hub-and-spoke distribution system allowed Wal-Mart to build the leanest supply chain in the industry.[10]

The firm's brand and market management, supply-chain management, and customer value focus distinguished it in the industry. These corporate abilities or distinctive competencies, coupled with locational assets and unique cultural attributes, served it well throughout the 1990s. Insiders wondered whether these historical strengths alone were sufficient to build a trillion-dollar enterprise over the next decade, with $200 to $500 billion in sales outside the Americas. Furthermore, how could Wal-Mart appease external stakeholders as its influence magnified? For example, concerns with Wal-Mart's purchasing practices resurfaced in December 2003.[11]

> There is no question that doing business with Wal-Mart can give a supplier a fast, heady jolt of sales and market share. But that fix can come with long-term consequences for the health of a brand and a business.

Resource	Industry Average Cost/Wal-Mart Cost (Percentage of sales)
Tangible: Store locations	0.3% Store rental space
Intangible: Brand reputation Employee loyalty	1.2% Advertising expense 1.1% Payroll expense 0.7% Shrinkage expense
Capabilities: Inbound logistics	1.2% Distribution expense

Total advantage: 4.5 percent*

Exhibit 3 Wal-Mart's Competitive Advantage

*Wal-Mart's cost advantage as a percentage of sales. Each percentage point advantage is worth $500 million in net income to Wal-Mart.

Source: Pankaj Ghemawat, "Wal-Mart Stores' Discount Operations," Harvard Business School case 9-387-018.

Wal-Mart is legendary for forcing its suppliers to redesign everything from their packaging to their computer systems. It is also legendary for quite straightforwardly telling suppliers what it will pay for their goods.

Many companies and their executives frankly admit that supplying Wal-Mart is like getting into the company version of basic training with an implacable army drill sergeant. The process may be unpleasant. But there can be some positive results.

Future Questions

CNN described the coming extinction of American malls as the "Death of an American Icon." In 2000 PricewaterhouseCoopers and the Center for the New Urbanism first identified "grey fields," or dying malls, as those with annual sales of less than $150 per square foot—less than a third of sales at successful malls. Their study found that 7 percent of existing regional malls qualified as grey fields, and another 12 percent were headed in that direction. Increasingly, these grey fields were being redeveloped into lifestyle centers or "main street centers," which mimicked traditional villages of the past—with lots of open-air space, attractive landscaping, outdoor sound systems, park benches, artistic fountains, and attractive building facades. Regardless of the fate of American malls, Wal-Mart and its rivals wondered:

- What would the retail industry look like by the year 2010?
- Would the economy return to the growth rates of the mid-1990s?
- Would consumers worry about inflation or deflation?
- Would aging baby boomers still be driving consumer spending or would they be tapped out by their overextended credit card debt and devastated retirement accounts?
- By 2010 would Wal-Mart take a larger share in existing product categories or leap into new categories like banking and auto retailing?

The five dominant trends that could alter the face of the retailing industry in the remaining years of the decade were:[12]

1. Removal of the "one size fits all" premise that would be replaced by a system in which individual retailers employed a more robust multi-format or portfolio strategy.
2. A very unique concept of "Wal-Mart always smiling" would be even more successful by 2010, with the company's continued focus on the customer shopping experience, customer care, customer intimacy, and customer value.
3. As consumers searched for greater shopping efficiency, their preferences would shift away from traditional supermarkets and discount department stores toward super centers. Some supermarkets would expand their one-stop shopping appeal while others would tap into emerging trends such as natural/organic, ethnic, gourmet, and health food products.
4. The days of mass-merchandised specialty chains with multitudes of outlets delivering the same narrow and deep assortment of goods to the market, regardless of location, would be over. Specialty retailers would manage a portfolio of different concepts, each operating a small chain of stores in order to address multiple market opportunities.
5. Customers would embrace technologies that gave them more control over the shopping process. These would include Web-enabled store kiosks that give shoppers access to a retailer's full inventory, wireless technology that provides shoppers with product information on handheld devices, smart carts that draw on shoppers' buying history to alert them to products and promotions, radio frequency identification (RFID)-enabled checkout where all items in a cart are scanned at once; and contactless payment solutions that use RFID-enabled smart cards or transponders.

Other Retail Industry Trends

By 2003 the consolidation wave that started in the United States had caught on in Europe too. With the largest retail space per capita, the U.S. market was a prime candidate for consolidation owing to the proliferation of retailers in the previous two decades that led to the paring down of margins and intense undercutting of prices. The inevitable shakeout was precipitated by Wal-Mart's takeover of many small retailers.

Wal-Mart's acquisition of the U.K. food retailer ASDA in 2002 marked the international entry of American retailers into the United Kingdom. Until then, U.S. retailers had concentrated on domestic expansion only. However, globalization had hit Europe much earlier and the French firm Carrefour had long ago struck roots in South America and Mexico. Similarly, Royal Ahold struck firm roots in the U.S. retail arena with its Stop & Shop chain and the takeover of the ailing Peapod.com.

Many retailers had started vending fuel adjacent to their outlets. This not only came as a boon to the time-starved customer but also provided an opportunity for retailers to cross-subsidize merchandise sales with fuel sales. A similar phenomenon happened at gasoline stations where convenience stores catered to the basic needs of customers. "Buying the product from the cheapest and most efficient source" was the retailer credo.

To reduce time in queues, retailers had given self-checkout authorization to customers. Initially, this was done only for frequent shoppers or loyalty cardholders. The reduction of cycle time (between ordering and physical arrival of the merchandise) was a critical cost driver in the retailing industry. Retailers looked for ways to cut inventories. The most common facilitator was an accurate demand and sales forecast as well as rapid replenishment.

Technology Trends

Enterprise integration, or linking all the different systems used by a retailer to provide seamless information flow and better resource management, was an important trend emerging in the retail industry.

Smart cards that contained detailed customer information provided a wealth of information to the retailer about customers' buying habits and patterns. Also, they helped in tailoring the offering to specific needs. They integrated many operations and one card could be used across locations and functions. To avoid the risk of obsolescence, many retail software vendors provided Web-based packages updated in real-time.

Radio frequency data communication had become a standard in the retail fulfillment industry. Handheld radio frequency devices provided an excellent tool to perform inventory tracking and order-picking activities.

Large retailers had relied on intranets and extranets for information sharing within the organization and with external entities, respectively. Extranets had long been a preferred way of carrying out electronic data interchange with suppliers. However, with the Internet becoming omnipresent, their efficacy would decrease, and virtual private networks that offered a secure pipeline for information flow using the Internet would become increasingly employed for the exchange of information.

Consumer Trends[13]

Single-serve, "easy-pour," and portable packaging had all been on the scene awhile. However, these were expected to become the norm for most products in addition to required enhancements in temperature-control, spill-proof, lifestyle, and alternative-usage packaging.

Obesity and the problems associated with it were expected to increase. Manufacturers and retailers would have to deal with this issue by offering healthier foods and increased information relating to health and nutrition. Products oriented toward wellness and an improved life would continue to emerge in numerous categories beyond the traditional health and beauty aid (HBA) and drug categories. These products made numerous claims and required significant communication with the consumer to ensure their success. This trend began with the aging population, but was fueled by manufacturers seeking any avenue available to develop and market new products ahead of the continued growth of private labels.

Shoppers continued to decrease the amount of time they spent on each shopping trip. Grocery shopping continued to be viewed as "need to do" instead of "want to do." As such, consumers desired to travel fewer aisles on any one shopping trip and ultimately spend less time in the store. The implications of these views would be continued modification of store layouts and limits on the absolute size of new stores built.

In the future, loyalty card programs and, more importantly, the processing of related data would be performed by third-party companies. These dedicated research firms focused on linking databases across industries. The result would be far more valuable marketing information, both within and outside the grocery industry. Due to the inability of most retailers to provide truly individualized services to loyalty cardholders, their future use would be questioned, if not eliminated, by some retailers and refocused by others. This trend would be exacerbated by consumer privacy concerns or plain indifference.

Wal-Mart's Future

In January 2007 Wal-Mart was still at the top of Fortune 500 list. By anyone's reckoning, it had dominated an industry for three decades and grown into one of the most influential corporate enterprises in history. To maintain its phenomenal growth in the future, it needed to sustain growth in the Americas and address development and profitability issues internationally.

With market saturation looming in the United States and the absence of any truly international retailer, how would Sam's successors allocate future resources to ensure Wal-Mart's global dominance across disparate global markets?

Endnotes

1. Wal-Mart Stores, Inc. 1999. *International Directory of Company Histories,* vol. 26 (St. James Press). Reproduced in Business and Company Resource Center, 2003 (Farmington Hills, MI: Gale Group), www.galenet.com/servlet/BCRC.
2. The material in this section is based on information from the official Wal-Mart Web site, www.walmart.com.
3. The material in this section comes largely from the official Wal-Mart Web site, www.walmart.com.
4. Knorr, A. & Arndt, A. 2003. Why did Wal-Mart fail in Germany? *IWIM,* University of Bremen, June 24.
5. *KPMG/EHI.* 2001. 15.
6. Knorr & Arndt, 2003. Why did Wal-Mart fail in Germany?: 18.
7. Retail Forward, comp., The top 100 retailers worldwide 2002.
8. "The world's largest retailers cannot expect a stable business environment going forward," commented Geoff Wissman, vice president with Retail Forward. "Slow economic recovery in the U.S. combined with weak economies in Japan, Latin America, and Western Europe, are forcing many retailers to seek alternative outlets for growth outside their home countries. . . . Retailers will find themselves battling for market share rather than relying on growing markets," Wissman stated. "The recent difficulties faced by some of the world's largest retailers—including Kmart, Royal Ahold, and Sears—reinforce the fact that retailers of any size can experience serious financial strain."
9. Sam Walton's approach to implementing Wal-Mart's strategy, in Walton, Sam. 1992. *Made in America.* New York: Doubleday.
10. The case "Wal-Mart's Mexican Adventure."
11. Fishman, Charles. 2003. The Wal-Mart you don't know (Why low prices have a high cost). *Fast Company,* December.
12. 2003, *Retail Merchandiser,* 43(5): 4.
13. The material in this section is provided in large part by MJH & Associates, July 2003.

Appendix 1A Fortune Rankings

Rank	Fortune 2003	Value (in $ millions)	Rank	Fortune 2007	Value (in $ millions)
1	Wal-Mart Stores	246,525	1	Wal-Mart Stores	351,139
2	General Motors	186,763	2	Exxon Mobil	347,254
3	ExxonMobil	182,466	3	General Motors	207,349
4	Ford Motor	163,630	4	Chevron	200,567
5	General Electric	131,698	5	ConocoPhillips	172,451
6	Citigroup	100,789	6	General Electric	168,307
7	ChevronTexaco	92,043	7	Ford Motor	160,126
8	International Business Machines	83,132	8	Citigroup	146,777
9	American International Group	67,723	9	Bank of America Corp.	117,017
10	Verizon Communications	67,625	10	American International Group	113,194
11	Altria Group	62,182	11	J.P. Morgan Chase & Co.	99,973
12	Conoco Phillips	58,394	12	Berkshire Hathaway	98,539
13	Home Depot	58,247	13	Verizon Communications	93,221
14	Hewlett-Packard	56,588	14	Hewlett-Packard	91,658
15	Boeing	54,069	15	International Business Machines	91,424
16	Fannie Mae	52,901	16	Valero Energy	91,051
17	Merck	51,790	17	Home Depot	90,837
18	Kroger	51,760	18	McKesson	88,050
19	Cardinal Health	51,136	19	Cardinal Health	81,895
20	McKesson	50,006	20	Morgan Stanley	76,688

Appendix 1B Wal-Mart Stores: Five-Year Financial Summary

Fiscal Year Ended January 31,	2007	2006	2005	2004	2003
	(in $ millions except per share data)				
Operating Results					
Net sales	344,992	308,945	281,488	252,792	226,479
Net sales increase (percentage)	11.7	9.8	11.4	11.6	12.6
Comparable store sales increase (percentage)	2	3	3	4	5
Cost of sales	264,152	237,649	216,832	195,922	175,769
Operating, selling, general and administrative expenses	64,001	55,739	50,178	43,877	39,178
Interest expense, net	1,529	1,178	980	825	930
Effective tax rate	33.6	33.1	34.2	34.4	34.9
Income from continuing operations	12,178	11,408	10,482	9,096	7,940
Net income	11,284	11,231	10,267	9,054	7,955
Per share of common stock:					
Income from continuing operations diluted	2.92	2.72	2.46	2.08	1.79
Net income, diluted	2.71	2.68	2.41	2.07	1.79
Dividends	0.67	0.6	0.52	0.36	0.3
Financial Position					
Current assets of continuing operations	46,588	43,146	37,913	33,548	28,867
Inventories	33,685	31,910	29,419	26,263	24,098
Property, equipment and capital lease assets, net	88,440	77,865	66,549	57,591	50,053
Total assets of continuing operations	151,193	135,624	117,139	102,455	90,229
Current liabilities of continuing operations	51,754	48,348	42,609	37,308	31,752
Long-term debt	27,222	26,429	20,087	17,088	16,545
Long-term obligations under capital leases	3,513	3,667	3,073	2,888	2,903
Shareholders' equity	61,573	53,171	49,396	43,623	39,461
Financial Ratios					
Current ratio	0.9	0.9	0.9	0.9	0.9
Return on assets	8.8	9.3	9.8	9.7	9.6
Return on shareholders' equity	22	22.9	23.1	22.4	21.8
Other Year-End Data					
Discount stores in the United States	1,075	1,209	1,353	1,478	1,568
Supercenters in the United States	2,256	1,980	1,713	1,471	1,258
Sam's Clubs in the United States	579	567	551	538	525
Neighborhood Markets in the United States	112	100	85	64	49
Units outside the United States	2,757	2,181	1,480	1,248	1,163

Source: Wal-Mart Annual Reports.

Appendix 2A   Number of Wal-Mart Stores

Year	2003	2004	2005	2006	2007
Store Type	Domestic	Domestic	Domestic	Domestic	Domestic
Regular Discount Store	1568	1478	1353	1209	1075
Super Centers	1258	1471	1713	1980	2256
Sam's Club	525	538	551	567	579
Neighborhood Markets	49	64	85	100	112
Total	3400	3551	3702	3856	4022

Source: Wal-Mart Annual Reports.

Appendix 2B   Wal-Mart's EBIT and Net Income, 1998–2007

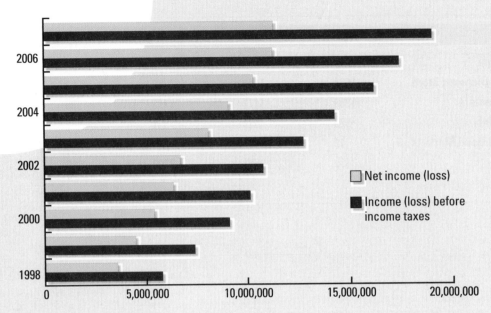

Source: Wal-Mart Annual Reports.

Appendix 3   Wal-Mart Timeline

1962	Sam Walton and his brother opened their first Wal-Mart Discount City in Rogers, Arkansas.
1969	Brothers had opened 18 Wal-Mart stores throughout Arkansas, Missouri, Kansas, and Oklahoma. They still owned 15 Ben Franklin franchises.
1970	Wal-Mart went public.
1972	Company was listed on the New York Stock Exchange for the first time.
1976	The Waltons phased out Ben Franklin Stores.
1977	The company made its first significant acquisition when it bought 16 Mohr-Value stores in Missouri and Illinois.
1977	Based on data from the previous five years, *Forbes* ranked the nation's discount and variety stores. Wal-Mart ranked first in return on equity, return on capital, sales growth, and earnings growth.
1978	Wal-Mart began operating its own pharmacy, auto service center, and jewelry divisions, and acquired Hutchinson Wholesale Shoe Co.
1979	With 276 stores in 11 states, sales rose to $1.25 billion.
1983	The company opened its first three Sam's Wholesale Clubs and began its expansion into markets in larger towns.
1985	"Buy American" program was launched.
1987	Wal-Mart's first Hypermart USA store was opened.
1987	Prices were reduced as much as 40 percent below full retail level; sales volume averaged $1 million per week.
1987	100,000 independent representatives initiated a public campaign to fight Wal-Mart's effort to remove them from the selling process, claiming that their elimination jeopardized a manufacturer's right to choose how it sells its products.
1988	Concentrated in the South and Midwest, Wal-Mart operated in 24 states.
1990	The first stores opened in California, Nevada, North Dakota, South Dakota, Pennsylvania, and Utah.
1990	Wal-Mart agreed to sell its nine convenience store–gas station outlets to Conoco Inc.
1990	Acquired the McLane Company, Inc., a distributor of grocery and retail products based in Temple, Texas.
1991	A new store brand, Sam's American Choice, was introduced.
1991	The company owned 148 Sam's Clubs.
1992	April 5: Founder Sam Walton died.
1992	The company opened 150 new Wal-Mart stores and 60 Sam's Clubs. Some of these stores represented a change in policy for the company, opening near big cities with large populations.
1992	Wal-Mart entered into a joint venture with Cifra in Mexico.
1993	A television show revealed child laborers in Bangladesh producing merchandise for Wal-Mart for five cents an hour. The program further alleged that foreign-made products were being sold under "Made in USA" labels.
1993	Wal-Mart introduced another private label called Great Value and channeled the proceeds from its American Choice label into the Competitive Edge Scholarship Fund.
1993	Wal-Mart's 1,914 stores included 40 Super Centers in 45 states and Puerto Rico, 208 Sam's Clubs in 42 states, and four Hypermart USAs. Retailers Dayton Hudson, Kmart, and Meijer complained about Wal-Mart's misleading price comparisons.
1994	Purchased 122 Woolco stores in Canada from Woolworth Corporation.

(continued)

(continued)

1994	Wal-Mart signed an agreement with the State of Michigan promising various changes in the way it compares prices to those of its competitors.
1994	Announced plans to expand into Argentina and Brazil.
1994	A joint venture was formed to open three to four stores in Hong Kong and to operate discount stores in China.
1995	David Glass received *Chief Executive* magazine's 1995 Chief Executive of the Year Award.
1996	Tested the sale of stock items on the Internet.
1996	Wal-Mart opened its first Super Center and Sam's Club in Shenzhen, China.
1997	Wal-Mart entered Europe for the first time when it acquired the 21-unit Wertkauf hypermarket chain in Germany.
1998	In an effort to accelerate growth, Wal-Mart began testing a new format, the Wal-Mart Neighborhood Market.
1998	Opened 32 Super Center stores, bringing the total number in operation to 542; opened two stores in New Hampshire. Operations spanned 29 states.
1998	Wal-Mart entered Korea through its acquisition and conversion of four Makro stores.
1998	A Wal-Mart expansion under a franchise agreement into a troubled Indonesia appeared to have stalled.
1999	Purchased the 230-store ASDA Group PLC, the third-largest food retailer in the United Kingdom. Named one of the Most Admired Companies in America by *Fortune.*
2000	Glass stepped down as CEO and president, and was succeeded by H. Lee Scott, Jr.
2000	Became the largest retailer in Mexico and acquired full ownership of 194 stores and 205 restaurants from its former partner Cifra SA.
2000	Became union-free in North America and converted the last of its remaining Hypermarket USA stores to a Wal-Mart Super Center.
2002	Wal-Mart purchased a 34 percent stake in Seiyu, Ltd., a leading Japanese retailer. Seiyu operated over 400 supermarkets in Japan and employed 30,000 associates.
2002	When fiscal year sales reached $220 billion, Wal-Mart became the largest company in the world.
2002	Planned to invest $2 billion in international expansion.
2003	Was announced number 1 on *Fortune* magazine's annual survey of Most Admired Companies in America.
2004	Wal-Mart was presented the Corporate Patriotism Award, which is presented to a company that exhibits exceptional dedication to raising awareness and support of U.S. service members and their families.
2005	Acquired Sonae Distribuicao Brasil S.A. (Sonae), a retail operation in Southern Brazil consisting of 139 hypermarkets, supermarkets, and warehouse units. The purchase price was approximately $720 million.
2005	In McKinney, Texas, and Aurora, Colorado, Wal-Mart creates experimental stores that save energy, conserve natural resources, and reduce pollution.
2006	Wal-Mart disposed of its South Korean retail business to Shinsegae Co. and its German retail business to Metro AG.
2006	Announced the launch of the new and improved Walmart.com.

Appendix 4   Sam's Rules for Building a Business

Sam's 10 Rules for Building a Business

People often ask, "What is Wal-Mart's secret to success?" In response to this ever-present question, Sam Walton compiled a list of 10 key factors that unlock the mystery in his 1992 book *Made in America.* These factors are known as "Sam's Rules for Building a Business."

Rule 1: Commit to Your Business. Believe in it more than anybody else. I think I overcame every single one of my personal shortcomings by the sheer passion I brought to my work. I don't know if you're born with this kind of passion, or if you can learn it. But I do know you need it. If you love your work, you'll be out there every day trying to do it the best you possibly can, and pretty soon everybody around will catch the passion from you—like a fever.

Rule 2: Share Your Profits with all Your Associates, and Treat Them as Partners. In turn, they will treat you as a partner, and together you will all perform beyond your wildest expectations. Encourage your Associates to hold a stake in the company. Offer discounted stock, and grant them stock for their retirement. It's the single best thing we ever did.

Rule 3: Motivate Your Partners. Money and ownership alone aren't enough. Constantly, day by day, think of new and more interesting ways to motivate and challenge your partners.

Rule 4: Communicate Everything You Possibly Can to Your Partners. The more they know, the more they'll understand. The more they understand, the more they'll care. Once they care, there's no stopping them.

Rule 5: Appreciate Everything Your Associates Do for the Business. A paycheck and a stock option will buy one kind of loyalty. But all of us like to be told how much somebody appreciates what we do for them. We like to hear it often, and especially when we have done something we're really proud of. Nothing else can quite substitute for a few well-chosen, well-timed, sincere words of praise.

Rule 6: Celebrate Your Successes. Find some humor in your failures. Don't take yourself so seriously. Loosen up, and everybody around you will loosen up. Have fun. Show enthusiasm—always.

Rule 7: Listen to Everyone in Your Company. And figure out ways to get them talking. The folks on the front lines—the ones who actually talk to the customer—are the only ones who really know what's going on out there. You'd better find out what they know. This really is what total quality is all about.

Rule 8: Exceed Your Customers' Expectations. If you do, they'll come back over and over. Give them what they want—and a little more. Let them know you appreciate them. Make good on all your mistakes, and don't make excuses—apologize.

Rule 9: Control Your Expenses Better than Your Competition. This is where you can always find the competitive advantage. For 25 years running—long before Wal-Mart was known as the nation's largest retailer—we ranked No. 1 in our industry for the lowest ratio of expenses to sales.

Rule 10: Swim Upstream. Go the other way. Ignore the conventional wisdom. If everybody else is doing it one way, there's a good chance you can find your niche by going in exactly the opposite direction.

Other Important Rules and Policies

The Sundown Rule: One Sunday morning, Jeff, a pharmacist at a Wal-Mart store in Harrison, Arkansas, received a call from his store. A store associate informed him that one of his pharmacy customers, a diabetic, had accidentally dropped her insulin down her garbage disposal. Knowing that a diabetic without insulin could be in grave danger, Jeff immediately rushed to the store, opened the pharmacy and filled the customer's insulin prescription. This is just one of many ways your local Wal-Mart store might honor what is known by our Associates as the Sundown Rule.

The Ten-Foot Rule: One of Wal-Mart's secrets to customer service is our "10-foot attitude," handed down to us by Wal-Mart Founder, Sam Walton. During his many store visits, he encouraged associates to take a pledge with him: ". . . I want you to promise that whenever you come within 10 feet of a customer, you will look him in the eye, greet him, and ask him if you can help him."

Pricing Policy: Sam's adherence to this pricing philosophy was unshakable, as one of Wal-Mart's first store managers recalls:

> Sam wouldn't let us hedge on a price at all. Say the list price was $1.98, but we had paid only 50 cents. Initially, I would say, "Well, it's originally $1.98, so why don't we sell it for $1.25?" And, he'd say, "No. We paid 50 cents for it. Mark it up 30 percent, and that's it. No matter what you pay for it, if we get a great deal, pass it on to the customer." And of course that's what we did.

Source: The official Wal-Mart Web site, www.walmart.com.

Case 32   FreshDirect: Delivering The Goods?*

With a bold promise on their 2007 Web site entry page Fresh-Direct claimed, "Our food is fresh, our customers are spoiled. . . . Order on the web today and get next-day delivery of the best food at the best price, exactly the way you want it, with 100% satisfaction guaranteed."[1] Operating out of its production center in Long Island City, Queens, Fresh-Direct offered online grocery shopping and delivery service to selected zip codes in Manhattan, Queens, Brooklyn, Nassau County, Riverdale, Westchester, and New Jersey. FreshDirect also offered pick-up at its Queen's Long Island City facility, as well as corporate service to selected delivery zones in Manhattan, and summer service to the Hamptons on Long Island. When it was launched in July 2001 by Joseph Fedele and Jason Ackerman, FreshDirect pronounced to the New York area that it was "the new way to shop for food." This was a bold statement given that the previous decade had witnessed the demise of numerous other online grocery ventures. However, the creators of FreshDirect were confident in the success of their business because their entire operation had been designed to deliver one simple promise to grocery shoppers: "higher quality at lower prices."

While this promise was an extremely common tagline used within and outside the grocery business, FreshDirect had integrated numerous components into its system to give real meaning to these words. Without a retail location, FreshDirect didn't have to pay expensive rent for a retail space. To offer the highest-quality products to its customers, FreshDirect had created a state-of-the-art production center and staffed it with expert personnel. The 300,000-square-foot production facility located in Long Island City was composed of 12 separate temperature zones, ensuring that each piece of food was kept at its optimal temperature for ripening or preservation—kept colder and cleaner than in any retail environment.

Further quality management was achieved by an SAP manufacturing software system that controlled every detail of the facility's operations. All of the thermometers, scales, and conveyor belts within the facility were connected to a central command center. Each specific setting was programmed into the system by an expert from the corresponding department, including everything from the ideal temperature for ripening a cantaloupe to the amount of flour that went into French bread. The system was also equipped with a monitoring alarm that alerted staff to any deviation from the programmed settings.

Another quality control element that had been made an integral part of the FreshDirect facility was an extremely high standard for cleanliness, health, and safety. The facility itself was kept immaculately clean and all

food-preparation areas and equipment were bathed in antiseptic foam at the end of each day. Incoming and outgoing food was tested in FreshDirect's in-house laboratory, which ensured the facility adhered to USDA guidelines and the Hazard Analysis and Critical Control Point food safety system, and that all food passing through Fresh-Direct met the company's high safety standards.[2]

System efficiency had been the key to FreshDirect's ability to offer its high-quality products at such low prices. FreshDirect's biggest operational design component for reducing costs had been the complete elimination of the middleman. Instead of going through an intermediary, both fresh and dry products were ordered from individual growers and producers, and shipped directly to FreshDirect's production center where FreshDirect's expert staff prepared them for purchase. In addition, FreshDirect did not accept any slotting allowances.[3] This unique relationship with growers and producers allowed FreshDirect to enjoy reduced purchase prices from its suppliers, enabling them to pass even greater savings on to their customers.

Each department of the facility, including the coffee roaster, butcher, and bakery, was staffed by carefully selected experts, enabling FreshDirect to offer premium fresh coffees (roasted on site), pastries and breads (baked on site), deli, cheese, meats (roast beef dry-aged on site), and seafood. Perishable produce was their specialty—by buying locally as much as possible and using the best sources of the season, they were able to bring food the shortest distance from farms, dairies, and fisheries to the customer's table.

FreshDirect catered to the tastes of its Manhattan clientele by offering a full line of heat-and-serve meals prepared in the FreshDirect kitchen by New York executive chef Michael Stark (formerly of Tribeca Grill) and his team. Partnering with chef Terrance Brennan of New York's French-Mediterranean restaurant Picholine, FreshDirect also sold "restaurant-worthy" four-minute meals. Made from raw ingredients delivered in a "steam valve system" package, these complete meals were not frozen, but delivered ready to finish cooking in a microwave.

The proximity of FreshDirect's processing facility to its Manhattan customer base was also a critical factor in its cost-effective operational design. The processing center's location in Long Island City put approximately 4 million people within a 10-mile radius of the FreshDirect facility, allowing the firm to deliver a large number of orders in a short amount of time.[4] Further cost controls had been implemented through FreshDirect's order and delivery protocols. Products in each individual order were packed in boxes, separated by type of item (meat, seafood, and produce packed together; dairy, deli, cheese, coffee, and tea packed together; grocery, specialty and nonrefrigerated product packed together), and placed on a computerized conveyor system to be sorted, assembled, and packed into a refrigerated truck for delivery.

---

* This case was prepared by Professor Alan B. Eisner of Pace University, Professor Pauline Assenza of Manhattanville College, Professor Noushi Rahman, and graduate student Keeley Townsend of Pace University as a basis for class discussion rather than to illustrate either effective or ineffective handling of an administrative situation. Copyright © 2004, 2007 Alan B. Eisner.

As of 2007, orders had to be a minimum of $50.00 with a delivery charge between $4.99 and $9.99 per order, depending on order dollar amount and delivery location. Delivery was made by one of FreshDirect's trucks and was available only during a prearranged two-hour window on weekdays from 2:00 p.m. to 11:30 p.m. and all day, starting at 7:30 a.m., on the weekends.

Competing with other online grocers, specialty gourmet/gourmand stores in Manhattan, and high-end chain supermarkets like Whole Foods, Trader Joe's, and Fairway, FreshDirect was trying to woo the sophisticated New Yorker with an offer of quality, delivered door-to-door, at a price more attractive than others in the neighborhood. Operating in the black for the first time in 2005,[5] by choosing to stay a private company, and expanding gradually, FreshDirect's owners hoped to turn a daily profit, steadily recovering the estimated $60 million start-up costs, silencing critics, and winning converts.[6]

Founding Partners

FreshDirect was launched in July 2001. Cofounder and former Chief Executive Officer Joseph Fedele was able to bring a wealth of experience with New York City's food industry to FreshDirect. In 1993 he co-founded Fairway Uptown, a 35,000-foot supermarket located on West 133rd Street in Harlem. Many critics originally questioned the success of a store in that location, but Fairway's low prices and quality selection of produce and meats made it a hit with neighborhood residents, as well as many downtown and suburban commuters.

Current Vice Chairman and Chief Financial Officer Jason Ackerman had gained exposure to the grocery industry as an investment banker with Donaldson Lufkin & Jenrette, where he specialized in supermarket mergers and acquisitions. Fedele and Ackerman first explored the idea of starting a large chain of fresh-food stores, but realized maintaining a high degree of quality would be impossible with a large enterprise. As an alternative, they elected to pursue a business that incorporated online shopping with central distribution. Using the failure of Webvan, the dot-com delivery service that ran through $830 million in five years of rapid expansion as their example of what not to do, Fedele and Ackerman planned to start slow, use off-the-shelf software, an automated delivery system, and pay attention to details such as forming relationships with key suppliers and micromanaging quality control.[7]

FreshDirect acquired the bulk of its $100 million investment from several private sources, with a small contribution coming from the State of New York. By locating FreshDirect's distribution center within the state border, and promising to create at least 300 new permanent, full-time, private-sector jobs in the state, FreshDirect became eligible for a $500,000 training grant from the Empire State Development Jobs Now Program. As its name implied, the purpose of the Jobs Now program was to create new, immediate job opportunities for New Yorkers.

CEO Successions

Although the press was mostly positive about FreshDirect's opportunities, growth and operational challenges remained. In the words of an ex-senior executive of FreshDirect, "The major problem seems to be constant change in Senior Management. I think they are now on their 4th CEO."[8] FreshDirect co-founder Joseph Fedele had remained CEO until January 2004, when cofounder Jason Ackerman succeeded him in that position. Since then, FreshDirect had experienced multiple CEO changes. Jason Ackerman stayed as CEO of FreshDirect for a little over seven months when Dean Furbush succeeded him in that position in September 2004. The tenure of Dean Furbush lasted a little over two years. Steve Michaelson, president since 2004, replaced him as the CEO of FreshDirect in January 2007.[9] Ackerman remained Vice Chairman and Chief Financial Officer. In 2007 it was reported that original CEO Joe Fedele was planning a new food retailing business.[10]

Business Plan

While business started out relatively slow, Fedele had hoped to capture around 5 percent of the New York grocery market, with projected revenues of about $100 million in the first year and $225 million by 2004. As of March 2003, FreshDirect had reached the milestone of 2,000 orders a day and was attracting around 3,000 new customers a day, for a total customer base of around 40,000.[11] FreshDirect service was originally slated for availability citywide by the end of 2002. However, in order to maintain its superior service and product quality, FreshDirect had chosen to slowly expand its service area. By the Spring of 2007 FreshDirect had delivery available to selected zip codes and neighborhoods throughout Manhattan and as far away as Westchester and the Hamptons on Long Island (in the summer only).

The company had employed a relatively low-cost marketing approach, which originally consisted mainly of billboards, public relations, and word of mouth to promote its products and services. In 2003 FreshDirect hired Trumpet, an ad agency that promoted FreshDirect as a better way to shop by emphasizing the problems associated with traditional grocery shopping. For example, one commercial stressed the unsanitary conditions in a supermarket by showing a grocery shopper bending over a barrel of olives as she sneezed, getting an olive stuck in her nose, and then blowing it back into the barrel. The advertisement ended with the question, "Where's your food been?" Another ad showed a checkout clerk morph into an armed robber, demand money from the customer, and then morph back into a friendly checkout clerk once the money was received. The ad urged viewers to "stop getting robbed at the grocery store."[12] As of 2007, FreshDirect enlisted celebrity endorsements from New York City personalities such as film director Spike Lee, actress Cynthia Nixon, former mayor Ed Koch, supermodel Paulina Porizkova, and chef Bobby Flay.[13]

Operating Strategy

FreshDirect's operating strategy had employed a make-to-order philosophy, eliminating the middleman in order to create an efficient supply chain.[14] By focusing its energy on providing produce, meat, seafood, baked goods, and coffees that were made to the customer's specific order, FreshDirect offered its customers an alternative to the standardized cuts and choices available at most brick-and-mortar grocery stores. This strategy had created a business model that was unique within the grocery business community. A typical grocery store carried about 25,000 packaged goods, which accounted for around 50 percent of its sales, and about 2,200 perishable products, which accounted for the other 50 percent of sales. In contrast, FreshDirect offered around 5,000 perishable products, accounting for about 75 percent of its sales, but only around 3,000 packaged goods, which comprised the remaining 25 percent of sales.[15]

While this stocking pattern enabled a greater array of fresh foods, it limited the number of brands and available sizes of packaged goods, such as cereal, crackers, and laundry detergent. However, FreshDirect believed customers would accept a more limited packaged good selection in order to get lower prices, as evidenced in the success of wholesale grocery stores, which offered bulk sales of limited items. Jason Ackerman identified the ideal FreshDirect customers as those who bought their bulk staples from Costco on a monthly basis and bought everything else from FreshDirect on a weekly basis.[16]

FreshDirect's Web site

FreshDirect's Web site not only offered an abundance of products to choose from, but also provided a broad spectrum of information on the food that was sold and the manner in which it was sold (see Exhibit 1). Web surfers could

Exhibit 1 FreshDirect Web site

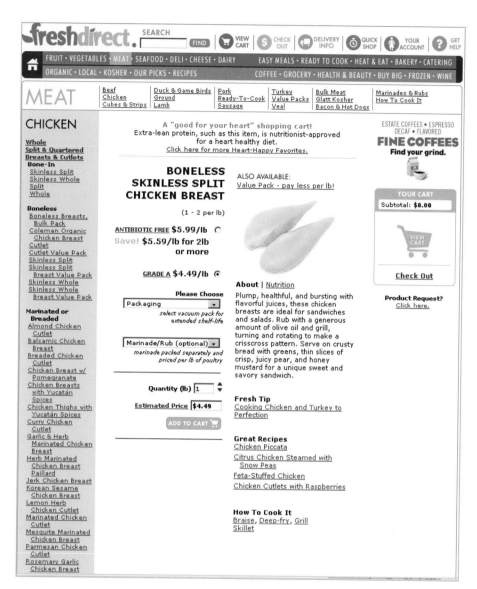

Exhibit 2 Example of FreshDirect Meat Selection Options

take a pictorial tour of the FreshDirect facility; get background information on the experts who managed each department; get nutritional information on food items; compare produce or cheese based on taste, price, and usage; specify the thickness of meat orders and opt for one of several marinades or rubs (see Exhibit 2); search for the right kind of coffee based on taste preferences; and read nutritional information for a variety of fully prepared meals. A large selection of recipes was available depending on the items chosen.

For example, if you wanted to purchase chicken, you were first asked to choose from breasts & cutlets, cubes & strips, ground, legs & thighs, specialty parts, split & quartered, whole, or wings. Once your selection was made—let's say you chose Breasts & Cutlets—you were given further

options based on your preference for skin, bone, and thickness. The final selection step offered you a choice of rubs and marinades, including teriyaki, sweet & sour, garlic rosemary, poultry seasoning, lemon herb rub, and salt & pepper rub. Throughout, the pages offered nutritional profiles of each cut of meat as well as tips for preparation and storage.

FreshDirect employed several different delivery models. Customers within the city were attracted to the FreshDirect service because it eliminated the need to carry groceries for possibly a substantial distance from the closest grocery store, or to deal with trying to park a car near their apartment to unload their purchases. Orders made by customers within the city were delivered directly to their homes by a FreshDirect truck during a prearranged two-hour delivery window.

Exhibit 3 FreshDirect at the Office

Suburban customers were serviced in a slightly different manner. Many suburban customers worked where corporations in the Tri-State area could arrange for depot drop off in the office parking lot, creating a central delivery station. FreshDirect would send a refrigerated truck, large enough to hold 500 orders, to these key spots during designated periods of time. Suburbanites could then exit their office building, go to their cars, swing by the FreshDirect truck, pick up their order, and head home. FreshDirect could also provide delivery to the parking lot of football or concert events to provide for tailgate or picnic needs. In addition to delivery, FreshDirect allowed customers to pick up their orders directly from the processing center. Orders were ready at the pickup desk within five to ten minutes after they were called in.

Business customers in Manhattan could also order for delivery at the office. Chef-prepared breakfast and luncheon catering platters, or restaurant-quality individual meals were available for business meetings and upscale events. FreshDirect provided dedicated corporate account managers and customer service representatives for these corporate clients, however FreshDirect only provided delivery, not set-up and platter arrangement services. Corporate delivery minimum order was $60, and delivery costs were $14.99 (see Exhibit 3).

The Retail Grocery Industry

In the United States in 2007, according to the U.S. Department of Commerce, supermarket chains made almost $500 billion in sales. The typical supermarket store carried

Exhibit 4   **2006 Top 10 North American Food Retailers**

Supermarket Chain	Stores	2006 Sales (In $ billions)	Comments
Wal-Mart Super Centers	2,981	$232.9	Includes Sam's Clubs
Kroger	4,276	66.1	Includes jewelry, 5% of TTL $
Costco Wholesale Corp.	458	59.0	Groceries were $36.6B
Safeway	1,767	40.5	Based in California
Supervalu	2,567	37.4	1,124 Albertson's stores
Loblaw Cos.	1,072	26.5	Based in Toronto
Ahold USA	827	24.0	Stop & Shop, Giant Foods
Publix Super Markets	885	21.7	Based in Florida
C&S Wholesale Grocers	0	19.4	Supplies products to above
Delhaize America	1,544	17.3	Food Lion, Hannaford Bros.

Source: *Supermarket News*, http://supermarketnews.com/top75/.

an average of 45,000 items, averaged just under 49,000 square feet in size, and averaged just over $18 million in sales annually.[17] The top 10 supermarket chains in the United States commanded a large amount of the total grocery industry business (see Exhibit 4).

The supermarket business had traditionally been a low-margin business with net profits of only 1 to 2 percent of revenues. Store profits depended heavily on creating a high volume of customer traffic and rapid inventory turnover, especially for perishables such as produce and fresh meat. Competitors had to operate efficiently to make money, so tight control of labor costs and product spoilage was essential. Online grocery retailers, like FreshDirect, because of the flexibility of information control, automated order fulfillment, and reduced real estate costs, could potentially have operating margins of up to 10 percent, rather than the 3 to 4 percent of traditional supermarkets.[18] Because capital investment costs were modest—involving mainly the construction of distribution centers and stores—it was not unusual for supermarket chains to realize 15 to 20 percent returns on invested capital.

The Online Grocery Segment

The online-grocery shopping business was still in the early stages of development in 2004, with this segment accounting for less than 1 percent of total grocery sales. Total online sales in 2004 were about $2.4 billion, but were expected to reach $6.5 billion by 2008.[19] In 2006 the numbers were expected to reach over $4.2 billion and double by 2010, but the five million people who shopped online for groceries still represented only 2 percent of the online population.[20]

Online grocery shopping had been slow to catch on, and industry newcomers had encountered high start-up and operating costs. Sales volumes and profit margins remained too small to cover the high costs. The problem, according to industry analysts, was that consumers had been largely disappointed in the service, selection, and prices they had gotten from industry members. This, coupled with the extensive investment needed in warehousing, fulfillment and inventory control, meant that the "pure play" e-grocery business models were risky. There was a belief that better success would come from those traditional grocery retailers that chose to venture online.[21]

However, some expected online grocery sales to grow at a rapid pace as companies improved their service and selection, personal computer penetration of households rose, and consumers became more accustomed to making purchases online.[22] An article in *Computer Bits* examined the customer base for online grocers, looking specifically at the types of consumers who would be likely to shop online and the kinds of home computer systems that were required for online shopping. An Andersen Consulting report, cited in *Computer Bits,* identified six major types of online shoppers (see Exhibit 5) and estimated that by the end of 2007, 15 to 20 million households would order their grocers online.[23] A MARC Group study concluded, "Consumers who buy groceries online are likely to be more loyal to their electronic supermarkets, spend more per store 'visit,' and take greater advantage of coupons and premiums than traditional customers."[24]

One of the problems with online grocery shopping was that consumers were extremely price sensitive when it came to buying groceries, and the prices of many

Types of Online Shoppers	Comments
Traditionals	Might be an older technology-avoider or simply a shopper who likes to sniff-test their own produce and eyeball the meat selection.
Responsibles	Feed off the satisfaction of accomplishing this persistent to-do item.
Time Starved	Find the extra costs associated with delivery fees or other markups a small price to pay for saving them time.
New Technologists	Use the latest technology for any and every activity they can, because they can.
Necessity Users	People with physical or circumstantial challenges that make grocery shopping difficult. Likely to be the most loyal group of shoppers.
Avoiders	Dislike the grocery shopping experience for a variety of reasons.

Source: Andersen Consulting study cited in Anderson, S. 2001. Is online grocery shopping for you? *Computer Bits*, April 11.

online grocers were above those at supermarkets. Shoppers, in many cases, were unwilling to pay extra to online grocers for the convenience of home delivery. Consumer price sensitivity meant that online grocers had to achieve a cost structure that would allow them to (1) price competitively, (2) cover the cost of selecting items in the store and delivering individual grocery orders, and (3) have sufficient margins to earn attractive returns on their investment. Some analysts estimated that to be successful, online grocers had to do 10 times the volume of a traditional grocer.[25]

Potential Competitors in the Online Grocery Segment

When online grocers started appearing within the industry, many established brick-and-mortar grocers began offering online shopping in an attempt to maintain and expand their customer base. Two basic models had been used for online order fulfillment: (1) to pick items from the shelves of existing stores within the grocer's chain, and (2) to build special warehouses dedicated to online orders. The demand for home delivery of groceries had been increasing, but in many market areas the demand had not yet reached a level that would justify the high cost of warehouses dedicated to the fulfillment of online orders.[26]

Safeway began an ambitious online grocery venture by establishing Grocery Works, an online shopping system that included a series of warehouses dedicated to filling online orders. Unfavorable returns forced Safeway to reevaluate its system, and it eventually chose to form a partnership with Tesco, a U.K.-based grocer. Tesco filled its online orders from the shelves of local stores in close proximity to the customer's home. Safeway and Tesco worked together on GroceryWorks in Portland, Oregon, where they received a positive initial response from customers.[27]

The craze over health food had created room in the grocery industry for organic food suppliers to enter as an attractive substitute to traditional groceries. When asked what kept him up at night, Fresh Direct's then CEO Dean Furbush said that Whole Foods or Trader Joes moving into a Freshdirect neighborhood was his biggest threat as that hurt Fresh Direct the most. Fresh Direct has focused on organic foods to respond to the threats of Whole foods and other health food stores.

Whole Foods, the Austin, Texas–based supermarket chain with the organic health food focus, had already threatened FreshDirect's sales in Manhattan. Trader Joe's, another specialty food retailer, was also opening a store in downtown Union Square, prime territory for FreshDirect.[28] Although commentators had believed there was enough room for all, including the street farm markets, Fresh-Direct had focused on organic foods to respond to the threats of Whole Foods and other specialty food stores.[29] With the shift among some customers to pay attention to local, sometimes organic suppliers, FreshDirect highlighted its support of and partnership with the local companies who provided produce, poultry, fish, cheese, milk, eggs, and specialties such as wine. (Exhibit 6). However, its efforts have been inconsistent in that area. For example, in order to facilitate shoppers and checkout operators to distinguish between organic and nonorganic produce, Fresh Direct wraps them in plastic, which in itself is not organic. Fresh Direct Chairman Jeff Turner recognized that such an approach seemed incongruous.[30]

Rivals in the NYC Online Grocery Segment—YourGrocer.com

FreshDirect's most geographically significant competitor in the online grocery industry was YourGrocer.com (see Exhibit 7 and Exhibit 8). YourGrocer was launched in New

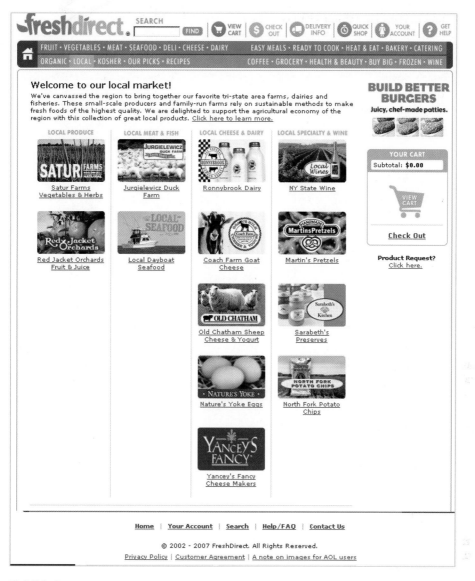

Exhibit 6 FreshDirect Local Market Offerings

York City in 1998 with the goal of being the leading online grocery service for the New York metropolitan area. By November 2001 the company ran out of money and was forced to shut down. In the spring of 2002 new capital resources were found and the company reopened for business. However, the second time around YourGrocer's approach was a little different.

YourGrocer was created with a bulk-buying strategy, believing that customers would order large, economical quantities of goods from the Web site and the company would make home deliveries in company trucks. During YourGrocer's first life, the ambitious business plan covered a large service area and included the acquisition of another online grocery company, NYCGrocery.com.[31]

But the business plan was modified in the second life. The company reduced the size of its staff, got rid of warehouses, decided to rent instead of owning its delivery vans, and scaled down its delivery routes.[32] Nassau County, and New Jersey were eliminated from the service area, leaving only Manhattan, the Bronx, Brooklyn, Queens, Rockland, Westchester County, and Fairfield County (Connecticut).

YourGrocer offered a limited selection of items that could only be purchased in bulk. Deliveries were made in varied time slots, depending on the customer's location in the New York area. There was a $75 minimum order with a $9.95 delivery charge (see Exhibit 9 and Exhibit 10).

Exhibit 7 Profiles of Selected Online Grocers, 2007

Name	Area Covered	Minimum Order	Delivery Charge	Delivery Method	Specialization
FreshDirect	Manhattan, Queens, Brooklyn, Nassau County, Riverdale, Westchester, New Jersey	$50	$4.99–9.99 depending on order size & destination; tipping optional	Trucks; available weekdays 2 p.m. –11:30 p.m. & all day on weekends	• Mostly perishables: fresh produce, meats, baked goods • Low prices because there is no middleman
YourGrocer	Manhattan, Bronx, Westchester, Greenwich, Brooklyn, Queens, Rockland	$75	$9.95 for orders > $75; $14.95 for orders < $75	Rented vans; available select days & times, depending on location	• Bulk orders of packaged goods
Peapod	Chicago, Boston, DC, Long Island, Connecticut, New Jersey, Rhode Island	$50	$6.95 for orders < $100; $9.95 for orders > $100; tipping optional	Truck; available 7 a.m.–1 p.m.; 3:30 p.m.– 10 p.m. weekdays, 7 a.m.–1 p.m. weekends	• Partner with Giant Foods and Stop & Shop; items picked from shelves of local warehouses near customer's home
NetGrocer	Lower 48 states, DC, special service to Alaska, Hawaii, APO/FPO	None	$5.99–$624.99, depends on order size & destination	FedEx; will receive order within 3–7 business days	• Only nonperishables; no fresh produce

Source: Company Web sites.

Exhibit 8 Comparison of Prices for Selected Online Grocers, May 2007

Grocery Item	Prices			
	FreshDirect	YourGrocer	Peapod	NetGrocer
Tide laundry detergent	$9.99/100 oz.	$24.88/340 oz ($7.31/100 oz.)	$7.69/100 oz.	$11.19/100 oz.
Wish-Bone Italian dressing	$1.89/8 oz.	$5.98/48 oz. ($0.99/8 oz.)	$1.89/8 oz.	$1.95/8 oz.
Cheerios	$4.69/15 oz. ($6.25/20 oz.)	$7.39/37 oz. ($3.99/20 oz.)	$4.19/20 oz.	$5.89/20 oz.
Ragu spaghetti sauce	$2.29/26 oz.	$7.99/135 oz. ($1.54/26 oz.)	$1.67/26 oz.	$2.69/26 oz.
Granny Smith apples	$4.99/4 pack (no per lb. price)	$7.69/5 lb.bag ($1.54/lb.)	$3.99/3 lb.bag ($1.33/lb.)	Fresh produce not available

Source: Company websites.

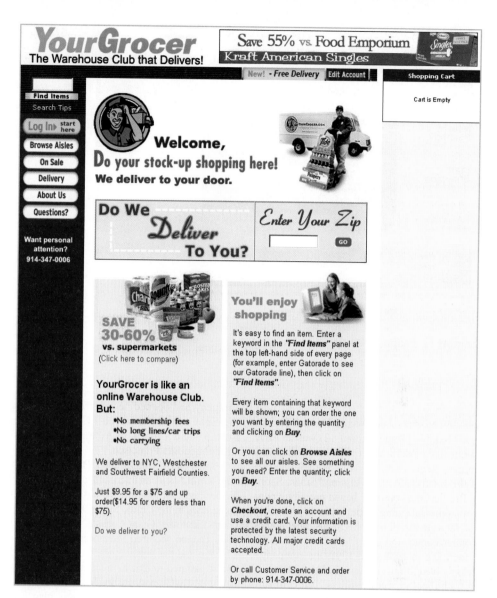

Exhibit 9 Yourgrocer.com Web site

Exhibit 10 Yourgrocer's Service Focus

New YourGrocer focuses on providing **three benefits** that families in the area most value:

1. **Easy ordering** over the Internet or on the phone to save hours of thankless shopping. You can use your last order as a starting point to save even more time.
2. **Delivery** right to the home or office, which eliminates the burden of lifting and transporting heavy and bulky items each month.
3. **Significant savings** with everyday low prices—not short-duration specials—which reduce what you pay for stock-up groceries and household supplies on average by 25 to 30% below local supermarkets.

Source: From http://www.yourgrocer.com/about_us.asp.

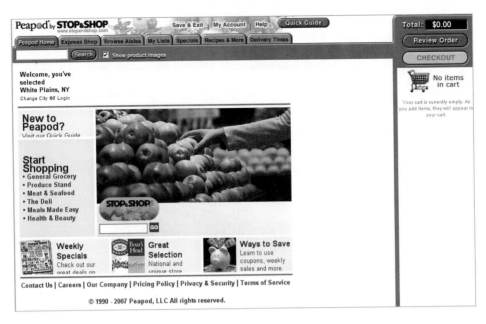

Exhibit 11 Peapod Web site

Peapod

Founded in 1989 by brothers Andrew and Thomas Parkinson, Peapod (see Exhibit 11 and Exhibit 12) was an early pioneer in e-commerce, inventing an online home-shopping service for grocery items years ahead of the commercial emergence of the Internet. With its tagline "Smart Shopping for Busy People," the company began providing consumers with a home-shopping experience in the early 1990s, going so far as to install modems in customer homes to provide an online connection.

From its founding in 1989 until 1998, the company's business model involved filling customer orders by forming alliances with traditional grocery retailers. The company chose a retail partner in each geographic area where it operated and used the partner's local network of retail stores to pick and pack orders for delivery to customers. Peapod personnel would cruise the aisles of a partner's stores, selecting the items each customer ordered, pack and load them into Peapod vehicles, and then deliver them to customers at prearranged times. Peapod charged customers a fee for its service and collected fees from its retail supply partners for using their products in its online service. Over the next several years, Peapod built delivery capabilities in eight market areas: Chicago; Columbus, Ohio; Boston; San Francisco/San Jose; Houston, Dallas, and Austin, Texas; and Long Island, New York.

In 1997, faced with mounting losses despite growing revenues, Peapod management shifted to a new order fulfillment business model utilizing a local company-owned and operated central distribution warehouse to store, pick, and pack customer orders for delivery. By mid-1999 the company had opened new distribution centers in three of the eight markets it served—Chicago, Long Island, and Boston—and a fourth distribution center was under construction in San Francisco.

In the late spring of 2000, Peapod created a partnership with Royal Ahold, an international food provider based in the Netherlands. At the time, Ahold operated five supermarket companies in the United States: Stop & Shop, Tops Market, Giant-Landover, Giant-Carlisle, and BI-LO. In September 2000 Peapod acquired Streamline.com, Inc.'s operations in Chicago and the Washington, DC, markets, and announced that it planned to exit its markets in Columbus, Ohio, and Houston, Dallas, and Austin, Texas. All of these moves were made as a part of Peapod's strategic plan for growth and future profitability. Under Peapod's initial partnership agreement with Ahold, Peapod was to continue as a stand-alone company, with Ahold supplying Peapod's goods, services, and fastpick fulfillment centers. However, in July 2001 Ahold acquired all the outstanding shares of Peapod and merged Peapod into one of Ahold's subsidiaries.

In 2007 Peapod provided online shopping and delivery service in many metropolitan areas, including Chicago, Boston, Rhode Island, Connecticut, New Jersey, Long Island, and Washington, DC. Peapod employed a centralized distribution model in every market. In large markets, orders were picked, packed, loaded, and delivered from a freestanding centralized fulfillment center; in smaller markets, Peapod established fast-pick centralized fulfillment centers adjacent to the facilities of retail partners.[33] Peapod's proprietary transportation routing system ensured on-time delivery and efficient truck and driver utilization.

Exhibit 12 Peapod Product Selection

NetGrocer

NetGrocer.com was founded in 1996 and advertised itself as the first online grocer to sell nonperishable items nationwide (see Exhibit 13 and Exhibit 14). NetGrocer serviced all 48 continental U.S. states and the District of Columbia with special service to Alaska, Hawaii, APO, and FPO destinations. All customer orders were filled in its single, 120,000-square-foot warehouse in North Brunswick, New Jersey. Orders were shipped by Federal Express and were guaranteed to reach any part of NetGrocer's service area within three to seven days.

NetGrocer offered its customers a large selection of brand-name and specialty nonperishable items that were difficult to find in a local supermarket. The key customer segment for NetGrocer's services were busy families, urban dwellers, special-needs groups (e.g., dieters, diabetics), and senior citizens. Customers purportedly enjoyed the benefits of convenient online shopping from home 24 hours a day, access to thousands of products, and delivery of their orders directly to their homes. Manufacturers also benefited from NetGrocer, as they were able to distribute their products nationwide, rapidly and easily.

Most Recent Challenges

As the online grocery retailing business continued to mature, all players needed to pay attention to customer perception. Online retailing giant amazon.com had entered the dry goods grocery delivery business, posing a threat to other online retailers because of its existing loyal customer base and legendary customer service. Creating a grocery section in 2006, Amazon offered over 10,000 nonperishable items including "long-time staples, from Kellogg's to Jiffy Pop."[34] The selection of dry goods rather than perishables meant Amazon, unlike FreshDirect and Peapod, didn't have to worry about delivery costs on time- and climate-sensitive items. However, even Amazon suffered grocery delivery failures. From out-of-stock problems, delivery glitches, and Web site technical outages, online grocery retailers needed to "serve their online customers just like they would serve the customers who come into their physical stores."[35]

Even though FreshDirect had been able to woo local New Yorkers, gaining a Fast Company "Local Hero" award in 2006, the company had to absorb "hundreds of thousands of dollars in parking tickets to get its customers its orders

Exhibit 13 Netgrocer.com Website

within the delivery window."[36] And, in early 2007, New York City government proposed a congestion charge for traffic entering Manhattan, adding to FreshDirect's delivery expenses. The rising cost of fuel was also a potential threat. Even though FreshDirect included a fuel surcharge to orders based on the average retail price of gasoline,[37] these expenses coupled with penalties accrued from parking violations might have put significant pressure on FreshDirect's ability to achieve its target profit levels.

Environmental concerns had also started to creep in as a major issue for FreshDirect. First, because of the conveyor packing system at the processing facility, FreshDirect was forced to use lots of cardboard boxes to deliver the groceries: produce came in one box, dry goods in another, and a single tube of toothpaste in its separate cardboard delivery container. Although FreshDirect had transitioned to the use of 100 percent post-consumer recycled paper,[38] the reusability of the cardboard boxes was very limited and the general public was increasingly becoming aware that their tax dollars were used to "collect and dispose of the huge stacks of cardboards that Fresh-Direct's customers leave in the trash."[39] As one environmentally conscious consumer observed, "I was baffled by

the number of boxes they used to pack things. Groceries worth $40 came in five boxes. And after I unpacked, I had to discard the boxes. There was no system of returning them to FreshDirect to be recycled."[40]

A second issue that environment conscious consumers had become concerned about was the additional exhaust fumes that FreshDirect trucks contributed to the urban atmosphere.[41] Third, FreshDirect trucks double-parked in busy city streets had only made the traffic congestion problems worse. "It's probably no exaggeration to say that FreshDirect has built its financial success on its ability to fob off its social and environmental costs on the city as a whole."[42] Lastly, some city dwellers had even expressed concern about FreshDirect's adverse effect on the overall makeup of their neighborhoods: "It is not just the impact they have on congestion, pollution, space, etc, but their very adverse impact on the best of businesses in neighborhoods that they can undersell because of their externalized costs. It is these small businesses, farmers markets and local grocery stores, that FreshDirect undercuts, that are some of the best businesses for supporting and preserving our walkable, diverse and safe neighborhoods."[43]

Exhibit 14 Netgrocer Shipping Charges

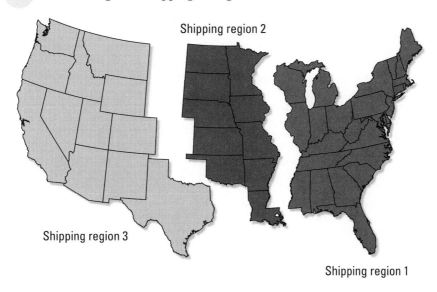

Shipping region 2

Shipping region 3

Shipping region 1

Order Total	Shipping Region 3	Shipping Region 2	Shipping Region 1
Brackets	**Rates**	**Rates**	**Rates**
$0–24.99	$ 9.99	$ 9.99	$ 5.99
$25–49.99	$ 15.99	$ 14.99	$ 9.99
$50–74.99	$ 21.99	$ 19.99	$ 13.99
$75–99.99	$ 27.99	$ 25.99	$ 15.99
$100–124.99	$ 33.99	$ 29.99	$ 19.99
$125–149.99	$ 39.99	$ 37.99	$ 24.99
$150–199.99	$ 59.99	$ 55.99	$ 29.99
$200–299.99	$ 88.99	$ 79.99	$ 44.99
$300–499.99	$116.99	$110.99	$ 59.99
$500–749.99	$218.99	$211.99	$119.99
$750–999.99	$319.99	$312.99	$179.99
$1,000–	$624.99	$613.99	$401.99

FreshDirect only served selected neighborhoods within New York City. As the neighborhood selection process is highly arbitrary, many people who live in neighborhoods that FreshDirect does not serve had started to accuse the company of discrimination. As one customer put it, "FreshDirect is the most convenient way to shop for groceries in NYC . . . unless you live in a Public Housing building—they won't deliver to you!."[44] Others have echoed similar concerns in terms of FreshDirect's decision to not serve specific neighborhoods: "These are neighborhoods that FreshDirect deems underserved, or in plain terms . . . not worth the bother."[45]

Looking into the future, there was speculation that FreshDirect might want to "seek public funding to underwrite growth possibilities."[46] In addition to the merger and acquisition activity, for instance Whole Foods Markets' pending acquisition of Wild Oats Markets, analysts felt that some private players in the New York market, such as FreshDirect, might consider pursuing investment capital through an initial public offering.

Endnotes

1. http://www.freshdirect.com/site_access/site_access.jsp.

2. Dubbs, D. 2003. Catch of the day. *Multichannel Merchant,* July 1, http://multichannelmerchant.com/opsandfulfillment/orders/fulfillment_catch_day/.

3. A "slotting allowance" is defined by the American Marketing Association as, "1. (retailing definition) A fee paid by a vendor for space in a retail store. 2. (sales promotion definition) The fee a manufacturer pays to a retailer in order to get distribution for a new product. It covers the costs of making room for the product in the warehouse and on the store shelf, reprogramming the computer system to recognize the product's UPC code, and including the product in the retailer's inventory system." http://www.marketingpower.com/mg-dictionary-view2910.php.

4. Laseter, T. et al. 2003. What FreshDirect learned from Dell. *Strategy Business,* Spring (30), http://www.strategy-business.com/press/16635507/8202.

5. Schoenberger, C. R. 2006. Will work with food. *Forbes,* September 18, http://members.forbes.com/global/2006/0918/041.html.

6. Smith, C. 2004. Splat: The supermarket battle between Fairway, FreshDirect and Whole Foods. *New York: The Magazine,* May 24, http://nymag.com/nymetro/food/industry/n_10421/.

7. Dignan, L. 2004. FreshDirect: Ready to deliver. *Baseline: The Project Management Center,* February 17, http://www.baselinemag.com/print_article2/0,1217,a=119342,00.asp.

8. *Chelsea-Wide Blogs,* 2006. http://chelsea.clickyourblock.com/bb/archive/index.php?t-128.html.

9. Michaelson named CEO at FreshDirect; Furbush resigns. *Supermarket News,* January 9, 2007, http://supermarketnews.com/retail_financial/michaelson_named_ceo_at_freshdirect_furbush_resigns_337/index.html.

10. FreshDirect co-founder considers new venture. *Supermarket News,* February 22, 2007, http://supermarketnews.com/retail_financial/freshdirect_co_founder_considers_new_venture_report_617/index.html.

11. Five months in Manhattan and FreshDirect passes the 2,000-order-a-day mark and has over 40,000 customers. *Business Wire,* February 12, 2003.

12. Elliot, S. 2003. A "fresh" and "direct" approach. *New York Times,* February 11, 2003.

13. Bosman, J. 2006. FreshDirect emphasizes its New York flavor. *New York Times,* January 31, http://www.nytimes.com/2006/01/31/business/media/31adco.html?ex=1182657600&en=14d9c9f5d468064f&ei=5070.

14. Laseter, op. cit.

15. Ibid.

16. Ibid.

17. Food Market Institute, *Supermarket Facts: Industry Overview 2006,* www.fmi.org/facts_figs/superfact.htm.

18. Leonhardt, D. 2006. Filling pantries without a middleman. *New York Times,* November 22, 2006, http://www.nytimes.com/2006/11/22/business/22leonhardt.html?pagewanted=1&ei=5070&en=102ea06150518b7a&ex=1182657600.

19. McTaggart, J. 2004. Fresh direction. *Progressive Grocer* 83(4): 58–60.

20. Koeppen, S. 2006. Online shopping: Way to go? *CBS News.,* July 28, http://www.cbsnews.com/stories/2006/07/28/earlyshow/living/ConsumerWatch/main1844539.shtml.

21. Kempiak, M. & Fox, M. A. 2002. Online grocery shopping: Consumer motives, concerns and business models. *First Monday,* 7 (9), http://www.firstmonday.org/issues/issue7_9/kempiak/.

22. Machlis, S. 1998. Filling up grocery carts online. *Computerworld,* July 27: 4.

23. Anderson, S. 2001. Is online grocery shopping for you. *Computer Bits,* April 11.

24. Woods, B. 1998. America Online goes grocery shopping for e-commerce bargains. *Computer News,* August 10: 42.

25. Fisher, L. M. 1999. Online grocer is setting up delivery system for $1 billion. *New York Times,* July 10: 1.

26. Online supermarkets keep it simple. *Frontline Solutions.* 2002. 3(2): 46–49.

27. Ibid.

28. Smerd, J. 2005. Specialty foods stores will go head-to-head at Union Square. *New York Sun,* March 4, http://www.nysun.com/article/10058?page_no=1.

29. NYC's FreshDirect launches street fight against Whole Foods. *Progressive Grocer,* March 3, 2005, http://www.allbusiness.com/retail-trade/food-stores/4258105-1.html.

30. We don't have time to waste. *New Zealand Herald.* 2007. February 3.

31. Joyce, E. 2002. YourGrocer.com wants to come back. *ECommerce,* May 15, http://ecommerce.internet.com/news/news/article/0,,10375_1122671,00.html.

32. Fickenscher, L. 2002. Bouncing back from cyber limbo: Resurgence of failed dot coms after downsizing. *Crain's New York Business,* June 24.

33. Peapod, Inc., Corporate fact sheet, http://www.peapod.com/corpinfo/peapodFacts.pdf.

34. Regan, K. 2006. Amazon dips toe into online grocery business. *E-Commerce Times,* June 15, http://www.ecommercetimes.com/story/51136.html.

35. Hamstra, M. 2007. Online stores may need to bone up on their execution. *Supermarket News,* January 29, http://supermarketnews.com/viewpoints/online-stores-bone-up-execution/index.html.

36. Danigelis, A. 2006. Customers first local hero: Fresh Direct. *Fast Company,* September, http://www.fastcompany.com/customer/2006/articles/local-fresh-direct.html.

37. See http://www.freshdirect.com/about/index.jsp, click on FAQs.

38. FreshDirect transitions to eco-friendly boxes. *Supermarket News,* May 11, 2007, http://supermarketnews.com/fresh_market/freshdirect_eco_friendly/index.html.

39. FreshDirect builds a grocery empire on free street space. *StreetsBlog,* November 22, 2006, http://www.streetsblog.org/2006/11/22/fresh-direct-builds-a-grocery-empire-on-free-street-space/.

40. Wadia, A. S. 2007. Is FreshDirect good for you? *Metroblogging NYC,* January 30, http://nyc.metblogs.com/archives/2007/01/is_freshdirect.html.

41. FreshDirect builds a grocery empire on free street space, op. cit.

42. FreshDirect builds a grocery empire on free street space, op. cit.

43. FreshDirect builds a grocery empire on free street space, op. cit.

44. Rodriguez, N. 2007. FreshDirect.com discriminates!!! *Metroblogging NYC,* February 7, http://nyc.metblogs.com/archives/2007/01/is_freshdirect.phtml.

45. Wadia, op. cit.

46. Merrefield, D. 2007. How different companies approach the growth challenge. *Supermarket News,* February 5, http://supermarketnews.com/viewpoints/how-different-companies-approach-growth-challenge/index.html.

Case 33   Nintendo's Wii*

When Nintendo released the Wii video game console, it was already in the midst of a very competitive market. The previous generation of video game consoles consisted of the Sega Dreamcast, Sony PlayStation 2, Nintendo GameCube, and Microsoft Xbox. These systems were all released between 1999 and 2001 in the United States, and although the GameCube sold more systems than the Sega Dreamcast, it fell into third place behind the PlayStation 2 and the Xbox. The PlayStation 2 sold more than 115 million units worldwide, more than twice the combined unit sales of the GameCube and Xbox (21 million and 24 million, respectively). The next generation of video game consoles was about to become even more competitive.

Not only did Nintendo sit behind Sony and Microsoft in terms of overall sales, but it derived most of its revenue from the video game business. Sony had more than 158,000 employees and its 2006 revenues were over $63 billion. Microsoft had more than 70,000 employees and its 2006 revenues were $44 billion. Nintendo was founded in 1889 but had only roughly 3,000 employees and 2006 revenues of $4.5 billion. Thus, Nintendo sat in the middle of two potentially dominating firms. Yet Nintendo was in the lead in video console sales growth and second in overall units sold to Microsoft, which had shipped its product a year ahead of Nintendo and Sony.

Background

Although Nintendo dates back to 1889 as a playing card maker, Nintendo's first video game systems were developed in 1979 and were known as TV Game 15 and TV Game 6.[1] In 1980 Nintendo developed the first portable LCD video game with a microprocessor. In 1985 Nintendo created the Nintendo Entertainment System (NES), an 8-bit video game console. The original NES was very successful, as its graphics were superior to any home-based console that was available at the time, and as a result more than 60 million units were sold worldwide.[2] The NES set the bar for subsequent consoles in platform design, as well as accepting games that were manufactured by third-party developers. As competitors began developing 16-bit devices, such as Sega's Genesis system or NEC's PC Engine, Nintendo knew that it had to respond and develop its own 16-bit system.

The Super Nintendo Entertainment System (SNES) was developed to stay current with the competitors. The Super Nintendo was released in 1991 and when purchased came with one game, Super Mario World. This was the successor to the previous Mario Brothers games that were played on the original 8-bit NES. In 1996 Nintendo

released Nintendo 64, which caused the popularity of the Super Nintendo to decline. The Nintendo 64 is Nintendo's third generation video game console and was named after the 64-bit processor. The retail price of the Nintendo 64 was $199.

The Nintendo 64, like its predecessors, used cartridges to play its games, but at the time, the competing systems of Sony and Sega were using CDs for game storage. Cartridges could store 64 megabytes of data, while CDs could store around 700 megabytes of data. Also, CDs were much cheaper to manufacture, distribute, and create, thus many game developers that traditionally supported Nintendo platforms began creating games that would support the other platforms to increase profits.[3] At the time, the average cost of producing a Nintendo 64 cartridge was cited as $25 per cartridge versus 10 cents per CD. Therefore game producers passed these higher expenses to the consumer, which explains why Nintendo 64 games tended to sell for higher prices than Sony PlayStation games. While most Sony PlayStation games rarely exceeded $50, Nintendo 64 titles could reach $70.[4] Third-party developers naturally switched to the systems that used a less expensive CD platform (such as the PlayStation).

In 2001 Nintendo released its GameCube, which was part of the sixth generation era of video game systems. These systems include Sony's PlayStation 2, Microsoft's Xbox, and Sega's Dreamcast. Although the GameCube no longer used cartridges, it began producing its games using a proprietary optical-disc technology. This technology, while similar in appearance to CDs, was actually several inches smaller in diameter and was unable to be played using a standard CD player.

Mr. Genyo Takeda, General Manager of Integrated Research and Development for Nintendo, explained that innovation and creativity were fostered by giving several different development teams "free rein to couple a dedicated controller or peripheral with a GameCube title, and then see whether or not the end result was marketable. This project gave rise not only to the Donkey Kong Bongos and the Dancing Stage Mario Mix Action Pad, but also to a number of ideas and designs that would find their way into the Wii Remote."[5]

As of 2007, Nintendo's revenues and income were on attractive upward trajectories (see Exhibits 1 and 2). Exhibit 3 shows that Nintendo's stock price was soaring relative to its larger competitions.

The Launch of the Wii

In 2006 Nintendo released its direct successor to the Game-Cube, the Wii (pronounced we). There have been many reasons cited as to why the name Wii was chosen, but perhaps the most compelling reason was "'Wii' sounds like 'we,' which emphasizes that the console was for everyone. Wii could be remembered easily by people around the world,

* This case was prepared by graduate student Eshai J. Gorshein and Professor Alan B. Eisner of Pace University. This case was based solely upon library research and was developed for class discussion rather than to illustrate either effective or ineffective handling of an administrative situation. Copyright © 2007 Alan B. Eisner.

Exhibit 1   Income Statements

(in ¥ millions except for per share items)	2007 03/31/07	2006 03/31/06	2005 03/31/05	2004 03/31/04	2003 03/31/03
Total Revenue	966,534	509,249	515,292	514,805	504,135
Cost of Revenue, Total	568,722	294,133	298,115	307,233	308,525
Selling/Gen/Admin. Expense	171,787	21,837	16,366	16,014	20,448
Labor & Related Expense	—	15,131	13,402	12,716	11,693
Advertising Expense	—	55,442	53,756	53,488	46,227
Sell/General/Admin. Expenses, Total	171,787	92,410	83,524	82,218	78,368
Research & Development	—	30,588	20,505	15,820	14,590
Depreciation/Amortization	—	1,764	1,621	1,846	2,526
Restructuring Charge	—	—	—	—	0
Impair-Assets Held for Sale	335	1,383	1,612	510	864
Other Unusual Expense (Income)	(338)	(3,610)	(1,735)	(2,575)	(117)
Unusual Expense (Income)	(3)	(2,227)	(123)	(2,065)	747
Total Operating Expense	740,506	416,668	403,642	405,052	404,756
Operating Income	226,028	92,581	111,650	109,753	99,379
Interest Expense, Net Nonoperating	—	(1)	0	0	(1)
Interest Income, Nonoperating	33,987	22,497	13,510	8,999	15,942
Investment Income, Nonoperating	26,632	49,017	18,336	(67,876)	(3,615)
Interest Income (Expense), Net Nonoperating	60,619	71,513	31,846	(58,877)	12,326
Gain (Loss) on Sale of Assets	(132)	(20)	(13)	761	(59)
Other, Net	3,087	2,398	1,924	1,335	1,677
Net Income before Taxes	289,602	166,472	145,407	52,972	113,323
Provision for Income Taxes	115,347	68,138	57,962	19,692	45,973
Net Income after Taxes	174,255	98,334	87,445	33,280	67,350
Minority Interest	37	46	(24)	(79)	(74)
Net Income before Extra Items	174,292	98,380	87,421	33,201	67,276
Net Income	174,292	98,380	87,421	33,201	67,276

Source: reuters.com.

no matter what language they spoke. No confusion."[6] Initially the system was known by its code name, Revolution, but later the name was changed to Wii. Nintendo stated that it wanted to make the Wii a system that would make anyone who tried it talk to their friends and neighbors about it.[7]

The Wii was created to establish a new standard in game control, using an innovative and unprecedented interface, the Wii Remote.[8] The Wii Remote was what made the Wii a unique home console. The remote acted as the primary controller for the Wii. Due to its motion sensor capabilities

it allowed the user to interact and manipulate objects on the screen by moving and pointing the remote in various directions.[9] It was the size of a traditional remote control, and was "limited only by the game designer's imagination."[10] For example, in a game of tennis it served as the racket when the user swung his or her arm, or in a shooting game it served as the user's gun. Not only did the remote serve as a controller but it also had a built-in speaker and a rumble feature for even greater tactile feedback and game involvement.

Exhibit 2   Balance Sheets

(in ¥ millions except for per share items)	2007 03/31/07	2006 03/31/06	2005 03/31/05	2004 03/31/04	2003 03/31/03
Cash & Equivalents	962,197	812,064	826,653	767,270	748,650
Short-Term Investments	115,971	64,287	20,485	17,375	8,266
Cash and Short-Term Investments	1,078,168	876,351	847,138	784,645	756,916
Trade Accounts Receivable, Gross	89,666	43,826	51,143	28,493	49,085
Provision for Doubtful Accounts	(1,886)	(1,514)	(1,880)	(3,028)	(5,463)
Total Receivables, Net	87,780	42,312	49,263	25,465	43,622
Total Inventory	88,609	30,835	49,758	30,955	104,524
Deferred Income Tax	35,631	24,170	19,513	24,911	31,158
Other Current Assets	104,483	45,061	28,217	24,784	33,088
Other Current Assets, Total	140,114	69,231	47,730	49,695	64,246
Total Current Assets	1,394,671	1,018,729	993,889	890,760	969,308
Land/Improvements	32,595	32,604	32,069	31,925	33,134
Construction in Progress	217	41	410	0	7
Property/Plant/Equipment Net	57,597	55,968	54,417	55,083	59,367
Intangibles, Net	505	319	354	245	225
Long-Term Investments	92,412	60,213	73,393	53,866	38,551
Other Long-Term Assets	15,991	15,156	277	883	3,352
Total Assets	1,575,590	1,160,699	1,132,485	1,010,026	1,085,515
Accounts Payable	301,080	83,817	111,045	57,945	96,475
Accrued Expenses	1,779	1,732	1,650	1,712	1,672
Income Taxes Payable	90,013	53,040	51,951	11,165	38,913
Other Current Liabilities	75,563	43,684	40,801	42,423	48,988
Other Current Liabilities, Total	165,576	96,724	92,752	53,588	87,901
Total Current Liabilities	468,435	182,273	205,447	113,245	186,048
Minority Interest	138	176	222	232	153
Pension Benefits—Underfunded	4,443	3,299	4,890	5,701	8,810
Other Long-Term Liabilities	698	861	461	602	135
Other Liabilities, Total	5,141	4,160	5,351	6,303	8,945
Total Liabilities	473,714	186,609	211,020	119,780	195,146
Common Stock	10,065	10,065	10,065	10,065	10,065
Additional Paid-In Capital	11,586	11,585	11,584	11,584	11,584
Retained Earnings (Accumulated Deficit)	1,220,293	1,096,073	1,032,834	964,524	950,262
Treasury Stock—Common	(155,396)	(155,112)	(129,896)	(86,898)	(81,521)
Unrealized Gain (Loss)	8,898	10,717	7,194	6,650	2,254
Other Equity, Total	6,432	762	(10,315)	(15,677)	(2,275)
Total Equity	1,101,878	974,090	921,466	890,248	890,369
Total Liabilities & Shareholders' Equity	1,575,592	1,160,699	1,132,486	1,010,028	1,085,515
Total Common Shares Outstanding	128	128	130	134	134
Treasury Shares—Common Primary Issue	14	14	12	8	7

Source: reuters.com.

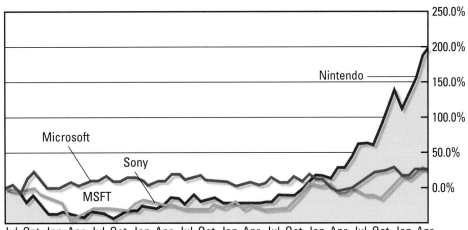

Exhibit 3 5-Year Stock Chart of Nintendo, Microsoft, and Sony, 2002–2007

Source: reuters.com.

The Wii remote came with an arm strap that could be tied to the user's wrist to avoid the remote flying away when being used. The remote was powered by two AA batteries, which could power the remote for approximately 30 to 60 hours.[11] Exhibit 4 shows the Wii and Wii Remote.

The second part of the Wii remote innovation was the Wii Nunchuk. The Nunchuk was designed to perfectly fit the user's hand, and connected to the remote at its expansion port. The Nunchuk had the same motion-sensing capabilities that the remote has, but it also had an analog stick to help the user move his or her characters. In addition to the analog stick, the Nunchuk had two buttons that gave the user quick access to other game functions. Thus the Nunchuk offered some of the benefits of a standard game controller coupled with the high-technology motion sensors of the remote. Users could hold a Nunchuk in one hand and the Wii remote in the other while playing the Wii Sports Boxing game and be transformed into the boxing ring with on-screen opponents. The game controls were intuitive for jabs and punches; however, a missed block did not hurt as much as if one were really in the boxing ring.

The ambidextrous nature of the Wii controllers was something seldom seen in other game controllers; the Wii controllers permitted the user to hold the remote and Nunchuk whichever way felt most comfortable.[12]

Features

In addition to the Wii Remote there were other features unique to the Wii. One of these features was the Wii Menu, which was the first screen that appeared on the television when the Wii was turned on. According to Nintendo, the Wii Menu easily integrates itself into the everyday lives of its users.[13]

The menu displayed several different icons, one of them was the Mii Channel (pronounced *me*). This channel gave the users the ability to create and personalize a 3-D caricature of themselves. Another icon was the Everybody Votes Channel, which permitted individuals to vote in national

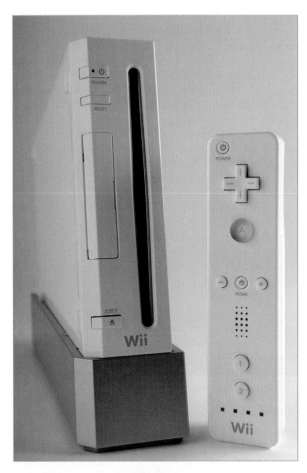

Exhibit 4 Wii Game Console and Remote.

and worldwide polls on a variety of topics. There was also a New Channel that gave the individual up-to-date breaking news from around the world organized into a variety of topics. The Forecast Channel was another icon displayed on the Wii Menu. This allowed the individual to view weather reports from anywhere around the world. Users had the ability to download older Nintendo games from the Wii Shopping Channel. A Wii Message Board allowed users to leave messages on the Wii for other users of the same console, or reminders for themselves. An Internet Channel allowed individuals to surf the Internet from their Wii. There was a Photo Channel that allowed the user to view photos stored on a standard SD memory card. And lastly there was a Disc Channel that gave the user the ability to play Wii games or Nintendo GameCube discs.[14] The Wii was backward compatible with the Nintendo GameCube's games, memory cards, and controllers.

Online Capabilities

Nintendo's Wii was the first Nintendo console that had online capabilities. The Wii could connect to the Internet in several different ways. The Wii could connect to the Internet via a standard wireless protocol—a consumer's home high speed Internet hookup (usually from a cable TV service or telephone company DSL). Another way the Wii could connect to the Internet was via the Nintendo DS, which had wireless capability built in. The Wii could also be connected to the Internet via an optional wired USB–Ethernet adapter.

According to Nintendo of America's president and COO, Reggie Fils-Aime, the Wii would "offer online-enabled games that consumers will not have to pay a subscription fee for. They'll be able to play right out of the box. . . . It will not have any hidden fees or costs."[15] However as of mid-2007, no such games existed. So far the only consoles to allow an individual to play games interactively with other users online were the competing products: Microsoft Xbox 360 and Sony PlayStation 3.

The Wii was released in North America on November 19, 2006, and sales as of March 3, 2007 were in excess of 2 million units (see Exhibit 5).[16]

However, although these numbers may seem quite large, Nintendo had been experiencing production problems with the Wii. Nintendo had been unable to meet demand during

Exhibit 5   **Wii Units Sold**

Region	Units Sold	First Available
North America	2,083,880	11/19/06
Japan	2,014,310	12/2/06
Europe	2,000,000	12/8/06
Australia	68,000	12/7/06
Total	**6,166,190**	

2007. In an interview on the Web site Game Theory, Perrin Kapaln, Nintendo vice president of marketing and corporate affairs suggested that shortages were expected for some time. "We are at absolute maximum production and doing everything we can . . . but demand continues to be really high."[17]

Demographics

According to Nintendo, one of the key differences between the Wii and the competitor's systems was the broad audience that the Wii targeted.[18] Many of the Wii games were able to be played by people of all ages, and were easier to control than the complicated controllers of the Sony PlayStation 3 or Microsoft Xbox 360. Nintendo's TV commercials of the Wii showed people of all ages and different social classes playing the Wii. According to Nintendo, the Wii remote allowed people of all ages to enjoy its use. Nintendo wanted to create a controller that was "as inviting as it was sophisticated."[19] Nintendo's goal was to create games that everyone could play, a system that would appeal to women and people who had never played video games in the past. Shigeru Miyamoto, a senior director at Nintendo explained, "Most of the game business is going down a similar path toward hyperrealistic graphics which recreate sports or movies. . . . We want to put a little more art into it in a way that casual consumers can enjoy the game."[20] The Wii offered something for both the advanced gamer and the person who had never played a video game before. The advanced gamer would enjoy the remote's unique features, whereas the novice gamer could use the remote as his or her hand and wouldn't need elaborate instructions on how to play a new game straight out of the box. Although the Nintendo games were easily played by a greater range of ages, the graphics were undoubtedly a relative weakness of the product.

Although Nintendo had been able to target a large range of age groups, it seemed to lack the lineup of games offered by other systems. Nintendo had focused on its proprietary Mario Brothers series games, as well as low graphic, low complexity games that could be played by a wide range of age levels. PlayStation 3's top-selling game was Resistance: Fall of Man, which had won many awards, but more importantly had a rating of *Mature* (a rating given by The Entertainment Software Rating Board), which meant that it was suitable for audiences of 17 and older only. Xbox's best-selling game was Gears of War, which also had a rating of *Mature*. The Wii's best-selling games were "The Legend of Zelda: Twilight Princess", which had a rating of *Teen,* which meant it's suitable for ages 13 and up, and "Wii Sports," which was rated *Everyone*, suitable for all audiences. One of the Wii's shortcomings was obviously its graphics.[21] It was widely believed that the Wii had 2.5 times the power of the GameCube, but hardly enough to compete with the Xbox 360 or PlayStation 3.

Although Nintendo hoped to target people of all ages, it has long been seen as a system that makes video games for children, as evident from its Mario, Zelda, and Donkey Kong series. It was going to be difficult for Nintendo to position itself as a console for gamers of all ages and tastes.

Gaining the Interest of Game Developers

As evident from the history of game consoles, game developers have tried to make games more and more complex with each new generation of systems. This meant that more money was invested in the production of each subsequent generation of games. Because game developers were spending more money on developing games, they were at great financial risk if games did not succeed. Thus, many developers felt more secure in simply creating sequels to existing games, which in turn restricted innovation. The Wii's innovative controller, the Wii remote, required a rethinking and reengineering of the human interface for game developers and programmers. Another issue with developing games for the Wii was that its graphics were not quite as good as those of the PlayStation 3 and Xbox 360, and therefore game developers were required to be more creative and develop special Wii editions of their games.

Many game developers use virtual machine software in developing new games. It was believed that game developers could develop games for the Wii and then make them for other platforms based on the same programming, thereby reducing production costs. However, while the Wii remote distinguished itself from its competitors, it created a hurdle for developers. When a developer created a game for the PlayStation 3, she could create the same game for the Xbox 360 and vice versa, whereas when a developer created a game for the Wii, it required significant rework to deploy the title for the other platforms. Converting a title from the Xbox 360 or PlayStation 3 also required significant work to modify the game to incorporate code for the Wii Remote's special features.

The Competition

The launches of the Wii and the PlayStation 3 in November of 2006 were the beginning of the battle for market share in the fierce competition of the seventh generation of video game consoles (see Exhibit 6). Although the Xbox 360 was released a year earlier, Microsoft intended to relaunch the Xbox 360 after some minor enhancements.

The price of $299 for the Wii included the Wii Remote, the Nunchuk attachment, the sensor bar, and the Wii Sports software title. The Wii sports title included tennis, baseball, golf, bowling, and boxing games. This retail price was much less than the prices of the PlayStation 3 and Xbox 360, possibly due to the fact that the Wii did not have as advanced a central processor unit or a high definition video player.

Exhibit 6   Game Systems Comparison

	Nintendo	Sony	Microsoft
Console Name	Wii	PlayStation 3	Xbox 360
Game Format	12 cm Wii Optical Disc	Blu-ray Disc, DVD-Rom, CD-Rom	HD DVD, DVD, DVD-DL
Hard Drive	None	20 GB or 60 GB	20 GB or 120 GB
Price	$249	$599 (60 GB)	$299 core, $399 premium, or $479 elite
Ethernet	Wi-fi standard	Wi-fi optional	Wi-fi optional
Online Services	WiiConnect24, Wii Channels, no online game play	PlayStation Network, has online game play	Xbox live, has online game play
Controller	Wii remote (wireless, motion sensing)	Max 7 SIXAXIS (wireless)	Wired or wireless
Backward Compatibility	Yes (Nintendo GameCube)	Yes (PlayStation 2)	Yes (certain Xbox games)
Game Count	235	150[22]	270

Sources: Company reports and author estimates.

Xbox 360

The Xbox 360 by Microsoft was released in November 2005, giving it a year lead over Nintendo and Sony's new systems. The Xbox 360 came in three different versions: Elite ($479 retail), Premium System ($399 retail) and Core System ($299 retail).

Although such prices were quite expensive to the retail consumer, in reality Microsoft was losing money on each sale. Take, for example, Microsoft's cost of producing the Premium System. It cost Microsoft $470 before assembly, and an additional $55 for the cost of the cables, power cord, and controllers, bringing Microsoft's cost to $526. Thus, Microsoft was losing $126 on the sale of each system. This was not only the case with the Xbox 360, but also with its predecessor, the Xbox. There too Microsoft was selling a system for $299 that cost Microsoft $323 to produce. Microsoft believed that through the sale of games and accessories it would turn a profit during 2007.[23]

One of the important features of the Xbox 360 was Xbox Live. According to Microsoft, Xbox Live was the "premier online gaming and entertainment service that enables you to connect your Xbox to the Internet and Play games online."[24] This feature allowed individuals to play online against other users from all around the world. Thus Microsoft had created a community of individuals who were able to communicate with one another by voice chats and/or playing against each other in a video game. It even allowed users to "see what their friends are up to at any time" and to look not only at their friends' list but also their friends' friends list.[25] Another service offered by Xbox Live was the Xbox Live Marketplace, which enabled users to download movies, game trailers, game demos, and arcade games. It is estimated that more than 70 percent of connected Xbox users were downloading content from the Xbox Live Marketplace, totaling more than 4 million members.[26] According to Microsoft there were more than 12 million downloads in less than a year and, due to this popularity, major publishers and other independent gamers had submitted more than 1,000 Xbox Live games.[27] Similar to the Wii, the Xbox 360 has a dashboard that showed up when the system is powered up. This gave the user the ability to either play DVDs or games.

The Xbox 360 had the capability to play High Definition DVDs.[28] The CPU of the Xbox 360 was a custom triple core PowerPC–based design manufactured by IBM, known as the Xenon. The Xbox 360 played all its games in 5.1-channel Dolby Digital surround sound, and along with the HD display, the Xbox 360 could truly display excellent picture and sound quality. However, a consumer who did not have a high-definition–enabled television set was not able to enjoy the high definition features of the system. The Xbox 360 played all its games on dual-layer DVDs which could store up to 8.5 GB per disc, but also had the ability to play many other formats.[29] The system had an Ethernet port and three USB ports but could also connect to the Internet via a wireless network.

Microsoft began production of the Xbox 360 only 69 days prior to the launch date.[30] This resulted in Microsoft being unable to supply enough systems to meet the initial demand, and therefore many potential customers were not able to purchase a console at launch.[31] However, according to Bill Gates, Microsoft had over 10 million units out in the market by the time Sony and Nintendo launched their systems.[32]

Sony Playstation 3

The PlayStation 3 was Sony's seventh-generation video game console. The PlayStation 3 had many advanced features including a Cell Broadband Engine 64-bit processor that features a main power-processing element and up to eight parallel processing elements. This was a multiprocessing unit that provided advanced support for graphics-intense games. Another notable feature of the PlayStation 3 was its ability to play Blu-Ray Discs. Blu-Ray was a form of high-definition video, which enabled game developers to create games of higher sophistication.[33] Another key feature of the PlayStation 3 was the SIXAXIS wireless controller. This controller had sensors that could determine when a player maneuvered or angled his or her controller to allow game play to become a "natural extension of the player's body."[34] Although this was a more advanced remote than a standard wired remote, it lacked the true motion-sensing capabilities of the Wii Remote in its first version.[35]

The PlayStation 3 could play music CDs, connect to the Internet, copy CDs directly to its hard drive, play Blu-Ray Discs and DVDs, connect to a digital camera, view photos, and more. However, a consumer who did not have a high-definition–enabled television set was not able to enjoy the high-definition features of the system.

Sales in North America were initially strong and tapered off rapidly with 1.3 million units sold during the first six months of sales (see Exhibit 7).[36] The United Kingdom also saw record-breaking sales of PlayStation 3 with more than 165,000 units (through heavy preordering) in its first two days on the shelves,[37] although the total European sales for the first six months of availability were only 920,000 units.[38] Sony CEO Howard Stringer attributed the slowing sales to a lack of software titles and said that Sony

Exhibit 7 **PlayStation 3 Units Sold During First Six Months**

Region	Units Sold	First Available
North America	1,370,300	11/17/06
Japan	870,492[40]	11/17/06
Europe	920,000	3/23/07
Australia	27,000[41]	3/23/07
Total	More than 3.25 million[42]	

expects at least 380 new PlayStation 3 games to hit the market by 2008.[39]

Part of the PlayStation Network's success was the ability to play games online. This allowed individuals to play other players who may be located in other parts of the world. The PlayStation Network allowed users to download games, view movie and game trailers, and text message and chat with friends. Users were also able to browse the Internet and open up to six windows at once.[43]

Since the launch of the PlayStation 3, there had been mixed reports about it. On the positive note, it was once called the "most important home entertainment device since the TV."[44] Also, MSN stated that the PlayStation 3 is a "versatile and impressive piece of home-entertainment equipment that lives up to the hype . . . the PS3 is well worth its hefty price tag."[45] However, *PC WORLD* magazine ranked the PlayStation 3 eighth out of The Top 21 Tech Screw-ups of 2006.[46]

Supply and Demand

When the Xbox 360 hit stores in November 2005, thousands of video game fans waited outside stores (some even in freezing weather) to be the first to purchase the console. And although the console quickly sold out, it became available several months later and there have not been problems purchasing one since. The same held true with the release of the PlayStation 3. Although it quickly sold out in stores, it was available thereafter, and anyone willing to spend the money is able to purchase it. However, Nintendo fans have had problems finding a Wii to purchase since its launch in November of 2006. Lucky customers might walk into a retailer at the moment the latest Wii shipment has arrived or wait in lines for hours for the privilege of paying the retail price of only $249. The unlucky customers had to search various auction Web sites such as eBay and pay premiums of double to triple the retail price.

There had been a great deal of speculation regarding the production problems with the Wii. Several analysts had argued that lack of availability of the Wii was a marketing ploy to create hype and increase demand. However, others have hypothesized that Nintendo was having production problems and was unable to meet the huge demand for the Wii. Billy Pidgeon, program manager for IDC's Consumers Markets claimed that consumers would have a difficult time purchasing the Wii through late 2008. Pidgeon stated that he believed that the Wii would continue to be a successful force in the gaming industry, and that Nintendo needed to start shipping out more consoles. Furthermore, he said that he didn't believe "supply will meet demand for the Wii until 2009."[47]

The supply problem was confirmed by Nintendo CEO Satoru Iwata during a company financial briefing and later on a Web site question and answer session in May of 2007. CEO Iwata said that "we are currently facing product shortages . . . we have been running short of inventories, and [the retailers] are getting after us."[48] Iwata said further,

"Making a significant volume of the high-tech hardware, and making an additional volume, is not an easy task at all. In fact, when we clear one bottleneck for a production increase, we will face another one."[49]

As evident from Exhibit 5 there are 235 games for the Wii. This number indicates that the Wii is obviously a successful system—one that has drawn a good amount of interest from game developers and gamers around the world. The production problem then is augmented because there is great interest in the Wii. However, if Nintendo did not meet the hardware demand, game developers might simply begin developing software for systems that were available to consumers.

CEO Iwata claimed that "shipments will increase and that we are trying to increase the shipments in order to comply with the needs of patiently waiting customers" as well as the number of software titles available for the system from Nintendo and third-party software developers.[50] However the question remained as to whether Nintendo's Iwata could manage to keep the Wii momentum rolling into the next generation of gaming systems.

Endnotes

1. Nintendo Annual Report 2006.
2. http://www.nintendo.com/systemsclassic?type=nes.
3. Bacani, C. & Mutsuko, M. 1997. Nintendo's new 64-bit platform sets off a scramble for market share. *AsiaWeek,* April 18, http://www.asiaweek.com/asiaweek/97/0418/cs1.html.
4. Biggest blunders. *GamePro,* May 2005: 45.
5. http://wii.nintendo.com/iwata_asks_vol2_p1.jsp.
6. Carless, S. 2006. Nintendo announces new revolution name—Wii. *gamasutra.com,* April 27, http://www.gamasutra.com/php-bin/news_index.php?story=9075.
7. Nintendo exec talks Wii Online, marketing. August 17, 2006, www.cnet.com.
8. Nintendo Annual Report 2006.
9. http://arstec hnica.com/news.ars/post/20060615-7067.html.
10. http://wii.nintendo.com/controller.jsp.
11. http://wii.ign.com/articles/718/718946p1.html.
12. http://wii.nintendo.com/controller.jsp.
13. See http://wii.Nintendo.com.
14. See http://wii.nintendo.com
15. Surette, T. 2006. Nintendo exec talks Wii online, marketing *GameSpot.com.* August 17, http://www.cnet.com.au/games/wii/0,239036428,240091920,00.htm.
16. Nintendo Consolidated Financial Statements, 1/25/2007.
17. http://livenintendo.com/2007/04/12/more-supply-problems-for-the-wii.
18. http://www.marketingvox.com/archives/2007/01/26/nintendo-wii-to-provide-ap-news-on-free-channel/.
19. http://wii.nintendo.com/controller.jsp.
20. En garde! Fight foes using a controller like a sword, *New York Times,* October 30, 2006, http://www.nytimes.com/2006/10/30/technology/30nintendo.html?ex=1319864400&en=135a11a72ad4a4f7&ei=5088&partner=rssnyt&emc=rss.

21. http://www.pcmag.com/article2/0,1895,2058406,00.asp.
22. Layne, N., & Hamada K. 2007. Sony promises more games to boost PS3 demand. June 21, *reuters.com*, http://www.reuters.com/article/technologyNews/idUST28081120070621?sp=true.
23. Microsoft's red-ink game, *BusinessWeek Online*, 11/22/2005. http://businessweek.com/technology/content/nov2005/tc20051122_410710.htm.
24. www.Xbox.com/en-US.
25. http://www.xbox.com/en-US/live/globalcommunity/fosteringcommunity.htm.
26. http://news.teamxbox.com/xbox/12028/Latest-Xbox-Live-Facts-and-Stats/.
27. Ibid.
28. http://arstechnica.com/news.ars/post/20061030-8108.html.
29. http://www.xbox.com/en-AU/support/xbox360/manuals/xbox360specs.htm.
30. http://money.cnn.com/2006/07/05/commentary/column_gaming/index.htm?section=money_latest.
31. http://news.bbc.co.uk/2/hi/technology/4491804.stm.
32. http://www.microsoft.com/presspass/press/2006/may06/05-09E32006BriefingPR.mspx.
33. www.us.playstation.com/PS3/About/BluRay.
34. http://www.us.playstation.com/PS3/About/WirelessController.
35. http://www.scei.co.jp/corporate/release/pdf/060509be.pdf.
36. http://www.cbsnews.com/stories/2007/01/07/ap/business/mainD8MGN9J80.shtml.
37. http://news.bbc.co.uk/1/hi/technology/6499841.stm.
38. http://news.bbc.co.uk/2/hi/technology/6499841.stm.
39. Layne, N., & Hamada, K. 2007. Sony promises more games to boost PS3 demand, June 21, *reuters.com,* http://www.reuters.com/article/technologyNews/idUST28081120070621?sp=true.
40. http://www.gamasutra.com/php-bin/news_index.php?story=12408.
41. http://au.ps3.ign.com/articles/778/778530p1.html.
42. Author estimates of units sold, approximately 5.5 million units shipped, but 3.25 million sold.
43. http://www.us.playstation.com/PS3/Network.
44. http://www.n4g.com/tech/News-35187.aspx.
45. http://tech.uk.msn.com/features/article.aspx?cp-documentid=4370234.
46. http://www.pcworld.com/article/id,128265-page,4-c,industrynews/article.html.
47. http://news.teamxbox.com/xbox/13335/Analyst-Supply-Wont-Meet-Demand-for-the-Wii-Until-2009/.
48. *Nintendo Investor Relations* Web site, http://www.nintendo.co.jp/ir/en/library/events/070427qa/02.html.
49. Boyes, E. 2007. Nintendo: Wii have a supply problem. *CNET.News.com,* http://news.com.com/Nintendo+Wii+have+a+supply+problem/2100-1043_3-6181842.html
50. *Nintendo Investor Relations* Web site, http://www.nintendo.co.jp/ir/en/library/events/070427qa/02.html.

Case 34 Reader's Digest: Inform, Entertain, and Inspire— Inspire Whom and for How Much Longer?*

The stockholders of The Reader's Digest Association, Inc. (RDA) made a decision on March 2 of 2007 to accept a $2.4 billion buyout offer from Ripplewood Holdings LLC. This transaction would finally return RDA to private status after a 17-year run as a public company. However, even with the installation of well-respected publishing executive Mary Berner as the new CEO, analysts once again had cause to question RDA's long-term viability, "It's a fabulous brand, but its equity is eroding daily. . . . Reader's Digest could fade into history if they don't make drastic changes."[1]

In 2004 the RDA Annual Report had contained the cautionary statement that there were "risks and uncertainties" relating to "our ability to attract and retain new and younger magazine subscribers and product customers in view of the maturing of an important portion of our customer base."[2] When that was written, Reader's Digest net income had yet to rebound from the downturn of 1996 (see Exhibit 1 and Exhibit 2). Extensive restructuring, reduction in staffing levels, acquisitions, and development of international ventures initiated by CEO Thomas O. Ryder in 1998 had produced an uptick that appeared to be heading in the right direction, but the subsequent years of 2005 and 2006 had failed to produce a significant improvement in earnings. Thomas Ryder's planned retirement in 2006 may have been a prelude for new directions. The return to private status might have given RDA breathing room out of the public eye, but more work still needed to be done. The new CEO and her management team were aware of the challenges ahead, and had requested that Ryder stay involved through 2007 as a special advisor to aid in the transition.[3]

Would strategic initiatives planned and executed by Ryder work in the long run? Would the future be able to report that Reader's Digest, once named one of the most successful magazines in the Western world,[4] had redefined its product line and found a new generation of customers to inspire? Would the implementation of nonpublishing revenue streams, like the online weight loss program Change-One help? Now that almost any type of information was available, online for free, what would that mean to a company whose flagship product was a 5- × 7-inch pocket-sized compendium of human interest stories, educational material, humor, and practical advice?

After the November 2004 sale of the 114-acre property in Chappaqua, New York, home of the company's corporate headquarters since 1939, an internal culture change at this well-known American institution had been inevitable. RDA old timers had said the founders DeWitt and Lila Wallace "would be turning over in their graves."[5] After a history of restructuring in business unit management ranks,[6] could leadership be expected to redefine a culture of quality and commitment, and sustain any improvement? Was the overall strategy sound?

Exhibit 1 The Reader's Digest Association, Inc. Stock Prices 1990 to 2007

Source: From http://phx.corporate-ir.net/phoenix.zhtml?c=71092&p=irol-stockquotechart.

Note: After private acquisition by Ripplewood Holdings LLC, RDA was delisted from the New York Stock Exchange on March 2, 2007.

* This case was prepared by Professor Pauline Assenza of Manhattanville College and Professor Alan B. Eisner of Pace University. This case was solely based upon library research and was developed for class discussion rather than to illustrate either effective or ineffective handling of an administrative situation. Copyright © 2007 Pauline Assenza and Alan B. Eisner.

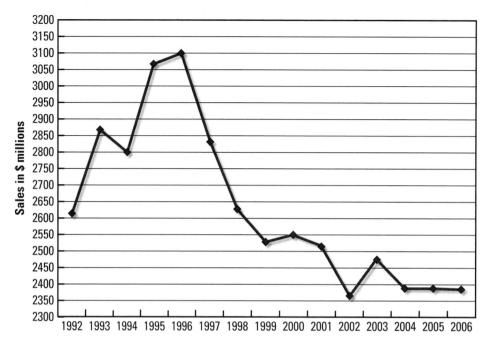

Exhibit 2 The Reader's Digest Association, Inc. Sales 1992 to 2006 (all products)

Source: From RDA 10K filings.

Background

In April of 1998, Thomas O. Ryder was recruited from American Express as Chairman and CEO of Reader's Digest Association, Inc. With Ryder's appointment came a formidable task of rebuilding and revitalizing the then 75-year-old company. When asked about what changes had to be made, Ryder, an unabashed fan, said he didn't feel the magazine was all that broken to begin with. "Any time magazines are grouped together for sale, the number-one seller is *Reader's Digest*. It ain't *Vanity Fair*. It ain't *Time*. It ain't *People*. That's also true in Brazil, Russia, and Hong Kong. It's true in a lot of places. This is a magazine of the people," he said.[7]

Ryder was to replace the interim CEO, George Grune, who had stepped back into the role of Chairman and CEO after James P. Schadt resigned in 1997. Grune's original tenure in the position lasted from 1984 to 1994. He was very successful, leading the company through the transition to become public, while doubling revenue and increasing operating profits ninefold. However, Grune's main concern during this stabilization period was to bring in a successor to put the company back on track.

Thomas Ryder seemed to be the answer. He came into the role a champion of RDA's flagship title. As Ryder said, he grew up reading *Reader's Digest*, and in his hometown of Alexandria, Louisiana, "*Reader's Digest* is pretty close to the word of the Lord."[8] As of 2006, after eight years in charge of some extensive changes to the business, he had tried to improve performance and lead the company back to the success that Grune had established during his first passage as Chairman and CEO. However, the question remained, could Reader's Digest continue to fulfill its stated mission to create "products that inform, entertain and inspire people of all ages and cultures around the world"?[9] And could it do this by continuing to rely on the *Reader's Digest* magazine?

Reader's Digest Association Business Mix[10]

Reader's Digest Association was a diversified publishing and direct-marketing corporation. They produced and distributed magazines, books, videos, music, and many other products in more than 60 countries throughout the world. The flagship magazine, *Reader's Digest*, was the world's most widely read magazine, reaching almost 100 million readers worldwide each month, delivered in 50 different editions in 21 different languages. In addition to the *Reader's Digest*, RDA published 27 other magazines worldwide on food, gardening, home improvement, country living, and other topics and sold approximately 50 million books a year.[11] Although much of the business was still in publishing, in 2004 Ryder had initiated a strategic plan to move away from what was considered the "core" business of the *Reader's Digest* magazine. This was a possible reaction to claims that the core Reader's Digest franchise was in a state of "perpetual decline" and was a possible way to shake the reputation as a "hinterlands magazine read by kindly grandparents."[12]

Reader's Digest's had been known for an extensive line of products, reaching customers on a global scale. The

Exhibit 3 The Reader's Digest Association, Inc. Business Segments as of FY2006

*Significant markets are in the United Kingdom, Germany, Central Europe, and France. Other emerging areas include Asia Pacific, Mexico, Brazil, Argentina, and the Middle East.

Source: From RDA 10K filing.

performance of the *Reader's Digest* magazines and other special interest publications had been driven primarily by circulation and subscription revenues and, to a lesser extent, by advertising sales worldwide. The international market segment had been more susceptible to changes in local market financial conditions due to the number of countries in which RDA had operated.

Ryder had divided RDA into three business units (see Exhibit 3). Reader's Digest North America consisted of the following products distributed in the United States and Canada:

Reader's Digest: RDA's flagship magazine publication, the world's largest monthly magazine. The U.S. edition had an approximate base rate of 10 million copies reaching approximately 40 million readers. A large-type edition and Spanish-language edition, *Selecciones,* were also published for U.S. distribution.

Reiman Media Group: Acquired in 2002, Reiman publications included magazines catering to "lifestyle topics" such as cooking and travel. *Taste of Home,* in 2004 the largest-selling food magazine in North America, was included in this category.

Special-Interest Publications: This category of products included other special-interest *Reader's Digest* magazines. RD Specials were one-time publications sold at grocery store checkout counters.

Recorded Music and Video: Individual box sets and series compilations in several musical and video genres were sold worldwide. Many Gold and Platinum certifications have been awarded to RDA's recorded music.

Reading Series/Select Editions: These books included Select Editions, which were specially edited novels by top authors. These volumes were sold worldwide in several countries and languages.

Young Families: Including some trade publishing relationships, this category marketed books and home entertainment products through direct and retail channels.

Illustrated Reference Books: Sold via direct mail and the publishing trade, products in this category included do-it-yourself, computer, travel, and health books.

Nonpublishing Products and Services: Products in this category included noncore ventures such as allrecipes.com and *Taste of Home Entertaining*, as well as financial and insurance services that were offered through marketing ventures with other companies.

Reader's Digest International consisted of products sold in more than 60 countries outside the United States and Canada, including Select Editions, music, video, and

Young Families products; special interest magazines in the Czech Republic; *The Family Handyman* in Australia; Books Are Fun operations in France, Mexico, and Spain; and financial services marketing partnerships and other nonpublishing initiatives in more than 30 countries. Local editions of *Reader's Digest* magazine in 50 editions and 21 languages were produced in various countries by local staff. *Selecciones,* the Spanish-language edition, was the number one magazine in most Spanish-speaking countries and, in 2006, reached over 3 million U.S. Hispanics.[13]

Consumer Business Services segment distributed products through nondirect marketing channels and utilized a specialized sales force. Businesses included:

> *Books Are Fun:* This category represented the marketing of books and gifts using product displays in North America. Established in 1999, it also served as an important marketing tool for products created in other parts of the company.

> *QSP:* This organization helped school and youth groups in the United States and Canada in their fundraising efforts.

Traditional revenues for the magazines and for books and home entertainment businesses had been principally driven by direct mail, and therefore were the most sensitive to changes in payment rates and returns. The Consumer Business Services businesses had been much less susceptible because the largest businesses in this segment collected most of their cash at the point of sale. This was another reason for diversifying away from the magazine core. In 2007, RDA had a varied array of products and services in addition to Books Are Fun and QSP, including several nonpublishing products such as ChangeOne, allrecipies.com, Taste of Home Entertaining, personal finance, and the Word Power Challenge contest.

Strategies, Goals, and Accomplishments

In November of 2004, signaling the end of an era, RDA sold the original Reader's Digest Chappaqua property, including the Georgian mansion built in 1939. Although mourned by long-time employees, this sale resulted in a one-time gain for RDA and reduced operating overhead in future years; the Reader's Digest corporate headquarters would continue to rent space for the approximately 800 corporate staffers who remained.

By 2006, Reader's Digest's goals had included reducing operating expenses and improving margins, stabilizing the customer base, expanding consumer acquisition channels, and increasing interdivisional selling to drive revenue growth. Since the 2002 acquisition of Reiman Publications, RDA had launched some significant new magazines: *Our Canada,* published by Reader's Digest Canada, *Backyard Living, Cooking for 2,* and *Birds & Blooms,* produced by Reiman, all exemplifying the Reiman Publications editorial formula. In addition, in 2005 RDA had produced a new magazine *Everyday with Rachel Ray,* featuring that popular author and TV personality.

RDA had also tested or launched Books Are Fun, Young Families, and other products elsewhere in the world. Eastern Europe had proven to be a profitable venture, with new publishing businesses in Slovenia, Croatia, Romania, Ukraine, Bosnia, Serbia, Bulgaria, Kazakhstan, and Lithuania, and new magazine releases in Russia, Germany, Finland, Australia, and Mexico. A book publishing business was also launched in the United Arab Emirates. The *Reader's Digest* magazine, under a new publishing team, had created an Indonesian edition and changed to a more prominent license partner in India in a move to expand circulation further in that populous part of the world. Children's Publishing had grown through partnerships with Disney, Nickelodeon, Hasbro, Mattel's Barbie, Fisher-Price, and NASCAR. It was thought that this division could help RDA reach young customers and their parents.

In 2006, RDA continued to expand their reach beyond publishing by acquiring allrecipes.com, a food Web site intended to connect cooks across the United States, and by creating *Taste of Home Entertaining,* an entertaining and party-planning business meant to extend the Taste of Home brand, which included the nation's largest-selling food magazine, cooking schools, and a best-selling cookbook. In 2007 RDA created a new brand, Reader's Digest Family Films, and partnered with Peace Arch Entertainment and Twentieth Century Fox Home Entertainment to produce and distribute *Ace of Hearts,* a full-length motion picture based on a true story published in *Reader's Digest* in 2002.[14]

Analysts in early 2005 were more positive regarding RDA's outlook, with some calling it a "solid pick," mostly encouraged by share prices in the $17 range, and the projected earnings growth in 2005, achieved mostly through expense and overhead cuts. This was the first time since the end of 2002 that the stock had showed some positive momentum.[15] In the 2005 Annual Report, Thomas Ryder, in his last letter to shareholders before his scheduled retirement on December 31, 2005, was still challenging the perception of the company as "*Reader's Digest* magazine, and some other stuff."[16] Eric Schrier, who succeeded Ryder as CEO in January 2006, had followed through on Ryder's strategic initiative by affirming three goals: to diversify and strengthen the core business, deepen customer relationships around selected affinities, and leverage global scale.[17]

In the fall of 2006, RDA announced talks with private equity firm Ripplewood Holdings LLC, and their intention to acquire RDA in a buyout of RDA's outstanding common shares and assumption of RDA's debt. The deal was worth $17 per share to RDA shareholders. With the acquisition completed in March 2007 for $2.4 billion, Ripplewood announced the appointment of Mary Berner as CEO. Included in the transaction was the integration of two of Ripplewood's portfolio companies: WRC Media, publisher of *Weekly Reader* magazine, the *World Almanac and Book of Facts,* the *Funk & Wagnalls Encyclopedia,* and *The*

World Almanac for Kids; and Direct Holdings U.S. Corp., exclusive worldwide marketer of TimeLife music, videos, DVDs and books. Eric Schrier would become an Industrial Partner with Ripplewood, and both Schrier and Ryder would continue to provide consultation to RDA through the transition.[18]

Berner's stated focus was on how to build on the platform that was already there. "The company has done an excellent job of diversifying both products and geography . . . with a depth and breadth of content that is one of its biggest strengths. How to leverage that digitally is one of our first initiatives," she said.[19] Berner also believed that the addition of the *Weekly Reader* and TimeLife product lines would provide more opportunities for growth, since now RDA would have "one of the largest music collections in the world."[20]

One of Berner's first acts was to restructure the company, reorganizing how the brands were marketed to consumers and advertisers by breaking them out of their corporate silos and grouping them by subject matter, such as food and entertaining and health and wellness. To aid in this, Berner recruited many of her former executives at Conde Nast/Fairchild Publications. Media observers commented that the new team must market the brands more aggressively, and since Berner was able to "lure these people to join Reader's Digest in its current incarnation . . . they must believe this company has a future as a major force in publishing."[21] Reaction within Reader's Digest was less than favorable, since Berner, even though highly regarded by the industry, had a reputation as being "fiercely smart and fiercely ambitious."[22]

The strategy to return RDA to its roots as a private company was not unique in media companies in 2006. Both Clear Channel Communications and the Tribune Company were undergoing talks with private equity firms, and there was speculation that a "large chunk" of the consumer media world would be privatized in coming years.[23] Commentators on publishing industry mergers and acquisitions noted, "companies that are valued the highest in the market are brands that are surrounded by multiple forms of media in good market positions that provide their readers and their advertisers with a comprehensive environment to interact."[24] Ripplewood's stated strategic approach was "to enhance the value of the businesses it acquires through a combination of strategic, operational, and financial actions."[25] A review of how *Reader's Digest* came to be and the strategy that drove its initial rise to popularity might provide some useful information for crafting future strategy.

A Source of "Enormous Popularity" for over 80 Years

History In 1920, DeWitt Wallace created a sample magazine containing condensed articles, which were intended to provide lasting interest and enduring significance.[26] He had long believed that much of currently published American journalistic content was "too verbose" and therefore escaped the attention of the public who didn't have the time to search for good stories. He submitted his sample digest-sized magazine to various publishers. When he was rejected by all of them, he published the magazine himself. In 1921 he established The Reader's Digest Association, selling 1,500 subscriptions to be delivered exclusively by mail. The magazine was intended to provide a reading service with selected material to "inform, enrich, entertain, and inspire." After marrying Lila Acheson in 1921, the two of them opened the first RDA office in their Greenwich Village apartment and published 5,000 copies of volume 1, number 1 of the *Reader's Digest* magazine in February 1922.

Later in 1922, the couple moved to Pleasantville (really Chappaqua), New York and in 1925 started a home and office there. (By 1939 they had finished building the majestic Georgian-style headquarters.) In 1929, *Reader's Digest* began selling at newsstands, and the circulation grew to 62,000. By 1935 circulation had passed the 1 million mark. Throughout the next decade, RDA continued to grow and expanded into different languages and countries for distribution. Starting with the United Kingdom edition in 1938, by 1945 the company had issued Brazilian, Swedish, Finnish, Australian, Danish, French-Canadian, English-Canadian, Norwegian, French, Belgian, German, Italian, Swiss-French, Swiss-German, and South African editions. The first foreign language edition was published in Spanish for distribution in America in 1940.

In the 1950s and 1960s, the Reader's Digest Association expanded into the publishing of condensed books, recorded music, and direct mail sweepstakes. In 1955, the magazine accepted its first advertising, but did not carry liquor ads until 1978 and has never carried cigarette ads. RDA also began to sponsor several educational funds and in 1963 founded QSP, Inc., an organization created to assist school and youth-group fundraising efforts in the United States and Canada. In 1973, the Wallaces gave up active management of the business, and after their passing, George Grune took over as chairman and CEO in 1984.

Under Mr. Grune's leadership RDA continued to thrive. A $15-million data center was opened at the RDA headquarters in Chappaqua. This operation allowed data to be collected and processed from all over the world. RDA entered the video business and had one of their books, *Household Hints & Handy Tips,* become number one on the General Books best-seller list. In 1990 Reader's Digest Association, Inc. became a public company trading on the New York Stock Exchange. The offering price was $21.50 per share.

In 1992, the company undertook its first global advertising campaign. The campaign included ads in 13 languages and appeared in 77 magazines and newspapers worldwide. A television commercial also aired on six continents. RDA established Young Families, Inc., in 1994. This new subsidiary created and marketed children's books and home entertainment products. On August 1, 1994, James P. Schadt succeeded Grune as president and CEO of RDA.

Under Schadt After assuming the role of president and CEO in 1994, James P. Schadt, former CEO of Cadbury Beverages, initiated a strategy to attract baby boomers to *Reader's Digest* and transition the company into a new phase. His specific strategy was to "get prices down . . . get a new variety of promotions and a new variety of products." Yet Schadt himself admitted "there's a lot of drama as the company comes face-to-face with the Information Age." He also said that he was "wrestling with a changing external world, and [had] a company that's unaccustomed to change."[27]

Despite the predisposition to "old-school" ways that Schadt felt he had to deal with at RDA, they were able to launch a Web site for Reader's Digest in 1996. The Web site was aimed at exposing new and younger consumers to RDA and "expand into new channels of distribution."[28] During Schadt's tenure, RDA also launched the Polish and Thai editions of *Reader's Digest* magazine.

However, by this point in time, it was common knowledge throughout the industry that RDA was struggling to move its content into the 21st century. One publishing industry analyst asserted that they had "lost their direction."[29] Some speculated that the largest hurdle for the *Reader's Digest* magazine, whose average reader at the time was 47 years old, was that it could not capture the interest of younger readers.

This same problem was evident with respect to the company's records, videos, and books, resulting in decreased earnings. Between 1994 and 1997, the company's stock price fell by 40 percent. Operating profits had fallen 31 percent, and revenue also decreased by 8 percent. Dividends were cut in half. Fiscal 1997 would not meet initial expectations. This was merely three months after Schadt had announced a $400 million plan for customer research, promotion, and product development.

Acknowledging the difficulties that RDA was facing and his failure to meet promises to attract a younger audience, Schadt said, "We were not successful, and we underachieved our goals." He sited an over abundance of mailings sent to customers, declining response rates, and seemingly stale products as a few of the issues contributing to RDA's problems.[30] James Schadt resigned as chairman and CEO on August 11, 1997.

Grune Returns After Schadt's resignation in 1997, George Grune was brought out of retirement to return as interim chairman and CEO of Reader's Digest. One of his major goals was to stabilize the struggling company. In one effort to do this, a joint venture between Reader's Digest Music and Warner Resound was established to bring RDA's music products into the $1-billion-a-year Christian bookstore marketplace.[31]

The second major activity under Grune's leadership was making editorial management changes at RDA. A number of senior appointments were made to strengthen the management teams in core business areas and aid in the transition.[32]

Another move toward modernization was a major change to the traditional appearance of *Reader's Digest* magazine. Forty-eight editions of the flagship magazine would replace their traditional front cover table of contents with photography and enhanced graphics. The table of contents was moved inside the magazine and expanded to cover two pages. It was also categorized by theme to make it more reader-friendly, modern in appearance, and hopefully more attractive to advertisers.[33]

Grune's final appointment and act as interim leader of RDA was to help find and appoint a new CEO and chairman for the company. The Board of Directors, aided by Grune, found what they considered the perfect candidate in Thomas Ryder.[34]

The "Quiet Revolution"—Ryder Steps in

After leaving American Express, where he was President of Travel Related Services and served on the Policy and Planning Committee, Ryder was excited about the task that lay ahead with RDA. He was not unfamiliar with the type of situation RDA faced. At American Express he had led the effort to strengthen the organization through a global re-engineering program, which helped redefine the organization's strategic direction. This was an experience that he could draw from in leading Reader's Digest.

There were many issues for Ryder to address, including assessing viability of products, broadening the customer base to include younger customers, overhauling the company's work processes and cost structure, addressing underperforming assets, and developing and acquiring growth businesses. He had to reassess overall strategy: an over-reliance on sweepstakes had lulled the company into failing to develop any other substantial means of generating business, and when subscriptions began to drop, there was no ready strategic response. His job would not be easy. One of Ryder's mantras became "no wimpy goals."[35]

After settling into his new role, Ryder's first order of business in July of 1998 was to redesign the corporate structure. He described this as the first step in a long-term strategy to build on the company's fundamental strengths and create new growth opportunities. He would create four domestic strategic business units in Books and Home Entertainment and three geographical units outside the United States, with each unit organized according to customer and business relationships. They would have specific product development and profit-and-loss responsibility.[36]

In September 1998, after profits and revenues continued to decline due to restructuring costs in the previous year, RDA refocused on gaining younger readers. This second phase of their restructuring included their acquisition of Rodale Press, Inc.'s woodworking group, including *American Woodworker* magazine. The company also sold some assets, including part of its art collection and some real estate holdings, for approximately $200 million. Some warehouse jobs were also moved outside the company. As a result, Ryder announced that several hundred employees were to be laid off.

In February 1999, Ryder announced the last phase of the restructuring that would focus the company's assets on five basic growing consumer interests: home, health, family, finance, and faith. The strategy was to expand RDA's nonpublishing products; diversify marketing channels, including the Internet; and broaden global operations.

In 1999, Reader's Digest Music, previously sold only by direct mail, made several instrumental albums by performers such as Henry Mancini available in Wal-Mart stores. Also RDA made an exclusive multiyear deal with CBS Productions to develop television movies and miniseries based on personal dramas that had been reported in *Reader's Digest* magazine. This collaboration would extend RDA's reach and publicity, it would afford them advertising opportunities, and RDA would control print publication and video distribution rights.

Your Family, a new magazine offering insight and emotional support to parents of children from infants to six years old, was also launched. The magazine was intended to promote RDA's values and traditions, yet include new ways of doing things that baby-boomer parents did not necessarily focus on. It would be sold via newsstands, supermarkets, and mass merchandisers such as Barnes & Noble.

A strong emphasis was placed on marketing and advertising resulting in a 9 percent increase in advertising revenues for fiscal 1998. RDA credited their magazines as the "front door" through which customers come in and become familiar with their products and services.[37]

Books Are Fun, Ltd. (BAF) was acquired by Reader's Digest in August 1999. BAF was the nation's leading display marketer of books and gifts. The acquisition was part of RDA's strategy to increase distribution channels for existing products and also add new products to their current offerings.

In year 2000, still continuing to pursue the strategies announced the year before, RDA acquired *Receptar,* a special interest do-it-yourself and gardening magazine in the Czech Republic. Their QSP arm also acquired the World's Finest Chocolate sales force. Lastly, the first volume of Select Editions was published in Russia. RDA experienced earnings and revenue growth for the second year in a row, with operating profits increasing 54 percent over fiscal 1999.

In 2001, Reader's Digest made several editorial and design changes to enhance publication and modernize their flagship magazine. In international business, RDA entered China. Also, RDA and Vanguard entered a marketing alliance to offer mutual funds and other financial services to Reader's Digest customers. This built upon RDA's strategy to focus on nonpublishing and financial products.

But in January 2001 the Internet bubble burst and lowered the value of RDA's Web holdings; then in September the 9/11 tragedy and anthrax scares focused the country's attention elsewhere and revenues plunged. Post office slowdowns affected the distribution of products and many direct mail customers never even opened their envelopes. In addition, lawsuits were causing regulatory agreements for all magazine sweepstakes promotions to be challenged, forcing a redefinition of this historic Reader's Digest practice.

The year 2002 brought with it two major events for RDA: the purchase of Reiman Publications LLC and approval of the recapitalization of the company. Reiman Publications was purchased for $760 million. Reiman's publications were being sold completely by direct mail and 77 percent of their readership had never purchased an RDA product before. These publications included *Taste of Home,* one of the best-selling food magazines in North America.

This acquisition was also part of RDA's effort to reduce reliance on sweepstakes sales for their magazines, since sweepstakes-generated subscriptions decreased from 92 percent in 1998 to 8 percent in 2002 as a result of regulatory changes and the attorneys' general's 2001 agreement to "dramatically change the way [RDA promoted] the sale of its products through the use of sweepstakes."[38] From 2001 on, the judgment read, all sweepstakes must provide "a clear and conspicuous" disclosure to recipients indicating that entry is free and a purchase won't help the recipient win sweepstakes prizes. In addition, RDA was to monitor sales and stop sending solicitations to consumers "who have purchased unreasonably high amounts of product."[39] Although this might have been perceived as a blow to RDA's marketing strategy, Ryder saw it as an opportunity to retool: "There was an over-reliance on sweepstakes," Ryder said. "When you overwhelm a limited audience with 50 mailings a year that are similar in all their aspects, you begin to blind them with similarities. You lost your sense of differentiation."[40]

After four years as Chairman and CEO, Thomas Ryder had made great efforts to get *Reader's Digest* back to its earlier success. What else needed to be done? With the acquisition of Reiman, RDA now had more than 23 million Gen X and baby-boomer readers aged 25 to 54, but attempts to gain younger readers' loyalty were not yet consistently successful. Even though Ryder noted that *Reader's Digest* had "nearly twice as many readers 18 to 34 as *Entertainment Weekly* and more professionals than *The Wall Street Journal, BusinessWeek, Forbes,* and *Fortune* combined," RDA*'s* stock price continued to fall. Net sales, revenues, and shareholder's equity were also lower.[41]

International business units, which accounted for 51 percent of RDA's revenues in 2001, fell to 20 percent in 2003 due to troubled economies in Germany and England. With RDA's reliance on direct mail, anthrax scares in the aftereffects of September 11, 2001, had additionally complicated North American and international business operations.

In 2003, the first full year of revenues for Reiman Publications only increased revenues by 5 percent. Although changes in the Books and Home Entertainment division were beginning to show a turnaround, revenues continued to fall there by 12 percent, reflecting the reduction in U.S. sweepstakes business.[42] Ryder's stated strategies for 2003 included a two-year plan to "achieve sustainable revenue and profit growth by Fiscal 2005" by, in part, reducing

Exhibit 4 The Reader's Digest Association, Inc. Income Statement 2004 to 2006

	Years Ended June 30,		
	2006	2005	2004
	(in $ millions, except per share data)		
Revenues	$2,386.2	$2,389.7	$2,388.5
Product, distribution, and editorial expenses	(997.1)	(970.9)	(972.9)
Promotion, marketing, and administrative expenses	(1,240.0)	(1,337.5)	(1,294.5)
Goodwill charge	(187.8)	(129.0)	—
Other operating items, net	(6.8)	14.1	(8.8)
Operating (loss) profit	**(45.5)**	**(33.6)**	**112.3**
Other (expense) income, net	(41.1)	(45.8)	(46.2)
(Loss) income before provision for income taxes	**(86.6)**	**(79.4)**	**66.1**
Income tax provision	(30.8)	(11.5)	(16.6)
Net (loss) income	**$ (117.4)**	**$ (90.9)**	**$ 49.5**
Basic and diluted (loss) earnings per share			
Basic (loss) earnings per share			
Weighted average common shares outstanding	95.9	97.4	97.1
Basic (loss) earnings per share	**$ (1.24)**	**$ (0.95)**	**$ 0.50**
Diluted (loss) earnings per share			
Adjusted weighted average common shares outstanding	95.9	97.4	99.2
Diluted (loss) earnings per share	**$ (1.24)**	**$ (0.95)**	**$ 0.49**
Dividends per common share	**$ 0.40**	**$ 0.30**	**$ 0.20**

Source: From RDA 2006 Annual Report, http://www.rd.com/corporate/2006/content.html.

marketing activity in the mature businesses to "'rest' customer bases, lower risk and improve margins," while investing in new products, expanding new customer acquisition channels, and providing more "inter-division selling opportunities to drive growth."

In 2003 RDA launched ChangeOne. With a book, weekly features, and a Web site for interactive support, ChangeOne was a weight loss program designed to improve eating habits over the course of 12 weeks and was meant to "inspire people of all ages."[43]

RDA also reorganized into the three divisions of Reader's Digest North America, Reader's Digest International, and Consumer Business Services to "combine related businesses under common leadership, reduce costs and improve . . . synergies." A decrease in revenues was noted for *Reader's Digest* magazine, stated as being "due to lower circulation and advertising revenues."[44] (Remember, for the first 35 years of its existence, *Reader's Digest*

didn't need to rely on any advertising.) In May 2003, RDA announced its first advertising campaign in 10 years to support the flagship magazine. Meant to attract media buyers, the campaign urged advertisers to "tap into the deep connection" readers have with the magazine.[45] In one analysis it was concluded that Reader's Digest's products were mature. The revenue reductions in core businesses that were not successful were outpacing the introduction of new and innovative products. The analysis stated that, "We are inclined to believe that the core Reader's Digest franchise is in a state of perpetual decline."[46]

Although 2004 was a hopeful year, fiscal 2005 showed a loss, with significant decline in profits for the Consumer Business Services (CBS) division. Although increased revenues and profits occurred in Reader's Digest North America and Reader's Digest International, CBS still had challenges, and profits for fiscal 2006 were basically flat (see Exhibits 4 to 8).

Exhibit 5   The Reader's Digest Association, Inc. Consolidated Balance Sheet 2005 to 2006

	Years end June 30,	
	2006	**2005**
	(in $ millions, except share data)	
Assets		
Current assets		
Cash and cash equivalents	$ 34.7	$ 37.7
Accounts receivable, net	261.9	233.9
Inventories	172.3	162.4
Prepaid and deferred promotion costs	62.3	53.8
Prepaid expenses and other current assets	173.1	144.9
Total current assets	704.3	632.7
Property, plant and equipment, net	119.3	119.3
Goodwill	744.1	880.9
Other intangible assets, net	134.4	137.8
Prepaid pension assets	324.6	307.9
Other noncurrent assets	95.4	102.0
Total assets	**$2,122.1**	**$2,180.6**
Liabilities and stockholders' equity		
Current liabilities		
Accounts payable	$ 128.2	$ 109.8
Accrued expenses	257.3	267.4
Income taxes payable	40.6	34.5
Unearned revenues	394.1	395.5
Other current liabilities	9.8	12.4
Total current liabilities	**830.0**	**819.6**
Long-term debt	695.0	559.2
Unearned revenues	131.2	133.0
Accrued pension	108.7	121.5
Postretirement and postemployment benefits other than pensions	94.2	96.7
Other noncurrent liabilities	87.9	84.4
Total liabilities	**$1,947.0**	**$1,814.4**
Commitments and contingencies		
Stockholders' equity	28.8	28.8
Preferred stock		
Common stock (par vale $0.01 per share; authorized 200,000,000 shares; 145,922,062 issued in 2006 and 2005; 95,047,776 and 99,256,958 outstanding in 2006 and 2005, respectively)	1.5	1.5
Unamortized restricted stock	—	(9.1)
Paid-in capital	208.1	206.8
Retained earnings	1,064.3	1,221.6
Accumulated other comprehensive loss	(67.4)	(84.1)
Treasury stock, at cost (50,874,286 and 46,665,104 shares in 2006 and 2005, respectively)	(1,060.2)	(999.3)
Total stockholders' equity	**175.1**	**366.2**
Total liabilities and stockholders' equity	**$2,122.1**	**$2,180.6**

Source: From RDA 2006 Annual Report, http://www.rd.com/corporate/2006/content.html.

Exhibit 6 The Reader's Digest Association, Inc. Consolidated Cash Flow, 2005 to 2006

	At June 30,	
	2006	**2005**
	(in $ millions)	
Cash flows from operating activities		
Net (loss) income	$(117.4)	$ (90.9)
Depreciation and amortization	36 .8	56.9
Magazine deferred promotion charge	—	—
Asset impairments	190.6	129.0
Amortization of debt issue costs	1.5	10.3
Stock-based compensation	14.3	11.2
Net gain on sales of long-term assets	(4.1)	(14.3)
Changes in assets and liabilities, net of effects of acquisitions and dispositions		
Accounts receivable, net	(19.1)	3.6
Inventories	(7.8)	(7.7)
Prepaid and deferred promotion costs (including the amortization of previously deferred promotion costs)	(7.5)	54.0
Other assets	(25.7)	13.6
Unearned revenues	(9.2)	(9.0)
Income and deferred taxes, net	(0.3)	0.1
Accounts payable and accrued expenses	1.9	(7.1)
Other liabilities	(6.3)	(10.7)
Net change in cash due to operating activities	**47.7**	**139.0**
Cash flows from investing activities		
Proceeds from sales of other long-term assets	0.9	6.7
Proceeds from sales of property, plant and equipment	3.7	62.8
Purchase of Allrecipes.com. net of cash acquired	(65.9)	—
Purchases of intangible assets	(0.5)	—
Capital expenditures	(19.9)	(23.5)
Net change in cash due to investing activities	**(81.7)**	**46.0**
Cash flows from financing activities		
Proceeds/(repayments) from borrowings, net	135.8	214.6
Proceeds from senior notes offering	—	—
Repayment of term loan	—	(377.0)
Cash paid for financing fees	(0.3)	(2.2)
Proceeds from employee stock purchase plan and exercise of stock options	2.2	3.3
Dividends paid	(39.9)	(30.5)
Treasury stock repurchases	(65.2)	(5.0)
Other, net	(3.7)	(3.0)
Net change in cash due to financing activities	**28.9**	**(199.8)**
Effect of exchange rate fluctuations on cash and cash equivalents	**2.1**	**2.2**
Net change in cash and cash equivalents	**(3.0)**	**(12.6)**
Cash and cash equivalents at beginning of year	**37.7**	**50.3**
Cash and cash equivalents at end of year	**$ 34.7**	**$ 37.7**
Supplemental information		
Cash paid for interest	$ 38.7	$ 36.8
Cash paid for income taxes	$ 34.1	$ 21.2

Source: From RDA 2006 Annual Report, http://www.rd.com/corporate/2006/content.html.

Exhibit 7 **Summary of RDA Reportable Segment Results 2002 to 2006**

Years ended June 30,	2006	2005	2004[1]	2003[1]	2002
Revenues					
Reader's Digest North America	$ 939	$ 917	$ 919	$ 932	$ 649
Reader's Digest International	1,031	1,012	970	1,008	1,078
Consumer Business Services	446	485	525	563	668
Intercompany eliminations	(30)	(24)	(26)	(28)	(26)
Total revenues	**$2,386**	**$2,390**	**$2,388**	**$2,475**	**$2,369**
Operating profit (loss)					
Reader's Digest North America	$ 115	$91	$ 71	$ 61	$ (2)
Reader's Digest International	78	76	57	49	106
Consumer Business Services	(3)	29	59	91	88
Magazine previously deferred promotion expense[2]	—	(77)	(27)	—	—
Goodwill charge[3]	(188)	(129)	—	—	—
Corporate unallocated	(40)	(38)	(44)	(22)	(7)
Other operating items, net[4]	(7)	14	(9)	(40)	(27)
Operating profit (loss)	**$ (45)**	**$ (34)**	**$ 112**	**$ 139**	**$ 158**
Intercompany eliminations					
Reader's Digest North America	$ (11)	$ (9)	$ (1)	$ (1)	$ (4)
Reader's Digest International	(6)	(4)	(4)	(4)	(6)
Consumer Business Services	(13)	(11)	(11)	(11)	(16)
Total intercompany eliminations	**$ (30)**	**$ (24)**	**$ (26)**	**$ (28)**	**$ (26)**

[1]In the first half of 2005, we made minor modifications to the composition of two of our reportable segments to reflect a change in the manner in which senior management and our chief operating decision maker internally manage certain smaller business units. Reader's Digest Young Families and Trade Publishing, which were included in Consumer Business Services, are now included in Reader's Digest North America.

[2]In connection with our change to expensing magazine deferred promotion costs when the promotion is mailed to prospective customers, our reportable segment operating (loss) profit in 2005 includes such expense as incurred. Amortization of previously deferred promotion costs in 2005 and our deferred promotion charge recorded in the fourth quarter of 2004 are not included in segment results reviewed by our chief operating decision maker. For the year ended June 30, 2005, amortization of previously capitalized magazine promotion costs related to: 81% to Reader's Digest North America and 19% to Reader's Digest International. For the year ended June 30, 2004, our magazine deferred promotion charge related to: 45% to Reader's Digest North America and 55% to Reader's Digest International.

[3]The goodwill charge related to Books Are Fun, part of the Consumer Business Services reportable segment, is not included in segment results.

[4]Other operating items, net in 2004, principally comprising severance and contract terminations, were attributable to: 12% to Reader's Digest North America, 22% to Consumer Business Services, 61% to Reader's Digest International and 5% to corporate departments that benefit the entire organization. In 2003, these items, principally severance, were attributable to: 13% to Reader's Digest North America, 6% to Consumer Business Services, 64% to Reader's Digest International and 17% to corporate departments that benefit the entire organization.

Source: From SEC 10K filing June 30, 2006, in $ million.

Cultural Factors and the Industry

Reader's Digest Cultural Impact The *Reader's Digest* magazine format and style, the features like "Word Power," "Everyday Heroes," "Life in These United States," and "Humor in Uniform," and the legacy of the Reader's Digest Condensed Books had all become part of the American experience and American culture. The brand name "Reader's Digest" had become the vernacular for a whole category of products. Even Garrison Keeler's Prairie Home Companion referenced the "reader's digest version" as part of Chatterbox Café lingo for "a condensed report on something or other."[47]

Exhibit 8　**RDA Revenue by Product and Geographical Area, 2002 to 2006**

Net Revenues by Product	2006	2005	2004	2003	2002
Books	$ 955.1	$ 971.6	$ 968.5	$ 982.9	$ 963.8
Magazines—subscription & other	$ 683.7	$ 689.8	$ 702.7	$ 750.1	$ 610.1
Magazines—advertising	$ 158.9	$ 153.2	$ 150.0	$ 151.0	$ 151.4
Music & videos	$ 264.1	$ 262.7	$ 240.3	$ 257.4	$ 328.8
Food & gift	$ 215.1	$ 215.0	$ 228.7	$ 244.9	$ 256.7
Fees from financial services marketing alliances	—	—	$ 16.9	$ 13.2	$ 20.8
Other	$ 109.3	$ 97.4	$ 81.4	$ 75.4	$ 37.0
Totals	**$2,386.2**	**$2,389.7**	**$2,388.5**	**$2,474.9**	**$2,368.6**

Revenues by Area	2006	2005	2004	2003	2002
United States	$1,202.6	$1,232.6	$1,291.3	$1,351.8	$1,176.7
International	$1,189.2	$1,162.6	$1,102.1	$1,124.6	$1,196.3
Inter-area	($5.6)	($5.5)	($4.9)	($1.5)	($4.4)
Totals	**$2,386.2**	**$2,389.7**	**$2,388.5**	**$2,474.9**	**$2,368.6**

Source: All data is from the RDA 10K filing of 2006, in $ million, years ended June 30th.

Even though some had wondered about an old-fashioned image, many readers, some in their 40s, liked the magazine just the way it was. Reviewers at Epinions in Books rated the magazine with 4 stars out of 5, calling it the "King of Magazines," "an enduring American institution and treasure," "good reading for people of all ages and backgrounds," and "one of the best overall magazines in publication today."[48]

RDA had acknowledged the importance of technology. Their Web site http://www.rd.com, launched in 1996, provided links to almost all their current products, and included shopping as well as information, citing over 14.5 million visitors to the site from around the world.[49] As of the winter of 2006, the user profile of Reader's Digest's RD Living online showed the median age of visitors was 47, with 84 percent of them college educated.[50]

Part of Thomas Ryder's "quiet revolution" to draw in "today's readers" was the engineered "subtle revamping process," developing ways to make the editorial content of the magazine younger without turning off loyal, older subscribers. Eric Schrier, hired by Ryder in 2000 to change the look and subtly upgrade the content, said Ryder warned him that it had to be done slowly, and that "this would be like changing the engine while the plane is flying."[51] In order to make that kind of change, employees had to change as well.

Regarding the internal view of the RDA culture, older employees had spoken wistfully about the paternalistic coddling, a legacy from DeWitt Wallace's days of raising salaries just because he was in a good mood;[52] of the "rides home for sick employees in the Wallace's limousine"; of the Georgian renaissance headquarters building's cupola, whose carillon bells would ring at 4 p.m. to signal the end of the work day; of Mr. Wallace walking from office to office "turning off workers' lights, urging them to go home"; and about giving workers Fridays off in May to work in their gardens. Now, thanks in part to Thomas O. Ryder, this was "a far leaner, more profit-oriented company where nobody can count on a lifetime job."[53] And the final blow to the old culture was the 2004 sale of the Wallace's elegant corporate headquarters.

The change of culture was inevitable, and Ryder said "I came at a time when people absolutely knew things had to change if the company was to survive." Some of many changes were the ones made in the executive team. Richard Garvey was hired as a Senior V.P. in 1996 by Schadt, and worked under three CEOs before being fired himself by Ryder in 1998. He is quoted as saying, "There must have been 25 vice presidents fired while I was there"[54] (see Exhibit 9).

Part of the culture change, and an overt strategy on the part of Ryder, was to use employee survey feedback, visualization workshops, a reconfigured benefits and retirement plan, and performance-based financial bonuses to create a younger, more ambitious workforce, a company that rewarded risk-taking, not conservatism; "in short, a place where someone like Mr. Wallace would be out of a job."[55]

Exhibit 9   Reader's Digest Executive Management Changes 1997 to 2007

1997

George V. Grune	CEO, President (retired in 1998)
Marcia Lefkowitz	Senior V.P., President Reader's Digest, U.S.A. (gone in 1998)
Richard Garvey	Senior V.P., Corporate Planning (gone in 1998)
Barbara Morgan	Senior V.P., Editor-in-Chief Books and Home Entertainment (gone in 1998)
Christopher Willcox	Senior V.P., Editor-in-Chief, *Reader's Digest* Magazine (gone in 2000)
George Scimone	Chief Financial Officer (gone in 2001)
John Bohane	Senior V.P., President International Operations (gone in 2002)
Peter Davenport	Senior V.P., Global Marketing (retired in 2003)
Clifford DuPree	V.P. Corporate Secretary and Associate General Counsel

1998

Thomas O. Ryder	CEO, President (retired in 2006)
Thomas Belli	President, QSP, Inc. (gone in 1999)
Gregory Coleman	Senior V.P., President U.S. Magazine Publishing (gone in 2001)
Elizabeth Chambers	V.P., Business Redesign (gone in 2002)
Robert Krefting	Senior V.P., President International Magazine Publishing (gone in 2002)
Michael A. Brizel	V.P. and General Counsel (gone in 2007)
Gary Rich	Senior V.P. Human Resources, in 2004 became President QSP
Thomas Gardner	V.P. Business Planning, in 2003 became Senior V.P., President, International

1999

Dominic Rossi	V.P. U.S. Publisher of *Reader's Digest* Magazine (gone in 2003)
Robert Raymond	V.P. Strategic Acquisitions, in 2003 became President, Consumer Business
Albert Perruzza	Senior V.P. Global Operations

2000

Michael Geltzeiler	Senior V.P., Chief Financial Officer
Eric Schrier	Senior V.P., Global Editor-in-Chief, became President/CEO in January 2006 (gone in 2007)
Jeffrey Spar	V.P., Chief Information Officer

2001

Richard Fontana, Jr	President, QSP, Inc. (gone in 2002)
John Klingel	Worldwide Circulation Director, General Manager *Reader's Digest* U.S. Magazines (gone in 2003)
Thomas Barry	Vice President and Controller

2002

Ian Marsh	Senior V.P., President, Reader's Digest Europe (gone in 2003)
Michael Brennan	Senior V.P., President Latin America and Asia Pacific
Richard Clark	V.P. Investor Relations, Global Communications (gone in 2007)

(continued)

2003	
	No additions
2004	
Giovanni di Vaio	V.P. Human Resources International (gone in 2006)
Francoise Hanonik	V.P. Human Resources North America (gone in 2006)
2005	
Bonnie Bachar	President, U.S. Publishing (promoted from V.P., at RDA since 1998)
Dawn Zier	President, North American Consumer Marketing & U.S. Books & Home Entertainment (promoted from V.P., at RDA since 1992)
2006	
Lisa Cribari	Vice President, Global Human Resources (promotion, at RDA since 1988)
2007	
Mary Berner	President/CEO (came from Conde Nast)
Suzanne Grimes	President, Food & Entertaining, new position (from Conde Nast)
Alyce Alston	President, Home & Garden/Health & Wellness, new position (originally from Conde Nast)
Eva Dillon	President/Group Publisher, Reader's Digest (from Conde Nast)
Mark Wildman	V.P. Integrated Sales & Marketing (from Conde Nast)
Andrea Newborn	V.P. General Counsel (promoted from within RDA)
William Adler	Chief Communications Officer (promoted from within RDA)

Source: Information derived from SEC 10K filings for each year.

Since 2004, the *Reader's Digest* flagship magazine had undergone several changes. It still reflected conservative, optimistic values, but with a new look and up-to-date content. For instance, RDA had hired CNBC Maria Bartiromo as a *Reader's Digest* "Money Talks" columnist.[56] In Asia, Reader's Digest English edition had gained the top spot in the Pan Asia cross media survey of nine markets, citing readership among affluent adults and business decision makers. Market share grew in the region from 9 to 11 percent, and some media directors believed that *Reader's Digest's* "mix of inspiration, drama and information clearly appealed to a younger and middle- to upper-class audience in Asia."[57]

Reader's Digest had been fighting for a long time against that image of being a magazine read only by kindly grandparents in Iowa. Even back in 2000, then publisher Dominic Rossi was saying "our median [readership] age is 47. Because we're so large, it pretty much reflects the population in general, which is 44. It's not like we have an ancient reader base." But media buyers weren't convinced, for, after all, how many of them—New York 20-somethings—read the magazine?[58] The median age of *Reader's Digest*

readers as of 2007 was 51.7, but the median age of *Reader's Digest Family Edition* was 45.6.[59] The challenge was convincing the media buyers to take a look at the statistics. RDA also had not been keeping pace with the overall publishing industry in terms of profit margins and other key ratios (see Exhibit 10). However, RDA was not the only magazine in trouble.

Publishing Industry Issues   In 2002 at the American Magazine Conference in Phoenix, some of the biggest players in the industry declared, "The business model for U.S. magazine publishing is broken and needs to be repaired to ensure the medium's survival." Thomas Ryder, CEO of Reader's Digest Association, said "We have no choice but to change," citing the industry's over-dependence on advertising, unwillingness to charge more for subscriptions, and the uncertain status of the newsstand distribution channel. No executive at the conference spoke of any visible turnaround for the industry, which had seen a major downward slide, especially since the terrorism threats of 2001.[60] The entire magazine publishing industry had had a steep reduction of over 10 million in circulation

Exhibit 10   Key Ratio Comparisons RDA to the Industry (Publishing–Books) and S&P 500

Growth Rates (%)	Company	Industry	S&P 500
Sales (quarter vs. year ago quarter)	0.20	8.20	10.20
EPS (YTD vs. YTD)	−48.20	7.00	19.00
EPS (quarter vs. year ago quarter)	−13.10	7.30	25.00
Sales (5-year annual average)	−1.29	2.94	4.25
EPS (5-year annual average)	−26.89	10.58	2.18
Dividends (5-year annual average)	0.00	4.54	2.89

Price Ratios	Company	Industry	S&P 500
Current P/E ratio	74.6	23.3	20.9
P/E ratio 5-year high	34.0	33.9	64.8
P/E ratio 5-year low	15.8	14.5	16.9
Price/sales ratio	0.72	2.02	1.57
Price/book value	3.41	4.61	2.98
Price/cash flow ratio	17.30	13.50	13.10

Profit Margins (%)	Company	Industry	S&P 500
Gross margin	62.7	63.1	47.1
Pre-tax margin	0.9	13.4	11.3
Net profit margin	1.0	8.8	7.6
5-year gross margin (5-year average)	62.2	61.2	47.4
5-year Pre-tax margin (5-year average)	6.2	12.6	9.3
5-year net profit margin (5-year average)	4.1	8.0	5.8

Financial Condition	Company	Industry	S&P 500
Debt/equity ratio	1.08	0.28	1.18
Current ratio	0.8	1.2	1.5
Quick ratio	0.4	0.7	1.0
Interest coverage	1.4	15.9	3.4
Leverage ratio	5.0	2.3	6.0
Book value/share	5.03	11.92	12.30

Investment Returns (%)	Company	Industry	S&P 500
Return on equity	4.8	20.1	14.4
Return on assets	1.0	8.6	2.4
Return on capital	2.3	15.7	6.6
Return on equity (5-year average)	22.7	20.7	11.9
Return on assets (5-year average)	4.5	7.9	2.0
Return on capital (5-year average)	11.1	14.9	5.5

Management Efficiency	Company	Industry	S&P 500
Income/employee	6,000	30,000	25,000
Revenue/employee	555,000	337,000	333,000
Receivable turnover	6.9	6.5	7.3
Inventory turnover	5.2	4.2	8.4
Asset turnover	0.9	1.0	0.3

Source: From http://moneycentral.msn.com/investor/invsub/results/statemnt.asp?Symbol=RDA.

Financial data in U.S. dollars. Presented in a Media General Financial Services proprietary format

Data is as of 2004. Since RDA is now private, comparative financial data is no longer available.

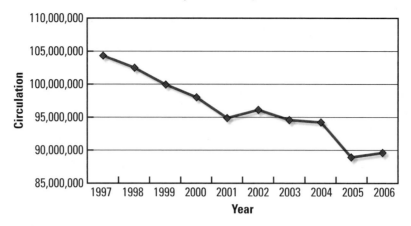

Total Top Ten U.S. Magazine Circulation

Exhibit 11 Total Top Ten U.S. Magazine Circulation, 1997 to 2006

Source: From Magazine Publishers of America Circulation Trends and Magazine Handbook,
http://www.magazine.org/circulation/circulation_trends_and_magazine_handbook/index.cfm.

since 1998 among the top ten U.S. magazine titles (see Exhibit 11).

Baird Davis, veteran consumer marketer and publishing consultant commented on industry market factors affecting the decline in circulation profitability of most mature consumer magazines during the years from 1999 to 2004. He believed the reasons for the decline could be traced to major market factors that drastically altered circulation economics: too many magazines chasing too few readers; the demise of sweepstake-generated subscriptions; a decrease in newsstand sales accompanied by an increase in newsstand marketing costs; the availability of free content, especially on the Internet; and other industry specific concerns such as audit bureau disclosure rule changes and a reduction in publishers' circulation staffs.[61]

Sarah Gonser of *Folio* warned that "publishers face the toughest ad market since the Great Depression, and there is little room for failure." She suggested that publishers were being maybe too cautious about looking for "ancillary revenue streams" that might be perceived as distractions from their core businesses. Citing Thomas Ryder's willingness to expand RDA into nonpublishing areas, she stated, "What might at first glance appear as an overwhelming hodge-podge of initiatives is in fact a highly organized, meticulously researched endeavor." There was no guarantee of success, but RDA appeared to be leveraging their brand strength, their 50-million person proprietary database, and their direct marketing expertise to try to find hidden profit sources.[62]

Regarding the Internet, most magazine publishers, including RDA, had made the shift to delivering timely content online, yet retaining their print product for its in-depth approach, its synthesis and analysis, and ability to satisfy the reader with a reliable, permanent, portable, and tactile alternative. Steve Adler of *BusinessWeek* said, "I'd even go so far as to say if the Internet didn't exist, we in this indus-

try would want to invent it," suggesting that the online version further attracts readers to the publisher's brand to see what else is available in the actual printed magazine. As Adler said, "there's still something extremely intimate and extremely powerful about settling down with a magazine and not knowing what you're going to get, page to page, and the experience of reading it."[63]

Thomas Ryder said he felt the "time was right to go on the offensive." He referred to the weakness in television advertising caused by TiVo and channel surfing. Even though the challenge was daunting, with "continuing circulation woes, looming postal rate hikes, and the specter of losing more ad dollars to the twin media of cable TV and a resurgent Web," print publishing represented a media in which ads were "bulletproof" from technology.[64] Jack Kliger, CEO of Hachette Fillipacchi Media U.S. said, "Magazines are the original on-demand medium, available on consumers' terms—whenever and wherever they choose to indulge. Magazines engage while other media interrupt."[65] In fact, studies had shown that the "influential" baby boomers were heavier readers of magazines, lighter viewers of television, and that for advertisers, adding magazine advertising to the marketing mix along with TV and Internet advertising offered a powerful punch. In fact, the "highest percentage of consumers find advertising in magazines to be more acceptable and trustworthy than advertising on network or cable TV or online."[66]

Where to Go From Here?

In 2000, after being asked why he had taken on such a big challenge at that time in his career, Thomas O. Ryder said, "I grew up reading *Reader's Digest*. The allure of trying to save an American icon was just too great to ignore."[67] At that time there had been rumors that Bertelsmann, the German privately held conglomerate with interests in

600 companies in 53 countries, was in informal talks to acquire Readers Digest.[68] And, at the time, Thomas Ryder's turnaround plan seemed to be on schedule. Since 2001, with the overall drop off in the publishing industry, these rumors had died down, but RDA could still have been an attractive takeover option.[69] In fact, Ryder had tried several times to interest buyers in a deal, even a joint venture, but was never successful. As far back as 1999 there was some serious talk with the Time Warner unit Time Inc., but a deal never materialized. There was some irony noted in the fact that the RDA takeover by private equity firm Ripplewood Holdings, first announced in November of 2006, occurred almost a year after Ryder's planned retirement.[70]

RDA's results for the second quarter of 2007 showed a $190 million increase in operating profits over the same period in fiscal 2006.[71] Things were looking like they might go in the right direction, assuming RDA could use the merger to provide time for refocusing the business out of the public eye and avoid all the risks and uncertainties facing most global businesses in 2007.

Endnotes

1. Flamm, M. 2007. New chief lures Conde Nast allies as she plots overhaul of old-line publisher. *Crain's New York Business,* May 14: 3.

2. From RDA 2004 Annual Report, http://phx.corporate-ir.net/phoenix.zhtml?c=71092&p=irol-IRhome.

3. SEC 14A Definitive Proxy Statement filing December 22, 2006, retrieved from http://yahoo.brand.edgar-online.com/EFX_dll/EDGARpro.dll?FetchFilingHTML1?SessionID=jC.Vhj7y2l3kef9x&ID=4839823.

4. Angeletti, N., & Oliva, A. 2004. *Magazines that make history.* University Press of Florida.

5. Rubenstein, C. 2004. As Digest goes the way of older readers. *New York Times,* Sunday Late Edition, August 29.

6. Romell, R. 2004. Management turnover at Reiman since sale; Several question new approach; New president calls some change inevitable. *Milwaukee Journal Sentinel.* Monday Final Edition, March 8.

7. Kaplan, M. 2000. *Reviving Reader's Digest. Folio,* July 1, 29(8): 70.

8. Kaplan, op. cit.

9. From RDA 2006 Annual Report, http://www.rd.com/corporate/2006/content.html.

10. Ibid.

11. Ibid.

12. Kaplan, op. cit.

13. *Selecciones* celebrates 35 years with the introduction of new editorial franchise issues and event. August 17, 2006, http://phx.corporate-ir.net/phoenix.zhtml?c=71092&p=irol-newsArticle&ID=896821&highlight=.

14. Reader's Digest, Fox Home Entertainment & Peach Arch Entertainment Combine to produce and release 'Ace of Hearts.' *Comtex News Network,* Filing Services Canada, May 30, 2007.

15. Tarsala, M. 2005. Under the radar—Reader's Digest. Market Report February 22, retrieved from http://www.briefing.com on March 13, 2005.

16. From RDA 2005 Annual Report, http://phx.corporate-ir.net/phoenix.zhtml?c=71092&p=irol-reports.

17. From RDA 2006 Annual Report, http://www.rd.com/corporate/2006/content.html.

18. Ripplewood Holdings announces completion of historic transaction to acquire Reader's Digest Association; Mary Berner appointed President and CEO. March 2, 2007, http://phx.corporate-ir.net/phoenix.zhtml?c=71092&p=irol-newsArticle&ID=969809&highlight=.

19. So what do you do, Mary Berner? Mediabistro.com, March 7, 2007, http://www.mediabistro.com/articles/cache/a9542.asp.

20. Kelly, K. J. 2007. Berner to help Digest. *New York Post,* March 3, http://www.nypost.com/seven/03032007/business/berner_to_help_digest_business_keith_j__kelly.htm.

21. Flamm. op. cit.

22. Fine, J. 2006. Conde Nast: Mary Berner out. *BusinessWeek Online,* January 4, http://www.businessweek.com/innovate/FineOnMedia/archives/2006/01/conde_nast_mary.html.

23. Fine, J. 2006. Media's new masters. *BusinessWeek Online,* November 13; Fine, J., & Lowry, T. 2006. End of the clear channel ear. *BusinessWeek Online,* November 16, see http://www.businessweek.com/innovate/FineOnMedia.

24. Steinmetz, M. 2007. M&A boomtown: How long will it last? *Publishing Executive,* February 1, http://www.pubexec.com/story/story.bsp?sid=47357&var=story.

25. Ripplewood Holdings announces . . ., op. cit.

26. Information in this section from Reader's Digest Web site "timeline" at http://www.rd.com and from *American Dreamers: The Wallaces and "Reader's Digest"* by Peter Canning, 1996, Simon & Schuster, NY, http://syracuseuniversitypress.syr.edu/encyclopedia/entries/readers-digest.html.

27. Leiberman, D. 1997. *Reader's Digest* wants baby boomers. *USA Today,* July 21: 3B.

28. Oneserver provides RDA with advanced Web site. *Telephone IP News,* December 1, 1996, 7: 1–8.

29. Berkowitz, H. 1997. Digest chairman out after turnaround fails. *Newsday,* August 12: A49.

30. Leiberman, op. cit.

31. Reader's Digest Music, Warner Bros. announce joint venture in Christian music retailing. *Business Wire,* September. 2, 1997.

32. Reader's Digest announces management changes. *Business Wire,* September 7, 1997.

33. *Reader's Digest* Magazine redesigns editions worldwide; bold cover photography replaces table of contents; eye-opening graphics inside create dynamic new look. *Business Wire,* March 29, 1998.

34. Reader's Digest names Thomas O. Ryder of American Express as chairman and chief executive officer. *Business Wire,* April 4, 1998.

35. Kaplan, op. cit.

36. Ibid.

37. Reader's Digest strengthens publishing arm. *Business Wire,* June 14, 1999.

38. Teague, M. 2001. Pryor reaches settlement with Reader's Digest regarding sweepstakes solicitations. March 9, http://www.ag.state.ar.us/prrecent11.htm.

39. Ibid.

40. Kaplan, op cit.

41. From RDA 2002 Annual Report, http://phx.corporate-ir.net/phoenix.zhtml?c=71092&p=irol-reports.

42. Craig Huber, Douglas Arthur, Lisa Monaco, analysis of RDA for Morgan Stanley, January 24, 2003.

43. Reader's Digest groundbreaking program for weight loss. January 7, 2003, http://phx.corporate-ir.net/phoenix.zhtml?c=71092&p=irol-news&nyo=0.

44. From RDA 2003 Annual Report, http://phx.corporate-ir.net/phoenix.zhtml?c=71092&p=irol-reports.

45. Reader's Digest launches first ad campaign in 10 years. May 15, 2003, http://phx.corporate-ir.net/phoenix.zhtml?c=71092&p=irol-news&nyo=0.

46. Mandana Hormozi, Kathryn Mak, analysis of RDA for Lazard Freres & Co., LLC, June 25, 2003.

47. Search the Chatterbox Café postings on http://prairiehome.forum.publicradio.org/.

48. Various reviews from Keith Pruitt, Bryan Carey and others posted during December 2004 at http://www.dealtime.com/xPR-Reader_s_Digest~.

49. Excerpted from the 10K filed by RDA on 9/9/2004.

50. From http://www.rd.com/content/advertise-with-us-on-the-web/.

51. Kilgannon, C. 2000. A workplace like no other painfully enters the real world. *The New York Times,* December 24.

52. Rubenstein, C. 2004. As Digest goes the way of older readers. *New York Times,* Sunday Late Edition, August 29.

53. Kilgannon, op. cit.

54. Ibid.

55. Ibid.

56. Reader's Digest adds CNBC anchor Maria Bartiromo as columnist. September 7, 2004, http://phx.corporate-ir.net/phoenix.zhtml?c=71092&p=irol-news&nyo=0.

57. Shaw, S. D. 2003. Reader's Digest's climb to the top of PAX may help it chip away at agency bias. *Media Asia,* January 10: 15.

58. Kaplan, op cit.

59. From the Reader's Digest Web site http://www.rd.com/mediakit/rd/circulation.jsp.

60. Fine, J. 2002. Magazines confront flawed business plan. *Advertising Age,* 73(43): 1.

61. Davis, B. 2004. Can't get no respect? Read this! *Circulation Management,* October.

62. Gonser, S. 2002. Looking inward for outside profits. *Folio,* 31(4): S4.

63. Business magazine editors identify trends that could affect your bottom line. Magazine Publishers of America, June 16, 2005, http://www.magazine.org.

64. Fine, J. 2004. Publishers finally unite to rally behind 'engagement'. *Advertising Age,* (Midwest region edition), Chicago, 75(44): 3.

65. Kliger, J. 2005. Magazine marketing coalition: Creating a movement. World Magazine Congress of the International Federation of the Periodical Press (FIPP), May 24, http://www.magazine.org.

66. Ibid.

67. Fine, J. 2000. Ryder pulls 'Digest' back from brink. *Advertising Age,* (Midwest region edition). Chicago, 71(44): S20.

68. Marcial, G. 2000. Buy Reader's Digest? *Business Week,* June 19.

69. Morais, R. 2003. Takeover bait. *Forbes,* 172 (1): 72.

70. Fine, J. 2006. Rader's Digest goes private, and the irony thereof. *BusinessWeek Online,* November 16, http://www.businessweek.com/innovate/FineOnMedia/archives/2006/11/readers_digest.html.

71. RDA Announces Higher 2Q Fiscal 2007 Revenues, Operating Profits, EPS and Cash Flow vs. 2006. January 25, 2007, http://phx.corporate-ir.net/phoenix.zhtml?c=71092&p=irol-news&nyo=0.

Case 35 UPS and Fedex in the Express Delivery Services Industry*

In January 2007, United Parcel Service (UPS) began its year-long celebration of 100 years of service.[1] More than just package delivery, UPS, and the express delivery services industry now included the synchronized movement of goods, information, and funds worldwide. Starting in February of 2005, Mike Eskew, chairman and CEO of the UPS had outlined the need for transformation:

> Think about how UPS was when you first met us. We had one kind of service: a reliable ground delivery business engineered for the masses. We had one way of doing things. Now we're going to be a one-to-one company— treating every package as if it's the only one we have, every customer as if he or she is the only one we have, every transaction as if it's the only one we have. UPS is also moving from satisfying the customer's small package needs to enabling global commerce.

In order to do this, Eskew believed UPS had to acquire assets to add capabilities, update the brand, upgrade technology, and get the message about change out to the employees. When asked about the competition posed by FedEx and DHL, Eskew replied, "They're aggressive. We've got to be better."[2] This message, and its implications, had not changed.

John Beystehner, UPS chief operating officer (COO) who retired in January 2007 after 36 years of service, underscored Eskew's beliefs by saying, "Our future rests on our continued ability to innovate and compete in a heated global economy."[3] UPS, although by all reports still one of the major players both in air and ground package delivery and supply chain solutions, had recently lost ground in the U.S. market to FedEx.[4,5] DHL, and parent Deutsche Post AG, with its recent purchase of Airborne in the United States and Exel plc in Europe, were making a big push worldwide, and several other strong niche competitors based in Europe such as TNT were posting impressive operating statistics (see Exhibits 1, 2, and 3.).

There had certainly been many changes in the package industry even over the last 10 years. Emery Air Freight used to be a case study example of efficiency, but Emery had stopped doing parcel deliveries in the early 1990s, shortly after being acquired by CNF Inc., the former owner of Consolidated Freightways.[6]

Industry consolidation through acquisition in the delivery arena appeared to be accelerating, with FedEx acquiring RPS and Viking Freight in 1998 and American Freight in 2001, DHL acquiring Airborne in 2003 and Exel in 2005, and UPS acquiring Menlo in 2004 and Overnite Transportation in 2005.

On the retail side, UPS bought out the Mailboxes Plus franchise in 2001 and FedEx acquired Kinkos in 2004. And these were only the headlines affecting the American market. Increasingly, the competitive arena was expanding beyond Europe and North America to South America, Asia-Pacific, and the Middle East and including not just overnight or expedited package delivery, but ground

Exhibit 1 Market Share

	UPS	FedEx	DHL	TNT	USPS	Other
			Market Share			
U.S.*	18%	32%	13%	0%	4%	33%
European**	19%	8%	30%	15%	0%	28%
Asia***	10%	22%	33%	7%	0%	28%
Emerging Markets****	10%	9%	47%	10%	0%	24%

*From the Colography Group, 2006 data.

**Comprises Germany, U.K., France, Italy, Netherlands, Spain.

From Market Intelligence, 2006 data.

***Comprises Singapore, Hong Kong, China, Japan, Taiwan, Thailand, Philippines, Indonesia, India, Australia, New Zealand, Malaysia, South Korea.

From L.E.K. Consulting, 2006 data.

****Comprises Turkey, Greece, Saudi Arabia, Russia, South Africa, United Arab Emirates.

Source: From Crescendo Partners/L.E.K Consulting, 2006 data, and Deutsch Post World Network, Annual Report 2006.

* This case was prepared by Professor Pauline Assenza of Manhattanville College and Professor Alan B. Eisner of Pace University. This case was solely based upon library research and was developed for class discussion rather than to illustrate either effective or ineffective handling of an administrative situation. Copyright © 2004, 2007 Pauline Assenza and Alan B. Eisner.

Exhibit 2   Customer Rate Comparisons

		Rate Comparisons			

From: Woodbury, CT 06798   To: Wimberley, TX 78676
Weight: 3 lbs   Package size: 12 × 12 × 12 box   Service: Business to Business

Carrier	Overnight	Next Day	2nd Day	Ground	Comments
DHL	$65.42		$33.36	$ 7.22	3 day total
FedEx	$65.08	$56.44	$32.92	$ 6.56	4 day total
UPS		$64.06	$33.89	$ 8.66	7 day total
USPS		$22.80	$10.50	$ 5.77	5 day total
TNT		$58.23	$38.14	$25.83	unknown

From: Woodbury, CT 06798   To: Kiev, Ukraine 04208   Value: $90
Weight: 3 lbs   Package size: 12 × 12 × 12 box   Service: Business to Business International

Carrier	Document	Priority Dutiable	Comments
DHL	$79.15	$249.95	3 day total
FedEx	$63.28	$219.24	5 day total
UPS	$81.58	$260.06	5 day total
USPS	$32.00	$206.00	3 day total
TNT	$42.85	$237.11	6 day total

From: Woodbury, CT 06798   To: Xiamen, China 361004   Value: $90
Weight: 3 lbs   Package size: 12 × 12 × 12 box   Service: Business to Business International

Carrier	Document	Priority Dutiable	Comments
DHL	$58.19	$161.27	3 day total
FedEx	$56.10	$139.36	5 day total
UPS	$40.52	$148.65	9 day document, 13 day box
USPS	$ 5.90	$116.00	3 day total
TNT	$42.85	$197.38	6 day total

From: Woodbury, CT 06798   To: Tustin, CA 92780
Weight 1.5 lbs   Package size: 6 × 6 × 6   Service: Business to Consumer, residential

Carrier	Overnight	Next Day	2nd Day	Ground	Comments
DHL	$39.93	$34.82	$17.14	$ 7.15	6 day total
FedEx	$40.19	$35.73	$17.28	$ 6.73	4 day total
UPS	$39.69	$36.14	$17.47	$ 8.82	6 day total
USPS		$19.60	$ 8.40	$ 7.24	7 day total
TNT	no residential delivery				

Sources: Company Web sites.

Exhibit 3   **Asset Data and Financial Comparisons**

	Overview of Assets—2006 estimates				
	UPS	**FedEx**	**DHL**	**TNT**	**USPS**
Number of employees	428,000	221,677	520,110	140,000	696,138
Number of vehicles	101,300	Approximately 41,200	72,000	23,462	216,004
Number of aircraft (leased & otherwise)	+600	671	420	44	0

UPS Product Line Revenue and Profit						
	2006	**2005**	**2004**	**2003**	**2002**	**2001**
Revenue (in $ millions)						
U.S. domestic package	$30,456	$28,610	$26,960	$25,362	$24,280	$24,391
International package	9,089	7,977	6,809	5,609	4,720	4,280
Supply chain & freight	8,002	5,994	2,813	2,514	2,272	1,650
Total revenue	$47,547	$42,581	$36,582	$33,485	$31,272	$30,321
Percentage Growth	11.7%	16.4%	9.2%	7.1%	3.1%	1.8%
Profit (in $ millions)						
U.S. domestic package	$ 4,923	$ 4,493	$ 3,702	$ 3,657	$ 3,925	$ 3,969
International package	1,710	1,494	1,149	732	338	139
Supply chain & freight	2	156	138	56	(167)	(146)
Total operating profit	$ 6,635	$ 6,143	$ 4,989	$ 4,445	$ 4,096	$3,962
Percentage growth	8.0%	23.1%	12.2%	8.5%	3.4%	−12.2%
Net income	$ 4,202	$ 3,870	$ 3,333	$ 2,898	$3,182	$ 2,399
Percentage growth	8.6%	16.1%	7.9%	−8.9%	32.6%	−18.2%

FedEx Product Line Revenue and Profit						
	2006	**2005**	**2004**	**2003**	**2002**	**2001**
Revenue (in $ millions)						
Express*	$21,446	$19,485	$14,365	$16,467	$15,438	$15,645
Ground**	5,306	4,680	3,447	3,581	2,918	2,565
Freight	3,645	3,217	2,374	2,443	2,253	993
Kinkos	2,088	2,066	1,513	—	—	—
Total Revenue	$32,485	$29,448	$24,710	$22,487	$20,607	$19,629
Percentage Growth	10.3%	19.2%	9.9%	9.1%	5.0%	
Profit (in $ millions)						
Express*	$ 1,767	$ 1,414	$ 629	$ 783	$ 801	$ 836
Ground**	705	604	522	494	337	113
Freight	485	354	244	193	185	61
Kinkos	57	100	39	—	—	—
Total Profit	$ 3,014	$ 2,472	$ 1,434	$ 1,470	$ 1,323	$ 1,010
Percentage growth	21.9%	72.4%	−2.4%	11.1%	31.0%	
Net Income	$ 1,806	$ 1,449	$ 838	$ 830	$ 710	$ 584
Percentage Growth	24.6%	72.9%	1.0%	16.9%	21.6%	

*Includes trade networks.

**Includes supply chain services.

Source: Annual Reports.

(*continued*)

Exhibit 3 Asset Data and Financial Comparisons (*continued*)

TNT/TPG Group Product Line Revenue and Profit					
	2006	2005	2004	2003	2002
Revenue (in $ millions)					
Mail	$ 5,365	$ 4,718	$ 3,900	$ 3,915	$ 4,005
Express	7,933	6317	4,696	4,251	4,175
Logistics*	(21)	934	4,081	3,735	3,610
Total revenue	$13,277	$11,969	$12,677	$11,901	$11,790
Percentage growth	10.9%	−5.6%	6.5%	0.9%	5.7%
Profit (in $ millions)					
Mail	$ 1,004	$ 920	$ 833	$ 765	$ 774
Express	765	561	322	223	194
Logistics**	(86)	(109)	90	(202)	85
Total operating profit	$ 1,683	$ 1,372	$ 1,245	$ 786	$ 1,053
Percentage growth	22.7%	10.2%	58.4%	−25.4%	6.5%
Net income	$ 885	$ 780	$ 667	$ 301	$ 604
Percentage growth	13.5%	16.9%	121.6%	−50.2%	2.7%

*Logistics was discontinued in 2006.

**Includes nonallocated losses of $122.

DHL Product Line Revenue and Profit (converted from Euros)				
	2006	2005	2004	2003
Revenue (in $ millions)				
Mail	$15,805	$15,320	$15,164	$14,864
Express	20,455	20,022	21,165	18,193
Logistics	27,050	11,816	8,073	6,992
Financial services	11,412	8,433	8,742	9,114
Other	—	—	—	—
Total revenue	$72,024	$53,049	$51,353	$47,604
Percentage growth	35.8%	3.3%	7.9%	
Profit (in $ millions)				
Mail	$ 2,443	$ 2,415	$ 2,480	$ 2,477
Express	387	−27	437	434
Logistics	906	412	334	245
Financial services	1,194	1,027	823	676
Other	—	—	—	—
Total operating profit	$ 4,606	$ 4,478	$ 3,541	$ 3,160
Percentage growth	2.9%	26.4%	12.1%	
Net Income	$ 2,279	$ 2,659	$ 3,067	$ 2,963
Percentage growth	−14.3%	−13.3%	3.5%	

delivery, supply chain and warehouse solutions, and logistics services.[7]

According to the *Financial Times,* certain analysts feared UPS had "not responded quickly enough to the shift in manufacturing to China and other low-cost countries, leaving it with too much infrastructure and cost in its slow-growing U.S. market and too little capacity in the fast-expanding international markets."[8] UPS, in a presentation to the international investment community in 2007, agreed that an international deployment strategy needed a "clear and deliberate path" to grow, especially in Asia, where 72 percent of companies worldwide were expected to source products and services by 2009.[9]

What business sectors should UPS and other expedited service delivery providers consider as major opportunities over the coming years and how should they position themselves to become the primary competitor in those sectors? What were the areas of concern, if any, in their current portfolios of business units? What should these providers do to continue to define their unique attributes and fulfill their value proposition to their customers?

As UPS entered its 100th year, additional and probably more important questions became: What was the nature of express package industry? Who were the customers? Where was the competition coming from?[10] (See Appendix A.)

What Can Brown Do For You?

Founded by James E. Casey in 1907 as a messenger company in Seattle, Washington, as of 2007, UPS was the world's largest package delivery company and one of the global leaders in supply-chain services, offering an extensive range of options for synchronizing the movement of goods, information, and funds.[11] Headquartered in Atlanta, Georgia, UPS delivered an average of 15.6 million packages each business day for 1.8 million shipping customers to 6.1 million consignees in more than 200 countries and territories worldwide. Since 1999, UPS's stock had traded on the New York Stock Exchange (UPS).

UPS's vision was to synchronize "the flow of goods, information and funds—the three flows of commerce."[12] UPS claimed to be the only company in the industry that had one operation network for all types of shipments: domestic, international, air, ground, commercial, and residential, making for economies of scope and scale that improved operating efficiency as well as customer service.

UPS's 100-year-old company culture was based on the owner/management philosophy through which over 30,000 active management employees had significant investments in UPS stock. With a large percentage of full-time non-management employees also having stock ownership, UPS claimed a decision-making mentality that had a long-term focus centered on achieving strong returns on invested capital and maintained a work ethic that was characterized by dedication, aligning employees' interests with the interests of public shareowners.

However, employee–management relations had been shadowed by uncertain union relationships, with the pilot union contract negotiation in 2004 to 2005 and driver negotiation starting in 2007. For instance, the 15-day strike by UPS's Teamster drivers in 1997 cost an estimated $750 million in revenue and caused previously loyal customers to search out and perhaps switch to competitors like FedEx and the United States Postal Service (USPS), among others. The 2001 union contract with drivers negotiated for wages, benefits, and new jobs that were estimated to increase UPS costs by $9 billion over the six years of the contract, which might contribute to larger increases in delivery rates over time.[13]

Overnite Transportation Company, acquired by UPS in 2005 and renamed UPS Freight in 2006,[14] was not unionized, and remained so because it was run as a separate operating company, part of UPS's Supply Chain & Freight Operations segment. Before acquisition, Overnite was a subsidiary of Union Pacific (UP), having been purchased by UP in 1986, and it was one of the 10 largest U.S. trucking carriers, operating from over 200 terminals, consolidating pallet-sized shipments in the labor-intensive sector of trucking known as less-than-truckload or LTL. LTL freight was "dramatically different from UPS small package operations," partly because it operated dock-to-dock.[15]

Although originally founded as a "common carrier" parcel post delivery service, since going public in 1999 UPS had expanded into retail shops with the purchase of Mail Boxes Etc., into logistics and freight forwarding, and then into heavy freight (see Appendix B and Appendix C). UPS had also focused a lot of attention on their Supply Chain Solutions Business Segment. In a Harris poll, 70 percent of executives surveyed believed that effective management of their supply chains would have "a large impact" on the ability of their companies to achieve their strategic goals, however, at the time; only 33 percent outsourced their supply-chain solutions. The remaining 66 percent admitted various problems with effective supply-chain management, and only 16 percent were comfortable extending their existing infrastructure to include China. This confirmed UPS's belief that having a supply-chain solution (SCS) was a strategically vital part of their business model.[16,17]

Supply Chain Solutions and Freight Operations enabled UPS to move any type of freight, by any mode, anywhere in the world. Through this business UPS managed warehouses and distribution networks and handled complexities of customs brokerage, frequently relying on UPS's small package network for package delivery.

UPS Supply Chain & Freight and other nonpackage businesses offered more than 60 products and services in transportation and freight management, logistics and distribution, international trade, financial services, and consulting. The infrastructure included facilities that oversaw global freight shipments, filled orders, performed technical repair, deployed critical parts, and managed customs brokerage.

Examples of Supply Chain Solutions' business included:[18]

- Repairing and returning laptop computers in as little as 24 hours from the Louisville, Kentucky hub, helping Toshiba distinguish its repair service from its competitors, saving on repair costs, and providing better customer service. This repair program utilized The UPS Store retail network for professional packaging and convenient drop-offs of customer laptops, UPS's package delivery network for movement of customer computers, and the UPS Supply Chain Solutions for parts management and technical repair. The specially designed repair center was a 2-million square foot campus adjacent to the UPS Worldport global air hub where certified repair technicians had access to parts to repair the entire laptop.

- Consolidating distribution of Honeywell automotive aftermarket products from five distribution centers into two facilities using sophisticated IT systems and automation that significantly reduced order cycle time and provided real-time order tracking from order entry to final delivery, with order accuracy near 100 percent on an annual total of about 400 million units. The facility included built-in flexibility to accommodate seasonal swings in demand as well as growth in business. UPS Supply Chain Solutions integrated the Honeywell Consumers Products Group information systems with advanced logistics software. Orders were sent through the UPS transportation management system, generating carrier options and consolidation opportunities for each order, minimizing transportation costs, and raising reliability of service. Customers consistently received orders on the requested dates, and the average number of shipments per purchase order had dropped from three to one.

UPS had estimated supply chain spending around the world at over $3 trillion in 2007, of which only about 10 percent was outsourced. Anticipated growth in this market was part of the reason that UPS had purchased Menlo Worldwide Forwarding. Menlo was a subsidiary of CNF, formerly Consolidated Freightways, Inc., another major freight and supply-chain management company, and had been losing money. But it was a well-established global air freight forwarder with international trade capabilities, providing ocean services and international customs brokerage in more than 175 countries and territories around the world, with customers in pharmaceuticals, apparel, high tech and consumer goods.[19] Menlo included the entity formerly known as Emery Air Freight, one of the dominant carriers of heavyweight air cargo in North America.

UPS's abilities in their supply-chain solutions business had gained them a top 10 rating in 2007 as one of an elite group of 3PLs (third-party logistics providers) increasingly dominating logistics outsourcing around the world. Expectations were that this "closed club" would become even more exclusive in years ahead as acquisitions concentrated the power among fewer but larger third-party logistics providers (see Appendix D).[20]

Even though this was a potentially important area for growth, UPS had had difficulty. Success in this area was contingent not only on efficient and technologically innovative communication, but on seamless and sustainable links to the overall air and ground transportation networks. These anticipated network synergies had not materialized in recent years, partly because of the difficulty integrating the acquisitions of Menlo and Overnite.[21]

Going forward, some of the factors that might affect the package delivery and expedited service industry as a whole included the following:

- Fuel charges, both in airline and truck (ground) segments, currently offset by an indexed fuel surcharge for both domestic and international air products
- Potential U.S. union contract negotiations, regarding funding for pensions and other benefits
- Fluctuating volume of U.S. mortgage refinancing activity, affecting overnight and next day air letter demand
- Growing e-commerce business worldwide, and keeping up with technology innovations both internally and in customer interface applications
- In addition to Asia and Africa, reaching out to be more of a force in the growing markets of Brazil, India, the Middle East, and Eastern Europe
- Careful financial management, including not only growth for shareholders, but operations that yielded enough free cash flow to finance capital expenditures and acquisitions in the future[22]

For UPS, its conservative culture and regimented work style might also become a hindrance.

When It Absolutely, Positively Has to be There Overnight

Major United States competitor Federal Express was founded in 1971, inspired by now famous CEO, Frederick W. Smith's undergraduate term paper about the need for a different distribution system for time-sensitive air shipments. It has traded on the NYSE as FDX since 1978.[23] FedEx was the first company to offer the overnight letter; the first to offer next-day delivery by 10:30 a.m.; the first to offer Saturday delivery; the first to offer time-definite service for freight; the first to offer money-back guarantees; and in 1990, the first service category company to win the Malcolm Baldrige National Quality Award.

In January 1998 Federal Express, the express delivery company, acquired the small package, freight, forwarding, logistics, and technology resources of Caliber System Inc., and in 2000, FDX Corp. was renamed FedEx Corporation. From its headquarters in Memphis, Tennessee, FedEx provided the following services:

FedEx Express: The mother of overnight, time-critical service provided time-guaranteed express shipping of small packages up to 150 pounds to every U.S. address and to more than 220 countries and territories. Express delivery of freight weighing from 151 to 2,200 pounds was delivered to any U.S. location and to 50 countries within one to three business days.

FedEx Ground: Using the automated sorting system introduced to the industry by Roadway Package System (RPS) in 1985, the ground segment of the business, initiated in 1998, handled 3 million packages on a typical day. Dan Sullivan, who retired as president of the FedEx Ground division in 2007, believed it was "critically important" to really create a work force that was entrepreneurial. Avoiding the threats of unionization, FedEx Ground drivers were independent contractors who purchased their white trucks with the FedEx logo and were paid by the stop and number of packages. This was part of FedEx Home Delivery, a business–consumer service designed to give catalog and online retailers evening and Saturday deliveries. FedEx SmartPost, which used the USPS Parcel Select program to give price breaks to large-volume retail customers who ship lightweight items that don't need expedited delivery, augmented this service. These packages were delivered by FedEx to bulk mail centers or post offices, and the USPS delivered them the "last mile" to the customer.[24]

FedEx Freight: American Freightways, a northeastern regional carrier acquired by FedEx in 2001, combined with Caliper System's Viking Freight, a regional LTL carrier serving the western United States, and Caribbean Transportation Services, an airfreight forwarding provider. This service offered coverage to the 40 contiguous United States and, via airfreight forwarding, to Puerto Rico and the Dominican Republic for LTL shipments.

FedEx Custom Critical: Based on the Roberts Express expedited model acquired in 1998, Custom Critical provided exclusive-use shipping via either air or ground for critical freight such as custom race cars, priceless art pieces, emergency equipment, temperature-sensitive items, and hazardous goods, door-to-door, internationally.

FedEx Trade Networks: Tower Group International and World Tariff Ltd., acquired in 2000, handled customs brokerage; global ocean and air cargo distribution; and trade information on duties, tariffs, and taxes for 118 countries, providing customer clearance solutions for international shippers.

FedEx Supply Chain Services and FedEx Services: Augmented by the acquisition of Caliper Systems Logistics and Technology solutions in 1998, this segment provided logistics management, consulting services, and data management and technology support for the package tracking capabilities of FedEx Express, Ground, and Freight services. Supply Chain Services had consistently ranked as one of the top 3PL providers.

FedEx Kinko's Office and Print Services: In 2003, FedEx CEO Fred Smith acknowledged that UPS had something FedEx did not—3,300 branded full-service retail stores. As Smith said then, "It is an area we are keenly interested in."[25] Therefore, it was no surprise that in 2004, FedEx acquired Kinkos, allowing them to provide copying, printing,

film processing, shipping, and other services to residential and commercial customers at more than 1,500 locations in 11 countries, many with 24-hour, 7-day-a-week operation. (For other milestones in FedEx history, see Appendix E.)

Donald Broughton, analyst for A.G. Edwards, believed there was a shift in momentum from UPS to FedEx, giving the advantage to FedEx, saying, "It's more entrepreneurial, more willing to take risk. And the model it's employing should produce better operating margins for it and steal the premium yield from UPS."[26]

Looking forward, FedEx CEO Fred Smith stressed the importance of expanding to provide service in Brazil, India, China, and Eastern Europe.[27] FedEx had some of the same operational challenges as UPS, plus these additional ones:

- Legal challenges to the FedEx Ground independent contractor status
- Competition for the "worksharing" arrangements FedEx had with the USPS
- Anticipation of additional capital spending for FedEx's extensive air fleet
- The need to expand FedEx capabilities in logistics and supply chain management
- Complaints from customers about unreliable and inconsistent service from the FedEx Ground delivery contract drivers[28]

Much had been written about the differences between the FedEx and UPS cultures. FedEx, which was nonunion except for pilots, was known for having an entrepreneurial culture, being innovative, and quick to respond, and providing lots of training opportunities for employees. Creativity was encouraged and employees were given latitude to make decisions on their own.[29] Risk-taking behavior was also reflected in aggressive expansion activity and sometimes heavy borrowing, but this had also paid off, especially in FedEx technology investments. FedEx had differentiated itself with many firsts in its first 20 years.

UPS's culture emphasized accountability and engineered efficiency (in the Frederick Taylor scientific management style[30]), with fairly rigid operational guidelines. This, plus a tradition of promoting from within, had given UPS one of the lowest historical turnover rates in the industry, and had generally pleased the union, which had also helped maintain service reliability.[31] UPS also had historically been fiscally conservative, rejecting debt, and subsequently had been the industry's cost leader (see Appendix F).

FedEx and UPS were basically neck and neck in the U.S. market, but how would they compare in global competition? In 2006, FedEx CEO Frederick Smith had commissioned a study of "access" from SRI International, detailing how people, businesses and nations around the world benefited from access to physical goods and information.[32] The study showed how increased access led to increased empowerment, connection, innovation, market reach, growth, and competitiveness in 75 countries. Smith detailed the challenges for business leaders and policymakers, and therefore for FedEx, as nuturing the environment; eliminating artificial trade barriers; securing "open skies" agreements; and helping developing countries obtain life essentials such as healthcare, and education, which lead to prosperity.[33] FedEx had continued to focus on international expansion, and had also continued to post steady growth compared to competitors, perhaps by following a socially responsible strategy (see Exhibit 3 and Appendix G).

Turning to the International Players, DHL Delivers

When considering the competition, both UPS and FedEx had to consider DHL, especially since it had acquired U.S. rival Airborne in 2004 to gain a ground delivery unit and access to the former Airborne air delivery operations, which were frugally run by original aircraft management company ABX Air, Inc. out of their private airport complex in Wilmington, Ohio.[34] From Albania to Zimbabwe, the DHL Worldwide Network delivered.

This subsidiary of Deutsche Post World Net was the world leader in cross-border express deliveries, ahead of both FedEx and UPS, and was a major provider of logistics and freight forwarding services. Overall, DHL's express service linked 120,000 destinations in more than 220 countries and territories. The company maintained about 5,000 offices, and it operated a fleet of some 72,000 vehicles.

The DHL brand had a powerful history.[35] Founded in San Francisco in 1969 by Adrian *D*alsey, Larry *H*illblom and Robert *L*ynn, DHL quickly turned its focus to the Far East and the Pacific Rim, providing expedited document services there by 1972 and initiating service in Europe in 1974. By 1979, when DHL began delivering packages in addition to documents, DHL had offices in Frankfurt, Germany, and London, with service to Latin America, the Middle East, and Africa. In 2002 DHL was fully acquired by Germany's Deutsche Post World Net.

DHL Worldwide Network S.A./N.V., was headquartered in Brussels, Belgium. Headquartered in Bonn, Germany, parent company Deutsche Post World Net had some 520,000 employees in more than 220 countries and territories worldwide, and generated revenue of €60 billion (approximately $72 billion) in 2006.[36] The divisions of Deutsche Post World Net were DHL Express/Logistics, Mail, and Financial Services. The business segments were organized under the Deutsche Post overall brand.

> DHL Express was the result of the consolidation of the former DHL Worldwide Express business and the Deutsche Post Euro Express parcels business. It offered Same Day, Express, Parcel, and Freight services, both by air and road.

> DHL Freight offered international and national transport solutions for part- and full-load shipments in Europe, moving goods by ground, rail, and a combination of the two. DHL Freight covered the former DHL's nondocuments and nonparcels business as well as the former Danzas Eurocargo road transport business.

> DHL Global Forwarding offered customized worldwide logistics solutions for air and sea freight, regardless of size and weight. It also provided specialist services such as integrated turnkey project forwarding for industry segments and cargo management services.

> DHL Exel Supply Chain provided tailor-made contract and industry-specific logistics solutions ranging from consulting to supply-chain design and including storage and sales logistics to production and order management. In 2005 Deutsche Post World Net had acquired Exel plc for €5.6 billion, creating the largest logistics company in the world.[37] They were now unique in that they had the geographical presence and operational scale to meet customer demand for a worldwide end-to-end supply chain, making this combined DHL/Exel unit far and away the largest 3PL provider in the world.

> Deutsche Post and DHL Global Mail delivered an average of 70 million letters throughout Germany each working day and offered international mail services, providing expertise in international direct marketing services and publication solutions. In 2006, 95 percent of all mail in Germany reached its customer the next day, despite a population of 82 million.

> Deutsche Postbank AG provided the whole spectrum of banking services to retail customers, including payment transaction services and selective finance solutions.

From 1995 to 2005 DPWN had gone through an unparalleled transformation. In a short period of time Deutsche Post evolved from a government-controlled, debt-ridden national agency into a publicly governed and profitable Global Player (see Appendix H).

Arthur Hatfield, at Morgan Keegan, said, "DHL has certainly spent a lot of money on ads, and they've said they're going to spend a billion or so to compete against FedEx and UPS, but I think to get the kind of network they're going to need to be on par with FedEx and UPS, they're going to have to spend a lot more than that. More like $3 billion or $5 billion."[38] Stories of delivery failures and poor customer service continued to point to integration troubles from the Airborne acquisition through 2007, and there were rumors of a management shakeup.[39]

Looking Further in Europe: Fulfilling Ambitions

Similar to Deutsche Post, but more focused on specific strategic segments of the industry, TNT N.V., headquartered in Amsterdam, included Royal TNT Post and TNT Express.[40] A third business, TNT Logistics was discontinued in late 2006. TNT was the Netherlands' largest private employer. The group employed over 140,000 people in 60 countries and served over 200 countries. The company was known for its caring culture, obtaining top rank in the Hewitt Associates Best Employer in Europe survey. Consistently, from 2000 to 2006, TNT had also been highly ranked in *Fortune*'s "delivery" industry category. For 2006 the company reported sales of €10 billion. TNT N.V. was publicly listed on the stock exchanges of Amsterdam and New York.

TNT had made a journey similar to Deutsche Post's. In 1799, the small individual postal services in the Netherlands were brought together to form the first Dutch national postal service. PTT Post remained a state-owned company until its incorporation on January 1, 1989, which allowed PTT Post to undertake new commercial activities. In addition to conventional postal services, the company developed national and international express-delivery and logistics services. In December 1996, PTT Post acquired the Australian company TNT and thus became a key player in the world market. In 1998 TNT and PTT Post became TNT Post Group (TPG). TPG was the first mail company to go public under the stock listing of TNT N.V.

TNT Post processed 16 million postal items addressed to more than 7 million locations in the Netherlands each day, collecting, sorting, transporting, and delivering letters and parcels. In 2006 TNT Post customers enjoyed a near 97 percent next-day delivery of letters. The company also specialized in data and document services, direct mail, e-commerce, and international post. In 2006 TNT launched a parcel delivery service to the U.K.

TNT Express was acquired in 1996, and was the world's leading business-to-business express delivery company. The company delivered 3.4 million parcels, documents, and pieces of freight a week to over 200 countries using its network of 857 depots, hubs, and sorting centers. TNT Express operated over 23,000 road vehicles and 44 aircraft and had the largest door-to-door air and road express business-to-business delivery infrastructure in Europe. Utilizing the mail and express networks in TNT N.V.'s portfolio allowed for cross-selling in both business-to-business and business-to-consumer markets.

Expansion into Brazil, India, and China, using TNT branded airplanes between China and Europe allowed for growth in those areas. In 2007 TNT launched the "fastest express deliver service in South East Asia using their network of providers to deliver emergency express shipments to major cities in Indonesia, Malaysia, Philippines, Singapore, Thailand, Hong Kong, and Japan within 6 to 16 hours rather than their competitors' 24 hours.[41]

Unlike UPS, FedEx, and Deutsche Post, TNT had adopted a closely focused strategy in 2005, electing to sell off its logistics segment and instead make investments that increased network coverage in selected markets. In 2006 this enabled them to upgrade service levels, standardize processes, and strengthen connections between express operations worldwide. By 2007, TNT had acquired express operations in Spain, India, and Brazil, and entered into a transfer agreement with a major Chinese provider. In the mail market, TNT continued to lobby for the opening of all European postal markets to full competition, and acquired mail companies in Germany, the U.K., and Italy, further positioning TNT's network in Europe.

Neither Snow Nor Rain Nor Heat Nor Gloom of Night . . .

The U.S. Postal Service was another legacy mail provider, an independent establishment of the executive branch of the U.S. government.[42] Unlike other federal agencies, it received no tax dollars for its operations. It was self-supporting, and had not received a public service appropriation since 1982.[43]

The USPS was a competitive force, especially in the overnight express and 2-day priority mail service niches. In fiscal year 2006, the USPS reported total revenue of $72.8 billion, of which $5 billion, or 924 million pieces, was Priority Mail; $2.2 billion, or 1,175 million pieces, was Package Services; $1.7 billion, or 774 million pieces, was International; and $0.9 billion, or 56 million pieces, was Express Mail.[44]

The USPS delivered more than 200 billion pieces of mail each year, but its future role was uncertain because customer needs were changing; electronic alternatives to mail were eroding volume; costs were rising faster than revenues, especially retirement and health benefit liabilities; fixed costs were high; giant private firms, some former national foreign postal services, and some privatized, were dominating global parcel and express markets, entering an increasing portion of the postal value chain; and finally, rising security concerns were requiring expensive and sophisticated countermeasures.[45] Although the USPS acknowledged that long-term restructuring of the legislative and regulatory framework was required, and although the USPS presumably had the historical field advantage in price, that advantage was eroding. The USPS was proposing either transforming into a privatized corporation, like TPG Post or Deutsch Post, or into a commercial government enterprise.[46]

The USPS interacted with various private partners such as UPS, FedEx, and DHL, in a worksharing arrangement where these carriers collected parcels from high-volume shippers, such as mail order and Internet retailers, and delivered these packages as deep into the postal stream as possible. USPS then carried the merchandise to the customer's door, thereby providing seamless service, but reducing the USPS's opportunity for productivity improvements.[47] However, opportunity for future alliances and innovation at the Postal Service interface had major potential in the future.

Other Players in the Industry—Con-way, Inc.: Heavy Freight Trucking and More

Born in 1939 as Consolidated Freightways and renamed in 2006, Con-way, Inc. traded on the NYSE as CNW, and was a $4.2 billion company and a leading provider of both less-than-truckload and full truckload heavy freight, re-builder of transportation equipment, and creator of global supply-chain solutions, including brokerage, logistics, and warehousing for a wide range of manufacturing, industrial, retail, and government customers.[48] The company and its subsidiaries operated across North America and in 20 countries.

While CNW transported freight for many of its customers, like many heavy freight companies it was taking on a much larger role.[49] Like others, CNW was assuming total management of the complex transportation and information networks required for companies to get all of the raw materials they needed in the door not just on the right day, but at the right time of day. CNW also managed warehouses, completed final configuration, packaged products, and distributed the finished goods.

Although CNW's roots were in heavy freight transportation, the nature of moving freight had changed and become so sophisticated that the movement of information was now as important as the movement of the products. CNW invested heavily in technology focusing its efforts on conducting customer transactions via the Internet; developing and implementing state-of-the-art dispatch, warehouse management, order fulfillment, and tracking systems; and optimizing the routing of its delivery vehicles to increase efficiency and reduce transit times.

Con-way's resources included more than 20,000 employees, and 32,000 tractors and trailers. Con-way maintained more than 440 service locations in the United States, Canada, and Puerto Rico and provided contract carriage services to and from Mexico. The company served more than 400,000 customers, providing them with 98 percent on-time, next-day delivery performance. Con-way increased earnings in the first quarter of 2005 by more than 30 percent, primarily from less-than-truckload growth across all regions of North America. By the end of FY 2006, earnings had continued to grow by over 20 percent.[50]

Ensenda: Delivery the Last Mile

Outsourced logistics was often associated with the large, global operators that managed vast, multimodal supply chains for the world's largest manufacturers and retailers; however niche players had emerged to prove that big wasn't always better.[51] Ensenda, based in San Francisco, was formed by two entrepreneurs in 2001 to serve what they perceived as a logistics vacuum: Ensenda was to be the leading last mile logistics provider in North America.[52] A nonasset company with national reach to oversee local delivery providers, Ensenda put their network of independent delivery experts—over 300 local delivery firms with 10,000 individual drivers—to work for their customers in over 135 markets across the United States and Canada, providing complete coverage for local domestic delivery needs and moving product between distribution centers and stores or branch locations or from branch locations and stores out to the end buyer.

Unlike the FedEx Ground model, Ensenda used a certification process to qualify each company, and tracked performance using key performance indicators on a weekly basis. Ensenda had redundant coverage in every market and changed the delivery network frequently, creating healthy competition between drivers. Customers only paid for the services they used on a per-transaction basis. Ensenda bought delivery services wholesale based on economies of scale and marked up the services to sell at retail. Customers could do the same but found it cheaper to use Ensenda rather than trying to manage such a network themselves. For the delivery companies, Ensenda bought unused capacity, making the delivery firm more efficient.[53]

Customers included outbound shipments from industrial supplier W. W. Grainger to restock their retail customers in 24 hours, delivery to residential customers of building supplies from The Home Depot, housewares and furniture from Ikea, and electronic products from Best Buy.[54] Ensenda boasted an average on-time delivery rate of over 99.2 percent.

Their comprehensive software suite of "last mile" local and regional logistics linked Ensenda with local drivers and customers, and customers could access delivery information real-time over the Internet. Services had helped shippers reduce shipping costs by 65 percent versus managing a proprietary fleet and had provided a faster, more cost-effective alternative to LTL. Ensenda had created one point of contact and one invoice for all North American last-mile deliveries and, therefore, was able to predict and control local delivery costs and accessorial charges. In summary, Ensenda had been able to respond creatively to customer special requests.[55]

Final Thoughts

Although the transportation services industry was over 100 years old, for express delivery services it had changed drastically (see Exhibit 4). Research analysts had been warning for years that a change was on the way, specifically the dominance of the transportation buyer,[56] the decline in average shipment weight, the shift from mode-specific to time-based shipping, and the shortening of the average length of haul.[57] This implied that carriers would be expanding regional distribution centers and partnering with other providers.

Global competition, customization manufacturing, increasing technology and information needs, expanded trade opportunities, and increased customer expectations had all exerted pressure on providers to make significant adjustments to their business and corporate strategies, so much so that the industry was difficult to categorize. Other players were emerging all over the world from previously separate niches. Major players had varying business unit structures, making it hard to do direct comparisons within service segments (see Exhibit 5). To compete, major players had to consider many factors before making strategic decisions. What could UPS and others take from this to help craft competitive strategy? More generally, where would the industry end up, and who would survive and prosper?[58]

Historical Stock Price Comparison

Exhibit 4 Relative Growth Chart, December 2001 to March 2007

Showing the increase in overall relative stock value for this industry, quarterly since 2001.

Note: TNT and DHL prices are from their relative European stock exchanges, Euronext Amsterdam, and Frankfurt/M, Xetra.

Source: TNT Share Monitor at http://qfx.quartalflife.com/clients/nl/tnt/sm6/Default.aspx.

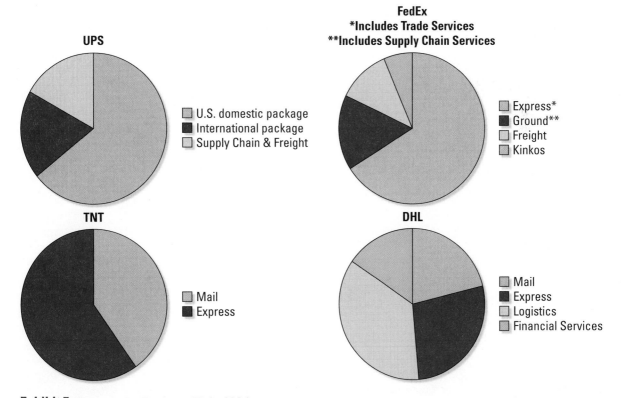

Exhibit 5 Revenue by Business Unit, 2006

Source: From financial data provided in Exhibit 3.

Appendix A

Air Cargo Services—Companies that provide delivery of freight by air.[59]

Express (or Expedited) Delivery Services—Companies that provide express delivery of parcels, letters, and documents.

Freight Forwarding Services—Companies that arrange the movement of freight by various transportation methods, including air, sea, and land, on behalf of exporters and importers. The companies may or may not own the assets themselves.

Less-Than-Truckload Carriers (LTL)—Companies that provide transportation of less-than-truckload shipments, in which freight from multiple shippers is consolidated into a truckload.

Logistics Services—Companies that engage in the process of planning, implementing, and controlling the movement and storage of raw materials, in-process inventory, finished goods, and related information from the point of origin to the point of consumption.

Postal Services—Companies that operate post offices and deliver parcels, letters, and documents.

Supply Chain Management Services—Companies that provide services that help companies manage the movement and storage of raw materials, in-process inventory, finished goods, and related information from the point of origin to the point of consumption.

Transportation Services (a general industry heading)—Companies that provide transportation of passengers and freight, arrange for transportation of freight, and manage transportation infrastructure.

Warehousing and Distribution Services—Companies that provide warehousing and distribution of freight.

Appendix B   UPS Milestones

- Founded in 1907, in 1922 UPS was one of the few companies to offer "common carrier" delivery service at rates comparable to those of parcel post, and in 1924 was the first to develop a conveyor belt system to handle packages.
- In 1975, UPS went international to Canada, by 1989 was serving more than 175 countries, with its own aircraft, and in 1990 began flights to Asia.
- In 1998 UPS Capital was founded to provide a comprehensive menu of integrated financial products and services to enable companies to grow their businesses.
- In 1999 UPS became a publicly traded security on the New York Stock Exchange.
- In 2001 UPS acquired Mail Boxes Etc. and in 2003 allowed franchisees in the 3,300 U.S. retail centers to convert to The UPS Store brand.
- In 2002 UPS consolidated UPS's Logistics Group, Freight Services, Capital, Consulting and Mail Innovations companies into UPS Supply Chain Solutions.
- In 2004, UPS was awarded 12 more frequencies to fly to China.
- In 2004 UPS acquired Japan's Yamato Express Co.
- In 2004, UPS acquired Menlo Worldwide Forwarding (including what was formerly Emery Air Freight) from CNF, providing the capability of guaranteed heavy air freight in North America, and Supply Chain Solutions in ocean shipping and customs brokerage services.
- Construction continued on UPS's highly automated hub in Cologne, Germany, their largest hub outside the United States.
- UPS acquired Overnite Transportation, allowing it to ship freight weighing more than 150 pounds using more of its own planes, and in 2006 Overnite became UPS Freight.
- In 2005 UPS acquires LYNX Express Ltd., one of the UK's largest independent parcel carriers, and Messenger Service Stolica, one of the leading express delivery companies in Poland.
- A new distribution and logistics hub opened in Singapore in 2006 as a logistics Free Trade Zone (FTZ), with plans for a new air hub in Shanghai in 2008.

Appendix C   Selected Awards Given to UPS and FedEx

Some of the many awards UPS has earned included:

- Top Performing Airlines Ranking, *Aviation Week and Space Technology*
- Number one on World's Most Respected Transport Companies Survey, *Financial Times*
- Most Valuable Corporate Brand, Best Big Companies in America, *Forbes*
- Among 50 Best Companies for Minorities, America's Most Admired Company in its Industry (21st consecutive year), World's Most Admired Company in its Industry (6th consecutive year), Fortune 500, Fortune Global 500, Blue-Ribbon Company, *Fortune*
- Technologies of the Year—Notable Innovations Award for UPS Package Flow Technologies, *Industry Week*
- Among top 25 Customer Service Champs and Best Global Brands *BusinessWeek;* among top 10 in online customer respect, *The Customer Respect Group*
- UPS Supply Chain Solutions top logistics provider, *Inbound Logistics;* best in class, *Consumer Goods and Technology Magazine*

FedEx's awards included:

- *Fortune*'s lists of Most Admired Companies (beating UPS), Best Companies to Work for in America, Best Companies for Minorities
- Among top 25 Customer Service Champs and Best Global Brands, *BusinessWeek*
- *Harris Interactive* U.S. Corporation Reputation Top 10 (2003 to 2006), Top 20 (2001 to 2002)
- *InformationWeek, Computerworld, Wired, CIO Magazine*—various awards for technological innovation
- Business Ethics Best Corporate Citizens List
- *Inbound Logistics, Logistics Management & Distribution Report,* Top 3PL Provider listings
- *Logistics Management & Distribution Report* Hall of Fame recognition as highest rating for customer service, 10-year top performer in LTL carrier category
- *General Motors* Supplier of the Year

Appendix D — Top 25 3PL (Third Party Logistics) Providers[60]

Rank	3PL	2006 3PL revenue (in $ millions)	Summary
	The Top 25 Global 3PLs		
1	DHL Logistics www.us.danzas.com	31,000	The integration of Exel into DHL has gone well. John Allan should be the right guy to lead logistics. Now let's see those margins improve. Global Forwarding has experienced management with a strong brand in Asia and Europe.
2	Kuehne + Nagel International www.kuehne-nagel.com	14,900	Kuehne + Nagel is a well managed company with high quality sea freight, airfreight and contract logistics. It is transparent and tough.
3	Schenker/BAX Global www.schenkerusa.com www.baxglobal.com	14,000	Schenker is one of the European big five. The BAX Global addition added muscle to Asia operations and a strong base in the U.S. It's moving out from under tight Deutsche Bahn control.
4	UPS Supply Chain Solutions www.UPS-SCS.com	8,000	Lots of capabilities and strong parent, but where are the profits? Does UPS SCS need non-Brown blood?
5	Panalpina World Transport www.panalpina.com	7,200	Panalpina is the largest pure freight forwarding player. It is profitable and transparent but difficult to acquire.
6	C.H. Robinson Worldwide www.chrobinson.com	6,600	CHR is still the most profitable with expanding international and intermodal business. Europe's atomized trucking industry is a good match for CHR's model.
7	Agility www.agilitylogistics.com	4,900	A well-run, very liquid company with politically stable operations in the Middle East.
8	CEVA Logistics www.cevalogistics.com	4,600	Apollo Management paid a lot for it, giving Dave Kulik and company great challenges and great opportunities. It needs freight forwarding capability to compete long term.
9	Expeditors www.expeditors.com	4,600	Expeditors is the dominant player between China and North America. It has excellent financial results and business model. A Rose is a Rose is a . . .
10	NYK Logistics www.nyklogistics.com	4,200	NYK is the Japanese company which has internationalized. It is now a competitor in non-Japanese markets.
11	UTI Worldwide www.go2uti.com	3,500	UTI's McFarland and company continue to grow, making the right acquisitions and opening the right way in the right markets. Contract logistics additions have been most successful here.
12	Nippon Express www.nipponexpress.com	3,400	Japan's dominant transportation company changes very slowly. Its international business needs stronger marketing and a new mind-set.

(continued)

Rank	3PL	2006 3PL revenue (in $ millions)	Summary
13	EGL Eagle Global Logistics www.eaglegl.com	3,200	Whither goest thou, Jim Crane? Eagle was acquirable. Is new ownership the path to major growth and profits?
14	Penske Logistics www.penskelogistics.com	3,050	Major non-automotive successes are an important change. How best to expand internationally is the challenge.
15	Ryder www.ryder.com	2,600	Ryder is adjusting well to non-automotive market. How to expand internationally and continue to improve margins are two questions. Upgrades in dedicated contract carriage are in the works.
16	Hellmann Worldwide Logistics www.hellmann.net	2,600	Hellman, a large privately held German-based freight forwarder, continues to grow.
17	CAT Logistics www.catliogistics.com	2,400	CAT is a moving machine. It is a master of inventory control and supply chain management for automotive, industrial, aerospace and hi-tech.
18	Kintetsu World Express www.kwe.com	2,300	Kintetsu is a major airfreight player between China and Japan. Worldwide forwarding operations are solid.
19	Schneider Logistics www.schneiderlogistics.com	1,500	What is really going on at Schneider is less clear all the time. This is the most private of private companies.
20	Menlo Worldwide www.menloworldwide.com	1,400	Menlo has lean logistics, multi-client operations and continuous improvement. Its a master of distribution center and network logistics.
21	APL Logistics www.apllogistics.com	1,300	APL has a new life and better results with Brian Lutt as CEO. Transparent financials to match operational improvements.
22	Toll Holdings www.toll.com.au	1,100	Toll is a major player in Southeast Asia and Australia. Let's see what the Aussies can do with this one.
23	Maersk Logistics www.maersk-logistics.com	800	A.P. Moeller, the parent company, needs to let management talk about this operation. It has some good operations and a lot of opaqueness. Maersk is still afraid to tell the public who its customers are.
24	FedEx Supply Chain Services www.fedex.com	739	FedEx SCS has strong customs brokerage, some freight forwarding and good IT capacities used to support FedEx's transportation operations.
25	Landstar Global Logistics www.landstargloballogistics.com	700	Landstar is putting together all the pieces of a true non-asset model.
	Total 2006 Logistics Revenue	**$131,589**	

*Most 2006 revenue numbers are derived from public records or company self-reporting. Where no such information was available (companies with *), these numbers are based on Armstrong & Associates' own research.

Appendix E   FedEx Milestones

- Federal Express installs its first Drop Box in 1975.
- In 1981, Federal Express introduces the Overnight Letter, also begins service to Canada and opens its "SuperHub" adjacent to Memphis International Airport.
- In 1984 Federal Express began shipping to Europe and Asia and in 1989 acquired Tiger International, becoming the world's largest full-service, all cargo airline.
- FedEx developed an innovative IT infrastructure, and was the first air express company in 1986 to provide customers a highly reliable tracking system.
- RPS was acquired in 1998 and became FedEx Ground in 2000.
- Acquiring Evergreen International Airlines in 1995, Federal Express, now officially "FedEx," was the first U.S.-based cargo carrier to obtain authority to service China, opening the Asia Pacific Hub at Subic Bay in the Philippines.
- Opened its European hub at Roissy-Charles de Gaulle airport in France in 1999.
- In 2000, FedEx acquired Tower Group's international logistics and trade information technology business, and WorldTariff, a customs duty and tax information company, forming the backbone of FedEx Trade Networks.
- American Freightways, a leading LTL freight carrier in the eastern United States, was combined in 2001 with FedEx's Viking Freight to become FedEx Freight.
- In 2001 FedEx Express and the USPS formed an alliance where FedEx provided air transportation of U.S. mail and FedEx Drop Boxes at post offices nationwide. In 2004 FedEx won the contract to be the international carrier for the USPS Global Express Guaranteed Service, winning over previous carrier DHL.
- In 2004, FedEx acquired Kinko's, providing document management services and shipping options to customers of all sizes, with 400 out of 1,200 stores open 24/7.
- Also in 2004, FedEx acquired Parcel Direct, a leading parcel consolidator, rebranding it as FedEx SmartPost to provide low-weight less time-sensitive service for e-tailers and catalog companies.
- In 2005 becomes the first carrier to launch overnight delivery from India to China and the first direct connection between mainland China and Europe. Plans to build the region's largest air cargo hub in Guangzhou, China.
- In 2006 acquires UK Express Company ANC, acquires Watkins Motor Lines in United States, expands long-haul less-than-truckload (LTL) services in the United States and Canada.
- December 18, 2006, is the busiest day in FedEx history.
- In 2007 acquires Flying-Cargo in Hungary, Express Business of China's DTW Group, Indian Express Company PAFEX.
- Beginning in June 2007, FedEx offers next-business-day, time-definite, or day-definite domestic service to more than 200 cities within China; has 30 weekly U.S.–China cargo frequencies.

Appendix F   UPS Mission

The UPS Charter[61]

Our Values—*Our enduring beliefs*

We believe that integrity and excellence are the core of all we do.

We believe that attention to our customers' changing needs is central to the success of UPS.

We believe that people do their best when they feel pride in their contributions, when they are treated with dignity, and when their talents are encouraged to flourish in an environment that embraces diversity.

We believe that innovation fortifies our organization through the discovery of new opportunities to serve our people and our customers.

Our Purpose—*Why we're in business*

We enable global commerce.

Our Mission—*What we seek to achieve*

We fulfill our promise to our constituents throughout the world in the following ways:

- We serve the evolving distribution, logistics, and commerce needs of our customers worldwide, offering excellence and value in all we do.
- We sustain a financially strong company, with broad employee ownership, that provides a long-term competitive return to our shareowners.
- We strive to be a responsible and well-regarded employer by providing our people with an impartial, rewarding, and cooperative environment with the opportunity for advancement.
- We build our legacy as a caring and responsible corporate citizen through the conduct of our people and company in the communities we serve.

Our Strategy—*The UPS plan of action*

Create the future through One company. One vision. One brand.

We will continue to expand our distribution and supply-chain solutions to synchronize the world of commerce—the flow of goods, information, and funds; We will expand our position as a trusted broker between buyers and sellers worldwide; We will harness the appropriate technology to create new services and to strengthen our operations and networks.

We will attract and develop the most talented people whose initiative, good judgment, and loyalty will help realize our company's mission. We will continually study customers' behavior, anticipate their needs, and design our products and services to exceed their expectations.

We will create a practice of innovation that leads to sustainable growth. We maintain an environment that enables us to treat every customer as if they are our only one. We will leverage the UPS brand to maximize brand loyalty among all constituencies.

Appendix G FedEx Mission

FedEx Mission:[62] FedEx will produce superior financial returns for shareowners by providing high value-added supply chain, transportation, business and related information services through focused operating companies. Customer requirements will be met in the highest quality manner appropriate to each market segment served. FedEx will strive to develop mutually rewarding relationships with its employees, partners and suppliers. Safety will be the first consideration in all operations. Corporate activities will be conducted to the highest ethical and professional standards.

Strategy: The unique FedEx operating strategy works seamlessly—and simultaneously—on three levels.

Operate independently by focusing on our independent networks to meet distinct customer needs.

Compete collectively by standing as one brand worldwide and speaking with one voice.

Manage collaboratively by working together to sustain loyal relationships with our workforce, customers, and investors.

Values:

People—We value our people and promote diversity in our workplace and in our thinking.

Service—Our absolutely, positively spirit puts our customers at the heart of everything we do.

Innovation—We invent and inspire the services and technologies that improve the way we work and live.

Integrity—We manage our operations, finances, and services with honesty, efficiency, and reliability.

Responsibility—We champion safe and healthy environments for the communities in which we live and work.

Loyalty—We earn the respect and confidence of our FedEx people, customers, and investors every day, in everything we do.

Appendix H   Deutsch Post World Net Values

Our corporate culture creates added value and leads us on the way to become stronger than our competitors. This is an obligation that we have to our shareholders. Our corporate culture unites the excellence of our individual subsidiaries and their unique company cultures to produce a shared strength.

An active, open corporate culture makes us an attractive employer for highly talented people and strengthens our position as a responsible global corporate citizen in this world. We are committed to the values defined in this corporate culture. They are both a challenge and a guide-post. They support the evolution of our business while we and they continue to develop. Our seven values are:

1. To deliver excellent quality.
2. To make our customers successful.
3. To foster openness.
4. To act according to clear priorities.
5. To act in an entrepreneurial way.
6. To act with integrity internally and externally.
7. To accept social responsibilities.

Source: From http://www.dpwn.de/dpwn?xmlFile=2006624&lang=de_EN.

Endnotes

1. See http://pressroom.ups.com/globalconnections/ and the centennial overview at http://www.100ups.com/index.html.

2. A conversation with Mike Eskew, interview by Walter Klechel, editor-at-large, Harvard Business School Publishing, 2/17/05, from http://www.pressroom.ups.com/execforun/speeches.

3. Driving growth through innovation, speech at Commerce & Industry Association of New Jersey, 3/32/05, http://www.pressroom.ups.com/execforum/speeches.

4. FedEx gained share across air, truck categories in 2004, 3/1/05, http://www.colography.com/press/2005.

5. Ward, A. 2005. UPS fades as global rivals deliver. *Financial Times,* January 25: Smith, R. 2007. FedEx flying fine. *The Motley Fool,* June 21, http://www.fool.com/investing/general/2007/06/21/fedex-flying-fine.aspx.

6. Emery became a subsidiary of the CNF logistics company Menlo Forwarding, and stopped doing business under the Emery name in 1996. Menlo, although a money-loser for CNF, was subsequently purchased by UPS in 2004.

7. United States International Trade Commission. 2006. Express delivery services: Competitive conditions facing U.S.–based firms in foreign markets. Publication Number 3678, August, http://www.usitc.gov/publications/abstract_3678.htm.

8. A. Ward, op. cit.

9. UPS European Investor Conference presentations by Alan Gershenhorn, President, UPS International; Scott Davis, CFO; Kurt Kuehn, SVP Worldwide Sales & Marketing, 3/6/2007, http://investor.shareholder.com/ups/news/webcasts.cfm.

10. Also see reports Competition within the United States parcel delivery market, http://www.postcom.org/public/articles/2003articles/parcel_competition.htm and The parcel service industry in the U.S.: Its size and role in commerce, 8/1/00, http://www.seas.upenn.edu/sys/logistics/parcelstudy.html.

11. What can Brown do for you? is the tagline for UPS's new branding push in 2004. Hearsay has it that the trucks are brown because that kept the mud from being seen when deliveries were made over the dirt roads in the 1900s.

12. This quote and the following summary is from http://investor.shareholder.com/ups/profile/charter.cfm and this and previous data is from the UPS 2006 Annual Report, http://investor.shareholder.com/ups/financials/annuals.cfm.

13. Brooks R., & Whelan, C. B. 2002. A tentative 6-year agreement with Teamsters stabilizes UPS. *The Wall Street Journal,* July 17.

14. Overnite becomes UPS Freight, 2/28/06, http://investor.shareholder.com/ups/news/releasedetail.cfm?ReleaseID=197291.

15. Nguyen, T. 2005. UPS deal sparks Overnite–Teamsters uncertainty. May 19, http://fleetowner.com/news/t.

16. Corporate Execs say supply chains a strategic key to their business future, 4/28/05, http://ups.com/pressroom/us/press_releases/press_release/0,0,4553,00.html.

17. Thuermer, K. E. 2004. Small package delivery goes global like the big boys. *World Trade Magazine,* July 1, http://www.worldtrademag.com.

18. See http://ups-scs.com/about/PR/04_27_2004_release.html?pr=true.

19. UPS to acquire Menlo Worldwide Forwarding. *Supply & Demand Chain Executive,* 10/5/04, http://www.sdcexec.com/article_arch.asp?article_id=6172.

20. Armstrong R. & Foster, T. 2007. Moveable feast of top 25 global third-party logistics providers. *Global Logistics & Supply Chain Strategies: SupplyChainBrain.com,* http://glscs.texterity.com/glscs/200705/; Foster T. A. & Armstrong, R. May, 2004. Top 25 third party logistics providers extend their global reach. May and 3PLs on the rise: Smaller firms prove big isn't always better. *Global Logistics & Supply Chain Strategies: SupplyChainBrain.com,* April 2004. http://www.glscs.com.

21. See CEO Letter to Shareholders, UPS 2006 Annual Report, http://investor.shareholder.com/ups/financials/annuals.cfm.

22. See *The Motley Fool* opinion on the importance of monitoring a company's free cash flow, at http://www.fool.com/investing/general/2007/06/21/fedex-flying-fine.aspx.

23. From http://www.fedex.com.

24. Also see J. McKay, Moon's FedEx Ground is booming and has become fierce rival to UPS. *Pittsburgh Post-Gazette,* 3/15/05, http://www.post-gazette.com.

25. Costello, T. Arch rivals: FedEx vs. UPS: Package shippers follow very different strategies. *CNBC,* 12/18/03, http://www.msnbc.msn.com.

26. Ibid.

27. See *BusinessWeek Online,* 6/3/05 at http://www.businessweek.com.

28. See http://www.epinions.com, search for "FedEx" and read all reviews.

29. Smith, S. S. Measuring the people side of FedEx Express. *Journal of Organizational Excellence,* 2001.

30. See http://en.wikipedia.org/wiki/Frederick_Winslow_Taylor for an overview.

31. Bowen, D. E. & Lawler, E. E. The Empowerment of Service Workers: What, Why, How and When. *Sloan Management Review,* Spring 1992.

32. See "The Power of Access," *SRI International,* 5/15/06, available at http://access.fedex.designcdt.com/sri.html.

33. See Frederick W. Smith speech, "Access: Changing what's possible," 5/23/06, at http://access.fedex.designcdt.com/sri.html.

34. See http://www.abxair.com.

35. See http://www.dhl-usa.com.

36. See http://www.dpwn.de.

37. "Deutsche Post World Net completes acquisition of Exel," December 14, 2005, http://www.dpwn.de.

38. Hesseldahl, A. DHL presence heats up shipping wars: UPS's no.1 position challenged by FedEx, other competitors. *Forbes,* 1/17/05, from http://www.msnbc.msn.com.

39. See http://forsalebylocals.wordpress.com/2006/10/04/the-myth-of-dhl-customer-service/.

40. From http://www.tpgpost.com/strategy/strategyanddata.html and http://www.tnt.com/tntgroup/en_corporate.html.

41. TNT Express launches the industry's fastest express. delivery service in South East Asia, 6/11/2007, http://www.ipc.be/index.php?option=com_news&task=view&id=154&Itemid=28.

42. Long believed to be the slogan of the USPS, "neither snow nor rain nor heat nor gloom of night" is rumored to actually come from Herodotus in 503 B.C.

43. From 2004 Comprehensive Statement of Operations, http://www.usps.com/strategicplanning/cs04/.

44. From USPS 2006 Annual report, available at http://www.usps.com.

45. For an insider's view of USPS reform, see Reisner, R.A.F. When a turnaround stalls. *Harvard Business Review, First Person,* February, 2002.

46. For an interesting discussion of the future of the postal market, see Diehl, H. M. Waller, P. Competing with Mr. Postman: Business Strategies, Industry Structure and Competitive Prices in Liberalized Letter Markets, 6/13/2001, from http://www.whu.edu/orga/geaba/Papers/2001/GEABA-DP01-22.pdf.

47. See http://postcom.org/public/articles/2004articles/USPS.Partner.with.DHL.htm.

48. From https://www.con-way.com/default.asp?bhcp=1.

49. See also Nagarajan, A. Canessa, E. Mitchell, W. White, C. C. E-commerce and the Changing Terms of Competition in the Trucking Industry: A Study of Firm Level Responses to Changing Industry Structure, 8/11/00, from http://e-conomy.berkeley.edu/conferences/9-2000/EC-conference2000_papers/mitchelbrie.pdf.

50. From Con-way consolidated financial statements, available at https://www.con-way.com/default.asp?bhcp=1.

51. Foster, T. A. 3PLs on the Rise: Smaller Firms Prove Big Isn't Always Better, 4/1/04, *Global Logistics & Supply Chain Strategies, SupplyChainBrain.com,* http://www.glscs.com.

52. From http://www.ensenda.com/why/index.html.

53. Mottley, R. Going the 'last mile'. *American Shipper, Journal of International Logistics,* 8/1/04, http://www.ensenda.com/about/gfx/AmericanShipper_080104.pdf.

54. Trunick, P. A. Best Practices in Transportation: Network in Progress. *Logistics Today,* 3/15/05, http://www.logisticstoday.com/.

55. For other "last mile" stories see Siegel, J. Nouveau niche, *Operations & Fulfillment,* 11/1/04, http://opsandfulfillment.com/mag/.

56. FedEx sweeps customer satisfaction awards for small package delivery service. *J. D. Power & Associates,* 12/10/02, http://www.jdpower.com/news/releases/ : reliability in pickup & delivery was most important for ground and international customers, 2nd on the list for air customers; "value for price paid" was most important for air service, and 2nd for international customers. Clear invoicing, driver relationships, reputation and tracking information were in the 2nd tier for both ground and air service; having access to helpful account executives, driver relationships and tracking information were 2nd for international customers.

57. Scherck, T. R. A View of the Future for the U.S. Expedited Transportation Industry, 11/14/03, http://www.colography.com/press/2003/futureview.html.

58. One final note: Qatar Airways, recently voted best cargo carrier, Middle East by *Asian Freight & Supply Chain,* was one of the fastest growing freight handling airlines in the world, in 2004 launching service to South Africa, see http://www.payloadasia.com/Magazine/archives/10_04/1004_supplement1.html.

59. See http://www.hoovers.com/transportation-services.

60. Armstrong R. & Foster, T. Moveable Feast of Top 25 Global Third-party Logistics Providers, May 2007, *Global Logistics & Supply Chain Strategies: SupplyChainBrain.com,* http://glscs.texterity.com/glscs/200705/.

61. From http://www.ups.com.

62. From http://www.fedex.com.

Case 36   Schoolhouse Lane Estates*

The supply of grapes crushed in California's 2006 harvest was an all-time record and it followed a record 2005 harvest. Quality is excellent—yet thousands of acres of vines are being pulled up across California with replanting of fruit trees. The *Santa Rosa Press Democrat* reported that Mondavi was cutting 10 percent of its workforce due to a reduced demand for wines selling above $25.00 per bottle at retail and to a projected quarterly operating loss for the first time since they became a public company in 1993. Several small wineries here in Sonoma County, notably DeLoach and Roshambo, have gone bankrupt in the last few years. How are things going for you on the East Coast, Jan?

Janess (Jan) Thaw had trouble responding to the information she had just received from her cousin, Stan White, during their telephone conversation in late January 2007. She had recently prepared a business plan for the expansion of her Schoolhouse Lane Estates winery, located in Cutchogue on the North Fork of Long Island. Her plans included the purchase of grape-growing acreage as well as expansion of the winery and construction of a retail store, new tasting room, and renovation of a special events facility. The estimated cost of these initiatives was $2.4 million and new construction would take approximately a year to complete. Her cousin Stan's information created a wave of uncertainty concerning not only these plans, but also the outlook for her current business strategy. Regardless of the financing options available to her, Jan knew that she'd first have to get the strategy right.

Company History

Jan and her twin brother Nick grew up on a 35-acre potato farm adjacent to Schoolhouse Lane, located on the North Fork of Long Island. Owned by her parents, the farm barely provided for family living expenses. While her father Harry plowed the fields, her mother Suzanne taught fourth grade at a nearby public school.

The experience of growing up on a farm had a very different impact on the adult lifestyles of the children. Jan loved the land. She enjoyed walking the fields with her Dad and seeing the animals that lived on the land, especially the birds nesting in the tall oaks on the periphery of the family property.

Jan attended the agricultural school at Cornell University. She worked during the summer at small wineries in the Finger Lakes region in upstate New York. Upon gradu-

* This case was prepared by Professors Raymond H. Lopez of Pace University and Armand Gilinsky, Jr., at Sonoma State University as a basis for class discussion rather than to illustrate either effective or ineffective handling of an administrative situation. All individuals and events have been disguised at the request of the host organization. Copyright © 2004, 2007 by Raymond H. Lopez and Armand Gilinsky, Jr. This case may not be reproduced without the express written permission of the authors. All rights reserved.

ation in 1985, she was offered an assistant winemaker position at the Glenora Winery in Hammondsport, New York. For three years she experienced all aspects of the wine-making process and saw a chance to combine her love for the land with a career path in this industry.

By contrast, her brother Nick, an avid reader and athlete, could not wait to leave the farm for college. With a full athletic scholarship to Yale, Nick thrived in what he thought was a "big city" (New Haven, Connecticut). After completing his BA in economics, he then went on to Columbia University for an MBA with a concentration in finance.

A few years later Harry and Suzanne told their children that they were ready to retire and move to Sedona, Arizona. They sold their farm to Jan and Nick for one dollar in 1988 and headed west.

In January 1989 Jan and Nick each unexpectedly inherited $3 million after the death of their uncle Garry. They had very different uses for these funds. Jan paid off her student loans and immediately embarked on a long-held plan to convert the potato fields to the growing of wine grapes. Nick paid off his loans and started a financial consulting firm for private equity investors in Manhattan. Although they spoke often on the phone, Nick had not been out to the farm for more than three years. Jan would occasionally meet him for dinner in Manhattan.

During the spring of 1989 Jan planted 20 acres of grapevines on the property and named her new business Schoolhouse Lane Estates. By fall 1994 her first harvest was completed and the grapes were crushed at a local winery. Production was 60 tons of grapes, resulting in 5,000 cases of bottled wine. Within six months, they were all sold locally to restaurants, catering firms, and local businesses for gifts and promotions. Revenues from cases sold were just over $250,000. The business seemed poised for growth.

Schoolhouse Lane Estates' wines—Cabernet Sauvignon, Merlot (red varietals), Meritage (a blend of red varietals), and Chardonnay (white wine)—were well received on their introduction to the local marketplace. Jan sold her wines at retail prices ranging from $10 per bottle for Merlot ($120 per 12-bottle case) to $36 per bottle for the Meritage ($432 per case). As demand grew, Jan decided to operate her own winery. There was a small winery on six acres of land just east of her vineyards. She had been speaking with the owner and sensed that he was ready to retire and move to Weaverville, North Carolina. After only three meetings, they agreed upon the terms of a sale and in the fall of 1996, Jan was now the proud owner of a winery. She invested $2.2 million, financed with a mortgage from a local Long Island bank, and was ready to oversee her first wine production in the fall of 1997. Having expanded its acreage, producing quality grapes, and using grape purchases from other vineyards, the renamed Schoolhouse Lane Estates generated just over $1.5 million in revenue.

Exhibit 1 Schoolhouse Lane Estates Income Statements, 2002–2006 (in $ thousands)

	2006	2005	2004	2003	2002
Net Sales	$5,416.4	$4,924.7	$4,296.6	$3,646.5	$3,040.4
Cost of Goods Sold	3,566.2	3,152.6	2,744.5	2,318.8	1,788.6
Gross Profit	1,850.2	1,772.1	1,552.1	1,327.7	1,251.8
Operating Expenses					
Marketing & Advertising	145.2	130.9	116.6	101.2	89.1
Selling & Administration	935.0	811.8	711.7	572.0	358.6
Total Operating Expenses	1,080.2	942.7	828.3	673.2	447.7
Operating Income (EBIT)	770.0	829.4	723.8	654.5	804.1
Interest Expense[a]	376.2	326.7	295.9	282.7	259.6
Net Income before Taxes	393.8	502.7	427.9	371.8	544.5
Income Taxes[b]	157.3	201.3	171.6	148.5	217.8
Net Income (Loss)	$ 236.5	$ 301.4	$ 256.3	$ 223.3	$ 326.7
Number of cases sold	36,109	32,831	28,644	24,310	20,269
Average wholesale FOB price per 12-bottle case	$ 150.00	$ 150.00	$ 150.00	$ 150.00	$ 150.00
Average retail price per 12-bottle case	$ 300.00	$ 300.00	$ 300.00	$ 300.00	$ 300.00

[a]Prime + 2% on average balance for a line of credit.
[b]Federal and state income tax rate of 40%.

Over the next five years through 2002, Schoolhouse Lane Estates expanded its presence in the local wine markets. About 35 percent of sales were to off-premises accounts, such as wholesalers and retailers, and 45 percent to on-premises accounts, such as restaurants and caterers. These trade intermediaries handled her products before they were resold to the final consumer, with a retail markup of 100 percent. Direct sales to consumers at retail prices by way of the tasting room accounted for the remaining 20 percent of Schoolhouse Lane's sales. Product acceptance translated into growing net revenues (Exhibit 1). Although her operating expenses for marketing and sales had grown rapidly, Jan felt that these expenditures were needed to differentiate her portfolio of fine wines from competitors' offerings and to stimulate demand from trade intermediaries.

Schoolhouse Lane's balance sheets (Exhibit 2) and statements of cash flow (Exhibit 3) reflected her efforts as well as the challenges of growing her business. Most significant among these challenges was the rapid and continuing expansion of inventories, as premium red wines and red wine blends require longer aging periods in oak barrels. Growing inventories were financed with an expanding line of credit from Goose Creek Savings, a local lending bank. Goose Creek Savings, however, maintained a lending limit for a business her size of up to $3 million based on the replacement value of fixed assets. Goose Creek Savings was also financing a small percentage of her inventories through a revolving line of credit. Either a larger bank would be needed within the year, or perhaps a more permanent source of financing would be needed. Laurel Durst, Jan's accountant and financial manager, had recently been exploring a number of working capital financing options with the North Fork Bancorp.

Evolution of Long Island's Wine Industry

How did it all begin? A small band of hesitant artisans and amateurs had pioneered the wine industry in converted barns and potato fields in the 1970s, in many cases because they sought a simpler agrarian lifestyle, or so they thought. In less than a third of a century, the profile of Long Island wine moguls had morphed to that of self-assured professionals backed by deep-pocketed investors who were also seeking a different lifestyle.

The migration to become owners of Long Island wineries was not unlike the one followed by "refugees" from the high-tech world of Silicon Valley, who bought or developed new Napa and Sonoma wineries in California in the late 1990s. Similar to what their California counterparts

Exhibit 2 Schoolhouse Lane Estates Balance Sheets, 2002–2006 (in $ thousands)

	2006	2005	2004	2003	2002
Assets					
Current Assets					
Cash	$ 244.2	$ 218.9	$ 231.0	$ 216.7	$ 210.1
Accounts Receivable	268.4	277.2	294.8	269.5	235.4
Inventories	3,279.1	2,839.1	2,568.5	2,183.5	1,925.0
Prepaid and Other Expenses	48.4	44.0	46.2	41.8	40.7
Total Current Assets	3,840.1	3,379.2	3,140.5	2,711.5	2,411.2
Property, Plant and Equipment	3,578.3	3,440.8	3,291.2	3,254.9	3,172.4
Less: Accumulated Depreciation and Amortization	216.7	191.4	183.7	191.4	216.7
Net Property, Plant and Equipment	3,361.6	3,249.4	3,107.5	3,063.5	2,955.7
Other Assets (Net)	16.5	15.4	16.5	15.4	13.2
Total Assets	$7,218.2	$6,644.0	$6,264.5	$5,790.4	$5,380.1
Liabilities and Capital					
Current Liabilities					
Accounts Payable	$ 298.1	$256.3	$ 217.8	$ 194.7	$ 170.5
Accrued Expenses	268.4	222.2	193.6	169.4	150.7
Line of Credit (bank)[d]	1,282.6	999.9	955.9	757.9	565.4
LTD (current portion)	33.0	33.0	33.0	33.0	33.0
Total Current Liabilities	1,882.1	1,511.4	1,400.3	1,155.0	919.6
Long-Term Debt Mortgage[c]	2,288.0	2,321.0	2,354.0	2,381.5	2,429.9
Equity					
Class A Common[a]	1,661.0	1,661.0	1,661.0	1,661.0	1,661.0
Class B Common[b]	0.0	0.0	0.0	0.0	0.0
Retained Earnings (Loss)	1,387.1	1,150.6	849.2	592.9	369.6
Total Equity	3,048.1	2,811.6	2,510.2	2,253.9	2,030.6
Total Liabilities and Equity	$7,218.2	$6,644.0	$6,264.5	$5,790.4	$5,380.1

[d]Class B Common Stock—1 vote.
[c]Class A Common Stock—10 votes.
[a]Prime + 2% on average balance for line of credit.
[b]Long-term debt (mortgage) at 7%.

had accomplished in the prior decade, the showcase Long Island wineries of the early 2000s burst on the New York culinary scene by making prize-winning and sought-after wines. While the production of world-class wines was still said to be some years away, the money, the wine-making talent, and the will to make them were now in place. It seemed just a matter of time before Long Island winemakers were regarded with the same status as their California counterparts, according to the Long Island Wine Council.

Exhibit 3   Schoolhouse Lane Estates Statements of Cash Flow, 2003–2006 (in $ thousands)

	2006	2005	2004	2003
Cash Flows from Operating Activities				
Net Income	$236.5	$301.4	$256.3	$223.3
Depreciation	25.3	7.7	34.1	24.2
Increase in Receivables (Net)	8.8	17.6	(25.3)	(34.1)
Increase in Inventories	(440.0)	(270.6)	(385.0)	(258.5)
Increase in Prepaid and Other Expenses	(4.4)	2.2	(4.4)	(1.1)
Increase in Accounts Payable	41.8	38.5	23.1	24.2
Increase in Accrued Expenses	46.2	28.6	24.2	18.7
Net Cash Provided (Used) by Operating Activities	(85.8)	125.4	(77.0)	(3.3)
Cash Flows from Investing Activities				
Purchase of Property, Plant and Equipment	(137.5)	(149.6)	(78.1)	(132.0)
Other Assets (Net)	(1.1)	1.1	(1.1)	(2.2)
Net Cash Used for Investing Activities	(138.6)	(148.5)	(79.2)	(134.2)
Cash Flows from Financing Activities				
Increase (Decrease) from Bank Line of Credit	282.7	44.0	198.0	192.5
Increase (Decrease) in Long-Term Debt (current portion)	0.0	0.0	0.0	0.0
Increase (Decrease) in Mortgage	(33.0)	(33.0)	(27.5)	(48.4)
Net Cash Provided (Used) in Financing Activities	249.7	11.0	170.5	144.1
Net Increase in Cash	25.3	(12.1)	14.3	6.6
Cash at the Beginning of the Year	218.9	231.0	216.7	210.1
Cash at the End of the Year	244.2	218.9	231.0	216.7

The land of the North Fork, where most wineries were located, was flat to slightly rolling, planted not only with grapes but also with potatoes, sod, and fruit trees. Craggy oaks shaded the villages of Greenport, Southold, and Cutchogue, small and quaint with 200-year-old houses and 100-year-old churches and plaques to show where the Pilgrims' punishment stocks used to stand on the village green. The water was never more than a few miles away, as the Long Island Sound lay to the north, and Peconic Bay and the Atlantic Ocean to the south.[1]

From its humble beginnings in 1973, the Long Island wine industry had developed steadily with growing numbers of vineyards, wineries, and acreage to produce quality wine products. Long Island wineries produced a broad variety of red varietals including Cabernet Sauvignon, Cabernet Franc, Merlot, Pinot Noir, and Shiraz, as well as white varietals such as Chardonnay, Gewürztraminer, Riesling, and Sauvignon Blanc. A few wineries, like Schoolhouse Lane, produced a Bordeaux-style blend of red wines called Meritage. All Long Island winery owners and their trade association, the Long Island Wine Council, anticipated continued growth and expansion into the 21st century.

Grape growing and wine production were located primarily on the eastern end of Long Island, which jutted more than 100 miles into the Atlantic Ocean, parallel to the coastlines of Connecticut and Rhode Island. The North and South Forks of eastern Long Island were a maritime region with a unique combination of climate, soil characteristics, and growing conditions ideal for quality wine production. Bays bordering the North and South Forks insulated the vineyards and trapped moist warm air. Along with rich sandy glacial soil, this combination created the perfect environment for growing grapes. Growing seasons were quite long (averaging approximately 200 days) and relatively mild winters encouraged the planting of Europe's noble vinifera grapes on almost all acres planted.

The Long Island wineries represented three appellations (American Viticultural Areas or AVA) approved by the Bureau of Alcohol, Tobacco and Firearms (BATF)—the North Fork of Long Island, the Hamptons, and, as of April 2001, Long Island AVA. This latest designation allowed for further expansion beyond the two forks of Long Island's east end, while at the same time protecting the overall integrity of the region's wines.[2]

New York State ranked third nationally in wine production. According to the New York Farm Bureau, the state had almost 1,000 family-owned vineyards that produced 175,000 tons of grapes annually—a $40 million industry. There were 160 wineries in the four main wine-producing regions of the state: the Finger Lakes, the Lake Erie region, the Hudson River Valley, and the Long Island region. All told, these regions produced over 100 million bottles of wine each year and attracted approximately one million tourists.[3]

Long Island wines were sold primarily in the New York metropolitan region. Products were found at most vineyards and in local wine retail stores, as well as in a broad variety of restaurants and catering establishments. Quality had been enhanced, resulting in higher ratings by wine magazines and in national taste tests, and the market broadened up and down the East Coast. Large regional distributors had in recent years shown a growing interest in carrying these wines. Several wineries already distributed their products in Florida, California, and Texas.

Anticipating that this trend would accelerate as knowledge spread of the rising quality of Long Island wines, the Long Island wine producers hoped that recent support from a New York U.S. congressional delegation would help to overturn the ban on direct shipments outside the state.[4] New York remained the nation's largest wine producing state that did not allow direct shipments. Current law prohibited wine producers from shipping wine directly to consumers in other states. Thirteen states already had reciprocal wine shipment laws enabling out-of-state shipments of wine, and eight had laws allowing the direct shipment of wine to customers.

Recent Developments and Industry Maturation

By 2006 Long Island boasted 60 vineyards and 41 wineries.[5] The remaining 19 vineyard owners who lacked production capacity either sold their grapes to other wineries or contracted with other wineries to produce wine.

A sure sign of the maturation of the industry on Long Island came with the announcement of a custom-crush facility to be constructed in Mattituck. This facility would cater to independent vineyard owners and grape buyers who lacked their own wine-making facilities.[6] The new custom-crush venture was led by Russell Hearn, the winemaker at Pellegrini Vineyards, along with investors Mark Lieb, a Connecticut money manager and owner of the 50-acre Lieb Vineyard, and Bernard Sussman, also a money manager and an associate of Lieb. The partners expected to fund 40 to 50 percent of the new winery with equity, borrowing the rest from a Long Island bank.

"The primary purpose of this venture is to make wines for a number of small and large producers which choose not to, or are unable to, build their own wineries," Hearn said. "Our service would allow someone to have small amounts of wine made and bring in their own consultant [winemaker] to set the style. The number of wineries that offered custom services in the past are approaching their maximum," Hearn added. Moreover, vineyards for commercial wine production in Long Island were expected to double in the next two decades, further expanding the customer base.[7]

The Long Island wineries drew more than 600,000 visitors in 2006 for wine tours. Although traffic congestion was increasing on the two roads that fed the North Fork, some locals felt that the trade-off was worth the price. Several local residents credited the vineyards as having preserved open space that might otherwise have been developed for housing.[8]

Wine Production in the United States

The internal structure of the U.S. wine industry similarly underwent fundamental changes after the early 1980s. In terms of product, the most significant developments were observed in table wine. After 1992, table wines represented the largest segment of production and value of shipments and accounted for more than 85 percent of total shipments annually. At the same time, table wine products responded to changes in the tastes and preferences of consumers for higher-quality premium wines.

Grapes used in the production of table wines were of varying quality. Varietals were delicate thin-skinned grapes whose vines usually took approximately four years to begin bearing fruit. As defined by the "truth in labeling" standards of the Bureau of Alcohol, Tobacco, and Firearms, one varietal—the name of a single grape—had to be used if more than 75 percent of the wine was derived from grapes of that variety, and the entire 75 percent was grown in the labeled appellation of origin. Appellation denoted that "at least 75 percent of a wine's volume was derived from fruit or agricultural products and grown in the place or region indicated."[9] Developing the typical varietal characteristics that resulted in enhanced flavor, taste, and finish could take another two to three years after the four years required for newly planted vines to bear fruit. These additional growing periods, in the pursuit of enhanced quality and value, increased both investment levels and operating expenses.

The wine industry was capital intensive. In addition to land and vineyards, a fully integrated firm needed investments in crushing facilities, fermentation tanks, barrels for aging their product, and warehouses to store the bottled and cased wine. Ownership was not essential for any of these activities. However, to control the quality and quantity of production, these investments became essential as a firm developed its brands and expanded its markets.

Since the wine industry was inherently capital intensive, as well as seasonal and cyclical, winery owners generally experienced low profit margins and limited options for outside capital, according to Dan Aguilar of Silicon Valley Bank, a major lender to the wine industry in Napa and Sonoma counties in California. Even under the best of conditions, working capital was under some pressure. Winery owners typically sought to fund continuing operations and business growth/inventory growth from limited retained earnings and bank debt, while at the same time satisfying the voracious appetites of their wineries for funds to finance some mixture of vineyards, production facilities, equipment, barrels, and tasting room and visitor facilities.[10]

Business risks were also substantial. Weather conditions could affect the quality and quantity of grape production. Insect damage and disease could affect the vines. Replanting of new vines required four to five years before commercial quantities of grapes could be expected.

In the fall of the year, usually late September to early November, depending on the weather, grapes were picked and carefully brought from the fields to the crushing facility. There was only one crop per year and crushing took from one to two months. Consequently, the investment in this facility stood idle at least 10 months of the year. Since all the grapes in a region matured at approximately the same time, there was no way to rent out crushing capacity to other wineries at other times of the year.

After crushing, the juice was pumped into the fermentation tanks. These stainless steel vessels were temperature controlled to balance the heat generated by the natural fermentation process. Fermentation lasted only a few weeks after the crush, so this investment was also idle more than 85 percent of the time.

From the fermentation tanks, the wine was pumped into oak barrels for aging. These barrels were expensive, costing $600 to $700 each. Due to quality concerns, they were used for only four or five years at which time their value was negligible (some were cut in half and sold as planters). A barrel-aging facility was a large open space that also had to be climate controlled. During the aging process, some wine was lost due to evaporation through the porous oak barrel. Every two weeks each barrel was refilled up to 3 inches from its top. For premium red wines that aged in barrels for two years or longer, about 5 percent of the original wine was typically lost to evaporation.

Table wines were defined as those with 7 to 14 percent alcohol content by volume and were traditionally consumed with food. In contrast, other wine products such as sparkling wine (champagnes), wine coolers, pop wines, and fortified wines were typically consumed as stand-alone beverages.

Table wines that retailed for less than $3 per 750 ml bottle were generally considered to be generic or "jug" wines, while those selling for more than $3 per bottle were considered premium wines.

Premium wines generally had a vintage date on their labels. This designation signified that the product had been made with at least 95 percent of the grapes harvested, crushed and fermented in the calendar year shown on the label, and used grapes from an appellation of origin (i.e., Napa Valley, Sonoma Valley, Central Coast in California; North Fork, the Hamptons, or Long Island AVA on Long Island). Within the premium wine category, a number of market segments emerged based on retail price points. "Popular premium" wines generally sold for $3 to $7 per bottle, while "super premium" wines retailed for $7 to $14. The "ultra premium" category sold for $14 to $20 per bottle, while any retail price above $20 per bottle was considered by the industry to be "luxury premium."

Changing Dynamics of the U.S. Wine Market

The value of alcoholic and nonalcoholic beverages consumed by Americans grew modestly from 1995 to 2005, according to figures compiled in *Adams' Wine Handbook, 2005*. For purposes of comparison, the largest beverage category was soft drinks, which in 2005 achieved almost double the dollar value of the next largest category, coffee. The consumption of wine produced domestically, as well as imports, grew steadily over the same period, but its volume remained significantly smaller, at less than 4 percent of soft drink volume in 2005. Wine consumption increased by 2.8 percent per year since 1996, trailing only bottled water at 10.8 percent per year and hard cider (an alcoholic beverage) at 8.8 percent per year. By contrast, overall beverage consumption grew at only 1.8 percent per year from 1996 to 2005. On a per capita basis, wine consumption rose steadily from 1.8 gallons per person per year in 1996, to just over 2.37 gallons in 2005.

Total wine consumption in the United States also reached an all-time high in 2005. At 703 million gallons, it exceeded the record consumption of 668 million gallons reached in 2004 (Exhibit 4). From those peak years in the mid-1980s, total consumption as well as per capita consumption trended downward for more than a decade. Since the early 1990s growth rebounded to record consumption and sales levels for table wine (Exhibit 5).

Reflecting the changing tastes and preferences of the American consumer, the growth performance of table wine sales by color also underwent dramatic changes. In 1991 white wine volume accounted for almost one-half of all wine sold in supermarkets, which sold 78 percent of all wine purchased in the United States (the remaining 22 percent of wine shipments were sold through specialty wine shops, tasting rooms, the Internet, or on-premises accounts such as hotels and restaurants). Approximately one-third of total wine sales by dollars in 1991 were blush/rosé, while

Exhibit 4 U.S. Wine Consumption, 1980–2005

Years	Total Wine (millions of gallons)[1]	Total Wine (per capita)[3]	Total Table Wine (millions of gallons)[2]	Total Table Wine (per capita)[3]
2005	703	2.37	619	2.09
2004	668	2.27	591	2.01
2003	643	2.21	574	1.97
2002	612	2.13	546	1.90
2001	572	2.01	512	1.80
2000	570	2.03	510	1.82
1999	551	2.02	482	1.76
1998	526	1.95	466	1.72
1997	520	1.94	461	1.72
1996	505	1.90	443	1.67
1995	469	1.79	408	1.56
1994	459	1.77	395	1.52
1993	449	1.74	381	1.48
1992	476	1.87	405	1.59
1991	466	1.85	394	1.56
1990	509	2.05	423	1.70
1989	524	2.11	432	1.74
1988	551	2.24	457	1.86
1987	581	2.39	481	1.98
1986	587	2.43	487	2.02
1985	580	2.43	378	1.58
1984	555	2.34	401	1.69
1983	528	2.25	402	1.71
1982	514	2.22	397	1.71
1981	506	2.20	387	1.68
1980	480	2.11	360	1.58

[1]All wine types including sparkling wine, dessert wine, vermouth, and other special natural and table wines.

[2]Table wines include all "still" wines not over 14% alcohol content.

[3]Per capita consumption in gallons based on the resident population of the United States.

Sources: The Wine Institute, www.wineinstitute.org; Gomberg, Fredricksen & Associates.

only 17 percent were red (Exhibit 6). By 2006 the market share of white wine and blush/rosé had declined to about 41 percent and 17 percent of total sales, respectively, but red wine grew to 42 percent. Still, most red wines were more expensive to produce and thus sold for higher prices than either white or blush/rosé. The net result was that rev-enues at the wholesale and consumer levels had grown more rapidly than the increase in case wine volume that was produced and then sold.

The latest forecasts from *Impact Databank 2005* indi-cated that strong advances from imported wine could be expected to drive much of the growth for the U.S. wine

Exhibit 5   Wine Sales in the United States (millions of gallons): Domestic Shipments and Foreign Producers Entering U.S. Distribution Channels, 1991–2005

Year	Table Wine[1]	Dessert Wine[2]	Champagne, Sparkling Wine	Total Wine	Total Retail Value (in $ billions)
2005	619	54	30	703	$26.0
2004	591	48	30	668	23.9
2003	574	41	29	643	22.2
2002	546	38	28	612	21.6
2001	512	35	25	572	20.2
2000	499	32	28	558	19.0
1999	475	31	37	543	18.1
1998	466	31	29	526	17.0
1997	461	29	29	519	16.1
1996	439	31	29	500	14.3
1995	404	30	30	464	12.2
1994	394	33	31	458	11.5
1993	381	35	33	449	11.0
1992	405	37	33	476	11.4
1991	394	39	33	466	10.9

[1]Includes all still wines not over 14% alcohol; excludes Canadian Coolers (made from malt).

[2]Includes all still wines over 14% alcohol.

Source: The Wine Institute, http://www.wineinstitute.org.

Exhibit 6   Table Wine Volume Share by Color (in U.S. supermarkets)

Color	1991	1995	2002	2003	2006
Red	17%	25%	39%	40%	42%
White	49	41	40	40	41
Blush/Rosé	34	34	21	20	17
Total	100%	100%	100%	100%	100%

Source: U.S. supermarket data from ACNielsen Beverage Alcohol Team.

market through 2010. Forecast growth in consumption of domestic wines was 3.3 percent to 193 million cases in 2003, 198 million cases in 2005, and about 211 million cases by 2010. For imports, a 12 percent increase to 65 million cases was projected for 2003, and case volume was projected to reach 90 million cases by 2010. California's dominant U.S. market share of domestic table wines was forecast to slip from 67 percent in 2003 to 63 percent in 2010, due in part to strong growth from imported varietals such as Shiraz/Syrah, Chardonnay, and Pinot Grigio. *Impact Databank* also forecast that the share of red wine in the U.S. market was expected to continue to gain at a more rapid pace than white or blush wine. Late projections held that red wine consumption would grow to 98 million cases in 2003 and 128 million cases by 2010. Projected annual compound growth rates for red wines were 5.9 percent for 2000 to 2005, and 3.5 percent for 2005 to 2010. White wine consumption was forecast to grow to 90 million cases by 2003 and 100 million cases by 2010. This translated into annual compound growth rates for white wines of 4.3 percent for 2000 to 2005, and further 1 percent annual increases from 2005 to 2010.

Competition

Since the 1960s there had been a substantial increase in the number of firms producing wine products in the United States. From hundreds of companies in the 1970s, the number exceeded 1,800 wineries by the turn of the century. Most were relatively small, each of the 50 states already had at least one winery, and about 800 were located in California. By 2005 the 20 largest firms produced approximately 90 percent of all American wines by volume and 85 percent by value at wholesale.[11]

The competitive structure of the industry could be classified into three types of stand-alone wineries: public conglomerates, private conglomerates, and multi-industry firms (primarily public). The largest publicly traded winery was Robert Mondavi, along with Chalone, a much smaller firm. Privately held wineries included the industry giant E&J Gallo, Kendall-Jackson, The Wine Group, and more than a thousand small- to medium-size wineries. The final group of competitors consisted of large publicly traded multi-industry firms. These included Allied Domecq, Brown Forman (Wine Estates Division), Foster's Group (Beringer Blass), Constellation Brands (Canandaigua Division), Diageo (Chateau and Estates Division), Fortune Brands, Louis Vuitton Moët Hennessey (LVMH), and UST (formerly known as U.S. Tobacco).

In addition to domestic competition, a growing percentage share of the U.S. wine market had been gained by imports. In addition to the traditional "Old World" supplies from France, Italy, Germany, Spain, and Portugal, a new group of countries had experienced growing acceptance of their wine production. Australia, Chile, and Argentina (the "New World" suppliers) increased their market share in the last decade, offering high-quality wines at very competitive prices.

Consolidation among wineries began to accelerate in the early 1990s, as larger producers decided to purchase smaller ones in order to achieve greater economies of scale in marketing and economies of scope in gaining access to more varied channels of distribution. These larger wineries could then become more effective in negotiating favorable selling terms with an increasingly small number of large regional distributors.[12] The "consolidators" were generally public firms that were able to offer predominantly family-run wine businesses a means to greater liquidity of their investment in larger, more diversified firms. Concurrently, the attractiveness of wine production across the United States resulted in a growing number of entrepreneurs purchasing or starting new, small operations.

Jan Meets with Her Team

The day after her conversation with cousin Stan, Jan set up a meeting with her operations manager Dan Henning and her accountant Laurel Durst. She also invited the executive director of the 14-year-old Long Island Wine Council, Nanette Hansen, to get her broader perspective of local conditions.

Jan began the meeting by presenting her plans for the expansion:

We have an opportunity to purchase additional grape-producing acreage across Schoolhouse Lane from our vineyard, that is, to buy 28 acres for $900,000. We have been

farming that land and now have the opportunity to purchase it. The winery needs expanded capacity, and I have estimates between $800,000 and $900,000 for the land. Our tasting room is overcrowded—even on weekdays—and its expansion would require $250,000. Finally, many of our neighboring competitors already have facilities for special events (weddings, birthday parties, anniversaries, business meetings, etc.), but I have a design in mind that is expected to cost $450,000. I estimate another $700,000 to $800,000 in working capital will be necessary as well, bringing the total investment up to about $2.4 million.

Dan supported Jan's plans:

The winery is operating at 100 percent capacity and I still had to ship some grapes over to the custom-crush facility in Mattituck. I'd like to bring all our production back here under our complete control.

The Schoolhouse Lane team was eager to hear Nanette's perspective, as she represented a broader regional industry viewpoint. Nanette was prepared for their questions, distributing copies of the information on Long Island wineries (see Exhibits 7 and 8) to the rest of the group.

At the Long Island Wine Council, our prime focus is the local producers and their markets. I can't tell you much about conditions in California such as how long the "glut" of grapes will last, but we have studied the markets extensively in the East Coast.

On the supply side, acreage and production have grown steadily over the last seven years through the harvest of 2006. Grape quality has risen consistently and yields per acre have grown slowly. A number of new owners have come to the area, bringing strong financial support to many vineyards and wineries. On the demand side, a major segment is event driven—celebrations of either a personal or business nature. For many local wineries, this represents 40 percent or more of their revenues and any weakness in pricing or volume will be felt quickly on cash inflows.

There has been a weakening in the last three years in business spending for events. While volume has held up reasonably well, the price points have deteriorated—moderately priced premium products ($10 to $15 per bottle) have been substituted for deluxe premium wines ($25 and up per bottle). Corporate and business budgets have been tightened and though it is likely that this trend will be reversed in the next few years. On a brighter note, on-premises sales have finally begun to rise this spring, as restaurant patrons are spending more on fine wine.

Will the Long Island wine industry be adversely or positively affected by these national trends? Will the regional extent of our markets shelter us from cyclical slowdowns in demand? From conversations with our members, the next few years are still likely to be quite challenging for our industry here on the East End.

Exhibit 7 Long Island Wine Industry Statistics (Selected years)

Year	Number of Vineyards	Number of Wineries	Planted Acres	Total Acres Owned	Value Per Acre ($)	Wine Production (Cases)
2006 (Estimated)	60	41	3,200	4,400	$22,000	550,000
2005	60	38				
2004	60	30				500,000
2002	52	29	3,000	4,000		500,000
2000		21	2,200	2,800	20,000	400,000
1999		21	2,100			
1998		21				200,000
1996	40			1,800		
1995		23	1,055		15,000	200,000
1989		14				
1987		12				
1985	16	7	600			
1984	12	4	700			
1975		1				
1973	1		17		4,000	

Sources: *The Wine Press, Underground Wine Journal, Wine East, Long Island Business News, Newsday,* and the Long Island Wine Council.

Exhibit 8 Estimated Values of Vineyards and Wineries on Long Island (Selected years)

Year	Name	Location	Winery Capacity (cases)	Total Planted Acres	Estimated Value ($)
2001	Raphael	Peconic	10,000	70	$6,000,000
2000	Gristina	Cutchogue	10,000	44	5,200,000
	Bedell Cellars	Cutchogue	8,000	50	5,000,000
	Pindar Vineyards	Peconic	80,000	42.5	
	Comtesse Thérèse	Mattituck		40	400,000
1999	Hargrave	Cutchogue	7,000	84	4,000,000
	Laurel Lake Vineyards	Laurel	5,500	23	2,000,000
	Corey Creek	Southold	4,000	30	2,500,000
	Peconic Bay Vineyards	Cutchogue		35	2,200,000
	Bidwell Vineyards	Cutchogue	15,000	34	2,900,000
1997	Laurel Lake Vineyards	Laurel		23	3,000,000
1993	Dzugas-Smith Vineyards	Cutchogue		29	245,000

Sources: *The Wine Press, Underground Wine Journal, Wine East, Long Island Business News, Newsday,* and the Long Island Wine Council.

From 2001 through 2004 New York City's financial services industry had experienced some of the largest declines in employment as well as reductions in salaries and bonuses. Special events sales volumes had also slowed due to cost containment at parties and declining expenditures for high-end wines at restaurants. Still, overall volume and revenues had been rising due to expansion of the geographic market for Long Island wines on the East Coast and growth westward through New York, Pennsylvania, Maryland, and Virginia. This geographic expansion, it was hoped by many local producers, could help offset the local trend toward lower prices to bolster sagging sales.

In response to Nanette's overview, Jan mentioned that she'd come across a *Business Week* article concerning the consumption profile of wine drinkers in the United States.[13] Forecasted trends for growth in U.S. wine consumption were hardly spectacular:

> One statistic I picked up was that in many European countries such as France, Germany, Italy, and Spain, wine is almost a necessity with meals—this is not the case here in the United States. Just over 10 percent of American adults account for 86 percent of wine consumed annually! We have not yet been successful at stimulating wine consumption to broader segments of the population. Until this occurs, perhaps our market strategy should be directed towards those consumers who are already drinking wine on a *regular* basis.

Ending the meeting, Jan thanked all present for sharing their ideas and expertise. She knew that she would have to prioritize each projected cost item and defend these expenditures when making a formal proposal for financing. Financing the proposed expansion as well as incremental working capital might have to be sourced by some form of equity, meaning that Jan would no longer own 100 percent of the Schoolhouse Lane Estates!

Jan Seeks Help

Jan decided it was time to call her brother Nick. Although he hadn't visited the North Fork in years, he had been to the Hamptons each summer, driving to his family's summer home on the beach. Jan began the call by saying, "Nick, how has your business and career been going this last year? I heard about all the reductions in financial services employment. Have you been affected?"

"My firm has maintained its competitiveness in these uncertain times," Nick assured her. "We are also diversifying our clients' portfolios from real estate and annuities into private and public equity positions. If you know of any interesting investment opportunities, we would examine the financial data."

Somewhat surprised, Jan responded, "Nick, did you know that at Schoolhouse Lane Estates, we have a financial proposal on the table? We need an equity investment

of approximately $2 million. Although the equity in the business is currently low, I will not be willing to give up control."

"Send me your business plan and financial statements," Nick replied, "and I'll contact you in two weeks with a proposal. The amount you are looking for is well within the range of my clients."

"Thanks, Nick," said Jan. "I'll fax you the documents tomorrow."

Two Weeks Later

"Jan, this is your brother. I received your materials and have a proposal for an investment of $2 million. Can we meet for lunch this Wednesday and I'll present the details? I also would like my wife to be at our meeting. As an equity strategist for a large investment banking house in Manhattan, Monica can provide some insight into the workings of the private equity market. She would also like to visit the winery."

Jan agreed and the three met for a long lunch at the Old Mill House in Peconic. After the salad, Nick presented details of his $2 million proposal to Jan.

"Although investment returns are low these days for fixed-income instruments, venture capital is still expensive. I could offer you a 10-year convertible note with interest at 6 percent," Nick began.

Sipping a glass of locally produced Gallucio Reserve Merlot, Monica added, "The note would provide the investor with potential capital gains up to his or her required return of between 20 and 25 percent per year, and then be converted into common stock with a par value of $1 per share. The holder would have the option over the next five years to convert the note into company stock at today's book value. If conversion did not occur, the note would be amortized from year 6 through year 10."

"Thanks," replied Jan, "I will have to speak with my accountant concerning the number of shares that would be granted should the note be converted, so that the required rate of return will be realized by your investor. By the way, who is this investor and when can I meet her or him?"

Nick smiled as Monica said, "Jan, you have known him all your life!"

The Bank Responds

The next day, Jan's accountant Laurel took Jan's projected capital expenditures of $2.4 million for expansion of the Schoolhouse Lane Estates operations, along with the business plan for the next five years, to the North Fork Bank. The projections included two scenarios: a "best case" for a revenue growth rate of 20 percent and a "base case" at a 15 percent growth rate. Both forecasts assumed enhanced operating efficiencies and expanded profit margins with no changes in prices and no introduction of new wine products.

The bank officer was skeptical of the most optimistic case, especially after speaking with a number of other winery operators in the area. North Fork's initial proposal was for a maximum $400,000 term loan with a small increase in the revolving line of credit to $3 million. The banker's implications and position were clear—Schoolhouse Lane needed permanent equity capital to sustain its growth plans. While the longer-term outlook for the industry was quite favorable, the banker was cautious about the trading conditions for wine over the next two years (2007 and 2008).

As she walked through the parking lot at North Fork Bank, Laurel relayed this disappointing news to Jan on her mobile phone. Although Jan understood why permanent capital was needed to support her growth strategy, she was not able to add to her personal investment in the business. Her husband, Tom, a professor of history at Stony Brook University, also believed that too large a percentage of the family's assets were already tied up in the business.

Nick's Position

After receiving Jan's fax, Nick responded by e-mail with some questions concerning the timing of the expenditures outlined in Jan's proposal. He was concerned about the "grape glut" and its impact on product pricing. In addition, the economic outlook in the near term appeared to be neither clearly defined nor strong. Therefore, could Jan construct forecasts using average annual growth rates in revenues of between 5 and 10 percent (less optimistic than Jan's 15 to 20 percent)? Nick did, however, agree with his sister that enhanced efficiencies could generate faster growth in net income than the growth in revenues.

With respect to Jan's concerns over maintaining ownership control, Nick was nevertheless very understanding. Monica had gently but firmly reminded him that the "last thing he should ever do was take over the operations of Schoolhouse Lane Estates." He thus approached this deal from a strictly financial point of view. Nick was looking for a viable and profitable investment of $2 million that would fit nicely into his portfolio. A current return of 6 percent, with a total expected return of 20 percent over at least a five-year holding period, was quite acceptable to him. While he might have expected a 25 percent total return on an investment with this risk profile some years ago, equity risk premiums had been trending downward in late May 2006, so a 20 percent return would meet or exceed his current portfolio needs.

Nick was aware of the lack of liquidity of an investment in Schoolhouse Lane Estate's operations. This investment would definitely have a "buy-and-hold" profile. Selling a private equity investment was traditionally accomplished through an initial public offering or an acquisition by another wine business, often years after the venture had developed into a viable, competitive, and profitable business. In evaluating his potential position in Schoolhouse Lane Estates, he was not confident that either of these scenarios would occur in the near term.[14] His only hope for monetizing his investment in the next five years would be to sell his shares back to Jan at a reasonable value or try to sell them to another private investor.

One More Meeting

After receiving her brother's proposal, Jan again met with Dan and Laurel. She opened the meeting by saying:

> I can't believe how expensive this funding could be even under the lowest cost presentation. Even given my most optimistic forecast of earnings growth for Schoolhouse Lane Estates and Nick's "cheapest" financing alternative, I will lose more than one-half ownership in the company. I surely do not want that to happen! Maybe we should defer our expansion plans or explore other options.

Dan countered by reiterating his desire to purchase the vineyard across the road and expand the winery's capacity:

> . . . that property has been owned by the O'Reilly family for 55 years. We may never get an opportunity to purchase it again if it is bought by another winery. We have managed it for the last six years and know the quality of grape production.

Laurel had planned what she would recommend. An integral component of her presentation was a summary of an appraisal report that had been prepared for Schoolhouse Lane Estates by a local firm specializing in wine industry asset valuations on Long Island (Exhibit 9). The appraisal clearly showed that the current value of the firm's two largest asset categories was considerably higher than their book values (approximately $9.5 million versus book values of $6.6 million). Adding the difference of nearly $2.9 million to the firm's equity value would surely enhance Jan's bargaining position in negotiating for new funds, possibly with other investors besides her brother. Laurel then summarized and prioritized the three components of the Schoolhouse Lane Estates' expansion plans:

> I agree with Dan that our highest priority at this time is the land purchase. We can produce larger volumes of wine, if the market so demands, at the new custom-crush facility. By postponing the other projects, Jan, you would reduce the volume of funds needed from your brother and, consequently, the dilution of your ownership position. If you really want to spend the entire $2.4 million in the next year, remember you can sell the Class B common stock that you already carry on the balance sheet.

After the meeting ended, Jan walked slowly back to her office. Almost there, she abruptly turned around,

Exhibit 9   Report of the Appraisal of Assets of the Schoolhouse Lane Estates

In response to the request of Ms. Janess Thaw, sole owner of the Schoolhouse Lane Estates, we hereby enclose our estimates of current market values for the firm's wine inventory as well as its fixed-asset position. Our personnel have carefully examined your inventories, land, winery building, and equipment and compared these assets with current market values that we have observed over the last six months. We are pleased to report to you that the quality of your inventory is excellent and your assets are in top operating condition.

With your firm's growing emphasis on the production of premium red wines (Meritage, Cabernet Sauvignon, and Merlot), our appraisal estimates that 30 percent of wine in barrels by volume has been stored for more than two years, resulting in a doubling of its book value at the time fermentation was completed in early 2006. Another 40 percent, also red wine and mostly from the 2006 harvest, has been in barrels for 14 months. Remaining wine volumes are a mixture of younger reds and white Chardonnay. We conclude that as of May 2007 the value of inventory, if sold in the local wholesale market, would result in receipts of $5.12 million.

In a separate analysis of property, plant, and equipment, our real estate expert on current market conditions estimates the value of company-owned land at $1,088,000 or $32,000 per acre on the 34 acres under cultivation by Peconic Bay. This is in contrast to $720,000, which is the current book value of this land on a historical cost basis.

The remaining $2,641,600 of depreciated book value of the winery plant and equipment has also increased in value since its original purchase. Its current replacement value is $3.35 million, according to our appraiser.

In summary, upon a sale of these three major asset categories, it is estimated that they would bring to the firm a total of $9,550,233, or $2,909,533 more than their current book value of $6,640,700. This additional value could be added to the firm's equity account of $3,048,100 at year-end 2006, bringing its total up to $5,957,633.

Summary Data			
Asset	**Book Value December 31, 2006**	**Adjusted Market Value April 30, 2007**	**Appraisal Difference**
Land—34 planted acres	$ 720,000	$1,088,000	$ 368,000
Plant & Equipment	2,641,600	3,347,233	705,633
Inventory	3,279,100	5,115,000	1,835,900
Totals	$6,640,700	$9,550,233	$2,909,533
Less: Liabilities	4,170,100	4,170,100	—
Equity Value	$2,470,600	$5,380,133	$2,909,533

It was a pleasure to provide you with the above data. If there is any additional information or clarifications that you may require, do not hesitate to contact us.

Respectfully submitted,

Sharon Brown, President

East End Associates

May 4, 2007

walked out of the building, and proceeded toward the vineyard. Strolling leisurely past the old oak trees with birds perching in the branches, she then ambled all the way down Schoolhouse Lane to the shore of Peconic Bay. Sitting on a large rock near the shore, she spent the next hour considering her alternatives. Should she continue the current strategy and focus on internal growth, borrow some money from the North Fork Bank, sell equity, and complete the expansion in order to sell the winery later down the road, or maybe sell all of Schoolhouse Lane Estates now? Jan knew that when she returned to the office, Dan and Laurel would be awaiting her decision.

Endnotes

1. *New York Times.* 2000. On the North Fork, dreams of Napa. July 26: F1.

2. To put this information in perspective, the California wine industry has been in business for more than 200 years and currently has 86 AVAs, www.wineinstitute.org.

3. States News Service. 2004. Washington, DC, February 5.

4. On January 29, 2004, U.S. Senators Hilary Rodham Clinton and Charles Schumer, along with U.S. Representatives Louise Slaughter, Tim Bishop, Maurice Hinchey, Sherwood Boehlert, Jack Quinn, and Arno Houghton, signed a letter calling on Governor Pataki and the New York State Legislature to overturn the direct shipping ban.

5. Canavor, N. 2003. Long Island continues to gain notoriety as wine-making region. *Long Island Business News,* April 4.

6. In contrast, nine custom-crush facilities served California's wine industry.

7. Walzer, R. 1999. Hearn pressing for $2M winery. *Long Island Business News,* October 1: 5A.

8. Johnson, K. 2003. Success is in the grapes; from a scruffy past, a winemaking capital emerges. *New York Times,* August 30: B1.

9. Bureau of Alcohol, Tobacco and Firearms, Regulatory Agency, U.S. Department of the Treasury, Title 27, Part 4 of the Code of Federal Regulations.

10. Aguilar, D. 2003. Working capital analysis for wine industry clients, working paper. Silicon Valley Bank Wine Group, December 26.

11. The Wine Institute, www.wineinstitute.org.

12. According to Vic Motto of Motto Kryla Fisher, a Napa, California, consultant to the wine industry, there were 10,940 distributors of wine in 1990 and 5,134 in 2000, but only two to three major distributors per state. The top 10 distributors accounted for 33 percent of wine sales in 1993 and 60 percent in 2003.

13. Himelstein, L. 2002. This Merlot's for you. *BusinessWeek,* September 30: 65–68.

14. Nick had read a *New York Times* article about the Gallucio Family Cellars in Cutchogue. That winery had been on the market for $7.5 million in the fall of 2003 with no takers. Gallucio had 82.5 acres, about 44 of them under vines, and had a 10,000-case annual production capacity. The Gallucios had purchased the property from Gristina Vineyards for $5.2 million in 2000. Vincent and Judy Gallucio had announced an ambitious expansion plan but in 2002 reversed their plan to transform the property from a boutique to a larger-scale winery. See Goldberg, H. G. 2004. Winery to feature state wines. *New York Times,* March 21: sec. 14LI, 12.

Case 37 General Motors*

General Motors was barely clinging on to its long-time status as the world's largest car company. By 2007, the costs related to the restructuring of Delphi, GM's largest supplier that it had recently spun off, were also not fully known. It has been estimated that the firm would have to spend around $7 billion to honor benefit guarantees for the employees at Delphi, which filed for bankruptcy protection in 2005.

However, there were signs that recent actions taken by G. Richard Wagoner Jr., Chairman and Chief Executive of the firm, had begun to turn things around for the troubled car manufacturer. GM had sold its stakes in Isuzu and Suzuki and 51 percent of its equity in the GM financial services arm, GMAC. Buyouts were offered to all of GM's hourly workers resulting in the elimination of almost 35,000 jobs, which allowed the company to drastically reduce its long-term labor-cost structure. Wagoner was also able to extract some reduction in GM's health care costs and it is believed that he will be able to extract still more cost savings during negotiations that are slated for fall 2007. To top things off, GM has also announced that it would cut its common stock dividend in half and slash the pay of its top five executives.

As a result of these actions, GM has been able to significantly reduce in its reported losses during 2006 down to a $2 billion loss (see Exhibits 1 to 3). The firm has actually been able to show some profits from its operations when the costs related to its restructuring are excluded. This represents a stark contrast to the $10.4 billion loss that GM had reported for 2005—it's largest loss since 1992. "Their track record over the last three quarters is really quite positive compared with the depths of the sewer they were in a year ago," said David Cole, chairman of the Center for Automotive Research.[1]

Critics still insist that the long-term prospects for GM will hinge on its ability to get consumers to buy its cars. The firm's market share has continued to drop, falling below 25 percent for the first time in several decades (see Exhibits 4 to 6). But the drop could be attributed in part to the big cuts that GM has made in low-margin sales to fleets like rental companies. Such a cut in fleet sales has also allowed the firm to reduce the rebates that it has offered for its cars by as much as 25 percent and to increase the resale value of its cars.

Wagoner has acknowledged that the firm's management mistakes over the last 30 years made his task much more difficult. Former heads from Frederic Donner to Roger Smith had built up a bloated bureaucracy that had cranked out boring, low-quality cars for many years. But Wagoner believes that his efforts are gradually turning things around, although he has refused to provide any specific timeline. As Chief Financial Officer Frederick "Fritz" Henderson stated, "There are signs that the turnaround is well under way, but there are no signs that I know of that the turnaround is done."[2]

* This case was developed by Jamal Shamsie, Michigan State University, with the assistance of Professor Alan B. Eisner, Pace University. Material has been drawn from published sources to be used for class discussion. Copyright © 2007 Jamal Shamsie.

Asserting Greater Control

As a longtime GM insider, Wagoner did possess some distinct advantages that he brought to his job as CEO. He knew what brutal facts needed to be confronted, and he was aware of the specific veterans who could handle key jobs. He assembled a new management team to help him turn around GM's performance, eventually placing the head of its profitable Asia Pacific region, Troy Clarke, in direct control of the firm's troubled North American operations. In order to start turning out more cars that consumers would buy, he brought Robert A. Lutz out of retirement and appointed him to head the firm's crucial product development. Lutz had sparked Chrysler's resurgence during the 1990s with cars such as the Dodge Viper and PT Cruiser.

Against all odds, Wagoner has also made real progress in energizing GM's torpid culture. Towards this end, he has begun to tear down the boundaries between the firm's free wheeling fiefdoms operating around the world. For most of its history, GM has been run as a collaboration of relatively autonomous geographical divisions that have catered to different markets. But many regions have seen a sharp decline in profits as they have had to respond to stronger competitors that have competed on a more global basis. The European division, in particular, has lost more than $3.5 billion since 2000.

Wagoner has been working with Lutz to restructure GM's four different geographical units to get them to collaborate with each other on designing, manufacturing, and marketing cars. Gradually, key decisions about the firm's product development are being made at GM's headquarters rather than at various far-flung subsidiaries. A global council in Detroit now decides how to allocate GM's $7 billion annual spending on new model development and serves as a check on units whose plans veer off course. The efficiencies that have been created by these changes are likely to reduce the firm's overall cost structure over the next few years.

Furthermore, Wagoner and Lutz have also tried to get the various functional areas to work more closely with each other. GM used to have different studios for each division working on car designs that would get passed on to marketing, then moved to engineering, and finally sent to manufacturing. Lutz has formed one committee that draws upon all of the functional areas to oversee the entire process from initial conception to final execution. Every Thursday, he and a small group that includes key top mangers from design and engineering hash out what vehicles should look like and which division will build them.

Wagoner also exerts control by imposing tough performance standards. As he rose up through GM's finance division, Wagoner developed a reputation as a legendary number cruncher who holds top managers to strict measures. Although GM, like most big companies, had performance goals, they never went nearly as deep or into as much detail. One of GM's executives has noted that Wagoner's use of measures to assess the performance of

Exhibit 1 Consolidated Statement of Operations (in $ millions except per share amounts)

Consolidated Statements of Operations			
	Years Ended December 31,		
General Motors Corporation and Subsidiaries	**2006**	**2005**	**2004**
Net sales and revenues			
Automotive sales	$172,927	$160,228	$163,341
Financial services and insurance revenues	34,422	34,427	32,010
Total net sales and revenues	207,349	194,655	195,351
Costs and expenses			
Automotive cost of sales	164,682	158,887	152,115
Selling, general, and administrative expenses	25,081	27,513	25,969
Interest expense	16,945	15,607	11,913
Provisions for credit and insurance losses related to financing and insurance operations	4,071	3,430	4,315
Other expenses	4,238	7,024	1,584
Total costs and expenses	215,017	212,461	195,896
Operating loss	(7,668)	(17,806)	(545)
Automotive interest income and other nonoperating income, net	2,721	1,066	1,400
Income (loss) before income taxes, equity income (loss) and minority interests and cumulative effect of a change in accounting principle	(4,947)	(16,740)	855
Income tax benefit	(2,785)	(5,870)	(1,126)
Equity income (loss) and minority interests, net of tax	184	562	720
Income (loss) before cumulative effect of a change in accounting principle	(1,978)	(10,308)	2,701
Cumulative effect of a change in accounting principle	—	(109)	—
Net income (loss)	$ (1,978)	$ (10,417)	$ 2,701
Basic earnings (loss) per share			
Earnings (loss) before cumulative effect of a change in accounting principle	$ (3.50)	$ (18.23)	$ 4.78
Cumulative effect of a change in accounting principle	—	(0.19)	—
Earnings (loss) per share, basic	$ (3.50)	$ (18.42)	$ 4.78
Weighted average common shares outstanding, basic (millions)	566	565	565
Diluted earnings (loss) per share			
Earnings (loss) before cumulative effect of a change in accounting principle	$ (3.50)	$ (18.23)	$ 4.76
Cumulative effect of a change in accounting principle	—	(0.19)	—
Earnings (loss) per share, diluted	$ (3.50)	$ (18.42)	$ 4.76
Weighted average common shares outstanding, diluted (millions)	566	565	567
Cash dividends per share	$ 1.00	$ 2.00	$ 2.00

Source: General Motors Annual Reports.

everyone working under him has been felt throughout the firm. Lutz was judged on 12 criteria last year, from how well he used existing parts to save money in new vehicles to how many engineering hours he cut from the development process.

Revamping Product Development

Since Wagoner delegated product development to Lutz, he has moved to reorganize the product development process to make it speedier, cheaper, and more effective. Lutz has been pushing GM to invest in styling, leaning on the engineering

Exhibit 2   Consolidated Balance Sheets (in $ millions)

Consolidated Balance Sheets		
	December 31,	
General Motors Corporation and Subsidiaries	**2006**	**2005**
Assets		
Current Assets		
Cash and cash equivalents	$ 23,774	$ 15,187
Marketable securities	138	1,416
Total cash and marketable securities	23,912	16,603
Accounts and notes receivable, net	8,216	5,917
Inventories	13,921	13,862
Equipment on operating leases, net	6,125	6,993
Deferred income taxes and other current assets	11,957	8,982
Total current assets	64,131	52,357
Financing and insurance operations assets		
Cash and cash equivalents	349	15,539
Investments in securities	188	18,310
Finance receivables, net	—	180,849
Loans held for sale	—	21,865
Assets held for sale	—	19,030
Equipment on operating leases, net	11,794	31,194
Equity in net assets of GMAC LLC	7,523	—
Other assets	2,269	25,157
Total financing and insurance operations assets	22,123	311,944
NonCurrent Assets		
Equity in net assets of nonconsolidated affiliates	1,969	3,242
Property, net	41,934	38,543
Intangible assets, net	1,118	1,869
Deferred income taxes	32,967	23,761
Prepaid pension	17,366	37,576
Other assets	4,584	4,864
Total noncurrent assets	99,938	109,855
Total assets	$186,192	$474,156
Liabilities and Stockholders' Equity (Deficit)		
Current Liabilities		
Accounts payable (principally trade)	$ 26,931	$ 26,402
Short-term borrowings and current portion of long-term debt	5,666	1,627
Accrued expenses	35,225	42,697
Total current liabilities	67,822	70,726
Financing and insurance operations liabilities		
Accounts payable	1,214	3,731
Liabilities related to assets held for sale	—	10,941
Debt	9,438	253,508
Other liabilities and deferred income taxes	925	26,325
Total Financing and Insurance Operations liabilities	11,577	294,505

(*continued*)

Exhibit 2 Consolidated Balance Sheets (in $ millions) (*continued*)

Consolidated Balance Sheets		
	December 31,	
General Motors Corporation and Subsidiaries	**2006**	**2005**
NonCurrent Liabilities		
Long-term debt	33,067	32,580
Postretirement benefits other than pensions	50,086	28,990
Pensions	11,934	11,225
Other liabilities and deferred income taxes	15,957	20,430
Total noncurrent liabilities	111,044	93,225
Total liabilities	190,443	458,456
Commitments and contingencies (Note 20)		
Minority interests	1,190	1,047
Stockholders' Equity (Deficit)		
Preferred stock, no par value, authorized 6,000,000, no shares issued and outstanding	—	—
$1 2/3 par value common stock (2,000,000,000 shares authorized, 756,637,541 and 565,670,254 shares issued and outstanding at December 31, 2006, respectively, and 756,637,541 and 565,518,106 at December 31, 2005, respectively)	943	943
Capital surplus (principally additional paid-in capital)	15,336	15,285
Retained earnings	406	2,960
Accumulated other comprehensive (loss)	(22,126)	(4,535)
Total stockholders' equity (deficit)	(5,441)	14,653
Total liabilities, minority interests, and stockholders' equity (deficit)	**$186,192**	**$474,156**
Reference should be made to the notes to consolidated financial statements.		

and design heads to work together and axing bureaucratic rules that turned sizzling concepts into dreary cars. He has forced design studios to compete with each other and tried to make better use of the firm's global resources. In the process, he has cut the time it takes to develop a new car from nearly four years to twenty months.

Since he has taken over, Lutz's biggest challenge has been to wean the GM culture away from a focus on engineering processes. New cars were designed to be built without any costly modifications on the firm's aging plants. Lutz has pushed designers to get more involved with the development process and for engineers to find ways to stick with the original car design. For the new Pontiac Solstice, Lutz ordered sketches from three different design houses and then created an engineering team to figure out how to manufacture these cars profitably. The changes have forced designers and engineers to work together more effectively, using weekly meetings to hammer out their differences. "It isn't a love-in," said chief designer Ed Welburn. "But in the last two years the laws of physics have changed."[3]

Furthermore, GM is trying to improve its product development process by adopting a practice that the Japanese have

perfected over many years. In past decades, only a small percentage of parts were reused from one generation of cars to the next. Now, Lutz is trying to raise that to 40 percent to 60 percent, about on par with the Japanese. As GM develops the next generation Chevy Silverado and GMC Sierra pickups for 2008, it aims to reuse much of the existing platform. The regular adoption of such practices should allow the firm to cut its development costs by almost half.

GM is also trying to imitate the Japanese by developing several models that share a similar chassis or frame parts. The new Chevy Malibu, for instance, uses the same platform and many of the same parts as the Saab 9-3 sedan. GM has also decided to reuse the skeleton beneath the sleek body of its Pontiac Solstice for its new Saturn coupe and possibly for the sporty Chevrolet wagon called the Nomad. "GM is managing its product development more efficiently than ever," Lutz recently declared.[4]

Although GM has been slow in its efforts, the firm is also working on several new technologies to compete with the hybrid cars that are currently being offered by Toyota and Honda. Those offered by the Japanese companies save on gasoline by supplementing internal combustion with

Exhibit 3   **Consolidated Statements of Cash Flows (in $ millions)**

Consolidated Statements of Cash Flows			
	For the Years Ended December 31,		
General Motors Corporation and Subsidiaries	2006	2005	2004
Cash flows from operating activities			
Net income (loss)	$(1,978)	$(10,417)	$ 2,701
Cumulative effect of a change in accounting principle	—	109	—
Adjustments to reconcile income (loss) before cumulative effect of a change in accounting principle to net cash provided by (used in) operating activities:			
Depreciation, impairments, and amortization expense	10,950	15,797	14,202
Mortgages: servicing rights and premium amortization	1,021	1,142	1,675
Goodwill impairment—GMAC	828	712	—
Delphi benefit guarantee	500	5,500	—
Loss on sale of 51% interest in GMAC	2,910	—	—
Provision for credit financing losses	1,799	1,074	1,944
Net gains on sale of credit receivables	(1,256)	(1,741)	(1,332)
Net gains on sale of investment securities	(1,006)	(104)	(52)
Other postretirement employee benefit (OPEB) expense	3,582	5,671	4,558
OPEB payments	(3,802)	(4,084)	(3,974)
VEBA/401(h) withdrawals	3,061	3,168	(8,618)
Pension expense	4,928	2,519	2,456
Pension contributions	(969)	(833)	(919)
Retiree lump sum and vehicle voucher expense, net of payments	(325)	(264)	(329)
Net change in mortgage loans	(21,578)	(29,119)	(2,312)
Net change in mortgage securities	427	(1,155)	614
Change in other investments and miscellaneous assets	(470)	(685)	104
Changes in assets and liabilities, net of acquisitions and disposals	(12,608)	(6,798)	(1,754)
Other	2,227	2,652	392
Net cash provided by (used in) operating activities	(11,759)	(16,856)	9,356
Cash flows from investing activities			
Expenditures for property	(7,933)	(8,179)	(7,753)
Investments in marketable securities, acquisitions	(25,530)	(21,800)	(15,278)
Investments in marketable securities, liquidations	28,549	22,537	15,911
Net change in mortgage servicing rights	(61)	(267)	(326)
Increase in finance receivables	(1,160)	(6,582)	(38,673)
Proceeds from sale of finance receivables	18,374	31,652	23,385
Proceeds from sale of 51% interest in GMAC	7,353	—	—
Proceeds from sale of business units/equity investments	10,506	846	—
Operating leases, acquisitions	(17,070)	(15,496)	(14,324)
Operating leases, liquidations	7,039	5,362	7,696
Investments in companies, net of cash acquired	(357)	1,355	(60)
Other	(15)	(863)	1,359
Net cash provided by (used in) investing activities	19,695	8,565	(28,063)
Cash flows from financing activities			
Net increase (decrease) in short-term borrowings	7,033	(10,126)	2,192
Borrowings of long-term debt	79,566	78,276	73,511

(*continued*)

Consolidated Statements of Cash Flows			
	For the Years Ended December 31,		
General Motors Corporation and Subsidiaries	**2006**	**2005**	**2004**
Payments made on long-term debt	(92,290)	(69,566)	(57,822)
Cash dividends paid to stockholders	(563)	(1,134)	(1,129)
Other	2,487	6,030	4,723
Net cash provided by (used in) financing activities	(3,767)	3,480	21,475
Effect of exchange rate changes on cash and cash equivalents	365	(85)	671
Net increase (decrease) in cash and cash equivalents	4,534	(4,896)	3,439
Cash and cash equivalents reclassified to assets held for sale	—	(371)	—
Cash and cash equivalents retained by GMAC LLC upon disposal	(11,137)	—	—
Cash and cash equivalents at beginning of the year	30,726	35,993	32,554
Cash and cash equivalents at end of the year	$24,123	$30,726	$35,993

Reference should be made to the notes to consolidated financial statements.

electrical power. GM's engineers have been working on the development of hydrogen fuel cells, and their efforts are now focused on cars that would run on a combination of ethanol and hydrogen. At the same time, GM and DaimlerChrysler have been working together to try and rush out some of the gasoline-electric hybrid versions of their own cars and SUVs. In December 2006, Wagoner also announced plans for the development of a hybrid electric vehicle that could be plugged in to be recharged, which would give his firm a step up on the Japanese rivals.

Generating More Consumer Interest

Wagoner had been relying on Lutz to push GM to develop cars and trucks that will have more appeal to buyers. This allowed the firm to reduce their emphasis on costly incentives that it has been relying upon to get its vehicles moving. In part, GM has also failed in its attempts to inject originality and styling into its new models because it has had to stretch its limited funds to develop models for eight different brands. In order to use its design efforts more effectively, the firm announced during 2005 that it would keep its successful Cadillac and Chevrolet as its only two full-line brands.

Brands such as Buick and Pontiac shouldered most of the cutbacks. Wagoner had been fighting off pressures to drop at least one or possibly both of these divisions. Instead, GM decided to shrink each of their lineups to a maximum of 8 vehicles, down from the 18 that each of them offered in 2005. A GM executive conceded that the firm had to accept that the growth prospects of these brands were limited: "The market tells you what to do; you don't tell the market."[5] But the firm is trying to improve the styling and performance of this limited lineup, pinning their hopes on the new Pontiac Solstice.

GM was finally trying to revive the sagging sales of Saturn, the much heralded division that was created to revive the firm's fortunes. The firm announced that it would try

Exhibit 4 U.S. Auto Manufacturer Market Share—December 2006

Source: Autodata.

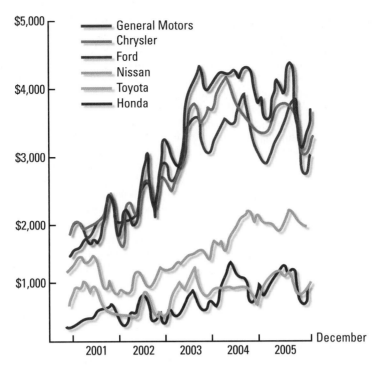

Exhibit 5 Incentive Spending per Vehicle

Source: Autodata.

to turn Saturn into a more upscale brand with more European styling and interiors. The Sky, a new sports car, was the first of a new crop of Saturns to be introduced over the next few years. Lutz was quite optimistic about the prospects for the

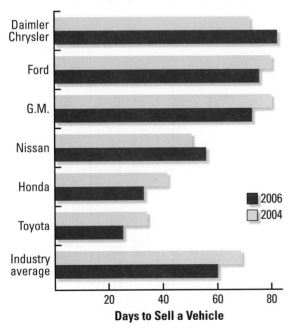

Exhibit 6 Dealer Turnover

Source: Ward's AutoInfoBank.

Aura sedan, which has generated some interest from potential customers. Under the new plan, however, Saturn lost its quasi-independence, with many of its operations being combined with those of GM's German Opel brand.

GM was developing its entries into crossover vehicles, which had shown the highest growth rates over the past few years as fuel prices have risen. Crossover vehicles were similar to larger SUVs, but they were built on car rather than truck platforms. The firm had high hopes for its Buick Enclave model, a six- or seven-passenger crossover that was nearly as large in terms of passenger space as a Tahoe truck. Lutz acknowledged that GM was a late entrant, but he felt confident that the Enclave would stand out from the crowd. "In retrospect, you wish you had everything earlier, but you can't," he said. "I like to adopt the philosophy that if you're going to be last in, you should be best dressed."[6]

In the meantime, Wagoner was taking the bold step of cutting the prices of its cars and trucks to bring them more in line with what the firm expected its customers to actually pay. Such a move allowed GM to cut back on the amount of the rebates that it had been using to attract buyers. There were risks attached to the cutback in rebates, even with lower sticker prices, unless the firm offered cars that had sufficient appeal for buyers. But both Wagoner and Lutz were optimistic about the potential of the new models that were being launched. Expressing his enthusiasm over the new additions that were being made to GM's lineup, Lutz recently stated; "All of the new stuff that's coming out is just a gigantic step in the right direction."[7]

Dealing with the Benefits Crunch

Wagoner's biggest challenge lay in dealing with the lavish health and retirement benefits that GM had accorded to its workers. The firm had agreed to these terms during the days when it was more profitable as a way to buy peace with the United Auto Workers. GM paid its UAW workers only slightly more per hour than Toyota, Honda, and Nissan pay their American factory workers. But the cost of pension and health care benefits had escalated, increasing by almost $2 billion from 2003 to 2006 (see Exhibit 7).

Over the past couple of years, these benefits added more than $2,000 to the cost of each car that GM rolled off the assembly line. Many Japanese competitors that build their cars in new, nonunion U.S. plants were paying considerably less. Costs for retirees had also escalated as a result of other recent decisions by GM's management. Underestimating the speed of its decline, GM agreed to pay workers for years after a furlough. As losses mounted, GM resorted to early-retirement offers, avoiding billions in unemployment benefits but adding thousands of retirees.

Those huge legacy costs explained why Wagoner had been reluctant to cut back on GM's production, even as he had been relying heavily on incentives to get these cars off the dealer's lots. Closing plants and accepting a smaller chunk of the U.S. market would have given GM fewer vehicles over which to spread those big pension and health care costs. Wagoner explained the pressures that he faced to generate revenues in order to meet the firm's cost obligations: "We have a huge fixed-cost base. It's 30 years of downsizing and 30 years of increased health care costs. It puts a premium on us running this business to generate cash."[8]

Wagoner had managed to negotiate with the UAW for some relief from the escalating health care costs. Under the new agreement, employees and retirees would pay for part of health care related costs for the first time. GM estimated that its spending on its health care plan has risen to almost $6 billion during 2006 but projected that these costs might drop by as much as 20 percent over the next few years. The firm was also planning to make some changes to its retiree pension program, although these would not affect its current retirees or their spouses.

But Wagoner was looking ahead a few years, when he expected the legacy costs to start to gradually diminish. Starting around 2008, the ranks of GM's elderly retirees would begin to drop, relieving some of the burden. After that, more of the incremental gains Wagoner had been achieving would fall to the bottom line rather than to retirees. The results could be dramatic. Nevertheless, he had to keep up cash flow to cover those benefit costs until they start to shrink. At the same time, he had to continue to rack up improvements in quality, efficiency, design, and brand appeal.

Firing on All Cylinders?

The visible signs of a turnaround in financial performance had given Wagoner some more time to push on his restructuring plans. Because of this progress, Kirk Kerkorian decided to back out of his effort to push GM into an alliance with two foreign automakers, Renault of France and Nissan of Japan. Kerkorian also sold off the $1.2 billion in shares that he had bought in the firm and his representative, Jerome B. York, gave up his seat on the board. Despite

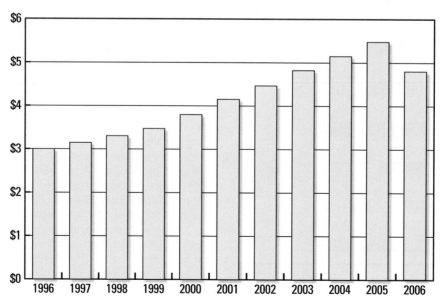

Exhibit 7 GM Health Care Spending (in $ billions)

Source GM, Standard and Poor's.

Exhibit 8 10-Year Stock Price History—General Motors (May 1997–May 2007)

Kerkorian's retreat, many analysts believed that GM still has a long way to go before it could stake out a long-term position in the competitive global automobile industry (see Exhibit 8).

Van Conway, partner at Detroit restructuring firm Conway, McKenzie & Dunleavy, was not sure if the team at GM could fully realize the seriousness of the situation that it still faced. "Most of the people there have been there for a long time, and I think there is some of the belief that 'Don't worry, we've been through this before and we'll get through it again,'" he explained.[9] However, there was a clear danger that if GM did not start making money soon on its lineup of cars and trucks, it could wind up staggering through a series of painful but insufficient cuts, restructurings, and reorganizations.

Wagoner was fully aware that GM's future depended on finding a way to stem the tide of losses racked up by its North American operations. Many of the firm's new products had been well received, but dealer inventories of its cars were turning over far more slowly since the cutbacks in rebates. GM had been relying on expanding in emerging Asian markets such as China and India to make up for the difficulties that it continues to face in its home market. "We need to keep the momentum going," said Hendersen. "We need to show what we can do on the revenue side."[10]

GM's efforts to push up revenues by selling more cars still faced formidable obstacles. In spite of significant advances that GM had made in the quality of its cars, none of its brands had been able to make the top 15 on *Consumer*

Reports' most-recommended list. Even if the firm was able to increase the attractiveness of its offerings, the image of most of its brands had been damaged by decades of cars that fell apart, lost their value quickly, or were just plain ugly. "GM management had built a case that they've taken action to fix the company, but it has not made a strong enough case to support a turnaround," said John Casesa, a veteran industry analyst with the Casesa Shapiro Group.[11]

Endnotes

1. Carty, S. S. 2006. GM loss shows plan is working. *USA Today,* October 26: 1B.
2. Bunkley, N. 2006. GM posts smallest loss in two years. *New York Times,* October 26: C13.
3. Welch, D. 2005. GM's design push picks up speed. *BusinessWeek,* July 18.
4. Welch D., & Kerwin, K. 2003 Rick Wagoner's game plan. *BusinessWeek,* February 10: 54.
5. Taylor, A. GM's new crop: Hot or not? *Fortune,* June 27: 32.
6. Terry Kosdrosky T., & Boudette, N. E. 2006. Paths diverge for Big 3 auto makers. *The Wall Street Journal,* January 9: A5.
7. Maynard, M., & Bunkley, N. 2006. GM applying its sales skills to its comeback story. *New York Times,* October 5: C12.
8. Taylor A. 2002. Finally GM is looking good. *Fortune,* April 1: 51–52.
9. Carty, S. S. Healey, J. R., & Woodyard, C. GM's broad cuts aim to share the pain. *USA Today,* February 8: 2B.
10. *New York Times,* October 26, 2006: C13.
11. *New York Times,* October 3, 2006: C12.

Case 38   Ford Motor Company on the Edge?*

Ford Motor Company was setting records, but, unfortunately, not encouraging ones. Although Ford's F-series pickups and the new Edge crossover vehicle were selling well, it had not been enough to stem the losses. The new crossover vehicle, the Ford Edge, was on track to sell 100,000 units in 2007, normally a success story. However, each Edge unit sold was less profitable than the larger sport utility vehicles (SUV) that they typically replaced according to Ron Pinelli of industry research firm Autodata Corporation. Ford's chief sales analyst, George Pipas, said that the company was "retaining Ford buyers who were in traditional SUVs that are moving into another category."[1]

On January 25, 2007, the struggling automaker posted a full-year net loss of $12.7 billion for 2006, the largest single-year loss in the company's history.[2] Ford's attempts at restructuring have been under way since 2001; however, it has been projected that the situation will not turn around until at least 2009.[3] In an attempt to stem the downward slide at Ford, and perhaps to jumpstart a turnaround, Alan Mulally was elected as President and Chief Executive Officer of Ford on September 5, 2006. Mulally, former head of commercial airplanes at Boeing, was expected to steer the struggling automaker out of the problems of falling market share and serious financial losses (see Exhibit 1).

Why Would Ford Invite in an Outsider?

The Ford empire had been around for over a century and the company had not gone outside its ranks for a top executive since hiring Ernest Breech away from General Motors Corporation in 1946[4] (see Exhibit 2). Since taking the CEO position in 2001, Bill Ford had tried several times to find a qualified successor, "going after such industry luminaries as Renault-Nissan CEO, Carlos Ghosn, and DaimlerChrysler Chairman, Dieter Zetsche."[5] Now Mulally had been selected and was expected to accomplish "nothing less than undoing a strongly entrenched management system put into place by Henry Ford II almost 40 years ago"—a system of regional fiefdoms around the world that has sapped the company's ability to compete in today's global industry and one that Chairman Bill Ford couldn't or wouldn't unwind.[6]

It had become more common to hire a CEO from outside the family or board. According to Joseph Bower from Harvard Business School, around one-third of the time for the firms comprising the S&P 500, and around 40 percent of the time when companies were struggling with problems in operations or financial distress, an outsider was appointed as CEO. The reasons may be to get a fresh point of view or to get the support of the board. "Results suggest that forced turnover followed by outsider succession, on average, improves firm performance."[7] Bill Ford claimed that to undertake major changes in Ford's dysfunctional culture, an outsider was more qualified than even the most proficient auto industry insider.[8]

An outsider CEO might also help restore faith in Ford management among investors, who had been discontented with the Ford family's high dividends and extravagant lifestyle. The Ford family controlled about 40 percent of the company's voting shares through their ownership of all its Class B stock and holdings of common stock. The class B family shares had almost the same market value as that of common stock, but the voting rights of the family shares are exceptionally high by industry standards (see Exhibits 3 and 4). The dividend stream had been an annuity, which over the years had helped various family members to own a football team, fund museums and philanthropic causes, and even promote the Hare Krishna movement. Given that the company was experiencing serious financial problems, these activities had raised stockholder dissent, as the annual retained earnings in the past were dissipated as dividends instead of reinvested in firm operations or acquisitions to increase the net value of the firm.

Mulally—The New Savior

Alan Mulally came from a metal-bending business, like automaking, that is influenced by global competition, has a unionized workforce, and was subject to complex regulations and rapidly changing technologies.[9] Although he is not an auto guy, he had a proven record in an industry that faces similar issues as the automobile industry, and a lot of his expertise and management techniques were highly transferable. In his own words "Everybody says, well, I'm not a car guy, so you couldn't make a contribution here. But I'm a product (guy) and I'm a designer."[10]

Prior to joining Ford, Mulally served as executive vice-president of The Boeing Company, and as president and chief executive officer of Boeing Commercial Airplanes. In those roles, he was responsible for The Boeing Company's entire commercial airplane programs and related services.[11] The advanced technology 777, which Mulally led the development of in the early 1990s, is now the most popular twin-engine jet in its class and was a testimony for Mulally's product and technology ingenuity. Under his leadership, Boeing regained its market leadership from Airbus. The appointment of Mulally at Ford had been seen by the market as a move to utilize his experience and success in managing manufacturing and assembly lines to help shape the future of Ford.

Bill Ford praised Mulally as "an outstanding leader and a man of great character."[12] He noted that Mulally had applied many of the lessons from Ford's success in

* This case study was prepared by Professor Helaine J. Korn of Baruch College, City University of New York, Ms. Naga Lakshmi Damaraju of The Ohio State University, and Professor Alan B. Eisner of Pace University. The purpose of the case is to stimulate class discussion rather than to illustrate effective or ineffective handling of a business situation. Copyright © 2007 Helaine Korn, Naga Damaraju, & Alan Eisner.

Exhibit 1   Income Statements

Ford Motor Company and Subsidiaries For the Years Ended December 31, (in $ millions, except per share amounts)	2006	2005	2004
Automotive			
Sales	$143,307	$153,474	$147,119
Costs and expenses			
Cost of sales	148,869	144,924	135,755
Selling, administrative and other expenses	12,359	12,738	11,564
Total costs and expenses	161,228	157,662	147,319
Operating income/(loss)	(17,921)	(4,188)	(200)
Interest expense	995	1,220	1,221
Interest income and other nonoperating income/(expense), net	1,478	1,249	988
Equity in net income/(loss) of affiliated companies	421	285	255
Income/(loss) before income taxes—Automotive	(17,017)	(3,874)	(178)
Financial Services			
Revenues	16,816	23,422	25,197
Costs and expenses			
Interest expense	7,788	7,197	7,250
Depreciation	5,295	5,854	6,618
Operating and other expenses	1,526	6,030	5,830
Provision for credit and insurance losses	241	483	1,212
Total costs and expenses	14,850	19,564	20,910
Gain on sale of Hertz	—	1,095	—
Income/(loss) before income taxes—Financial Services	1,966	4,953	4,287
Total Company			
Income/(loss) before income taxes	(15,051)	1,079	4,109
Provision for/(benefit from) income taxes	(2,646)	(845)	643
Income/(loss) before minority interests	(12,405)	1,924	3,466
Minority interests in net income/(loss) of subsidiaries	210	280	282
Income/(loss) from continuing operations	(12,615)	1,644	3,184
Income/(loss) from discontinued operations	2	47	(146)
Income/(loss) before cumulative effects of changes in accounting principles	(12,613)	1,691	3,038
Cumulative effects of changes in accounting principles	—	(251)	—
Net income/(loss)	$ (12,613)	$ 1,440	$ 3,038
Average number of shares of Common and Class B Stock outstanding	1,879	1,846	1,830
Amounts Per Share of Common and Class B Stock			
Basic income/(loss)			
Income/(loss) from continuing operations	$ (6.72)	$ 0.89	$ 1.74
Income/(loss) from discontinued operations	—	0.03	(0.08)
Cumulative effects of changes in accounting principles	—	(0.14)	—
Net income/(loss)	$ (6.72)	$ 0.78	$ 1.66
Diluted Income/(loss)			
Income/(loss) from continuing operations	$ (6.72)	$ 0.87	$ 1.59
Income/(loss) from discontinued operations	—	0.02	(0.07)
Cumulative effects of changes in accounting principles	—	(0.12)	—
Net income/(loss)	$ (6.72)	$ 0.77	$ 1.52
Cash dividends	$ 0.25	$ 0.40	$ 0.40

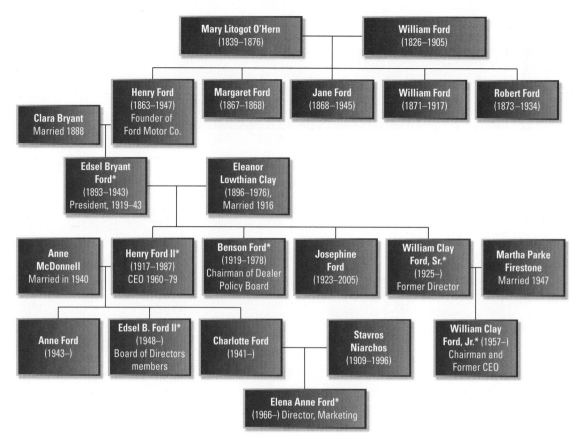

Exhibit 2 Ford Family Tree

*Ford Family members who have worked at Ford Motor Co.

Note: Family tree includes descendant of Henry Ford who worked at Ford Motor Co. and their children

Sources: Benson Ford Research Center, WSJ research, Wildpedia

developing the Taurus to Boeing's creation of the revolutionary Boeing 777 airliner. "Clearly, the challenges Boeing faced in recent years have many parallels to our own," said Bill Ford about Mulally's appropriateness for the top position at Ford.[13] In his e-mail to Ford employees announcing the appointment of Mulally, Bill Ford wrote, "Alan has deep experience in customer satisfaction, manufacturing, supplier relations and labor relations, all of which have applications to the challenges of Ford. He also has the personality and team-building skills that will help guide our Company in the right direction."[14]

Nonetheless, when Mulally took over the steering wheel, Ford was already poised to make significant structural changes as the company announced details of its accelerated "Way Forward" plan. Moreover, the company seemed to indicate that Mulally's appointment would not change the timelines and decisions associated with those restructuring actions, according to analyst Himanshu Patel of J. P. Morgan. This indicated that in spite of the appointment of Mulally as CEO, much of the decision making still remains with Bill Ford, who said he would remain "extremely active" in the business.

What Changes Has the New CEO Brought in?

In his effort to set Ford in the right direction, Mulally flew to Japan in January 2007 to meet with top executives of Ford's toughest competitor, Toyota, to seek their advice.[15] This was a huge break from the Ford tradition, and only an outsider CEO would have the courage and imagination to openly try to learn from foreign competitors.

Mulally has set his own priorities for fixing Ford: "At the top of the list, I would put dealing with reality."[16] In early 2007, Mulally signaled that "the bigger-is-better worldview that has defined Ford for decades was being replaced with a new approach: Less is More."[17] Ford needed to pay more attention to cutting costs and transforming the way it did business than to traditional measurements like market share.[18] The vision was to have a smaller and more

Exhibit 3   Sector Balance Sheets

Ford Motor Company and Subsidiaries (in $ millions)	December 31, 2006	December 31, 2005
Assets		
Automotive		
Cash and cash equivalents	$ 16,020	$ 13,388
Marketable securities	11,310	6,860
Loaned securities	5,256	3,461
Total cash marketable and loaned securities	32,586	23,709
Receivables, less allowances of $196 and $298	3,878	3,075
Inventories	11,578	10,271
Deferred income taxes	1,569	1,249
Other current assets	7,714	8,177
Total current assets	57,325	46,481
Equity in net assets of affiliated companies	2,029	1,756
Net property	38,236	40,348
Deferred income taxes	14,880	10,999
Goodwill and other net intangible assets	6,920	5,928
Assets of discontinued/held-for-sale operations	—	5
Other assets	3,244	8,308
Total Automotive assets	122,634	113,825
Financial Services		
Cash and cash equivalents	12,874	15,018
Marketable securities	10,162	3,812
Finance receivables, net	110,767	111,436
Net investment in operating leases	26,606	22,951
Retained interest in sold receivables	990	1,420
Goodwill and other intangible assets	17	17
Other assets	6,167	7,457
Receivable from Automotive	1,467	83
Total Financial Services assets	169,060	162,194
Intersector elimination	(1,467)	(83)
Total assets	$290,217	$276,936
Liabilities and Stockholders' Equity		
Automotive		
Trade payables	$ 17,069	$ 16,637
Other payables	4,893	4,222
Accrued liabilities and deferred revenue	28,995	28,829
Deferred income taxes	3,139	804
Debt payable within one year	1,499	978
Current payable to Financial Services	640	83
Total current liabilities	56,235	51,553

(*continued*)

Exhibit 3   Sector Balance Sheets (*continued*)

Ford Motor Company and Subsidiaries (in $ millions)		
	December 31, 2006	December 31, 2005
Long-term debt	28,514	16,900
Other liabilities	49,398	38,639
Deferred income taxes	441	586
Noncurrent payable to Financial Services	827	—
Total Automotive liabilities	135,415	107,678
Financial Services		
Payables	1,587	2,051
Debt	142,036	135,400
Deferred income taxes	10,827	10,747
Other liabilities and deferred income	4,125	5,579
Total Financial Services liabilities	158,575	153,777
Minority Interests	1,159	1,122
Stockholders' equity		
Capital stock		
Common Stock, par value $0.01 per share (1,837 million shares issued, 6,000 million shares authorized)	18	18
Class B Stock, par value $0.01 per share (71 million shares issued; 530 million shares authorized)	1	1
Capital in excess of par value of stock	4,562	4,872
Accumulated other comprehensive income/(loss)	(7,846)	(3,680)
Treasury stock	(183)	(833)
Retained earnings/(Accumulated deficit)	(17)	13,064
Total stockholders' equity	(3,465)	13,442
Intersector elimination	(1,487)	(83)
Total liabilities and stockholders' equity	$290,217	$275,936

profitable Ford. There were echoes in Detroit of Mulally's smaller-is-better thinking. G.M. was in the middle of its own revamping plan and Chrysler was also preparing a plan of cutbacks.[19] "Less is More" could be a new trend in the auto industry.

Mulally's cutback plan builds on the 14 plant closures and 30,000-plus job cuts announced by Ford in January 2007. Ford's new plan added two more North American plants to the closure list and targets $5 billion in cost cuts by the end of 2008, but pushed back a target for North American profitability by one year to 2009.[20] The company targeted seven vehicle manufacturing sites for closure and plans to have an optimum capacity at that point. At the same time, it also plans to increase the plant utilization and production levels in each production unit, while focusing more on larger, more fuel-efficient vehicles. The overall strategy seemed to be towards restructuring as a tool to obtain operating profitability at lower volume and with a changing mix of products that better appeals to the market.

Mulally also refocused the company on the Ford brand when he announced a formal review of Volvo in July 2007 as the first steps to putting the division up for sale. Volvo had been acquired eight years earlier to be part of the Premier Automotive Group of Ford among Jaguar, Aston Martin, and Land Rover.[21] However, Volvo's primary selling point of superior safety had been challenged as other manufacturers made advances in safety technologies in their own brands. Ford was also reviewing bids for Jaguar and Land Rover, both of which had lost money in four out of the last five years. Mulally said that the "real opportunity going forward is to integrate and leverage our Ford assets around the world," and decide on the best mix of brands in the company's portfolio.[22]

Exhibit 4   **Sector Statements of Cash Flows**

	Ford Motor Company and Subsidiaries For the Years Ended December 31, (in $ millions)					
	2006		**2005**		**2004**	
	Automotive	**Financial Services**	**Automotive**	**Financial Services**	**Automotive**	**Financial Services**
Cash flows from operating activities of continuing operations						
Net cash flows from operating activities	$ (4,185)	$ 7,318	$ 5,433	$ 6,912	$ 6,963	$ 7,963
Cash flows from investing activities of continuing operations						
Capital expenditures	(6,809)	(39)	(7,123)	(394)	(6,280)	(458)
Acquisitions of retail and other finance receivables and operating leases	—	(59,793)	—	(54,024)	—	(63,284)
Collections of retail and other finance receivables and operating leases	—	41,867	—	48,245	—	51,220
Net (increase)/decrease in wholesale receivables	—	6,113	—	4,751	—	2,882
Net acquisitions of daily rental vehicles	—	—	—	(1,988)	—	(2,492)
Purchases of securities	(4,068)	(19,610)	(5,714)	(6,169)	(7,590)	(4,177)
Sales and maturities of securities	4,865	13,591	5,106	3,629	7,615	9,033
Proceeds from sales of retail and other finance receivables and operating leases	—	5,120	—	17,288	—	6,481
Proceeds from sale of wholesale receivables	—	—	—	3,739	—	3,957
Proceeds from sale of businesses	56	—	280	7,657	125	412
Cash paid for acquisitions	—	—	(2,031)	—	(30)	—
Transfer of cash balances upon disposition of discontinued held-for-sale operations	(4)	—	—	(1,255)	(26)	(13)
Investing activity from Financial Services	1,185	—	8,407	—	4,361	—
Investing activity to Financial Services	(1,400)	—	—	—	—	—
Other	18	307	387	1,462	107	2,185
Net cash (used in) provided by investing activities	(6,157)	(12,444)	(688)	22,941	(1,718)	5,746
Cash flows from financing activities of continuing operations						
Cash dividends	(468)	—	(738)	—	(733)	—

(*continued*)

Exhibit 4   Sector Statements of Cash Flows (*continued*)

	Ford Motor Company and Subsidiaries **For the Years Ended December 31,** **(in $ millions)**					
	2006		**2005**		**2004**	
	Automotive	**Financial Services**	**Automotive**	**Financial Services**	**Automotive**	**Financial Services**
Sales of Common Stock	431	—	895	—	21	—
Purchases of Common Stock	(183)	—	(570)	—	(172)	—
Changes in short-term debt	414	(6,239)	(115)	(8,598)	(342)	5,227
Proceeds from issuance of other debt	12,254	46,004	385	24,174	469	21,754
Principal payments on other debt	(758)	(35,843)	(758)	(35,322)	(2,564)	(33,436)
Financing activity from Automotive	—	1,400	—	—	—	—
Financing activity to Automotive	—	(1,185)	—	(8,407)	—	(4,361)
Other	(147)	(192)	(177)	24	(39)	(97)
Net cash (used in/provided by financing activities	11,543	3,945	(1,078)	(28,129)	(3,360)	(10,913)
Effect of exchange rate changes on cash	104	360	(23)	(473)	117	388
Net change in intersector receivables/payables and other liabilities	1,321	(1,321)	(394)	394	1,258	(1,258)
Net increase (decrease) in cash and cash equivalents from continuing operations	2,626	(2,144)	3,250	1,645	3,260	1,926
Cash from discontinued operations						
Cash flows from operating activities of discontinued operations	2	—	(16)	71	(149)	464
Cash flows from investing activities of discontinued operations	—	—	17	(66)	137	(457)
Cash flows from financing activities of discontinued operations	—	—	—	—	—	—
Net increase/(decrease) in cash and cash equivalents	$ 2,628	$ (2,144)	$ 3,251	$ 1,650	$ 3,248	$ 1,933
Cash and cash equivalents at January 1	$13,388	$15,018	$10,139	$12,689	$ 6,853	$10,819
Cash and cash equivalents of discontinued/held-for-sale operations at January 1	4	—	2	679	40	616
Net increase (decrease) in cash and cash equivalents	2,628	(2,144)	3,251	1,650	3,248	1,933
Less cash and cash equivalents of discontinued held-for-sale operations at December 31	—	—	(4)	—	(2)	(679)
Cash and cash equivalents at December 31	$16,020	$12,874	$13,388	$15, 018	$10,139	$12,689

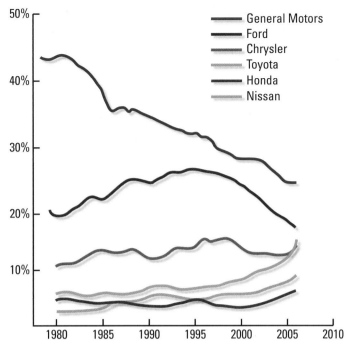

Exhibit 5 U.S. Market Share

Source: Autodata.

Since his appointment, Mulally had made some structural and procedural changes in the company. For instance, instead of discussing business plans monthly or semiannually as they used to do at Ford, executives now met with Mulally weekly. The in-depth sessions were a contrast to executives' previous efforts to explain away bad news, said Donat R. Leclair, Ford's chief financial officer. "The difference I see now is that we're actually committed to hitting the numbers. Before, it was a culture of trying to explain why we were off the plan. The more eloquently you could explain why you were off the plan, the more easy it was to change the plan."[23]

Mulally also did some senior executive reorganization at Ford and many of the newly appointed would report to him directly, including a global head of product development. In addition, the head of worldwide purchasing, the chief of quality and advanced manufacturing, the head of information technology, the chief technical officer, and the leaders of Ford's European division, its Asia, Pacific, and Africa units and its Americas unit would all report directly to him.[24]

About the Ford Motor Company

Ford Motor had been sinking since 1999, when profits had reached a remarkable $7.2 billion ($5.86 per share) and pretax income was $11 billion. At that time people even speculated that Ford would soon overtake General Motors as the world's number one automobile manufacturer

(see Exhibits 5–7). But soon Toyota, through its innovative technology, management philosophy of continuous improvement, and cost arbitrage due to its presence in multiple geographical locations, took over the giants—GM and Ford. Compounding this were Ford's internal organizational problems and a failed diversification strategy lead by Jacques Nasser, the CEO at that time, and Ford's market share began to drop—from 25 percent in 1999 to 18 percent in 2006, with major blows to market share in the light vehicle segment.

Moreover, in 2006, Chevrolet outsold the Ford division for the first time since 1986. Despite an extensive mechanical update, the much-improved Ford Explorer, which had been the world's best-selling sport utility vehicle, fell behind the dated Chevy TrailBlazer in sales. It did not help that the new Explorer looked just like the model it replaced. The long-neglected Ranger, which had been the top-selling small pickup, fell behind both Toyota Motor and Chevrolet, and despite 20 years of trying, the company has never been able to build a competitive minivan. Ford's most successful vehicles were the F-series pickup trucks (see Exhibit 8).

The company was also experiencing serious financial problems. Ford's turnaround plan aims to cut $5 billion in costs by the end of 2008 by slashing 10,000 white-collar workers and offering buyouts to all of its 75,000 unionized employees. The loss, including restructuring costs, was Ford's largest quarterly loss since the first quarter of 1992,

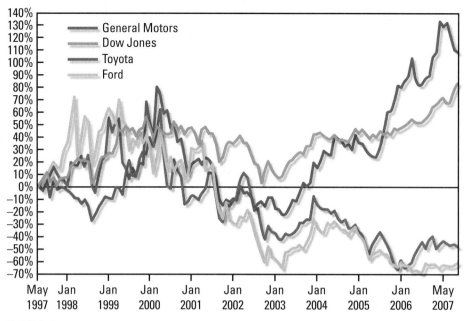

Exhibit 6 Ford 10-Year Stock Price History

when the company lost $6.7 billion due mainly to accounting changes. Ford said special charges for the third quarter of 2006 totaled $5.26 billion before taxes. The charges included $2.2 billion to revalue assets in North America and $1.6 billion to decrease the value of Jaguar and Land Rover assets.

Automobile Industry in the United States

The automotive industry in the United States was a highly competitive, cyclical business. The number of cars and trucks sold to retail buyers or "industry demand" varied substantially from year to year depending on "general economic situations, the cost of purchasing and operating cars and trucks, the availability of credit and fuel." Because cars and trucks are durable items, consumers could wait to replace them; industry demand reflected this factor (see Exhibit 9).

Competition in the United States intensified in the last few decades with Japanese carmakers gaining a foothold in the market. To counter the foreign problem, Japanese companies had set up production facilities in the United States and gained acceptance from American consumers. Production quality and lean production were judged to be the major weapons that Japanese carmakers used to gain an advantage over American carmakers. "The Toyota Motor Company of Japan issued a 2007 forecast that would make it first in global sales, ahead of General Motors, which has been the world's biggest auto company since 1931. Toyota, which had not even built its first automobile back then, expects to sell 9.34 million vehicles next year. That would exceed the 9.2 million vehicles that GM expects to sell worldwide this year."[25] For American consumers, Toyota vehicles have been "a better value proposition" than

Detroit's products, said Mulally, who was the first Detroit leader who readily said he was an avid student of Toyota.[26]

While there was a glut in the U.S. automobile market, the markets of Asia, Central and South America, and central and Eastern Europe all showed increasing promise for automobiles, and the automobile industry entered into an era of "global motorization."

Challenges Mulally Faces

Mulally was faced with a lot of challenges. He had considerable experience dealing with manufacturing and labor relations issues, but he did not have much background in finance. Given the cash drain at Ford due to restructuring costs and product development, and the B+ junk credit rating of Ford stock, cash was crucial to keep the company afloat and Mulally's abilities would be tested.[27]

"Mulally's fearlessness was well suited to pushing through projects at Boeing, but its suitability to Ford's culture remains to be seen. Like every new leader, he will have to move with confidence in his early days, but as an industry outsider, he will have to take care to avoid violating the long-standing industry norms."[28]

"Mulally's approach to management and communication hasn't been seen before in the halls of Ford, which have historically been the atmosphere of a kingdom with competing dukes."[29] Mulally was still in the honeymoon period but already clashes had surfaced between his management style and the "Ford way."

Mulally busied himself breaking down a global structure in which Ford Europe, Ford Asia, Ford North America, Ford Australia, and Ford South America had long created redundancies of efforts, products, engineering platforms,

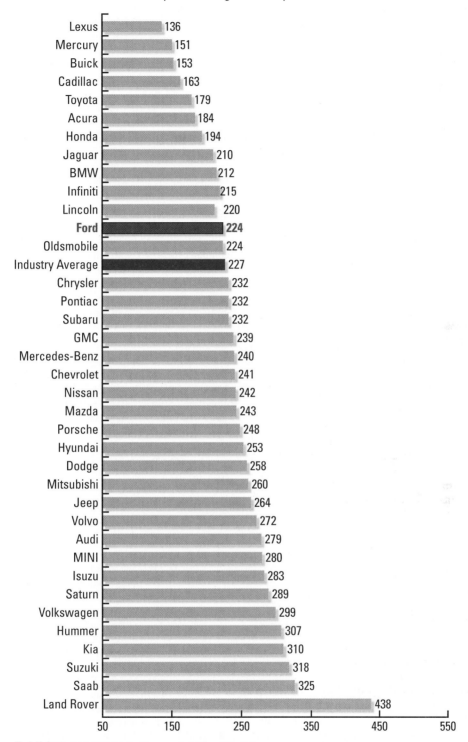

J.D. Power amd Associates
2006 Vehicle Dependability Study ^{SM} **(VDS)**
2006 Nameplate Ranking Problems per 100 Vehicles

Nameplate	Problems per 100 Vehicles
Lexus	136
Mercury	151
Buick	153
Cadillac	163
Toyota	179
Acura	184
Honda	194
Jaguar	210
BMW	212
Infiniti	215
Lincoln	220
Ford	**224**
Oldsmobile	224
Industry Average	227
Chrysler	232
Pontiac	232
Subaru	232
GMC	239
Mercedes-Benz	240
Chevrolet	241
Nissan	242
Mazda	243
Porsche	248
Hyundai	253
Dodge	258
Mitsubishi	260
Jeep	264
Volvo	272
Audi	279
MINI	280
Isuzu	283
Saturn	289
Volkswagen	299
Hummer	307
Kia	310
Suzuki	318
Saab	325
Land Rover	438

Exhibit 7 2006 Vehicle Dependability Rankings

Source: J.D. Power and Associates 2006 Vehicle Dependability Study.^{SM}

Exhibit 8 Top-Selling Vehicles of 2006

1.	Ford F-Series (includes F-150, F-250 Super Duty, and F-350 Super Duty)	796,039
2.	Chevrolet Silverado (includes 1500, 1500 Classic, 1500 SS Classic, 1500HD Classic, 2500HD, 2500HD Classic, 3500HD, 3500 Classic)	636,069
3.	Toyota Camry and Camry Solara	448,445
4.	Dodge Ram (includes 1500, 2500 and 3500)	364,177
5.	Honda Accord	354,441
6.	Toyota Corolla	318,123
7.	Honda Civic	316,638
8.	Chevrolet Impala	289,868
9.	Nissan Altima	232,457
10.	Chevrolet Cobalt	211,449

Source: *Automotive News* and Edmunds.com, http://www.edmunds.com/reviews/list/top10/120637/article.html.

engines, and the like as a way of perpetuating each division's independence.[30] Since the initial purpose of having an outsider CEO was to break the dysfunctional Ford culture, these clashes were expected and generally viewed as constructive.

However, the clashes also had their drawbacks. Unable to accept the Mulally management approach, some

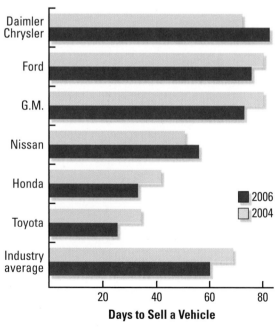

Exhibit 9 Dealer Turnover
Source: Ward's AutoInfoBank.

senior executives left Ford. International chief of the company, Mark A. Schulz, was one of them. "He had decided to retire this year after working for more than three decades at the company. Mr. Schulz is just the latest in a string of senior executives to leave since Mulally took over. Ford's second-ranking North American executive, its North American manufacturing chief and its chief of staff also all announced their departures after Mulally's hiring."[31] Ford had lost some of its most experienced leaders because of the outsider CEO.

Despite his rich experience and proven success in turning around the manufacturing operations at Boeing, Mulally was still not completely qualified or accepted as an auto guy. "He recently had to ask what the name of the auto industry's lobby group is (Alliance of Automobile Manufacturers) and what NADA stands for (National Automobile Dealers Assn., which he will address in a keynote speech in February)."[32] He had to learn the business and its unique terms on the fly. Speaking the auto language was still critical for an outsider CEO to be accepted in a giant company like Ford, which had a long and distinct tradition of promoting insider leaders.

Nonetheless, Mulally was confident that his years of experience running a big manufacturer and his technical background had prepared him for the challenges facing Ford.[33]

Looking Ahead

The year-end earnings report was not without some good news. Ford was out to cut operating costs by $5 billion by 2008. Mulally said that the more he learned about Ford's global operations, the more opportunities he saw to overshoot that target.[34] Maybe Mulally's smaller-is-better strategy was the lifesaver for Ford. Only time would tell whether bringing in an outsider was a good move for Ford and, more specifically, whether Alan Mulally was the right outsider for the job.

Endnotes

1. Bunkley, Nick. 2007. A crossover helps Ford, but not enough to hold its no. 2 spot. *New York Times.* May 2. www.nytimes.com.
2. Kiley, D. 2007. The record year Ford hopes to shake off. *BusinessWeek Online.* January 26. www.businessweek.com.
3. Kiley, D. 2007. Can this man save Ford? *BusinessWeek Online.* January 19. www.businessweek.com.
4. Knowles, F. 2006. Boeing exec flies the coop: Ford hires Mulally to turn things. *Chicago Sun-Times.* September 6.
5. Welch D., Kiley D., & Holmes S. 2006. Alan Mulally: A plan to make Ford fly. *BusinessWeek*
6. Kiley, D. 2007. Mulally: Ford's most important new model. *BusinessWeek Online.* January 9. www.businessweek.com.
7. Rakesh, K. 1998. The changing of the guard: Causes, process and consequences of CEO turnover.
8. Berfield, S. 2006. The best leaders. *BusinessWeek Online.* December 18. www.businessweek.com.
9. Levin, D. 2006. Mulally's hire by Ford may be too late. Bloomberg.com.

10. Crain, K. 2006. Mulally wants fewer platforms, fewer dealers. *The New York Times.* November 20.
11. Ford Motor Company, http://media.ford.com/article_display.cfm?article_id=24203.
12. Ford Motor Company, http://media.ford.com/article_display.cfm?article_id=24203.
13. Ford Motor Company, http://media.ford.com/article_display.cfm?article_id=24203.
14. Ford Motor Company, http://media.ford.com/article_display.cfm?article_id=24203.
15. Maynard, M. 2007. Ford chief sees small as virtue and necessity. *New York Times.* January, 25. http://www.nytimes.com.
16. Maynard, M. 2007. Ford chief sees small as virtue and necessity. *New York Times.* January, 25. http://www.nytimes.com.
17. Maynard, M. 2007. Ford chief sees small as virtue and necessity. *New York Times.* January, 25. http://www.nytimes.com.
18. Maynard, M. 2006. Ford expects to fall soon to no. 3 spot. *New York Times.* December 21. http://www.nytimes.com.
19. Maynard, M. 2007. Ford chief sees small as virtue and necessity. *New York Times.* January, 25. http://www.nytimes.com.
20. Stoll, John. 2006. Ford looks to reshape business model, executive says. *Dow Jones Newswires.* September 18.
21. Maynard, Micheline. 2007. Ford seeks a future by going backward. *New York Times.* July, 17: C1.
22. Bunkley, Nick and Maynard, Micheline. 2007. Ford breaks string of losing quarters, but says respite will be brief. *New York Times.* July, 27: C3.
23. Maynard, Micheline. 2007. Ford chief sees small as virtue and necessity. *New York Times.* January, 25. http://www.nytimes.com.
24. Bloomberg News. 2006. Ford reorganizes executives. *New York Times.* December 15. http://www.nytimes.com.
25. Maynard, M., & Fackler, M. 2006. Toyota is poised to supplant GM as world's largest carmaker. *New York Times.* December 22. http://www.nytimes.com.
26. Maynard, M., & Fackler, Martin 2006. Toyota is poised to supplant GM as world's largest carmaker. *New York Times.* December 22. http://www.nytimes.com.
27. Welch D., Kiley D., & Holmes S. 2006. Alan Mulally: A plan to make Ford fly. *BusinessWeek.*
28. Welch D., Kiley D., & Holmes S. 2006. Alan Mulally: A plan to make ford fly. *Businessweek.*
29. Kiley, D. 2007. Mulally: Ford's most important new model. *BusinessWeek Online.* January 9. www.businessweek.com.
30. Kiley, D. 2007. The record year Ford hopes to shake off. *BusinessWeek Online.* January 26. www.businessweek.com.
31. Bloomberg News. 2006. Ford reorganizes executives. *New York Times.* December 15. http://www.nytimes.com.
32. Kiley, D. 2007. Mulally: Ford's most important new model. *BusinessWeek Online.* January 9. www.businessweek.com.
33. Maynard, M. 2007. Ford chief sees small as virtue and necessity. *New York Times.* January, 25. http://www.nytimes.com.
34. Kiley, D. 2007. The record year Ford hopes to shake off. *BusinessWeek Online.* January 26. www.businessweek.com.

Case 39   Dippin' Dots Ice Cream*

Founded by Curt Jones and incorporated in 1988, Dippin' Dots, Inc., headquartered in Paducah, Kentucky, was the company that made the "ice cream of the future."[1] The company's chief operation was the sale of BB-sized pellets of flash frozen ice cream in some two dozen flavors to franchisees and national accounts throughout the world. As a Six Flags customer commented, "I gotta say, man, they're pretty darn good. . . . Starts off like a rock candy but ends up like ice cream."[2]

Dippin' Dots was the marriage between old-fashioned handmade ice cream and space-age technology. Dippin' Dots were tiny round beads of ice cream that were made at supercold temperatures, served at subzero temperatures in a soufflé cup, and eaten with a spoon. The supercold freezing of Dippin' Dots ice cream, done by liquid nitrogen, cryogenically locked in both flavor and freshness in a way that no other manufactured ice cream could offer, since the process virtually eliminated the presence of trapped ice and air, giving the ice cream a fresh flavor and a hard texture. Not only had Jones discovered a new way of making ice cream, but many felt his product proved to be much more flavorful and richer than regular ice cream. According to Jones, "I created a way . . . [to] get a quicker freeze so the ice cream wouldn't get large ice crystals. . . . About six months later, I decided to quit my job and go into business."

Jones was a microbiologist by trade with an area of expertise in cryogenics. His first job was researching and engineering as a microbiologist for ALLtech Inc., a bioengineering company based in Lexington, Kentucky. During his days at ALLtech, Jones worked with different types of bacteria to find new ways of preserving them so they could be transported throughout the world. He applied a method of freezing using supercold temperatures with substances like liquid CO_2 and liquid nitrogen—the same method used to create Dippin' Dots.

One method Jones developed was to "microencapsulate" the bacteria by freezing their medium with liquid nitrogen. Other scientists thought he was crazy because nothing like this had ever been done before. Jones, however, was convinced his idea would work. He spent months trying to perfect this method, and continued to make progress. While Jones was working over 80 hours a week in ALLtech's labs to perfect the microencapsulating process, he made the most influential decision of his life. He took a weekend off and attended a family barbeque at his parents' house. It just so happened that his mother was making ice cream the day of the barbeque. Jones began to reminisce about homemade ice cream prepared the slow, old-fashioned way. Then Jones

began to wonder if it was possible to flash-freeze ice cream. Instead of using a bacteria medium, was it possible to microencapsulate ice cream?

The answer was yes to both questions. After virtually reinventing a frozen dessert that had been around since the second century BC,[3] Jones patented his idea to flash-freeze liquid cream and opened the first Dippin' Dots store.[4] Once franchising was offered in 2000, the "Ice Cream of the Future" could be found at thousands of shopping malls, amusement parks, water parks, fairs, and festivals worldwide. Dippin' Dots were transported coast-to-coast and around the world by truck, train, plane, and ship. In addition to specially designed cryogenic transport containers, Dippin' Dots were transported in refrigerated boxes known as pallet reefers. Both types of containers ensured the fastest and most efficient method of delivery to dealers around the globe. The product was served in 4-, 5-, and 8-ounce cups, and 5-ounce vending prepacks.

Product Specifics

Dippin' Dots were flash-frozen beads of ice cream typically served in a cup or vending package. The ice cream averaged 190 calories per serving, depending upon the flavor, and had 9 grams of fat. The ice cream was produced by a patented process that introduced flavored liquid cream into a vat with liquid nitrogen. The liquid cream was flash-frozen in the $-325°$ vat to produce the bead or dot shape. Once frozen, the dots were collected and either mixed with other flavors or packaged separately for delivery to retail locations. The product had to be stored at subzero temperatures to maintain the consistency of the dots. Subzero storage temperatures were achieved by utilizing special equipment and freezers and supplemented with dry ice. Although a challenge for international shipping, the beads could maintain their shape for up to 15 days in their special container. To maintain product integrity and consistency, the ice cream had to be served at 10 to 20 degrees below zero. A retail location had to have special storage and serving freezers. Because the product had to be stored and served at such low temperatures, it was unavailable in regular frozen food cases and could not be stored in a typical household freezer. Therefore, it could only be consumed at or near a retail location, unless stored with dry ice to maintain the necessary storage temperature.

Industry Overview

The frozen dairy industry was occupied by family-owned businesses like Dippin' Dots, full-line dairies, and a couple of large international companies that focused on only a single sales region. The year 2006 had been marked by a slight increase in the production and sale of ice cream, as volume in traditional varieties remained flat and new types of ice-cream forms emerged. Despite higher ingredient costs, manufacturers were continually churning out new products ranging from super-premium selections to good-for-you

* This case was prepared by Professor Alan B. Eisner of Pace University, Professor Pauline Assenza of Manhattanville College, and graduate student Brian R. Callahan of Pace University as a basis for class discussion rather than to illustrate either effective or ineffective handling of an administrative situation. Copyright © 2007 Alan B. Eisner and Pauline Assenza.

varieties to co-branded packages and novelties. Most novelty ice creams could be found together in a supermarket freezer case; small freezers in convenience stores; and in carts, kiosks, or trucks at popular summertime events. Ice-cream makers had been touched by consolidation trends affecting the overall food and beverage industry that extended beyond their products, as even the big names were folded into global conglomerates.

The ice-cream segment in the United States had become a battleground for two huge international consumer products companies seeking to corner the ice-cream market. Those two industry giants were Nestlé SA of Switzerland, the world's largest food company with more than $69 billion in annual sales, and Unilever PLC, of London and Rotterdam, with over $52 billion in annual revenues. Both had been buying into U.S. firms for quite awhile, but Nestlé, which already owned the Häagen-Dazs product line, upped the ante with its June 2003 merger with Dreyer's Grand/Edy's Ice Cream Inc., of Oakland, California. But even as these two dominated the U.S. ice-cream industry, about 500 small businesses continued to produce and distribute frozen treats. As one commentator said, "like microbrewers and small-scale chocolate makers, entrepreneurs are drawn to ice cream as a labor of love."[5] Some of the better known brands were regional ones, such as Blue Bell, based on Brenham, Texas (see Exhibit 1) .

The International Dairy Foods Association reported that, of the $21.6 billion total spent on ice cream in 2005, ice cream and related frozen desserts were consumed by more than 90 percent of households in the United States.[6] Consumers spent $8.2 billion on products for at-home consumption while $13.5 billion went toward away-from-home purchases. In the first half of 2006, overall ice-cream sales in supermarkets were down 4.3 percent, with sales down in most categories, but the reduced-fat segment showed significant growth, increasing 15 percent from January to June 2006.[7] Harry Balzar of the market research firm NPD Group said about ice cream in general, "It's not a small category, but one that has remained flat for more than a decade, and is not likely to grow."[8]

The challenge was to woo customers away from competitors, and sustain a loyal fan base by continuing to innovate. The trend toward more healthy treats had spurred the major players Nestlé and Unilever to develop reduced-fat product lines that still had the taste and texture of full-fat ice cream. Edy's/Dreyer's, Breyers and Häagen-Dazs had all continued to experiment, and the "Slow Churned," "Double Churned," or "Light" products were seeing increased sales since their introduction in 2004.[9]

In October 2002, it was announced that Good Humor–Breyers Ice Cream of Green Bay, Wisconsin, and Ben & Jerry's of Vermont had formed a unified retail sales division named Unilever Ice Cream. The new organization brought together both companies and represented the five Unilever North American ice-cream brands, which include Ben & Jerry's, Breyers, Good Humor, Popsicle, and Klondike. Good Humor–Breyers had created several new co-branded

novelties specifically for convenience store and vending locations. The company had also set out to expand the availability of single-serve novelties by placing freezers of its products in Blockbuster video stores and Breyers-branded kiosks in 30 Chicago-area Loews theaters. In addition to prepackaged products, freshly scooped ice cream was served at the kiosks. The new sales team would focus exclusively on the out-of-home ice-cream business and, therefore, exclude grocery channels.

Another novelty product delivery system in the independent scoop shop was the "slab" concept. Employees at franchises such as Marble Slab Creamery, Cold Stone Creamery, and Maggie Moo's worked ingredients on a cold granite or marble slab to blend premium ice cream with the customer's choice of tasty additives such as crumbled cookies, fruits and nuts before serving in a cup or cone. The novelty was in the entertainment of watching the preparation. All three chains had ranked in *Entrepreneur's* list of top 500 franchise opportunities in 2006, but commentators were skeptical of sustainability once the novelty wore off, especially since the average price was $5 for a medium serving.[10]

Industry Segmentation

Frozen desserts come in many forms. Each of the following foods has its own definition, and many are standardized by federal regulations.[11]

Ice Cream consists of a mixture of dairy ingredients, such as milk and nonfat milk, and ingredients for sweetening and flavoring, such as fruits, nuts, and chocolate chips. Functional ingredients, such as stabilizers and emulsifiers, are often included in the product to promote proper texture and enhance the eating experience. By federal law, ice cream must contain at least 10 percent butterfat, before the addition of bulky ingredients and must weigh a minimum of 4.5 pounds to the gallon.

Novelties are separately packaged single servings of a frozen dessert, such as ice-cream sandwiches, fudge sticks, and juice bars, which may or may not contain dairy ingredients.

Frozen Custard or **French Ice Cream** must also contain a minimum of 10 percent butterfat as well as at least 1.4 percent egg yolk solids.

Sherbets have a butterfat content of between 1 percent and 2 percent, and a slightly higher sweetener content than ice cream. Sherbet weighs a minimum of 6 pounds to the gallon and is flavored either with fruit or other characterizing ingredients.

Gelato is characterized by an intense flavor and is served in a semifrozen state. Gelato contains sweeteners, milk, cream, egg yolks, and flavoring.

Sorbet and **Water Ices** are similar to sherbets, but contain no dairy ingredients.

A **Quiescently Frozen Confection** is a frozen novelty such as a water ice novelty on a stick.

Frozen Yogurt consists of a mixture of dairy ingredients, such as milk and nonfat milk, which have been cultured, as well as ingredients for sweetening and flavoring.

Exhibit 1   Top Brands

Top 10 Ice Cream/Sherbet Brands*				
	$ Sales (In Millions)	% Change vs. Year Ago	Unit Sales (In Millions)	% Change vs. Year Ago
Total Category	$4,403.0	−0.3%	1,370.0	−0.4%
Private Label (Ice Cream)	812.8	−2.7	285.9	−0.4
Breyers	638.8	7.5	196.7	10.0
Dreyer's/Edy's Grand	445.1	−1.0	130.9	−4.7
Häagen-Dazs	287.3	12.1	83.4	7.2
Dreyer's/Edy's SlowChurned	284.0	100.8	76.8	93.3
Blue Bell	253.2	2.0	75.0	1.0
Ben & Jerry's	207.6	8.7	67.8	10.1
Wells' Blue Bunny	122.0	14.0	34.6	17.1
Turkey Hill	116.9	13.8	41.8	14.1
Private Label (Sherbet/Sorbet/Ices)	59.8	−4.0	27.3	−2.7

*Total sales of all forms of ice cream/sherbet brands in supermarkets, drug stores and mass merchandisers (excluding Wal-Mart) in the 52-week period ending December 31, 2006.

Source: Information Resources Inc.

Top 10 Frozen Novelty Brands*						
	Sales (in $ millions)	% Change vs. Year Ago	$ Share	Unit Sales (in millions)	% Change vs. Year Ago	Unit Share
Total Category	$2,470.7	2.3%	100.0	819.4	−0.1%	100.0
Private Label	317.9	−4.0	12.9	134.5	−3.2	16.4
Nestlé Drumstick	131.3	−0.6	5.3	38.0	−3.8	4.6
Weight Watchers	127.4	57.3	5.2	28.9	54.1	3.5
Klondike	126.2	−5.0	5.1	42.7	−7.5	5.2
Popsicle	113.3	10.4	4.6	41.5	5.0	5.1
Dreyer's/Edy's Whole Fruit	103.4	−1.3	4.2	31.6	−9.9	3.9
Carvel	93.2	6.0	3.8	5.9	2.4	0.7
The Skinny Cow	84.3	16.2	3.4	19.5	12.8	2.4
Dreyer's/Edy's Dibs	83.6	97.8	3.4	25.2	91.6	3.1
Häagen-Dazs	57.4	7.6	2.3	19.0	8.1	2.3

*Total sales of all forms of frozen novelty brands in supermarkets, drug stores and mass merchandisers (excluding Wal-Mart) in the 52-week period ending December 31, 2006.

Source: Information Resources Inc.

Dippin' Dots Growth[12]

The growth of Dippin' Dots Inc. had been recognized in the United States and the world by industry watchdogs such as *Inc.* magazine, which ranked Dippin' Dots as one of the 500 fastest-growing companies two years in a row in 1996 and 1997. Most recently, Dippin' Dots Franchising, Inc., ranked number four on *Entrepreneur* magazine's 2004 list of the top 50 new franchise companies and achieved the 101st spot on

Exhibit 2 Dippin' Dots Franchise Growth

Year	U.S. Franchises	Canadian Franchises	Foreign Franchises	Company Owned
2006	448	1	0	2
2005	635	1	0	2
2004	618	1	0	2
2003	598	0	0	2
2002	580	0	0	2
2001	569	0	0	3
2000	525	0	0	1

Source: http://www.entrepreneur.com/franchises/dippindotsfranchisinginc/289468-1.html.

Entrepreneur's "Franchise 500" for 2004. In 2005, Dippin' Dots ranked number two as a top new franchise opportunity and climbed to number 93 on the Franchise 500 list. Exhibit 2 shows the growth of franchises for Dippin' Dots.

However, the success of Curt Jones and Dippin' Dots has not been without obstacles. Once Jones perfected his idea, he needed to start a company for the new process of flash-freezing ice cream. Like many new entrepreneurs, Jones enlisted the help of his family to support his endeavor. It was essential to start selling his product, but he had no protection for his idea from competitors.

The first obstacle confronting Jones was to locate funding to accomplish his goals. He needed money for the patent to protect his intellectual property and seed money to start manufacturing the ice cream once the patent was granted. At the same time Jones was perfecting the flash-freezing process for his ice cream, he was also working on a small business association (SBA) loan to convert the family farm into one that would manufacture ethanol. However, instead of using the farm to produce the alternative fuel, Jones's parents took out a first, and then a second, mortgage to help fund Jones's endeavor. Thus, Jones initiated the entire venture by self-funding his company with personal and family assets.

However, the money from his parents was only enough to pay for the patent and some crude manufacturing facilities (a liquid nitrogen tanks in his parent's garage). Jones always believed that his ice cream would sell, but with the patent he felt reassured by the protection it offered from any competitors. He next had to open a store to validate his faith that consumers would buy his product, but opening the store required more money—money that Jones and his family did not have. They were unable to get the SBA loan because, while the product was novel and looked promising, there was no proof that it would sell. So Jones and his newly appointed CFO (his sister) went to an alternative lender who lent them cash at an exorbitant interest rate that was tacked onto the principal weekly if unpaid.

With the seed money they needed, Curt Jones and his family opened their first store. Soon after the store opened in the summertime, there was a buzz in the community—and the store was mobbed every night. Dippin' Dots was legitimized by public demand. Through the influx of cash, Jones was able to move his manufacturing operation into a vacant warehouse. There he set up shop and personally made flash-frozen ice cream for 12 hours every day to supply the store.

Once the store had been operating for a few months the Joneses were able to secure small business loans from local banks to cover the expenses of a modest manufacturing plant and office. At the same time, Jones's sister made calls to fairs and events to learn if Dippin' Dots products could be sold there. Luckily for the Joneses, the amusement park at Opryland in Nashville, Tennessee, was willing to have them as a vendor. Unfortunately, the first Dippin' Dots stand was placed in front of a roller coaster and people generally did not want ice cream before they went on a ride. After a few unsuccessful weeks, Jones moved the stand and business picked up considerably. Eventually, they were able to move to an inline location, which was similar to a store, where Dippin' Dots had its own personnel and sitting area to serve customers.

Just by word of mouth, the speculation about Curt Jones and Dippin' Dots spread. Soon other entrepreneurs contacted Jones to open up stores to sell Dippin' Dots. In 1991 a dealership network was developed to sell ice cream to authorized vendors and provide support with equipment and marketing. During that time, Jones employed friends to assume corporate jobs. Dippin' Dots grew into a multi-million dollar company with authorized dealers operating in all 50 states and internationally (see Exhibit 3).

By the end of the 1990s Jones was happy with his company, but felt as if Dippin' Dots had hit a plateau and needed to reach the "next level" to continue to prosper. He began working with his friend and now controller and director of franchising, Chad Wilson, to develop the franchise system. By January 2000, all existing Dippin' Dots dealers were required to sign a franchise agreement and pay the associated franchise fees for any location they operated or planned to operate.

A franchised location was any mall, fair, national account, or large family entertainment center. According to the franchising information in 2007, the initial franchise fee was $12,500, with an estimated initial investment range from $80,428 to $235,250.[13] The result was a cash inflow for Dippin' Dots franchising. Franchisees were required to pay a 4 percent royalty fee and contribute a half-percent of their gross incomes to an advertising fund, which Jones said had greatly enhanced marketing.

The Future

Dippin' Dots was counting on youthful exuberance to expand growth.. "Our core demographic was pretty much 8- to 18-year-olds," said Terry Reeves, corporate communications director. "On top of that, we're starting to see a generation

Exhibit 3 **Milestones**

1988	Dippin' Dots established as a company in Grand Chain, Illinois.
1989	First amusement park account debuts at Opryland USA in Nashville.
1990	Production facility moves to Paducah, Kentucky.
1991	Dealer network established for fair, festival, and commercial retail locations.
1994	First international licensee (Japan).
1995	New 32,000 sq. ft. production facility opens in Paducah.
1997	Production facility expands by 20,000 sq. ft.; earns spot on *Inc.* 500 list of fastest-growing private companies in the United States.
2000	Dippin' Dots Franchising, Inc., established and first franchise offered; initiation of litigation against competitors to protect patent.
2001	Dippin' Dots enlists 30 new franchisees. *Franchise Times* magazine lists Dippin' Dots third nationally behind Baskin Robbins and Dairy Queen in number of franchises.
2002	Dippin' Dots Franchising, Inc., achieves 112th spot on *Entrepreneur* magazine's Franchise 500 list. Dippin' Dots Franchising, Inc., ranked 69th on *Entrepreneur* magazine's list as Fastest Growing franchise company. Dippin' Dots Franchising, Inc., ranked the number one New Franchise Company by *Entrepreneur*. Dippin' Dots becomes a regular menu offering on menus at McDonald's restaurants in the San Francisco Bay area.
2003	Dippin' Dots Franchising, Inc., achieves 144th spot on *Entrepreneur* magazine's Franchise 500 list. Dippin' Dots Franchising, Inc., ranks number four on *Entrepreneur's* magazine's list of the Top 50 New Franchise Companies. Dippin' Dots' opens the Ansong manufacturing plant, 80 miles south of Seoul, South Korea.
2004	Dippin' Dots Franchising, Inc., ranks number four on *Entrepreneur's* list of the Top 50 New Franchise Companies. Dippin' Dots Franchising, Inc., achieves 101st spot on *Entrepreneur* magazine's Franchise 500 list. Curt Jones and Dippin' Dots featured on a segment of the *Oprah Winfrey Show* appearing in 110 countries. Dippin' Dots featured among the Top 10 Ice Cream Palaces on the Travel Channel. Curt Jones quoted in Donald Trump's best-selling *The Way to the Top* (p. 131).
2005	International Dairy Foods Association names Dippin' Dots Best In Show for Dot Delicacies. Dippin' Dots also wins three awards for package design. Dippin' Dots Franchising, Inc. ranks number one on *Franchise Times* magazine's Fast 55 list of the fastest growing young franchises in the nation. Ice cream cake and ice cream sandwiches (Dotwiches) introduced to launch the "Dot Delicacies" program.
2006	Company leadership restructured. Curt Jones becomes Founder/Chairman of the Board. Tom Leonard becomes President, Dippin' Dots, Inc. Dots 'n Cream, conventional ice cream enhanced by beads of Dippin' Dots, is introduced for testing market in Kroger stores in the Midwest. 200th Franchisee begins operations.

Source: Company Web site, http://www.dippindots.com/company/history/.

of parents who grew up on Dippin' Dots and are starting to introduce the products to their kids."

Although Dippin' Dots seemed to appeal more to youngsters, the product still had to have staying power as customers grew older. As one individual commented, "How can this stuff keep continuing to call itself the 'ice cream of the future?' Well the future is now folks, and they have been pushing this sorry excuse for ice cream off on me at amusement parks and zoos since I was a little kid."[14]

In 2002 McDonald's reportedly spent $1.2 million on advertising to roll out Dippin' Dots in about 250 restaurants in the San Francisco area. Jones called the deal "open-ended" if it works favorably for both firms. "I think both companies are proceeding with the impression that nothing was going to be overcommitted," he said. "We're growing at a 10 to 15 percent annual rate and we're excited about the potential of McDonald's, but it's too early to tell." By mid-2007 Dippin' Dots was only available at a few McDonald's franchises in southern California. Storage and transportation issues were problematic, and the price of the product, 5 ounces for $5, was too steep for all but the die-hard Dippin' Dots fans.

In other marketing efforts, Dippin' Dots ads had been running in issues of *Seventeen* and *Nickelodeon* magazines. Reeves said the company had been "inundated with e-mails" once the June 2002 issue of *Seventeen* hit the newsstands. Additionally, Dippin' Dots had hired a Hollywood firm to place its ice cream in the background of television and movie scenes, including the 2003 *Cheaper by the Dozen*. In 2002 the Food Network's "Summer Foods: Unwrapped" showcased Dippin' Dots as one of the most unique and coolest ice cream treats. 'N Sync member Joey Fatone ordered a Dippin' Dots freezer for his home after seeing a Dots vending machine at a theater the band rented in Orlando. Caterers also sought Dippin' Dots for their star clients. A recent birthday party at the home of NBA star Shaquille O'Neal featured Dippin' Dots ice cream. Dippin' Dots continued to pursue the celebrity word-of-mouth route by serving Dippin' Dots products at events such as the MTV awards and celebrity charity functions.

According to Jones, in 2006 almost half of Dippin' Dots sales came from national accounts such as stadiums, theaters, and theme parks like Six Flags; the rest of the estimated $50 million income came from approximately 150 franchisees, many with multiple locations.[15]

Dippin' Dots had met increased competition in the out-of-home ice-cream market. The major threats to Dippin' Dots were other franchise operations such as Ben & Jerry's, Haagen-Dazs, Baskin-Robbins, Carvel, Dairy Queen, and newcomers such as Cold Stone Creamery, Maggie Moo's, and Marble Slab Creamery (see Exhibit 4). In addition, a very similar type of flash-frozen ice cream called Frosty Bites was introduced in the spring of 2000 by eight disenfranchised former dealers of Dippin' Dots. Another company, Mini Melts, located in the United Kingdom was also manufacturing a similar product, and two brothers who were formerly part of the Dippin' Dots dealer network brought this flash frozen ice cream to the United States.

In 2002 Jones had thought that introducing a formal franchising agreement would provide protection against copycats and unify the company's public image, since Dippin' Dots was often unrecognizable under its unstructured dealership network of locations.

Terry Reeves, corporate communication director, said: [T]he stronger and more unified Dippin' Dots retail offering became through franchising, the more [franchisees] were able to be considered for better retail properties (high-end malls, better locations, and so on). This obviously strengthened our system and bolstered overall sales for the company and for our franchisees. While franchise fees and royalties were a new income source, much of the profit was put back into the business to promote future growth.

Although one dealer commented that Dippin' Dots used incoming franchise fees from royalties on sales for their own corporate means rather than to improve franchise support, most dealers did convert to the new franchise system. Dippin' Dots Franchising, Inc., grandfathered existing dealers' locations by issuing a franchise and waiving the franchise fee for the first contract period of five years. Many dealers had to renew their contracts in 2004; while many were initially apprehensive of converting to a franchised system, less than 2 percent left the system, and the firm showed franchise growth.

In an attempt to counteract the copycat threats from Frosty Bites and Mini Melts, Dippin' Dots brought a patent infringement lawsuit against them in 2005. However during the jury trial, Dippin' Dots testimony in support of the original patent revealed that Jones had made sales of the beaded ice cream product to over 800 customers more than a year before submitting the patent application. Even though Jones argued that these sales were for the purpose of market testing and that the production method may have subsequently been further refined, therefore deserving of a patented process, the court rendered the patent nonenforceable since these sales were not disclosed to the Patent Office. An appeal by Dippin' Dots was denied in 2007, and the patent was declared invalid.[16]

Mini Melts, released from the lawsuit, continued to expand manufacturing facilities throughout the world, and had plants in South Korea, Philippines, the United Arab Emirates, Hong Kong, and China as well as the United Kingdom and the United States. Instead of franchises, Mini Melts sold vending carts and kiosks. One of the brothers who originally brought Mini Melts to the United States had been successful with this vending operation, being nominated "Entrepreneur of the Year" by *Inc.* Magazine in 2006.[17]

In spite of these challenges, Jones, always the inventor, was investing in R&D to create a conventional ice cream product that had superfrozen dots embedded in it. He was developing a new product that could withstand conventional freezers while preserving the superfrozen dots in the ice cream. Called Dots 'n Cream and available in vanilla, chocolate, mint chocolate chip, or banana split, this product was introduced for market testing in Kroger stores in the Midwest in 2006. Thus, Dippin' Dots could finally have a take-home ice-cream option.

However, the company's experience and resource base were clearly in the ice-cream manufacturing and scoop shop retailing businesses. Dealing with supermarket chains, packaging, and distributors would be a challenge for this relatively small firm. On the other hand, opportunities might still be pursued by enlarging the franchise and national accounts businesses for scoop shops and vending machines. Jones continued to assess his company's situation, identifying and choosing among the best strategic options for Dippin' Dots' growth. In 2006 Jones was also working to develop an unrelated business; an ethanol plant in southern Illinois.[18] He had retained his role as founder/chairman of the board, but relinquished the presidency of the company to Tom Leonard.

Exhibit 4   Ice Cream Franchises at Entrepreneur.com as of 2007

Franchise Name/Description	Startup Costs ($ thousands)	Number of 2006 Franchises
2 Scoops Cafe Ice cream parlor/cafe	$99–175	1
Abbott's Frozen Custard Frozen custard	$120–126.8	20
All American Specialty Restaurants Inc. Ice cream, frozen yogurt, deli sandwiches	$171–281	30
Applegate Inc. Ice cream	$137.7–322	7
Baskin-Robbins USA Co. Ice cream, frozen yogurt, frozen beverages	$135–522	2,279
Ben & Jerry's Ice cream parlor	$127–396	420
Blue Sky Creamery Ice cream, gourmet coffees, desserts	$138.8–373.9	5
Bruster's Real Ice Cream Homemade ice cream	$172–1,200	249
California Quivers Carts serving fruit ices, hot dogs, & coffee	$45–149.3	2
Carvel Ice cream & ice cream cakes	$46.9–388.7	576
Cold Stone Creamery Ice cream, Italian sorbet	$294.3–438.9	1,328
Culver Franchising System Inc. Frozen custard & specialty burgers	$340.4–2,900	326
Dairy Queen Soft-serve dairy products & sandwiches	$655–1,300	4,743
Dippin' Dots Franchising Inc. Specialty ice cream, frozen yogurt, ices	$70.2–215.95	448
Frats Ices Italian ices & fried ravioli	$89–132	0
Haagen-Dazs Shoppe Co. Inc. Ice cream & frozen yogurt	$86.8–397.1	220
Happy Joe's Pizza, pasta, ice cream	$98.2–1,100	56
La Paletera Paletas, fruit cups, smoothies, ice cream	$144–199	40
Little Scoops Retro '50s-style ice cream party	$99.7–160.2	5
MaggieMoo's Int'l. LLC Ice cream, smoothies, cakes	$237–336.7	174

(*continued*)

Franchise Name/Description	Startup Costs ($ thousands)	Number of 2006 Franchises
Marble Slab Creamery Inc. Ice cream, frozen yogurt, baked goods	$205.2–313.3	347
Melt Inc. Gelato, Italian coffee, crepes	$200–400	8
Paciugo Italian Gelato Gelato	$78.5–377.6	27
Ricky's Candy, Cones & Chaos Candy, ice cream, parties	$378.5–563.8	8
Rita's Franchise Co. LLC Italian ices, frozen custard, gelato, pretzels	$166.3–347	384
Ritter's Frozen Custard Frozen custard	$249–818	62
Shake's Frozen Custard Frozen custard	$168–800	39
Strickland's Homemade ice cream & related products	$224.5–337	14

Source: http://www.entrepreneur.com/franchises/categories/ffqicecr.html.

Endnotes

1. Information unless otherwise stated is derived from the Dippin' Dots Web site. www.DippinDots.com, the Dippin' Dots 10-year anniversary video, or from the self-published Dippin' Dots Corporate Profile.
2. Associated Press. 2006. Business blazing for supercold Dippin' Dots. July 23, http://www.msnbc.msn.com/id/14001806/.
3. Ice cream's origins are known to reach back as far as the second century BC, although no specific date of origin or inventor has been indisputably credited with its discovery. We know that Alexander the Great enjoyed snow and ice flavored with honey and nectar. Biblical references also show that King Solomon was fond of iced drinks during harvesting. During the Roman Empire, Nero (AD 54–86) frequently sent runners into the mountains for snow, which was then flavored with fruits and juices. Information from Ice Cream Media Kit, International Dairy Foods Association.
4. The idea of using liquid nitrogen to make ice cream had been around in scientific circles for some time. See http://www.polsci.wvu.edu/henry/icecream/icecream.html for how to make this at home, from an article in *Scientific American*, April 1994, pages 66–71. See also http://www.subzeroicecream.com/press/coldfacts2006.pdf.

5. Anderson, G. 2005. America's favorite ice cream. *CNN/Money.com,* July 29, http://money.cnn.com/2005/07/25/pf/goodlife/summer_ice_cream/.
6. See http://www.idfa.org/facts/icmonth/page2.cfm. Ice cream consists of a mixture of dairy ingredients, such as milk and nonfat milk, and ingredients for sweetening and flavoring, such as fruits, nuts, and chocolate chips. Functional ingredients, such as stabilizers and emulsifiers, are often included in the product to promote proper texture and enhance the eating experience. By federal law, ice cream must contain at least 10 percent butterfat, before the addition of bulky ingredients, and must weigh a minimum of 4.5 pounds to the gallon.
7. Source, 2006 Dairy Facts/International Ice Cream Association, available at http://www.idfa.org/facts/icmonth/page2.cfm.
8. Murphy, K. 2006. Slabs are joining scoops in ice cream retailing. *New York Times,* October 26, http://www.nytimes.com/2006/10/26/business/26sbiz.html?ex=1319515200&en=5f77555844021708&ei=5088&partner=rssnyt&emc=rss.
9. Moskin, J. 2006. Creamy, healthier ice cream? What's the catch? *New York Times,* July 26, http://www.nytimes.com/2006/07/26/dining/26cream.html?ex=1182916800&en=501180740dd57a44&ei=5070. Note: Slow-churned and double-churned each refer to a process called low-temperature

extrusion, which significantly reduces the size of the fat globules and ice crystals in ice cream.

10. Murphy. 2006. Slabs are joining . . . op. cit.
11. All definitions taken from the IDFA Web site, www.idfa.org/facts/icmonth/page4.cfm.
12. Dippin' Dots 10th Anniversary Promotional Video.
13. http://www.dippindots.com/franchise/information/.
14. Michelle, S. 2006. *Yelp Reviews–Chicago,* November 17, http://www.yelp.com/biz/qnA4ml7Lu-9W4SDJOF1YPA.
15. Associated Press, op. cit.
16. Undisclosed prior sales doom Dippin' Dots patent. *IP Law Observer,* May 1, 2007, re Dippin'Dots, Inc. v. Mosey (Fed. Cir. 02/09/07—No. 2005-1330, 2005-1582, http://www.iplawobserver.com/2007/05/undisclosed-prior-sales-doom-dippin.html.
17. See http://www.minimelts.com/usa/usindex.html.
18. Associated Press, op. cit.

Case 40   McDonald's*

On January 24, 2007, McDonalds CEO Jim Skinner stated that the total revenue for the fast food chain had risen by 11 percent during 2006 to $21.6 billion. Net profits had climbed by 36 percent to $3.6 billion. These results indicated that the firm had managed to make significant improvements to its performance since announcing its first quarterly loss ever in early 2003. The stock for McDonald's had risen to almost $45, representing a threefold increase in value since pulling out of a nosedive three years ago. "To state the obvious, McDonald's is on a bit of a roll," the firm's chief financial officer Matthew Paull told analysts[1] (see Exhibits 1 and 2 for income statements and balance sheets).

Skinner was the second person to take over the company since James R. Cantalupo had died unexpectedly of a heart attack in 2004. Cantalupo had been replaced by Charlie Bell, who also resigned a few months later in order to fight his recently discovered cancer. In spite of these changes in leadership, the firm has continued to push on the turnaround strategy that had been initiated by Cantalupo in order to address McDonald's lackluster performance. The strategy, commonly refereed to as the "Plan to Win" tried to target various critical areas that needed to be addressed.

In fact, Skinner attributed the firm's consistent growth in sales and profits to the successful development of Cantalupo's early turnaround efforts. As a result of these, McDonald's has managed to achieve 44 straight months of higher same-store sales. Much of the momentum has been generated in the United States, the firm's single largest market, where new menu items, refurbished outlets, late-night hours and cashless payments have boosted sales. The firm has also shown some improvement in its sales in Europe, where it had failed to show much growth for several years.

But Skinner was acutely aware that the problems at McDonald's went way beyond cleaning up restaurants and revamping the menu. The chain has been squeezed by long-term trends that are threatening to leave it marginalized. McDonald's is facing a rapidly fragmenting market, where changes in the tastes of consumers have made once-exotic foods like sushi and burritos everyday options. Many of its fast-food customers are also looking for food that is healthier and better tasting. Furthermore, competition has been coming from quick meals of all sorts that can be found in supermarkets, convenience stores, and even vending machines.

Many analysts believe that McDonald's must continue to work on its turnaround strategy in order to meet these challenges. But they acknowledge that the firm has pushed hard to transform itself, and they are encouraged by the results that it has achieved over the last three years. "They have experienced a comeback the likes of which has been pretty unprecedented," said Bob Golden, executive vice-president of Technomic, a food service consultancy. "When restaurants start to slide, it really takes a lot to turn them around."[2]

Experiencing a Downward Spiral

Since it was founded more than 50 years ago, McDonald's has been defining the fast food business. It provided millions of Americans their first jobs even as it changed their eating habits. It rose from a single outlet in a nondescript Chicago suburb to become one of the largest chains of outlets spread around the globe. But it had been stumbling over the past decade (see Exhibit 3).

The decline in McDonald's once-vaunted service and quality can be traced to its expansion of the 1990s, when headquarters stopped grading franchises for cleanliness, speed, and service. By the end of the decade, the chain ran into more problems because of the tighter labor market. McDonald's began to cut back on training as it struggled hard to find new recruits, leading to a dramatic falloff in the skills of its employees. According to a 2002 survey by market researcher Global Growth Group, McDonald's came in third in average service time behind Wendy's and sandwich shop Chick-fil-A Inc.

McDonald's also began to fail consistently with its new product introductions, such as the low-fat McLean Deluxe and Arch Deluxe burgers, both of which were meant to appeal to adults. It did no better with its attempts to diversify beyond burgers, often because of problems with the product development process. Consultant Michael Seid, who manages a franchise consulting firm in West Hartford, pointed out that McDonald's offered a pizza that didn't fit through the drive-through window and salad shakers that were packed so tightly that dressing couldn't flow through them.

In 1998, after McDonald's posted its first-ever decline in annual earnings, CEO Michael R. Quinlan was forced out and replaced by Jack M. Greenberg, a 16-year veteran of the firm. Greenberg did try to cut back on McDonald's expansion as he tried to deal with some of the growing problems. But his efforts to deal with the decline of McDonald's were slowed down by his acquisition of other fast food chains such as Chipotle Mexican Grill and Boston Market.

On December 5, 2002, after watching McDonald's stock slide 60 percent in three years, the board ousted Greenberg. He had lasted little more than two years. His short tenure had been marked by the introduction of 40 new menu items, none of which caught on big, and the purchase of a handful of nonburger chains, none of which helped the firm to sell more burgers. Indeed, his critics say that by trying so many different things and executing them poorly, Greenberg allowed the burger business to continue

Exhibit 1 Income Statement

Consolidated Statement of Income			
	Years Ended December 31,		
	2006	**2005**	**2004**
	(in $ millions, except per share data)		
Revenues			
Sales by Company operated restaurants	$16,082.7	$14,726.6	$13,755.2
Revenues from franchised and affiliated restaurants	5,503.7	5,105.9	4,838.8
Total revenues	21,586.4	19,832.5	18,594.0
Operating Costs and Expenses			
Company-operated restaurant expenses			
Food & paper	5,349.7	5,004.9	4,698.2
Payroll & employee benefits	4,185.4	3,860.4	3,586.5
Occupancy & other operating expenses	4,006.6	3,709.2	3,403.2
Franchised restaurants—occupancy expenses	1,060.4	1,021.5	1,002.7
Selling, general, & administrative expenses	2,337.9	2,167.1	1,939.1
Impairment and other charges (credits), net	134.2	(28.4)	281.4
Other operating expense net	67.1	105.3	145.0
Total operating costs and expenses	17,141.3	15,840.0	15,056.1
Operating income	4,445.1	3,992.5	3,537.9
Interest expense—net of capitalized interest of $5.4, $4.9 and $4.1	402.0	356.1	358.4
Nonoperating income, net	(123.3)	(38.0)	(21.2)
Income from continuing operations before provision for income taxes	4,166.4	3,674.4	3,200.7
Provision for income taxes	1,293.4	1,088.0	923.2
Income from continuing operations	2,873.0	2,586.4	2,277.5
Income from discontinued operations (net of taxes of $96.8, $0.4 and $0.7)	671.2	15.8	1.0
Net income	$ 3,544.2	$ 2,602.2	$ 2,278.5
Per common share—basic:			
Continuing operations	$ 2.33	$ 2.05	$ 1.81
Discontinued operations	0.54	0.01	—
Net income	$ 2.87	$ 2.06	$ 1.81
Per common share—diluted:			
Continuing operations	$ 2.30	$ 2.03	$ 1.79
Discontinued operations	0.53	0.01	—
Net income	$ 2.83	$ 2.04	$ 1.79
Dividends per common share	$ 1.00	$ 0.67	$ 0.55
Weighted-average shares outstanding—basic	1,234.0	1,260.4	1,259.7
Weighted–average shares outstanding—diluted	1,251.7	1,274.2	1,273.7

Source: McDonald's.

Exhibit 2 Balance Sheets

Consolidated Balance Sheet		
	Years Ended December 31,	
	2006	**2005**
	(in $ millions, except per share data)	
Assets		
Current assets		
Cash and equivalents	$ 2,136.4	$ 4,260.6
Accounts and notes receivable	904.2	793.9
Inventories at cost, not in excess of market	149.0	144.3
Prepaid expenses and other current assets	435.7	640.2
Discontinued operations		380.0
Total current assets	3,625.3	6,219.0
Other assets		
Investment in and advances to affiliates	1,036.2	1,035.4
Goodwill net	2,209.2	1,924.4
Miscellaneous	1,307.4	1,236.7
Total other assets	4,552.8	4,196.5
Property and equipment		
Property and equipment, at cost	31,810.2	29,482.5
Accumulated depreciation and amortization	(10,964.5)	(9,909.2)
Net property and equipment	20,845.7	19,573.3
Total assets	$29,023.8	$29,988.8
Liabilities and Shareholders' Equity		
Current liabilities		
Notes payable	$ —	$ 544.0
Accounts payable	834.1	678.0
Income taxes	250.9	569.6
Other taxes	251.4	233.1
Accrued interest	135.1	158.5
Accrued payroll and other liabilities	1,518.9	1,158.1
Current maturities of long-term debt	17.7	658.5
Discontinued operations		107.9
Total current liabilities	3,008.1	4,107.7
Long-term debt	8,416.5	8,934.3
Other long-term liabilities	1,074.9	851.5
Deferred income taxes	1,066.0	949.2
Shareholders' equity		
Preferred stock, no par value, authorized—165.0 million shares issued—none		
Common stock, $.01 par value authorized—3.5 billion shares; issued—1,660.6 million shares	16.6	16.6
Additional paid-in capital	3,445.0	2,720.2
Retained earnings	25,845.6	23,516.0
Accumulated other comprehensive income (loss)	(296.7)	(733.1)
Common stock in treasury at cost 456.9 and 397.4 million shares	(13,552.2)	(10,373.6)
Total shareholders' equity	15,458.3	15,146.1
Total liabilities and shareholders' equity	$29,023.8	$29,988.8

Source: McDonald's.

Exhibit 3   McDonald's Milestones

1948	Brothers Richard and Maurice McDonald open the first restaurant in San Bernadino, California that sells hamburgers, fries, and milk shakes.
1955	Ray A. Kroc, 52, opens his first McDonald's in Des Plaines, Illinois. Kroc, a distributor of milk shake mixers, figures he can sell a bundle of them if he franchises the McDonalds' business and installs his mixers in the new stores.
1961	Six years later, Kroc buys out the McDonald brothers for $2.7 million.
1963	Ronald McDonald makes his debut as corporate spokesclown using future NBC-TV weatherman Willard Scott. During the year, the company also sells its 1 billionth burger.
1965	McDonald's stock goes public at $22.50 a share. It will split 12 times in the next 35 years.
1967	The first McDonald's restaurant outside the United States opens in Richmond, British Columbia. Today there are 31,108 McDonald's in 118 countries.
1968	The Big Mac, the first extension of McDonald's basic burger, makes its debut and is an immediate hit.
1972	McDonald's switches to the frozen variety for its successful french fries.
1974	Fred L. Turner succeeds Kroc as CEO. In the midst of a recession, the minimum wage rises to $2 per hour, a big cost increase for McDonald's, which is built around a model of young, low-wage workers.
1975	The first drive-through window is opened in Sierra Vista, Arizona.
1979	McDonald's responds to the needs of working women by introducing Happy Meals. A burger, some fries, a soda, and a toy give working moms a break.
1987	Michael R. Quinlan become chief executive.
1991	Responding to the public's desire for healthier foods, McDonald's introduces the low-fat McLean Deluxe burger. It flops and is withdrawn from the market. Over the next few years, the chain will stumble several times trying to spruce up its menu.
1992	The company sells its 90 billionth burger, and stops counting.
1996	In order to attract more adult customers, the company launches its Arch Deluxe, a "grownup" burger with an idiosyncratic taste. Like the low-fat burger, it also falls flat.
1997	McDonald's launches Campaign 55, which cuts the cost of a Big Mac to $0.55. It is a response to discounting by Burger King and Taco Bell. The move, which prefigures similar price wars in 2002, is widely considered a failure.
1998	Jack M. Greenberg becomes McDonald's fourth chief executive. A 16-year company veteran, he vows to spruce up the restaurants and their menu.
1999	For the first time, sales from international operations outstrip domestic revenues. In search of other concepts, the company acquires Aroma Cafe, Chipotle, Donatos, and later, Boston Market.
2000	McDonald's sales in the United States peak at an average of $1.6 million annually per restaurant, a figure that has not changed since. It is, however, still more than at any other fast-food chain.
2001	Subway surpasses McDonald's as the fast-food chain with the most U.S. outlets. At the end of the year it had 13,247 stores, 148 more than McDonald's.
2002	McDonald's posts its first-ever quarterly loss, of $343.8 million. The stock drops to around $13.50, down 40 percent from five years ago.
2003	James R. Cantalupo returns to McDonald's in January as CEO. He immediately pulls back from the company's 10 to 15 percent forecast for per-share earnings growth.
2004	Charles H. Bell takes over the firm after the sudden death of Cantalupo. He states he will continue with the strategies that have been developed by his predecessor. Jim Skinner subsequently takes over from Charles H. Bell, as Bell resigns to fight a bout with cancer.

Source: McDonald's.

with its decline. According to Los Angeles franchisee Reggie Webb, "We would have been better off trying fewer things and making them work."[3]

Pinning Hopes on a New Leader

By the beginning of 2003, consumer surveys were indicating that McDonald's was headed for serious trouble. Measures for the service and quality of the chain were continuing to fall, dropping far behind those of its rivals. In order deal with its deteriorating performance, the firm decided to bring back retired Vice-Chairman James R. Cantalupo, 59, who had overseen McDonald's successful international expansion in the 1980s and 1990s. Cantalupo, who had retired only a year earlier, was perceived to be the only candidate with the necessary qualifications, despite shareholder sentiment for an outsider. The board had felt that it needed someone who knew the company well and could move quickly to turn things around.

Cantalupo realized that McDonald's often tended to miss the mark on delivering the critical aspects of consistent, fast, and friendly service and an all-around enjoyable experience for the whole family. He understood that its franchisees and employees alike needed to be inspired as well as retrained on their role of putting the smile back into McDonald's experience. When Cantalupo and his team laid out their plan for McDonald's in the spring of 2003, they stressed getting the basics of service and quality right, in part by reinstituting a tough "up or out" grading system that would kick out underperforming franchisees. "We have to rebuild the foundation. It's fruitless to add growth if the foundation is weak," said Cantalupo.[4]

To begin with, Cantalupo cut back on the opening of new outlets, focusing instead on generating more sales from its existing outlets. In fact, he shifted his emphasis to obtaining most of the growth in revenues to come from an increase in sales in the over 30,000 outlets that are already operating around the world (see Exhibits 4 through 7). In

Exhibit 4   Number of Outlets

	Total	Company Owned	Franchised	Affiliated
2006	31,667	8,785	18,687	4,195
2005	31,397	8,802	18,326	4,269
2004	31,152	8,811	18,240	4,101
2003	30,824	8,661	18,125	4,038
2002	30,876	8,773	17,859	4,244
2001	29,916	8,204	17,392	4,320
2000	28,603	7,548	16,795	4,260
1999	26,272	6,022	15,949	4,301

Source: McDonald's.

Exhibit 5   Distribution of Outlets

	2006	2005	2004	2003
United States	13,774	13,727	13,673	13,609
Europe	6,403	6,352	6,287	6,186
Asia Pacific	7,822	7,692	7,567	7,475
Latin America	1,656	1,617	1,607	1,578
Canada	1,391	1,378	1,362	1,339

Source: McDonald's.

Exhibit 6   Breakdown of Revenues

	2006	2005	2004	2003
	(in $ millions)			
United States	$7,464	$6,955	$6,525	$6,039
Europe	7,638	7,072	6,737	5,875
Asia Pacific	3,053	2,815	2,721	2,447
Latin America	1,659	1,327	1,008	859
Canada	1,081	948	898	778

Source: McDonald's.

Exhibit 7   Breakdown of Operating Income

	2006	2005	2004	2003
	($ millions)			
United States	2,657	2,422	2,181	1,982
Europe	1,610	1,449	1,471	1,339
Asia Pacific	364	345	200	226
Latin America	55	30	(20)	(171)
Canada	198	156	178	163

Source: McDonald's.

part, McDonalds tried to draw more customers through the introduction of new products. The chain has had a positive response to its increased emphasis on healthier foods, lead by a revamped line of fancier salads. The revamped menu was promoted through a new worldwide ad slogan, "I'm loving it," which was delivered by pop idol Justin Timberlake through a set of MTV-style commercials.

But the biggest success for the firm came in the form of McGriddles breakfast sandwich which was launched nationwide in June 2003. The popular new offering consisted of a couple of syrup-drenched pancakes, stamped with the Golden Arches, which acted as the top and bottom of the sandwich to hold eggs, cheese, sausage and bacon in three different combinations. McDonald's has estimated that the new breakfast addition has been bringing in about 1 million new customers every day. In 2006 the firm also launched its Premium Roast Coffee with considerable fanfare to enhance its breakfast offerings.

With his efforts largely directed at a turnaround strategy for McDonald's, Cantalupo was thinking of divesting the nonburger chains that his predecessor had acquired. Collectively lumped under the Partner Brands, these have consisted of Chipotle Mexican Grill and Boston Market. The purpose of these acquisitions had been to find new growth and to offer the best franchises new expansion opportunities. But these acquired businesses had not fueled much growth and had actually posted considerable losses in recent years. Skinner was finally able to dispose of the firm's investment in Chipotle Mexican Grill in 2006.

Striving for Healthier Offerings

As Skinner took over the reins of McDonald's in late 2004, he expressed his commitment to Cantalupo's plans to pursue various avenues for growth. But Skinner felt that one of his top priorities was to deal with the growing concerns about the unhealthy image of McDonald's, given the rise of obesity in the United States. These concerns had recently been highlighted by the release of a popular documentary, *Super Size Me,* made by Morgan Spurlock. Spurlock vividly displayed the health risks that were posed by a steady diet of food from the fast-food chain. With a rise in awareness of the high fat content of most of the products offered by McDonald's, the firm was also beginning to face lawsuits from some of its loyal customers.

In response to the growing health concerns, one of the first steps McDonald's took was to phase out supersizing by the end of 2004. The supersizing option allowed customers to get a larger order of French fries and a bigger soft drink by paying a little extra. McDonald's has also announced that it intends to start providing nutrition information on the packaging of its products. The information will be easy to read and will tell customers about the calories, fat, protein, carbohydrates, and sodium that are in each product. Finally, McDonald's has also been pledging to gradually remove the artery-clogging trans fatty acids from the oil that it uses to make its french fries.

But Skinner must also try to push out more offerings that are likely to be perceived by customers to be healthier. McDonalds has continued to build upon its chicken offerings, using white meat with products such as Chicken Selects. It has also placed a great deal of emphasis upon its new salad offerings. The firm's latest addition, an Asian style salad with chicken, was added in 2006. Although the firm had failed to attract many customers in the past with its salads, McDonald's carried out extensive experiments and tests with its new premium version. It chose higher quality ingredients, from a variety of lettuces and tasty cherry tomatoes to sharper cheeses and better cuts of meat. It offered a choice of Newman's Own dressings, a well known higher-end brand.

McDonald's has also been trying to include more fruits and vegetables in its well known and popular Happy Meals. It has been testing Happy Meals for grownups with items such as an entrée salad, a bottle of Dasani water, and a "stepometer." And in many locations, the firm is offering apple slices or carrot sticks in place of French fries in the children's Happy Meal. The addition of fruits and vegetables has raised the firm's operating costs, because these are more expensive to ship and store because of their more perishable nature.

But Skinner believes that the firm had to push more heavily on fruits and salads. "Salads have changed the way people think of our brand," said Wade Thoma, vice president for menu development in the United States "It tells people that we are very serious about offering things people feel comfortable eating."[5] The addition of items that are perceived to be healthier makes it easier for people to continue to eat at McDonald's, even though the vast majority of them still order a hamburger and fries.

Revamping the Outlets

Skinner is also aware that most of McDonald's outlets are beginning to look and feel outdated. About a quarter of its 1,400 outlets in the United States are, in fact, more than 25 years old. Without any changes to their décor, the firm is likely to be left behind by other more savvy fast-food and drink retailers. Under Skinner, McDonald's is pushing harder to refurbish, or re-image, all of its outlets around the world. "This is all part of becoming more relevant to our consumers," said company spokesman Walt Riker. "When a customer enters our restaurant, they enter our brand."[6]

The re-imaging concept was first tried in France in 1996, and has been gradually expanded to other European countries. Dennis Hennequin, president of McDonald's Europe, felt that the effort was essential to revive the firm's sagging sales. "We were hip 15 years ago, but I think we lost that," he said.[7] McDonald's is now applying the re-imaging concept to its outlets around the world, with a budget of more than half of its total annual capital expenditures. In the United States, the changes cost an average of $150,000 per restaurant, a cost that is shared with the franchisees when the outlet is not company owned.

One of the prototype interiors being tested out by McDonald's has curved counters with surfaces painted in bright colors. In one corner, a touch-activated screen allows customers to punch in orders without queuing. The interiors can feature armchairs and sofas, modern lighting, large television screens, and even wireless Internet access. The firm is also trying to develop new features for its drive-through customers, which account for 65 percent of all transactions in the United States. They include music aimed at queuing vehicles and a wall of windows on the drive-through side of the restaurant allowing customers to see meals being prepared from their cars.

Beyond these ideas, Skinner is also looking for new ideas from some of the better performing franchisees. He insists that its franchisees must feel free to respond to their own markets, although they must adhere to specific parameters that are set by corporate headquarters. One of its more innovative franchisees, Irwin Kruger recently opened a 17,000-square-foot showcase unit in New York's Times Square with video monitors showing movie trailers, brick walls, and theatrical lighting. Similarly, Bob and Julie Dobski have been remodeling their outlets around Illinois, trying to create a different atmosphere in each of them. One of their outlets even has a fireplace in the front lobby.

The chain has even been developing McCafes inside its outlets next to the usual fast food counter. The McCafe concept originated in Australia in 1993 and has been rolled out in many restaurants around the world. McDonald's has just begun to introduce the concept to the United States as it refurbishes many of its existing outlets. McCafe offers espresso-based coffee, gourmet coffee blends, chicken wraps, fresh baked muffins, and high-end desserts. Customers can consume these while they relax in soft leather chairs listening to jazz, big band, or blues music. Commenting on these types of changes, Marty Brochstein, executive editor of *The Licensing Letter* said, "McDonald's wants to be seen as a lifestyle brand, not just a place to go to have a burger."[8]

A New and Improved McDonald's?

Even though Skinner's efforts to transform McDonald's have led to improvements in its sales and profits, there are questions about the future of the fast-food chain. The firm is trying out a variety of strategies in order to increase its appeal to different segments of the market. Through the adoption of a mix of outlet décor and menu items, McDonald's is trying to target young adults, teenagers, children, and families. In so doing, it must ensure that it does not alienate any one of these groups in its efforts to reach out to the other. Its new marketing campaign, anchored around the catchy phase "I'm loving it," takes on different forms in order to target each of the groups that it is seeking to attract.

Larry Light, the head of global marketing at McDonald's since 2002, insists that the firm has to exploit its brand through pushing it in many different directions. The brand can be positioned differently in different locations, at different times of the day and to target different customer segments. In large urban centers, McDonald's can target young adults for breakfast with its gourmet coffee, egg sandwiches, and fat-free muffins. Light explains the adoption of such as multiformat strategy, "The days of mass-media marketing are over."[9]

As McDonald's expands upon its concept of fast food, it is moving beyond its staple of burgers and fries to a wider variety of offerings. It is also trying to find a balance between the reliably cheap food for which it has become known and the newer items for which it can charge a premium. Many analysts are wondering just how far McDonald's can stretch its brand while keeping all of its outlets under the traditional symbol of its golden arches. Film maker Spurlock insisted, "People go to McDonald's to eat burgers."[10]

Chief financial officer Paull acknowledged that burgers continued to be the main draw for McDonald's. "There is no question that we make more money from selling hamburgers and cheeseburgers," he recently stated.[11] The chain must make sure that it keeps its established customer base from bolting to the growing number of competitors such as the California-based In-N-Out chain. The long-term success of the firm may well depend on its ability to compete with rival burger chains. "The burger category has great strength," added David C. Novak, chairman and CEO of Yum! Brands, parent of KFC and Taco Bell. "That's America's food. People love hamburgers."[12]

Above all, Skinner is aware that McDonald's may not have many shots at trying to get its strategy working. The recent improvement in performance has taken some of the pressure off to turn things around. It has allowed Skinner to respond to disgruntled shareholders, some of whom have suggested that the firm should spin or sell off its company-owned restaurants in order to raise its stock price. But the firm must figure out what steps it needs to take in order to ensure that it does not encounter another meltdown like the one that it faced a few short years ago. "They are at a critical juncture and what they do today will shape whether they just fade away or recapture some of the magic and greatness again," said Robert S. Goldin, executive vice-president at food consultant Technomic Incorporated.[13]

Endnotes

1. Carpenter, D. 2006. McDonald's stock soars on 4Q earnings. *Associated Press,* January 24.
2. Buckley, N. 2004. McDonald's shares survive resignation. November 24: 18.
3. Gogoi P., & Michael Arndt, M. 2003. Hamburger hell. *BusinessWeek,* March 3: 106.
4. *BusinessWeek,* March 3, 2003: 105.
5. Warner, M. 2005. You want any fruit with that Big Mac? *New York Times,* February 20: p. 8.
6. Horovitz, B. 2003. You want ambiance with that? *USA Today,* October 30: 3B.
7. Grant, J. 2006. McDonald's to revamp UK outlets. *Financial Times,* February 2: 14
8. Horovitz, B. 2003. McDonald's ventures beyond burgers to duds, toys. *USA Today,* November 14: 6B.
9. Big Mac's makeover. *Economist,* October 16, 2004: 65.
10. *Economist,* October 16, 2004: 65.
11. *Economist,* October 16, 2004: 64.
12. *BusinessWeek,* March 3, 2003: 108.
13. *BusinessWeek,* March 3, 2003: 108.

photo credits

Chapter 1: page 8, Photo by Jocelyn Augustino/FEMA; page 21, Royalty-Free/CORBIS

Chapter 2: page 42, Getty Images; page 65, The McGraw-Hill Companies, Inc./John Flournoy, photographer

Chapter 3: page 81, The McGraw-Hill Companies, Inc./Lars A. Niki, photographer; page 94, Royalty-Free/CORBIS

Chapter 4: page 128, © Digital Vision/Punchstock; page 143, Royalty-Free/CORBIS

Chapter 5: page 164, The McGraw-Hill Companies, Inc./John Flournoy, photographer; page 182, The McGraw-Hill Companies, Inc./Andrew Resek, photographer

Chapter 6: page 197, The McGraw-Hill Companies, Inc./Christopher Kerrigan, photographer; page 209, B. Drake/PhotoLink/Getty Images

Chapter 7: page 234, © David Zurick; page 253, Cartesia/PhotoDisc Imaging/Getty Images

Chapter 8: page 266, Royalty-Free/CORBIS; page 279, JupiterImages

Chapter 9: page 310, The McGraw-Hill Companies/Jill Braaten, photographer; page 329, Royalty-Free/CORBIS

Chapter 10: page 353, © Flying Colours Ltd / Getty Images; page 361, The McGraw-Hill Companies, Inc./Jill Braaten, photographer

Chapter 11: page 388, © imageshop - zefa visual media uk ltd / Alamy; page 401, The McGraw-Hill Companies, Inc./Rick Brady, photographer

Chapter 12: page 412, Royalty-Free/CORBIS; page 427, © image100/PunchStock

Chapter 13: page 461, Digital Vision/Getty Images

Case 33: page C297, Product courtesy of Brian, Willy, Taylor, and Carly. The McGraw-Hill Companies, Inc./Jill Braaten, photographer

company index

Page numbers followed by n indicate material found in notes.

Page numbers followed by n indicate material found in notes.

subject index

Page numbers followed by n indicate material found in notes.

Internet auction sites, C235
to C243
Internet gambling, C200
Internetnews, C242
Internet service providers, C158
to C164
Internet usage, 51
in Asia, C237
growth 1996 to 2007, C236
by region, C237
Internet World Stats, C236
Intrapreneuring, 422
Introduction stage strategies,
177–179
first-mover advantage, 177
late-mover advantage, 178
Inventory management at Ann Taylor
Stores, C109
Inventory turnover, 98, 456, 476
Investext Plus, 483
Investment decisions
and agency theory, 431
real options analysis, 428–432
Investments, transaction-
specific, 204
Investors Business Daily, 327
Iraq, 182
Irrational escalation of
commitment, 432
Israel, global start-ups, 352
Italian footwear industry, 232

j

Japan
business groups, 331
commuter-generated
electricity, 84
just-in-time systems, 231
population size, 235
Wal-Mart in, C265
Job creation by small businesses, 268
Joint ventures
Caribou Coffee, C230 to C231
Claire's Stores, C209
for cost reductions, 215
definition, 214
to develop new technologies, 216
to enter new markets, 214–215
example, 255
for market entry
benefits, 254
risks and limitations,
254–256
QVC and AOL, C90
reasons for failure, 216
Sun Life Financial, C34 to C35
Just-in-time systems, 78, 231
competitive advantage, 91

k

Keiretsu, 331
Key competitors, comparison of
financial ratios, 99–100
Knowledge
central role in economy, 116–119
codified for competitive
advantage, 139–140
explicit, 118, 139
intellectual capital, 142–143
redistributing, 392–393
tacit, 118, 139
transforming, 123

using technology to leverage,
137–140
Knowledge-based Gross Domestic
Product, 116
Knowledge economy, 116–119
definition, 117
explicit knowledge, 118
human capital, 118
intellectual capital, 117
social capital, 118
tacit knowledge, 118
Knowledge-intensive corporations,
117–118
Knowledge management, through
social networks, 131–136
Knowledge management
systems, 140
Knowledge sharing, 137
Knowledge transfer, 249
Knowledge workers, 115, 119

l

Labor supply, power of, 56
Las Vegas, Nevada, casinos, C197
to C202
Late-mover advantage, 178
Later-stage financing, 272
Latin America, slow growth, 229
Leaders, involved in developing
human capital, 123
Leadership
activities of, 378–384
challenge in global marketplace,
7–8
as change agent, 379
charisma problem, 276
and culture of ethics, 381
definition, 379
designing the organization,
380–381
development of vision, 25–26
doing the right thing, 379
drawbacks of emotional
intelligence, 389
emotional intelligence, 384–389
for empowering employees, 391
entrepreneurial, 276–277
and ethics, 397–398
external view, 7–8
Goolsby Leadership Model,
404–405
in innovation, 382
interdependent activities,
379–380
learning from mistakes, 377–378
managing relationships, 386
nurturing a culture of
excellence, 381
and organizational success, 85
overcoming barriers to change,
381–383
process, 377
at Procter & Gamble, C192
to C193
qualities needed for, 8
role models, 400
romantic view, 7
self-management skills, 386
setting direction, 380
Southwest Airlines, C142 to C144
types needed in organizations,
23–24
unethical behavior, 397–398
use of power, 383–384
Leadership traits, 384
Learning, 390
Learning from mistakes
Airbus Industrie, 339–340

Boston Scientific, 191–192
Coors Brewing, 37
ESPN, 265–266
Ford Motor Company, 5–7
Goodyear Tire & Rubber
Company, 75–76
KB Home, 303–304
Krispy Kreme, 377–378
at Polaroid, 411–413
profiting from failure, 396
Starbucks Corporation, 155–156
Wal-Mart in South Korea,
227–228
Wildflower Group, 115–116
Learning organization, 17
changing status quo, 395–396
creating, 468–469
definition, 390
empowering employees, 391–392
enabling creativity, 395–396
integrating external information,
393–395
key elements, 391
requirement, 390–391
sharing internal knowledge,
392–393
Learning perspective, in balanced
scorecard, 101
Learning tool, Internet as, 111
Legacy costs, 171
at General Motors, C364
Legal environment, 47–48
Legitimate power, 383, 384
Leveraging core competencies,
195–196
LexisNexis Academic, 483
LexisNexis Statistical, 484
Licensing, for market entry
benefits, 253
definition, 253
risks and limitations, 254
Licensing agreement, 275
Licensing Letter, C393
Life insurance, C34
Life insurance business, C32 to C41
Liquidity ratios, 98, 456
cash ratio, 456, 474
current ratio, 456, 473–474
quick ratio, 456, 474
Listening skills, 394
Litigation
on noncompete contracts, 149n
patent infringement, C383
Research in Motion case, 143
Local adaptation
backfiring, 248
versus cost structure, 247–248
evolution over time, 248
for multidomestic strategy,
246–248
in packaging, 247
pressures for, 242–244
Local line leaders, 23
Locating Company Information, 481
Locating Industry Information, 481
Logistics
inbound, 78–79
outbound, 80
third-party providers, C335 to
C335
Long- and short-term
perspectives, 11
Long-term solvency ratios, 98, 456
Los Alamos National
Laboratories, 270
Los Angeles Police Department, 385
Losses
by General Motors, C357, C365
Louvre Museum, Paris, 382
Low-cost strategy, 134
and blue ocean strategy, 281
Southwest Airlines, C140

m

Magazine publishing, C316
to C318
Maintaining, 182
*Making the Grass Greener on the
Other Side* (Melrose), 391
Malcolm Baldrige National Quality
Award, 82, 217
Management
at Caribou Coffee, C226
changes at Ford, C366 to C372
changes at Reader's Digest
Association, C315 to C316
at Claire's Stores, C219
at McDonald's, C391 to C392
at Panera Bread, C134 to C135
at Procter & Gamble, C192
to C193
at Reader's Digest Association,
C308 to C310
Management information systems,
at Panera Bread, C135
Management of global start-ups,
351–352
Management restructuring, 206
Management risks, 238–239
Managerial conceit
illusion of control, 431
irrational escalation of
commitment, 432
overconfidence, 431
Managerial role models, 316
Managers
and agency theory, 431
ambidextrous behavior, 12
back-solver dilemma, 431
bargaining power, 96
competitive vs. local
pressures, 243
credibility and ego, 213
defenses against takeovers, 326
erosion of value creation
antitakeover tactics, 219–220
egotism, 218–219
growth for growth's sake, 218
incentive and reward systems for,
323–324
opportunistic behavior, 325
profits obtained by, 96
risk taking, 439
tradeoffs by, 11–12
of virtual organizations, 365
Managing relationships, 386
Manufacturing
automated, 169
Crown Cork & Seal, C24 to C25
metal container industry, C17
offshoring, 240–242
outsourcing, 240–242
by Rocky Mountain Chocolate
Factory, C173 to C174
Manufacturing alliances, 275
Maquiladoras, 236
Market capitalism, 229
Market commonality
Intel and AMD, 289
in threat analysis, 287–189
Market dependence, 293
Market entry
for international expansion,
251–257
by exporting, 252–253
by franchising, 253–254
Häagen-Dazs procedure, 257
joint ventures, 254–256
by licensing, 253–254
strategic alliances, 254–256
wholly owned subsidiaries, 256
by joint ventures, 214–215
by strategic alliances, 214–215

The Reviewer Hall of Fame

We would like to thank the dedicated instructors who have graciously provided their insights since the inception of *Strategic Management: Creating Competitive Advantages* and *Strategic Management: Text and Cases.*

Acquaah, Moses — University of North Carolina-Greensboro
Alessandri, Todd — *Syracuse University*
Alexander, Larry — *Virginia Polytechnic Institute*
Amason, Allen C. — *University of Georgia*
Anders, Kathy — Arizona State University
Antoniou, Peter H. — *California State University, San Marcos*
Arnott, Dave — *Dallas Baptist University*
Azriel, Jay — *Seton Hall University*
Bailey, Jeffrey J. — *University of Idaho*
Barringer, Bruce — *University of Central Florida*
Beal, Brent D. — *Louisiana State University*
Beggs, Joyce — University of North Carolina-Charlotte
Bell DeTienne, Kristen — *Brigham Young University*
Bernstein, Eldon — *Lynn University*
Bodie, Dusty — *Boise State University*
Bogner, William — *Georgia State University*
Calhoun, Mikelle A. — *Valparaiso University*
Cappel, Samuel D. — *Southeastern Louisiana State University*
Carini, Gary — *Baylor University*
Carraher, Shawn M. — *Texas A&M University, Commerce*
Caruth, Don — *Amberton University*
Castrogiovanni, Gary J. — *University of Tulsa*
Chaganti, Radha — *Rider University*
Cho, Theresa — *Rutgers University*
Coffey, Betty S. — *Appalachian State University*
Coggins, Wade — *Webster University, Fort Smith Metro Campus*
Coombs, Joseph — *University of Richmond*
Cordeiro, James J. — *SUNY Brockport*
Covin, Jeffrey — *Indiana University*
Datta, Deepak — *University of Texas at Arlington*
Davis, James — *University of Notre Dame*
Deresky, Helen — *State University of New York, Plattsburgh*
DeWitt, Rocki-Lee — *University of Vermont*
Dial, Jay — *Ohio State University*
Dobbs, Michael E. — *Arkansas State University*
Doh, Jonathan — *Villanova University*
Douglas, Tom — *Clemson University*
Down, Jon — *Oregon State University*
Engle, Clare — *Concordia University*
Evans, William A. — *Troy State University, Dothan*
Fabian, Frances H. — *University of North Carolina, Charlotte*
Fanelli, Angelo — *Warrington College of Business*
Fathi, Michael — *Georgia Southwestern University*
Fausnaugh, Carolyn J. — *Florida Institute of Technology*
Ferguson, Tamela D. — *University of Louisiana at Lafayette*
Flanagan, David — *Western Michigan University*
Fox, Isaac — *University of Minnesota*

Frankforter, Steven A. — *Winthrop University*
Fried, Vance — *Oklahoma State University*
Gardberg, Naomi A. — Bernard M. Baruch College
Geringer, J. Michael — California Polytechnic State University
Gilbertson, Diana L. — *California State University, Fresno*
Gilley, Matt — *Oklahoma State University*
Gilliard, Debora — *Metropolitan State College of Denver*
Godiwalla, Yezdi H. — University of Wisconsin-Whitewater
Goel, Sanjay — *University of Minnesota, Duluth*
Gough, Sandy — Boise State University
Hatfield, Donald — Virginia Polytechnic Institute
Harrison, Niran — *University of Oregon*
Harveston, Paula — *Berry College*
Hester, Kim — *Arkansas State University*
Hironaka, John — *California State University, Sacramento*
Hoffman, Alan — *Bentley College*
Holbein, Gordon — *Northern Kentucky University*
Hough, Jill — *University of Tulsa*
Humphreys, John — *Eastern New Mexico University*
Ibe, James G. — *Morris College*
Janney, Jay J. — *University of Dayton*
Jauch, Lawrence — *University of Louisiana - Monroe*
Johnson, Dana M. — *Michigan Technical University*
Katzenstein, James — *California State University, Dominguez Hills*
Kellermanns, Franz — *Mississippi State University*
Kelley, Donna — *Babson College*
Kelley, Craig — *California State University, Sacramento*
Ketchen, Dave — *Florida State University*
Kilpatrick, John A. — *Idaho State University*
Korn, Helaine — Bernard M. Baruch College
Kowalczyk, Stan — *San Francisco State University*
Kraska, Daniel — *North Central State College*
Kreps, Donald E. — *Kutztown University*
Kroeger, Jim — Cleveland State University
Kulkarni, Subdoh P. — Howard University
Lant, Theresa — New York University
Legatski, Ted — *Texas Christian University*
Lengnick-Hall, Cynthia — *University of Texas at San Antonio*
Lester, Donald L. — Arkansas State University
Lester, Wanda — *North Carolina A&T State University*
Lemak, David J. — Washington State University-Tri-Cities
Lichtenstein, Benyamin — *University of Massachusetts at Boston*
Lockhart, Dan — *University of Kentucky*
Logan, John — University of South Carolina
Lowe, Kevin — University of North Carolina-